BIRDS AND PEOPLE

Birds and People

MARK COCKER and DAVID TIPLING

With specialist research by and the support of Jonathan Elphick and John Fanshawe

JONATHAN CAPE
LONDON

Published by Jonathan Cape 2013

2 4 6 8 10 9 7 5 3

First published in Great Britain in 2013 by
Jonathan Cape
Random House, 20 Vauxhall Bridge Road,
London SW1V 2SA

www.vintage-books.co.uk

Addresses for companies within The Random House Group Limited
can be found at: www.randomhouse.co.uk/offices.htm

The Random House Group Limited Reg. No. 954009

A CIP catalogue record for this book is available
from the British Library

ISBN 9780224081740

The Random House Group Limited supports the Forest
Stewardship Council®(FSC®), the leading international forest-
certification organisation. Our books carrying the FSC label are
printed on FSC®-certified paper. FSC is the only forest-certification
scheme supported by the leading environmental organisations,
including Greenpeace. Our paper procurement policy can be found at
www.randomhouse.co.uk/environment

MIX
Paper from
responsible sources
FSC® C008047

Designed by Peter Ward

Printed and bound in China
by C&C Offset Printing Co., Ltd

Birds and People is dedicated to all
those 650 contributors from 81 countries
who submitted materials for the book

CONTENTS

INTRODUCTION

This is an unusual bird book, in that it is as much about human beings as it is about birds. As the title suggests, it attempts to explore the common ground where these two very different organisms meet. It is about how people's lives are entwined with, and are very often shaped by, their encounters with birds. It is not a book of biology, although some explanations of bird behaviour have entered its scope. Nor does it seek to identify birds, which is the stock purpose of most ornithological guides.

Birds and People inevitably contains many stories of our exploitation of birds, both in the past and in the present. Birds have provided a seemingly inexhaustible supply of meat for human consumption. Indeed, one species – the Red Junglefowl with all its myriad domesticated forms – is the biggest single source of human protein on Earth; bigger than cattle, goats, sheep or pigs. Yet we have consumed many other species and also very specific parts of birds. The Romans ate parrots' tongues and flamingos' brains. The emperor Caligula even bathed in flamingo blood.[1] Modern humans retain an almost cult-like taste for the artificially enlarged livers of ducks and geese in pâté de foie gras. There is a parallel Asian cult centred on the nests of various species of swift, nests that are actually constructed from the birds' own dried saliva. However unprepossessing the raw materials might seem, birds'-nest soup is one of the most expensive dishes in the world and is now at the heart of an Asia-wide multi-million-dollar industry.

We should recall also that birds have supplied us with their eggs; not only to eat, but as vessels in which to carry liquid or from which to drink. Eggs have served equally as decorations. The Christian tradition of painted eggs offered as part of the religious ceremony of Easter, to mark the death and resurrection of Jesus, is just one instance of a much wider pattern. As far back as 3000 BC, Sumerians exchanged the carved and decorated eggs of ostriches at funeral ceremonies. So too – 6,400 km (4,000 miles) away – did the San people of the Kalahari Desert. These perfect porcelain-like forms, ripe with the potential for new life, have long commended themselves to us as a means to express the inexorable continuity of the living, even at moments of crisis, such as the death of a loved one.

With this we touch on a theme that is fundamental to *Birds and People*. The entire class of birds has occupied more of the Earth's surface, on terra firma and at sea, than any other vertebrate life form. Emperor Penguins lay their eggs and rear their chicks in the depths of the Antarctic winter on thick beds of sea ice, enduring temperatures of –60 ºC (–76 ºF). Their breeding colonies represent one of the extreme climatic outposts for all warm-blooded life on Earth. Yet birds are not just ubiquitous upon our physical planet. They are fellow travellers of the human spirit, and have also colonised our imaginations, as if we were one further habitat to conquer and exploit.

Birds and People explores and celebrates, perhaps more than any other theme, how birds live within us – and how they have been, in the words of the great French anthropologist Claude Lévi-Strauss, 'good to think' and to reflect upon.[2] Birds dwell at the heart of human experience, furnishing us with an imaginative and symbolic resource that is as limitless as their fund of flesh and feathers. Look around. You will see birds' images everywhere: on our currencies, on our stamps, our flags, our national emblems; on our televisions, in our writing, our music, in all our art forms, in fact, but equally in our commercial spheres with their advertisements, logos and jingles. They are even more important than all these examples suggest. Birds are part of the very language we use to express ourselves about life and about our encounters with life. Why should this be so?

I think part of the answer lies in their biology. Birds often seem so much more intensely alive than we are. Birds walk the Earth on two legs just as we do, but then they perform something we never have. They rise up and fly away. In so doing they unleash a special characteristic of their basic physiology, which supports the notion of their greater dynamism. In their bones, birds have special air sacs that reduce density to aid flight, but which also connect to the avian respiratory system. Birds would be at risk from the excess heat generated by their muscular activity while flying, but these air sacs increase the surface area from which heat is dissipated. Their enhanced respiratory system not only regulates temperature during the exertions of flight, it also improves the efficiency with which they extract oxygen from the atmosphere; in fact, their rate of absorption is twice that of mammals'.[3]

In taking flight, this two-legged creature – which earlier seemed to share so much of our own gravity-bound condition – is instantly transformed. It is life quickened and intensified beyond our range. The bird, in fact, has become almost everything we are not. But this relationship is not confined to the precise moment of passage. Birds' appeal goes deeper and we often feel compelled to make imaginary journeys with them. When this happens we also submit to their other key properties: their richer sense of geographical location and their more complete ability to reach their destinations. When we ourselves try to achieve the same arrow-like directness we suggest that we are going 'as the crow flies'.

Birds seem to know precisely where they are going. In the past we were mesmerised but utterly confounded by bird migration. Some authorities even believed that their disappearance in autumn stemmed from the fact that they flew to the moon. Migrating birds are in many ways living journeys. No wonder we watched their formations overhead to foretell the future. Specialised Greek and Roman priests once observed the motion of birds to advise their political leaders about state policy and its potential outcome.

To give just one compelling instance of the unfathomable ability of birds to navigate time and space: there are records of a seabird called the Manx Shearwater, ringed as a chick in its Welsh nest burrow. Fourteen days later that same three-month-old bird, unaccompanied by any relative, arrived for the first time ever in the species' customary winter quarters off the coast of Argentina. It is a distance of 8,000 km (5,000 miles). An individual bird may repeat that same oceanic journey, back and forth, 100 times in the course of its world-wandering life.

Birds in the sky or birds flying over the waves offer us a way of comprehending and articulating two of our most fundamental but fundamentally inaccessible experiences: the passage of time and the interior workings of our imaginations. To take these phenomena in turn, time is that elusive essence which is as insubstantial as air. Yet we are as certain of its reality as the flight of a bird across the heavens. Famously, Bede, the British monk of the eighth century AD, likened the brevity of human life between birth and death to a sparrow passing from door to door through the fire-lit hall of the king on a winter's night (see page 487).

It is surely no coincidence that we call our most creative moments – of which the above metaphor is a perfect example – 'flights of imagination'. What better way to conjure the elusive and magical wanderings of our own creative impulse than as a bird moving through the intangible weightlessness of mid-air? What simpler way to convey our journey into the farthest recesses of our minds and spirits than a bird?

Birds make such powerful appeal as metaphors for these fundamental parts of life, that they have been treated repeatedly as symbols for our most heightened experiences. We use birds to express ideas of transformation, such as when we fall in love or achieve other intense emotional states, or when we are turned from an animate person into a disembodied soul. Sometimes birds have come to stand for our ultimate values. To the Sufi mystics of the Middle East, God was sometimes known as 'the unnamed bird'.

Birds and People seeks to document the multitudinous ways in which we are indebted to birds for their life-enhancing gifts. As far as possible, I have tried to focus on living lore and beliefs about birds. Many books dealing with folklore discuss bird-related ideas or beliefs as if they all still coexist now, often without presenting evidence for that assumption. Here I have attempted to differentiate between archaic and living myth. Yet I have made reference to older ideas, especially where they throw into sharp relief modern responses, or where they demonstrate continuities between the past, occasionally a remote past, and the modern context.

Humans have a particular need for birds. The ancient Hindu epic poem the Harivamsa suggested that 'an abode without birds, is like a meat without seasoning'. The following contribution to *Birds and People* suggests that intrinsically people love birds even when they hate them:

> From a very young age I had a fear of birds that became worse as I got older. By the time I was in my thirties I could not be in the garden if there was a bird nearby and I would have to turn back if there was one on the pavement. In 1996 we were on holiday in Turkey and were invited to a person's house. When we arrived they had chickens and I was absolutely terrified and went hysterical. It ruined the day for the whole family. They suggested to me that I get some help on my return from holiday and early the next year I began some sessions. They only lasted a couple of months but what a difference it made to my life. We now have feeders in our garden and get great joy from watching the wonderful selection of 'our birds' that visit. I never

knew before that such beautiful birds as European Goldfinches, Common Chaffinches and Long-tailed Tits existed. I have even been to St Mark's Square in Venice, which would previously have been unthinkable.[4]

Many bird books do not concern themselves with the subject of birds' wider cultural significance, except for the specific and compartmentalised issue of bird conservation. This is ironic because environmentalists cannot by themselves oversee the protection of birds. It is only when whole societies collectively believe in the goal that it is attainable. *Birds and People* does not set out to be another environmental lament or standard account of conservation, rather it is a source book on why we cherish birds. It is an anatomy of what they mean to us and what we owe them culturally and materially. In truth, it goes further. It celebrates our own part in the shared relationship – that fundamental human role of telling stories to ourselves about birds. More than 650 people in 81 countries have sent their stories. Many hundreds of them are reproduced here. One contributor argues:

> Observing birds makes us feel all the more human. For I cannot imagine anything greater in our nature as human beings than our cognitive ability to appreciate things. If nature existed without humanity, would it be beautiful at all? For beauty lies in the eye of the beholder, and if there's no one to behold it, then would it be beautiful? We humans are the admirers. We behold the beauty in the world. Despite all our faults, human nature brings so much joy to the world, as much as it does grief.[5]

Traditional societies everywhere, from the San of the Kalahari to the Aborigines of Australia, know this fundamental truth. They appreciate how we have our place in the order of things. We are the keepers of the Earth's tales. With that privilege now comes huge responsibility.

As far as we know, this is the only planet proven to hold life in any solar system. Life has unfolded across the surface of the Earth in all its vertigo-inducing complexity. The best guess for the entire biosphere is between 3–10 million different species, but there are possibly as many as 100 million, of which we are just a single example.[6] This 3.5 billion-year-old flush of life extends seamlessly to a depth beneath the sea of just 11 km (7 miles); it continues into the atmosphere for little more than the highest peaks (8.85 km: 5.5 miles). Compared to the limitless dark emptiness of the galaxy, life is a diaphanous sheet of silk wrapped around one small precious head.

We are woven into this miraculous light-loving fabric. Yet surely one fundamental measure of our civilisation, now and always, is our devotion to the living and to the maintenance of that living fabric – birds and people, flowers and insects, trees and butterflies, bumblebees and bush crickets, mammals and fishes in all their teeming diversity. To assume that we alone are all that matter and to contemplate with any kind of equanimity the loss of these other species, or a part of them, is to risk losing our very souls and silencing our own imaginations. A world without birds would lay waste the human heart.

STRUCTURE OF THE BOOK

We need to emphasise from the very outset that this book is in no way exhaustive of its subject. It is a personal view by two people. I suspect that if one set out to do full justice to the relationships between birds and people worldwide one would easily fill 20 volumes of this size.

There are about 10,500 species of birds in the world, subdivided into just over 200 recognised families. The book is broken down into different sections according to these families. The taxonomic order and nomenclature for the families follow the systematic list established by Frank Gill and Minturn Wright in their book *Birds of the World: Recommended English Names* (2006). Only on the rarest occasions have I felt it necessary to deviate from their decisions on names (for instance I preferred the widely used picathartes rather than their choice, bald crows. These twins of the African rainforest just seem too wonderful for so prosaic a construction).

In a few places I have felt compelled to cite two names simultaneously for the same species. An example is the section on the species of grouse known in North America and elsewhere as Willow Ptarmigan (Gill and Wright's preferred choice). Unfortunately in Britain this same bird, which is of huge historic and contemporary cultural significance, is well known by a completely different name (Red Grouse). Rather than choose one or the other and baffle a part of the book's intended audience, I have constructed a somewhat cumbersome combined version, Willow Ptarmigan (Red Grouse). It is, incidentally, a perfect measure of the importance we attach to names that when I wrote to an English grouse-moor owner asking him to dilate on the joys of grouse shooting, he refused, perceiving in my version of the name some kind of ornitho-anarchist's plot to subvert the whole Glorious Twelfth and all its complex meanings.

The main body of text is broken down according to family, but not all bird families were judged to be of cultural importance. Appendix III comprises a list of 59 families, many of which contain only a few species (in total they add up to 602 species) that received no coverage. I treat in detail the remaining 144 families as well as two extinct families that retain powerful cultural associations. These are the elephant birds of Madagascar and the moas of New Zealand. Each family text is further divided by separate subject headings and on first mention of any single family member, that species appears in red bold type together with its italicised scientific name. The latter is omitted thereafter. All full species names appear throughout the book with initial capitals, as is customary in works of natural history.

As I mention above, an unusual aspect of the book is that we invited anyone from anywhere in the world to contribute their observations, reflections and experiences of birds. In the event, we received many thousands of separate pieces from 600–800 people. More than 600 of these contributors are listed in the acknowledgements, while the stories and thoughts of about 300 are included in the book. The names of these various individuals are cited in the endnotes. Receiving these wonderful observations was a truly inspiring part of the book's assembly and they add immeasurably both to its authenticity and its comprehensive coverage. In total our contributors form a worldwide chorus, involving 81 different countries, on how birds enrich our lives. The book is dedicated to them all.

However, managing such a vast correspondence over many years, involving tens of thousands of emails, and having to store contributions for long periods (the earliest submissions featured in *Birds and People* were sent to me in 1997) before incorporating them into the text was a major undertaking, taxing my organisational skills to the limits. If anyone feels they have been omitted or their name has been incorrectly listed then please contact us. We will endeavour to correct any errors.

Each personal contribution is cited in the endnotes with the name of the author, their nearest major city or their province / state / county and then their country of residence. Some people moved during the course of their various contributions and the notes may reflect their geographical wanderings. Books and journal sources are listed in the endnotes only by the name of author(s), date of publication and page number of the cited reference. The full bibliographic details appear in the Select Bibliography.

Tinamou family *Tinamidae*

The rather evocative name is said to be an onomatopoeic version of the call, coined by indigenous Americans possibly in Argentina or French Guiana.[1] Almost all the 49 tinamou species are small- to medium-sized (23–46 cm: 9–18 in), short-legged birds of dense vegetation. They are found right across the Neotropics from Argentina to Mexico and, in appearance, most conform to a single basic 'gamebird' pattern – rotund, slender-headed and cryptically coloured.

They have been much favoured for the cooking pot and after thousands of years of human predation, tinamous have acquired an exacting secrecy. As one expert noted wryly: 'Learn the call; dozens will be heard for every bird glimpsed.'[2] Others have described them as 'vexing and elusive'.[3] The European colonists quickly appreciated the tinamous' furtive ground-dwelling habits and referred to them as: *perdiz*, 'partridge'; or *codorna*, 'quail'. However, their similarity to Old World gamebirds illustrates convergent evolution: they are, in fact, among the most primitive birds on Earth and are most closely related to the ratites, the group which includes ostriches and rheas.

Despite the family's culinary excellence – the flesh is tender, flavoursome and 'oddly transparent' – there was no attempt at domestication by indigenous Americans.[4] Nevertheless, tinamous will breed in captivity and now hand-reared birds are being used to reintroduce some species to areas from which they had been extirpated. In addition there have been several historical attempts to establish them in North America, in various states from Oregon to Florida. The only successful scheme was in 1885 and involved the **Chilean Tinamou** *Nothoprocta perdicaria* on Easter Island, where they persist today. A key factor that probably discouraged hunters in their release efforts is the tinamous' reluctance to fly, which would have made them poor sport. The birds are noisy in take off, rather bad at steering and dangerous when landing. Once flushed, they can crash and kill themselves by hitting branches, posts, wires and even houses.[5]

In many forms of South American landscape, particularly forest, tinamous supply a vocal backdrop that is often melodic, invariably haunting and deeply atmospheric. The whistled notes peak at dawn or dusk and some tinamous call at night, especially on a full moon. The great Brazilian ornithologist Helmut Sick told a legend that touches on the affecting melancholy in their voice. Two species, the **Red-winged Tinamou** *Rhynchotus rufescens* and **Undulated Tinamou** *Crypturellus undulatus*, were once said to be inseparable friends, but a fatal argument caused them to part, the former for the open sunlit grassland and the latter for the forest shadows. However, the Undulated Tinamou eventually repented of the tiff, and from the forest edge called out a mournful four notes to his lost friend: *Vamos-fazer-as-pazes?* ('Shall we make peace?'). The Red-winged Tinamou replied, *Eu, nunca mais* ('Me, never again').[6] The two species' post-quarrel habitat choices reflect their genuine ecological differences, while the Portuguese phrases are imitative of the birds' true calls.

A grimly familiar double act of habitat loss and human pressure, particularly hunting, now bears down heavily on almost all the tinamous. They are routinely pursued with dogs and guns, or trapped with snares, while another technique involves use of a hunting whistle to lure them out, which has given rise to a small handicraft industry in parts of Brazil.[7] Some of the available statistics on the size of the historic slaughter are as grievous as they are revealing. Between 1890 and 1899, 18 million tinamous were shipped from Buenos Aires alone. In North America they were often imported under the catch-all name of 'South American partridge'.[8] Today BirdLife International deems 11 species to be threatened or near-threatened, while the Peruvian endemic **Kalinowski's Tinamou** *Nothoprocta kalinowskii* is known from just two specimens, the last collected in 1900.

A male Somali Ostrich has grey legs and neck rather than the pink of a Common Ostrich, but both species share all the fine plumes and towering grandeur of their family.

Ostrich family *Struthionidae*

The **Common Ostrich** *Struthio camelus* is the giant of the avian world. Big males weigh as much as 150 kg (331 lb), stand up to 2.75 m (9 ft) tall and are the world's largest living birds (see also Moa family, page 27). The trapping of a single adult would have delivered a major supply of meat to the earliest hunters. So too would a 'nestful' of ostrich eggs, which can number as many as 78 in a single scrape. Images of adult birds feature regularly among Neolithic portraits of hunt scenes from southern Africa and the Saharan region. Some of these petroglyphs, which have a striking and elegant simplicity, are contenders for the oldest portrait of a recognisable bird species found anywhere on Earth.

Size alone cannot explain the richness of our cultural responses to ostriches. The adult male is substantially larger than the dowdier, predominantly grey-brown hen, and in breeding dress, when his lacy white wing and tail plumes contrast with his jet black body, he is a magnificent-looking bird. To boot, the ostrich is the fastest animal on two legs

and can top 70 kph (43 mph). All of this sheer physical power has helped to cement its cultural prominence.

By appropriating just small associated parts of an ostrich, humans have sought to acquire symbolically the enormous life force of the living creature. In many ways the whole cultural history of the bird is the story of how we have obtained these representative portions and of the various ways they have then been deployed. Two key items – feathers and eggs – dominate the story of ostriches.

Each egg is the equivalent of two dozen chicken eggs and weighs 1.5 kg (3.3 lb), the largest produced by any species. The internal capacity is more than half a litre (1 pint) and this accounts for what was probably their earliest usage as water carriers. San hunter-gatherers of the Kalahari were among the last to use them in this way. Blown eggs were sealed with grass wads and held in specially designed bags or could be buried at marked locations and left as emergency supplies.

This elaborately carved ostrich egg in the British Museum was originally found in a tomb near Rome and is at least 2,600 years old.

Yet ostrich eggs would have appealed to us simply on account of their beauty. The shell is smooth, creamy in colour and porcelain-like in texture. Like whales' teeth or elephant ivory they seem to have presented a perfect three-dimensional canvas for human creativity. Even eggs used as water pots were often decorated. Examples, which are held in the British Museum, London, and the American Museum of Natural History, New York, often bear abstract patterns or figurative designs. Today blown eggs are routinely displayed as exotic curios, many carefully carved or inscribed with pictures, then marketed as ethnic art in Africa's major tourist countries. They are even sold as super-sized Easter eggs.

These ostrich products are often kept in countries far distant from the bird's natural distribution. One unusual arrangement I have seen in the UK involved an entire bowlful, all au naturel and looking like some immutable display of ivory fruit. A negative consequence of this Western appetite is described in east Africa: 'I'm afraid the most obvious use of ostrich products these days is young boys standing on the side of the road, holding out eggs for sale to unthinking tourists. Logic dictates that rural Tanzanians will not be choosy about the provenance of the eggs they sell.'[1]

Given these developments, it is perhaps to be welcomed that glass is fast replacing ostrich eggshell as a traditional

source material for African jewellery. Yet items made from ostrich, such as necklaces, head- and waistbands are still important to some communities, partly for their symbolic attributes. These derive from a peculiar characteristic of the ostrich mating system. The nest includes not only eggs produced by a dominant 'pair', but also those from up to 18 other 'minor' hens (normally between two and five). Nest duties are divided between the dominant couple, but they incubate only as many of the eggs as they can cover and some laid by the 'minor' hens are pushed into an abandoned periphery. The advantage of this egg surplus to the dominant female is that they serve as a decoy should the nest be visited by predators.

These biological facts were long obscured from humans and our conclusion based merely on the nests' appearance was of the bird's huge sexual potential. Superior fertility was thus added to the various attributes of ostrich. In parts of Kenya women who wear ostrich-shell jewellery are thought to enhance their own fertility, while mothers wear ornaments on their foreheads as proof of maternal status. Such items are particularly important at marriage ceremonies.[2]

The ornamental use of the eggs has provided some of the best evidence for the bird's long-standing cultural importance, as well as the wide reach of ostrich lore. Egg fragments have been found at the ancient city of Kish in Iraq (near the site of Babylon and also the modern town of Al Hillah) which date to about 3000 BC. Restoration work has enabled the reconstruction of these 5,000-year-old eggs and shown us how the 'tops' were cut off to leave a fluid-bearing vessel or drinking goblet. These were then placed as grave goods in Sumerian cemeteries, like the one at Kish, but similar eggs have also been unearthed at prehistoric tombs in Carthage and Spain (Punic), Italy (Etruscan), Greece (Mycenaean) and ancient Egypt.[3]

It is striking that 6,000 km (3,700 miles) away and only last century, ostrich eggs were also exchanged as death gifts by the San people. Is it possible that in all these hugely varied contexts, the ostrich egg retained much the same symbolic importance? Certainly one senses that a huge and beautiful ivory-coloured egg makes an intrinsic appeal to our imagination as an emblem of life's continuity that might be powerfully appropriate in such funereal rites.[4]

A very different symbolic value of the ostrich egg has survived elsewhere in Africa and around the world. They are still widely kept as display items in places of worship for both Muslims and Christians, and ostrich eggs were once hung above the lamps in the Church of the Holy Sepulchre in Jerusalem.[5] Are they still? (Another suggestion for this practice – although it may be no more than a good tour-guide tale – is that the eggs are placed on chains or cords from which are suspended olive-oil candles, and the eggs act as a barrier preventing rodents climbing down the rope to eat the nutritious oil.)[6]

Another specific power attributed to ostrich eggs was an ability to ward off lightning. In Ethiopian churches the eggs are arranged on a seven-pointed star, each representing the virtues of truth, benevolence, brotherly love, harmony, spirit, justice and peace.[7] In the 1980s the widespread nature of this custom was thought to exert substantial pressure on Ethiopia's wild population, which is now considered a completely separate species called the **Somali Ostrich** *Struthio molybdophanes*. One estimate suggested 15,500 ostrich

eggs were being taken a year to replenish displays in Coptic churches.[8]

For 2,000 years the ostrich was one of only two flightless birds well known in Europe (see also Great Auk, page 224) and its lack of aerial ability caused deep confusion. Even today its strangely un-avian bulk means that many naturalists think of it differently to other birds:

> Ostriches are bizarre creatures – perhaps even honorary mammals, being taller and more vigilant than many grazing companions. I saw them first in Nairobi National Park, Kenya, and was struck by their large eyes, shabby, duster-feathering, super-fat drumsticks, and their curiously gentle way of dipping to browse. Great birds, or mammals, or confusingly, a bit of both distilled.[9]

That uncertainty has a long pedigree. In one of the oldest written accounts, Aristotle was unsure how to classify ostrich – the Greek name *strouthiokamēlos* means 'sparrow-camel' – and he noted how 'it has some of the characters of a bird, some of the characters of a quadruped'.

> It differs from a quadruped in being feathered; and from a bird in being unable to soar aloft, and in having feathers that resemble hair and are useless for flight. Again, it agrees with quadrupeds in having upper eyelashes, and the parts about the head and upper portion of the neck are bare – so that its eyelashes are more hairy; and it agrees with birds in being feathered in all the parts posterior to these. Further, it resembles a bird in being a biped, and a quadruped in having a cloven hoof.[10]

The passage may reveal the philosopher's confusion, but there is no doubt that he was intimately acquainted with the living creature.

By the time of ancient Greece, the keeping of ostrich already had long traditions in the Mediterranean and elsewhere. A beautiful Greek bowl from the sixth century BC (now in the Museum of Fine Arts, Boston) depicts young jockeys on ostrich-back and suggests that racing the birds was an established sport. Another important ostrich portrait occurs in a large mosaic fragment discovered at the Roman settlement of Thuburbo Maius in modern Tunisia (now held in the Bardo Museum in Tunis). It dates from the fourth century AD and shows an ostrich flock being hunted with greyhound-like dogs.

Perhaps the most memorable, if bizarre, references to

The Romans looked upon the ostrich as a strange source of sport, as a quarry for hunters and as an exotic subject for their mosaics. This remarkable fragment is in the Bardo Museum in Tunis.

ostrich from the classical world are written accounts from imperial Rome. The mad emperor Commodus (AD 161–192), whose mental disintegration was so powerfully evoked by Joaquin Phoenix in the film *Gladiator*, once had ostriches chased around the Coliseum; the crowds were apparently entertained to see the birds continue the run even after their heads had been cut off.[11] Equally weird was Elagabalus (AD 203–222), an emperor noted for gluttony, who served his fellow guests with the brains from 600 ostrich crania. In this species the eye is larger than its brain, and what became of the other 60 tonnes of ostrich flesh is not recorded.[12]

The harvesting of wild birds for their flesh and eggs almost certainly played a part in the slow shrinkage of numbers, which has seen the bird vanish from all of western Asia and north Africa (with the exception of one possible enclave in southern Egypt). Yet a far more important cause of decline was the use of ostrich feathers in human costume. The huge size of some of these plumes as well as their fine, soft, bushy, filamentous structure were key to their appeal. Even today ostrich feathers are used worldwide and in a bewildering range of social contexts, from tribal ritual to high-society costume, and from the formalities of the parade ground to the high-camp of Broadway musical. They have been worn to convey both masculine power and also feminine allure. As one commentator notes, 'we have borrowed ostrich glamour and used it to signal sexual and imperial power, seductive spectacle, hyperbole, escape'.[13] If a single common denominator could be discerned in all these heterogeneous situations, then it is the theme of prominent social display.

The oldest usages of ostrich feathers are probably African. The ancient Egyptians certainly held the birds in high esteem. The barbules on each side of the vane are of exactly equal length in an ostrich feather, which is unlike most other birds. The Egyptians appropriated this natural symmetry as a metaphor for justice and ostrich feathers were used in ceremonial contexts. They were the sacred emblem of Maat, goddess of truth, justice and order, who was always depicted with a feather in her hair.

Ostrich feathers were also reserved for royal usage. One of the oldest surviving ostrich-feather artefacts is the base of a gold fan used by Tutankhamun (1341–1323 BC). When it was found the remains of alternating dark and white feathers were still attached and the base itself bears a description of how the young king hunted the birds from which the feathers were taken. There is also an embossed picture of the hunt scene.[14]

In parts of Africa the feathers were and, to some extent, still are a classic adornment for men of various ages. Just as ostrich-shell jewellery is still prized as a symbol of female fertility, the long white-and-black plumes of the cock bird are traditionally valued as a means to convey masculine virility. Ostrich males are among only a small number of birds (including swans and ducks) with a penis, which is a bizarre appendage looking rather like a slender pink boxing glove, up to 40 cm (16 in) long. William Harvey, the seventeenth-century naturalist, likened it to a cow's tongue.[15] The perceived power of a cock ostrich to command a harem of hens had particular resonances for a society where multiple wives is often a reflection of a man's wealth and status.

For the Marakwet people of western Kenya there is also a strong connection between ostrich and cattle, a traditional currency for measuring success. To hear the male bird make his strange booming note at dawn is a sign of good luck, predicting the ownership of a large herd.[16] For the Nandi, near-neighbours to the Marakwet, the association was enshrined in an old riddle: 'What is the thing which, though so weak that it is blown by the wind, is able to herd oxen?' The answer was an ostrich feather: in the tall vegetation his plumed headdress was often the only visible part of a man guarding his cattle.[17]

The loose structure of the feathers and their tendency to wave and ripple in response to movement are undoubtedly key to their popularity in formal costume. (Although it is worth noting that the softness also has hard application. 'One very functional use by the Hadza hunter-gatherers [from Tanzania], which capitalises on the ostrich feather's wavy structure, is to put a feather on the backside of the firestick and use to monitor wind direction while hunting.')[18]

In Africa it is in the context of military dress that ostrich feathers have made their largest impression, both in life and, subsequently, on camera. Perhaps the most impressive of all pictures are those of the Maasai moran, the warrior class of the famous east African pastoralists, in which each Adonis sports a seemingly contradictory mix of spear and headdress of frizzy black-and-white plumes. Such images are as much a world archetype of tribal grandeur and martial prowess as portraits of the Zulu impi at their height, or of Sioux and Cheyenne braves in eagle-feather war bonnets. Today, however, as cash replaces conflict as a test of manhood, the Maasai usage of such gear has acquired fresh meaning. In Tanzania 'you occasionally see ceremonial ostrich head-dresses among the Maasai, but more often roadside types, posing for a photo opportunity. Whether they do this in response to a perceived demand, or they have the headdresses at home anyway, I can't say.'[19]

The power of public statement intrinsic to ostrich plumes was not lost on Europeans. From the age of imperial Rome, the feathers were routinely found in the ceremonial regalia of high-ranking military leaders. But it was at the other extreme of social display that the bird really achieved its greatest popularity. It was said that Marie Antoinette, the doomed wife of French king Louis XVI, triggered the original craze in the eighteenth century. She happened to decorate her coiffure with a particularly fine spray of ostrich and peacock feathers. The king complimented the look, the fashion caught hold at court, and for more than a century it blazed across Europe and North America.[20] During the French Revolution she was even known as the 'Ostrich bitch', a pun on her Austrian background.

Initially there was no large supply of high-quality feathers, although in the Sahara and on the Arabian Peninsula (where the bird went extinct in the 1960s) the role of ostrich hunter had long been traditional. The British Arabist and author Charles Doughty reported an encounter with one of these figures in the late nineteenth century. The man claimed to kill just two birds a year, itself a reflection of the ostrich's extreme rarity in Arabia, and then sold the skins for a high price in Damascus, whence they were exported to London milliners and Parisian *plumassières*.[21]

The huge value placed on feathers soon unleashed a holocaust upon hundreds of species of bird, whose breeding plumage happened to include fashion-friendly plumes (see also Herons and the Feather Industry, page 131) But the popularity of ostrich outstripped all others. A single first-

Today the lacy plumes of ostriches are largely worn to express the essence of human femininity. Historically, the feathers were important in military or male costume, such as this Maasai headdress worn by Kitkung Nampaso of Kenya.

class feather could be over half a metre in length (22 in) and some of the resulting hat arrangements worn in London or New York measured almost 2 m across (6.5 ft).[22]

In many parts of Africa there had been numerous independent efforts at domestication, but the demand for feathers resulted in the first industrialised farming. Ranching took hold as far away as California and Australia, with birds being transported to the latter in 1869 (even today a tiny feral population remains in southern Australia), but the real centre was the Karoo region of South Africa, where there were said to be a million ostriches at the peak.[23]

South African dominance in the market was strengthened after the Trans-Saharan Ostrich Expedition of 1911, led by an adventurer called Russell Thornton. He and his team returned to the Karoo with breeding stock of the finest north African birds called Barbaries, whose plumes were especially magnificent. To find and transport 156 ostriches cost the government over £7,722 (more than $900,000 by today's values) but the rewards were huge. A half-kilo of feathers (1.1 lb) peaked at £500, while a single prime plume could be £12, about the equivalent of the fare for the month-long sail from Cape Town to London.[24]

The capital of the business was the town of Oudtshoorn, where ostrich barons grew enormously prosperous. Out of the Karoo desert they conjured 'feather palaces' that were noted for vulgar display as much as architectural eccentricity ('Baroque parapets, pyramidal turrets, gazebos and Spanish arches ... red fish-scale tiling and odd borrowings from the dreamlife of a Byzantine potentate').[25] One such mansion boasted a lion-footed bath that could hold 1,300 litres (286 gallons) of water. By 1913 total exports had risen to 45.4 tonnes of feathers, which sold for £2.75 million ($320 million in contemporary prices). Only gold, diamonds and wool were more important to the South African economy.[26]

Yet an empire founded on feathers seems almost inherently transient, and the Victorian styles which had inspired such extravagance on the streets of Paris – as well as in the Karoo – vanished almost overnight, outmoded by world war and the close-fitting fashions demanded by the motor car. Yet at its height the taste for ostrich gave rise to a look that is still considered the epitome of feminine ostentation and female sexual allure. It was made famous by risqué nightspots such as Les Folies Bergère in Paris, in shows where women could appear on stage wearing little but ostrich feathers. That same style has since been copied by some of the most glamorous queens of world entertainment, from Marlene Dietrich and Marilyn Monroe, to Elton John and Kylie Minogue.

The bird's large size and high-quality meat, which is deep red, hugely flavoursome and not unlike beef in texture, mean that ostrich has probably been a part of the human diet since the origins of our species. Today ostrich meat has acquired fresh cachet. Since it is now recognised to be low in calories, cholesterol and fat, it is marketed as a healthy alternative to more conventional meat sources and sells online for prices comparable with prime beef.

Rhea family *Rheidae*

Of all the eight ostrich-like flightless birds occurring right across the southern continents, the two species of rhea drew the longest straw on the issue of English and scientific names. Rhea was the name of a female Titan from Greek mythology and was, therefore, large like the bird itself. She was also mother to Hades, Poseidon and the great Zeus, and for once the name conveys something of the size, specialness and visual grandeur of the wild creature.

Rheas are endemic to South America and fossil specimens from the Eocene (*c.*40 million years ago) suggest that they are among the continent's oldest birds. Both ostrich and rhea probably had a common ancestor, which split into the American and African forms when Gondwana, the southern supercontinent, broke apart 120 million years ago. The two recognised species in South America are the larger and more widely distributed **Greater Rhea** *Rhea americana* and **Darwin's Rhea** *Pterocnemia pennata*.

Today they are called *ñandú* in much of their Spanish-speaking range, a name derived from the Guaraní people of Paraguay and northern Argentina. The Brazilian is *ema*, a Portuguese word with a complex history, which has been used, in turn, as a name for the crane (or ostrich), then the cassowary and finally the rhea (see Emu family, page 23).[1] 'In Brazil it is also a word for drunk – *montado na ema* means "mounted on the rhea" (I imagine because of the way the bird runs brings to mind a swaying drunkard). There is also an expression for a coward, *bunda de ema*, which means literally "the arse of a rhea".'[2]

Behind the patronymic for the smaller species, the Darwin's Rhea, there is an intriguing anecdote. Charles Darwin encountered rheas during his four-and-a-half-year journey (1831–6) mainly around the coasts of Brazil, Uruguay, Argentina and Chile. In his subsequent account of the travels, *The Voyage of the Beagle*, the young scientist referred to rheas as 'ostrich', a translation of a widely used Spanish name *avestruz*. The gauchos from the Argentinian pampas south of Buenos Aires told Darwin that there was not only the 'ostrich' that he had seen for himself, there was also a hitherto undescribed second species which was smaller and darker.

Several months later in January 1834, Darwin happened to be onboard ship and sitting down to dine on 'ostrich', which one of his colleagues had earlier shot and shown to him. Suddenly, in the middle of the meal, Darwin leapt to his feet recalling the gauchos' earlier conversations, and realised what he had just done. He had eaten a species new to science (see also Udzungwa Forest Partridge, page 55). Fortunately the head, neck, legs and one wing had all survived among the kitchen scraps and Darwin preserved them for his return to England where, in 1837, John Gould, then taxidermist to the Zoological Society of London, was able to patch together a serviceable skin. With Darwin, he then described the bird, naming it after the 'discoverer', *Rhea darwinii*. Neither part of the scientific name has remained and today the species is often known by an alternative English version, 'Lesser Rhea'.[3]

The bird weighs as much as 25 kg (55 lb) and stands up to 1 m (3.3 ft) tall, but the other species can reach 50 kg (110 lb) and 1.5 m (4.8 ft) in height.[4] Both are birds of open habitats.

Greater Rhea is more tolerant of tree cover and occurs from Argentina to north-east Brazil. The Darwin's Rhea is more exclusively southern in range but also occurs on the arid upland heaths of the altiplano in southern Peru and Bolivia, where it forms a separate race sometimes called the 'Puna Rhea'. This form is now critically endangered, largely as a consequence of over-hunting, and numbers only a few hundred birds.[5]

Rheas have probably been hunted since the arrival of humans in South America, and in the northern Brazilian state of Piauí there are prehistoric cave images of rheas dating to 12,000–8,000 BC.[6] The rhea has been enormously prized for the amount of meat represented by a single bird. However, the most famous of rhea hunters were the legendary gauchos of the pampas, who developed a remarkable technique using a bolas. This device comprises three joined straps, which were themselves often made from rhea sinew, weighted with a small ball of wood or metal, about the size of a pigeon's egg. The gauchos threw them with immense skill and with a heavier version could bring down livestock and other game, the straps wrapping around the legs and disabling the creature, from over 70 m (230 ft).[7] The rhea meat was prized but the leather was also used for bags and salt containers, the whole skins were made into mattresses and the fat reputed to have medicinal properties.

Historically the slaughter inflicted on rheas for their plumage was as intensive as that for almost any species at the height of the feather trade (see also Herons and the Feather Industry, page 131). In the second half of the nineteenth century between 300,000 and 500,000 birds were killed annually and in 1872 alone 61 tonnes of feathers were exported through a single Buenos Aires custom house. The rather drab grey-brown plumes were not deemed high enough quality for women's hats and boas, but were used to make feather brooms and dusters. Today in South America the market for this very specific product still exists.

> In the centre of Chile's capital, Santiago, I encountered four or five rather scruffy street sellers, all greying swarthy men in vests. They had plastic buckets at their feet full of feathers. On closer inspection these were obviously rhea feathers for use as dusters.[8]

The first 'official' record of Darwin's Rhea involved both science and savour. Charles Darwin discovered the species while he was eating it.

Greater Rheas are kept in a semi-wild state on private estancias and there are some rhea farms where they are raised for meat and eggs, and undoubtedly the feathers are made directly into dusters. Rhea-feather dusters can occasionally be seen on sale in hardware shops but are much more commonly sold by ambulant salesman trading to shops, house-to-house and to drivers halted at traffic lights. These guys specialise exclusively in selling dusters and carry large numbers of them attached to a tall pole. The dusters are commonly used by taxi drivers here in Buenos Aires, and many people own one at home.[9]

Cassowary family *Casuariidae*

With their deep-cobalt-blue facial skin, drooping crimson throat wattles and a raised bony helmet-like knob on their heads, cassowaries are extraordinary-looking creatures. Their body plumage is black and the hair-like feathers coarse and dense. The birds are mainly distributed on New Guinea but one of the three species, the **Southern Cassowary** *Casuarius casuarius* – the world's heaviest bird after the ostriches – is more widespread and occurs in northern Queensland, Australia, and on the Indonesian islands of Aru and Seram (it was probably introduced by human settlers to the latter two places).

Cassowaries, a name that came from an original Malay word, *kasuari*, weigh up to 60 kg (132 lb) and, like most ratites, have represented a prodigious catch to any hunter. In fact, they are the largest of all forest animals on New Guinea. Throughout the island, cassowaries have played a full suite of roles, important as a source of myth and story, but also as functional products that are entwined with the social life of New Guinea's enormously diverse peoples. The island – the world's second largest – is divided politically between West Papua (Indonesia) and Papua New Guinea, but it is home to the most complex human mosaic on Earth.

It would be virtually impossible to summarise the cultural profile of cassowaries for such a heterogeneous society. Another caveat is that ethnographic portraits are rapidly moving pictures. Customs and conditions evolve. In Papua New Guinea, especially, stone and bone tools have given way to steel, bark cloth to cotton and pearl-shell to minted coin (incidentally, 'there is a cassowary on the PNG 20-toea

The extraordinary bony casque and bare warty neck and wattles on a Southern Cassowary make it seem one part dinosaur and one part bird.

piece' [pronounced 'toyah']).[1] Modern Papuans prefer mobile phones to cassowary-bone daggers.

However, the birds are still eaten and Joseph Ando, a hunter turned wildlife guide, describes how he once caught this formidable bird:

> We would look for the places where the cassowary feeds and make a trap on the trail where the bird walks. We would dig a small round hole and put round the whole thing a bush rope. When the trap was set we would cover the hole over with dried leaves that we had previously brushed from that very same spot. The bird would come along and put its foot into the trap and the rope, which was attached to a long stick rooted into the ground at the side, would close and tighten around the cassowary's leg. The big stick would spring back and the bird would be caught with one leg in the air and its head facing towards the ground. I caught about six **Dwarf Cassowary** *Casuarius bennetti* like this when I was a young hunter.[2]

The increase in hunting pressure has severely affected numbers so that now both **Northern Cassowary** *Casuarius unappendiculatus* and Southern Cassowary are considered vulnerable to extinction (estimates are 2,500–10,000 and more than 10,000 birds, respectively), while the upland Dwarf Cassowary is near-threatened.[3]

There are common themes in the relations between New Guinea people and cassowaries. The bird's distinctive hair-like feathers are still widely used for adornment and headdresses throughout the country, but the bare quills that once served as nose-pins or earrings are seldom encountered.

A single large individual is sufficient to feed a small hamlet for a couple of days and the birds are hunted and eaten wherever they occur. No community has succeeded in domesticating them, although the chicks are often taken and reared in the village to be eaten later. Or they are traded across New Guinea and also function as part of the monetary system, frequently being sent around the country on planes, sometimes when rather too large for the other passengers' peace of mind.

In New Guinea we were once about to board a small plane when we noticed that lying among the luggage waiting to be loaded was the head of a well-grown cassowary. The feet and body were encased in a sack which was tied up round the top so that the head just poked out. Sure enough when all the bags were onboard the cassowary was tossed on top. The passengers climbed in and we were all really relieved to see that between us and the bird was a curtain and between us and the pilot nothing. Had the bird decided to struggle and get free it could have caused havoc. Small planes have a history of falling from the sky in New Guinea. Is this the reason?[4]

Among Papuan ethnic groups, the Kukukuku (known also as the Angu), who live largely among the forested mountains of the Morobe Province of Papua New Guinea, are notable because their very identity is derived from the cassowary. At one time they were warlike cannibals and the very essence of what Westerners considered primitive savagery. Even to their Papuan neighbours, who coined the striking name (pronounced 'cooker-cooker'), they were

It pays to be cautious in the presence of a male Southern Cassowary, which has a reputation as the most dangerous bird on Earth. Yet the species is also a garden familiar at places like Cassowary House in Northern Queensland, Australia.

a people as free-roaming and wild as the *kokokoko*, the cassowary.[5]

In the traditional life of the Kukukuku, cassowaries were ubiquitous. The metatarsal bone was fashioned into a blunt-ended tool. Among married men, two cassowary thigh bones were worn around the waist as a symbol of their status.[6] A new wife can be acquired with a bride price of cassowary meat. (The custom is still widespread and presumably considered a reasonable trade for a European woman too: 'I was once offered five cassowaries, five pigs and 5,000 kina for my 15-year-old English daughter when we were up in the Highlands!')[7] In a nose-piercing ceremony for young boys, the septums were punctured with cassowary-bone implements, and in a separate initiation rite, adolescent males were ceremonially wounded on the face and arms with the bird's wing bones.[8]

The cassowary's sharpened tibia made a dagger-like awl and throughout New Guinea it was used as a lethal weapon. The Australian naturalist Tim Flannery, writing of the Miyanmin tribe, describes how, once they had selected and surrounded an opponent's village, the war party would often attack at dawn and kill all the adults, dispatching them with a cassowary blade thrust down between the shoulderblade and collarbone. 'Anaru mimed a demonstration using an old blood-stained dagger, with me as a mock victim. The feeling of his sinewy arms round my neck pinning my body to his, and the point of the bone biting into my skin, sent a shiver down my spine.'[9] The adult bodies were then butchered for eating, but these Miyanmin cannibals would often carry off their victims' offspring, raising the children lovingly as if they were their own.

One famous usage of a body part seems to combine simple practicality with a symbolic appropriation of the bird's innate aggression. Cassowaries are armed with long pointed

toes, and the inner digit bears a stiletto-like appendage that can be 12 cm (5 in) long. These formidable points were used to tip Papuan arrows and were also 'attached to angle-headed fighting sticks which can do a lot of damage when brought down hard on an opponent's head'.[10] For their original owner the claws are no less lethal. Competing male birds can do serious injury to one another, but they are also quite capable of inflicting fatal wounds on other animals, such as dogs or pigs, and occasionally on humans.

The inner claw is the one characteristic widely known about this otherwise rather enigmatic, shy forest bird. It is almost always highlighted in written accounts by Western commentators, even in authoritative works of science, and often to the exclusion of other facts:

'armed with a long sharp claw – a deadly weapon in combat'[11]

'Wounds from the claws can be terrible . . . a likelihood of massive bleeding'[12]

'very dangerous if cornered . . . big kicking strokes . . . can disembowel an enemy in no time. They are quite capable of tearing man apart'[13]

The repetitions have cemented the cassowary's renown as the world's most dangerous bird. Fatalities in New Guinea are said to be regular but are largely unrecorded and a modern Papuan suggested to me personally that deaths are probably extremely rare. However, the death of a teenage boy, Philip Granville, in Northern Queensland in 1926 has been recounted for many decades. The contemporaneous newspaper report described how Granville, having struck at the bird with his bridle, 'was kicked in the base of the neck. The bird's toe, penetrating into the throat, severed the jugular vein. The unfortunate lad ran towards home for about 200

Cassowary bone was once an important material for making tools in New Guinea, such as this lethal dagger.

yards and then collapsed and died.'[14] Sixty years later, a secondary account felt compelled to add how, 'According to his sister . . . he had staggered and crawled "until he ran out of blood".'[15]

Exaggeration may be part of the poor cassowary's lot, but caution in the presence of such a bird is never misplaced, as one of its close neighbours makes clear:

> Cassowaries are usually quite wary and retiring, but when they become accustomed to people they have to be managed carefully. We have them most days at Cassowary House in Kuranda, far north Queensland, and have to be particularly wary when the male first brings the chicks to visit. We always warn people not to approach too closely, and above all not to run away if they meet the birds unexpectedly. The best thing to do is simply stand quietly, or position a tree between you and the birds. Cassowaries are often very inquisitive birds; when we do gardening or maintenance here, they come and see what is going on and may suddenly appear at your side without warning, watching with interest before wandering away again.
>
> We had an elderly English couple staying who knew our local cassowaries well and were familiar with how to behave around them. One day we sent them off up to the Crater National Park on the Atherton Tablelands, and they came back clearly very shaken and somewhat scratched-up and torn. They claimed to have been attacked by a cassowary, which was surprising. They'd been standing in the forest by the bower of a Golden Bowerbird and the cassowary had come towards them. Instead of standing still and savouring the meeting, they panicked and tried to run away, getting scratched by the wait-a-while vines and falling over and smashing the camera, whilst the bird of course followed to see what was happening! It came right by them, then wandered off; had they just stood still or gone behind a tree

nothing more would have come of it. A waste of a great encounter basically!

> You can also never legislate for stupidity and the unexpected, and just before we took over here one of the wildlife tour leaders suddenly decided to pick up one of the small stripey chicks. The male bird of course did attack, rushing straight at him and making him release the bird.
>
> I once got caught myself with one of our dogs right by our back door, which was unexpectedly locked just as the male and his family came around the corner. Dogs and cassowaries are a bad mix so we segregate them very effectively, but in this case I was bailed up without exit, so all I could do was push the dog up against the screen and keep myself between it and the bird whilst yelling to get the door opened! Happily the bird was more interested in what was going on than being in full defence mode, so I got away with it after an uncomfortable couple of minutes jammed up against the screen subduing a squirming dog and keeping the bird at bay!
>
> Another time I met the male along a track when I had a dog with us, but luckily I had a very sensible and well-trained dog, who obeyed without question, and I was carrying a spade, which I used to keep the bird back whilst hastily retreating. He was very determined to get at the dog and kept bumping against the bulwark as we backed up. All part of the joys of living in the wet tropics![16]

Cassowaries are now seriously threatened in Australia by loss of rainforest, but they are also regular victims of road collisions, especially in towns like Mission Beach, Far North Queensland. Today there may be as few as 1,200 adults left.

Emu family *Dromaiidae*

Emu *Dromaius novaehollandiae*. The name of this stately Australian endemic is not, as one might imagine, derived from one of the numerous and highly variable Aboriginal words for the bird. (Yet to give a sense of this large synonymy, the Aborigines from the state of Victoria alone call the Emu *coura*, *myoure*, *barrimal* and *bigourumgar*.) There are two likely sources for 'emu'. It either comes from *ema*, the Portuguese word for a very large bird, originally a crane or an ostrich, or it comes from the Arabic *na'ama* (or *na'ema*) for ostrich.[1] Given the long Moorish residence in Iberia, this Arabic word could itself have been the source for its Portuguese equivalent.

Whichever was the primary source, *ema* seems to have been used firstly as one of two interchangeable titles for

Emus are highly inquisitive and can be drawn in with jangling keys or shiny objects.

A 'woolly cushion on the top of two poles' rather nicely describes the Emu's appearance.

another New Guinean ratite, the Southern Cassowary. Portuguese merchants would certainly have been among the first Europeans to encounter this latter bird in the Moluccas in the sixteenth century. It strengthens the idea that the name was of Portuguese origin and was transferred first from the crane (or ostrich) and then to the cassowary.

When English-speaking naturalists reached Australia two centuries later, they were able to pass on the name *ema* to a third type of bird. Since 'cassowary' already existed as a perfectly adequate word for the New Guinea bird, they were able to reattach the anglicised version, 'emu', to the other large flightless species when Emus were themselves encountered on the Australian continent. (To make matters more complicated the original *ema* also became fixed as a Portuguese/Brazilian name for yet a fourth ratite species, the rhea of South America.) [2]

The word 'emu' may come from elsewhere, but the bird itself is deeply embedded in Australian identity.

The Aboriginal paintings at Carnarvon Gorge, Queensland, Australia, are thought to be 2,000 years old. Among the boomerangs and stencilled human hands are images of Emu footprints.

Since 1912 a rather beady-eyed example has stood, with a Red Kangaroo, either side of Australia's coat of arms. It is de facto the national bird and a trademark symbol for numerous Australian products, as well as for the arid landscapes to which it is so beautifully adapted. The bird's image has become subliminally familiar to many millions through the Emu motif on the official kit of Australia's once all-conquering cricket team. Modern Australians also carry the bird in their pockets, featured on the 50-cent coin. Since 1901 it has also been the title and logo for the country's top ornithological journal. [3]

Yet the bird's cultural importance long pre-dates a European presence in Australia. Emus have made an enormous contribution to Aboriginal society, both as food and as an emblem of their identity. Emu images feature even now in an enormous range of artworks. One early example is the 'bird tracks', usually considered to be footprints of Emu, which were pecked into rock surfaces as long as 15,000 years ago and constitute some of the most ancient 'bird' images anywhere in the world. [4] The Emu looms equally large in living myths and legend. For instance, a creation story of the Yuwaalaraay in New South Wales describes how the sun was made by throwing an Emu egg into the sky. [5]

The bird's practical applications are legion. The Emu is among the largest species in the world – the biggest are 1.9 m (6.2 ft) tall and weigh 50 kg (110 lb) – and Aborigines still eat its high-quality beef-like meat and eggs. They once used the feathers for ceremonial decoration, the bones as implements and weapons, while the empty shells served as water vessels. Unlike the ostrich's egg, those of the Emu have a dark olive-green outer surface with progressively paler layers within. This makes them an especially rich medium for carved designs; worked Emu eggs are both an Aboriginal art form and, now, a highly saleable commodity. Often one finds them with hand-painted designs by Aboriginal artists

(alongside kangaroo-claw backscratchers) in a particular kind of Australian souvenir shop. Another valuable by-product is Emu oil or fat, which was applied as a lubricant to Aboriginal weapons and equipment, and as a medicine for their aches and pains. It is used therapeutically today and may have genuine anti-inflammatory properties.

Many of the Aboriginal techniques for catching the birds exploited their highly inquisitive nature. They can be drawn towards humans by waving a red cloth or hat, and shiny objects seem to exercise an almost infallible attraction. Emus in zoos will peck at the buttons on the clothes of their human visitors, and tame birds will eat 'nuts and bolts, small pieces of machinery, car keys, jewellery, money' and bits of broken glass. [6] With domestic stock it is even advised how they can be 'captured by standing in the pen and rattling a key chain until the bird approaches to investigate'. [7]

One of the Aboriginal ploys was to dig a pit filled with sharpened stakes. The covered trap was then seeded with some attractive bright object to bring the birds to it. Another technique involved an artificial head and neck, which was manipulated to mimic the movements of a real Emu and bring it within range of a spear or net. Or they were lured in by a ball of feathers dangling from a thread on a twig. A highly imaginative strategy, widely used in Aboriginal society, was to poison a waterhole with *pituri*, a drug made from the nicotine-bearing leaves of *Duboisia*, and wait until the birds were stupefied. [8]

White settlers in Australia also shot and ate Emus, but the species was perhaps blessed in its dull brindled brown-grey plumage – likened memorably to 'a woolly cushion on the top of two poles' – which meant that it never suffered the kinds of exploitation inflicted on the fancy-feathered ostrich (see page 16). [9] If anything Emus have benefited from the spread of European-style settlement and agriculture, and particularly from the creation of artificial watering holes.

They also eat arable crops and were long considered a major pest species in wheat-growing areas. Although flightless, the birds perform seasonal journeys – two Emus bearing leg rings were retrapped 900 km (560 miles) from their original capture point – in search of rain-freshened country.[10] These can build into mass movements involving as many as 70,000 birds, whose impact upon crops can be devastating.

THE EMU WAR

This potential menace, in turn, triggered one of the most notorious plans for intended mass slaughter devised for any Australian bird. Mercifully it is best remembered today for the note of high farce that accompanied its implementation. Often referred to as the 'Emu War' of 1932, itself a name heavy with irony, it originated from Australia's ministry of defence as an exercise combining target practice for the troops, with vermin control for depression-afflicted farmers in Western Australia. The plan was to drive part of an estimated 20,000-strong Emu flock along a 35 km (21 mile) front towards an ambush point on the No. 1 Rabbit-proof Fence.

The waiting troops were armed with rifles, with two Lewis machine-guns able to discharge 500 rounds a minute and a Fox Movietone cinematographer as audio-visual reinforcements. In the event, the Emus proved a far more subtle and treacherous foe than the authorities had imagined. Rather than the mass cull intended, the Australian troops inflicted only a few hundred casualties in more than a month. The commanding officer, Major G P W Meredith, complained that Emu had the 'invulnerability of tanks' and reported birds that were still alive with as many as five bullet wounds. He also noted the birds' capacity for camouflaged withdrawal and likened them to that most feared of all Anglo-imperial enemies, the Zulu impi. Nor did the struggle close without the bird themselves inflicting casualties: 'a truck belonging to one of the local farmers pursued and ran down a lone emu with the unfortunate result that the bird "became entangled in the steering gear". The vehicle veered off the road out of control, in the process destroying "a whole half a chain of fence before it was finally brought to a standstill".'[11]

The immediate outcome of the Emu War was acute official embarrassment, but the birds eventually succumbed to a more efficient plan based on government bounty payments. In 1935–6 the slaughter in Western Australia topped 72,000 birds.[12] In Queensland, where Emus were implicated in the spread of the invasive prickly pear, 121,768 birds were killed between 1926–8.[13] On three of Australia's offshore islands, earlier settler exploitation may have been less systematic but its impact was far worse. It resulted in the extinction of three distinct races of Emu: on King Island (before 1802), Kangaroo Island (1820s) and Tasmania (1865). The mainland population, concentrated on the western and eastern sides of the continent, is now currently stable and numbers c.675,000 birds.

Despite its reputation among Australian cereal producers as a pest, the species is generally considered docile and tractable. Emu farming has been developed since the 1970s and is valued for a variety of products including the meat, oil and high-quality leather. There are also ranches in Peru, China and North America, the latter with an estimated population of a million birds. The American Emu Association even holds an annual week-long event to broadcast the health-giving properties and versatility of Emu-derived products.[14]

There was one Emu export to Europe and the USA in the 1970s which was infamous not for its docility, but for its frequent acts of random violence. The late entertainer Rod Hull developed a puppet character while resident in Australia and seems to have based his bird 'Emu', both in appearance and personality, less on the real *Dromaius novaehollandiae* than on the Southern Cassowary, whose own reputation for aggression is well founded but often exaggerated (see page 22). Hull's bird had a predominantly bluish-black plumage and red throat, which are suggestive of the Southern Cassowary's colours, but it has to be admitted that the strands of silver thread in the body plumage, the banana-yellow bill and the mustard legs are all pure invention.

While the bird was inspired by Australia and its avifauna, it is worth noting that neither Rod Hull nor his Emu register at all with the Australian public. However, the bird and the Englishman were extremely well known for attacking two great television institutions on both sides of the Atlantic: America's Johnny Carson and Britain's much-loved Michael Parkinson. Emu's humiliation of the latter in the show broadcast in November 1976, when he forced Parkinson to the ground and savaged the TV legend's head, leg and foot, was subsequently voted one of the great moments of British television. In the Johnny Carson attack, the bird abused both the show host and his guest, the comedian Richard Pryor, who had just undergone reconstructive surgery on his face after he set himself on fire while freebasing cocaine. In this instance, Emu's attack alternated between the comic's plastic surgery and his groin, but it should be added that Pryor was as much overcome by laughter as fear. Another wonderful moment of unscripted madness came in 1972, when Emu ate the bouquet of the Queen Mother during a Royal Variety Performance. Somewhat perversely, Hull's creation was one of the best-loved bird puppets of the modern era.

Elephant Bird family *Aepyornithidae*

The now extinct **Elephant Bird** *Aepyornis maximus* of Madagascar was formidable in scale, standing 3.5 m (11.5 ft) tall and weighing as much as half a tonne – the heaviest bird ever to have lived. The latest morphological evidence suggests that in deportment elephant birds were more horizontal than vertical, tending to stoop the head low, and felt no need to pull themselves up to their full height. They were the largest terrestrial species on their island and may have thrived, flightless and invulnerable, for 75 million years. Within a few centuries of human arrival on Madagascar, they had been hounded to oblivion.[1]

It might then seem eccentric to give space to a bird which became extinct as long as 1,150 years ago, but *Aepyornis* has been almost impossible to ignore either while it lived or after its passing.[2] The way it continues to stir scientific conjecture mirrors closely the manner in which the bird conjured fantastic speculations from the medieval imagination. Tales about Elephant Birds were recounted in places thousands of kilometres from their native shores and among peoples who would never know the unadorned, yet equally remarkable, facts.

It is now generally agreed that the fabled creature known as the *roc* (also *rokh*, *rukh*, *rucke*, *peng* and, in some European texts, griffon) had its origins in this magnificent Malagasy endemic. The *roc* surfaces most notably in four of the *Tales from the Arabian Nights*. In one of these, Sinbad the Sailor wanders ashore on a tropical island to find a great shining dome without an entrance. As he marvels at the sealed edifice, he happens to look skywards and observe the 16 m (53 ft) long wings of an enormous bird blotting out the sun. He quickly realises that the dome before him is the creature's fabulous egg. When the *roc* settles to incubate, Sinbad finds himself trapped beneath, but binds his turban to its feet and is later carried aloft towards a skyline of heroic adventure.

The *roc* resurfaced in works of natural history for several centuries and various museums claimed relics from the creature – a feather or a claw – until the seventeenth century.[3] However, the best-known European account of the bird, post-dating the *Arabian Nights* and yet comparable in the way that it gives a wide berth to the truth, is in that model of the traveller's tale, Marco Polo's *Il milione*. One overlap between the bird of Sinbad and that of the Venetian traveller is its vaunted capacity to kill and eat elephants. Reporting the testimony of Arabian informants, Marco Polo wrote:

> in build [rukhs] are just like eagles but of the most colossal size . . . that one of them can pounce on an elephant and carry it up to a great height in the air.

Then it lets go, so that the elephant drops to earth and is smashed to pulp, whereupon the gryphon bird perches on the carcase and feeds at its ease. They add that they have a wingspan of thirty paces and their wing-feathers are twelve paces long and a thickness proportionate to their length.[4]

The egg of the Elephant Bird may not have been, as Sinbad reported, 50 paces in circumference, but it was immense – seven times the size of an ostrich's, with a capacity of 9 litres (2 gallons), and the equivalent of 200 chicken eggs. Engineers have suggested that it would be structurally impossible for an egg to be bigger.[5] Several intact examples, which had long been prized by the Malagasy as objects of extreme rarity, eventually surfaced in the mid nineteenth century and provided the best evidence that behind the *roc* legend there was a genuine bird. Today about 30 unbroken eggs exist.[6]

With the subsequent discovery of bone fragments palaeontologists were able to establish that there were between six and 12 large flightless species on Madagascar. They were almost entirely vegetarian and were exterminated by a combination of habitat loss and hunting pressure. Radiocarbon dating of eggs suggests a date of AD 850–1150 for the last, although seventeenth-century tales of the *vouroupatra*, a Malagasy name for an ostrich-sized species, raises the possibility of survival of at least one species of elephant bird until the French colonial period. Warren King, author of *The Endangered Birds of the World*, thought the eyewitness accounts sufficiently credible to include it with the Dodo (see page 232) in a list of birds extinct after AD 1600.

Moa family *Dinornithidae*

The extraordinary moas of New Zealand played out much the same drama of extinction on these Pacific islands as the elephant birds once did in Madagascar. Endemic, flightless and ranging upwards in size to the gigantic 3.6 m (12 ft) tall **Great Moa** *Dinornis maximus*, the whole family had enjoyed millions of years as New Zealand's largest organisms. Prior to the arrival of Polynesian settlers (from about AD 800 onwards) they had never encountered a terrestrial mammal larger than a tiny mouse and knew just a single predator, the massive (also extinct) Haast's Eagle.

Under these relatively benign conditions, moas had assumed the roles of large herbivores, with about ten species radiating out to fill this and other ecological niches. The tallest have invariably seized the headlines but some moas had the squat proportions, if not quite the small size, of New Zealand's other endemic bird family, the kiwis (see page 28). In fact, the word 'moa' comes from the Polynesian name for the domestic chicken.

Maori colonisation of New Zealand unleashed a period of intense hunting pressure, and subsequent archaeological investigation has revealed about 300 locations across the islands where the birds were trapped and butchered. At the largest of these processing sites, the cumulative catch may have been as many as 90,000 birds.[1] By the time that Europeans arrived in the region, the moas' physical presence

in New Zealand had been largely reduced to mere bone and egg fragments in hunting middens.

It seems remarkable how quickly the Maoris' collective memory of the giants was largely erased once the birds were extinct. Victorian studies of Maori sayings, poems and myths unearthed only a small number of references to moas. One of the best known, an old saying, itself suggesting regret at their own terminal impact upon the birds, ran as follows:

> *Ka ngaro I te ngaro a te Moa*
> Lost, as the Moa is lost [2]

Not until the reign of Queen Victoria did British settlers start to appreciate that they had just missed out on some of the world's most extraordinary birds. In 1838 a single bone fragment was the cause of a desperate and, at times, embittered colonial quest for moa that has not ceased even today. An intriguing aspect of this search, which has recently evolved into a specialism for cranks and crypto-zoologists, has been a wish to force our gaze beyond the horizon of possibility.[3] Some of the most recent moa 'sightings' in 2007 involved the discovery of the 'nest' and 'tracks' of **Small Scrub Moa** *Anomalopteryx didiformis* in the Urewera Range, near Hawke's Bay, North Island.[4]

The persistence of these 'eyewitness' accounts of a species long considered to have been extirpated may shed real light, not so much on the birds, but on human nature. The recent parallel claims of Ivory-billed Woodpecker sightings in North America may reflect a similar desire, deeply rooted in some of us, to defer or circumvent the desolate finality of extinction (see page 340).

There is one intriguing postscript to the moa's tale. A team from Oxford, UK, and New Zealand's Otago University have managed to sequence the mitochondrial DNA of two moa genera from bone remains.[5] One of the proposals – at a putative cost of NZ $50 million – which flowed from this DNA work, was to isolate moa genes and clone them with

ostrich and Emu genes, to reproduce large moa-like birds. However, the Ngāi Tahu Maori community of South Island has contested the right of the scientific team to the genes, claiming that all New Zealand's flora and fauna are under Maori ownership. There is a leaven of irony in this claim, given that the Maori brought extinction to the moas, yet there is another intriguing facet to the row. The notion that a bird's identity is a phenomenon susceptible to cultural possession, or control, suggests how sometimes we are incapable of disentangling the imagined version we hold of birds in our (collective) heads from the living creatures themselves.[6]

Kiwi family *Apterygidae*

The five flightless, nocturnal species that comprise this remarkable family are endemic to New Zealand and rank among the most unusual of all the world's birds. The kiwi's face is heavily whiskered, the legs are short but stout, and the whole body cloaked in fine hair-like feathers. As one commentator noted, it seems like 'a bird trying to be a mammal'.[1] Kiwi heads are small proportional to their bodies, the eyes and vestigial wings are tiny and the tail is non-existent. If you plucked the largest species, the **Great Spotted Kiwi** *Apteryx haastii*, its 2–3 kg (4.5–6.5 lb) body would have the smooth swollen contours of an immense gourd or pear.

The long awl-like bill is unusual for bearing nostrils at its hooked tip which, exceptional among birds, give the kiwi an acute sense of smell. When the famous British naturalist David Attenborough encountered a kiwi, he found a novel means to thwart the bird's usual powers of detection. He was standing on a beach at night when a kiwi, looking like 'a small hunched homunculus no more than a foot high, stalked cautiously out of the bush'. When it began to walk towards him, feeding along the wrack line, Attenborough

had the presence of mind to lie down and drape himself in several rotting fronds of seaweed. The 'creature's mammalian inclinations' were thus neutralised by the weed's sulphurous foetor and it proceeded to walk right past him. 'I had the privilege', he wrote later, 'of allowing one of the world's most extraordinary birds to pick up its food a few inches in front of me'.[2]

It is a source of acute anxiety to New Zealand environmentalists that all five species of kiwi are now threatened with extinction. While the **North Island Brown Kiwi** *Apteryx mantelli* (35,000 birds) and **Southern Brown Kiwi** *Apteryx australis* (27,000 birds) are the two most common species, in the last half-century they have suffered declines of around 90 per cent. Meanwhile, the total numbers for the **Little Spotted Kiwi** *Apteryx owenii* (1,100 birds) and **Okarito Kiwi** *Apteryx rowi* (several hundred) are perilously small. A major problem, aside from habitat loss, is predation by non-native mammals, such as dogs, cats, stoats and brush-tailed possums. At one site in 1987 a single feral German Shepherd killed 500 kiwis in less than two months before it was shot.[3] One solution, and a mainstay for some

North Island Brown Kiwis have such extraordinary powers of smell they can sniff out earthworms deep in the soil, but their sight is so poor they can bump into things as they run away.

kiwi populations, has been the transfer of birds to smaller offshore islands, such as Kapiti and Little Barrier Island, where the alien predators are absent or have been eliminated. New Zealand environmentalists have pioneered techniques in the control or complete extermination of unwanted non-native animals and now lead the world in this critically important field. Another scheme being explored is kiwi-aversion training, which involves dogs being given a mild electric shock if they show an unhealthily high response to kiwi stimuli.[4]

Given the kiwis' scarcity or inaccessibility it is hardly surprising that most modern New Zealanders will never once see the real thing in the wild. Yet in view of these facts, it may seem curious that the kiwi is not just the national bird, it has become a part of the very identity of the country and its citizens. The euphonious disyllable, which is an onomatopoeic rendering of the birds' call first coined by the Maori, has become the key alternative name for the human population.

The Bank of New Zealand (1861) and New Zealand Insurance Company (1859) had already adopted kiwi imagery at a very early stage in their commercial development. However, its international application as a catch-all term for New Zealanders probably originated with the army. All of the country's early regiments had a kiwi on their regimental insignia. Eventually the part became a symbol for the whole, and New Zealand troops were known collectively as 'kiwis'. As one kiwi notes:

> There were grounds for our servicemen identifying with the bird. In both world wars, most of them had originally been farm boys, like my father, and they would have been familiar with the character of the bird, since the kiwi was more prevalent then. Farmers would have been aware of its pugnacious, combative nature, and known that it was quite capable of giving the farm dogs a hard time.[5]

A modern Maori scholar gives her slant on its current symbolic connotations:

> The NZ $1 coin is sometimes called a 'kiwi dollar' because on one side it features a kiwi and the silver fern – both prominent NZ icons. I can also think of *kiwi bacon* (pork, not kiwi meat!), and *kiwi saver* (a New Zealand superannuation scheme). I think the kiwi has also become a symbol for conservation – predation from stoats, cats and dogs have had such a devastating impact on this bird, we have come to admire its determination to survive against such odds. I guess this is how most New Zealanders see themselves – as underdogs that overcome many obstacles to succeed. Sir Edmund Hillary, Dame Kiri Te Kanawa and Jonah Lomu all symbolise what it means to be a 'kiwi'. Most New Zealanders do in fact see themselves as 'kiwis' – particularly those overseas.[6]

It's a measure of the dominance of the association between endemic bird and the people in general that the Auckland telephone directory lists 180 businesses with the bird's name. The New Zealand Rugby League team is officially called the Kiwis (the cricket team is the Black Caps, but the Kiwis is a common nickname) and the female team is the Kiwi Ferns. In a recent dictionary of New Zealand slang, there were several kiwi listings, including 'kiwified' (immigrants who became indistinguishable from the average New Zealander), 'kiwiana' (popular cultural items) and 'kiwi green' (home-grown cannabis).[7]

The name – even the bird's own distinctive silhouette – has been helped to worldwide fame through two other global products with strong New Zealand connections. The first is 'Kiwi' shoe polish, which was first developed in Melbourne by a Scots-born Australian called William Ramsay at the beginning of last century. He gave the name to his new shoe-cleaning agent in honour of his New Zealand wife, Annie Elizabeth (née Meek). Ramsay died in 1914 leaving an estate of £11,500, but his Kiwi brand is now a household name in 150 countries.[8] Sixty years after Ramsay launched one of his best-selling lines, I can well recall wondering about the weird bird on the tin lid, as I applied dark-tan to an eight-year-old's school shoes.

The other near-universal kiwi is the sweet, watery, green-fleshed fruit with a hairy skin. In fact it is conceivable that there are many people, particularly in non-English-speaking countries, who know and enjoy the fruit without realising that its name derives from a flightless bird. The fruit itself was originally an Asian plant *Actinidia deliciosa*, popularly known as Chinese gooseberry. Its global conquest was initiated by the redoubtable Isabel Frasier, the principal of Wanganui Girls' College, who brought back seeds from its native China in 1904. These were developed by a local nurseryman (the first fruits were gathered in 1910) and eventually marketed to the UK (13 tonnes were exported in 1952). Six years later a fruit-packing company in Auckland dallied briefly with the idea of calling it 'melonette', but changed tack when they heard of high tariffs on imported melons, and quickly settled on the name by which it has become world famous.[9]

One of the more bizarre by-products of this implicit identification of New Zealand's national bird with its citizenry is a gigantic white kiwi in the heart of the southern English countryside. It measures 127 m (419 ft) tall – over

The world's largest kiwi artefact is in the English countryside at Bulford, Wiltshire. It was carved after the First World War by 'kiwi' soldiers homesick for their native New Zealand.

▶ Maori cloaks
adorned with kiwi
feathers were items
of immense value and
ritual importance.

twice the height of Nelson's Column and three times that of the Statue of Liberty – and has a beak 45 m (148.5 ft) long. After the end of the First World War, Kiwi troops stationed in Wiltshire vented their deep frustration at not being repatriated by rioting in their barracks. To give them a more patriotic outlet for their thwarted energies, the authorities had them carve the great bird into the chalk hillside above Bulford in 1919. For years its maintenance was paid for by the producers of Kiwi shoe polish, but it has long since been taken to heart by Wiltshire people, as a cherished landmark that has given its name to Bulford's Kiwi pub and Kiwi primary school. Thus, the white chalk flightless ratite has become both an English icon of local distinctiveness, but also a monument to a New Zealand sense of exile, 20,000 km (12,000 miles) from its native land.

The bird's relations with humans long pre-date the arrival of white colonists. New Zealand Maori referred to kiwi as the 'hidden bird of Tāne' (after Tāne Mahuta, Maori god of the forest) due to its nocturnal and secretive nature. They had sustainably hunted kiwi for more than a thousand years and it is a measure of how their tracking skills combined with exceptional natural-historical ability that they had names for at least five kiwi species or subspecies.[10] The bird's flesh seems to have been an acquired taste. One writer likened it to eel or wild boar, while another compared the meat to 'pork boiled in old coffee'.[11] The eggs were also prized and noted for their fine flavour and while the clutch often comprises just a single egg, proportionate to the size of the adult female, that egg is the largest produced by any of the world's birds. Sometimes it is as much as a quarter of her weight. A human equivalent would be a 57 kg (9 stone) woman bearing a 14 kg (31.5 lb) baby.

The bird's feathers are notable for their simple structure and kiwis were initially spared the kind of persecution suffered by other gloriously plumed ratites, such as the ostrich. However, during the second half of the nineteenth century, Maori craftsmen and -women became skilled at fashioning traditional woven garments of flax (*Phormium tenax*) into stylised and highly valued feather cloaks (*kahu huruhuru*). Along with the brown kiwis, the brightly coloured plumages from other birds, such as the New Zealand Pigeon (*kererū*), the striking New Zealand Kaka, an endemic species of parrot, and the Tui were also used. Of all the feather cloaks, garments covered entirely with kiwi (*kahu kiwi*) or kākā (*kahu kura*) feathers were considered the most prestigious and were immensely prized by Maori chiefs, particularly those *kahu kiwi* with patterns or borders that included a trim of unusual white albino kiwi feathers.

Western costumiers were soon alerted to the unusual quality of the kiwi's plumage and exploited the birds to make modern female fashion accessories such as muffs and scarves.[12] Another specialised usage of the feathers was in the making of tied flies for trout fishing.[13] All of these later industrialised forms of exploitation took a heavy toll on the wild kiwi population and completely swamped the more moderate harvest of traditional Maori hunters. Today kiwis are entirely protected by law: 'even feathers from deceased birds are distributed to Maori weavers by the government-owned Department of Conservation.'[14]

Megapode family *Megapodiidae*

This small but economically important family includes a group of ground-dwelling medium-sized birds with rather plain grey or brown plumage. The 22 species are Indo-Australian in distribution. Essentially they are spread across the numerous islands scattered between mainland Asia and the south Pacific to Australia's east coast, with the highest diversity in eastern Indonesia and New Guinea. Megapodes have been a traditional food for humans across the region, yet the hunting was usually small scale, and few species now occur in sufficient numbers to represent a major harvest. Several, including the **Biak Megapode** *Megapodius geelvinkianus*, **Micronesian Megapode** *Megapodius laperouse*, **Nicobar Megapode** *Megapodius nicobariensis* and **Tongan Megapode** *Megapodius pritchardii*, are restricted to just one or to a handful of tiny islands and have world ranges of less than 3,000 km² (1,158 miles²).[1]

Despite their plain looks and isolated localities, the megapodes are widely considered one of the most fascinating

The megapode family including this Scrubfowl are some of the most industrious of all the world's birds and are equipped with feet to match their mound-building labours.

of all bird families. They have excited scientific and cultural interest comparable with the world's ultimate glamour creatures, the birds-of-paradise (which, incidentally, share a good deal of the megapodes' distribution; see page 396). At the heart of our preoccupations lie their extraordinary breeding arrangements, which are unlike those of all other birds and more closely resemble those of crocodiles or turtles.

Megapodes do not physically incubate their eggs but bury them in mounds of decomposing vegetation, or excavate pits so that they can be warmed by geothermal energy. The unusual mode of incubation explains the origins of their rather odd name: 'megapode' is of Greek derivation and means 'big foot', a reference to the stout legs and powerful toes that are used in their earth-moving activities.

In some species their very particular requirement for volcanically heated soils leads to many thousands of birds converging on a relatively small traditional 'nest' area. In turn this concentration of breeding activity can result in a massive seasonal deposition of eggs, and while adult megapodes may not have represented a major source of food for humans, these buried clutches certainly have. One of the best examples involves the **Melanesian Megapode** *Megapodius eremita*, a species that inhabits the chain of Pacific islands to the north-west of New Guinea, including the Bismarck and Solomon archipelagos. In 1978, at one site called Pokili on New Britain island (Papua New Guinea), there were an estimated 53,000 breeding birds present. In the past, wars were sometimes fought to secure the strange fruits of these tropical beaches, which can run to millions of eggs, while the ownership and management of such sites were sometimes a royal prerogative.[2]

Before giving an account of their economic importance and the conservation emergencies that have resulted from

excessive human consumption, it is worth making a short tour through the basic facts of megapode reproduction. There are three methods of incubation. Most of the family (probably 13 species) construct mounds of vegetation, in which the heat is generated by microbial decomposition. Three other species – the **Maleo** *Macrocephalon maleo*, Tongan Megapode and **Moluccan Megapode** *Eulipoa wallacei* – use either solar-heated beaches or geothermal sources, while six species use a combination of two or three of these various strategies.

One of the most industrious in the family is the **Scrubfowl** *Megapodius reinwardt*, which is spread west to east, from the Indonesian island of Lombok, through southern New Guinea and along Australia's northern coastal fringe. It is notable for its prodigious digging capacity and one nest mound found in Australia's Northern Territory was 18 m long, 5 m wide and 3 m high (59.4 x 16.5 x 9.9 ft). Another was reported to be 8 m high and 51 m in circumference (26.4 x 168.3 ft). Some of the largest constructions, which are often communal and used for several generations, are calculated to include more than 50 tonnes of material.[3] Perhaps even more impressive is the Scrubfowl recorded to have dug out a stone weighing 6.9 kg (15.3 lb) and to have moved it 70 cm (27.5 in). To give a sense of its Sisyphean efforts, a 77 kg (12 stone) human would have to move a rock weighing over 600 kg (1,322 lb) for almost twice their body length.[4]

The male megapode does most of this building work, leaving the female to devote herself to the production of her marvellous eggs. Each is about one-sixth the weight of the mother and in the Maleo it can be anything up to 250 g (8.8 oz). There is an Indonesian folk tale describing how the female Maleo faints after laying such a prodigy. Unlike chicken eggs, in which the yolk represents less than a third of the contents, megapode eggs have a yolk that is 50–67 per cent of total volume. They are thus seven or eight times richer than hen's eggs and have been described as 'super eggs', which helps to explain the large human appetite for them, as well as the chick's advanced state of development when it hatches as much as 80 days after being laid.

Once the young megapode is ready to emerge, it pushes with its legs and back on the thin shell and then digs upwards through the earthy mound. This 'unpleasant, dark journey' to the surface, which is the chick's first experience of independent existence, causes it to lose the protective waxy sheath enclosing its feathers. Once it finally breaks free, the young bird resembles a quail or small partridge and is entirely ready for its solitary life, receiving no form of parental care whatsoever. 'I have seen Maleo chicks on several occasions fly straight away into the rain forest immediately after they have emerged from the ground.'[5]

Although human exploitation of the eggs is long-standing, it is mainly in recent decades that the impact has been so negative. Habitat loss and increased human populations are important factors, but just as significant is the changing cultural context of the egg harvests. Formerly, collecting was a privilege reserved for certain castes and among those communities it was governed by strict ceremony. The ritual tended to ensure that the birds were allowed to maintain self-sustaining numbers, and consumption was limited to local communities. Since the 1950s, however, these patterns have broken down. At the height of unregulated collection in the late 1970s, the Melanesian Megapode site at Pokili was a place of industrial activity, with 200 people working the burrows at any one time. Eggs were excavated and wrapped in palm leaves then loaded on to lorries for local distribution. A conservative estimate of the resulting annual harvest was 4.89 million eggs.[6]

Yet the harvest of megapode eggs is not without its hazards. At one site where Melanesian Megapodes lay in the black sands of an active volcano, Mount Tavurvur in East New Britain, the egg hunters have to be aware of the huge stray boulders occasionally spewed out by the volcano and also of the risk posed by their own excavations collapsing and burying them alive.[7]

If the risks are high, so are the rewards. In the case of the Maleo of Sulawesi, harvested eggs are traded at five times the price of chicken eggs and as far away as Jakarta, 1,350 km (840 miles) from the site of harvest. They are particularly popular around Christmas, when they are given away as gifts to friends and family.[8] The Maleo's wider fortunes are in many ways indicative of the whole family's recent history. In 2000, of the 131 known nest grounds, 42 had been abandoned, 38 were severely threatened, 34 were threatened, 12 were of unknown status and just five were considered viable. The Maleo is now one of the nine megapode species deemed at risk of extinction.[9]

However, the answer to megapode conservation may not lie in stopping all forms of collecting, as this fascinating account suggests:

> The villagers of Kailolo, a town on Haruku – one of Indonesia's Spice Islands – harvest nearly 40,000 Moluccan Megapode eggs a year. The species lays in sun-warmed sand and, with the exception of ten or so locations visited by a few birds, all the world's

population nests on two beaches: at Kailolo and at Galela on the island of Halmahera, 575 km to the north. One of the current owners at Galela asserts that his grandfather founded the nest beach by seeding it with 40 eggs he brought back from another site. The egg harvesters at both places hold the belief that the more eggs they take the more the megapodes lay. But this goes against all conventional conservation wisdom. How can it be that the more eggs they take the more there seem to be?

During a weekend spent with the egg collectors I came up with a few ideas, but one of my abiding memories on arrival was the village head offering me a meal of fried megapode egg. The yolk was enormous and I wasn't sure whether it was protocol to take the whole egg or just part. Being hungry I ate the lot and subsequently had difficulty sleeping because of the protein overload. This incident alerted me to the fact that this was more than just an egg – it was an egg with agency and imbued with cultural meanings.

Over dinner the village head revealed how only residents of the village were allowed to bid and a village committee set a sale price for eggs prior to the auction. The price for selling eggs was low, whereas the price paid by the successful bidder to harvest them was high. It was hard to see how he could make any money! Indeed it sounded more like a subsidy than a business opportunity, not least because the three- to four-man collecting team was the same irrespective of who acquired the rights and seemed to be working full time. My host also mentioned that eggs were given as gifts to the regent of Ambon.

I wonder now whether this auction was tied up with traditions of status and politics in the village. In the feudal sultanates that once governed the Moluccas, megapode eggs, being a rare, localised and oversized version of something normal, would have had considerable currency as a gift. It seems likely that Kailolo elders would have given megapode eggs in tribute to powers on Ambon and received favours in return. From this perspective, the auction is not so much about purchasing the right to harvest eggs, but about bidding for the privilege to give tribute and to advance or maintain a position in the echelons of local power structures. The bidder repays this privilege in the form of the auction price, which goes into the village coffers to finance needy projects.

The following morning I went out to look at the beach forest. I was interested in this habitat because it is one of the rarest forest types in Indonesia, and probably one of the most threatened on account of the amount of settlement along the coast. Yet it rarely appears in conservation plans because it occurs in linear bands that are too narrow to appear on larger-scale maps. The beach forest at Kailolo was the best I'd encountered on extensive travels in eastern Indonesia. The forest was tall and dense, and although it was sandy underneath and there were crabs scurrying around, there was nowhere really for a megapode to lay its eggs.

I started thinking about how it must have been for megapodes before people had settled the coasts during the Muslim diaspora of 400 years ago. Moluccan

Megapodes must have been dependent on disturbances such as a tree fall or sea surges to create gaps in these forests where the sun could warm exposed sand. This suggests that Moluccan Megapodes were originally adapted to find and utilise nest grounds with a limited lifespan. This idea seemed consistent with the reports on megapodes flying long distances at night. Indeed people told me that birds nesting on Haruku were flying from neighbouring islands and possibly even from Buru some 120 km away. It was not hard to imagine how a group of settlers, finding a megapode nest ground, decided to clear, tend and extend it. As the nest ground became larger and more stable it attracted more and more of the megapodes flying around looking for a good place to nest.

Whilst I was entertaining these thoughts a monitor lizard rustled into view. Of course! Not only would the megapodes have had difficulty finding a nice bare sand patch, they would also have had to contend with monitor lizards digging up their eggs. Perhaps the reason they'd evolved a large egg and chicks that can fly on hatching is to escape these lizards. In short, these birds must be adapted to high predation levels and erratic hatching success. It transpired that the Kailolo egg team are more site managers than collectors who, as well as maintaining a large, clear sandy patch, exterminate all monitor lizards and feral dogs. If my conjecture is true then the villagers are, in effect, concentrating and then utilising a natural redundancy in megapode breeding ecology. In other words, they are harvesting lots of eggs but no more than would otherwise be lost through all the natural hazards which

megapodes face at unmanaged nest sites. The team believed that they were not over-harvesting because there are always eggs laid which they miss, or which are laid too deep or at an odd angle from the disturbed patch, or laid on nights when they don't turn out.

How might these thoughts extend to ideas on how to conserve Moluccan Megapodes? One thing that seems clear is that conservationists should not object to the harvesting and trade of megapode eggs; indeed reviving traditions of megapode eggs being given as symbols of loyalty, friendship and respect might be a good thing. Alternatively, it might be simpler for conservation bodies to buy a patch of beach and create their own megapode nest ground, rather than trying to coerce villagers into some notion of a science-based sustainable harvest. [10]

Given the levels of threat suffered by many family members, it may seem strange that one megapode, the **Australian Brushturkey** *Alectura lathami*, was once considered a pest. It occurs along the east coast from New South Wales to northern Queensland and, while it is mainly a bird of forest and scrub, it quickly adapted and fed upon the fruits of the widely introduced prickly pear. When this plant enjoyed a plague-like proliferation in the early twentieth century, the bird too expanded in range. It is typical of the *ex post facto* reasoning which accompanies the scapegoating of many wildlife species that angry farmers, rather than appreciating how the bird followed its food plant, blamed the brushturkey for the spread of the prickly pear.

More recently the species has endured a secondary wave of controversy because it has also adapted to the kind of open

In its home country the Australian Brushturkey is a bird of rainforest, scrub and – in some areas – of suburban gardens and streets.

woodland habitat represented by the gardens of Australian suburbia. In places like Noosa on the south Queensland coast, brushturkeys are habitual pedestrians on the town's busiest streets, dodging in and out the cars and patrolling the waste bins. Problems arise when brushturkeys choose someone's back garden as a suitable location for their heaps of decomposing vegetation. A nest mound can include 2–4 tonnes of material and, as one highly tolerant host describes, the best place for the brushturkey might not always be the most convenient for its human neighbours:

> A few years ago, Far North Queensland experienced a rare drought. For the first time in living memory our creek dried up and the local firemen had to revise the firefighting protocol. We were ready for evacuation, cat basket to hand, vital documents on top of the cat box. We were not the only ones to be affected. Brushturkeys are mound builders and rely on a combination of heat and rain to get the mound composting nicely so the eggs are kept at the optimum temperature for incubation. This year there were piles of dead leaves to be raked up into mounds, the drought-stricken trees were shedding them like mad, but no moisture to start the composting.
>
> Our dominant male turkey made a lovely mound. He cleared the forest floor of leaves for metres around it. It was about 1.5 m in diameter and about half a metre high. Nothing happened. After a few days he decided to move the mound. He raked it all up and within two days there it was again in an entirely different spot as he searched for better conditions.

In all he made at least ten position changes, the most inconvenient of which was immediately outside our son's bedroom door. He came home from school and found a turkey mound blocking the way into his room. He had to sleep on the sofa in the living room for the next three nights and to dive into the ironing basket for a change of clothes. He couldn't get into his room at all. During the fourth day our male decided that that position wasn't going to work either and when our son got back from school that night the way into his room was unblocked. [11]

Brushturkeys quickly become habituated to human presence and will readily mount outdoor staircases or enter verandahs to forage right by the house. They will sometimes show aggression towards perceived intruders, such as the garden's human owners, and will try to see off much larger adversaries including horses. The species has given rise to one of the very rare cases of weapon use by an animal: showering a potential predator such as a monitor lizard in a barrage of sticks and debris. [12]

The rather droll blend of truculence and offhand sociability has appealed to the Australian sense of humour, launching brushturkeys – 'chooks' as they are often called – into cyberspace. In 2008 there were at least 17 clips of the species on the video website YouTube, including one of a bird pecking a crocodile's tail, another burying a small tethered terrier under a cascade of vegetation and a third assembling a nest mound similar to the one described above.

Chachalaca, Curassow and Guan family *Cracidae*

The 52 species in this largely Central and South American family are primitive gallinaceous birds that are often referred to collectively as cracids (pronounced 'crassids'). Together with the tinamous they have played much the same cultural role as gamebirds in the Old World – as food, sport and pets or captive trophies. They will quickly acclimatise to life in the backyard or the aviary, but they have never been fully domesticated partly because, unlike some of their European counterparts, they are highly arboreal and do not easily reproduce in captivity.

The cracids are long-tailed, long-necked birds with relatively short, broad, rounded wings befitting a need for manoeuvre in dense vegetation. While they can be weak fliers, most have the long (spurless) legs of a rooster (and, in some, fleshy crimson wattles and dewlaps) and they can run and leap through the canopy with startling speed. A modern author recently suggested that their individual names 'conjure . . . images of misty forests dominated by moss, lianas and great-buttress-rooted trees, dimly lit spaces where drops of water glint from every leaf'. [1]

They are blessed with an extraordinary variety of names. 'Curassow', for instance, is thought to be a version of Curaçao, the largest of the Lesser Antilles and the port from which the first live cracids were exported to Europe in the seventeenth century. Ironically, while the place gave a name to the birds (and the delicious orange-based liqueur) curassows were never resident on the island.

More arresting still among cracid names, and a personal favourite for any of the world's birds, is 'chachalaca'. It is a word from Nahuatl, one of the indigenous languages of Mexico, and is a wonderfully onomatopoeic rendering of their calls. [2] It seems somehow suffused with music, even dance, and fitting for a bird from Latin America, but any suggestion of vocal harmony is misleading. In Central America today, *chachalaca* means a chatterbox.

Many male cracids have elongated tracheae that act as resonating chambers to increase the volume of their calls, and these are often delivered in concert by several birds, sometimes for hours on end. A number of chachalacas and guans are credited as the loudest bird species on Earth. 'Ear-splitting cacophony' and an 'almost indescribable din' are two memorable verdicts. [3] Other indigenous names are equally suggestive of the sounds, such as *aracuã/aracuan* (Brazil), *Wakago* (Suriname for the **Little Chachalaca** *Ortalis motmot*), *guacharaca* (many parts of South America), and *Yacu-Caraguatà* (Guaraní for the **Chaco Chachalaca** *Ortalis canicollis*). The persistently repeated phrases of this last bird, said to carry for up to 2 km (1.3 miles), have commended themselves to the residents in Brazil's Mato Grosso region as *Quero casar pelo natal*: 'I want to marry by Christmas'. A more macabre interpretation is *Quero matar*: 'I want to kill', perhaps an allusion to the nightmare-like repetitions. [4]

For the Q'eqchi' Maya in the central Guatemalan highlands, chachalaca vocalisations are a source of weather lore

– a whole suite of birds known as 'rain-sayers' are especially important to them.

The **Plain Chachalaca** *Ortalis vetula* is as dominant in the soundscape of the montane forests as it is prevalent in the cultural landscape of the Q'eqchi' Maya. The most common of the cracids in central Guatemala, this bird has an interesting cultural profile for the Q'eqchi', whose name for it – *Jaykettzo* – is onomatopoetically derived from the raucous three-syllable note. Half an hour before dawn they begin to call and keep it up until dawn. When a flock of chachalacas (known, incidentally, as a 'collaboration') breaks out into a cacophony of cries, Q'eqchi' farmers hear in them the distress of the hungry. They plead that the mountain and the sky would provide enough of all the needed elements: moisture from the clouds, light from the sun and nutrients from the soil, so that fecundity, goodness, balance and abundance will reign.[5]

Today across much of the cracids' range the most widespread name, a clear reference to their importance as food, is *pavo* or *pava*, the Spanish for turkey, or variations of it such as *pavilla* ('little turkey') and *pavo de monte* ('forest turkey').[6] *Pavo* originally derived from *pavón*, the name for the peacock, the only exotic galliform which the Spanish would have known before their arrival in the New World. The cracids' dark meat is said to be very tasty, but in many countries the consequences of intensive hunting have been catastrophic. They are among the world's most threatened bird families with 23 species, just under half of the entire group, deemed at some risk.

As one correspondent from southern Peru notes:

Several Amazonian species have been almost eaten to extinction by humans. They were once a sustainable food source for native peoples, but invasion by colonists with firearms and population growth have put pressure on them, especially those that live along rivers in varzea [seasonally flooded] forest such as the **Wattled Curassow** *Crax globulosa*. The commonest species here, the **Razor-billed Curassow** *Mitu tuberosum*, is the preferred food source of native peoples and its feathers are also deemed the best to fletch arrows.[7]

The threats are unevenly distributed across the family. The curassows are the most vulnerable and seem unable to survive even light hunting pressure. Yet the chachalacas can be common in the most 'man-infested habitats', withstand high levels of predation, and sometimes thrive in cultivated areas or on the edge of small villages.[8]

As an illustration of how human population growth and colonists with firearms can bring a bird to the brink of extinction, the story of the **Black-fronted Piping Guan** *Pipile jacutinga* is one of the most compelling. The bird was once spread widely in northern Argentina, through southern Brazil and into eastern Paraguay, but it enjoyed an unenviable reputation for being fearless of firearms and also for making a high-quality stew. In a report to Charles Darwin, the great German naturalist in Brazil Fritz Müller wrote:

I myself saw how half a dozen jacutingas [the Brazilian name] were killed, one after the other, in the same tree. A neighbour told me that, two years ago, he had killed about 100 jacutingas in just one guarajuva tree. During the cold winter of 1866 so many jacutingas appeared

The vocalisations produced by the cracids including this Common Piping Guan are some of the most distinctive sounds in the Latin American landscape.

in the lowlands of the Rio Itajaúí that in a few weeks approximately 50,000 were killed.

Photographs from the first half of the twentieth century depict hunters standing proudly by the side of a *jacutinga* pyramid.[9] Now the world total may be as low as 2,500 birds.[10]

Yet a more recent story from the Upper Paraná region of Paraguay also demonstrates how a bird's cultural familiarity – even its reputation for good eating – can be turned upside down and to the species' advantage. A major project that combines organic farming of watermelons and soya beans with forest conservation and a challenge to the agri-business methods of big landowners, all under the direction of another Paraguayan rarity, a municipal mayoress, has chosen the Black-fronted Piping Guan as both a symbol of social change and environmental improvement. The scheme's long-term goal is to protect the forest that this beleaguered bird inhabits.[11]

Another reason why the cracids are so perilously placed is their popularity as cagebirds or as free-roaming pets. Although they have never been truly domesticated, they will adapt well to living around humans. The practice is ancient and widespread. In the 1850s the English naturalist and explorer Henry Bates delighted in the 'absurd tameness' of a pet Razor-billed Curassow that he encountered in an Amazonian farmhouse on the Rio Tapajos:

> It seemed to consider itself as one of the family: attended at all the meals, passing from one person to another round the mat to be fed, and rubbing the side of its head in a coaxing way against their cheeks or shoulders. At night it went to roost on a chest in a sleeping-room beside the hammock of one of the little girls, to whom it seemed particularly attached, following her wherever she went about the grounds.[12]

In the 1990s Helmut Sick of Brazil added that 'there is not now and never was an Indian village without some cracid as a mascot'.[13] The eggs are often placed under domestic chickens and the poults tended by their surrogate mothers. The chachalacas are thought to be the easiest to raise in this way and although noted for their aggression are also among the most useful, the birds' ear-splitting calls serving as an early warning if there is disturbance around the farm.[14] In Honduras hand-reared birds are known as *madre de gallina* (mother of the chickens), possibly because of the behaviour observed in a chachalaca elsewhere in Central America:

> It had the self-appointed position of police to all the poultry population, and any slight disturbance among the fowls was instantly a signal for the arrival of a tornado in gray, that put to flight any and all fighting cocks in the pueblo … Never to my knowledge did a cockfight continue after the chacha had given notice … I never saw the chacha follow the retreating cocks, he seemed to consider his duties had been fulfilled when the fight had been broken up.[15]

It is perhaps easy to see how the chachalaca's dominance over the domestic roosters could lead to a notion that a hybrid of the two would produce a champion fighting bird. The myth that cracids were cross-bred for this purpose was widely held across Central and South America. Judging from the following from a Panamanian contributor, it is still: 'I have heard from several people that chachalacas are sometimes bred with fighting cocks to produce a particularly aggressive bird used in cockfighting.'[16] Unfortunately it appears to be without foundation.[17]

If chachalacas are generally kept by rural inhabitants as working fowl, then the more beautiful, extravagantly crested and invariably rarer curassows are definitely prized as show birds. They are illegally trapped and widely traded for the cagebird industry. One species, the Brazilian **Alagoas Curassow** *Mitu mitu*, is now completely extinct in the wild, one of the earliest victims of biofuel production. Its future now completely relies on just 44 birds, divided between two well-known aviculturists in Rio de Janeiro.[18]

Guineafowl family *Numididae*

The wide array of cultural connections with these beautiful birds could serve as the basis for a good riddle. Which exclusively African bird family, once famous for its fertility associations across much of that continent and now a worldwide domestic fowl, links the Greek legend of Meleager, the modern centrepiece on the Christmas dinner table and the country of Turkey?

The thread of association begins with that striking appearance. The six species in the family are predominantly grey or black, medium-sized, ground-dwelling birds of forest and grassland, but four of them have an elaborately white-spotted plumage. Even individual feathers demonstrate the overall delicacy and complexity of this patterning and one part of the myth about Meleager trades on that aspect of their looks.

The tale is of a young heroic prince who takes part in a hunt for a monstrous boar, sent by the goddess Artemis to terrorise his father's kingdom of Calydon. Meleager sets out and slaughters the beast, but also kills members of his mother's family during the chase. In revenge she then contrives her own son's death and, in the way of Greek legend, adds to its tragic theme by hanging herself, while Meleager's two grief-stricken sisters are inconsolable. Their clothes become liberally bespattered with shining teardrops – like the genuine plumage of *Numida* – and the women are then turned by Artemis into guineahens (known in Greek as *mĕlĕagrĭdĕs*).[1]

Myth coincided with history on the Dodecanese island of Leros, off Turkey's south-western coast, where a genuine shrine dedicated to Artemis was populated by a free-roaming, white-spotted flock of her sacred birds.[2] The Meleager connections also eventually inveigled themselves into modern ornithology, through the scientific name for the best-known member of the group, the **Helmeted Guineafowl** *Numida meleagris*.

No one knows how or when the Greeks first obtained their white-spotted birds, but the Egyptians had kept them as domestic fowl at least 1,500 years before the birds

crossed the Mediterranean. There are several notable images of guineafowl from Pharaonic times, and one well-known stone-relief hieroglyph carved into a temple at Karnak dates from about 1900 BC. These particular temple walls are devoted to images of foreign plants and animals, suggesting that the guineafowl was also considered exotic and probably obtained from beyond Egyptian borders.[3] Certainly the Romans acquired their domestic guineafowl from the red-wattled race *Numida meleagris sabyi* from Numidia (whence, incidentally, came its modern family and generic names *Numididae* and *Numida*), the region to the west of Egypt and roughly coincident with modern Algeria.

It seems that with the fall of Rome the birds died out as an item on the European dining table. It was only in the Late Middle Ages and the quest for gold and slaves down the west coast of Africa that guineafowls were 'rediscovered'. Several African communities, including the Hausa of Nigeria and Mali's Dogon people, are said to have long domesticated Helmeted Guineafowl.[4] When European traders brought back some of this west African stock, of the blue-wattled *Numida meleagris galeata* race, guineafowls finally embarked on the journey that has since spread them across the world as farmyard familiars. It is this blue-wattled form of the species that is now domesticated worldwide.

Their arrival in Britain occurred in the early sixteenth century, just a short while before transatlantic mariners returned from the Americas with another domestic species. The latter bird, which had once strutted the back streets of Tenochtitlan, the glittering capital of pre-Columbian Mexico, would eventually eclipse all other domestic birds in Europe, except the chicken and farmyard goose. But on its first arrival in Tudor Britain, the turkey and the guineafowl became inextricably muddled in the popular imagination.

The sequence of confusion appears to have run as follows. An early name for the guineafowl was 'turkey-cock' or 'turkey-hen', either as a way of simply denoting an exotic or remote origin, or because some birds arriving in England had actually come, or were believed to originate, from domestic stock in the eastern Mediterranean.[5] This same name was then used interchangeably for both the African white-spotted import *and* for the newly arrived American galliform. In time the more accurate name 'guineafowl' was settled on the first bird, but the fowl which became central to Thanksgiving and Christmas celebrations entered the English language as the turkey (see page 41). One wonders how many of us sitting down to dinner on 25 December ever stop to reflect on the oddness of this name, or understand

Traditionally the Helmeted Guineafowl was a bird of the African bush and savannahs, but its domesticated forms are now found worldwide.

The white teardrop spots on guineafowl feathers have long appealed to humans as a source of symbol and story. Here they adorn the headdress of a young Kikuyu man at Thomson's Falls, Kenya.

I was in Texas and the camp I was living on had a petting farm, and on the farm were guineahens. They were intended to keep the grasshoppers in check. They were very, very noisy. A friend of mine had a flock in Newfoundland, but had to get rid of them because of neighbours' complaints . . . They were too noisy (proof that they make a good alarm system).[7]

The contributor alludes to a final practical benefit of guineafowl husbandry: their capacity to suppress certain invertebrate populations. In parts of North America this has been especially valuable where Lyme disease is a major problem, because guineafowl reduce the numbers of blood-sucking ticks that carry the illness.[8]

The other main incentive for keeping the birds is simply for their looks. Humans have been captivated by the almost mesmerising effect of guineafowl spotting. The feathers have been widely used as adornments not only in Africa, but also wherever they have been subsequently cultivated. In the nineteenth century they were highly prized in female fashions, although more recently their usage seems to have switched genders. Now they are a frequent feature in the hats of safari professionals – guides and rangers, etc.

Testament to the specific aesthetic attached to guineafowl feathers is the way that the birds' names have entered a variety of languages as a means to describe elaborately spotted or chequered patterns. For instance the scientific name for the European flower the fritillary is *Fritillaria meleagris*, which refers to the plant's vermiculated bell-like bloom (two old vernacular names were 'guinea-hen flower' or 'ginny flower'). In Spanish the guineafowl is known as *pintada*, which has a secondary meaning of 'graffiti', while *pintado* means 'mottled' or 'spotted'. An alternative name for the Cape Petrel, whose plumage is chequered with black and white, is 'Pintado Petrel'. In South Africa the Xhosa name for the guineafowl, *Impangele*, has been transferred 'to objects coloured – that is dotted or spotted – like the bird'. It has also acquired an additional meaning to describe anything 'with white spots or dots, as if marked by hail'.[9]

Aside from these plumage details, a secondary aspect of their physical appeal is the remarkable shape, which is distinguished by a pronounced keel-like slump to the mid belly. At times guineafowl look almost spherical. The sculptural possibilities of this gravid bulge definitely accounts for the birds' recurrence on the shelves of paperweights and decorative ornaments that fill the souvenir shops in tourist parts of sub-Saharan Africa.

One also wonders if the shape helps to explain the guineafowl's widespread status as a bird of power and magic, often associated with fertility. (There is little doubt that the female's prolific egg production is also at work in this symbolism.) In Ghana guineafowl eggs were once used in purification rituals at the beginning of the year to bless both crops and state. Among west Africa's Hausa people, guineafowl eggs were also smashed against the front door of newlyweds as a good luck charm, while a lonely wife could apparently summon a wayward husband by placing an egg on the roof and willing his return.[10] A Zimbabwean folk tale, which taps into similar themes, tells of a downtrodden, childless wife who adopts a guineafowl as her child and eventually seeks revenge through the bird on her neglectful husband.[11]

that the missing link in the chain of confusion is an African bird once sacred to Artemis.[6]

There is one incidental linguistic addendum. The Guinea region of Africa was the source of the precious metal from which golden guineas were minted, and these multiple associations were compressed into the term 'guinea-hen', which was slang for a woman available only on due payment – the prostitute. This vernacular usage surfaces in Shakespeare's play *Othello* (Act 1, Scene 3), where Iago, the play's evil genius, excoriates his friend Roderigo for his slavish attachment to Desdemona: 'Ere I would say I would drown myself for the love of a guinea-hen, I would change my humanity with a baboon.'

Today a number of other family members, including the **Crested Guineafowl** *Guttera pucherani* and the curiously long-necked **Vulturine Guineafowl** *Acryllium vulturinum*, are kept worldwide. However, Helmeted Guineafowl are hugely popular in countries such as France, where over 55 million are said to be reared annually. This is primarily for their high-quality meat and eggs but also for their loud calls. In concert, guineafowl flocks produce a raucous, rather metallic cackle, with repeated and slightly creaking or clucking notes. In Africa the collective racket produced by wild birds is a sign of an approaching predator; in the farmyard this early warning system is valued as a defence against intruders, human or otherwise.

New World Quail family *Odontophoridae*

The 32 species in this group were originally placed among the Old World galliforms, although more recent DNA studies have shown them to be a distinct bird family. However, most fit the standard quail model and have plump, rounded, small-headed shapes with subtle, even exquisitely beautiful patterning and colours. The birds are concentrated in a roughly hour-glass shaped section of the Americas, between latitudes 30° N and 10° S, with more than one-third (11 species) found in Mexico. Most of the culturally significant quail are inhabitants of grassland or bush, a preference beautifully evoked in a Native American name for one of their number, the **Scaled Quail** *Callipepla squamata*. The Tewa word for the species means 'sagebrush softness'.[1]

New World quail have a similar pattern of cultural reference to the other American game families, the tinamous and chachalacas. They were, for instance, widely introduced into other countries because of their popularity with hunters. This was especially the case with the two best known and most intensively pursued of the group, the **Northern Bobwhite** *Colinus virginianus* and **California Quail** *Callipepla californica*. The first of these, whose name is an onomatopoeic echo of its cheery two-note call, was released into regions of North America where it had never previously occurred (i.e. British Columbia and Oregon), as well as Hawaii, several Caribbean islands and a number of European countries (Italy, France, Croatia and Spain). If anything, releases of California Quail have been even more successful. There are now substantial numbers in New Zealand, where it can be an agricultural pest, while in Chile the total is thought to exceed the population native to the USA.[2]

If these releases are typical of human interactions with gamebirds, then there is one facet of their cultural exploitation which is unusual. It has led to New World quails becoming familiar to several billion human beings, although it should be added that the impact is largely subliminal. A close relative of the California Quail, the **Gambel's Quail** *Callipepla gambelii*, is a species largely found in the four south-westernmost states of the USA as well as northern Mexico and west Texas. Both California and Gambel's Quail have a characteristic song of three or four high, clear, boldly whistled notes (often rendered as *chi-ca-go*). The two birds are hugely evocative of the open desert scrub country which they inhabit and were – and still are – endlessly used as part of the background acoustic atmosphere in Western films and television programmes.

In fact, they were once almost a signature sound for the whole genre, and utilised even when the film was set where the birds themselves did not occur. An example is *The Virginian*, the cowboy series which ran from 1962–1970 and starred James Drury, about a ranch community in Wyoming in the 1890s. Unfortunately this is well north-west of the quails' true distribution. It is a measure of how bird sounds can acquire and then transmit automatic connotations – in this instance of gun-toting horsemen on the range – even when they have little connection with the genuine places of California and Gambel's Quail.

Quails prefer to run rather than fly and if approached will crouch tightly until the last second, when they will literally explode at your feet. This sudden, unpredictable mode of escape calls for the fastest reflexes – not to mention strong nerves – from hunters, and the exacting challenge is the very essence of their sporting appeal. Arthur Bent noted that it was a good shot who put 'two quail in his pocket for

◄◄ The aptly named California Quail is the avian symbol for the Golden State.

◄ New World quail such as the beautiful Gambel's Quail are among the most exacting and sought-after gamebirds in the Americas.

every four shells fired'.[3] A modern quail hunter suggests that even Bent's mathematics were rather optimistic:

> I have hunted bobwhite quail. Historically in Nebraska they were likely only native to the south-east corner of the state and along waterways but now – owing to the development of irrigation canals, farm ponds and the increase of forested areas through suppression of fire – they are found state-wide. While growing up I never shot at one. When the covey rises, it is explosive. A thunder of wings erupts from the cover and then each of the birds, in a blur, flies in a different direction. They would flush, I would raise my shotgun but would never fire because I couldn't quickly decide which one to take aim at. I have since shot some but I usually pass on the quail because of the little meat on them. In Nebraska they are mostly taken by hunters who come across them incidentally while hunting pheasants.[4]

Those who have experienced quail or bobwhites erupting from their path will understand Bent's memorable description of them as 'feathered bombshells'.[5] They will likewise appreciate a riddle recorded in Honduras:

I am completely humble	*Soy enteramente humilde*
And I fight no one	*No sé pelear con nadie*
But I can scare the bravest one,	*Ero asusto al màs valiente*
Even though I never even think of hurting him.	*Aunque ni pienso pegarle.*

The answer is the *perdiz*, a generic name for New World quails and their close relatives in Central America.[6]

A single bobwhite may weigh just 100–150 g (4–6 oz), but what it may lack in size is more than made up for in quality. The bird was long regarded as a 'delicious morsel for the table', an opinion that appears to have lost none of its savour.[7] According to a modern American hunter, 'they make an excellent meal and are easy to cook. Just throw them in a crock pot and add cream of mushroom soup and water to cover. Cook for four to five hours and you can eat them over rice.'[8]

The prospect of bobwhite for dinner was said to draw an estimated 500,000 hunters into the field in the early twentieth century. In parts of south-east USA, its dominance as a sporting target was so uncontested it was known simply as 'the bird'.[9] While it is still popular, it is now only for the dedicated (it costs anything from $375: £230 for half a day's organised quail shooting, to $750: £465 for a full day, depending on bag size) and is tightly regulated, particularly since Northern Bobwhites have declined dramatically over much of their range. In the last 40 years the species has suffered a 75 per cent fall in numbers, mainly because of habitat loss or deterioration in habitat quality in agricultural areas.[10]

Given that quail are essentially birds of open country and well suited to corn or other arable crops, these declines reverse an earlier trend during the original settlement of North America. Bobwhites were said to have 'followed the plough westwards', while other quail species also benefited from agricultural expansion. At the turn of the twentieth century the great pioneer environmentalist John Muir believed that the California Quail had 'vastly increased in numbers since the settlement of the country, notwithstanding the immense numbers killed every season by boys and pot-hunters'.[11]

A sense of this bird's abundance, described as 'almost unbelievable to-day', is indicated by the scale of the harvest. There was a vast trade in key Californian cities such as Los Angeles and San Francisco, where quail on toast was on almost every restaurant menu at 30 cents a dish. In 1881–2 the total shipped to San Francisco was put at 384,000 birds. In 1883 two market hunters in Los Angeles and San Bernardino counties took 3,600 California Quail in 17 days – an average of a bird every two minutes – while a pair targeting quail that came to a single wet spring shot 8,400 in one week.[12]

Long before white settlers chased bobwhites or quail, Native Americans hunted the birds with a wide armoury of traps and snares. In California the Pomo people, inhabiting the lake area north of San Francisco, were especially attached to them. A secondary value came from the California Quail's luxurious topknot, the long forward-curving crest (the scientific name *Callipepla* comes from the Greek *kalos*: 'beautiful'; and *peplos*: 'ceremonial robe'), which was worked into the Pomo's exquisite basketry or employed as personal decoration.[13] In volume XIV of his masterwork, *The North American Indian*, the great early-twentieth-century photographer Edward Curtis took an image of a Pomo girl with a spray of California Quail feathers in her ear pendant.

The state as a whole seems to have embraced the Pomo's attachment to this glorious little bird, which combines a hugely endearing mix of humour and beauty: 'I love these birds. Their bustling run and appearance is so comical. They remind me of a cross between Charles Dickens' Mr Pickwick and something out of Gilbert and Sullivan's *Mikado*.'[14] Their adoption as the state bird in 1931 has inspired one recent Californian to the following poetic reflections:

> All my sightings of them have been in the beautiful Marin Headlands across the bay from San Francisco. Here the scenery is on a grand scale. Towering redwood forests give way to magnificent vistas across the Pacific flanked by imposing hills. I last saw a quail here in early April when the hills had burst into their technicolor glory before drying to their summer brown. The bird seemed to echo in its small form every colour that blazed in this huge landscape: the blues and violets of the sky and the lupins that covered the hills, the white flashes of the patches of wild garlic and the bright surf of the ocean, the golds and sun-bleached yellow-whites of sand and driftwood and the rich red-browns of the redwoods' soft bark. Its face was the deep charred brown-black of the burnt trees and scrub left by past wild fires. At first I felt surprise that California should have picked so diminutive a specimen as its state bird. I suppose I rather expected a condor, or an eagle or some other equally grand symbol of power and strength. Now, however, I see an aptness in the choice of this small, more (literally) down-to-earth bird. California is, after all, the place where the little guy can make it big.[15]

Pheasant, Fowl and Allies family *Phasianidae*

Although this group embraces a huge diversity of species, from finch-sized quail to peacocks whose feather trains are 2 m (6.6 ft) long, the gamebirds have a basic unity. They are ground-dwelling birds with stout legs, rotund bodies, disproportionately small heads and a propensity to run rather than fly away from danger. Once airborne, many of them are powerful fliers with a loud thrumming wingbeat.

The birds are known collectively by a more technical term, the galliforms (see Glossary), and are without cavil *the* most important for humans worldwide. This significance does not rest exclusively on the family's inclusion of the domestic chicken, which is derived from the **Red Junglefowl** *Gallus gallus* of Asia, yet it is worth reiterating that the species has become the most numerous bird on the planet, and out-competes sheep, goats and cattle as our main source of protein.

The group also includes another key cultural and economic icon, the **Wild Turkey** *Meleagris gallopavo*, with all its commercially significant domestic forms. If that were not enough, the galliforms, especially some of the Asian pheasants, provide examples not just of the most beautiful birds on Earth, but of the most beautiful of all living organisms.

Then there is the wide sweep of gamebirds – grouse, partridge, francolins, etc. – which have only ducks or geese as rivals in the context of sport shooting and wild-caught protein. It is no exaggeration to suggest that large parts of European and North American landscapes have been shaped to provide habitat for these sporting totems.

The taxonomic issues concerning galliforms are complex.

There are currently assumed to be 179 species spread over 51 genera. For the purposes of exploring the vast spectrum of their cultural associations, I have divided them under seven headings: Turkey; Grouse; a larger, rather amorphous category, which I have called the Old World Partridge, Francolin and Snowcock; Old World Quail; Pheasant; and Peafowl. While technically one of the pheasants, the Red Junglefowl requires completely separate treatment. It is, appropriately, the longest account of any bird in the book.

TURKEY

A male turkey in full display is among North America's most impressive birds. Audubon called it the 'noblest game bird in the world'.[1] However distinguished it may appear, it is perhaps curious to note that, in the English-speaking world, it bears another bird's name. 'Turkey' or 'turkey-cock' originally described the Helmeted Guineafowl from Africa. How it was transferred to the American bird is explored in full under the other species account (see Guineafowl family, page 36). Nor was the confusion confined to the English language. The French *dindon* is a corruption of *coq d'Inde*, 'the Indian cock', and stems from the same misapprehension that it came from the east.[2] Ironically modern Turks share this error: their name for their eponymous bird is *hindi* (after India, *Hindistan*).[2] The original entanglement is still manifest in the turkey's scientific name: *Meleagris* was the old Greek word for guineafowl.

While most people may be familiar with the Wild Turkey which is widespread across North and Central America, and

The Ocellated Turkey may be rare and timid over much of its Central American range, but at the magnificent Mayan ruins of Tikal in Guatemala it is a strolling familiar.

from which all the domesticated stock has derived, there is another lesser-known sibling. **Ocellated Turkey** *Meleagris ocellata* is arguably the more beautiful bird, but it has had a far smaller cultural role and was apparently never domesticated. Endemic to the Yucatán Peninsula, it is still hunted which, in part, explains its general scarcity and wariness. A notable exception, however, is around the Mayan ruins of Tikal in Guatemala, where Ocellated Turkeys are remarkably tame and common, even around the public car parks. There is a rather satisfying congruity in the fact that this quintessentially Mesoamerican bird should be such a strolling familiar in the most magnificent of pre-Columbian places. With its lustrous iridescence and its weird 'infestation' of orange facial warts, the bird seems almost an analogue of the splendours (and the incidental barbarities) of Mayan civilisation.

SYMBOLIC TURKEYS

There may be two species, but there are also multiple symbolic versions of the turkey. There is, for instance, the bird that is a byword for ineptitude. Today 'a turkey' is slang for almost any kind of dud or failed enterprise, especially a theatrical flop, as well as a stupid person. The French names, *dinde* (female) or *dindon* (male), similarly means something like 'silly goose'; while *dindonner* means 'to dupe'.

A much older strand of symbolism sheds an intriguing light on these modern pejorative connotations. The great Spanish historian of pre-Cortesian Mexico Bernardino de Sahagún recorded that the soft red fleshy 'snood', which dribbles down over the cock turkey's face, had magico-medicinal properties for the Mexicans, and could induce the ultimate form of (masculine) failure. If a victim could be secretly made to drink or eat it, then he would suffer impotence.[3] That symbolism meshes closely with ideas in a number of other cultures, such as the Cheyenne and sections of the Apache people. They believed that to eat turkey flesh would make them cowards. Even the feathers were not used in making arrows for much the same reason.[4]

The birds are often considered not just cowardly but proverbially brainless. A modern urban myth holds that turkeys can drown by looking up into the rain. One US contributor notes the tale's prevalence: 'It's just one of those things you take in as a child without thinking about it too much. In fact, it wasn't till I was in the middle of telling my wife that I stopped to think and realized: well, that actually can't be true, can it?'[5] The rather humorous anxiety that seems inherent in the turkey's quivering call is part of the bird's image as fool. The word 'gobbledegook', meaning pompous or unintelligent jargon, draws directly on the turkey's own gobble.

One wonders if the modern associations – gobbledegook dates from just the 1940s – derive mainly from experiences of birds already emasculated by captivity.[6] If domestication does bring with it a desensitised response, then these debased versions of the turkey will become ever more entrenched, given that most people now do not even see the free-roaming farmyard bird. The typical turkey encounter is with a plastic-wrapped frozen block, while the living antecedents to that supermarket experience are the anaemic overcrowded fowl of the hermetically sealed poultry unit. The image of the bird as stupid and cowardly seems somehow implicit in these intensive methods and it perhaps lies behind the horror stories of British factory-farm workers, themselves degraded by the concentration-camp environment, who were caught throwing turkeys in the air as sport, and then beating them to death with baseball bats.

Yet there is also a diametrically opposite vein of symbolism. It is the turkey as emblem of fertility, strength and even of the plainly spoken facts. (For the antithesis of 'gobbledegook' is the unvarnished truth as expressed in 'talking turkey'. 'Cold turkey' has its origins in the same no-nonsense bird: it means the realities of life without the junkie's narcotic prop.) Even some of the names given to male turkeys convey a sense of the bird's honest-to-goodness vigour. Americans call old wild cocks, 'toms', and young birds, 'jakes'; while Europeans know the domestic equivalent as a 'stag'.[7] A saltier play on this potency is the slang phrase for the penis, 'turkey-neck', much loved by Charles Bukowski and used by Sylvia Plath in *The Bell Jar*.[8]

Wild 'tom' turkeys are infamous for their aggression and can terrorise whole communities that fall within 'their' territory, even chasing off 'rivals' as large as automobiles. This fine strutting bird of the woods made a comparable appeal to Native American cultures. The central tuft of bristly feathers that emerges from the cock turkey's chest, known as a 'beard', was once an emblem used in weaponry or ceremonial clothing to denote virility. An early-nineteenth-century head ornament incorporating this part of the bird is in the British Museum, where the associated caption describes how the Oto chief who wore it did so by right of having killed his enemy in his own lodge.

It was the turkey's grander aspects which led Benjamin Franklin to consider it a more fitting symbol for the newly created American republic than the species that was finally selected, the Bald Eagle. In a letter to his daughter Sarah in January 1784, Franklin wrote:

> For in truth, the turkey is in comparison a much more respectable bird, and withal a true original native of America. Eagles have been found in all countries, but the turkey was peculiar to ours . . . He is, besides, (though a little vain and silly, it is true, but not the worse emblem for that,) a bird of courage, and would not hesitate to attack a grenadier of the British guards, who should presume to invade his farmyard with a *red* coat on.[9]

One contributor notes that the old idea is not without its modern support:

> I regularly heard people tell that story of Franklin's preference for the turkey. I always assumed that they thought perhaps we might have been better off if he had carried the day, because our national mascot would have been a dumb, peaceful, gentle, delicious bird instead of the aggressive, militaristic, carnivorous eagle. But that is no doubt because I grew up in California, surrounded by hippies.[10]

TURKEY TRADITIONS IN EUROPE

Before exploring in more detail the turkey's rich cultural heritage on its native continent, we should consider one striking anomaly. The genetic strains of domesticated stock are probably older in Europe than they are in America. In fact the bird's journey towards domestication by white

We are so accustomed to turkeys as frozen blocks of meat from the supermarket that we can easily overlook how weirdly magnificent the Wild Turkey can be.

Roast turkey may now be a staple of the British Christmas, but the same is not true in many European countries.

aspect of this ancient swan lore survives (see *Birds Britannica*, pages 60–64).

The rearing of turkeys became a speciality of poulterers in East Anglia, where the Norfolk Black and Cambridge Bronze are two ancient breeds. The artist Thomas Bewick described the traditional methods by which turkeys were walked sometimes for 200 km (120 miles) to the English capital at Christmas. 'Great numbers are bred in Norfolk, Suffolk and other counties', he wrote, 'whence they are driven to the London markets . . . The drivers manage them with facility, by means of a bit of red rag tied to a long rod, which, from the antipathy these birds bear to that colour, effectually drives them forward.'[12]

Although the bird forms the main dish of the British Christmas – the country produces a quarter of a million tonnes annually – the following snapshot indicates that roast turkey is far from universal as a part of Christian Europe's cultural celebrations during December:[13]

France: 'Turkey: yes, we now eat it as a traditional meal on Christmas Day, generally at lunchtime. I'm not sure when it dates back to!'[14]

Germany: 'Turkey (*Truthahn* or more commonly *Pute*; strictly speaking the latter refers to females and the former to males) is not a Christmas tradition. It is goose – the poor thing being reared to yield the highest possible amount of fat.'[15]

Greece: 'Yes turkey (*gallopoula*) is the traditional meat for Christmas and it's usually filled with rice and chestnuts. Some people who don't like turkey meat use chicken but the traditional is turkey!'[16]

Italy: 'No turkey (*tachinno*), it is capon, a castrated rooster. But not everybody in the whole of Italy cooks this for Xmas.'[17]

Russia: 'No, not in my region (Novosibirsk), at least; goose is the traditional meat at Christmas. I never ate turkey (индейка, *indeyka*) until I was about 18.'[18]

Serbia: 'We don't eat turkey (*ćurka*) for Christmas. Indeed, turkey doesn't figure large in Serbia (and it doesn't in most Balkan countries). There is no standard Christmas day meal, and Christmas Eve is more important than Christmas Day – but people eat fish then (mostly carp), dried fruit cakes, walnut pies, sweetmeats, drink much wine, and call it fasting. On Christmas Day, my family and many others would have a roast suckling pig, small enough to fit in the oven, crackling as thin as paper.'[19]

Sweden: 'No, in Sweden turkey (*kalkon*) is most certainly not a traditional dish at Christmas. A specially cured ham still has pride of place on the huge buffet table (*smörgåsbord*) that Swedes gather round on Christmas Eve. (It includes meatballs, several kinds of pickled herring, liver paste, cabbage dishes, etc.) Traditional is also a very rich rice pudding (sometimes with cinnamon and milk, sometimes with a berry sauce). Recently quite a number of Swedes have taken to serving chicken or turkey as a Xmas meal, but I suspect that the ham and the rice pudding are the only dishes that most Swedes consider traditional Xmas fare.'[20]

colonial settlers in North America was not, as might be imagined, from the backwoods to the backyard. It involved turkeys in an international odyssey from Mexico to Spain then England, and finally to the Atlantic colonies. Turkeys are thought to have arrived in Spain by the early years of the sixteenth century, and in England during the reign of Henry VIII. While the bird's first appearance was five centuries ago, the following contribution suggests that the event is still a part of modern family lore:

One of my Mother's relations, William 'The Navigator' Strickland, commanded one of Sebastian Cabot's ships as a young man during an expedition to the New World. William is believed to have brought the first turkeys from America to England via Spain. In 1550 he was granted arms and a crest, the latter consisting of 'a Turkey Cock Argent beaked and legged Sable combed and wattled Gules'. There is a rough sketch of a turkey, probably the first ever made in Britain, supporting this grant in the records of the College of Arms.[11]

With Strickland's importation, possibly in 1524, turkeys quickly became a culinary favourite. One of the more striking consequences of this was the cultural demotion of another iconic bird. Roast swan had once been the centrepiece at most English high days and holidays. A complex system of husbandry had delivered wild swans to the dining tables of the landed classes since Saxon times. Yet ease of supply – not to mention the superior quality of turkey meat – meant that swan inexorably lost ground. Today only a single notable

AMERICAN TURKEY TRADITIONS

In a classic study, *The Wild Turkey: Its History and Domestication*, A W Schorger underscores how large a role the turkey played in indigenous American society. The meat was widely eaten and throughout much of the bird's range its plumage was intricately woven into cloaks, blankets and quilts, which were renowned for their durability, warmth and visual appeal.[21] The spurs were used for arrowheads, the bones as awls, sewing needles and tubular beads.[22] The feathers also had ritual significance for many communities, especially for the Pueblo Indians in south-west USA. What is more difficult to pinpoint is the precise symbolic valency attached to the bird, although its plumes were abundantly deployed in religious rites associated with rain, fertility and death.[23]

The raw materials for these ritual practices derived from both wild and tame birds, with the turkey's domestication occurring in south-west USA as early as AD 700. Yet the best evidence for the economic importance of domestic birds comes from a later period in Mexico. When Cortés led his Spanish *conquistadores* into the capital, Tenochtitlan, in 1519 the bird was central to national life. A classic illustration is the numbers of turkeys consumed by the imperial household of Moctezuma, a high percentage of which went to feed the carnivores in the emperor's menagerie. (One huge raptor – can we assume that it was a Harpy Eagle? – daily ate a whole bird.) Schorger suggests an annual minimum consumption in Moctezuma's palace of 365,000 turkeys.[24]

Although these traditions were far in advance of domestication elsewhere on the continent, it was with the seventeenth-century foundation of European colonies further north that the bird acquired its pre-eminent ritual significance. Thanksgiving is now as embedded in the annual cycle of national holidays as anything in the American calendar. While it was first celebrated as early as 1621, neither the event, nor the role of turkey therein, became a fixture until the early nineteenth century. The official proclamation of a Thanksgiving holiday (designated as the last Thursday in November) was not made until 1863.[25]

Two modern celebrants reflect on some of the Thanksgiving rituals, as well as how the day unfolds:

> One Thanksgiving memory that is practically universal for Americans is being taught in school to draw a turkey by tracing around their splayed hand, making the thumb into the neck and head, and the palm and fingers into the body and tail feathers. It is probably the first bird most Americans draw.[26]

> It's a very special day for me and my family. Most businesses close for the day and schools are dismissed. A traditional Thanksgiving meal always is a beautiful roasted turkey with cornbread stuffing and cranberry sauce. I prepare my family's favorites including fresh turnip greens, squash casserole, mashed potatoes and, of course, pumpkin pie with whipped cream for dessert. We sit around a big table sometimes set with our best china and linens and always a special grace is said giving thanks to God for all the blessings He has given us. It is a day for togetherness.

> The day before Thanksgiving is the most traveled day of the year and the day after Thanksgiving is the most crowded day in the stores and shops, as the Christmas shopping begins this day. There is a field

surrounded by woods west of town inhabited with Wild Turkeys. I've seen them feeding late in the afternoon. A friend of ours who hunts turkey has brought them home. His wife, however, says they taste different from supermarket turkeys. I've never eaten one of them.[27]

Yet the presence of turkey on the modern table echoes a time when the wild bird was a vital source of food for settlements along the eastern seaboard. Sometimes it was a dietary mainstay until a colony could harvest the first crops.[28] Initially birds were so abundant that they 'were obtainable for a pittance', and Audubon describes how in Kentucky they were so numerous that they sold for less than a barn-fowl.[29] In Carolina, colonists noted flocks of 500 emerging from the swamps at sunrise.[30] Gradually, however, numbers dwindled and prices rose. These incremental changes allow us to track not only the wild bird's role as food, but the way that demand inexorably outstripped supply. The price per pound (450 g) in Northampton, Massachusetts, went from 1 pence in 1730, to 2.5 pence (1766), to three pence (1788) and to 4–6 pence (after 1800). Within half a century Wild Turkey had been extirpated completely from the state.[31] In fact, Audubon expressed fear for the species' complete extinction.[32]

This situation has long since been reversed, with widespread captive-release programmes allowing Wild Turkeys to recolonise their entire historic range and even acquire territory they never formerly held. The return of turkeys to sites like Mesa Verde National Park, Colorado, in 1944 gave clear insight into how the species might originally have been domesticated. The birds, initially wary and elusive, gradually came to dominate the food provided by park staff at bird feeders, then commenced roosting in the park's residential areas, despite efforts to scare them off that eventually encompassed use of fireworks ('cherry bombs') and gunfire. Nothing would shift them. As one author noted, 'There is little reason to believe that prehistoric humans at Mesa Verde were not tormented by turkeys in much the same manner. Eventually people realised that a bird which could not be driven or frightened away, might just as easily be corralled and cropped.'[33]

Turkeys now occur in every state except Alaska, and numbers have climbed from 30,000 to 4.5 million since the 1930s.[34] Hunting this emblem of American plenty is now as widespread as it is exciting:

The Wild Turkey is a key part of Thanksgiving festivities but if Benjamin Franklin had got his way it might also have been a symbol for the entire United States of America.

I remember my first turkey hunt over a hen decoy. I called and got a response from an ol' gobbler. As I sat waiting I kept hearing a *bong* sound. Being a novice at this sort of hunting I was curious as to what it was, but patiently waited while it grew louder. I was close to a farm and wondered what the farmer could be pounding on; after all, I was trying to hunt and wanted quiet.

Then suddenly something appeared out of the corner of my eye. I turned slightly and there he was, a gobbler as big as a 55-gallon barrel. I heard the *bong* sound again and then I realised it was him doing it. He was drumming and strutting to impress my hen decoy. My heart was pounding so hard I was actually having trouble catching my breath. And then it happened. He pounced on my hen decoy and gave her a whirl, tipping her over and looking at her with disgust. I gave him a little *putt putt* (an alert call for turkeys) from my caller and his head popped up and . . . well . . . he was dinner. [35]

The current estimate for annual American consumption of turkey is 250–300 million birds, with about one-fifth of the total eaten on the last Thursday in November. The vast majority, reared in intensive facilities, have an average life of 105 days for females and 133 days for toms. A typical 150 m by 15 m (500 ft x 50 ft) barn holds approximately 10,000 hens or 7,000 toms, giving each bird an average living space of 0.28 m^3 (3 ft^3). In these conditions they are unable to move comfortably and confinement leads often to conflict. To minimise each turkey's damage to its neighbour, its beak and toes are often cut off. [36]

I close with an image of the bird, not as victim of modern industrial agriculture, but as it should be seen – as an astonishing force of nature. In his poem, 'Turkey-Cock', D H Lawrence manages somehow to capture the fantastic otherness and complex aesthetics of a male wild turkey, partly by comparing it to the by-products of industrial metallurgy (as well as a more dubious stereotype of Native America). Lawrence's unforgettable phrase is 'Slag-wattled turkey-cock'.

You ruffled black blossom,
You glossy dark wind.

Your sort of gorgeousness,
Dark and lustrous
And skinny repulsive
And poppy-glossy,
Is the gorgeousness that evokes my most puzzled
   admiration.

Your aboriginality
Deep, unexplained,
Like a Red Indian darkly unfinished and aloof,
Seems like the black and glossy seeds of countless
   centuries.

Your wattles are the colour of steel-slag which has been
   red-hot
And is going cold,
Cooling to a powdery, pale-oxidised sky-blue . . .

Why do you have wattles, and a naked wattled head?
Why do you arch your naked-set eyes with a more-
   than-comprehensible arrogance?

The vulture is bald, so is the condor, obscenely,
But only you have thrown this amazing mantilla of
   oxidised sky-blue
And red hot over you.

The poem excavates the living creature from its otherwise smothering humus of domestic reference and association. It resurrects a primal turkey in all its grotesque splendour, allowing us to imagine how it might once have been when the bird stepped freshly minted from what Lawrence called 'the furnace of creation'.

GROUSE

Everybody knows that the autumn landscape in the north woods is the land, plus a red maple, plus a ruffed grouse. In terms of conventional physics, the grouse represents only a millionth of either the mass or the energy of an acre. Yet subtract the grouse and whole thing is dead. An enormous amount of some kind of motive power has been lost. [37]

In his reflections on what he called 'the physics of beauty', the American ecologist Aldo Leopold could not name precisely what it was about the bird's presence that exalted the landscape, but he gave voice to something which we have felt for millennia. Grouse are deeply special.

They have undoubtedly been important food since the Palaeolithic times and remain among the northern continents' most cherished sporting birds. In Britain the Red Grouse has the reputation as the 'King of Game Birds'. (NB: Red Grouse and Willow Ptarmigan are respectively the British and American names for the same species, albeit the British bird is a separate race *scoticus*. Both names are long established and the bird is referred to throughout as **Willow Ptarmigan** (**Red Grouse**) *Lagopus lagopus*.) Approximately 405,000 ha (1 million acres) of English upland are managed to support grouse. In Scotland the figures are double that. Yet in the early twentieth century the sport had such cachet and social importance for the politicians in both chambers of the British parliament that they looked upon the house sittings as a deep inconvenience if they did not coincide with the dates of the grouse season. [38] This still opens in August on what is known as the 'Glorious Twelfth'. Across the Atlantic, its counterpart is Aldo Leopold's totem of the north woods, the **Ruffed Grouse** *Bonasa umbellus*. 'I think most sportsmen will agree', wrote one commentator, 'that the ruffed grouse . . . is the unrivalled king of North American upland game birds.' [39]

Yet it is not just their sporting qualities that distinguish grouse. A remarkable feature of grouse behaviour is their congregation at communal mating grounds, where males compete in elaborate displays or 'dances'. These traditional sites have become the focus of deep human interest, as tourist attractions, business opportunities and as places of pilgrimage for wildlife enthusiasts. They have also been a much older source of inspiration. Native Americans have drawn on the ritualised behaviour of the birds as a model for their own ceremonies. Often known simply as the Chicken Dance – after its principal grouse model, the **Greater Prairie Chicken** *Tympanuchus cupido* – it is performed

The display of the Greater Prairie Chicken is a spectacle that combines compelling sexual theatre with a strong dash of the bizarre.

by tribes in the USA and Canada and is a significant part of their evolving cultural identities.

Regardless of their capacity to compel us, many grouse species are now in full retreat because of human changes to the landscape. There are 18 grouse worldwide, nine in Eurasia and 11 in North America, mainly north of latitude 40° N. Many thrive best in some of the most austere environments – montane and upland bog, boreal forest, prairie grassland and the open tundra of the high Arctic. The **Rock Ptarmigan** *Lagopus muta* has the most northerly range of any terrestrial bird and is frequently cited as one of the species most acutely at risk from climate change. For now, however, this bird and the Willow Ptarmigan (Red Grouse) are among the most abundant species and have distributions which entirely encircle the northern hemisphere. The population of Rock Ptarmigan is estimated to rise as high as 3.7–24.3 million birds in autumn, while the spring population for Willow Ptarmigan (Red Grouse) is put at 12 million globally.[40]

The position of the **Gunnison Grouse** *Centrocercus minimus*, which was only 'discovered' in the 1990s and is the first North American *nova avis* since the nineteenth century, could not be more contrasting. The bird is almost entirely confined to one valley (Gunnison) in south-west Colorado. Both the Gunnison Grouse (4,000 birds) and the **Lesser Prairie Chicken** *Tympanuchus pallidicinctus*, which is found in five US states (*c.*17,500 birds), are classified as threatened with extinction.[41] (To give a sense of the calamitous decline of the latter, a flock seen in 1904 in a single Kansan grain field was said to number 15,000–20,000 birds.)[42] Equally, Asia's **Siberian Grouse** *Falcipennis falcipennis* and **Severtov's Grouse** *Tetrastes sewerzowi* are listed as near-threatened.[43]

While several other grouse may not meet the criteria of

these formal designations, they have, nevertheless, suffered massive irreversible losses. The Greater Prairie Chicken was once numbered in millions from the Atlantic coast right across the central American prairies. Early explorers described single flocks of 30,000 birds.[44] Now the world population is 460,000 and is largely restricted to six key states. The **Black Grouse** *Lyrurus tetrix* is in some ways its Old World counterpart, having suffered declines in 21 of 25 European countries. Yet it was once abundant and widely hunted. In Edwardian Britain sportsmen probably shot more Black Grouse a year (approximately 38,000 birds) than today's total national breeding population (*c.*15,000 pairs).[45]

HUNTING GROUSE

Although killing and trapping of grouse have had a part in the decline of some populations, there is no simplistic causal relationship between subsistence or sports hunting and the grouses' fortunes. The fate of the Willow Ptarmigan (Red Grouse) in Britain in many ways exemplifies an almost symbiotic relationship between grouse hunters and the bird itself. During the Victorian age, after the development of the railways (for transportation to the northern moors) and the breech-loading shotgun, grouse shooting acquired the status of a national mania among the wealthy. By 1910 there were 3,157 grouse shoots in Scotland alone.[46] The tens of thousands of hunters pouring north for the season led to the laying on of special trains out of London. In the course of a single season this cadre of landowners and urban industrialists or professionals killed as many as 1.5 million grouse.

In so doing they created an ancillary economy in costume, guns and the associated paraphernalia of outdoor sport (nor should we forget the Scottish single malt whiskies and all the other increasingly ritualised comestibles that went

The Willow Ptarmigan (Red Grouse) is still one of the commonest and most widely hunted of all the world's grouse.

with shooting). They also visited a policy of extermination upon natural predators – crows, raptors, foxes, etc. – which might otherwise have helped themselves to the artificially high stocks of gamebirds. Yet grouse have almost certainly never fared better in Britain. One and a half million may have ended up on the dining table, but there was a stable breeding population of more than 1 million pairs. In our own age, when killing grouse is neither so popular, nor so economically viable, the national total is 155,000 pairs.[47]

Regardless of the synergy between grouse and hunters, the scale of the human harvest is remarkable. In his book, *The Grouse of the World*, the eminent American ornithologist Paul Johnsgard assembled the most comprehensive worldwide figures on grouse shooting, albeit from a generation ago. They are deeply revealing. Only the bag figures for Russia, which are substantial, are missing from his census. They gave a global figure for the late 1970s of just over 9 million birds a year. This equates to roughly 5,900 tonnes of grouse, all of it obtained from entirely wild stock. By contrast, many, if not most, partridge or pheasant bags comprise birds reared by hand. Although Johnsgard gave figures for 13 species, two birds accounted for the vast majority – Willow Ptarmigan (Red Grouse) and Ruffed Grouse. In fact the total yearly harvest of the latter in North America was 5.7 million birds.

Geographically the census was equally revealing. It showed that the world epicentre for the pastime is the mid-west cluster involving a single Canadian province, Ontario, with three adjacent US states – Michigan, Minnesota and Wisconsin. Between them they accounted for 2.9 million grouse a year, 36 per cent of the entire North American bag, which was just under 8 million birds.[48]

There are several grouse which, while shot in good numbers at the time of Johnsgard's estimate, are now no longer or barely harvested as the species have declined. This is particularly the case with the Greater Prairie Chicken, **Sage Grouse** *Centrocercus urophasianus* and **Sharp-**

tailed Grouse *Tympanuchus phasianellus*. However, the key targets – Ruffed Grouse and Willow Ptarmigan (Red Grouse) – remain common and commonly hunted. If anything some bags have increased. In Norway, for instance, the combined harvest of Rock Ptarmigan and Willow Ptarmigan (Red Grouse) has gone from 423,000 (1975–80) to 500–750,000 (1998).[49] The estimates concerning grouse hunting in Russia, which were unavailable to Johnsgard, have also now been established, putting the national total for the last-named species at 8 million birds.[50] It suggests a current world harvest possibly as high as 15–20 million grouse.

We should try, perhaps, to visualise that behind each cold statistic stands a hunter, warmed by the exertion of his or her efforts and confronted with a flock of birds whirring away through the landscape. While there is a generic simplicity and inherent excitement to the activity, it has carried very different meanings according to time and place. The eminent novelist and poet Margaret Atwood reflects on the importance of grouse shooting to her family as she grew up in 1940s Canada.

I lived in those woods as a child. My dad – a crack woodsman and subsistence expert – hunted grouse. So did my brother, with a bow, before he was of firearm age. The grouse were somewhat easy to track because of the drumming they do – usually on hollow logs, using the log as an amplifier and beating with their wings. We didn't have any dogs. We only ever hunted grouse in order to eat them. (They are delicious but we had to watch for pellets.) It was the war. It was the woods – there were no grocery stores. The alternate animal proteins were Spam and Klick and smoked bacon. We fished for the same reason – to eat. The idea of killing any animal or fish for sport and then throwing it away is repugnant to me. My dad said in later years that he regretted his grouse shooting after a point; he kept on with it – in his opinion – longer than necessity strictly warranted. He was good at it, and people enjoy doing things they're good at.

The North American Ruffed Grouse doesn't go about in flocks, nor is it an open-country bird. Its territories are larger than those of [Red Grouse] in Britain, so the beating-the-fields techniques used there would be useless here: the idea of platoons of ghillies plodding through boreal or sub-boreal young growth in order to flush Ruffed Grouse in huge flocks is ludicrous. (Impenetrable, that stuff. Also, no flocks. Also, the grouse would hear you falling over and swearing, and would hide.)[51]

A modern hunter with 40 years' experience of grouse shooting reflects on how the sport has changed in parts of North America in the years since the Second World War.

I know of no one for whom grouse hunting is now a 'subsistence activity'. It is sport hunting. Certainly the sport hunters do eat their birds, although there is a percentage that enjoy the hunting more than the eating, probably because the only way they know to prepare them is as my mother did – pan-fried – resulting in shoe-leather eating.[52]

If North American grouse hunting has become more purely recreational in character, nevertheless it remains a socially broad-based activity that requires only modest financial outlay. A lapsed Nebraskan hunter writes on the economics and logistics of grouse shooting in that state:

Here Sharp-tailed Grouse and prairie chickens can be hunted with a small game license. A habitat stamp is also required. Total cost: $30 ($14 for license, plus $16 for habitat stamp). The place I hunted was government land. Typically a hunter would see likely grouse habitat, and track down the owner via a map that shows the property lines, names of owners, as well as contact information. Or one would just drive to the nearest house and ask permission. Every one who hunts must abide by the harvest limit set by the state, which is three birds – either three of one species, or a combination of the two Nebraskan grouse.[53]

In Britain a similar informal model of hunting occurs, known as 'walking up' the birds. It involves small parties of shooters taking moderate bags during the course of a day's hilltop tramp, with trained gun dogs often 'pointing' out the grouse as they crouch in the heather. However, even this style of hunting is usually a 'product', purchased by the day or through the costs of accommodation by non-local customers from the owners of the grouse moor or sporting estate. (The same is true for some hunters in North America, although invariably at lower cost.) In Britain a day's shoot of this kind for ten brace involving four guns costs approximately £880 ($1,410) or £220 ($350) per person.[54]

A second and almost exclusively British model of hunting grouse, alluded to in Margaret Atwood's piece ('platoons of ghillies plodding'), is the driven shoot. It follows traditions established during the Victorian age and has a highly organised structure, in which several, even dozens, of flag-waving beaters drive birds across the moor towards the guns. They, by contrast, travel by all-terrain vehicles and then stand in lines of open, walled structures known as

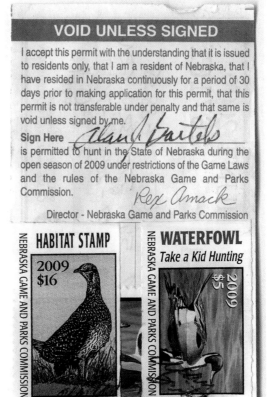

In the US state of Nebraska a hunting licence and habitat stamp are required by law, and entitle the holder to shoot three grouse a day and to hold no more than six at any one time.

butts where they are served by loaders – those reloading the guns with cartridges while another is being fired – and other support staff. Here the bags tend to be considerably larger. The expense is also higher. Typically a driven shoot taking 50 brace by eight guns, costs £7,050 ($11,000) a day, or £881 ($1,400) per person.[55]

While it involves a high degree of sporting challenge and while the grouse are usually eaten, with some going to beaters and other employed personnel, the activity's exclusivity is obvious. Its very structure is a carefully choreographed ritual about social dominance (the beaters are invariably low-paid locals while the 'guns' are the moor owners, friends of the owners or privileged non-locals) and ascendancy even over the landscape and nature itself (often the only physical exercise for the 'guns' is the bird killing). It bears no resemblance to subsistence hunting, but is rather a form of conspicuous consumption for the wealthiest in society.

GROUSE NAMES

The word 'grouse' is of obscure derivation. Dating from at least the sixteenth century it is widely held to have its origins in the Old French *grouchier*.[56] From the root word has come the English verbs 'to grudge' or, in older form, 'to grutch', meaning to murmur or grumble.[57] Of more modern coinage – dating to the early twentieth century – are 'grouch' and 'grouchy'.[58] 'Grouse' as a verb has a similar sense of making complaint and suggests that the name described the bird's vocalisations. Certainly the call of the Willow Ptarmigan (Red Grouse) has a particularly bad-tempered quality and

The traditional sites where Sharp-tailed Grouse perform their remarkable foot-stomping displays can be in continuous use for hundreds of years.

is often transliterated as *go-bak, go-bak, go-bak*, which nicely combines irritation with protest.

The most singular name for the family is 'ptarmigan'. It originates with the Gaelic *tarmachan* (itself from a root *tarm*: 'murmur') and meant something like 'croaker'.[59] The name evokes the weird creaking calls of rock ptarmigan but, adding a touch of neoclassical confusion in 1684, the Scottish naturalist Sir Robert Sibbald gave a silent 'p' to the new version to falsely suggest a Greek construction. This made it ptarmigan. What is particularly striking is how this chance error by a single individual has become embedded in modern ornithological nomenclature and accepted usually without us ever stopping to reflect how such an odd word came to pass.[60]

Some of the earlier alternatives to the word 'grouse' indicate the exploitative character of our interactions, and even two current names, Greater and Lesser Prairie Chicken, spell out our culinary intentions. Another tendency in North America was for the first colonial settlers to recycle Old World names that carried implications of game, food and hunting. Both 'pheasant' and 'partridge' were used, for instance, for the Ruffed Grouse.[61] Perhaps the ultimate slight, which combines a sense of the bird as food with a slur on its intelligence, is 'fool hen', used interchangeably for Ruffed Grouse, **Blue Grouse** *Dendragapus obscurus* of western USA, or the largely Canadian **Spruce Grouse** *Falcipennis canadensis*. Yet the name is not without justification:

> My father grew up in a small town in Newfoundland, Canada, where hunting for your meal was common. They hunted many Spruce Grouse with guns, but he's always said you didn't really need one and that sometimes you could get so close that all you had to do was carry a big stick. I guess this was better, because you didn't have to worry about picking shot from your stew.

I'm not sure how true it all is, but he has eaten his fair share of grouse . . . and gulls and American Robins.[62]

The stories that turn on how easily grouse can be captured were commonplace in the past, but referred essentially to birds unschooled in the ways of humans. In Labrador an old method involved slipping a noose around the necks of Spruce Grouse before jerking them off their perch. Sometimes, if a noose touched the grouse without looping cleanly over its head, the bird's only response was to nudge the rope away with its bill, and stay put until the hunter's efforts succeeded.[63] One commentator wrote that he climbed up a small pine and grabbed one bird by its feet 'just to see if I could do it'. Another noted how a bird 'sat sedately on a limb while a revolver was emptied at her. The shots having missed, roots and stones were thrown, which she avoided by stiff bows or occasional steps to the side.'[64]

GROUSE DISPLAY AND HUMAN DANCE

Grouse behaviour achieves its most bizarre form in the breeding season, when many species gather on a communal display ground or arena, known as a 'lek'. The word functions as both verb and noun. It originates with the Swedish *leka*: 'to play'; although there is an archaic English term 'lake' signifying 'play' or 'sport' that comes from Old Norse (*leik-r*: 'play'), and has corresponding words in Old English (*lác*: 'warlike activity') and Gothic (*laik-s* 'dance'). All of these meanings converge nicely in that simple monosyllable. On the lek, male grouse indulge in a mixture of hormonally charged posturing and weird far-carrying vocalisations that are at once arresting, dramatic, sometimes humorous and always astonishingly beautiful.[65]

In Europe the leks of both Black Grouse and **Western Capercaillie** *Tetrao urogallus*, which is the largest family member, are major draws for birders (their displays are

The Western Capercaillie is one of Europe's most magnificent birds, but across that region the species is succumbing to the wholesale simplification of its wooded habitats.

described in detail in *Birds Britannica*; see pages 158–62). Yet the behaviour is equally compelling in five North American species – the two species of prairie chicken and the Gunnison, Sage and Sharp-tailed Grouse. In the latter species the display area is frequently referred to as a 'dancing hill', while that of the two prairie chickens is more usually termed a 'dancing' or 'booming ground', after the birds' deep resonant calls, which can carry several kilometres.

Some of these traditional locations are very ancient; one Albertan farmer noted in the 1930s that a site on his land frequented by Sharp-tailed Grouse dated back beyond the tribal memory of the local Native Americans.[66] In fact the ancestry associated with many leks draws into question the very notion of human ownership. The power of the site to compel its grouse attendants is also legendary. No example is more poignant than a place used by a now extinct subspecies of Greater Prairie Chicken, the Heath Hen. The last lone male returned faithfully to an hereditary booming ground year after year, until its own abysmal end.[67]

The Greater Prairie Chicken population is one of the classic examples where market hunting did play a part in the contraction of a grouse species' range and numbers. There are stories of New York dealers receiving 20 tonnes of them in a single consignment.[68] Aldo Leopold described 25,000 birds being shipped to market in 1896 from one Wisconsin village.[69] Fortunately sufficient numbers of this grouse survive in central USA, where their display grounds are a major draw.

At rest, long feathers fall from the male prairie chicken's crown like a cloth-rabbits' floppy ears, but at the height of the performance these tufts are pressed forwards. The tail is cocked vertically. The flight feathers, like outspread hands, curve round a swollen white bustle of under-tail coverts at the bird's rear. The head droops and the chicken advances, the elongated crown feathers now thrust up like horns in a priapic gesture of challenge. It also emits a soft, penetrating dove-like *woowing* sound, which it continues as it performs an accelerated foot-stomping action (up to 20 steps per second).[70] The so-called 'booming' notes then synchronise with an awkward, almost convulsive jerk of the whole head downwards. It occurs as the bird gulps in air to inflate skin sacs on the neck. These quickly swell up and become visible as orange bladders on the breast sides with an outer margin of an exquisite pale-magenta colour. With all these emblems of sexual ripeness on display the cock then literally deflates, only for the actions to begin again. The whole performance looks at once ritualised, ancient and ecstatic. For any human observer it is compelling theatre.

The leks used by various species of grouse have become an attraction for birders and tourists in Colorado, Nebraska, Texas, Kansas, Utah and New Mexico ('listed in descending order of signficance').[71] Photography is often a part of the human focus. Sometimes a lek can be an important source of income for the landowner, the new ecotourism justifying both the preservation of the birds and their habitat. As one Nebraskan notes, 'As the birds have become rare, people are willing to pay to observe them. It's like a trophy for some to say, "I went to Nebraska and saw prairie chickens dancing, it was amazing."'[72]

One of the most remarkable responses to prairie chicken displays is their inspiration for a wide range of Native American ceremonial dances. (To a lesser extent the equally remarkable display of the Sharp-tailed Grouse and Sage Grouse inspired similar human imitations.) These rituals are ancient and were historically encountered among various communities including the Cree, Ojibwa, Blackfoot and Lakota nations.[73]

Today, however, the practice has achieved much wider cultural diffusion through the nationally or regionally organised pow-wow gatherings attended by many different

Native American communities. These fundamentally modern expressions of Indian identity have created new spaces and opportunities for traditional cultural activity. At pow-wows the dances are often competitively organised, with substantial prize money for individual winners in separate dance categories. The chicken dance is particularly popular and now occurs well beyond its place of origin.

Another good illustration of its wider incorporation into the 'mainstream' of modern Native American culture is its appearance in Ledger Art. This peculiarly dynamic form of visual expression had its own origins in images first painted or drawn on to account books obtained by native peoples through trade. George Flett, a contemporary exponent of ledger art from the Spokane Reservation in Washington state, has repeatedly returned to the subject of chicken dancers in his own acclaimed paintings.[74] Flett's work, in turn, represents a reinterpretation of the dance as a traditional subject among earlier ledger artists. Yet it is worth noting that no genuine prairie chicken ever danced in the state of Washington. Nor would Flett's people originally have performed it. One wonders, indeed, how many modern chicken dancers have ever seen a bird perform the original display?

There is a huge variety of costume and styles associated with the chicken dance, but a number of characteristics are recurrent and suggest how the human choreography continues to mimic the original avian performance. These include the dancers wearing a prominent bustle of feathers at the rear, a pair of taller feather horns, while the dance itself often incorporates intricate stepping or foot-stomping actions.

This is not the only example of a grouse-inspired dance. The *Schuhplattler*, which claims to be one of the oldest surviving European dances, is a folk dance performed in German Bavaria and Austria. It is famous (even, perhaps infamous) for the way leather-clad men slap their thighs and the soles of their shoes alternately. One of the pioneers of ethno-ornithology, E A Armstrong, believed that the dance borrowed from the ritualised actions of the Black Grouse, suggesting that there was proof of the claim in the large tuft of Black Grouse tail feathers often worn by the dancers in their hats.[75] However, a section of the dance known as the *Nachsteigen* suggests another more impressive grouse as the key inspiration. In this stage of the performance:

> The young man does not simply dance with his maid, but with wooing movements, clicking his tongue, hissing, and clapping the hands, he jumps along behind her or, if space is lacking, next to her, stamps on the floor, take [sic] a couple of leaps, or perhaps even turns a somersault. Finally, with his arms outspread or hanging close to the ground, he rushes towards his partner or leaps suddenly in a curve towards her, after he has struck the ground hard with one or both hands.[76]

These distinctive gestures and sounds invoke the other grouse of European uplands, Western Capercaillie. It is interesting to compare the hissing and tongue clicking with the following description of a capercaillie's vocalisations during display: 'begins with notes . . . "klick-*kleck*" sounding like knocking together of two small sticks at intervals . . . but getting quicker at end, followed without break by sound like drawing of cork and ending with one represented as "sch-scht-ssts-pss-sch-scht" . . . like twittering of bird or grinding of knife.'[77]

This bizarre performance is often a moment of intense aggression (the bird goes momentarily deaf during the display, a fact once exploited by human hunters). The competing males sometimes die of their wounds and in one encounter, famously caught on television, an especially irate Finnish capercaillie floored David Attenborough, then badgered him into ignominious flight.

OLD WORLD PARTRIDGE, FRANCOLIN AND SNOWCOCK

The partridge – like the goose or duck – is a classic model of the wild-caught bird for the pot. Collectively these gamebirds are of major cultural significance as a source of meat and recreation, but also in terms of land management. Fondness for game has left parcels of rough country at the margins of agricultural fields all over the partridge-shooting world. In so doing it has led to habitat conservation across several continents. Even so, 26 species of partridge and francolin – one-quarter – are threatened or near-threatened.

The birds have also inspired much literature and art. One of the most powerful modern representations of the group occurs in that quintessential American art form, the Western. Sergio Leone's masterpiece *Once Upon a Time in the West* (1968) is now regarded as one of the genre's finest examples. This reputation owes much to the hauntingly beautiful if violent opening scenes. In one of these an Irishman, Brett McBain, and his young son Timmy wile away the moments before the family's al fresco picnic with a spot of partridge shooting. The birds repeatedly flushed from the surrounding brush hurtle upwards with startling impact. This action, which is so typical of partridge, explains much about their worldwide reputation as game, demonstrating how hunting them with firearms requires marksmanship and extremely steady nerves.

Leone used this unpredictable eruption of the birds to heighten the scene's atmosphere of almost inexplicable menace. (We should not overlook how the sounds of two other galliforms, the clucking chickens and gobbling turkeys, reinforce this subliminal edginess.) The partridge shoot reaches its dramatic climax with the sudden, shocking slaughter of the whole McBain family and culminates in the emergence of five cattle-coated murderers from that same brush whence the partridge had earlier burst forth. Contrary to all expectations, Henry Fonda, the archetypal good guy, is cast here as psychopath-in-chief.

In many ways the scene exemplifies a second core theme in our interactions with partridge. The birds in the film should never – and, in fact, have never – been flushed from the sagebrush of Arizona. They are **Red-legged Partridge** *Alectoris rufa*, a bird endemic to western Europe. Their appearance in the film is typical of the natural-historical inconsistencies that are commonplace in cinema, and in this case reflects the likelihood that Leone shot the 'Arizonan' scenes in Spain, where Red-legged Partridges are common.

Grey Partridges are declining across 25 European countries. What are often understated in these biological losses are the vanishing cultural riches accruing from the birds' subtle beauty and wonderfully atmospheric creaking calls.

PARTRIDGE INTRODUCTIONS

However, Leone's birds are emblematic in this sense: many partridge species are now located precisely where they should *not* be. Such is the family's reputation on the dining table or in the hunter's covert that, if a place did not originally hold partridge, humans have tended to contrive their presence (except in South America, where tinamous, chachalacas and other indigenous 'gamebirds' have served as replacements). Thus, one of the dominant cultural engagements with the group is their introduction into many parts of the globe. Two of the most highly prized sporting birds of Eurasia, for instance, the **Grey Partridge** *Perdix perdix* and **Chukar Partridge** *Alectoris chukar*, now have large ranges in North America (with additional toeholds in New Zealand and South Africa). About a million chukars were being shot each year in the 1960s.[78]

Perhaps the most extraordinary example of these Old-to-New World transplants involves the **Himalayan Snowcock** *Tetraogallus himalayensis*, an inhabitant mainly of Tibet and western China. They are impressive high-altitude grouse-like birds and, like Asia's other four snowcock species, inhabit snowfields and rocky crags up to 5,000 m (16,500 ft), flourishing amid the lowest oxygen levels enjoyed by any bird family on Earth. America's snowcocks were released in Nevada in 1963, with the intention of providing a new, if highly challenging, quarry for US sportsmen.

A total of 2,045 birds, taken from Hunza in Pakistan, were liberated mainly in the Ruby Mountains and breeding was confirmed by 1977. This rather strange project, which involves a species confined to altitudes above 3,000 m (9,900 ft), has left an estimated 250–500 birds marooned, as one authority notes, 'on an alpine island at the centre of

the Great Basin'. Yet the snowcock has since been admitted to America's national list and birders take helicopter rides to the tops to tick them off. The scheme bore its officially intended fruit in 1980, when the first shooting season was declared. However, today, one of the figures central to the release project suggests that more birders than hunters make the effort to go to see them.[79]

Just as remarkable was the parallel attempt to introduce the species on Hawaii; snowcocks being liberated on the slopes of the dormant volcano Mauna Kea. The project failed, but it confirmed the unofficial status of these islands as the gamebird-transplant capital of the world. Originally Hawaii had none at all. Over the centuries the release of 22 non-native species has been attempted with varying degrees of success. Today Wild Turkeys, **Grey Francolin** *Francolinus pondicerianus*, **Black Francolin** *Francolinus francolinus*, **Erckel's Francolin** *Pternistis erckelii*, Chukar Partridge, Red Junglefowl and Indian Peafowl all flourish on Hawaii, compressing into one small Pacific-lapped territory the ornithological sights, sounds – and sporting experience – of four distant continents.[80]

Although ecologists frown upon the deliberate spread of non-native species, sometimes the introductions bolster a bird's overall population. A classic case involves the scene-setting bird from Leone's film. Red-legged Partridges were brought to Britain in the seventeenth century, and have established themselves as far north as Scotland. Yet the species' world distribution is relatively small, essentially comprising Spain and France. With recent declines in those countries, the British population (335,000 pairs) has come to represent 10 per cent of the world's total.[81]

The Romans considered partridges as pleasing on the eye as they were satisfying to the palate. This mosaic image, probably of a Barbary Partridge, was on the floor of a villa at Carthage in modern Tunisia.

PARTRIDGE VOCALISATIONS

Today the same birds may also be kept for their distinctive voice. Like all species in the genus and, like partridges in general, chukar produce a sound that is often one of the most atmospheric in the entire landscape. This guttural, rattling cock's crow has given identity to the species for millennia, as shown by the sweep of onomatopoeic names across almost its entire range: *kakkabē* (ancient Greek; the modern name is *Nisiotiki Perdika*: 'island partridge'), *keklik* (Turkish), *kabk* (Persian), *zarkar* (Pashto) and *chukōr* (Hindi).[84] Allan Octavian Hume heard the bird in India and thought that the harsh notes were announcing: *I'm here, I'm here; who's dead, who's dead; oh lor, oh lor.*[85]

The Black Francolin, which shares much of the latter's Asiatic range, has a similarly loud advertising call. Across the continent it is one of the most popular sporting birds.[86] Its reputation also appears to be ancient. Its name appears in Sumerian cuneiform texts, which were inscribed on clay tablets and subsequently found in Mesopotamia (now Iraq). Including more than 30 identifiable species, this 4,000-year-old text must be the oldest bird list in the world.[87] Like the chukar, Black Francolins have a habit of giving away their presence through their vocalisations. In fact the rasping six-note crow commended itself to the ears of Babur, the Mogul emperor, as *Sūbhān-tēri-qūdrāt* ('Omnipotent, thy power'). A more humorous version, which may glance at the racket's self-betraying quality, interprets the sound as *Lehsān-piāz-ădrăk* ('Garlic, onion, ginger'). The bird is, apparently, fine eating.[88]

The list of examples of partridge or francolin calls reproduced as fragments of human speech probably spans every country where the family occurs. It indicates the arresting power of the vocalisations. The calls are loud, or, at least, penetrating, vigorous, sometimes rather asthmatic in quality, and tending to run on an emotional axis between excitement and irritation. For these reasons partridge calls often have a Proustian effect, capable of awakening deep memories, especially a rich sense of place.

My own version of the experience comes from the strange creaking notes of Grey Partridge. That sound is absolutely synonymous with my birthplace and the moment in early spring when a distinctive, smoky, evening light descends on the snow-burnt hills of Derbyshire. The following contributions on two francolin songs suggest how the association between bird sound, moment and place is widespread, if not universal:

> The call of the bird we called the yellowneck (**Yellow-necked Spurfowl** *Pternistis leucoscepus*) is a major part of my childhood. They were quite common around Nairobi; in my mind their call is associated with walking in the early morning, in wild places, the sun low and my socks soaking with dew and full of burrs! Yellownecks are mad keen on potatoes, especially cooked ones! I found this out when we camped in the Serengeti, many years ago, and we put potatoes in silver foil in the fire. We couldn't see them in the dark and missed a number, and at dawn I saw the yellownecks digging in the embers and pulling the potatoes out of the foil. Old Kenya hands would put out some small potatoes at dusk, and in the morning have the shotgun handy when the francolin came . . . breakfast![89]

CAPTIVE PARTRIDGES

One unforeseen consequence of releasing a second partridge into Britain (the only native was the Grey Partridge) was to introduce confusion to the famous carol. The first verse in 'The Twelve Days of Christmas' includes the oft-referenced line, 'a partridge in a pear tree' (see also *Birds Britannica*, page 164). This tree-dwelling galliform has long perplexed birdwatchers. 'Pear tree' may be a corruption of the French word for partridge, *perdrix* (the song is thought to have originated with a French forfeit game that appeared in England about 1780). Even with this fresh gloss the line is no more coherent, but it would at least confirm the lyrics' wider theme of whimsical wordplay (e.g. 'ten lords a-leaping').[82] A more intriguing theory centres on 'pear tree' as the old name for a type of wicker or fruit-wood (pear) domed cage, in which live gamebirds were held until ready for the pot.[83] This interpretation is highly persuasive, but the bird's precise identity remains beyond evaluation.

However, in parts of southern Europe, Red-legged Partridges and their more easterly relative, Chukar Partridges, are still kept in cages exactly like this, where the birds have almost no room to turn. The prisoners are held partly for the bold, simple, almost graphic design of their markings, which have evidently appealed to us for thousands of years. In the classical period chukars were a common motif in all sorts of art forms from ceramics to mosaics. Typically, on the island of Rhodes, Greece, the archaeological museum houses a virtually intact, painted urn that dates to 600 BC. On each side are seven exquisitely painted chukars. There is also a fine image of a chukar (or its lookalike sibling **Rock Partridge** *Alectoris graeca*) in a mosaic housed in the Palace of the Grand Masters in Rhodes Town.

Nothing brings back east Africa's savannah quicker than the distinctive calling of the little **Crested Francolin** *Dendroperdix sephaena*. It takes me right back to my early days in Kenya travelling around in the back of a Land Rover with my father – and our nights out in the field with those heavy canvas tents. As with Hemingway, I never woke up in the morning without feeling an immense energy for life – and happy – aided by reassuring, familiar birdsong. But it is the evocative loud screeching utterances of this bird that makes me feel 'back home' more than any other. This is partly due to the fact that I've attended many wonderful field programmes in Kenya and Tanzania, where large flocks of francolin dominate the morning chorus and sunset. I suspect that the enormity of the savannah landscape would feel very odd without its incessant call. [90]

In many ways the **Udzungwa Forest Partridge** *Xenoperdix udzungwensis* is the antithesis of the 'yellowneck' or the Crested Francolin. This intriguing bird was only revealed to science in 1991 and occurs on just two peaks, Ndundulu and Nyumbanitu, in the Udzungwa Mountains of south-central Tanzania, a world range of 190 km² (73 miles²). How it managed to escape detection until so late in the twentieth century is remarkable, but more extraordinary still was the manner of discovery. On 4 June 1991 a group of Danes were birdwatching in this endemic-rich part of east Africa:

Supper was, as always, a most welcome interruption. During the fight to get hold of the remaining bits of . . . [meat], two small chicken-like feet suddenly appeared at the bottom of the pot . . . what species did these 'spare parts' belong to? The guides from the local village, Udweka, were smiling roguishly due to the white people's excitement and we knew by then that they were the promoters of this unexpected diet contribution.

It turned out that it had been caught in a snare just behind the camp. It was a 'kwale ndogo' . . . presumably some kind of francolin . . . As the checklists of the Udzungwa Mountains did not mention any forest-dwelling francolins or the like, we were very eager to get a closer look at this bird – preferably alive. During the next two days we caught only glimpses, but on the third day we saw a small flock at close range.

. . . On our way back to Dar es Salaam we were naturally bubbling with expectancy like a shaken bottle of champagne. The cork went off next morning as we were unable to find anything like it in the literature. The people of Mbezi Beach got an abrupt awakening by the sound of 'ornithooligans' yelling, bawling, jumping – the pack of Danes were back with a major discovery. [91]

The beautiful, delicate, flame-throated bird turned out to be without close relatives and, if anything, is more closely allied to the hill-partridges (*Arborophila*) of Asia than other species in Africa. The species may have escaped European notice, but it was well known to local people. When the Danes tried to catch Udzungwa partridge, they mist-netted 1,000 birds of 58 species, but trapped not a single *kwale ndogo*. As they freely acknowledge, it took real Tanzanian expertise to catch a male and female partridge as final proof of 'their' discovery.

OLD WORLD QUAIL

There are seven species in the genus *Coturnix* and all are to some extent migrants, moving particularly in response to rainfall and the growth of the lush grassland vegetation which they love. They occur across a vast region, from the middle latitudes of Europe to much of Asia, Africa and Australia. The **Common Quail** *Coturnix coturnix* is the most widespread; its breeding range extending from Mongolia to Portugal.

It is a tiny, shy, cover-hugging bird that is seldom observed and notable for its long-distance seasonal journeys. Its spring movements out of sub-Saharan Africa into Eurasia are inextricably linked to the Common Quail's history as food. The celebrated cook and writer Claudia Roden, member of an old Egyptian Jewish family, captures something of this in her recollection of childhood picnics on the dunes near Alexandria. They were 'timed to coincide with the arrival of migrating quails on the beaches', she writes: 'The birds fell exhausted, to be caught in large nets and collected in baskets. They were cleaned and marinated in a rich cumin and coriander sauce and grilled on the beach over small fires.' [92]

Subsistence hunter-gathering of this kind has probably occurred in Egypt since the early Holocene. Certainly there is a remarkable carved relief from Saqqara dating to the middle of the third millennium BC that depicts ancient Egyptian trappers using draw nets to catch quails in the cornfields. [93] The bird was important enough for them to fashion an ideogram – or hieroglyph – depicting a quail chick (denoting the phoentic sound 'w'), which suggests that they may also have domesticated the species. However, the most revealing portraits of migrant quails in the ancient world are textual.

One of these is in Pliny's *Natural History* (see Appendix II), where he writes of migrant quail: 'They too get here by flying in the same way as the cranes, not without danger to seafarers when they have come near to land: for they often perch on the sails, and they always do this at night, and sink the vessels.' [94] The observation of nocturnal migration across the Mediterranean is certainly accurate, but the claim of flocks so vast that they could crash into and capsize a boat is an extraordinary assertion.

There were other classical European claims of boat-sinking quails, but the best description of their mass

The hunting of Common Quail is recorded in the Old Testament and in ancient Egyptian frescoes. This one is in the tomb of Nebamun at Thebes and dates to *c*.1350 BC.

Common Quail were once caught in huge numbers in the Mediterranean region using nets that stretched along whole coastlines.

" Blinded decoy quail are placed in a large cage, often as many as sixty or seventy together, and the cage is placed on a platform elevated by poles about seven or eight feet from the ground in the centre of the netted part. These decoys call, making a noise like a man knocking two stones together, and the quails in passage hear it and are attracted to the spot"

QUAIL-NETTING IN SOUTHERN ITALY

DRAWN BY HORACE FISHER

movement during migration is in the Old Testament.[95] The first of two references is Exodus 16:13. When Moses led the Jews out of Egyptian enslavement, God relieved their starving condition as they tramped across the Sinai by delivering flesh in the evening and manna the following dawn: 'And it came to pass that at even the quails came up, and covered the camp.' (The story also appears in the Qur'an, Surah Al-Baqarah, v. 57.) In Numbers 11:31–34, there is much more detail on this event:

> And there went forth a wind from the Lord, and brought quails from the sea, and let *them* fall by the camp, as it were a day's journey on this side, and as it were a day's journey on the other side, round about the camp, and as it were two cubits high upon the face of the earth.
>
> And the people stood up all that day, and all *that* night, and all the next day, and they gathered the quails: he that gathered least gathered ten homers: and they spread *them* all abroad for themselves round about the camp.
>
> And while the flesh was yet between their teeth, ere it was chewed, the wrath of the Lord was kindled against the people, and the Lord smote the people with a very great plague.
>
> And he called the name of that place Kibroth-hattaavah: because there they buried the people that lusted.

For all its wrath-filled visitations from Jehovah, to which we will return later, the passage includes some accurate natural history. The appearance of the flocks on a spring evening in the Sinai meshes closely with genuine quail migration. Even the reference to birds coming in off the sea and landing in profuse numbers suggests first-hand experience of their habits. (It is precisely the birds' exhaustion after a long flight which leaves them easy prey for Mediterranean hunters.) Once again, however, the striking feature is the sheer number. Birds arranged on either side of the camp to a depth of 2 cubits or 91–111 cm (36–44 in) were calculated by the British ornithologist Hugh Gladstone to number 9 million.[96]

Questions have been raised over whether the passage meant that the quail flew at 2 cubits' height over the ground, or accumulated to that depth of bird flesh. This is largely immaterial to the calculations. However, the text does specify that 'he that gathered least gathered ten homers'. A homer was an ancient Hebrew measurement roughly equivalent to 365 litres (80 gallons). If one worked on a basis of two quail per litre – an average quail weighs 100 g (4 oz) and measures just 16–18 cm (6–7 in) – then the total number of birds harvested by Moses and his stated party of 600,000 'footmen' would be 4.4 billion. However, Gladstone argued that this estimate of the Jewish population as it was fleeing Egypt is far too high, hence his much smaller figure of 9 million birds, which he arrived at from a calculation based on just 600 'families', not 600 'thousand' men.

Even his much more conservative total seems like, and

surely *is*, a piece of biblical fantasy but, as in Pliny's reference to quail flocks capsizing boats, there may be more to it than just ludicrous exaggeration. Other sources on historical quail catches suggest the large scale of the birds' movements. In his classic work, *A History of Fowling*, the Reverend Hugh Macpherson gives a detailed account of the varied and ingenious devices by which Europeans caught quail. Macpherson suggested that the annual catch on the southern Italian isle of Capri alone was 56,000 birds.[97] Another nineteenth-century source recorded a single day's quail haul – along an 8 km (5 mile) stretch of southern Italian coastline – that numbered more than 100,000 birds.[98]

Today both the trapping operations and the birds' numbers have declined. Even so, until the 1990s the trammel nets deployed along Sinai's northern coast were thought to stretch continuously for 179 km (111 miles). Every autumn thousands of people flocked to the coast to man this vast wall of mesh. In 1990 the season's catch was 205,000 birds, with an estimated success rate of 87.5 per cent of all the migrant quails passing. It is worth recording the words of one old trapper, Haj Eid, who was over 100 years old. He recounted 'with great emotion the days when he was a young boy . . . "great flocks of Quail came from the sea and darkened the horizon . . . our nets would collapse from the weight of the Quail, a kilometre of nets would catch a thousand Quails in a day or even an hour . . . not a whole season"'.[99]

It seems relevant to the theme of this quail account that Eid's interviewers thought his statement 'might be slightly exaggerated'. It is known, however, that a 1926 report on quail exports from Egypt recorded an annual average of well over a million birds for the 40 years before the First World War. The document offered few figures for the kind of local, incidental domestic consumption described earlier by Claudia Roden, but suggested it could have been as high as the entire annual export total.[100]

Moreover, the report only documented catches for Egypt, yet its author noted elsewhere that intensive trapping occurred along Africa's entire northern coast.[101] In fact quail were harvested in similar fashion wherever they occurred, from the European Mediterranean to the Indian subcontinent. To give a single example, between the 1960s and 1970s, the quails shot in Russia dropped in number from 2.5 to 1.6 million. The figures indicate the scale of the recent catch, but also the size of the bird's continent-wide fall in population, perhaps partly because of hunting.[102]

The overall picture from a variety of sources is of the use of intensive methods and an ever-diminishing quail harvest along a massive front stretching for thousands of kilometres. The battue has continued unabated not just for centuries, but for millennia; and not only in the spring as the birds migrate north to breed. It is repeated each autumn when they return to Africa.

As the present quail numbers diminish, so our capacity simply to imagine the past size of the quail migration or the human bag becomes ever more impoverished. The caution displayed over the memories of a modern Egyptian trapper helps us to understand our own incredulity when confronted with the seemingly fabulous numbers cited in ancient texts: in short, we tend to disbelieve what we have never witnessed. Yet, if we cannot endorse the poetic imagery of the Old Testament, then we can at least infer how in the remote past – when human populations were minimal and habitat at its

maximum – the quail numbers were so vast that they *explain* the exaggeration, if not confirm it.

Returning briefly to Pliny's report of birds cascading on to the decks of a boat until the vessel sank, one can catch a glimpse of the phenomenon in a relatively recent ornithological paper on migrant birds in the Mediterranean. During a thunderstorm on 27 September 1962 off the Greek island of Skyros, a large 'blizzard' of quail came onboard a ship, and more than 100 birds were killed in the collision.[103] There were also reports from earlier in the twentieth century of boats which passed through 'masses of drowned Quails' following rainstorms just south of the Greek island of Crete.[104] These modern observations at least hint at the kind of storm-tossed events which might help us to understand Pliny's more extraordinary claims.

Finally we should return to that part of the Old Testament account which describes how Jehovah, lavishing quail flesh upon the Israelites, then smote his people with a terrible plague. Something of the bird's cultural identity is entwined in that strange, seemingly unrelated retribution. For the quail was not just delicious to eat, it was said to inflame other physical appetites. A people who craved a bird, which was itself a symbol of sexual desire, were presumably all the more deserving of divine wrath.

The fertility and sexual associations were partly rooted in the quail's connection with spring. This was dramatised not only in the bird's migration, but also in its propensity to appear after or during rain which, as noted previously, is connected with the family's ecological attachment to grassland. Several species in Africa and Asia make seasonal movements in response to patterns of rainfall. The species found in India is actually called the **Rain Quail** *Coturnix coromandelica*. One wonders if the same underlying link is manifest in old vernacular names once used for Common Quail in parts of Britain, such as 'Wet-my-feet', 'Wet-my-lips' and 'Wet Weather'.[105] The first two are partly echoic of the male's three-note song, but the repeated references to wetness are striking.

Like other gamebirds, quail were also thought to be over-sexed because of their polygamous breeding arrangement. In his book, *Ornithology*, John Ray wrote of the species: 'The Quail is a bird no less salacious than the Partridge, infamous also for obscene and unnatural lust. The Cocks are of high spirit and courage; and therefore by some are wont to be trained up and prepared for the combate, after the manner of Cock[erel]s: and *Aelian* [see Appendix II] tells us, that of old times at *Athens* Quail-fightings were wont to be exhibited as shews; and . . . that there was as great flocking to them as to a spectacle of Gladiators.'[106] Rearing and keeping quails for sport is both ancient and widespread and, at one time, occurred from Europe to Japan.

In ancient Greece the associated gambling was so widespread they had a phrase – 'Quail Madness' – to describe those who were particularly addicted. However, the great Greek statesman, philosopher and lawmaker Solon (*c.*640–559 BC) is said to have considered quail fighting a wholesome spectacle for the Athenian youth, because the bravery of the fighting birds inspired the young men's courage.[107]

It is strange that the name of a bird renowned for its pluck and aggression should later acquire a secondary sense as a word meaning to cower in fear. In fact there is no obvious connection between the bird and the verb 'to quail', the identical spelling being a matter of simple coincidence.[108]

THAUMALEA AMHERSTIÆ.

This painting of Lady Amherst's Pheasant by Joseph Wolf is from D G Elliot's *A Monograph of the Phasianidae*, one of the most expensive bird books in the world.

PHEASANT

There is another apocryphal tale about Solon which tells of the occasion he met the Lydian king Croesus (595–*c.*547 BC). He was asked whether he had seen anything more splendid than this Asian potentate and his magnificent court at Sardis. Wishing to deflate such vanity, Solon replied, 'Yes, I have seen cocks and pheasants, and peacocks; for they are adorned with natural colours, and such as are ten thousand times more beautiful.'[109]

Today the story probably falls a little flat, the anticlimax shaped by our more prosaic responses to pheasants, which have been debased by the birds' sheer abundance. In Europe, America and elsewhere approximately 50 million **Common Pheasant** *Phasianus colchicus* may be reared and released annually by sporting communities.[110] Only when we catch a glimpse of a lesser-known species – perhaps a **Reeves's Pheasant** *Syrmaticus reevesii* with its extraordinary 1.6 m (5.2 in) tail, or even the dazzling, improbable colours of a **Temminck's Tragopan** *Tragopan temminckii* – can we revive Solon's appreciation of these sumptuously beautiful birds. For they are without cavil among the most radiant of all living creatures. In the avian world, perhaps only birds-of-paradise and hummingbirds compare.

For better or worse, this beauty has been at the heart of human engagement with pheasants. So too has their culinary reputation. They are shot and eaten wherever they occur. Their feathers have been worn as adornments. In the past their skins were collected. Eventually so too were the living birds. Pheasant keeping arose as a pastime in the nineteenth century. In the 1870s a single pheasant of a scarce form could reach a premium price equivalent to thousands of pounds today.[111]

Yet from these exploitative activities have grown more benign responses. The UK-based World Pheasant Association, devoted entirely to galliforms and their conservation, had its origins with a group of like-minded collectors. The beauty of pheasants has also inspired us to celebration in the visual arts and literature. The work of Chinese artist Wang Yuan, whose dates are unknown but whose extant paintings were completed in the 1340s, are among the earliest detailed images of pheasants. In terms of their mastery of bird physiology, the drawings exceed

anything in Western art up until that period (the exception, while not 'western' in provenance, are some of the magnificent murals found in ancient Egypt; see page 81).

Recent representations of pheasants have formed part of one of the most sumptuously produced of all ornithological publications. Daniel Giraud Elliot's two-volume *A Monograph of the Phasianidae* (1870–72) is the supreme model. Elliot was a wealthy American zoologist and one of the founders of the American Museum of Natural History in New York. His work on pheasants was self-published after years of meticulous study and featured the paintings of a man described as 'one of the greatest of all bird illustrators', the German-born Joseph Wolf.[112] Their combined efforts produced a book that was as rigorous in quality as it is now expensive. In 2004 a copy went to auction with a guide price of $120,000–$180,000 (£75,000–£112,500).

Our sense of beauty in pheasants is not simply a matter of colour, although it plays a major role. Typical is a species of the high mountains, **Himalayan Monal** *Lophophorus impejanus*. Memorably compared to 'a humming-bird enlarged to the size of a fowl', it is the national bird of Nepal, where it is called *Danphe* (pronounced 'Da-fé') meaning 'nine colours'.[113] The name refers in part to the metallic iridescence on a male's upperparts, which grades from brilliant copper to grass then emerald green and finally royal blue shot through with deep bronzed purple. In addition the rump is white, the tail rufous and the belly black.

A bird like the **Great Argus** *Argusianus argus* of Malaysia, Sumatra and Borneo is superficially rather plain, (albeit with a tail that renders the male 2 m: 6.6 ft in length). The bird is essentially grey-brown, but the male's elongated flight feathers, especially the secondaries, bear a sequence of green ocelli (Latin for 'eyes') that are enmeshed by the most exquisite tracery of shading and counter-shading. The beauty here is of an entirely separate order to that of the Himalayan Monal, yet no less compelling. One author spoke of the 'indescribable marvel' of the Great Argus, while Charles Darwin explored its very peculiar aesthetics in his arguments for the concept of sexual selection (see below).[114]

Another part of the pheasants' allure is the way the birds sometimes cease to resemble birds at all and just look bizarre. The Temminck's Tragopan is a classic example. The male has a body of dried-blood red overlaid by hundreds of white spots edged with black, and in display he beats his wings and produces a sound like marbles clicking together, while distending a bare-skin flap at the throat until it flares to the size of a plate. This quivering shield is predominantly electric blue finished in patterns of scarlet and indigo. In these moments the pheasant assumes a beauty that is difficult to pinpoint, one that is aesthetically moving and yet simultaneously primitive, even unearthly. We might presume that this extraordinary moment would be most appreciated in our own age of recreational birding. In fact, there is a beautifully accurate ink-and-wash drawing of a displaying Temminck's Tragopan by Wang Yuan from the 1340s.[115]

It is often historical responses which help us to appreciate how even the one pheasant we take for granted, the Common Pheasant, moved and affected people when they saw it. After Constantinople fell to the Turks in 1453, Philip the Good, Duke of Burgundy – foremost European prince of his age and founder of the Order of the Golden Fleece – held a banquet where he pledged himself and his nobles to the task of retrieving the ancient Byzantine city. The sacred oath swearing them to this mission was taken in the name of God and the Virgin, but also on a living pheasant (and a peacock) borne on the arms of the herald for Philip's chivalric order of knights. This genuine event underscores how the emblazoned beauty of a pheasant could galvanise the medieval imagination.[116]

The same story glances at the pheasant's Asiatic origins, because the fabled Golden Fleece was originally located in Colchis on the Black Sea (now a part of Georgia). The Common Pheasant, which was first obtained in exactly this area, was possibly intended to represent for the Burgundian court a precious, beautiful substitute for the fleece itself. Both parts of the Common Pheasant's modern scientific name (*Phasianus colchicus*) commemorate the geographical connection. The generic name comes from the River Phasis (now called Rioni, also in Georgia) and gives us in turn the versions in English, French (*faisan*), German (*fasan*), Greek (*phasianos*) and Italian (*fagiano*).

With one singular exception (see Congo Peacock, page 74), the area once known as Colchis is the most westerly point in the native distribution for any pheasant. The family's true home is eastern Asia, with the vast majority occurring in China and Tibet (24 species), the Indian subcontinent – including Myanmar and Sri Lanka – (14 species) and Indochina (12 species). In total there are 50 pheasant species and technically it includes the three peacocks and four junglefowl. However, since the latter are treated in detail under separate headings, references to 'the pheasants' mean only the residue 43 species.

Of these, no fewer than 32, nearly three-quarters, are considered to be threatened or near-threatened.[117] This places the pheasants among the most imperilled large bird families in the world (see also Parrot family, page 246). Even those not in immediate danger are affected by forest clearance, habitat loss or persecution. Perhaps just five birds – **Blood Pheasant** *Ithaginis cruentus*, Temminck's Tragopan, **Kalij Pheasant** *Lophura leucomelanos*, **Silver Pheasant** *Lophura nycthemera* and **Koklass Pheasant** *Pucrasia macrolopha* – can be considered plentiful. Only the Common Pheasant and **Green Pheasant** *Phasianus versicolor*, the national bird of Japan – where, ironically, up to half a million are shot each year – can be judged invulnerable.[118]

Rarity and extreme beauty are a heady combination, but stirred into the mix is another potent ingredient. They have been hunted for thousands of years and many have adapted by becoming supremely elusive. The great American naturalist William Beebe, author of a classic four-volume work *A Monograph of the Pheasants*, described the patience needed to watch the **Crested Fireback** *Lophura ignita* in Borneo. These birds, whose males are a glorious blue-black with copper-red rump and a bizarre electric-blue facial mask, were active in an area of forest that served as a cemetery for the local Dayak people. Beebe lay there for hours concealed by a thatched mat placed across a grave. Unfortunately, he wrote:

> I had disturbed a populous city of ants – innocuous as to bites or stings, or I should not have been able to lie still for a moment – but afflicted with an inordinate curiosity as to the meaning of this strange intruder. They certainly left no portion of my clothing

unexplored, and it took all the will-power I possessed to restrain myself and disregard the scrambling host. Then I realized that certain nerves in my body were going to sleep under the unaccustomed pressure, and it was not until I rose and shook the dirt from my person that I learned the fact that every centre of drowsy sensation had been a hungry leech who had feasted to repletion while my attention was distracted by the pheasants.[119]

Beebe evokes perfectly the challenge of observing pheasants in lowland rainforest. Unfortunately that sweaty, leech-tormented, bone-aching stillness of the subtropics is probably less demanding than the alternative trial entailed in watching pheasants of high-altitude habitats. Allan Octavian Hume once wrote: 'Unless you are a man of iron, able to walk 40 or 50 miles up and down without fatigue, and able to go uphill just as well as downhill, it is all nonsense going pheasant-shooting in the Himalayas.'[120]

Ironically, a beauty that was both rare and difficult of access made the pheasants' plumage a hugely desirable fixture in ceremonial costumes or as an insignia of elevated social rank. Typically, the **Blue Eared Pheasant** *Crossoptilon auritum* from central China sports long, filamentous, central tail feathers that were used as an official decoration in the hats of military mandarins in the imperial government.[121]

Some of the pheasants including this male Temminck's Tragopan are surely among the most radiantly colourful of all living organisms.

Until the twentieth century, Chinese generals wore the tail feathers of the male **Brown Eared Pheasant** *Crossoptilon mantchuricum* in their helmets.[122]

Another type of feather with an exact social purpose was the tail plume of the male Reeves's Pheasant, which has an inherent theatricality. (It is probably this species that was recorded in Marco Polo's *The Travels*, where he described it as having a tail that was 'fully ten palms in length'.)[123] In China the feathers were worn in the hats of actors when they played military roles and one assumes, therefore, that earlier still they were a part of genuine martial regalia.[124] Certainly the scalp feathers of the Himalayan Monal were used in Pakistan as a regular cap badge by the Gilgit Scouts, until the unit was disbanded in the 1970s. Today they are still worn, often after they are presented to young Pakistani men at the time of their wedding. Similar practices extend across the bird's entire Himalayan range.[125] In northern Nepal, for example, some of the region's Buddhist communities 'use a single monal feather (obtained by non-lethal means) as a spray tool of holy liquid (water or oils) during prayer'.[126]

The one rather serendipitous benefit arising from the Asian habit of sporting pheasant plumes was the 'discovery' of at least two new species. One of these was the intensely beautiful **Mikado Pheasant** *Syrmaticus mikado* in 1906. It is an endemic of Taiwanese montane forests and it came to the attention of Western science in the person of Walter Goodfellow, when the Briton spotted the distinctive black tail feathers in the headdress of a man who had come to carry his baggage.[127]

An even more remarkable piece of detective work, based on a handful of feathers, was the 'discovery' of **Mrs. Hume's Pheasant** *Syrmaticus humiae*. In 1879 the spouse of the eponymous lady, Allan Octavian Hume, visited the kingdom of Manipur in north-east India. The official sent to escort Hume to the maharajah bore, as a symbol of rank, three or four tail feathers from a pheasant species Hume did not recognise. When he finally persuaded his hosts to send a group of indigenous hunters to the pheasant's hitherto inaccessible home, they subsequently returned with a skin and a healthy living specimen. It was the first moment that any official in Manipur, let alone anyone in the outside world, had ever seen the bird alive.[128]

The Great Argus pheasant, whose feathers are among the most astonishing in size and pattern of any bird, were always likely to attract our cupidity. The abnormally huge secondaries bear a sequence of startling patterns known as ocelli. While many ocelli are just spots, those in the wings of the Great Argus have a more complex 'ball and socket' pattern. However, the full aesthetic impact is only evident during display, when the feathers are tilted to form a vertical plane. In his book, *The Descent of Man*, Charles Darwin reasoned that, since the feathers' beauty was hidden at all other times and the full impact of the ocelli manifest only when the feathers are inverted from their usual position, it proved the display was a calculated appeal to the female's aesthetic judgement and that her recognition of beauty played a key role in mate selection.[129]

In some ways just as remarkable as Darwin's theory on these exquisite plumes is the manner in which Malaysian and Sumatran hunters once obtained them for their own use. Their technique showed an insight into bird behaviour that was as precise and revealing as Darwin's own. Male argus

pheasants display in a special forest glade known as an 'arena', some of which can be used for decades if not centuries, the birds constantly clearing and re-clearing the area of any intrusive debris. The hunters would therefore embed razor-sharp flakes of bamboo deep into the arena floor. In their unremitting efforts to clear these deadly obstructions from their ceremonial space, the pheasants would literally stab and often bleed themselves to death. Beebe recorded some Dayak tribes who reported catching birds at the same arenas for several (human) generations.[130]

The precise usage made of Asian pheasant feathers could entail high levels of exploitation, but historically it was when they became a generic form of female adornment in the West, that the harvest had its deepest impact (see also Herons and the Feather Industry, page 131). One of the worst-hit species was the *Danphe*. A British friend of William Beebe acknowledged that he had personally trapped or shot 30,000–45,000 male Himalayan Monal between 1850 and 1880. Beebe suggested a single skin of this pheasant was achieving a price in London of between $5–$20 (about £1–£4). It explains why the monthly shipment in the late nineteenth century was 200–800 birds and why, after the trade was outlawed, British customs officials made 1,930 seizures of prohibited pheasant feathers in the decade after 1923.[131]

Fortunately not all humans have responded to the beauty and colour of pheasants with naked acquisitiveness. In Daocheng County, in China's western Sichuan province – where ethnic Tibetans are the largest minority – some pheasants are protected by sacred aura. A beneficiary of Buddhist attachment to the colour white, which stands for holiness and virtue, is the strikingly beautiful **White Eared Pheasant** *Crossoptilon crossoptilon*. At a significant number of Sichuan monasteries and their associated 'sacred groves', which are themselves religiously significant areas of woodland (and now also important reservoirs of biodiversity), the pheasants are routinely fed and become exceptionally tame. Flocks of up to 80 will peck around the monastery compound, where they are oblivious of monks and motorbikes alike. One notable development, as the Chinese authorities slacken their restriction on religious practice, is the expansion of both feeding and the habituation of White Eared Pheasants at other monasteries nearby.

The World Pheasant Association (WPA) has supported research on the birds and their relationship with Sichuan Buddhist practice. In 2006 the links forged between modern conservation and an ancient religious civilisation gave rise to a very strange but heart-warming cultural hybrid. In that year the WPA's fund-raising Christmas card featured an image of a local monk hand-feeding White Eared Pheasants. Christianity, Buddhism and the New-Age reverence for nature were all jumbled together in one delightful token of human goodwill.[132]

Similar religiously inspired behaviour occurs elsewhere at religious houses in China, Tibet, Nepal and Bhutan. It also embraces other Himalayan wildlife such as musk deer and blue sheep, which become so tame they too can be hand-fed. One of the more compelling instances involving galliforms is the flock of **Tibetan Eared Pheasant** *Crossoptilon harmani* (together with Blood Pheasants and **Tibetan Snowcock** *Tetraogallus tibetanus*), which find year-round food supplies at Xiongse Nunnery in Tibet. This religious centre, just 30 km (19 miles) from Lhasa, has stood for 800 years, and it is thought possible that the practices have continued since the twelfth century.[133] Every morning about eight o'clock the female occupants call out to the birds 'a kind of *coo-loo coo-loo coo-loo* sound, while various other nuns stand and watch if they have the time to do so.' They are fed mainly barley and scraps at a set area just next to the monastery ('a door opens and there they are') and even directly from the nuns' hands.

> They are not scared of people and come very close. The birds tend to roam around the monastery throughout the day, but I didn't see them going inside and they had a fairly set route through the buildings that eventually led to a wilder spot just above the monastery itself. I think they spend the night and breed around this area.[134]

This simple act of human charity, which is all the more powerful for occurring amid some of the most austere mountain scenery in the world, seems a model of compassion towards another living creature.

In his book, *The Botany of Desire*, the American ecologist Michael Pollan turns on its head our standard perception of plant domestication. Rather than seeing ourselves as the ecological slave masters coercing species like the apple, tulip or potato to do our bidding without recompense, Pollan suggests that we should consider it a bilateral arrangement. In return for the tulip's beauty or the apple's sweetness, humans have carried plants that were once geographically confined to the four corners of the Earth. Humans exploit plants, but plants have used humans to spread and increase. If birds could be said to have replicated that model of ecological partnership, then the Common Pheasant is among the best candidates.

With our assistance the species has added to its original Asiatic range a set of territories including most of Europe, large parts of North America, New Zealand, Tasmania and lesser areas, such as the islands of St Helena (since the sixteenth century), Cuba, the Bahamas and Hawaii. It is the most numerous pheasant on Earth, probably outnumbering all the other 42 species combined. Some of these have been similarly transplanted. The Kalij and Silver Pheasants (eastern Himalaya and China to Argentina, where they now hybridise), **Golden Pheasant** *Chrysolophus pictus* (China to Argentina and Britain), **Lady Amherst's Pheasant** *Chrysolophus amherstiae* (China to Britain) and Reeves's Pheasant (from China to the Czech Republic, France and Germany) have all been attempted, but seldom with outstanding success.[135]

The Common Pheasant's global spread has taken 2,500 years and has hinged on two separate patterns of introduction. The initial importation was during the ascendancy of classical Greece, the bird being known in Athens in or before 425 BC.[136] From there it was eventually passed to Rome and, under the auspices of the empire, it was carried Europe-wide, where it was highly prized as a table fowl. However, the bird may well have vanished from most of the continent with the empire's subsequent collapse.

One enduring Roman art form in which early pheasant images have survived is the mosaic. Aside from their obvious beauty, the birds were a motif of luxury and gastronomic pleasure, which would have been especially appropriate on

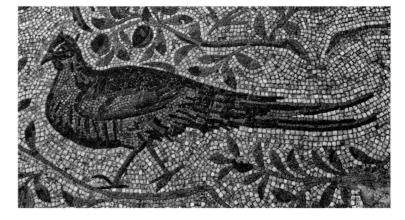

the tessellated floor of the dining room. The Bardo Museum in Tunis holds one of the world's most important mosaic collections and pheasants feature in some remarkable pieces. One particularly accurate image clearly reveals the racial affinities of the Roman pheasants. Today most cock birds in Europe, North America and elsewhere show a white collar and brow, because they derive wholly or in part from eastern Chinese races, such as *torquatus*, imported from the late nineteenth century onwards. However, the bird in the Bardo Museum is without the white collar because it was of the nominate dark-necked race *colchicus* from the Black Sea region.

It was this same subspecies which began a second advance during the medieval period. Now it is virtually impossible to gain an accurate sense of its abundance, yet the exalted status of the pheasant at Philip the Good's banquet in 1453, mentioned above, suggests a creature of considerable scarcity; while a household kitchen book from early-sixteenth-century England put a price on a single pheasant of 12 pence – as much as six partridges or ducks, a dozen woodcock, two dozen chickens and the equivalent of a peacock.[137]

Ironically it was when the price of the individual bird fell that the overall social and economic importance of pheasants soared. During the nineteenth century only the Willow Ptarmigan (Red Grouse) competed as the main sporting totem of rural Britain (see Hunting Grouse, page 47). One author suggested that the pheasant probably had more impact on the English countryside than any other creature with the exception of the horse (or perhaps cattle and sheep).[138]

However, the preservation of game also carried negative consequences, such as the massive slaughter of all predatory animals classified as 'vermin'. Sometimes the term was loosely applied: W H Hudson claimed to know English country estates where they killed nightingales because the celestial song kept the pheasants awake.[139] (Even in the mid twentieth century one gamekeeper acknowledged that 'my job was to kill everything that his Lordship couldn't eat'.)[140] During the Georgian era humans fell squarely within the vermin category. A third of prisoners in English jails by 1823 had been convicted under the Game Acts (although Stephen Tapper points out that it may have been because more serious criminals were hanged or deported). Conversely from 1833–43, 42 gamekeepers lost their lives to poachers.[141]

The socially divisive pheasant is largely a motif of Europe's past. Today, pheasant shooting is enjoyed by hundreds of thousands and is now ingrained in the region's

The Common Pheasant was a regular subject in Roman mosaics. This beautiful example from the third century AD is at the Villa of the Aviary in Carthage, Tunisia.

What transformed the hunting of gamebirds, including the Common Pheasants introduced to Europe and North America, were developments in the breech-loading shotgun.

landscape, with six countries – Britain, Denmark, France, Germany, Hungary and Romania – holding almost 90 per cent of the entire continental population.[142] This social and economic importance is manifest in the retention of otherwise 'uneconomic' woodlands and other pheasant habitats. The land management practices are, in turn, good for wildlife. A large survey of British woodlands found that those with pheasant release pens held 22–32 per cent more birds, especially warblers and pigeons.[143]

In Britain pheasants are now relatively more important than in their Victorian and Edwardian heyday, the birds having risen as a percentage of the total game bag from 15 to 55 per cent.[144] In 1981 an estimated £400 million was spent on British game hunting, with at least half focused on pheasants. The sum outstripped by a factor of ten the total annual budget of the government's own agency charged with all environmental conservation.[145] Even more edifying is to compare this figure expended on the killing of a single super-abundant pheasant, with the annual income of the World Pheasant Association, which devotes itself to securing all the planet's galliforms. In 2007–8 its revenues were £125,000 ($200,000). Perhaps it is high time we reconsider our priorities.

In North America the story of the Common Pheasant's introduction is even more dramatic, in terms of the rapidity of spread and the way it achieved centrality in the affections of American hunters. Attempts at naturalisation had been made as early as 1733 but none resulted in success until the American consul-general in Shanghai, O N Denny, imported about 100 pairs of the white-collared Chinese race *torquatus* in 1881 (the birds were originally referred to as 'ring-necked pheasants' and are often known now simply as 'ringnecks', or 'roosters').[146] They were released in Oregon's Willamette Valley and the first open season was held a decade later.

The phenomenal success of the experiment was soon

followed by releases across the USA. By the mid twentieth century the bird was legal wild game in 34 states, with a heartland in the northern prairie states (roughly it includes North and South Dakota, Iowa, Minnesota and Nebraska).[147] The birds were intimately associated with the conversion of grassland to arable crops and were said to have 'flourished like the corn' itself.[148] In the decade beginning 1940 more than 82 million Common Pheasants were shot in these states alone.[149] South Dakota specifically, where it was made the state bird in 1943, is considered the 'old Mecca of avid pheasant hunters'.[150] It has remained at the forefront of the sport and in 2007 the total bag (2.1 million birds) was more than twice that of its nearest rival and geographical neighbour, North Dakota.

Although modern pheasant hunting, regardless of nationality, is essentially the pursuit of a non-native galliform with a firearm, the ethos of the American model is closer to its subsistence roots. This contrasts with the history of the sport in Europe where large bags – occasionally so large that thousands of unwanted pheasant carcasses are bulldozed into specially dug pits – are highly prized. The largest bag ever is the total slaughtered in Hungary by Count Károlyi and his guests on one day in 1909 – 6,125 birds. Yet the record that seems most extraordinary, mainly for the sheer tedium it must have entailed, not to mention the obsessive arithmetic, is that of the Marquess of Ripon who, over 56 years, shot 556,813 gamebirds including a quarter of a million pheasants.[151]

The great financial crash of 2008 provided an intriguing modern sidelight on the role played by pheasants as a form of ritualised conspicuous consumption. In Britain pheasant shooting suffered a major decline, particularly on estates formerly patronised by city bankers, whose mismanagement was widely viewed by the public as the cause of the wider economic crisis and whose institutions had been saved

The chicken delivery service New Delhi style.

with public money. One pheasant-shoot owner said, 'It's hopeless. People don't wish to be seen to do it. Banks can no longer budget for it and, if they have been bailed out by the taxpayer, senior people can't be seen to leave the office.' This reluctance intensified after a high-profile scandal in the USA. Even after it had been saved from bankruptcy with government money, the bosses of insurance giant AIG went on a partridge-shooting weekend in England. New York's attorney-general threatened to sue them for repayment of the £60,000 ($97,000) spent on the jaunt.[152]

The incident, however, is not truly representative of America's broad-based pheasant culture, where the focus has been on the wild bird (not on pen-reared stock) with a daily bag limit in most states of two to four birds. The possession limit at the end of a four-day hunt is just a dozen birds, with no hens permitted.[153] (These limits are legally enforceable and people found breaking them can be fined and, if repeat offenders, can incur loss of weapon, revocation of their hunting licence or potential impoundment of their vehicle.) Sometimes even this modest total is not required for a good day's shooting:'There's nothing like the experience of walking through a cattail marsh on a frigid winter morning when a rooster pheasant erupts, his wings striking the dry stalks, all the while cackling as he gains altitude. It is a rush. The shot rings out and often, in my case, the bird escapes unscathed. Even then, I can consider the hunt a success.'[154]

Pheasant shooting is now undergoing significant change in the USA. The days of national bags totalling 30 million birds may well have ended (in 2007 the figures were under

6 million). For a variety of reasons young people are less keen on outdoor pursuits such as shooting. Agricultural intensification and loss of formerly pheasant-friendly habitats are leading to widespread declines of the birds themselves. Another particular aspect of the sport under pressure from recently proposed state legislation is put-and-shoot pheasant hunting. It involves pen-reared birds, raised often at public expense and released on public land, which have no experience of wild conditions and are incapable of sustaining themselves once liberated. Opponents of this form of hunting, such as The Humane Society of the United States, challenge it partly on the grounds that it is unsustainable and has no value for wildlife management. Sometimes the birds are shot down (in scenarios condemned as 'canned hunting') even as they attempt to fly from captivity. If the legislation were passed, then the release of as many as one million pen-reared birds would eventually cease.[155]

RED JUNGLEFOWL

This is the longest species account in the book but it could easily be expanded to fill several volumes. The bird's domesticated form, familiar all over the world as the chicken, has helped shape human civilisation. William Beebe suggested that the only community unable to profit from its companionship was the Inuit.[156] Today even they eat chicken products. The bird is, in some ways, more important now than at any time in its history. It is certainly more abundant; in fact, it is the most numerous on the planet. There are at least 12 billion chickens, almost two birds to each human.

63

CHICKEN AND THE FAST-FOOD INDUSTRY

In the USA alone 24 million are killed and prepared for the table every day. Chicken represents half of all meat eaten worldwide, making it the greatest source of protein we possess. If the old maxim – we are what we eat – were true, then we are more chicken than any living creature. For all of these reasons, our custody of this most precious fellow citizen could be considered a good index for our care of the entire biosphere. Yet should we choose it as measure of our conduct, then we stand condemned.

According to a 2007 estimate the total consumption of poultry was almost 90 million tonnes worldwide. (Egg consumption in 2001 was 57 million tonnes, the British consuming 26 million eggs a day.)[157] The vast majority were chicken eggs. The vast majority of chickens are reared in intensive poultry units.[158] One author described the broiler industry, 'in both magnitude and severity, the single most severe, systematic example of man's inhumanity to another sentient animal'.[159]

The basic unit of industrial production is a creature that has just six weeks to journey from egg to table. Almost all of its 42 days are spent in a hot, crowded chamber filled with the smell of the bird's own ammoniacal faeces. In many countries low lights are maintained to discourage movement. Not that there is much scope for activity. Dust bathing is impossible. They cannot even stretch their wings or preen with ease. The average individual, weighing 2 kg (4.4 lb) before plucking, has the space equivalent to the page you are now reading for its entire life.

If anything, matters are worse for hens kept for egg production. They enjoy no more liberty but endure it for far longer. Egg laying is the entire purpose of their existence, and as soon as they stop producing – 'spent' is the industry's word – they are slaughtered. They are, in effect, egg machines. (The very fact of their confinement with so many of their kind was judged deeply unnatural by the German biologist Konrad Lorenz. He suggested that forcing a hen to lay in the presence of others violated the bird's fundamental instincts, equivalent to obliging humans to defecate in front of one another.) The aggression that is equally innate among galliforms, and which is still exploited for sporting purposes in some countries, has grim penalties in the battery unit. To stop fights or self-harm in the cramped cages, birds often have their beak ends cut off.[160]

In poultry units organised for meat production, many countries have regulations tolerating 19–20 birds per m² (10.8 ft²). Most of the birds' short lives are spent lying down. In Britain, where mortality is low, 3–5 per cent die of a mixture of conditions resulting from these constraints. Small in percentage terms, it represents in absolute numbers about 45 million birds. One major cause of death, ascites, is a malady as unpleasant as its common name suggests, 'leaking liver'.

> Before they die, their hearts have been frantically trying to pump enough blood through their arteries to supply their bodies with oxygen. In order to achieve that the blood becomes more viscous, and the heart chambers dilate in an attempt to force the thick blood through. When it simply can't be pushed on, blood begins to go backwards. It fills the veins, the organs swell and blood leaks from the liver. Eventually the abdominal cavity fills with fluid as the bird suffocates.[161]

The corpses of dead birds are weeded daily from intensive units like bad apples from a tray. A mortality rate of 3–5 per cent may be deemed tolerable, given that as many as 97 per cent suffer no such fate. What seems brutal is a statistic of serious leg disorder among the British national flock of over one-quarter. In some companies the figure rises to 72 per cent. Even the lower fraction translates into hundreds of millions of birds enduring chronic pain, often resulting in an inability to walk, for a third of their short lives. One further source of suffering is the layer of litter on which the birds sit. This can become so steeped in their own waste that the ammonia burns their backsides, which are swollen and discoloured yellow, and blisters the breast and hocks. Even eyes and lungs are seared in the constant levels of vaporised pollution.

The interior of a single poultry unit is a distressing vision, but the wider story of the industry's exponential growth possesses, at least, a kind of ferocious vitality. In the USA the genesis was in Delaware, on the Atlantic coast, where a small state-wide cottage industry accounted for just 50,000 birds in 1925. Within less than a decade it had risen to 7 million.[162] Through the Second World War, chicken was given a federal push by the absence of rationing – unlike pork or beef – and by the maintenance of government-authorised high prices, which encouraged fresh producers into the market. The stimulus seemed beneficial not just to the nation's economy, but also to the American diet.

Chicken, a white meat low in fat or cholesterol, had been no more than a luxury item prior to the industry's expansion. In the 1920s politicians chose it as a symbol of social improvement to entice voters. Putting 'a chicken in every pot and a car in every garage', was a slogan for Herbert Hoover's presidential campaign.[163] By the 1980s what had seemed a dream of national progress had been fulfilled. Chicken was a staple of daily life. At the end of the century the average person ate 100 times more of the meat than their grandparents during the Depression. The associated fall in price and the expansion in availability of a healthy, nutritious, delicious food seemed like a wholly beneficial double achievement – a triumph of capitalist enterprise and of government-targeted production.

Unfortunately it has been predicated on what one author calls 'the dangerous transformation of America's favourite food'. The latter quotation, the subtitle to Steve Striffler's book *Chicken*, derives from the central place the bird now occupies in a deeply troubling social and cultural matrix afflicting modern America. This links the meteoric rise of the fast-food industry, based on systems of chicken production described above, with a national epidemic of obesity. Striffler suggests two out of every three Americans are overweight. About one-fifth – 60 million people – are clinically obese.[164] One in three American children now eats fast food every day.[165]

Yet the USA is merely in the vanguard of processes set to sweep the developed world, if not the whole planet. Indeed the lag is only marginal in Europe. Already in Britain the crisis has arrived, with a third of children overweight or obese, and a quarter of adults obese.[166] The problem is also set to deepen. In France, where the national average for being overweight is 42 per cent, obesity rates are rising among adults at 6 per cent and in children a staggering 17 per cent annually. By 2020 French people could be as fat as Americans.[167] The most alarming of all perhaps are the figures for China. By 2000, obesity rate among male students in Beijing had reached 15 per cent, and had doubled since 1990.

A major element in this vast health problem has been the exponential rise in fast-food chains. By the 1980s the seemingly benign, avuncular visage of Colonel Saunders in the logo for Kentucky Fried Chicken was the second most recognised face on the planet. KFC's major rival, McDonald's, have matched this ubiquity by opening 30,000 restaurants in over 100 countries.[168] In China the steep rise in obesity levels has been correlated directly with the recent appearance of the fast-food giants: the country now has over 1,200 KFCs and McDonald's. Collectively the purveyors of industrially produced fast food open a new outlet somewhere in the world every two hours, and the total service-sector food industry has an estimated value of £1.07 trillion ($1.7 trillion).[169]

Under their care the white, tender, wholesome flesh of the junglefowl has become an engineered and reconstituted pulp less healthy than red meat. Striffler calculated that six of the fried lumps known in McDonald's argot as the McNugget, contain the equivalent fat of a double cheeseburger.[170] To combat any public reaction to such baleful revelations, the fast-food companies maintain a relentless campaign of persuasion that costs the sector about £20.6 billion ($33 billion) in advertising.

As Striffler makes clear in his compelling, even nightmarish, analysis of the contemporary role of chicken, the fast-food giants, if left unchallenged, could bring about a wholesale re-ordering not just of a society's diet and health, but also of our entire value system. The industrially produced broiler chicken will become a metaphor for a whole way of life – one in which the fast-food outlet is the central nexus between an individual and the nutrients sustaining them. He or she will be incapable of basic human skills such as cooking. In fact, they will consider themselves too busy for food preparation when set against the demands of work, shopping and electronic entertainment. They will, in turn, consume values shaped mainly by television and will pass their lives desensitised across large areas of their personal experience, and cut off completely from the real nature and the origins of the food they place in their mouths.

The fortunes of this prospective world lie, of course, entirely in our hands. It stands or falls with consumer choice. We can each pinpoint the suffering behind those fried flavours and conclude that the incarceration of billions of birds and their brief lives of boredom and distress are a future too inhuman, too unhealthy and too dangerous to endure.

THE ORIGINS OF DOMESTICATED CHICKENS AND THEIR GLOBAL SPREAD

The extraordinary journey we have made with our foremost avian companion began about 8,000 years ago somewhere in Asia. The initial archaeological evidence for a domesticated galliform arises in the Yellow River valley of China around 5400 BC. However DNA evidence indicates that domestication began earlier still, possibly in Thailand or Vietnam or at multiple sites, and also that the Red Junglefowl and **Grey Junglefowl** *Gallus sonneratii* were both involved in the original ancestry. The genotype for the production of yellow skin, which is such a conspicuous character of the

farm bird, is solely found in the latter species. (Yet running counter to the claim is the fact that junglefowl hybrids are almost always infertile and the Grey Junglefowl now only occurs in south India, and distant from the presumed source of domestication.)

The dates for the chicken's spread become more precise as the bird travelled through time and towards the west. By the third millennium BC it was reared in settlements of the Indus civilisation (now in Pakistan). Based upon textual evidence, there are claims for an arrival in the Mesopotamian city of Ur by about 2000 BC. Stronger proof – four rooster images carved on an ivory vessel (1300 BC) – comes from Ur's Assyrian neighbour Assur.[171] From the Fertile Crescent the species journeyed into Egypt and then to Europe. It is noteworthy that the cockerel's crow is heard neither in the Old Testament, nor those other grand references of the ancient Mediterranean world, Homer's *The Iliad* and *The Odyssey*.[172] Yet the bird was regularly arriving in Greece during the seventh century BC and cockfighting itself is mentioned in Aristophanes' play *The Birds* (*c*.415 BC), where the species is called the 'Persian bird', suggesting its eastern origins.[173]

Subsequently Europeans played a major role in the chicken's territorial advance. There is a notable exception however. It is now thought that the first appearance in the Americas was not as a result of early Spanish or Portuguese explorers. The earliest domestic fowl on that continent, often called the 'Araucana' (after an indigenous Chilean people of the same name, now known as the Mapuche), originated with those who travelled steadily eastwards from Asia to South America. Bones found in northern Chile have been radiocarbon-dated to about a century before Columbus' Atlantic crossing.[174] The bird itself is interesting not just as proof of the extraordinary trans-Pacific odyssey achieved by Polynesian navigators, but also for its lack of a tail and the production of light-blue or green-blue eggs.

One striking detail which links the bird's original journey out of Indochina to both east and west is that wherever it travelled it had a combined status as food, but also as a bird of magical rite or theatrical entertainment – in the form of cockfighting (see below) – and as a source of elegant plumes for ornamentation.[175] During its first centuries in Europe the cockerel appears also to have been very much associated with divination.

A chicken stall in Belen market, Iquitos, in the Peruvian Amazon; but this same scene is played out wherever the planet's 7 billion humans and 12 billion chickens converge.

This relief carving of a cockerel was found in a Lycian tomb (modern Turkey) and dates to c.470 BC. It was common practice to sacrifice the bird when the deceased were interred.

In Rome chickens were kept as a means of fortune telling, especially during times of war. They were known as the *auguria pullaria* ('chickens of augury') and Pliny emphasised their central importance: 'These . . . birds . . . give the Most-Favourable Omens; these birds daily control our officers of state . . . these send forward or hold back the Roman rods of office, and order or forbid battle formation, being the auspices of all our victories won all over the world.'[176] Yet one who ignored their advice was Publius Claudius Pulcher. During the First Punic War, as the Roman fleet sailed to meet the Carthaginian enemy, the birds were consulted and refused to touch the grain cast before them. The official seer (*pullarius*) advised the consul not to engage his forces, but Publius slung the birds overboard, announcing that if they would not eat then they could drink. He went on to suffer a heavy defeat.[177]

THE CHICKEN'S THERAPEUTIC AND SYMBOLIC IMPORTANCE

For the ancient world the chicken's predictive powers readily spilled over into symbolic and therapeutic values. The most compelling instance of this was the habit, prior to seeking medical help, of ritually sacrificing a cockerel to Aesculapius, the Greek god of medicine. The rite drew on the fundamental association between the bird and vitality, but there was a secondary symbolism in play. Aesculapius was the son of Apollo (by a princess, Coronis), who was the classical world's primary sun god. The ultimate solar bird (see below) was clearly the right offering to a solar deity. (It was, incidentally, this sacrificial custom that gave rise to one of the most grimly ironic jokes in Western civilisation. After he was condemned to death by poisoning for his corruption of public morals, Socrates announced to his friend as the hemlock triumphed over him, 'Remember we owe a cock to Aesculapius.' The great philosopher had been cured of humanity's one inescapable affliction – life.)

A striking aspect of these ancient Greek customs is the way they echo contemporary cultural practice in radically different contexts. A good example is the role played by domestic fowl in voodoo, that ancient, occasionally sinister, blend of religion and magic, which is found in west Africa (ranging from Nigeria westwards to Ghana) as well as

Brazil, Haiti and other areas of Afro-Caribbean culture. During consultations with the voodoo priest, the applicant is invariably required to sacrifice a chicken as a token of payment. The bird is often black or white, depending on the nature of the magic required.

Chickens have a similar sacrificial place in many other cultures across Africa, occasionally acquiring a very specific curative purpose. The herpetologist Stephen Spawls notes:

An old friend of mine, a snakebite expert and chameleon enthusiast, treated a lot of snakebite victims among the Zulus in KwaZulu-Natal, and he told me that the usual treatment was to split a chicken and clap it on to the wound; it was then strapped there (it was believed to suck the venom out, I think), so victims usually arrived at hospital with a split chicken lashed to a limb![178]

This practice may now seem bizarre, yet it finds a precise European parallel in an old Estonian ritual associated with pregnancy. To alleviate birth pain, a hen was slaughtered and its still-twitching body clapped to the belly of the mother-to-be, so that the affliction passed from human to bird. Examples of these old magic spells involving domestic fowl, many of which had protective or therapeutic intention, could fill a sizeable book. In fact, Ernst and Luise Gattiker in their compendium of European bird folklore, *Die Vögel im Volksglauben*, filled 50 pages with just such remedies, superstitions and ancient quackery. Many now seem ludicrous, such as the recommendation made to Bavarian parents to lay chicken guts, freshly boiled in milk, on the stomachs of their colic-suffering offspring. Or the Saxon cure for painful corns: walk barefoot in a puddle where hens have bathed, replace socks and refrain from washing the dirty extremities for a further fortnight.[179]

The practices may seem quaint and even farcical, but running through so much archaic chicken lore was a theme central to our entire engagement with the species for eight millennia. Our closest avian companion has come to represent, in some fundamental sense, ourselves. The Greek philosopher Plato once suggested that a human was a biped without feathers. The chicken could be said to be a human *with* feathers – hence its vital emblematic place in religions and cultures right across the world.[180] It was at once a precious possession, a producer of eggs and meat, a bird integral to our own well-being, and yet, like every scapegoat and substitute, it could also be sacrificed so that we might not.

Among the rituals of penitence associated with the festival of Yom Kippur is a moment when ultra-orthodox Jews – 'orthodox Jews (like me) use money now instead of chickens, or do not do it at all'[181] – having read religious texts to one another, hold a chicken (a cockerel for men or a hen for women) above their heads and circle it nine times with a recitation: 'This is instead of me, this is an offering on my account, this is in expiation for me.' Then the bird is slaughtered.

The many virtues associated with the chicken's ritual death readily spilled over into a belief in the bird's status as a kind of medicine. Aldrovandi, the great sixteenth-century Italian naturalist, once asked, 'Which condition of the body, internal or external, does not obtain its remedy from the chicken?'[182] The flesh was regarded as an immensely beneficial food long before the discovery of cholesterol or the value of a low-fat diet. Yet perhaps the place where chicken has achieved its ultimate restorative power is in Israel. Jewish attachment to chicken soup is now both legend and cliché. In fact the term has become a synonym for any kind of panacea and also a brand name for a type of self-help book. However, as we have seen, the original magico-medicinal rites involving chicken lie deep in Hebraic culture.

One wonders if the expiatory powers of the bird are in some ways entailed in the deep Jewish faith in chicken soup as a catch-all remedy. Certainly it is still the standard diet for convalescents, although arguments may rage between Jewish mothers and families over the key active ingredients in a really good soup. General agreement seems to exist on the benefits of invoking support from the chicken's larger, more powerful American cousin: 'Turkey neck is one of the secret ingredients in the traditional chicken soup – one of the most potent Jewish medicines for most diseases known to mankind.'

> Take great care with chicken soup. It's a matter of life and death. I nearly divorced my wife (French Algerian) because she stuck two cloves in the two onions that are placed carefully in the soup. She actually said 'to add taste', while I was on the brink of death from a nasty cold. There is only one way to make chicken soup. If you go wrong with this crucial and major topic you will have to deal with eastern European Judaism and may be even God will intervene.[183]

We could easily assume that the modern world has advanced beyond the kinds of sympathetic magic manifest in the sacrifice of fowl in voodoo ritual or, indeed, the Jewish faith in chicken soup, but many in Western society encounter the bird's deep, mysterious and powerful symbolism on a daily basis. It is just that we have ceased to notice.

THE CALL OF THE COCKEREL

This emblematic role originates in the cockerel's pre-eminent gift to humankind. Wherever we have kept male fowl, his clarion call has notified us of dawn. That heraldic sound, which first visits us in our collective dream state, signifies the single key environmental precondition that determines all human occupancy: the presence of the sun. *Homo sapiens* is quintessentially a diurnal primate and an inhabitant of daylight. Conversely our status as the dominant species is neutralised by night's advance. These underpinning ecological truths about the human condition have invariably been expressed in moral form. What was most necessary for us was also most virtuous. It is for this reason that we have projected on to the sun's chief envoy an associated sense of intrinsic and indivisible virtue. An idea that is exceedingly rare, and possibly absent entirely, from all cultures is the notion of the chicken or cockerel as emblem of evil. The creature may be promiscuously sexual (Little Red Rooster), selfish or stupid (Chicken-Licken). There may even occasionally be taboos against eating chicken:

> In highland Ethiopia orthodox Christians have strict rules about what they can eat and when. According to a teaching colleague of mine they are not allowed to eat anything that has hair between its toes, and really strict believers will not eat anything that does not have cloven hooves. Many people will eat chickens, but a high

churchman can insult a lower one by saying that that individual eats chicken. This then cascades downwards, as some country people (especially Oromo farmers) will eat guineafowl or francolin, which are seen as 'relatives of chickens'. Such people are then looked on with contempt by most orthodox townspeople.[184]

Yet fundamentally our key avian companion stands for life and the inherent goodness of life. A classic illustration is found in Chinese astrology: the rooster, the only bird among the 12 animals of the Chinese zodiac, represents good luck and virtue.[185] In Chinese the word 'luck' and 'cock' have the same pronunciation – *Ji*.[186] Henry Thoreau showed profound insight into the way we have conflated the bird's fortunes with our own when he wrote: 'I hear the cockerels crow through [the fog], and the rich crow of young roosters, that sound indicative of the bravest, rudest health . . . That crow is all-nature-compelling; famine and pestilence flee before it.'[187]

An ancient myth trading precisely on this cluster of ideas was recorded by the Roman author Aelian. He wrote that the lion or basilisk (also known as a cockatrice, a beast hatched by a serpent from a cock's egg – itself a quintessential inversion of natural order – whose very look or breath was fatal) could be banished by a cockerel. Merely the sound of the bird caused these two archetypes of nocturnal terror

With chest out, neck arched and extended, beak held wide open and its scarlet fleshy crown raised high, a crowing cockerel is truly the king of the dawn.

to convulse and expire. For these reasons, Aelian added, travellers in Libya carried a cockerel with them as a guarantee of safe passage.[188] The story of the basilisk has resurfaced in the most popular of all modern story cycles. In J K Rowling's *Harry Potter and the Chamber of Secrets*, a basilisk haunting the bowels of Hogwarts castle is unleashed by the Heir of Slytherin. As a precondition of this evil release, the cockerels living in Hagrid's vegetable patch must all first be killed.[189]

Yet perhaps the most famous statement of the cock's powers of exorcism occurs in the first scene of the most famous play by the most famous playwright in the English-speaking world. In *Hamlet*, Bernardo, Horatio and Marcellus hold the following exchange on the sudden vanishing of the king's ghost:

BERNARDO:
It was about to speak, when the cock crew.

HORATIO:
And then it started like a guilty thing
Upon a fearful summons. I have heard
The cock, that is the trumpet to the morn,
Doth with his lofty and shrill-sounding throat
Awake the god of day; and at his warning,
Whether in sea or fire, in earth or air,
Th' extravagant and erring spirit hies
To his confine; and of the truth herein
This present object made probation.

MARCELLUS:
It faded on the crowing of the cock.
Some say that ever 'gainst that season comes
Wherein our Saviour's birth is celebrated,
This bird of dawning singeth all night long;
And then, they say, no spirit dare stir abroad,
The nights are wholesome, then no planets strike,
No fairy takes, nor witch hath power to charm,
So hallow'd and so gracious is that time.

It was inevitable that this pre-eminent attribute ascribed to the cockerel should have been adopted by the major religions. It was, for example, part of Islamic tradition, the cock's crow being a herald of God, while his silence presaged the Day of Judgment. (Arabic folklore held that a white cock with a divided comb could keep the devil away.)[190] The theme is also embedded in the New Testament, where it acquired an additional layer of moral instruction, entreating Christians to be vigilant and attentive in pursuit of their faith. The story of the Passion and particularly St Peter's denial of Christ three times before the cock crowed (Matthew 26:75) accounts in part for the presence of metal cockerels crowning the spires of cathedrals and churches across all Christendom. Yet the omnipresence of this symbol in the Western landscape, and the way in which the bird restates an ancient primal human myth about the triumph of light over darkness, of good over evil, can easily be overlooked.

The fact that the range of the domestic fowl is almost coterminous with our own lends a sense of deep universality to the cock's clarion. Once again, Henry Thoreau showed singular awareness of the way in which the birds he enjoyed had their echoes right across the globe. In a diary for 25 July 1852 he wrote: 'As I came along, the whole earth resounded with the crowing of cocks, from the eastern unto the western horizon, and as I passed a yard, I saw a white rooster on the topmost rail of a fence pouring forth his challenges for destiny to come on. This salutation was travelling round the world.'[191]

Perhaps the most elaborate imagining of the cockerels' chorus is by the British travel writer Patrick Leigh Fermor. Its inspiration was an incident recorded in a letter by the novelist Lawrence Durrell to his friend Henry Miller, the arch pagan of twentieth-century American letters (who reproduced the letter in his book, *The Colossus of Maroussi*). Durrell wrote to the latter about their mutual Greek friend George Katsimbalis, a larger-than-life Rabelaisian figure who, during World War Two, went with others to the Acropolis at night. Drunk on cognac and poetry, Katsimbalis looking like 'a heavy black faery queen, in his black clothes, threw back his head . . . and sent out the most blood-curdling clarion I have ever heard'. Time after time, veins proud on neck and face, the great Greek character 'screamed himself hysterical' until, as Durrell wrote, 'The whole night was alive with cockcrows – all Athens, all Attica, all Greece, it seemed, until I almost imagined you [Henry Miller] being woken at your desk late in New York to hear these terrific silver peals.'[192]

In his own book about Greek culture, *Mani*, Patrick Leigh Fermor revisited the story and imagined, in a bravura four-page reconstruction, how the cockerel song-torch might have been passed from the Acropolis, one bird to another, until it spanned the Earth's entire land surface:

Now it spread like a jungle-fire through the southern hemisphere and a strident spark of sound leapt the swift-flowing narrows of Trinidad to ignite the whole Caribbean chain, jolting the rum-sodden slumbers of the Barbadians and touching off, in the throats of sacrificial birds in Haiti that the dark fingers of Voodoo priests were soon to silence, a defiant *morituri te salutamus* ['we, about to die, salute you']. In the dank unexplored recesses of the Amazonian hinterland, aboriginal and unclassified poultry were sending up shrill and uncouth cries and high in the cold Andean starlight gleaming birds were spreading their wings and filling their breasts on the great tumbled blocks of Inca palaces. The volume of the call was swelling now, sweeping south across the pampas, the Gran Chaco, the Rio Grande; and then dwindling as the two great oceans inexorably closed in . . . Now the dread moment came, the final staging-point and terminus of those great Katsimbalis lungs; the last desperate conflagration of sound in Tierra del Fuego with the ultimate chanticleer calling and calling and calling, unanswered but undaunted to the maelstroms and the tempests, the hail and the darkness and the battering waves of Cape Horn . . .

For there was no hope here. It was the end. We thought with sorrow of the silent poles and the huge bereaved antipodes . . . of combed heads tucked in sleep under many a speckled wing that no salutation from the Parthenon would ever wake: the beautiful cocks of the Easter and Ellis and the Gilbert islanders, of the Marquesas, the Melanesians and the Trobrianders, of Tristan da Cunha and St. Helena.[193]

If the song can never travel like this as a single fantastical and self-perpetuating pulse of sound, nevertheless it is intriguing to reflect that our profound attachment to the junglefowl has genuinely authorised one of the great song cycles of our planet. The daily rotation of the Earth finds its parallel in a continuous 24-hour canticle of cockerel calls, wherever the species occurs and whenever dawn first breaks. That never-ceasing song has perhaps orbited our world for 150 years.

I have located the sound's transliterated form in as many languages as possible (please feel free to add to it). The versions of the cockerel travel west to east, beginning in northern USA and passing south through the Americas, through Africa and on across Eurasia and finally down into south Asia and Australasia.

'Here in Nebraska it would be described as *cockle doodle doo*. I've also heard it as *You're a fool too* and *Don't you have work to-do*?' From Arizona: 'We said *cock-a-doodle-doo* as children, and I think that's very much the standard in US English; primary stress on the first syllable, secondary on the last.' In Mexico 'the consensus seems to be the *quiri quiri / kiri kiri* sound (like *KI kiri KI! KI kiri KI!*)'.

Coo-ka-roo-koo (Bahamas and Bermuda); *ki-kiri-kí* (Guatemala); *kí-kiri-ki* (Honduras). There is slight variation further south: 'We have two calls in Panama for cocks: if it is a young one the call is *kikiriki* ("keekeereekee") and if it is an old cock the call is *kukuruku* ("kookoorookoo").' *Quiquiquiriqui* (Peru); *kiki-rikiiii* (Bolivia); *kiki kiri kiiii* (Argentina).[194]

From west Africa the following were submitted: *cocoroiko* (Sierra Leone); this is the title, incidentally, 'of the country's biggest and most widely read newspaper'. '*Cucu ru cuu* in Ogoni land' (Nigeria); *co clo cooh* (Nigerian Pidgin); *cock-co-cooh-coooh* (Bafut, northern Cameroon). From the other side of the continent I received the following: 'A Chagga friend (the dominant tribe thereabouts) tells me that "on the verdant slopes of Kilimanjaro (Tanzania), the Chagga cockerel says *ijokoo*" (i.e. 'jogoo')'; while 'in Kikuyu (Kenya) it is transliterated as *cocococo uuuuuuuuuu*'. I have also resorted to versions found in regional dictionaries (assembled by an expert):

Bantu languages:
Swahili: *koromiko, kokoikoo, kokowiko, kokowiku* (the first four all from Zanzibar, the last from the northern Kenya coast)
Giryama: *kokoikoo* (central Kenya coast)
Matengo: *ngou ka le kye ng'oo* (south Tanzania)
Chewa: *kokoliko* (Malawi)
Shona: *kokorigo, kukurigo* (Zimbabwe)

Other Niger–Congo languages:
Kisi: *kukuluukuu* (Sierra Leone, Liberia)
Dagaare: *konkoliirikoo* (Ghana)

Austronesian languages:
Malagasy: *kokoriko* (Mayotte in the Comoros)
Malagasy: *kekehoke, kekeoke, kekeoake, kakaoake* (Madagascar)

These words are all ideophones (words that represent sounds), and can be described as onomatopoeic ideophones (ideophones that imitate sounds). Linguists are fond of citing *cock-a-doodle-do* in different languages as an example of this. As Swahili and Malagasy show, you can get variants in the same language and/or dialects of it. Some terms are clearly linked historically,

and not just independently copied from the cock's crow. They are also often related to the verb meaning 'to crow' (e.g. Swahili *wika*) and names for the birds themselves (e.g. Swahili *kuku*: 'chicken', from a widespread Bantu root).

Further north in east Africa comes *Waa-Na-Soo-GaaaaadH* (Ki-Somali); 'it is saying, "dawn has arrived"!'[195]

Coco rococo (Portugal); *quiquiriquí* (Spain); *coquerico* (France); *cock-a-doodle-doo* (UK); 'the cockerel says *mac na hóighe slān* which means "the son of the Virgin is safe". Isn't that lovely!' (Ireland); *kikeriki* (Germany); *kykelikyyy* (Norway); *kuckelikuuu* (Denmark and Sweden) 'which rhymes with the well-known Swedish phrase *klockan är sju*, literally "it's seven o'clock", so it's time to get out of bed. I remember grown-ups telling me that when I was a child, living in a small village, that staying in bed longer than the cock meant you were lazy!' *Kukko kiekuu* (Finland); *kikuyu*, pronounced 'cookooricoo'(Poland); *chicchirichi* (Italy); *quqqu-QU-qu* (Malta); *kukuriku* or *kukurikuku* (Serbia); къ-ки-гн-guuu (koo-koo-ree-goo, Bulgaria); *Ko-Ko-Rii-Kouu* (Greece); кукареку (*kukarekú*, Russia).

Koo koo ri koo (Israel): 'in Hebrew it is also used to describe someone who's a bit loony – "so Mark Cocker is a bit *koo koo ri koo*."' 'It is *koko . . . kooko . . . koko . . . kooko* [repeated]' (Arabic, Qatar); *Ghoo-Ghooli Ghoo-Ghoo* (Farsi, Iran); *cokr-roo-coo, kukduu koooo, kuk-ru ku* (Hindi, Urdu and several other Indian languages). Elsewhere in Asia: *O-O* (Chinese); *kokekokkō* (Japanese). 'My colleague tells me that the cockerel says *Ba co nha khong*. The literal translation would be "Wife at home or not?" And she replies "co, co, co, co" or "yes, yes, yes, yes". Vietnamese has many personal pronouns and the one used for the woman here is *Ba*, which is for an older woman, generally a grandmother' (Vietnam). *ku-ku-ruyuk* (Indonesia); *Kokore Ko'oo* in Tok Pisin (Papua New Guinea); *kukureko* (West New Britain, Papua New Guinea); 'the rooster's call is *cock-a-doodle-do*' (Australia); *kēkē kü* (Maori, New Zealand).[196]

COCKFIGHTING

Humans have always been captivated by the outright vigour of male chickens. In particular the cockerel's innate hostility towards others of its kind was exploited in formal sport, whose pedigree dates to the Iron Age and possibly earlier. In ancient China the Red Junglefowl shared its sporting status with another intensely aggressive, albeit pocket-sized galliform, the quail (see page 57). Yet in Europe the cockerel was pre-eminent. Cockfighting was widespread in classical Greece – the bird's name *alektōr* meant 'repeller' – while at Pompeii the volcanic lava from Vesuvius has preserved until today Roman murals depicting roosters in combat.

The sport, now outlawed across most of the domestic bird's global range, still exists in certain areas and is often not just a tired cultural tradition dwindling towards extinction. Cockfighting flourishes. In Mexico and the Philippines it is pursued with passionate devotion. In the latter it has deep social roots and was a national sport long before the Spaniards arrived in the region (although the overlap between former Spanish colonial territories and the present distribution of cockfighting is intriguing). In the USA it was legal in several states until the twenty-first century, Louisiana and New Mexico being the last to outlaw it in

▶ Condemned for its cruelty in some parts of the world, cockfighting is still legal in the Philippines, where many view it almost as a religion.

2008 (it continues as an underground activity, partly boosted by its popularity among Hispanic communities). In Bali, Colombia, Cuba, Dominican Republic, Haiti, Nicaragua, Panama, Peru, Puerto Rico, Thailand and Venezuela it is still legal, while in Cambodia and Honduras it flourishes despite government prohibition.

It is impossible here to chart the entire history of cockfighting. The aim is to illuminate some of the deeper continuities across time and space – near-universal charact-eristics, which suggest how the species has elicited common responses regardless of location or cultural context. Essentially cockfighting involves the release of two or more male birds in a way that is likely to result in a fight. A piece of open level ground encircled by a press of human spectators has probably sufficed as a makeshift locus for millennia. However, eventually the sport acquired its own specific place – the cockpit. At Redruth in Cornwall, UK, an open-air example was thought possibly to date to the Roman era.[197] In the Philippines almost every small town still has a purpose-built cockpit – usually a wooden beamed structure with a corrugated-iron roof over a raised circular arena.

The birds themselves are often remarkably beautiful with elongated coppery neck plumes, known as hackles, and glossy iridescent green- or blue-black tails and wings that bear resemblance to the original plumage of wild junglefowls. (In fact, it is easy to miss, because of the over-familiarity flowing from domestication, how often chickens and cockerels are among the most striking birds in any landscape.) Unlike their native ancestor, gamecocks can be as much as 2.4 kg (5.3 lb) in weight, two and a half to five times bigger than a junglefowl).[198] Another key difference is the absence of the coarse red fleshy wattles and comb: gamecocks have these sexual characteristics removed in an operation once known as 'dubbing'.

While the feathers are often sculpted to bring out their owner's innate aggressive aura (as well as sharpened pinion shafts with the power to blind), birds cannot be forced to fight. Occasionally they refuse, when the retreating individual is said to 'show the white feather', a phrase which became a general term for cowardice. (Hence the white plume given to conscientious objectors during times of war. By contrast the vocabulary for human bravado owes much to the male chicken. 'Cocky' and 'cocksure' are just two such borrowings.) The very fact of confinement is normally enough to initiate combat, often prolonged and to the death. The tethering of pointed metal spurs to a cockerel's hind leg was intended to raise the likelihood of fatalities and to satisfy a lust for blood among the highly aroused audience.

Spurs were first introduced in ancient Greece and examples have been unearthed at Roman archaeological sites as far away as Britain. Metal spurs are no more than an artificial (if more lethal) version of the cockerel's natural armoury. Those seeking to defend the sport often claimed that spurs made the fight less drawn out. In places where they were habitually *not* used, birds still fought to the death but sometimes for hours on end. In the Philippines, as in Mexico and other Latin American countries, the spur has an additional razor-sharp bladed edge and is known as a 'slasher'.

The Filipino cockpit is invariably surrounded by three wooden sheds. One of these is known as the gaffing area, where cocks are fitted with the slashers by a gaffer. The other

two sheds are in many ways there to mitigate their effects. One is where the owners sit with their cocks and match them to opponents to ensure a fair contest; the other shed houses men attempting to patch up the wounded survivors. An argument against the slasher (as opposed to the simple sharp-pointed spur) was the element of arbitrary chance it introduced to the fight. As one modern witness to a Filipino cockfight indicates, a single blow can decide the outcome:

> Amid much shouting, cheering and jeering, two roosters were paraded around the ring, owners and supporters alike calling out their strength, their aggressiveness, their killer instinct. A fury of betting took place until, at a signal from the judges, the birds were released. As the owners stepped back, the birds flew at each other, and in less than five seconds, one had slashed at the other with its spur, breaking its neck, or cutting its jugular – I'm not sure which – amidst a flurry of feathers. Fight over. The victorious owner paraded his cockerel again, acknowledging the yells and cheers. The vanquished scooped up what remained of his bird and left the ring, as winners lined up at the betting booths to claim their returns.[199]

The cockpit has always been a place of intense human, invariably masculine, speculation and eventually of high-stakes betting. In England, where the sport was fanatically pursued until outlawed in 1849, large sums were often wagered on birds and, as if to confirm the axiomatic link with gambling, cockfights often took place at horse-racing fixtures. The highest figure staked in a single fight – the entire contest, involving dozens, occasionally hundreds, of cocks was known as a 'main' and mains were divided into 'battles' – was said to have been fought in Lincoln in the early nineteenth century. It involved 1,000 guineas for each of seven battles and 5,000 guineas for the whole main. These were massive sums of money, equivalent to hundreds of thousands of pounds today.[200]

Such an expensive sport attracted the very wealthiest in society. Henry VIII had a royal cockpit built in Whitehall, London, while James I was an enthusiastic cocker – the name for those who rear or own fighting birds – and appointed his own official 'cockmaster'. However, British royalty was completely outdone in its devotion to cocking by one of its subjects, the twelfth Earl of Derby (1752–1834). This Lancastrian noble reared as many as 3,000 birds a year, bred his own champion strain known as the 'Knowsley' (after the family seat) and reputedly had a fight staged for his entertainment even as he lay dying.[201]

Yet cockfighting was by no means exclusively a pastime for the socially prominent. The diarist Samuel Pepys, visiting a London cockpit in the mid seventeenth century, noted: 'It is strange to see how people of the poor rank, that look as if they had not bread to put in their mouths, shall bet three or four pounds at a time, and lose it, and yet bet as much the next battle, so that one of them will lose £10 or £20 at a meeting.'[202] (To put those monetary figures in context, when William Shakespeare died in 1616 he owned a substantial town house that was the largest property in Stratford. It cost him £60.) There was a strict code about the honouring of debt and those who failed to pay – welshers – were sometimes suspended in a basket above the cockpit.

Little has changed in 350 years. The links between

cockfighting and high-stakes betting thrive today in the Philippines. The pot for international fights in Manila can exceed 10 million pesos (£141,000: $227,000) and owners fly their cockerels to the arena by helicopter to limit travel stress. The betting is organised by figures known as 'cristos', who make a living from commissions and, as one eyewitness explains, are as much a part of the spectacle as the competing birds.

> I arrived at the cockpit just before 2 p.m. with Chicoy my Filipino helper and another local cristo, who bet for us. They act rather like bookmakers but also bet against each other. It seemed a complicated business with a lot of hand signals and shouting. The noise of their shouting and that of spectators prior to the start was incredible. The cristos reminded me of a scene from the dealing floor of the Wall Street Stock Exchange. Domingo Gutterez, a cristo from Palawan, told me, 'When I bet on a cock I am looking at the owner's reputation as much as the cock, the cock must have a good stance, strong legs and wings.'
>
> The first fight I witnessed wasn't the savage spectacle I'd imagined. It was over in 30 seconds with one of the cockerels administering a fatal blow with his slasher. The cock had been killed instantly and would be taken home and eaten by his owner's family. My cristo had chosen the right bird and I was up 400 pesos. Once the fight was over the cristos settled their bets and money was screwed into balls and thrown around the ring from losers to winners, never once did I see a dispute. Filipinos say there is never any dishonesty when it comes to betting at a cockpit. They said it was a sacred place where a man's word is king.[203]

The widespread opposition to cockfighting, the pitting of one animal against another unto the death, seems as straightforward as the historical case against bear baiting, or the modern condemnation of bullfighting. Many would agree with a Western eyewitness to a Filipino cockfight, who concluded: 'I couldn't believe what my eyes had just seen. The intensity and ferocity of both the birds and the crowd stunned me. After watching a few more handsome cockerels meet a similar savage, bloody end, I'd had enough.'[204]

Yet others have noted a strange but powerful emotional paradox at the very heart of the enterprise. The birds may be destined for mortal combat by their owners, but in the course of their training they are by no means treated as dispensable assets. Another Western eyewitness reflects:

> It seems far more cruel to feed a chicken in an artificially lit shed and kill it after eight weeks of life, than it does to rear a cockerel for two years for fighting. These birds are often the most precious possession of a rural Filipino. This was summed up for me by a man I met on the island of Bohol. He told me, 'Each morning I wake up and immediately go to see my cock. I sit and hold him for often up to an hour. My wife is jealous of my cocks. I would rather spend money on them than on my wife.'[205]

Setting aside such contentious priorities, there is little doubt that many cockers are utterly devoted to their birds. Not only do they lavish emotional energy on them, the birds are virtually smothered in material comforts. The old obsolete verb 'to cocker' meant to indulge or pamper or treat with excessive tenderness and care.[206] (It is proposed as one source of the old name for Londoners – 'Cockneys' – those accustomed to the pampered life of the city.) The historical treatments intended to ensure first-rate fighting birds are remarkable for their eccentricity as well as their variety. English cocks were sparred, sweated and stoved – a bizarre ritual that involved burying the bird to its neck in a straw basket. While forced to fast before a fight, at other times they were indulged with rarefied forms of 'cock-bread' made of fine oatmeal flour, eggs, butter, mixed sometimes with ale or white wine, and flavoured with aniseed, carroway, liquorice, 'Syrup of Clove-gillyflowers . . . a Date or two, with some Candyed Eringo Root'.[207] The cock's drinking water also might be infused with herbs such as wood-sorrel, ground ivy, feverfew, dandelion and borage.

One practice, apparently pursued until the twentieth century and advocated by some of the most famous exponents – which suggests a desire for some deeper, almost transubstantiation-like conversion of owner to bird – involved feeding the birds bread steeped in the cocker's own urine. The same liquid was widely used once battle was over; the bird's eyes and wounds were licked by the owner, until all the blood was sucked away – even sometimes from the inside of the cock's mouth – after which cuts were washed in his urine.[208]

These archaic practices and decoctions have now long gone, replaced today in the Philippines by a hi-tech regime that combines exercise, hygiene, scrutiny of the bird's bowel movements, a battery of medicines for everything from avian pox to stress, and a suite of dietary supplements including bee pollen and cod liver oil.[209] Despite the lavish care expended in the two years of the cock's development, all of it comes to a close – and such a fate is absolutely implicit in the long months of preparation – with the chance strike of a slasher. The eighteenth-century poet George Crabbe explored the moral and emotional tension embedded in cockfighting in his long poem *The Parish Register*:

> Here his poor bird th' inhuman cocker brings,
> Arms his hard heel and clips his golden wings;
> With spicy food th' impatient spirit feeds,
> And shouts and curses as the battle bleeds.
> Struck through the brain, deprived of both his eyes,
> The vanquish'd bird must combat till he dies;
> Must faintly peck at his victorious foe,
> And reel and stagger at each feeble blow:
> When fall'n, the savage grasps his dabbled plumes,
> His blood-stain'd arms, for other deaths assumes;
> And damns the craven fowl, that lost his stake,
> And only bled and perished for his sake.[210]

In a sense the killing of the bird, which is routinely swift, is not the central moral problem with cockfighting. Many legal bird-centred sports entail a far less efficient means of death. Rather it is the responses aroused in the humans who witness it. In a penetrating survey, *The History of Cockfighting*, George Ryley Scott came to the following conclusion in 1957:

> The outstanding evil of the sport is not concerned with the combatants; it is concerned with the spectators.
> And this would appear to be a point which enthusiastic

cockers overlook or ignore. To call cockfighting cruel, in all but exceptional circumstances . . . is perhaps not strictly correct. But it is brutal. It arouses and develops brutality in the onlookers. This is *the* evil of cockfighting.[211]

This is not the place to debate the morality of blood sport, which is defended by its proponents with other arguments. Namely, that their particular version is a codified re-enactment of nature's own intrinsic brutality; or that it is an ancient pursuit enabling humans to return to their first roots; or that it is a process through which the spectator is given cathartic release from his or her own brute condition. Advocates of blood sports argue further that the momentary violence of the creature's death is held, cherished even, and given new meaning by a cradling infrastructure of ritual.

This much, however, one may conclude – that the cockfight and the mass-production chicken facility coexist in this world. One or the other brings the suffering and pain of our most precious bird into the homes of virtually every human on this planet, and the modern lives of domestic junglefowl surely require that each of us examines our own conscience.

PEAFOWL

The fabulous eye-spotted plumes in the peacock's 'tail' are among the longest feathers possessed by any bird and can measure 1.6 m (5.2 ft). Technically they are massively elongated upper-tail coverts which, at rest, overlay the true tail and sweep behind the male bird rather like a bridal train. In display they rise and spread as a shimmering hemisphere of green, liberally sprinkled with copper discs that are themselves studded with royal-blue ocelli.

It is not just the colours which wow the human observer but the total spectacle inherent in the display. Few ornithologists have more accurately or beautifully conveyed the blend of theatre, choreography and artifice implicit in a peacock's dance than the Indian Salim Ali:

His half-open chestnut wings are drooped at the sides and go through a continuous shaking or quivering. In this posture he faces the hen (or hens), and with legs partly flexed struts and prances from one foot to the other in mincing steps as if stalking her . . . From time to time he goes through violent paroxysms of shivering the erected train, the quills producing a 'zizzing' sound, and

The Mor Chowk at the City Palace in Udaipur reflects the enormous cultural importance of Indian Peafowl in its eponymous country.

thus slowly pivots round to exhibit his posterior – the greyish under tail-coverts and black rump surmounted by the radiating glistening white shafts of the fanned-out train.[212]

It is not surprising that the dance known as the 'pavane' (from the Spanish for peacock, *pavón*), was thought to mimic the grave posturing flux of these stately movements and to have given the dance its name (although this may not, in fact, be true).[213]

The male's extravagant colours and luxuriant form have made it one of the classic measures of all avian beauty and a fixture for the human imagination for thousands of years. The bird is embedded in religious traditions and mythologies from China to the Atlantic, while its inspiration for art, literature and cultural reference is a global phenomenon. In truth it is intergalactic: 183 light years from Earth there is a constellation visible in the southern sky named Pavo (from the Latin for the bird). The largest of its stars is the peacock's eye.[214]

We talk routinely of *the* peacock, when technically it is simply a name for the male bird, while 'peahen' is a word for the female. In scientific nomenclature the birds are called peafowl, of which there are three species. The **Green Peafowl** *Pavo muticus*, spread in a disjunct range through Myanmar, southern China, Indochina and Java, is little known and now threatened with extinction, yet it is as beautiful as its more celebrated relative. Even less familiar is the **Congo Peacock** *Afropavo congensis*, which was only 'discovered' (for science) in 1936, despite thriving in Africa and diverging from its Asian cousins about 26 million years ago. It is a more compact creature lacking the train of its relatives and in shape resembles a pheasant. The way in which this extraordinary African bird revealed itself to Western eyes involves a wonderful story of natural-historical detective work.

The bird is endemic to forests at the heart of the Democratic Republic of the Congo, where it was well known (under the names *ngowe* and *itundu*) to local people. Yet it had eluded recognition by the white colonial community and only gave a clue to its existence in 1913, via the headdress on a Congolese hunter in the Ituri Rainforest. A young American naturalist, James Chapin, happened to spot, tucked into this headgear, a black-barred rufous feather that suggested some type of pheasant or peacock, neither of which was known to occur in Africa. Chapin nursed his silent inklings for decades until, one day in 1936, in the Congo Museum of Tervuren, Belgium, he came across two dusty skins that had lain wrongly identified for years. Chapin noted the similarities between 'his' 1913 feather and these Belgian specimens and soon afterwards named the species for science.

Chapin never made great claim for what was indubitably a remarkable piece of forensic observation by him and generously acknowledged that the species would have been 'found' by other colonial officers, even had he not divined its existence from the scant clues. Yet secondary accounts of his discovery written by other people have tended to reduce the detail to enlarge the myth, which suggests that he saw the first live bird.[215] In fact by the time Chapin himself observed a wild bird in the Congo in July 1937, several good specimens had already been obtained and the bird's distribution was partly mapped. Moreover the story of scientific discovery

needs to be set alongside the fact that Congolese people had probably been eating the bird for millennia. It is apparently still trapped but is also partly protected by local lore.[216]

PEACOCKS IN INDIA AND CHINA

The word 'peacock' is almost invariably intended to conjure the last of the three species, the **Indian Peafowl** *Pavo cristatus*, found wild throughout the subcontinent and since 1963 the national bird in India. It was originally a forest dweller, but it has become so entwined with the religion, folk culture and destiny of India's Hindu population that peacocks are now birds of scrub, cultivation and even of the village. In a country famed for its tolerance of wild animals, peacocks are widely cherished and protected so that in many parts they behave like domestic birds. For visitors to India they possibly have their largest impact at sites with some historical or cultural status, especially temples, forts and palaces. The beauty of the semi-tame peacocks then seems a natural extension to the monument's wider aesthetic appeal.

The birds have also acquired a secondary role in shaping an outsider's stereotypic impression of India. The sight and sounds of peacocks – those wonderful, high, wailing, emotionally laden cries – have almost guaranteed background roles in films or television programmes with an Indian subcontinental setting, so that they permeate the foreigner's sensory encounter with the place:

> The cry of the peacock must be one of the most evocative sounds in the Indian jungle. It is particularly used as a background detail on documentaries about tigers, helping to set the scene and heighten the sense of drama. Indeed some of my strongest memories of searching for real tigers in parks such as Ranthambore revolve around being wrapped in a blanket in the back of an open jeep at dawn with a high sense of anticipation about finding and photographing tigers, all played out to the haunting cries of peacocks. Those calls, coupled with the other ingredients that make daybreak in Indian forests so special, somehow give me more pleasure than finding the actual tigers, the very reason for my being there.[217]

Peacock calls have another role in visual media when used in non-Asian, frequently European or American, settings, where the implied presence of domestic birds evokes ideas of style, wealth and horticultural leisure.

Two contributors from the peacock's native region outline the bird's place in ancient Indian mythology:

> Many Hindu deities such as Lakshmi, goddess of fertility, Brahma and Kama are portrayed riding upon peacocks. Saravati, goddess of poetry and wisdom, also has her sacred peacock mount. The Hindu god Skanda was depicted riding a snake-killing peacock. So too was the god Kartik (son of Lord Shiva and Parvati and brother to the elephant god Ganesh), who rides on its back. Peacocks always accompany images of Lord Krishna. And the beautiful peacock feather is also part of Lord Krishna's crown.[218]

Ananda Banerjee confirms the peacock's rich part in Hindu mythology, but also explores some of the tension between this and everyday treatment of the real bird:

Peacock-feather fans are a common tourist sale item in India and may lead to the illegal slaughter of the country's national bird.

The Mayur dance in the Braj region of India celebrates Lord Krishna and takes full advantage of his key avian symbol, the Indian Peafowl.

The peacock is the bird which carries Shanmukha or Kartik, son of Lord Shiva, and the colourful feathers are associated with Lord Krishna. Indian artists always show Krishna as wearing a feather in his hair. The peacock population is higher in the arid zone of Rajasthan where, in spite of their damage to crops, they are not killed because of the element of divinity attaching to them. It is also believed that the presence of peacocks near homes keeps away snakes from the surroundings. In former time tribal peoples like the Bhils (of west-central India) wore garments made of feathers and even today they play an important part in tribal dances. Peacock feathers are also collected and sold after the birds have shed them. Fans and dainty short-handled 'brooms' are prepared from the feathers and religious sanctuaries, puja or worship-rooms, etc. are often swept with them. The peacock is a common theme and design in both traditional and modern Indian jewellery as well as in paintings.

Poaching of this national bird is still rampant, scores of peacock deaths have been reported from the Indian state of Uttar Pradesh. Many also die through the direct intake of pesticides which are sprayed in the fields. Another thing is that, while their sale is illegal in India, peacock feathers are still found on the open market for Indian tourists, who put these plumes as decorative items in their living rooms. [219]

One intriguing by-product of the Indian and specifically Hindu attachment to the species is its vestigial population in Pakistan. Once found extensively in the southern half of the country, peacocks were exterminated in many parts by Muslim hunters after Pakistan's creation in 1947. Today the bird survives only in the extreme eastern border areas, where it is protected by Hindu communities living in this Islamic state. [220]

It was perhaps inevitable that a creature of such exalted cultural association and beauty would be exported beyond its genuine range both as a natural wonder and exotic luxury. Captive examples or skins of Indian and Green Peafowls journeyed to the Chinese imperial court, where their various feathers were once used to denote the graduated ranks in the empire's civil and military administrations. They were also frequent insignia of the royal family itself, and one extraordinary imperial garment was a type of female cape made entirely from peacock tail feathers and silk. Such robes were worn at least from the seventeenth century and an example from the late Qing Dynasty owned by the Empress Dowager Cixi (1835–1908) sold at auction in 2008 for $32,403 (£20,252). [221]

It was also said that China's Tang Dynasty (AD 618–907) was founded when the daughter of a distinguished general, who herself frequently painted and embroidered peacock designs, was offered in marriage to the man who could shoot an arrow through one of her painted peacock's eyes. The victor, Tang Gaozu (better known as Li Yuan), secured his bride but also founded a dynasty in his adopted name. [222]

PEACOCKS IN THE WEST

In western Asia, awareness of 'domesticated' peacocks dates at least to 745 BC, when the court records of Tiglath-Pileser III indicate how this Assyrian ruler received the birds among royal tribute. [223] The species then travelled to Europe by at least 500 BC, Greek writers often referring to it as 'the Persian bird', confirming their awareness of its Asiatic origins. One measure of the extraordinary impact of peacocks on Greek society is the story of Demos, son of an Athenian ambassador, who brought them back from Persia in the second half of the fifth century BC. Demos then charged the public entrance fees to see his birds on the first day of every month, attracting sightseers from as far away as Thessaly and Sparta. At a time when a skilled workman earned a drachma a day, a pair of peacocks was valued at 1,000 drachmas. [224]

It is a further index of the peacock's powerful visual impact that this foreign bird eventually became entwined with the Greeks' own religious thought and practice. It was an avian motif for the goddess Hera, consort to Zeus and the Hellenic queen of heaven, and free-roaming peacocks were said to wander her temple precinct on the Greek island of Samos. Later the bird acquired a similar symbolic role for the goddess Juno (Hera's Roman equivalent), the harnessed peacocks drawing her chariot across the sky.

Rome was possibly the place where the deep reverence that had accompanied the peacock in its journey westwards began to mingle with darker associations. The birds had always been the epitome of exoticism. In late-Republican Rome that rarity value morphed into social prestige when roasted birds started to grace high-society dining tables. Eventually it became so de rigueur at Roman banquets that Cicero suggested it was actually 'daring' to omit it from the menu. [225] The first major Roman dealer in peacock was said to have earned 60,000 sesterces a year, but the ultimate glutton for them was the emperor Aulus Vitellius, who reigned for just seven months in AD 69. [226] Before being murdered he was a byword for indulgence, the historian Edward Gibbon suggesting that he spent the equivalent of £6 million (at eighteenth-century values) in mere eating. [227] Vitellius' brother feted him during one banquet that achieved notoriety as the Shield of Minerva. It was the ultimate culinary statement of power and political reach, incorporating 7,000 gamebirds from a territory that stretched from Spain to modern-day Iraq. Among the vast effluent of flavours were peacocks' brains and flamingos' tongues. [228] It is not perhaps surprising to find that in the satires of the poet Horace (65–8 BC) the bird had already come to suggest vanity's human embodiment, the coxcomb. [229]

Thereafter cultural connections with peacocks seem to take two divergent paths. One strand of association in Western literature has deployed the bird as a symbol for conceit and self-regard. The link is now embedded in many European languages. 'Proud as a peacock' is proverbial in English, while 'peacock' (in the sense of an overdressed beau), 'peacockery', 'peacockish' and 'peacockishness' are part of a large synonymy to denote ostentatious male display or strutting foppery. The pattern is repeated in modern Greek, Serbian, Spanish, Portuguese and Italian. [230]

In Italy we say: *Fare il pavone* ('To act like a peacock'). It means that you are proud. There is also a verb: *pavoneggiarsi*, which comes from the word *pavone* ('peacock') which means 'to strut'. [231]

In Serbia and Croatia people say *Šepuri se kao paun* – 'he struts like a peacock' – the implication being of showing off rather than pride. *Paun* ('peacock') is also a rather old-fashioned male name, but you won't find anyone called that now, but Paunovic – the correspondent family name – is relatively more common (more so than Peacock in the UK).[232]

It is worth adding that even the English surname Peacock – and possibly its Serbian equivalent – was itself coined to describe a person noted for their dandyism.[233]

Another European idea further tainting the bird's name was a belief that the evil eye resided in the ocelli of the tail feathers. William Beebe, the great scholar of pheasants, was at a loss to explain its origins, but noted how it was completely absent from India and China.[234] A modern observer confirms that no derogatory ideas of any kind have a place in contemporary India. 'There are no negative connotations attaching to the peacock. Indian girls are still named Mayuri and boys Mayur (they mean peacock). Obviously they would not be popular if there were any connections to cockiness and pride.'[235]

Yet I can testify personally to the power that these superstitions once held over a Western imagination, in the form of my indomitable Derbyshire-born grandmother, Cicely Cocker. As a child I was given a number of glorious peacock feathers and, while they were the proudest exhibit in my bedroom's collection of natural curios (along with a ram's skull and owl pellets), they were there very much against my Grandma's wishes. She thought them an omen of disaster.

English actress Lisa Goddard confirms the superstition among her fellow thespians:

Peacock feathers are bad luck in the theatre and in houses too (aren't they?). Real flowers on stage are also bad luck. Although butterflies, real or not, are good luck, and they frequently fly round the stage during a performance. I think that it is the heat of the lights that brings them out.'[236]

Another actor wrote: 'Anything to do with peacocks is fatal . . . I put on a play called "Cage me a Peacock" which lost me every penny I had.'[237]

The unluckiest of all peacock tail feathers have to be the 98 jewel-bedecked plumes belonging to a trio of birds worked into the front cover of what became known as the Great Omar, a unique edition of Edward FitzGerald's *The Rubáiyát of Omar Khayyám*. Although peacocks do not appear in this cycle of poems (yet nightingales do, see page 478), they were seen as a suitably Oriental motif to complement FitzGerald's famous translation of this Persian work. The Great Omar was commissioned by a London binding firm, Sangorski and Sutcliffe, and completed by a master craftsman, G F Lovatt, who worked the front and inside covers using 1,500 separate pieces of finest morocco leather. The eye-spots in the three peacock tails were each encrusted with 98 unhappy garnets and their crests finished with six tragic turquoises.

The spectacular book eventually sold to an American buyer for £400 (well below its hoped-for price of £1,000; about £71,000: $106,000 by modern standards) and was shipped across the Atlantic. Alas, the luckless vessel bearing the Great Omar was entitled SS *Titanic* and the book became legendary as one of the most important treasures lost on that tragic night of 14/15 April 1912. However, the misfortunes of the Great Omar were by no means finished. Francis Sangorski drowned shortly afterwards and Lovatt succumbed to consumption in 1918 (in the book trade it

was said that he died of grief at the loss of his masterpiece). Undeterred, Sangorski and Sutcliffe then commissioned a second version, working from original drawings and taking seven years to complete it. During the Second World War, the German blitz on London meant that it was too dangerous to store the Great Omar II at the bindery and it was removed to a warehouse, which then took a direct hit. In the intense heat the book melted, leaving just the 98 garnets. A third version of this remarkable work was finally completed in 1989 and is on display in the British Library.[238]

Perhaps more intriguing, in view of how dominant the negative themes have become in European peacock symbolism, is the continued and parallel spiritual attachment to the bird. Early Christians borrowed some of the religious feeling that had evolved in Asia and then in Greece. Various civilisations had associated peacocks with fertility and specifically with rain and sunshine. The first link is a classic piece of *ex post facto* reasoning. Peacocks breed during the Indian monsoon and since they vocalise more in the nuptial season, their calls were eventually taken as an omen of rainfall. It is remarkable to find how that connection endured for thousands of years and across an immense span from south Asia to the Atlantic edge of Europe. The Ulster-born scholar Edward Armstrong recalled how, during his childhood, peacock screams prophesied rain in his native Northern Ireland.[239]

The solar association is easy to understand when one has witnessed the shining eye-studded corollas of peacocks in display, and their strong resemblance to the rising sun. Roman potters apparently stamped their ceramic lamps with a peacock motif to signify that their wares turned darkness into light.[240] Early Christians connected the bird with dawn and the theme of resurrection. This idea was reinforced by both the peacock's annual moult cycle, in which the sun-like fan of feathers is lost and renewed, but also by a widespread belief in the imperishable quality of peacock flesh. This was viewed as a living symbol of the incorruptibility of Jesus Christ. (It sheds an incidental light on the bird's renown as a delicacy, not to mention the peculiar tastes of Roman epicures. Apparently the meat can be as hard as leather, one critic describing it as 'excessively tough and with no distinguishable flavour'.[241] William Beebe thought the tongue in particular – once among the most prized morsels – a 'hard, gristly, bony affair' that could have been no more satisfying than the scales on its legs.)[242]

Christian attachment to peacocks resulted in a striking piece of bird-centred ritual that survived in Rome for centuries. Until recently the pope, during formal procession, was flanked by a pair of chamberlains bearing *flabelli* – great ostrich-feathered fans tipped with peacock plumes. The remarkable and beautiful objects brought an Aztec-like flourish to Catholic ritual, but they also had a precise symbolism. The ostrich was an ancient emblem of justice (see page 14), while the peacock represented both immortality and the all-seeing vigilance of the church.[243] The Vatican chose to set aside its *flabelli* during the pontificate of John XXIII, although at his own coronation in 1958 they were prominently on display (as demonstrated in the YouTube footage listed in the references).[244]

The linking of Christian concepts to the peacock provided Western artists with one of several recurrent justifications to include the most gloriously colourful of all birds in their paintings. Either it was there to evoke the very specific religious ideas outlined above (such as in Jan Brueghel the Elder's *Christ the Gardener*, c.1610, currently on display in the Musée des Art Décoratifs in Paris), or it was added as a colourful detail connoting expensive luxury. (A good example of this is a work entitled *A Poulterer's Shop*, c.1670, by the Dutchman Gerrit Dou in the National Gallery, London.) Alternatively it served as a motif in paintings of classical mythology, especially scenes involving the appropriate Greek or Roman goddesses (e.g. Pieter Lastman's *Juno Discovering Jupiter with Io*, 1618, also in London's National Gallery). One constant throughout all these multifarious Western depictions is for the peacocks to look static (sometimes actually dead) and two-dimensional (invariably with tail spread at the moment of display).

THE PEACOCKS OF J M WHISTLER

Notable departures from this convention are the paintings of the birds by the artist James McNeill Whistler (1834–1903). Whistler was American-born but spent most of his working life in Paris and London. His peacock paintings were done between 1876–7, at an early stage in his career for a client, Frederick Leyland, a wealthy shipping magnate, who was also a great lover of Oriental art. The businessman wanted to develop rooms at his home in Prince's Gate, London, to house a valuable ceramics collection, and he employed Whistler to complete the designs.[245]

He even invited the artist to move into the house during his absence. Unfortunately, with Leyland away, Whistler was inspired to go well beyond his original brief. The entire room from ceiling to skirting, which Whistler, with his idiosyncratic bent for ellipsis, entitled *Harmony in Blue and Gold*, was completed in colours and motifs drawing on the Asian bird. It is the conceptual integration manifest in the whole interior as well as the vibrancy of the actual bird paintings that makes the room among the most important of all peacock-inspired artefacts. Ironically, when Leyland finally returned to London he was as displeased by the

artistic liberties expressed in Whistler's avian tour de force, as he was by the enlarged bill for 2,000 guineas (probably in excess of £150,000 or $240,000 today). The quarrel was finally settled with a payment of £1,000.

Whistler then returned to the house to complete the commission, sometimes working from six in the morning until nine at night, painting in the process his *pièce de résistance* in the Peacock Room. The image, taking up a whole wall, is a major departure from the usual European peacock tradition. For Whistler was himself a great student of Japanese art and on the shutters in the room he had completed peacock images that closely suggest the influence and the shimmering fluid lines of the great Japanese printmaker Ando Hiroshige.[246] Oriental artists drew on an ancient tradition of bird-and-flower paintings in China and Japan, where peacocks were a favourite subject, not simply for the open fan-like corolla of displaying birds, but for the lithe, sinuous, cascading sweep of peacocks in motion.

In Whistler's main painting, a magnificent tableau of two fighting birds, there is no suggestion of the static stereotype beloved of the West. Instead one has the conventions of the Far East, the tails twisting round the posturing birds in glorious dynamic curves. In truth Whistler combined the best of both traditions. One bird, head uplifted and crowing triumphantly, has its wings and tail half open, while the other pivots, train swishing extravagantly, round its opponent. Together they create an unforgettable image of contending males, at the heart of which is a whirling gyre of peacockish antagonism.

Whistler, originally educated for a military career at West Point, was nothing if not combative. Yet his final revenge on his employer was an exquisitely aesthetic affair. He inserted into the painting, completed in gold and silver leaf, a number of coins at the feet of one of the birds. It was intended to mock the mercenary attitudes of Leyland and just in case the money-grubbing magnate missed the point, Whistler entitled the piece *Art and Money*. These final details gild this

This magnificent peacock painting by J M Whistler might have been part of a room he designed and named *Harmony in Blue and Gold*, but its creation involved a tale of financial squabbling and personal acrimony.

remarkable, semi-autobiographical ensemble and ensure that Whistler's Peacock Room is almost a recapitulation of all human symbolism projected on to the species. Here in one space are vanity, wealth, excess, self-indulgence but also – and most memorably – vaulting artistic aspiration inspired by one of the most radiantly beautiful of all living organisms.[247]

There is an intriguing coda to the story of Whistler's loose and free-flowing peacocks. His original working cartoon is now on display in the Hunterian Gallery in Glasgow, Scotland. Yet after Leyland's death the Peacock Room was sold to an American art collector, Charles Lang Freer (1854–1919). During his lifetime the whole thing was moved lock, stock and barrel to his Detroit home. Then on Freer's own death Whistler's peacocks migrated once more, and eventually came to reside in the Freer Gallery (opposite the Smithsonian Natural History Museum) in Washington, DC, where recent restoration work has returned the Peacock Room to something remarkably close to Whistler's initial bird-inspired vision.[248]

Screamer family *Anhimidae*

These three curious, heavily built goose-like birds are unlike any other species in the world, but are now thought to be most closely related to wildfowl. They are found exclusively in South America: the **Northern Screamer** *Chauna chavaria* is endemic to Venezuela and Colombia (and is now considered near-threatened mainly because of habitat loss), but the **Horned Screamer** *Anhima cornuta* and **Southern Screamer** *Chauna torquata* are widespread, and often common on lowland marshes, swamps and wet grassland, with the former occurring across much of the northern continent and the latter concentrated in a south-central region between Bolivia and Argentina.

One of the screamers' stranger features is the dense series of air cells beneath the skin, which allows them both to swim buoyantly, and to soar majestically when they take to the sky. It also causes them to 'crackle' and 'pop' like bubble wrap if they are physically handled. They can hiss menacingly like a snake when threatened and are even capable of a ventriloquial *boo* sound that comes directly from the spongy skin within their chests.[1] But it is the more conventional vocalisations which have given screamers their unmistakable name and, in addition, a certain notoriety.

The names in various languages for the two widespread species are echoic of the family's basic trumpet notes. *Tach* and *chajá* are respectively the Brazilian and Argentinian words for Southern Screamer; while in Guyana, where the Horned Screamer was once abundant, it was called *mahooka*. The great American naturalists William and Mary Beebe considered this trisyllable an almost exact rendering of the call.[2] Hunting has now extirpated the species from Guyana, but the name is enshrined in two neighbouring coastal regions of the country, Demarara-Mahaica and Mahaica-Berbice, while a town just east of the capital, Georgetown, is called Mahaicony.[3]

Hunters are said to dislike the birds because of their readiness to raise the alarm for every living creature within earshot. In Argentina gauchos get very annoyed since their incessant racket is capable of spooking cattle.[4] Quite how loud the birds can be is revealed in a long and wonderful passage by W H Hudson, which is still the most evocative account of screamers in the English language. In *The Naturalist in La Plata* he described a ranch on the Argentinian pampas where the birds, which he calls by another local onomatopoeic name, *chakars*, gathered in huge numbers. As he and his host ate their supper, the birds suddenly 'burst forth into a tremendous evening song'.

It is impossible to describe the effect of this mighty rush of sound; but let the reader try to imagine half-a-million voices . . . bursting forth on the silent atmosphere of that dark lonely plain. One peculiarity was that in this mighty noise, which sounded louder than the sea thundering on a rocky coast, I seemed to be able to distinguish hundreds, even thousands, of individual voices. Forgetting my supper, I sat motionless and overcome with astonishment, while the air, and even the frail rancho, seemed to be trembling in that tempest of sound.

As it ceased the host noted resignedly: 'We are accustomed to this, señor – every evening we have this concert.'[5]

Hudson went on to express concern for the future of the species because of over-hunting, noting that screamers were good eating and flavoured like goose. This accords closely with a modern verdict submitted by an Argentinian who lives remarkably close to Hudson's frail rancho: 'I have eaten Southern Screamers and they are really good. Usually you only eat the breast, and a lot of people make what we call here 'milanesas' [schnitzels], which involves cutting the meat thinly and putting it in breadcrumbs.'[6]

This judgement, however, is not universal. 'I was canoeing once through a huge expanse of marshy wetlands north of Buenos Aires, and I came across my first pair of Southern Screamers. I asked whether they were good to eat: after all, they munch aquatic vegetation so might taste like huge ducks. No, she responded, they taste awful.'[7] It is widely repeated that the strange texture of the skin makes screamers repugnant and for that reason they are seldom hunted.[8]

If the sponginess of screamer flesh is not to everyone's taste, it has at least found fame by association.

Noticing *Torta Chajá* on the dessert menu, and knowing that a *chajá* is a Southern Screamer, I asked the waiter to explain the name. A baker called Clemente in the small village of Paisandu used to make a cake, especially for birthdays. It quickly became popular among local residents, who called it *torta chajá* on account of the spongy texture resembling that of *chajá* meat (this also suggests that screamers are indeed eaten and a friend tells me that he has seen chicks on sale, because their meat is nice and oily!). Realising that he was on to a good thing, Clemente patented both name and recipe, and the cake is now cooked – presumably under licence – all over Uruguay.[9]

Duck, Goose and Swan family *Anatidae*

This family of medium to very large birds – including some of the heaviest of all those with the powers of flight – comprise 161 species spread through the six upper continents, with a bias towards the northern hemisphere. Eurasia and North America each have 46 species. South America, meanwhile, holds 33, but the Australasian and Afrotropical regions have just 22 apiece.

These figures do not tell the full story, however, and take no account of wildfowl movements outside the nesting season. The African total is typical. While there might be only 22 reseident wildfowl mainly south of the Sahara, the continent as a whole is visited by 50 species, many of them migrating to Africa during the non-breeding period from northern latitudes. Then one must consider that underlying the distribution of wild ducks, geese and swans is their ubiquity as domesticated stock.

If gamebirds represent the family of greatest cultural and practical value to humankind, then wildfowl command an undisputed second place. They have yielded two of the most economically important birds on Earth, the **Mallard** *Anas platyrhynchos* and the **Greylag Goose** *Anser anser*, from which we have developed almost all of our multifarious farmyard ducks and geese. Yet two other species have also undergone full domestication. They are the **Swan Goose** *Anser cygnoides*, primarily of China and Russia (whose wild populations, ironically, are now considered at acute risk of extinction), and the **Muscovy Duck** *Cairina moschata* (see page 86). Wildfowl have meant more to us than their

wonderful gifts of meat, eggs and feathers. They entwine our history in so many ways that it is almost impossible to find a form of human activity that does not involve them. After grouse and partridge, they are the hunter's wild birds of choice. They are also often beautiful creatures and while their colours have long been appreciated, it is sometimes underestimated when measured against their utility or flavour. The following contribution reminds us how impressive wild ducks can look and sound, especially in winter landscapes that are otherwise drained of colour and purged of other living creatures:

I have lived in the same remote, partially ice-free bay of Alaska and have the honour of sharing this area with the wintering sea ducks. These are long-lived birds that show strong site fidelity to their habitats so we meet each year when they return from the breeding grounds and I from summer work. As I walk down the beach a raft of **Barrow's Goldeneye** *Bucephala islandica*, **Surf Scoter** *Melanitta perspicillata* and **Harlequin Duck** *Histrionicus histrionicus* accompany myself and my dogs. The incredible squeaks, whistles and bubbling noises fill my heart with joy. The intense beauty of their blues, greens, golds, orange browns, purples, whites and shimmery blacks is a delight to behold in the midst of a south-westerly blizzard.[1]

Adding to their mastery of air, water and dry land, wildfowl have also colonised the interior world of our collective imaginations. They are symbols in art and

This image of a Northern Pintail reminds us how impressive wild ducks can look, especially in winter landscapes that are drained of colour and purged of other living creatures.

literature, music and ballet, story and folklore. Yet the birds have acquired further modern roles. They have this wonderful habit of congregating in prodigious numbers at key wetland sites, where the sheer spectacle of tens, sometimes hundreds, of thousands of birds has alerted us to the restorative power of nature. In short, ducks, geese and swans have made us feel deeply and then think hard. They have become symbols for the human spirit and the need for our imaginations to enjoy free play in wild spaces. Often wildfowl have been catalytic in the development of an environmental awareness in many countries. The interconnecting threads of their cultural roles could fill a multi-volume book by themselves.

DUCKS IN THE ANCIENT WORLD

One striking aspect of duck physiology, indeed of all wildfowl, is that they possess an external sex organ, which is unlike most other birds (the ratites, including ostriches, are a classic exception; see page 16). The fact was appreciated by Aristotle (in reference to geese), although he could never have known, for instance, that the prodigious penis belonging to the predominantly Argentinian **Lake Duck** *Oxyura vittata* is 42 cm (16.5 in) long and almost the length of the bird itself.[2]

It seems more than coincidence that these physical attributes run parallel with the wider and older status of wildfowl as symbols of fertility and sexuality. As we will see, it is a recurrent theme across the whole family. It is mere speculation but one wonders if their apparent potency can help to explain the frequency of duck images in artefacts that had links to the enhancement of human beauty, such as perfume and cosmetics. In London's British Museum, for example, there are both ancient Egyptian spoons for applying make-up and cosmetic and perfume holders shaped in duck form. One of the most beautiful wildfowl objects of the ancient world – with a slender neck, head and beak that are highly suggestive of **Northern Pintail** *Anas acuta* – is a 3,400-year-old ivory cosmetics vessel found in Assyria (now in the Ashmolean Museum,

This 3,360-year-old Egyptian painting of Nebamun hunting in the marshes is surely one of the great treasures of the British Museum.

Oxford, UK; and similar to the Egyptian artefact pictured below). Did wildfowl have an inherent sexiness for the ancients?[3] Or, conversely, was it that pairs of ducks suggested an ideal companionability as they sailed serenely together across the water? Or was it much more prosaic? Did ducks simply have nice rounded shapes that lent themselves to the design of containers and vessels of all kinds?

Certainly we know that older still than any erotic lore was the duck's status as a classic test of masculine prowess. Men must have pitted their wits against the birds almost since humans acquired a capacity for collaborative foraging. The payback has always been substantial – that moist reddish meat which falls off the breastbone where the birds' powerful wing muscles are enfolded. The other core asset of

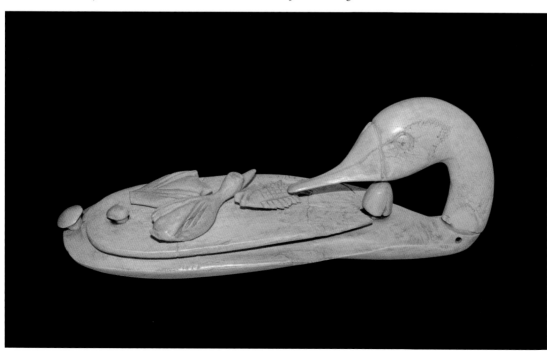

This Egyptian cosmetics holder in the form of a duck bearing a fish, flower and duckling on its back reflects the ancient world's linkage of wildfowl with natural fertility and, by association, with human sexuality.

This is a facsimile of an Egyptian painting of Red-breasted Geese. More than 4,500 years old, the original is so accurate and modern in style it looks as if it could have been painted yesterday.

wildfowl is their gregariousness. Often they can be caught en masse: sometimes several scores at a time, even hundreds, and, occasionally, by the thousand.

Some of our best evidence for the ingenuity of the early fowlers and also for our compulsive need to celebrate the atavistic thrill of duck hunting, is from ancient Egypt. Two paintings in particular are justly ranked among the best known of all bird-centred artworks produced by that eternally fascinating civilisation. Yet both are by unknown artists. The older is at Beni Hasan, on the walls of a tomb that is about 3,700–3,900 years old (see also page 376). The image memorialises the life of a high-ranking official called Khnumhotep II. It shows this grand vizier indulging in the pastime of duck trapping with the use of a clap net (an excellent facsimile of the painting is housed in the Metropolitan Museum of Art, in New York).

Khnumhotep's political importance is emphasised by the fact that he is twice the size of his servant, but one senses that this is a painting less about rank and political status. Rather it celebrates life lived intensely and happily. It is overflowing with vibrant nature, a point underscored by the abundance of ducks. The clap net closes tightly over 38 wildfowl, but outside the mesh on the wider marsh is a larger flock of mainly Northern Pintail; fearful, desperate and densely packed, some of them rising skywards in a bid to escape. They are beautifully delineated so that one can easily recognise not just male pintails, but also **Eurasian Teal** *Anas crecca*, **Eurasian Wigeon** *Anas penelope*, **Ruddy Shelduck** *Tadorna ferruginea* and Mallard.[4]

If anything the other work, a later painting produced in about 1350 BC, is even more wonderful. It was cut out and taken by a grave robber from an unknown tomb wall at Thebes and eventually entered the British Museum in London, where it is still housed. It illustrates a middle-

ranking official called Nebamun punting his reed skiff through the marshes of the Nile, his daughter crouched at his feet to stabilise the vessel. All around them throngs wild nature; and not just wildfowl, but other birds and animals: butterflies by Nebamun's elbow, fish beneath the boat. In his hand, clamped by their legs, he holds three pintail-like ducks. Another fleeing bird shows characteristics of a female Mallard, while a third has elements of a **Greater White-fronted Goose** *Anser albifrons*.

One striking detail in the painting is the presence of a large tame cat, which is thought to have been Nebamun's trained pet, used to recover birds much as later wildfowlers would use spaniels and retrievers. The cat is leaping upwards, seizing a duck in mid-flight. Another fascinating detail is the presence of a fourth wildfowl, an **Egyptian Goose** *Alopochen aegyptiaca*, at the skiff's prow, close to Nebamun's feet. The bird is mysterious. It is assumed to be a decoy, a tame bird, whose presence allayed the fears of wild prey and lured them within range. (One further interpretation, which returns us to an earlier theme, is that the bird is in some way a sexual symbol. Marshes and water, with their teeming lotus flowers and associated upwelling of fecund nature, were often artistic subjects that were supercharged with erotic connotations in ancient Egypt.)[5]

Whatever the exact and, most likely, multi-layered meanings of this painting and the earlier Khnumhotep masterpiece, one cannot avoid their shared sense of natural plenty and of human life intensely fulfilled. Can one also infer that these glorious artworks carried a subtler, subversive message about the real meaning and value of our lives? High politics and power and status are all fine: far better, however, to go duck hunting in the marsh. They are themes embedded in the entire history of wildfowling.

METHODS OF WILDFOWLING

The two Egyptian paintings demonstrate the ingenious efficiencies of our wildfowling methods. While Khnumhotep reveals the quiet capabilities of a clap net, Nebamun illustrates how a simple throwing stick can be used with deadly impact. Other fowling techniques have sometimes been so brutally successful that they were outlawed or, at least, have been condemned morally. Helmut Sick cited several unacceptable practices in modern Brazil, including the use of a cannon loaded with special shot that downed 'ducks by the ton.' Another ruse of unsustainable efficiency was to catch the birds during moult when they are flightless. On a single ranch in 1964, one drive caught 60,000 **Black-bellied Whistling Duck** *Dendrocygna autumnalis*.[6]

Sometimes it is the notoriety of these huge single tallies that highlights the excesses of wildfowling. Yet it also casts an oblique light on the paradisiacal abundance of birds at some of these wetland sites. A good example is Bharatpur in Rajasthan, India. In the 1890s the local maharajah established this now world-famous wetland as a hunting preserve (sadly its once massive wetland-bird populations have been severely reduced by water shortages inflicted by irrigation in surrounding farmland). At the far end of Bharatpur's central causeway bisecting the large man-made pools, there is a series of ageing stone plaques commemorating famous bags from major duck shoots. On 12 November 1938, a party of 39 'guns' accompanying the British Viceroy, Lord Linlithgow, downed 4,273 in one day. Almost 3,000 ducks were killed before lunch.[7]

This slaughter pales into insignificance when measured against that recorded at the flooded rice fields of Albufera, south of Spain's coastal city of Valencia, where in a single morning in the early twentieth century as many as 23,000 duck and Eurasian Coot were taken. It equated to *c*.20 tonnes of roasted fowl. However, the guns at Albufera could have been as many as 3,000. For individual determination not many can equal the Archduke Franz Ferdinand. Eleven years before he was murdered with his wife in Sarajevo in 1914 (and triggered the First World War), he went fowling on the Danube and brought down 238 ducks in two hours. The only thing that prevented him killing more was a shortage of cartridges.[8]

A remarkable aspect of wildfowling is the ingenious insights that hunters have somehow gained into duck psychology. Perhaps the most bizarre is revealed in Iran on the string of wetlands along the southern shore of the Caspian Sea. Vast numbers of ducks and geese, 'almost unequalled in the western Palearctic', spend the winter at these sites and are at the heart of ancient fowling operations.[9] The traditional method involves two boats working in tandem during the hours of darkness. On the bow of the first is a burning flare placed on a platform of earth which is hooded with a screen of rush matting so that the rest of the boat is kept in darkness. On the second boat are two men: one poling the vessel, while a partner sits in the prow banging non-stop on a brass gong. The catching is done from the boat with the flickering light. Dazzled by the flare, the ducks do not notice a man with a long-poled net, like a huge butterfly net, that he uses to scoop the birds as they come within range. What is most remarkable is that this mixture of light and din seems irresistible to the victims, which remain mesmerised by the boats until it is too late. In perfect conditions the teams can take 600 duck in a night.[10]

At one major location where the method is used, the wetland of Anzali Mordab, the annual harvest during the 1990s was 100,000 waterfowl (with a similar number falling to 1,000 hunters licensed with shotguns).[11] In the 1950s the total catch along the entire Caspian littoral was estimated at 1.2 million birds a year, while the figure for Anzali Mordab was 875, 000.[12]

It is no surprise that places once famous for hunting, including Bharatpur and Albufera, are now often celebrated as wildfowl refuges. Yet Iran's Caspian marshes have a special symbolism in the entire development of conservation. Close to Anzali Mordab is the city of Ramsar. In 1971 it was host to a meeting that signed into international law one of the key agreements on habitat protection. Today, with 160 contracting parties and 1,967 sites listed, covering 1.9 million km^2 (737,000 miles^2) of the richest marsh and aquatic habitats, the Convention on Wetlands of International Importance – better known as the Ramsar Convention – helps to protect wildfowl worldwide.

DUCK DECOYS IN EUROPE AND NORTH AMERICA

If a gong and lamp seem strange tools for trapping duck, then the decoys once used across much of Europe relied on an equally peculiar mechanism. The decoy, a word from the Dutch *eende kooy* or *eende-coy* ('duck cage'), was striking in physical structure and singular in its exploitation of avian psychology (for a fuller account, see *Birds Britannica*, pages 94–6).[13]

A decoy was a large octopus-shaped trap with a central open flight pond as the body, from which spread tentacle-like arms, each enclosed by net and ending in a capture pen. The ducks were seized in these traps, but what slowly drew them from the safety of the uncovered pond into the decoy's covered limbs was a peculiarity of their behaviour. When confronted by a terrestrial predator, such as a fox, wolf, or dog, swimming wildfowl actually follow the mammal's course along the lake-shore, while keeping to the safety of the open water. The decoy dog enticed the birds in exactly this way, gradually leading them along the channels of water to their final doom at the end of the netted pipes.

Until supplanted by the shotgun, the delicate arts of duck decoying were a fundamental part of Europe's rural economy, shifting vast quantities of birds from the misty stillness of the continent's fringing wetlands, to the bustling centres of population. The Netherlands alone once had 1,000 such traps, and even in the 1950s, after decades of decline, Dutch decoys were still supplying 300,000 fresh duck to market every year.[14] In the 1880s there was also a series of them along the Baltic coast that were said to have taken 106,000 birds, mainly Mallard, in a season.[15]

It is intriguing that while these hugely efficient devices were not transplanted to North America, the word 'decoy' itself did take firm root on the continent. However, in its journey across the Atlantic it acquired very different connotations. Rather than a type of trap, an American decoy is a model bird, originally made of wood (now usually of synthetic materials), shaped by a wildfowler and placed upon the waters where he is intending to hunt. Often they are used in small flotillas known as 'rigs'. The purpose of these floating lookalikes is to allay the suspicions of their wild counterparts and lure them to the shooting ground. The Egyptian Goose pictured on Nebamun's painted skiff was possibly a form of live decoy.

Yet the use of artificial birds was never a major element of wildfowling in the Old World, as it was, and indeed, still is, in America. The decoy's roots, in fact, pre-date European settlement. The oldest found in the USA were made by indigenous Americans and unearthed in a Nevadan cave in 1924. They are constructed from painted rushes and, despite being 1,000 years old, they are beautiful objects and easily recognisable as a widespread North American duck, the **Canvasback** *Aythya valisineria*.[16]

Decoys were adopted by colonial settlers and eventually became an integral element of the fowlers' practice, with their golden age between 1850 and 1950. Some makers were said to have carved 200,000 such birds in their careers. Some nineteenth-century hunters, meanwhile, armed with decoys and guns, were estimated to have shot 7,000 Canvasbacks in a single season.[17] More recently these often beautiful wooden carvings have acquired status as a quintessentially American art form and as a symbol of a pioneer history that is just now vanishing over the horizon of memory.

Collectors spend substantial sums on originals made by particularly celebrated carvers. A record was established in September 2007 for a drake Northern Pintail that fetched $1.13 million (£706,000) at auction. Its creator, Elmer Crowell (1862–1952), was from Cape Cod, Massachusetts, and his career typified those of other makers, whose own models now sell for five- and six-digit figures. Crowell was a market hunter by the age of 14, but eventually switched to carving decoys, living modestly and in close contact with the hunters who bought and used his 'birds' as working tools, 'akin to a hammer or a shovel'.[18] Such men would be astonished by the high regard in which their works are now held.

What makes decoys such attractive collectors' items is not merely their beauty, or their verisimilitude, or the vibrant life stories entailed in many of these working 'birds'. A key factor is the sheer variety of ducks and other wetland species – waders and even gulls – that were represented.

Popular table birds, such as Mallard and **Canada Goose** *Branta canadensis*, were obvious subjects for decoy makers. Yet they also crafted models of species that now have little or even adverse reputations for their meat: species such as **Common Goldeneye** *Bucephala clangula*, **Red-breasted Merganser** *Mergus serrator* and the subject of that record-price Crowell decoy, the Northern Pintail.[19]

The noted US birder and author Clay Sutton explains this facet of decoy making. His paternal grandfather, Frank Harold Sutton, was a market hunter in New Jersey during the Great Depression, when appetites were far less choosy than today. For Sutton Snr the key fowl of choice was the large gamey **American Black Duck** *Anas rubripes*, both for its size and savour. Clay Sutton adds:

> My Grandfather, and his son (my Uncle) Frank Jnr after him, each made and deployed decoys not just of their favored target, but of other ducks too, particularly the perky and beautiful **Hooded Merganser** *Lophodytes cucullatus*. These birds weren't eaten or even shot, but lent realism to the decoy 'spread'. The underlying rationale was to lull the main species into a false sense of security and lure it within range of an awaiting gun. Gull decoys were frequently used in this manner. Gulls, at least back then if not today, were flighty and nervous creatures, and therefore decoys of these birds were calculated to inspire trust in the black ducks. In addition to gulls, heron and egret decoys were also used by many gunners. All of these were collectively known as 'confidence decoys'.[20]

Today decoys are just as likely to be deployed in the living room as on the flight pond, but the revival of interest at least ensures that the art of making them has been kept alive. One tradition sustaining them is the decoy-making competition, which began in the 1920s and is now widely popular. However, makers are perhaps a little more evasive about the mysteries of their craft. Asked once how to perfect a decoy, one noted maker said, 'The secret to carving is to take a piece of wood and then remove anything that doesn't look like a bird.'[21]

GOOSE DECOYS

One of the great successes of North American conservation, spearheaded partly by wildfowling organisations such as Ducks Unlimited and Wildlife Forever, is the major increase in wildfowl numbers. The **Snow Goose** *Chen caerulescens*, which breeds in Arctic Canada and winters in the southern USA, is a classic exemplar of these reviving fortunes. Since the 1950s its numbers have grown dramatically from *c*.600,000 to 9–10 million. In fact the upsurge is so great that the hunting season and bag limits for wildfowlers have been increased to reduce the birds' own deleterious impact on the Arctic tundra habitats where they nest.

The North Platte River area of central Nebraska lies on a major fly-way for migrant Snow and Canada Geese, where decoy hunting is still a flourishing tradition. The following description is based on a personal account from a dedicated wildfowler, whose own deployment of goose decoys is exceptional.

Rick Halcott has hunted for most of his life using decoys, some of which he made himself from fast-drying foam. The full rig is now far smaller than when he was really keen. Some

New Jersey birder Clay Sutton with duck decoys made by his grandfather Frank Harold Sutton in the 1920s or 1930s.

winters he and his friends spread up to 6,000 birds across the 1.2–1.6 ha (3–4 acres) of his 8 ha (20 acre) stretch. He has traded and bought decoys from makers throughout the North Platte area. The earliest examples, which date to the 1930s and which are still 'working birds', were sewn together in canvas, then stuffed with straw and painted. They have since been laminated with fibreglass to protect them and increase their longevity. In the 1930s, when hunting geese was a vital source of food, decoys were sometimes made out of stove-pipe steel and the cut-steel head and neck would be soldered on to a metal body.

The modern decoys vary with conditions. If it is windy and cold then Halcott uses decoy birds that appear to be sleeping with legs tucked in and head and neck resting across the back. The more varied and lifelike they are, the more they are able to bring wild geese into the pool. It is important to have models that simulate movement, including birds with rotating radio-controlled wings, especially when hunting for Snow Geese, which are very active and seldom settle for long. The decoy birds vary in price. Rick now makes and sells many himself, which can cost around $250–$300 a dozen.

The other important part of decoying is to create sounds similar to those of live geese. Rick has a variety of callers and he uses both their contact flight calls and the more contented feeding grunt notes. The latter sounds calm the birds' nerves, suggesting to others passing overhead that it is safe to land. At certain times Rick is able to broadcast taped versions of goose calls and these also help to lure the birds within range.

There is now an open season on Snow Geese, because

of their excessive numbers, and it is possible to hunt them without a permit. In a year Halcott hopes to shoot about 150 Canada and 250–300 Snow Geese. These would be either frozen or converted to jerky for personal consumption, or given away to friends and to people who permit him to shoot on their land. Most years the supplies last until the following season, and the meat provided by hunting offsets some of the costs incurred on shells, decoys, maintenance of the decoy pond and other expenses.

Rick draws a distinction between Snow Goose meat, which has a finer texture and, if anything, a less 'wild', more domesticated flavour, and Canada flesh, which is more stringy and gamey. However, the latter makes good jerky, which he shares with friends as a snack while waiting in the shooting pit. Rick feels positive about eating goose, because it is organic and there is a natural wholesome relationship between the birds he shoots himself and eats, unlike those who buy it pre-prepared from a supermarket.

Rick exercises strict morals in the sphere of hunting. The challenge is to get the birds to fly into his pool. If they are able to sneak in without him noticing then he does not shoot them. The essence of the sport is in luring them to descend and hitting them as they come down. Rick would not shoot into a large group of geese because the intention is to make a clean kill, bringing down a bird in one go, nor does he allow other people to shoot into flocks.[22]

The hunting of geese is continent-wide in North America. It is at once sporting recreation, harvest of wild food and spiritual exercise. No one has expressed this relationship between hunter and wildfowl, and the

The Snow Goose can now be found in flocks numbering hundreds of thousands and is a great success story of North American conservation.

Surrounded by his decoy Snow Geese, many of which are home-made, Nebraskan wildfowler Rick Halcott demonstrates the subtle arts of goose calling.

underlying connections to place that are created by these glorious migrant birds, better than Aldo Leopold. In his classic *A Sand County Almanac*, he wrote:

> By this international commerce of geese, the waste corn of Illinois is carried through the clouds of the Arctic tundras, there to combine with the waste sunlight of a nightless June to grow goslings for all the lands in between. And in this annual barter of food for light, and winter warmth for summer solitude, the whole continent receives as net profit a wild poem dropped from the murky skies upon the muds of March.[23]

DOMESTICATED DUCKS

At a very early stage, people learned that they did not have to resort to the silky skills of the hunter if the birds were unable to fly. Ducks may have been tamed more than 3,500 years ago and probably first in China. A separate domestication subsequently occurred in Europe, but involved the same wild bird, the hugely plastic Mallard. Under our carefully selecting hands, this duck has morphed into hugely diverse breeds. The British-bred Khaki Campbell, for instance, can produce 363 of its large chalky eggs in a year, while the Rouen duck, developed in France, can acquire body mass like few others. Some of them are 4.5–5.6 kg (10–12 lb), more than three times the weight of their largest wild counterparts. A third famous breed is the all-white Pekin duck of Chinese

origin that dates to the Ming Dynasty (AD 1364–1644). It is familiar to anyone dining in an authentic Chinese restaurant, where it invariably hangs on display, a compact 'four-limbed' fowl with distinctive honey-coloured skin.

The other key domesticated species is the Muscovy Duck. After the turkey, it is pre-Columbian America's second great avian gift to humanity (see page 41). The wild bird has a wide Central and South American distribution, but is often shy because of hunting pressure. It was probably first tamed in pre-Incan Peru, where one of the core benefits was its partly insectivorous diet and, thus, its pest-disposal services around the house. Today it is less valued as a source of meat and eggs, but it has been transported right across the planet. In the West it sometimes serves merely as a farmyard mascot or as a curious adornment on the park lake, where people may see the birds daily without ever reflecting on the species' origins or the misleading implications of the name.

The classic assumption is that 'Muscovy' is a corruption of 'musk duck', on account of the bird's strong odour.[24] The presence of any smell is keenly disputed, with several authorities arguing that the bird has 'no musk aroma whatsoever', while others suggest that only old birds have any taint.[25] The other more likely explanation is that 'Muscovy' derives from the Russian capital, Moscow. When the first examples of the species arrived in Europe, they were assumed to have originated in Russia or to have been brought by Russian-owned ships. A range of other early names equally misconstrued the bird's true origins but they share an identical form of name construction: 'Indian duck', 'Turkish duck' and 'Guinea duck'.[26] The scientific name enshrines the same historic error: *cairina* means 'from Cairo'.[27]

Today Muscovy Ducks are routinely hybridised with Pekin ducks and other Mallard-derived races. These sterile cross-bred birds, often known as 'Mules' or 'Moulards', are a hugely important commercial strain, especially in Asia where China is the main duck-breeding nation. In 2004 an estimated 1.7 billion birds, many reared in intensive conditions, were produced in the country. It represents about three-quarters of the world total, with the other 'major' duck-keeping nations, Vietnam and France, contributing just 3.3 per cent and 3.6 per cent respectively. Nevertheless, each of these last countries rears more than twice the entire domestic duck stock of North America.[28]

WILDFOWL IN THE BEDROOM

I woke one day to hear a scratching noise from within the wardrobe in my bedroom at Baringo. Thinking it was a rat, I very quietly got up and stalked to the cupboard, sweeping brush in hand. I then flung open the door and was amazed to see my cat (a large male tabby called Isaac) sitting perfectly calm and friendly with an Egyptian Goose. I picked up the goose and took it outside – where it flew off without any problem. I've always wondered, however, just how did that goose (and cat) come through my bedroom, get inside that wardrobe, and close the door, without waking me?[29]

Unlike Terry Stevenson in Kenya, most people only encounter wildfowl in their sleeping quarters in a metaphoric sense. For domesticated ducks and geese have supplied the luxurious sense of warmth of a cosy bed for millennia. Yet one other key source of down for bedding and pillows has been a wild bird. The hugely handsome **Common Eider** *Somateria*

mollissima (along with the **King Eider** *Somateria spectabilis*, **Spectacled Eider** *Somateria fischeri* and **Steller's Eider** *Polysticta stelleri*) has a distribution that entirely circles the Arctic region. The bird's body feathers have no equal in terms of their insulatory properties (an eider-down sleeping bag provides warmth at –35 °C: –31 °F or even lower, while synthetic fill is adequate only to –7 °C: 19.5 °F).[30]

The species has given us not only many of our warmest night-time comforts, but also some of the very vocabulary for the bedroom. An 'eiderdown', meaning one of those old satin feather-filled quilts that our grandmothers used to own, is the best-known example. It may now be a thing of the past but even its modern replacement, the duvet, has wildfowl associations. Despite the fact that the product is usually made of synthetic materials, *duvet* means 'down' in French: the name for the Common Eider in France is *Eider à duvet*, the 'eider with down'.

The Inuit almost certainly used eiders for insulation before Christ was born, lining dog- or sealskin parkas with as many as 22 birds, especially in garments for women and children.[31] Today, however, one of the main countries producing commercial eider down is Iceland, with smaller cottage industries in Norway, Greenland and Russia. Icelandic eiders were theoretically protected by law from the tenth century AD, but in the nineteenth century there were strict penalties for killing eiders, while protection of breeding colonies at coastal farms led to a large increase in the harvest of the female ducks' down.

The birds can be encouraged to nest by the exclusion of ground predators but also by the presence of numerous flapping white flags (they are thought to mimic the appearance of gull's wings, among colonies of which eiders often choose to nest for the protection it provides). One modern strategy for keeping foxes at bay is to play loud music dawn until dusk, which the sitting birds seem not to mind.[32] The down is taken twice a season and other insulating materials such as straw are substituted by farmers.

The tiny feathers in this duck's nest have probably given us more cosy nights than any other bird product: they are the breast down of a Common Eider.

The industry's heyday was in the early twentieth century, with a maximum yield of 4.29 tonnes of feathers in 1915, representing the fluff plucked from 282,000 individual eider breasts.[33] The export total has steadily decreased, partly because of social changes in Iceland, but also because of the high cost of the raw product. Today the total Icelandic output of eider down, much of which goes to Japan, would probably fit on a single truck (c.2.5 tonnes in the twenty-first century) with a retail value of £26.7 million ($43 million).[34] Once converted to the retail product, a single king-size duvet can sell for an eye-watering £3,593 ($5,783).[35]

DOMESTICATED GEESE

There are relief carvings from the Old Kingdom of ancient Egypt (c.2649–2150 BC) that are assumed to depict domesticated Greylag or Egyptian Geese being fed and reared on grain.[36] However, discussion of this latter species calls into question the whole nature of what is a 'goose'. Theoretically there are 27 species worldwide that bear this name, but not all are really geese. The so-called **African Pygmy Goose** *Nettapus auritus* is actually a duck that can be as small as 27 cm (10.5 in). Technically the Egyptian Goose is part of a wildfowl group called the Tadornini, which includes six species that are all known as shelducks. Like the Egyptian Goose itself, the Tadornini are intermediate between our conventional images of goose and duck.

While it is likely that Egyptian Geese were one of the first wildfowl to be artificially reared, they lost ground even among the Egyptians to the Greylag Goose. (The six other members in its genus *Anser*, together with five species of *Branta* and three in the genus *Chen*, are predominantly inhabitants of northern boreal latitudes. These 15 birds are the ones many people think of when the word 'goose' is invoked.) Thanks to the pioneering efforts of ancient Egyptians the greylag became *the* goose, from which modern agriculture derives almost all the domesticated stock.

The bird eventually crossed the Mediterranean and Homer, in *The Odyssey*, is among the first to mention geese being reared in Europe. He refers to a tame flock on Ithaca being tended by Penelope as she awaits the return of her wandering husband, Ulysses. It is likely that geese had symbolic functions for the Greeks as well as gracing the dining table, because the birds were sacred to the Hellenic deity Aphrodite. The linkage touches upon the recurrent connection between wildfowl and human sexuality, Aphrodite being the goddess of fertility and love.

The Romans later transferred the associations to another divine female, Juno, who was the patron goddess of marriage. It was geese sacred to Juno, kept in her temple on the Capitoline Hill that ultimately spared Rome from defeat in 390 BC, during a devastating attack by the Gauls. Greylag Geese produce a vile honking note that has lost none of its powers of irritation during millennia of captivity. However, the racket has one undisputed merit. Few unwanted visitors or, indeed, honoured guests, can approach a goose-occupied farmstead without being loudly serenaded and even physically threatened. (Their insatiable aggression was exploited in Russia, where there was a tradition of the birds fighting in special goosepits.)[37] In Rome the birds' ear-splitting alarms alerted the soldiers to the Gauls' surprise attack and so saved the city for future greatness.[38]

In more peaceful times, the Gauls and other tribes from what are now modern France and Germany acquired their own goose traditions. Pliny the Elder records one of the most remarkable commercial odysseys of classical times, when he wrote of the Morini people from Belgica (today French Normandy and west Belgium) driving their herds of geese to market in Rome. It was a journey of at least 1,660 km (1,031 miles) and involved walking the birds right across the Alps. Who knows how long it took, but in nineteenth-century Britain geese were walked to the London markets at an average speed of just 13 km (8 miles) a day.[39]

Some of the most important and enduring strains of domestic goose originated in central Europe. Breeds such as the Toulouse (France) and Embden (Germany) can acquire extraordinary bulk as well as weird ship-like profiles, with some reaching as much as 18 kg (40 lb). Roasted goose, basted in its own luxurious fat, was the traditional dish of European high days and holidays, and especially at Christmas (see also Turkey Traditions in Europe, page 42). However, its most famous – or perhaps, infamous – product is derived from just one part of the bird.

PÂTÉ DE FOIE GRAS

Pliny was among the first historians to describe the delicacy. 'Our countrymen . . . know the goose by the excellence of its liver,' he wrote. 'Stuffing the bird with food makes the liver grow to a great size, and also when it has been removed it is made larger by soaking in milk sweetened with honey.'[40] It is among the first descriptions of a food that some celebrate and others curse as pâté de foie gras. Yet much of its real history began in seventeenth-century France, where the name was first coined. *Foie gras* means 'fat liver' and refers to the soft, pale, smooth, creamy texture of its enlarged organ.

The method by which it is forced to swell is called gavage (from the verb *gaver*, 'to cram'), a technique that was developed in the Franco-German border region of Alsace, although some aspects of it may have been used in ancient Egypt. There are relief images that depict bird keepers feeding cranes by hand with their beaks forcibly held open.[41] (Even more remarkable is the image of a Striped Hyena being force fed with goose flesh to fatten it for sacrifice in a way that anticipates gavage.)[42] In France it became the duty of the farm wife to insert a feeding pipe into the goose's opened beak and pour corn mush or other liver-fattening foods – a speciality of ancient Rome was mashed figs – straight down the bird's oesophagus. In the process the liver swells up to many times its natural size; as much as 1.14 kg (2.5 lb) in a 6.5 kg (14.5 lb) goose. It is this very technique that lies at the heart of the impassioned moral debate surrounding pâté de foie gras.

To its detractors gavage is a form of torture that leads to breathlessness and overheating, as well as causing disease to the inner organs, so that the overstuffed bird can hardly walk without pain. To those who cherish foie gras and support its production methods, gavage is no more than tube feeding, to which the birds show no serious aversion.[43]

There is apparently very little evidence that the goose does suffer particularly in the final weeks of rearing, when the procedure is repeated two or three times a day. However, that lack of data does not reflect an absence of stress, rather the absence of adequate research into how stress might be properly measured in the goose's neurological system. When investigated by a team of specialists established by the European Union, their report found little scientific proof of suffering, but it concluded overall that 'force feeding, as currently practised, is detrimental to the welfare of the birds'. More specifically it recommended a ban on the cages in which the individual birds were held while subjected to gavage.[44]

Opposition to foie gras has a long pedigree. Roman poets such as Horace viewed the eating of goose liver as morally questionable, on the grounds that it was a food exclusively for the super-rich. Little has changed. Today a tin of 40 g (1.4 oz) of best Strasbourg-goose pâté can cost £7.30 ($11) in the UK. Public disapproval of luxury easily blends, in the case of foie gras, into class-based social politics, but it also merges with long-established questions over animal welfare. The Victorian chef Mrs Beeton complained in the 1860s about geese and ducks having their feet nailed to the ground and 'in that position plentifully supplied with food and water. In a few days, the carcase is reduced to a mere shadow, while the liver has grown monstrously. We would rather abstain', she added, 'from the acquaintance of a man who ate *pâté de foie gras*.'[45] Pope Benedict XVI has more recently condemned the product as 'degrading of living creatures'.[46]

The fact remains, however, that goose-liver pâté is a much-loved foodstuff and a cherished aspect of European culture, particularly in France, the country that accounts for 80 per cent of the world's output and where it was declared a 'protected national product' in 2005. Perhaps the real moral questions entailed in this singular food are the same as those in all intensive poultry farming; while some may have an image of pâté de foie gras as the fruits of a cottage industry presided over by the motherly farm wives of France hand-feeding 'their' birds, in truth, most production is done on an industrial scale.

In the 1960s the French switched from goose- to duck-liver foie gras and now have a Moulard duck population of 35 million birds (compared with 800,000 geese). The Chinese, the largest of all poultry producers, have also focused on foie gras' economic potential, and plan to increase output to 1,000 tonnes annually.[47] Who knows what standards of welfare are deemed acceptable in China's industrial duck-rearing units, but it is highly unlikely that international scrutiny will be a high priority.

While this ultimate cuisine looks set to enjoy a long future, an increasing number of countries have banned force-feeding methods in animal husbandry, including Austria, Croatia, Denmark, Germany, Italy, Norway, Poland and Israel, the latter country despite once being a major producer of foie gras. There is, moreover, a vociferous international opposition lobby, drawing on the likes of Paul McCartney and Kim Basinger for celebrity support, and restaurants in many countries are often nervous of featuring this delicious fatty food on their menus, for fear of adverse publicity.[48]

SWANS

There are seven species worldwide and some might be surprised to learn that two swans are found only in South America: (the rather goose-like **Coscoroba Swan** *Coscoroba coscoroba* and the **Black-necked Swan** *Cygnus melanocoryphus*). The more famous **Black Swan** *Cygnus atratus* is also a bird of the southern hemisphere and was originally confined to Australia (it is now routinely kept

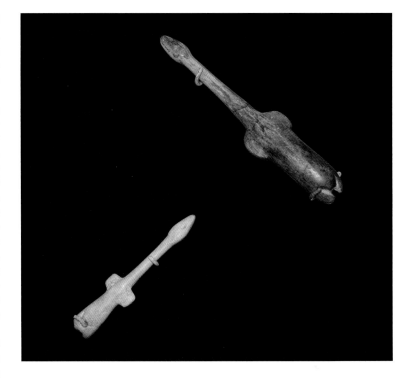

worldwide in ornamental collections, and introductions in New Zealand have led to a substantial feral population in that country). Yet it is perhaps a trio of swans dwelling at the fringes of the northern hemisphere that have appealed most to our imaginations.

The **Trumpeter Swan** *Cygnus buccinator*, **Tundra Swan** *Cygnus columbianus* (known as Bewick's Swan in Britain) and **Whooper Swan** *Cygnus cygnus* breed in Arctic or boreal regions among some of the wildest and least-populated places on Earth. After they nest, however, the birds move south to spend their winters at temperate wetlands from California to China, and from Japan to Ireland. Flying in family parties aligned in V formation, pure white in colour and some of the largest birds ever to take to the air, migrant swans suddenly appear above us in the winter skies. As if their visual impact were not enough, the birds possess elongated tracheae that wind round their breast cavities to give them great horn-like organs of sound. Accompanying their heraldic passage is a grandiose swan music, often delivered in chorus, that is full of a sense of boreal wilderness.

Some of the oldest bird artefacts ever found on Earth are carved images of these northern species. They are as much as 15,000 years old and are made from mammoth ivory. Found at a site called Mal'ta (near Irkutsk) in eastern Siberia, they now reside in the Hermitage Museum in St Petersburg, Russia (facsimiles of some can be seen at the American Museum of Natural History in New York). The figures' enormously long necks and the rotund body of one of the standing birds have identified them as images of swans.[49] One of the carvings, depicting a flying bird, was retrieved from a child's burial site.

It seems deeply moving that more than 10,000 years later, in *c*.4330 BC at a place called Vedbaek in Denmark, a Mesolithic community interred the bodies of a teenage mother with her tiny infant. The grieving community had laid the huge white wing of a swan on the ground beneath

These are facsimiles of what are thought to be flying swans. The originals were found in Siberia and are c.15,000 years old.

The triumphant bugling calls of Whooper Swans create one of the great songs of the Eurasian winter.

the child, a cradle perhaps for his delicate head and body.[50] No matter how faintly the light comes to us over so many intervening millennia, and no matter how ambiguously we might now receive their messages, these various artefacts illuminate the enduring psychological impact of swans.

These wonderful birds are entwined with the entire history of ideas and are as meaningful in the age of cyberspace as they were at a time of woolly mammoths. Fused with our vision of them are notions of death and transcendence. In fact a huge stately white bird seems almost purpose-made to act as a symbol for the human soul. In Japan the Whooper Swan is known as 'the angel of the winter'. One cannot avoid the assumption that at sites such as Mal'ta and Vedbaek, these ideas had already begun to take shape. Yet, as we shall see, swans have also been central emblems in music and, indeed, all artistic endeavour.

None of the exalted associations, however, excluded the possibility of swans as meat. Each individual bird, especially Whooper, Trumpeter and **Mute Swan** *Cygnus olor*, represents a massive protein bonus, albeit of almost black, rather unyielding flesh. One particularly obese Mute Swan, twice its species' usual weight, was said to have been 23 kg (50.7 lb), which would make it one of the heaviest flighted birds ever recorded.[51]

For 1,000 years all of the Mute Swans in the UK were prized as food and subjected to a complex system of management that placed the entire population at the disposal of the British diet (for an account of swan husbandry, see *Birds Britannica*, pages 61–4). With their wings clipped, Mute Swans were regularly captured and marked, and eventually acquired the semi-domesticated personality that we associate with the birds today. This has made them the swan export of choice and led to introductions in Africa, North America (where they are widespread), Australia, New Zealand and Japan.[52] The Mute Swan is so docile a species that until the nineteenth century it was even called the 'Tame Swan' in Britain, to differentiate it from its migrant counterparts in the Old World, the Tundra and Whooper Swans. Yet even these wilder, unapproachable birds were hunted, their bones being routinely found in Stone Age middens. In modern times the Trumpeter Swans of North America were hounded almost to extinction, although the harvest was as much for their valuable skins as for their flesh.

SWANS IN ART AND MUSIC

One compelling story that has never lost its magical appeal for us, and remains proverbial in many languages as a means to describe a person's last great defining achievement, is connected to the hunted swan. The bird transfixed by arrow or bullet and at the point of death, was said to sing as it expired. This sublime notion of the 'swansong' was widely believed in the ancient world and claimed Aristotle and Plato among its supporters, who envisioned it as a music of triumph and celebration, rather than the bird's tragic lament for life's passing.[53] The idea was to some extent enshrined in Greek mythology because swans were considered sacred to Apollo. He was the god of light, but he was also god of music, and in winter Apollo was said to retire to the mythic region of the Hyperborei, a people who dwelt beyond the north wind. Apollo was sometimes depicted with his famous sun chariot drawn by great white birds.

Yet the myth of the swansong had its doubters even in classical times. Pliny the Elder was sceptical on the matter, although in the same passage that he dismissed the belief, he also condemned swans for their cannibalism.[54] In truth, he may have been as wrong about swans eating each other as he was about swans *not* singing at their deaths. Genuine experiences described by a number of modern naturalists, such as the nineteenth-century American Daniel Giraud Elliot, are cited now as a means to explain the origins of this fable. After shooting a Tundra Swan in North Carolina, he wrote:

> On receiving his wound the wings became fixed and he commenced at once his song, which was continued until the water was reached, nearly half a mile away . . . never before nor since have I heard any [notes] like those sung by this stricken bird. Most plaintive in character and musical in tone, it sounded at times like the soft running of the notes in an octave, and as the sound was borne to us, mellowed by the distance, we stood astonished and could only exclaim, 'We have heard the song of the dying swan'.[55]

The last expiring and uncontrolled passage of air through that French-horn-like trachea, which gives swans their clamorous voices in life, is now considered a key to understanding the ancient Greek legend of a swan music performed in death.

The classical world also issued us with one of the most challenging of ideas, not only in association with swans, but in our relations to all birds – that of sexual congress. In his convoluted amorous career, the god Zeus adopted various animal guises to seduce his paramours, including that of a cuckoo and an eagle. None of his conquests, however, has exercised the same fascination as his lovemaking to Leda of Aetolia while disguised as a swan. From the liaison between this divine bird and his beautiful queen there hatched a figure at the heart of Greek thought and indeed of all Western culture, Helen of Troy; she who inspired both the Trojan War and Homer's great poetic works *The Iliad* and *The Odyssey*.[56]

For some largely inexplicable reason, this affair between the swan god and Leda seems to have haunted Western artists (largely male artists, it must be said) like few other divine one-night-stands. For almost three millennia it has been endlessly portrayed and referenced by sculptors, painters, poets and photographers. Leonardo da Vinci, Michelangelo, Titian, Raphael, Cézanne and Dalí are among the illustrious names who have tackled the theme. Mingled with our fascination is surely the possibility – both repugnant and compelling – of their interspecific coupling. Swans are such large birds that they can seem at times to be of human scale. Some sculptures from the classical period (this powerful relief carving is in the British Museum in London) envisioned not some consensual union between an airy winged creature and human lover; rather, they are images of urgent physicality, as if the rape of a woman was within the physical bounds of so powerful a bird.

Most famous of all perhaps is the work of Leonardo da Vinci usually known simply as *Leda and the Swan*. In truth it is one of the 'lost' Leonardos: we have several surviving preparatory cartoons and then a finished painting, now in the Uffizi in Florence, that was possibly completed by a student of da Vinci's, Cesare da Sesto.[57] It is nevertheless a compelling image, but less for any eroticism than for its gentle, sensuous evocation of the motherhood endowed upon a fecund and beautiful Leda by her divine liaison. At the other end of the spectrum is the French artist François Boucher (*c*.1740), whose image of this same bird–woman congress manages to convert both the swan god himself, and all who subsequently view Boucher's painting, into lecherous voyeurs.

All these heterogeneous strands of swan lore seem now almost a wider cultural preparation for the greatest of all swan-inspired artworks, *Swan Lake* by Tchaikovsky (1876). It is, in addition, among the best known, best loved of all ballets. To shape the story the composer drew on an additional and vibrant part of the cultural swan – present in his native Russia as well as Celtic, Siberian and even Chinese folk traditions – the idea of the swan maiden. In *Swan Lake* she is manifest as Odette, who is both a beautiful young woman and also the swan queen. Her dual form is the result of a spell cast on her by an evil sorcerer, Von Rothbart. (It is worth pausing to note, in relation to another much-mythologised bird, that Von Rothbart has a capacity to mutate into an owl; see also page 276.)

The themes of duality, transformation and of the possibility of love that can transcend difference, even the differences between separate species, are at the heart of *Swan Lake*. A further pattern of duality is at work because Odette, as well as being binary in nature – maiden and swan – has her evil counterpart in Von Rothbart's daughter, Odile. The latter is Odette's rival for the heart of Tchaikovsky's leading man, Prince Siegfried, and the glorious symmetry of the ballet is completed by Odile's own representation as a swan, but a black swan.

Swan Lake tells the story of how Siegfried encounters and falls in love with Odette while out hunting by the lake. The two central figures then swirl and entwine to one of Tchaikovsky's most bewitching melodies, a moment in which both music and choreography mimic the sinuous curves and the serene motions of swans on water. Yet they also manage to express, amid all this exalted snow-white grace, a darker brooding undertow of melancholy. While the dance-framed love affair is cemented, Odette tells Siegfried that only his avowal of enduring devotion can break the curse inflicted upon her by Von Rothbart.

Before he can publicly declare his love for his swan maiden, however, Siegfried must submit to a ball in his honour, at which he must dance with six potential brides. During these revels, Siegfried is tricked by Von Rothbart, when Odile comes to dance with the prince disguised as Odette. Siegfried falls for the subterfuge of father and daughter and the seductive charms of a black swan bring the story to its tragic climax. For Odette and Siegfried, tortured

The classical myth of Leda and the swan, in which Zeus in bird form mated with a Spartan queen, has compelled the Western imagination for millennia. This Roman relief carving dates to the third century AD.

by a realisation of this deception and the prince's momentary faithlessness, vow suicide to finally break the sinister magic. At the close of the ballet, the two lovers perform the final *pas de deux* that is at once an acceptance of their tragic fate, but also an avowal of their love.

In many ways *Swan Lake* draws together and brings to their apotheosis all the ideas contained within the swansong, as well as the more difficult, erotically charged notions of love between man and swan. Its composer and its unknown librettist (probably the director of Moscow's Imperial Bolshoi Theatre, Vladimir Begichev) embedded in the ballet some of our most ancient responses to these magical creatures, and managed somehow to take us right back even to that Mesolithic graveside in Denmark. For at the end of *Swan Lake* we are like those mourning that child at Vedbaek, confronted by the tragedy of death yet somehow consoled, with our hopes resting like an infant's head on a wing of pure-white feathers.

Penguin family *Spheniscidae*

Instantly recognisable and immensely popular, the penguins are without dispute one of the most familiar of all bird families. Yet sitting in downtown Paris or New York, we should not assume that awareness of penguins is universal:

> To go to an average person in downtown Hargeisa [in Somalia] and ask: *Adeer, ma taqaan shimbirta la yidhaa [Af Ingriiska]* 'penguin' ('Please sir, would you know about a bird with the [English] name of "penguin"?') the answer would invariably be 'No'. Remember there is no Somali word for nearly 98 per cent of the birdlife in our midst here, let alone a penguin![1]

Yet it is remarkable how the penguin's perky image has penetrated the most closed societies. 'In Iranian supermarkets there is a brand of plastic bags called "penguins" and it has a picture of one on the cover.'[2]

There is an intriguing gulf between public recognition of them as subjects for cinema and television, as images on billboards or product brands, in zoos or theme parks, newspaper cartoons or (the fluff-filled versions of) children's playrooms, and our highly limited experience of wild penguins. In truth they are among the least accessible of all birds. Encounters with them in their genuine habitat – usually a mixture of sea, windswept rock and ice – are reserved for the (often privileged) few.

Three penguins live exclusively on or around Antarctica itself – the **Emperor Penguin** *Aptenodytes forsteri*, **Chinstrap Penguin** *Pygoscelis antarcticus* and **Adelie Penguin** *Pygoscelis adeliae* – but nine others occupy a largely uninhabited scatter of islands far-flung across the Southern Ocean and beyond the 45th parallel south. Just four are predominantly birds of continental distribution: the **Fairy Penguin** *Eudyptula minor* in Australia; the **Jackass Penguin** *Spheniscus demersus* of African coasts; and the **Magellanic Penguin** *Spheniscus magellanicus* and **Humboldt Penguin** *Spheniscus humboldti* of South America. One anomalous family member is the **Galapagos Penguin** *Spheniscus mendiculus*, found exclusively on that single equatorial archipelago. Of the world's 17 species, only the Fairy Penguin could be said to have a mass audience as a wild bird. Some breeding sites, such as Phillip Island south of the Australian city of Melbourne, attract half a million visitors annually.[3]

The fact that even this locality is run as a theme park that blends 'real' nature with contrived entertainment is indicative of our underlying attitudes towards the family. The returning parent Fairy Penguins emerge from the surf and pass a nightly gauntlet of ticket-buying spectators arranged in raked seating and illuminated by floodlight. In microcosm the place reflects how penguins have been incorporated into modern human experience, and how we have come to think of the birds as entertainers and smaller, invariably comedic versions of ourselves.

Yet this anthropomorphism is not just easy to understand, it seems unavoidable. Like ourselves penguins are flightless and bipedal. The wings are reduced to featherless flippers of a length proportionate to human arms. Their upright gait more closely resembles our own than that even of chimps and gorillas. The biggest species have both a size and weight comparable with small children. The penguin's waddle invites almost irresistible comparison with one of the Western archetypes of comedy, Charlie Chaplin and his flat-footed stroll. Their plumages, a mixture of dark black or blue above, white below, often with colour detail that evokes a sash, headdress or bow tie, famously suggested to the Antarctic explorer Edward Wilson the 'dress tail coat and white waistcoat' of formal costume. The idea of penguins as birds in smart evening wear is now the stuff of cliché.[4]

They are among the very few bird families to inspire the following kinds of statement: 'Penguins are habit forming and I am an addict'; or, equally noteworthy, 'I have *met* most of the world's . . . penguins [my italics].'[5] In the context of advertising, their popularity creates its own self-reinforcing syndrome. Companies love to use penguins in logos or commercials because the birds are so cherished. We then fall in love with them all over because they appear so funny. The products sold with penguin assistance are legion, from a global brand of paperback (ten books were launched in 1935 at sixpence each, including Ernest Hemingway's *A Farewell to Arms* and Agatha Christie's debut novel, *The Mysterious Affair at Styles*), to a type of chocolate biscuit in Britain, air-conditioning equipment in Australia and a kind of beer in Brazil 'with its logo two King Penguins and called "Antarctica".'[6]

> Before the 1940s 'Antarctica' was called *Pinguim* ('Penguin'). There is also a nationally famous pub in Ribeirão Preto (a city in São Paulo state) that is called *Pinguim*. The link between beer and penguins is almost natural, because the Brazilian people like to drink their beer very cold.[7]

Penguin images are frequently used to stress low temperatures. Ice cream or frozen desserts are perennial favourites. Quite what link these flightless birds might have with either commercial aviation or the Arabian Desert is more difficult to fathom, but nevertheless an Emperor

Penguin appeared in an Emirates Airline advertisement in *The Times*, 6 October 2009. A further bizarre anomaly is the use of penguins to conjure Arctic associations. There are even boats called 'Arctic Penguins'. Ultimately one senses that advertising agencies, regardless of how tenuous or inaccurate the link, will choose penguin images to sell their clients' product simply because we bear an imperishable fondness for their seeming 'humanity'.

The same underlying anthropomorphism is strongly at work in our modern preoccupation with one penguin species. The breeding cycle of the Emperor Penguin is one of those marvels of adaptation that strains the human imagination. To coincide the chick's development with the spring abundance of krill and squid, the parents begin their incubation of a single egg in the depths of the Antarctic winter. They select areas of sea ice free from the risk of thaw (which might break up and float away) and have to reach these breeding 'rookeries' by walking sometimes up to 150 km (90 miles). (In 1957 Emperor Penguin tracks were found 400 km: 250 miles from the nearest sea.)[8] Once laid, the egg is transferred from the female's feet to the prospective father, who then incubates it through two months of midwinter darkness and cossets the emerging chick until his partner's return. During his vigil the male emperor can withstand winds of over 160 kph (100 mph) and temperatures of –60 °C (–76 °F). Throughout the whole breeding cycle he may not feed for 120 days and in the process loses at least 40 per cent of his body weight (from 38 kg: 83.5 lb to 23 kg: 50.5 lb).[9]

Equally wonderful, if less well known, is the emperor's ability to dive to sea depths greater than 450 m (1,476 ft), more than the height of the Empire State Building including its topmost 60 m (197 ft) pinnacle. On a single breath the bird can remain submerged for 18 minutes.[10] Regardless of repetition in print or visual media, these details have yet to achieve the anonymity of cliché. Their capacity to astonish us is matched by few other sets of data, such as the dimensions of a Blue Whale (a male's penis weighs 1 tonne) or the temperatures at the core of the sun (15 million °C: 27 million °F). Emperor Penguins carry the range of warm-blooded vertebrate experience to one of its outermost limits on Earth. In a curious way, it is our endless identification with penguins as avian versions of ourselves that makes the bird's lifestyle so fundamentally compelling. We are driven to imagine their world as an extension of our own; all the while we are assailed by the bottomless terror of their everyday routine.

If so sublime a theme could be said to have yielded a human product of commensurate depth and richness, then it is probably the book by Apsley Cherry-Garrard entitled *The Worst Journey in the World* (1922). It is widely acknowledged as one of the great works of travel writing and among the finest ever on polar exploration. Cherry-Garrard ('Cherry' to his friends) was a member of the British Terra Nova expedition led by Captain Scott; a venture which saw Scott reach the South Pole with four colleagues, only to find that a party under Roald Amundsen had planted the Norwegian flag days earlier. All five Britons died on the return leg in 1912.

Penguins were a recurrent motif of the whole expedition. Serving almost as a surreal collage of human experience in

The breeding cycle of the Emperor Penguin, which begins in the depths of the Antarctic winter, forms one of the most remarkable stories in the world of birds.

Penguins seem almost purpose-made for comedy, as in this image by Herbert Ponting.

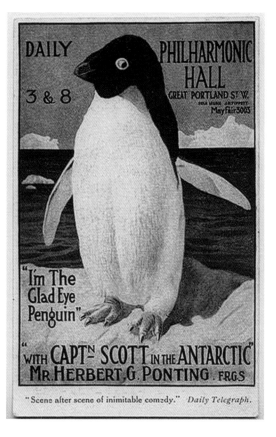

Antarctica were the open copies of *Illustrated London News* and the half-stuffed Emperor Penguin on Scott's desk at base camp exactly as he left them when he set off for the pole. They are still there today, but are probably part of a reconstruction.[11] When the expedition's photographer, Herbert Ponting, later toured with an exhibition of his work he used a funny image of an Adelie Penguin (the photo was known as 'The Glad Eye' and became a popular postcard) to sell his slideshows. It also appears on the dust jacket of his own book, *The Great White South* (1921). One wonders, incidentally, if Ponting chose this light-hearted picture to avoid the bass note of sadness which otherwise entombed the whole Scott adventure.[12]

However, the most important penguins were the birds which Cherry went to find in 1911 with Henry 'Birdie' Bowers and Edward Wilson. It involved an extraordinary five-week trek to study the breeding behaviour of emperors. A rookery at Cape Crozier lay just 108 km (67 miles) from Scott's base camp and the intention was to walk there to study the colony and return with a series of eggs. The latter were needed to test a popular scientific theory, known as the biogenetic law, which held that sequential developments occurring inside an egg recapitulated in microcosm the entire evolutionary history of birds as a life form.

As Cherry's biographer, Sara Wheeler, has noted, since 'the Emperor Penguin was at that time thought to be the most primitive bird, the logical conclusion was that a study of its embryology would reveal the origin of birds and their relationship to other vertebrates'.[13] In fact the theory was wrong, but on 27 June 1911 it launched what Cherry called 'the weirdest bird-nesting expedition that has ever been or ever will be'.[14]

Dragging a sledge weighing 343 kg (757 lb), Bowers,

Cherry and Wilson set off for the emperor's world. In measured, balanced, classically informed prose, Cherry lovingly evokes the nightmare of their journey. If they touched metal for a fraction of a second with naked fingers they were frostbitten. The daily opening and re-threading of straps or cord ties was agony, but to handle items such as the cooker, mugs, spoons, primus or oil-can was worse. Bowers managed to keep a perfect meteorological log despite the fact, Cherry noted, that 'as you breathed near the paper it was covered with a film of ice through which the pencil would not bite.' The temperatures at their lowest dropped to –60 °C (–76 °F) but Cherry fingered the dark as the greatest villain.[15]

It took them 19 days to reach Cape Crozier, where worse was to come. After scaling down the treacherous cliffs on to sea ice to secure the precious eggs and two Emperor Penguin skins, the trio climbed back to their camp where Wilson, never one to exaggerate, suggested that their fortunes had reached bed-rock and 'things must improve'. That night they were struck by a storm. Bowers, even less given to overestimation than his colleague, logged winds of force 11. Cherry demurred: 'I think it was blowing a full hurricane.' Weighing 45 kg (100 lb), nevertheless their outer tent flew away almost 1 km (0.6 miles) and they were forced to lie in the dark, without food, for 48 hours, exposed to the full fury of a winter tempest in Antarctica. In his exquisitely precise style, Cherry weighed the odds against them:

> We had spent days in reaching this place through the darkness in cold such as had never been experienced by human beings. We had been out for four weeks under conditions in which no man had existed previously for more than a few days, if that. During this time we had seldom slept except from sheer physical exhaustion, as men sleep on the rack; and every minute of it we had been fighting for the bed-rock necessaries of bare existence, and always in the dark. We had kept ourselves going by enormous care of our feet and hands and bodies, by burning oil, and by having plenty of hot fatty food. Now we had no tent, one tin of oil out of six, and only part of our cooker. When we were lucky and not too cold we could almost wring water from our clothes, and directly we got out of our sleeping-bags we were frozen into solid sheets of armoured ice. In cold temperatures with all the advantages of a tent over our heads we were already taking more than an hour to thaw our way in. No! Without the tent we were dead men.[16]

The miracle is not just that the trio found the tent, walked back to base camp and survived, the miracle is also that, as they suffered, so too the penguins had remained calmly huddled against the hurricane, incubating eggs in a parallel world of quotidian ordinariness. Adult male emperors may repeat that same winter-long exercise at least seven times in their 20-year lives.

There are two affecting addenda to the winter trek to Cape Crozier. In 1913 Cherry called at the British Museum in London to hand over the emperor eggs, where the gift was met by an official indifference colder than the South Pole. Then 26 years after the trek, Cherry met Angela, his future wife, on a cruise to Norway. As an opening expression of his intentions he picked up a quartz pebble and handed it to her. Years later she learned that pebble-giving formed part of (Adelie) penguin courtship rituals in their Antarctic colonies.[17]

We must acknowledge that consideration of Cherry's book as an insight into a penguin's life is based on a fallacy: that we can measure another organism's experience by our own. We cannot. Yet in the hell that Cherry draws out so tenderly in *The Worst Journey* we sense a sharp, oblique ray of light cast on a bird's benighted world. A more direct attempt to explore and reveal the emperor's behaviour comes in a recent award-winning film, *The March of the Penguins* (in its original French, *La marche de l'empereur*: 'The March of the Emperor'), 2005. This documentary, shot by two French cinematographers, Laurent Chalet and Jérôme Maison, and written and directed by fellow countryman Luc Jacquet, covers the annual breeding cycle of a colony near the French research station on Antarctica.

The images are intimate, beautiful, uncompromising, astonishing. They dwell in particular on the bond of trust implicit in the relationship between emperor couples. A 'love story' is the tag frequently used to convey its central theme. The French version intensified the anthropomorphic element by overdubbing human voices on to individual birds. However, the English-language film involved only a documentary-style narration by Morgan Freeman, the Hollywood voice most associated with emotional sincerity and thematic gravitas. *The March of the Penguins* was translated into numerous other languages, screened almost worldwide, won an Oscar for the best documentary film and took the largest box-office return of any film of its kind except Michael Moore's *Fahrenheit 9/11*.

Human relations with penguins have not always been so benign. In fact our modern endearment is really the exception. Indigenous peoples living in southernmost Africa and America killed and ate the flesh or used penguin skins (some to make soft, strong baby carriers for their offspring) from Palaeolithic times.[18] The name 'penguin', in fact, comes from another forlornly persecuted, now extinct species, the Great Auk (see page 224). There was once a Penguin Island (now known as Funk Island) where the penguins of the deep south never swam, off the east coast of Canada's Newfoundland. Why this word served as a title for the extinct auk is not known, but one argument holds that it comes ultimately from *pinguis*, the Latin for 'fat'. An intermediate source word could have been the Spanish (or Portuguese) *pingüe* (meaning 'fat' or 'rich'), which Iberian mariners attached to the plump flightless auk of the north Atlantic. The name was then carried south and on encountering similar rotund black-and-white flightless seabirds, the Europeans gave it anew to these other 'penguins'.[19]

Their flightlessness and supreme approachability may cement our modern bonds with penguins, but to the early European sailors they just made the birds a convenient target. Breeding rookeries were often treated like a cost-free commissariat. Stored in casks and immersed in oil, penguin eggs could last nine months and were sometimes more popular among the crew than chicken eggs.[20] In 1520 the Portuguese chronicler for the expedition of Ferdinand Magellan mentioned that at one subantarctic island, 'full of geese and sea-wolves', they took enough of these 'geese' ('black and unable to fly') to fill five ships.[21]

In 1775, during Captain Cook's second world voyage, he wrote of his own penguin-killing and cooking operations: 'We . . . got on board a little after 12 o'Clock with a quantity of Seals and Penguins . . . I was now for the first time heartily tired of salt meat of every kind and prefer'd the Penguins, whose flesh eat nearly as well as bullocks liver, it was however fresh and that was sufficient to make it go down.'[22] One wonders whether, had Cook suffered no scarcities, his opinion would have been so favourable. Another explorer described penguin meat as a 'combination of beef, a piece of cod and a duck carcass, stewed in a blood and cod liver oil sauce'.[23]

The sporadic slaughter of penguins for onboard stores was trivial compared with later systematic operations by the animal-oil hunters of the nineteenth century. Very often penguins became a target once commercial sealing had inflicted virtual extinction on its mammalian victims. However, the highly concentrated distribution of penguins, especially when on their breeding islands, must have whetted appetites and suggested commercial possibilities long before the birds became an object of desire. One major centre for penguin oil was the Falkland Islands, where the **Gentoo Penguin** *Pygoscelis papua*, **Rockhopper Penguin** *Eudyptes chrysocome* and **Magellanic Penguin** *Spheniscus magellanicus* abounded. It followed the typical boom–bust pattern of so many maritime harvests and reached its peak in the early 1860s. Over their short 16-year span the Falkland operations probably killed well over 2 million birds. The majority was that endearing, punk-crested, endlessly entertaining creature the rockhopper, which yielded about a half-litre (1 pint) of oil a bird.[24]

Another island where industrial processing achieved notorious levels was on Macquarie, south-west of New Zealand. **King Penguin** *Aptenodytes patagonicus* had been exploited there from the early nineteenth century, but a lease was granted to a London-born New Zealand operator, Joseph Hatch, in 1891 and over a six-week season in late summer, his hired team dispatched about 150,000 penguins annually. Killing at a rough rate of four birds a minute, the men herded them into wire-netted yards, picked out the fattest chicks and clubbed them over the head to load into digesters and boil them down to oil. The final product was used initially by rope and twine manufacturers, later for soap and tanning.[25]

When he had finished off all but the last of the King Penguins – he blamed 'sealers' for their decimation – Hatch focused on the smaller **Royal Penguin** *Eudyptes schlegeli*. However, a campaign led by the Antarctic explorer Douglas Mawson signalled the end of Hatch's empire on Macquarie. One of the allegations made against his workers was that they drove the compliant penguins up a ramp and on to the lip of the digesters, where the birds pitched involuntarily straight into a vat of their own boiling oil. If this Dantesque scene was not actually true, then Macquarie was verily a penguin hell on Earth. Its human agents freely acknowledged that the four digesters processed about 3,500 Royal Penguins a day, while a further 500 birds were consigned directly to the flames to fuel the fires below.[26] By 1919, when Hatch's licence was terminated, he had probably killed several million birds. It is intriguing to find that our unavoidably anthropomorphic responses to penguins had finally come to their aid in this decision. One correspondent in a Sydney newspaper noted how in the faces of the doomed birds he could recognise 'the familiar human emotions of fear, affection, curiosity, anxiety and solicitude'.[27]

With Macquarie's closure as a killing field the writing

was on the wall for the whole era of penguin exploitation, although its final gasps included a 1940s proposal from a Romanian company to process Magellanic Penguins for wallets and shoes. As late as the 1980s a Japanese company sought a licence for Argentinian birds. The intended products included oil and meat, while the skins were to be used for top-of-the-range golf gloves.[28] If direct persecution has now receded, less obvious forms of man-made hazard may be even more threatening. One modern scholar suggested that 'their future has never looked so grim'.[29] Penguins are in the first rank of wildlife imperilled by climate change. On Campbell Island, south of New Zealand, Rockhopper Penguins have declined by 94 per cent in half a century, from 1.7 million to 105,000 in the 1990s. Warmer seas are the primary cause of the losses.[30]

The recent fortunes of Africa's Jackass Penguins in many ways exemplify the revolution in attitudes, but also the complexity of new challenges. This species was among the most severely affected by direct harvest, with 13 million eggs gathered in just one area over a 30-year period. This ceased in 1969, but the numbers have fallen from 575,000 pairs (1900), to 180,000 (1990) and now 72,000 (2008).[31] One major problem is that the human harvest of the bird's fish prey is so severe it may have shifted distribution of anchovy and sardine stocks to sea areas that lie beyond the range of feeding parents. Quite simply, the adult birds cannot reach the fish and return to the onshore colonies, so their young – and the entire species – are slowly starving to death.

A second threat is from oil tankers. One major spill in

2000 off western South Africa caused the contamination of 19,000 birds, one-fifth of the world's jackass population. Remarkably about 19,000 were taken into protective custody, cleaned and released, but a further 19,500 unoiled penguins were also gathered up from rookeries on Dassen and Robben Island (where Nelson Mandela was incarcerated for nearly two decades) and moved 800 km (500 miles) to a release site near Port Elizabeth, giving the oil time to disperse. Satellite telemetry informed the organisers of this pre-emptive mass-evacuation that the birds took 18 days to navigate back.[32] Arguably only a bird as cherished as a penguin could have commanded this level of human support.

Yet the initiative is not alone as an expression of public affection. Faced with oil spills off their own coast, the Tasmanian Conservation Trust (TCT) launched a scheme to help Fairy Penguins in 2001. The Penguins Jumper Project requested people to knit woollies to fit this sprite-sized species. The plumages of oiled birds lose their insulatory properties and the sweaters help both to prevent penguins brought into care from getting cold and from ingesting the toxic oil while preening. The TCT hoped for 100 jumpers. However, a group of women from the Church of Jesus Christ of Latter-Day Saints in Coffs Harbour, Tasmania, ran up 1,000 jumpers and, with a knitting pattern broadcast on the web, the project received in excess of 15,000 penguin-sized jerseys from all over the world. These have now been stockpiled in Oil Spill Response Kits for when the next disaster strikes the island.[33]

Loon (Diver) family *Gaviidae*

This family of five large, immensely handsome aquatic birds breeds on the lakes and coastal waters of northern latitudes, especially in Russia and Canada, but also in the USA, Scandinavian Europe, Iceland and Greenland. They are fish-eating birds with extraordinary powers of underwater propulsion. Early ornithologists noted they were occasionally caught in Scottish herring nets, while the American author Henry Thoreau wrote: 'It is said that loons have been caught in the New York lakes eighty feet beneath the surface, with hooks set for trout.'[1] In a classic piece of Thoreauvian imaginative sympathy, he added, 'How surprised must be the fishes to see this ungainly visitor from another sphere speeding his way amid their schools!'[2] In fact the birds can speed their way down to over 70 m (230 ft).[3] In Britain the five birds are actually called 'divers'.

Until the advent of modern birders (for whom the five species present an acute identification challenge, especially in non-breeding plumage) loons impinged mainly on the consciousness of those thinly dispersed communities dwelling beyond the 60th parallel. From these northern peoples have come the original words that have given us the family's singular name and, in turn, its associated confusion. 'Loon' (and, at one time 'loom' or 'lumme') is derived from the much older Norse *lóm-r* and Icelandic *lómur* names for the birds.[4] However, the meaning of these original Atlantic versions is disputed. One theory is that it meant 'lame' or 'helpless', invoking a creature that was as awkward and clumsy as loons genuinely are once they come to dry land. The birds are highly adapted to life on water and have legs set so far back on their bodies that the best they can manage on terra firma is a hobbling shuffle. In Scotland an old word for lame or crippled, referring to humans or livestock, is 'lameter'.[5]

The other suggestion is that *lóm-r* or *lómur* meant wailing or moaning, in imitation of the birds' extraordinary and atmospheric vocalisations.[6] Whichever of these explanations is correct, the name is certainly *not* associated with the words 'lunatic' or the more colloquial 'loony'. These both derive from the moon (and its Latin equivalent *luna*), and the ancient idea that our states of mind were governed by lunar cycles. There is therefore no truth in the claim that the bird gave us a name for a madman.[7] The link is simply a linguistic coincidence. However, this has not stopped people deploying the double entendre: 'Our friend is also mad about loons. Her house on Lake Michigan bears the name "The Loony Bin" together with a lovely wooden carving of a loon!'[8]

As others have also suggested, the connection is fitting even if it is technically inaccurate.[9] Graeme Gibson, Canadian author and neighbour of nesting **Great Northern Loon** *Gavia immer*, writes of their eerie and strangely beautiful voices:

Loons are indeed special, mostly I think because we hear them on their breeding lakes. We've just returned from the Atwood log house (her father built it without a chain saw) on a glacial lake in northern Québec, where great restless loon choruses abound in late summer. The only thing to compare with them is a family of howling wolves in the dark.[10]

Another Canadian ornithologist agrees: 'The voice is loud, resonant and greatly varied. It has been variously described as maniacal, blood-curdling, horrible, beautiful, and thrilling. Three basic calls are (1) a laughing tremolo, (2) a weird yodel, (3) a wolflike wail.'[11] The sound is so remarkable that it has almost inevitably found its way into the special-effects department of Hollywood. Loon recordings are widely deployed in films and dramas to create a sense of place or to suggest mystery. The reason the calls are so affecting is that they have a residual human quality, but only a human undergoing some extreme experience – agony or ecstasy. It is pure speculation but perhaps it was the power of the vocalisations to impel our attention that explains why loons were (and perhaps still are) so deeply rooted in the cultural life of many northern people. The sounds seemed so emotionally loaded that loons had to be announcing something important.

The great scholar of bird folklore Edward Armstrong located an interconnecting pattern of cultural tales from lands encircling the Earth's northern crown which portray loons as participants in creation myths or as helpers to the shamans in these animist communities. For the Ojibwa (once known as Chippewa) dwelling around Lakes Huron and Superior, the loon dived down to the bottom of the water after a great flood, bringing back mud from which dry land was first formed. The Samoyede (from the Yenisey region of north-central Siberia) have a remarkably similar myth describing how seven men in a boat were aided by a loon (presumably either a **Black-throated Loon** *Gavia arctica* or **Red-throated Loon** *Gavia stellata* since they are the two local species). When the bird retrieved mud from the depths, the humans cast it into the water and dry land appeared.[12]

However, the key role that loons have played is as helpers to the shaman. Uniting the roles of medicine man and spiritual guide for many Arctic or sub-Arctic communities, the shaman is uniquely able to travel into the spirit world, where he can affect issues of fortune and health for both the community and the individual. Typically illness is thought to have its roots in this other realm and is attributed to a person's loss of soul.

By achieving an altered state of consciousness, the shaman enters the spirit world, but he requires animal spirits to assist and, as one authority notes, the loon is specially endowed for this purpose: 'The essential uses of the zoomorphic spirits are as mounts and sentinels. Swans, geese and eagles carry the shaman up to the higher world. Loons, reindeer and bears carry him down to the lower world . . . The animals most preferred for use are those which belong to several elements and are thus most able to facilitate passage from one world to the next. Thus, the loon, the characteristic spirit of Tungus [Evenki] shamans, swims as well as it flies . . .'[13] One can appreciate not only why so adept a diving bird would be important, but also how an underwater realm could easily stand as a metaphor for the human subconscious.

In effect the loon confers on the shaman the gift of seeing beyond the material world and it is with this power of sight that the birds are often associated. The most compelling historical evidence was found at an ancient Inuit

▶ To mark the twenty-fifth anniversary of the 'Loonie', the Canadian $1 piece, the national mint issued a special Two Loons silver coin. The iconic birds were painted by First Nations artist Richard Hunt.

site called Ipiutak in northern Alaska. Human skulls were unearthed that had had ivory-and-jet eyeballs inserted into their sockets. Also among the grave goods was a loon skull treated in similar fashion. The archaeological inference is that the human skull was that of a shaman, while the bird had been included among his grave furnishings as guide for the deceased in his darkened journey through the afterlife.[14]

This quality of loons' eyes may be a further factor predisposing shamans to a relationship with this particular bird family. Shamans themselves are often noted for the penetrating nature of their gaze. The eyes of a Yakut shaman in Siberia were said to have 'a peculiar unpleasant dull glare, and . . . their persistent stare . . . excited and disturbed those upon whom he fixed it'. In their youth, those individuals destined to become shaman among the Chukchee people may be recognised first by the quality of their stare.[15] What links these common shamanic attributes to the loons themselves is the birds' extraordinarily luminous crimson eyes, whose glow is most fiery during the breeding season.

The bird with magical gifts of sight both in this world and the next appears regularly in stories of northern origin. Commonly the loon is portrayed as a bird able to restore the vision of blind human companions. The myth was widespread among the Inuit and other Native Americans and in 1949 it was given powerful expression in a cultural form that brought the story to an audience of millions. An award-winning Canadian film, *The Loon's Necklace*, retells a traditional tale of the Tsimshian people about a blind medicine man, Kelora, and his relationship with 'his father' the loon. In the film's denouement, the bird restores the man's sight by carrying him beneath the surface of a lake four times. In return Kelora thanks him with his dearest possession, a necklace of dentalium shells that catches around the loon's neck and scatters white shells across his back. The old myth depicts a fundamental transaction between human and bird: the loon grants its sacred visionary power to humankind and, in exchange, man gives to the loon the pattern of delicate white fretwork on its summer plumage.[16]

The Loon's Necklace, written by Douglas Leechman and produced and directed by Frank 'Budge' and Judith Crawley, features real people, but they and other animal characters are

depicted in authentic West Coast First Nations ceremonial masks (except the loon itself, which is represented through footage of wild birds), and it has the atmosphere and character of an animation. It lasts just ten minutes yet it had a major impact, particularly in Canada, and became a much-loved staple of school, library and community film events. More than half a century of enduring popularity has, in turn, cemented attachment to a bird already prominent and well loved across many Canadian lakes.

The species has since been chosen as Canada's national bird and the provincial bird in Ontario. In 1987 an image of the species took its place on the currency, appearing on the reverse side of a CAN $1 coin, and soon gave rise to its nickname, the 'Loonie'. In Francophone Canada it is the *huard*, the French name for the same bird. A $2 coin brought out in 1996 was quickly rebranded the 'Toonie', and in time the whole currency has taken part of its identity from the shaman's fiery-eyed avian helper. The Canadian dollar is sometimes known in financial circles as the 'Loonie', to distinguish it from the 'greenback' of its southern neighbour.

Albatross family *Diomedeidae*

Westerners are now so familiar with moving images of albatrosses gliding effortlessly through the waves as the ultimate expression of avian freedom (reinforced perhaps by Fleetwood Mac's hit instrumental track 'Albatross') that we can overlook how the bird's impact on the majority of humanity is relatively recent.

The word 'albatross' was not even recorded before 1769 and its derivation is confused and intriguing. It originated with an Iberian word *alcatraz*, which has been identified as an early name for the pelican and a reference to that bird's capacious pouch (the Spanish came from the Arabic *al-câdous* meaning 'water-carrier'; see page 142). However, the *Oxford English Dictionary* associates 'albatross' not with the pelican, but with the frigatebird. There is support for a connection with either bird. It is notable, for instance, that in modern Portuguese, *alcatraz* is still the word for frigatebird. Also, an

old alternative name for the **Wandering Albatross** *Diomedea exulans* was 'man o' war bird', which was originally an English name for the frigatebird. It reinforces the possibility that words used for that family were then applied to albatrosses.[1]

There is an interesting link between pelican and frigatebird physiology that may also inform our understanding of the name's original usage. Both birds have large expandable pouches. In the case of frigates it is a curious skin bladder on the neck that the males inflate like huge crimson balloons during sexual display. Since both pelicans and frigatebirds seemed to have a 'water-carrier' at their throats, perhaps *alcatraz* was used interchangeably for them. Certainly we know that bird names in former centuries were applied in a highly fluid way. Whichever was first, it is indubitably true that the name was later transferred

to the birds in the family *Diomedeidae*, and also that the word *alcatraz* itself morphed on the English tongue to 'alcatras', 'algatross' and eventually to 'albatross'. Its only contender as a name for the long-winged seabirds is a word of Dutch origin, 'mollymawk', (from *malle*: 'foolish', *mok*: 'gull'), an old title for a type of petrel, the Northern Fulmar. 'Mollymawk' was later employed to describe several smaller albatross species and still has some currency.

Albatrosses comprise a family of 13 species mainly inhabiting the oceans south of the Tropic of Capricorn. There are however three central Pacific species – the **Black-footed Albatross** *Phoebastria nigripes*, **Laysan Albatross** *Phoebastria immutabilis* and **Short-tailed Albatross** *Phoebastria albatrus* – that occur as far north as the Arctic Circle. Another, the **Waved Albatross** *Phoebastria irrorata*, is a near endemic to the Galápagos archipelago. The country regularly cited as the albatross capital of the world is New Zealand, although exactly how many species it holds is a moot point. The family's taxonomy – for once a subject of critical cultural importance – is a theme to which we will return later.

If ever an avian family should liberate us from our curious but ingrained sense of national ownership of birds, it is this one. Albatrosses are the ultimate nomads. Their true home is not any terra firma but the open ocean. Their flight is both supremely beautiful and endlessly fascinating. The American author Peter Matthiessen taps into something fundamental when he writes, 'One can watch albatrosses for hours, like rough surf or fire.'[2] We have long known that they have the greatest wingspan of all birds – Wandering Albatrosses

can measure 3.5 m (11.5 ft) – but at one time we routinely exaggerated, stretching it to more than 5 m (17 ft).[3]

Our understanding of their nomadic lifestyle may once have been a matter of subjective impression, but not any more. Satellite telemetry has tracked one Wandering Albatross that covered 25,000 km (15,500 miles) in about nine weeks, almost the entire Atlantic and Indian Oceans from west to east. Another in Australian waters moved 8,000 km (5,000 miles) to the south Pacific in 17 days. Recent work suggests a mean speed of 55 kph (34 mph) but for almost a tenth of their journeys they travel at over 85 kph (53 mph).[4] It is surely a recognition of the birds' extraordinary aerial feats that in golf, a hole achieved in one under par is a 'birdy', two under par is a mere 'eagle', but to sink the putt and go three under is an 'albatross'.

One of the most striking aspects of the English-speaking world's engagement with albatrosses is the absolute dominance of a single artistic representation. Indeed it is hard to think of another animal where one cultural image has so engaged and almost trapped our imaginations. Samuel Taylor Coleridge's *The Rime of the Ancient Mariner*, published in 1798, profoundly affects how the bird is perceived in popular culture but – strangely – it has also muddled our understanding of how albatrosses were viewed in the past. Even today it is a poem shrouded in confusion, perhaps partly because Coleridge steeped the bird in a powerful and highly refracted symbolism.

Essentially the work is about an old mariner who narrates the story of his voyage to the Southern Ocean. There his ship is driven by storm into a zone of terrifying

With a wingspan of 3.5 m, the Wandering Albatross is the world's longest-winged bird and one of the most wonderful of all flying creatures. Yet it can also be a formidable scavenger.

The aerial grace of
the Light-mantled
Albatross is often
considered the most
perfect in a peerless
family.

cold. Miraculously the vessel is visited by an albatross and simultaneously released by a south wind from the region's icy grip. Day after day the bird follows the northbound boat, whose crew regard the creature's presence 'As if it had been a Christian soul', and 'hailed it in God's name'. As suddenly and inexplicably as the albatross appears, the Mariner then mindlessly slaughters it with his crossbow.

Initially the crew turn on the Mariner for killing the creature 'That made the breeze to blow!' Then as the warm southern wind continues to bless the ship they change tack and, as one, declare that it was the bird that brought the fog and mist and therefore killing it was right. That pivotal moment spells catastrophe for all onboard. In verse that was once committed to memory by almost every English-speaking schoolchild, the ship becomes marooned and the crew dies. Yet before expiring they hang round the neck of the Mariner the corpse of the albatross as an irrevocable expression of his guilt. Sole survivor of his crime, the Mariner then endures a kind of hell on Earth until the poem's second key moment. Gazing out, he sees water snakes rippling across the sea surface. These conventional emblems of evil trigger a moment of epiphany and the poem's core message, the Mariner declaring:

> O happy living things! no tongue
> Their beauty might declare:
> A spring of love gushed from my heart,
> And I blessed them unaware:
> Sure my kind saint took pity on me,
> And I blessed them unaware.
>
> The self-same moment I could pray;
> And from my neck so free
> The Albatross fell off, and sank
> Like lead into the sea.

The Mariner, understanding now the blessed unity running through all living things – human, albatross and even serpent – is forgiven and returns to his homeland, there to repeat his tale of albatross killing, of guilt and of redemption to anyone who will listen.

The English playwright Alan Bennett defined a classic as a 'book everyone is assumed to have read and forgets if they have or not'.[5] The *Ancient Mariner* is an indisputable candidate for Bennett's version of the classic. Misrepresentation of the central symbol in Coleridge's poem is systemic now in Western thought. The poet almost certainly intended the bird to be seen not as a curse, but as a blessing – a benign expression of life's fundamental unity. Certainly Coleridge's modern biographer, Richard Holmes, sees in the symbolic killing of the bird 'what might be called a "green parable", the idea of man's destructive effect on the natural world, so that human moral blindness inadvertently introduces evil into the benign systems of nature'.[6] It is intriguing to find that Coleridge expressed that unity of nature by invoking both albatross and sea snake. The winged serpent, a mythic being embodying these two polar opposites of earthly life, is a recurrent motif in world mythologies (see also Trogon family, page 312).

Little of this intended symbolism concerning the bird is now manifest in popular culture. Instead the word has become proverbial for an unwanted thing or heavy burden. In modern dictionaries the second definition of

albatross is something like 'an encumbrance (in allusion to Coleridge's *The Rime of the Ancient Mariner*)'.[7] An example of similar confusion is to be found on the same page as the earlier quotation by Peter Matthiessen. The American writer notes: 'Both birds [Wandering Albatrosses], as befits those harbingers of death that plagued Coleridge's Ancient Mariner, are white as bone.'[8] Rather than the Romantic poet's intended symbol of life, the albatross has become its diametric opposite, a portent of doom.

A secondary misunderstanding relates to Coleridge's source for his representation of the albatross as a bird loaded with cultural meaning. The following is typical of numerous modern statements about the bird's historical significance: albatrosses 'figure in many marine legends (see, for example, Coleridge's *The Rime of the Ancient Mariner*)'.[9] The assumption is that Coleridge was drawing on a long tradition of mariners' superstitions and the poem was therefore a reflection of those earlier beliefs.

There is strong circumstantial evidence that Coleridge, while composing the poem, read an eyewitness account of someone killing an albatross. It was his friend and fellow Romantic poet William Wordsworth who both proposed the albatross as an element to be incorporated into the *Ancient Mariner* and who also owned a book entitled *Voyage Round the World by the Way of the Great South Sea* by Captain George Shelvocke (1726). In it is the following passage:

> Southwards of the streights of *le Mair*, nor one sea-bird, except a disconsolate black *Albitross*, who had accompanied us for several days, hovering about us as if he had lost himself, till *Hatley*, (my second Captain) observing, in one of his melancholy fits, that this bird was always hovering near us, imagin'd, from his colour, that it might be some ill omen. That which, I suppose, induced him the more to encourage his superstition, was the continued series of contrary tempestuous winds, which had oppress'd us ever since we had got into this sea. But be that as it would, he, after some fruitless attempts, at length, shot the *Albitross*, not doubting (perhaps) that we should have a fair wind after it.[10]

Did Coleridge borrow Wordsworth's copy of this text? Certainly one senses in broad outline one of the inspirations for the work, but it is explicitly *not* a statement confirming a superstition felt generically by sailors for albatrosses. It was one man's fancy. It is true that many seabirds had predictive qualities or powerful psychological associations for mariners. The fears aroused by some petrel vocalisations (see Petrel and Shearwater family, page 104), the very name applied to several storm petrels – 'Mother Carey's chickens' (see page 112) – and the widely held idea that seabirds of all kinds could be the reincarnated souls of lost sailors are typical examples. Yet there is little evidence that albatrosses were singularly important in this pattern of beliefs.

On the contrary, the historical material prior to Coleridge's poem provides abundant testimony on how albatrosses were treated like almost any wild marine animal – as an al fresco commissariat. The birds were exploited for food in the form of their eggs, young and the adults. Their webbed feet were made into tobacco pouches, while the long hollow wing bones were converted into pipe stems. Other bones were used as darning needles. The feathers were woven into rugs and feet warmers. An old name for

The Black-browed Albatross is among the many family members still considered at risk of extinction, although the population in the Falkland Islands is at last showing some signs of recovery.

Wandering Albatross, 'Cape sheep', is presumed to arise from this regard for the plumage as a type of wool.[11] There is a strong suggestion that catching albatross with a baited hook was even a kind of recreation. In later years shooting them with rifles was definitely thought of as sport.[12]

If any albatross could be said to arouse more specific superstitions it would be either of the two gloriously beautiful species **Light-mantled (Sooty) Albatross** *Phoebetria palpebrata* or the **Sooty Albatross** *Phoebetria fusca*. Their consummate flying skills are widely regarded as the most perfect in a peerless family.[13] The nineteenth-century English bird artist John Gould noted how they are 'the only species that passes directly over the ship . . . often poising itself over the masthead, as if inquisitively viewing the scene.'[14] It was perhaps the close 'inspection' of a vessel's seaworthiness performed by sooties that led some sailors to think these albatrosses embodied mariners' lost souls coming back for a final check. It was probably one of these two sooty albatrosses that Captain Shelvocke described and which later helped to give wings to Coleridge's imagination. Yet even these dark birds were not completely immersed in taboo. They were shot and eaten like others of the family.

In trying to summarise the impact of Coleridge upon attitudes towards albatrosses we should recognise that prior to his poem the birds were not the focus of intense and uniform beliefs. While the two dark species and, to some extent, the others were the object of mariners' lore, they were no more so than other seabirds. What beliefs there were dwelled in individuals. They were not general, and they coexisted with widespread and often dominant utilitarian attitudes to the birds that would allow of no strict taboo. If any single generalisation can be imposed on this highly fluid body of evidence then it is the point that Coleridge's poem, rather than drawing on old folklore, in fact gave rise to the idea that there had been ancient superstitions and that the poem was itself a reflection of those pre-existing ideas, often without anyone ever bothering to check the veracity of that assumption. One might go further. Such was the huge popularity of the verse that it subsequently gave rise to a form of taboo. A classic example is the Scottish sailors who refused to strike a light on a famous brand of matches (Swan Vestas). The stated reason for this was that the box featured an image of a swan, and that bird was said 'to symbolise the albatross in the Ancient Mariner'.[15]

There is one final link to consider between Coleridge's poetic bird and the real creature. Despite having never seen a wild albatross, Coleridge somehow divined in the bird its potential as a symbol for all nature. It is hard now to imagine a better candidate. On encountering the living birds today one is moved by the wonderful 'softness' – an almost inherently benign aura – in their facial expressions, and touched by the knowledge of their deep faithfulness towards their partners (they can remain paired for decades), so that one could almost believe that they have the higher feelings so cherished in our own species. Yet one is also in awe of their supreme adaptation to survive, alone and unaided, in an environment utterly inimical to a naked human: the open ocean. Since our world is primarily covered in salt water – there are 350 million km² (135 million miles²) of ocean compared with 148 million km² (57 million miles²) of land – these birds seem among the truest and most exalted citizens of our planet. Given these qualities, Coleridge's characterisation of a slain albatross as a symbol of human folly and unthinking abuse of nature could not have been more prescient. Today, this avian family is the most threatened bird group in the world.

In 1992 an agreed cessation was finally implemented on what had become known as the 'walls of death', a type of nylon fishing mesh, single lengths of which could stretch for 50 km (30 miles). During the 1980s in the Pacific Ocean alone, these drift nets could run cumulatively to 50,000 km (30,000 miles) each night. As well as a phenomenally valuable fish catch, particularly of tuna, the walls of death were killing millions of marine animals including large numbers of albatross. Drift nets used in the north Pacific in 1990 were estimated to kill 500,000 seabirds, of which 21,000 were albatross.[16]

Their eventual withdrawal in favour of what became known as 'dolphin friendly' methods involved fishing fleets switching to a system of 'longlines'. Paid out from trawlers for anything up to 100 km (62 miles), the longlines bear at short intervals secondary lines carrying hooks baited with fish or squid. As these hooks enter the water many seabirds, particularly petrels and albatrosses, attend the operations in hope of a free meal. Despite our common image of them as free-spirited nomads of the deep, they are also inveterate scavengers. The reason they featured so routinely in the early mariners' diet was the ease with which they could be caught with hook and line, rather like massive winged fish.

Even the Wandering Albatross will slum it among the fish guts and squabble over offal like some great ocean-going vulture. The birds were once habitual visitors to whaling stations, where they could be a serious nuisance. The whalers often used to inflate the whales with compressed air to make them float, while plugging the dead beast's blowhole with cloth to stop the air escaping. Wandering Albatross were partial to these rags, especially after they had become soaked with oil from the whale's blubber, and would sometimes pull them out and cause the whale to sink.[17]

Around modern fishing vessels the same scavenging appetite often means that albatross seize the baits and are snagged and dragged under, to be retrieved only hours later when the fishermen recover their longlines. The euphemism applied to this inadvertent death is 'by-catch'. What it means in reality is that each trawler crew, as it processes the fish, builds up an ancillary heap of drowned seabirds. For the fishermen they are nothing but an inconvenience. Each dead and worthless albatross caught on a hook means one less valuable fish for the hold. In a single fishery for bluefin tuna off the Australian continental shelf, Japanese trawlers were estimated to be losing AUS $7 million annually because of birds.[18]

The practical solution for the fisheries has been to find ways to pay out the lines without seabirds being allowed to steal the bait and affect the catch. The fairly simple measures include the release of baits (from 'setting tubes') only when they are underwater and out of harm's way, the weighting of baits so they sink quicker and present less temptation, dying baits to make them less visible, using brightly coloured streamers that scare the birds from the danger area and setting at night when most seabirds are inactive.[19] Proof of the efficacy of these mitigation measures came in a French fishery in the Indian Ocean where the by-catch was reduced by 75 per cent in one season.[20]

The problems have lain in securing agreement across multiple national fisheries, and also in the deterrent effect of assumed additional costs and labour for the fishermen. These do not take into account the general complacency of their governments, and the far bigger issue of a huge illegal fleet of unlicensed operators inaccessible to official monitoring or agreement. Together, the obstacles to albatross-friendly fishing methods have visited catastrophe on the world's population in under two decades.

The first unequivocal evidence of a crisis came in a 1991 paper by an Australian biologist, Nigel Brothers, who examined by-catch of **Shy Albatross** *Thalassarche cauta* in a Japanese fishery off Tasmania. His conclusions were stark: around 44,000 albatross were being killed annually.[21] There was hardly much comfort when this estimate was reduced to 39,000 birds. Data from many other albatross breeding grounds supported a picture of worldwide losses. Some species had declined by 90 per cent in 60 years.

It is in this context that the complex issue of albatross taxonomy assumes major cultural and political significance. Several so-called species of albatross comprise highly distinct and widely spread sub-populations. The Wandering Albatross is a class example. Five different recognised forms breed on scattered islands or archipelagos spread throughout the southern Indian, Pacific and Atlantic Oceans. One such sub-population breeds only on Amsterdam Island, a pinprick in the southern Indian Ocean, where in 2001 there were just 120 individuals and only 15 breeding pairs.[22]

The deep natal loyalty shown by sub-populations and the highly restricted gene flow between these recognised 'races' of Wandering Albatross, mean that colonies, such as that on Amsterdam Island, represent a unique form – in essence, a proto-species – that may have been isolated for millennia. Hadoram Shirihai, one of the world's leading experts on the group, recommends that they be regarded as 'more than "just" subspecies. Each merits . . . conservation measures because all populations, whether species or subspecies, are under immediate threat and in sharp decline.'[23] If one applies this precautionary principle worldwide then 18 of 22 recognised albatross 'species' are now considered at some risk of extinction. The figure for losses to longlining and other anthropogenic causes much used in media reportage

The recurrent tragedy of seabirds killed by human fishing operations is depicted here in Bruce Pearson's watercolour and pencil image of a Shy Albatross being cut to shreds by a trawl cable off South Africa.

is 100,000 dead birds annually.[24] Coleridge's symbol for the unity of all life is now facing oblivion worldwide, while the campaign to save albatrosses is one of the highest-profile conservation stories of our age.

Longlining is by no means the only issue. A lesser-known problem arises in the Pacific Ocean in a central region equal in area to the whole of Africa, more than 26 million km² (10 million miles²). Absence of notable tides or winds has made this central Pacific gyre a vast doldrums where all the plastic polymers jettisoned over decades into the sea have accumulated. As they break down under the effects of sunlight they form an indigestible soup of plastic molecules and studies suggest that for each 0.5 kg (1.1 lb) of plankton there are 2.7 kg (6 lb) of this toxic flotsam. In this region albatrosses mistake floating plastic pieces for their natural prey and the 'stomach contents of Laysan Albatross look like the cigarette lighter shelf at a convenience store they contain so many of them'. Predictions about the ongoing build-up of plastic suggest that there may eventually be 60 times more of it at the surface than plankton.[25]

Ironically, those looking for hope in this vast dark oceanic panorama can possibly take comfort if they examine what must rank as one of the bleakest episodes in all human encounters with albatrosses. The events occurred on the southern Japanese island of Torishima (it means 'bird island' in Japanese) where nineteenth-century entrepreneurs spotted a lucrative market. Its massive breeding population of Short-tailed Albatrosses was systematically clubbed to death and converted into feathers or rendered down for oil. For its rapid, almost mindless, depletion of a valuable crop, the slaughter of 'shorties' on Torishima ranks with the very worst examples of exploitation of a marine resource. Its

agents kept hammering their wooden clubs into the flocks – estimated to number 5 million – until they were all gone.[26] By the Second World War, the Short-tailed Albatross was judged to be extinct.

However, albatrosses, like ourselves, are what are known as K-selected species. Their strategy for survival in a largely stable environment, but with an unpredictable food supply, involves low adult mortality but also slow recruitment to the population. The often long-lived individual members do not reach sexual maturity until after a decade or more. Some individual albatross do not nest until they are 22 years of age, but can go on to breed until they reach 50, occasionally even 60, years old.[27] ('Grandma', a **Royal Albatross** *Diomedea epomophora*, at Taiaroa, New Zealand, had her last chick at 62 and was the subject of an award-winning documentary.)

The last few immature Short-tailed Albatrosses were probably out over the open Pacific, oblivious that the rest of their species was being battered into extinction. Some of that final handful of young adult 'shorties' eventually returned from their ocean-wandering adolescence and started to breed on Torishima in 1951. This minuscule number, this tiny spark, gave rise eventually to a flame of hope. Today, there are now about 2,400 Short-tailed Albatrosses.[28]

The almost miraculous resurrection on Torishima has obvious implications for the present longlining crisis. The birds on the Japanese island, like all of their family, required only the slenderest of chances. Perhaps by managing somehow to organise ourselves, and to redesign our fisheries to shorten the odds for survival of the world's albatrosses, we can simultaneously redeem some of the long, dreary past in our relations with these remarkable and charismatic sea creatures.

Petrel and Shearwater family *Procellariidae*

The family's 79 species are intermediate in size between the albatrosses and the diminutive storm petrels. They are among the most strictly maritime of all seabirds but, notwithstanding this exclusivity, the group is probably more widespread across the surface of the Earth than any other bird family. Several, such as the **Great Shearwater** *Puffinus gravis*, **Sooty Shearwater** *Puffinus griseus*, **Flesh-footed Shearwater** *Puffinus carneipes* and **Short-tailed Shearwater** *Puffinus tenuirostris*, make annual trans-hemispheric journeys from the southernmost oceans to offshore waters around Europe and North America, and travel as far as the Arctic Circle. There is barely a square metre of sea that is not, at some point, darkened by the long-winged shadows of these wanderers.

The family is most abundant in the Southern and Pacific Oceans, while just 13 species occur predominantly or exclusively in the Atlantic region. The pelagic lifestyle means that they fall within the ken of one distinctive branch of humanity: sailors and fishermen (and now ocean-going birders). Several petrels are notable scavengers upon human harvests at sea, whether fish or crustaceans and, at one time, whales, seals and even other birds. In many stretches of ocean there has seldom been a sizeable fishing vessel without petrels following in the hope of discarded offal.

My most powerful encounter with this petrel behaviour

came at an abattoir on the outskirts of Port Stanley, East Falkland in 1989. A flock of 200 **Southern Giant Petrel** *Macronectes giganteus*, the biggest family member with each bird the length of a medium-sized albatross, rested offshore in the shallows where the severed heads of cattle and a million livestock bones were crystal clear beneath the waves. From the slaughterhouse there was an intermittent discharge of unwanted viscera into the open water. Instantly the pale-eyed, hook-billed dark petrels converged in a seething melee of blood, guts and wrangling birds. Occasionally two individuals contested the same length of intestine, the pair back-paddling and clattering the sea surface with their 2 m (6.5 ft) wingspan in a ferocious tug of war. An older scientific name for the species is *ossifraga* ('bonebreaker'). Four archaic sailors' names for it were 'glutton', 'stinker' or 'stink-pot' (because of the musty odour of the egg) and, among Peruvian fishermen, *gallinazo marino*, 'sea vulture'.[1]

One can only begin to imagine the squabbling chaos when they flensed the great whales at the old whaling stations in the Southern Ocean. Regardless of their gluttony, the capacity of giant petrels as described by Bishop Stanley, a fabulous purveyor of divine falsehoods, cannot help raise an eyebrow. He noted an occasion when 600 birds ate over 20 tonnes of blubber in six to eight hours; that equates to 34 kg

(75 lb) of flesh per bird and roughly seven times their own body weight.[2]

A stranger impact upon human cultures arose in the places where these ocean-going birds come to land. Petrels and shearwaters might be among the most consummate fliers, but they are virtually helpless when they fly ashore to nest. To reduce any predator threat they often arrive under cover of darkness and breed in subterranean burrows or among rocks on remote offshore islands, where land mammals are (or were) absent. This return to the nest colony is often performed en masse and enveloped in some of the strangest vocalisations produced by any bird.

Such nocturnal invasions left a deep impact not only on their human neighbours, but ultimately on the landscape itself. Nowhere is this more apparent than on the Caribbean island of Dominica in the Lesser Antilles. This was once part of the breeding range of the **Black-capped Petrel** *Pterodroma hasitata*, a now endangered family member, whose three repeated calls have been described as 'a drawn-out wailing *aaa-aw* . . . a drawn-out *ooow* . . . and yelps like "a hurt puppy".[3] The sounds must have seemed so disturbing that the two peaks where the birds nested were called Morne Diablotin ('Little Devil's Bluff', the island's highest relief) and Morne au Diable ('Devil's Knoll'). The creature itself was named *Diablotin* and is still known as such in parts of the Caribbean.[4]

Environmentalists now seek out folklore or place names with supernatural associations to try to locate the whereabouts of rare petrels. One example was the search of a montane area in Cuba called La Bruja ('the witch'). Black-capped Petrels have been seen offshore near La Bruja, but breeding is yet unproven.[5] Another example involves the even rarer **Zino's Petrel** *Pterodroma madeira* of Madeira (world population, *c*.60). Naturalists were helped to relocate some of the handful of known nests by a shepherd, Lucas, who recognised recordings of petrel calls on tape. However, he had originally believed that the sounds were being 'made by ghosts!'[6]

Extraordinary claims have also been made for the sounds of another Caribbean petrel, the **Cahow** *Pterodroma cahow*, whose name even suggests the weirdness of the call. This supremely rare bird is endemic to the Atlantic island of Bermuda, where it once bred in large numbers. The associated cacophony around their burrows was so unnerving to Spanish sailors that they refused to settle such a haunted landscape. Bermuda was even dubbed the 'Isle of Devils' because of the stories of demons and nocturnal spirits. (One wonders if the island's enduring reputation for supernatural presences seeped through slowly into the larger surviving myth of the Bermuda Triangle as a zone of occult mystery and nautical mishap?) It fell to the English to settle the island, particularly after a small flotilla was shipwrecked there in 1609. On encountering the Cahow the early colonists noted its 'strange hollow and harsh howling . . . There are thousands of these birds . . . and for their cry and hooting, we called the "sea owl".'[7]

What is intriguing about such responses to petrels and shearwaters is how widespread they were. A classic example comes from the once great (now almost lost) colony of **Manx Shearwater** *Puffinus puffinus* on the Calf of

Like vultures on a kill, Southern Giant Petrels in a feeding frenzy create a scene of visceral power and drama.

Shearwaters and petrels may be birds of consummate grace in the air, but on land they are clumsy and helpless. These breeding Manx Shearwater wait until dark before venturing to their nest burrows in Wales.

Man in the Irish Sea. These cliffs held tens of thousands of shearwaters and the site found its way into the Icelandic *Njáls saga* as a place where a Viking party landed before an assault upon Ireland in 1014 (written down in the thirteenth century, the saga describes events of more than 200 years earlier). While they rode at anchor in their long ships, the ill-fated forces were not only unnerved by what they called ravens, but came under attack and lost 20 men to the evil birds. The British scholar Kenneth Williamson, while acknowledging the poetic exaggeration in *Njáls saga*, argued that 'the nightly clamour and the "ravens" of ill omen is [*sic*] too strong to be denied as the earliest historic record of a Manx Shearwater colony in the British Isles'.[8]

Williamson located supernatural associations embedded in other ancient place-names where Manx Shearwaters nest. These included two sites on his wife's native Faroe Islands – Tröllanes ('troll foreland') and Trölhøvdi ('troll hill' or 'head').[9] However, the most extraordinary colony is on the Scottish isle of Rum. It holds almost a quarter of a million breeding birds (more than a third of the world population). The call from an individual Manx Shearwater has been described as 'the crying of insane spirits'. To my own ears, it evoked a cockerel crowing after a deep breath of helium on the point of being strangled. Who knows how it impacted upon the original Norse-speaking settlers of Rum, but they named the mist-shrouded slopes, which the birds still honeycomb with their burrows, Trollaval ('troll hill').[10]

Today we are less likely to ascribe supernatural origins to the sounds of shearwaters, but they still have the power to surprise us.

I was on a business trip to Hawaii in June 1995 and had the opportunity to stay a couple of nights on Kauai. The cottage was part of a very secluded complex (located on the US Navy's Missile Test Facility at Barking Sands). Only two cottages were occupied. I went to dinner the first evening, returned around 10 p.m., and was confronted by a shearwater sitting in the middle of the drive, adjacent to another cottage. I eased past, obtained my bins and a flashlight and returned for a more relaxed look at the bird. As I approached it, I heard some very weird noises. My first thought was that the adjacent cottage was occupied, probably by a honeymoon couple. As I drew closer, the number of voices increased dramatically, leading to speculation as to exactly how many honeymooners (or honey 'moaners') were present. I then noticed that the sounds were coming from the beach, where I encountered a sign that read:

Do Not Disturb
Wedge-tailed Shearwater Nesting Colony
US Fish and Wildlife Service

I spent the better part of an hour being serenaded. It was a truly magical experience. The Hawaiian name for the **Wedge-tailed Shearwater** *Puffinus pacificus* is *Ua'u Kani*, to 'call out'. The vocalisations could be described as moaning, groaning, wailing, a baby crying, or . . . well . . . orgasmic.[11]

Our historic fear of these nocturnal wailings was often tempered by a realisation that the breeding birds were a major source of protein. Shearwater and petrel colonies

have been exploited for food or feathers worldwide. In the Westman Islands (Iceland), for example, 20,000–30,000 young **Northern Fulmar** *Fulmarus glacialis* were taken annually before 1844, and between 1850–1900 the figures rose to 40,000–50,000 (fowling ceased in 1939). Equally, in the Danish-speaking Faroe Islands, 80,000–100,000 young Northern Fulmars were harvested each year until 1935.[12] On Nightingale Island, part of the Tristan da Cunha group (in the southern Atlantic), 10,000–20,000 young Great Shearwaters were taken yearly as food, with over 1,000 eggs, until the late twentieth century.[13]

Before it ended in the 1970s, the harvest of **Cory's Shearwater** *Calonectris diomedea* was deeply embedded in the cultural life of the Portuguese island of Madeira. Each year, around 25 September, a party of about 20 fishermen would sail 267 km (166 miles) to the uninhabited island of Great Salvage, where they would stay for about 20 consecutive days of work, dawn till dusk.

The daily round involved them working in teams across the island's barren rocky terrain throughout the morning, hauling out single *cagarra* chicks (the adult birds were often present but never killed). Each youngster, weighing about 900 g (2 lb), was winkled from its burrow by hand or with a hooked stick if the tunnel was long. The chick was bitten through the back of the head to dispatch it, and the precious oil in its stomach drained into a bucket, when the gullet was plugged with a feather swatch to prevent leakage. Others workers gathered up all the carcasses and carried them to a designated plucking spot. Once the chicks had been stripped and the saleable feathers collected, the men took their midday meal before dividing the catch into portions. The party then dipped skins into a cauldron of boiling water for a final clean, before they were gutted, salted and stored in barrels. The feathers were sold to England for eiderdowns (see Wildfowl in the Bedroom, page 87), while the fishy meat was sold locally in Madeira. A typical harvest for a month's labour in the nineteenth century might be 85 barrels of *cagarra* (perhaps 30,000 birds in good years), 17 bales of feathers, eight barrels of limpets (sold as far away as the Caribbean), 29 boxes of shellfish and three barrels of rabbits.

The work was rough and conditions unforgiving, but the rhythms of the hunt had been honed by decades of practice. A detailed description was made of the 1892 expedition by Ernesto Schmitz, a German pastor living in Madeira. Fishermen who made the trip in the 1950s (it ceased in 1969) and who had read Schmitz's 60-year-old account, confirmed that little had changed in their methods over the intervening period. Schmitz noted that among the 1892 party was a man who had been to Great Salvage every autumn for four decades. Inured through long years of elemental toil, this old hunter recorded an intimate detail of life on Great Salvage.

In his youth the fowlers had been accustomed to sleep in a cave that had been walled in at one end. At the far side of this chamber was an ancient *cagarra* nest and every night the parents arrived at the cave mouth, fluttered over the sleeping bodies, and entered the burrow to feed their offspring. The old salt described how, even when he visited in the 1850s, this nest was thought to have been used since 'time immemorial'. It had always been a tradition among the sleeping men to spare the shearwater that shared their cave.[14]

Once hunted for its feathers and flesh, the Northern Fulmar has now hugely expanded its breeding range and increased its numbers.

In the 1970s, poaching by non-Madeiran fishermen, unrestrained by tradition, eventually reduced the Cory's Shearwaters to virtual extinction. Great Salvage's designation as a nature reserve and a ban on fowling have since seen the birds recover almost completely.

One of the last examples of shearwater hunting may now be the largest legal harvest involving a wild seabird anywhere in the world (see Exploitation of Auks, page 227). It occurs in the Furneaux Group and other islands in the Bass Strait between Australia and Tasmania, and involves Short-tailed Shearwaters, a species better known as the 'muttonbird' (thought to derive from its sheep-like flavour, or from the subcutaneous fat resembling the tallow visible on lamb carcasses). From the early nineteenth century until 1925 about 1.1 million birds were taken for meat, feathers and oil (credited with medicinal properties) in both subsistence and commercial operations. However, the combined off-take declined to a little over 600,000 birds by the 1980s, and in 2008 the catch stood at 120,000 birds. While this is only about one-tenth of the nineteenth-century maximum, muttonbirding is still an important expression of Tasmanian cultural identity.

The bird is uniquely bound up with the history of the first peoples on Tasmania – a community isolated from the Aborigines of Australia for 10,000 years. In that prolonged solitude the approximately 4,000 Tasmanians had lost many aspects of the Stone Age technologies available just across the Bass Strait, leaving them with 'the simplest material culture of any people in the modern world'.[15] When all the paraphernalia of industrial Europe came sweeping across their island in the form of a Victorian British penal colony, Tasmania's Aborigines were overawed. Within 70 years its full-blooded population succumbed to a mixture of disease, brutal violence, habitat loss, decimation of key prey species such as kangaroos, starvation and Victorian charity. When a diminutive female figure known as Truganini passed away in 1876 she was viewed by the island's white colonial community as the 'Last of the Tasmanians'.

However, this legend overlooked the complex social interactions between the tough white male sealers inhabiting the islands of the Bass Strait and female Aborigines. The resulting offspring from these relationships gave rise to a community of mixed race, which did not fit neatly into the racial stereotypes dominating the mindset of a British colony. During decades of official denial and mistreatment, this surviving Aboriginal people was sustained partly through its maintenance of muttonbirding, one of a suite of hunting activities that were at the core of their lives until the twenty-first century. Muttonbirding was both economic resource and rallying point for a culturally fused Aboriginal identity. While it has now lost some of this centrality and while muttonbirding is also a white Tasmanian pastime and enterprise, the taking of Short-tailed Shearwaters is still embedded in the life of the Bass Strait community.[16]

Today muttonbirding is controversial and under pressure from wildlife charities, but its overall impact on numbers of Short-tailed Shearwaters is probably negligible. There are an estimated 11.4 million muttonbird burrows in Tasmania and 23 million birds in Australia overall, making it one of the most common seabirds in that region.[17]

By contrast, it was almost a defining characteristic of other shearwater and petrel hunts established by colonial settlers, including Europeans and Polynesians, that they were entirely unsustainable. (This was not the case, however, with petrel harvests developed either in Europe by indigenous inhabitants – e.g. Northern Fulmar on St Kilda and Faroe Islands – or by those after long-standing residence – e.g. Madeira – which were usually managed to ensure sustainability.) Another core problem initiated by colonial spread was the introduction of non-native terrestrial animals, particularly pigs, goats, cats and rats, to island ecosystems where they had a devastating impact on physically inept, burrow-nesting seabirds. There are 45 taxa among the petrels and shearwaters deemed at some risk of extinction. The **Jamaican Petrel** *Pterodroma caribbea* has probably already crossed that threshold, having not been seen since 1879. Before that it was hunted relentlessly, although introduced rats and mongooses may have issued the *coup de grâce*.[18]

A frequent pattern has been for petrels to find their names entered on ornithology's official lists and then for the birds to disappear almost immediately, so discovery of their existence and mystery at their whereabouts virtually coincide. A single example of the **Magenta Petrel** *Pterodroma magentae* (known to Polynesian inhabitants of the Chatham Islands as *taiko* and probably severely harvested by them) was collected at sea in the southern Pacific in 1867 and then never seen again until 1978. The **Fiji Petrel** was discovered on its native island in 1855, loaded with its unwieldy official title – firstly *Pterodroma*, then *Pseudobulweria macgillivrayi* – and only refound in 1983. The bird that takes all prizes in this field is the Bermudan endemic mentioned earlier for its central role in that territory's legend as an 'Isle of Devils'.

The Cahow's nocturnal calls may have discouraged the Spaniards from early settlement in Bermuda, but nothing could stop European mariners from hauling the oil-rich chicks from their burrows and eating them. There are seventeenth-century accounts of 300 of these 'well relished Fowle, fat and full as a partridge', being taken in an hour, and of 4,000 caught, skinned and salted down in a single night.[19] By 1621 the Cahow was already considered extinct. At intervals, in the early twentieth century, examples of unidentified dead petrels were found in Bermuda giving hope that all might not be lost. Finally in 1951, after a full-scale search by the American Robert Cushman Murphy, the Cahow flew back phoenix-like into human ken. A tiny cluster of islets in Castle Harbour, just 1 ha (2.5 acres) in extent, was found eventually to hold 18 pairs.[20]

The mission to restore a bird lost for 330 years has largely been the life's work of one Bermudan resident, David Wingate. He had been present as a 15-year-old boy at the initial rediscovery, an event that he identifies as one that 'determined the course of my career'. Since that moment he has coaxed and supported Cahow numbers until they now approach 100 pairs (2010). Here is just one extraordinary detail from that lifetime of effort:

> 1958 was a banner year for me. I had succeeded in saving four chicks and was looking forward to witnessing that inevitable point when the fledgling makes its first flight to sea to face life on its own. Until then it had never been witnessed and I had already missed the first three departures through poor timing. I knew from footprint evidence that the fledglings are abandoned a

few days before they begin their nightly wing-exercising excursions, but this was becoming ridiculous. It was now fifteen nights since this chick had been fed and I was in the fourth consecutive night of all-night vigils, but if anything its wing exercising was becoming feebler and its wanderings between the burrow and cliff edge more frantic.

The full moon was waning and the fireworms had just completed their spectacular display of monthly mating. Silver-lined cumulus drifted slowly by, casting dark shadows over the chaos of eroded cliff and boulders that characterised this outermost fragment of Bermuda. Waves surged in and out of the sea caves thirty feet below and the tinkling notes of the crickets echoed out into the starry vault like some secret form of intergalactic communication. I was beginning to nod off when the bird came out of the burrow for the last time. Once more it waddled to the cliff and peered over with much head bobbing. 'Come on, come on,' I muttered, not sure if I could stay awake much longer. There was desperation in its manner now and I could feel the tension building.

Then suddenly it was gone. I dashed to the cliff edge and shone my light but instead of flying as expected it had just jumped straight down into the water. 'Is this the way it's supposed to happen?' I wondered. But there was no time to ponder that now. I had a lot of cliff to scramble down to get to my boat – a fragile twelve foot moulded plywood hull – and then I had to move it around to the seaward side where the fledgling had jumped. It was still there swimming in circles so I dropped the anchor to watch. That was a bad idea because when it finally began to head to sea I found the anchor hitched and had to disconnect the chain and tie it to a float to follow. At that point my sole intention was to find out what the bird was going to do, even if it took the rest of the night.

Obeying the call of the open ocean my fledgling swam steadily seaward as I paddled behind. Soon it was near the scragged rocks off Outer Pear islet. Near at hand I could see and hear the breaking surf on those rocks but, far more ominous, was the deeper roar of the boiler reef barrier further out, which was taking the full brunt of the ocean swells. I could see long black lines as the waves rose up before them and then an eerie phosphorescent glow as they cascaded over the top.

Incredibly my bird led the way through one of the few narrow passages but on either side I could clearly see the hard black lips of the boilers exposed in the wave troughs. This was the most frightening moment of all, but once clear of these shoal areas the choppiness was replaced by a smooth rolling swell that lifted and fell in the moonlight.

The boiler reefs were far behind us now but still my bird paddled on towards an uncertain destiny. Soon we were over mile-deep waters where William Beebe and Otis Barton had made their famous half-mile descent in the bathysphere three decades before. The setting moon now cast shadows off the swells, which seemed

to race ahead of them making visual contact more and more difficult. Disturbingly, too, my occasional checks by flashlight suggested that the fledgling was becoming waterlogged.

It must have been after 3 a.m. when I finally lost contact but by then I had come to the realisation that it was probably doomed: one of those unfortunates that for whatever reason had failed to build up enough fat reserves to survive the transition to independence. Following age-old instincts it had thrown itself to the mercy of the fates. This chick was one of the last of its kind and I realised then that its own fate might well determine the fate of the Cahow species as a whole! In that chilling moment of epiphany I found myself staring at the face of extinction.

Suddenly I felt dreadfully alone – and terrified! It was time to think about my own predicament. Tiny Bermuda was already below the horizon and but for the night glow from lights on land and my knowledge of the stars I might not have had a clue how to find my way back. Then there was the barrier of the boiler reef line to negotiate again, this time without the instinctive wisdom of a Cahow to guide me through.

With heart still pounding I finally made it back to the comparative safety of my hitched anchor and tied up to wait out the rest of the night dozing uncomfortably in a very wet boat. It never occurred to me then that I could have quite safely freed the anchor right away by pulling myself down its chain using the light from phosphorescent plankton to see my way. Indeed, there was so much I still had to learn in those heady early days of the recovery program. In the decades ahead as my ability to help the Cahow improved I would be rewarded with more and more successful fledgling departures. By then I knew the way it was *supposed* to happen: the pressure of warm, webbed feet as robust and confident birds climb up your arms and on to your head to find the highest unobstructed point; the powerful downdraft as they exercise their long wings to a peak of perfection and then the final burst of power as they helicopter straight up to locate the horizon before heading directly out to sea . . .[21]

In 2009 a major milestone was reached when Cahows bred for the first time on nearby Nonsuch Island, after a long-term translocation project carried out by Wingate's successor, Jeremy Madeiros, who moved chicks from their low-lying and vulnerable rocky crags to the higher, biologically restored nature reserve on Nonsuch.[22]

The Cahow story is truly remarkable. It describes not just a key development in the fate of one seabird. It is also an extraordinary moment in human history with implications for all life on Earth. It is surely the first occasion in 4 billion years of evolution that one species – represented by a single remarkable man – masterminded, intentionally and with unremitting dedication, the continued survival of another species. It is a model of hope for our planet and for humankind.

Storm Petrel family *Hydrobatidae*

▶ Its weird vocalisations and nocturnal habits once made the European Storm Petrel and other members of its family creatures of superstition and mystery.

This family of 21 species includes the smallest, yet simultaneously some of the most remarkable, ocean-wandering birds on Earth. They are proportionately long-winged, often with brown-black plumages broken by variable quantities of white on wing, rump, tail or, in several species, on the underparts.

A common family characteristic is their distinctive manner of flight, which is close to the water even in the most violent conditions, and characterised by long elastic swoops or glides, broken by sudden twists, erratic changes of direction and even vertical leaps. A speciality of some is to stall, fluttering just above the waves with legs outstretched, so that the webbed feet touch the sea surface. It is this action from which the word 'petrel' is derived. Various archaic spellings include *pitteral* and *petteril* and all suggest the attempted onomatopoeic rendering of the light rhythmic flutter of their feet on water.

An alternative origin was proposed by the British mariner and pirate William Dampier who wrote, 'As they fly, they pat the Water alternately with their Feet, as if they walkt upon it; tho' still upon the Wing. And from hence the Seamen give them the name of Petrels, in allusion to St. Peter's walking upon the Lake of Gennesareth [the Sea of Galilee].'[1] The creation of names is such a complex process of word, sound and thought association that both ideas could easily have been at work in the formation of 'petrel'. The scientific name *Hydrobatidae* is a Greek construction with a similar reference – meaning roughly 'water treader'.[2]

The birds range in size from the **White-throated Storm Petrel** *Nesofregetta fuliginosa* of the western Pacific, which measures 26 cm (10.2 in) and has a wingspan of about half a metre (20.8 in), to the **European Storm Petrel** *Hydrobates pelagicus*, whose dimensions are those of a large swallow. In fact several species have names associating them with hirundines. For instance the similarly tiny **Wilson's Storm Petrel** *Oceanites oceanicus* is known as *Golondrina del mar* ('sea swallow') in parts of Spanish-speaking America, but the rather lovely Brazilian name, *Andorinha-das-tormentas* ('storm swallow') is a poetic construction (of the German Brazilian ornithologist Emilie Snethlage) without wide currency.[3]

The small size of most storm petrels has meant that they have seldom been judged worthy of human consumption, although one singular purpose they have served was in the Faroe Islands (belonging to Denmark; located between Iceland and Britain). The birds are so rich in oil that the Faroese would decapitate the young of European Storm Petrels (*drunnhviti*), dry them and thread a woollen wick through their bodies. They were then burned as night lights and one tradition among these hardy crofting and fisherfolk was to gather in the farmhouse, tell tales (see also The Northern Gannets in Faroese Folk Tale, page 148), sing old ballads (and presumably drink alcohol) until the *drunnhviti* had burned through.[4] The same usage of storm petrels, possibly until the early twentieth century, has been recorded among the fishermen of Shetland, Britain's northernmost archipelago (examples are held in the Pitt Rivers Museum in Oxford).

It is instructive to compare the biggest albatross with Wilson's or European Storm Petrels, because they are all part of the same seabird order (Procellariiformes). The petrels weigh 25–45 g (0.9–1.6 oz) and less than one-three-hundreth of a Wandering Albatross. Regardless of the disparity, the albatross and Wilson's Storm Petrels inhabit the same formidable southern oceans beyond the roaring forties. Storm petrels are sometimes as long-lived as albatrosses, while their world-wandering journeys are just as inspiring. Given the birds' own Lilliputian scale, they are perhaps more impressive. A European Storm Petrel found dead on a South African beach in 2002 had been ringed as an adult in Scotland in 1975. The distance between the two places was 10,391 km (6,457 miles). If one assumes it made the journey at least 28 times, that 25 g (1 oz) bird covered 581,896 km (361,573 miles). To get a sense of this individual's entire lifelong Atlantic odyssey one would have to multiply the figure many times.[5] The ordinary ocean-going lives of storm petrels are truly a challenge to the human imagination, and similar to those made by such mysteries of the ocean floor as the coelacanth and giant squid.

Storm petrels only ever come to land when they breed. Then their dancing grace is exchanged for a curious terrestrial helplessness. Some species are so weak-limbed they literally crawl to move around. To mitigate the obvious vulnerability the birds nest underground in burrows or crevices between rocks, with European Storm Petrels in Britain apparently showing a 'particular fondness' for prehistoric ruins known as Pictish brochs.[6] Storm petrels also arrive on shore during the hours of darkness. The nocturnal visitations have helped cement the family's wider aura of mystery and strangeness, because storm petrels use their voice as a communication guide to help locate both burrow and partner. In turn the calls are an unearthly blend of chuckling, clicking, purring, bubbling squeals and gurgles. One memorable description of **Leach's Storm Petrel** *Oceanodroma leucorhoa* at a North American site evokes nicely the disorientation felt by a human visitor, which arises not just from the random movement of the birds; it is the fact that, during their assault upon our senses, storm petrels have so little frame of reference within the rest of organic life.

> Here within Night's dominion in the midst of a . . . throng of flitting forms, seeming to speak most earnestly in a subhuman, unknown tongue . . . the mind may readily picture a . . . gathering of the black elves of old, hurrying to and fro . . . ere dreaded Day begins . . . As each flying bird passes over its nest, it calls in a hurried gibberish, to be answered by its brooding mate in an energetic purr often ending with a coaxing wail; the flying bird . . . swings away to leeward again and again . . . until it finally drops to the entrance of its burrow to meet its anxious mate. Now from the dank weeds and grass, like great June bugs others are rising, or crawling to a convenient place to rise. One is in the very midst of their activities. From one's feet . . . they swarm, often dashing against one's person in their haste.[7]

The author notes their similarity to insects, but another regular comparison is to the flickering movement of bats. Both suggest the unnerving impact of storm petrels, and it

Until 2003 the New Zealand Storm Petrel had gone 175 years without being recognised, yet it lives just a few hours' sail from the 1.4 million 'kiwis' resident in Auckland.

still survive, two British birders watching in a nearby area of the same Hauraki Gulf took numerous pin-sharp images confirming the earlier supposition. Now the species has been seen and recorded on scores of occasions, and even caught and fitted with super-lightweight transmitters. Yet the local nest grounds still await discovery. One remarkable aspect of this story is the bird's general location. It lies just a few hours' sail from the 1.4 million inhabitants of the country's largest city, Auckland, yet New Zealand's eponymous storm petrel had persisted for 175 years without ever being noticed.[9]

It is the unfathomable aura surrounding storm petrels that has shut them off from most of mankind and, in turn, converted some naturalists into complete devotees. John J Borg, curator of the National Museum of Natural History in Mdina, Malta, explains the appeal of a bird once known in his native language as *Bu nittien* 'father of the stinker or the stinking one' – a reference to the deep musty odour that emanates from the European Storm Petrels' burrows. (Sometimes the smell of a whole colony is so strong it can be detected 25 km: 15 miles out to sea.)[10]

> When I was extracting my first storm petrel from a mist-net in the middle of a balmy night on a tiny rocky islet, it was love at first sight. That first encounter goes back to the summer of 1980 when I formed part of a bird-ringing expedition to the island of Filfla located some 5 km south of Malta. This outcrop had served for over a century as a bombing target by the British forces and lying around among the rocks and boulders one could still see several unexploded bombs and shells. After putting up a couple of mist-nests we waited for nightfall. As soon as it got dark I became aware that the air was filling up with flying birds not unlike bats; the storm petrels were coming back from a day at sea. After an hour or so, amidst all the rubble and boulder screes around me there were thousands of birds scrambling and calling. This hubbub kept on till about an hour before first light. On that night we caught and ringed over 444 storm petrels. Since then I have visited this colony every year sometimes twice a year, ringing over 20,000 birds.
>
> The anticipation of finding a new nesting site is usually preceded by goose pimples all over and a blood-rush to the head. This feeling was never as strong as in 1994 when I discovered a new colony on Gozo. The last breeding record on that island was in the eighteenth century. Winning the lottery jackpot would not have made me happier. Needless to say, after 29 years these birds still occupy more than half of my waking hours, if not some of my sleeping ones as well.[11]

The sound on Borg's mobile phone notifying him of the receipt of text messages is the contact call of his totem bird. One can only imagine the surreal impact of this wonderfully individual ringtone – an intense rhythmic purr punctuated by a convulsive gulp that has been likened to a 'fairy being sick' – when it happens to go off in the museum or, better still, at the cafe.

seems that the effect is felt not only by our own species. 'Let a hawk or an owl appear in . . . gull or tern colonies,' wrote the American Edward Forbush, 'and the war cry is sounded . . . Let a cat appear in a colony of Herring Gulls in the daytime, and its appearance is the signal for general attack . . . But the small and apparently inoffensive petrel is avoided as if it were ghost or banshee.'[8]

Storm petrels are sometimes attracted to bright lights and one can imagine how their sudden nocturnal appearance onboard a ship, the spectral forms fluttering over the decks or entangled in the sails and rigging, could have affected a breed as superstitious as the old mariner. The sailors' archaic name for storm petrels was 'Mother Carey's chickens', possibly a corruption of 'Mother Mary's chickens' and an index of their taboo status for seamen. The birds were said to be the souls of drowned or dead sailors, and taken as an omen of disaster.

If storm petrels do not come back from beyond the grave, they can at least *seem* to return from the dead. The **New Zealand Storm Petrel** *Oceanites maorianus* was known from just three skins collected in the 1820s. Thereafter it vanished completely and was deemed extinct by many specialists. Yet on 25 January 2003 two kiwi (see also page 29) ornithologists, Sav Saville and Brent Stephenson, were on a pelagic birding trip off New Zealand's North Island, when they spotted a storm petrel showing strong resemblances to the lost species. Several months later, after an article by them proposing that the New Zealand Storm Petrel may

Diving Petrel family *Pelecanoididae*

Common Diving Petrel *Pelecanoides urinatrix*. It is the most widespread in a family of four small seabirds, which are all found in the oceans of the southern hemisphere, especially around New Zealand, southern Australia and the coastlines of Argentina and Chile. The quartet are all plump, long-winged birds, predominantly black above and white below, and rather resemble 'miniature penguins' in body shape.

Although diving petrels generally fall within the ken of just a small part of humanity, none the less they have the capacity to affect us deeply, as proven by the senior surgeon on RMS *Canberra* during the Falklands War of 1982:

> A result of coastal action, in particular the sinking of vessels, such as HMS *Antelope*, was that several quite large oil slicks lay in wait for the unwary in the relatively sheltered bays near Port Stanley, Falkland. Many birds became badly oiled and sought refuge on or about the decks of the *Canberra*. As is customary at sea, these poor unfortunates became the responsibility of the medical fraternity. The birds were almost exclusively

Common Diving Petrels, although we did process one Snowy (American) Sheathbill. They would arrive at the hospital facility reception at any time. A thorough cleanse with washing-up liquid after rubber-banding the bill and then a blow-dry with a hairdryer seemed to do the trick, with a recovery period of 24 hours or so for cod liver oil feed while the feathers dried and were preened to be waterproof. We started counting but lost our records and probably had some return visits, but I would guess about 50 were treated.

> It was an act of caring that just became part of our normal onboard duties, which themselves had been extended beyond our own forces to include Argentinian or Patagonian troops (they made up 90 per cent of our patients). It gave us a change of focus away from the destruction of war and into the close-up world of a small innocent. As such it helped return all involved to a true sense of proportion.[1]

Grebe family *Podicipedidae*

Often exceptionally beautiful and possessed of elaborate nuptial displays, in which some species perform almost balletically synchronised dancing movements, grebes have long held human attention. There are 21 species spread right across six continents from the Siberian Arctic to Chile's Tierra del Fuego. Some have massive transcontinental ranges, such as the **Little Grebe** *Tachybapytus ruficollis* (Europe, Asia and Africa) and **Great Crested Grebe** *Podiceps cristatus* (Europe, Asia, Australasia and parts of Africa).

Yet the grebes' wide distribution and adaptability should not disguise their acute specialisation. They are supremely designed for an exclusively aquatic life, possessing dense, silky, water-resistant plumages, lobed feet that function like flippers under the water, and legs set far back on the abdomen to aid the birds' propulsion both at the surface and when diving. It is this peculiar arrangement that renders grebes awkward on land and gave rise to a deeply unflattering original name. *Podiceps* roughly translates as the old English word for the grebe, 'arsefoot'.[1]

In a sense it was these aquatic adaptations that also gave the birds their practical function for humans. The body is so densely feathered, especially on the underside – a Great Crested Grebe has 20,000 feathers compared, for example, with an eagle that has just 7,000 – that the plumage closely resembles a mammal's pelt.[2] In fact it was known as 'grebe fur' and exploited probably from ancient times, but certainly since the Middle Ages. One of the localities where grebe trapping was an enduring tradition was around the Swiss lakes. In the 1540s the naturalist Conrad Gesner described how in his native Zurich they used to target Great Crested Grebes in August on a day that became known as *Tuccheltag* ('Grebe Day'). It was the moment when their annual moult left the grebes – reluctant fliers at the best of times (and several species are flightless) – incapable of taking off and

they could be more easily driven into nets. After the final body count the fowlers sat down to a celebratory feast.

The hunt's real purpose was not so much the meat, which has, at best, an ambivalent reputation. In the late twentieth century, a British couple, Shelagh and Jonathan Routh, recreated some of the recipes listed in Leonardo da Vinci's kitchen notebooks. One was 'boiled loon' (an old name for Great Crested Grebe). The great Renaissance artist had recommended that first the loon be hung for six weeks. Unfortunately after just 14 days the Rouths found the bird had acquired a greenish hue and 'looked so unhappy' that they decided to wait no longer. After 90 minutes of boiling and the addition of garlic, pepper and a sprinkling of rosewater, the grebe was 'quite inedible – tough and tasteless'.[3] The judgement of a modern Argentinian contributor meshes closely with this verdict and with the opinions of the old European fowlers, who thought Great Crested Grebes difficult to shoot and not worth the effort: 'I tried the meat of **White-tufted Grebe** *Rollandia rolland* on one or two occasions in my youth and it was smelly and strong.'[4]

The main target for hunters, including the fowlers from Zurich, was the grebe's wonderfully soft, lax, silvery-sheened belly feathers. (An old name for the species was 'satin grebe', just as a particularly soft downy cotton cloth was known as 'grebe-cloth'.)[5] Their skins were cut into strips and used as trim on the cuffs or collars of dresses and cloaks, and eventually on almost any fashionable female clothing; grebe fur was a speciality fabric for making muffs. This exploitation probably suppressed grebe numbers, but without drastic effect until the nineteenth century when feather adornments of all kinds became a global fashion (see also Herons and the Feather Industry, page 131).

For the Victorians the birds seemed purpose-made

to complete the headgear for the stylish belle, because in spring species such as the **Red-necked Grebe** *Podiceps grisegena* and **Horned Grebe** *Podiceps auritus* of North America and Eurasia, as well as the Great Crested Grebe, acquire a thickened corolla of neck and crown feathers. As if to confirm their function for the millinery and couture industries, these elongated feathers and the garment details into which they were inserted were known equally as 'tippets'.[6] The industry's rapacious demand for wild grebes eventually exhausted the commercial possibilities of most populations. In places such as central Europe and Britain, the Great Crested Grebe was reduced to the point where regional extinction seemed imminent.[7] Faced with this collapse, the feather merchants widened operations, importing fur from wherever the larger species could be targeted. Just before the trade was outlawed in North America, plume hunters went after the beautiful **Western Grebe** *Aechmophorus occidentalis* for its sparkling white belly skins and shipped them from California to the New York fashion houses for 20 cents apiece.[8] It is a measure of how desirable it was as a fashion fabric that after the ban there was a 1924 British court case in which customs officers seized a shipment of 135,956 grebe skins (of three unnamed species).[9] Mercifully the birds gradually recovered after protective legislation was introduced, and today the European population of Great Crested Grebe stands at about 300,000 pairs.[10]

Not all grebes have been so fortunate. Two-thirds of the world's species are found in North and South America, with eight (and, until recently, ten) found on the latter continent alone. Five of these exhibit (or exhibited, since two are now extinct) extraordinary levels of endemism, appearing on a handful of high-altitude lakes, sometimes on just one lake alone. Inherently vulnerable because of these narrow ranges, the birds have suffered grievously, if often inadvertently, at human hands. The classic example is the **Atitlan Grebe** *Podilymbus gigas*. It was confined exclusively to one Guatemalan water body of the same name. Sadly it was driven to oblivion by the lake's tourist exploitation, including the use of speedboats, introduction of non-native predatory fish (for angling) and the over-harvest of reed for thatch (for weekend houses). A last bird was apparently shot in 1990.[11]

The **Colombian Grebe** *Podiceps andinus*, which was once found at a handful of montane lagoons in that country, suffered a similar fate and has not been seen since 1977. The **Junin Grebe** *Podiceps taczanowskii* is equally at risk, because all of the world's 100–300 birds grace the one wonderfully named Laguna Chinchaycocha de Junín of west-central Peru. Now it faces additional threats from

toxins released by mining and from water extraction for a hydroelectric scheme. Its neighbour, the **Titicaca Grebe** *Rollandia microptera*, if not limited to its eponymous wetland, is flightless, rare (2,000–6,000 birds) and occurs nowhere outside the Peruvian and Bolivian altiplano.[12] It is worth noting, incidentally, how the appeal of grebe fur was as strong on the Andean páramo as it was in the salons of Manhattan: the local people used to use Titicaca Grebe skins as saddle blankets.[13]

The last of the Neotropical quintet is the **Hooded Grebe** *Podiceps gallardoi* of southern-western Argentina, where it is restricted to open lagoons in the high Patagonian steppe, and is both scarce and severely declining.[14] However, to this species attaches an intriguing story with its own quirky, touching coda. It was only discovered in 1974 after extraordinary good fortune on the part of two naturalists. During a joint trip Maurice Rumboll had offered to introduce his field assistant Edward Shaw to the arts of skinning and preparing a museum specimen, but they had been unable to find a suitable roadkill corpse to serve their training purposes. Eventually they stopped at a high, wind-blasted Patagonian lake where Shaw targeted one of the many grebes visible just offshore. He managed to hit one but then had to watch it being blown further out by the ferocious winds and only claimed the prize after stripping down and swimming out to retrieve it.

When the two examined what they assumed was an example of the **Silvery Grebe** *Podiceps occipitalis* – the abundant species of the region – they sensed its oddity (it proved to be twice the weight of a Silvery Grebe), and after careful consultation of museum skins in Buenos Aires and New York they finally realised their achievement. They had discovered a new bird for the world. Strangely, however, they now believe they were not the first ever to see 'their' grebe.

One of Rumboll's friends later unearthed a reference in a book, *Through the Heart of Patagonia* (1902) by the explorer, marksman and naturalist Hesketh Hesketh-Prichard, in which the author mentions seeing unidentified grebes – he was familiar with the other Argentinian species – in an area now associated with Hooded Grebes. Like Rumboll and Shaw, Hesketh-Prichard very probably saw a new species for the world but, unlike these two, he did not know it and he never knew it. His own possible achievement passed him by and now his account of unnamed grebes at an unknown lake (on page 187 of his book) seems imbued with a fresh and rather poignant sense of opportunity unfulfilled.[15] (Mercifully Hesketh-Prichard is immortalised in the name of a species he did find – *Poa prichardii*, a type of grass.)[16]

◀ At one time the head plumes of Great Crested Grebes were favourite adornments for women's hats, while the densely feathered bodies were made into muffs and collars.

Flamingo family *Phoenicopteridae*

There are six flamingo species worldwide with at least a single representative on five continents (Australia is flamingo-free), and a concentration of four in South America (**American Flamingo** *Phoenicopterus ruber*, which also occurs in Central and North America, **Andean Flamingo** *Phoenicoparrus andinus*, **Chilean Flamingo** *Phoenicopterus chilensis* and **James's Flamingo** *Phoenicoparrus jamesi*).

Yet the image of the family that is now engrained in the Western imagination is of vast flocks breeding on the

soda lakes of east Africa. Comprising mainly **Lesser Flamingo** *Phoeniconaias minor*, these congregations represent the largest assemblage of non-passerine birds on Earth. Flocks of a million are not exceptional and a gathering on Lake Magadi, Kenya, in the 1960s is thought to have included 2.4 million birds. Aerial photographs reduce the prodigious numbers to a simple abstract design – quaking planes of pink set within a larger white-and-blue matrix of crystallised soda and water. Such images take their place

Lesser Flamingos on the soda lakes of the African Rift Valley region form the biggest flocks of large birds found anywhere on Earth.

among the most sublime expressions of natural plenty on our planet.

To see the flocks from the air is one thing. To experience on foot the hellish conditions in which flamingos thrive is to appreciate the extraordinary – and even surreal – beauty of these gloriously roseate birds. For few other organisms can survive in this intensely alkaline environment. One notable exception is the algae (*Spirulina platensis*) on which Lesser Flamingos mainly feed, and from which the birds obtain the carotenoid pigments that turn them rose red. The flock on Lake Magadi was probably consuming *c.*160 tonnes of the algae every day. The only other large living organisms in the entire ecosystem are a handful of avian scavengers – African Fish Eagles and Marabou Storks – that kill and eat the flamingos themselves.

The Kenyan ornithologist Leslie Brown once attempted to walk out across the seeming terra firma of a soda lake. Only with extreme good fortune and after exertions that would have defeated a lesser man did he escape to recount the experience. One problem is the highly alkaline water, which burns human skin but from which flamingos are protected by the thick scales on their legs. (Brown found birds on Lake Natron wading in geothermally heated water that was close to boiling temperature.)[1] Another challenge is the lake's crusted substrate, over which the flamingos glide untroubled. For Brown it was a thick black stinking mire, 'gelatinous in texture and extremely sticky, [that] gripped my feet in their protective boots with a tenacity I had never before encountered. The effort of wrenching one boot out was often sufficient to imbed the other so deeply that it, in turn, required several jerks before it would come free.'

> I found I could take five or six steps before I was brought up short, plunging in the filth and gasping for breath. At each halt I could only allow myself a momentary respite, for I sank slowly into the black foul mud beneath the crust, and I dared not sink too far for

fear that I would be unable to wrench my boots free again.

> . . . If I had not been a strong man and an experienced mud-walker I should be there yet, the flesh dissolved from my bones and the skeleton stuck in the mud like those dried heaps of locusts. It was partly the thought of the beastliness of this way of dying, and partly anger at my own stupidity, that kept me going.[2]

Fortunately Brown survived. It was his book *The Mystery of the Flamingos* (1959) that revealed not only his ordeal, but also the whereabouts and staggering numbers of the birds nesting in east Africa.

It is not merely the austerity of their habitat that sets flamingos apart. Even their physique seems to confirm a central human idea that they are deeply special. The **Greater Flamingo** *Phoenicopterus roseus*, the most widespread of the six species and found across Africa, Asia and Europe, can stand 1.6 m (5.2 ft) tall, only two-fifths of which is body. At times the bird can look like nothing more than a long pink neck (and head) curving in a gentle S-shape, perched above pink stilt-like legs. It joins a select group of birds – the others being parrots, penguins and pelicans – that are instantly recognisable to most people, even in silhouette.

The overall aesthetic effect is of elegant beauty with an added dash of the bizarre. (Yet they may not appeal to all our senses, as one contributor observes: 'Have you noticed how badly flamingos smell?')[3] The short thick decurved bill can give a blunt, even stoved-in, effect to the face. The limbs and neck are so long they can look ludicrously disproportioned. This in many ways increases once they take wing. The US ornithologist Frank Chapman wrote: 'Flamingos in flight resemble no other bird known to me. With legs and neck fully outstretched, and the comparatively small wings set halfway between bill and toes, they look as if they might fly backward or forward with equal ease.'[4] I once saw a distant line of Greater Flamingos in eastern Turkey and it was

Lesser Flamingos typify the family's collective reputation for exquisite colour and bizarre physical form.

several minutes before I could work out in which direction they were actually facing and flying.

The curiousness of flamingos has only added to their allure as captive adornments for parks and gardens. It is partly this tradition, which goes back thousands of years, that has led us to think of them as an adjunct to our world. The best-known, best-loved version of this humanised creature is the flamingo as croquet mallet in the nineteenth-century fantasy of Lewis Carroll, *Alice's Adventures in Wonderland*. Less familiar is the masterly poem by the Austrian writer Rainer Maria Rilke, 'The Flamingos'. It was inspired by encounters with birds in a Parisian menagerie and while it clearly references the way humans have attempted to possess the birds and their beauty, Rilke's flamingos somehow manage to elude physical confinement and even our attempts at imaginative appropriation.

> With all the subtle paints of Fragonard
> no more of their red and white could be expressed
> than someone would convey about his mistress
> by telling you, 'She was lovely, lying there
>
> still soft with sleep.' They rise above the green
> grass and lightly sway on their long pink stems,
> side by side, like enormous feathery blossoms,
> seducing (more seductively than Phryne)
>
> themselves; till, necks curling, they sink their large
> pale eyes into the softness of their down,
> where apple-red and jet-black lie concealed.
>
> A shriek of envy shakes the parrot cage;
> but *they* stretch out, astonished, and one by one
> stride into their imaginary world.

THE QUEEN'S GARDEN

Lewis Carroll's conjuring of the flamingo as a substitute croquet mallet is one of the more surreal ways in which the birds have been incorporated into human experience.

One imaginary world where flamingos have featured prominently for many hundreds of years is in the enduring myth of the phoenix. This fictional bird achieved prominence in Western thought through the writings of the Greek historian Herodotus (*c*.484–425 BC), and it has haunted our imaginations ever since. As the author Beryl Rowland notes, 'Few fabulous creatures have any popular currency today, but the phoenix, like its myth, never dies.'[5] On Google the

From its original source in Egypt the myth of the phoenix has expanded its range to include almost all the world. This one is on a door in the Forbidden City in China's capital, Beijing.

word elicits 650 million hits. It is, famously, the motif used by D H Lawrence to encapsulate his literary philosophy. More recently the phoenix has found its way into that modern digest of human fancy, the work of J K Rowling (e.g. *Harry Potter and the Order of the Phoenix*, 2003). At Hogwarts Professor Dumbledore has a pet phoenix called Fawkes.

The fable as told by Herodotus was encountered during his travels in Egypt. 'I have not seen a phoenix myself,' he wrote, '. . . for it is very rare and visits the country (so at least they say at Heliopolis) only at intervals of 500 years, on the occasion of the death of the parent-bird.'

> To judge by the paintings its plumage is partly golden, partly red, and in shape and size it is exactly like an eagle. There is a story about the phoenix; it brings its parent in a lump of myrrh all the way from Arabia and buries the body in the temple of the Sun. To perform this feat, the bird first shapes some myrrh into a sort of egg . . . puts its father inside and smears some more myrrh over the whole . . . finally it is carried by the bird to the temple of the Sun in Egypt.[6]

Other classical writers added a mass of detail to the initial description and subsequent accretions continued even into the modern age. Among the huge miscellany encircling the tale were certain constants, such as the phoenix's eastern origins (Arabia, Ethiopia or sometimes India), its longevity (500–7,006 years), and its return to one particular sacred location for its death and simultaneous restoration to life, invariably achieved in a crucible of flame.[7]

There have been many attempts to link the story of the phoenix to a living bird, and the flamingo was almost unavoidably swept up into the blaze of fancy, partly because of the Greek language. *Phoenix* was the original Greek name for the mythic bird of Herodotus, and *phoinikopteros* (literally 'red-winged') was that for the flamingo. Both names are derived from the same root word (*phoenix*; meaning deep purple or red) but the bird – the phoenix – is not the source of the name for the flamingo. (The Greek survives, of course, more or less intact in the flamingo's scientific name, while

'flamingo' itself derives from Latin – *flama*: 'flame'.)[8] The association between the mythic bird and the flamingo was strengthened when early Christian writers seized on the phoenix as a metaphor deeply redolent of their own religious beliefs about a god who died and was reborn. The striking cruciform outline of the flamingo in flight seemed only to confirm its identity as the real bird behind the story.

Other candidates, however, have been proposed as the source of the myth, including an African bird of prey called the Bateleur, and the Purple Heron, in part because it spans the range of colours supposedly shown by the phoenix. Another contender was the Golden Pheasant, partly for its radiant plumage but also because representations of the phoenix in the Far East, where the myth had a parallel enduring appeal for the Chinese, resembled a galliform such as a pheasant or peacock.[9] These attempts to find a genuine avian identity to fit the phoenix are intriguing and perhaps reflect our own age and its concern to root speculation in rational and material soils. Yet it is the sheer mutability of historical representations of the phoenix that ultimately enable us to understand it more clearly.

The phoenix is a bird whose principal habitat has always been the human imagination. The real constants in the story are not the creature's physical attributes, but rather the idea of its death and resurrection. The phoenix myth endures because it encapsulates a deeply felt human need that somehow an individual being can escape the bounds of mortality and live for ever.

Why this powerful metaphor found expression through the life of a bird is perhaps explained by the mythology of the country in which the phoenix first came to prominence. For the ancient Egyptians the idea of rebirth was a cardinal element in their entire belief system. One may even speculate that the civilisation's absolute dependence upon the annual flow cycles of the River Nile predisposed them to this dominant metaphoric language about death and rebirth. In Egyptian art the idea of rebirth was often represented by a bird named *bnw*. Egyptian hieroglyphic writing had no vowels and it is better known in Western literature as *bennu* or *benu*.

This symbolic bird had prominence in the theology of Heliopolis and occurs in Egyptian papyrus texts such as the *Book of the Dead*. The *benu*, which was identified with Ra the sun god and with Osiris the god of the underworld, became an image of the sun's resurrection in the morning, but also of human reawakening after death. In Egyptian art the bird that used to represent this central idea was a heron, and often specifically the Grey Heron.[10] (Note that the Egyptians distinguished between the metaphoric heron [*benu*] and the real heron that lived on the waters of the Nile, which was called *shenty*.)[11]

Is it perhaps possible, even likely, that Herodotus described (and confused) some of this mythology when he revealed the idea of the phoenix to a wider audience? This is not to propose that the heron is the true phoenix. (Although that claim is regularly made and herons in Egyptian art are sometimes referred to as images of the phoenix.)[12] Rather it is to suggest that the heron-centred ideas of the Egyptians lay behind and unleashed one important Greek representation of the legendary bird. However, the full phenomenon of the phoenix myth is an amalgam of diffuse cultural ideas from many sources, all of which roughly converge in the notion of a bird as an expression of eternal life. The Egyptian heron symbolism served as one ingredient, but the phoenix was a larger imaginative entity into which successive societies poured their own interpretations. And, importantly, we continue to pour meaning into it; even if it serves now only as an advertising slogan for an insurance company, or a fictional character in a children's novel. In a sense our more recent attempts to fix the identity of the phoenix as a flamingo are reflective of some of the deepest impulses of a scientific, rational, materialist society.

If the flamingo did not inspire the phoenix myth, it has certainly long enjoyed a place in human affairs which associate it with heightened rarity and luxury. Nowhere was this expressed more fully than in the classical age. The epicures of ancient Rome ate the birds roasted or boiled, and considered a dish of their pickled tongues a real delicacy. Early volumes on French, Italian and Spanish cuisine all included recipes for flamingo.[13] Judging from the experience of a modern flamingo scholar, one can understand why: 'On opening a freshly dead bird in order to investigate the stomach contents (it was a big male), a friend and I discovered the wonderful meaty breasts the size of a good steak which we fried the same day.'[14] A particularly acquired taste of the epicurean and brutally corrupt emperor Elagabalus (AD *c.*203–222) was flamingos' brains.[15] Others kept the live birds in gardens as a statement of wealth and power, while the emperor Caligula is said to have sacrificed flamingos to his divine self and anointed his body with their blood on the day before he was assassinated.[16]

The bird is still writ large in a number of contemporary landscapes that are synonymous with themes of fantasy, extravagant wealth and, at times, violence. Flamingo colours, motifs and associations are dominant in Florida, particularly along Miami's art deco South Beach, where a proto-Flamingo Hotel was a resort for the super-rich by the 1920s. Nearby at Hialeah Park, the owners of this famous racetrack – 'that boasted private boxes for the Vanderbilts and Kennedys' – incorporated a flock of flamingos into its attractions. One of its best-known races (1926–2001) was actually called the Flamingo Stakes.[17] Southern Florida is one of the very few

US locations where wild American Flamingos can be seen and there is still a feral flock in Hialeah Park – 260 at the last count (2009) – even though the racecourse has now closed.[18]

Yet the part of the USA most familiar with the bird as a motif of luxury is that rarest of all desert blooms, Las Vegas. Before being gunned down by his gangster friends, Benjamin ('Bugsy') Siegel opened a hotel in 1946 furnished with pink leather fittings and a pink neon sign. In so doing he gave rise to a whole dynasty of flamingo-related establishments not just in Nevada's Sin City, but across the USA and even worldwide. Siegel's original building was called The Pink Flamingo Hotel and Casino, but it was subsequently renamed The Fabulous Flamingo, the Flamingo Hilton and now the Flamingo Las Vegas. This last avatar, a 3,626-room structure, has its own flock of Chilean Flamingos (and, at one time, live penguins). The original source of the name is intriguing. Siegel once owned a stake in the Floridan flamingo-adorned racetrack at Hialeah but, while that may have inspired him, credit is usually given to the long legs of his girlfriend, Virginia Hill, whom he nicknamed 'Flamingo'.

In holiday resorts worldwide the flamingo has become a stock motif for grandeur, artifice and perhaps a hint of decadence.

Stork family *Ciconiidae*

The world's 19 stork species are among the Earth's most charismatic birds. Long-legged, long-necked and often black-bodied (or, at least, black-winged) with contrasting white underparts, storks also possess heavy cone-shaped beaks that are invariably black, red or yellow in colour. All of them are large birds: the smallest, the **African Openbill** *Anastomus lamelligerus*, is 60 cm (2 ft), but several of the tallest – the **Jabiru** *Jabiru mycteria* (Latin America), **Greater Adjutant** *Leptoptilos dubius* (India), **Saddle-billed Stork** *Ephippiorhynchus senegalensis* (Africa) and **Black-necked Stork** *Ephippiorhynchus asiaticus* (south Asia and northern Australia) – stand as high as some people (1.5 m: 4.9 ft).

The size is clearly at work in a whole suite of localised names. In Sri Lanka the Black-necked Stork is known as *Ali-kokka*, 'man heron'.[1] In Australia it was once called the 'policeman bird', presumably because of the civil-uniform-like smartness of the pied plumage and the long-striding gait. (Another colloquial alternative for the Australian population of this species is 'jabiru', a name borrowed from its South American relative, which has given title to the town Jabiru in the Northern Territory.) Two Asian species – the Greater and **Lesser Adjutant** *Leptoptilos javanicus* – were named for their resemblance to the strutting military figure of the same rank. Similarly the **Marabou Stork** *Leptoptilos crumenifer* comes from the Arabic *Murabit* for a Muslim holy man or hermit. It is sometimes claimed that the bird itself is considered holy, but this may arise more from the marabou's solitariness and aura of inward contentment, rather than from any genuine spiritual association. Yet certainly in Somalia it is a species of proverbial calmness: '*Sabir Xuureed* means the "patience of a stork" (referring here to the marabou), while *Sabir Xuurleh* is "(He who has) the patience of a stork".'[2]

The habit of ascribing human names to storks has worked equally well in reverse. 'Both Serbs and Croats have a habit of using *roda* (our word for the **White Stork** *Ciconia ciconia*) to describe a particular type of tall, bony woman.'[3] Several other species with bare unfeathered heads are infamous for their raw unappealing looks. In Brazil *jabiru* is a word used to describe an ugly or awkward person.[4] The marabou of sub-Saharan Africa, which is considered a candidate for the world's least-attractive bird, has the same metaphoric place in Somaliland. '*Ali Xuur* – 'Ali the stork' – would imply someone who was tall, skinny and small headed; in other words ugly.'[5]

Storks may vaguely resemble people in size and in their long-legged stride, but they thrive by eating what few humans wish even to touch. Their diet of snakes, lizards, toads, frogs, scorpions, insect pests and rodents is a list of everything we have conventionally loathed. Just as societies long reviled these other creatures as bad, so the human-like birds that cleared them from the landscape were almost inevitably viewed as good. The storks' preference for creatures inimical to human agriculture meant that many communities were in a state of symbiosis or mutualism with the birds for millennia. Only in the twentieth century did that ancient partnership begin to break down.

Before recounting some of our shared history with storks, it is worth exploring their extraordinary diet a little further. The birds are formidable predators, tackling species and even inanimate objects that test credulity. The **Wood Stork** *Mycteria americana* of North and Central America regularly eats baby alligators, while South American Jabirus take young cayman and snakes the size of small anacondas. Some are not even that small. 'On one occasion a gigantic bird standing near me was seen to toss a writhing serpent fully 6 feet . . . into the air, catch it, thrash it on the ground a few times, shake and generally maltreat it before finally placing it on the ground where it was doubtless then torn into segments.'[6]

White Storks have been recorded to devour 44 mice, two hamsters and a frog in one hour. One bird took 25–30 crickets every minute.[7] This last statistic gives insight into their pest-disposal capabilities. For example, in 1987 in Tanzania, 100,000 White Storks and 40,000 **Abdim's Stork** *Ciconia abdimii* were observed feeding on a massive infestation of moth caterpillars known as armyworms.[8] At the cricket-per-minute rate noted above, the Tanzanian flock could eat 230 million armyworms an hour. In fact young storks have been observed at locust swarms where they have consumed so many insects they cannot fly and fall victim to predators themselves.[9]

Perhaps the ultimate in the stork's catholicity of diet is manifest in the three species of the genus *Leptoptilos*. Until their devastation by habitat loss, pesticide use and direct exploitation, the Greater and Lesser Adjutants were urban scavengers with habits closely resembling vultures. The adjutants were habitual residents of Asian cities such as Kolkata (Calcutta), where they could be seen 'on the highest point of almost every home' and where their refuse-disposal services were highly valued.[10] The eccentric miscellany noted in the diet of these two species includes a leg of mutton, maimed ducks or live chickens (swallowed intact), a whole family of live kittens (gulped down one at a time), a shoe well shod with iron and lengths of buffalo vertebral column measuring 30 cm (12 in).[11]

If anything their African relative is more remarkable. The marabou is equipped with a heavy, lethal beak that is credited with an ability to kill children or to pierce elephant hide, with a flock of 200 birds once observed on a single jumbo carcass. In one gulp the stork can tackle chunks of meat weighing 600 g (21 oz) and tear apart and eat a whole adult flamingo in three or four minutes. A measure of its invincible alimentary system is the bird attending a Kenyan abattoir that swallowed a bloody butcher's knife: 'days later the knife, digested spotlessly clean of all blood and residue, was found in the grass nearby, where it had been regurgitated'.[12]

Sadly the world's storks are increasingly emblematic of an older, more unstructured agricultural dispensation and also of an untidier and less intensively managed inner-city landscape. The classic model of a change to modern methods, which brought an attendant slump in stork numbers, is in Assam and Bengal. The Greater Adjutant (the world population is 700–800 birds today) and Lesser Adjutant (5,000 birds) were once present in hundreds of thousands. These scavengers have now joined three other Asian storks – **Milky Stork** *Mycteria cinerea* (6,100), **Storm's Stork** *Ciconia stormi* (250–1,000), and **Oriental Stork** *Ciconia*

boyciana (2,500) – as being among the most threatened birds in the world.[13]

Yet in Africa, at least, storks remain deeply familiar and firmly integrated into the urban landscape. In the Kenyan city of Nairobi breeding marabous are prominent even as one drives from the main airport. The six-lane highway into the heart of the capital has acacia-lined boulevards where their nests cover the treetops. The birds seem as indifferent to the thick diesel fug from endless *mutatu* minibuses as the local residents are tolerant of the stork guano whitewashing the pavements below. On the imposing Nyayo Stadium (Freedom Stadium), even during match days, the tops of the stands are often crowned with the birds' gothic silhouettes.[14] However, our urge for metropolitan tidiness is giving rise to an uneasy relationship with storks and is even starting to impact upon Africa's formerly invulnerable populations. Marabous are habitual in the Ugandan capital, Kampala, but in 2007 nests in trees on downtown traffic islands were cut down and the chicks left to starve.[15]

In many ways the full spectrum of human interactions with storks – both ancient and modern – is most intensely expressed in the recent fate of White Storks in Europe, north Africa and south-west Asia. If this particular bird has suffered some of the most acute pressures from industrialised society, it has also long enjoyed the most exalted status of its family. The attachment, however, is notably absent in those European countries where White Storks do not breed. Vagrant birds in Britain were routinely shot. Yet even in this country the folkloric link between storks and fertility is evident. In 1987 a woman attending a London clinic with her newborn baby noted small red marks on the infant's nape. She was told they were 'stork' marks where the bird carried the child in its beak. 'Don't worry', she was reassured, 'they go in about a year.'[16]

White Storks are also talismans in other parts of their migratory range. One contributor writes:

> In west Kenya White Storks visit the area on their
> southern migration. Every year in November,
> around the third week, we watched for their arrival.
> They would settle overnight in the Kakamega Forest and
> near North Nandi escarpment, and next morning they
> would wait and catch the thermals before disappearing
> high and out of sight. We loved it, and again waited for
> their return, usually in mid March. One African told
> me that when they saw the storks arrive in November, it
> was a sign to start tilling the land (which they did over
> the drier months of December, January and February),
> and when the storks returned, it was time to start
> planting, the long rains usually starting in April / May.[17]

The Greater Adjutant is now threatened with extinction, but at one time the species was an abundant scavenger of east Indian cities.

White Storks and
human fertility are
now permanently
paired in the
European imagination.

Hearty Congratulations.

The underlying elements that explain why this bird is
such a talismanic species in Europe (and elsewhere) include
the fact that it is one of the largest, predominantly white
birds in a region where the lexicon of colour associates white
with purity and virtue. It is also, like other storks, a valuable
ally to the farmer and would have been encouraged regardless
of other associations. Yet, centrally, it is a migrant, moving
between Eurasia and Africa every year. There are few clearer
statements about the annual reawakening of the Earth than
the dramatic spring appearance of great white benign birds
clattering their red bills in nuptial ceremony, while perched
on the roof of the farmhouse or even an inner-city residence.

The White Stork's fertility associations are still widely
felt: 'In Serbia and Croatia a lot of nurseries and playgroups
will either be called *roda* or have the bird in the logo. The
connection between storks and babies is embedded in the
Serbian language too – *roditi* is the verb "to give birth".'[18]

White Storks are not common in Italy but there are
several introduction programmes in the north of the
country and the bird is closely associated with childbirth.
I can think of the pink or light-blue rosettes that people
hang on the door when a baby is born; sometimes there
are images of storks with the name of the baby. There are
also cards with storks to send as congratulations for the
newborn. There are also many nurseries or baby-clothes
shops with *la cigogna* (the Italian name) in the title and I
found online an association for the adoption of children
from Chernobyl (http://www.associazionecicogna.
it/). There is a similar website for people who hope to
become parents and would like to be able to choose the
sex of their baby-to-be.[19]

The Bulgarian belief that storks bring health to people
is at the root of an old ritual. The moment one sees a
stork for the first time in spring, he or she takes off the
martenitza [a special spring adornment made of red and
white yarn] and throws it in the direction of the stork's
flight. People believe that this symbolic exchange will
protect them from illnesses, especially from back pain.
If you greet the storks standing on your feet, your work
on the field will be easy. But if the first time you see the
bird it is perched, then this means languor and tiredness
during the agricultural season. There are still old people
who predict the weather looking at the first storks. If
the wings of the storks are dirty with mud, it means the
year will be rainy. All the Bulgarian myths and beliefs
protect storks. It is forbidden to kill one or destroy a
nest. It is so deep-seated even nowadays. The fact that
every year the stork come to its nest makes it a symbol
of a 'solid' family. If someone destroys a stork nest the
human home will be blighted; the kids will become
orphans, or they will leave home and settle far away.
Because the stork couple is so devoted, it is believed that
storks can be used in a love charm: a girl takes a piece of
straw from the nest to kindle the love of her sweetheart.
There are no beliefs in Bulgarian folklore that storks
bring babies. These birds are only symbols of the spring,
love, health, strength, fertility.[20]

Some of the most profound feeling for the birds and
perhaps the richest body of ancient folklore centred on
storks arose in the German-speaking parts of central Europe.
As early as the fifteenth century the future Pope Pius II
recorded one of the central themes in their attachment, when
he noted how the residents of Basel counted birds nesting
on their houses as an omen of good health and luck. This
benediction was widely considered to confer protection from
the standard medieval hazards – fire, ill health, infertility and
infidelity. In the seventeenth century the historian Johann
Leopold Cysat (1601–1663) noted that around Lake Lucerne
the birds were so revered that anyone who harmed storks
could even be placed under a sentence of death.[21]

It is hardly surprising that throughout large parts of
Europe encouragement has long been given to their nest
building. The full suite of structures and sites exploited by
storks reads like an inventory of all human architecture,
from palaces to factory chimneys and grass huts. Churches,
mosques and other religious buildings are a common
location. One nest taken off a French cathedral weighed
800 kg (1,763 lb), although this is by no means the record.
Successive generations of White Storks can continue using
a site for a century or more. Such super-nests can weigh
2 tonnes and measure 2.5 m (8.2 ft) deep, although the
ultimate nest in terms of longevity is German, 'on a small
tower in Langensalza, Thuringia, which was already inhabited
in 1549 and it still was in 1930 . . . There is an old bill from 1593,
in which a sum is mentioned for the repair and upkeep of this
particular nest, so already at that time people were keeping up
Stork's [*sic*] nests in order to preserve them.'[22]

However, not everyone who hosts the White Stork loves
the birds. This is from a reluctant Spanish landlady:

I have two pairs on our roof, they are beautiful and
spectacular but I hate them! They are a big problem,

they shit on my washing, on my grass, on my car and they are very noisy *clack-clacking* with their bills at night. The biggest problem is that the weight of the nest is cracking our roof and causing cracks in our walls. The 150 euros a year the government gives us for this is not enough and if we remove the nests it is a big offence.[23]

A standard engineered alternative to the rooftop site is the stork nest perched on specially erected poles, which were traditionally capped by disused wagon wheels (now often with old tractor tyres). A postmodern sculptural version of this is the German stork nest resting on a metal girder crowned with that infamous piece of communist transport technology – the Trabant car. A second variation was a site constructed for an injured Danish White Stork in 1968, which was a cartwheel and pole, with a ladder giving the female pedestrian access.[24] This solicitous attention is often met with remarkable tameness on the part of the birds themselves. In the nineteenth century the White Storks of Europe were said to stalk 'about in perfect confidence along the busy streets and markets of the most crowded towns'.[25]

One widely believed preference for which it is more difficult to account was an old notion that storks bred only in republics or countries without sovereigns. No one has explained it but, as the seventeenth-century naturalists John Ray and Francis Willughby found, it was straightforward to disprove: 'this we found to be false, observing them in the Territories of some Princes in *Germany*'.[26] Yet the supposed political preferences shown by the birds occasionally led to their persecution.

The British traveller Charles MacFarlane visiting the Ottoman Empire during the nineteenth century claimed that while the storks:

> built on the mosques, minarets, and Turkish houses, their nests were never erected on a Christian roof. In the Turkish quarters they were met in all directions, strutting about most familiarly, mixing with the people in the streets, but rarely entering the parts of the town inhabited by the Greeks or Armenians, by whom, possibly they may be occasionally disturbed.[27]

It was claimed that in nineteenth-century Smyrna the penalty for any Christian caught killing a White Stork (*leylek* in modern Turkish) was death, and it is interesting to find that this Islamic feeling for storks persists across the border in modern Iran:[28]

> The stork (called *lak-lak* in Iranian) is a very important bird in our culture. I was on vacation in Tabriz city, close to Turkey, and I asked the village people about their beliefs. In the past they used to call it *Haji*. It is a phrase Iranian people use for a person who has travelled to Mecca and who has visited God's House and he or she is a very important religious person. During the months when it was not around, people used to believe that the stork travelled to Mecca.[29]

In the past it was exactly Islamic attachment to storks that helped to explain, in turn, Greek hostility to them during the period of Ottoman Turkish rule in Greece. Several nineteenth-century travellers in the country

The San Miguel Collegiate Church in Alfaro, Spain, serves as both baroque house of God and bustling nursery for Europe's classic symbol of spring – the White Stork.

123

The Marabou Stork has a reputation as the least lovely of all the world's birds.

bird: Lithuania (2009) which has some of the highest stork densities in the world, and Germany, where affection for the bird has deep social roots.

One hot summer after walking with friends across baking fields and ecstatic after spotting White-tailed Eagles, we entered Goldenbaum, a typical east German village. Nothing moved, nothing happened, as usual, except for a stork nest (atop a long pole) with two birds. In a garden opposite sat an old man contemplating life and maybe these village interlopers. We asked him about the two birds and if they were too hot under the sun. He said that the two were young ones waiting for the parents to bring them a snack and they weren't too hot. Heat doesn't bother them, and if it did he wasn't going to climb up and give them suncream.

It struck me how important these birds are to the locals, so much so that they become an integral part of village life. People fret when the birds are late returning from Africa, if it is too cold for the chicks, why nests are abandoned. Village records are proudly kept on the side of barns. Naturally there are bird experts recording and analysing all the data, but most of the interest and quirky observations come from the locals. In essence the birds become a part of the village and keep it alive during the summer months (and even in winter when nests are repaired and restored).[32]

These national gestures have helped galvanise a marked revival in fortunes with an increase in Europe's population from 135,000 to 166,000 pairs by 1995. Although no overall figure is yet available, the picture in Europe and north Africa since that date is of further rapid increase.[33]

One curious boost for the region's White Storks has been the benefits brought by the most recent technological developments. Electricity pylons and telecommunication towers now serve as important nest sites. It is fairly common to see their nests in some European towns crowning both medieval architecture and adjacent satellite dishes. In Armenia in the late 1980s half of all stork nests were on telephone poles or other telegraph-wire supports. Similarly, in Algeria the birds' revival of fortunes has been matched by a switch to pylons by a third of the national population.[34] Unfortunately accidents in which storks crash into the wires are a major source of mortality region-wide.

reiterated the deep feeling for the birds felt among Muslims. One striking act of public charity was an edict issued by the cadi of Ioannina (western Greece), whereby all storks that failed through injury to migrate had to be taken into custody and fed until the following spring. (This echoed practices in Morocco, where there were similar 'hospitals' for storks in Fez and Marrakesh.) During the war of independence Greek soldiers took revenge on this avian emblem of their oppressors, and in Athens Greek liberators shot storks nesting on chimney tops or on ancient monuments. One famous Greek leader, Kolokotronis, on entering Tripoli, ordered a large plane tree used as a nest site by storks to be cut down.

As the author of a study suggests, there were possible sound ecological reasons to explain how people like Charles MacFarlane could construe the storks' preference for Turkish property over that of their Greek subjects. As rulers the Turks would command the tallest buildings (especially the minarets of mosques) and occupy the highest parts of towns (fortifications, etc.) – precisely the places where storks would choose to nest. Equally the large plane trees located in the central squares of many Greek towns were both likely stork-nesting sites and exactly the place for public hangings of Greek opponents to Ottoman authority. Cutting down the stork-haunted gallows, therefore, carried a double political meaning for the Greeks.[30]

Today European storks have acquired a much more benign symbolism almost in direct proportion to their declining ecological fortunes. The species retreated rapidly during the twentieth century as a consequence of intensification; agrochemicals often performing the tasks once done by this avian pesticide. Typical of a widespread collapse in range was the reduction in Denmark of breeding numbers from 4,000 pairs in 1890 to nine in 1991. In Holland the comparable figures were *c.*500 pairs (1910) and fewer than ten (1980). A fall in Spain (14,500 to 6,700 pairs) between 1934–84 represented the most significant national loss in western Europe.[31]

An almost continent-wide response to the disappearance of this cherished bird has been intensive environmental action. Stork reintroduction programmes have occurred, for example, in France, Italy, Germany and Sweden, while two other countries with important populations reinforced their efforts by adopting the stork as their official national

WHITE STORKS
AND THE ISRAELI AIR FORCE
However, the collision with modern technology has had its greatest impact on storks and humans in Israel. More than 2,600 years ago, the prophet Jeremiah noted the regularity of their passage over his country. 'Yea, the stork in the heaven knoweth her appointed times;' he wrote, 'and the turtle and the crane and the swallow observe the time of their coming.' (Jeremiah 8:7) (see also Swift family, page 291). The narrow isthmus of land between the Sinai Peninsula and the Mediterranean, which links Africa to Asia, is a migratory bottleneck through which approximately 600,000 White Storks (85 per cent of the world population) migrate each spring and autumn.

Unfortunately this annual benediction of white birds carries with it a major problem for civil and military aviation in the region, especially the latter, which is accustomed to flying at altitudes used by the migrant flocks. In the last 30 years White Storks and other large passage species, including pelicans and birds of prey, have been involved in approximately 6,600 collisions over Israel. Many have resulted in no or little harm to life or equipment, but 75 strikes resulted in £625,000–£6,250,000 ($1–$10 million) worth of damage to Israeli aircraft. In addition nine fighter planes have been completely destroyed – three of them wrecked by strikes with White Storks – and three pilots have been killed since 1974. Dr Yossi Leshem, the former director of the Society for the Protection of Nature in Israel, pioneered a strategy for reducing the incidence of collisions. As he himself noted, 'If a plane is flying at 1,000 km per hour . . . a ten kilo pelican hits it with the force of a 100 metric tonnes . . . [it is] like taking two tanks and throwing them into the pilot's face.'[35] A somewhat pat observation on the issue is that birds have destroyed more of the Israeli Air Force than any of its enemies in air-to-air combat.

Yossi Leshem's research into migration pathways over Israel and neighbouring countries has led to detailed mapping of the main routes and a halt to military operational flights below 1,000 m (3,281 ft) during the migration season, and to a no-fly policy in what are termed 'Bird-Plagued Areas'. A constant radar-based early warning system on daily movements of migrants now covers the whole of Israel and has paid massive dividends. To date the scheme has led to a 76 per cent reduction in collisions and an estimated saving of £401 million ($646 million) since 1984. In 2007 and 2008 the cost of bird collisions had declined to about £307,000 ($495,000) for each year.[36]

Yossi Leshem's long-term goal is a regional system that involves Egypt, Israel, Jordan, Lebanon, Syria and Turkey, each country notifying its immediate neighbours depending on the season of migration and the direction in which the birds are flying. White Storks and other migrant birds may yet prove to be a source of international trust and cooperation in a region where conventional peace symbols have been in very short supply.[37]

Ibis and Spoonbill family *Threskiornithidae*

Medium-sized to large, with long thick legs and heron-like body shapes, these birds are most notable for their distinctive beaks. Those of the 27 species of ibis are broad-based and sickle-shaped, but the six distinctive family members known as spoonbills have, as their names indicate, a peculiar appendage laterally flattened at the tip like a spatula, that they sweep back and forth through water to sieve out aquatic invertebrates.

Ibis and spoonbills are extremely widespread but show a tendency to be sun-loving, with just ten species occurring north of the 30th parallel (a line of latitude that runs roughly through the USA–Mexico border, northern Egypt, New Delhi and Shanghai). The southern hemisphere – Africa (12 species), South America (ten species) and Australia (five species) – supports all but three of the family. This exclusively northern trio, by contrast, is distinguished by extreme rarity and the threat of extinction. In 2009 their population estimates were 200 for **Giant Ibis** *Pseudibis gigantea* (Cambodia and Laos), 500 **Crested Ibis** *Nipponia nippon* (China and now Japan after a release programme on Sado Island) and 2,041 **Black-faced Spoonbill** *Platalea minor* (China, North and South Korea).

The family is synonymous with fresh water of some kind, including lakes and rivers, but they particularly love that unstable zone where seasonal flooding meets low-lying terra firma. River deltas, wet grasslands and open marshes are favourite habitats. The huge ibis flocks (mainly **White-faced Ibis** *Plegadis chihi* and **Bare-faced Ibis** *Phimosus infuscatus*) that gather on the last pristine pampas of Argentina make these vast grasslands perhaps the last place on Earth where one can have a sense of ibis before the impacts of humankind.

Global loss of untrammelled wetland has led to a decline of many species, yet the birds can still be closely associated with human habitation. The **Hadada Ibis** *Bostrychia hagedash* of sub-Saharan Africa is often a conspicuous bird of towns and inner cities, picking over lawns and flowerbeds, even probing the turf on traffic islands in the middle of

The Hadada Ibis typifies the family's attachment to wetland habitats but also its ability – the strongest among the ibises – to thrive in dense urban centres.

The Sacred Ibis was at the heart of an extraordinary religious cult for the ancient Egyptians.

rush hour. Often referred to simply as hadada or hadeda (pronounced with accent on the second syllable), the bird takes its unusual name from the loud laughing vocalisations, which have conferred cultural associations in many places and also affection: 'My favourite bird sound must be the screaming of the hadada; even though it's not very beautiful (ha-ha-hadada!), but it makes me happy every morning when it wakes me up, knowing I am in Africa again!'[1]

In southern Africa the bird's presence is taken as a good omen.[2] In east Africa, among the Marakwet, the calls of the hadada (known as *kibang'ang'*) are likened to a whining or mischievous child. An infant crying in this way is told to 'quit acting like the kibang'ang'.[3] The **Wattled Ibis** *Bostrychia carunculata*, an endemic to the Ethiopian highlands, has a similar raucous rolling note and in the southern Oromigna-speaking part of the country, the bird is known as *gaganu*; 'the same name is applied to any excessively talkative person!'[4]

The African region where ibises lived in most intimate connection with humans was on the banks of the Nile in Egypt. There they became the subject of one of the most extraordinary interactions between birds and people found anywhere on Earth. The modern name of the key species involved, **Sacred Ibis** *Threskiornis aethiopicus*, indicates the character of this relationship. The species is still widely found throughout sub-Saharan Africa but not, strangely, in Egypt itself. (It may yet re-establish itself in the Mediterranean and even more widely, given the pace of expansion achieved by an introduced Sacred Ibis colony on France's Atlantic coast. From just a handful of released birds, these ibises have multiplied to 1,100 breeding pairs and a total population of over 3,000 since 1975.)[5]

While many may be aware of the ancient reverence once shown towards Sacred Ibis, few will be familiar with the exceptional measures they inspired. Equally few will perhaps appreciate that the word 'ibis' itself originates from the Egyptian language. The ancient name for the bird was *hb(j)* (the written language had no vowel signs), and was spelt as 'ibis' not only in original Greek and Latin, but ever since in English and virtually all other European languages.[6]

Exactly why Egyptians felt such deep attachment to ibises is more difficult to pinpoint.[7] One of the first Western interpretations of ibis worship was by the Greek traveller and author Herodotus. In his *Histories* (*c.*435 BC) he suggested that Egypt was invaded in spring by winged serpents that poured into the country through certain mountain passes. Fortuitously these creatures were met by an army of ibises, which set about eating them.

> According to the Arabians, this service is the reason for the great reverence with which the ibis is regarded in Egypt, and the Egyptians themselves admit the truth of what they say. The ibis is jet-black all over; it has legs like a crane's, a markedly hooked beak, and is about the size of a landrail [corncrake]. That, at any rate, is what the black ibis is like – the kind namely that attacks the winged snakes; there is, however, another sort, more commonly found in inhabited districts; this has a bald head and neck and is white except for the head, throat, wing-tips, and rump, which are jet-black; its legs and beak are similar to those of the black ibis.[8]

Like much in Herodotus, the passage confuses as much as it clarifies. He was correct in suggesting that there was more than a single ibis in Egypt. His all-black species is very probably **Glossy Ibis** *Plegadis falcinellus*, the most widespread of all the family, occurring today on six continents. (The account may also refer to **Northern Bald Ibis** *Geronticus eremita* which is now exceptionally rare [*c.*210 birds] and confined largely to Morocco.) Yet the bird that Egyptians held in highest regard was the larger white Sacred Ibis. Of this species Herodotus does, at least, offer an accurate physical description.

The intriguing detail is the Greek historian's rationale for Egyptian attachment. It is possible that underneath his account of Arabia's winged serpents eaten by ibises on mountain passes is a garbled interpretation of the role which the birds might have played in devouring pests of arable crops. Were the winged serpents actually locusts, as some have suggested? Certainly both Glossy and Sacred Ibises eat swarming locusts, as well as other insects, frogs, snakes and even the eggs of crocodiles.[9]

It is striking how the ancients' perception of the birds as eaters of filth is borne out by field science. The South American species the **Buff-necked Ibis** *Theristicus caudatus*, as well as enjoying rats, spiders, snakes and lizards, can eat the poisonous toad *Bufo granulosus*, which is fatal to most other animals. Another Brazilian ibis, the sumptuously beautiful **Scarlet Ibis** *Eudocimus ruber*, is similarly renowned for its consumption of pests and is kept tame in gardens to dispose of bugs. Its beauty is legendary, but the purity of the bird is proverbial: *limpo como um guará* – 'as clean as a scarlet ibis' – is a Brazilian saying.[10] In South Africa the Hadada Ibis is valued on golf courses for its good offices in clearing out destructive beetle larvae.[11]

Wherever birds benefit humans through their diet or behaviour – our relationships with storks and swallows are excellent examples (see pages 120 and 415) – then those ecological services often underpin deep cultural, even spiritual, attachments. The Greek writer Strabo (64 BC– AD *c.*21) confirmed that ibises were regarded as important refuse-disposal agents – 'they seek out every noxious creature' – and noted how deeply integrated the birds were into domestic urban life ('Every square in Alexandria is full of them'), where they were prominent scavengers outside butchers' shops.[12]

It is intriguing to note that 2,000 years after Strabo's comment the species is true to its calling. One of the sources of rubbish and offal chosen by introduced Sacred Ibises in southern France is a local McDonald's restaurant (from the dustbins outside).[13] (The remarkably similar **Australian White Ibis** *Threskiornis molucca* is a commonplace sight of inner-city Australia, probing the brick-enclosed flowerbeds in the heart of Brisbane's busiest shopping mall, where they are surrounded on all sides by weary shoppers, mobile-phone conversation and even the sonic blare of a brass band. Another common feeding strategy for the species is to dodge about the dozer on the Australian rubbish dump.)

There is a strong likelihood that the Sacred Ibis' predominantly white plumage (see White Stork, page 122) predisposed Egyptians to their reverence. Yet the detail that may have clinched it was the bill. The sickle shape mimicked the sweet curves of a new moon and the ibis was sacred to Thoth, the key lunar deity, god of wisdom, patron of scribes and of secret knowledge. (In Greece Hermes acquired attributes of his Egyptian predecessor; his Roman avatar was

The ibis-headed Thoth was the ancient Egyptian god of wisdom and of the moon.

Mercury.) Thoth was sometimes represented as a baboon, but frequently depicted in ibis form and an ibis hieroglyph was often incorporated into his written name. A curator at the British Museum explains:

> The flexibility of hieroglyphs allowed names, including those of gods, to be written in a variety of ways. A common short form of Thoth is with the Sacred Ibis bird, but it could also be shown as a baboon-sign, or with a phonetic spelling of the consonants (Dj, Hu, t, y) followed by a determinative (whether the ibis or a generic divine determinative). A very typical writing is with the ibis followed by the phonetic complements (t) and (y).[14]

Representations of ibis have been recorded from Egypt's IV Dynasty, more than 4,500 years ago, but it was during a later age, approximately 330 BC–AD 390 (the Ptolemaic and Roman Periods), that their social importance blossomed. Why ibises and other animals became such a central part of religious life in this period is difficult to fathom. One possibility is that as the country became ever more politically dominated by outside powers – Assyrian, Greek, Roman, etc. – its society retreated into cultural practices that stressed its unique indigenous identity. One of these expressions of Egyptian nationalism was animal cults.

They involved a range of religious practices including the sacrifice of animals held sacred to particular deities – cats to the goddess of pleasure, Bast; dogs to Anubis, god of mummification and travel. Following the ceremony the animals were embalmed and stored as mummies as perpetual expressions of religious duty. Salima Ikram, one of the leading experts on animal cults, notes: 'Votive mummies acted much in the same way as the candles purchased and burned in churches, except they were longer-lasting.'[15] Eventually the cults acquired their own community and even an associated industry to service public need. Each had its own priesthood to perform rites and serve as oracles at the shrine. In effect, a supplicant expected divine payback for his or her votive animal in the form of advice, or priestly intervention with the deity to request health, good fortune or to reveal the future. The priests were the mouthpieces for these heavenly communiqués. The animal cults also employed a range of attendant shrine openers and doorkeepers, along with bird keepers who reared, fed and supplied the ibises themselves. There was an ancillary army of embalmers and stewards to manage the offerings and finally to store them in their subterranean catacombs.

Ibises were treated in this fashion at various important temple complexes, including the necropolis at Saqqara (just south of Cairo), Abydos and Thebes (near Luxor), and Tuna al-Gebel, which lies roughly midway between the two modern Egyptian cities, and was close to the ancient town of Hermopolis. These animal cemeteries were nothing short of astonishing. Sanctioned by pharaonic decree, an endless procession of mummified ibises flowed from all over Egypt to the administrative centre at Hermopolis. Beneath the surface temples, and branching off from a series of underground causeways, was a vast complex of subterranean galleries that ran blind into the soft underlying limestone rock. Into these darkened cavities, for more than 700 years, the priests carried ceramic pots filled with ibis remains, embalmed in linen bandages and often smelling of resinous unguents. We know that some of the mummies were still dripping with these fragrant preservatives, because the stairways into the vaults at Tuna al-Gebel are even now stained darkly with the oils.[16]

Despite damage inflicted by grave robbers, time, earthquakes and other vandals there are still hundreds of thousands of embalmed ibises beneath the ground at Tuna al-Gebel. In the animal cemetery at Saqqara to the north there are probably more than 1.5 million mummified birds.[17] It is hard now to appreciate how each of these surviving bundles of rag and dust, which have lain in the silent darkness for more than 2,000 years, bore the fervent hopes of individual living people when the ibis mummies were first interred. Today they are the focus of long-term research programmes that have uncovered startling aspects of the cult.

Around Hermopolis, for instance, there were nearly a dozen captive ibis breeding centres (known as 'ibiotropheia') where the birds were hand-reared to meet religious demands. However, there may at times have been problems with supply, because many mummies have proved to contain merely parts of ibis. Very often there are also bones of completely different birds in the mummies and altogether the desiccated remains of 59 species have been identified at Tuna al-Gebel.[18] Occasionally there are few real bird parts at all, except bits of feather or just dried grass (presumably from nests). The assumption is that when the embalmers removed birds from pits where they had been placed to reduce them to skeletons, they took anything that was present and, unable to identify

one bird bone from another, simply bundled it up for transfer to Tuna al-Gebel. It suggests that the symbolism of the act was everything, rather than specific anatomical accuracy. Or perhaps the paying supplicants were simply victims of that time-honoured vice: religious fraud. Some wrapped bundles found in the ibis cemetery have proved to contain parts of three cats, small bits of fish, a single Glossy Ibis bone, the skull of a mongoose and some birds of prey.[19]

How should we perceive Egypt's ibis cult? The elaborate measures involving mummification and storage of ibises at centres such as Tuna al-Gebel now seem otherworldly and bizarre, if not completely incomprehensible. Yet are they really that distinct from our own behaviour? The annual rearing, slaughter, distribution and consumption of hundreds of millions of turkeys – even the ceremonial pulling of its furcula (better known as the wishbone and, once, the 'merry thought') in the crook of a little finger – are taken for granted across large parts of the Western world as essential components of Christmas formalities (yet not everywhere; see Turkey Traditions in Europe, page 42).

These modern rituals involve birds in what seems now a much more straightforward, practical role of physical consumption, but nonetheless there is a symbolic associative element in the specific choice of the turkey. The ancient Egyptians would no doubt have counter-argued that their ibis served functions that were entirely practical. Filtered through their own cultural norms, the elaborate bird-centred practices furthered both their social and personal well-being in a manner not too different from the ritualised eating of a bird at the communal table. They may even have suggested that their ibis use had an intrinsically more important purpose: permitting direct communion with divine power.

The symbolic incorporation of ibis into their religious life certainly reflected the way in which Egyptians placed natural phenomena, such as the sun, moon, etc., and native species – Egyptian Cobra, crocodile and vultures – at the heart of their most exalted beliefs and ideals. This cultural celebration of the natural world closely chimes with values expressed by modern environmentalists. There may have been a gulf between the reverence for the symbolic bird and the often brutal treatment of real ibises, yet we should recall that turkey rearing today shows few advances on methods once practised on the banks of the Nile. We might also surmise that the cult probably had little overall effect on native ibis populations, since most of the votive birds came from captive-breeding stock. Wild ibises, by contrast, were shielded from harm by order of the pharaoh – perhaps the first protective legislation for any bird species on Earth – which made it a capital offence to kill them.[20] Ironically the Sacred Ibis did become extinct in Egypt but for unknown reasons and only during the modern era, in about the 1850s.

The Egyptian cult of the ibis has left its legacy in our scientific age, firstly in the name of the Sacred Ibis, but also in the title of the journal for the British Ornithologists' Union. The *Ibis* reached its 150th birthday in 2009. Thoth was, of course, a bird god of knowledge and wisdom.

Heron and Bittern family *Ardeidae*

The 65 species of heron and bittern range from the pocket-sized American **Least Bittern** *Ixobrychus exilis*, which is no bigger than a street pigeon, to the African **Goliath Heron** *Ardea goliath*, a bird that stands over 1.5 m (4.9 ft) and is as tall as some adult humans. The family includes some of the most widespread, best-known large birds in the world, but herons have also long commanded our attention for their beauty. One aspect cementing their appeal is a frequent aura of inner poise. The classic mode of hunting among this predominantly fish-eating family is to wade or wait at the water's edge, where the birds' physical stillness suggests an almost spiritual quietude; at least, until the moment of that final lethal strike.

However renowned the birds might be for their refinement, they can at times suggest diametrically opposite qualities. As one ornithologist noted, their breeding sites can be the source of a 'constant cacophony of croaks, growls and other coarse sounds'.[1] Equally, herons can appear laboured and even clumsy in their actions. In his tragic novel *Tess of the d'Urbervilles*, the author Thomas Hardy perfectly captures the same machine-like awkwardness in herons when the birds are encountered by Tess and her suitor, Angel Clare, as they savour their brief summer of love at Talbothays farm. Hardy gives us not only the mechanical heron but, lest we forget, also the exquisite grace of his heroine (she is depicted at dawn with 'minute diamonds of moisture from the mist' upon her eyelashes and hair 'like seed pearls').

At these non-human hours they could get quite close to the waterfowl. Herons came, with a great bold noise as of opening doors and shutters, out of the boughs of a plantation which they frequented at the side of the mead; or, if already on the spot, hardily maintained their standing in the water as the pair walked by, watching them by moving their heads round in a slow, horizontal, passionless wheel, like the turn of puppets by clockwork.[2]

The American author and naturalist Henry Thoreau noted similar toilsome characteristics in the movements of two heron species near his home at Concord, Massachusetts. In flight the birds often have a ponderous rhythmic wingbeat and Thoreau wrote of the **American Bittern** *Botaurus lentiginosus* 'digging his way through the air' and 'plowing the air with the coulter of his breast-bone'. Of the even heavier **Great Blue Heron** *Ardea herodias* he noted: 'It was a grand sight to see them rise, so slow and stately . . . They are large . . . and seemed to oppress the earth, and hush the hillside to silence, as they winged their way over it.'[3]

Perhaps the most aesthetically captivating of all the family is a range of medium-sized, rather attenuated, usually all-white herons in the genus *Egretta*, whose 14 members are spread across all continents (except Antarctica). Known mainly as egrets in English, they frequently nest at communal sites and can be observed in large aggregations. One modern

The Eurasian Bittern was once an omen of doom; now it is a symbol of wetland conservation.

For the Japanese, images of egrets and lotus blossoms have implicit associations with summer and fertility.

egrets' wetland associations the compound metaphor has ecological veracity, but it also evokes the idea of human copulation. In Japan the symbolism may be less explicitly sexual, but the birds are frequently painted in conjunction with hibiscus or other flowers which, like the birds, are emblems of summer and fertility. This conjunction of motifs occurs in a poem, 'Egrets', by the Chinese poet Du Mu (AD 803–853):

> Snowy robes and snowy hair,
> beaks of darkest jade:
> A flock of them go catching fish
> in reflections on the stream.
> Startled, they fly, set far against
> the green hills as they leave –
> A tree's worth of pear blossoms
> scatters in the evening breeze.

A particularly captivating representation of egrets (and crows) appears on a nineteenth-century Japanese wooden box used for holding letters or poetry, which is housed in the British Museum, London. The egrets are rendered in crushed eggshell, the crows painted in black lacquer (with mother-of-pearl eyes) and are designed so that one occupies the negative space left by the other's outline. This alternating pattern makes it challenging for the eye to retain a sense of both species simultaneously. The temptation is to assume that the artist's intention was a reconciliation of opposite values associated with the birds – black and white, day and night, good and bad, ying and yang, etc. Unfortunately the traditional Japanese symbolism attaching to the two species may not quite fit that interpretation, and perhaps the work is no more than a witty visual conceit.

PRACTICAL HERONS

As well as serving as a perpetual source of metaphor and image, herons have long played practical roles for humans. None is perhaps more straightforward nor more widespread than their consumption as food. In Britain and more widely in Europe **Grey Heron** *Ardea cinerea* was a classic bird of the civic banquet, although this may well have lapsed because of its increasingly dubious culinary reputation. Yet throughout the early modern period landowners were known to manage heron breeding colonies in order to make 'good profit of the young'.[8] Roast heron survived as a country dish well into the nineteenth century.

Similarly in Sind, in southern Pakistan, a caste of fisherfolk known as the Mohanas used herons in multiple ways. They kept Grey and **Purple Heron** *Ardea purpurea* tethered to their boats and ate the birds as a delicacy until the late twentieth century. (One wonders if they still do?)[9] Even more intriguing is their deployment of herons as decoys in their fowling operations (they also used pelican skins for the same purpose). Quite how the herons facilitate a close approach to other waterbirds is not clear – and may never have been studied – but it is a technique which is thousands of years old. In *The Birds of Ancient Egypt*, Patrick Houlihan writes: 'There is scarcely a scene in Egyptian art picturing the pursuit of the fowlers in the swamps that does not include at least one of these tamed aquatic birds wading in the shallows alongside of their clap-nets.'[10]

Western recreational anglers also tried to harness herons to their cause, but in much more symbolic ways. For

ornithologist, writing of South American species, suggests that, 'Few sights in the world of birds are as memorable as a flock of egrets passing . . . the backdrop of a setting sun.'[4]

Egrets are particularly important and auspicious in the cultures of China and Japan, where they are a recurring motif both in literature and in the visual arts. The immaculate appearance of the white birds lends them associations with Buddhist purity. Often they are placed in conjunction with other emblems of flawlessness such as snow-capped peaks. The patience manifest in the egret's feeding strategy even suggests the solitude and inwardness of meditational practice.[5] A Chinese contributor writes: 'In my language the character for "egret" sounds the same as those for "road" and for "salary", cementing the bird's associations with both the future and with material fortune.'[6]

The slender form of the egret also has additional phallic associations for the Chinese. The composition of paintings or embroidered images often places the birds in association with a feminine sexual symbol, the lotus flower.[7] Given the

instance, an oil distilled from heron fat was rubbed on the worm by fishermen in the assumption that it would enhance the effectiveness of the bait. (In Europe an oil made from the **Great Egret** *Ardea alba* had alternative use: it was said to cure wind.)[11] A fall-back strategy was to keep a heron's foot in a pocket as a good luck charm. This may have been an adaptation of an even older British practice that involved the long hind claw of **Eurasian Bittern** *Botaurus stellaris*. The appendage was apparently set in silver and carried as a reusable toothpick. [12]

HERONS AND THE FEATHER INDUSTRY

There is one other pre-eminent use of herons that could, with some justification, be said to have changed the world: the wearing of heron feathers as a part of female costume. It is perhaps in keeping with Marie Antoinette's wider status as the epitome of amoral frivolity that she has a lead part in the story of how feathered headgear became a global fashion. Legend has it that the French queen happened to draw compliments one night from Louis XVI for a nice arrangement of ostrich and peacock plumes in her hair. The Versailles court noted the royal approval and a craze was born almost overnight. Eventually the feather displays on the tops of their heads were so absurdly elaborate that women of style, to avoid spoiling them, had to ride in their carriages kneeling or with their coiffures out the window.[13] The passion for plumes and other bird-part adornments continued to expand throughout the nineteenth century, until an almost complete collapse in the market at about the time of the First World War (1914–18).

The most prized feather during the entire period was the extravagant bushy plume taken from adult male ostriches, which were eventually farmed in South Africa on an industrial scale to supply the global demand (see Ostrich family, page 18). Yet there was also a parallel market in wild birds, and the species at the forefront of this were the various white egrets. With the onset of the breeding season the birds acquire an array of lacy filamentous back feathers, which are known technically as scapulars. The Indian ornithologist Salim Ali aptly described these diaphanous plumes as spreading 'out in "showers"' like 'a halo of mist'.[14] Among the millinery workers and traders in the business, the very same feathers were known as 'aigrettes', the French name for the birds themselves. (Bizarrely, an alternative was 'osprey' because of a mistaken belief that the fish-eating raptor was a prime source.)

The fundamental linkage between the beautiful white birds and the standard jargon of the plume trade expressed the heron family's centrality in the entire history and development of the industry. In turn, the popularity of aigrettes in the fashion salons of Manhattan or London's West End launched a veritable holocaust of collecting and killing on the breeding grounds of herons almost across the entire world.

The tale of the trade's impact is now embedded in the wider history of the environmental movement and is well summarised in books such as Robin Doughty's thorough and exact *Feather Fashions and Bird Preservation* (1975). The details he recounts take their place alongside a suite of other horror stories about human exploitation of natural resources. The various episodes of what might be termed industrialised slaughter fall roughly within a hundred-year period after

1850, and include the near-extinction of the American Bison, the total extermination of Passenger Pigeons – once the most abundant bird ever to have lived (see page 241) – the world collapse of tigers (for sport) and African Elephants (for ivory), as well as a string of sea-borne quests for animal oil, fur and flesh that decimated the world's seals, penguins (see page 95) and the great whales.

What is most extraordinary about all of them is not just the scale of the killing, but the apparent nihilism, the seemingly complete disregard for any sustainability in the harvest. Perhaps we should see these episodes in the same

To the ancient Egyptians the heron was a real bird of the Nile marshes (*shenty*) but also a bird of the soul (*benu*) that is sometimes thought to have given rise to the myth of the phoenix (see also Flamingo family, page 119).

We hope to show you our line of
Fall and Winter Millinery
which is now ready
Miss Mary Lehr
Main 322   1700 W. 25th St.

The demand for feathers in female hat fashions launched a worldwide slaughter of herons in the late nineteenth century but also gave rise to the modern environmental movement.

In the nineteenth century bird feathers were so sought after that these lacy plumes on a Great Egret were worth twice their weight in gold.

light as we now partly view the key human conflict of the same period, the First World War. It was essentially a failure of political or moral authority to understand, let alone control, the new technologies of death and destruction that had recently been acquired. Forces were set loose upon the Earth like the uncontrollable powers of a sorcerer's apprentice.

In a similar manner the wanton killing of birds for hats involved a failure to foresee how rapidly or how completely birds breeding in some of the world's most remote wilderness could be killed using the latest weaponry and then inserted into international networks of transportation and economic activity. (To give just one brief indication of the trade's global tentacular reach, between 1899 and 1912 the feathers from an estimated 3–15 million herons were exported alone from Argentina, Brazil and Venezuela.)[15] Without exonerating anyone from responsibility, we should perhaps concede that neither the hunters, nor the traders, nor the female customers who placed feather hats on their heads could quite appreciate the carnage they had unleashed on the world's birds.

There is no way now of measuring the total slaughter except in the roundest possible figures. Yet the sheer tonnage of feathers – a conjunction that seems almost a contradiction in terms – moving between the far corners of the Earth and the centres of the plume industry – London, New York and Paris – has its own brutal eloquence. Between 1870 and 1920, 18,400 tonnes of wild bird feathers were imported

into Britain. In France (between 1890 and 1920) the figure was 45,360 tonnes, although this number probably included commercially farmed ostrich.[16] The USA measured imports only in cash value, which gives less insight into the scale of slaughter, but between 1891 and 1910 the figure was $16,975,000 (approximately $354 million today).[17] At the height of the industry a single ounce (28 g) of top-quality feathers was worth $30, twice the value of gold.[18]

Some sense of bird numbers killed is possible if you realise that a single Great Egret, the biggest of the group of white herons, yielded just 40–50 aigrettes. To the hunters who decimated this beautiful creature the species was known simply in commodity terms – as 'the long white' – and it required an estimated 150 Great Egrets to produce 1 kg (2.2 lb) of long whites. (Other authors argue that it took twice as many, 300 adult birds, to harvest 1 kg.) Thus, a tonne represented a minimum of 150,000 Great Egrets. Of the far smaller (American) **Snowy Egret** *Egretta thula* or the (Eurasian and African) **Little Egret** *Egretta garzetta*, it may have required a straight million corpses to accumulate the same amount of feathers.

This, of course, was the visible harvest, but each aigrette implied a secondary chain of fatality. Plumes were at their best at the height of the nuptial season and each adult breeding egret shot usually left a nestful of failed eggs or chicks. To get a crude sense of total mortality, one could perhaps simply double the figure. That is 2 million Little Egrets for every tonne, or 300,000 Great Egrets.

One needs also to bear in mind that the species involved in the hat-plume industry spanned the entire class of birds, from hummingbirds weighing 1–2 g, to huge storks, cranes and even vultures. In an impromptu census on the streets of New York, the eminent American ornithologist Frank Chapman found that 75 per cent of 700 hats included feathers. These had come from at least 40 native species. Nor were the feathers just in the hats. Gowns might have their hems trimmed in swallow wings or the heads of finches.[19] The overall numbers of birds killed to let women think themselves stylish is probably in the billions, while the numbers of herons killed is estimated in the hundreds of millions.[20]

As the author Jennifer Price has noted it is quite remarkable, given the other pressing issues of the age – deforestation, water pollution, etc. – that it was the fight to end this abuse of herons and other birds that triggered the formation of a new environmental community. Lobbying to end the whole business began as early as the 1860s, but it did not achieve its larger goals until the early decades of a new century. Important legal changes on both sides of the Atlantic required 30 years of sustained social agitation. In the USA there had been piecemeal state-based bills to limit the killing of birds and trade in their plumes, but these regional initiatives were given federal reinforcement with the Lacey Act of 1900 and finally by the Tariff Act of 1913. This last bill included a clause prohibiting finally all US importation of wild bird plumes. In Britain the same level of sanction did not come until after the First World War and royal assent to the Importation of Plumage (Prohibition) Bill (1921).

Establishing a framework of protective legislation that safeguarded wild herons and shut down the plume trade was by default a male preserve since their married partners had no vote. Yet the more enduring social movements which had lobbied so long and hard to secure these legal ends can be seen as largely female initiatives. A striking aspect of the story of feather fashions is the centrality of women, not just to its origins, but also to its demise. This dimension is all the more noteworthy given the marginal political status enforced upon their gender during the same period.

A classic symptom of this was the frequent reference to the key female figures of early conservation only by their husbands' names. Yet typical of the remarkable (and also remarkably long-lived!) women who fought and defeated the plume trade were Harriet Hemenway (1858–1960), founder of the Massachusetts Audubon Society in 1896; Margaretta Louise Lemon (1860–1953), secretary for 47 years of the UK's Society for the Protection of Birds; and Winifred Dallas-Yorke, the Duchess of Portland (1863–1954), who was that organisation's president for 65 years. Nor was it simply a case of the efforts made by a small coterie of high-born ladies. Eighty per cent of the membership and half the leadership for the various new state Audubon societies that proliferated after Hemenway's inaugural Massachusetts branch were female.[21] In a little over 30 years these redoubtable women laid the foundations for two of the world's most important wildlife NGOs, the National Audubon Society and the RSPB, with respective modern memberships of 800,000 and 1.1 million. In 1922 they joined a federation of global partners that became the International Committee for the

Protection of Birds. Today it is called BirdLife International, the organisation that has aided this book.

THE RANGE EXPANSION OF THE CATTLE EGRET

With the cessation of hunting pressure in the early twentieth century most herons rebounded from the years of devastation. Yet one in particular, the **Cattle Egret** *Bubulcus ibis* which had been only marginal to the plume trade, not only recovered, but benefited from deliberate human attempts to widen its distribution. The bird has an ancient feeding relationship with large grazing mammals: it accompanies the animals to snatch invertebrates stirred up by their movement. Scores of Cattle Egrets can dash in and out the path of a single set of trampling hooves. In Africa massive flocks sometimes attend wild buffalo herds, even indicating to safari-style tourists where they might find them. In the nineteenth century the birds were credited with a more baleful role – helping elephant poachers to find their victims.[22]

Ranchers encouraged their attendance on domestic stock because it was widely believed that the egrets picked parasites off the animals' bodies. Indeed, Cattle Egret was known as the 'tick-bird' in many countries.[23] Nor were the assumed benefits restricted to cattle. Studies in Egypt suggest that three-quarters of the bird's diet comprises

In large parts of the world there is hardly a domestic herd or a group of wild ungulates that doesn't have its attendant flock of Cattle Egrets ready to snatch insects from under the trampling hooves.

insects harmful to agriculture. Its Egyptian name is *Abuu Qurdaan*, although in most Arabic-speaking countries the bird is *Sadeeg Almuzareh* (both apparently mean 'friend of the farmer').[24] A locust swarm in Tanzania once attracted what must have seemed a heaven-sent rainstorm of white birds that included 40,000 mixed egrets.[25] Another of the bird's specialities is the city dump and other places of human waste, even slaughterhouses, where they associate with vultures or crows and feed on the superabundance of insects. Their immaculate plumages can often become heavily soiled with urban grime.

It was once assumed that the benefits of Cattle Egrets led to them being actively introduced into South America in the early twentieth century. In fact their arrival was probably a natural range extension (as early as the 1880s), although benign responses from farmers can only have helped what has since become a global expansion. Cattle Egrets are now widespread on six continents and it must be a candidate for the most successful heron on Earth.[26]

Not all have been so fortunate. The **Chinese Egret** *Egretta eulophotes*, once a beneficiary of the deep cultural attachments shown towards egrets in the Far East, became one of the easiest to kill during the worst years of the plume trade, because it had long been encouraged to nest above temples or in town gardens. In the late nineteenth century profit triumphed over those ancient cultural responses and Chinese Egrets were hounded relentlessly. Sadly the species has never truly recovered and is still classified as vulnerable to extinction.

BITTERNS AND THE BIBLE

Some of the most distinctive of all the herons are the four species in the genus *Botaurus*: American Bittern, North and Central America; **Australasian Bittern** *Botaurus poiciloptilus*, Australia and New Zealand; Eurasian Bittern, Europe and Asia, wintering in Africa; **Pinnated Bittern** *Botaurus pinnatus*, Central and South America. The quartet is characterised by large size (76 cm: 30 in), highly secretive behaviour and rather dull buff-brown plumages overlaid with complex vermiculations that confer an almost magical gift for invisibility on the birds.

Another shared feature is the male bittern's strange, even unearthly, vocalisations, which have inspired universal responses. The sound is a short, repeated, far-carrying moan-like hoot that is often described as a 'boom', and is frequently compared to a cow's lowing. (Each male's individual boom is subtly different and in Eurasian Bitterns the vocal musculature producing the sound can be one-fifth of the bird's total body weight.) *Botaurus* means to 'roar like a bull'. The Australasian Bittern was once known as 'bull-bird', the Eurasian Bittern as 'bull o' the bog' (in Scotland), while the American Bittern is called *Ave torro* ('bull bird') in many parts of Latin America.[27] In Brazil the Pinnated Bittern is called *Socó-boi-baio*; the words *boi-baio* roughly translate as 'buff bullock'.[28]

The bitterns are also birds with great gifts for ventriloquy. Henry Thoreau paid careful attention to the call of the American Bittern, noting how, after hearing one, 'I immediately went in search of the bird, but, after going a third of a mile, it did not sound much nearer, and the two parts of the sound did not appear to proceed from the same place.'[29] This seemingly disembodied and fundamentally

inhuman noise was long steeped in mystery and inspired fear or the persecution of bitterns in many parts of the world. To some it signified the imminence of death or doom. Australian Aborigines, for instance, told early colonial settlers that it was the sound of a marsh-dwelling, 'blackfellow-eating monster known as "bunyip"!'[30] Similarly in Europe there is an apocryphal fifteenth-century tale of an army led by King John II of Aragon engaging in battle at Amposta near Spain's Ebro Delta and then retreating in terror at the sound of the Eurasian Bittern's boom.[31] It is also on account of the bird's forbidding reputation that it found its way erroneously into the Old Testament.

The details are deeply illuminating. In the Book of Isaiah the text describes God's wrath upon Edom for its inhabitants' part in the capture of Israel. The Edomites, occupying a region south of the Dead Sea, were to be visited with destruction, and in the *King James* version of the Bible, the text outlines the ornithological consequences of this desolation:

> But the cormorant and the bittern shall possess it; the owl also and the raven shall dwell in it: and he shall stretch out upon it the line of confusion, and the stones of emptiness. (Isaiah 34:11)

In the Book of Zephaniah parallel prophesies of catastrophe were made on the consequences of Assyria's moral corruption:

> And he will stretch out his hand . . . and destroy Assyria; and will make Nineveh a desolation, *and* dry like a wilderness. . . . both the cormorant and the bittern shall lodge in the upper lintels of it; *their* voice shall sing in the windows . . . (Zephaniah 2:13–14)

The translations made by the seventeenth-century authors of the *King James Bible* are now deemed in error, most explicitly in the rendering of Zephaniah. The consequences of desertification could never be an invasion of wetland birds such as the cormorant or bittern. There are two possible explanations for them citing the 'wrong' species. Either the authors calculated that the wetland birds, though technically inaccurate, would strike the right emotional note because they had sinister reputations among a northern European audience. Or, much more likely, it is a classic case of a British mindset projecting its own experience, falsely and unwittingly, upon the original Middle Eastern texts. The English-speaking scholars mistranslated the bird names given in the original biblical source because bitterns and cormorants were the birds of ill omen with which they were familiar.

However, the original authors of the Old Testament knew much more intimately the real ecological context of civilisation between the rivers Tigris and Euphrates in ancient Mesopotamia. These city-states were entirely dependent on the river systems supplying the key deficit of such a desert environment. The way to bring ruin to these places was water's withdrawal. Desertification, not flood, was exactly the background to send forth the horned owl or the ruffed bustard into Edom and Assyria. It is these alternative desert species that now appear in the translations used in *The New English Bible*, commissioned and written in the mid twentieth century.

Tropicbird family *Phaethontidae*

These three elegant, predominantly white seabirds are well named, occurring in a broad band around the Earth's middle latitudes and coming to shore in many hot countries of Africa, Asia, the Pacific, and South and Central America, causing them to feature in scores of national field guides. Yet for much of the year tropicbirds are essentially creatures without country – inhabitants of anonymous open stretches of ocean.

Early names for the family were plainly coined by seamen. 'Boatswain' or 'Bo'sun bird' was meant to draw on their sharply whistled calls, 'like the trilling of boatswain's pipe'.[1] Even the scientific name touches on nautical matters: Phaëthon was the son of Apollo who, unable to control the sun god's gleaming chariot, careered into the deep. Another archaic vernacular version – 'marlin-spike' – continues a maritime theme, but also emphasises the tropicbirds' singular outstanding feature.

The adults have massively elongated central tail feathers, which can equal or even exceed their entire body length (the largest species, **Red-billed Tropicbird** *Phaethon aethereus*, found in the Caribbean, west Atlantic and east Pacific, is 48 cm: 18.9 in without and up to 106 cm: 42 in with its streamers.) These ribbon-like feathers give tropicbirds a lithe, sinuous, even ethereal and occasionally fantastical quality, especially when the birds are in sexual display, which is characterised by steep dives and chases. Even in normal flight tropicbirds are creatures of huge aesthetic appeal.

A passage by the great American seabird specialist Robert Cushman Murphy evokes the character but also the sudden unexpected beauty of tropicbirds:

After weeks . . . in tropical blue waters where birds are scarce, the voyager may sometimes be electrified by hearing the shrill whistle of the Boatswain-bird. Looking aloft, he may see . . . a pair of the gleaming, long-tailed creatures passing high in air on steadily and rapidly beating wings. On such occasions . . . the visitors are likely to show a certain brief curiosity in the ship, and will turn off their course in order to fly in an oval orbit around it once or twice before streaking away like animate comets. They are well named after Phaëthon, the son of Apollo, who hurtled from the far sky into the sea. I remember the July day long ago when, at a point to eastward of Martinique but out of sight of land, I first saw one of a pair of Red-billed Tropic-birds dive from the height of the 'Daisy's' masthead into the quiet, transparent water. For several seconds it remained below and, after reappearing, shook a shower of pearls from its feathers, rested at the surface with wings spread and raised, and tail plumes cocked up, and finally leaped into the air as lightly as a tern.[2]

The birds' gorgeous plumes have long inspired cupidity in humans of all cultures. In the **Red-tailed Tropicbird** *Phaethon rubricauda* the feathers even come with a crimson stripe. During the great Victorian vogue for hat feathers, tropicbirds were much desired and slaughtered. In Polynesia they also had similar cachet, the streamers being worn as a head plume or through a pierced nasal septum. In the Pacific, however, they plucked the feather without killing the bird.[3]

This sixteenth-century image by the Englishman John White is one of the earliest Western illustrations of a Red-billed Tropicbird.

Frigatebird family *Fregatidae*

The five species in this family of tropical seabirds are as variable in plumage as they are problematic to separate. One noted marine-bird specialist suggested that they are 'perhaps, the most difficult identification challenge in any seabird group'.[1] Adults have dark oily-black plumages with variable strengths and tones of iridescence, but sub-adults possess a bewildering array of essentially pied patterning so that two birds seldom, if ever, look the same.

In terms of movement frigatebirds have the lithe, supple aerial grace of giant terns, but in overall shape they possess some of the angular menace of flying pterodactyls. The long arched wings – up to 2.5 m (8.2 ft) in **Magnificent Frigatebird** *Fregata magnificens* – have the greatest surface area proportional to weight of any bird. Yet strangely the family lacks the oil gland which confers waterproofing on the plumage. Frigatebirds can thus spend weeks at sea, sometimes hundreds of kilometres from shore, yet never land and they even sleep on the wing. One frigatebird fitted with a satellite transmitter made a non-stop 26-day 4,000 km (2,500 mile) return journey to Christmas Island in the Indian Ocean, travelling via Sumatra, Borneo and across Java, and probably never ceased flying in the entire 624 hours.[2]

The low wing-loading and consummate manoeuvrability are adaptations to a kleptoparasitic lifestyle, in which they chase and harry other seabirds until they regurgitate their catch. Pelicans and boobies are regular victims. Although the birds also find food for themselves, plucking it off the sea surface with dextrous skill, their particular technique of robbery with menace has often been highlighted by human observers. Christopher Columbus, himself not averse to taking what belonged to others, noted the behaviour in 1492; the first European ever to do so. Prior to their present name, frigatebirds were often known as 'man o' war birds', which carries similar associations of ocean-going speed and violence. Even early ornithological texts found it difficult to resist morally charged descriptions ('well known buccaneer' . . .'a pirate and a freebooter') yet the quality few have failed to highlight is the frigatebirds' astonishing aerial grace ('the

admiring observer . . . longs for the eloquence to describe it; but words are powerless to convey the impression that it creates.')[3]

Words are powerless, unless chosen by a great poet.

> Thou who hast slept all night upon the storm,
> Waking renew'd on thy prodigious pinions,
> (Burst the wild storm? Above it thou ascended'st,
> And rested on the sky, thy slave that cradled thee,)
> Now a blue point, far, far in heaven floating,
> As to the light emerging here on deck I watch thee,
> (Myself a speck, a point on the world's floating vast.)
>
> Far, far at sea,
> After the night's fierce drifts have strewn the shore with
>   wrecks,
> With re-appearing day as now so happy and serene,
> The rosy and elastic dawn, the flashing sun,
> The limpid spread of air cerulean,
> Thou also re-appearest.
>
> Thou born to match the gale, (thou art all wings,)
> To cope with heaven and earth and sea and hurricane,
> Thou ship of air that never furl'st thy sails,
> Days, even weeks untired and onward, through spaces,
>   realms gyrating,
> At dusk that look'st on Senegal, at morn America,
> That sport'st amid the lightning-flash and thunder-cloud,
> In them, in thy experiences, had'st thou my soul,
> What joys! What joys were thine!

Walt Whitman's poem 'To The Man-Of-War-Bird' contains mannered archaisms ('thou ascended'st'), showy alliteration ('prodigious pinions') and poetic embellishment ('At dusk . . . Senegal, at morn America'), but it still beautifully captures a frigatebird's mastery of wind and thermal. It also distils that strange atmosphere of calm after a night of storm ('rosy and elastic dawn') when the almost miraculous reappearance of frigatebirds – as if nothing had really happened – allows one to appreciate even more emphatically what incredible powers of flight they possess. (In the Caribbean, where it is the Antiguan national bird, an old name for the Magnificent Frigatebird was 'hurricane bird'.) Yet for succinct precision on the family's aerial gifts, there is perhaps nothing more perfect in the English language than Herman Melville's closing couplet in his poem 'The Man-of-War Hawk':

> No arrow can reach him; nor thought can attain
> To the placid supreme in the sweep of his reign.

The place where frigatebirds have had their deepest impact on human cultures is in the Pacific, especially in the Solomon Islands, but also in other neighbouring groups, such as the Kiriwina (also known as the Trobriand) Islands, made famous through the work of the great Polish anthropologist Bronisław Malinowski. Both archipelagos lie east of Papua New Guinea.

The seven large forested volcanic islands and array of outlying atolls and islets which make up the Solomons are inhabited predominantly by Melanesians speaking at least 60 languages. Across this cultural complex, the **Lesser**

The frigatebird is a creature of great symbolism in the western Pacific. Some wooden carvings, such as this from the Trobriand Islands, are so schematised they are barely recognisable as birds.

Frigatebird *Fregata ariel* and **Great Frigatebird** *Fregata minor* have enjoyed important symbolic status because of their deep association with bonito tuna. Between March and June these large striped fish, which are integral to the islanders' diet and economy, are at the heart of an extraordinary marine event. Bonito pursue smaller fish shoals and as they feed in frenzied fashion, churning the sea surface, so they often draw in a menacing penumbra of hungry sharks and an overhead swarm of clamorous seabirds, including many frigates. One speciality of the latter is to seize flying fish when they take to the air to flee the jaws below.

Western writers have found it difficult to put a precise symbolic value on the Solomon Island use of frigatebird imagery, suggesting it may have multiple meanings. However, the birds' instinct for locating tuna seems to be central, and through the images the birds' guiding powers were being invoked. Certainly the birds appear, often in elaborately stylised form, as carved images in a wide suite of older Solomon Island artefacts including ceremonial bowls (used to hold mashed taro pudding at feasts and initiation rituals), weapons, ornaments and on the posts of ritually important custom houses.[4] Since the initiation of young boys was closely allied to their induction into the arts of bonito fishing, the birds had parallel emblematic status in these important rites of passage.[5] A contemporary Solomon Islander notes: 'Today, we still see frigatebird designs used as motifs carved on to the prows of canoes or small canoe carvings, handicrafts, woven into traditional bags, and even on t-shirts or body tattoos.'[6]

The artefacts on which the image was traditionally most prominent were the various accoutrements of fishing. In addition to the boat prow, it appeared on paddle-heads

A food bowl from the Solomon Islands in the form of a frigatebird.

and on bamboo scoops used to beat the water to attract fish. Sometimes the entire canoe was shaped and exquisitely painted to resemble a highly schematised frigatebird head.[7] The fact that the motifs also once appeared on weapons and ritual artefacts associated with headhunting suggests that the sheer elan of their movements and predatory grace made their appeal in the west Pacific, as they have in so many other parts of the frigatebirds' vast oceanic range.

A recent expansion in the distribution of frigatebird artefacts has occurred in the pockets of many millions of Peruvians. The currency in Peru, the *Nuevo Sol* ('new sun'), acquired a five-denomination bi-metal coin in 1994, which features on its reverse side a rudimentary version of the bird. However, the original image for this modern coin design was created at least 1,500 years earlier and is one of the famous Nazca Lines, those mysterious geoglyphs carved into the parched earth of the Nazca Desert in south-western Peru. This particular outline, which measures *c.*130 m (426 ft) long, must be the largest image of a frigatebird anywhere on Earth.

Hamerkop family *Scopidae*

The **Hamerkop** *Scopus umbretta*, which occurs commonly across sub-Saharan Africa and occupies most kinds of freshwater habitat, is exceptional in every sense. It is endemic to this single continent and while it has affinities with the storks, it has been placed in its own separate family and is judged to have no 'particularly close relationship with any other living bird so far studied'.[1] Essentially it looks like a small (50 cm: 1.6 ft tall) completely matt-brown heron. As one author noted, however, 'No other bird in Africa possesses so few characteristic colour markings and yet is so easy to identify almost up to the limit of visibility.'[2]

The most distinctive feature is the head. The bird's scientific and common names draw on this peculiarity. Hamerkop is Afrikaans for 'hammerhead', while *scopae* is Latin for a broom made of twigs. Both invoke the long loose feathers protruding at the rear of the crown. The word *umbretta* refers to the umber or earth-brown colour of its whole body.

However, the Hamerkop's odd appearance only hints at the deeper, more radical strangeness of its behaviour. This centres on the nest. A pair spends about six weeks constructing these domed fortresses, locating them most often high in the fork of a tree or occasionally on cliff ledges or rock columns. Sometimes they will devote much of an

entire year to creating multiple nests. They are assembled from sticks and branches – some individual pieces are 1.6 m (5.2 ft) long and weigh 230 g (8 oz), half the weight of the bird itself – and have an interior circular chamber where the eggs are laid. Both the entrance tunnel and inner walls are smoothly plastered with mud and the whole thing can weigh 25–50 kg (55–110 lb) and comfortably take the weight of an adult man.

During the course of construction the birds also like to embellish the interior with a wide range of what might loosely be called ornamental items. These depend on availability and can be nothing more distinguished than discarded rags, corn cobs and other waste food products, paper, old bones, empty tins, stones, desiccated bird and mammal skins, dead frogs, sloughed snakeskins, tortoise shell, dried lizards, and faeces from various sources, including cattle, human or other birds. One author noted around a Hamerkop nest 'a definite odor of human excrement'.[3]

An extraordinary and far more modern version of this original miscellany was found in a Zimbabwean nest documented in 1985. Along with 100 kg (220 lb) of grass, twigs and sticks were a pan brush, a broken cassette tape, a glove, a plastic dish, a plastic cup, two peacock feathers, chicken feathers, two socks, rabbit fur, 45 rags, four corn

▶ The Hamerkop's penchant for collecting and adorning its massive nest with almost anything, from cotton underparts to human ordure and from shed snakeskins to typewriter ribbons, has made it a bird rich in human story and superstition.

cobs, one piece of glass, four bits of wire, a plastic comb, one pair of underpants (male), a typewriter ribbon, a piece of leather belt, four bits of stocking, two bits of tin, two bits of foam rubber, seven bits of hose pipe, nine bits of plastic pipe (electrical), six bits of asbestos (roofing), 11 bones (one the remains of a T-bone steak), 12 pieces of sandpaper, four lengths of insulation tape, ten plastic bags, nine pieces of paper, 56 scraps of tinfoil, six bicycle tyres and six lengths of insulating wire.[4]

Another witness to the extraordinary aspects of 'Hamerkopian nest-building', records the following:

Whilst working on a South African game reserve, I received an account of the bird's ingenuity. One of the rangers had found a nest containing, amongst other items, a t-shirt and a shoe. History does not relate whether, at the reserve's reception desk, there stood an irate guest, semi-shod, stripped to the waist and demanding the return of his garments.[5]

A creature possessed of this eccentric sensibility and such industriousness was perhaps ever likely to attract our attention, but the Hamerkop is immersed in human superstition and story. One belief in southern Africa – among both white and black communities – holds that the nest is divided into chambers with one kept clear for the brood, while another is defiled with bones and other half-eaten refuse. In fact a rationale for the whole super-structure is as a store and charnel house.[6]

Another misconception is that the bird creates multiple entrances, so that it can never be caught inside the nest. Among the Zulu it is proverbially difficult to catch, and a human who is particularly slippery is (or, at least, was) likened to an *uThekwane* (the Zulu for Hamerkop).[7] In fact the birds have no escape route but they do exit or enter the smooth mud-lined nest entrance at high speed: 'They emerge . . . Like a cork out of a popgun and return . . . with an "upward dive" . . . like a dart.'[8] This mode of access has also entered folklore.

The Lungu in south-west Tanzania call it *Kanfune*. They say it is a special bird chiefly because of its huge nest. They do not generally kill it. They have a saying as follows: *Kanfune mwamukula ing'anda, nukuilala atailala.* This means, 'The Hamerkop builds a house but does not sleep in it.' This is a reference to the fact that sometimes a pair will spend months building a huge nest then abandon it for no apparent reason and start building another somewhere else. The Lungu say it is because the Hamerkop applies a test as to whether the nest is suitable or not. When it has finished the nest it flies away some distance then flies back towards the nest at full speed. If it cannot make it through the nest entrance at high speed on the first pass, it deems the nest unsuitable and moves away to build another.[9]

'In fact,' as this contributor notes, 'what usually happens is that a Barn Owl, cobra or Grey Kestrel takes up residence and evicts the builders.'

The full suite of other tenants in Hamerkop nests means that they are virtually an ecosystem in their own right. Verreaux's Eagle-Owl, Egyptian Goose, Knob-billed Duck, African Pygmy Goose and Speckled Pigeon all reuse the nests, along with small mammals like genets. Monitor

lizards, pythons and spitting cobras are regular squatters.[10] Bees also take them over, but even when the original builders are in residence the presence of so much decomposing matter attracts a wide range of invertebrates. As one author noted, 'Old nests are rich collecting grounds for the entomologist.'[11]

Much of this background ecology is at work in the superstitions that were once widely held about the Hamerkop. Two specific ideas – that it was a bird of power, even a kind of witch, and that it was a bird of prophetic omen – still have a strong hold over the African imagination. They hinge on the Hamerkop's noted habit of collecting household items or detritus, because this behaviour closely resembles one of the standard practices in African sorcery. In order to exercise control over a person, a witch doctor must first get hold of some item that is intimately connected to the victim. Possessions, clothing, even perhaps waste products like hair or nail clippings, are all preliminaries to influence. The Hamerkop nest is full of such materials. In fact the first inventory listed above reads like a witch doctor's pharmacopoeia. That a Hamerkop nest might subsequently be taken over by a python, spitting cobra or bee swarm may only seem to confirm that the bird keeps company with other creatures of the occult.

The resulting taboos against harming Hamerkops have probably spared the species from persecution. Certainly it was once considered dangerous to interfere with the nest or the bird, and the person who did so was obliged to make instant use of a witch doctor to counteract the consequences. Otherwise they were fated either to die, or to suffer a loss of cattle or house directed often from the heavens: 'In parts of northern Botswana (especially along the Chobe River) there is a belief that the Hamerkop draws lightning down from the sky, and if it lands on your house it will bring bad luck; you need to move house.'[12] To questions posed by the Reverend Godfrey, during compilation of his book *Bird-Lore of the Eastern Cape Province*, one respondent dwelled on similar themes: 'If you destroy its nest, you will see the sky overcast on the spot as the bird keeps on calling; and if you run into the hut for refuge, it will sit on the roof and call till you are struck by lightning, and then it will go away.'[13]

The links with lightning and rain are intriguing and difficult to explain, except perhaps that the species' whole lifestyle is intimately connected to a wider freshwater ecology. One theory is that Hamerkops occupy a very specialised niche and are dependent upon certain frogs and tadpoles (of the genus *Xenopus*).[14] The birds are inevitably most conspicuous – gathering their heterogeneous nest materials and feeding their chicks most actively – during the rainy season. A fundamental unconscious association between these background conditions and the Hamerkop would be natural. A classic instance of *ex post facto* reasoning is at work in the belief that the bird's call foretells (or foretold) rain. Reverend Godfrey also recounted an incident during a period of drought, when a Hamerkop was killed and hung from a tree upside down in an attempt to bring on rain.[15] These more innocent but essentially understandable connections between a bird and its favoured meteorological conditions may in time have fed into the Hamerkop's darker reputation as a practitioner of magic.

The exact distribution of beliefs about Hamerkop is

unclear. It is sometimes stated that the ideas are Africa-wide: for example, 'Never persecuted by Africans who regard it as having magic powers.' Such a simple blanket assertion needs qualification.[16] Superstition was particularly strong in South Africa, although old beliefs are now succumbing to more modern attitudes or values.

> I recently discussed the Hamerkop with a young Zimbabwean (aged 27) and he confirmed that urbanised Africans no longer subscribe to beliefs about it, but in rural areas it is still considered a bird of ill omen, especially if it calls near your home. Superstition is still only just below the surface, even in urbanised situations. The body parts of vultures are still sold to give insight into where to place one's bets at the horse races (the presumption being that its superior eyesight gives insight into the right choice).[17]

Elsewhere Hamerkop superstitions appear not to have taken hold. 'I have quizzed people I work with in Zambia about Hamerkops a number of times, but they don't seem too bothered about them at all. They just say they have good meat!'[18] In Kenya among the Kikuyu people at least four names for the bird (e.g. *karogi ngunu*: 'witch of the red cows') link it with sorcery, although another strand of association portrays Hamerkops as lazy and foolish creatures. This stems from its supposed habit of catching frogs and then allowing them to escape almost immediately. Among the Mbeere, a community closely related to the Kikuyu, the bird is proverbially stupid. While there are taboos against eating Hamerkops in Kenya, these arise from the bird's unclean diet of frogs and tadpoles, and not from anxiety over its occult powers.[19]

Pelican family *Pelecanidae*

Physically huge (they are among the world's largest birds) with that great pouched scoop of a beak, the eight species of pelican are among the most easily recognised animals on the planet. However, our sense of living-room familiarity doesn't necessarily arise out of contact with the real creature. Their singular shape and profile have been endlessly recycled in modern media and commercial iconography. Penguin's Pelican Books (founded 1937), an imprint that published works on contemporary issues until the mid 1980s (see also page 92), is just one example of a worldwide range of products.

Perhaps it is also the comedy inherent in their grotesque disproportions that has given them a parallel life in the world of cartoons. Among the most recent crop is the **Australian Pelican** *Pelecanus conspicillatus*, which, contrary to its usual behaviour, helps to reunite the eponymous clownfish with his father in the film *Finding Nemo* (the world's biggest-selling DVD). For much the same reason the birds have been perennial favourites at zoos or parks for centuries. Sometimes they also occupy a halfway house between captivity and wild status.

Individuals of a variety of species – notably **Great White Pelican** *Pelecanus onocrotalus* in southern Europe, **Brown Pelican** *Pelecanus occidentalis* in North America or the Caribbean (it is the state bird in Louisiana, USA, and the national bird on St Kitts and Nevis) and Australian Pelicans – become permanent residents, either after injury or through habituation, in seaside docks and harbours. There they can be found pottering between the mooring ropes or the fishing nets, invariably cherished as a kind of local mascot and fed by their human neighbours, who are themselves often catchers of fish. I have personally witnessed semi-tame Great White Pelicans on the Greek islands of Lesbos, Mykonos and Rhodes.

Entertaining and humorous they may be, but these tamed versions are nothing compared with pelicans seen en masse and in the wild. They can occur in huge congregations, sometimes standing at lake edges in great white crowds that quake and shimmer in the heat haze. The biggest examples of the largest species, such as the Great White and

Dalmatian Pelican *Pelecanus crispus*, can weigh 12 kg (26.5 lb) and have wingspans measuring 3.5 m (11.5 ft). Despite the bulk they are consummate fliers: 'the flat-keeled underside to their body is beautifully streamlined for buoyant flight and is reminiscent of the float of a flying boat'.[1] Birds have been known to make daily round flights of up to 500 km (300 miles) when seeking prey to feed their young. On return to the nest the adults and chicks often perform a bizarre feeding routine that has been beautifully evoked by US ornithologist William Finlay (here in the case of the **American White Pelican** *Pelecanus erythrorhynchos*):

> The old bird backed up as if she were getting a good footing and slowly opened her mouth to admit the bill of the little pelican. She drew her neck up till the ends of the upper and lower mandibles were braced against the ground and her pouch was distended to the limit. Jonah-like, down the mother's throat went the head of the child till he seemed about to be swallowed had it not been for his fluttering wings. He remained buried in the depths for about two minutes, eating everything he could find. Nor did he withdraw from the family cupboard voluntarily, but when the supply was exhausted or the mother thought he had had enough she began slowly to rise and struggle to regain her upright position.[2]

PELICAN SYMBOLISM

Perhaps it was this compelling vision of entangled, even ambiguous, intimacy between parent and chick, or perhaps it was the intense colours sometimes present on the gular pouches of breeding birds (in Dalmatian Pelicans it can be livid purple, while the cutting edge on the beak of the Great White Pelican is cherry red), but early naturalists came up with a version of this exchange that was bizarre beyond measure. In a bestiary known as the *Physiologus*, a collection of pious fables loosely drawn from the natural world and compiled in the second century AD, an early Christian writer described the pelican's feeding routine as follows:

They love their young very much. When the young are born, and as soon as they are a little grown, they strike back and kill them. But presently the parents begin to have compassion on the young and, after they have mourned three whole days over the children they killed, the mother opens her side and drops her blood on the dead bodies of the young and arouses life in them.[3]

In another version of the myth the chicks are killed by a serpent and the parent then performs the blood-letting rite that restores them to life.

However misguided we may now judge this version of feeding pelicans, it gathered strength, partly because of the popularity of the *Physiologus*, until the whole of Christendom held it to be a cardinal truth. It was, of course, an idea calculated to make a deep appeal to the medieval psyche, because it echoed in microcosm the central story of their religious faith. Christ's redemption of humankind through his own sacrifice was manifest in the life of a bird. The myth flourished for well over 1,500 years – in fact versions of it survive still, such as on the state flag of Louisiana – and it was endlessly recycled. The great thirteenth-century Italian theologian Thomas Aquinas made the link between Christ and bird explicit in a quatrain that was itself variously translated and reproduced:

Pie pellicane, Jesu Domine
Me immundum munda tuo sanguine
Cuius una stille salvum facere
Totum mundum quit ab omni scelere.[4]

Pelican of Piety, Jesus, Lord and God,
Cleanse thou me, unclean, in thy most precious
   blood,
But a single drop of which doth save and free
All the universe from its iniquity.

Another aspect of the myth was its reinvention over the centuries as writers applied new layers of fantasy to the original claim, presumably without one of them ever going anywhere near a genuine pelican. Typical was a version appearing in a twelfth-century book, *The Bestiary of Philippe de Thaon*:

Of such a nature it is, when it comes to its young birds, and they are great and handsome, and it will fondle them, cover them with its wings; the little birds are fierce, taking to pecking it – desire to eat it and pick out its two eyes; then it pecks and takes them, and slays them with torment; and thereupon leaves them – leaves them lying dead – then returns on the third day, is grieved to find them dead, and makes such lamentation, when it sees its little birds dead, that with its beak it strikes its body that the blood issues forth; the blood goes dropping, and falls on its young birds – the blood has such quality that by it they come to life.[5]

The notion that young pelicans viciously attacked their own parents surfaces in Shakespeare's work, when King Lear refers to his paragons of filial ingratitude, Goneril and Regan, as 'Those pelican daughters' (Act 3, Scene 4).

Strange as it may now seem to a world more accustomed to the bird as a cartoon character, the pelican, because of this symbolic representation, was one of the most abundant

Human and avian catchers of fish, such as these fishermen and Brown Pelicans, often share the same quayside space.

The pelican in its piety, a commonplace Christian image for centuries, is the subject of this stained-glass window at St Cuthbert's Chapel on Inner Farne Island, Northumberland.

Animal behaviour – especially that of birds – was often drawn upon to illustrate these anecdotes, which derived from Aesop's fables and other myths or legends. The pelican was one of the species which was used repeatedly in emblem books.

Emblems also found their place in ornithological works of the early modern period. Naturalists such as the Swiss Conrad Gesner (1516–1565) or the Italian Ulisse Aldrovandi (1522–1605) quoted them and related as true the strange and wonderful behaviour of birds such as the pelican. The presence of emblems in apparent works of fact demonstrates the blurred boundaries between myth and natural history in the period. For some early modern naturalists the pelican did indeed pierce its chest in order to revive its chicks, just as they believed in the existence of the phoenix. One of the last ornithological encyclopedias in which we find the pelican feeding chicks on its own blood is a book from 1650 (John Jonston's *De avibus*). The English naturalist John Ray [see Appendix I] was really the start of a more empirical approach to natural history and he explicitly omitted such references from his books. In fact the popularity of the pelican emblem is important, because the way in which the author dealt with it was a useful marker for the level of 'science' in their work. By 1781, the French naturalist Buffon was describing the symbol of the pelican as the 'religious emblem of ignorant peoples'.[6]

avian symbols in churches, monasteries and cathedrals over the whole of Europe. It featured repeatedly in illuminated manuscripts. What is fascinating about these two- or three-dimensional versions of the Christian pelican is the way that they – just like the literary accounts on which they drew – lost any kind of mooring in genuine fact. Often the pelican shed its massive bill and pouch, it acquired a body shape reminiscent of an eagle (presumably a form deemed more suitable to its sublime theme), and the posture became increasingly dramatic or cruciform as if to emphasise the religious message. A pelican of the strangest proportions appeared even as late as *c.*1744 in a painting by Francesco de Mura entitled *Allegory of Charity* (now held in the Art Institute, Chicago, USA). While the human figures in the image are powerfully and sensually evoked, the pelican has the head of an ibis, the build of a rooster and offspring resembling young chickens.

The history of the 'pelican in its piety', as this parent–chick scenario came to be known, is fascinating for what it tells us about early Christian understanding of the natural world. Isabelle Charmantier, a scholar of natural-historical writing during the Renaissance and early modern period, explains how birds were viewed and treated:

> In the sixteenth and seventeenth centuries a type of publication called an 'emblem book' became highly popular. These were an expression of the widespread belief that nature was full of symbols which had been placed there by God and, once interpreted correctly, would guide people to lead a good life. An emblem consisted of a title (or motto), generally quite obscure, complemented by an illustration and a poem which both shed light on the moral message conveyed by the motto.

There are several strange ironies arising out of the pelican's long if now largely submerged history as a Christian emblem. One surfaces in San Francisco Bay on that famous landmark colloquially known as 'The Rock'. Yet the word 'Alcatraz' had its roots in an old Spanish and Portuguese name for the pelican (see also Albatross family, page 98). In turn alcatraz is thought to derive from the Arabic *al-câdous*, 'water-carrier' (it may equally come from the Greek *kados*, 'water pot'). There is a notable seabird colony still on Alcatraz Island, but pelicans may well never have bred there.[7] However, *alcatraz* became a general Spanish term for various large seabirds and is used as part of the current names for several members of the gannet and booby family. Ironically it is no longer a part of modern Spanish nomenclature for pelican (now *pelicano*). Regardless of the lapse, the prison of Alcatraz, which has become a popular emblem for man's inhumanity to man, ultimately acquired its name from a bird that was once the pre-eminent symbol of Christ.

A second notable anomaly is the near absence of pelican iconography in modern Christendom. Yet it does appear, as previously noted, on the flag of Louisiana. Unfortunately, in the mid twentieth century, American pelicans were especially susceptible to poisoning following the widespread use of pesticides such as DDT. Louisiana's entire Brown Pelican population was a classic victim. Fortunately the species rose again from regional extinction once the toxic compounds were withdrawn and pelicans are now widespread on the Gulf of Mexico, giving a peculiarly modern and genuine resonance to the theme of rebirth depicted on the state's pelican-emblazoned flag.[8] Pelicans also assumed fresh symbolic power with the Gulf oil spill of 2010, when these iconic birds were shown helplessly

flapping and shrink-wrapped into their slimy film of crude oil. Television images of such slow-dying birds were screened worldwide as a metaphor for man's casual inhumanity to the natural environment.

It is intriguing that no European country has adopted the pelican as a central national symbol except the small Muslim state of Albania, where there is a tiny population of Dalmatian Pelicans (the bird is called *Pelikani kaçurrel*: 'curly pelican', a reference to the mop of feathers on the adult's head).[9] However, it should be noted that the species may have had Islamic resonances, since a pelican was said to have brought water in its pouch for the fourth caliph Ali as he lay exhausted on the battlefield.[10]

PELICANS AND FISHERMEN

The sheer size of the bill pouch – it can hold 9–13.7 litres (2–3 gallons) of water depending on species – may well have led to the many claims made about pelicans as prodigious catchers and devourers of fish. In fact the daily catch is a more modest 10 per cent of body weight and probably just 900–1,200 g (32–43 oz) even in the largest species.[11] Yet pelicans can display great coordination and teamwork in their methods. 'Occasionally several hundred gather in [a] milling swarm, flapping frantically over one another to trap shoals of fish; or a long semi-circular line may form, bills open, held below water, moving slowly shorewards, trapping fish against land like animated seine-net.'[12]

Regardless of this prowess, some modern estimates of their capacity are extraordinary. Recently, Romanian fishermen alleged a daily diet of 23 kg (50 lb) per bird to justify persecution of them.[13] Until the 1980s Dalmatian and Great White Pelicans were shot or their nest sites trampled and destroyed. Even in 2009 there was a case reported in

Romania of Dalmatian Pelicans and Pygmy Cormorants shot in the Danube Delta Biosphere Reserve. The world's most abundant species, the **Peruvian Pelican** *Pelecanus thagus*, has faced similar treatment, especially when its human competitors needed a convenient scapegoat. In the 1970s a combination of over-fishing and the effects of El Niño massively reduced anchoveta harvests in the east Pacific, and Peruvian fishermen instinctively blamed pelicans and other seabirds for the collapse (see also Gannets as Fertiliser, page 147).[14]

However, well-publicised educational programmes have led some to adopt more enlightened approaches.

In Greece we have both Great White and Dalmatian Pelicans breeding, with a colony of the former at Lake Mikri Prespa and two colonies of Dalmatian at lakes Mikri Prespa and Kerkini. The last one is quite new and the birds nest on man-made platforms. On both these lakes the pelicans (mostly Dalmatian and fewer Great Whites) are accustomed to the local fishermen and they seem to be able to identify certain individuals. The birds are accustomed to hang around the fishermen's cottages especially in winter, and every time the fisherman goes to check his nets the whole group follow the boat.

Usually the fishermen throw them some low-price fish, mostly crucian carp (*Carassius auratus gibelio*). The young birds are braver. But the birds are still wild and if you are not a fisherman or you don't have fish to offer them they quickly swim or fly away! During the breeding season the birds spend more time on the platforms (which are located in the heart of the protected area) and they do more fishing on their own. During this season they are much more difficult

Their conspicuous pouches have probably fuelled the many exaggerations about pelicans' appetites. Several species including the Dalmatian Pelican have been persecuted because of these false claims, especially by fishermen.

to approach. The fishermen respect the pelicans and admire their beauty. They say that they have always had respect for pelicans and know that they feed on surface fish and don't affect the fisheries. Moreover they understand that the birds attract tourism and the whole local community benefits from that. By contrast, they hate cormorants because they believe that those birds are the cause for the loss of high-price fish.[15]

The affinity described between this Greek lakeside community and its pelicans is a reflection of a very ancient relationship between human and avian catchers of fish. In Egypt at the sun temple of Niuserre at Abu Gurab, there is a 4,500-year-old wall relief depicting fishermen hauling in their catch and interacting with pelicans in much the same manner.[16]

Gannet and Booby family *Sulidae*

The family comprises ten large seabirds, whose torpedo-like body design has been shaped to suit their signature fishing method. Often gannets and boobies hunt communally in response to the shoaling behaviour of their prey, when hundreds, and occasionally thousands, of birds fly high above an area of sea and rain down like a relentless shower of missiles. Prior to each dive, the birds seem to stall, and then collapse with wings trailing like a comet's tail behind their bodies, the thick long spear-like bill foremost as they strike the water at 100 kph (60 mph), the impact cushioned by a spongy air-filled layer of bone in their heads.

The family is spread unevenly through the world's oceans with the seven booby species concentrated in the tropics, especially across the Pacific. The **Blue-footed Booby** *Sula nebouxii*, **Nazca Booby** *Sula granti* and **Peruvian Booby** *Sula variegata* are exclusive to that ocean. However, the distributions of **Masked Booby** *Sula dactylatra*, **Red-footed Booby** *Sula sula* and **Brown Booby** *Sula leucogaster* encircle the Earth's middle latitudes, while the three gannet species occur, in turn, around the coasts of Australia and New Zealand (**Australasian Gannet** *Morus serrator*), southern Africa (**Cape Gannet** *Morus capensis*) and on both sides of the north Atlantic (**Northern Gannet** *Morus bassanus*). The exception is **Abbott's Booby** *Papasula abbotti*, a species at risk of extinction, whose entire population nests on one Australian-controlled territory, Christmas Island, in the Indian Ocean south of Java.

Gannets and boobies are judged among the most impressive of seabirds, while their breeding colonies or feeding concentrations in certain marine hotspots are deemed among the planet's great natural spectacles in places as remote and diverse as the Galápagos Islands, coastal Peru, Scotland or southern Africa. Bryan Nelson, who has studied the family for more than half a century, beautifully captures the visual spectacle (as well as the olfactory impact and occasional horrors) of a typical island colony, in this case an ancient breeding site for Northern Gannets at Ailsa Craig, Scotland:

Its soaring, cathedral columns rise in tiers, clear silver, green and ferric orange. The white crosses of wheeling gannets against granite and an azure sky are Ailsa's imprint on the mind. As Gurney remarks, 'the whole Craig is a marvel of life, and, given fine weather, one of the most enjoyable spots in the world'. But, as always, there is another side. The gloomy, dripping water caves, green with slime, the blackened boulders from which the nettles and rank vegetation rise on a tide of debris, feathers and corpses; the broken gannets lying there . . .

Seabird islands are a potent mixture of the rhapsodic and the repellent.[1]

Colonies of gannets and boobies may be considered major attractions today, but the birds' names reflect a less awestruck age. 'Booby' is a word of Spanish or Portuguese origin (*bobo* in either language) meaning 'a fool' or 'buffoon'. Even today in the Dominican Republic the Brown Booby is known as *Bubí pardo*, while its corresponding title in French-speaking Haiti is *Fou brun* – 'brown idiot'. *Morus*, the scientific name for the three gannets, is originally a Greek word and has given us an English synonym, 'moron'. The lack of intelligence credited to the family derives from a time when humans moved among breeding colonies to harvest eggs and wring the necks of plump fat-filled chicks, and neither the victims nor their parents showed a requisite level of fear. The array of pejorative names thus added insult to the injury of human predation.

GANNETS AS FOOD

The anonymous harvesting of gannets or boobies for their salt-savoured meat and large eggs probably occurs sporadically, especially when hard-pressed fishermen are short on supplies. A modern Solomon Islander describes the current use of Red-footed Boobies in this Pacific archipelago: 'Seabirds are important to traditional societies, especially in remote parts of the Solomon Islands. Some boobies are kept as pets and taken out with fishing expeditions. If the canoes are lost at sea, they help the fishermen navigate back to land. In cases, where storms and high seas blow voyaging canoes off course, these boobies are a last source of food for the sailors.'[2]

Elsewhere the family has been subjected to extraordinary levels of historic persecution, from which one species is still continuing to recover. The Northern Gannet, the largest of the group with a wingspan tipping 1.8 m (6 ft), is the exemplar of a bird that can retrieve its former range and numbers, even after centuries of intense depredation.

In some ways its scientific name enshrines the old exploitative relationship, because *bassanus* is a reference to the Bass Rock, a volcanic plug in the Firth of Forth, just east of Scotland's capital, Edinburgh. It was known as a place for gannets by the fourteenth century, although Bryan Nelson suggests that it is likely to have been a colony 'before modern man (*Homo sapiens*) existed'.[3] The Bass Rock's early mention in the written records almost certainly hinged on its economic importance, the site being rented for its yield of seabird flesh.[4] When Charles I visited the rock in 1641 his companion noted that it was so smothered in gannets 'that

Northern Gannets often hunt in dense flocks and shower down on fish shoals like fin-winged missiles.

you can scarcely find free footing anywhere'. Yet by the early nineteenth century the 'marvellous multitude' had fallen to just 3,500–4,000 pairs because of a relentless cull.[5]

Once the harvest ceased in 1885, numbers of nesting birds rose steadily, the Bass Rock morphing over the decades from basalt black to a guano-and-gannet brilliant white. The most recent estimate (2008) is 50,000 pairs, involving a mixture of natural increase and immigration from other colonies. Nelson concludes that gannets here, 'like the species as a whole, are simply climbing steadily back to their former numbers following wholesale depletion by humankind; they are not "exploding" in any demographic sense'.[6]

Yet the recovery has not been universal. One historic colony in Canada, in the Gulf of St Lawrence, was probably the largest congregation of any member of the *Sulidae* anywhere in the northern hemisphere. It was visited by European mariners as early as the sixteenth century; Jacques Cartier, the French explorer, noting that 'These Ilands were as full of birds, as any field or medow is of grasse, which there do make their nestes: and in the greatest of them, there was a great and infinite number of those that wee call Margaulx.' It was a French name for a gannet.[7] The islands were known simply as Bird Rocks (ironically there is a cluster called the Gannet Islands off the south coast of Labrador in Canada, but the species has probably never bred there).[8]

Almost exactly 300 years later, when the great French American artist John James Audubon visited the same eroding shelves of limestone, he is thought to have seen a colony of 250,000 birds (Nelson suggests it may well have been more).[9] Thereafter Bird Rocks were subjected to a model of resource depletion that brings to mind the extinction of the Greak Auk on nearby Funk Island, or the slaughter of the great whales in the southern oceans during the twentieth century (see also Exploitation of Auks, page 227). Audubon himself recorded how six men in a single

hour harvested 540 gannets to use as bait for cod hooks. The killing continued at much the same pace until the end of the century and, although the site received government protection from 1904, the damage had been done. In 1932 the colony numbered 1,000 birds (although a 1994 estimate was 9,868).[10]

Given that the entire world population has only ever bred at 20–40 sites, it was perhaps inevitable that such super-abundant concentrations of protein would be magnets for hunters. Almost all gannetries were subjected to some level of harvest, but the colony on Bird Rocks is the exception in terms of its profligate waste of a self-renewing resource.[11] Elsewhere collectors tended to exercise self-restraint or bound the taking of seabirds within social structures that ensured continuity of supply. The classic sustainable harvest occurred on St Kilda, the most remote of the Scottish archipelagos. The tiny Gaelic-speaking community, one of the last exponents of a hunter-gatherer lifestyle in Europe, persisted on these islands until 1930 and may have enjoyed continuous occupation for 5,000 years.[12] They certainly took gannets for hundreds of years and when fowling for this species effectively ceased at the end of the nineteenth century, St Kilda held one of the largest colonies in the world. Today it is *the* largest (60,000 pairs).[13]

Gannets, salted and stored in barrels, were not just a source of St Kildan winter protein. The birds were plucked and their feathers sold for stuffing pillows or furnishings, 300 carcasses being used to fill a single featherbed. The islanders paid their rents with these barrels of white down, the landlord making in mainland Scotland three times on resale what he had paid his tenants.[14] In 1874 feathers fetched 18 shillings (old British pounds were divided into 20 shillings) for a Scottish stone (10.9 kg : 24 lb), and even at the turn of the twentieth century a London merchant was getting 10 shillings a stone. In order to rid gannet feathers of their unmistakable odour of the Atlantic they had first to be baked or aired in direct sunlight.[15]

Another important crop – aside from the gannet necks worn as short-lived (female) slippers, breastbones for lamp wicks, and webbed feet as tobacco pouches which the men filled with dried moss if tobacco ran out – was the oil derived from the carcasses. St Kildans converted the bird's own stomach into an expandable container both for this liquid fat and other fluids. The habit of utilising every conceivable part was a reflection of their waste-free economy, yet one possible side effect of this scrupulous recycling may have been an inadvertent check on their own numbers. The islanders suffered very high levels of tetanus and one suggested cause was the anointment – at the arrival of any newborn baby – of the freshly cut umbilical cord with gibben, an oil obtained from Northern Fulmars, that had been stored in a gannet's stomach. This peculiar form of baptism into the life of the seabird community may have contributed to the high infant mortality rates and, ultimately, helped doom the island to its final abandonment in 1930.[16]

After St Kilda's evacuation the taking of Atlantic gannets continued at just three sites: on the island of Eldey off southwest Iceland (less than 70 km: 43 miles from the capital Reykjavík) where it was discontinued in 1939; at Mykines in the Faroes (the archipelago lies equidistant between Iceland and mainland Scotland but is politically part of Denmark), where it exists today on a small scale; and at Sula Sgeir (which means 'gannet skerry' in Gaelic), a group of tiny islets north of the Outer Hebrides. This last is now the only other surviving vestige of the once Atlantic-wide harvest of gannets. The 'guga hunt' (*guga* is Gaelic for the brown chick) at Sula Sgeir has been in existence at least since the sixteenth century and involves an annual off-take of *c*.2,000–3,000 birds, the hunters setting sail each September from the Outer Hebridean island of Lewis, 100 km (60 miles) to the south. The size of harvest is prescribed by licence from the Scottish office of the British government.

GANNETS AS FERTILISER

One of the least known instances of uncontrolled, even frenzied, human consumption of wild seabirds did not centre on any flesh that might have fallen from the breast- or thigh bone. It focused on products evacuated from the avian cloaca. Yet the story of our harvest of seabird dung is among the most bizarre and edifying in modern history. In its capacity to illuminate a pattern of consumption without limit, and appetite without self-restraint, it appears now almost as a metaphor for the entire impact of capitalism upon the biosphere.

It has its origins in coastal South America. The Inca people of the high Andes had long exploited a form of bird-derived manure that they had named *huana*. The original Quechua word was modified in its journey to Europe and we now know the product as 'guano'. The Inca obtained their supply of this high-quality fertiliser, which was uniquely rich in phosphates and nitrates, from a series of islands close to the current Peruvian coast. These offshore sites were thickly populated with nesting seabirds involving a wide range of species but dominated by three – Peruvian Booby, Guanay Cormorant and Peruvian Pelican. The first of these species is the most populous gannet on Earth.

The dung middens amassed by these seabirds are

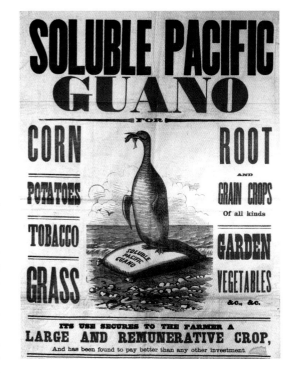

Seabird guano is one of the richest of all agricultural fertilisers and was once ruthlessly exploited to the detriment of both its human harvesters and its avian producers.

uniquely fertile because of desert-like precipitation levels, which minimise leaching of the precious nitrate content. In keeping with the Inca's rigorous social and economic control, the birds that gave rise to this precious commodity had been scrupulously protected. Yet with the empire's sixteenth-century collapse under the weight of Spanish steel, the old self-restraint gave way to a different pattern of consumption, especially once the potential of guano had been widely advertised by Alexander von Humboldt (1769–1859). The great German explorer had given impetus through his writings on South America, firstly to European and American agricultural trials with guano, then to the arrival of the first transport ships off Peru.

In 1841, 2,000 tonnes were dispatched to Liverpool. Within a decade the main centre for guano mining, the seabird colonies on the Chincha Islands, supported a small town of 3,000 inhabitants and an export industry involving nearly half a million tonnes annually. A potent fertiliser it may have been, but guano was a nightmare to mine. It lay in rock-like cap deposits up to 50 m (164 ft) thick and, once loosened from its substrate, the fine stinking white powder was so noxious it caused the nose or lips to blister and burn. Colonial entrepreneurs found a solution to the appalling conditions and the ferocious heat by employing first convicts, then native Pacific labourers and finally Chinese coolies under black gangmasters. All of them were regarded as utterly disposable, which was perfectly in keeping with a back-breaking regime that entailed the men shovelling four tonnes of shit over a 17-hour day. Many of them, deceived, abused and without hope, overdosed on opium or threw themselves off the cliffs.[17] Of the 30,000 Asians duped into taking contracts few went home, and their descendants now form a significant Peruvian minority. Somehow the guano mountains were dismantled, shovelful by shovelful, and between 1848–75 an estimated 20 million tonnes were exported. The Chincha deposits, which had accumulated over hundreds if not thousands of years, were scraped down to bare rock and by the end of the century Peru's guano reserves were virtually nil.[18]

Completely overlooked in the scramble for profit was the underpinning ecology from which the wealth derived. It has its origins in the Humboldt Current, a great northward-thrusting bloom of cold water that brings up to the surface off the coasts of Peru and Chile a vast reservoir of nutrients. In turn this fuels the anchoveta, a tiddler that occurs in spectacularly large numbers (the Peruvian fishing fleet caught 14 million tonnes in 1969–70 – an estimated 13,000,000,000,000,000 fish). In fact, the guano is anchoveta processed by the alimentary systems of boobies, cormorants and pelicans. The seabird populations flourishing in this place of oceanic luxuriance are some of the highest anywhere. The Peruvian Booby and Peruvian Pelican, for example, are the most numerous species of their respective families, while the population of Guanay Cormorant is estimated in the millions. Bryan Nelson masterfully conveys the visual impact of this ecosystem, which is surely one of the great natural wonders on Earth:

> Sea-lions, boobies, cormorants, pelicans and Humboldt Penguins loll in a soup of fish; the limits to their catch are imposed only by the time it takes to grab their prey which, moreover, is on their very doorstep. Thick black skeins of seabirds snake everywhere through the mist, above the oily swell; rafts of them mat the sea and, here and there, hailstorms of diving piqueros [Peruvian Boobies] lance the water, so densely that it appears miraculous that they avoid spearing each other.[19]

At the eleventh hour the Peruvian government recognised not only the nihilism inherent in the methods of European and American merchants, but also its own complicit folly. In 1909 it instituted protection for the seabirds and over a matter of decades the measures restored most of their numbers and revived guano production. In fact the bird populations naturally fluctuate – from less than 3 million to 28 million – in response to the effects of El Niño, a periodic incursion of warm water that chokes off the diatom-rich Humboldt Current and leads to a temporary breakdown of this east Pacific nutrient cycle.[20] (In 1983 this was thought to have caused a 85 per cent mortality in the key guano species.)[21]

However, not all parts of the ecosystem have rallied. Seabirds such as the Humboldt Penguin and the Peruvian Diving Petrel have never recovered. The guano caps that had been the boobies' and cormorants' middens, served the other birds as their nurseries. The wholesale removal of the guano, into which they dig their nest chambers, helped to trigger steep declines which neither species has reversed. Today both are at risk of extinction.[22]

In many ways the exemplar of a bird assailed by the human appetite for its guano is another family member, the Abbott's Booby. This curious rainforest-nesting single-species genus is confined to one Indian Ocean island, after guano extraction had earlier destroyed its other far-flung nest colonies. Its last stand against extinction is maintained by the 2,500 pairs on Christmas Island, which they share with another parlously rare endemic seabird, the Christmas Island Frigatebird (3,200 pairs).[23] There is some dispute whether the phosphate on this coralline limestone reef originated with seabirds but, whether true guano or not, its removal was ongoing and relentless. The Australian government and the mining company cut down the forest and dug out the soils until large parts of Christmas Island resembled the scorched red, deadened landscapes of Mars. Between 1965 and 1987 they destroyed a third of the rainforest. Now, fortunately, a more enlightened regime has come to pass after decades of environmental pressure. Approximately 60 per cent of the island has been safeguarded as a national park, covering many of the main colonies of Abbott's Booby. There is a ban on the removal of further pristine forest and permits are required for clearance of regrowth forest.[24]

THE NORTHERN GANNETS IN FAROESE FOLK TALE

It is intriguing to compare this unsustainable depletion of a precious resource – a characteristic of human interactions with seabirds right around the world (see also Petrel and Shearwater family, page 108), with an old Faroese folk tale that originated in an era long before the idea of official state quotas.

It tells of a giant called Tórur who coveted the Faroese island of Mykines (where the gannetry was located), and who decided to slay the community's headman and chief sorcerer, Óli. The latter, fearful for his life, retreated to the island's high cliffs where the physical manoeuvrings of these two magical beings caused the formation of a number of geological features that can still be seen in the Faroese landscape today.

After several days' battle, Óli gained the upper hand by gouging out an eye from his opponent. Tórur, sensing defeat, begged for mercy and promised the islanders three gifts if Óli spared his life. His offer was hedged by a single condition: the residents should never laugh or mock the good things he gave. His proffered trio included a large whale as meat, a huge piece of driftwood for boat timber, and a bird that would be found nowhere else in the Faroes.

Tórur was true to his promise and thereafter he and Óli became fast friends until death. However, with time the people forgot the old giant's central condition and one year they laughed at their whale because it had only a single eye. The next year they laughed at their driftwood because it was all twisted and gnarled. As the giant forewarned, no whale ever sailed to their shores and no huge driftwood log supplied the islanders with fine timber again. Fearful lest they lose their last gift, their special seabird and its supplies of meat, eggs and oil, the people of Mykines never mocked the stately gannets soaring above their cliffs.[25]

This resonant folk tale, with its fantastical central characters and their deeds, is typical of traditional myths anywhere in the world, in that it presses an ancient moral argument. This truth runs entirely counter to much of our historical engagement with boobies or gannets and speaks of the need for respect, even when the source of human plenty seems there simply for the taking, and when it seems not just guileless, but to yield itself up for human consumption. Yet even boobies have power. As Tórur foretold, they can disappear. Seabird hunters would have done well to heed this timeless message.

Cormorant family *Phalacrocoracidae*

'Cormorant' is an anglicised contraction of the Latin name *corvus marinus*: 'sea crow' – a reference to the birds' size, colour and very probably the ambiguous moral qualities that we have long projected on to them.[1] Yet the association has resonances that transcend cultures. In Hindi cormorants are known also as *Pān-kowwa* or *jal-kowwa*, 'water crow', while an old Chinese name ('aquatic old crow') trades on this same linkage.[2] Half of the family draws its identity from a completely different association – the prominent tuft of crown feathers – that has given rise to the alternative name, 'shag'.

These large dark birds, with serpentine necks and often with wings outstretched in heraldic postures, are quintessentially inhabitants of that liminal space where rocky cliffs and outcrops meet the ocean waves. In total there are 38 species occupying much of the world's available shoreline, and reaching 73° N in the case of the **Pelagic Shag** *Leucocarbo pelagicus*, or the Antarctic mainland in that of **Imperial Shag** *Leucocarbo atriceps*. Yet the family is by no means dependent upon salt water. The **Neotropic Cormorant** *Phalacrocorax brasilianus* in Latin America occurs throughout the immense forested river basins of the Orinoco and Amazon, while Australia's **Little Pied Cormorant** *Phalacrocorax melanoleucos* thrives even in wooded billabongs or short-lived lakes at the heart of the continent's desert interior.

Somewhat ungainly on land, and looking heavy-bodied and broad-winged in flight, cormorants are transformed utterly once they enter their true element. Birds seen underwater have an almost piscine litheness and we have long admired or envied this sub-aquatic grace and the associated fishing proficiency. These emotions have had their deepest cultural impact in the Far East, where ancient trappers learned to exploit **Great Cormorant** *Phalacrocorax carbo* as proxy fishing rods.

The use of tame birds occurs still in both China and Japan (in the latter country they use another species, **Japanese Cormorant** *Phalacrocorax capillatus*) but which nation was the originator of the custom is not clear. The first recorded evidence in China dates to 317 BC, with an initial possible reference in Japanese literature as early as 600 BC, although detailed Japanese accounts are generally much later (about the tenth century AD). Regardless of its origins, the practice is much more widely pursued in the southern half of China and is more deeply rooted in its contemporary rural life.[3]

The techniques are very different in each country. In China the best-trained birds, which can be as 'docile and obedient as dogs', are bred in captivity, brooded by chickens and hand-reared by the trainer. (A recent development has been the increased collection of eggs from the nests of wild birds to meet domestic needs.)[4] There is an amusing description of the affections which cormorants can display towards their human 'owners' written by a nineteenth-century French practitioner: 'The cormorant becomes

Black in colour and predatory in mien, the fish-eating Great Cormorant has often been an object of human enmity, mingled no doubt with a dash of envy.

The art of cormorant fishing has flourished in east Asia for millennia and is one of those human–bird collaborations that never fails to capture our imaginations.

'know' when they are due their reward and refuse to budge until the collar is removed and they are allowed to feed. The inference is that the birds can count.[6]

Cormorants enjoy a secondary cultural role in China and Japan as a frequent poetic motif in the literature of both countries. In haiku the bird's name is a season word used to connote summer. Cormorants are conspicuous in 'Country Cottage', a work by one of China's foremost poets Du Fu (AD 713–770), whose oeuvre is notable for the frequent allusions to birds and rivers. After his enforced retirement from imperial court life, Du Fu passed his last years largely in Sichuan. He remained a man of substance but, like many writers of this and later dynasties, affected a form of literary and aesthetic rusticity. Here, cormorants – observed in that post-feeding posture with wings outstretched, which is almost the family's calligraphic signature – along with the other physical details at day's end fit the poem's wider theme of regret and of an emotional ebb tide:

A house in the fields at the clear river's bend:
A ramshackle gate by the old path's edge:
Thick weeds: they hide the hamlet's well;
A rustic place: I'm too lazy for formal dress.
Elms and willows, branches young and frail;
Each medlar tree spreads its fragrance.
And cormorants, against the westering sun's light
Bask their wings as they flock on the fish-weir.

In contrast to the subsistence character of cormorant fishing in China, a deep formality has entered the Japanese version of the activity, especially after it was taken up by the educated gentry. The fishermen operate at night, with the cormorants held on leashes (traditionally of spruce fibres) and as many as 12 birds per boat. Occasionally a number of boats collaborate to enable all the birds to fish collectively, which mimics the natural behaviour of wild cormorants when confronted with shoaling fish. (Flocks of 1,000 birds have been observed feeding together.)[7] Today the practice is protected and maintained as a tradition by the Japanese royal family and in more recent years it has become a commercial spectacle, attracting local visitors and foreign tourists, who often sail alongside the fishermen in traditional boats while dining and drinking sake.

One visitor was presumably British author Ian Fleming, creator of James Bond, who features the bird in his Japanese-located novel *You Only Live Twice*. The Japanese cormorant is almost as beautifully evoked as its owner, Kissy, Bond's suitably gorgeous Japanese companion. Her cormorant, known as 'David' (after David Niven, whom Fleming was possibly teasing in a private joke), sits in her boat alongside Bond 'opening its wings to the full extent of their five-foot wingspan and flapping them with gentle grace. Then, with a final shimmy through all its length, it settled down and gazed out to sea with its neck coiled backwards as if to strike and its turquoise eyes questing the horizon imperiously.'[8]

Mark Brazil, another Englishman in Japan, offers an eyewitness account that perfectly captures the fuller ritualised spectacle of fishing with Japanese Cormorants, especially the powerful chiaroscuro created by the open flame torches during these nocturnal sessions.

A paper lantern, yellow light gleaming from within, cast a strong silhouette of a painted bird on its surface – black,

rapidly familiar; if you feed him out of your hand, you will have trouble to prevent him from following you everywhere, ascending the stairs behind you, perching on your furniture, and leaving on all pieces incontestable traces of his rapid and abundant digestion.'[5]

Taking advantage of the intimacy developed between bird and human, Chinese fishermen simply encourage the free-flying birds into the water, the only signal for the cormorants to dive being a stamp of the foot or smack on the water with a pole. The birds are often fitted with a small bamboo float on their legs, so that they can be caught with the pole should the owner wish to retrieve them, and sometimes with a neck ring to prevent the birds swallowing the catch. Even where multiple boats work together or when boats operate singly but in close proximity, the cormorants show remarkable ability to find and fly back to their owners.

In China the system of reward varies. Sometimes the neck ring is large enough to allow the bird's consumption of small fish, or the bird is fed directly with titbits as it rests on its boat perch. Among the cormorant-fishing communities that live south of Guilin city in Guangxi province, the standard practice, which may well have persisted for centuries, involves the neck ring being removed after the bird's seventh catch. Observations of these fishermen suggest that the cormorants

long scrawny neck, wings spread, a cormorant! It was a hot, humid summer evening outside Kyoto. I reached the river before dark, in readiness to watch as the owners of long narrow boats prepared for their evening's fishing. Empty metal baskets were hung from bow hooks, woven bamboo baskets were stacked mid-ships, and the fishermen changed into dark cotton leggings and loose jackets. Many lanterns were strung along the riverside and more boats with lanterns were moored against the shore, but these were for revellers, the appealing clink of full glasses carried across the water – summer heat and cold beer and sake make a great match.

Once the boats were out on the river, the fishermen lit fires in the metal baskets at their bows, the wood crackled and snapped, burning brightly and reflected in the river water. The master fisherman at the bow added a roughly woven, thatch-like skirt to his outfit then began lifting cormorants from baskets and casting them into the water. He had them tethered like a sled-dog team on a fan leash. The birds quickly went into action, diving after fish drawn to the light, only to be yanked back to the boat by their fisherman. They were quickly divested of their catch – which they couldn't swallow because of the roped ring around their necks – then cast back to fish again.

The scene was busy with the sound of tipsy partygoers enjoying 'the show', the crackling of the flames, the splash of the boats and of the birds, and a steady beating, which I was never quite sure of – perhaps a boatman beating a drum, or just knocking a pole against the side of his boat. I was concerned for the birds, at first, but after a while each boat moved away from the revellers and let the birds out on to a gravel bar in the river to air-dry their wings.[9]

One of the key Western scholars on the subject, Berthold Laufer, observed in an important paper of 1931 how extraordinary it was that, despite the wide distribution of cormorants across six continents, only the Chinese and Japanese have brought any species into full domestication.[10] Yet there were notable attempts. The most enduring involved a cormorant relative, the Darter (see page 152), in modern-day Assam. The one other intriguing effort was launched simultaneously by James I in England (1566–1625) and Louis XIII of France (1601–1643).

Quite how these European monarchs acquired the interest is not known – contesting theories include the importation of the hobby via a British diplomat sent to the Chinese court, or through Dutch Jesuits who brought the birds back to Flanders – but James invested a small fortune in cormorants until he died, keeping a large stock of birds in London and taking them with him on hunting expeditions to Cambridgeshire and Norfolk (see also *Birds Britannica*, page 37).[11] He even tried to export the art, sending birds to Venice presumably as a gift to the doge, but the Duke of Savoy intercepted the king's Master of the Royal

Cormorants and stole them.[12] Yet James' son, Charles I, kept the tradition alive and in 1678 John Ray included the following passage in his book *Ornithology*, suggesting that it was at least a royal pastime for several decades.

> They are wont . . . in England to train up Cormorants to fishing. When they carry them out of the rooms where they are kept to the fish-pools, they hood-wink [place a hood over their heads] that they be not frightned by the way. When they are come to the Rivers they take off their hoods, and having tied a leather thong round the lower parts of their Necks that they may not swallow down the fish they catch, they throw them into the River. They presently dive under water, and there for a long time with wonderful swiftness pursue the fish, and when they have caught them they arise presently to the top of the water, and pressing the fish lightly with their Bills they swallow them; till each Bird hath after this manner devoured five or six fishes. Then their Keepers call them to the fist, to which they readily fly, and little by little one after another vomit up all their fish . . . When they have done fishing, setting the Birds on some high place they loose the string from their Necks, leaving the passage to the stomach free and open, and for their reward they throw them part of their prey they have caught, to each perchance one or two fishes, which they by the way as they are falling in the air will catch most dextrously in their mouths.[13]

It is clear from this description that while the training closely followed many aspects of the methods used in the Far East, the retrieval of the cormorants to a gloved fist reflected the powerful influence of falconry upon the European version.

A more constant, if far less positive, engagement with cormorants that seems almost universal arises because of the birds' supposed effect upon fisheries. This antagonism often manifests as a deep personal hatred of the birds. In Britain, fishermen recently ran websites explaining why cormorants should be exterminated, referring to them as the 'black death' or 'black plague'. Even in parts of China where domestic birds are not utilised for fishing, wild Great Cormorants are disliked and persecuted.[14]

Nor is it just the Great Cormorant. In south-west Britain from 1900–1950 a bounty system of rewards was used to cull regional populations of **European Shag** *Phalacrocorax aristotelis* and Great Cormorant.[15] In South Africa during the 1950s, so-called experts on local Atlantic fisheries proposed systematic culling of three piscivorous birds – **Cape Cormorant** *Leucocarbo capensis*, Cape Gannet and Jackass Penguin – to counter their assumed effect on pilchards and other commercial stocks.[16] In the late twentieth century Canadians have used flame-throwers on **Double-crested Cormorant** *Phalacrocorax auritus*; in New England the birds' nest sites were sprayed with an emulsion of oil and formalin, while in the southern states of the USA cormorant killing seems to have entered the space age: their roosts have been fired on with laser guns.[17]

Anhinga family *Anhingidae*

▶ An Osprey diving for its fish creates a sense of drama that is virtually unequalled by any other predatory bird.

There are just two species in this family and both are freshwater birds, dwelling particularly on rivers and channels through forest. The **Anhinga** *Anhinga anhinga* occurs in south-eastern USA and widely in Latin America south to Argentina. The **Darter** *Anhinga melanogaster*, has a massive world range across sub-Saharan Africa, south Asia and Australia.

The scientific names for both species and the common name for the American bird derive from a Tupi word (pronounced 'an-yeen-ga' and translating as 'small head'). It has long been mistaken to mean 'water-turkey', a name that was current in the USA even until the twentieth century.[1]

Both family members resemble cormorants but with strikingly attenuated upperparts so that often, when the birds are swimming with body almost entirely submerged, the pipe-like neck and head protrude above the water surface rather like the foreparts of a slender snake; hence the Darter's alternative name, 'snake-bird'.

One intriguing development was the use of Darters by itinerant fishermen on the Brahmaputra River (around the Indian town of Dhubri in Assam). It seems highly likely that this was borrowed and adapted from China, and is noted here mainly as an example of the highly restricted diffusion of Chinese cormorant-fishing practices. How the Hindi and Muslim fisherfolk of Assam first encountered the parallel use of Chinese birds is not clear (see also Great Cormorant, page 149). Nor is it known why they chose the Darter rather than the Great Cormorant, which is better suited to catching fish for human consumption. (The Darter's fine neck restricts its diet to small fry.) The use of Darters was noted in 1948, but has since been assumed to have died out.[2] Certainly there is no contemporary awareness of them in neighbouring parts of Myanmar or Bangladesh, where the Darter is now rare.

A curious symbolic appropriation of the species has occurred in Israel, a country where a tiny population of Darters was extirpated by wetland drainage in the 1950s. Notwithstanding this extinction, the Darter, under its Hebrew name *Nahshon* (*nahash* is 'snake' in Hebrew), became the title for a make of aircraft for the Israeli Air Force. 'The jet is also actually named after the first person that crossed the Red Sea when it parted. Since then the first person to do something is always called a Nahshon. It's also true that IAF planes carry a bird's name. The jet named Nahshon is used for intelligence, so it always leads the way.'[3]

Birds of Prey *Cathartidae, Falconidae* and *Accipitridae*

Universally distributed across all biomes (except in Antarctica), birds of prey are among the best-known avian groups in the world. Yet this has not always been reflected in our accurate scientific understanding of them. They have probably been a greater source of muddle than any other bird family. The males of many species are routinely smaller than their partners, while the young birds are frequently different in plumage to their parents and change as they mature. Unfortunately one must also contend with massive colour variations across whole species. Members of the genus *Buteo* are classic sources of confusion, including the European **Common Buzzard** *Buteo buteo* and the American **Red-tailed Hawk** *Buteo jamaicensis*, which can be completely white or black, with almost every colour morph in between.

Early naturalists mistook these gender- and age-related differences to be the distinct features of entirely separate species. Even now mastering raptor identification is a milestone in the career of any ornithologist, while raptor taxonomy remains a knotted issue, with authorities dividing them between as many as five families. Gill and Wright recognise three: the New World Vultures (*Cathartidae*: seven species), the Caracaras and Falcons (*Falconidae*: 64 species) and then the Kites, Hawks and Eagles (*Accipitridae*: 242 species). Since so many cultural responses to raptors overlap substantially or are common across the whole order, irrespective of which theoretical division is applied, I treat them as a single unit. So vast is the history of raptor–human interactions that I have attempted to illustrate just the broad but essential themes: their ongoing symbolic importance, the human debt to birds of prey and our gifts to them.

THE DISTRIBUTION AND BIOLOGY OF RAPTORS

Raptors are not just conspicuous and eye-catching, their prominence is also a product of culture. Such is their commanding hold over our imaginations that we tend to observe them more acutely and to prioritise (or demonise) them before other birds. Yet there is an intrinsic bias in their distribution, with a strong tendency towards the tropics. Two centres of diversity are South America and Africa, each holding almost a third of all the world's 313 species. Both continents have large resident communities, but they are also the recipient territories for millions of migrant raptors pouring annually out of the northern hemisphere. The latter region, by contrast, holds a small percentage of the world total, with just 34 species found in America north of Mexico and 39 species in Europe.

Most people have an immediate sense of a raptor's core features. Irrespective of size the birds possess strong legs and feet with sharply hooked talons for killing and manipulating prey, as well as relatively massive heads with arresting eyes. As if reflecting their sharpness of vision, many species have brightly coloured irides – intense orange or yellow – and for the birds' overall size, the eyes themselves are huge. A **Peregrine Falcon** *Falco peregrinus*, a bird weighing no more than 1.3 kg (2.9 lb), has eyes that are larger and heavier than a man's. The corresponding acuity of sight is legendary and partly derived from the densely packed colour-sensitive cones on the falcon's fovea. Where humans have 200,000 cone cells per square millimetre in this most sensitive part of the retina, a peregrine has 1 million.[1]

Raptors compel our attention like few other bird families and Steller's Sea Eagles wintering in Hokkaido have made the ice-girt Japanese island a dream destination for many birdwatchers.

The other singular feature on the raptor's face is that extraordinary beak. In a bird of prey the upper mandible curves down and round the lower mandible, terminating in a hard hooked nail. The lower mandible is short but often possesses a distinct notch or notches that correspond with interlocking patterns on the upper mandible. These 'tomial teeth' aid the raptor's beak in its primary task of cutting, holding or tearing flesh.

One of the foremost expectations we have of birds of prey is that they live by catching and eating other animals. Power, speed and agility are all implicit in a carnivore's lifestyle and most raptors possess these attributes, although the prey itself is not always so fleet-footed. There is even the ultimate oxymoron: the vegetarian bird of prey. The **Palm-nut Vulture** *Gypohierax angolensis* of sub-Saharan Africa lives largely on the pericarp of palm tree nuts. Other species are equally finicky, including the **Snail Kite** *Rostrhamus sociabilis* of Central and South America which feeds only on molluscs. The list of insectivorous raptors is also long. There are specialists like the **European Honey Buzzard** *Pernis apivorus* that feeds by excavating social-insect nests to eat the grub-rich comb. They have thick blunt nails, not for handling live prey, but for digging and raking bare soil.

The largest of all raptors, the **Andean Condor** *Vultur gryphus* of South America and the **Himalayan Vulture** *Gyps himalayensis*, seldom take live prey of any kind. They are scavengers dependent upon dead carcasses. The heaviest individuals of either species weigh around 12 kg (26.5 lb), although the condor averages a shade heavier and shaves it on wing length, with a span of 3.2 m (10.5 ft), against 3.1 m (10 ft) for the vulture. Both are among the longest-winged birds in the world but their spans are a little shorter than that of the Wandering Albatross (see page 99), and a good deal less than we once believed.

In the eighteenth century the great French naturalist Comte de Buffon accepted reports of condors with wings of 5.5 m (18 ft).[2] Such exaggerations persisted in the ornithological literature for centuries and one wonders what these early fantasists might have done with the real measurements of an extinct raptor called *Argentavis magnificens*. This lost giant flew the heavens above modern Argentina in the Late Miocene, more than 5 million years ago. Its wings measured 7 m (23 ft) and it weighed five times more than an Andean Condor. What a world it must have been![3]

There is general agreement that for sheer aura, the grandest of all living species is the **Harpy Eagle** *Harpia harpyja* of South and Central America. Leslie Brown described it as 'unquestionably the world's most formidable bird'.[4] Its spread talons equal the span of a man's hand; the legs are the thickness of a child's wrist. Weighing 9 kg (19.8 lb), the adult female Harpy Eagle can catch and carry away monkeys or sloths, some of which are almost as heavy as she is.

Yet we should not overlook the proportionate powers of the harpy's smaller relatives. The **Eurasian Sparrowhawk** *Accipiter nisus* weighs 103–350 g (3.6–12.3 oz), but the bird has the daring of a fiend.

> A friend told me this morning that a neighbour of his heard a big bang in her house yesterday and when she went to investigate discovered two sparrowhawks locked together in a fight on her bed! They had come through her (closed single-pane) window, with glass shattered on the floor. Fetching her gardening gloves she managed to pick them up and release them outside. They must have been travelling at a terrific speed actually to break through the window glass. I guess if it had been a double-glazed window they would probably both have been killed.[5]

I was in the doorway on a warm summer's morning with my kitchen door wide open, when two seemingly huge-winged birds flashed in and came at me at eye level. I put my hands up so they jinked sideways and ended up clawing at the windows each side of the stove but entangled in vases, wooden spoons, muesli, herbs, fruit, oils and all that makes for good cooking. My dog was leaping up and down trying to get at them. I quickly shut the door, grabbed a garden coat and after clearing away as many of the hazards, managed to enfold each beautiful, fiercely powerful bird and watch it fly away unfazed. The sparrowhawk's powerful yellow beak, its piercing eyes and enormous claws the size of my hand were thrilling to see so close and what a treat for any bird lover. But the story isn't over. Pip, my dog, was still leaping up and down near the stove and I saw that a Barn Swallow – the bird we all love the most – was trapped in one of the vases. I gathered it up and popped it carefully among some shrubs to recover and hopefully make it to Africa. So the birds didn't get me, the dog didn't get the sparrowhawks and they didn't get the swallow.[6]

One of the pixies among the raptors is the **Collared Falconet** *Microhierax caerulescens* of India and south-east Asia. Some individuals measure just 14 cm (5.5 in) – only twice the length of the Harpy Eagle's hind claw – yet a Collared Falconet has its own brand of vest-pocket ferocity. Asian potentates reared falconets to take sparrows in the palace gardens, or they were used specifically to fly at the heads of cranes, whereby the huge befuddled birds were seized by hand.[7]

RAPTORS AND POLITICO-MILITARY SYMBOLISM

Humans have long admired this aggressive potency in raptors. It is precisely these qualities that have made a number of the very biggest species some of the most frequently deployed symbols, especially of military and political power. The exemplar is the eagle. Modern Iraq, Egypt, Albania, Mexico, Poland, the Philippines and the USA are just a few of the heterogeneous countries holding the bird dear as a national emblem. Eagles probably feature on more flags and coats of arms than any other kind of bird.

What is striking about such symbolism as a means of expressing our collective power is its almost irresistible appeal to humans – demonstrated as strongly among the possessors of nuclear weapons as it was once among the lance-bearing Indians of the North American plains. Eagle symbolism is found among the simplest political entities, such as the Amerindian tribes of the rainforest, as it is among the world's greatest empires. Eagles graced the corridors of power in ancient Rome, but are also found in the Yanomami's thatch.

Some of the earliest examples of bird-of-prey imagery are found among the cluster of city-states in the Sumerian and later the Assyrian empires, centred on the confluence of the Tigris and Euphrates rivers (in modern Iraq). Images representing large raptors have been found on objects and buildings that are almost 5,000 years old. Such birds were often shown in conjunction with the ultimate mammalian predator from the region, the lion, as if the bird and the

This relief sculpture of an eagle-headed protective spirit was found at the Assyrian capital of Nimrud and is almost 3,000 years old.

cat were the aerial and terrestrial counterparts of the same natural majesty. Feathered creatures resembling eagles were sometimes given lion heads, or were shown with eagle heads but taloned paws.

These mythical beasts should alert us to one of several fascinating aspects of ancient 'eagle' symbolism. Historical societies in no way possessed, nor were they concerned to conform to, the kind of natural-historical accuracy that we often consider important. When we speak of eagle symbols – such as the relief carvings of eagle-headed spirits (from the Assyrian city of Nimrud, *c*.865 BC) that greet visitors walking through the doors of the British Museum in London – we need to introduce a major caveat. The likelihood is that many of the huge ravenous birds that we try to designate as 'eagle' or 'vulture' or 'hawk' symbols were an amalgam, synthesised from various large raptors present in that particular historical territory.

Ancient beliefs about the birds often owed nothing to genuine natural history. A classic example occurs in the Roman writings of Pliny the Elder. He noted how 'the eagle' is the only bird never to have been killed by a thunderbolt.[8] The reason eagles were unaffected by thunderbolts was because the birds were emblems of Jupiter. For Pliny's contemporaries the eagle was as truly an embodiment of this Roman deity as it was a bird of the air, and since lightning was also a manifestation of Jupiter, it was logical to assume that the eagle and the thunderbolt were on amicable terms.

When all the caveats have been entered, we can still acknowledge how important eagles were as political symbols for the ancient world. Greek temples to Zeus, like Roman shrines to Jupiter, featured spectacular eagle images on their facades. It was the pre-eminent bird of power and divinity. At state funerals for Rome's rulers, a live eagle was released at the emperor's burning pyre as a metaphor for the soul's

A vulture of beaten gold was found on one of the mummified wives of Thutmose III at Thebes. It represents the goddess Nekhbet, whose avian symbol is omnipresent in ancient Egyptian funerary artefacts.

final flight to the heavens. Most memorable of all, however, was the eagle imagery emblazoned on the standards for the imperial legions. Rome once fought and conquered its enemies under the eagle's gaze.

It was Rome's own bid for world domination that bequeathed the symbolic-eagle habit to many subsequent political dynasties with expansionist goals both in Europe and beyond. This was the case for the Byzantine Empire centred on Constantinople (a double-headed eagle motif, which is still manifest on Greek civic and Greek Orthodox religious buildings today), as it was for Tsarist Russia and Napoleonic France. Even the Founding Fathers of the USA could not resist the eagle's dark gravitational hold upon the European political imagination. When the fledgling state established independence and proclaimed a radically different dispensation in the New World, it still opted for the ancient motifs of the Old. This was despite Benjamin Franklin's suggestion that the US Founding Fathers adopt the Wild Turkey as their national mascot (see page 42).

During the early twentieth century, the Nazis in Germany adapted eagle symbols that had been central to political imagery in Prussia and the Austro-Hungarian Empire for hundreds of years. Surviving footage of Nazi rallies frequently shows flags bearing that diagnostic German symbol – the black eagle, talons down-stretched, with a ragged rosette-like spread of open wings all about it. Yet they also deployed a specifically fascist eagle – a cold, lean, angular cruciform bird often emblazoned on the Führer's breast pocket or on his peaked cap – whose obvious Christian connotations now seem grotesquely ironic. (It is striking how the trenchantly democratic modern Germany has retained the same motif, but expanded the girth of its new eagle to make it a rather replete, seemingly satisfied, somehow unrapacious bird of prey. As one Berliner notes, 'in the vernacular it is called the *Fette Henne*, 'fat hen'.)[9]

The sinister qualities of the earlier Nazi version of the German eagle, to which people may still have visceral adverse reactions, brings to the fore a third facet of this raptor imagery. Throughout history any one of these imagined birds might have brought a reassuring sense of historical

legitimacy, and proclaimed the power and majesty of those nations that had taken a symbolic eagle to their hearts. For all its opponents, however, it was – and sometimes still is – nothing more than a terrifying predator.

Political symbols are double-edged. They are loathed as much as they are loved. One can only imagine the kind of fear inspired among the subject peoples by the eagle standard of the Roman army as it marched inexorably over Europe; or the sense of foreboding which a prisoner felt as the odious Nazi harpy stared down upon them in the SS cell. Our responses to symbols of power are conditioned by its realities – boots, guns, bombs, injury, servitude and death. One wonders, in fact, whether the inevitable binary nature of this politico-military symbolism has itself shaped some of our complex and deeply ambivalent responses to the flesh-and-blood creatures themselves. For, as we will explore, no birds-related stories are more emotionally charged or socially divisive than those involving birds of prey.

Proof of our deeply ambiguous attitudes is the fact that the same people who cherish the symbol can still despise the living bird. Despite the centrality of the **Bald Eagle** *Haliaeetus leucocephalus* to so much national symbolism in the USA, the species was persecuted for decades. In Alaska alone bounties were paid on 41,812 eagles between 1917–27 and by the late 1930s the figure may have been as high as 70,000 birds.[10] In Texas and New Mexico between the 1940s and 1960s the **Golden Eagle** *Aquila chrysaetos* was shot from the skies by hunters in small aeroplanes to counter the species' presumed depredations on sheep farms. Before the Golden Eagle was given legal protection in 1963, these so-called 'control' measures killed 1,000–2,000 birds annually.[11] Sometimes the slaughter continues, regardless of legislation. In Scotland, where the Golden Eagle is the ubiquitous if unofficial symbol of the country's northern Highlands, illegal persecution by landowners is so intense that today 'increasingly large areas of suitable breeding habitat are unoccupied'.[12]

Sometimes the acute contradictions between care for the imaginary bird and indifference to the real creature assume tragic proportions. Perhaps the most threatened of all eagle symbols is the **Philippine Eagle** *Pithecophaga jefferyi*. This magnificent endemic, only a shade less dramatic than the Harpy Eagle, is the national bird of the Philippines with a presence on all the country's banknotes. Alas, none of this symbolic ubiquity really counts when set against the devastating realities of deforestation. One-third of all Filipino forest, on which the eagle is entirely dependent, has been cleared since 1990. It continues to be lost at an annual rate of 2 per cent and will drive the surviving population (350–670 birds) towards inevitable extinction, unless massive remedial efforts are taken soon.[13]

Eagles on German coinage: note how the bird on the left (a one-euro piece) has acquired a fuller, somehow less predatory, girth compared with its wartime predecessor.

Brutal and cruel it may be, but the Yawar Fiesta of the Peruvian Andes is a completely compelling piece of political theatre.

THE YAWAR FIESTA IN MODERN PERU

Modern South America is witness to an extraordinary ritual that demonstrates how raptors have lost none of their capacity to express our most fundamental political values. The event is now known to the outside world as the 'Yawar Fiesta' and is held in towns and villages throughout the Peruvian Andes. One such place is Cotabambas, a town to the south-west of the old Incan capital, Cuzco.

The exact nature of the celebrations varies from place to place, as does the date. The events are regularly held between 26–30 July, to coincide with wider festivities associated with Independence Day (28 July), when the country commemorates its liberation from the old

imperialist government. However, Yawar Fiestas can also take place at the time of other important religious festivals, such as Christmas. One recurrent feature is the baiting and occasionally the killing in ritual form (in the past this slaughter was central) of a bull by poncho-wielding locals, for whom this ancient but quintessentially European import serves as symbol for the Peruvians' former Spanish masters.

One of the first people to offer a detailed description of these events was the Peruvian writer José María Arguedas (1911–1969), in his ground-breaking novel *Yawar Fiesta* (1941). It documents a version of the ritual as practised in Puquio, the highland town of his youth. In the early twentieth century the place was home to a deeply stratified community. Yet, as the novel rises to its climactic scenes in the bullring, one gains a sense not only of the profound social

157

The Andean Condor
is the largest bird of
prey on Earth.

injustices inflicted on the predominantly 'Indian' population by the white *mistis*, the Westernised landowners, but also of the perverse interdependence of the oppressed and the oppressors. In Puquio's festival the community's strange unity is consummated when a bull is caught and brutally slaughtered, its chest blasted apart with dynamite.

A modern resident in the Peruvian Andes describes the impact of this important novel and the way in which Arguedas' writing has helped shape today's version of the bullfight:

> The festival currently happens in some 40 or so remote villages in the Apurímac Region. The event was originally known as *Toropucllay* (loosely translated as 'games with the bull') but it has generally become known as the 'Yawar Fiesta' after the book of the same name by Arguedas, who is often called the 'Hemingway of the Andes', incidentally, because he also blew his brains out. The key moment of the modern festival involves the tying of an Andean Condor to the back of a bull. The people then fight the bull for a few minutes, after which the latter is lassoed and the condor is set free. This is undoubtedly cruel to both animals. The bull gets holes punched through its skin so that the condor's legs can be tied to it. The condor spends a few days or weeks tied up in someone's yard; it is paraded through town; it is given beer to drink; it is tossed around on the back of the bull, and, if all goes well, it is then tossed off a cliff with ribbons tied to it. However, not infrequently the bird is injured or killed.
>
> People almost unanimously insist that a condor features in this way in Arguedas' book (the covers in most Spanish-language versions have an illustration of this) and they mistakenly say that this struggle between the two creatures is his metaphor for the

indigenous Andean peasants overcoming the repression of Spanish-originated landowners. Yet Arguedas himself did not write this. In his novel the bullfight does not feature a condor. That notion comes from the masses of people who should have read the novel at school, but skipped it because they were lazy, or because they found his use of Quechua grammatical structures with a Spanish vocabulary tortuous (as it is). They assume they know all about a book that they have never actually read completely. This misinterpretation of Arguedas' book is probably the main reason the festival grows in popularity and the number of events increases annually even as the condor population continues to decline.[14]

The word 'condor' is derived from the ancient Quechua (the Inca language) name *kuntur*.[15] However, the bird's cultural importance long pre-dates the Incas, with early representations from 2500 BC.[16] Today traditional Andean communities still view the bird as a form of divine messenger, able to traffic between the realm of humans and the Peruvian gods of the high peaks. (It is partly on account of its semi-sacred status that it is the national bird in four Andean states: Bolivia, Colombia, Chile and Ecuador.) At Cotabambas a delegated group climb into the mountains prior to the fiesta to capture a wild condor lured down with bait. The giant bird is rushed and caught at high risk of injury to its human assailants. In a glorious piece of modern religious syncretism, the bird of the ancient Incan deities is blessed in church by a Catholic priest. It is also adorned with pennants that express its psychological link to Andean society. (This same ritual is described by Arguedas, who writes of a condor months after the fiesta 'flying from snowy peak to snowy peak, trailing his streamers'.)[17]

A modern eyewitness of a Yawar Fiesta comments on the deep contradictions at the heart of this remarkable event:

Black Kites can gather in their tens of thousands at Ghazipur rubbish dump near New Delhi, India.

Before I went to Cotabambas, I was sure that, as a conservationist, I would hate being there and hate the people doing this, yet it was not like that. It is, however, one of the weirdest spectacles I have ever witnessed. Drunks and show-offs vie for the bull's attention and the free beer offered, and get in the way of the more skilled bullfighters, whilst dogs wander through the makeshift bullring in the village square. The struggle of the condor only lasts minutes but the process of capture, parades, fight and release may take two months or more. It seems a bloody strange way to treat your sacred bird, yet they have an almost religious devotion to the condor, they really care what happens to it, and if it comes to any harm this is considered a seriously bad omen for the village. I suspect they are some of the best allies for saving this magnificent bird, which is rapidly disappearing from the Peruvian Andes – certainly without their involvement there will be no chance, no more condors, and no more Yawar Fiestas.[18]

Animal welfare groups object to this raw, if powerfully expressive, piece of political theatre on the grounds of its brazen cruelty to bird and bull. At one time, in fact at least until the 1970s, there were parallel rituals practised in the Peruvian Andes in which condors were deliberately sacrificed. At villages such as Cashapampa in the Callejón de Huaylas, an Andean Condor would be caught in a special pit trap and then ritually suspended upside down. The villagers would then ride beneath the bird and beat it with their fists until it eventually expired. As many as ten to 15 birds were thought to be killed annually in this manner, which was known as *arranque del condor*, the 'pulling of the condor'. Dead condors are still valued for their wing bones, from which are made even now the *quena*, the Andean flute.[19]

At today's Yawar Fiestas the real dangers are largely human. Wherever they are held, the celebrations entail injuries to those alcohol-fuelled men who brave the fury of an angry bull. Some are gored and tossed, even killed. That, indeed, is an intrinsic element of the fiesta's power. The word *yawar* means 'blood', and this spilling of human blood is viewed as a blessing upon the event and upon the community. For all its primitive character and complicated symbolism, this Andean ritual illuminates as emphatically as any other human enterprise how predatory birds continue to shape and express our ideas about political conflict and social triumph in all its multifarious physical and spiritual guises.

THE BLACK KITE

Owing to their presence at the top of the food chain, many birds of prey are extremely sensitive to human alterations to their environment. More than one-fifth (70 species) of all raptors are now considered at some risk of extinction, including species with high cultural status such as the Andean Condor. Yet, remarkably, other raptors seem almost immune to the wholesale human destruction of the natural environment, thriving even amid our squalor and pollution. Possibly the most abundant and successful of all is the **Black Kite** *Milvus migrans*.

This immensely graceful, long-winged bird has a world range across vast areas of southern Eurasia, all of Africa (except the Sahara Desert) and large swathes of Australasia. It is as comfortable over virgin rainforest as it is over the choked metropolis. It may well have adapted to urban living at about the same time as humans built the first cities. Certainly there is a striking, highly accurate image of a Black Kite hanging around a butcher's stall at Thebes (*c.*1100 BC), and even older, and just as redolent of their modern behaviour, is the bird hoping for titbits from an ancient Egyptian fisherman (*c.*1500 BC).[20]

This was once one of the quintessential sights of rural India, but not any more: a veterinary painkiller called Diclofenac has wiped out 40 million vultures in the last 20 years.

Black Kites are adept scavengers and are occasionally despised for the habit – old names include 'pariah kite' and 'shitehawk' – yet the species is not without its own brand of courage. In 2004 a kite in KwaZulu-Natal was reported to have attacked a light aircraft, its high-speed dive embedding its whole body in the plane, forcing the pilot almost into a crash-landing.[21] The bird has a more established reputation for stealing poultry and general larceny, talents which have their origins in the Black Kites' breathtaking aerial agility. This enables them to seize much of their food from off the surface of open water or from busy roads amid heavy traffic – patrolling for roadkill is a common kite strategy – without ever landing.

In many cities they have adapted these skills, snatching meals from market stalls and vendors or from people's hands and plates. I lost a chapatti once to a kite in Kathmandu, Nepal. They have also been recorded to take cheroots out of people's mouths and hats off heads.[22] As long ago as the seventeenth century John Ray complained that 'Courts, or Yards of houses are not secure from their ravine. For which cause our good Housewives are very angry with them.'[23] Yet some of us have good reason to be grateful for this kind of mischief:

> The Black Kites at Debre Libanos in Ethiopia are well used to tourists. When groups of visitors stop to admire the old Portuguese Bridge, it's not long before the kites begin circling expectantly overhead. On one occasion a bold bird swooped down and removed a sun hat from a lady's head, much to our amusement. But the following year, we were all standing around eating our picnic lunch, when one of the kites swooped down and grabbed a whole chicken leg from my hand. I was furious at the time, but the following day everyone in the group who had had a chicken leg on that picnic was violently ill – those who had had chicken breasts were

fine. Clearly the undercooked legs were to blame, and I had been spared a dose of food poisoning by a Black Kite – my guardian angel.[24]

What is truly remarkable are the sheer numbers of Black Kites that can find a good living in some tropical conurbations. Kolkata (Calcutta), Mumbai, Cairo and Istanbul are among the cities with huge kite populations. In the 1540s French naturalist Pierre Belon reported the vast flocks, many of them autumn migrants returning from Asia to Africa, that were visible over the Turkish Bosphorus. '[W]e could not conceive', he wrote, 'where such a multitude of Kites could get themselves food. For should they for but fifteen days space fly continually that way in such numerous squadrons, I dare confidently affirm, they would exceed the number of men living upon the Earth.'[25]

Belon's claim sounds exaggerated but there are modern equivalents to his Bosphorus multitudes. On the eastern outskirts of Delhi in India is Ghazipur, the capital's main landfill site. Aside from the noxious foetor from burning debris and gaseous rot, the place is a hub of vibrant activity.

> Children in colourful rags scavenge for recyclable litter while feral packs of dogs roam menacingly over the top of this mountain of rubbish, which is a mile across and stretches as far as the eye can see. On the street below there are chickens being gutted by people that perch precariously over open sewers. You could not imagine a more hellish place. Yet swooping to pluck entrails and swarming over the Ghazipur dump, like a scene from Hitchcock's *The Birds*, are tens of thousands of Black Kites. The surrounding forest of electricity pylons is smothered in them. An estimated 150,000 kites call this stinking suburb home.[26]

This is surely among the largest semi-permanent congregations of raptors to be found anywhere on Earth.

Wherever Black Kites congregate, there are often so many of them that one is assailed not only by the grace of their aerial evolutions and their perpetual whinnying calls, but also by that same thought that struck Belon in Ottoman Turkey. How on Earth do so many large predatory birds find a living in one place? At Ghazipur the question is overwhelming. Yet there, also, eloquently articulated in the gyring thousands, is the kites' answer. They do, they can, they will.

The Black Kite seems truly a bird of prey for any human future. So too do several other carrion-eating raptors that have flourished amid the rubbish produced by people worldwide. These species include the **Black Vulture** *Coragyps atratus* and **Turkey Vulture** *Cathartes aura* across much of the Americas, as well as the **Hooded Vulture** *Necrosyrtes monachus* and **White-backed Vulture** *Gyps africanus* in Africa. At one time, the **White-rumped Vulture** *Gyps bengalensis*, **Slender-billed Vulture** *Gyps tenuirostris* and **Indian** (Long-billed) **Vulture** *Gyps indicus* of Asia would automatically have been on this list. Just 20 years ago the first of these species vied with the Black Kite to be the world's most numerous large bird of prey. Its Indian population alone was estimated in tens of millions, while single flocks of 15,000 birds had been observed.[27] Now it is threatened with extinction, having suffered a 99.9 per cent decline. Today it may number 11,000 in total.

The carcasses that Asian people have supplied for millennia to these formerly superabundant raptors have become contaminated with a common veterinarian painkiller called Diclofenac. In a generation this seemingly innocuous compound has killed all but a few thousand pairs of the three threatened species. The reversal of fortune of the White-rumped Vulture is a measure of how precarious it can be to have such reliance on humankind.

THE CALIFORNIA CONDOR

The issue of often inadvertent poisoning that has resulted from our ever-increasing arsenal of modern chemical agents – herbicides, fertilisers, insecticides, industrial disinfectants, etc. – has been central to the story of birds of prey for nearly a century. In the case of the **California Condor** *Gymnogyps californianus*, however, it has determined much of its recent history and casts a long shadow still over the bird's future.

This magnificent and magnificently ugly bird, with its massive sable wings and livid red goitrous neck, is the largest bird of prey in North America. In many ways it is the antithesis of the Black Kite and its entire population numbers 394 birds (April 2011). Most were born in captivity and more than 200 still live in zoos. Yet just a generation ago the entire population was 23 individuals, and in 1986 there remained a single wild breeding pair in the world. It was the rarest raptor on Earth. The only bird to have reached such a nadir and to have avoided extinction was the Black Robin of the Chatham Islands in New Zealand (see page 403).

Yet this much the condor shares with the superabundant Black Kite. The lessening rarity of the first bird and the vast numbers of the second are products of human action. In a sense, the future of both species lies squarely in our hands. No raptor, in fact, no other bird species of any kind, has received more dedicated attention than the California Condor. The financial sum spent on saving the species is impossible to calculate, but it has long been measured in tens of millions of dollars, and very soon it will be hundreds of millions. Its recent history highlights the new meanings that we have invested in birds of prey as the supreme symbols for their wider environment.

Many people are so accustomed to the condor's connection to the Golden State that it is hard sometimes to recall how it once flourished across all of North America. Its heyday was the Pleistocene, when condors fed on carcasses of now-extinct megafauna such as mammoths and ground sloths. By the time of European colonisation, it had already begun its descent towards oblivion. In the nineteenth century it was largely confined to the west coast from Baja California to Vancouver in Canada. By the 1890s there was even an article on the species entitled 'A Doomed Bird', and when the great American naturalist William Beebe contemplated its fate in 1906, he wrote, 'within a few years at most, the last individual will have perished'.[28]

The shared sense of inevitability about the condor's extinction became, in some ways, a self-fulfilling prophecy. Collectors, intent on a final relic of a 'lost' soul, further subtracted from the survivors by shooting adults for museum skins and by stealing eggs. The prediction of its doom also seemed to render unnecessary any scientific research into the causes of the decline. Even now the reasons for the slump in numbers during the nineteenth and twentieth centuries are open to conjecture. One of the more unusual factors, however, was the widespread killing of condors for their great wing quills, which were used to hold gold dust by California's successive waves of prospectors.[29] Other issues included deliberate persecution, habitat loss, disturbance at nest sites and, especially, inadvertent poisoning of various kinds.[30]

In the early years it was strychnine baits set to rid Californian cattle ranches of their stock-stealing predators. By the 1920s bane for vermin – thallium sulphate put down to clear farms of ground squirrels – may have been an unseen killer. Yet the most serious problem was almost certainly lead. Bullets lodged and left in deer carcasses and other game were ingested by flesh-eating condors, where they acted as a slow-release poison. Even now the issue is an unresolved threat.

Between 1946 and 1982 the bird's population shrank from about 150 to 21–24 individuals. This final phase of decline also overlapped with the widespread deployment of a so-called wonder chemical, DDT, a pesticide with broad-based application. It was so gleefully embraced as a cost-free cure-all in agriculture that one of its advertising jingles contained what seems now an extraordinarily crass rhyme – 'D-D-T is good for me'. In the area where condors staged a final battle for existence this lethal chemical was applied at a ratio just a fraction under 1 kg/1 ha (1 lb/1 acre) over 77,000 ha (190,000 acres) of the species' prime habitat.

Steadily the evidence accrued that DDT, a stable compound persisting often at sub-lethal levels in the body tissues of herb- or grain-eating birds and mammals, accumulated with devastating effect in predators higher up the food chain. One problem it triggered was the laying of eggs with unnaturally thin shells. During the ordinary business of incubation, the sitting parents cracked and destroyed their own clutches. Condors were known to have produced thin-shelled eggs in this period, but the extent to which DDT was implicated in the species' last years of nest

The California Condor may not be pretty but it is immensely valuable. Its salvation from extinction has involved the most costly conservation project ever mounted for one species.

failure is less clear than it was in the case of its most famous victim.[31]

This particular raptor, the Peregrine Falcon, is arguably the most successful on Earth. Yet from the 1950s, especially in Europe and North America where DDT was used with greatest concentration, the falcon plunged wildly downwards in number. The dark race of peregrine found on the east coast of the USA, *Falco peregrinus anatum*, was actually driven to near-extinction. Such losses precipitated fears for the entire world population of the species but also for other birds of prey.

The story of how environmentalists unravelled the tangled skein linking DDT to calamitous declines in predatory birds, from peregrines to pelicans, has now entered the annals of conservation (see *Birds Britannica*, pages 149–50). For some it is part of the creation myth of the entire environmental movement. One of its key patron saints was Rachel Carson, scrupulous scientist and fiery activist, whose 1962 publication, *Silent Spring*, is widely credited with lifting the lid on the pernicious side effects of agrochemicals. It was thanks largely to the crisis telescoped into the story of the Peregrine Falcon that DDT and similar pesticides were banned or voluntarily withdrawn from agricultural usage in many countries from the 1970s onwards.

By the mid 1980s activists in the field of California Condor conservation had grouped into two deeply opposed camps. On the one side were those who believed the condor was a relict from America's Pleistocene past; the last essence of wild nature, a creature that shrank from human contact and for whom the last best hope was to leave it sequestered in glorious isolation and to pray that it would somehow pull through this bottleneck crisis of a poisoned landscape. Central to that strategy had been the declaration in 1947 of a condor park, the Sespe Sanctuary, which eventually comprised 21,450 ha (53,000 acres). In the other camp was a group of environmentalists who felt that the only way to save a species down to its last wild pair was all-out hands-on intervention. This plan involved taking all of the wild condors into protective custody and then housing them in special breeding facilities at two Californian zoos. Supported by the highest levels of veterinarian care and scientific expertise, the condors would slowly be able to build up the bird numbers, through pair manipulation, artificial incubation and hand-rearing techniques, so that they could be released into the wild at a later date.

For nearly 20 years, environmentalists, many of them experienced falconers, had been hacking peregrines back into the wild, especially on the North American east coast, in a parallel bid to save that endangered bird of prey. The scheme had been a massive success, described as 'one of the most positive and far-sighted wildlife conservation projects yet attempted anywhere in the World'.[32] By the early 1980s more than 100 peregrines were being released every year. Today the species has recovered almost all its former haunts continent-wide and now breeds in most major US east-coast cities. This 'landmark recovery' of the poisoned peregrine offered a model for the Californian environmentalists, except their raptor was nine times bigger.[33]

Despite impassioned debate and even legal challenges from the condor's hands-off lobby, it was this version of the bird's future that was eventually implemented. In many ways it has been a second astounding success story. Protective custody of all the remaining condors was finalised in 1987, with the capture of a diehard named Igor. Artificial breeding had its first triumph – a chick called 'Molloko' – in 1988. By January 1992 the first two California Condors were loosed once more above their old rangelands. Since that time several hundred birds have been introduced back into the wild, not only in central and northern California but also in Baja California and Arizona, the latter population in a vast expanse of former condor habitat around the Grand Canyon. As insurance against catastrophe, there is still a captive population split between San Diego and Los Angeles Zoos.

As things turned out, California Condors were absent from their former rangelands for just the period between 1987 and 1992. For many this short-lived spell of human wardship was the necessary price to relaunch the magnificent bird on a new and secure trajectory. For some, however, those five short years have changed everything. What ended with the spell of collective internment was the condor's 11-million-year heritage as a free-flying species. In those 57 months, the essence of the wild bird died. What emerged from the release pens on 29 January 1992 was something entirely different. As one critic put it, the zoo-reared condors had been bred 'as we produce poodles and we will manage them like domestic stock'. Some of this seemed to be immediately justified. Of the first two released individuals in 1992, one was taken back into custody because it was 'acting tame'; the other died after drinking a puddle of bright-green anti-freeze.[34]

The issue of the birds becoming imprinted on humans in the years of captive rearing is a major problem for the condor recovery teams. So too has been the challenge of getting condors to act, feed or breed entirely for themselves. Yet, no matter how slowly it has occurred, the birds have regained necessary survival skills and have even begun to breed successfully in the wild without intervention. The one remaining hurdle – in fact, the very problem that has dogged our shared history with birds of prey for the last century – is that of environmental poisoning.

All condors bear numbered tags on each wing to aid recognition, and are fitted with radio transmitters to enable researchers to locate and, if necessary, re-trap the birds. So far, it has been essential to retrieve and subject some of them to detoxification treatments to stop the condors succumbing to the lethal effects of ingested bullets. If such recurrent, complex and expensive interventions are what define an animal as being managed as domestic stock, then the condors are truly being tended like free-range cattle. Certainly the large black creatures with the 2.9 m (9.5 ft) wingspan and the raw-liver-red heads seen flying freely over the last untamed landscapes of the American West seem somewhat less than genuinely wild birds.

Yet they are still indubitably *there*. It is for us to choose whether their presence, however compromised or dependent upon our assistance, is a good thing – a better thing – than otherwise. What some struggle with, in the case of the California Condor, is not just the continuing threat from lead poisoning, but their very notions of how a massive wild predator should live and have its being. Noel and Helen Snyder, outstanding condor specialists, have put it thus:

> One cannot escape the impression that for many people
> involved, preserving habitat and preserving an image
> of the condor as a paragon of wilderness have been
> more important than saving the condor itself. These are
> important and attractive goals . . . but they have turned
> out to be ones that have often conflicted with preserving
> the condor as a viable biological species.[35]

More than perhaps any other raptor, the California Condor has dramatised the challenge faced by this order of birds in a world almost universally affected by our chemical agents. Yet its history also illuminates how we are sometimes as fixated by our imaginative versions of raptors, as we are by the real creatures themselves.

FALCONRY

There is arguably no more intimate and subtle relationship between a human and any bird on the face of the Earth than that attained by a falconer with his falcon or hawk. Essentially it involves the pursuit of wild quarry with a wild raptor, and originally it had as its end the eminently practical goal of meat for the table. Yet around this utilitarian operation humans have assembled a temple-like complex of ritual, knowledge, lore, superstition and passionate, almost religious, devotion to predatory birds.

The precise origins of falconry are still disputed, but it

Hooded falcons in an Arab hunter's camp form the centre-piece to a cultural activity that has been sustained for thousands of years.

probably began somewhere in the Middle East or central Asia as early as the second millennium BC. It then travelled eastwards into China, where there was already a substantial written account by the Zhou Dynasty (1046–256 BC).[36] Falconry also made its way steadily westwards into Christian Europe in the early Middle Ages where it flourished for 1,000 years. So many different raptors have been used across the entire northern hemisphere, including as we shall see full-sized eagles in Mongolia, that it makes the word 'falconry' seem overly specific. Regardless of the bird deployed, however, the essentials are the same.

It involves taking a wild and initially overwrought raptor that panics at the merest touch or sound, and gradually acquainting it with human presence (today birds are often bred in captivity). The acclimatising process is called 'manning' the bird and it continues until the creature will sit upon a gloved fist and fly to take prey at the urging of its human partner. To move from the raw bundle of nerves to the self-confident hunter involves the use of several key items. There is a pair of leather gauntlets or wristbands to take the lethal impress of the talons. The bird's eyes are 'seeled' with a stitch through each lid or, more usually, a 'hood' is placed over them to soothe the bird's fears in temporary darkness. A pair of leg straps called 'jesses' enable it to be held and manipulated, while small bells tied to these help the falconer find his bird once it has flown freely. A long lead known as a 'creance' is used as the bird flies after a 'lure' – a live or dead imitation bird or mammal – to rehearse the act of catching prey on the wing in controlled settings. Eventually the bird matures from these contrived simulacra to real pursuits in a natural setting.

The myriad variations in technique that have been used to advance through these stages have given rise to a body

Members of a Kazakh family pose in traditional costume with their Saker Falcon, which they have brought to the eagle hunters' festival at Bayan-Ulgii in western Mongolia.

of writing that would fill a library. One falconer suggested that a reasonably complete collection would be 1,000 titles in 24 languages.[37] The complexities they reveal indicate the spectrum of regional tradition, but also the infinitely diverse ways in which birds of subtle temperament respond to their instructors. The watchwords of all falconry, however, are self-control, dedication and exacting patience. Falconers are often said to be as devoted to their birds as to a spouse. If the intention is always to exert a kind of control over a wild raptor, nevertheless the relationship is likened to one between mistress and slave, in which the bird, not the human, is dominant. One modern practitioner writes, 'Far more than "just" hunting, falconry is in essence a commitment to a life of service to the bird.'[38]

Part of this is an almost obsessive concern for the birds' well-being. Every expression on its face, every movement of the bowel is noted. Today in the Middle East, where falconry has retained far more of its cultural pre-eminence, the birds are objects of immense expenditure. It is claimed that the oil-enriched Arab devotees of falconry indulge an annual sum of $2 billion on their passion. Yet what is now measured in cash was once expressed in a fantastic kind of falcon quackery. A stock theme of the Arabic falcon literature is an inventory of ailments and their remedies. Some medicines had ingredients such as the oil of earthworms mingled with dragon's blood, or the flesh of a rabid wolf, or dry pounded tiger's heart. Reminiscent of the elixirs once deployed by obsessive cockers on their beloved fighting cocks, some falcon recipes included human urine or medicines dampened with a mother's breast milk.[39] One means to stimulate the raptor's appetite involved a blend of crayfish, maggots and the head of a black snake all buried in a dung heap.[40] Today, Arab sheikhs are far more likely to rely on hi-tech veterinarian services to oversee their treasured birds, and to track their movements with expensive satellite equipment.

The species most cherished in falconry vary according to

region. Yet several members of the genus *Falco* have never lost their historical appeal. In fact, some of our passion for falcons pre-dates even the advent of falconry. If the eagle has long been recognised as the king of birds, then the falcon is its prince and heir. Horus in ancient Egypt (and later Apollo in Greece) was a god of the sun whose sacred bird was a falcon. The animal cult of Horus involved the mummification of hundreds of thousands of wild falcons in exactly the way that Sacred Ibises were ritually slaughtered and embalmed as votive offerings to the god Thoth. Since Horus and Thoth were respectively deities of the sun and the moon, their two sacred birds were often found together as a pair in these religious catacombs (see Sacred Ibis, page 126).

Three species have been supreme in the art and science of falconry. The peregrine has been almost universally treasured, and in Persia and elsewhere in Asia it was known as *Shaheen* (*shah* was the Farsi name for the Iranian king). If anything its hold over the imagination of the Christian West has been even more intense. It is famous as the fastest predator on Earth, with a top speed of 322 kph (200 mph). For some it is *the* bird and a measure of all winged freedom. The British writer J A Baker suggested in his great book *The Peregrine* that, 'You cannot know what freedom means till you have seen a peregrine loosed into the warm spring sky to roam at will through all the far provinces of light.'[41]

Yet to the Arabs, where peregrines are largely non-resident migrants and wanderers (as the name itself implies), *the* falcon is the **Saker Falcon** *Falco cherrug*. In Arabic *saker* or *saqir* means simply 'falcon'. It is the predator most adapted to their arid grassland and the best equipped to tackle the desert game that Arabs love to eat, which includes *Karawan* or *Karouwan*, the Eurasian Stone-curlew and, especially, the houbara (see Stone-curlew and Thick-knee family, page 194 and Houbara Bustard, page 170). It is often claimed in the Arabic and Persian literature that desert falconers also took gazelle and even wolves with their sakers, loosing a

Powerful in body and ferocious in expression, the Northern Goshawk is a truly formidable predator.

'cast', a pair of falcons, to distract and delay the antelopes until the long-limbed hunting dogs, their Salukis, overtook them.[42] Yet modern proof of sakers tackling anything as large as a gazelle or as fearsome as a wolf is actually rare. The frequency of reference to such quarry, as opposed to the paucity of evidence, touches on the element of high poetry that is often heard whenever the falconer's campfire is lit.

The bird generally agreed to be the most impressive of all is a species of the far north called **Gyrfalcon** *Falco rusticolus* (from Old Norse, *Geirfaki*: 'excellent falcon').[43] The biggest individuals stand 60 cm (24 in) tall, with a wingspan of 1.6 m (5.2 ft); as much as a small eagle. Gyrs, in fact, were regularly trained to take eagles or kites. The Elizabethan courtier Sir Thomas Monson was said to have spent £1,000 (a fortune in the seventeenth century) on training a cast of gyrs to hunt for kites.[44] More usually in Europe these supreme hunters were flown at the key quarry for the medieval banqueting table: cranes and herons.

Gyrs vary in colour from charcoal grey to white. This latter form is perhaps the most impressive and at one time it was an almost mythic creature with occult power. In India even the touch of a white Gyrfalcon was thought to cure a patient of fever.[45] Its value, both in cash terms and as a status symbol, was immense. In 1396 the French were negotiating ransom for captives after their defeat by the Turks in the Battle of Nicopolis. The victorious Sultan Bayezid I is said to have initially spurned the European offer of 200,000 ducats. What clinched the deal for this falconry fanatic was an offer of 30 prized birds, including a number of white gyrs.[46]

In India white birds were sometimes not so much a bargaining chip for peace as a cause of war. The sixth Sikh Guru Hargobind Sahib came into possession of a prized white bird of prey that was said to have been a present to the Mogul emperor Shah Jahan from the Shah of Persia. The Guru refused to yield his heaven-sent gift, and after the Indian ruler had tried twice to retrieve it in heavily armed

skirmishes, Shah Jahan's followers pleaded with him not to expend human lives for a mere bird.[47]

In truth white Gyrfalcons are best adapted to the boreal tundras that encircle the planet's northern crown. Nests have been found in Greenland where the guano is piled up 30 cm (12 in) deep and carbon dating has shown the lowest layers to be 2,500 years old. The white falcons of the Arctic are often not equipped to cope with, let alone to hunt in, the desert heat. Across much of Europe and Asia, however, gyrs were kept often for the sheer elan of the beast, as well as for the prestige of ownership. For falcons were not only important in the international language of diplomacy and as expressions of conspicuous consumption: they were metaphors of personal power. Some eastern potentates were surrounded by a veritable flock of hunting birds. Shah Jahan was reputed to have at court 100 female Eurasian Sparrowhawks, 40 female and 30 male **Northern Goshawk** *Accipiter gentilis*, 20 female Peregrine Falcons, and ten **Laggar Falcon** *Falco jugger* and Saker Falcons.[48] (Yet not every falconer believed that size mattered: Shah Jahan's grandfather, the great emperor Akbar, favoured before all other birds the Eurasian Sparrowhawk, of which males weigh no more than a small apple.)

The most extreme of these raptorial statements of human power was the vast entourage at the disposal of Kublai Khan. Marco Polo suggested that China's thirteenth-century Mongol emperor 'was accompanied by fully 10,000 falconers and takes with him fully 5,000 gerfalcons and peregrine falcons and sakers in great abundance, besides a quantity of goshawks for hawking along the rivers'.[49] Such a massive number of hunting birds could have decimated the entire breeding population of these species in his territories. Yet we should not assume that such exhaustive consumption was impossible. In Pakistan, where oil-rich Arabs of the Middle Eastern principalities are accustomed to slake their hunting tastes, sakers have been virtually wiped out by an

The Kazakh hunter Dal Han with his Golden Eagle, which caught all the foxes in his fur coat.

illegal trade that hiked prices in the 1980s to as much as $50,000 for a good female.[50]

Cupidity of this kind is ever likely to surface in a pursuit that arouses some of our deepest instincts. Yet the norm in falconry is a profound respect not just for the bird on the gloved fist, but for the natural world of which it is such a supreme component. When the Peregrine Falcon suffered its calamitous decline in North America during the 1960s it was primarily falconers who developed techniques of both breeding and releasing captive birds that rescued the species from extinction. This practice, long known to falconers, is called hacking – a returning of trained birds back to the wild. It reflected the long-standing utilitarian ethic implicit in falconry. Once the hunting season was done the birds were set free. Then the complex rituals would all begin again the following autumn. Falconry at its best is not a process involving ownership and capture, it is a collaboration of equally free hunters.

There are still a few places where birds of prey and humans forge these kinds of elemental partnerships. Until recently in Korea there were men who sold the birds and game caught by their falcons (do they still?).[51] In western Mongolia today there are Muslim Kazakh nomads who catch and train Golden Eagles for hunting purposes. In an attempt to preserve their vanishing traditions, the hunters have established a festival in the town of Bayan-Ulgii where they take part in competitions to demonstrate their skills and equipment. It is in many ways like any form of rural show, but instead of prize cattle and trained dogs, it is a display of huge predatory birds and horseback hunters wearing wolfskin. With their birds fastened upon their saddle rests,

the nomads ride across the steppe for 160 km (100 miles) to attend the festival. One of these nomads, Dal Han, explains the importance of hunting and the values that inform his relationship with the birds:

I have been hunting for 20 years, I started when I was 26, but my uncles were hunters and so I really started at 13 or 14 about 120 km from here, where I still live. I have owned seven eagles. Some have characters that are really wild and they won't train so we release them back. Some are like people – silly and stupid – so we release those back too. Some die because they go from the warm *ger* [felted wool tent] out to the cold and this is not good for them. The old-aged ones are released back into the wild. The Kazakh tradition holds that the eagle lives to about 30. We release at a maximum age of 12, maybe 13 or 14 if it is a really good eagle. When we send the eagle back to the wild we climb one of the highest peaks, butcher a sheep and leave the eagle on the sheep. Other eagles will come and join the feast. Sometimes they get caught again by mistake by others. If it is taken by an elder he will release it, but some younger hunters might catch and keep it.

Firstly we catch some by taking from the nest. Eagles hatch in April and fly by August. Secondly we use a trap wire on a pile of rocks placed near a carcass, such as a rabbit. We know the eagle will land on high ground next to the carcass to look. We are waiting, we cushion iron parts of the trap with cloth so as not to hurt the bird. Thirdly we sometimes use a cotton net that's the diameter of a *ger* and we tie live bait

In the 1990s Eurasian Sparrowhawks could still be found for sale in the Beijing bird market. The birds were sold as a delicacy and had both wings broken while still alive.

like a rabbit or fox, and when the bird lands the net is triggered.

I hunt from September normally twice a week, sometimes every day if there's time. Nowadays there is no longer an economic benefit to hunting with an eagle so it is mainly a hobby among us. There were Kazakhs who became wealthy by hunting foxes and small ibex for fur and skins. Our main prey are Pallas's Cat, rabbit, gazelle and fox. The Altai steppe once held abundant game but no longer. My coat is from all the 14 foxes I caught last year and was made by my wife. Some years I catch pretty much nothing. My best year was 15 foxes. Most of the time the fox gets away because they are tricky. We hunt eagle-owls too. They are hard to spot on the cliffs but hunters know where to go. We scare the owl off the cliff then release the eagle to catch the owl. The feathers are distributed among friends and family.[52]

PEOPLE EATING BIRDS OF PREY

Using raptors to catch meat for the table is one way that humans have capitalised on birds of prey. Less familiar is the manner in which some communities convert raptors themselves directly into protein. Consuming a meat-eating bird is unusual, but by no means unknown. In New Britain (Papua New Guinea) I was told that some local people eat the fish-eating **Osprey** *Pandion haliaetus* (*Taragau*). Another classic modern example is the trade in Eurasian Sparrowhawks and also some falcon species in China, where they were sold, albeit illegally, until at least the 1990s.[53] The practice may still continue, given that sparrowhawks were considered a delicacy and featured on the menus at civic banquets for local state officials.

Even more unusual is the inclusion of vultures in the modern human diet. The Bandas of southern India number about 300 families in two districts of Andhra Pradesh state. While largely small-scale farmers and followers of Hinduism, the Bandas also trapped vultures in nets that had been baited with livestock carcasses. Otherwise young birds and the eggs were taken directly from vulture nests. (Nor was this the only carrion-eating bird enjoyed by the Banda community. They are also partial to crow stew.) Prior to the wider disappearance of India's vulture populations as a consequence of poisoning by Diclofenac, these scavengers were largely absent from the two districts inhabited by Banda communities, almost entirely because of the latter's dietary habits.[54]

A relish for vulture meat may be exceptional, but public acceptance and even civic encouragement of these extremely useful birds is commonplace, especially in countries such as India. Such attitudes are striking, not only because they express the region's deep ancient tolerance of other life forms, but also because they stand in marked contrast to the Judaeo-Christian tradition of the recent past.

In ancient Europe vultures could be birds of auspicious status, classically illustrated by a myth associated with Rome's foundation, when Romulus chose the site on seeing a flock of 12 vultures above the Palatine Hill.[55] Yet the birds had also been expressly identified as unfit for consumption since the time of the Old Testament. 'You may eat all clean birds,' read the Book of Deuteronomy, 'These are the birds you may not eat: the griffon-vulture, the black vulture, the bearded vulture, the kite, every kind of falcon, every kind of crow' (14:11–14). What had essentially been a precautionary principle of hygiene evolved in the West as a statement of the vulture's wider moral degeneracy.

For medieval Christians the birds were seen literally as agents of hell. A German expression *hol dich der Geier* translates as 'may the vulture seize you', but it actually refers to Satan. Nor were naturalists immune to this vituperation. The eighteenth-century writer Oliver Goldsmith described

how 'the sloth, the filth and the voraciousness of these birds almost exceeds credibility'.[56] Even in the 1980s one can find a natural history book where the **Egyptian Vulture** *Neophron percnopterus* is identified as 'perhaps the most loathsome of all the scavenging birds'.[57] It is hardly surprising that one of the dictionary definitions of vulture today is a 'person of a vile and rapacious disposition'.[58]

BIRDS OF PREY EATING PEOPLE

It is intriguing to see how these prevailing views shaped understanding of some of the most arresting and important vulture images ever discovered. The paintings were at Çatalhöyük in southern Turkey and formed part of a remarkable Neolithic site excavated by the British archaeologist James Mellaart in the 1960s. They date to *c.*6000 BC and are some of the oldest bird images painted on to a prepared surface anywhere in the world. They are highly schematic with bodies flattened and elongated, while the wings are depicted as 11–17 thick lines running parallel with the body to represent the main span of flight feathers. The strongly hooked beaks and upstanding feather ruffs on the base of the birds' long thin necks suggest that they are vultures.

What clinches the identification is the fact that each bird is flying towards and is poised over the headless body of a man. The notion of consumption is clearly implied by the spatial relationships between the corpses and the predatory birds. These fragile images, for so long preserved by the damp compacted clay, began to dry out and crack once they were exposed, the red pigment sometimes turning grey or going mouldy. Those he was able to remove, Mellaart cut out and transferred to the museum in Ankara, but some were lost irretrievably.

In his book on Çatalhöyük the British archaeologist characterised part of the vulture frieze as 'a gruesome scene of an enormous vulture attacking small headless human figures'.[59] Another modern archaeologist has written of the birds 'viciously attacking headless people' and described the imagery at Çatalhöyük as a 'Neolithic hell' and 'a nightmare vision of the world that farming has brought to these

particular members of humankind'.[60] Yet these classically Western interpretations seem at odds with the widespread presence and presumed importance of vultures and other large birds of prey to Neolithic communities across the region.

Small sculptural models of vultures, including birds taking hold of human figures, were found in other parts of Turkey, notably at Nevalı Çori and Göbekli Tepe, both about 500 km (300 miles) to the south-east. Vulture images or actual remains also came out of two other archaeological sites further to the east, both on the edge of the Zagros Mountains in north-eastern Iraq. One was a place called Shanidar Cave, where the American archaeologist Ralph Solecki uncovered a large pile of carefully severed wing bones. These were eventually identified as the remains of the following species: the **Bearded Vulture** *Gypaetus barbatus* (four), **Griffon Vulture** *Gyps fulvus* (one), **White-tailed Eagle** *Haliaeetus albicilla* (seven), and a small unidentified eagle (four).[61]

All were covered in red ochre, itself a material of symbolic importance to Neolithic communities, and were thought to have played a role in shamanic practice. It is assumed that key members of the Neolithic group at Shanidar donned the birds' wings as part of their ritual dances. James Mellaart also assumed that the 'shrines' containing the vulture paintings at Çatalhöyük were the location for comparable funerary practices, in which 'priestesses' cloaked themselves in garments resembling the vulture's plumage. Other archaeologists suggest that the significance of the vulture images was metaphoric, reflecting ritual practices in which a shaman was symbolically dismembered but reborn as a bird.[62]

It is impossible to know precisely what the Çatalhöyük images really meant to their creators but there is powerful circumstantial evidence that they were not considered evil or ghoulish in any way.[63] To both the east and west of Turkey vultures were of immense spiritual importance. In fact one of the most famous of all ancient Egyptian artefacts has a vulture motif. We may normally be too distracted by the dazzling beauty of the thick sheet-gold face of Tutankhamun's mask to notice that there, unmistakably, above the king's right temple is a vulture's head. Between the eleventh and twelfth layers of bandages upon his mummified body there was another famous vulture treasure – his glorious gold and lapis lazuli pectoral with its image of an open-winged **Lappet-faced Vulture** *Aegypius tracheliotus*. Tutankhamun may well have worn it in life.[64]

It is an image of the goddess Nekhbet, one of two Egyptian deities – the other was Mut – which ancient Egyptians represented in vulture form. The former was the patron deity of Upper Egypt, with a cult centred on the predynastic town of Nekheb (known still today as El Kab). Nekhbet's origins may go back to 6000 BC, a time contemporary with the existence of Çatalhöyük. One notable aspect of both Nekhbet and Mut is their association not just with femininity, but with motherhood. Nekhbet played an important role assisting at the delivery of divine and royal births. It is thought that the queens of Egypt wore a Nekhbet headdress and in paintings and engravings of queens in labour, the goddess was sometimes shown hovering above the royal family. Similarly 'Mut' (or 'Mwt') was very close to the ancient Egyptian word used for mother,

The celebrated Neolithic site at Çatalhöyük contained this remarkable image of a vulture, one of the oldest bird paintings on a prepared surface to be found anywhere on Earth.

and some Egyptologists consider her to be, like Nekhbet, a mother goddess.

Images of both of these deities with their wings outstretched were intended to symbolise maternal protectiveness and love. One intriguing discovery at Çatalhöyük, a relief sculpture that depicts a female breast from which extrudes a vulture's skull, explicitly makes this same link between human femininity and the birds. One archaeologist has called the artefact 'motherhood itself violently defiled', but could the profoundly positive vulture symbolism recurring throughout ancient Egypt be more indicative of how the residents of Çatalhöyük viewed the birds all those millennia ago?

To the east of Turkey is yet another engagement with vultures that not only persists today, but reveals a degree of intimacy that has few equals in the entire spectrum of bird–human interactions. Remarkably, the process of exposing the human dead for vultures to feed upon, as illustrated at Çatalhöyük, survives in modern India. The Parsees are a small community, concentrated now in the city of Mumbai, where there is a population of 46,000 adherents. It includes some of the wealthiest families in Asia, such as the Tata dynasty, founders of the powerful industrial conglomerate the Tata Group. They are a long-established minority having arrived in the subcontinent as refugees from Islamic persecution in their original Persian homeland (the word 'Parsee' reflects these Persian origins) in AD 936.[65]

They brought with them both their ancient Zoroastrian faith and their tradition of *dokhmenashini*. This enduring facet of Parsee social custom involves the disposal of their dead in *dokhma*: round, relatively low-rise (9 m: 30 ft), fortress-walled religious structures that have come to be known as 'towers of silence'. These remarkable buildings, of which there are still three functioning in Mumbai and which once stood in other Asian cities occupied by the Parsee diaspora, are erected in compliance with elaborate religious rites and fulfil a Zoroastrian belief that the elements – earth, fire and water – should not be defiled by the corruption of human flesh.[66] Instead of interring their dead, the Zoroastrians developed sky burials in which the remains of relatives are eaten by flesh-eating birds – corvids, kites and, historically, vultures.

The first *dokhma* were probably built around the early ninth century and there is no continuous link between the scenes depicted at Çatalhöyük and those in the leafy suburbs of modern Mumbai.[67] Nevertheless the traditions of *dokhmenashini* demonstrate a remarkably enlightened acceptance of the role of flesh-eating birds that is wholly distinct from the attitude towards vultures prevalent in medieval and even modern Europe. Yet not even Parsees see inside the towers of silence, except for the corpse bearers (known as *nassasalars*), who carry the white-sheeted body to the exposed upper tier, where it is laid out on three concentric platforms, one each for men, women and children.

When all the family members had finally left, the *nassasalars* would alert the awaiting vultures to the presence of a corpse by clapping their hands. After the birds had then fed – and they were once reputed to devour all the flesh in 60 minutes – only a dried skeleton was left and this was deposited in the *dokhma*'s central well, where purified rainwater would eventually wash out the crumbled dust of the bones. At its most efficient the tradition of *dokhmenashini*

BOMBAY PARSEE TOWERS OF SILENCE.

was an odourless, clean and near-instant processing of the departed. As one modern British eyewitness notes: 'It produced no false sentimentality, no fuss, no monuments, no epitaphs, no urns . . . and it was cost-free.'[68] Surveys across the Parsees' global diaspora indicated that even until the 1980s a high percentage of those living in places as far away as London (26 per cent), California (33 per cent), Melbourne (40 per cent), and Kenya (27 per cent) wished to have a traditional *dokhma* funeral.[69]

In their heyday the towers of silence disposed of thousands of corpses annually, giving rise to a large, healthy, well-fed vulture population that bred in the surrounding grounds, which were often developed as beautifully tended gardens. An eyewitness account from the early twentieth century suggested a population around Doongerwadi in Mumbai of 500 birds.[70] However, those numbers were unheard of even long before the crisis wrought by Diclofenac. A contemporary Parsee writes of his own childhood:

> I have seen quite a few sky burials at the towers of silence in my younger days, when vultures were present in reasonably large numbers. As food was plentiful, they would roost on the trees nearby and during the breeding season I have seen at least seven or eight White-backed Vulture nests in the grounds.[71]

One incidental aspect, which leaves one in awe of the vulture's digestive tract, was the bird's capacity, at one time, to devour many people who had died of a whole suite of contagious illnesses – cholera, typhoid, smallpox and the plague. Many flesh-eating birds of prey, including not just the three Asian vultures but also the Black Kite and Black Vulture of the Americas, are reputed to be immune to highly toxic pathogens, such as *Clostridium botulinum*, salmonella and anthrax. The disposal of infected waste by carrion-eating birds is just one aspect of the birds' 'yeomanly service as unpaid garbage men'.[72]

Alas, the catastrophe inflicted on Asian vultures by Diclofenac, traces of which have even shown up in human body tissue, has now effectively terminated this 1,200-year-old funeral rite. While sky burials still take place in Mumbai, the flesh is disposed of slowly and inefficiently by House Crows and Black Kites, or the bodies are desiccated by a new system of mirrors that reflect and intensify the effects of sunlight. A proposal to establish a captive-breeding

This Victorian postcard of the towers of silence, built by the Parsee community of Mumbai to allow vultures to eat their dead, indicates our long-standing fascination with this remarkable bird-and-human collaboration.

169

programme for vultures attached to the towers of silence has received mixed support from the Parsee community and many wish to switch from their tradition of *dokhmenashini* to alternatives such as burial or cremation.

There is now only one surviving vestige of those scenes so graphically retold on the walls of Çatalhöyük. In Tibet people still lay out and dismember human corpses at special ceremonial grounds for vultures and other carrion-eating birds to devour. The communist Chinese forces that have occupied the country since 1949 have sought to eliminate the extraordinary religious life of this former Buddhist theocracy, but these burial traditions have survived both within Tibet and in neighbouring regions where similar cultural and ecological conditions prevail, such as Indian-administered Ladakh.

The Tibetan name for processing the dead in this way is *rir skyel* ('to carry to the mountain') and formerly *bya khyir ster-ba* ('to give to the birds and dogs'), reflecting the fact that the latter animals also played a major role in the post-mortem rites. Some of the earliest documentary evidence for them actually comes from a Western source. The fourteenth-century Italian Friar Odoric (1286–1331), who spent several years travelling in Asia, reported on Tibetan funerary customs and mentioned the feeding of corpses to vultures and eagles.

Unfortunately he also added that the grieving relatives themselves partook of the dead person's flesh. Despite his false allegations of cannibalism, his testimony does confirm some of the basic facts and indicates the longevity of these practices. His account also reflects the enduring fascination felt in the West for the strangeness of these Tibetan customs.

However, as the author of a recent anthropological study argues, the custom seems less strange when one reflects that only 0.2 per cent of Tibet's total land area is suitable for cultivation, while 88.4 per cent of the country lies above an altitude of 4,300 m (14,100 ft) and is permanently frozen for up to 10.5 months of the year. Given the high premium on agricultural land and the virtually complete absence of combustible wood fuel, the idea of cutting up bodies for vultures to eat starts to look eminently sensible. The author Dan Martin goes on to suggest that, given 'an increased sense of ecological responsibility (even in the absence of Buddhist altruistic motivations), the world at large will learn to see the positive value of sky burial and perhaps eventually adapt it – assuming that the birds will cooperate'.[73] One wonders finally how many lovers of birds might themselves also cooperate, and volunteer to make the ultimate donation to raptor conservation?

Bustard family *Otidae*

'In 1947 . . . we went out one day and shot forty-seven gazelles in the span of one kilometre. Today I am ashamed of this. I am also angry to think that a few years ago I saw a party of rich city men with automatic rifles killing thirty or forty gazelles in one hour near here. Now the desert is empty. I used to fly my beautiful Saker Falcons after Houbaras and Sandgrouse, but now there are scarcely any left. I caught the migrating falcons myself with a net, when they came after tethered pigeons. There is no point in keeping them today. Yes, I am ashamed to think of this; but are the men from the city ashamed too?'[1]

The confessions of Ali Kerasha, an old Jordanian sheikh, lamenting the slaughter of local wildlife and his role specifically in the decimation of his country's **Houbara Bustard** *Chlamydotis undulata*, could serve as a microcosm for the whole story of human interaction with this bird family. Like the remorse-filled words of this aged Arab, the bustards' tale is one of continuous exploitation, descending on occasions into senseless nihilism.

Yet bustard hunting has also given rise to an extraordinary body of lore, literature and visual imagery. Perhaps the old sheikh's sense of shame was inspired as much by the loss of these cultural riches – in his case the whole art and rationale for his falconry – as it was by the vanished magnificence of the birds themselves. In the last three decades, humans have sought to reverse their impact upon bustards in a range of conservation projects, but it may prove too little too late. Bustards are among the most imperilled large birds on the planet with all 27 species probably in retreat, and 11 of them either threatened or near-threatened with extinction. Two Asian species, **Great Indian Bustard** *Ardeotis nigriceps*

and **Bengal Florican** *Houbaropsis bengalensis*, number less than 1,000 each.[2]

Bustards are primarily inhabitants of wide open space – steppe, desert grassland, savannah – and, less frequently, of thicker bush country, with Africa representing the main area of distribution. All but four have occurred or still occur there, yet six species are now found largely in Eurasia, with just a single representative, **Australian Bustard** *Ardeotis australis*, on that other great desert continent. None occurs in the Americas.

Most of the family are tall, long-legged terrestrial birds that are slow to take flight, often preferring to rely on camouflage and to walk cautiously away from potential danger. There is a striking heraldic poise to almost all their movements that is matched nicely by an up-tilt in the carriage of their heads, so that they look to possess an innate hauteur. Even in flight the larger bustards have a deep rhythmic wingbeat, which has a slow-motion solemnity. Despite the vaguely humorous sound, the word 'bustard' draws on this gravitas. The Roman natural historian Pliny used the name *aves tardas*, 'slow birds', when he wrote about them.[3] It subsequently entered various European languages in modified form – *bistarda* (Italian) and *bistarde* (French) – and eventually gave us the present English version.[4]

Bustards range in size from the **Little Bustard** *Tetrax tetrax*, barely bigger than a stout-legged rooster, to the massive male **Kori Bustard** *Ardeotis kori* or **Great Bustard** *Otis tarda*, which weigh up to 20 kg (44 lb) and share the prize as the largest flighted birds in the world. The last two, along with the Australian and the appropriately named Great Indian Bustard, are among the most impressive species in their four respective regions. It is hardly surprising that the quartet has acquired wide symbolic status. The

The transfer of 'surplus' Great Bustard eggs from Russia to the UK is part of an ambitious reintroduction scheme, which reflects the cultural grip that bustards hold over our imaginations.

Great Indian Bustard is the state bird in Rajasthan, while the Great Bustard is Hungary's national bird. In Britain, the latter occurred until it was hunted to extinction in the early nineteenth century, and it still features in the county crests for Wiltshire and Cambridgeshire.

It is a measure of the Great Bustard's enduring hold over our imaginations that Wiltshire is now the site for a reintroduction project 180 years after its disappearance. To date, 91 Great Bustards, taken from Russian nests that would otherwise have been affected by agricultural activity, have been reared and relocated. The project plans to maintain releases until the end of 2013, when they will total 200 birds. The laying of a single infertile clutch in 2007 and the fledging of four wild-bred chicks in 2010 are the most notable developments so far, reflecting the patience needed with such long-lived, slow-breeding species.[5]

While Pliny supplied us with the modern family name, it is to be regretted that we did not take from him a culinary judgement on bustard flesh. He thought it was revolting: 'When the marrow is drained out of their bones a disgusting smell . . . follows.'[6] Alas, the majority has long held a very different view.[7] Quite how long is impossible to calculate, but the stone sculpture of a bustard found at Nemrik near Mosul in Iraq dates to around 9000 BC.[8] Since then most people have tended to agree with Babur, the Mogul emperor of the sixteenth century, and his comment that in many birds either the leg or breast was to be preferred, but in bustards the whole roast was delicious.[9] The royal reputation still flourishes: 'Anywhere I have been in sub-Saharan Africa the bustard is held up as the golden standard of bird flesh. This is considered by far to be the most tasty bird.'[10]

However, it was in 1770 that the bustard's culinary reputation was immortalised. Captain Cook, navigating the *Endeavour* off the modern Queensland coast, dined on an Australian Bustard that had been shot on shore. In his diary Joseph Banks noted how all of them agreed that it was the best bird they had eaten since leaving England. In honour of its savour, Captain Cook declared the adjacent inlet 'Bustard Bay', a name which it bears to this day.[11]

Another enduring strand of observation that originated in the classical period is the bustard family's deep tolerance of domestic stock, possibly because of the large invertebrates that their trampling hooves disturb. The Roman naturalist Aelian noted that 'when [the bird] catches sight of a horse, it delights to fly up to it and to keep it company'.[12] Quite how the Greek writer Oppian arrived at his claim that bustards were even capable of mating with horses is more difficult to fathom.[13] Yet it is undoubtedly the case that the birds' habituation to livestock enabled hunters to use them as a form of blind to get within shooting range. Horse- or ox-drawn carts were often exploited in Europe. In Africa even today a stratagem not dissimilar is used:

> The traditional method of catching a bustard was to use a leg-hole snare (*Lukoti*) set near a place where the bird frequented, such as a termite mound where a male was displaying. With the advent of shotguns, another method is used to get close enough to shoot it. A hunter will 'borrow' a herd boy's cattle and drive them towards a bustard he may have seen on the grasslands. If he maintains a low profile and drives the cows close, the bird will not flee as it would from an approaching human. Once he gets close enough, the hunter sits or lays down in the grass and lets the herd move off, then shoots the bird. This method of hunting also works for Spur-winged Goose, which you cannot approach to within 300 metres otherwise.[14]

In India camels were specially trained to get close to Houbara Bustards. Salim Ali, the great Indian ornithologist (see Appendix II), hunted them using this technique, noting

The Great Bustard
vies with its relative
the Kori Bustard as
the largest flighted
bird in the world.

the 'consummate skill and judgement in the preliminary manoeuvring of the camel on the part of its shikari-camel driver', and also the man's 'truly phenomenal' eyesight:

> The shikari pulls up the camel and nudges you excitedly to shoot, but for you the bird is simply not there. In desperation he points to that dried cow pat at the base of yonder bush and urges you to fire at that, which you reluctantly do, more in order to allay his disgust. It is only when the pat turns over with the shot that you notice the outspread wings and recognize it as your quarry![15]

The sheer range of techniques used to catch bustards is testament to the high reputation of the meat, but also to the ingenuity, even devilish cunning, of the hunters. One trick, part of the wider dismal tale of Great Bustard extinction in Britain, involved the use of greyhounds in Wiltshire. It was said to have taken place in dank drizzling conditions when the birds were incapacitated by soaked flight feathers and was considered unsporting even in the Victorian age.[16] A Russian technique (reported by the eminent travel writer Norman Douglas, in his earlier incarnation as a diplomat in St Petersburg) was actually to wait until the outer feathers froze. A group of peasants were said to have caught 63 Great Bustards – representing over half a tonne of meat – in this way, and took them to market in Kiev.[17]

In Somalia local people used a ploy that resembled fishing, in which the **Arabian Bustard** *Ardeotis arabs* was hooked on a line baited with mice or locusts.[18] Yet by far the most extraordinary method of hunting (once used widely

across Africa and Asia to catch bustards, cranes or Saker Falcons) is a stratagem recorded in Chad.[19] A child is buried right next to the nest of an Arabian Bustard with just a hand freely positioned underneath the eggs in the sand. When the female returns to incubate she is grabbed by the feet and the child tries to hold tight until the adult hunters arrive.[20]

The method of capture that should involve the greatest skill, and offer the fairest sport, has ironically been one of the most grievous factors in the family's recent declines, and has attracted widespread condemnation. Falconry has been associated with bustards, especially in the Middle East, almost as long as the falconer's art has been known. For many Arab practitioners, the contest between saker and houbara has or, at least, *had* a near-sacred quality. (Recently the houbara was split into two taxa: the north African population retaining the existing English and scientific names, and the Asiatic populations being retitled **Macqueen's Bustard** *Chlamydotis macqueenii*. However, for simplicity's sake, and since all the references used in this account refer only to 'houbara', it is treated as if a single taxon.) The arrival of migrant houbaras in the Middle East once unleashed a sense of national holiday and excitement commensurate with the start of the British grouse season on the Glorious Twelfth (see page 46). Houbaras, however, add a dash of sexual allure to the already testosterone-charged business of hunting, because the flesh of the bird is widely held to be an aphrodisiac. Some contemporary sheikhs are credited with eating it every day.

The socio-economic developments in the Middle East that accompanied Arab independence in the twentieth century, and the simultaneous realisation of fantastic oil wealth, meant that the hunting of Arabia's desert wildlife both widened its appeal and deepened its impact. By the time that Sheikh Ali Kerasha – quoted at the beginning of this account – had lamented the empty desert in the 1960s, Houbara Bustards were virtually extinct in the Arabian Peninsula.

Rather than giving the initiative to desert conservation, the loss of Arabian houbaras transferred the locus of their hunting elsewhere. From the 1960s a foremost destination was Pakistan, where the houbara is both a resident breeding species and a formerly common winter visitor from central Asia. The man credited with establishing his country as the primary holiday camp for the houbara-hungry sheikhdoms and principalities of the Middle East was Agha Hassan Abedi, the millionaire founder of the Bank of Credit and Commerce International. Abedi introduces the themes of big money and international politics to an already complex nexus of sporting indulgence, illegality and high-level corruption. At the heart of the human tangle is a bird that resident Pakistanis have been forbidden to hunt since 1972.[21]

Regardless of its protected status in that country, the houbara has been pursued for decades in Pakistan by exalted Arab dignitaries, who draw in their respective wakes an entourage of luxury that sounds like something out of a hi-tech *Arabian Nights*. Scores of desert-equipped vehicles are serviced by fleets of fuel tankers and water bowsers, each holding more than 8,000 litres (1,750 gallons). In the 1950s one Saudi entourage on home soil comprised 482 vehicles.[22] Some expeditions to Pakistan even bring drilling equipment to create their own water wells.

Among the more recent plane-borne cargoes that are then shifted into columns of land cruisers are mobile palaces complete with fortress walls. The late King Khalid of Saudi Arabia even transported his own dancing camels with him, while a defence minister in the Saudi kingdom slaughtered 70 sheep and lambs every night to feed his guests. Mary Anne Weaver, eyewitness to a 1990s caravan following Crown Prince Fahd, described an encampment patrolled by scores of guards bearing Kalashnikovs. Some royal visitors, who rent concessions covering hundreds of square kilometres, establish what are, in effect, autonomous fiefdoms in the middle of Pakistan, complete with worldwide satellite communications. In the 1990s the average expenditure on a single royal hunting trip was said to be $10–$20 million.[23]

At the heart of each tented facility are as many as 150 falcons to meet the needs of a single dignitary, his family and friends (see also Falconry, page 164). These raptors are themselves worth a small fortune. A highly rated falcon can fetch $8,000, and the top price paid for a Balochistan peregrine was $120,000. (Political power is also part of the chain that links falcons and money with wealthy Arabs. Thus one finds that the main falcon dealer in Pakistan in the 1990s was a former minister in the short-lived government of the late prime minister Benazir Bhutto.) It is perhaps not surprising that the hunting falcons are equipped with super-lightweight French-developed radar homing devices, which are attached to the bird's tail and offer a tracking radius of 13 km (8 miles).[24]

It goes without saying that the hunting of bustards in the old days, as practised by the likes of the Jordanian sheikh Ali Kerasha, was an all-embracing contest that pitted the almost mystical relationship between bird and falconer against a wary, powerful quarry. The art acquired an additional lustre against its backdrop of harsh and unforgiving landscapes. But the margin for failure has been so squeezed by the sheer welter of hi-tech gadgetry and equipment at the disposal of the new multi-millionaires that it is difficult not to agree with one Pakistani dignitary who observed that, 'The poor bird doesn't stand a chance'.[25]

The degraded character of the hunt fits a pattern of wider psychological alienation among its practitioners. Wealth, luxury and power have uprooted royal Arab falconers from the real traditions of their own rich culture and abolished any genuine connection with desert places, the people or the magnificent wildlife. Instead of showing respect for a delicate ecosystem, they have unleashed across large parts of Africa and Asia a meaningless abuse of landscape and wildlife.

The statistics are fragmentary but compelling. In 1984, 25 Arab parties in Pakistan killed more than 5,000 houbaras, giving an average of 200 bustard fatalities per group. In other parts of the world that tally has been exceeded. A relatively small Saudi royal team in Sudan killed 3,000 bustards in 83 days of 1989.[26] Cumulatively, and since their overseas forays began, Arab hunting parties have killed tens of thousands of bustards of various species, including the near-threatened **Nubian Bustard** *Neotis nuba* and range-restricted Arabian Bustard (today that name has been rendered anomalous by the virtual extinction of the species on mainland Arabia).[27]

For the houbara specifically the hunting pressure has driven it towards localised extinction from the Atlantic to the borders of China. The one surprise is that the species has sunk only to near-threatened status, which suggests that the central Asian populations are more resilient than previously thought. Yet bustards are not the only wildlife to suffer. Major losses have been inflicted on a wide range of Asian and African ungulates, especially gazelle, the other traditional focus of Arabian culture. Typically the same record-breaking Saudi hunt in Sudan accounted for 1,660 Dorcas Gazelle.[28]

It is important to note that Arab exploitation of another country's wildlife merely replicates, at its worst, the nineteenth- and early-twentieth-century mania for hunting that was once commonplace among imperial Europeans. Secondly, some wealthy Arabs have repented of their excesses, and set up houbara reintroduction schemes. By 1995 there was one locality (a protected area of about 14,000 km²: 5,400 miles²) for resident houbaras in the Saudi kingdom with a population of 70–300 birds, and another reserve established as a refuge for migratory houbara and as a breeding facility for reintroducing captive birds.[29] Yet this has to be compared with the estimated $2.4 billion spent on falconry each year. Moreover the laudable schemes to reintroduce houbara to the Arabian Peninsula run alongside a more shadowy flow of captive houbaras to the Gulf region. An estimated 500 eggs and 8,000 birds are smuggled annually from Pakistan to the Gulf.[30]

Sometimes this export of foreign wildlife to the Arabian Peninsula from poorer African and Asian regions is greeted with outrage by indigenous environmentalists. Witness an impassioned complaint from a resident Somali:

> I was flying from Mogadishu to Dubai about four years ago and boarded the plane in Hargeisa, Somaliland. An hour into the flight, I saw through a partition towards

the front of the aisle a couple of Spotted Hyenas bounding among a jumble of what looked like wooden crates. One of the animals was about to get into the pilots' cabin where a white-shirted crew member was trying to shoo the hyena out and shut the door. I was trying to get the attention of fellow passengers over the strange drama and some of us got up and approached the partition. By then a few guys managed to corner both hyenas and manhandle them into crates. I tiptoed forward and saw the terrible sight occupying that half of the plane.

There were many dead and dying birds because of the terrible heat (there was no air conditioning). I saw Crowned Lapwings, Spotted Thick-knees, bustards, including a few Kori Bustards, before they managed to push me back. I also saw many types of antelope including dik-diks and Lesser Kudus, a Cheetah, mongoose and a crateful of snakes. By then I was raving mad about the scale of the cruelty. Almost all the passengers resented the scene I was creating, especially the airline crew. A few passengers said that this kind of wildlife cargo going to Arabian countries was normal. The crew began manhandling me and making all kinds of threats as to what they would do when we landed in Dubai. A passenger in the back section pointed to a fat gentleman seated near him saying that the guy was a minister in the government. I tried to get him to get up to take a look at the carnage. He just waved me away. I can still see the disdainful look on his face.[31]

Wider conservation efforts to secure the Houbara Bustard are necessary, but mercifully the bird is not without defences of its own. In Bedu culture it appears to have a reputation for bravery (and also, rather curiously, for stupidity: 'in Arab culture a person described as an idiot is said to be more stupid than a houbara').[32] Various Middle Eastern treatises on falconry noted the houbara's special capacity to fight back by ejecting faeces with singular accuracy and volume at its assailants. The excrement is notably foul smelling and mucilaginous and even falcons merely traumatised by the experience of these 'mutes', the technical term for the guano, can forsake bustard hunting thereafter. Less fortunate falcons have been known to suffer a worse fate; the glutinous mess fouling their plumage and even causing them to crash-land.[33]

In view of the latter's remarkable defecatory prowess it is intriguing to discover the name for another bustard in east Africa:

In south-western Tanzania there are only two species, the commoner **Black-bellied Bustard** *Lissotis melanogaster* (known by three names, *Namume*, *Talanye*, and *Ntasilalupweko*), and the rare **Denham's Bustard** *Neotis denhami* (*Chimilamatuze*). The name *Namume* does not appear to have an extant meaning, but *Talanye* and *Ntasilalupweko* both refer to the bird's habit of defecating a streak of liquid faecal matter as it takes off while escaping a predator or approaching person. *Talanye* means literally 'first let it shit' and *Ntasilalupweko* means 'my diarrhoea never ends'.[34]

Seriema family *Cariamidae*

The family's two members – **Red-legged Seriema** *Cariama cristata* and **Black-legged Seriema** *Chunga burmeisteri* – are large, distinctive inhabitants of east-central South American scrub woodland and tree-dotted savannah. They are well known for their weird, loud and, at a distance, musical calls ('like maniacal laughter') and are among the few Amazonian birds benefiting from deforestation and its consequent extension of open habitats.[1]

Although seriemas are elegantly proportioned with extremely long legs and necks and slender bodies, the birds nevertheless possess a quintessential strangeness. In the case of the Red-legged Seriema this centres on the face and its piercing silver eyes with enormously elongated 'eyelashes'. Both species also carry their head with bustard-like upward tilt to the bill, suggesting an innate dignity or, as one writer proposed, a resemblance to 'immensely superior feathered camels'.[2]

The intriguing name is of unresolved origin. The *Oxford English Dictionary* repeats the idea that *çariama* is a word of Tupi origin, the language once spoken by a large section of Amazonia's indigenous population. It means 'upright', 'standing crest' or 'erect cockscomb', which is actually a reference to those bizarre lashes.[3] A contending Brazilian claim proposes the combination of *siri*, a native diminutive, with *ema*, the ancient Portuguese name for South America's other long-legged resident of grassland, the rhea (see Emu family, page 23). Hence 'little rhea', which does in some ways describe the seriema's tall leggy shape.[4] It is conceivable that

both these explanations are true, but the phonetic similarity of *çariama* and 'seriema' is so obvious it suggests that one of the theories, and probably the latter, is a secondary *ex post facto* rationalisation.

Large and palatable, seriemas are still hunted and eaten, although their widespread reputation as snake-killers – 'thus, the saying "where there are seriemas there are no snakes"' – is believed to serve as a brake on persecution in country areas. Unfortunately, snakes do not truly form a large part of the diet, nor are the birds immune to snakebites as many people believe.[5] However, there is a Brazilian saying, *Quem mata seriema é perseguido pelo azar* ('Who ever kills the seriema is pursued by bad luck').[6]

The birds are kept in captivity, especially in zoos and parks, partly for that charismatic visual appeal, but it is also regularly repeated that they are held by rural Brazilians as 'pets' among the domestic fowl to act as a form of early warning system against potential intruders.[7] Modern eyewitness accounts of this claim are rare, but the following proves that it still happens, albeit in Brazil's south-western neighbour: 'I can tell you that just this summer I got my feet and ankles viciously pecked by a seriema kept by a Guaraní household in the Paraguayan Chaco (a group known in the older literature as the Chiriguano). I had dropped by when no one was at home and the bird took it badly.'[8]

Seriemas are well known for their omnivorous appetites and their habit of seizing live prey then worrying or beating it to death with violent strokes on the ground. Sometimes, however, their catholic appetites have baleful consequences. While on an expedition in the Gran Chaco, the semi-arid lowland region shared between Bolivia, Paraguay and Argentina, the naturalist John Graham Kerr was given a captive seriema called Tum-um-hit, who became a charming pet.

> Poor Tum-um-hit came to a sad end. One morning he was found lying dead . . . the post-mortem disclosed in his gizzard the skin of a rat which had been preserved with arsenical soap. Tum-um-hit had in fact been the bane of my colleague Budgett's life, for as he sat at his laboratory table, making dissections or preparing some rare specimen, Tum-um-hit would keep walking around at a distance. . . . Then when Budgett, having turned away to consult a book, turned back again to his dissection, he would find it gone, snapped up by Tum-um-hit whom he could see disappearing in the distance.[9]

Kagu family *Rhynochetidae*

With their elaborate bonnet-like crests, limpid red eyes and strange pale-grey plumage, **Kagu** *Rhynochetos jubatus* 'are fantastic' according to one enthusiast.[1] A local name, the 'ghost of the forest', evokes the sense of mystery and strangeness which still surrounds the bird.

It is a rooster-sized, flightless, forest-dwelling species that has all the qualities of a modern ornithological celebrity. It is exceptionally rare (fewer than 1,000 birds). It is endemic to one Pacific island (Grande Terre in the New Caledonia group). It belongs to a monotypic family (while its long-legged shape, size and habits have suggested affinities with a range of families including herons and pigeons, the Kagu's closest relatives are the cranes or Sunbittern). Even just the name seems somehow suggestive of unique status. In fact it is a word of Kanak origin, the original inhabitants of New Caledonia, and is thought to be onomatopoeic of the Kagu's weird dog-like notes.

Prior to the colonial period, the bird appears to have been hunted and eaten, kept as a pet or mascot, and the feathers used to adorn the chief's headdress. Kanaks even named children after it. Yet the introduction of dogs by Europeans in the 1850s made its capture easier and expanded the forms of persecution. These included their slaughter to provide plumes for the millinery trade, and their live export to satisfy the curiosity of zoo- and aviary-going Europeans.[2] Over-hunting helped initiate a serious contraction in the Kagu's range and numbers. However, predation by non-native mammals, including dogs, rats and feral pigs, now forms one half of an ecological pincer movement that is completed by habitat loss and forest clearance.[3]

Its cultural status in New Caledonia is mixed:

> On the one hand the bird is everywhere, from stamps and cuddly toys to business logos and company names. It is the symbol for the national post office, all the sports teams and was the morning call of the local radio for decades. However, while Kagu is used symbolically in New Caledonia, it doesn't seem to have such an important place in local indigenous culture. It is not – or very rarely – seen as a totem and is not cited first when talking about birds. Kanaks usually mention the *Notou*, New Caledonian Imperial Pigeon, which is a very important gamebird here, killed for new yam ceremonies. Kagu is not eaten or only very occasionally. However, *Notou* is a delicacy, which is probably why people pay much more attention to it.[4]

Sunbittern family *Eurypygidae*

The family has just a single representative, yet the **Sunbittern** *Eurypyga helias*, an inhabitant of forest streams in Central and South America, is one of the region's most charismatic birds. It is a hugely prized desideratum for birders in the Neotropics: one commentator recently named it in his list of the 'world's ten sexiest birds'.[1] This is not just because of the unique taxonomic status; the bird is also arresting in appearance, combining a delicate heron-like form with a plumage of exquisite crypsis. Complex vermiculations and chequering create that strange but compelling form of beauty which enables Sunbitterns not to stand out boldly, but to melt into the forest shadows.

The most eye-catching detail, visible in flight and used as part of a threat display, is the bright ocelli located in the centre of each outspread wing. When flashed at a potential predator, including humans, these semicircular chestnut 'eyes' are intended to confuse and frighten. They have also inspired one modern ornithologist to poetry – 'like a sun darkly glowing in a sunset-tinted sky'. They do, however, explain the repeated sun references in the bird's nomenclature (the Greek word *helias* means 'of the sun').[2]

Sunbitterns are said to be easily tamed and widely kept around villages in Brazil and other parts of South America as a natural means of pest disposal. Once again (see also Seriema family, page 174), there are few contemporary eyewitness descriptions of this usage.[3] However, the following may at least imply their status as village familiars:

> The Tacana people of tropical western Bolivia believe that if you want to put a spell on a woman to fall in love with you, you must kill a Sunbittern. They don't regularly eat them. The long hollow leg bone creates a whistle tone. When it is cleaned, you must then spy the girl you want through the hollow of the bone, and this will make her fall in love with you. I haven't tried it, but I have heard this story from three different sources when we saw the bird.[4]

The bird's dried bones are also said to be a powerful talisman in parts of Brazil.[5]

Rail, Crake and Coot family *Rallidae*

Spread across the six 'upper' continents, this varied family comprises 128 species that are predominantly southern in distribution: Latin America (48 species), Africa (18 species) and Australasia (38 species). However, many rails and crakes are confined to just a single island or archipelago, and barely more than a handful have transcontinental ranges.

This cosmopolitan minority includes probably the best known of all the family: the **Common Moorhen** *Gallinula chloropus* (found on five continents and replaced by the similar **Dusky Moorhen** *Gallinula tenebrosa* in Australasia), the **Eurasian Coot** *Fulica atra* (all Eurasia, north Africa, the Indian subcontinent and Australasia) and **Purple Swamphen** *Porphyrio porphyrio* (southern Europe, widely in Africa, the Middle East, the Indian subcontinent, Asia and Australasia). In the Americas the last two are replaced by similar species – **American Coot** *Fulica americana* and **Purple Gallinule** *Porphyrio martinicus*. In their respective regions these birds, especially the coots and moorhens, are present in almost all wetland habitats, from drainage ditches to inland seas.

For all our near-global familiarity with a few species, the rest of the family is characterised by a shyness that can intensify to pathological secrecy. It is manifest in the birds' wide preference for tangled vegetation, which is frequently made more inaccessible by muddy or swamp-like substrates. Rails are also routinely nocturnal or crepuscular in lifestyle. When disturbed they prefer to walk away from danger and many slink wraith-like through the tight jungle so that they have acquired laterally compressed bodies.

THE ALLURE OF RAILS

All of the above factors mean that rails have a marginal place in human cultures. The one glaring exception is in the realm of ornithology. The elements that make it easy for most of us to ignore them have galvanised specifically the birding imagination. They are sometimes among the most sought-after birds. A classic example is the **Black Rail** *Laterallus jamaicensis* of North and South America, which is barely bigger than a sparrow. The US ornithologist Frank Chapman perfectly evoked not just its elfin size (it can weigh just 29 g: 1 oz) but also the perverse enchantments of such a bird when he suggested that it was 'about as difficult to observe as a field-mouse'.[1] Adding to the allure is the fact that many rails are strikingly beautiful.

A more elusive part of the pleasures of rails is the contrast between the vibrancy of the living birds and the forbidding, punitive character of their chosen habitat. For many observers the finding of a fellow vertebrate in surroundings that are inaccessible, and even inhuman, lends to the encounter a powerful sense of discovery. It is as if life itself, manifest in these subtle and sensitive creatures, has revealed some of its inner mystery. (See also Pitta family, page 345 and Tapaculo family, page 354.) Seeing them can feel like a quest fulfilled. Yet there is often a further gloss to the impact, which dwells in the rails' gift for unpredictability. Frequently shy, individual rails or crakes can sometimes just walk into view and act as if nothing were more natural. This strange flux in their behaviour adds zest to the whole group.

As a way of compensating for their reticence, rails

◄ The Sunbittern has a whole family to itself and is one of the most captivating of all Latin American birds.

The American Coot typifies the group's salient features – black plumages, white frontal shields and a distinctly irascible form of sociability.

For centuries some indigenous people in South America believed that the strange vocalisations of the Grey-necked Wood Rail were produced from its cloaca!

frequently have loud and highly arresting calls. One characteristic of many of the sounds is their veritable weirdness. The South African ornithologist Barry Taylor, an authority on the family, notes how their vocalisations 'include screams, squeals, trills, whistles, whines, hoots, moans, booms, rattles, clicking and ticking notes, snoring noises, humming and buzzing sounds, trumpets, roars, grunts, barks, frog-like croaks and snake-like hisses; calls of some of the smaller species may be very insect-like'.[2] One kind of noise production omitted from Taylor's list is that of the **Grey-necked Wood Rail** *Aramides cajanea* from Central and South America.

The eminent Brazilian naturalist Helmut Sick recalled how, 'In central Brazil the Tupi Indians tried to convince me that the noisy calling of [Grey-necked Wood Rail] was not only a chaos of voices but was accompanied by the noise resulting from gas expelled from the cloaca!' Sick observed that a sixteenth-century author, Fernão Cardim, had also recorded this quaint belief of the Tupi. Cardim wrote that the wood rail 'makes another sonorous, intense, loud, but not very smelly tone with its rear end, which can be frightening'.[3] What is extraordinary about the myth is its longevity. The story of the farting rail clearly survived for 400 years and there is every possibility that it had already been recycled by Amerindians for millennia.

Mystery has long surrounded one of the most charismatic of all Eurasian rail sounds – the monotonous, incessant and completely wonderful *arp-arp* of the **Corncrake** *Crex crex*. Despite massive declines, this is a migrant species from Africa that spreads to breed in 42 countries from Ireland's Atlantic coast to China. In one night, concealed by vegetation, a single male of this predominantly brown crake can repeat its basic monosyllable 20,000 times.

In English letters there is a long tradition of Corncrake poetry that dwells on the strange, compelling nature of the disembodied song and the mystery of its meaning. Foremost among these was the great nineteenth-century nature poet John Clare, who recorded Corncrakes when they were abundant birds of croplands in his native Northamptonshire. One poem is called 'The Landrail' (the bird's old name):

We hear it in the weeding time
When knee deep waves the corn
We hear it in the summers prime
Through meadows night and morn

And now I hear it in the grass
That grows as sweet again
And let a minutes notice pass
And now tis in the grain

Tis like a fancy every where
A sort of living doubt
We know tis something but it neer
Will blab the secret out

If heard in close or meadow plots
It flies if we pursue
But follows if we notice not
The close and meadow through

Boys know the note of many a bird
In their birdnesting bounds
But when the landrails noise is heard
They wonder at the sounds

They look in every tuft of grass
Thats in their rambles met
They peep in every bush they pass
And none the wiser get

And still they hear the craiking sound
And still they wonder why

It surely cant be under ground
Nor is it in the sky

And yet tis heard in every vale
An undiscovered song
And makes a pleasant wonder tale
For all the summer long

In recent times the Corncrake's almost complete extinction in Britain (not because it was such a highly regarded table bird – 'two Landrails are said to be a present for a queen' – but because of mechanisation of harvest techniques) has added a note of sadness to Clare's meditation on its mysterious invisibility.[4] Echoing his idea that the call was a 'sort of living doubt', the Scots poet Norman MacCaig (in 'A Voice of Summer') suggests how the Corncrake's disappearance from the local soundscape was, 'As though the language of a subtle folk / Had lost a word that had no synonym.'

RAILS AS PETS AND FOOD

Many of the family, particularly coots and gallinules, are infamous for their intense and noisy squabbling (an old Spanish name for the Eurasian Coot was *pájaro diablo*, 'devil bird').[5] In the case of the strikingly handsome **Watercock** *Gallicrex cinerea*, a large gallinule-like bird from south Asia, the propensity for aggression was exploited by rural communities (in what is now Bangladesh). Until the early twentieth century it was commonplace to raid Watercock nests and raise the chicks as fighting birds, on which their owners would gamble large sums of money. The incubation technique, used also in the case of the Swamp Francolin, a partridge reared for the same purpose, involved swaddling the eggs in cotton and placing them inside one half of a coconut, which was held permanently against the waist. For 24 days the individual was unable to bathe, sleep or work without his precious charges strapped to his middle.[6] How the eventual Watercock contests were scored or whether the birds could be induced to scrap to the death is not clear, but in the wild their scuffles seldom result in serious injury.[7] The practice has probably died out, but Watercocks are still widely caught and eaten in Asia.

At the other extreme of human regard for a rail is perhaps the most touching and bizarre of all cultural engagements with the family. In the classical world, the Romans had a unique tradition of keeping Purple Swamphens as pets. The species is among the largest and most beautiful of its family, distinguished (in the European race) by a deep rich sheeny, purplish-blue body and red legs and bill. There were undoubtedly special factors predisposing the Romans to this bird. Yet the reaction of a nineteenth-century naturalist, Philip Gosse, on seeing the similarly beautiful Purple Gallinule in Jamaica, is noteworthy. 'I could not help thinking', he wrote, 'what a beautiful addition it would make to an ornamental water in an English park; and the more so, because its confiding tameness allows of an approach sufficiently near to admire its brilliancy.'[8]

The Romans clearly shared this generic human delight in swamphen beauty, but infusing their particular fascination was a fixation with the sacred magic of the colour purple. In fact their name for the bird was itself striking: *Porphyrion* means simply 'the purple' or 'purple thing'. The Greek adjective *porphyreos* – widely used, by Homer especially, to describe the sea – carried an additional sense of 'shining', a quality manifest in the swamphen's glorious plumage.[9] In the classical world's lexicon of colour, purple was the ultimate expression of status and power.

It was the mark of magistrates, senators, members of the equestrian order and, above all, of imperial majesty. The purple of the Roman toga was derived from Mediterranean shellfish famously exploited by the Phoenicians of Tyre in modern-day Lebanon. Only a double-dyeing process yielded Tyrian purple. The resulting colour was similar to dried blood and, when looked at superficially, seemed merely black, but when held to the light it glowed magically. In Caesar's day a pound of violet wool cost 100 denarii, but Tyrian purple wool was ten times more expensive. Despite repeated attempts to prevent the ordinary citizen from wearing it, purple-trimmed robes became hugely popular. Eventually purple of the finest quality was an imperial privilege protected by legislation. The private individual who assumed it could be guilty of high treason.[10]

One highly revealing observation by the author Aelian was that not even the most indulgent epicures seem to have eaten Purple Swamphens. That is saying much in the context of Roman attitudes towards all things avian (see Peacocks in the West, page 76). Instead the birds were kept as treasured pets that enjoyed the freedom of the house, even at the wealthiest villas. They also wandered temple precincts without any particular religious significance being ascribed to them. Yet they were thought to be quaintly prudish in matters of sex, never mating in public; one claim repeated by several authors was that the male acted as a kind of keeper of domestic morals. If the mistress of the house should take an illicit lover the swamphen would hang itself out of shame.[11]

A more tangible legacy of Rome's fascination with swamphens is the presence of their image in many surviving mosaics. It seems almost a part of the rails' overall gift for surprise that such an unlikely species is so regularly found in these remarkable artworks. Yet there are beautiful depictions of the birds among the collection of Roman mosaics in the British Museum (London), the Bardo Museum (Tunis), the museum in El Jem (Tunisia), at the Palace of the Grand Masters (on the Greek island of Rhodes) and among the series of remarkable wall paintings unearthed at Pompeii.[12]

The Purple Swamphen is a surprising but regular subject in Roman mosaics. This one is from Carthage, Tunisia.

Perhaps the strangest of all Roman swamphen images appear in what is known as the 'Little Circus', a scenario depicted at the Villa Romana del Casale. This UNESCO site in central Sicily is noted for its outstanding late Roman mosaics, the most famous of which is a tableau of young women dressed only in bikinis. The swamphens are part of a scene showing four chariots driven by children, with teams of birds as the beasts of burden. One chariot is drawn by a pair of swamphens and is defeated in the four-corner race by the green team, represented by the pigeons (there are also teams of flamingos and white geese in harness). It is possible that each bird team represents a season, with the swamphens, garlanded with grapes, representing autumn. It seems typical of our wider modern bafflement over why exactly these birds should have been so important to the Romans that on a modern website featuring the Villa Romana the swamphens are misidentified as plovers.[13]

These ancient images are among the oldest accurate portraits of a rail species anywhere on Earth. Yet older still are the carved reliefs of Purple Swamphens in Egypt. Often incorporated into larger Nilotic hunting scenes, these images, dating to *c*.2500 BC, are the earliest in a much wider human response to the rail family.[14]

Worldwide the commoner species have been a long-standing source of protein. The older names given to the birds – and even much of the current nomenclature: 'swamphen', 'moorhen', 'Watercock' – betray a perception of rails as being closely allied to domestic fowl. The ground-dwelling lifestyle and rounded body shapes of both bird groups predisposed us to the transfer of names and suggested to our earliest ancestors that rails were good to eat. In Spanish, for example, the Purple Swamphen was *gallo azul* ('blue cock'), while the Common Moorhen is still *polla de agua* ('water chicken') and the same in French (*poule d'eau*).[15] In the Americas a similar pattern exists. The second part of Purple Gallinule derives from *gallinula*, a diminutive of the Latin word *gallina*, 'hen'.[16] In Brazil this species is known as *Frango-d'água-azul* ('blue water-chicken').[17] The bird is apparently still hunted throughout much of its South American range and forms the basis of an esteemed dish in some Brazilian regions.[18]

Rails remain an important food in Asia and South America, but our appetite for their meat tends to be strongest in areas with ancient hunting traditions and where rural poverty is commonplace. There were once major driven shoots for Eurasian Coot in parts of south-west England and southern France, but both have now ceased. Yet around the Mediterranean the birds are still hunted (in ancient Greece they were trapped and pickled, while the Romans reared them specially for the table).[19] In Egypt the Eurasian Coot, Common Moorhen and Purple Swamphen are widely eaten today despite their reputation for strong fishy flavours. As many as 25,000 moorhens are killed on a single Egyptian lake each year, while the average number of Eurasian Coots offered at market in Port Said over a single season (between 1979 and 1986) was estimated at 30,000–32,000.[20]

Similarly, in south Asia the Eurasian Coot is highly prized and eaten in vast numbers.[21] They are, for example, caught by fishing tribes (Mirbars) in the wetlands of Sind, Pakistan; the fowlers driving them with boats into flight nets suspended on bamboo poles. Individuals also walk in water up to their necks to stalk coot, disguised by a clay pot on their heads, over which a coot skin has been crudely

stretched. They mingle with the birds and pull them under one by one, fixing them into a belt, the other coots seemingly oblivious that when their fellows 'dive' they never return to the surface.[22]

Across the Atlantic, the annual American Coot harvest over several decades until the late 1980s was 880,000 birds for the USA (with a figure of just 8,000 for Canada).[23] However, among the premier sporting targets of former centuries were two far smaller rail species: the **Clapper Rail** *Rallus longirostris* and the **Sora** *Porzana carolina*. The first is famous for its loud, ventriloquial cackling notes (these mechanical sounds, which fall in pitch and slow towards their close, explain the bird's name), its weak flight and, at one time, it was renowned for its fine flesh. Spread around the coastlines of North and South America, the species was hunted intensively in the USA, with large numbers being supplied to market in coastal cities such as San Francisco or Charleston. A secondary harvest of the bird's eggs was also on a grand scale. John James Audubon recalled professional eggers who could gather 1,200 in a day, but the artist's own private tally of 864 eggs in one collecting bout was a reflection of the Clapper Rail's former abundance.[24]

Rather strangely for a bird so small – it weighs about 90 g (3 oz) – the Sora had an even stronger reputation as a fine table bird (its nickname was 'ortolan'; see The Cult of the Ortolan, page 520). Even today there is a substantial harvest, especially in the southern states such as Louisiana. However, the primary factor in population decline among North American rails is adumbrated in a lovely passage by Arthur Bent (see Appendix II). His account of student egg forays evokes the feral joys of the hunter-gatherer lifestyle, but also the central and devastating impact of habitat loss on human and bird alike.

> In my college days, in the late [eighteen] eighties, such a bog still existed near the centre of Brookline, where a friend and I used to wade around in the mud up to our waists, collecting rails eggs; then dripping with mud and water, we would return to his house, jump into the bath tub with our clothes on and wash off the mud, much to his mother's disgust. In those days the Fresh Pond marshes in Cambridge [Massachusetts] were an oasis of wilderness in a desert of civilization and both the **Virginia** [**Rail** *Rallus limicola*] and sora . . . nested there in abundance. Both of these marshes were filled in and obliterated by human 'improvements'.[25]

RAILS AND EXTINCTION

The gradual worldwide shrinkage of wetland habitats as they have been drained and converted to farmland has inflicted major losses on this bird group. In fact, extinction has borne down with greater, disproportionate weight on rails than on any other family. The total number lost in the last 500 years is impossible to calculate, but we know that at least 22 species have vanished since AD 1500. The family's powers of flight, or, rather, their lack of them, are an issue at the heart of this pattern.

It seems part of the wider unpredictable element in this family's personality that, while they take to the air with reluctance, once airborne – with legs dangling and short, rounded wings battling vigorously – rails seem uncertain how to stop and can fly huge distances. The Corncrake is the exemplar of long-distance rail travel. Birds summering in eastern Siberia migrate more than 9,000 km (5,500 miles) from Africa. (A striking part of this behaviour is that they often accompany another anomalous traveller to Eurasia – the Common Quail [see also page 55]. The frequent link between the two species led to names in several countries that suggest how one acted as leader for the other. In German, Corncrake is still known as *Wachtelkönig*, 'quail king', while in Spanish it was *rey de las codornices*, 'king of the quails', and is still called *guión de codornices*, 'guide of the quails'.[26] Today both birds are caught together and eaten in Egypt.)

It is typical of their ungainly flight that migrant rails are frequent victims of collisions. Travelling at night, they are often confused by the metropolitan dazzle of cities or the blinding beam of lighthouses. They can crash into floodlights, towers, power lines, or impale themselves on barbed wire. Yet these rather uncertain airborne powers have carried rails to some of the most isolated islands in the world, such as Ascension Island (**Ascension Flightless Crake** *Atlantisia elpenor*, St Helena (**St Helena Rail** *Porzana astrictocarpus*, **St Helena Crake** *Atlantisia podarces*), and Gough and Tristan da Cunha (**Inaccessible Island Rail** *Atlantisia rogersi*, **Gough Moorhen** *Gallinula comeri*, **Tristan Gallinule** *Gallinula nesiotis*), all in the middle of the Atlantic; as well as the Hawaiian archipelago (**Hawaiian Crake** *Porzana sandwichensis*, **Laysan Crake** *Porzana palmeri*, **Hawaiian Coot** *Fulica alai*) in the very heart of the Pacific Ocean. The first of these islands is the nearest to a continental landmass at 1,400 km (870 miles), and the last is no less than 4,500 km (2,800 miles) from North America and 8,300 km (5,200 miles) from the Asian mainland.

Once they have made landfall and colonised such places, the birds regularly resort to type. So a seemingly perverse pattern among island rail species is that they fly to an isolated refuge, take to the undergrowth, gradually abandon their means of arrival and become flightless. The combination of tiny world ranges and flightlessness has then become a severe disadvantage when humans arrive. Island rails are susceptible not merely to hunting, but also to the impact from a suite of introduced animals including rats, pigs, cats and dogs.

The overlapping pattern among these ground-dwelling birds is stark. Of all the world's rails and crakes, almost a third (40 species) is threatened or near-threatened, and 21 of these are endemic inhabitants of islands or archipelagos. Equally, there are 20 flightless rails on Earth; just two of them are (for now) considered secure. Of the nine island rails named above, only three (Inaccessible Island Rail, Gough Moorhen and Hawaiian Coot) are not already extinct, and this surviving trio is judged to be at risk of extinction.[27]

One of the family, the remarkable **Takahe** *Porphyrio hochstetteri* of New Zealand, has suffered the indignity of 'extinction' more than once. The bird is closely related to the Purple Swamphen, but during its long separation on New Zealand it became flightless, endemic and massive. It is the largest of the family and about the size of a moderate turkey (males can weigh 4 kg: 8.8 lb). It was hunted by the Maoris for centuries, but European colonists only stumbled upon the bird in 1849, when it was first described from subfossil bones by the brilliant but venomous British biologist Richard Owen. Even at its naming the species was assumed to be extinct, and while additional records of live birds occurred

The Takahe of New Zealand is the world's largest rail.

at lengthy intervals, they always seemed to leave the species half sunk in shadow. A final sighting in 1898 was followed by nothing but darkness for half a century and Takahe was assumed to be another lost rail.[28]

Then in 1948 the discovery of a completely unknown population in the montane scrub of Fiordland on South Island reacquainted humankind with this remarkable bird. The finder, a kiwi doctor called Geoffrey Orbell, was feted for his discovery and made the cover of *Time* magazine. Since then the species has been the subject of a concerted effort to provide the 200 or more survivors with permanent security from the risks of introduced stoats or possums and habitat loss. The area where Orbell found them is now a national park, and the place where the good doctor and the bird initially met is called Takahe Valley.[29]

While the Takahe's vicissitudes over the last two centuries are in many ways emblematic of the plight of so many rails, its discovery through subfossil evidence touches on a theme most revealing about this strange family. Palaeontologists have suggested that our ability to understand exactly how many rail species have slipped into oblivion is concealed underground on the world's oceanic islands. One expert, working with excavated bone evidence, suggests that the birds' long history of globetrotting carried them to every oceanic island in the world. Another proposes further that the real total of extinct rails in Oceania alone could be anywhere between 1,000 and 3,000 species. The Polynesian and then European colonists moved, with their domestic livestock, from island to island, encountering flightless endemic rails, hunting them and eating them and finally extinguishing them without leaving so much as a name. Whatever the true number of lost rails, it is indisputable that the family has paid the heaviest price of all birds for man the hunter and man the master mariner.[30]

Finfoot family *Heliornithidae*

The shyness of the three widely spread finfoot species is so intense that the family has been listed among 'those that have had least impact on the lives of men'.[1] They have long grebe-like bodies which can be submerged in the manner of a cormorant or Darter, until only the serpentine neck and head are visible above the water.

The family's scientific name is an oddity. It comes from the **Sungrebe** *Heliornis fulica*, the South American representative of the trio (the others are the **Masked Finfoot** *Heliopais personatus* of Asia and **African Finfoot** *Podica sengalensis*). The Greek-derived word *Heliornis* means 'sun bird', despite the fact that the finfoots are,

at best, creatures of sun-dappled shadow cast by overhanging waterside vegetation. The birds rarely offer prolonged views, almost never venture far from dense cover and seldom give an observer cause to reflect if the plural is 'finfeet' or 'finfoots' (it is the latter).

The family's introverted personality means that it is seldom hunted, although roast Masked Finfoot has been described as 'delicious'.[2] However, the real reason for the species' threatened status is loss of mangrove habitat and other human works, such as dam construction, aquaculture and boat traffic.[3]

Trumpeter family *Psophiidae*

The trumpeters comprise three similar forest-dwelling frugivores that inhabit the Orinoco and Amazonian basins from Guyana and central Brazil west into Bolivia, Peru and Colombia. The plumage is predominantly black with fine violet or royal-blue details, and paler velvet-textured 'sashes' on the lower mantle. The legs and neck are long and the head is rather small, particularly in proportion to the pronounced sphere of the trumpeter's body. This swollen somewhat chicken-like shape can be further emphasised by the birds' exaggerated postures, which can allow them to change, in the words of one commentator, from 'looking rotund and sedate into a speeding ball of apparent fury in an instant'.[1] The slightly hunched appearance is reflected in a local name in Suriname, *kamikami* (or *kamee-kamee*) which is derived from the Dutch, *kameel*, for 'camel'.[2]

Trumpeters resemble chickens not only in build and

ground-dwelling lifestyle, but in their reputation as fine eating. All three are widely hunted, although their secondary value is as a popular addition to village life. Birds are taken from the wild as eggs or young chicks and reared by a brooding hen, after which trumpeters can become important members of any settlement, providing a range of domestic services. 'Trumpeters are kept as pets in villages in Peru. I have seen it often and they make great pets. They are used as "guard dogs" much like geese in farmyards – they make a racket when there is an intruder – particularly if there is a snake and will peck and kill a snake. I have seen them do that.'[3] In addition trumpeters are reputed to take care of the other poultry, in much the same way that has been described in various chachalaca species (see page 36).[4]

In the wild, trumpeters are gregarious, probably polyandrous in breeding arrangements and appear to

A Grey-winged Trumpeter looks for leftovers at a Peruvian lodge. In Amazonia trumpeters are often kept as household familiars for their affectionate personalities, their pest-disposal services and sometimes for their sporting prowess.

have complex social lives, in which 'play' has an important function. This includes 'mock fights . . . rowdy chasing, "attacks" on twigs and leaves, "bragging" over food'.[5] A trumpeter seems to feel the same urge for sociability and recreation even after it has been domesticated, but simply transfers its attention to the humans on which it has become imprinted. The result is a domestic bird with immense personality.

> I have seen them in various villages in Brazil. I do not know if I would use the word 'pet' – I haven't found that the indigenous people I've worked with, view animals in the same way as many Westerners. The birds are very smart and loving and will play all sorts of games with you. They are the best company in the world, so intelligent, so interested in things, such loyal companions and so much fun to play hide and seek and chase with. I also love their contact vocalisations and the way they always want you to preen their head. I just can't say too many superlatives about how wonderful they are. They are my favourite Amazonian bird and they alone would be reason enough to preserve tropical forests forever! I almost wept when I had to leave my trumpeter friends – I wished so much that I could get some chicks or adult birds for a country place I have in the US and may look into this after I retire.[6]

On a trip to the Ecuadorian Amazon in 2002, we stayed at Pañacocha Lodge, which had a semi-tame **Pale-winged Trumpeter** *Psophia leucoptera* that acted as a 'guard dog'. When we arrived by boat, the trumpeter and dog rushed down to the river to 'greet us', the trumpeter fluffed out in display. We were told that local forest-dwelling people often kept the species around their huts, as it was a dab hand at snaring snakes. Our experience was restricted to the trumpeter killing the many tarantulas that ventured in and around the accommodation.

But this particular trumpeter had a gift; it was also a fantastic footballer – and had earned the name Valentino after a famous soccer player. Shortly before dawn, Valentino would wake up and locate the semi-deflated football that lay around the grounds. The bird would then peck at the football and push it around for hours, until someone came to play. Somewhere I have a few slides of Valentino tackling me.[7]

There was a delightful old misconception about trumpeters that their calls were emitted from the cloaca. The idea persisted until the twentieth century, with a book from 1908 including the remark that, 'Long before science discovered it, natives knew the booming call . . . was made by the anus and not the beak.' The authors cited in support the belief of Guyanan Indians that trumpeters stole the trick from the rooster, who complained every morning about its theft.[8]

Crane family *Gruidae*

If we ever had to vote for a family to serve as a symbol for the entire 10,500 species of bird and even for whole panoply of life on Earth, then cranes would probably make the shortlist. A book equal in length to this one could easily be written about their multitudinous cultural connections. Almost every aspect of the cranes' physique, lifestyle and behaviour has captured our attention. Like the cockerel, dove, crow and eagle, the crane seems an avian archetype for the human imagination. Particularly in the northern hemisphere they have served as a kind of psychological compass that has helped to orient us in our entire relationship with nature.

They are long-legged, long-necked, cloak-winged birds and, if not human-shaped, they at least suggest what we might have looked like had we been birds. Some cranes, in fact, are as tall as people. The **Sarus Crane** *Grus antigone* reaches 1.7 m (5.6 ft) and often stands higher than its human neighbours in south Asia. Just as impressive are their vast trumpeting calls and their slow, stately mode of progress, which somehow manages to suggest both intense caution and innate dignity.

Their long legs are adapted to movement in flat wet environments and many cranes nest in some of the most remote, inaccessible places on Earth. The breeding or wintering localities for at least two species – **Siberian Crane** *Grus leucogeranus* and **Whooping Crane** *Grus americana* – were not found until the second half of the twentieth century. The world's 15 cranes are widely but unevenly distributed with just five in the southern hemisphere: four species in sub-Saharan Africa, one in Australasia and none in South America or Antarctica. Ten species inhabit Eurasia and North America, where they perform lengthy migrations often between the circumpolar boreal forest and tundra, south as far as the Tropic of Cancer. In so doing cranes link some of the most important, wildlife-rich wetland environments left in the northern hemisphere.

At one time the sight of migrant cranes on genuine passage to and from unknown territories seemed to echo larger human mysteries. In Asia, where the cranes' cultural importance is perhaps most fully developed, the birds became a symbol of the ultimate journey. They were said to carry the souls of the departed on their ascent to heaven. Yet alongside these transcendent notions is a far more modern and profane usage of crane imagery. A good example is their appearance in a glossy advertisement for Greek cigarettes. It involved an entirely anomalous photograph of **Red-crowned Crane** *Grus japonensis*, exclusively a species of the Far East, to market the 'Ultra One' brand of cigarette, complete with its 'bio-filter' (just 0.1 mg of nicotine). The linkage of the bird with an infamous carcinogen is difficult to fathom. Perhaps a subliminal awareness of the crane's role in trafficking the souls of the dead was at work in this otherwise surreal conjunction.

Despite the image abuse inflicted by modern capitalism, cranes retain a genuine capacity to illuminate some of the most important political issues of our age. There is no finer example than the story – one is almost tempted to call it the parable – of Whooping Cranes in North America. At one time this magnificent species was hounded towards extinction until, by the 1940s, the world population stood at 29 birds. Three-quarters of a century later, the concerted efforts to save it are still ongoing and have probably incurred greater financial cost than that spent on any other single bird (except perhaps the California Condor, see page 161). Arguably only a white crane could have so stirred the human imagination. In the process it has become a central emblem for all North American conservation.

The great American ecologist Aldo Leopold, striving to convey the exalted character of cranes, wrote: 'Our ability to perceive quality in nature begins, as in art, with the pretty. It expands through successive stages of the beautiful to values as yet uncaptured by language. The quality of cranes lies, I think, in this higher gamut, as yet beyond the reach of words.'[1] In the light of this passage, it seems bizarre to report that nine of the 15 cranes, including all four mentioned above, are at risk of extinction, while another, the **Black Crowned Crane** *Balearica pavonina* of Africa, is near-threatened.

This account is largely an exploration of the family's enormous importance as a cultural symbol, set against descriptions of frequent neglect and routine persecution. The material is so rich that it is presented under four headings: Africa, Europe and West Asia, East Asia, and North America. However, many of the stories overlap from region to region. In fact one of the striking characteristics of human–crane interactions is how, regardless of place or species, they have often inspired us to the same ideas.

AFRICA

Cranes are writ large in the official symbolism of a number of modern African states. Unfortunately the birds' prominence tends to illuminate the curious contradiction between reverence for the imaginary crane and neglect of the real creature. The status of the Black Crowned Crane in Nigeria is typical. It is the country's national bird, but is now virtually extinct there because of habitat loss and hunting for bushmeat.[2]

I once did a radio interview on the crane and nobody I spoke to then or since was aware that it was the national bird. In the early 1970s we arrested a bird trapper with about 50 Black Crowned Cranes in NE Nigeria. As we had nowhere readily available to keep the birds prior to the court case, the then expatriate manager of the Standard Bank in Nguru agreed to keep them in the dry swimming pool in his compound. As you can imagine, he was none too pleased when he had to clean out the pool afterwards. After the case, we shipped them all to Maiduguri and a small zoo, where they were allowed to wander freely until their flight feathers re-grew and they were allowed to fly off.[3]

The closely related **Grey Crowned Crane** *Balearica regulorum* has a key part in the state insignia of Uganda, appearing in the coat of arms, on the flag and on Uganda's currency, including a lovely illustration on the 20,000-shilling note. So far this species has not suffered the same troubling decline as its close relative.

The **Blue Crane** *Anthropoides paradiseus* has also enjoyed high esteem in southern Africa. The feathers, particularly the long gracefully curved tertials, were once an important emblem of masculine power for both the Xhosa and the Zulu peoples. The plumes were awarded to senior leaders and warriors as recognition of prowess in battle. A vestige of the custom has

survived into the modern era, and on ceremonial occasions the present Zulu King Goodwill Zwelithini wears Blue Crane feathers on his head. The modern Republic of South Africa, to which the species is virtually endemic (Namibia has a dwindling and isolated group of under 60 birds), paid careful attention to the ancient symbolism and adopted the Blue Crane as the national bird. Unfortunately recent conversion of grasslands in KwaZulu-Natal for intensive agriculture has severely reduced numbers and the species' plight is worsened by inadvertent poisoning with agrochemicals. A current estimate of 21,000 for the whole of South Africa represents an 80 per cent decline since the 1960s.[4]

EUROPE AND WEST ASIA

There are just two species in the region: the **Common Crane** *Grus grus* and the smaller, predominantly Asian **Demoiselle Crane** *Anthropoides virgo*. Of the two the first has probably always been more numerous and widespread. Certainly it has played the larger cultural role. Flying in conspicuous formation and with their robustly metallic notes acting as an adhesive, migrant flocks have impressed themselves upon us since our first footsteps on a northern landmass. Given that they also represented a major source of protein, it is hardly surprising that Common Cranes account for a series of cultural 'firsts'.

Birds thought to be of this species are depicted on Neolithic stone columns at a south-eastern Turkish site called Göbekli Tepe (9500 BC) and are among the oldest relief carvings of birds in the world.[5] The cranes featured on the stucco walls of Çatalhöyük (6500–5600 BC), the archaeological site near the city of Konya, most likely represent the oldest identifiable bird paintings on a prepared surface found on Earth (see also Exploitation of Auks, page 227). Then there are the migrant cranes invoked in Homer's *Iliad* to convey the tumultuous roar of Greek forces on the plains of Troy:

Their clans came out like the countless flocks of birds
– the geese, the cranes or the long-necked swans – that
fore-gather in the Asian meadow by the streams of
Cayster, and wheel about, boldly flapping their wings
and filling the whole meadow with harsh cries as they
come to ground on an advancing front.[6]

This is one of the oldest references to an identifiable bird species in the whole of Western literature, pre-dating even those for the domestic chicken.

The inexorable two-way rhythm of crane migration eventually impressed itself upon early Europeans as a kind of slow-swinging metronome that marked the seasonal round. In ancient Greece, cranes in full flight southwards were taken as a farmers' index for the moment to plough in late autumn.[7] The birds were also indicators of weather. According to Aelian, the Roman writer of the second century AD, cranes making tranquil progress across the heavens presaged fine weather, but if a flock turned back from a sea crossing then it was a sign of impending storm.[8]

The notion that cranes can predict both season and climate has retained its hold on the European imagination, as illustrated by these two contributions:

In the past in south or central Sweden there was a saying *Tranan bär ljus i säng* ('the crane carries a light

Common Cranes
at dawn at
Hornborgasjön.

to bed'), which meant that when the cranes arrived in spring it was time to go to bed even though the sun was still up.[9]

In Finland the Common Crane is called *kurki* and there used to be a belief that the bird held up the sky so it didn't fall down. In log houses even today the strongest, highest log in the roof is known as *kurkihirsi*, 'the crane log'. There are several crane sayings that are still used: 'When you hear the call of the crane, you shouldn't go to the lake ice anymore.' In parts of Finland the crane is replaced with the Eurasian Curlew, but both species are migrants and arrive in spring about the same time that the ice melts. So this is a serious warning about weak ice!

For Finns, cranes are very important spring messengers and people get very excited about them. All of us have heard the word *kurkiaura*, which is a special name for the V formation of migrating cranes. (What they don't know is that other species fly in V formation, so occasionally there are early spring 'crane' records that may relate to cormorants or gulls.) Today – and especially in the past – people carefully follow crane behaviour and have attached beliefs to it. Early migration in autumn indicates that winter will arrive early. If migrating flocks fly high over an area there will be heavy snowstorms. If cranes leave the area in noisy flocks, there will be a good crop but if they leave quietly then the harvest will be bad.[10]

Wherever cranes have occurred they represented a substantial protein source, but in the Mediterranean area they were particularly prized. At one time the ancient Greeks scooped out the brains from the minuscule skull to use as a type of aphrodisiac.[11] In Egypt there are impressive relief sculptures dating from the middle of the third millennium BC. These depict the hand-feeding of cranes – it is one of the

few places where captive management (as opposed to true domestication) was ever attempted – in the same way that geese are still forcibly engorged to produce pâté de foie gras (see page 88).[12]

Subsequently cranes were prized as a highly wary quarry for hunters, especially for the feudal aristocrats of the Middle Ages, who hunted with horse and hounds and magnificent falcons fastened to their leather-clad arms. The cranes' central place in the sporting life of medieval Europe led to one notable 'first' for the literary bird, when it formed the subject of Book IV in the remarkable work *De Arte Venandi cum Avibus*, better known as *The Art of Falconry*. It was written by Frederick II (1194–1250), the Hohenstaufen Holy Roman Emperor, and has good claim to be considered the first work of scientific ornithology, although it was not properly known until the early eighteenth century.

The whole of Book IV in *The Art of Falconry* is devoted to the hunting of Common Cranes, one of Frederick's favourite sports in southern Italy and on Sicily. The heart of the challenge was to get his bird – usually a Gyrfalcon; the largest, rarest and most powerful of its family (see page 165) – over the top of the crane quarry. Hunter and hunted would then strive to gain ascendancy. Usually the falcon worked in a partnership with hounds to seize the grounded prey. The trial involved a superb predator against its largest adversary and as a preliminary required exacting patience to impart the silkiest of skills. If it did not express the exalted value of cranes as envisaged by Aldo Leopold, then it implied a magnificence of sorts.

Cranes were a popular if rather unwieldy favourite for the European banqueting table, and the relentless pincer movement operated by aristocratic sportsmen and medieval culinary fashion, not to mention a gradual loss of wetland habitat, eventually squeezed them out of former breeding areas such as Britain, Hungary, Ireland and Spain. In the former they continued to be caught and eaten until the late

A Common Crane
serenades the return
of spring.

seventeenth century, but the last proven breeding record was 1543. There is, fortunately, a pleasing symmetry to the story of Britain's cranes. The site of the last capture became the location to which they returned – unexpectedly and without assistance – exactly 439 years later. Since an initial nest in 1982, the population has increased at Hickling, Norfolk, until there are now about 50 birds.

The Common Crane's British resurrection fits a wider modern pattern of environmental protection across the whole continent. Although the species' numbers endured declines almost from the time of Frederick II, recently the population curve has been upwards. Today the Common Crane is among the most secure of all the family, with a total population of over 250,000. That such a specialist of wide open spaces has flourished in one of the world's most crowded regions has underscored its symbolic status for the whole environment. The underlying assumption is that if cranes and humans can coexist in this context, then there is hope for all.

The sheer cacophony of movement and sound produced by migrants has converted several resting places into major attractions. From Spain to Sweden, tourist organisations have erected an infrastructure of road signs and interpretation boards, blinds and viewing platforms, to enable people to enjoy the spectacle. Several sites have now acquired international reputations, such as Laguna de Gallocanta (up to 50,000 birds) in the Spanish province of Zaragoza; the Lac du Der-Chantecoq, east of Paris (up to 40,000 birds); and the Hortobágy National Park in eastern Hungary, where the autumn peak of 60,000 cranes occurs in mid-late October.

Among the most visited is Hornborgasjön in south-central Sweden. Crane numbers are not as high as at the other places, yet the spring arrival is sufficient to generate the key ingredients of a crane spectacle, which involves a battery upon the senses that almost obliterates attempts at description. The underlying impression, as arriving and departing sub-flocks intersect amid a cacophonous din of trumpet notes, is of visual and audible chaos. Paradoxically, the cranes also resolve into a kaleidoscopic harmony of colour, movement, drama, grace and rhythmic, slow-motion beauty.

At Hornborgasjön there is a further symbolism underpinning the inherent power of the scene, because the peak numbers occur in the first week of April, when birds perform a courtship dance to establish and cement pair bonds. Each micro-part of the panorama thus involves a display of wild sexual excitement. The gathering at Hornborgasjön came to public attention in the 1950s after a celebratory film by Arne Sucksdorf and has grown ever since.[13]

I believe the crane dance at Lake Hornborga is THE biggest bird-related crowd-drawing spectacle in Sweden. And it's attracting increasing numbers of international visitors. Among hard-core birders it's not fully accepted as a 'real' birdwatching experience. However, a lot of people keep coming back year after year, and the managers have a busy time throughout the calendar.

As cranes depart from their wintering grounds, Swedish newspapers, radio and television keep track of their progress and when the birds close in on Sweden, the wardens at Lake Hornborga are expected to make educated guesses about when they will arrive. Earlier, cranes were drawn here to feed on waste potatoes from local distilleries. Today, barley is spread on the feeding grounds, lowering the pressure on close-by farmland.

The daily count features in local newspapers and record-breaking tallies make it on to national television. To date the all-time record is 15,300 on 2 April 2008. How they arrive at the figure is one of the most frequently asked questions. A long-standing joke tells how the legs are counted and divided by two. In truth, it is hardly as difficult as it sounds. During the evening, small parties leave the feeding grounds for their roost and all the flocks are added up. There you have the daily total.[14]

The Demoiselle Cranes at Kheechan in Rajasthan symbolise a world in which birds and people coexist as part of one enlarged mutually tolerant community.

These bronze cranes in the Forbidden City in Beijing, China, exemplify the family's huge cultural importance in the East.

EAST ASIA

It is perhaps among the ancient civilisations of India and China that crane symbolism and wider cultural responses to the birds reach their apotheosis. Images of the birds are ubiquitous in art, literature and in a full suite of cultural artefacts, from ceremonial clothing to advertising billboards. Yet it is in ordinary people's engagements with the real birds that one finds some of the most powerful expressions of human attachment, not just to this family in particular, but to any birds.

One story, which has a worldwide reputation in ornithological circles, centres on a small village in the heart of the Thar Desert in the Indian state of Rajasthan.

Kheechan is more than 500 years old, an ancient caravan stop-over on the Silk Route from Kabul. Many families of the Rakhecha (Jain), Ravana Rajput, Darji, Suthar, Nai and Meghwal communities settled and laboured to create a beautiful oasis by digging several ponds and wells. The village thus had ample drinking water to attract the Demoiselle Cranes, which are primarily birds of dry grasslands.

What is now known as the 'Bird Feeding Home' or *Pakshi Chugga Ghar* began with one Ratan Lal Maloo and his wife, who used to sprinkle grain in their huge backyard for pigeons, peafowl, sparrows and crows. The Demoiselle Cranes started visiting this feeding site and had no problem interacting with local species. Maloo spread more grain for the new visitors and gradually enlarged his backyard into a feeding centre in 1983. Now the cranes swoop down here in thousands. About a million rupees' worth of grain is fed to the birds every year. And Kheechan is a fully fledged birdwatching centre, a perfect example of the tourist economy leading conservation efforts.

One of the village's great crusaders for crane welfare is the now octogenarian Seva Ram. During our visit we caught him at sunset, easing sacks of *jowar* and *bajra* one by one on to his back, bending hips and knees and scattering them in a 50 m x 40 m enclosure. He told us that about 15,000 cranes arrive by January from the plains of central Asia after crossing the high mountains of Afghanistan and Pakistan.

On a crimson dawn at about seven o'clock we went to Seva Ram's terrace. The cranes have already started arriving, rows of Vs coming in from everywhere, each flock looking like a collage of a giant bird. Their discipline startles me, not one of them is out of line, not one of them intends to stray. Soon, they crowd the enclosure so that all you get to see are specks of grey and white, the other birds are almost pushed to the fringes. After the feeding is over, the cranes fly away in batches to the village ponds where they drink and spend the afternoon, unperturbed by tractors and labourers working in the adjacent fields. Even the local stray dogs have a very different attitude towards these birds, hardly scaring or bothering them.

The birds are referred to in many local folk songs and fables. The most common song refers to the Demoiselle Crane as a messenger for lovelorn ladies, whose husbands work in faraway lands. Parents also call their daughters *kurjadi* (derived from *kurjan*, the local name for the bird), no doubt seeing them as slender, graceful, elegant and beautiful. When a daughter gets married, the family likens her journey to her new life to the flight of the bird. Be it joy or tragedy, the villagers feed the birds to mark any event in their isolated lives. This explains the many grain enclosures scattered around the village, shrines to good karma. We read a memorial slab near one of them: it had been built by one Nathmal Kochar in 1970 in memory of his mother.

The desert people believe in *Vasudeva Kutambakam*, the philosophy that all species living on Earth are part of one big family, and it is reflected in their religion and culture. This is the reason that some of the most unique forms of wildlife flourish in this otherwise hostile region where even humans have a tough time sustaining themselves. Even during the severest drought, villagers collect donations to arrange for water, food and fodder for wildlife. Almost all the villages in this belt have a patch of groves called *Oran* which they protect and preserve with religious ardour. They consider it God's munificence in an arid land and so felling of trees, hunting of animals or encroachment in the *Oran* are the worst sins you could commit.

The cranes know they can't have a better home. Satyanaryan Singh Rajpurohit, Managing Director of Marwar Crane Foundation, has got the Rajasthan High Court to restrain the change in land use of a patch of village land, commonly used by the cranes to rest in the afternoon. Villagers have stopped a hotel from encroaching on bird habitat. They fill up dry ponds with tankers and tube-wells during drought so that the birds don't go thirsty. They have even rubberised live and naked electric cables. The demoiselles appreciate their concern and hospitality and keep coming back every winter.[15]

A very similar story attaches to another of the Asian species, the globally endangered Red-crowned Crane. Despite the *japonensis* component of the scientific name, two-thirds of the species' minuscule population (2,700 birds) is found in China or Korea. However, its huge cultural profile in Japan, and particularly in the northernmost island, Hokkaido, is at the heart of conservation efforts for the bird.

Red-crowned Cranes call and dance in the sunlit winter air of Hokkaido.

In fact it is one of those heartening examples where a species' wider symbolic significance has finally come to the rescue of the living creature.

By the 1920s the resident breeding population in southern Hokkaido had fallen to just 20 birds. Concern for the crane, known locally as *tancho* (literally 'red top'), gradually increased until the severe winter of 1952, when a local farmer began feeding them on his land. This simple act of human kindness caught the attention of the public and the practice has been maintained ever since. In the 1960s the crane became a Special Natural Treasure and an expanded area of the neighbouring Kushiro Marsh, where the birds breed, was declared a reserve and then a national park in 1987.[16]

Throughout, *tancho* tourism has gone from strength to strength, and now no visitor to Hokkaido could easily avoid its image. The nearest airport is known officially as Tancho Kushiro Airport. Immediately outside, at either end of a bridge, are two large crane sculptures, and there are symbolic *tancho* heads embedded in the hand rail.[17] Hokkaido's ice

Sandhill Cranes at their evening roost in Bosque del Apache, New Mexico.

John Abbott's early-nineteenth-century painting of a Whooping Crane was completed in his home state of Georgia and reflects a time when this iconic species was widespread in the USA.

Whooping Crane.

hockey team is called The Cranes and, lest we forget, *tancho* forms part of the backdrop to the local television news studio. At Akan itself, where the *tancho* feeding first began in 1952, the surrounding hotels are packed each winter with visitors specifically there to see the birds. Each day an impromptu press pack of about 100 photographers gathers to record the daily handout of grain. All in all, this endangered bird and its associated industry have marched forward in complete lock step. The Hokkaido crane population now numbers over 1,000 birds, while the benefits to the local economy are valued at $50 million.

Tancho's local celebrity is only one part of a much larger national attachment to cranes. A modern aspect of this preoccupation is especially noteworthy – the cranes' role as a Japanese symbol of peace. The making of paper cranes dates from 1798, with the publication of an Origami instruction manual, *How to Fold a Thousand Cranes*. This magical number was itself drawing on an ancient Confucian belief that cranes could live for a round millennium. There is also a classic of Japanese art, *A Thousand Cranes*, painted by Sōtatsu in 1611, that measures 15 m (49 ft) in length.[18] The endurance test involved in folding 1,000 paper cranes achieved wider cultural importance through the story of a young girl, Sadako Sasaki, a victim of the Hiroshima atomic bomb. In 1955, as this 12-year-old lay dying in hospital of leukaemia, she set herself the task of folding 1,000 birds. When death cut short her goal, Sadako's friend Chizuko Hamamoto completed the total.

In so doing she galavanised the nation's imagination and the birds, often completed in multicoloured papers and threaded on to strings, have become a symbol of peace hung frequently in temples and at other ceremonial sites. The

most celebrated of these is the Peace Park in Hiroshima where paper cranes can be numbered in their hundreds of thousands. There is also a memorial shrine celebrating the life of Sadako Sasaki.

The symbolism has now acquired international resonances and has spread to the West, where strings of 1,000 cranes are given to cancer victims, or feature on graves and in funerals. Perhaps this recent association with ideas of universal harmony partly explains the claim that the crane gave rise to the widely recognised peace symbol adopted by, among others, the Campaign for Nuclear Disarmament. While this motif does indeed resemble a bird's footprint enclosed within a circle, it is in fact formed by the semaphoric signals for the letters N and D – Nuclear Disarmament.

NORTH AMERICA

There are two cranes in North America: the **Sandhill Crane** *Grus canadensis* and the Whooping Crane. As in Europe, one of the pair is much more numerous. However, in the case of North America it is the rarer species, the Whooping Crane, that has seized the headlines for much of the last 75 years.

The Sandhill Crane is notable for being the world's commonest family member. There are now an estimated 80,000 birds – and six recognised subspecies – breeding widely across northern boreal America, south as far as California and Colorado. This widespread and common species was a source of story and myth for a range of indigenous American peoples. To diverse communities, such as the pueblo-dwelling Zuni and the semi-agricultural Ojibwa of the lake region, it was a totem of communal identity. Both peoples had crane clans.

With the arrival of Old World colonists a pattern of exploitation and numerical decline mirrored the birds' fortunes in Europe. However, the North American version of the story intensifies and distils the elements to create one of the great sagas of environmental history. Whooping Cranes were once found thinly from Texas to Florida in winter, and breeding in a wetland belt running north-west from Illinois to Canada's Great Slave Lake. Whooping Cranes – or 'whoopers' as they are known – are strikingly beautiful and stand more than 1.5 m (5 ft) tall. They are all white but for black primaries, a black facial slash and a crimson crown. The species was never common and some population estimates for the early colonial period have been placed as low as 1,500 birds.[19]

Even worse was the fact that, when settlers first encountered it in the eighteenth century, the Whooping Crane was already noted for its good eating and the way that the hollow wing bones made a pleasant flute.[20] Even the bird's iconic whiteness was a handicap, because it gave it an additional lustre for the early collectors. Persecution by naturalists, taxidermists, plume hunters, zoologists and sportsmen was bad enough. What converted the Whooping Crane's lot to near tragedy were the hopelessly optimistic population estimates in the twentieth century. As late as 1941 the American Ornithologists' Union had a working figure of 300 birds; in fact, there were just 14–18 left.[21]

Many forces had brought the Whooping Crane to the brink of catastrophe, but what blocked its route across the threshold into oblivion was President Franklin D Roosevelt's signature on a federal order on 31 December 1937.

It authorised the purchase of 191 km² (74 miles²) of coastal grass, lagoon and sandbank that protruded like a fingertip into the Gulf of Mexico, near the Texan town of Corpus Christi. The site was the wintering grounds for the survivors and proved to be just enough at the eleventh hour. It has since acquired fame as the Aransas National Wildlife Refuge.

For three-quarters of a century it has supplied protection for Whooping Cranes in winter. Over the same period a sister site in Canada has buffered the birds while they nested. However, the whereabouts of the breeding whoopers was only uncovered in 1954, by chance, when an aerial reconnaissance of a fire revealed the presence of white cranes with rusty-coloured fledglings in Wood Buffalo National Park, an area of 44,515 km² (17,186 miles²) straddling the borders of Alberta province and the Northwest Territories – one of the remotest parts of Canada.

These twin sanctuaries have been the foundation of the species' rescue, but the journey towards security has involved constant setbacks. In a sense it is the real journey performed by whoopers between the two sites, a biannual flight of 4,083 km (2,537 miles), which has been problematic. Hunters, power lines, barbed-wire fences, pollution, hostile weather and the natural vagaries of migration have been a constant drain on numbers. As late as the 1950s a group of disgruntled Saskatchewan farmers, angry at the money devoted to a bird, suggested that the best way to resolve 'the whooper problem' was to shoot the lot and save the taxpayer further expense.[22]

Fortunately such nihilism never gained wide appeal. Instead Canadian and American naturalists collaborated in the most ambitious programme of conservation efforts mounted for any species, except perhaps for that other paragon of American wilderness, the California Condor

(see page 161). This included massive educational projects to deflect the guns of wildfowlers along the migration route. Another scheme, by which much was learned if not exactly achieved, involved 'surplus' whooper eggs being placed under wild nesting sandhills in Idaho. In 1975 the hope was that the chicks would be fostered and eventually create a self-sustaining whooper population. The plan foundered, however, on the 'identity crisis' suffered by the offspring, which were imprinted on the other crane species and often behaved as if they too were sandhills. It was disbanded in 1990 and the birds died out in 2002.[23]

A development that has underpinned all modern efforts involving Whooping Cranes, as well as conservation initiatives for cranes around the world, was the establishment in 1973 of the International Crane Foundation (ICF) at Baraboo, Wisconsin. Typical of the way that cranes have helped us to transcend political boundaries was the collaboration between ICF staff in the USA and natural scientists from Soviet Russia and an Ayatollah-led Iran, at a time when their respective governments were deadlocked in political enmity. In the 1980s the first two of these nations cooperated in a project to transfer captive-bred Siberian Cranes back into the wild.[24]

Another ICF-supported project was the re-establishment of a captive-release non-migratory Whooping Crane population in Florida. Like the Idaho cross-fostering project, the reintroduction has suffered major setbacks. In 2003 just 68, a third of the birds released, survived after ten years. Attention has now turned to perhaps the most ambitious hi-tech intervention ever mounted for Whooping Crane. It drew first breath in the early 1990s, when two small-plane pilots trained a group of captive-reared Canada Geese to

Migrating Sandhill Cranes rest at nightfall on the Platte River, Nebraska. They create the largest concentration of this bird family to be found anywhere on Earth.

follow their light aircraft on a migration route from Ontario to sites in Virginia and South Carolina. The plane and pilots took the place of wild adult geese that would, in a normal context, guide less-experienced birds on such a journey. Juvenile Sandhill Cranes then became the focus of an interim parallel project, before the organisers finally embarked on Operation Migration.

In this scheme, Whooping Cranes are hand-reared at a site in Wisconsin, but their carers are disguised in costumes resembling real adult whoopers, to avoid the crane chicks becoming sexually imprinted on humans. (In the Idaho cross-fostering scheme, it was the whoopers' imprinting on their sandhill foster parents that thwarted success.) On fledging, the young cranes are conditioned to follow an aircraft on a 2,000 km (1,250 miles) route between Wisconsin and a coastal reserve in Florida. In the trial spring of 2002 all of the plane-led whoopers found their own way back to the Wisconsin natal area. In subsequent years more plane-led cranes have been introduced to this new fly-way and in 2006 the hand-reared birds (known as 'ultracranes' after their ultra-light aircraft guides) successfully bred for the first time.

Despite the seemingly inescapable human desire to intervene and speed up the recovery, it has been the agonisingly slow increase of whoopers on the Wood Buffalo–Aransas fly-way that has offered consistent hope. Yet ten years on from the first conservation attempts this population had risen by just a dozen cranes, and in a quarter of a century it had not even doubled its 1938 baseline figure. To reach a total of 100 took 45 years. By 2008 it was 261 birds. The projected date to reach 500 is 2020. There is still a 1 per cent chance of extinction.[25] Who exactly can take credit for averting such disaster is perhaps best left to the verdict of Robert Allen, one of the founding figures in all the recovery efforts:

> This is a bird that cannot compromise or adjust its way of life to ours. Could not by its very nature; could not even if we had allowed it the opportunity, which we did not. For the Whooping Cranes there is no freedom but that of unbounded wilderness, no life except its own. Without meekness, without a sign of humility, it has refused to accept our idea of what the World should be like. If we succeed in preserving the wild remnant that still survives it will be no credit to us; the glory will rest on this bird whose stubborn vigor has kept it alive in the face of increasing and seemingly hopeless odds.[26]

Allen touches upon something that perhaps explains much of our deep feeling for all cranes. The birds seem completely unaware of human aspiration or design. Yet simultaneously cranes are so large and noisy, gathering often in such conspicuous numbers that we, by contrast, are unable to ignore them. Allen himself believed that cranes offered a 'brief and unexpected look at the World as it was in the beginning', a sentiment echoed by this contributor:

> It is hard to choose one birdsong, since so many elicit a range of emotions – the lonesome, soothing call of the loon, the sassy *chickadee-dee-dee*, the comical Blue Jay's *be-boop-boop* deep knee bends – but what lightens my heart is hearing a flock of migrating sandhills flying overhead. It is a primal connection to something that has occurred for hundreds of thousands of years. To see the sandhills

reunite and reconnect with family and friends at the Platte River in Nebraska before continuing home, is to witness what was occurring on Earth before there were people to name the Platte River, or Nebraska, or North America.[27]

Certainly, fossil evidence found in Nebraska indicates that Sandhill Cranes (or a taxon remarkably similar) have held connections with the region since the Miocene, almost 9 million years ago; a continuous genetic heritage twice that of the genus *Homo*. The notion that the birds encapsulate something largely lost to the modern world is perhaps a key ingredient in the deep human response to migrant cranes both in Nebraska and more widely. Various wildlife organisations host crane festivals in 13 states across North America, often associated with important populations such as Bosque del Apache, New Mexico; Monte Vista, Colorado; and Aransas, Texas. None, however, involves a more spectacular crane concentration than that at the Rowe Sanctuary on the Platte River, Nebraska.

During spring a total of *c.*600,000 cranes now pass across a narrow front of about 200 km (124 miles). For several weeks in March and April they fatten up in the region's vast cornfields and roost each night in the braided stony bed of the Platte River. As they congregate during the evenings, sometimes in concentrations of 50,000 birds, they create one of the great avian spectacles of North America and, indeed, on the entire planet. (The cranes are only some of the approximately 10 million large waterbirds that use this important migration fly-way; see also Snow Goose, page 84).

People converge from many parts of the state and elsewhere in North America to witness the passage. Some of these human visitors are on momentous journeys of their own:

> As a volunteer at Rowe and an admitted 'craniac', I have led many groups of visitors to see the Sandhill Cranes. One day, I was told that I had a special visitor. I was also informed that she had terminal cancer. She wouldn't be able to stand at the windows so I asked a visitor to move from one of the lower windows and I found a stool for her to sit on. The ill woman did not mind the cold weather. Several times her sister suggested that she take a seat on a bench and cover up but the lady was content from her window. Occasionally she would make a moaning sound. At first I thought it was delight but it was soon apparent that it was pain she was expressing. The crane 'show' is always magnificent but something about that night seemed different, almost spiritual. The sun set in a collage of orange, pink and amber. A beaver swam right next to the blind, directly underneath the ill woman's window. Cranes filled in closer to the blind than I had ever seen them and three whitetail deer walked through the huge flock of birds, paused for a moment and then vanished into the surrounding woods.
>
> When it was nearly dark I drove them right up to the car and they allowed me to help the sick woman into the vehicle. I bid them goodnight and started to walk away when the healthy sister thanked me profusely. The sick woman thanked me also and I again thanked them. Three days later I received a phone call at work telling me that the woman had passed away and that her sister

specifically wanted to again thank me for my help a few days before. I became emotional and had to step outside, much to the consternation of my fellow factory workers. My mother works with the elderly every day. I called her and told her about what had happened. She said that it was common for elderly people to hold on just long enough for a special event like a wedding, a birth or a graduation. I knew that the cranes were special. The fact that the last thing the sick woman wanted to experience on this Earth before she died was to once again see the Platte River full of Sandhill Cranes taught me just how special the birds and their magnificent migration truly are.

To see the wonder on people's faces, their emotional outpouring at seeing the cranes and to experience their genuine gratitude (as if I had anything to do with what nature provided them) has helped me realise that cranes are here for people on a physical but also spiritual level. I cannot say what each person thinks, but for me the cranes represent the possibility that there is at least, in one small segment of central Nebraska, something that mankind has not totally destroyed . . . yet.[28]

Limpkin family *Aramidae*

This is one of only nine monotypic bird families in the Americas and while it is related to the rails and cranes, the **Limpkin** *Aramus guarauna*, with its long legs and long decurved bill, more resembles a large ibis. It is a bird of marsh and swamp found from Florida right across the continent to northern Argentina.

The rather odd name is meant to capture the bird's high-stepping gait, although an older and perhaps more appropriate alternative was 'courlan'. It is now obsolete but, together with the far more explicit 'wailing bird' or 'crying bird', it was meant to echo the fantastically weird vocalisations, which are noted for their ability to 'make your hairs stand on end'.[1] The same eerie note is reflected in a spectrum of onomatopoeic names used in Latin America, such as *Carão* (Brazil), *Carau* (Argentina and elsewhere in Spanish-speaking regions) and *Carrao* (Dominican Republic).

The volume and range of a Limpkin's vocalisations are made possible by the French-horn-like convolutions in its trachea. Attempts to convey the sound have inspired some wonderfully imaginative descriptions. They ascend in tone from the restrained ('loud . . . varied wailing screams' or 'Loud guttural screams and yaps that carry for long distances'),[2] to the merely fanciful ('a hoarse rattling cry like the gasp of a person being strangled'),[3] and finally into the realms of the absurd (like 'little boys lost in the swamp forever' or 'some lost spirit on the swamps, or Nickar the soulless himself, shrieking and crying').[4]

The birds are easily approached and readily feed in the vicinity of human settlements. However, they have lost an earlier trustfulness, which once allowed them to be shot with immoral ease, or to be snatched up even as they sat on their nests. Their wide reputation as a gamebird resulted in a number of early Limpkin accounts, which are of familiar and depressing tone: 'Natives along the river told me the bird was excellent food and some years ago it was not an uncommon custom to shoot 20 or 30 before breakfast.'[5] In Florida the Limpkin was almost exterminated in the early twentieth century, although legal protection has now enabled it to increase to about 5,000 pairs. The recovery, as well as the bird's earlier emblematic status, is still reflected in the Limpkin logos and *Limpkin* newsletters used by various local chapters of the Audubon Society in the USA.

The Limpkin is a taxonomic oddity and has the weirdest vocalisations.

Stone-curlew and Thick-knee family *Burhinidae*

The nine waders in this family are highly cosmopolitan and occur on six continents, but are most widespread in the southern hemisphere: South America (two species), Africa (four species) and Australia (two species). The family's presence is limited on the North American continent to those **Double-striped Thick-knee** *Burhinus bistriatus* that extend from the Neotropics as far as southern Mexico, while the **Eurasian Stone-curlew** *Burhinus oedicnemus* is Europe's only representative.

No matter where they occur, thick-knees possess a compelling aura of otherness. The birds' nocturnal or crepuscular lifestyle, their powerful and often haunting vocalisations and their large, menacingly bright yellow eyes are all involved. Yet their style of movement is undoubtedly a further factor. Thick-knees have highly cryptic vermiculated plumages and are slow to fly, preferring to avoid detection by remaining stock-still, sometimes for hours on end, where they blend perfectly into the surroundings.

Even when animated they proceed in a slow, deliberate, halting manner. They trot a few steps then pause. Turn their heads, and pause again. A few more steps, perhaps a peck at the ground, and they stop completely. It is a blend of movement and stillness that seems somehow as reminiscent of a lizard as of a bird. Their long legs are adapted to a ground-dwelling existence and several are specialists of open treeless landscapes where, despite the lack of cover, the birds' camouflage makes them hard to spot.

For all this reserve, thick-knees can become highly tolerant of human presence. The **Bush Stone-curlew** *Burhinus grallarius* of Australia will wander on to the streets of quiet outback settlements. (The small Queensland town of Quilpie is said to derive its name from an Aboriginal word for this species.) Much of the time, however, Bush Stone-curlews are heard rather than seen, even when living in closest proximity to us:

> Haunting, mournful and eerie are words often used to describe the night-time calls of the enigmatic [Bush Stone-] curlew. If you walk quietly across our lawn, and cast your eyes into the orchard, there by the pile of fallen branches you'll find a family of them. We know they're around when a typical evening's squabbles and hoots are suddenly silenced by a supernatural keening. It's the cheerful dirge of curlews courting on our moonlit lawn. Later their frenzied screaming is accompanied by the doleful falsetto of chicks exploring the upper ranges of their spine-chilling repertoire. We creep around in the dark, delighted to catch the occasional glimpse of them skulking, dashing and freezing, like a family of feathered ghouls.[1]

Another speciality of this is residence right in the city centre:

> Bush Stone-curlew are one of those entirely unexpected creatures that look too big and too weird just to turn up in an inner-city park but there they are. Even for Brisbanites, who accept the presence of big birds like brushturkeys and ibis instead of sparrows, an encounter with a thick-knee (still almost universally called 'stone curlews') that has been sitting spectre-like under a nearby bush, is always a bit alarming. It's those huge alien eyes, their eerie silence and particularly the lack of alarm at being close to humans that are especially unnerving. They seem oblivious to the proximity to people. Indeed, that's the key issue for me and many others: while some urban birds have grown used to people and cohabit with us to exploit things we provide, these birds seem to be here anyway – not so much tolerating us, as ignoring us. It's quite creepy.[2]

In South America the Double-striped Thick-knee was actually caught and 'domesticated' in rural areas – it may well be still – and it became utterly fearless around the farm. As well as acting as a natural pesticide, these strange household pets, like several other bird species (see also page 36 and page 182), served as a kind of 'watchdog' that gave notice of any nocturnal intruder, human or otherwise, with their far-carrying calls.[3]

The place where humans and thick-knees come into closest proximity is probably in the heart of Africa's largest city, Cairo. **Senegal Thick-knee** *Burhinus senegalensis* has a wide distribution across the whole of central Africa, from the Atlantic to the Indian Oceans, but the extensive delta zone where the River Nile debouches into the Mediterranean is their most northerly outpost. Here the birds have adapted in extraordinary ways, breeding right in the heart of built-up districts and utilising, as an alternative to the open sandy wastes of Egypt, the flat mud roofs of a million Cairene buildings.

As many as 21 birds, 'their nests almost touching', were counted once on an old store-room roof at the Delta Barrage (20 km: 12 miles north of Cairo). There appear to be no detailed observations of how the chicks descend from their elevated nurseries, but it is assumed that the parents carry them down.[4] Since the environs of the Nile have been intensively settled for more than 5,000 years, one also wonders when the local thick-knees first acquired the roof-nesting habit.

Sherif Baha El Din, long-time resident of Egypt's capital, describes the bird's accommodation to metropolitan Africa.

> Senegal Thick-knees nest on roofs in Cairo and elsewhere in urban Egypt. I have seen chicks myself on roofs. But they only nest on secure and inaccessible roofs that are flat and enjoy some shade, preferably from an overhanging tree, so they do have a special 'roof habitat'! With the recent introduction of satellite dishes, human access to these roofs has dramatically increased and I notice that there is a much-reduced population of this bird, certainly in Cairo itself. Yet they used to be so common right in the middle of the city and their loud call is well known to locals and is a prominent part of the cultural landscape. They are still there but in smaller numbers. The nest usually contains only two young and they seem to be quite territorial, although post-breeding congregations are common.[5]

Another resident of the city adds:

The thick-knee is very much alive and well in suburbs like El Ma'âdi, and of course has to be a resident breeder, and is heard crying at dusk and at night. It is also heard in Garden City, which is virtually downtown Cairo, but the sound of their calls has definitely decreased in recent years.[6]

The species has a prominent place in Egyptian culture, where it is known as *Karawan* or *Karouwan*. (One interesting sidelight on this Arabic word, which is used to refer to both Senegal Thick-knee and Eurasian Stone-curlew, is its similarity to the Spanish and Portuguese equivalents. Even today the lookalike Eurasian Stone-curlew is known in Spain as *alcaraván* and in Portugal as *alcaravão*, indicating that these words are direct borrowings from the Arabic, probably from the time of the Moorish occupation. Since the Moors arrived in those countries in the eighth century AD, it suggests the longevity of Iberia's Islamic-derived names for this bird and also the even greater age of the Arabic original.)

In Cairo itself the nocturnal sounds of *Karawan* are enshrined in the title to a novel by the Egyptian author Taha Hussein (1889–1973). Published in 1934, *Du'a' al-Karawan* was translated into English as *Curlew's Prayers* (or sometimes as *The Call of the Curlew*). However, it was subsequently made into a film that, rather confusingly, carried an entirely new title in the English version, *The Nightingale's Call*, 1959 (but not, it should be noted, in the Arabic film version, where it was still *Du'a' al-Karawan*). What seems a rather curious switch of identities from the wader to the more celebrated

songbird derives from the fact that among French-educated Egyptians the Senegal Thick-knee is sometimes known as the 'nightingale', partly for its mournful nocturnal vocalisations.[7] As Sherif Baha El Din notes, 'people in Egypt might think *Karawan* is a cute little fluffy ball since they have never seen the bird and are surprised to learn that the big-eyed long-legged creature is the source of all that romantic allure!'[8]

Perhaps the strangest of all connections with this strange bird family is an old piece of lore in the land just across the Mediterranean from Egypt. It involved the Eurasian Stone-curlew, which was known to several classical writers, including Plato, the historian Plutarch and Aelian. Their interest centred on the therapeutic power of the *charadrios*, as it was known, to cure jaundice. It was a classic piece of sympathetic magic that centred on the flaring yellow colour of the bird's irides. Aelian described this medical usage as follows:

> The Stone-curlew, it seems, has this gift, which assuredly is by no means to be despised. At any rate if a man who has become infected with jaundice gazes intently at it and it returns the gaze without flinching, as though it were moved by jealousy against the man, this retaliatory gaze heals the man of the aforesaid complaint.[9]

Alas, this blessing upon the patient was a very poor deal for the stone-curlew, because the condition was thought then to pass from human to bird (see also Finch family, page 501).

The Spotted Thick-knee of sub-Saharan Africa has all the classic family traits: long legs, staring yellow eyes, weird vocalisations and that strange aura of quietude.

Sheathbill family *Chionidae*

There are two sheathbill species (the family also includes another wader oddity, the **Magellanic Plover** *Pluvianellus socialis* of Argentina) and both are found in the very deep south. The more widespread **Snowy Sheathbill** *Chionis albus* breeds from the Antarctic Peninsula to South Georgia, but moves north in winter to the coasts of the Falkland Islands and the South American mainland, where very occasional sightings in Brazil represent the family's approximate northern limits. The more restricted **Black-faced Sheathbill** *Chionis minor* occurs only on the subantarctic islands of the Indian Ocean, including Marion and the Crozet and Kerguelen archipelagos.

Sheathbills are entirely white in plumage, but they also seem as if they have been assembled from the different parts of other species, 'with the general appearance, gait, and flight of a pigeon, with the beak and voice of a crow, with the habits of a wader . . . and with the pugnacity and familiarity with man of a [gamebird]'.[1] Even this understates the sheathbills' oddity. Norwegian whalers used to call them 'ptarmigans'; a British seabird expert felt that they looked like domestic fowl; while an old seaman's name for them was 'paddy', because of an assumed similarity to small herons or egrets found in Asia.[2] An odd, fat, short-legged, white dove of the subantarctic shoreline probably best describes the sheathbill's appearance (the Argentinian name is *Paloma-Antarctica*, 'Antarctic pigeon').

They are well known as scavengers and have long attended human settlement for any discarded waste products. In Antarctica itself, 'they love hanging around people, landing on them, investigating rucksacks and the contents of Zodiacs'.[3] They are also notorious for waiting upon seal and penguin colonies, relishing dead carcasses, unattended eggs, even faeces or afterbirth. As one former resident of the Falkland Islands notes: 'I must admit, I was always amazed that such a pristine white bird should wait at the wrong end of a sea lion for a liquid lunch and come away looking just as pristine.'[4] One sheathbill was observed to start on an umbilical cord even while it was still attached to the baby seal. In his book *Oceanic Birds of South America*, Robert Cushman Murphy recorded how a nineteenth-century explorer, James Eights, described:

> Sheath-bills which had become practically domesticated at the South Shetland Islands elected to remain on the ship when it departed! It would be hard to credit such a story were it not for the support of Moseley . . . who writes that a Kerguelen [Black-faced] Sheath-bill attached itself to the 'Challenger' during the southward voyage to Heard Island, occasionally leaving the vessel to fly around and then return.[5]

The prince of all stowaways, however, was a Snowy Sheathbill that joined a Royal Fleet Auxiliary tanker, *Plumleaf*, in the Falkland Islands (after the war in 1982). Fed by its Chinese crew for the whole journey, the bird sailed the 13,300 km (8,300 miles) all the way back to naval dock in Britain. Sadly it enjoyed only the briefest of residences in Plymouth harbour (it died of botulism after an outbreak that badly affected local gulls) but still managed to make a lasting impression, if only for its somewhat guileless habits, and among the locals it acquired a nickname, 'Wally' (British slang for a fool).

The first person to recognise Wally as a sheathbill and one of the bird's chief admirers noted how the creature was the subject of many amusing anecdotes:

> A small bowl, which had been provided as a source of drinking water for Wally, was once used by it as a bath. Squeezing its lower body into the tight space, the bird then began to make the action of flicking water over itself with its wings. In reality it was moving nothing but fresh air because the wings couldn't actually fit into the bowl. After much vigorous flicking it extracted itself from the pot to preen and shake itself 'dry'.
>
> On another occasion while stealing ragworms that were being used as fish bait by local anglers on the quayside, Wally saw a really large 'worm' and began energetically tugging at it, determined not to let it escape. Finally the angler shooed Wally away and was then able to tie up his bootlace.[6]

Many of the local boat owners delighted in feeding scraps to Wally and the two choicest morsels he loved most during his brief and tragic career in the wrong hemisphere were streaky bacon and cheese.

The Snowy Sheathbill is a scavenger of the deep frozen south.

Oystercatcher family *Haematopodidae*

From at least the 70th parallel north as far south as Tierra del Fuego there is hardly a coastline that does not play host to one of the world's ten species in this family. Only the shores of south-east Asia are largely barren of oystercatcher sounds and colours. Elsewhere they are as adapted to high cliffs, low-lying rocky islands or strandlines of shingle and pebble as they are to vast open stretches of estuarine mud. In terms of species diversity they tend to be concentrated in the southern hemisphere with two species confined to South America (**Blackish Oystercatcher** *Haematopus ater* and **Magellanic Oystercatcher** *Haematopus leucopodus*), one to Africa (**African Oystercatcher** *Haematopus moquini*) and three to Australasia (**Pied Oystercatcher** *Haematopus longirostris*, **Sooty Oystercatcher** *Haematopus fuliginosus* and **Variable Oystercatcher** *Haematopus unicolor*, the last being restricted to New Zealand shorelines).

All ten species are unmistakable. They are large, heavy, highly sociable waders with broad wings and long bills. They may vary from all-black through to the strongly pied plumages of the **Eurasian Oystercatcher** *Haematopus ostralegus* and **American Oystercatcher** *Haematopus palliatus*, but across all ten there are several constants. They possess bright-red thick beaks, red or orange orbital rings of skin round equally bright irides, and they have loud ringing voices that the birds themselves seem to delight in using. Their conspicuous and simple colours have resulted in oystercatchers being used in motifs, advertisements and logos for commercial companies worldwide, especially for enterprises associated with the coast.

When they fly en masse in synchronised formations, with the birds' black and white surfaces revealed alternately to the observer, there is a wonderful graphic beauty to oystercatcher flocks. The following contribution stresses the affecting power of these birds, when the clarity of their sights and sounds often seem to be an integral part of the wider bracing atmosphere of coastal landscapes. Yet the passage also illuminates the generic capacity of birds to lift our spirits, even in the darkest moments. Their movement between different elements, land to air – or, in the case of oystercatchers, land, sea and air – seems a metaphor for our own capacity for transcendence:

> My husband died from cancer in November 2006 at the age of 51. We had been together for 24 years; I was 19 when we met at university and we loved each other very very much. Walking the beaches where I live became my only solace. It brought a calmness and peace, as well as a place to cry alone.
>
> As I walked, I also started to watch and to listen and I began to learn about the life on the seashore. The oystercatchers made me laugh and I went regularly to visit the large winter colony, just a ten-minute walk from my house, on Swansea Bay, Wales. One day as I approached they started to hop away; I'd never seen them hopping before! Well over a hundred oystercatchers hopping towards the sea; it was hilarious. I started to photograph them and other seabirds: redshank, curlew, dunlins, turnstones, an egret. I often saw oystercatchers at the edge of the road on the golf course or playing fields; I used to look out for them as I passed on the bus to work. Once I saw oystercatchers

Eurasian Oystercatchers slowly milling in their thousands at a high-tide roost in the UK.

stamping on the ground like seagulls, attracting worms to the surface.

The oystercatchers became my companions, a great source of comfort and amusement and I really loved them. Even when the tide was out, and they were too far away to be seen, I'd listen to them piping at the edge of the sea. They are such busy birds! I found out that they are also called 'sea pies'.

I once visited Teignmouth and just had to stop at a pub there called The Oystercatcher. It was painted outside with oystercatchers, inside an entire shelf of singing toy oystercatchers sat in a row. I bought one and he now sits beside my bed. The waitress, who was wearing an oystercatcher t-shirt, sweetly asked if we'd heard them say *peep-peep*.

I miss them in the summer when the migrant flocks have gone, leaving just a small indigenous population. But they will return again in the autumn; in time for November.

I continue to walk the beaches.[1]

Stilt and Avocet family *Recurvirostridae*

Both groups in this family – the stilts (six species) and avocets (four species) – are largely pied and immensely elegant, almost fragile-looking birds with needle-fine bills and remarkably long thin legs. In fact, proportionate to their size, they have the longest legs of any birds on Earth. The great eighteenth-century naturalist Comte de Buffon lamented the 'enormous defects' of nature in equipping the stilts with limbs of such length, which, he felt, left the birds barely able to reach the ground. The Frenchman was clearly overlooking, however, the advantages offered in deep water and also the leg's acute flexibility whenever a stilt requires to bend down.[1]

Both stilts and avocets are found on every continent except Antarctica, although the stilts show a bias towards the southern hemisphere and overall both groups have a strong presence in Australasia. The **Red-necked Avocet** *Recurvirostra novaehollandiae* is endemic to the continent. So too is the **Banded Stilt** *Cladorhynchus leucocephalus*, while the **Black Stilt** *Himantopus novaezelandiae* (*Kaki* is its Maori name) occurs only in New Zealand. One of the world's most threatened waders (largely because of predation from introduced mammals), in 2008 there were 78 Black Stilts of both captive and wild origin, including just 20 breeding pairs, and that minuscule figure represented a substantial improvement on the situation a decade earlier.[2]

Stilts and avocets are all wetland birds with wide tastes in a range of fresh- and salt-water habitats. However, what is almost their signature landscape as a breeding location is that curiously atmospheric mix of white bleached flats and dazzlingly blue or dull pink shallows associated with salt production. Salt works and saltpans, which are as old as civilisation itself, must have been cherished by these birds for thousands of years.

Stilts and avocets are one of the few wader groups to derive food from such hostile conditions, feeding on the invertebrates or brine shrimps and other crustacea that are able to thrive in the intensely alkaline water. In such places, where the heat haze can become an eerie blurring of colour and light in the first torrid metre above the surface, stilts and avocets appear even more ethereally delicate. When seen from any distance they often seem to be floating over the pools.

If saltpans are their signature landscape then the persistent calls of these birds, especially when breeding with eggs or young to defend, are the signature sound of such places. High, shrill and agitated, the dogged monosyllables of mobbing avocets and stilts have given rise to colourful names in several languages. The Dutch, who hold more **Pied Avocets** *Recurvirostra avosetta* than any other European nation, call them *Kluut* (an almost perfect rendering of its call), while the **Black-winged Stilt** *Himantopus himantopus* is known as *Steltkluut*. In Brazil, the local **White-backed Stilt** *Himantopus melanurus* (known as *pernilongo*) has another vernacular name *Quero-quero-da-praia*, meaning literally 'I want, I want of the beach', although *Quero-quero* is also the name of Southern Lapwing (see page 199) so the full name actually means 'beach lapwing'. What plover and stilt have in common is the importunate quality in their endless alarm notes. An old North American alternative for the **Black-necked Stilt** *Himantopus mexicanus* – a name that suggests a sense of humour, rather than being onomatopoeic – was 'lawyer', because the bird was so persistently voluble.[3]

Black Stilts made by local artist Noel Gregg adorn the town centre of Twizel, New Zealand, where a captive-breeding programme is part of the rescue plan for this critically endangered wader.

Plover family *Charadriidae*

The world's 67 plovers have the long-legged, long-necked form of all waders, yet among this already charismatic group the plovers are widely acknowledged as special. They often possess bright or contrasting colours, as well as ample curves and an overall symmetry that make them especially pleasing to the eye.

They occur on six continents, and in many regions of grassland or marsh they are among the most conspicuous of all wild creatures. Their preference for open habitats once meant that forest clearance in the name of agriculture was a key benefit. The **Northern Lapwing** *Vanellus vanellus* is the archetypal coloniser of farmland. It now occurs from the Mongolian steppe to the Atlantic coast of Ireland and nests in 40 countries, where originally it can only have been marginal until Neolithic tree felling cleared the path. Today, however, we are taking back what we once gave: Northern Lapwings are declining in 24 countries from Ireland to Armenia, primarily because of agricultural intensification.[1] In western Europe its numbers have more than halved in 25 years.

Plovers thrive equally in places where trees are naturally absent or sparse, including Australia's arid interior (**Masked Lapwing** *Vanellus miles*), although we should not omit this bird's love for suburban parks, bowling greens, cemeteries, 'sports field, school yards and in fact any flat bit of grass'.[2] Plovers also have a strong presence on the African savannahs (**Blacksmith Lapwing** *Vanellus armatus* and **Crowned Lapwing** *Vanellus coronatus* are probably the most common of 11 African species), the once-vast pampas of South America (**Southern Lapwing** *Vanellus chilensis*), and the open tundras of North America (**American Golden Plover** *Pluvialis dominica* and **Grey Plover** *Pluvialis squatarola*) and Eurasia (**European Golden Plover** *Pluvialis apricaria* and **Pacific Golden Plover** *Pluvialis fulva*).

THE SOUNDS OF PLOVERS

Like many ground-dwelling birds, they are often cryptically patterned with black bands or counter-shading to disrupt their outline and are often extremely difficult to spot even in featureless terrain. The one thing that brings them to our attention is their nesting. Plovers often have intense vocalisations that can be loud and persistent. The calls are intended as a vocal assault and a means of distracting would-be predators, as well as a simultaneous warning to their young, yet they commend themselves to human ears as forms of speech.

The **Red-wattled Lapwing** *Vanellus indicus* – a bird found on roads, cricket pitches, polo grounds, pavilion gardens and airfields as well as farmland – ranges from Turkey east to the Indian subcontinent. There it enjoys a rich synonymy of local Indian names (*Titeeri, Titai, Titi, Titori, Tateehar, Hatatut* and *Hatatertu* are just a sample) and these are derived from an endlessly repeated four-note alarm call, which is rendered in English as *Did-he do it?*[3] The predominantly African **Spur-winged Lapwing** *Vanellus spinosus* has a four-note call that seems to pronounce exactly the same question. In Arabic, however, this bird is known by the wonderfully resonant name, *Zik Zak* '(it's a heavy k) but in Egyptian dialect it would be "Ze^ za^" (no pronounced k sound)'.[4]

Other plover species have acquired onomatopoeic names based on their calls. In North America the **Killdeer** *Charadrius vociferus* (which means the 'clamorous' or 'noisy plover') has a name that is a faithful rendering of what the author Peter Matthiessen calls 'its shrill and strident cry, *kill-dee, kill-dee*'. In Brazil *Quero-quero* (literally 'I want, I want') and *Téu-téu* are names for the Southern Lapwing and suggest its importunate, repetitive notes.[5] In Argentina the same bird is known simply as *Tero*, a direct echo of the sound (described in field guides as *tay-roh* or *tero-tero*).[6]

In south Asia, Red-wattled Lapwings occur on almost any open space, from farmers' fields to cricket pitches.

Big flocks of
European Golden
Plovers arrive from
their northern
breeding grounds in
early winter. Their
appearance at a time
of bad weather led
to deep associations
with rain.

However, the richest vocabulary attached to the call of any plover is probably that inspired by the Northern Lapwing. Today in Britain alone it has at least 22 surviving vernacular names ('peewit' and 'teewhup' are typical), while the inventory of archaic versions runs into several score (see chapter 14 of Ken Spencer's work of gloriously catholic scholarship *The Lapwing in Britain*, 1951). Even now it probably has more local names than any other native British bird (William Tait thought the same true in Portugal).

A great many of these echo the high, pleading double note of Northern Lapwing which, to the Moroccan ear, once suggested the name *beebet* (whence, incidentally, the formerly Moorish-occupied Portuguese presumably derived the species' local name in the Algarve, *bibes*).[7] To the French it gave an old name, *dix-huit*, and even now to the Dutch it suggests *kievit*, to the Germans *kiebitz* (and *kiewitt* in north Germany, while *giebitz* in the south), to the Swiss *kievitz* (also *kiwit*, *ziefitz*, *giritz*, *gifiz*, *gibiz* and *giwix*), then *Ijip or Iiip* to the

Friesians, *Vivak* (pronounced 'vee-vaa') to Serbians, *chibis* (чибис) to Russians and *vipa* to Swedes. (Technically it is *Tofsvipa* – *Tofs*: 'crest' – but as a Swedish birdwatcher explains, 'Sometimes people just say *vipa* because we have only one species. *Vipa* is pronounced "vee´pa" with a short a, the Norwegian is *vipe*, like Swedish but with e pronounced as e in "Ben", while the Danish is nearly the same but with b instead of p: *vibe*.')[8] The extraordinary similarities revealed in this transcontinental naming pattern is one of the best examples I know of the psychological processes underpinning much avian nomenclature. The birds really do call out to us their own names.

PUGNACIOUS PLOVERS

While all of these various plover sounds are the birds' early warning system against intruders, some species have more than their voice to deter the unwanted. The Spur-winged Lapwing (*spinosus* in its scientific name means 'thorny plover')

The Southern
Lapwing is a bird
of bold colour,
loud voice and rich
cultural association.

possesses sharp spines on the front edges of the wings, which it raises when threatened to emphasise its armoury. Several other plovers have similar appendages and they are particularly impressive in the Masked Lapwing of Australasia (still well known in that country as the spur-winged plover) and the Southern Lapwing of South America. Both are noted for their aggressive airborne assaults, accompanied by hysterical calls, when the birds dive-bomb the luckless intruder and frequently strike dread into the human heart but, actually, seldom strike physically.[9] As Darryl Jones notes of the Masked Lapwing: 'In the zillions of incidents I have witnessed over the years, I have never even heard of an injury. Plenty of terror but no contact made.'[10]

James Lowen notes much the same about Southern Lapwing: 'I have never seen any contact between spurs and person, although my wife would say that she came very close the first time she encountered the birds – at a cricket match in Buenos Aires – she ran shrieking from the boundary rope, having strayed a little too close to chicks.'[11]

SOUTHERN LAPWING FOLKLORE

South American gauchos, far from objecting to the Southern Lapwing's formidable capabilities, cherish this hugely handsome bird. Helmut Sick suggested that it is among 'the most celebrated birds of Brazil' and that ranchers 'know it to be a better sentinel than dogs'.[12] Unusual among waders (although not unknown; see Senegal Thick-knee page 194) is the Southern Lapwing's habit in Argentina of perching on the tops of roofs in country towns. One piece of regional lore, believed especially by an older generation, holds that a bird heard shrieking over one particular house is a sign of an impending visitor. A local practice south of Buenos Aires is to take a young Southern Lapwing, remove some of its vital flight feathers and rear it as a farmyard familiar. The resulting adult then becomes a fierce guardian for the farmstead, raising alarm at the approach of strangers.

A resident of Patagonia recalls the following:

> Although the eggs were famed for being tasty, my grandfather would not allow any collecting of them at all. Yet my grandma was a keen pet owner and she had a pet *tero*, something rather common in those days. They acted as an alarm, because they'd scream if someone unknown arrived. They'd sky dive them and show the spikes on their wings. But I do remember them extracting long juicy worms from the lawn and then wiggling their bottoms on the paved road that led to the gate to produce amazingly copious amounts of white guano, something my grandma wasn't so keen on![13]

There is a strong folklore surrounding the taking of Southern Lapwing eggs, which apparently have clear whites and strong yolks. It is customary to look for eggs with the pointed end facing outwards (rather than into the centre of the nest) because these are thought not to have developing embryos. Children who bring eggs home must wait for them to be immersed in water (those that float are not good) and they are encouraged to leave at least some fertile eggs, because it ensures that there are lapwings to breed next year.[14]

The sights, sounds and lore of resident plovers may be integral to the atmosphere of one place, yet the birds can also carry radically different associations. W H Hudson, who himself once lived on the pampas and even recalled a childhood harvest of 64 Southern Lapwing eggs in one morning ('In those distant days the birds were excessively abundant all over the pampas where sheep were pastured . . . and nobody ever thought of killing a lapwing for the table'), recorded the impact upon him of a very different plover.[15]

At his childhood farm on the grass plains, Hudson was accustomed to listen for the sweet resonant contact notes of migrant plovers and other waders as they moved south:

> In September, and even as early as August, they begin to arrive on the pampas, the golden plover often still wearing his black nuptial dress; singly and in pairs, in small flocks, and in clouds they come – curlew, godwit, plover, tatler, tringa – piping the wild notes to which the Greenlander listened in June, now to the gaucho herdsman on the green plains of La Plata, then to the wild Indian in his remote village; and soon, further south, to the houseless huanaco-hunter in the grey wilderness of Patagonia.[16]

Hudson's passage makes the case beautifully. Plovers can be embedded in the spirit of one spot and, in another way, they can be inhabitants of no particular place at all. Or perhaps it would be most accurate to say that the extraordinary migrations of some plovers inspire us to see the whole world as a single locality. The American Golden Plover (the bird referred to in Hudson's passage) is typical. Its two-way movements between the American Arctic and Argentinian pampas comprise an annual odyssey of 26,700 km (16,600 miles). However, some Pacific Golden Plovers pass between the Russian Arctic and New Zealand, a round journey of more than 28,000 km (17,400 miles).

PLOVERS AND WEATHER

Perhaps it was partly out of a sense of their sudden and almost miraculous abundance that some human hosts to wintering plovers viewed the birds as gifts from heaven. Or, rather, they viewed them as gifts of the weather. It has been claimed that in the Middle Ages it was even believed they lived on the wind.[17] More certainly, the appearance of migrant plovers was closely linked to autumn or winter conditions and specifically to rain. The word 'plover' itself is derived from *pluvia*, Latin for rain, while *Pluvialis*, the scientific name for the four most impressive world-wanderers, means 'relating to rain' or 'bringing rain'.[18] Today in Germany the same quartet are known as *regenpfeifer*, 'rain pipers'.

The link was almost certainly a classic instance of *ex post facto* reasoning, in which our forebears presumed that since plovers arrived at a time of (likely) bad weather, they had actually caused it. An alternative for the rain connection – dismissed by the *Complete Oxford English Dictionary* – is that the birds were more easily caught in wet weather.[19] There is no evidence for this claim, and the recurrence of similar weather links in the names for other plovers suggests that it was their seasonality which was uppermost. The Spaniards, for instance (and the Portuguese), know the Northern Lapwing as *avefriá* (or *avefria*), the 'cold bird', an indicator of their large-scale irruptive movements into Iberia during times of snow and hard weather. In South America similar weather lore attaches to the Southern Lapwing.

> My hometown has very cold winters and the ponds freeze and stay frozen for days. Most birds migrate, like

The glorious song and sky-dance routine of breeding Northern Lapwings was once a commonplace drama of European farmland. Not any more: half the birds have been lost in one generation because of agricultural intensification.

the Southern Lapwings. They are a much-loved bird by farmers, because the sight of their return means the worst has passed. Although there's the so-called *nieve de los teros* or 'snow of the lapwings', the one last dusting of snow *after* they arrive, which makes them look miserable and out of place. When they flock in the autumn I can't help it but feel a bit blue. They flock and flicker around like butterflies, screaming in unison. Then one day, they're gone.[20]

PLOVERS AS FOOD

One almost inevitable consequence of the birds' temporary abundance was their subjection to hunting. The pedigree of roast plover in the human diet is probably as old as our species, but the oldest proof is more recent. At Saqqara, near Cairo, there is an ancient Egyptian relief carving of a young

girl holding a Northern Lapwing she has just trapped. The sculpture is beautifully rendered, right down to her braided pigtail and the curved crest of her captive. More than 4,500 years later the arts of plover catching are still alive, not just in the Mediterranean, but across all of Europe.

In the winter of 1983–4, the French alone shot 1.6 million Northern Lapwings. Restrictions on season and a decline in the popularity of hunting saw this national total fall to 436,000 by 1999, but the Europe-wide figure was still estimated at about 1 million birds (including 250,000 in Italy and 100,000 in Greece).[21] Through all that roar of gunfire there is still a small community devoted to a quieter set of skills. One of the last places where flight nets are used is in the provinces of Friesland and Groningen (and to a lesser extent Noord-Holland) in northern Netherlands. Known as *wilsterflappers* in Dutch, these plover catchers draw on a tradition dating at least to the Middle Ages. *Wilster* is a

Maltese author Natalino Fenech displays old plover decoys used by hunters on his native island.

name for European Golden Plover, but the men also caught a suite of edible waders, including Northern Lapwing, Ruff and Bar-tailed Godwit. In the past the birds were lured down with special whistles. Another stratagem was to seed the surrounding area with 'stales' (stuffed plover skins) or live birds that were tethered but still able to flap and draw the attention of passing flocks. As soon as wild plovers flew in close, the trapper, concealed in a blind adjacent to his laid net, would pull a cord and release it, catching the birds in mid-air.

The life of a *wilsterflapper*, who was often a fisherman or farm labourer at other times, was invariably tough, cold and lonely, but equally rich in folklore and practical skill. Families passed on their knowledge from generation to generation. One remarkable aspect of their expertise was their sophisticated understanding of their quarry. *Wilsterflappers* readily identified rare vagrant Pacific Golden Plovers among their usual catch of European Golden Plovers long before ornithologists had acquired this ability. They also recognised the distinct races of Common Redshank before science even knew that they existed.[22]

Over the course of last century this time-honoured Dutch community yielded to the modern world, while the total harvest declined from *c.*100,000 birds to *c.*18,000 by 1969. Commercial netting was eventually banned in 1978, and the shooting of European Golden Plover halted in 1993, yet *wilsterflappers* have continued to practise, placing their skills at the disposal of scientific ringing schemes to study the plovers' migration and population dynamics.[23]

Similar vestiges of the old ways survive on that last bastion of bird hunting in Europe, the island of Malta. The best account of this now controversial practice is in Natalino Fenech's wonderfully rich study of his country's ornithology and birdlore, *A Complete Guide to the Birds of Malta*. For its adherents the Maltese hunting of birds is a glorious maintenance of ancient traditions. To its opponents it comprises a ruthless and unnecessary decimation of migrant

populations. Nevertheless, the specific harvest of European Golden Plover is probably marginal – Fenech suggested a total annual bag of 4,000–6,000 birds – when compared with the gross historic numbers of European Turtle Doves once shot on Malta (see page 244), or the enormous flocks of finches trapped (see page 503).[24]

What is most striking about the plover practices is the complex lore surrounding the whistles used in imitation of the soft, sweetly melancholic notes produced by the birds. They are used to entice migrant European Golden Plovers as they fly over so that they settle on open fields long enough to be shot or netted. The instruments are cut from dried reed stems or bamboo and are completed in a matter of hours. Hunters carry as many as eight, partly because they often lose tone as they become wet with saliva, but also because whistles of higher pitch are used specifically as the birds come closer. A good whistle is viewed among the cognoscenti as a work of art, whose construction and proper usage are jealously guarded secrets. Favourite whistles are adorned with images of birds and finished in silver, even gold.

A whistle of highest quality is a thing of legend and an old Maltese adage asserts that such a plover whistle is inherited, not bought. Fenech tells the amusing story of a hunter, whose 'dying' wish – to express gratitude to his doctor – was the gift of his favourite whistle. When the man subsequently lived to hunt another day, the doctor found his patient at the front of his house shuffling with embarrassment: since he had survived he wondered if he could buy the whistle back. After the doctor returned the treasured object, the hunter then suffered a relapse. He again made a gift of his precious lure with the cautious proviso that in the event of a further recovery he wanted it back from his doctor, no questions asked.

Today the Maltese traditions associated with home-made whistles are being lost and supplanted by illegal use of electronic bird callers.[25]

HARVEST OF PLOVER EGGS

Plover catching and killing was once a major occupation, but the spring collection of the eggs of Northern Lapwing was an industry on an international scale. It is worth recounting a little of its history, if only to indicate the vast scope of this harvest and the former size of the birds' numbers. The British had an inordinate fondness for lapwing eggs which, lightly boiled for five minutes, yield a rich orange yolk framed within a white 'of a translucid mauvy shade of mother-of-pearl appearance'.[26]

Eating them was as much a matter of aesthetics as it was culinary. The shell has a striking pyriform shape with a ground colour varying from buff or stone, through olive, reddish brown and even blue. Over this base hue is a rich grafitti of dark scribblings and splashes. A dozen of these beautiful eggs fetched between 3–10 shillings during the Victorian era and, as the birds declined in numbers, so the egg peaked in value at 18 shillings a dozen (for the first clutches of the season). This was considerably more than the weekly wage of a nineteenth-century farm labourer and it is hardly surprising that dogs were specially trained in some areas to sniff out the precious nests.

The exact size of the egg harvest is difficult to estimate. One authority, citing Denmark, the Netherlands (where the first eggs of the season were traditionally presented to the Dutch queen) and Britain as the main countries involved, placed the annual total at between 100,000 and 1 million eggs.[27] However, the great nineteenth-century British ornithologist Alfred Newton cited a figure of 800,000 eggs that were imported annually to London exclusively from Friesland during the 1870s.[28] Given that the whole of the British Isles was itself a major source, it would imply a total harvest in the countries encircling the North Sea of several million eggs a year. Whatever the precise figure, it was marked declines in Northern Lapwings that triggered the introduction of legislation, such as the British Lapwing Act of 1926. The Dutch placed progressively stricter time limits on egg collecting (only until 30 April before 1914, until 28 April in 1914, and then 19 April by 1937) and in the early twentieth century many Friesian villages appointed guards to stop poachers taking eggs after the legal date.[29]

It should be acknowledged that pre-dating and even running alongside the apparently unsustainable commercial practices of the nineteenth century there had always been a much more piecemeal but continent-wide tradition of gathering Northern Lapwings' eggs by local landowners and farmers. In some places it continues. Yet this probably had little impact on the species' abundance. For the bird has long been a popular neighbour and at one time, when ploughing practices involved a more intimate style of husbandry, farmers showed instinctive care for these and other birds.

A Swedish contributor probably speaks for all European farmers where lapwings once bred.

> I was raised on a small farm in the Skaraborg region in the lower half of Sweden. This was just prior to, and during, World War Two, and things were often done a bit differently from now. Corncrakes and partridges were common birds, now we seldom find them on the land surrounding the farm (which we no longer own). My father was very strict about us taking responsibility for the birds and mammals living on our land. In order not to ruin the nests of skylarks, lapwings, corncrakes and curlews, we walked the fields and marked with a stick all the nests we could find. In this way, during mowing or harvest, at least a patch of grass or crop around the nest was spared, which hopefully lowered the impact of our farming practices. I don't know how common this practice is today, around here it seems to be gone.[30]

A modern British environmentalist reflects on the past, but also illuminates how the story has evolved:

> Through my job over the last 12 years I've come across one or two old farm labourers, who used to plough the fields with horses, which was hard heavy work aligning the plough. They told me that when they came to a lapwing's nest (or skylark) they would stop to move it to one side, plough, stop and move it back to where it was and continue ploughing. Apparently the lapwings would always return to the nest and breed successfully.
>
> The lapwing is a truly wonderful bird and it is so sad now to see their numbers fall each year. Today whenever I have seen a successful nest of lapwings I take the farmer some beer and wine and thank them. This also lets them know someone is watching and cares.[31]

Jacana family *Jacanidae*

Jacanas have a basic physical blueprint that combines small crake-like body shapes with short beaks, short wings and enormously long legs and toes. The eight species, which are spread across the world's tropical regions from South America to Australia, are the quintessential inhabitants of marshy fringes to rivers or lakes, where they come as close as any bird to walking on water. Proportional to a jacana's body weight (the **Lesser Jacana** *Microparra capensis* of sub-Saharan Africa is just 40 g: less than 2 oz), the elastic, spider's-web spread of toes is gigantic and enables it to thread a passage across the flimsiest vegetation. The habit earned the birds an older and increasingly abandoned English name – 'lily trotters'. A lovely Australian alternative for their **Comb-crested Jacana** *Irediparra gallinacea* is 'lotusbird'.

Jacana is a Portuguese word taken from their name in the indigenous South American Tupi language. While the English-speaking world pronounces it 'jakána', some Spanish- and Brazilian-speaking Americans say 'yaçaná', with soft c and emphasis on the final syllable. However it may be articulated, the name evokes birds of rather unusual but undeniable beauty. In fact, jacanas seem integral to the wider and rather elusive aesthetic appeal of tropical wetlands. These are invariably sultry environments of moist air and saturated colour, manifest in the intense greenery and brilliant dragonflies and in deep-blue skies mirrored in sluggish waters, often with a choking surface tangle of white flowers and shiny plate-like leaves.

While people often cherish these fascinating and

inoffensive birds, jacanas have made little mark on our collective consciousness. Even the usual common denominator of human predation barely functions: their flesh is apparently rather poor and they are seldom eaten.[1] Probably for these reasons, jacanas are often very common. One small measure of how much we notice them is the rich array of vernacular names for some species. In India, Salim Ali recorded 22 regional alternatives for the **Pheasant-tailed Jacana** *Hydrophasianus chirurgus*, including one that hints at deeper cultural connections. In Assam it is known as *Rani didao gophita*, 'Little White Water Princess'.[2]

Sandpiper and Snipe family *Scolopacidae*

For many of us this family of 91 species is at the margins of our attention, primarily because they occupy the periphery of the physical landscape. They are birds of intertidal mud, shoreline and marsh, and often they appear merely as distant shapes huddled at the water's edge. Their remoteness, however, is not just a matter of location.

The sandpipers can be bewildering in their similarities. Identification often rests on subtle plumage variations in grey or brown, or in the length of leg, wing or bill, especially the latter. In many books about ecology, the sandpipers are often used to illustrate the process of adaptive radiation. The classic image is of a spectrum of waders arranged to illustrate increased bill length as they probe beneath the surface to differing depths. In effect, the various strata of subterranean prey made accessible by these extraordinary appendages represent each particular wader's distinct ecological niche. The adaptations are invariably shown to culminate in the enormous decurved probe of a curlew. In the case of North America's **Long-billed Curlew** *Numenius americanus* it can be 22 cm long (8.7 in), longer than many of its relatives in their entirety (e.g. **Sanderling** *Calidris alba*). The scientific name for curlew, *Numenius*, a word of Greek construction, actually means 'new' (*neos*) 'moon' (*mēnē*), connoting its vast sickle-shape beak.

This huge range in wader forms is not their only identification challenge. A compound problem is that the birds making up a single species can have strikingly different plumages from one another, according to age or season. The best example is the **Ruff** *Philomachus pugnax*. Males are a completely different size to females, which are even known by a different name, 'reeves', and there is such variety among male Ruffs when breeding that it is often said no two birds are alike. Another conundrum is a wader occurring across the entire northern hemisphere, the **Dunlin** *Calidris alpina*, which typifies the differences between breeding and non-breeding plumages. Dunlins can be sparkingly bright rufous and black in summer with linen-white underparts; by autumn they have no more colour than the grey mud they walk upon (the name 'Dunlin', often heard and seldom understood, derives from a medieval English dialect word, *dunling*, i.e. the 'little dark one' or, perhaps, most appropriate, 'little dull one').[1]

Waders can be so difficult to separate that for many they are routinely lumped together as 'shorebirds' or – to use a pithy North American collective that somehow conveys their anonymity – as 'peeps' (for the smallest species). However, those qualities that confound the ordinary person, compel bird specialists. Waders and their identification often

The world-wandering Sanderling joins an elite group of shorebirds that have appeared in more countries – even those that have no shoreline – than almost any other bird species.

The Bar-tailed
Godwit is truly one
of the world's great
navigators.

represent a rite of passage precisely because of this challenge, and they attract passionate devotees. One source of fascination that draws the attention of novice and aficionado alike is the mystery of wader migration.

THE UNIVERSALITY OF THE WIND BIRDS

If people were asked to name the most widespread birds on Earth, the likelihood is that most would suggest the Common (Feral) Pigeon or the House Sparrow, species that thrive in urban environments and which are probably the most abundant. Very few of us would think to nominate a wader, such as the Sanderling, **Ruddy Turnstone** *Arenaria interpres* or **Whimbrel** *Numenius phaeopus*. Yet if one were to compare the national bird lists for every country in the world, then this trio or some of their close relatives – such as the **Red Knot** *Calidris canutus*, **Curlew Sandpiper** *Calidris ferruginea* or **Red-necked Phalarope** *Phalaropus lobatus* – would appear as often as almost any other species.

The universality of waders seems all the more anomalous if you look at the breeding distributions for these six candidates. They cluster in what looks like a tiny area – that Arctic halo of ground at the frozen crown of the planet. Five, in fact, of the six birds nest together on the shores of the Laptev Sea, beyond the 75th parallel north in the Arctic Ocean. The odd one out, the Whimbrel, breeds in central Siberia. Typical of many species in this extraordinary family, these six favour the most hostile and marginal of habitats to rear their young.

Yet once the Arctic's briefest season of superabundance has ended, waders fan out across the globe for nine of every 12 months of the year. This world-wandering aspect to waders was beautifully summarised by the American author Peter Matthiessen, who named his book about them *The Wind Birds*. The individual lives of some species are narratives of

unending passage that challenge our imaginations in a way that only the most extreme seabirds – albatrosses or storm petrels (see respectively pages 98 and 110) – can surpass.

The Sanderling is a classic example. In summer the adults have a beautifully warm peachy buff on their breasts, and upperparts of chequered fox-red, to blend to the tundra on Canada's Ellesmere Island or Russia's Arctic Siberia, at the very northern limit of terra firma. By autumn, however, Sanderlings metamorphose into white bundles of energy that can be seen on beaches throughout the entire temperate and tropical latitudes. Matthiessen called it a 'tireless toy bird' in honour of its rhythmic clockwork-like motion back and forth in synchrony with the tide. Despite the comic air to this small sandpiper, a Sanderling that breeds on Ellesmere may winter in Tierra del Fuego. A Sanderling born in Arctic Russia can migrate to western Europe, then to South Africa. Others may cross Asia to fly to Tasmania or New Zealand – a round trip of 30,000 km (18,600 miles).[2] Yet the individuals undertaking these journeys weigh less than 100 g (3.5 oz). As Matthiessen notes, 'One only has to consider the life force packed tight into that puff of feathers to lay the mind wide open to the mysteries – the order of things, the why and the beginning.'[3]

Perhaps the true Ulysses (or the Amelia Earhart) among all waders, the one that covers the greatest distance in a single passage, is the **Bar-tailed Godwit** *Limosa lapponica*. The species breeds mainly in northern Eurasia with an outlying population in Alaska. It is twice the length of a Sanderling and possesses a long slightly upturned beak for deep-probing estuarine silts. In flight the blade-like wings, which often shine white in the blue sky as the bird sails high overhead, have an easy, compact action that looks well suited to endurance. This was demonstrated in 2007, after a number of godwits had been surgically implanted with transmitters by researchers in New Zealand and Alaska.

Red-necked Phalaropes typify the waders' mastery of land and water. They breed in the northern polar rim and spend their winters out on the Pacific Ocean or the Arabian Sea.

The devices, acting like an aeroplane's black box (and costing £1,800: $2,700 apiece), emitted signals that enabled New Zealand and US scientists to monitor bartail movements across the Pacific Ocean between their 'winter' grounds (actually they are in New Zealand during the austral summer) and their breeding areas in Alaska. A female, known as E7 to the scientists (after the number on her plastic leg-tag) and later christened 'Miranda' (after the place where she was caught), demonstrated how she had made a 16,800 km (10,440 mile) curving journey via the Yellow Sea coastlines of Korea or China as she headed north to breed.

Yet her return-leg southward was a direct non-stop flight of 11,690 km (7,264 miles) from Alaska to New Zealand. It was completed over eight days at an average speed of 60 kph (37 mph) and probably resulted in the loss of half her body weight, from *c.*500 g to 250 g (17.6 oz to 8.8 oz).[4] In the period before her marathon flight the bird will have stored body fat, her own internal organs (kidneys, liver and intestines) all shrinking by as much as a quarter to reduce weight and create space for more fat. These physiological adaptations equip her to perform the longest, non-stop journey recorded by any bird other than a seabird, which, unlike Miranda, can at any time pause to rest on the sea surface.[5]

The godwits' collective arrival on New Zealand's shorelines is a classic sign of spring and some people have taken to welcoming these glorious heralds in a special ritual. Islay McLeod, originator of this wader-centred event, describes its origins:

'The Return of the Godwits' celebration started in 2004. Today the bells of the venerable Christchurch Cathedral ring out for half an hour to welcome the birds home. The city also marks their departure and it was this 'Farewell' event that came first and inspired the 'Welcome' to publicise the story of the Bar-tailed Godwits' epic non-stop journey to Christchurch every September. These birds are a much more inspirational and indigenous harbinger of spring's arrival than the usual postcard lambs and daffodils!

Every year I've been working with the council park ranger, Andrew Crossland. Some godwits over-winter in Christchurch but the new arrivals are easy to spot in September by their emaciated and bedraggled condition. Andrew notifies me as soon as he sees the first birds and I call the Cathedral to arrange for the bells to ring out and then we alert the media. The New Zealand press, radio and television cover the bells ringing and usually include an interview with Andrew. It's an event that has captivated the people of Christchurch and, indeed, the rest of New Zealand – and all the world really – because of media coverage. Sadly, in China there has been a constant incursion of industrial development and aquaculture ponds into wetland habitats and this is destroying the areas where the birds stop-over during their journey north. This is an ominous threat to the Bar-tailed Godwits' survival.[6]

The celebrations reflect a deeper cultural attachment to the species in New Zealand. The bird was enshrined in a novel, *The Godwits Fly*, written in 1938 by the poet Robin Hyde (her real name was Iris Guiver Wilkinson). It is now recognised as a major work of kiwi literature in the early twentieth century, dwelling on themes central to that country's experience as its colonial status drew to a close. The godwits of the title are an emblem for the author's autobiographical character, who herself feels the magnetic pull northwards (in Hyde's case for England) to fulfil her literary potential and escape the perceived provincialism of 1930s New Zealand.

Wader flocks –
here of Red Knot
and Eurasian
Oystercatchers –
assault the senses in
the sensuous turmoil
of their movements,
in the rush of mixed
colours and in the
woodwind music of
their collective flight.

Hyde, who sadly killed herself shortly after the novel's publication, may have been wrong about the specifics of the godwit's journey (to Russia and Alaska, rather than to Europe); but, nevertheless, she tapped into the genuine, powerful imaginative appeal of wader migration as a commentary on the nature of home and our attachment to place, or, conversely, our sense of exile from it.

Another compelling aspect of wader migration is the way that the birds progress to the accompaniment of their own hauntingly beautiful contact notes. One can track waders in their world-wrapping journeys in the dead of night as they pass overhead. There seems something even more moving about sounds so redolent of remote places when heard in the middle of towns or cities.

Like Robin Hyde, W H Hudson was a writer who felt compelled to leave the elemental landscapes of his childhood (in Argentina) to travel to Europe. It seems fitting therefore that he should have written about the bittersweet impact of calling waders. In his deeply nostalgic account of his youth, *Far Away and Long Ago*, he describes the sounds of **Upland Sandpiper** *Bartramia longicauda*, the gloriously subtle grassland wader that breeds in central North America and winters on the southern pampas.

And, lying there, I would listen by the hour to the three-syllable call-note of the upland or solitary plover, as the birds went past, each bird alone far up in the dim sky, winging his way north. It was a strange vigil I kept, stirred by strange thoughts and feelings, in that moonlit earth that was strange too, albeit familiar, for never had the sense of the supernatural in Nature been stronger. And the bird I listened to . . . the most graceful of birds, beautiful to see and hear when it would spring up before my horse with its prolonged wild bubbling cry of alarm and go away with swift, swallow-like flight

– what intensity and gladness of life was in it, what a wonderful inherited knowledge in its brain, and what an inexhaustible vigour in its slender frame to enable it to perform that annual double journey of upwards of ten thousand miles!

By their leaving, Hudson's Upland Sandpipers somehow emphasise our gravity-bound link to place. As the author testified, their sounds are a glorious affirmation of life, yet they remind us of an existence beyond ourselves and out of reach. Their calls, he wrote in this same passage, were 'a momentary intense joy, to be succeeded by ineffable pain'.[7] Peter Matthiessen, in his book *The Wind Birds*, suggests that the fleeting migratory presence of waders invites questions that eventually bring the witness full circle to the mystery of his or her own mortal passage 'under the sun and sky'.[8]

THE ABUNDANCE OF SANDPIPERS

A striking aspect to the life journeys undertaken by many species of wader is that they often move simultaneously in spectacular numbers. While they may spread widely, waders also concentrate in specific places. There are sites, often some of the least-visited wilderness areas on the planet, where they gather in prodigious numbers to rest and refuel. Such localities are sanctuaries for non-breeding waders, and occasionally they accommodate entire international populations. One of the most important in the southern hemisphere is the remote Eighty Mile Beach in Australia. This extraordinary place is described by Clive Minton, who was among the first to recognise its importance for waders:

Our first real exploration of the shores of northern Australia took place in 1981 using two light aircraft and a ground support team armed with a cannon net [to catch the birds]. We couldn't believe what we found: 150,000 waders in Roebuck Bay at Broome and nearly half a million spread along the 220 km of Eighty Mile Beach (incorrectly named!) about 200 km south of Broome (where the Great Sandy Desert meets the sea). Some 400,000 of these were concentrated in an 80 km stretch of unbroken sand adjacent to Anna Plains Station. At high tide, when the 3 km-wide mudflats were covered and the birds were concentrated in the upper part of the 100 m-wide beach, birds were grouped in flocks of 1,000 to 10,000 every few hundred metres.

Driving along the beach and counting them was one of the most memorable experiences of my life, with a never-ending carpet of birds stretching away into the mirage horizon. Altogether 55 species of waders have now been recorded in the Broome/Eighty Mile Beach area – a greater diversity than anywhere else in the world. Since 1981 I've returned at least once each year to continue the counting and ringing studies. Unfortunately now wader numbers are reduced (perhaps 300,000 on Eighty Mile Beach) because of the severe loss of habitat at migratory staging areas in the Yellow Sea (China and Korea) owing to huge amounts of 'reclamation'.[9]

In the northern hemisphere there is an equally little-known desert place called the Banc d'Arguin in Mauritania, a World Heritage Site and the most important place on Earth for non-breeding waders. This landscape comprises 11,700 km^2 (4,500 miles^2) of coastal shoal, creek and intertidal flat that either shimmers under tropical African skies or is sand-blasted by desert winds. Yet the site plays host to 900,000 Dunlin, 540,000 Bar-tailed Godwits, 365,000 Red Knot, 220,000 Curlew Sandpipers and 100,000 **Common Redshank** *Tringa totanus*. In all, the Banc d'Arguin accommodates 2.25 million waders, not to mention a vast number of other wetland birds.[10]

In some ways it is hard to imagine a place less like the Arctic tundra, where many of these species breed. Yet, in one sense, all of these wader-rich localities are deeply similar. Whether polar or tropical, they represent some of the most naturally fertile localities on the planet. A common tendency is to associate natural richness with forest, especially rainforest, where the teeming abundance of life is manifestly obvious. Shoals, sandflats, intertidal mud and expanses of saltmarsh – all those heat-hazed, sea-levelled featureless places that cluster in a narrow zone where ocean and land intersect – have a fertility that is less accessible. It is their superabundance of arthropods – worms and crustacea – beneath the shallows and glistening mud; and underpinning even that hidden bounty is the teeming efflorescence of marine micro-organisms. Yet waders in their prodigious numbers dramatise the whole glorious mass of that unseen life. The birds lose individual identity and merge – dissolve almost – into flocks that are super-organisms, whose flight suggests choreographed smoke, whose onrushing clamour of wings resembles thunder and whose impact can be moving beyond words.

While some of the largest wader congregations may seem like flocks without number, they are not infinite. In fact dependence upon prolific but localised ecosystems can make waders especially vulnerable. The recent history of Red Knot in Delaware Bay, on the USA's Atlantic coast, is a classic example. Most of the birds calling at this large wetland site breed in the high Arctic and belong to a separate subspecies (*Calidris canutus rufa*). A large percentage of the population makes an annual two-way journey totalling 29,000 km (18,000 miles) to spend the 'winter' in South America's Tierra del Fuego.

In early May, during their return leg to breed in the Arctic, the *rufa* race of Red Knot pauses at Delaware Bay to take advantage of another teeming concentration of marine life – the horseshoe crabs which spawn in the adjacent waters. The Red Knot fatten on the billions of crab eggs swilling in this vast sea creek. However, this season of ancient plenty (fossil remains show that horseshoe crabs were on Earth 450 million years ago) has been equally enticing to local fishermen, who use the adults as bait for their eel- and conch-fishing industries. A tenfold increase in the catch of crabs between 1990 and 1998 is thought to lie behind a recent collapse in knot. From an original population of 100,000–150,000, the birds slumped to a maximum of 33,000 in a little over 20 years.

The declines at Delaware Bay may be compounded by parallel problems in the southern hemisphere at equally important staging sites for the Red Knot during their trans-American journeys. For some inexplicable reason, the birds from Tierra del Fuego are arriving later than expected at Delaware, making it increasingly difficult for them to feed up and complete the final leg to the nesting grounds in peak condition to breed.[11]

RUSSIA AND ITS SANDPIPERS

If any one country could be singled out as the ultimate landscape for the sandpiper and snipe family, it would be Russia. At least 49 species, more than half of the family, nest within its political boundaries. Nine breed nowhere else on Earth (such as the Curlew Sandpiper, **Sharp-tailed Sandpiper** *Calidris acuminata* and **Great Knot** *Calidris tenuirostris*). A further six (including the **Red-necked Stint** *Calidris ruficollis*, **Marsh Sandpiper** *Tringa stagnatilis* and **Pin-tailed Snipe** *Gallinago stenura*) are almost endemics. There are also waders that extend into other parts of Europe, nesting, in some cases, even in a dozen other countries; birds like the **Common Greenshank** *Tringa nebularia*, **Green Sandpiper** *Tringa ochropus*, **Wood Sandpiper** *Tringa glareola*, Bar-tailed Godwit, and even **Eurasian Woodcock** *Scolopax rusticola* and **Common Snipe** *Gallinago gallinago*. Yet the lion's share of these widespread birds are essentially Russian in origin. Overall the country is a vast reservoir for all the world's sandpipers. Birds that pass their non-breeding months on the shores of Australia or New Zealand, Namibia and South Africa, even Chile and Argentina, might have begun their lives under Russian skies.

Russia is also the source of two modern causes célèbres among the waders. The **Spoon-billed Sandpiper** *Eurynorhynchus pygmeus* is another Russian endemic and has captivated wide conservation attention, not only because of its dramatic collapse in numbers, but also because of a bizarre quirk in its physiology. As the name suggests, the bird – unique among all waders – possesses a curiously flattened spatulate tip to the bill. It is a tiny sandpiper, but with the beak of a spoonbill.

The other great Russian mystery, and judged now the rarest bird in Europe, has exercised conservationists for the last three decades. The **Slender-billed Curlew** *Numenius tenuirostris*, about the same size as a Bar-tailed Godwit, is a bird of troubling anonymity in terms of colour, pattern and form. The one marginally engaging feature, aside from the slenderness of that down-curved beak, is a sequence of tear-shaped dark spots along the adult's flanks. Otherwise it is an undistinguished medium-sized wader whose one striking feature is behavioural. Instead of migrating south after breeding, Slender-billed Curlews journey east-to-west from the Russian steppe to spend the winter around the shores of the Mediterranean.

In the light of its catastrophic decline, the descriptions of flocks in the nineteenth and early twentieth centuries have about them an agonising casualness. 'At times they come in great numbers,' reads one Italian account from Tuscany. 'Very abundant,' noted another from Tunisia, to which was appended an ominous rider, 'caught until June.' In neighbouring Algeria there was a late-nineteenth-century description that spoke of 'incredible flocks' of Slender-billed Curlews '. . . as big as Starling flocks'.[12]

It was perhaps the species' peculiar misfortune to have selected as its winter quarters a zone where the hunting and eating of waders were time-honoured traditions. The carved reliefs of ancient Egypt are a rich source of imagery of these practices and the Mediterranean harvest of shoreline birds, such as curlews, is certainly many thousands of years old. Yet the extent to which the shooting and trapping of Slender-billed Curlew is specifically implicated in the species' near (or complete) extinction is still unclear. In a way, the mystery of why the bird has slipped to the edge of oblivion intensifies the whole tragedy.

Another painful aspect is the manner in which the bird's plight went unnoticed until just 25 years ago. What adds a sharply ironic edge to the omission is that it occurred in a region with more wildlife observers than almost any other – western Europe. Yet the revised edition of *The ICBP Bird Red Data Book* (1979) missed the curlew from its inventory of threatened species, and the problem was only recognised in 1988, when a figure of less than 1,000 was suggested as a world total.[13] Within five years this was reduced to between 50 and 270 birds. In truth probably no one had seen flocks to indicate such a population since the 1960s.[14] One modern searcher for the lost curlew, Nicola Crockford, now proposes that the 1995 report of two birds at Merja Zerga in northern Morocco (a site at which it was seen each winter from 1987 until 1995) is the last incontrovertible record. There is a wider category of tantalising but unverified sightings of migrant slenderbills from the whole Mediterranean and parts of the Middle East, yet none of these has yet given solid grounds for hope.

There is a last element to the curlew's story that makes it the ultimate Russian mystery. However numerous the species was assumed to be across wintering areas in Europe, only a single birdwatcher ever saw its breeding grounds. The Russian naturalist Valentin Ushakov was the one ornithologist ever to find both the nest and eggs of Slender-billed Curlews. Between 1909 and 1925 this remarkable Russian made searches in the taiga marshes around Tara in south-western Siberia, culminating, on 20 May 1924, in his location of 20 birds and 14 nests on a small island in the midst of a wet bog. Even on the occasion of this momentous find, Ushakov concluded that his bird was already deemed 'a dying-out species'.[15]

One of the few western Europeans to follow in Ushakov's footsteps is Adam Gretton (who, sadly unsuccessful in his search for curlews, met his Russian wife during the quest). He adds the following:

There are so many mysteries regarding the Slender-billed Curlew, but without this extraordinary Russian the mystery would be all the deeper. Valentin Ushakov ('a humble and ordinary nature-lover', in his own words) wrote four articles in hunting journals that provide the sum total of confirmed information about the species' nesting grounds.

I feel very lucky to have been able to visit 'Ushakov's marsh' near Tara twice, and spent many days watching the species at Merja Zerga in Morocco in 1989, 1990 and 1994. Returning to Merja Zerga in January 2010, as part of the region-wide final search for the bird, was a deeply melancholic experience. No Slenderbills were present, yet the local guide Hassan Dalil goes on searching and has not given up hope. (Incidentally, Hassan met his wife through his work on Slenderbills. The story is recounted in the Lonely Planet Guide for Morocco 2009, page 134.)

When I first started in 1988 I realised that it might already be too late. However much Ushakov may have identified habitat loss as a factor in its decline I am sure that excessive hunting played a major part in bringing the species to catastrophe. It is with deep sadness that I'm close to concluding the species has gone. For thousands of years this curlew crossed most of the Western Palearctic twice a year, but we've wiped it out less than two centuries after the species was recognised (in 1817). While specialist reports and books lament such losses, there seems to be a striking lack of gut-level passionate responses (songs and poems) about this snuffing out of life. Perhaps these would provoke a more real and raw sense of grief at such a profound loss.[16]

THE ESKIMO CURLEW

There are many examples of extinction that could have acted as warning with regard to the Slender-billed Curlew. What gives devastating force to the tale of the Russian bird is the fact that throughout we had before us the older story of its relative, the **Eskimo Curlew** *Numenius borealis*. The prior downward spiral to destruction endured by this American species means that conservationists have twice travelled much the same dreary path.

Technically, the Eskimo Curlew is classified by BirdLife as 'critically endangered (possibly extinct)', but it would be truer to say that it has already entered a kind of limbo state and is closer to a condition of myth rather than flesh-and-blood bird. Only perhaps the Ivory-billed Woodpecker (see page 340) has attained the same fabulous realm. It is highly telling that most recent North American field guides do not include the Eskimo Curlew. Yet it still features in some (*The National Geographic Complete Birds of North America*, 2006), and most notably in an illustrated checklist: *Birds of Southern South America* (1998). For the Eskimo Curlew was a genuine pan-American citizen and as true a wind bird as any of its relatives. While it bred in north-west Canada, and almost certainly in Alaska, it spent its non-breeding seasons on the South American pampas.

At the close of the breeding season the Eskimo Curlews' migration first carried them eastwards towards Labrador. There they congregated and stored up energy reserves for the onward journey, gorging often on an abundant fruit crop that is now called crowberry, but was once equally known as 'curlew berry'.[17] Sometimes stained purple across the whole of their underparts, these small curlews then made an Atlantic crossing, apparently to the east of Bermuda and non-stop for 4,000–5,000 km (2,500–3,000 miles), until they reached South America.[18] Occasionally they could encounter fierce storms in the hurricane season and in the nineteenth century some were blown to Europe, one appearing for sale in a Dublin market in Ireland (1870).

It has been claimed that in the autumn of 1492, as the curlews made this time-honoured passage, their route intersected the voyage of an Italian navigator heading into the unknown. On 7 October, moved by the sight of immense flocks of birds travelling south-west, the man known to the world as Christopher Columbus decided to follow them in the hope of striking dry land, and five days later he discovered a New World. The circumstantial details have suggested to some authors that the explorer had witnessed flocks of Eskimo Curlews, or, perhaps, American Golden Plovers, the bird described as their 'boon companions'. Some of the birds were even snared by the crew and were recognised as land birds, unable to rest on water.[19]

One detail that seems absent from the Columbus diary is a verdict on the birds' flavour. For the factor that helped consign Eskimo Curlew to its subsequent fate was the excellence of its flesh. One commentator noted how 'they are found to be exceedingly plump and delicate, and far surpassing any of our English Game in richness and flavour'.[20] When the birds arrived on the shores of Labrador or New England, they laid down such layers of body fat that when shot they would fall to the ground and their breasts burst apart. Hunters called them 'doughbirds' in honour of this sweet plumpness. An alternative spelling, 'doe-bird', seems to hint at something inherently benign in the curlew's nature. It was said that whenever one bird had been killed, its fellows would congregate round almost presenting themselves as fresh targets for the next shot.

Ominously perhaps, the unnumbered flocks – said by many to involve millions of birds – were routinely likened to another lost species of superabundance, the Passenger Pigeon (see page 241). In truth the link between the two was deeper and more tragic than a comparison of numbers. Once the pigeon flocks had been largely destroyed, the hunters turned to the curlew as substitute.

Like many migrant waders, but especially the American Golden Plover, they followed one route south and another more westerly route as they came north. This South American passage in spring carried them over the Andes and eventually into Texas, then on across the Great Plains. What finally sealed the bird's fate was that during this last leg of their journey, the market hunters were waiting. In fact, intense killing dogged them everywhere – in Labrador and New England during fall, again in Argentina where they passed the winter, then relentlessly in the American West as the birds tried to reach the nesting grounds. Hunting devastated the species largely in a single generation, between 1865 and 1890, and by 1915, when the first obituary was written (entitled 'The Eskimo Curlew and its disappearance'), its

author, Professor Swenk, described the hunt scenes on the plains of Nebraska as 'appalling and almost unbelievable'.

The core image, which has come to summarise the species' fate, is Swenks' description of a vast heap of curlews – 'as large as a couple of tons of coal' – that was left where it had been dumped, because the hunters who had killed them lacked the time or opportunity to transport them to market. Their response was simply to leave the curlews to rot and go back out to the plains to kill wagonloads more.[21]

While Swenk fingered this kind of profligate behaviour as a key driver, it was perhaps extinction's customary double act that crushed the Eskimo Curlew: hunting on one hand and habitat loss on the other. The American plains, where the curlews had once fed, were converted wholesale to farmland as the vast exodus of settlers spread to the West. Today just 4 per cent of the original prairie system is left.

Very little redeems the sadness of this tale. We cannot even say we learned our lesson. The Slender-billed Curlew's parallel fate is dismal proof. Yet at least a second and more fitting obituary for the Eskimo Curlew did justice to the splendour of the bird. The Canadian author Fred Bodsworth wrote a novel in 1955, entitled *Last of the Curlews*. It has been in print ever since and is acknowledged today as a major work that helped to raise environmental awareness, in the manner of Aldo Leopold's *A Sand County Almanac* (1949) or Rachel Carson's *Silent Spring* (1962).

Bodsworth's novel, which has sold more than 3 million copies in a dozen languages, tells the simple affecting story of an Eskimo Curlew and his mateless journey from Arctic Canada to the Argentinian pampas. There, miraculously, he meets another of his kind, a female, and after their relationship is cemented, the curlew couple sets out to brave the odyssey of their trans-American journey. In its final stages, on the prairies of Canada, the female is brought down by stray shots and the male, alone once again, carries on his barren journey into the north.

The novel is remarkable for the way it solves the problem of how to evoke the obvious pathos of the birds' plight without recourse to a sentimentalised anthropomorphism, which had been a conventional mark of nature writing in preceding decades. His solution, reminiscent of the works of Henry Williamson (*Tarka the Otter* and *The Phasian Bird*), was to avoid emotion altogether. Instead the author creates, as faithfully as possible, the interior world of an animal that is incapable of conscious thought, but is moved

All the beauty and the tragedy of the Eskimo Curlew are caught forever in John James Audubon's famous painting.

The wonderful courtship music of the Eurasian Curlew is a song of joy edged with boreal melancholy.

and shaped by instinctual drives. It is the author's forensic attention to the observable detail of a bird's world, guided by a strictly scientific interpretation of behaviour – yet blended with poetic evocations of habitat, climate and the wild creatures with which the curlew shared the landscape – that somehow conveys the beauty of another species and the implied tragedy of its loss. To force home a moral message, Bodsworth intercut the tale with excerpts from scientific journals, contemporary nineteenth-century newspaper accounts and works of early natural history. These narrate the other side of the curlew's fate – human greed, human ignorance and human folly.

In 1972 *Last of the Curlews* inspired the film company Hanna-Barbera to make an hour-long cartoon with the same title, which was shown repeatedly on American television as part of series called 'After School Specials'.[22] As fellow-Canadian author Graeme Gibson notes, Bodsworth's story has also moved trained scientists as well as children: 'I personally know two field ornithologists who say that it was the reading of this book that led them into their profession.'[23] The authors of a third obituary of the bird, a book entitled *Eskimo Curlew: A Vanishing Species?*, published in 1986, even wondered whether the Canadian novelist had had a direct impact on the curlew itself. 'It would not be an exaggeration', they wrote, 'to say that some of the few remaining Eskimo Curlews owe their lives to Fred Bodsworth and Terry Shortt [the artist who drew the book's illustrations].'[24]

What is fascinating about this sentence is the implied hope of the species' survival. For one of the most challenging aspects of the Eskimo Curlew story is the century-long state of uncertainty about whether it was extinct, and whether it might, even at an eleventh hour, be saved. Numbers may have collapsed by 1915, yet reports have continued to surface of possible sightings. Even after Bodsworth's ominously titled novel, there were two confirmed records: two birds that were photographed – the world's only photographs of Eskimo

Curlew – at Galveston Island, Texas, in March 1962, and one of a curlew shot in Bermuda in 1963. There have since been 30 other sightings in North America – one remarkable and widely accepted claim involved 23 birds in 1981, also in Texas – but none has been incontrovertible and while they nourish our dreams, they give us small hope. The Eskimo Curlew exemplifies a common theme in cases of extinction: its emotional messiness, where the pain of loss is blurred and enveloped by the confusion of never quite knowing.

THE MYSTERIOUS PLEASURES OF WADERS
Nothing, of course, can redeem the stories of these extinct curlews. Yet at minimum it should ensure that we save two further magical North American species, the Long-billed and the **Bristle-thighed Curlew** *Numenius tahitiensis*, which are now also deemed at risk of extinction. Equally, it should oblige us to take proper remedial steps for the **Eurasian Curlew** *Numenius arquata*, which is in serious decline from Ireland to Russia.[25]

It is not easy to define exactly what is forfeit when such birds vanish from their former haunts, but it is more than the affecting narrative of their journeys, more than the utilitarian profits from their flesh and feathers or the excitement of the chase, and more than the moral lessons drawn from our own inept exploitation. One part of the loss that seems beyond category is the silencing of their voices. While waders seldom register on a list of the world's favourite birdsongs, curlews in particular are praised for their profoundly moving vocalisations.

Eurasian Curlews deliver their song during a high, stylised courtship flight, so these wild sounds are broadcast across the open and invariably windswept moors and pastureland that they favour. The drawn-out, tremulous, bubbling notes are often a signature for such places and they have an intriguing emotional ambiguity that is somehow perfectly apt for the landscape. It is a sound of joyous release edged with a darker boreal melancholy. It evokes the strongest responses, like the following:

> For me no bird's song can compare with the curlew's. I found this anecdote in *The Birds of Northumberland and the Eastern Borders* of 1912: 'A country gentleman from the west of Scotland on a visit to England was invited out by his friend to hear the nightingale. When the friend asked if he was not delighted with the song he replied: "It's a' very gude, but I wadna gie the wheeple of a whaup [Scots dialect for curlew] for a' the nightingales that ever sang."' Up on the moors on a fine April day, listening to a curlew in full bubbling flow, who would ever disagree with him?[26]

In 1972 the Finnish composer Einojuhani Rautavaara wrote a piece of music entitled *Cantus Arcticus*. It is also known as the *Concerto for Birds and Orchestra* and was originally commissioned by the University of Oulu on the Gulf of Bothnia. Although even Finland's Eurasian Curlews are now in steep decline, that country still has one of the largest populations in all of Europe and the species was common at the nearby marsh of Liminka, where Rautavaara recorded their songs. In the opening sequence to the first movement both oboe and clarinet repeatedly evoke the simpler disyllabic contact notes of the bird (or do the instruments mimic another glorious wader, the Northern Lapwing?).

However, floating above the piece are the unmistakable sounds of real Eurasian Curlews in song display. Together with the clashing bugle notes and softer crooning noises of Common Cranes in flight, the songs of the curlews swell and fuse with the whole orchestra. It is a remarkable blend of human and natural music – surely one of the most successful attempts to make art directly from birdsong – and it is filled with a sense of space and of northern sunlight, and the open watery quaking places of Rautavaara's homeland. If we want to understand what the loss of curlews means, then this wonderful piece of music is a good place to start.

Another sub-group of waders, the eight species of woodcock, further illuminates the complex and multifaceted pleasures that people everywhere have derived from this family for millennia. Between them, the two most widespread, the Eurasian and the smaller **American Woodcock** *Scolopax minor*, occur across a vast belt of the entire northern hemisphere (the other six are all in eastern Asia). Chunky, barrel-chested, with broad wings, woodcocks are exceptional waders for being nocturnal (or at least crepuscular) and inhabitants of damp or boggy woodland. A further striking character is their remarkable invisibility.

Both species are among the commonest birds that birdwatchers on either side of the Atlantic seldom and often *never* see well. It is straightforward to spot them in flight. To find woodcocks on the ground is exceptional. In the dappled conditions of the woodland floor, the birds are so beautifully camouflaged that they look to have bulbed up spontaneously from the Earth, mushroom-like, ready cloaked in the colours of leaf litter. Their sombre and obliterative patterns of counter-shading have been nicely summarised by one writer as a 'book of browns'.[27] Yet on the living bird in its true place, these complex earth colours are illegible against the crazy scribbled lines of dead leaf and withered bracken. Henry Thoreau was one unfailingly acute observer who deciphered

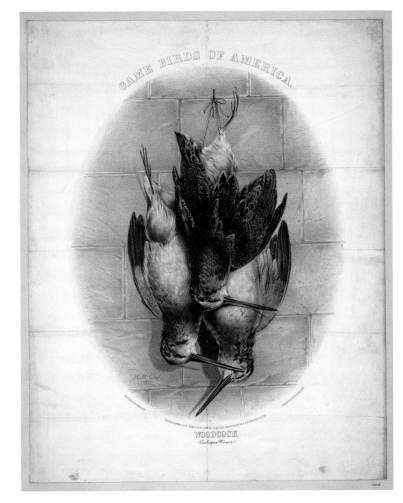

a resting woodcock in the field. His account perfectly illuminates the challenge:

> My attention was drawn to a singular-looking dry leaf or parcel of leaves on the shore about a rod off. Then I thought it might be the dry and yellowed skeleton of a bird with all its ribs; then the shell of a turtle, or possibly some large dry oak leaves peculiarly curved and cut; and then, all at once, I saw that it was a woodcock, perfectly still, with its head drawn in, standing on its great pink feet. I had, apparently, noticed only the yellowish-brown portions of the plumage, referring the dark-brown to the shore behind it.[28]

It is the wider shoal of mystery encircling woodcocks that creates a cult around the whole bird. It is the one wader that has inspired special clubs dedicated to the sport of hunting it. Arthur Bent described the American Woodcock as 'An aristocrat among game birds!' and its flesh 'a delight to the palate of an epicure'.[29]

Both American and Eurasian Woodcocks are migrants, like many of their family. However, people were once deeply confused about where exactly these enigmatic waders came from, in both a geographical and a genetic sense. In France, for instance, the native species was once thought to be the spawn of a mustelid, the polecat (whose name was *père de la bécasse*, 'father of the woodcock').[30] In England the muddle was on a similar scale, as the poem the 'Shepherd's Week', by John Gay, illustrates:

Woodcocks have long been regarded as one of the trickiest targets as well as one of the finest sources of wild meat.

Eurasian Woodcock as we seldom see it. The subtle crypsis in the plumages of woodcocks makes the birds some of the most difficult to observe well.

He sung where woodcocks in the summer feed,
And in what climates they renew their breed;
Some think to northern coasts their flight they tend,
Or to the moon in midnight hours ascend.

The seemingly wild notion of the woodcock as a moon-dwelling bird hinged partly on the fact that all its comings and goings took place under cover of darkness. A further cause of our confusion was the almost mystical inexplicability of their abundance once they arrived from the north in autumn. Woodcocks can materialise anywhere, including on the decks of passing ships. A British naval officer of the nineteenth century is reputed once to have shaken several Eurasian Woodcocks out of the rigging of a sail vessel.

The birds' presence even in woods where they are traditionally hunted can be just as unexpected. There have been occasions when 1,000 American Woodcock have been shot in a single day's hunt (on 17 November 1924 at Cape May, New Jersey).[31] Equally a group of six hunters in the Peloponnese, Greece, took a bag of 1,026 Eurasian Woodcocks

in six days, while near Izmir, Turkey, one hunter shot 168 in one day.[32] Yet the morning before, these same areas may have held few if any woodcocks at all. Their arrivals are called 'falls', reflecting the birds' mysterious and sudden appearance like a fall of snow overnight. 'Fall', in fact, is still the collective noun for woodcocks (and was first recorded in 1486), while 'fall' has entered the modern birdwatcher's vocabulary to describe the large arrival of any migrants.

It was customary to hunt this 'Owl among Snipe', as one American ornithologist called his native species, at dusk or during the hours of darkness.[33] A widespread practice was to lay vast nets across specially cut rides through the woods. The catching and eating of this beautiful wader was so deep-rooted in British culture that the broad glades in which they were caught were known as 'cock-shoots', or 'cock-shuts', while the dusk period when the nets were operational was called 'cock-shut time'.[34] For hundreds of years these woodcock-catching strategies were as commonplace in Britain as they were in France, Holland, Germany and Italy. A Tuscan ruse was to dazzle the birds by lantern and then shoot them before they could fly. (A similar method on the cottonfields of the American South was to blind them momentarily with lighted torches and either fell them with a pole or stake, or shoot them.[35] Using the latter technique, a single gun could bring down a 100 in a night.)[36]

All of this ingenuity reflected one thing: the wide taste for a meat that is dark, rich, savoury and exalted still above the flesh of all other waders. While woodcock is common fare in the country cottage, the bird holds its own at the most expensive tables. In the great Sicilian novel of Giuseppe di Lampedusa, *The Leopard* (*Il Gattopardo*, 1958), the author describes in exquisite detail the central place of this earth-brown wader in the aristocratic palaces of late-nineteenth-century Palermo.

> Beneath the candelabra, beneath the five tiers bearing towards the distant ceiling pyramids of home-made cakes that were never touched, spread the monotonous opulence of buffets at big balls: coraline lobsters boiled alive, waxy *chaud-froids* of veal, steely-lined fish immersed in sauce, turkeys gilded by the ovens' heat, rosy *foie-gras* under gelatine armour, boned woodcocks reclining on amber toast decorated with their own chopped guts, dawn-tinted gelantine and a dozen other cruel, coloured delights.[37]

Even when plucked and roasted the 'mysterious hermit of the alder' manages to retain a pinch of its gift for mystification.[38] Woodcocks were indeed prepared, as Lampedusa indicates, with their entrails (known as 'trail') presented as a garnish. Not everyone, however, has recognised the fine thread-like intestines exactly for what they are. A not infrequent error is that the birds are served, not with their entrails, but with the arthropods found within the gut; hence this claim: 'In more epicurean times these wholesome worms from the woodcock's stomach were prized as a delicacy.'[39]

Nor is gastronomy the only field with its residual woodcock mysteries. There are puzzles even now in the science of ornithology. It centres on the claimed behaviour of parent birds with small young. Adults of both American and Eurasian Woodcocks have been observed to fly off, carrying their chicks away from potential danger, most often by bracing the offspring between the tail and feet. The first recorded observation was made by an Italian naturalist, Giovanni Scopoli, in the late eighteenth century and given wider coverage in Gilbert White's *Natural History of Selborne* (1789). Since that time, hundreds of people on both sides of the Atlantic have claimed to see woodcocks either holding young beneath their feet (said to resemble 'a shrike carrying off a small bird'), clasped in their beaks or even with the chick sitting on the parent's back.[40] As one commentator notes, 'Thousands of words have been written about it and countless hours of discussion and argument have been spent by generations of woodcock-minded sportsmen in debating it.'[41]

It is part of the birds' ongoing fascination that this piece of woodcock lore is still a contested field more than 250 years after it was first recorded. As a small measure of the controversy I conducted a straw poll, canvassing ten professional ornithologists (anonymously) of various disciplines, from four countries on three continents. They could answer only yes or no. I found that five do not believe it to be true. Five believe it is. One person even had personal experience of the phenomenon and wrote:

It is a great surprise to get this question and I am very pleased because it evokes memories from 1985. I was walking along the eastern shore of Krankesjön [Skåne, Sweden]. Suddenly, I was startled by a bird flying up in front of me. A woodcock. But I thought what a strange way to fly. I had never seen it before: arched back, tail right down, heavy take off. And then, I thought is she carrying a young? She flew 25 m or so, then landed, and I walked towards her. She took off again but in normal flight. And, with my blood pressure rising, I found three woodcock babies on the ground. Cute small fellows! Had I really witnessed what has been reported many times over the years but was and is still disputed? I tell you, at that moment I was convinced that I had! What a discovery!

On my way back, I tried to analyse this wonderful moment. But honestly, I had *not* seen the young really hanging between the legs of the mother woodcock. She must have tried to fool me, like woodcocks can do in this way of taking wing. And she landed where her young were lying motionless in the grass. I must say it was easy to come to the conclusion of thinking that woodcocks can carry young. Totally impossible? Maybe not, but unlikely. So I have to vote no.[42]

Yet here is the sighting of an additional eleventh observer:

It must have been 34 years ago now when I had a sighting I shall never forget. I was working as a gamekeeper on the Cornbury Park estate in Oxfordshire. I was doing my daily rounds at that time of year in early spring. As I was walking along a ride in the forest, I was taken aback as a woodcock rose about 10 ft in front of me, and I could see clearly the bird had a young woodcock between her legs, she carried it about 30–40 yards, landed and then took off again. I could see the young woodcock chick on the ride and as I got near it ran into the cover. In all my years as a gamekeeper I have found many woodcock nests and seen newly hatched chicks; although I've only ever seen the young get carried the one time.[43]

These wonderful birds, like most waders, dwell in those marginal places between solid ground and bog, between dry land and water, but also in a border zone between what we can see and know firmly, and things of which we are uncertain. This is part of the indefinable thrill and joy of waders. Through their mysterious companionship, or the sounds of their voices, or the steady rhythmic beat of their tireless wings, they conduct us to an appreciation of the vast and unfathomable grandeur of the Earth.

The plain facts of their habits license our imaginative capacity both to shrink the planet – from Alaska to Argentina, or from the Arctic Ocean to the Banc d'Arguin – but also to appreciate our own infinitesimal smallness within it. Yet a Bar-tailed Godwit, that pound-bag of a bird, can span the entire Pacific Ocean, alone, unaided, and without stopping. What could that possibly be like? How would we possibly feel ourselves? We can only clutch at the idea. But what is lost when any wader is lost is our ability to share in the compelling stories of their lives and our chance to participate in the real and genuine magic of this world.

The inappropriately named Egyptian Plover may be the source of an enduring myth about a bird that picked its food from the crocodile's teeth.

Courser and Pratincole family *Glareolidae*

This wader family of 18 species is split more or less evenly between two types of bird – the coursers (nine species) and pratincoles (eight species) – but all have a strong reputation for physical elegance. The coursers are long-legged, slender, upright, ground-dwelling creatures with soft pastel colours that blend well with the arid environments they favour. The pratincoles, by contrast, are invariably associated with wetlands and appear rather weak-legged, even awkward and dumpy if seen perched on the ground. However, they instantly acquire a long-winged grace when they take to the air. Pratincoles often feed in flight, sometimes swooping and twisting en masse in a manner that suggests a flock of giant swallows.

Both coursers and pratincoles are birds of the Old World (none occurs in the Americas) with a strong bias towards Africa. Six coursers and three pratincoles are exclusively found on this continent, while the last member of the family, the species that has the most striking cultural profile, is itself an African endemic. The **Egyptian Plover** *Pluvianus aegyptius* is actually neither a plover nor is it any longer found in Egypt, but breeds right across Sahelian Africa with outlying populations as far south as the Congo River. It is a bird famed for its beauty, with pinkish-buff belly and lavender-grey upperparts, emphasised by a longitudinal black stripe over the mantle and crisp black gorget around the lower breast. Each wing bears a curving black bar that unfolds as an inverted archer's bow across the whole span when the bird takes flight.

The graphic purity of colour and design has helped make the Egyptian Plover one of the key target species for birdwatchers in Africa. As a consequence it appears with disproportionate regularity on books, brochures and other ornithological advertisements. (It is, for example, the logo of the African Bird Club.) Yet it also has an engaging myth attached to it. When the Greek historian Herodotus (484–425 BC) visited Egypt he encountered and retold a story of apparent symbiosis between the Nile crocodile and some type of bird. A modern translation of the relevant passage reads:

> Other animals avoid the crocodile, as do all birds too with one exception – the sandpiper, or Egyptian Plover; this bird is of service to the crocodile and lives, in consequence, in the greatest amity with him; for when the crocodile comes ashore and lies with his mouth wide open (which he generally does facing towards the west), the bird hops in and swallows the leeches. The crocodile enjoys this, and never, in consequence, hurts the bird.[1]

The identification of this crocodile bird as the Egyptian Plover was never part of the original text by Herodotus. This detail was added by the translator, E V Rieu, and was based on evidence (or perhaps, more accurately, the conjecture) first supplied by a French naturalist, Étienne Geoffroy Saint-Hilaire (1772–1844). It was he who, accompanying the Napoleonic expedition to Egypt in 1798, proposed the Egyptian Plover as the bird in question. He suggested that the plover fed not on leeches, but on a kind of gnat which swarmed into the reptile's mouth, turning it black and half choking the poor beast.

In truth, this strange and ancient tale has never been satisfactorily resolved with indisputable proof. The only real advance made by modern science is to dismiss the leech element of the story: there are no such parasites in a croc's mouth. Yet the idea of a bird entering that giant maw to feed has survived as a tantalising possibility that has teased and challenged ornithologists for almost two and a half millennia. One can understand why it should have excited our imaginations, given the crocodile's status as one of the most pitiless predators, which routinely includes humans in its range of prey. The idea that such a formidable beast could show tenderness to a small bird has all the necessary psychological appeal to act as seed for an enduring myth.

A further candidate for the Herodotus story was another species of wader, the Spur-winged Lapwing, found in Africa and southern Eurasia, which was proposed by two Victorian naturalists in the 1860s. However, it has always been second favourite for the role. Not only Geoffroy Saint-Hilaire, but also a German naturalist, A E Brehm, claimed to have witnessed repeatedly Egyptian Plovers in the act of feeding inside the mouth of the huge reptile.[2] What is intriguing about the crocodile–bird story is the kind of witnesses and supporters it has acquired during its long history. It was viewed as 'strictly true' by none other than Edward Stanley, a man who never let the facts stand in the way of a great tale, despite (or, perhaps, because of) his other role as the Bishop of Norwich.[3] Another ornithologist partial to the traveller's tale was the legendary British figure Richard Meinertzhagen. This immensely colourful man made other

equally questionable claims for a number of birds and, most notoriously, he has now been exposed as having stolen a significant percentage of his own once-celebrated bird-skin collection from a truly international suite of natural-historical institutions, including the British Museum, London, to which he eventually donated (or, some would say, gave back) the entire ensemble.

Meinertzhagen entered the fray in his entertaining book *Pirates and Predators* (1959), suggesting that he had seen the behaviour north of Khartoum, Sudan, when a large crocodile rose on to a sandbank and opened its jaw with eyes shut: 'Three *Pluvianus* who had been feeding near by at once flew to it, one perching on the outer gums and pecking at the teeth, the other remaining on the ground and inspecting the mouth . . . and pecking the teeth.' Meinertzhagen further claimed that he had seen Blacksmith Lapwing perform the same mouth-cleaning service in 1907, and suggested that the Water Thick-knee was another associate; he finally proposed that the 'crocodile bird' of Herodotus was, in fact, a composite involving a range of different waders.[4]

Sadly no modern ornithologist has either corroborated or utterly dispelled the myth and it remains a fascinating possibility, but little more. There has been no modern sighting and few major ornithological works give it credence.[5]

Gull and Tern family *Laridae*

The family includes perhaps the best known of all seabirds. This familiarity is partly because gulls and terns are not so much inhabitants of open ocean; rather, they occupy that place which exercises a peculiar and dominant attraction for humans. Like us they love the often flat, shifting, sun-sparkled beaches and shoals where terra firma meets the sea. In fact, the birds' calls are as integral to our internal sense and memory of the shoreline as the lapping of the waves themselves.

Gull and tern images are constantly recycled as logos or product names by companies and institutions with a link to the sea. There must also be a vast fleet of every form of sea-going vessel each bearing a name drawn from these birds. Their hugely atmospheric voices are now widely used in film, theatre, radio or television, and often as a signature sound to alert the listener that the setting is coastal. In some gulls the calls closely resemble human laughter. A good example is the **Common Black-headed Gull** *Larus ridibundus*, a species with a massive trans-Eurasian range, from easternmost Russia to Iceland and south into Africa and Asia. In truth – and despite the scientific name (*ridibundus* means 'laughing') – only some of the vocalisations have a coarse chuckling quality. The arch humorist of the family is undoubtedly an inhabitant of North America's east coast, the aptly named **Laughing Gull** *Larus atricilla*. The calls are variable, but all genuinely evoke comedy, from a short, sharp noise like a squeaky toy worried by a dog, right through to a loud manic laughter of theatrical hilarity.

Yet perhaps the most familiar gull sound is known as the 'long call' and is performed by a number of much larger species such as the **Herring Gull** *Larus argentatus* and **Great Black-backed Gull** *Larus marinus*, which are found on both sides of the Atlantic. The birds even deliver

the long call with enormous flourish, throwing back their heads and firing the notes upwards like a wolf howling in triumph at the moon. All the gulls that perform the long call – and these various species wrap round the entire northern hemisphere – produce a gloriously pagan music that is loud, ringing and emotionally complex, mingling laughter with a dash of menace. It is indubitably *the* sound of the seaside. Sometimes, however, the relentlessness of gull calls can be trying. In France there is an expression – *Vos geueles les mouettes* – 'which is impolite slang to make a group of people shut up so someone can talk'.[1]

The family comprises 100 species in total, spread worldwide, but with particular concentrations in the northern hemisphere. The region with greatest diversity is North America, which holds more than two-fifths of the family (42 species), albeit with ten that occur only as vagrants. Western Europe has 39 species with an even higher proportion of marginal residents or occasional visitors (13 species). Sea and sand are such basic constituents of the world's coastlines that several of the family have colonised every continent except Antarctica, including the **Gull-billed tern** *Sterna nilotica* and **Caspian Tern** *Sterna caspia*. The **Arctic Tern** *Sterna paradisaea*, however, goes one better and visits almost every shoreline on Earth. Each year some of the breeding population makes a biennial passage between the two polar regions, completing a journey in the order of 35,000 km (21,750 miles).

What distance an individual Arctic Tern might cover in the course of its entire life (the oldest ringed birds have been in their 30s) beggars the imagination. Yet the species' Arctic-to-Antarctic odyssey has become the clichéd tale of wonder in many books about bird migration or behaviour. What licenses the lifestyle itself is the bird's remarkable physiology:

The Arctic Tern's annual migration from the Antarctic to the Arctic is one of the great odysseys in all nature.

the average Arctic Tern weighs 107 g (3.8 oz), has a wingspan of 80 cm (31.5 in) and is little more than a heart enclosed in wing muscle, arced around by shining flight feathers. It is a bird of exquisite attenuated beauty, a notion that is enshrined in the scientific name: *paradisaea*, 'of paradise'.

Nor is it alone among the family. The aptly named **Angel Tern** *Gygis alba*, of tropical islands mainly in the Indian and Pacific Oceans, is surely one of the most beautiful of all seabirds. One contributor, encountering them in the Seychelles, writes:

> They are, by any standards, bewitching birds, light as gossamer in the blue sea air, translucent in sunlight, glowing like angels in the clear tropical light. If, like William Blake, you fancy you can see heaven in a wild flower, then you will also see it in these birds, the angel pose adding to the effect.[2]

The smaller terns have long been praised for beauty, a quality that seems implicit in their old nickname, 'sea swallow'. Yet it is sometimes easy to overlook the aesthetic qualities of the larger family members. We are so habituated to images of gulls roiling over fish guts sluiced from rusty trawlers, or hungry mobs swaying back and forth with a dozer as it drives the moraine of trash across the dump, that we forget what glorious creatures they really are. At first glance the chromatic range in both gull and tern plumage seems narrow – usually some tone of grey mingled with white. Yet the birds redeem these colours from their common associations. To see a flock of **Whiskered Tern** *Chlidonias hybrida*, dipping to feed in wild free sorties over a nest marsh, or a flock of Herring Gulls afloat on updraughts above sea cliffs, the birds rising in long loose shoals high into the blue, is to appreciate grey unlocked from any residual sense of concrete, bureaucracy, conformity or boredom. Gulls and terns make grey beautiful.

SYMBOLIC GULLS

The white in gulls and terns is no less special. As Helmut Sick noted, the shimmering silvery tint on tern flight feathers 'comes from the refracted light in the microscopic structure of the feathers which lack pigmentation in this area'.[3] Gulls can possess exactly the same glittering quality. In fact the Herring Gull's scientific name, *argentatus*, means 'ornamented with silver'.[4] In sub-zero conditions their whiteness can outshine snow. Henry Thoreau described the light reflected by gulls as like 'candles in the night'.[5] Our ancestors, free of any psychological link between gulls and modern human detritus, clearly saw this translucent beauty in the birds.

The great Welsh poet of the fourteenth century Dafydd ap Gwilym caught perfectly the gull's light-refracting properties in his love poem *Yr Wylan* ('The Seagull').

Fine gull on a warm tide-flow,	*Yr wylan deg ar lanw dioer*
Colour of snow or pale moon,	*Unlliw gan eiry neu wenlloer,*
Flawless is your beauty,	*Dilwch yw dy degwch di,*
Sun-shard, sea-gauntlet,	*Darn fel haul, dyrnfol heli.*
Weightless on the wave-flood,	*Ysgafn ar don eigion wyd,*
Swift proud fishfeeder,	*Esgudfalch edn bysgodfwyd.*
Close flying to the anchor,	*Yngo'r aud wrth yr angor*
Close to my hand, sea-lily,	*Lawlaw a mi, lili mor.*
Bright sheet's semblance,	*Llythr unwaith llathr ei annwyd.*
Nun of the tide's swell.	*Lleian ym mrig llanw mor wyd.*

As Jim Perrin, the poem's modern translator, explains, the gull serves the author as both a messenger to his beloved but also as a metaphor for her own beauty. (He adds: 'Dafydd's poetry is very dense in its echoes, allusions, alternative senses and sound-architecture. I can remember asking my Welsh lecturer, a wonderful old maiden from Llanfair Caereinion, 40 years ago if she'd give me some help in understanding Dafydd's verse and her blushing and telling me that she'd rather not, he being something of a libertine.')[6]

Many people are now so familiar with gulls' wholesale invasion of inland areas, especially in major centres of human population – on reservoirs, sewage works and rubbish dumps – that the non-coastal encounter has been drained of any real significance. Yet this was not always the case. Gulls were once rare away from the seashore. Henry Thoreau perfectly conveyed both his axiomatic connection of gulls with the sea and, conversely, his sense of nature out of joint when he saw a group of Herring Gulls near his hometown of Concord in 1855. It is worth noting that the latter is just 37 km (23 miles) from the Massachusetts shore. 'To see a gull beating high over our meadowy flood', he wrote, 'is akin to seeing a mackerel schooner on the coast. It is the nearest approach to sailing vessels in our scenery . . . Oh how it salts our fresh, our sweet watered Fair Haven all at once to see this sharp-beaked, greedy sea-bird beating over it!'[7]

These occasional and dramatic gull appearances were once taken as a prophesy of bad weather, in which there was possibly a grain of truth. Yet they were also perceived as a wider portent of human disaster or individual mishap. Equally the ghostly whiteness of the birds triggered its own kind of psychological associations. Gulls were connected to the older common superstition that seabirds could become the embodied spirits of lost sailors. All these ideas now seem deeply archaic and highly fanciful but, as the following

There has seldom been a human catch of fish that did not attract its roiling, squabbling mob of beautiful gulls.

contributions make plain, they are not quite below the horizon of memory:

> To the inhabitants of rural north Norfolk, UK, in the early years of the twentieth century, the Great Black-backed Gull was known as the 'Land Gull'. It was a term also used to describe any other large gull, particularly a Herring Gull in its dark immature plumage. Both my father, Maurice Bloomfield (shepherd at Holkham for 30 years and a stock man and farm labourer from his youth in the 1930s at Egmere), and his parents (his father worked a team of horses at Egmere) had strong feelings about the Land Gull, feelings that I was led to believe were quite widespread amongst the rural communities. Although the 'Saddlebacks' (another local name but more restricted to the coast) were well known along the seashore during that period, the species was obviously not as frequently encountered inland as it is today. Consequently the Land Gull was known as a sign of ill omen, particularly if one lingered for any length of time on a field. The threat of bad weather and, perhaps more strangely, the view that some unexpected tragedy was imminent in the neighbourhood, were both cited commonly as reasons for the suspicious mistrust and hatred that were levelled at the Land Gull. Another belief was that they had come inland because they were sick and were looking for somewhere to die. I remember as a boy bringing home a sick Great Black-backed Gull and putting it in an old disused stable. An hour or two later I found it had mysteriously disappeared. The answer I received from my father was that it would only bring bad luck – 'they ent n' good to hev about!'[8]

Over several years I had a special relationship with a male Herring Gull. He would follow me around like our cats. He used to come into the house, walk through the open door, through the sitting room, into the porch where I fed the cats. He (Pop) would eat any cat food, walk back the way he came in, sometimes perching on the coffee table like a beautiful sculpture, ignoring the cats, who usually hid under chairs and beds when they saw him coming, and go out the door again. After he swallowed a fish-hook and line, he came as usual to be fed, and took kitten-food – all he could manage – from my hand, for several days before he flew off never to be seen again. He was called Pop after my late father, a Royal Navy man, who always said that he, like all mariners, would come back as a gull. Pop 2 even had the same bitter and pissed-off expression that Pop 1 habitually wore.[9]

Some of this lore was surely at work in a play by the Russian author Anton Chekhov, *The Seagull* (1895). In fact the playwright also deployed an additional strand of psychological association that is commonplace in many representations of gulls and which is possibly rooted in those plaintive long calls. It is the idea of the gull as the lonely wandering spirit. In Chekhov's play the bird is a complex leitmotif standing for several of the key characters, especially Nina the would-be actress. Equally it stands for the central figure of Konstantin, who is both Nina's would-be lover and himself a would-be author. His own tragic destiny is foreshadowed in his shooting of a 'real' gull, of which he makes a macabre gift to Nina. Laying the bird at her feet, he announces: 'Soon I shall kill myself in the same way.' The venue where *The Seagull* first rose to international prominence was the Moscow Art Theatre. It was staged to huge acclaim in 1898 and the theatre adopted a seagull as its emblem and retains it to this day.

One might imagine that the novelist Daphne du Maurier (1907–1989), as well as the film director Alfred Hitchcock (1899–1980), drew on the same residual foreboding and

The high, laughing wail of the Herring Gull or one of the other large gull species is part of the soundtrack to the seaside in many parts of the world.

kiosk. Eventually they take human lives, pecking out the lovely green eyes of the actress Suzanne Pleshette.

The wider sense of chaos – and, it must be said, of humour because the whole plot is ludicrous and the writing singularly flat in atmosphere – is more heavily underscored in du Maurier's story. She implies that birds not only attack a few isolated farms in Cornwall, but that they invade British towns and cities everywhere. When eventually we realise that they have somehow silenced the dogged dependability of news bulletins by the British Broadcasting Corporation we are left to infer that birds have somehow wiped out most or all of the population of London.

Gull-inspired gore may be central to both book and film, but neither du Maurier nor Hitchcock makes any reference to the old superstitions. Nor do they explicitly refer to any sense of ancient foreboding about gulls away from coastal locations. In fact, both artworks do not so much revisit these older layers of perception; instead they reflect the new meanings that gulls had acquired in the twentieth century. In that period the birds' ecology shifted radically in many parts of the Western world. One key change was in their population size. Almost everywhere gulls increased in numbers, partly because the harvest of their eggs, which had been practised for millennia, was discontinued as the birds were given protection or the wild-gathered protein was no longer deemed necessary or appealing. It was also because gulls found fresh feeding opportunities in the abundant leftovers of consumer society. What both versions of *The Birds* really drew upon to give a veneer of credibility to their shared plot was the audiences' collective encounter with gulls as the major new scavengers upon modern urban life.

This process of inland invasion continues even now. It is manifest in the gulls' ever-expanding roof-nesting habits; in their willingness to enter the most enclosed urban spaces, including people's balconies or back gardens, and even to enter buildings to steal food off supermarket shelves; in their capacity to perch comfortably on telegraph poles and, in the case of smaller gull species, to balance on the actual wires. 'And since when', asks one Mediterranean contributor, 'did Common Black-headed Gulls go all continental and eat olives? They are plucking them off the trees like it is what gulls have always done. They will be drinking Martinis next.'[11]

And if not quite cocktails, then at least gulls have acquired a taste for life's little luxuries, not to mention the signature dish of consumer society, junk fried food on a white polystyrene takeaway dish.

menace when, between them, they created the great gull fiction of the twentieth century. We know it as *The Birds*. Du Maurier's short story was published in 1952, while Hitchcock's film of the same name, loosely drawing on the novelist's tale, was shown in cinemas worldwide in 1963.

Gulls are absolutely to the fore in both works. Hitchcock's film opens with a shot of the San Francisco skyline and the words: 'Have you ever seen so many gulls? What do you suppose it is?' In the case of du Maurier's story, what, 'it is' eventually is a frenzied suicide attack by tens of thousands of gulls on Nat Hocken and his family in their small Cornish cottage. In Hitchcock's film the same murderous assault is transferred to the Brenner family and the other good citizens of Bodega Bay in northern California, after the Brenners are visited by a gift-bearing Californian socialite, Melanie Daniels (played by Tippi Hedren).

In both works gulls create some of the most memorable scenes and, although other species participate in the avian vendetta upon humankind, the sheer brute size and strength of the seabirds are constantly emphasised. In the novella Nat Hocken watches a Nazi-like gull rally involving so many birds offshore that before they make their mass attack they cover 'the bay like a white cloud, head to head, body packed to body'.[10] In the film gulls batten on young children at a birthday party, pecking their bare necks or prostrate bodies, and unleash terror attacks on Melanie Daniels while she is trapped in the birdcage-like claustrophobia of a telephone

On one sunny afternoon in the late 1990s I took my Mum and her friend on holiday. We were walking along the promenade and my Mum was eating an ice cream with a chocolate flake in it when, suddenly, she gave a small cry of surprise and then said 'My flake has gone!' We looked to see if she had accidentally knocked it on to the floor and in her handbag. Mum said that she thought she had seen a brief flash of white in front of her face, but neither I nor her friend had seen anything. It could have remained a mystery apart from a serendipitous event that occurred later that afternoon. I left my Mum in a tearoom, while I continued to walk the promenade. In the near distance a young couple was walking towards me. The man had a tray of fried chicken and chips and was eating and admiring the sea view, when suddenly I saw a Herring Gull fly down, at an angle and speed I had previously thought was only possible by birds of prey, and take the man's piece of chicken.

What happened next explained what had happened to my Mum's ice cream, as the man gave a start (but didn't realise why), looked down at the tray and exclaimed, 'My chicken's gone.' The couple proceeded to look around the ground to see if he had accidentally dropped it. It was incredible they had absolutely no idea what had just happened. I was astonished and didn't quite believe my eyes, but had anyone else witnessed what I had just seen? I turned to my right and saw that a stallholder had also observed the event but with considerably less astonishment than myself. 'Did you just see what that Herring Gull did?' I asked, 'Oh yes,' came back the resigned reply, 'They're a menace! And just look out there!' I followed his direction and saw a group of juvenile Herring Gulls sitting in a row on the roof of a shed opposite and evidently watching the whole proceedings. 'That's how they learn the technique,' he said. I went away amazed at the dexterity of this bird to steal food without the person concerned seeing what had happened. I hurried to the tearooms to tell them what I had discovered.[12]

Finally, it is intriguing to see how in the aftermath of *The Birds*, and even in the city where Hitchcock's film is partly set, his tale of horror has not quite dislodged our wider, older sense that gulls are beautiful. A San Franciscan reflects on the birds' most recent symbolism:

In this city gulls glide on scimitar wings, arcs of white high up over the wharfs and docks of the Bay. They also hang about inland, like the delinquent crows, scavenging fast-food detritus and roadkills. In their cheeky aggression they resemble the crows but their large size makes them a little more fearsome, a mixture of beauty and thuggishness. Gulls have a habit here of perching on top of street lights and dropping down to rise and fall amongst cars that are waiting at lights. It's a spectacular, almost angelic sight as they move in and around each other. Sometimes, as I sit in my car, they fly close enough that I can see the sun glow through individual feathers. In the bright light they are a dazzling white but their backs are the colour of the famous San Francisco fog. They seem very much a part of this place but there is also about them something universal.[13]

THE HARVEST OF GULL AND TERN EGGS

If the fictional gulls of *The Birds* had needed to spell out their motives for hatred of humankind, then our long history of exploitation might have served nicely. The harvest of gull and tern eggs was global, systematic, relentless and, in some cases, is ongoing. It was also ancient. (In fact our modern preoccupation with the seaside as a recreational space is probably rooted partly in its 100,000-year-old importance as the perfect hunter-gatherer habitat.)

Yet the taking of gull and tern eggs was sometimes managed like any other valuable, self-renewing agricultural resource. In the mid seventeenth century Sir Thomas Browne described how the eggs of Common Black-headed Gull were transported every spring to London from a breeding colony at Scoulton in Norfolk.[14] Almost 260 years later it was still being husbanded in this way, and between 1840 and 1919 Scoulton yielded an annual average of 9,236 eggs, with a grand total of 729,659 over the 80-year period.[15]

In Russia an old name for seabird nest colonies translates as 'bird bazaars'.[16] Unfortunately a perception of such resources as little more than cost-free department stores where customers simply helped themselves was not conducive to long-term sustainability. One such site, mainly of auks in Novaya Zemlya, was so severely abused it declined from 1.6 million to 290,000 birds in 21 years.[17] However, the most extreme examples involved the harvest of tern eggs.

The **Sooty Tern** *Sterna fuscata* is a large black-backed species, which is notable for a lack of proofing in its feathers that leaves the bird at risk of becoming waterlogged if it lands at sea. It compensates, however, for the deficiency by being able to fly without landing sometimes for months, even years, at a stretch. This oceanic wanderer breeds in the Seychelles Islands and other tropical paradises in the Indian and Pacific Oceans. In the former archipelago its massive breeding colonies were looted on a grand scale. In the 13-year period 1939–1951, the total egg count reaching the capital, Victoria, on Mahé was 15.6 million and that did not include a harvest of 120 tonnes of egg yolks processed during the same period. At one of the sites being systematically robbed, there were *c*.250,000 pairs of Sooty Terns in 1937. Yet this extraordinary colony was but a shadow of its former self. Just six years earlier there had been 5 million pairs at the site.[18]

When the old mariners first encountered these great protein bonanzas in the tropics they added insult to injury and labelled the birds whose eggs they took as fools for being so trusting. The name they coined – used as early as 1578 – was 'noddy', meaning an 'idiot' or 'simpleton'.[19] (We should recall that the word 'gull' itself carries associations of folly and reflects the way that those birds too were hapless victims of our thievery.) Later, the same term of abuse was officially reapplied to five other close relatives by ornithologists. To this day they are all known as noddies, including the **Brown Noddy** *Anous stolidus* whose scientific name translates roughly as 'silly dullard'.[20] Another old name that was used in similarly loose fashion served not only for Brown Noddy, but also for the Sooty Tern and another lookalike species called **Bridled Tern** *Sterna anaethetus* (the latter word itself means 'senseless'). To the Caribbean people who exploited them this trio was all of a piece. They were just 'egg birds'.

They were egg birds because, until the early twentieth century, the Jamaican fishermen harvested up to 600,000 eggs each breeding season. Between March and July it was once a common sight to see the girls offering 'booby' eggs for sale on the streets of Kingston ('booby' was another pejorative name for both Sooty and Bridled Terns, but has now come to signify a very different avian family; see page 144). Over the years the trade steadily declined in line with the birds themselves. In 1929 the take from important tern colonies in eastern Jamaica was 630,000. By the 1970s the harvest was 70,000 annually. Yet the collection of Sooty and Bridled Tern eggs has continued, albeit on a much smaller scale, partly because, mixed with wine, condensed milk and spices, they are drunk as a punch with aphrodisiacal powers.[21]

A nesting Gentoo Penguin responds to the marauding presence of a Subantarctic Skua.

Skua family *Stercorariidae*

These seven, dark, gull-sized, brutally powerful, if often elegant, seabirds are concentrated at the opposite ends of the Earth. Three species nest around the Antarctic continent or on the subantarctic islands across the Southern Ocean, and the four others breed in high northern latitudes. However, if their nesting places are largely polar in range, the birds themselves, especially the northern quartet – **Great Skua** *Stercorarius skua*, **Pomarine Skua** *Stercorarius pomarinus*, **Parasitic Jaeger** (**Arctic Skua**) *Stercorarius parasiticus* and **Long-tailed Jaeger** *Stercorarius longicaudus* – are extraordinary world wanderers. There is barely a shoreline on Earth that is not graced seasonally by these wonderful birds. Equally the skuas can turn up almost anywhere on the open sea.

Their anglicised names are rather complicated. The word 'skua' comes from the Faroes, the Danish archipelago between Iceland and northernmost Scotland (*Skúir* was the original Faroese for the Great Skua and one of the smaller islands is still called *Skúvoy*, meaning 'skua island').[1] This name was transmitted into wider usage during the seventeenth century and while the British still use 'skua' for all seven species, North Americans adopted the name 'jaeger', a word of German or Dutch origin (the latter spell it *jager*) for several of the smaller northern species. Jaeger means 'hunter' and is deeply apt for all the family.

On the Faroes another local word for skua is *kjóvgi*, meaning 'thief'. This too could not be more appropriate. One of their main feeding strategies is known technically as kleptoparasitism, but most people would know it better as robbery with menace. The birds are often likened to the ultimate thieves of the sea, pirates or buccaneers. They are specialists in harrying other seabirds, sometimes staying in hot pursuit for several minutes, until their victims disgorge their fish catch to lighten their escape. As soon as the food is dropped, the chasing skua spirals down to snatch it off the water.

A good pair of binoculars would probably have enabled our ancestors to see this chase scenario a little more clearly. Unfortunately to their eyes it seemed as if the skuas were taking not what came out the victim's mouth, but what was ejected from the cloaca. An old English name for some of the skuas was 'dung bird' or 'dirt bird', while in Spanish they were known as *estercorario* or *cágalo* (*estercolar* means 'to manure', *cagada* means 'shit').[2] Most ornithologists are probably unaware that these scatalogical associations are still embedded in modern nomenclature. *Stercorarius* derives from *stercus*, the Latin for dung.

If skuas are not often copraphagous, they are, nevertheless, frequent scavengers. In the Antarctic they will gobble up afterbirth and stillborn carcasses of Weddell and Crabeater Seal pups. Skuas were also perpetual attendees at the old whaling and seal-processing stations scattered across the Southern Ocean. Occasionally this refuse-disposal work was put in the service of science. 'I learned how useful I could make [**Subantarctic Skua** *Stercorarius antarcticus*],' wrote the ornithologist Robert Cushman Murphy of his time on South Georgia, 'in cleaning the fat from the inside of penguin skins.'

> The skuas would pick off the blubber as cleanly as it could have been done with a scraper, and in much less time . . . On one occasion I had 35 skuas ready to work, each attempting to perform on my behalf this fundamental and arduous taxidermic process.[3]

Rather as in *Paradise Lost*, where, despite Milton's moral intentions, Satan somehow emerges as his poem's most compelling figure, so skuas tend to captivate us through sheer devilment. Murphy added a passage on his penguin-cleaning birds that describes many of our feelings about this family's magnificent meanness:

> In spite of their voracity, rapine, and cannibalism, the skuas quickly make themselves the beneficiaries of a peculiar, sentimental, anthropomorphic interest. When they crowd around you, and look up with bright, fearless, unsuspicious, brown eyes, accept the bounty you offer them, and show no more concern over the loudest shouts, whistles, or handclaps than if they were stone-deaf, you succumb to their charm, and subscribe to the principle that their supremacy of might must be deserved.[4]

Skuas are much more than scavengers and thieves. The bigger species, such as the Great Skua or **South Polar Skua** *Stercorarius maccormicki*, are major predators, routinely killing lambs and birds far bigger than themselves. They can swallow whole eggs as large as those of the White-chinned Petrel, a morsel measuring 8.3 x 5.3 cm (3.3 x 2 in). It has also been proven that skuas function like cattle ranchers, or, as one contributor puts it:

> Southern skua pairs 'own' penguin rookeries, a bit like mafia dons 'own' sections of cities. And they don't like outsiders muscling in on their patch. Naive young skuas often learn this the hard way. At Danco on the Antarctic Peninsula, I watched a juvenile South Polar Skua land next to a Gentoo Penguin colony and start to scan for absent-minded penguin parents. The rookery's Subantarctic Skua owners were unimpressed. The pair flew in quickly and launched a vicious attack on the young pretender. For several minutes the juvenile flailed and yelped as the adults took it in turns to stab and grapple before liberating the interloper to beat a retreat.[5]

Skua pairs can police territories that incorporate between 90 and 2,011 penguin nests. When the territory-holding birds are not defending their patch from other skuas, gulls or sheathbills (see also Sheathbill family, page 196) they will harvest their own penguin 'wards', either to eat themselves or to feed to their offspring.[6]

All seven skuas are notorious for the vehemence with which they protect their young from almost any intruder, as this account from the Falkland Islands makes plain.

> It means a merry Christmas for any human being or dog who dares to approach anywhere in their vicinity, either for business or for pleasure; if the latter, it is mostly on the skuas' side. Gathering sheep for shearing in a [skua]-infested area is no joke.
>
> These birds are always labouring under the delusion . . . that all men and dogs seen are after their little ones. This makes them croak with rage and sail at top speed straight for the head of the unfortunate dog or man – which they miss by inches as a rule, but occasionally hit. If they hit, it is worse than unpleasant, for they are exceptionally strong on the wing and are capable of making one see stars by daylight with their terrific biffs on the back of one's head.

> Men have been knocked down by them and dogs so terrified that they take refuge from them under the friendly lee of the horse's heels . . . At times the air is so full of these birds that the only way to progress at all is to lash a sheath-knife to a stick and hold it above one's head. There is no second innings for the skua that strikes the knife.[7]

At one time this predatory relationship was turned on its head. In some areas the birds were kept tethered and fattened for the pot. The old name for the Subantarctic Skua – 'sea hen' – reflects this former consumption.

In flight Arctic Skuas combine the aerial grace of a tern with the predatory menace of a hawk.

The Least Auklet of the northern Pacific is the smallest of its family and not much bigger than a sparrow.

Auk family *Alcidae*

These seabirds breed exclusively in the northern hemisphere, where they subsist on a diet of small fish, plankton, jellyfish or crustacea, and occupy much the same ecological niche as the penguins of the southern oceans. A fundamental difference between these two unrelated families is that the auks have retained their powers of flight. There are 23 species clustered mainly in a broad belt round the Arctic, with just six family members found in Atlantic waters and 19 breeding on either the North American or Asian shores of the Pacific Ocean. In fact, more than two-thirds of all auks (16 species) occur nowhere else, with the greatest diversity centred on the Aleutian Islands, the US-controlled archipelago which, together with the Komandorskiye (Commander) Islands of Russia, arc between southern Alaska and Siberia's Kamchatka Peninsula.

This drawing of a Great Auk is the only known image that was taken from a live bird. It was a pet, complete with its little 'dog' collar, belonging to the seventeenth-century Danish collector Ole Worm.

The auks' ability to fly has meant that none has acquired the size and weight achieved by penguins. In fact the smallest, the appropriately named **Least Auklet** *Aethia pusilla* of the northern Pacific region, is barely bigger than a sparrow and weighs 85 g (3 oz). Even the world's heaviest auks are only about 1 kg (2.2 lb) and are relative featherweights compared with an Emperor Penguin, which can tip the scales at 40 kg (88 lb).

Yet there was once an auk that stood as tall as most penguins, which dwarfed all its relatives – it was said to be 'hardly less than a tame goose' – and which possesses still a name that seems in keeping with its tragic story.[1] It was the **Great Auk** *Pinguinis impennis*. The remorseless slaughter of this seabird is one of those heartbreaking yet rather commonplace examples of how humanity has boiled down to nothing but salt the teeming life of the world's oceans. Of Great Auks there were once millions; now there is none. Many were converted to oil, but the birds' own oily bodies were also fed directly into the flames that rendered down the rest of their species. Before its demise in the mid nineteenth century it was this singular creature that gave us the word 'penguin', which is retained still in the bird's scientific

The extraordinary
facial characteristics
of the Atlantic Puffin
somehow manage to
convey sadness and
humour all at once.

name. European mariners of the sixteenth and seventeenth centuries, who harvested the benign and flightless birds, had originally christened it 'the penguin'. They then carried the name with them and reused it when they met other ocean-going birds of similar appearance in the southern hemisphere (see also page 95).

Today the Great Auk's largest relatives are three species, the Atlantic-dwelling **Razorbill** *Alca torda* and two close cousins with extensive ranges across both the northern Pacific and Atlantic Oceans. They are the **Common Murre** (**Common Guillemot**) *Uria aalge* and the **Thick-billed Murre** (**Brünnich's Guillemot**) *Uria lomvia*. The English name 'murre', a word pronounced to rhyme with 'fur', is of obscure derivation, but is probably onomatopoeic; 'murr' is an archaic dialect verb meaning to make a harsh sound.[2] Ironically, while murre may have been the birds' original name it was eventually abandoned in Britain in favour of 'guillemot', but murre was successfully transplanted in the New World. I have given both names to avoid confusion.

A characteristic that auks share with penguins is an apparent gift for humour. One perpetual source of comedy is the fact that auks have their legs set far back on their bodies for underwater propulsion. Yet when they come to land they walk in a somewhat awkward, upright manner which, if not suggestive of our own gait, does evoke a kind of hominid form, like a gnome or dwarf. An old Scottish name for the **Atlantic Puffin** *Fratercula arctica* was *tommie-* or *tammie-norie* meaning 'literally a roundish little chap'.[3] The birds also possess a mix of colours – black, grey and white – that is reminiscent of formal male Western costume. Small, waddling and besuited, auks can even sound a bit like people.

The exemplar is the Atlantic Puffin, whose vocalisations include a rather self-satisfied and very human sigh. One ornithologist noted how the 'note of the puffin is very peculiar – sepulchrally deep, and full of the deepest feeling.

Another note is more commonly heard . . . a long deep slowly rising *Awe* uttered in something of a tone of solemn expostulation, as though the bird were in the pulpit.'[4] It seems more than coincidence that in the Danish-speaking Faroe Islands, where Atlantic Puffins are abundant, they are known by a humorous nickname, *Prestur*; 'priest'.[5]

If this bird family has regularly amused, it can also impress. In a curious way, it is our tendency to anthropomorphise auks that emphasises, by contrast, the otherness which they encompass. They may be awkward on land, but when they enter the sea they are transformed into creatures of consummate grace and speed. Auks use their stiff, narrow wings to propel themselves and literally fly underwater. They have been recorded to make 20 consecutive dives with less than a minute at the surface before the next descent. While most of these sub-aquatic forays reach no more than 60 m (197 ft), some of them can last three minutes and have been recorded to depths of 210 m (690 ft).

When away from their breeding grounds, auks persist for months on the open sea in conditions of relative isolation. It is our intermittent ability to intersect the individual life of an auk that helps us to appreciate its essential mystery. From time to time the encounters also allow us to calculate an auk's remarkable longevity. One Atlantic Puffin, for instance, was ringed on the Outer Hebrides in Scotland on 28 June 1975, and on 10 July 2009 the same bird was caught again. It was 34 years old and one of those people who retrapped it was the very person who first placed the ring round its leg. Less conclusive but even more suggestive is the testimony from two generations of Faroese bird hunters, who reported an albino Atlantic Puffin that was 60 years old.[6]

AUKS AS PHYSICAL LANDSCAPE AND AS CULTURAL BEDROCK

There is another dimension to this bird family that is also immensely impressive. In the places where auks breed, they can be present in such numbers that they seem not just part of the surroundings, but a landscape unto themselves. Sea cliffs are locations of inherent drama and of immense conflicting natural forces; the relentlessness of the sea waves matched only by the millennial stubbornness of the rock. These sites are sometimes tourist attractions with mass appeal. Auks can smother the tiered cliffs in their tens and sometimes hundreds of thousands and these gatherings have a rather wonderful technical name, a 'loomery', a word originating with the old Norse for one of the most abundant species, the Common Murre (Common Guillemot). This bird is known even today as *Lomvie* in Danish and Norwegian, or *Lanvía* in Icelandic.

The most northerly of all family members, the **Little Auk** *Alle alle* has loomeries on the cliffs of Greenland's east coast that were once calculated to hold 5 million birds.[7] In the Thule district of western Greenland there are several colonies of more than a million pairs and 10 million in aggregate. In summer the flocks are so large that 'when they take flight they actually darken the sky'.[8]

Each Little Auk stands no taller than a Common Starling and weighs 160 g (5.6 oz), yet as it breeds, so it traffics to the mainland a fraction of the vast life-soup teeming in the Arctic waters. Through the cumulative deposition of their red-coloured excreta and through the flesh of their own bodies, the birds conjure a terrestrial ecosystem where none otherwise would exist. This central part in Arctic life was noted by an eyewitness of the early twentieth century:

> Its vast colonies on these north-west Greenland shores . . . play an important part in the ecology and human economy of the region. They furnish the food for the many foxes . . . without these birds the foxes would be so few that the natives could not secure adequate clothing, and these 'Arctic Highlanders' could not have persisted here as the most northern people of the world. No trading would have been established by the Danes; one of the chief incentives to some of Peary's and other expeditions of the coast would have been missing. The grass slopes about the rookeries, the luxuriant herbage being due to their dung, support the largest numbers of hare and ptarmigan, and probably afforded the richest pastures for the Caribou before the introduction of firearms effected their extermination from some of the areas along the coast.[9]

The passage underscores how the birds are at the core of a great living arc running through the region's history, which rises upwards from the seabed to the land – from the simple phytoplanktonic organisms to the terrestrial birds and beasts, and on eventually as the subsistence bedrock for the local Inuit and their entire cultural world.

One exceptional cultural service into which Little Auks are still pressed in Greenland is known as *kiviaq*. One contributor describes her less-than-enthusiastic excursion into the pleasures of this particular delicacy: 'Have you ever eaten an extremely strong cheese that somehow combines the essence of liquorice with the consistency of wet rubber? And would you ever want to?'

> Over the course of several visits to Greenland my adopted Inuit family showed me how they create *kiviaq*. In spring they catch and stuff up to 500 Little Auks into a bag made from sealskin and blubber. The bulging furry bag is then buried underground and left to rot for many months. When it was time to dig up this stinky spread, which gave me a sinking feeling in my belly, the whole family gathered amid an air of excitement. The stench of *kiviaq* is so strong that the meal is served outdoors. I watched with strange anticipation as the seal bag was laid on the ground and soggy, fully feathered birds were pulled from within. First it was given to the elders of the family, then to the small kids who were grabbing at it with glee. A lady called Tuko easily dismembered a slimy leg between her thumb and index finger and pointed it in my direction. I tried to accept the bird but I couldn't. Tuko jabs her rotted-bird-covered finger closer to my mouth, but again and again I shied away. Finally I closed my eyes and swallowed the tiny bit of meat. It tasted as bad as it smelled and, try as I might, I couldn't help but grimace. When I opened my eyes again I looked around and something much bigger than the taste hit me – it was a feeling of appreciation, both for the birds and for the ingenuity of the people. For centuries Inuit families in this area have relied on the annual migration of millions of seabirds. Their feathers have been used for children's clothing and the clever preservation of their meat has helped generations of families to survive the lean Arctic winters.[10]

It is not too far-fetched to suggest that at one time, if not now, the birds and the people were intrinsically part of the same system, separate only as different stages in a single upwelling of life. Barry Lopez, author of *Arctic Dreams* and witness to the autumn passage of 10 million Greenland-breeding Little Auks through Lancaster Sound, pays homage to their flowing riverine potency. 'The outcry of birds', he writes, 'the bullet-whirr of their passing wings, the splashing of water, is, like the falling light, unending.'[11]

It is hardly surprising that people have often used auks to define their geography and orient themselves in the landscape. There are many specific localities whose names originate with auks. In Iceland there are several places called Lundey, while in southern England there is an offshore pinprick, Lundy. Christened by Norse mariners, they translate as 'puffin island'. In Canada the early geographers were equally direct in their place naming. On the east shore of Newfoundland is a site known as Funk Island. At one time, however, it was 'Penguin Island', and, earlier still, just the 'Isle of Birds'. (In Iceland and the Danish-speaking Faroe Islands there are small islets – respectively Fuglasker and Fugloy – whose names mean 'Bird Island' for much the same reason.) All these titles were a straight reference to the auks and other edible seabirds that were, or are still, present there. The rather odd 'Funk' appears to have no avian connection, but even that word, an archaic English expression meaning 'to blow smoke' or 'create a foul smell', referred to the ammoniacal stench produced by the hundreds of thousands of fish-eating residents.

The early mariners sailing from Europe to the New World alerted their fellow travellers to the presence of these same birds: 'Know that when you approach close to land, about 100 leagues,' wrote one sailor in 1579, 'you will find large black birds that are not able to fly.'[12]

EXPLOITATION OF AUKS

Great Auks were a navigational aid during an uncertain passage across the Atlantic, but for many European sailors they were also the essential provisions that ensured their survival. This taking of birds on Funk was no innovation. Humans had eaten auks and their eggs for millennia. In fact, there is an extraordinary image in the Cosquer Cave near Marseille, France, that is now accessible only from under the sea (its entrance was flooded by the sea-level rise at the end of the last ice age). This charcoal outline depicts a flipper-winged bulbous bird that looks strikingly like a Great Auk. It has been carbon-dated to at least 16,000 BC, when the northern Mediterranean was presumably part of the Great Auks' winter range, and when the bird, in turn, was part of the Palaeolithic diet. This remarkable cave painting is a strong candidate for the oldest bird image of a recognisable species on Earth.[13]

The family in general has often been hunted using techniques that take full advantage of the birds' somewhat guileless characters. However, few strategies can have been as basic or have shown as little regard for the future as those deployed on Funk Island. Some mariners bragged that they herded the flightless Great Auks down the gangplank into the waiting boat. If this is rather unlikely, the following excerpt from 1534 by the French explorer Jacques Cartier stresses what easy victims they were: 'In less than halfe an houre we filled two boats full of them, as if they have bene stones, so that besides them which we did eat fresh, every ship did powder and salt five or sixe barrels full of them.'[14]

During the early period of exploitation there may have been 200,000 Great Auks breeding on Funk and to mariners they looked inexhaustible. So, over the course of the next three centuries everyone operated on much the same lines, latterly in order to process the birds for their feathers to fill pillows and mattresses. There were, however, dire warnings for the species' future as early as 1785, when a trapper called Captain George Cartwright predicted that, 'If a stop is not soon put to that practice the whole breed will be diminished to almost nothing.'[15]

There was even legislation to control the harvest, but it offered little break from the killing. By the 1820s the Great Auk was gone from Funk, although the event usually recognised as the *coup de grâce* for the entire species is sited elsewhere. In June 1844 a party of 14 fowlers sailed out to Eldey, a small isle off southern Iceland, where a surviving remnant of the birds had persisted. There the fowlers found and strangled two Great Auks to death. They were eventually recognised as the last historically verified examples.[16]

What had almost certainly doomed the Great Auks on Funk Island was the absence of a local human community that could stake proprietorial rights over the breeding colonies. The nearest human settlements had been those of the Beothuk people, who had once sailed out from Newfoundland, risking the 56 km (35 miles) of treacherous open seas in their birch-bark canoes for the seasonal bounties of eggs and flesh. Such expeditions had probably been made for millennia. Nearby there are burial chambers created by the Beothuk's ancestors that date back 3,000–4,000 years. In one of these there was a single body covered with 200 Great Auk beaks.[17]

In many ways the fate of the Great Auk reflected a wider pattern of exhaustive exploitation of the whole family along

North American shorelines. Seabird eggs were especially desirable. In 1833 John James Audubon described how four men from Halifax in Nova Scotia took 40,000 auk eggs in a single spring, selling them in their home town and other local ports for 25 cents a dozen. 'In less than half a century,' he predicted, 'these wonderful nurseries will be entirely destroyed unless some kind government will interfere.'[18] It was deeply prescient. In 2009 a nesting Common Guillemot was discovered on an island off the coast of Maine. It involved the first egg laid by this species on the USA's Atlantic coast since 1883.

NORTHERN PEOPLE AND AUKS

All Inuit communities living in proximity to breeding colonies have valued auks both as sources of food and of insulating feathers for their clothing. The inhabitants of the Pribilof and Aleutian Islands in the north Pacific used the skins of **Horned Puffin** *Fratercula corniculata* and **Tufted Puffin** *Fratercula cirrhata* to make their famous parka coats. The birds were sewn together with the skins facing outwards and the feathers forming the coat's inner lining, with as many as 45 being used on a single man's garment. Aleutian women would gather with their neighbours to drink tea and gossip, while pulling a puffin skin from the folds of their coats. An eyewitness to these proceedings described how they would

The island inhabitants of the northern Pacific once used the skins of Tufted Puffins to insulate their famous parka coats.

This nineteenth-century painted apron of the Haida or Tsimshian peoples of the Pacific Northwest is a perfect expression of their hugely distinctive art (see also The Wise Crow, page 393). While the central design features a beaver, there are about 45 puffin bills sown into its fringed hem.

then chew the flesh of these dead birds to prepare them for use, as complacently 'as our country dames will draw out [their] knitting . . . to wile away the time'.[19]

The yellow crest plumes of the Tufted Puffins added a touch of decorative colour to Inuit parkas, while on mainland Alaska the fabulous multicoloured beaks were sewn on to huge sealskin mittens that were worn during ritual dances.[20] A simple percussive musical instrument was also made by the Inuit of the northern Pacific using 30–50 puffin mandibles tied by sinew on to a circular tambourine-like frame.[21]

One striking method of catching auks eventually diffused around almost the entire Arctic crown of the Earth and is still used even today by biologists wishing to catch live auks for study purposes. The implement is often referred to by its Faroese name, the *fleyg*, and is used today not only in that archipelago, but on Iceland, Greenland, Arctic Canada and the Aleutian Islands. It resembles a small bag-net fitted on to a pole that can be as much as 4 m (13 ft) long (and known as the *fleygastong*). The classic victims were the three puffin species, which nest in burrows on grassy clifftops. Two other methods for extracting the fat-filled downy chicks from these warrens included the use of a hooked gaff, rather like a shepherd's crook, with which the bird was winkled out like a grub (Faroe Islands), and the employment of *lundehund*, a small long-bodied fowling dog (northern Norway), of which a bird hunter might once have owned up to 16 for this specialised activity.[22]

However, the technique involving the highest skill is the *fleyg*. The art lies in raising the pole at the last minute, as the bird comes closest to the fowler's location, and positioning the net exactly in line with the bird's flight trajectory, so that it has no time to adjust and becomes caught in the mesh. Then the pole is lowered, the bird is extracted and its neck instantly broken.

In the Faroe Islands the catching of Atlantic Puffins was once a mainstay of the local economy, a social ritual and a regional sport all in one. The fowlers would set off for the

fuglabørg ('bird-mountains') and wait on the clifftops at traditional catching places where, in the mid twentieth century, they were thought to take as many as 500,000 birds throughout the whole archipelago. A decent average for a single catcher was 200–300 birds a day but if all the conditions were perfect then he might take 900.

Most of the birds were salted down for the winter with 200 deemed a suitable store for a family of five, while two birds were deemed sufficient for a man's dinner. The British ornithologist Kenneth Williamson, who married a Faroese woman and lived on the islands for several years, thought puffin 'delicious meat – rich and tender, and very tasty'. Yet he also noted that his birds were served 'Danish fashion', which involved a more refined dressing of the carcass and removal of its various striking 'appurtenances'. Native Faroese, however, enjoyed their puffins with the skin, the orange feet and that striking parrot's beak all intact. 'All is devoured with gusto,' he added, 'save the larger bones.'[23]

The harvesting of Atlantic Puffins now survives only in Iceland where it has been a traditional part of the country's cultural life for centuries. However, in recent years both the attitudes and activities centred on the puffin catch have shifted in the wake of major breeding failures. In the late 1990s the average annual Atlantic Puffin harvest throughout Iceland was estimated at 183,816 birds.[24] Today the catch is 15,000 and some experts believe even this is too high. The picture in one of the major strongholds of seabird catching, the Westman Islands off the country's south coast, is even more dramatic. Puffin breeding success in this archipelago has fallen virtually to nil so that local people have reduced the hunting season from 45 days (2007), to 20 days (2008), five days (2009) and finally banned it altogether (2011). The cause of breeding failure is as yet unknown. The main hypotheses centre on the interference in the birds' food supply, possibly because of sea-temperature rises, and, while hunting could become a drain on the puffin population, it is not considered the main threat.[25]

However, in Greenland, home to one of the last hunter-gatherer economies on Earth, human error and excess slaughter by local people is thought to lie behind a massive collapse in auk numbers. A combination of over-generous open seasons on the country's loomeries of Thick-billed Murres (Brünnich's Guillemots), illegal killing and the annual drowning of an estimated 200,000–500,000 birds in salmon nets along the east coast has triggered a decline that is little short of catastrophic.

One of the sources of the problem is the demographic shift among the Greenland people. The population quadrupled in the twentieth century to 49,369, and of these more than one-fifth (10,663) are either professional or leisure hunters. Between them they have access to 1,469 motorboats, compared to 288 in 1949.[26] The net effect of these changes is a massive increase in their off-take of native fauna. Whole colonies of Thick-billed Murres (Brünnich's Guillemots) on the country's east coast have been decimated. On sea cliffs where there were once 500,000 birds there are now a few thousand.[27]

The Danish journalist Kjeld Hansen suggests that one of the major issues is not just a false understanding of the birds' ability to withstand these harvest levels. Much more damaging is the very myth of this hunter-gatherer community, at one with nature and in balance with its environmental resources, which somehow stops outside agencies and environmentalists recognising or responding more forcefully to the bitter truth of over-exploitation. 'We seem to want to keep this dream', Hansen argues, 'of an unspoilt Greenland alive in our hearts.'

> The man in a kayak with raised harpoon, the camouflaged hunter inching across the ice, the woman flensing a seal on the beach holding the traditional *ulo* – we all have our image of a Greenland Inuk in our minds' eye. Yet we continue to cling to these traditional images

of Greenlanders despite the advent of Yamaha engines, fibre-glass dinghies, Remington rifles, snow-scooters, GPS navigators, helicopters and Tenson clothing.[28]

The truth is that the native fowler can modernise, and he can abandon the ethic of sustainability and replace it with an aggressive market-driven appetite for profit. He can, in short, destroy bird populations as easily as he substitutes the *fleyg* and the skin-lined kayak for the automatic rifle and the speedboat.

Sandgrouse family *Pteroclididae*

Sandgrouse are pigeon-sized birds of Old World desert and semi-desert, and are absent from the Americas and Australia (although deliberate introductions to both regions have been attempted). They occur widely across the Middle East and Asia, including the high-altitude steppes of Mongolia (**Pallas's Sandgrouse** *Syrrhaptes paradoxus*) and Tibet (**Tibetan Sandgrouse** *Syrrhaptes tibetanus*), but the family's heartland is Africa. Thirteen of the world's 16 species occur, where they show a strong bias towards the Sahara and Kalahari Deserts. Despite the name, sandgrouse have no affinity with real grouse, but are probably most closely related to pigeons or waders. Yet convergent evolution has conferred on them some of the characteristics of gamebirds, such as a ground-dwelling lifestyle, a largely seed diet, densely feathered legs and a plumage range that centres on shades of brown.

This might suggest that they are dull-looking, but their

basic colour is overlaid by exquisitely cryptic barred or vermiculated patterns. In addition, areas of warm orange or yellow, frequently arranged in successive bands, intergrade with shades of blue-grey and are then often edged with white or black. The total effect is a deeply harmonious union of function (camouflage) and aesthetics. In sandgrouse there seems a perfect adjustment of beauty to the exactions of an arid landscape and, although there is barely a primary colour among them, they have a good claim to be one of the most uniformly attractive bird families on Earth. Every single species is beautiful.

A secondary element in the appeal of sandgrouse is their voice. They have loud, bubbling, even chuckling and explosive notes that serve as an adhesive for flocks in flight. They are, in fact, wonderful fliers with a direct, swift, rhythmic action (the generic name, *Pterocles*, actually means 'notable' or 'splendid winged').[1] One necessity of their desert

SAND GROUSE.

The mass irruptive wanderings of Pallas's Sandgrouse across Europe in the nineteenth and early twentieth centuries were as mysterious in purpose as they were dramatic in impact.

lifestyle is to drink regularly and this can involve sandgrouse in daily round trips of 160 km (100 miles) to traditional waterholes. These journeys, completed at about 70 kph (43 mph), are invariably the first chore of every morning and as the birds near the precious source they accumulate. Flocks of several hundred are commonplace. Occasionally they gather in thousands and in Mali, at Lake Kabara about 100 km (62 miles) south-west of Timbuktu, regular congregations of 50,000 **Chestnut-bellied Sandgrouse** *Pterocles exustus* have been recorded.[2]

In the stillness of the desert morning the calls of the birds are far-carrying. Invariably one hears them rippling out of the pastel-toned horizon long before the sandgrouse themselves come into view. It is hardly surprising that several of them have onomatopoeic names. The **Pin-tailed Sandgrouse** *Pterocles alchata*, one of two species to breed regularly in western Europe (the other is **Black-bellied Sandgrouse** *Pterocles orientalis*), is confined in that region to the grass steppe of Iberia with a small outpost in southern France. There the bird is called *Ganga cata*. More than 6,000 km away (3,700 miles), in the Pakistani province of Balochistan, the same bird is known as *kătău*. Both *cata* and *kătău* are close approximations to the bird's rather grumpy flight notes and the link between the two is almost certainly the Arabic language, whose speakers once occupied all the intervening territories. Their word for sandgrouse is *Qataa* and it is echoed even in this bird's scientific name: *alchata*.[3]

Even more accurate are the Asian names for the **Spotted Sandgrouse** *Pterocles senegallus*, which occurs right across the Saharo-Sindian region from Africa's Atlantic shore to the Pakistan–Indian frontier. In the Sind dialect it is called *gūtū*, and in the Rann of Kutch it is known as *wăku*. The latter name is an almost exact rendering of this bird's flight call. The British ornithologist Claud Ticehurst found an image that was perfectly apposite for the bird's geographical territory as well as its human landscapes when he suggested that, in the distance and in chorus, the sounds of these glorious birds reminded him of a hookah or hubble-bubble pipe, as the gloops of smoke were being drawn down through the water.[4]

Several species of sandgrouse – including the **Four-banded Sandgrouse** *Pterocles quadricinctus* (Sahelian Africa), **Lichtenstein's Sandgrouse** *Pterocles lichtensteinii* (north Africa and the Middle East) and **Painted Sandgrouse** *Pterocles indicus* (India) – buck the family's trend of drinking shortly after dawn. These others come to water at dusk or once night has fallen. They are otherwise remarkably tolerant of intense heat and can persist, barely moving for hours, even in direct sunlight at temperatures of 50 °C (122 °F).[5] Very often the only way to see these species is when they come to their water source at sunset. Birdwatchers love to gather and watch them arrive (Eilat in southern Israel holds one such site). Waiting there in the semi-darkness as the birds fly in from some unknown daytime haunt, despite seeing little more than dark silhouettes plumping down through dusk's orange afterglow, is an immensely moving experience. One has a deep sense of being witness to something mysterious and solemn, like an ancient rite.

Humans have long exploited the unavoidable quest for water in the sandgrouse's daily routine and, indeed, like many other predators, have waited to catch them as they drink. The birds are cherished targets for Arabic falconers and they were also caught in nets or snares to supply local Asian markets. The nets stood almost 2 m (6.6 ft) high and were held erect by sticks, but the whole thing was intended to collapse once hit by the flying birds, so that they became quickly entangled in the mesh. The flesh, which includes brown and white meat, is of mixed reputation, although the Black-bellied Sandgrouse has some devotees, with one old critic calling it 'the finest game-bird for the table in India'.[6]

For the colonial British, sandgrouse also became a prominent source of sport. The density of their flocks means that a single shot can bring down as many as a dozen birds. However, they are not easy targets. The eminent ornithologist Allan Octavian Hume once wrote: 'It takes a straight eye, No. 3 shot, and a hard-hitting gun to bring down a clean-killed right and left out of a party going over you, 30 to 35 yards high, at the pace these birds can go.'[7]

Some of the most developed practices were as sophisticated as they were wasteful. A single day's slaughter during these so-called 'prestige shoots' in the early part of the twentieth century could account for 2,000 sandgrouse. With barely concealed contempt, the great scholars of Indian ornithology Salim Ali and Dillon Ripley detailed methods used to ensure a record bag of 5,963 sandgrouse at a watering hole called Gajner close to the Rajasthani city of Bikaner. This total was brought down in just two mornings, but the preparations stretched over a much longer period and involved the sandgrouse being denied access to water at pools all around the intended killing zone. On the allotted morning, the hunters even prevented the sandgrouse using this single source that had been open to them hitherto and the birds' extreme thirst fuelled, what Ali and Ripley called with bitter irony, the 'fine sport'.[8]

Ali and Ripley give no specific dates for this shoot ('in 1919 or thereabouts') and Hugh Gladstone in *Record Bags and Shooting Records* (1922) passes on the achievements of another 48-hour period in 1922, when the Maharajah of Bikaner and his guest Lord Rawlinson, together with their party, killed 6,113 head of game, mainly Black-bellied Sandgrouse. The maharajah's son, then only 18 years old, shot 558 sandgrouse on the second day alone. 'So I think you will all agree with me', wrote the *Field* correspondent, 'that his performance is a very fine one.'[9]

Even today the birds are highly prized targets and they have given rise to a lucrative business in southern Africa. However over-hunting by local and overseas sportsmen has led to international conservation agreements between Botswanan, Namibian and South African parties to protect three endemic species – **Namaqua Sandgrouse** *Pterocles namaqua*, **Burchell's Sandgrouse** *Pterocles burchelli* and **Double-banded Sandgrouse** *Pterocles bicinctus*.[10]

One intriguing outcome of a wider passion for sandgrouse hunting was an attempt to introduce them into Australia in the late nineteenth century.[11] This failed almost immediately but subsequent efforts in the USA were more successful. The sites selected were Nevada and Hawaii; while the former state possesses the desert landscapes that sandgrouse might have been assumed to favour, a tropical archipelago in the mid Pacific was a more unlikely choice. In the event, however, it is the Hawaiian birds that have persisted. The Nevadan initiative, involving a release of 2,030 Chestnut-bellied Sandgrouse from 1959–61, as well as an experimental release of Black-bellied Sandgrouse, very quickly came to grief. By 1962 hardly a single bird could be found and the project was discontinued.[12]

On the Pacific islands an initial batch of 378 Chestnut-bellied Sandgrouse from India was liberated on Molokai (137 birds), Kauai (118) and Hawaii itself (123), followed by a further 370 birds exclusively on the latter in the following year (1962).[13] This last population has survived for half a century, mainly in the north, and the project has even reached its intended outcome, with a sandgrouse season between November and January, and a bag limit of ten birds per person.

One of the earliest descriptions of a sandgrouse in Western literature is Marco Polo's reference in *Il milione* (*The Travels*, c.1299). On his way to the court of Kublai Khan, the thirteenth-century Venetian came upon a creature he called *bargherlac*. The bird was said to be a frequent victim of the large Asian falcons and to be the size of a partridge, with parrot's feet and the tail of a swallow.[14] These peculiarities converge in the one sandgrouse that is, in some ways, the most extraordinary member of the family. We know it today as Pallas's Sandgrouse (named after the intrepid German explorer and naturalist Peter Pallas, 1741–1811) and it occurs in innermost Asia, roughly from the Aral Sea in Kazakhstan eastwards across Mongolia and Russian Siberia. (An attempt to introduce them into Washington state, USA, in 1928 was a failure.)[15]

The most striking physical aspect of the bird, aside from its fine thread-like tail, is probably those parrot's feet. The whole of the legs to the toes are densely feathered and this broadens the feet so that they function almost like snowshoes. The nineteenth-century French traveller Abbé Évariste-Régis Huc was captivated by this when he wrote his *Travels in Tartary, Thibet and China, 1844–1846*. Even in his own day he was one of the few Europeans ever to have seen Pallas's Sandgrouse, and he described it in a tone of wonderment mingled with a dash of the sensational:

its legs, instead of feathers, are covered with a sort of long, rough hair, like that of the musk-deer; its feet

are totally different from those of any other bird; they exactly resemble the paws of the green lizard, and are covered with scales so hard as to resist the edge of the sharpest knife. This singular creature, therefore, partakes at once of the bird, of the quadruped, and of the reptile. The Chinese call it *Loung-Kio* [*lung-chio*] 'Dragon's Foot'. These birds make their periodical appearance in vast numbers from the north, especially after a great fall of snow.[16]

It was, in fact, this last characteristic of the Dragon's Foot that has come to dominate the interests of modern ornithology. Their invasions encompassed not only Tartary and east into China as far as Beijing; rather like the Tartars themselves and the other horsebacked peoples of Asia, Pallas's Sandgrouse temporarily irrupted from their breeding range to spread widely across western Europe.

The trigger for their wider excursions across 5,300 km (3,300 miles) of otherwise alien countryside is little understood even today. However, the largest arrivals occurred in 1863 and 1888, with lesser incursions in 1872, 1876 and 1908. The most impressive of all, involving thousands of birds, was in the spring and summer of 1888, when the sandgrouse reached Norway, the Faroe Islands, Ireland, Italy (near Rome) and Spain (Albufera marsh near Valencia). Pallas's Sandgrouse even temporarily bred in Belgium, France, Germany, the Netherlands, Sweden and the UK, and especially in Denmark.

The reaction of European naturalists to this extraordinary visitation was deep excitement blended with an even more powerful cupidity. As one ornithologist in northern England noted: 'sand grouse pie was indulged in . . . and the wings and feathers of a good many were turned to account in the Sunday bonnets of the fisher-lasses'.[17] The barrage of gunfire was so destructive that the British parliament passed special legislation outlawing the slaughter. Sadly the law was passed in 1889 and too late for it have any real protective value. Even more unfortunate is the fact that these irruptions of Pallas's Sandgrouse have now largely ceased, possibly because of habitat loss and the bird's reduced population.

Pigeon and Dove family *Columbidae*

This is a very large bird family – there are 306 species worldwide – and they are present in almost every terrestrial habitat, from snow-capped peaks and dense rainforests to waterless desert. It is not just that pigeons are virtually omnipresent. They are frequently among the most abundant and successful birds in all these habitats. Yet in addition to this central ecological role, pigeons have colonised the human imagination.

In *Birds Britannica* I suggested that the dove or pigeon was part of a great trinity of avian symbols for Western civilisation (with the raven and eagle). Yet perhaps the dove should be thought of as an avian archetype for almost all humanity. With a small number of other equally significant birds – notably the domestic chicken, crane and swallow – the dove has helped frame our whole imaginative encounter

with life. It is impossible to overstate its importance. A work of this length could be devoted entirely to dove symbolism. Indeed, books have been written on the theme (*Die Taube* by Daniel Haag-Wackernagel, *The Pigeon in History* by Jean Hansell).

A frequent misconception to dispel before considering the group is the idea that doves and pigeons are separate and distinguishable from one another. The version of this family which dwells in our imaginations and which has performed multiple cultural roles – the 'inner dove', as it were – is usually known by that name, and hardly ever as a 'pigeon'. However, in the realms of natural history there are no distinctions. 'Pigeon' and 'dove' are merely interchangeable words for different members of the same family.

PIGEONS AND EXTINCTION

The ideas associated with the birds cluster around two essential themes. Pigeons have been used for millennia as symbols of life, fertility, peace and love (both physical and sacred), as well as of transcendental notions such as the Christian concept of the 'Holy Spirit'. On the other hand, pigeons have come to stand for a set of ideas that are, in many ways, the polar opposite of life and love. History has produced several episodes in which we have persecuted pigeons to the point of their extinction. The exemplar is the flightless endemic to the Indian Ocean island of Mauritius, the **Dodo** *Raphus cucullatus*, which was hunted to oblivion in the 1660s. (Another flightless relative and lookalike was on a neighbouring island and called the **Rodrigues Solitaire** *Pezophaps solitaria*. It went extinct in 1791.)

These pigeon associations with death and species extinction are in shallower cultural soil than the dove connections to life and love, and are also more limited in geographical range. Yet in the context of the natural history of pigeons, and even in the entire field of biology, the pigeon links with death are substantial. In fact the short, tragic history of the Dodo gave us, arguably for the very first time, an inkling of our own potentially devastating impact upon the rest of life on Earth. In short, extinction as an idea really begins with the Dodo.

The hard facts about the bird are rather few in number and contentious in character. The word 'dodo' may originate with a Portuguese word *doido* meaning 'stupid' or 'crazy'. Two alternatives are that it derived either from an old Dutch word *dodoor*, meaning 'a sluggard or lazy person', or from *dodaars*, literally 'a fat or lazy arse'.[1] The creature itself was indisputably a large heavy-bodied flightless bird about 1 m (3.3 ft) long and about 12.5 kg (27.5 lb) in weight, although accounts of individuals weighing as much as 23 kg (51 lb) would justify the claim of Oliver Goldsmith, the eighteenth-century writer, that three or four dodos 'are enough to dine a hundred men'.[2]

One possibility, to explain these weight discrepancies, is

that captive Dodos were overfed on the wrong food and it caused them to become hugely obese. It may also account for the grotesquely misshapen creatures depicted in some contemporaneous artworks (e.g. the 1651 portrait in the Oxford University Museum of Natural History, UK, by Johannes (Jan) Savery). The wild birds appear to have been solitary in habit, possibly coastal in distribution and fruit-eating in diet. However, the fact that Dodos could survive a journey to Europe eating presumably anything, including ships' biscuits, suggests that they were not strict frugivores.[3]

One indisputable truth was the Dodo's susceptibility to human contact and Western civilisation. Portuguese sailors had used Mauritius intermittently as a source of fresh food and water since 1508, while Dutch navigators recorded landings on this Indian Ocean island in 1598. The Dutch then colonised Mauritius by the 1640s, and the last reliable sighting of a Dodo was in 1662.[4] The unwary birds were hunted by Europeans for food, but they also fell victim to introduced predators including pigs, monkeys and rats. Much of the evidence – and a good deal of the confusion – derives from written descriptions and illustrations completed in Europe and based on a small number of live Dodos (or their skeletal and plumage remains) that were transported there from Mauritius. However, no single complete skin has survived and today bones retrieved from a Mauritian swamp are probably the best physical evidence for the bird's true appearance.[5]

In a way, it is not what this pigeon really looked like but how we have come to envision it that is the real moral of the story. A primary source for all modern Dodo impressions are the paintings of Jan Savery's more famous uncle, the Dutch artist Roelandt Savery (1576–1639), who completed drawings from live specimens held in a menagerie belonging to Prince Maurice of Nassau (now in Germany). Although these artworks are a major source of data, and while they are well executed for their time, they inevitably obey the representational conventions of the seventeenth century.[6] These unforgettable images have helped create what might be called the Dodo 'archetype', of which all subsequent portraits are variations. The legs are stumps, the eyes expressively sad, the body swollen, the bill – perhaps the most compelling of all Dodo features – is more a grotesque, Macawberesque bulbous nose. Recent research has suggested that, in fact, Dodos were longer legged, swifter and more graceful than was once assumed, yet these revelations cannot now dislodge the established stereotype.[7]

To our own contemporary sensibilities, the original seventeenth-century versions and even many much later Dodo images are caricature-like and anthropomorphised. Their faces are like human faces. The lost, lonely and sad Dodo – and perhaps the individuals marooned in Europe were truly all of those things – is now part of our fundamental sense of the bird. The only other strand that was added subsequently, particularly in the Dodo images completed by Sir John Tenniel to illustrate the species' famous appearance in Lewis Carroll's *Alice's Adventures in Wonderland* (1865), was comedy. The Dodo is almost unavoidably an object of humour. As the great African naturalist Jonathan Kingdon has suggested, had the Dodo 'never existed it might very well have been invented by a cartoonist'.[8]

Somehow we cannot 'see' Dodos as they might have appeared to a twenty-first-century witness, had the bird

George Edwards' eighteenth-century Dodo image has all the hallmarks of Europe's stereotypic portrayal of the extinct pigeon – as grotesque, overweight and somehow faintly comic.

survived into our own age. Other strange, even grotesque, creatures have survived and therefore escaped deeply negative historical portraits, such as the California Condor (see page 161), Sperm Whale and Great White Shark. But the Dodo can never become a vibrant, compelling or even just a 'worthy' fellow inhabitant of this Earth. Living (and dying) before the advent of photography, or even accurate natural-historical illustration, has consigned the species to a state of perpetual anachronism and fantasy.

Maybe that is how we have coped with, or subverted, the bird's real message. We have trivialised it. Or, perhaps, we should view our attempts to portray the Dodo as lazy, clumsy, foolish and comic – even Linnaeus named it *Didus ineptus*, 'silly dodo' – as simple projection.[9] The Dodo got the fate it deserved. Whatever the precise truth, it is so lost in these humanised versions that, even while it is the first widely recognised victim of extinction and is often cited as the first documented example in the modern era, its story carries less moral weight than it should. It has left us a proverbial expression to summarise the abysmal totality of deadness. However, the phrase 'as dead as a dodo' has very little resonance beyond the English-speaking world (it means nothing, for instance, to the French, Italians and Germans), and, rather curiously, even among anglophones the phrase is barely used in an environmental context.[10]

> I am sure that but for Lewis Carroll's *Alice* (the book is so immensely popular) the Serbians would not have heard of the dodo! [11]

> No, I don't think 'as dead as a dodo' is a well-used Dutch saying. We say 'as dead as a rainworm' (*zo dood als een pier*), which is used when somebody is truly, totally dead – but don't ask me why.[12]

> In Russia it belongs to 'encyclopaedic' knowledge and although the phrase is known, it is not widely used, and perhaps only by a few 'boffins'.[13]

The American birder and writer Rick Wright notes:

> The phrase is current and common in the US and Canada. But we don't use it in reference to literal extinctions: I'd never say, for example, that the Labrador Duck is as dead as a dodo. Instead, I hear it in the US only in description of ideas or plans or possibilities that are definitively excluded from the possibility of fruition.[14]

The modern impotence of the Dodo story to arouse any genuine sense of shame is unfortunate, given how much its individual fate adumbrates that of its whole family. Today 34 pigeon species are considered near-threatened, while another 61 are deemed at direct risk of extinction. It means almost a third of all pigeons are in some state of jeopardy, and there are now many other potential Dodos. Among the most critically threatened are the **Pink Pigeon** *Nesoenas mayeri* (it is another Mauritian endemic and its present total of *c.*370 is a huge improvement on that in 1990, when there were just ten), **Polynesian Imperial Pigeon** *Ducula aurorae* (*c.*300), **Marquesan Imperial Pigeon** *Ducula galeata* (249), **Blue-eyed Ground Dove** *Columbina cyanopis* (*c.*150), **Grenada Dove** *Leptotila wellsi* (96), **Socorro Dove** *Zenaida graysoni* (*c.*90), and **Negros Fruit Dove** *Ptilinopus arcanus* (fewer than 50).[15]

The last three emphasise the extent to which the Dodo's fate foretold that of its wider family. For this trio are all single-island endemics plagued by the combination of hunting, introduced predators and habitat loss that pushed Dodos into the abyss. However, the Grenada Dove highlights peculiarly modern forms of nihilism. Confronted with the plight of their island's most threatened bird, the government in Grenada degazetted the national park, which was the dove's primary hope of salvation, and sold the land to developers in order to construct a major hotel resort.

PIGEONS AS SYMBOLS OF PEACE, LOVE AND FERTILITY

The dove associations with peace and fertility are much more ancient than their connotations of death, and are closely linked to the bird's history of domestication. The Fertile Crescent (running from Palestine and Israel through Syria, southern Turkey and south into Iraq) is usually cited as the place where the **Common Pigeon** (also known as Rock Dove and Feral Pigeon) *Columba livia* – the bird best known for its urban-adapted lifestyle in almost every town and city on Earth – was first brought within the human fold as a source of meat, eggs, feathers, dung (for fertiliser), sacrificial victims, beauty and companionship. Given the species' granivorous lifestyle and its willingness to nest in buildings, it is not difficult to contemplate how the Neolithic inventions of agriculture and urban society attracted Common Pigeons into human settlement.

Yet even during an earlier phase of our existence, based upon cave dwelling (the far longer period of the Palaeolithic), one can imagine close connections between our species and Common Pigeons. The wild birds routinely nest in caves and the discarded seeds on middens associated with human occupation would have been an obvious setting for the earliest encounters. This ancient intimacy would have made the pigeon's journey from wild commensal to full-blown domesticate all the more likely once free-standing mud structures had supplanted caves as our main place of dwelling. The Common Pigeons simply acquired the habits of civilisation alongside us.

Sumerian archaeological sites have yielded some of the earliest material evidence – dove figurines dating to about 4000 BC – for both domestication and the fundamental link between pigeons and fertility.[16] Doves were familiars in temples dedicated to a Sumerian deity called Inanna, and also in those of a subsequent Assyrian incarnation, Ishtar. Eventually the birds were treated as symbols for this mother goddess, who intervened in human affairs on matters of love and fertility. Virgin women dedicated to the cult of Ishtar were themselves known as *hu*, 'doves'.[17] The connection between bird and both female and Earthly bounty was then inherited by successive civilisations, including the Phoenicians (Astarte), the ancient Greeks (Aphrodite) and Romans (Venus), with the dove serving, in turn, as symbol for each version of the same fertility goddess. It is equally noteworthy that in Latin (*columba*), modern Italian (*colomba*), ancient Greek (*pelēa*), modern Spanish (*paloma*), Portuguese (*paloma*), French (*colombe*), Arabic (*hamama*) and Hebrew (*yona*) the word 'dove' is a feminine noun.

It is worth pausing to reflect on the fundamental predisposition among humans to associate love with both fertility and peace. These abstract ideals are not technically

This fresco in the Holy Trinity Russian Orthodox Cathedral in Jerusalem, Israel, typifies the way in which doves – here representing the Holy Spirit – are so often subliminal extras in Christian imagery.

the same, although we can easily appreciate how fertility and peace flow from love, and vice versa. Nor is there a single English word to capture all of the qualities symbolically manifest in doves. Perhaps the way to summarise what the birds mean to us, and how they express the deep linkages between this constellation of ideas, is to say that doves symbolise that moment when these various elements of life are in their right relationship and are properly ordered.

This complex of associations between doves and fertility is similarly rooted in the Judaeo-Christian tradition and is exemplified by the dove's role in the Book of Genesis and the story of Noah's Ark (8:6–11). (Note, incidentally, the bird's gender.)

And it came to pass at the end of forty days, that Noah opened the window of the ark which he had made:

. . . Also he sent forth a dove from him, to see if the waters were abated from off the face of the ground;

But the dove found no rest for the sole of her foot, and she returned unto him into the ark, for the waters *were* on the face of the whole earth: then he put forth his hand, and took her, and pulled her in unto him into the ark.

And he stayed yet other seven days; and again he sent forth the dove out of the ark;

And the dove came in to him in the evening; and, lo, in her mouth *was* an olive leaf pluckt off: so Noah knew that the waters were abated from off the earth.

Together with the olive, the bird has since become the pre-eminent emblem of peace between different human societies. Yet in the story of Noah itself the bird represents a more generic kind of peace, which is the resumption of harmony in the Earth's own affairs, after the turmoil of the flood, and the restoration of good relations between humans and the rest of the natural world.

Dove symbolism permeates Christianity and is used most significantly to connote the abstract notion of the Holy Spirit. The bird is an important symbol at key moments in the Christian story.

In Italy the dove, *colomba*, is associated with innocence and purity and at Easter it is a symbol for Christ. We eat an Easter sweet cake known as *colomba pasquale*, which we just call *Colomba*. It is bird shaped.[18]

The dove is also particularly present in representations of the Annunciation, the moment when the Angel Gabriel foretold Mary of her pregnancy with Jesus. In early versions of the Immaculate Conception, Mary is impregnated by a dove through her ear, or through a dove settling in her lap. Similarly a dove was said either to have escaped from Joseph's groin and settled on his head, or to have emerged from his staff, before fertilising Mary with the holy child. In each of these scenarios the sexual and spiritual symbolism is obvious.[19]

People of Western background are so familiar with the way doves pervade their lives as a means to evoke notions of peace, fertility or erotic love, as well as spiritual devotion, that they seldom stop to reflect on the ancient heritage behind this symbol. It is often simply assumed that the Genesis references mark the starting point, but, in truth, the dove released by Noah was already an emblem with thousands of years of accumulated associations.

It is impossible to detail the full extent to which the symbol's Sumerian rootstock has branched outwards to entwine almost every aspect of our lives. Yet even a brief sample can suggest the spectrum of dove connections. One obvious contemporary indicator is the 425 million hits for 'dove' on Google, not to mention the 104 million additional links with 'paloma'. In the commercial businesses associated with love, the white birds are superabundant inhabitants – for example, on Valentine's and wedding cards, on all manner of other wedding accoutrements and shops selling wedding garments, especially dresses. The establishments are routinely named 'Paloma' or have the word in the title. Real doves and their symbolic counterparts often come together in the context of Egyptian weddings:

In our country pigeon meat is very popular and cooks, as well as common people, clean out the viscera and stuff the abdominal cavity with a mixture called *Freek* in Arabic. The dish is called *hamām bi'l-farīk* (pigeon stuffed with green wheat). It's so familiar and a lovely meal for the bride and bridegroom on their wedding night and during the honeymoon, because it is thought of as a general and sexual tonic.[20]

In many countries commercial businesses exist specifically to trade in live white doves for release at weddings or funerals. The entire enterprise is founded on two interconnecting facets of the symbolism. Wedding doves reflect the connection with romantic love, but the white birds set free at gravesides draw on their ancient association with the human soul. Dove motifs are ubiquitous in churchyard stonework across the Christian world to signify the salvation of the departed.

Doves also feature in the legends of various Christian saints, sometimes emerging from their mouths to represent the ascending spirit of the beatified.[21] St Eulalia, a Spanish girl of the third century AD, was said to have been brutally tortured after refusing to worship the Roman gods, until a white dove issued from her mouth. A rather bowdlerised painting of this gruesome scene, by the nineteenth-century

The Soviet communist astronaut Yuri Gagarin and the Christian dove of peace are rather strange bedfellows in this 1970s mural from the Mongolian capital, Ulan Bator.

artist J W Waterhouse (in the Tate Britain Gallery, London), illustrates the girl's broken body, yet here associated not with a single dove, but surrounded by 12 birds.

The birds have also retained their more profane connotations – 'pigeon' was an ancient Greek euphemism for a prostitute, while 'soiled dove' was its English equivalent and 'pigeonhole' an old slang term for the vagina.[22] In a painting by the French eighteenth-century artist Louis-Jean-François Lagrenée (J Paul Getty Museum, Los Angeles), entitled *Mars and Venus*, the same erotic connection is blended with the other standard associations of peace and fertility, but all are represented with great tenderness and wit. The work shows Mars gazing in wonderment at the lusciously beautiful sleeping form of Venus, as she lies in post-coital bliss, while beneath the gods' shared bed, where Mars' sword and shield lie abandoned, a pair of white doves has made a nest in his discarded helmet. The male bird carries to his incubating mate an ear of ripening corn.

It is striking how the full ancient constellation of ideas orbiting around these birds makes fresh appeal to successive generations of writers or artists, thereby creating its own self-sustaining universe of symbolic doves. An extraordinary modern instance of the pattern was a sculpture made in Mozambique in 2004. This south-east African state suffered 16 years of bitter civil war until the early 1990s, which had sucked into the country a vast arsenal of weapons. After a fragile truce was established an estimated 7 million guns remained hidden in people's homes or buried in the ground.

The extraordinary lacy plumes from the Victoria Crowned Pigeon feature here on another kind of headdress, worn by a participant at the Mount Hagen sing sing in the highlands of Papua New Guinea.

The feeding of Common Pigeons is underpinned by many cultural and psychological motives; at Jodhpur in India it is a religious rite.

The weapons blighted the prospects of lasting peace and in 1995 the Mozambican Bishop Dom Dinis Sengulane initiated a project entitled Transforming Arms into Tools (TAE). The scheme found visual expression in a remarkable sculpture by four artists – Christovao Canhavato (Kester), Fiel dos Santos, Adelino Serafim Mathé and Hilario Nhatugueja – entitled *The Tree of Life* (British Museum, London).

Rising above this totemic symbol is an unmistakable dove on outstretched metal wings. Yet there is a whole new power to this traditional set of motifs when you realise that the rust-coloured bird, like all the other components in the Tree of Life, is made from fragments – barrels, stocks, magazines, triggers – of old firearms. It is difficult to imagine a more transcendent image of human hope than a dove of peace constructed out of the very same AK-47s that had previously inflicted such appalling misery, death and injury.

Another classic example of the bird's deployment in a contemporary cultural context is the doves quietly nestled within Jim Crace's award-winning novel *The Pesthouse* (2007). It is set in North America and in an unspecified but post-apocalyptic age, when the technology has somehow been reduced to one more primitive than that possessed by the Pilgrim Fathers. Instead of these white Americans expanding westwards, the traditional orientation of their lives is inverted: the settlers retreat to the east to escape by ship. During his own flight, the central character, Franklin, suffers a leg injury and retires to a shack called the 'pesthouse', where victims of some unspecified plague ('the flux') are quarantined by relatives far from town, until they either recover or die.

There, Franklin meets and tends to its sole occupant, the convalescent Margaret. He treats her by holding and massaging her feet in his hands, an action which mimics a time-honoured nostrum of this old-new world, where pigeons are clapped to a sick person's foot until the illness transfers from human to bird. (Pigeons were, indeed, once genuinely considered medicinal: their flesh, blood, dung and feathers being used by ancient Greeks to treat burns, jaundice, ulcers and cases of poisoning. One remedy involved tearing out the dove's still palpitating heart and sticking it to the patient's thigh.[23] The application of a live pigeon, split down the middle, to the feet, exactly as in Crace's novel, was a recommended medical procedure until the seventeenth century. One specific application among Muslims was for scorpion stings.)[24]

Following her recovery, Margaret renames Franklin as 'Pigeon' for his form of therapy, after which they set out as companions and lovers to trace the pilgrims' route across America to its eastern shore. However, their adventures intervene to reshape their shared destiny. Franklin is captured by a group of slave traders, while Margaret acquires unintentionally a baby girl, Bella (she renames her Jackie, short for Jackson). Eventually this makeshift 'family' unit is reunited when Franklin escapes from his captors, and possessed of a single horse, they turn their faces against the eastward trend of their neighbours, and return to the west, to construct a new life of hope in a blighted land.

Jim Crace comments on the symbolism that has been so lightly feathered into his narrative:

> You are correct to make the connection to the Holy Family, though it was only meant as a nudge rather than an essential component. It's the same with the pigeon in *The Pesthouse*. I'm prompting the readers to make a connection with the pigeon/dove in the Bible story and then go on to align the Holy Family on their

flight into Egypt (parents, donkey, child via immaculate conception delivered by dove) and *The Pesthouse* family on their final flight west (adoptive parents including one called Pigeon, horse, child via immaculate kidnap). I'm just being playful, mischievous, wide ranging, throwing out hints by the handful. It's random rather than architectural. I was thinking of **Passenger Pigeon** *Ectopistes migratorius*, too. And the doves in the Noah story. And the dove of peace. And the association of pigeons and doves with loving, cooing couples.[25]

PRACTICAL PIGEONS

An obvious question arising from any consideration of this complex dove symbolism is why exactly should these birds lend themselves to this kind of association? One answer may be the pure and seemingly contented quality of most pigeon vocalisations, which are usually purring or peacefully droning in character. Another obvious answer is pigeons can be astonishingly fertile. The family is spread across almost the entire surface of the Earth except the permafrost zone of northern latitudes and the frozen wastes of Antarctica. Common Pigeons even occur beyond the Arctic Circle in the Swedish mining town of Kiruna at 68° N; they also breed in Ushuaia, the Argentinian city that is the most southerly in the world (55° S). It must vie with the House Sparrow as the most widespread 'wild' bird on the planet. The street-dwelling form of this complex and highly elastic species is often now the only bird encountered daily by large swathes of humanity, and also the only bird with which they will have shared any kind of intimacy, including physical contact.

The Common Pigeon's extraordinary adaptability is manifest in its breeding cycle. As long as food is available the birds will breed at any time of the year, with only their moult period of August–September intervening.[26] It means that pigeons can be seen mating year-round; a reproductive strategy that more closely mirrors the human open season on sex than that of any other widespread animal, and a constant reminder of a link between pigeons and procreation.

Their willingness to nest continuously was one reason why early societies developed artificial breeding sites. The pigeons supplied fresh meat, in the form of full-grown squabs, that was almost instantly replenished. Domestic birds were selected for their fertility and for early breeding and now commercially managed birds can produce 16–22 squabs a year (six in the wild), while female homing pigeons can start to lay eggs at just 95 days.[27]

Some of the earliest evidence for dovecotes dates to the Greco-Roman period in Egypt (*c.*330 BC–AD 395), where today pigeon is still considered to be almost a national dish.[28] An inhabitant of modern Cairo reports on how things stand almost two and half millennia later:

> Breeding pigeons is still a popular hobby in Egypt, especially among young men. Lofts, called *Gheeya* in Arabic, are a common sight on the blocks of flats and houses in different areas all over Egypt. (Pigeon coops are called *Burg*, which means a 'tower'.) I remember when we were teenagers many of my friends and myself had a great passion for raising pigeons, and learning more about the different breeds, competing to create the best-decorated loft, and training certain birds to fly very long distances from all over Egypt. We would travel with a caged pigeon, for example, from Alexandria where we had the loft, to Aswan (840 km away) and then let it go and calculate the bird's return time to the

Common Pigeons are as much a part of street life in New York as the yellow taxi or the hotdog stand.

loft. The amazing thing is that sometimes it reached the loft before we did![29]

The Romans also made wide use of these pigeon houses (known by them as *columbaria*) throughout the empire, but they were developed to an even higher degree in medieval Europe. Some British dovecotes, of which there are very fine surviving examples, can house several thousand pairs at one time, while the country as a whole may have held 26,000 such structures. In both Britain and on the European continent the right to own a dovecote was reserved for the landed classes, who could impose harsh penalties on anyone caught killing domestic birds. These feudal privileges were resented by the rural population and have been cited as one of the many factors behind the 1789 revolution in France.[30]

What may have been the original form of dovecote – an innovation that probably accompanied the first ever domestications – is still found in places like Cappadocia. The inhabitants in this region of south-central Turkey carved out cave-like houses directly from outcrops of very soft volcanic rock. Above these troglodyte dwellings, many of which are still occupied today, one finds repeat rows of smaller niches that were used to encourage nesting Common Pigeons. The hollowed-out cavities are the original pigeonhole. The birds' fertility was valued twice over: once as meat and then as dung, which is apparently still used as fertiliser on local fields. The pre-ninth-century AD churches at Zelve (near the celebrated open-air museum at Göreme), which was only abandoned by its resident population in the 1950s, still hold good examples of the prototype dovecote.

The initial motive for domestication may have been high-quality meat and eggs, but humans eventually found other purposes for the living birds. The extraordinary gift of domesticated pigeons to navigate their way back to their dovecote eventually inspired their use as messengers. The tale of Noah's olive-bearing bird during the flood reveals an early application of the system although, as yet, experiments suggest that an ability to relocate a mobile home, such as a floating ark, is largely beyond the pigeon's internal compass. An event that is often cited as the earliest example of homing birds is the acclamation of Rameses II's coronation in 1279 BC, but Jean Hansell, the pigeon scholar, suggests that the fresco depicting this scene is equivocal.[31]

Some of the earliest proven testimony is from Pliny (see Appendix II) on the birds used to carry intelligence for Rome's Republican forces, when Mark Antony besieged their army at Modena in 44 BC. 'What use to Antony', Pliny wrote, 'were . . . even the barriers of nets that he stretched in the river, when the message went by air?'[32] There is a long history of European messenger pigeons in times of conflict. At the Siege of Paris during the Franco-Prussian War of 1870–71, pigeons were thought to have flown over 2 million missions. In World War Two homing birds were dropped by parachute to resistance forces in occupied Europe and were also carried by pilots. In October 1943 one crew that ditched in the sea off the Hebridean islands in Scotland released White Vision, who flew 97 km (60 miles) against a force 6 headwind with visibility down to 90 m (300 ft). For this feat and her crew's rescue, White Vision received the Dickin Medal, one of 32 pigeons to be honoured.

Pigeon post has also been important in times of peace. The region under medieval Islamic rule enjoyed a communication network based on pigeons that was particularly sophisticated. The twelfth-century caliphate maintained postal links from its capital in Baghdad as far as Egypt, while in fourteenth-century Turkey, pigeon towers were erected at intervals and sentinels could pass intelligence via a relay of birds – with duplicate messages sent two hours later as a safeguard – that could traverse the entire country. In Asia generally the system was used for both political and commercial purposes. Merchants sailing into port released birds to give advance notice of their cargoes. In China they were used until the nineteenth century to ferry news concerning business transactions, particularly between bankers or money changers.[33]

It seems, however, that some pigeon messengers come from further and deeper within the mysteries of life than others:

> My uncle Stanley was a well-known ornithologist and I must have inherited my passion for birds from him. They are magical creatures, many believe them to be God's messengers but here is a story which really happened to me. Many years ago I wrote a poem for a dear friend that ended in the line 'and I would send a Dove to you and bid you come and stay awhile'. Some years later a white dove flew in, alighted on my shoulder and would not leave me. On close inspection I saw that it had a ring on its foot (it was, in fact, a racing pigeon). Wishing to trace its owner, I removed the ring and found to my astonishment the name of the friend I had written the poem for (it was a namesake – John Shelly). I telephoned the gentleman who was delighted to have his pigeon back. It had been lost for five years. Then remembering the poem, I telephoned *my* John Shelly. We had been out of touch for years. He answered the phone. 'Suzy,' he said, 'how did you know to contact me? I went blind last night!' God's messengers? – I truly believe so.[34]

It is probably in the realms of recreation or sport where the relationship between humans and pigeons has achieved levels of intimacy equalled only perhaps by the bizarre tenderness shown by the devotees of cockfighting for their prized birds (see page 72). Pigeon breeding has produced an astonishing array of specialised forms that meet almost every practical and aesthetic demand placed upon the birds. Indeed, it was the sheer plasticity of the Common Pigeon, morphing occasionally into breeds of grotesque disproportion, that inspired Charles Darwin to become himself a pigeon fancier and to make it one of the key themes in his work *Animals and Plants under Domestication*. However, not everyone is so driven or goal-oriented in their attachment to the loft of fluttering birds.

The company of pigeons has been both a source of aesthetic delight and even therapy for a huge cross section of human types. One aspect of this is surely the birds' irrepressibly soft and sedative bubbling notes. As one Iraqi devotee observes: 'Their sound is so full of emotions and warmth and it makes you feel that you are very close to them and that you are surrounded by their wings. You feel that it comes from their heart not from their syrinx.'[35]

The voices of other pigeons frequently have this same power of soothing reassurance, as the following makes plain:

The call was the first thing I noticed about **Common Wood Pigeon** *Columba palumbus*, when I was staying with my grandparents in Holland. I was in my grandmother's bedroom when I first heard it, but it was years before I knew what was making that sound. For years I thought the bird only existed in Holland, I so associated the song with my cosy Easter visits. It's not easy to find a phrase which mimics the rhythm of their song. 'I like artichoke, I like artichoke, I like artichoke: Yum!' Instantly there's sunshine: the first warmth creeping into the air after the winter months, bulbs beginning to show, the light matching the golden yellow of the crocuses. And I am sitting in the garden with my grandparents, not having to say anything because we know how much we love each other. There is something so calm and reassuring about those puffed up little bodies and that even, steady call.[36]

Being enfolded in this emollient song is surely one part of the appeal of pigeon keeping. Yet the hobby has also claimed among its devotees the Nazi SS leader Heinrich Himmler; Pablo Picasso's father, Don José Ruiz y Blasco; the rock musician and composer Frank Zappa; the film-maker Walt Disney; and the actor Yul Brynner.[37] The self-proclaimed attachment to pigeons of 'the baddest man on the planet', the great and infamous boxer Mike Tyson, is striking yet also, in many ways, typical of the pastime. (He once wrote: 'They're very soothing and they keep me out of the strip clubs.') For the birds have had a special appeal for people of deprived social background, regardless of nation or continent. Tyson himself acquired a pigeon habit during his Brownsville childhood in that notoriously tough ghetto of Harlem in New York. Today at his home in Phoenix, Arizona, he is said to maintain a collection of 350 different breeds.[38]

Among the most important pigeons today are those used in racing competitions which require a graceful bird built for speed and endurance. The pastime began in Belgium in the nineteenth century, where it is still the national sport, but has since attracted a worldwide following. In Britain it rose steadily from obscurity to a peak in the 1950s, when two-fifths of an estimated half-million people keeping pigeons did so to race them.[39] Today there are 60,000 fanciers spread over 3,000 clubs, but the sport is still most popular in areas of social deprivation – such as south Wales, central Scotland and northern England. The poet Katrina Porteous reflects on the deep connection between poverty, industrial dereliction and the places of the modern pigeon loft:

This was the backdrop to my maternal family in County Durham – a landscape of red-brick council terraces, allotments and, beyond them, the pit-head, with its mysterious, towering wheel, the black slag-heap, then miles of green fields, cow-parsley, hawthorn hedges, open skies. It was a landscape peopled by characters as contradictory as the place itself: rural people who had suddenly, only a few generations earlier, found themselves defined by the blackest of industries; people who derived their whole identity, their pride, from belonging to a coal-mining community, yet who were determined that their children should escape from it. Inextricably woven into the thread of their lives were birds of many kinds, but chief among the pitmen's birds, ever-present, wheeling overhead or purring from the

ledges of their brightly painted crees, were the racing pigeons. Pigeons played a hugely dramatic role in the communal imagination of the mining community. Their circling flight was as much part of the landscape as the pit wheel. As a child, I was touched by the tenderness with which some craggy-voiced old miner would cradle a soft pigeon in his hand. For the men who laboured underground, in the dark, these creatures of the sky were more than flesh and blood and feathers, more than the race, its prize-money and status. Years after the last pit closed in County Durham men still race pigeons. It is one of the last vestiges of a culture born out of such harsh experience and conflict that I can sense the depth beneath the words of one former pitman: 'Say what tha likes aboot me or ma lass, but dinna say owt aboot me pigeons.'[40]

The place where pigeon racing has achieved its most extreme form is in Sun City, the casino resort established to meet white gambling habits in the former homeland territory of Bophuthatswana and now a part of the modern Republic of South Africa. It is the site of the richest pigeon race in the world, known as the Sun City Million Dollar Race, which attracts over 5,000 participants each paying $1,000 to enter three birds to the contest. The $200,000 prize for the winner has led to participation by the British monarch, Elizabeth II, as well as those dwelling in the traditional territories of the fancier. According to the author Mark Collings, this is a landscape of 'concrete tower blocks, scowling teenagers wearing black tracksuits, and spindly old men with faces the colour of their intestines shuffling along clutching cans of turbo-strength lager'.[41]

SUPERABUNDANT PIGEONS

If the Common Pigeon is the most widespread and best known of its family, it is not necessarily the most abundant. Other pigeon species can be present in extraordinarily high numbers, even forming a high percentage of the total bird biomass in a given habitat. The exemplar, to which we shall return, was the Passenger Pigeon, whose gargantuan flocks were surely one of the great natural wonders on Earth, and which qualified the bird as one of the most abundant ever to have lived. The species' pre-eminent biographer, the wonderfully fastidious William Schorger, suggested that it might have represented 25–40 per cent of the total bird population in America.[42]

Other pigeons are good candidates for the world's most abundant wild non-passerine. The **Ring-necked Dove** *Streptopelia capicola* occurs from South Africa north as far as the Sudan. It is supremely adapted to dry savannah and, at some waterholes much favoured by game, the dawn flocks of Ring-necked Doves can completely envelop the herds of wandering herbivores like some additional deep layer of animate dust. Indeed, anyone who has ever watched wildlife television programmes with an African theme knows the vocalisations of this species, if only subliminally. Its soporific hoarse three-syllable drone is an almost unavoidable part of the African bush soundscape. To many humans, the sounds of Ring-necked Doves – rather like a wide range of calls produced by African pigeons – commend themselves to our ears as words. In a number of places the bird appears to proclaim its nationality, such as *zim-Bab-we, u-Gand-a, ma-Law-i* and, perhaps most perfectly, *bot-Swan-a*.

involved **White-winged Dove** *Zenaida asiatica* or a chorus of this bird and the aptly named **Mourning Dove** *Zenaida macroura*.[45] To the singer Bob Dylan, in 'Shelter From The Storm', the sound of the latter suggested the crying of newborn babies.)

Another pigeon that is superabundant occurs right across the northern hemisphere. The **Eurasian Collared Dove** *Streptopelia decaocto* was originally an inhabitant of the largely desert belt running east from Iran to northern India. In this hot arid zone, the dust-coloured bird produces a sound more monotonous than its African relatives. An English mnemonic for the dozy three-note song is 'u-Nit-ed' ('like a bored football fan'). In Bosnia-Herzegovina it is equally prosaic (*Ku-puj kruh, ku-puj kruh . . .*: 'buy bread, buy bread').[46]

For some, as yet, inexplicable reason the Eurasian Collared Dove began a westward push into the marches of Europe by the early twentieth century. What is striking about the bird's initial expansion, until the early 1950s, was its overlap with the catastrophic disruption to the continent's human population caused by two major wars. As vast crocodiles of advancing and retreating armies or civilian evacuees zigzagged across the region, so the spread of this bland symbol of peace was as relentless as it was unobtrusive. When one hears the catalogue of countries and the dates of their annexation by collared doves, the linkages trigger a cascade of human associations that are wholly other than the ornithological story: Greece (1928), Hungary (1932), Czechoslovakia (1936), Austria (1938), Poland (1940), Germany (1943), the Netherlands (1947), Denmark (1948), Sweden and Switzerland (1949), France (1950), Belgium and Norway (1952), Britain (1955) and Ireland (1959).[47]

By the 1970s Eurasian Collared Doves had reached Iceland and also begun a rapid onslaught across Iberia. By the 1980s Africa's Mediterranean shoreline was included in the next wave of expansion.[48] So too was Russia's Volgan steppe and western Kazakhstan, while across the Atlantic it was almost as if the febrile locust-like spirit of increase had been picked up by collared doves introduced to the Bahamas in 1974. From these islands, the species spread first to Cuba and then to Florida, establishing a breeding outpost in Dade County by 1982. A few years of consolidation were the prelude to a second continental advance even more rapid than the settlement of Europe. Invariably it is described as an 'explosion', which is ironic, perhaps, for a beige drowsy-voiced symbol of peace. Yet it is justified. By the 2004–5 Christmas bird count, the species was found in 32 states and four Canadian provinces including British Columbia.[49] Should the Eurasian Collared Dove penetrate South America – and it is hard to think why it will not – then it must surely qualify as one of the most abundant and successful birds on Earth.

However, on that continent it will have to compete with the remarkable **Eared Dove** *Zenaida auriculata*, a species in the same genus as the most familiar of all its North American family members, the Mourning Dove. Ranging from the southern Caribbean islands almost to Tierra del Fuego, Eared Doves achieve extraordinary densities in parts of Brazil and Argentina. In the former country they are hunted especially at drinking holes and in 1959 one poor site in Ceará, close to the Atlantic coast, was reported to yield *c*.100,000 birds a week. Salted and dried (each bird weighs 60 g: 2.1 oz), they were packed into 50 kg (110 lb) bales. A

From the Middle East to the West Coast – the Eurasian Collared Dove's spread across much of Europe and North America represents one of the most dramatic modern range expansions of any bird.

Or if you may prefer the less nationalistic version, *drink lager, drink lager . . .* or even *work harder, work harder . . .* Whichever local alternative you choose the Ring-necked Dove is a rather monotonous sound which fills the air from dawn to dusk, eventually driving its listeners mad. Fortunately this species isn't the only sound echoing across this landscape. There is for instance the call of **Red-eyed Dove** *Streptopelia semitorquata* – *I am a red-eyed dove, I am a red-eyed dove . . .* which is self-explanatory, but its tiny cousin, the **Emerald-spotted Wood Dove** *Turtur chalcospilos* has a far sadder tale to tell. It's supposed to be saying *I've lost my father, I've lost my mother, I've lost my brothers, my sisters, and now there's nobody at all, at all, at all . . .*[43]

(Before returning to other pigeon species of huge number, it is worth noting that the theme of sadness in dove notes is widespread. The great American novelist John Steinbeck could hear in the doves' voices of Baja California 'a quality of longing . . . One wishes to walk toward the sound – to walk on and on toward it, forgetting everything else.'[44] What Steinbeck described as 'a song of homesickness' probably

single truck could carry away 100,000 birds and roughly 6 tonnes of pigeon meat. Local people once held that the birds were crossing the Atlantic from Africa to breed in Brazil and that the more they killed, the more the birds would appear.[50]

The same fantastical sense of abundance underpins a massive modern harvest of the species in Argentina, where the population explosion is closely linked to intensive agriculture, on which the birds are judged to be a serious pest. The province of Córdoba is one of the major Argentinian destinations for overseas sportsmen, drawn by the possibility of shooting more than 1,000 Eared Doves a day per person. Images of what is called 'high-volume dove hunting' usually involve white men in combat khaki standing proudly behind the day's bag – high-piled heaps of dead doves. Some establishments claim local populations of 20–30 million birds and advertise as key attractions the absence of a bag limit, the ongoing increase in the dove population, and the opportunity to undertake responsible pest-control measures while indulging in a dawn-to-dusk orgy of killing.

Clients can expect to loose off about 2,000 cartridges which means, on an assumed basis of six hours' actual firing during the day's recreation, that the sportsmen are discharging their guns every 11 seconds. One substantial issue is the grinding impact on the rifle shoulder. The almost unavoidable monotony of the slaughter is not apparently a problem. Website testimonials describe it as the best-ever dove hunting experience, during which the 'Killing of 16,000 birds as a group was pretty cool too!' There are stories of nine-year-old children from California killing 1,000 doves over ten hours. One wonders what kind of educational or formative experience that might be for a small child?[51]

So far Eared Doves have sustained what seem invulnerable numbers, regardless of these hunting excesses. Yet it is in the context of such environmental stories that the tale of the Passenger Pigeon assumes all its contemporary force and resonance. It is odd that the ultimate icon of extinction is often said to be the Dodo, rather than its formerly superabundant North American relative. For it is the contrast between seemingly limitless numbers of Passenger Pigeons and their rapid descent into oblivion that confronts any modern observer with such awful dismay. On hearing this species' life story one cannot but feel that it is among the most powerful bird-centred parables ever. It is the sort of ecological tale that should be imprinted on the consciousness of every single person. For this reason alone, I feel entitled to recapitulate some of the detail.

The basic biological facts of the species are fairly standard. The Passenger Pigeon was a medium-sized dove, measuring about 40 cm (16 in), with a noticeably long tail. Its plumage was predominantly beige-grey with dark spots on the wings and a lovely vinous blush on the male's upper breast. It nested in April–May. It laid one white egg. Its main food was the fruit of several deciduous trees, but especially beech mast, oak acorns and chestnuts. It was the periodic and localised abundance of these natural crops that determined the pigeon's nomadic lifestyle.

What separated the Passenger Pigeon from most of its family and, indeed, almost all other land birds (except, perhaps, the Red-billed Quelea; see page 490) was the size of the congregations. These vast protean flocks represented a concentration of life usually associated only with oceanic shoals of fish or the rains-oriented game on the African

No amount of the taxidermist's art can bring back for us the real-life beauty and drama of the Passenger Pigeon.

plains. The Scottish-born American naturalist John Muir recalled the birds in his adopted homeland of the 1850s:

> Of all God's feathered people that sailed the Wisconsin sky, no other bird seemed to us so wonderful. The beautiful wanderers flew like the winds in flocks of millions from climate to climate . . . I have seen the flocks streaming south in the autumn so large that they were flowing over from horizon to horizon in an almost continuous stream all day long . . . like a mighty river in the sky, widening, contracting, descending like falls and cataracts, and rising suddenly here and there in huge ragged masses like high-plashing spray.[52]

In Kentucky, another Scottish-American pioneer naturalist, Alexander Wilson, saw a flock and basing his calculation on the speed at which it passed worked out the length at 400 km (250 miles) with a total number of 2,230,272,000 birds. In fact he overestimated the speed at 100 kph (62 mph), when it was probably half that figure. Even so, he felt his guesstimate of the flock's width to have been highly conservative and he had certainly seen well over a billion birds.[53]

This speed gave the species its nickname – the 'blue meteor'.[54] En masse, however, they were avian tornados. Their impact was astonishing and traumatic. One hunter was said to have been so overcome he threw himself to the ground in terror. As they passed, their droppings fell like rain and their outspread wings turned day instantly to night, so that chickens went prematurely to roost as in an eclipse. A geologist in Arkansas noted how, 'Our horse, Missouri, at such times has been so cowed by them that he would stand still and tremble in his harness, whilst we ourselves were glad when the flight was directed from us.'[55]

The flock's appearance was sometimes taken as a kind of prodigy, foretelling cataclysm. 'It is a common observation in some parts of this state,' wrote one eighteenth-century

Audubon's famous painting of the Passenger Pigeon depicts a species whose flocks were once numbered in billions.

Audubon saw a roost that stretched for 67 km (42 miles). Places where the flocks gathered nightly were deluged in dung sometimes to a depth of 30 cm (1 ft). The blanket wiped out ground vegetation and poisoned trees. However, there was increase as well as ruin. An old roost near Troy in Geauga County, Ohio, was eventually the site of the town's most fertile farmland. In addition, the crust of guano was used in the production of saltpetre (to make gunpowder). 'Thousands of wagonloads' was the assumed yield at a Mississippian roost. One intriguing speculation is how old some of these traditional sites might have been. An example in Scott County, Indiana, was known to have been occupied for at least 40 years, but usage of such places could have been hundreds, even thousands, of years old. Now all we have to remind us of that immense backbeat of wings is the echo of an echo: the nearby settlement in Scott County is still known as Pigeon Roost.[61]

Such a prodigious natural plenty was taken as a benediction by human communities wherever the pigeons alighted. For North America's indigenous people, the birds were food, feathers, fat, and, in the imaginations of the Huron, they ferried the souls of the departed to heaven.[62] Usually killing only squabs and not breeding adults, the Seneca made offerings of wampum (shell beads) and tobacco for the divine blessing, then whole communities would wigwam by the pigeon nest trees and gorge on the plenty. 'When the marauders departed,' complained an eyewitness after one Native American harvest, 'they left the ground blue with dead birds, having killed twice as many as they knew how to dispose of'.[63]

White settlers also treated the birds as limitless heaven-sent manna. They were stored in barrels of their own fat, or smoked for pigeon jerky, or salted, or pickled in spicy apple cider, and Alexander Wilson said he never ate one of any age that was not delicate or delicious. Their fat, sweet and buttery, was rendered down and poured into tubs that kept a whole year long, while the feathers filled a fine soft mattress. Around St-Jérôme, Quebec, it was said that no girl went to the altar without a pigeon-feather bed and pillows for a dowry.[64]

The haphazard battening upon Passenger Pigeon flocks by settler or Native American communities was probably no more than a temporary drain on numbers, while the Seneca people's focus on squabs rather than adults suggested a harvest ethic that may well have been sustainable. However, all changed when the killing morphed into decades of systematic commercial exploitation.

At its peak during the last third of the nineteenth century there were large business houses with buyers and trappers following the movements of the birds relentlessly wherever they flocked. Some nesting sites attracted thousands of hunters. Meticulous in his ability to drill down through the hearsay of pigeon history, William Schorger suggested that most of the estimates for birds shipped to market from these specific hunting episodes were exaggerated. Typically, a major nest flock in Van Buren County, Michigan, was said by the pro-conservation naturalist William Hornaday to have yielded 11.88 million birds. A game dealer, by contrast, working from more reliable figures, gave a total cull of just 7.56 million. Schorger thought even this an overestimate.[65]

While the specifics may have been enlarged, it is difficult to understate the remorseless, cumulative,

Pennsylvanian, 'that when the Pigeons continue with us all winter, we shall have a sickly summer.'[56] On some occasions the damage to crops was so feared, communities sought divine intervention. The dove may have been the enduring symbol of the Holy Spirit, but with this species they were taking no chances. More than once the Bishop of Quebec excommunicated Passenger Pigeon flocks.[57] In a rather bizarre reversal of the quackery described in Jim Crace's novel *The Pesthouse*, some Canadian communities viewed pigeon not as a cure for the flux; they thought eating them spread cholera.[58]

The birds across an empty sky elicited images that were aqueous, flowing and riverine. Yet birds at roost among the forest or in their nesting congregations, which could cover as much as 2,460 km² (950 miles²), demanded a language that somehow bridged scenes of impossibly random, noise-filled chaos and which yet resolved into a kind of functioning whole. John James Audubon wrote of one roost in Kentucky:[59]

> The noise which they made, though yet distant, reminded me of a hard gale at sea, passing through the rigging of a close-reefed vessel. . . . The Pigeons, arriving by thousands, alighted everywhere, one above another, until solid masses as large as hogsheads were formed on the branches all around. Here and there the perches gave way under the weight with a crash, and falling to the ground, destroyed hundreds of the birds beneath, forcing down the dense groups with which every stick was loaded. It was a scene of uproar and confusion. I found it quite useless to speak, or even to shout to those persons who were nearest to me. Even the reports of guns were seldom heard, and I was made aware of the firing only by seeing the shooters reloading.[60]

grinding, inexorable impact of all these separate episodes of depredation. The pigeons faded, and faded fast; so fast, in fact, that most could not believe in the idea of their extinction. Right to the very end, some preferred a mythic solution, such as the possibility that the birds had all flown off to South America. Even Schorger remained a little perplexed. While he sifts the data with great thoroughness, the Passenger Pigeon's most exacting scholar cannot really summarise the ecological mechanisms by which the world's most abundant land bird was steered down into the abyss at human hands. The best guess we can muster so long after the events is that they succumbed to multiple factors, but especially over-exploitation and systematic loss of habitat. Here is a momentary glimpse of how eternal oblivion is achieved:

> Day and night the horrible business continued. Bird lime covered everything and lay deep on the ground. Pots burning sulphur vomited their lethal fumes here and there suffocating birds. Gnomes in the forms of men wearing old, tattered clothing, heads covered with burlap and feet encased in old shoes or rubber boots went about with sticks and clubs knocking off the birds' nests while others were chopping down trees and breaking off the over-laden limbs to gather the squabs. Pigs turned into the roost to fatten on fallen birds added their squeals to the general clamor . . .
>
> Of the countless thousands of birds bruised, broken and fallen, a comparatively few could be salvaged yet wagon loads were being driven out in an almost unbroken procession, leaving the ground still covered with living, dying, dead and rotting birds.[66]

It cannot have helped the species' plight that sportsmen took to using Passenger Pigeons for an activity known as trapshooting. It was a pastime inherited from Europe and it involved a mechanical device by which pigeons were simultaneously encouraged to take to the air and present themselves as targets for waiting guns. It began about 1830, had its spiritual home in Cincinnati, Ohio, and, at its peak, may have accounted annually for 500,000 birds nationwide. There is a story from Chicago of a single trapshooter, a hero called Captain Adam Bogardus, who killed 500 pigeons for a $1,000 wager in 528 minutes.[67] By the late 1880s, with the Passenger Pigeon all but finished as a commercial or recreational product, the wit of man finally came up with a substitute for the live target. The disk-like ceramic alternative to the bird, known ever after as a 'clay pigeon', came into use as the species' flame guttered.[68]

When the last female pigeon passed in 1914 – the individual famously known as Martha – the bird was gone. Yet the environmental historian Jennifer Price argues that something uniquely human died too. The phenomenon known as the 'pigeon year', that short exalted moment when birds arrived in a neighbourhood in all their prodigious numbers, was an event that engaged the whole of the human spirit. It triggered consequences that were at once social, political, economic, recreational, cultural and aesthetic. These wider responses were central to the whole meaning of the bird and with their end, Price concludes, 'we lost . . . a wonderfully complex, integrated human connectedness to pigeons'.[69]

Yet cultural responses to the Passenger Pigeon – essays,

histories, articles, books, children's stories – have never ceased since the moment of its demise. One of the most recent and important is by the Canadian novelist and environmental activist Graeme Gibson. His work *Perpetual Motion* (1982) is set in late-nineteenth-century Ontario. Even through its location Gibson reminds us of something crucial. The 'onrushing phalanx of victorious birds, sweeping a path for spring across the March skies', as Aldo Leopold so beautifully described the migrant flocks, knew no national boundaries.[70] Passenger Pigeons were as much a gift to Canada as they were to the USA.

The novel's central character is Robert Fraser, a farmer with a taste for invention. His consuming passion is a machine that is intended to harness the effects of gravity and achieve a state of perpetual motion 'merely by the Power of its own Balance and Pivots'.[71] This machine's proffered dream of limitless energy makes it a powerful symbol for our wish that Passenger Pigeons could be a resource without end. There is a theme of unbridled appetite – emotional, sexual and material – recurring throughout the disparate parts of Gibson's novel. But at its heart is the insatiable desire of Fraser himself. Ironically – given we all know that which Fraser cannot: namely, that the Passenger Pigeon is no more – his own material security, and the wealth underpinning his efforts to create the perpetual motion machine, derive from profits acquired during the local pigeon hunt. Just as the pigeon fell short of the hunters' dreams of profit without limit, so the machine eventually self-destructs in a devastating implosion.

Graeme Gibson illuminates his response to the Passenger Pigeon story and how it offers commentary upon wider and fundamental human themes:

> My sense of the perpetual motion machine is our old (and continuing) human dream of something for nothing. The birds dramatise our commercial destruction of what is natural in order to build abstractions. It is true, I think, that Fraser assumes the pigeons are an endless resource, but all so-called 'developed' societies assume that about everything in Nature. A fellow called René Dubos points out that 'the word "wilderness" occurs approximately three hundred times in the Bible, and all its meanings are derogatory.' (See *The Wooing of Earth*.) We mercilessly exploit life in order to pursue our dreams, either of avarice and power, or benevolence and comfort. In his book *The Failure of Technology*, Friedrich Georg Jünger writes: 'Everything mechanical cuts deeply into life,' and, 'The exploitation of Nature produces not wealth but scarcity.' All of the above is analytical, rational, and more proper to an essay, a rant, or lecture. The task of a novelist, indeed the primary responsibility of a novelist, is to bundle these kinds of intellectual observations into a convincing story of lives lived.[72]

Jennifer Price identifies another aspect of the Passenger Pigeon story with deep resonances for a modern audience. Rather than the Aesopian fable entailed in the idea of superabundance mindlessly squandered, Price is intrigued by the fundamental disconnection between consumers who ate Passenger Pigeons in city restaurants remote from the scenes of dove slaughter. She argues that this late-nineteenth-century lack of genuine relationship with the living birds,

The European Turtle Dove may be a bird of subtle beauty and renowned savour, but it is also becoming a species of major conservation concern.

except as a processed plate of food, anticipates our own experience. 'All of us', Price writes, 'consume nature from within cities or markets, where nature arrives commodified, transformed, already dead, and way out of ecological context. ... And this, as much as the avarice of man, is the moral of the pigeon's story: the specific modern constellation of intensive overuses of nature, urban long-distance connections and strangely unmoored meanings.'[73]

Just in case anyone might wish to project the Passenger Pigeon's story of extinction as an exclusively New World issue, we should close with a short coda on the **European Turtle Dove** *Streptopelia turtur*. It is one of the most beautiful of all Eurasian pigeons, whose emollient purring song I have described as the 'colour of ripening grain made audible'.[74] It is an exceptional columbid, like the Passenger Pigeon, for being a migrant; behaviour that was appreciated even by the prophet Jeremiah: 'Yea, the stork in the heaven

knoweth her appointed times; and the turtle and the crane ... observe the time of their coming ...' (8:7).

There seems something even in the turtle dove's aesthetic appeal that hints at the fine quality of its flesh. Across almost its whole Eurasian range, this 125 g (4.4 oz) bird has been relished as food. There are Egyptian wall reliefs of doves being trapped in nets that are about 4,500 years old and, with the development of new technologies, the slaughter has intensified.[75]

In Portugal, where the species' mass movements might once have been more spectacular than anywhere else, the ornithologist William Tait noted (in 1924) how, near the River Douro, there was 'a continuous fusillade . . . from shortly after sunrise until about 10 o'clock in the morning'.[76] The practice of trapping turtle doves goes back to the fifteenth century in north-west Portugal. However, there are other traditional localities where turtle doves were killed – or,

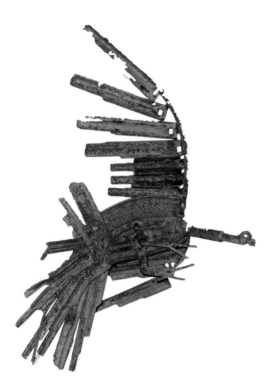

indeed, are still killed – in large numbers including Cyprus, Malta, the Gironde in southern France and central Iberia.

The place most notorious for dove hunting is probably Malta. The small Mediterranean island has a sophisticated attachment to bird trapping and hunting, which, for many male Maltese, are a source of recreation, a statement of both national and gender-oriented identities and a way of maintaining long-established cultural traditions. While hunting was once a major source of subsistence protein, rising standards of living have not seen the activity substantially diminish. For the last quarter of a century there have been between 14,000 and 17,000 registered hunters or trappers (in a total population of *c*.350,000). Their cumulative bag, scattered indiscriminately across scores of species, most of which are not eaten, was assumed in 1990 to be between 2.6 million and 5.8 million birds.[77] In that year, the annual turtle dove kill was put at 160,000–480,000 birds, although this has since declined substantially and this part of the bag at least enjoyed the rationale of the cooking pot.

What is most striking about the continuing slaughter of turtle doves – estimated across the whole European Union at 2–4 million birds annually – is its conflict with the logic generated by the species' massive systemic declines. These have probably been ongoing since the glory days of Portugal's spring-long fusillade recorded by William Tait, but in the last 30 years the turtle dove across 16 European Union countries has suffered a 70 per cent reduction on its 1980 population. In Britain it is 90 per cent.

Yet under pressure from the highly vocal and important hunting lobby, the Maltese government has sought, since 2004, an exclusion from legislation that bans hunting of declining species. What seems most striking is the frame of argument used to justify the killing of protected species both at a national level and also at the point where the man pulls the trigger. For its part, the Maltese government argued that the turtle dove, while it may be in plight locally, had large (and, it should be added, largely unknown) numbers in countries such as Russia and Turkey. At a global level, therefore, this rendered it a species of least concern. In 2009 the argument was rejected and Malta judged in breach of international legislation by the European Court.

For his part, the Maltese hunter on the ground applied much the same logic. 'If I don't shoot it, someone else will, so I'd rather shoot it myself,' one individual explained when asked why he killed as he did.[78] The argument is revealing for drawing its primary meaning from competition among the hunters, and also for its utter lack of reference to the prey itself. It is, in truth, not a rationale for hunting. That surely requires some imaginative transaction, some ecological linkage, between the hunter and his target. To justify the killing as a means to pre-empt one's predatory competitors is little more than a charter for the quarry's eventual extinction.

To return once more to the Passenger Pigeon, in the light of the turtle dove's recent history, is to see both species' fate in sharper focus. To take the lost American bird first. One factor possibly undervalued when assessing how such a superabundant species could have collapsed to zero is the psychological response that was engendered in hunters by the bird's migratory behaviour. As is now the case with the turtle dove, it was the shooter's inability to understand the cumulative total effect of his local actions, and that of all his peers wherever they may have operated, that made a highly abundant but seasonally distributed pigeon so vulnerable to over-hunting. To turn back finally to the European Turtle Dove, perhaps the most shocking thing is our inability to learn from the past and our dismal capacity to repeat it.[79]

◀ The ultimate dove of peace – made by Mozambican sculptors from parts of old weapons that were used in the country's prolonged civil war.

▲ On Malta the hunters use tame decoy birds to lure other wild European Turtle Doves to their deaths.

Cockatoo and Parrot family *Psittacidae*

With perhaps the exception of some Caribou-herding Arctic communities, it is hard to imagine that there are many humans on Earth who are not aware of parrots. The birds are among an elite group of avian families which almost all of us recognise instantly.

Parrots have been present in our arts and literature for thousands of years. For many centuries they have also been a constant source of imagery in the multifarious products of capitalist society, from ceramics and tapestries, to television advertisements and children's fluffy toys. The living birds are themselves a major money-making commodity, and today millions of them are kept as pets all over the world. With the exception of the finches, no other avian family has equally appealed to our sense of ownership. In fact, our desire to possess them is so intense it represents one of the major threats to wild parrots everywhere. Fortunately, important legislation controlling the sale of live birds (firstly in Australia in 1960, then the USA's 1992 Wild Bird Conservation Act and a European Union trade ban in July 2007) has acted as a major cap on this flow of parrots out of the wild and into Western captivity.[1]

There are 359 species in total – one of the largest of all non-passerine families – and despite our universal awareness of parrots, their own natural distribution is heavily biased to the southern hemisphere. Their northern limits across the Americas, Africa and south Asia approximate to the 30th parallel. They reach a peak of diversity close to the Equator, with countries such as Colombia and Peru holding over 50 species each. However, the Brazilian rainforest, the ultimate treasure house of terrestrial life, claims the highest number of parrots of any state (69 species). There is then a secondary

centre of diversity in the west Pacific, with Australia claiming 53 and the island of New Guinea holding 49 species. The whole of Africa, by contrast, has just 23 parrots.

This species diversity then dwindles towards the southern fringes of the Americas and Australasia to a small cluster that are tolerant of temperate conditions. Yet it includes two parrot oddities that are endemic to New Zealand. The acutely threatened **Kakapo** *Strigops habroptila* (world total of 120 birds) is flightless, ground dwelling and the heaviest parrot of all (males weigh up to 2.5 kg: 5.5 lb). The **Kea** *Nestor notabilis* is one of the only carnivorous members of a largely fruit-and-grain-eating family. This high-altitude, fun-loving species (Keas are known to sledge repeatedly down snow slopes or corrugated-iron roofs) is also partial to the fat on live sheep and digs into the area around the kidneys where it creates deep festering wounds. These offences led to a long history of persecution, and by the date of the last bounty payments in 1970 approximately 150,000 Keas had been killed. Today the survivors (*c.*2,000 birds) have turned their attentions to the rubber seals on car windscreens or caravan windows, tyres, tents and their camping contents, walking boots or ski gear, and edible scraps of any description.[2]

The Kea's notoriously destructive antics glance at an aspect of parrot physiology that is manifest in all species – the extraordinarily powerful bill. It is always deep, often spanning the entire height of the head, has a hooked nail and is backed by a massive facial musculature that enables some macaws to crack palm nuts, the hardest seeds in the world. (In a macaw, one-fifth of its entire weight is entailed in that head and bill.)[3] Aside from their bright colours, which invariably include some element of green, parrots also possess zygodactylic toes (two facing forwards and two back like an opposable thumb), which is one reason for their legendary dexterity.

Despite this suite of constant features, which render all species instantly recognisable as members of one family, the parrots encompass a spectrum of sizes and forms. The **Buff-faced Pygmy Parrot** *Micropsitta pusio* of New Guinea measures just 8.4 cm (3.3 in) and weighs about 13 g (0.5 oz), while the South American giant of the family, the spectacularly beautiful **Hyacinth Macaw** *Anodorhynchus hyacinthinus*, is 1 m (3.3 ft) long and its beak alone is bigger than its New Guinean relative.

One other aspect to parrots that is now almost a defining characteristic of the family is the scale of the human threat to them. There are 94 species deemed at risk of extinction, and a further 30 are considered near-threatened.[4] A frequent claim is that this is the most imperilled bird family in the world. However, what appears to be a categorical statement hides a degree of ambiguity. It depends on what is judged to be a species or, indeed, what comprises a bird family. There are groups like the albatrosses in which 18 of 22 taxa are considered at some level of risk (see page 103). Equally, all but three of the world's 23 Hawaiian honeycreepers are in some state of jeopardy (see page 504). However, if the figure is calculated simply as the highest absolute number of a bird family, then parrots can rightly claim the dubious honour. They are the ultimate expression of how we have endangered so much of the natural world.

The Kea of New Zealand is famous for its curiosity, its love of play and its gift for mischief.

Nor is it just the statistics. It is the speed at which the threat has escalated. The periodic audit of all the world's birds by BirdLife International initially identified 41 parrots at risk (1981), then 71 (1988), 89 (1994) and now 94 (2001) – roughly a quarter of all the family. That overall figure contains even more alarming details within it. The macaws – arguably the most totemic of all rainforest birds – and certainly the Neotropical region's largest, most famous and among the most exquisitely coloured parrots – face particularly acute problems. Nine of the world's 16 species are red listed. A further five are already extinct.

PARROTS AS PESTS

It seems almost bizarre to reflect that parrots sometimes present a diametrically opposite facet to humans. They can achieve levels of extraordinary abundance, partly because of their adaptation to man-modified landscapes with all its attendant opportunities, and sometimes the birds become major agricultural pests. The exemplar, probably the world's most numerous parrot, is the **Rose-ringed Parakeet** *Psittacula krameri*. This medium-sized species, with a coral-red bill and pink necklace, occurs across the Indian subcontinent and much of Sahelian Africa to the Atlantic coast. A secondary population has also developed from escaped caged birds in more than a dozen countries from the USA to China, and today they can be heard issuing their shrill raucous flight notes over the streets of Los Angeles, London, Antwerp or Amsterdam. These naturalised Rose-ringed Parakeets are among the most northerly free-flying parrots in the world.[5]

However, it is in the places where this species is native that the bird creates the most lasting and powerful impression. In India the sights and sounds of Rose-ringed Parakeets are almost a background precondition of all human experience. They can be heard from the city centre to the most remote tiger-haunted forest, and from the moment that dawn breaks until the sun sets blood red through the evening layers of dust and wood smoke. Each of these key solar events is accompanied by an intensification of parakeet music, because the birds move in vast flocks either from or to their roost sites.

Ananda Banerjee describes the way in which birds are embedded in so many Indian landscapes:

Against the backdrop of a crimson sky and the cacophony arising from congregations of storks, egrets, ibises, herons and other waterbirds, there are often great aerial manoeuvres at evening time in the famed Keoladeo Ghana National Park in Bharatpur. In fact the returning cormorants and ducks create such an array of Vs and Ws over the Rajasthani sky, it seems a typographers' delight. Perhaps this cannot be said of the thousands of parakeets which arrive in a sudden burst of speed like a set of arrows, in one great *whoosh*. Their beaks shine like red arrowheads as they all dive into the thick canopy over the wetland marshes. Some take up hollow cavities on the bald date palms that line the only road running through the park and engage in a peek-a-boo warble with the passers-by. The occasional screech gives away the other flocks' stealthy flight, about which there always seems a sense of urgency. I have seen it even at much higher elevations in the Himalayan

forests. Looking from above, one notices how the parakeets look ribbon-like, fluttering silently over the gorges, a dazzling near-fluorescent green against the oak and pine forests.[6]

One inevitable consequence of the bird's Indian ubiquity is a deep familiarity with its harsh cacophony among all Western society. Many of us never register it consciously, but Rose-ringed Parakeets are perpetual extras in television programmes or films with an Indian setting. They are, for instance, in the Richard Attenborough biopic of the father of the nation, *Gandhi* (1982). Similarly they are present in the Oscar-winning *Slumdog Millionaire* (2008). However, the more baleful aspect to the birds' huge numbers is beautifully evoked by the Indian ornithologist Salim Ali:

they descend in swarms upon ripening fields of food crops, biting into the ears of grain or cutting off the heads completely and flying to a nearby tree where it is raised up to the bill with one foot and after a nibble or two wastefully discarded . . . Frantic shouts and stones hurled from slings by the ryot [peasant] from

The Rose-ringed Parakeet is one part emblem of tropical exoticism and one part screeching nuisance.

An Australian King Parrot on the arm of a visitor at Lamington National Park, Queensland – such moments of intimacy with a completely wild bird can have an enormous and lasting impact upon people.

beneficiary at outdoor cafes, restaurants and parks, where the wild birds exchange the beauty and vibrancy of their close living presence for scraps of food.

This powerful and moving transaction between parrot and human has offered opportunities to profit-oriented 'nature' centres in Australia, such as the Currumbin Wildlife Sanctuary and O'Reilly's on the edge of Lamington National Park, both in southern Queensland. Seed and fruit are laid on at regular feeding times to encourage the birds' tameness. The first location, which features flocks of Rainbow and **Scaly-breasted Lorikeet** *Trichoglossus chlorolepidotus*, receives 500,000 human visitors annually, while the O'Reilly's hotel (where, at a price, visitors can hand-feed **Australian King Parrot** *Alisterus scapularis* and **Crimson Rosella** *Platycercus elegans*) is among the country's best-known wildlife attractions.[10] Although commerce is at the heart of these feeding events, the 'hands-on' benediction offered by the parrots seems both compelling and life enhancing for many visitors. Up to 800 birds descend at one time and they readily clamber on heads, arms or shoulders in their quest for food. 'I even had a Crimson Rosella fly on to my shoulder trying to get at the Magnum [ice cream] I was eating, and that was supposed to be a wild bird.'[11] These moments of intense intimacy may perhaps be the only occasion in many people's lives when they are in such close contact with another wild vertebrate animal.

However, there is another side to the steady rising arc of the rainbow:

> There are growing issues associated with the extraordinarily noisy (and nasty) impacts of the gigantic roosts, which are frequently situated in very disturbed places such as supermarket car parks, etc. There is also evidence that they are dramatically out-competing the smaller species such as Scaly-breasted and **Musk Lorikeet** *Glossopsitta concinna*. Away from the cities, they are definitely a major issue for fruit and grape growers.[12]

Yet the rainbow's pest status is neither as infamous nor as long-standing as that attaching to a relative, the **Sulphur-crested Cockatoo** *Cacatua galerita* (this striking word is from the Malaysian *kakatúa* for several closely related family members in Asia).[13] This fellow Australian species is one part national emblem, one part public scourge, an ambiguous status that seems to be entailed in the bird's widespread nickname, 'cocky'.

Cockies – since they are almost never solitary – are broad-winged and look wholly white, while their solemnly measured flight is more suggestive of a large egret than a parrot. Airborne flocks of another widespread Australian relative, the **Red-tailed Black Cockatoo** *Calyptorhynchus banksii*, are even more massively impressive. With their deep, slow, deliberate wingbeats these bigger, longer-winged and largely black parrots have an almost proprietorial air in flight: 'We call them the "mafia of the skies", because they are black and fly around surveying the scene, as if they are keeping an eye on everything.'[14]

This physical beauty is not matched by the bird's voice. The red-tailed black has a loud, guttural rolling note, but the Sulphur-crested Cockatoo produces a noise that is Jurassic in its harshness. Ugly and grating, the sound has also appealed to the indigenous sense of humour. 'That

his machan [bed] amidfield only serve to move the destructive horde to a different corner of the field where the depredation complacently continues.[7]

Studies conducted in the Punjab indicated that Rose-ringed Parakeets could be responsible for the loss of as much as a fifth of the region's sunflower crops, while in 1986 the loss of trade earnings caused by parakeets was estimated at 146 million rupees (£8.5 million).[8]

Another country where some parrots are present in huge numbers is Australia. The **Rainbow Lorikeet** *Trichoglossus moluccanus* is commonplace in the eastern third of the country and thrives in suburban environments: 'It is now the most abundant bird in most large cities but certainly Brisbane, Sydney and Melbourne and they are extremely common even in Perth where they are introduced.'[9] With plasticine-red beaks, glistening powder-blue heads and underparts that blend squamated lines of yellow, crimson and navy, they are glorious creatures. They are especially attracted to the nectar and pollen from trees or shrubs widely grown in Australian gardens, such as bottlebrush, grevilleas, banksias and eucalypts. The lorikeet is also a conspicuous

ear-shattering screech has led to the colloquial name of "Australian nightingale". The largest flock I encountered numbered at least 5,000 and as they rose above the fields the noise was like a sky full of audible barbed wire.'[15]

Yet when perched, cockatoos will raise about a dozen forward-curling lemon crown feathers that spread over their heads like a crested helmet, a display that renders the species a gift for graphic designers. Its image is regularly used as a logo on Australian business stationery, or in shop fronts and other commercial insignia. The **Gang-gang Cockatoo** *Callocephalon fimbriatum* (the unusual first name is of Aboriginal origin) has a more exalted symbolism as the state bird for the Capital Territory (the administrative area around Canberra). The strangest of these appropriations of the cockatoo image is the use of the word 'cocky' as an affectionate name for the Australian farmer. It may date back more than 100 years, but today it has a deeply ironic ring.

Many farmers, especially those cockies producing wheat, nuts and fruit, look upon their namesake as vermin and take heavy toll of their seemingly irrepressible numbers. Many of Australia's cockatoo species, including the beautiful **Galah** *Eolophus roseicapilla* with its rich dark-pink breast and silky grey upperparts, are killed, sometimes illegally, and occasionally in huge numbers. In the state of Victoria a recent six-year campaign of gassing and trapping accounted for 80,000 birds.

Although there are official mass captures of (mainly) **Long-billed Corella** *Cacatua tenuirostris* and innumerable birds shot by irate farmers literally everywhere grain is grown, the truly impressive and appalling slaughter is entirely illegal and unspoken. While working on crop damage by cockatoos, Galahs and **Cockatiel** *Nymphicus hollandicus* in sunflower and sorghum crops in the 1980s, it was common practice to cross the aftermath of a mass poisoning of hundreds, sometimes thousands, of the larger species, who had feasted on grain soaked in cattle drench (pesticide meant for ectoparasites). Huge numbers certainly died in excruciating pain but many more were sat around or attempted to fly, most to die a prolonged and presumably agonising death. Of course, no one knew anything about who was responsible. Such practices would be harder to get away with today, one hopes.[16]

One can, however, sympathise with some of the victims of cockies. A pecan-nut grower in New South Wales claimed to spend AUS $15,000–$20,000 on aeroplanes and pilots to scare cockatoos out of his 70,000 trees, saving him possibly as much as 3–4 tonnes of nuts per harvest. A domestic example of their destructive potential comes from Melbourne, where a band of Sulphur-crested Cockatoos over two days in May dismantled large parts of a wooden house. 'They'd chewed large holes in every wall, pulled out windows and turned much of the woodwork into a fine layer of mulch.'[17]

THE FIRST PARROTS IN EUROPE

It is striking how the parrots' capacity for mischief has been an enduring theme among Western observers from the times of Europe's earliest encounter with the birds. Aristotle suggested that those individuals reaching Greece from the east were already being allowed to indulge in alcohol. After 'drinking wine', he wrote, 'the parrot becomes more saucy

than ever'.[18] (It seems this vice is not entirely a matter of bad habits picked up in their misspent captivity: 'In Queensland the wild lorikeets and rosellas fed on the over-ripe pears in a neighbour's garden and were so drunk they fell on the ground. They also do it on the sugar from gum trees. They love it and sometimes fall out of the tree.')[19]

By the time that captive parrots – and invariably they were Rose-ringed Parakeets or its close relatives from India – had become a more widespread plaything for wealthy Romans, they had been trained to perform a variety of party tricks. There was a bizarre painting found at Herculaneum (the settlement near Pompeii buried by the eruption of Vesuvius in AD 79) of a parakeet placed in harness and drawing a tiny chariot manned by a grasshopper.[20] It suggests how the birds had been adopted as a symbol of novelty, exoticism and, perhaps above all, wealth – themes that are still engrained in attitudes towards, and treatment of, the whole parrot family today. However, the Romans had a way of pushing these values to their outer limits. It seems supremely of a piece with their voraciously materialist mindset that they should eventually get around to eating parrots. There were various Roman recipes for cooking them, but their tongues were apparently prized titbits for the banquet. The exquisitely corrupt emperor Elagabalus found a way to outdo even his subjects. He fed parrots to his captive lions and parrot heads to his staff.[21]

One intriguing development in the West's regard for the birds came about after Rome fell and Christian Europe began to reacquaint itself with parrots in the Age of Discovery. Colonial expeditions to both Africa and the Americas led to increased contact with new parrot-rich areas. In fact during the early years of Portuguese exploration along the Atlantic coastline of South America, the whole country was featured on the original sixteenth-century maps as the 'Land of Parrots' (*Brasilia sive terra papa-gallorum*).[22]

The Red-tailed Black Cockatoo is one of the largest and most impressive parrots in all Australasia.

As well as the ongoing connection with tropical exoticism, parrots acquired very specific associations for medieval Europeans that are now rather more difficult to comprehend. Yet early Christian texts dwelled on the birds' supposed cleanliness and the dense waterproof quality of their plumage. This was deemed analogous to the Holy Family, who were seen as similarly pure, and, just as the birds were unaffected by rain, so were they untouched by sin. A further connection, which more than one commentator has judged to 'defy rational explanation', drew on the parrots' gift of speech and their common training to announce *Ave* (the Latin for 'hail'): the very word used by the Angel Gabriel when he first greeted Mary with news of her immaculate conception.[23] 'Ave Maria' was (and still is) an important Catholic prayer to the holy mother.[24]

This religious attachment to parrots found expression in the birds becoming highly valued pets for a number of popes. In 1418, Pope Martin V had two employees specifically tasked with accompanying his parrots on their travels. More than 40 years later, one of Martin's successors was paying wages to a similar custodian for his birds, while Pope Leo X, scion of the Medici family and son to Lorenzo the Magnificent, had his South American parrots – gifted to him by the Portuguese king Manuel I – paraded through the streets of Rome.[25]

Yet another outcome of this version of the parrot as a paragon of virtue and intelligence was a long history of European artworks that depict important moments in the Christian story, where these birds are featured. In paintings of the Garden of Eden, for instance, parrots were habitual extras. (It is intriguing to find that the appeal has not dimmed 500 years later. In images of Paradise featured in *Awake!* and *Watchtower*, the magazines of the Jehovah's Witnesses,

the birds have reclaimed their long-standing residence: e.g. *Awake!*, 22 November 1996, page 10.)

In the Late Middle Ages they were often depicted with the Virgin Mary, either sitting in her lap or on her shoulder. The theme was treated by, among others, Jan van Eyck (*The Madonna with Canon George van der Paele* in the Groeninge Museum, Bruges, Belgium), Albrecht Dürer (*Madonna and Child with a Multitude of Animals* in the Albertina, Vienna, Austria) and Peter Paul Rubens (*The Holy Family with Parrot* in the Museum of Fine Arts, Antwerp, Belgium). One wonders, incidentally, if it was this medieval and Renaissance link between the Virgin Mother and the bird that led people regularly to call their pet parrots 'Mary', and which then bequeathed us 'Polly' as a stock English name for the bird (Polly being a familiar version of Mary). Or was Poll / Polly simply a diminutive of the word 'parrot' itself?[26] It is noteworthy that there are no links with Polly (or Mary) in France or Italy. In these countries the names for the conventional pet parrot are respectively 'Coco' and 'Loreto'.[27]

With the growing traffic of parrots from all parts of the tropics to Europe the birds underwent a twofold change in status. On the one hand, the increased frequency of parrots as pets dislodged them from their exalted role as an amusement for princes and pontiffs. However, they were also uprooted from their connection to piety and religious values. This loss of rank was mirrored by the changed meaning of the word 'popinjay'. Derived from the medieval French, *papegei*, this had been the original word for the birds. Yet by the time of Shakespeare it had been replaced by 'parrot' as the name for the actual creature, while popinjay became merely figurative – an expression of abuse for a showy and empty-headed person (see *Henry IV*, I, Act 1, Scene 3).

What was left once parrots had been stripped of their scarcity and their metaphoric link to virginal purity were the same old qualities that had been projected on to them since classical times and even earlier. They were exotic. They were frivolous. Possession of a parrot signified that the owner could afford life's luxuries and had social access to people who traded such items. From these connections to wealth and caprice flowed their natural bedfellow. Parrots became sexy. A secondary but strong trend in European artworks is the parrot as metaphor for erotic temptation (in west Africa the red tail feathers of the **Grey Parrot** *Psittacus erithacus* are even now considered an aphrodisiac).[28]

A classic image of the sexual parrot is a painting by the Dutch artist Nicolaes Berchem, *A Moor Presenting a Parrot to a Lady* (c.1660), which is now housed in the Wadsworth Atheneum in Hartford, Connecticut, USA. It shows a well-dressed woman of wealth, both restrained and urged on by her maid as she confronts a black African dealer proffering for sale a South American parrot species, **Red-and-green Macaw** *Ara chloropterus*. The woman, in a posture that is at once coquettish and scalding, seems to restrain her male supplicant who, though dressed in equally extravagant costume, is caught in a gesture of tradesman's servility, while at the same time holding his hand suggestively to his open mouth. The picture's meaning has been disputed, but the sexual subtext is undeniable. To one side of the main characters stands a soldier looking on, a part-eaten peach and glass of wine to hand. Behind him a minstrel strums love songs to his maid. Above them all stands Venus, the goddess of love, her fingers caressing her fulsome left breast. (Note,

Nicolaes Berchem's *A Moor Presenting a Parrot to a Lady* is rather mysterious in content, but it typifies the centuries-old trade in wild-caught macaws.

The requirement for minerals to aid their digestion leads some parrots to gather in large numbers. At Tambopata National Reserve in Peru the clay lick attracts Blue-and-yellow Macaws, Mealy Amazons, Blue-headed Parrots and Chestnut-fronted Macaws.

incidentally, the other birds which complete this seductive tableau of Western luxury: the bird-of-paradise feather [see page 402] tucked in the Moor's turban, the ostrich plumes [see page 16] arrayed above the soldier's hat, as well as that of the minstrel, and finally the doves of love billing and cooing at Venus' naked feet [see page 233].)

The overarching point to make, drawing on all these reflections of the parrot as religious emblem or as sexual motif, is the way in which the birds served (and still serve) Western imaginative ends without any regard for their living reality, or their status as genuine inhabitants of a real landscape. (In the Berchem painting this absolute disconnection from true geography could not be more emphatic: a north African trader offers a South American bird in a Mediterranean Christian port.) What all these deployments of parrots

underscore is how they were treated as adjuncts to our world. It is this fundamental appropriation of the birds that is at the heart of almost our entire experience of the family, and hinders any real understanding of them as wild birds even today. Parrots are held in cages, but they are trapped in our imaginations.

Of all birds only perhaps the penguins have been so thoroughly humanised. In each case, one can understand the anthropomorphism. Penguins – upright, two-legged, flightless, arm-like flippers for wings and dressed in 'evening wear' – look like us (see page 92). Parrots, however, sound like us. They have the gift that (we assume) separates humankind from the rest of nature. Parrots talk.

One cannot overlook the importance of their glorious colours, nor the ways that parrots affect our other senses. As

As well as being creatures of enormous beauty, Red-and-green Macaws are rich in cultural meanings, especially for the people of Amazonia.

Amigo, a Yellow-naped Amazon, is the star of Jurong Bird Park, Singapore, and can sing in three different languages.

I am aware, only one comparable example of a bird preserving memory of its lost human neighbours (see Lyrebird family, page 360).[30]

As well as explaining the deep human attachment to keeping parrots, their gift of mimicry illuminates aspects of their own natural history. Their speech has become an important measure of their own brainpower. Of all birds – and the **Blue-and-yellow Macaw** *Ara ararauna* has the highest among parrots – they have the largest intra-cerebral weight index. In the latter species it is 28.07; while in the chicken, the lowest of its class, it is just 2.7.[31] Despite the words 'parrot-fashion' suggesting a kind of rote learning that owes little to real aptitude, parrots are widely recognised for their intelligence, and none more so than Alex, the African Grey Parrot belonging to the renowned American scholar of animal communication, Irene Pepperberg.

This stocky powder-grey bird of west African rainforest has long been recognised for its linguistic ability, but Pepperberg's studies from the late 1970s until Alex's death aged 31 in 2007 (his passing was marked by an obituary in the magazine *The Economist*) revealed the cognitive powers that underlay its mastery of human sounds. While his vocabulary may not have been huge, Alex recognised the relationships between the approximately 100 words he had mastered and 23 separate objects, five colours, four shapes and five numbers. Alex could use language to express his recognition of form, number, colour and difference between the objects that he was shown.

When confronted with pairs of items – such as a green piece of wood with four corners and a blue piece with four corners – he would be asked, 'What's same?' or, 'What's different?' Choosing between 'shape' and 'colour', Alex would give the correct answer 75 per cent of the time. When he was presented with new, previously unseen, objects, in colours that he had not acquired a label for, he actually scored correct answers 85 per cent of the time. He could even combine his established words to express new concepts. Confronted for the first time with an apple, he conflated the initial part of 'banana', which was a fruit flesh he knew of comparable quality, and 'cherry', which shared the outer skin colour of the new item, to form 'banerry'. It remained his name for the food.

Another series of tests examined his numeracy. He would be shown two cups under which would be concealed varying numbers of nuts. He would then be asked for a total and over six months he was right on 85 per cent of occasions. When then shown either three blue wooden blocks or a green plastic figure in the shape of a number 5, Alex would be asked, 'What colour bigger?' He was right again to a high degree of accuracy, demonstrating that he understood the value of the number, regardless of whether it were expressed in an equivalent amount of actual objects or through its symbol. These tests demonstrated an intelligence comparable with the primate brain of chimpanzees or a four- or five-year-old human child.[32]

One obvious purpose to which humans have put these avian capabilities is business. Parrots have been trained to lie on their backs and play with small stones using their feet, to screw a nut on and off a large bolt, to fly through hoops, to roller-skate, ride a bicycle, play dead and come back to life, to twirl torches lighted at both ends, and to load and fire a tiny cannon.[33] In India they have also been schooled in the arts of prognostication.

well as touch and taste, they have appealed even to our sense of smell, because the birds often have a distinctive odour – in macaws it is detectable at 2 m (6.5 ft) – and honey-like in some species.[29] Yet it is their powers of speech that are their central attractant and explain why we have kept the birds captive for many thousands of years.

The earliest-ever European eyewitness account of the family, by the Greek scholar Ctesias in the late fifth century BC, concerned a **Plum-headed Parakeet** *Psittacula cyanocephala* that could speak words of a south Asian language. Almost all literary pet parrots have had their famous phrases: from Poll, the desert-island bird tamed in Daniel Defoe's *Robinson Crusoe* ('Poor Robin Crusoe'), to the 'Pieces of eight' fired by Captain Flint from Long John Silver's shoulder in Robert Louis Stevenson's *Treasure Island*. Flint bequeathed us, incidentally, not just those immortal psittacine words, but also an axiomatic link between pirates and parrots.

However, perhaps the most moving of all the vocabularies spoken by a bird was the one encountered by Alexander von Humboldt during his early-nineteenth-century journeys in modern-day Venezuela. The great German explorer came across a parrot on the Orinoco which was the last living keeper of a language spoken by the Atures people, a race which, in the manner of so many Amerindians (and American parrots) under European influence, had become extinct. In the annals of bird–human stories there is, as far as

The roadside fortune-teller (in white dhoti and shirt with his forehead smeared with holy ash and vermilion) has a series of pre-written cards (27 fortune cards based on the Indian cosmic system) predicting what the future will be (mostly they are optimistic messages). The lovable parakeet, known as *tota* in Hindi, with wings clipped so it cannot fly away, walks daintily across and digs into the pack of cards or picks up one of the tarot cards with its beak which are neatly displayed on a small table/stool and the fortune-teller takes it from there to interpret the prediction in exchange for a small sum of money.[34]

The party trick that has appealed to us before all others, however, is simply the gift of speech. Parrots like Alex have become star performers with national or, in the latter's case, international reputations. Another avian celebrity was a British-born **Budgerigar** *Melopsittacus undulatus* called Sparkie (1954–1962), who was able to reproduce ten nursery rhymes, 383 sentences and 531 words and was the winner of the 1958 BBC Cage Word Contest. The following year he was disqualified because he was just too good. His contract selling bird feed left Sparkie with a post-mortem bank balance of £1,000 (in excess of £16,000: $25,000 today), and record sales of over 20,000. Television and newspaper appearances were commonplace. In 2009, almost half a century after his death, this remarkable bird was the subject of a musical performance, *Sparkie: Cage and Beyond*, by British composer Michael Nyman and German artist Carsten Nicolai. The Berlin performance of the show even featured a 'live' appearance by Sparkie himself, albeit as a stuffed skin, which is normally housed in Newcastle's Great North Museum: Hancock.[35]

An incidental benefit possessed by the talking parrot is an ability to suggest the way home should it ever get lost:

When I was a little girl over 50 years ago we found a blue Budgerigar in our back garden. Having a vacant cage, since we had just lost our latest budgie, my Father caught the bird and put it in, but it immediately started to talk about Monica. Saying 'Monica's going to church', and other expressions relating to her. We looked in the local paper under 'Lost and Found' and saw an advert from a lady living some five miles away who had lost her treasured budgie that talked about 'Monica'. We rang her and she told us her address and we all piled in the car and delivered the budgie back to its grateful owner. She was over the moon to have located her little feathered friend.[36]

Even more impressive was an American Budgerigar called Puck who earned a place in the *Guinness Book of World Records* by reproducing 1,777 words or phrases. One extraordinary aspect of this vocabulary was that Puck had only been taught about 50 words by his owner. The rest of his repertoire had been picked up from the radio or from overhearing conversations. Eventually Puck himself was an active participant in this household repartee. Once, when a pair of veterinarians arrived to record his precise verbal output, the observer grew very frustrated with the bird's quick-fire delivery. 'Please slow down. You talk too fast', she said, to which Puck responded: 'What's wrong, stupid?'[37]

It is in these moments – when parrots seem to transcend

Sparkie the Budgerigar had a vocabulary of 531 words.

species boundaries and communicate directly with us, either by coincidence or, as most owners would claim, because the birds understand the significance of both the words and their context – that their linguistic skills are most compelling and affecting. The Canadian author Graeme Gibson records just such a moment of deep pathos:

Early in the autumn of 1964 I bought a parrot in Oaxaca, Mexico. He was a handsome creature, very healthy and full of life. I named him Harold Wilson. He scarcely said anything at all, but he barked like two dogs at once, made roaring noises like a vacuum cleaner, and spoke my sons' names. He was bright and affectionate, and soon became an amusing and responsive member of the family.

However, back in Toronto a year later I became increasingly uneasy about Harold's situation. As winter cold and darkness set in I saw that the bird was miserable: diminishing daylight must have been bad enough, but I also sensed that he was lonely. By spring I'd arranged to give him to the Toronto Zoo, a modest operation back then. The director led us to the aviary himself, where a congenial cage had been prepared. Waiting inside was a female parrot named Olive. Watched by my sons and a gathering crowd, I entered the cage, with Harold on my wrist. When I placed him on the main perch, Olive shuffled away. I said my goodbyes and turned to leave. Then Harold did something that astonished me. For the very first time, and in exactly the voice my kids might have used, he called out 'Daddy!' When I turned to look at him he was leaning towards me expectantly. 'Daddy', he repeated.

I don't remember what I said to him. Something about him being happier there, that he'd soon make friends. The kind of things you say to kids when you abandon them at camp. But outside the aviary I could still hear him calling 'Daddy! Daddy!' as we walked away. I was shattered to discover that Harold knew my name, and that he did so because he'd identified himself with my children. I now believe he'd known it all along, but was using it – for the first time – out of desperation. Both Konrad Lorenz and Bernd Heinrich mention instances of birds calling out the private names of intimates when threatened by serious danger. I am no longer surprised by such information. We think of our captive birds as our pets, but perhaps we are theirs as well.[38]

THE TRADE IN PARROTS

All those people who love parrots and particularly cherish the richness of their companionship as pets must acknowledge that this gift to humankind has come at an extraordinarily heavy cost for the wild birds. The loss takes two forms. The first concerns the conversion of vibrant wild rainforest communities – since most parrot species are intensely sociable creatures – to captive stock held often in conditions that approximate to solitary confinement. In the 1990s one estimate suggested 50–60 million parrots were in captivity around the world.[39] Another puts the figure at 50 million for the USA alone.[40] While a substantial percentage of these may be cage-bred Budgerigars and Cockatiels, which are two species that are secure and widespread in their native Australia, many parrots now threatened with extinction are still illegally traded as part of a multi-billion-dollar pet industry. Just a single **Golden Parakeet** *Guaruba guarouba* of Brazil, for example, was selling for as much as £10,000 ($15,000) by 1980.[41]

As all those parrot paintings by European old masters indicate, this export business is centuries old. However, we should not assume that Europe was the only civilisation in the market for such glamorous creatures. Pueblo Bonito in Chaco Canyon is the site of some of the most spectacular structures built by the Anasazi people in the twelfth century AD. This complex in north-western New Mexico contained 600 rooms and housed about 1,000 people – until the 1880s, it was North America's largest apartment building – but it also included accommodation for ceremonially important **Scarlet Macaw** *Ara macao*, whose feathers were used in Anasazi rituals. Today the nearest wild birds are 1,700 km (1,060 miles) away in the forests of southern Mexico and the subfossil macaws embedded in 24 cm (10 in) of accumulated guano at Pueblo Bonito provide evidence of a pre-Columbian trans-American trade that flourished for hundreds, if not thousands, of years.[42]

However, it is industrial society that has developed the most rapacious appetite for captive parrots. This zeal reached a crescendo during the last century. As early as the 1930s there were reports of 36,000 of the largest, most charismatic South American parrots being sold, but the trade gathered pace in the post-war years. Given that a lot of the traffic ranged from merely unmonitored transactions or semi-clandestine dealings, right through to outright criminality and smuggling, it is difficult to give a precise picture of the whole enterprise. Yet the data, however fragmentary and localised, are compelling: such as the 200,000 parrots imported into the USA in the nine months from October 1979.[43] In the 1990s the annual legal figure for the USA alone rose to 250,000 birds (worth about $300 million), and in the same decade an estimate for the worldwide legal sales over a five-year span was 4.2 million parrots.[44]

One figure beyond dispute is that for every parrot traded, another one dies in transit. The famous Monty Python 'parrot' sketch by British comedians John Cleese and Michael Palin, in which a 'Norwegian Blue' is deceased even before leaving the pet shop, reflects a tragedy that should actually make us weep. The total mortality by the time they reach the final marketplace is thought to be about 60 per cent. So, for example, between 1994 and 2003, records show that 360,000 Grey Parrots were traded legally. Yet the actual loss to wild populations, after factoring in deaths during transit and adding to this the illegally smuggled birds, may easily have been closer to a million.

The trapping methods are as crude and brutally wasteful of parrot lives as the transportation. The avian commodity is 'free' in its wild form so there is little incentive for attentive care to the raw product. However once it reaches the middleman, a scarce species can be more valuable than illegal narcotics. As an example of disparity in profits achieved by the country trapper as against the city merchant, Mira Tweti, in her book *Of Parrots and People* (2008), suggested that Guyanese locals were receiving $8 for a parrot of the genus *Amazona* and $25 for a Scarlet or Red-and-Green Macaw. In her native USA, Tweti suggested a retail price for these wild-caught Guyanan birds of $1,000 and $1,500 respectively.[45] In Africa during the 1990s a Grey Parrot earned the trapper $5, the middleman $20, but the importing retailer was selling it at $500.[46]

It is the more circumscribed history of the macaws that illuminates the human story of parrot trafficking at its most intense – a saga of widespread corruption, selfishness, greed, but also of people with an emotional commitment to parrots and their ownership that morphs into passionate, even pathological, obsession. Many who have witnessed these large long-tailed birds sailing in rainbow colours over the forest canopy recognise them as the most glorious representatives of their family. Macaws mate for life and they are so tightly bonded that whenever one sees a pair flying, their deep, rhythmically coordinated movements seem to express not just physical synchrony but emotional harmony.

Perhaps the *most* beautiful of the most beautiful parrots are the blue quartet – the Hyacinth, **Lear's Macaw** *Anodorhynchus leari*, **Spix's Macaw** *Cyanopsitta spixii* and **Glaucous Macaw** *Anodorhynchus glaucus*. The last of the group is almost certainly extinct; a victim partly of their young being taken as pets, but more especially of hunting and habitat loss. Most of the verifiable sight records referred to captive birds and date to the nineteenth century. In the wild it had occurred along wooded river systems threading between south-western Brazil, southern Paraguay and north-eastern Argentina and Uruguay. A record by locals in the Brazilian state of Paraná from the 1960s is probably the last ever sighting.[47]

Extensive illegal trapping and trading have reduced the two other Brazilian species, the Hyacinth Macaw (over 6,000 but decreasing) and Lear's Macaw (375 but increasing), to their present paltry world totals. What is so striking about the declines is the way their shrinking numbers run in inverse proportion to their monetary value as pets and to the intensifying cupidity of parrot fanciers. People are said to be willing to pay $75,000–$100,000 for a pair of Lear's Macaws.[48] In 1979 a single German dealer held 200

ARA hyacinthinus.
Le Perroquet à couleur changeante de Saphir
Tab. XXIII.

belong to their pets, rather than vice versa. One challenging aspect of this is the birds' frequent longevity.

In Stevenson's novel *Treasure Island*, Long John Silver suggests that 'they lives for ever mostly' and speculates whether Captain Flint was not already 'two hundred years old'. More plausible was a parrot belonging to the Maharajah of Nawanagar that was said to have an international passport, travel by Rolls-Royce and to be 115.[52] Beyond dispute are the birds that survive above 50 years of age. A South-American-held Scarlet Macaw was known to have lived through four generations of one human family, while Professor Darryl Jones reports:[53]

> I remember a bald 82-year-old cocky (Sulphur-crested Cockatoo) very well. 'Syd' was his name, the same as his owner. The joke went: 'So which one is the real Syd?' Punch line: 'The one with no teeth!' (the human Syd had lost all his teeth decades earlier). This cockatoo outlived his owner by at least five years and after switching to seed from his porridge diet, actually started to re-grow some feathers. His vocabulary was limited to 'Struth!' and 'What you lookin' at!' But the others captured the style of a lost generation: 'Bloody hell it's hot!', 'Trouble and strife!', 'String 'im up, Guvna,' and, 'Shut ya bleeding gob.'[54]

A common occurrence is for parrots *not* to survive the death of their owners, indicating how strongly bonded bird and human can become. A famous example was a Grey Parrot belonging to Frances Stuart, Duchess of Richmond and mistress to the British king Charles II. She apparently kept it for 40 years and when she died in 1702 it outlived her for four days (it is now the oldest surviving bird skin in Britain).[55]

However, not all birds and their owners are as strongly attached to one another. Longevity and intelligence may be factors that make parrots absorbing and satisfying pets, but they also ensure that they are the most demanding. Parrots can be easily offended if ignored or can become highly jealous of other pets, or of other humans who take the owner's attention from themselves. In the wild their mimicry and vocalisations are reflections of a highly complex social life and while in nature the solitary parrot is almost a contradiction in terms, in captivity it is the norm. Studies suggest that many of the verbal phrases mastered by pet birds are the ones most likely to secure them notice from human companions.

When parrots are habitually ignored they show recurrent symptoms of stress, such as plucking their own feathers. In the USA this behaviour is known to occur in 10 per cent of all parrots seen by a veterinarian, but since a little under one in six birds ever visits a clinician, the actual total may be far higher. The writer Mira Tweti suggests that possibly three-quarters of avian pets live a life of neglect or abuse, and that it is 'not uncommon' for parrots to be fed anti-depressant drugs to control *their* dysfunctional behaviour.[56]

One result of a huge increase in parrot keeping in the USA is a parallel rise in the number of rescue centres – charitable institutions that look after the ever-expanding flock of unwanted, abandoned or psychologically disturbed pet birds. Another correlated outcome is the expansion of non-native parrots that are set loose and are now flying freely in the USA, as people rid themselves of their 'problem' birds. One area particularly affected is southern Florida. Within

Hyacinth Macaws, almost certainly all trapped in Brazil.[49] In the 1980s the drain on wild numbers of that species was running at 1,000 a year. One measure of how well the world's biggest parrot takes to a life behind bars is the story of the Paraguayan dealer who received 300 young Hyacinth Macaws in 1972. He had every incentive to keep them alive, given that each one would have traded in the USA for about $2,000. Yet all but three died soon after.[50]

It is the Spix's Macaw, however, that illuminates the ultimate dead end of all this nihilism. The smallest of the blue quartet was confined to gallery woodland in a restricted arid zone of east-central Brazil. First collected for science in 1819 by Johann Baptist Ritter von Spix, the parrot that bears his name actually went unrecognised among this German naturalist's collections until after his death. When it was finally described in 1832 the species was already deemed scarce and local. During the twentieth century, however, the limited numbers were subjected to ceaseless assault by trappers. By the late 1970s it was down to a mere handful, and extinction an outcome obvious to everyone concerned should the depredation continue. Yet the depredation did continue, and when the total was down to three birds, trappers twice smashed clutches of eggs in trying to snare the would-be parents.[51]

In 1987, seizure of two of this remaining trio condemned the species to the ultimate cul-de-sac. For 13 years there was a single male Spix's Macaw left in the wild. He vanished from this Earth in 2000, leaving his species to a peculiar and morbidly ironic fate. The only hope now is the eventual re-release of birds held in captivity (120 in 2010) – birds bred and held sometimes by the very individuals who connived at the total decimation of wild Spix's Macaws.

Mass mortality and population declines among wild species are only one portion of the cost paid by the family for our love of pet parrots. The other part is the birds' life of incarceration once they make it through the trade system and into private ownership. Parrot keepers are often passionately devoted and frequently describe how they feel as if *they*

The first image of Spix's Macaw was painted in 1824 by the man after whom the species is named, Johann Baptist Ritter von Spix. Ironically, he did not realise that it was a new species for science and called 'his' bird a Hyacinth Macaw.

▶ A shaman of the Bora people from the Peruvian Amazon, Guillermo Rodriguez Gomez sports his headdress of macaw tail feathers.

a short distance one could encounter a truly multinational selection (each bird's natural range is in brackets) including: **Monk Parakeet** *Myiopsitta monachus* (mainly Argentina), **Nanday Parakeet** *Nandayus nenday* (central South America), **Mitred Parakeet** *Aratinga mitrata* (Peru and Bolivia), **Blue-crowned Parakeet** *Aratinga acuticaudata* (South America), **Red-crowned Amazon** *Amazona viridigenalis* (Mexico), **Chestnut-fronted Macaw** *Ara severus* (Amazonia), **Yellow-chevroned Parakeet** *Brotogeris chiriri*, **Red-masked Parakeet** *Aratinga erythrogenys* (Ecuador and Peru), **White-eyed Parakeet** *Aratinga leucophthalma* (Amazonia), Budgerigar (Australia), Rose-ringed Parakeet (India) and just conceivably Blue-and-yellow Macaw. Parts of southern Florida and California (where there may be even more non-native species) probably have the most diverse parrot assemblages of anywhere outside of the family's genuine range.[57]

PARROTS AND AMERINDIANS

While the subject of keeping parrots as pets looms large in the whole history of our relations with this family, one aspect that receives less attention is the importance of the birds to the people who first tamed them. The Amerindians of South America have probably kept them as household companions and taught them to speak for at least 10,000 years, surely one of the oldest ongoing intimate relationships between people and birds on Earth.

Although parrots, like most other products of the rainforest, can be treated as utilitarian objects by these tribal communities, they are sometimes accorded a central place in the tribe's overarching belief system. Charged with complex cultural meanings, the birds are appropriated as symbolic entities, but they are also recognised and valued as genuine neighbours – as separate wild communities – whose parallel

This rock drawing from the Petroglyph National Monument in New Mexico probably represents a macaw. The birds were sourced from southern Mexico and their feathers had ceremonial value as symbols of the sun and of fertility.

lives in the forest canopy or in their cave nesting sites are a wished-for expression of the wholeness of life. It is this sense of shared destiny between indigenous people and parrots, woven into Amerindian mythology, which Western society, for all its sophisticated traffic and supposed devotion to pet birds, would do well to heed.

A key characteristic of birdlore among Amerindians is the extent to which each detail of these cultural responses relates to a much larger philosophical whole. A physical object, even of the most practical kind, is seldom just a material object. It is imbued with multiple symbolic meanings. A perfect example is the gourd rattle, the so-called *hebumataro*, possessed by shamans among the Warao people of the Orinoco Delta in Venezuela.

The shaman is a central figure in indigenous life, combining roles that approximate to those of priest, psychiatrist and doctor, but he is also a general keeper of shared cultural values. For the Warao shaman, known as *wishiratu*, his calabash rattle is at one level just a gourd with a wooden handle and sparse macaw-feather adornments. Yet it is also a sacred item and each of its components is obtained through trials of the shaman's courage, power and ability. In assembling a *hebumataro* he also creates a model of the Warao's vision of the Earth, with its haft standing for the world's central axis. The whooshing sound it creates when whirled round helps the shaman contact the higher powers, and the stones inside that produce the sacred noise – 250–300 pieces for an experienced shaman but fewer for a novice – are thought of as his 'family' of spirit-helpers. Obtaining these small quartzite stones is itself a trial and expense, since they come from the neighbouring countries of Trinidad or Guyana.

Key elements of this precious object are the feathers taken from Scarlet and Blue-and-yellow Macaws by the shaman himself. The quest for these all-important plumes involves him locating a particularly tall palm tree that is selected not merely for the macaws that feed on its fruits, but because the shaman uses the stipules off the leaves on this specific palm to create his sacred cigars. These 30–60 cm (12–24 in) rolls of tobacco are no mere super-smokes: they are the ritual drugs which, gulped down in huge draughts, help the shaman achieve his ecstatic trances. To secure macaw feathers the shaman climbs 36 m (118 ft) into the canopy of the giant tree and waits, precariously balanced, risking death even, to snare the wild birds as they come to feed. However, he takes only what he needs. And it involves the painstaking capture of several birds because each must be released unharmed, except for the handful of plucked feathers that are too few to impede the macaw's flight.[58]

The same kind of inter-relationship between the part and the whole – the individual action or physical object and its wider context of spiritual and philosophical values – is manifest in the life of the Bororo people of the Mato Grosso region in central Brazil and on the fringes of the Pantanal, one of the richest wetlands on Earth. The Bororo are known as 'the crowned ones' for their magnificent feathered diadems, key components of which are macaw feathers.

The Bororo's religious values and ideas of cosmic order are expressed even in the structure of their own dwellings. The village comprises a precisely configured circular pattern of huts ordered around a larger middle house (the *baito*). The outer dwellings are designated as female and the inner

A little girl of the Yahua people with her pet White-winged Parakeet reflects a tradition of parrot keeping by Amerindians that probably dates back 10,000 years.

▶ Parrot body parts, such as these macaw (and oropendola) feathers, are still an important element in Amerindian ceremonial costume and ritual.

building as male. The *baito* is temple, school, workshop and place of secret ritual, while the semicircular plaza to the west side of the *baito* is a site for public ceremonies. The outer circle of female houses is further divided in precise order among the different clan elements of the tribe, while the eastern and western sections of the village, which is split in half by the path of the sun along its east–west axis, have additional physical and spiritual associations. The west side of the village is linked with the moon, black, death, night and male, but the east side is connected to the sun, brilliant red, fertility, daytime and female.

These domestic arrangements seem to have taken us far from the subject of the parrots' cultural importance, but such is the ecological linkage between each part of Bororo life to its cosmic whole, that almost everything is connected to everything else. The psychological relationship between certain colours and particular values finds expression in the spectrum of bodily ornaments – crowns, diadems, headbands, facial paintings, lip plugs, earrings, bracelets, necklaces, pectoral pieces, and arm- and legbands – worn by the Bororo in the course of their ritualised lives. The macaws, particularly two species, the Red-and-green (known as *nabure*) and Scarlet Macaws, are at the heart of these feather-expressed cultural ideas, since they are the source of the long crimson plumes that are considered so important to the tribe.[59]

The birds are caught as youngsters, and named and raised in the village by the women, to whom they are symbolically linked. They are never killed and even when an individual pet dies it is a source of great sadness; its anointed featherless body being buried with careful ritual. While different elements of the community have priority to wear some colours and types of bird feather, all the separate clans and

subdivisions of Bororo society wear macaw feathers. Indeed the people believe that they are themselves *nabure* (Red-and-green Macaws). In real life the species nest in caves or cavities in cliffs where the Bororo once buried their dead. The spirits of these ancestors are thought to come back to the terrestrial world embodied as macaws to eat the nuts and other foods that the Bororo themselves enjoy.

A classic illustration of the part played by both the symbolic macaws and by the birds as manifest in their all-important crimson wing and tail feathers is in the rite of passage conducted on the naming of a Bororo child. The anthropologist Elizabeth Netto Calil Zarur suggests that these rituals, like that performed at a person's death, 'are metaphors of a spiritual bond that exists between the Bororo and *nabure*':

> In the naming ceremony, the infant, decorated like a newborn macaw, first receives public recognition as a member of Bororo society. The chanting during the naming ceremony invokes the similarities between *nabure*'s baby bird and the Bororo infant . . . At the end of each verse in the chant, reference is made to a rocky mountain where the baby came from . . . The metaphorical link between the bird and the Bororo is reinforced by recalling the common birthplace of the child and bird, a nest in a rocky mountain.[60]

South America's enormously diverse spectrum of indigenous communities also hunt parrots, eat them and utilise their body parts as personal adornments. The fantastic headdresses worn by Amerindians, which are surely some of the most beautiful of all avian artefacts, frequently incorporate the tail and wing feathers of parrots, especially macaws. (One incidental development flowing from this has been an acquired ability to make live birds produce plumes with specific colours. By rubbing parts of the body with ointments that include animal fat and frog's blood the parrot artificially generates feathers of the desired hue, which is often yellow.)[61]

Indigenous use of these parrots is increasingly affected and caught up in their wider environmental context in South America. Nowhere more so than in the Beni department of north-eastern Bolivia, an area of tropical savannah enormously rich in wildlife. One cultural donation to the rest of the country is the Beni dance of the *macheteros*, a blend of post-colonial Christian ritual strongly infused with indigenous elements, that is performed at key ceremonies including Christmas and Easter. Part of the costume worn by *macheteros* is a spectacular headdress of macaw feathers (*plumaje*) shaped like the rays of a dawning sun. These glorious corollas of avian colour are deeply rooted in local life and feature in regional cultural insignia, such as the coat of arms for the Beni capital, Trinidad. It has also acquired wider Bolivian representation, as well as achieving a huge leap of cultural context, as part of the costume worn by Miss Bolivia in the Miss World competitions. (This link affirms, incidentally, both the specifically psittacine and the generically avian connections between parrots and human sexuality.)

While the headgear might be rooted in local life, it has also long taken toll of at least five macaws. Birds are shot and hunted for their feathers, including the critically endangered **Blue-throated Macaw** *Ara glaucogularis*, of which there are just *c*.250 left in the wild (it was once widely traded for captivity). A single headdress can involve killing ten macaws. In an attempt to uncouple the *machetero* traditions from their damage to wildlife, without disrupting the activities' cultural centrality for Beni people, the environmental group Asociación Armonía has tried to find substitutes for feathers of hunted macaws.

Feathers made from cloth and the parts of palm fronds, the registration of all existing macaw headdresses and the cessation of local-government payments for hunted macaw skins (for use in *plumaje*) are part of a concerted effort to make good environmental practice an integral element of this Beni tradition. These new developments are typical of the kinds of social accommodation that are required to protect parrots in their increasingly stressed native landscapes. To date there has been a 30 per cent reduction in macaw mortality, but the aim is a total voluntary cessation.[62]

Hoatzin family *Opisthocomidae*

It seems deeply appropriate that the **Hoatzin** *Opisthocomus hoazin* has such a strange name (pronounced 'hwatsin'), because this is one of the world's genuine avian eccentrics. Sixty centimetres (24 in) in length and bizarre in shape – a tiny head 'mounted by a great unruly crest' on a heavy pheasant's body, with a long broad tail – the bird is further distinguished by loud raucous calls and a lethargic, clumsy manner.

Hoatzins are awkward in flight (resembling 'grotesque chachalacas') but they also use their wings almost as hands to clamber gracelessly through the dense forest that they inhabit.[1] As chicks they even possess, rather like the celebrated fossil bird the *Archaeopteryx*, two hooked claws on the wing edge that help them to cling on to the branches (the claws are lost as they mature). If they cannot escape from danger using these vestiges of their dinosaur past, then

The strangeness of the Hoatzin from the South American rainforest is recognised in it having a bird order all to itself.

259

young Hoatzins fall into the water and swim from trouble, climbing back into the canopy once it has passed.

The great American naturalist William Beebe witnessed this extraordinary behaviour. In writing of it he bore witness not just to the impact of the Hoatzin, but to those feelings aroused in us occasionally by birds, when their living reality seems somehow equally eloquent of a very ancient past.

> The young hoatzin stood erect for an instant, and then both wings of the little bird were stretched straight back, not folded, bird-wise, but dangling loosely . . . For a considerable fraction of time he leaned forward. Then without effort, without apparent leap or jump he dived straight downward, as beautifully as a seal, direct as a plummet and very swiftly. There was a scarcely-noticeable splash, and as I gazed with real awe, I watched the widening ripples which undulated over the muddy water – the only trace of the whereabouts of the young bird.
>
> It seemed as if no one, whether ornithologist, evolutionist, poet or philosopher could fail to be profoundly impressed at the sight we had seen. Here I was in a . . . very modern boat, with the honk of motor horns sounding from the river . . . in the year nineteen hundred and sixteen; and yet the curtain of the past had been lifted and I had been permitted a glimpse of what must have been common . . . millions of years ago. It was a tremendous thing, a wonderful thing to have seen, and it seemed to dwarf all the strange sights which had come to me in all other parts of the earth's wilderness.[2]

As the nineteenth-century British ornithologist Alfred Newton put it, the Hoatzin has 'long exercised the ingenuity of classifiers'.[3] Over the centuries ornithologists have proposed its relationship with eight separate bird orders. Today it is deemed most closely related to the African group called turacos (see below), but the Hoatzin has been placed in its own separate order, Opisthocomiformes. To give a sense of how exceptional that is, the world's entire list of over 10,500 species is divided into just 30 orders. The Hoatzin has one of these to itself.

The Brazilian naturalist Helmut Sick called it 'the most notable product of bird evolution in the world's greatest river systems, the Amazon and the Orinoco'.[4] Sick not only restates the Hoatzin's singularity, he also maps out its basic range across the South American rainforest. Its suitably odd diet mainly comprises the foliage of trees, a preference that has earned it the description of an 'arboreal cow'.[5] Its greens are pre-digested in a massively enlarged muscular crop that can account for a third of its entire body weight.

These peculiarities of diet and digestive tract – in which ferments what Sick has called a 'great deglutinated vegetable mass' – help to explain the Hoatzin's reputation as a smelly bird.[6] Its Brazilian name, *Catingueiro*, derives from the verb *catingar*, 'to stink'. The odour has been likened to 'that of a cow house', but far more telling is another comparison: 'musk combined with wet hides'. Anyone who has ever encountered the noxious blast from a working tannery will know exactly what is implied.[7]

Remarkably perhaps, that unusual name, which is said to be derived from an original Nahuatl word (an indigenous language of pre-Cortesian Mexico, where the species does not occur), is not a reference to any of the Hoatzin's abundant oddities.[8] It is said to be onomatopoeic of the call.[9] Equally strange is the fact that, despite the wide reputation for being foul-smelling, the bird is still apparently hunted for its flesh and the eggs are prized, while its feathers are used to make fans, or as medicine.[10] Bennett Hennessey, a contemporary Bolivian conservationist, questions the bird's edibility: 'I think the meat is supposed to be horrible to eat – really the only way for the species to survive, because Hoatzins live right on the river-edge vegetation, and are slow clumsy fliers (with guts full of vegetable matter and bacteria).'[11] Ironically those microbes in the foregut may possibly help to save the Hoatzin's habitat. They are being studied to see if the enzymes, which neutralise the toxins in rainforest vegetation, could be transferred to domestic grazing stock and therefore permit these mammals to forage on native vegetation, rather than just deforested pasture.[12]

Turaco family *Musophagidae*

The turacos are a distinctive group of fruit-eating arboreal birds with pigeon-sized bodies and very long cuckoo-like tails, but with relatively small heads crowned by a distinctive topknot or conical crest. There may be just 23 species in this entire order (the Musophagiformes) and they may be exclusively African in range, but they go by various names in English-speaking areas, including 'lourie', 'turaco' (and formerly 'tauraco'), 'plantain-eater' and 'go-away-bird'.

Several of these are anomalous. Lourie, a name still used for a number of the group in southern Africa, was originally a Malay word (pronounced 'looree') for members of the parrot family. Similarly, plantain-eater was based on an assumption that turacos were lovers of bananas. The idea is manifest still in the scientific nomenclature, because *Musophagidae* derives in part from *musa* (Latin for banana and originally from the Arabic word *môza*). Yet, in truth, turacos seldom eat the fruit.[1]

'Turaco' (with the stress on the first syllable) and 'go-away-bird' are said to be onomatopoeic renderings of the

family's croaking calls, but they serve now also to separate the two groupings within the family. The turacos proper are rather shy inhabitants of dense tropical forest and are characterised by their rich colours. By contrast, their relatives, the three members of the genus *Corythaixoides* – the **Grey Go-away-bird** *Corythaixoides concolor*, **Bare-faced Go-away-bird** *Corythaixoides personatus* and **White-bellied Go-away-bird** *Corythaixoides leucogaster* – together with the **Western Plantain-eater** *Crinifer piscator* and **Eastern Plantain-eater** *Crinifer zonurus* are rather dull-brown or grey creatures of dry open woodland. They are the family members most often seen on safari, and are frequently among the subliminal extras to people's encounters with zebras, giraffes and lions.

Yet go-away-birds can sometimes force themselves on to our attentions, when they sit atop the tallest acacias and deliver a gloriously atmospheric, almost sheep-like, nasal bleating note. The exact sound varies with species but the

Ceremonial headgear featuring the Bannerman's Turaco plays a key role in local ceremony in the Mount Oku region of western Cameroon.

vocalisations are almost always engaging and suggestive of human speech, from the 'wonderful drawn-out *gu'way*' of Grey Go-away-bird (from which they get their names), to 'the rather surprised *corr!*' of the Bare-faced Go-away-bird.[2] As well as resembling actual words, these strange sounds were once thought in east Africa to be an indicator of coming rain. They were also considered to be an attempt at communication; not with ourselves, but with the game animals around them. There was a further belief among hunters in southern Africa that the birds were deliberately trying to warn the neighbouring mammals of the danger.[3]

The gruff frog-like barking notes of the turacos may not be quite so arresting. Yet their physical beauty certainly is. They are among the most brilliantly colourful of all Africa's avifauna and in the magazine literature of birdwatchers, turacos feature with disproportionate regularity in all sorts of advertisements. Rather like other bird families of glamorous colour – the motmots (Latin America) and pittas (Asia) – turacos instantly conjure notions of far-flung tropicality and exoticism.

Perhaps the most memorable part of this aesthetic impact is the element of surprise. Many of the 14 species in the genus *Tauraco* have body plumages dominated by rich moss greens. When they are glimpsed high in the dense forest canopy they invariably look completely green. Then they swoop down and instantly unfold wings of magical hue. This sudden blaze of deep blood red is both beautiful and unique, because it is derived from a copper complex called uroporphyrin-III, a pigment found nowhere else in the Animal Kingdom. This has been the subject of a remarkably tenacious false myth (it was recently recounted to the author and is now 150 years old) that the colours dissolve if the bird gets wet.[4]

These same feathers are the focus of powerful cultural attachment for various African communities. Even today many turacos are utilised as part of the different magico-medicinal systems found widely on the continent, such as the ju-ju of west Africa and muti in southern Africa. Exactly what values are ascribed to their body parts is still not fully understood, although turacos are usually omens of good fortune. One place where the birds have distinct value is in the Bamenda Highlands of Cameroon. Mount Oku, the second highest peak in west Africa, is home to **Bannerman's Turaco** *Tauraco bannermani*, named after the prolific British ornithologist David Bannerman (1886–1979).

Unfortunately its former range has shrunk dramatically as the region's rich volcanic soils are pressed into agricultural usage, and as its forest habitat is exploited for firewood and other timber needs. The species is now endangered with a world population of fewer than 10,000 birds. It has been the subject of a high-profile conservation project and, for once, the bird's priority status in environmental terms coincides with its cultural significance. Bannerman's Turaco is known locally as the 'king of the birds' or 'king of the forest'. To the Oku people it goes by the strikingly pithy name, *fen* (elsewhere in the region it is called *fungu*). Hearing or observing the bird is deeply auspicious. Finding its nest is particularly lucky. One part of the special relationship with local people is its role as a timekeeper. A Cameroonian conservationist, born within the historical range of Bannerman's Turaco, writes:

> In my own village Bambili the bird was used as a 'watch' because it announced the time. It signalled (through its unique song) the top of the hour every hour from about midday until 5 p.m. My father demonstrated that to me and I took pleasure in following this amazing pattern. Now its habitat around Bambili has been destroyed and the tale about a bird signalling the time must sound to modern generations as nothing more than a fiction.[5]

The Great Blue
Turaco of tropical
west Africa is
sometimes a garden
bird of glorious
colour but also a
source of feathers
associated with
courage and wisdom.

Local farmers were once said to regulate their working days by the *fen*'s hourly calls.

The bird has other significance for locals. A key means of expressing social merit in the Mount Oku area involves a literal interpretation of that well-known phrase about a feather in one's cap. The red wing plumes are presented by a local dignitary called the *Fon* and are worn by any member of the community who has earned public distinction. The BirdLife campaign for Bannerman's Turaco has reinforced all of the existing local cultural attachments. Yet it has also now broadcast the bird as a national symbol and the giving of red feathers as a mark of respect, sometimes using those of the more widespread **Great Blue Turaco** *Corythaeola cristata* or **Guinea Turaco** *Tauraco persa*, has itself increased elsewhere in Cameroon.[6]

Kabiri Serge Bobo has studied this wider Cameroonian engagement with the birds and writes:

> Turaco skulls, feathers, bills and claws are seen in strategic corners of houses in the west, north-west and south-west regions of Cameroon. Feathers of the Great Blue Turaco are always seen on the door posts of certain hunters in the south-west region, as a sign of wisdom and courage. Just as the red feathers of Guinea and Bannerman's Turacos are fixed on caps as a mark of courage and high esteem for members of traditional societies in these same areas, so are the glossy blue feathers of the Great Blue Turaco put on the caps of some elders for the same purpose. The red feathers of the Guinea Turaco are also placed on the jug of palm wine as

a sign of respect to the palace in the north-west region.

In most rural areas of Cameroon, the appearance or the calls of certain wild species are significant to local people. The Great Blue Turaco is known to call at particular hours, i.e. at about 6 a.m., 1 p.m. and 5 p.m. Hunters and farmers said that when the call of this turaco species is heard at 5 p.m., they have to stop everything and start going back to the village to avoid passing the night in the forest. Hunters also reported that the call of the Guinea Turaco at any moment during the day is an alarm call provoking other animals like monkeys to run away from potential danger like a hunter. Other uses of feathers of the Guinea and Great Blue Turacos include personal adornments and general decorations, as well as making dresses especially the juju dresses.[7]

Although the harvest of *fen* feathers now relies on naturally moulted plumes, the various social and cultural values placed on Bannerman's Turaco almost certainly meant that it was hunted in former times (turacos are also said to be excellent eating). Another usage to which the feathers are put is medicinal. The wing plumes are still collected and employed by Mount Oku's traditional healers (apparently any part of the plumage may be used) as an element of their plant-based medicines to give 'respect' to the remedy. A local magico-medicinal practitioner can even 'own' a free-flying Bannerman's Turaco and his special spirit connections with the bird enable him to summon it magically if he requires it for medicinal or occult purposes.[8]

Cuckoo family *Cuculidae*

This well-known, often well-loved and hugely fascinating family is found almost worldwide and comprises 144 species that are spread across every continent except Antarctica. In size they often fall between 25–41 cm (10–16 in), although the smallest, such as the widespread Australian **Shining Bronze Cuckoo** *Chrysococcyx lucidus*, is just 14 cm (5.5 in). At the other end of the spectrum is a giant of the north Australian bush, the **Channel-billed Cuckoo** *Scythrops novaehollandiae*, which can measure 70 cm (27.5 in) and is the world's biggest cuckoo. Many are birds with long tails, short wings and plumages of grey, brown or similar sombre tone with dense transverse bars across the underparts.

CUCKOOS OF SEXUAL BETRAYAL, LUST AND STUPIDITY

Although the family has become inseparable from the behaviour known as 'brood parasitism', which involves the laying of eggs in other birds' nests – where the young are reared by the unrelated 'foster' parents – by no means all cuckoos behave in this way. Several birds, notably two widespread species of North America, the **Yellow-billed Cuckoo** *Coccyzus americanus* and **Black-billed Cuckoo** *Coccyzus erythropthalmus*, occupy a reproductive halfway-house, hatching and rearing their own young, while in years of high food abundance laying extra eggs in the nests of conspecifics or other species. Yet a majority of the cuckoo family incubate eggs and rear chicks exactly

like most birds. Only about 40 per cent, 57 species, have no other reproductive strategy and are defined as 'obligate brood parasites'.

The sight of a cuckoo chick dwarfing the nest and begging relentlessly from its foster parents, as they, in turn, try to satisfy the needs of their insatiable 'offspring' – their heads sometimes vanishing down its vast maw as they stuff in more victuals – is one of the great tragicomedies of the avian world. In truth, the young bird can test even human capabilities:

> It wasn't until an orphaned cuckoo was brought into the wildlife hospital where I worked and I found myself playing 'mother', that I truly understood the demands they make upon their surrogate parents. Nestled in a tea-towel-lined shoebox the cuckoo gazed up at me, its head held coquettishly on one side as he gave me the once-over with his golden-rimmed eye. Swiftly deciding that I would make a suitable parental guardian, he allowed me to scoop him up, immediately deposited a faecal sac in my palm, then stretched his neck and gaped like an opera singer. From dawn to dusk my infant cuckoo petulantly teetered at the edge of his incubator, bobbing his head and begging, until I obliged him by easing a waxworm into the yawning pink chasm. Sated for mere seconds, he would resume his tortuous cries that, far from mimicking a brood of hungry

Thomas Bewick's woodcut depicts something Europeans more often hear than see – a Common Cuckoo in full song.

chicks, seemed more akin to the sound of a car alarm blended with a whistling kettle. For two weeks I played nursemaid, darting to and fro with choice larval morsels until he had doubled in size and was bursting from his margarine-tub nest. Then, overnight, a transformation occurred. Gone was the gawky, pouting powder puff and in his place a sleek, barred beauty ready for the flight aviary. After a fortnight he was ready for release. As I tossed him into the sky, the glint of his leg ring caught the late afternoon sun as he headed for the coast.[1]

The most widespread of all the world's migrant cuckoos, the appropriately named **Common Cuckoo** *Cuculus canorus*, has been responsible for much of the family's global celebrity. It breeds across Eurasia, from Japan and the Kamchatka Peninsula in Siberia (occasional visitors even reach the USA in mainland Alaska and its offshore islands) across to the Atlantic coast of Ireland and Morocco – roughly two-fifths of the Earth's land surface. Over this vast range it has been recorded to lay eggs in the nests of 108 bird species, including the Great Grey Shrike, which fed its surrogate offspring on pieces of vole flesh. Apparently the ravening chick readily accepted them.[2]

Aristotle was the first ornithologist to describe key aspects of Common Cuckoo behaviour. He noted, for instance, that it built no nest, but laid eggs in those of other birds. He also grappled with the issue of its seasonality and, while he never knew of the species' transcontinental journey from Africa to Eurasia, he dismissed a widely held alternative theory – which survived in rural pockets of Europe for more than two millennia – that the Common Cuckoo transmuted into a hawk during winter (the birds actually do resemble small *Accipiter* hawks). Aristotle also reflected upon what happened once the cuckoo egg hatched in the alien nest:

> Eye-witnesses agree in telling most of these stories, but are not in agreement as to the destruction of the young. Some say that the cuckoo itself comes and devours the brood of the rearing mother; . . . others says that, by its superior strength, it actually kills the other ones whilst it is being reared up with them. The cuckoo shows great sagacity in the disposal of its progeny; the fact is, the

mother-cuckoo is quite conscious of her own cowardice and of the fact that she could never help her young . . .[3]

As in so much of this extraordinary philosopher's work, the passage raises many of the key themes that have been writ large in European and Asian cultures for thousands of years. One element found in his account is the vexed issue of conflicting opinion. As one Victorian naturalist noted, 'No single bird has . . . had so much written about it, as this, and of no bird perhaps have more idle tales been told.'[4]

An enduring uncertainty was how the young Common Cuckoo came to monopolise all the food resources brought by the unsuspecting parents. It would take at least 2,135 years before the English scientist Edward Jenner confirmed one of Aristotle's theories and proved that the chick uses a special hollow in its mid back to heave its rivals to their doom out of the nest. When Jenner submitted the record of his meticulous observations in 1788, Sir Joseph Banks, the President of the Royal Society, was even then loath to believe it and rejected Jenner's paper.[5]

Aristotle's passage also adumbrates subsequent attitudes towards cuckoos in its tone of moral ambiguity. While the Greek author saw it as a creature of 'great sagacity', he also emphasised its 'cowardice'. That ambivalence has been at the heart of our anthropomorphic responses right through to our own times. The Serbian writer and poet Vesna Goldsworthy illuminates these continuities:

> In Serbia, Croatia, Bosnia and Montenegro, the name for cuckoo is *kukavica*, which is also the word for 'a coward' (both male and female). Its etymological root is the verb *kukati* ('to cry' – as in to keen or to ululate rather than to howl – i.e. to cry continuously). You can encounter *kukavica*, particularly in Croatia, as a family name, but I suspect, in so far as it is possible to tell, that the derivation is from coward rather than cuckoo.[6]

The dominant ethical issue associated with cuckoos was sexual betrayal. The bird has given rise to a rich vocabulary connected to human infidelity. It seems to have mattered little that in the real world it is the avian female who deceives; in the human context the cuckoo-derived name was transferred to the deceived male. In English we still have 'cuckold' as both verb and noun and while it is perhaps slightly archaic or self-consciously formal, it is still used.

The *Oxford English Dictionary* locates a mid-fifteenth-century cognate form in Old French, *cucuault*, but suggests that the link between cuckoos and marital betrayal is much older. The French today use *cocu* (from the bird's name *coucou*) for the person who is betrayed, and *faire cocu* for the verb. Two French contributors add the following:

> I think most people would use *trompé* nowadays. *Cocu* is a bit more colloquial. But I would say that it's an expression still very much in use. Agony aunt columnists probably use it a lot.[7]

> The verb *cocufier* is regularly used in science as a verb, especially to talk about extra-pair copulation. My PhD thesis on the *Mésange bleue* (Blue Tit) seems to contain a staggering number of the terms *cocufiant*, *cocufier*, etc.[8]

Symbolic cuckoos have extended their territory into associated areas of several European languages.

In Belarus we call a mother who doesn't care for her child and gives it to the orphanage or to other people a 'cuckoo'.[9]

In Swedish we don't have, as far as I know, a noun with the same meaning as 'cuckold'. Instead we have the verb *göka* from the cuckoo's name (*gök*), which means 'to have sex'. It does not necessarily refer to having sex with

another man's wife but simply refers, in a slightly jocular way, to making love. All the same, I suppose it originates in the fact that a male cuckoo obviously has kids all over the place.[10]

Two old English slang names for the organs of procreation (and betrayal) were 'cuckoo' for the male member, while 'cuckoo's nest' served for the vagina.[11] Neither seems to be

The Common Cuckoo chick being fed by its diminutive foster parent (a Reed Warbler in this instance) is one of the great tragicomedies of the avian world.

current. Nor, fortunately, is that gruesome cuckoo-named test of female fidelity, the 'cucking-stool', by which a victim could be lowered underwater. It was also a punishment for the scold and disorderly woman, but also, notably, for a fraudulent tradesperson of either sex.[12]

Other moral failings ascribed to the cuckoo have surfaced extensively in literature. It was, for instance, once proverbial in French (*ingrat comme un coucou*) to talk of the bird's ingratitude.[13] In 'The Knight's Tale' of Geoffrey Chaucer's *The Canterbury Tales*, the fourteenth-century poet made the species a symbol of distrust, seating a cuckoo on the arm of a character called Jealousy. Another frequent conceit of Elizabethan and early modern English poetry was to place the nightingale in juxtaposition to the cuckoo, each bird symbolising different forms of love. If the first represented true devotion, the second was an emblem of faithless lust. Milton in one such work ('Sonnet to the Nightingale') wrote of the 'shallow Cuccoo's bill' and 'the rude Bird of Hate'. Shakespeare too, in *The Rape of Lucrece*, asks:

Why should the worm intrude the maiden bud?
Or hateful cuckoos hatch in sparrows' nests?

In addition to all this immorality, cuckoos have enriched the English repertoire of insults, mainly as synonyms for an idiot. This may have been partly because the cuckold was also an object of contempt, but teasing out exactly why the bird became a symbolic simpleton is more complex. There are a number of sources suggesting an ancient association, such as *The Birds* by the Greek playwright Aristophanes (*c.*448–388 BC), whose town of unattainable ideals assembled by the birds in the clouds, Cloudcuckooland (*Nephelekokkygia*), is now proverbial for any ridiculously optimistic state or aspiration. Was Aristophanes drawing upon pre-existing notions of the bird's stupidity when he coined the title?

Certainly we know that both 'gowk', an old British name for the Common Cuckoo, and the word 'cuckoo' itself describe a person who is simple-minded or actually insane. My mother-in-law, Christine Muir, points that, 'Huntygowk is what older Scots would still call April Fool's Day'.[14] More recently the connection between bird and madness was embedded in the otherwise rather mysterious title for Ken Kesey's novel about life inside an American mental institution, *One Flew Over the Cuckoo's Nest* (1962), and for the subsequent Oscar-winning film (1975). The most likely link between the bird and the idea of the fool is the sound itself. 'Cuckoo' may be one of the most exact transcriptions of a bird's call in the English language, but there is indubitably something simple, even something of the simpleton, in the endless repetitions. Perhaps cuckoos announce to us again and again that they are a little half-witted.

BLESSED CUCKOOS OF SEASON AND TIME

There is, however, a wholly other personality to this most human of birds. In Europe and Asia the songs of several cuckoo species have been the sound of new life, hope, happiness, joy and, rather perversely, even of love. One intriguing aspect of this near-universal affection for cuckoos is the extent to which it relies upon the voice, a reflection of the fact that cuckoos can be remarkably difficult to see or to locate, because of their tantalising ventriloquy. Across a vast geographical territory the names for the species are onomatopoeic in origin and include *cuach* (Irish Gaelic),

cuco (Portuguese and Spanish), *coucou* (French), *kuckuck* (German), *koekoek* (Dutch), *culuco* (Italian), *kukulka* (Polish), *kukačka* (Czech), *käki* (Finnish), *kakukk* (Hungarian), *kukavica* (Serbo-Croat), *kukuvica* (кукувица; Bulgarian), *koúkos* (Greek), *guguk* (Turkish), *gugoo* (Azerbaijani), *kuku-ye* (Iranian), *Shakuk*, *Kuku* and *Kukil* (Kashmiri), *Kukku* (Sikkimese), *Akku* (Bhutanese).

Across Eurasia it rivals the equally widespread Barn Swallow as the key bird symbol of spring (see also page 414). While the latter may be the more significant emblem of the season's first arrival, the Common Cuckoo denotes high spring or summer. In the Czech Republic there is a saying: 'Swallow brings the spring, but the Cuckoo brings warm days.'[15] Nor is it simply a symbol of the summer to come. Very often it conjures all our remembered summers, especially those from the halcyon days (see also Kingfisher family, page 316) of our childhoods. In this context the cuckoo still evokes joy, but it is often salted with deep nostalgia.

It is exactly this bitter-sweet mixture that characterises William Wordsworth's (1770–1850) famous poem 'To the Cuckoo', in which he calls the bird a 'wandering Voice':

The same, whom in my schoolboy days
I listened to; that Cry
Which made me look a thousand ways
In bush, and tree, and sky.

To seek thee did I often rove
Through woods and on the green;
And thou wert still a hope, a love;
Still longed for, never seen.

And I can listen to thee yet;
Can I lie upon the plain
And listen, till I do beget
That golden time again.

O blessèd Bird! The earth we pace
Again appears to be
An unsubstantial, faery place;
That is fit home for Thee!

Wordsworth composed the poem in 1802. Here is proof from a contributor, writing 207 years later, that the species has lost none of its capacity to evoke lost innocence:

The air was warm, the water sparkled. And cuckoos
– lots of cuckoos – shouted, yes shouted, from tree to tree. Never before or since have I heard such a glorious racket: clear, bell-like notes bringing the morning alive with joy. It was one of those moments when everyone wears a silly grin and nothing needs to be said. This was nearly 40 years ago and the people I shared this with have passed away, but I write this with a smile on my face, and tears in my eyes.[16]

For some there is now a twofold melancholy infused with that sound, as the Common Cuckoo suffers deep troubling declines across western Europe. 'I have long been anxious', writes one contributor, 'about the non-appearance of the cuckoo, fearing that it will slip out of consciousness, and be no more a messenger of peace and joy.'[17]

Yet where the species persists it retains its status as a talisman in several core spheres of human fortune – romance, health and economics.

The first cuckoo heard in Sweden is still said to tell your fortune. These sayings are still part of a living tradition. It says: *Norr-gök är sorggök* ('a cuckoo in the north brings grief'), *södergök är dödergök* ('a cuckoo in the south means death'), *östergök är tröstergök* ('a cuckoo in the east is for solace'), *västergök är bästergök* ('a cuckoo in the west is best').[18]

My girlfriend's French family believe that if you have money in your pocket when you hear your first cuckoo of spring, you'll not go short all year. This, apparently, is a well-known French saying or folk belief. I'm not sure whether there is an English equivalent, or, indeed, whether it works with English cuckoos, but I find now that it gives me added incentive to listen out for the first cuckoo of the year! And I always try to keep a few coppers in my pocket, just in case.[19]

It is a habit in Germany that when you hear the first Common Cuckoo of the year you shake your wallet. This guarantees you a prosperous year (I do it every year – with mixed success!).[20]

According to popular Bulgarian belief, if you've eaten and you're full and you have a coin in your pocket when hearing the first cuckoo, the year will be good. People believe that if you don't have any money with you when you hear it, you will never have them. Others believe that you should have coins made of iron with you to guarantee possession and riches, but you will also be strong and healthy as iron. It is also a good sign if you count money at that time – this means that you will do the same year round. Girls see in the cuckoo's call a forecast of their forthcoming marriage. For the young men from the village it means the end of flirting with the girls and the beginning of the working season.[21]

In the Czech Republic there are two main superstitions connected to cuckoo. Its voice (especially the first being heard in spring) predicts the lengths of a person's life or their future fortunes – 'How many times will cuckoo call, so many years will one live.' Or 'the more will cuckoo call, the more money will one earn'. The cuckoo occurs in many folk songs especially for children. 'Raining, raining' is one of the most famous that almost all people know:

> Raining raining, down it's pouring
> My little horses, where are we going?
> We shall go to meadows
> When the cuckoo calls.

> Cuckoo has just called
> My girl has just cried.
> Don't call cuckoo any more,
> Don't cry my girl any more.

> Little cuckoo, where have you been (in this song the cuckoo's folk name is used, *žežulička*)
> Little cuckoo where have you been,
> That you have not called so long
> Cuckoo cuckoo cuckoo-cuckoo-cuckoo

> On a fir tree I've been sitting
> On the hunter I've been calling
> Cuckoo cuckoo cuckoo-cuckoo-cuckoo.[22]

The links between human health and the cuckoo are very much alive in the Greek countryside. If you hear the first cuckoo's song in spring after you have eaten something then it is taken as a prediction of good health until next spring. Some people also work out the age they will live to by counting the number of 'cuckoos' they hear. First they ask of the bird: 'Cuckoo my little cuckoo, how many are my years?' In old traditional songs cuckoos are bringers of good news and places without cuckoos are a synonym for unhappiness and old people wish to live until next year to hear the cuckoo again.[23]

There are lots of Ukrainian beliefs and superstitions. If a cuckoo is first heard at dawn and the trees are already green, then the harvest will be good, but if it's at twilight and the trees bare, then expect a poor harvest, even famine and epidemics. If the bird cuckoos for the first time after the nightingale, then summer will be nice, but if the nightingale comes after the cuckoo then times will be hard. If you hear the cuckoo when you have an empty stomach, you will have bad luck. Once you've first heard the bird cuckooing in spring, shake coins in your pocket, and money will be with you throughout the year; or if you happen to have no money at that moment, you won't have any for the whole year. If the cuckoo calls near the house – especially if it's sitting on a guelder-rose (*Viburnum opulus*), which is the national symbol of the Ukraine – then it foretells a wedding.[24]

Armenian villagers believe that cuckoos start to call more often in early summer, which means that the time for harvesting the corn is getting closer. In Armenia the number of cuckoo calls predicts how many more years are left for a person to live.[25]

The Common Cuckoo can look rather raptor-like in flight and people once accounted for its annual disappearance by suggesting that the quintessential bird of summer actually turned into a hawk in winter.

This short sample simply glances at the vast body of lore that has rooted the bird in our sense of summer and the season's wider gift of natural plenty. A secondary facet is the inventory of flowers, insects and birds that have (or had) names with cuckoo associations. Some derive from their own brand of cuckoo-like brood parasitism (e.g. the Cuckoo Weaver of Africa; see page 494). Many, however, are linked to the bird because of their coincidental seasonality.

In his wonderful study of plant folklore, *The Englishman's Flora* (1958), Geoffrey Grigson listed 38 botanical names drawing on the bird. Many of them served for a number of different plants. There were 13 separate species, for instance, that are, or were once, all known simply as 'Cuckoo-flower'.[26] A personal favourite, for its precise observation of plant morphology and its insight into the rural imagination, is the northern Scots name 'cuckoo's shoe' for the tubular blooms of Common Bluebell (*brog na chuthaig* in its original Scots Gaelic).[27] There were also many birds that had cuckoo-derived names, from the migrant woodpecker, the Eurasian Wryneck (the 'cuckoo's mate' – UK), to the Eurasian Hoopoe ('cuckoo's verger': *kuckuckküster* and 'cuckoo's lackey': *kuckucklakei* – Germany) and Egyptian Vulture ('cuckoo's horse': *to alogo tou koukou* – Greece).[28]

CLOCKS AND OTHER CUCKOOS

The question hovering behind all of this ancient, hydra-headed cuckoo lore is why exactly should this particular bird be so singled out for special attention? Paradoxically, perhaps, it is best answered by examining the parallel ideas attaching to other cuckoos, including the mechanical bird inside the famous clock.

In Africa, where the Common Cuckoo is present only as a largely silent 'winter' visitor, the role of seasonal herald has devolved on to a relative, the intra-African migrant **Red-chested Cuckoo** *Cuculus solitarius*, which is widespread across the continent south of the Sahara. In the breeding season the bird has a loud, penetrating piping song of three evenly spaced notes, which are repeated with typical cuckoo-like monotony. For many African communities it is associated with the coming of the rains at the onset of the agricultural season. To the Marakwet people of western Kenya its name *Kwetkweton*, which is an almost perfect rendering of the sound, means 'voice which predicts rain'. It is particularly taken as a herald of termite emergence, when these small but nutritionally valued insects swarm in their millions.[29]

Among other Kenyan communities the bird is similarly an omen of rain. For the herdboys it signals the need to shelter livestock, and to the ploughmen it presages that they must soon prepare the ground for seed (exactly as the song of the Common Cuckoo once did in ancient Greece). To the Kikuyu the three-note phrase is thought to repeat *Ngwikia ku*, 'Where do I sow the seed?'[30]

A Zulu contributor from KwaZulu-Natal makes the following observation:

> The Red-chested Cuckoo was once considered a bird of crop planting (in the old days there were no calendars, or radio and television to tell what time of the season it was). They waited for the summer migrants and the Red-chested Cuckoo was the bird that they used to recognise the arrival of spring. There was a big ceremony

for planting which was celebrated as soon as the cuckoo started to call. The Zulu name for the species is *Phezu Komkhono Amageja* (it means 'time to carry the hand hoe on your shoulders for planting').[31]

In India another family member has assumed many of the roles ascribed to its European and African siblings. The **Asian Koel** *Eudynamys scolopaceus* is a large all-black brood parasite that exploits the nests of House Crows and, unlike the Common Cuckoo, may lay multiple eggs in the same nest. One such super-clutch contained 11 Asian Koel eggs, almost certainly deposited by different females.[32] It is only one among several cuckoos in the Indian subcontinent, but:

> This one is the most widely known and most popular cuckoo. It's the star. Indians refer to it as just 'koel'. It's the bird for spring and romance. What the Common Nightingale is to the British, the koel is to us in the subcontinent. The melodious call is described by the great poet Kālidāsa in his epic Meghadoot. A number of other poets have also used it and it is in numerous lyrics from Bollywood blockbusters, to regional folk tunes to Tagore songs. All are linked to spring, romance, melody, the fresh breeze of life, new season, etc. The koel is often found calling from mango orchards and it is believed that as long as he sings the mango ripens accordingly. Koel is also a popular female name in India and is directly linked to the bird's melodious voice.[33]

Strangely enough the cuckoo that perhaps best explains why all of these diverse family members have had this fundamental role in announcing seasonal change is the little bird inside the cuckoo clock. These somewhat humorous and now unfashionable timepieces were once immensely popular. It is claimed that between their invention in the early eighteenth century and 1975, a total of 50 million cuckoo clocks were manufactured.[34] Contrary to the famous remark of US actor and film director Orson Welles (while playing Harry Lime in *The Third Man*), associating their origins with Switzerland, they were actually invented in the Black Forest region of western Germany.

One of the major inspirations for using a mechanical bird to call the hour was a singing cockerel on the astronomical clock in the nearby Strasbourg Cathedral (see The Call of the Cockerel, page 67 for its Christian symbolism).[35] However, the crowing of a rooster was a more difficult sound to achieve with mechanical bellows and reed pipes than the simple, disyllabic notes of a cuckoo. The early German manufacturers therefore opted for this unmistakable spring songster. (In some clocks the quarter hours are marked by a fellow spring migrant, the Common Quail, albeit with a rather atypical four-note call.) The mechanical birds – some made eventually from real feathers, or with moving wings, heads and beaks, usually popping out from tiny shuttered windows or occasionally triggering the march-past of miniature tin soldiers – have had a tendency to become ever more elaborate as the German craftsmen set themselves more exacting technical challenges.[36]

Yet it is surely with the arch simplicity of the cuckoo's sound that we begin to approach not only why the bird was so attractive to clock manufacturers, but also why it has this fundamental timekeeping role in human folklore. The

African Red-chested Cuckoo may be trisyllabic, but both Asian Koels and Common Cuckoos issue just two notes, and all three birds yield sounds as fundamental, memorable and as redolent of time's passing as the 'tick-tock' of the clock's own relentless mechanism. In short, cuckoo song is ready-made to tell us the time. It also pronounces on that moment which humanity longs to feel at hand – the arrival of spring and the end of winter. It is this coincidental appearance with that precise season and the unmistakable clarity with which they herald its coming that have surely made cuckoos the archetypal birds of spring, of new life and of future happiness.

ROADRUNNERS AND COUCALS

The cuckoos as a family may be most famous for brood parasitism and all the cultural connections that flow from this behaviour, but there are non-parasitic species that have had an equally large impact upon their human neighbours. The exemplar is the **Greater Roadrunner** *Geococcyx californianus*. Like its close relative, the **Lesser Roadrunner** *Geococcyx velox*, it is found widely across Mexico, but the larger bird also spreads north into the USA as far as southern Kansas and northern California.

It is an oddly shaped, long-legged, ground-dwelling cuckoo with features that are 'compounded of a chicken and a Magpie'.[37] Greater Roadrunners also seem creatures of immense character and have been writ large in regional culture. For the pueblo-dwelling Hopi of Arizona, for instance, roadrunners were associated with rituals that celebrated or invoked qualities of strength, endurance and courage. One factor that may have predisposed local people to ideas of great stamina is the distinctive footprint left by

these pedestrian cuckoos in the desert sands. Since the birds hardly fly the tracks seem to go on for ever.

Greater Roadrunners were also incorporated into the extraordinary and mysterious rock art of the remarkable Anasazi Indians, who pecked images either of whole birds or their footprints into complex designs, such as in El Malpais National Conservation Area, New Mexico. In the latter petroglyph a roadrunner is shown devouring a lizard, although the bird's legendary ability to tackle rattlesnakes (one old name in the USA was 'snake-killer') must have further cemented its reputation for courage.[38]

Images of Greater Roadrunner tracks are a common motif in rock art. In life the species has two toes pointing forwards and two back, an arrangement in all cuckoos and technically known as zygodactylous. Pueblo Indians depicted the striking X-shaped footprint rather like an aberrant form of swastika. They were used as a symbolic evocation of the birds' strength, but since real roadrunner tracks often criss-cross in maze-like complexity, it is thought that they may also have been invoked as a symbolic means of confusing the Anasazi's opponents, both animal (in the hunt) and human (in war).[39]

The bird's stranger qualities have not lost their appeal in the modern era. If now perhaps familiar only to audiences of a particular vintage, there is a wonderful cartoon series featuring two characters called Road Runner and Wile E Coyote. The films portray the same violent mayhem and predator–prey rivalries of Tom and Jerry, but transferred from the urban interior to the desert landscapes of the American Southwest. Road Runner was famous for his perpetual evasion of Coyote's devilishly cunning ruses,

The Greater Roadrunner is well known for its serpent-killing ability and will even tackle rattlesnakes.

mainly by dint of his legendary speed; his legs worked so fast they were shown as a circular blur, accompanied by his beep-beep motor-horn note. In truth the Greater Roadrunner's top speed is a more modest 24 kph (15 mph).

An Old World cuckoo group that has attracted similarly strong responses are the 30 species of coucal in the genus *Centropus*. They inhabit a vast tropical zone from Africa to Australasia, and are often familiar birds around African and Asian villages. Typically cuckoo-like in shape, with especially long, broad dark tails and bright chestnut wings, coucals have a rather loose plumage that makes them seem somehow irredeemably 'scruffy'.

They also possess highly distinctive hooting calls that are rapidly repeated and are midway between an owl's and a pigeon's in quality. They have been memorably likened in some African species to the glugging sound of 'liquid being poured from a long-necked bottle'.[40] Coucals possess one further trait that is found among many other cuckoos: they are renowned for their weak flight. Many prefer to scramble over the bushes, with outstretched wings used almost like hands, or they scuttle on the ground in a somewhat gamebird-like fashion.

In keeping with the birds' dishevelled appearance, coucal nests are noted for being untidy structures. In west Africa the **Senegal Coucal** *Centropus senegalensis* has a reputation for laziness. Among the Bassar people of northern Togo it is called *natu*, which means the fool or idiot. Its weak flight enables it only to move short distances in straight lines and it is thus easily caught.[41] The bird is also the subject of a *Just So*-like folk tale explaining this indolence. It tells of how a coucal once jeered at a sunbird for boasting of its own physical strength (in real life the sunbird metabolism does indeed seem to function at the other end of the spectrum to a coucal's; see page 480). Sunbird challenged the larger bird to remain fasting in his house and see who could last the longest without food. Unbeknownst to the coucal, his opponent was slipping out of his house by night to feed. When coucal finally conceded defeat he was so exhausted he was never able to recover his strength, and to this day he remains feeble and weak-winged.[42]

In contrast to this implied slur on coucal energies, the birds are also creatures of magic for some west African people. The Senegal Coucal is a tribal totem for communities in Benin, while the species is routinely among the commonest bird skins found in the country's fetish markets, although exactly what ideas or values are conjured by the birds in these contexts is as yet largely unexplored.

In India there is a similar and intriguing aura of magic attaching to the most widespread of the country's species, the **Greater Coucal** *Centropus sinensis*. This bird, incidentally, shares the Senegal Coucal's reputation for poor flying ability and has a vernacular name – 'common crow-pheasant' – that reflects its own semi-terrestrial lifestyle. It is also the object of the following remarkable folk belief that

has been recorded directly from modern informants among the Toda, a pastoralist people of the Nilgiri Hills in southern India.

> The *Kegoor fehll* or Greater Coucal has the uncanny ability to locate rare herbs from remote mountaintops that are inaccessible to the Toda people. They have thus used these birds traditionally to bring them such medicinal plants. This is done by locating a nest and tying an iron wire-mesh round the eggs in the absence of the parents. The mother bird then sets out in search of the *sanjeevini* root that is mentioned in Indian mythology as being able to protect a person (wearing it on the body) from physical harm. After bringing this or a similar root, the bird is said to place it on the mesh so as to release her clutch. The person who had enclosed the eggs returns later to retrieve the invaluable herb.[43]

A sidelight on this strange tale is the existence of corresponding stories associated with other species. The classic myth of a bird utilising a magic herb relates to the Eurasian Hoopoe in south-west Asia (see page 325). Then there is an extremely similar if somewhat later European belief concerning a woodpecker. In the case of the Eurasian Hoopoe the herb, often identified as sesame, had the power to split open rock. In the woodpecker versions of the story the bird used the plant to free its nest if humans had deliberately sealed the chamber with a stone or metal spike. The tale of a herb-seeking woodpecker was recorded by both Pliny and Aelian.[44] Remarkably, the folklorist John Aubrey described how the same myth was still going strong in seventeenth-century Britain:

> Sir Bennet Hoskins . . . told me that his keeper at his parke at Morehampton in Herefordshire did for experiment sake, drive an iron nail thwert the hole of a woodpecker's nest, there being a tradition that the damme willl bring some leafe to open it. He layed at the bottome of the tree a cleane sheet, and before many houres passed the naile came out and he found a naile lying on the sheete . . . They say moonewort [*Botrychium lunaria*] will doe such things.[45]

There seems to be little doubt that the origins of the woodpecker folklore lie in the older story concerning the Eurasian Hoopoe. However, the existence of a presumably ancient Indian tale of a magical herb found by Greater Coucals (the Indian ornithologist Salim Ali mentions other versions of this same story elsewhere in southern India) raises the possibility of some proto-myth that was older still, that was widespread in oral tradition across southern and south-west Asia in the mid Holocene.[46] This myth then evolved over time and space and gave rise to distinct versions, invoking quite separate birds, which drew on the earlier basic legend. All redound, however, to that same core human association of birds with magical powers of transformation.

Barn Owl family *Tytonidae* **and Owl family** *Strigidae*

Of all bird families, the owls and their diurnal counterparts, the birds of prey, are probably the only ones that every human will recognise as culturally significant. (Technically there are two owl families but I treat them together because their cultural profiles are inseparable.) In the case of owls their primacy is all the more striking, given that most species roost by day and are active when we ourselves are asleep. In a sense, it is this 'inverted' nocturnal lifestyle that explains the owls' universal significance.

OWL AS PORTENTS OF MYSTERY AND EVIL

Owls inhabit our unconscious dream-world almost as completely as they blanket the Earth's land surface. This imagined bird is the quintessential emblem of darkness. Or to be precise it conjures the more compelling moral darkness that humans associate with night – that unfathomable zone of mystery from which emanate our base anxieties about misfortune, disorder, evil and death.

A good example of this symbolism is found in *The Grapes of Wrath*, John Steinbeck's classic novel about the fate of rural communities in the American Midwest at the time of the Great Depression. As the Oklahoman families are driven out by debt, so the piecemeal degeneration of their homesteads is set in train.

> When the folks first left, and the evening of the first day came, the hunting cats slouched in from the fields and mewed on the porch . . . When the night came, the bats, which had stopped at the doors for fear of light, swooped into the houses and sailed through the empty rooms . . . And the mice moved in and stored weed seeds in corners, in boxes, in the backs of drawers in the kitchens. And weasels came in to hunt the mice, and the brown owls flew shrieking in and out again.[1]

In Steinbeck's evocation of the home once filled with human warmth, now echoing to the cries of predatory night birds, he emphasises the owls' fundamental indifference to our lives. Yet his sonorous monosyllabic repetitions also trade on more famous Old Testament passages about the coming of owlish desolation, such as that in Jeremiah (50:39) on the fall of Babylon:

> Therefore the wild beasts of the desert with the wild beasts of the islands shall dwell there, and the owls shall dwell therein: and it shall be no more inhabited for ever; neither shall it be dwelt in from generation to generation.

Another example is in the Book of Isaiah (34:11), when Jehovah smites down the enemies of his people and visits catastrophe on their lands:

> But the cormorant and the bittern shall possess it; the owl also and the raven shall dwell in it: and he shall stretch out upon it the line of confusion, and the stones of emptiness.

This old version from the *King James Bible* has now been modified in *The New English Bible* to:

> Horned owl and bustard shall make their home in it,

The Eurasian Eagle-Owl is a magnificent bird and the largest of its family.

271

Sheila Kett of Norfolk, UK, admires a small sample of her 'owl' collection, which includes about 2,000 items. Her 30-year passion for owlish knick-knacks reflects how this bird family can command our fascination, and even our obsession, like few others.

Screech-owl and raven shall haunt it.
He has stretched across it a measuring-line of chaos,
And its frontiers shall be a jumble of stones.

Gone from the modern text are the cormorants and the bitterns (and also, sadly, much of the wonderful poetry), but the owls persist as perhaps the most universally recognised avian symbol of human misery and moral disorder.

The Finnish owl expert Heimo Mikkola suggests that owls are among the first birds towards which humans developed easily recognisable cultural responses.[2] Certainly there is an owl image of indeterminate species in the Chauvet Cave in southern France that is one of the first depictions of a bird ever found and is about 30,000 years old.[3] Since that time, and with increasing frequency, they have been writ large in literature and art, in music and sculpture, in folklore and popular culture.

However, almost with the same breath that we acknowledge their fundamental role as portents of evil and disaster, we need to stress that there is another version of the imagined owl, which has made a more recent but deeply positive appeal to humankind. This is partly the benign and revered bird of wisdom, but it is more than that. In our own age we have been enlightened by a rich scientific appreciation of the birds' genuine natural history, so that they have been drained of anxiety and refilled with a sense of wonder. Beyond this mere fascination with the known parts of their biology is the owls' ongoing appeal to our sense of mystery. They have become, in short, some of the most popular of all birds, starring endlessly in television documentaries, in cartoon films and children's stories; or repackaged as ubiquitous household items for the living room, kitchen and nursery.

Strictly for convenience I tackle separately the two opposing halves of the owl's image; first the owl of death

and then the bird of life. Yet the real picture we must hold before us is of a bird family that simultaneously arcs through our full moral compass, from reviled omen to cherished symbol. Sometimes the birds can be all these things at once. The following contribution stresses how they tap into our deepest feelings, yet these can be hugely ambivalent and complicated:

A friend of mine used to live in Zimbabwe and she would frequently travel across the bush roads at night with her young autistic son, and they would often see nightjars and thick-knees in the headlights. On one occasion a grey blob appeared in the headlights and my friend slammed on the brakes, stopping a few feet in front of a **Verreaux's Eagle-Owl** *Bubo lacteus* that was sat slap-bang in the centre of the road. Dazzled perhaps by the headlights, it refused to move, blinking slowly to show off its startling pink eyelids. After a short while she and her son emerged from the car and crept towards the bird, unsure if it was injured, to see if she could make it fly. All the while her son, an animal lover through and through, sat spellbound and transfixed – and then terrified – as the enormous bird suddenly took flight, making his mum jump back as its broad wings swept so close to her face she could feel the displaced air prickle her skin.

She has told me that for the rest of that journey he spoke of nothing else, and since that time, perhaps because of his autism, he has become fixated on owls, reading all he can about them, asking again and again when he is out in the countryside which owls might be present. He is fascinated and frightened of these predatory birds all at once, and he cannot break his compulsion. Once, when I heard **Tawny Owl** *Strix aluco* calling outside his house, I went and watched as an

owl in silhouette flew from roof apex to garden fringe, with the boy clutching my arm and peering round me in awe, fear, delight as the bird became cloaked by the blackness.[4]

THE RELATIONSHIP BETWEEN OWL PHYSIOLOGY AND OWL FOLKLORE

How should we understand this complexity or begin to explain it? One place to start is with their physical attributes. For our fears, rather like our more recent admiration of owls, are rooted in the birds' appearance. In turn key aspects of this physiognomy are integrally connected to their status as nocturnal predators.

There are 202 owl species worldwide, with just 16 in Europe and 19 north of Mexico's border with the USA. Yet there is a strong bias towards both the American continents – together they hold 75 species – with an even stronger concentration in the tropics. The Oriental (44 species), Afrotropical (37 species) and Australasian regions (37 species) have almost equal shares and there are only ten species of owl that have ranges entirely outside of the tropical zone, with the extremes represented by the **Snowy Owl** *Bubo scandiaca* of the Arctic north and the **Morepork** *Ninox novaeseelandiae* of the far south (Tasmania and New Zealand).

The family varies in size from the **Elf Owl** *Micrathene whitneyi* of Arizona, Texas and northern Mexico, which is little larger than a sparrow and weighs just 40 g (1.4 oz). The biggest of all, the appropriately named and continent-wide **Eurasian Eagle-Owl** *Bubo bubo*, can be 100 times heavier than its minuscule relative (4.2 kg: 9.3 lb). Yet all owls bear much the same family traits: short tails, thickset bodies, huge heads and disproportionately large staring eyes.

Owls' eyes are set in the upper head and face forwards to give them the greatest binocular field of vision among all birds. Yet their eyes are also rather immobile with a narrow field of view of just 110°, which is considerably less than humans (180°). The unseen portion of the eyeball is tubular in structure, giving them the largest possible retinal surface to further enhance visual acuity. The owl retina also has a much higher preponderance of light-sensitive receptors known as rods – those most useful in low-light conditions – compared with humans or with other diurnal birds. A Tawny Owl, for instance, has 100 times the light-gathering capability of a pigeon. It is these remarkable eyes, which in the biggest species are as large as an adult man's, that help to explain our owl fixations.

Yet there is a further compounding factor. Owl vision is matched by remarkable audio sensitivity that enables the birds to pinpoint the source of sounds with uncanny precision. The **Great Grey Owl** *Strix nebulosa* found in North America and Eurasia can hear, locate and pounce upon rodents that are buried under 30 cm (12 in) of snow. A **Barn Owl** *Tyto alba* can find and catch a mouse in conditions of

Eerily silent and ghostly pale, the Barn Owl is a glorious spirit of dusk almost worldwide.

total darkness, merely by its exquisite radar-like hearing. These auditory powers are enhanced by a prominent disc of feathers on an owl's face, which channels the sounds to the ears rather in the way that a parabolic reflector guides sound towards a microphone. In combination these seemingly magical sensory gifts have engineered a bird with forward-facing large eyes in a flat rounded or oval-shaped disc. The overall result is a facial structure that closely resembles our own.[5]

Notwithstanding these similarities, owls produce sounds – quavering hoots, wails, screeches, moaning bass notes, shrill piercing screams and, in the case of the most widespread and familiar of all, the Barn Owl, an intense breathy hissing, gargling and caterwauling – that no human produces except in emotional and physical extremis. The birds then choose as home that place in which we feel least comfortable – the night. Finally they do that thing which we can only undertake in our wildest fantasies. They fly. So owls are both like us in their appearance, but fundamentally unlike us in every other way. And that, in short, is what we find so troubling and exciting about them. As a consequence we have identified owls with all those human forms that are essentially inhuman – spirits, goblins, demons, ghosts, witches, vampires, ghouls and devils. Owls have come to symbolise the imagined versions of ourselves that cleave to the darkness of our unconscious and dwell furthest from the light and the warmth of the family hearth.

It is almost uncanny how the birds seem to have been designed specifically to fit our deepest nightmares. Take, for instance, a fascinating aspect of owl kinetics. Because of the largely immobile nature of the eyes, the birds compensate by being able to turn their heads through an enormous arc. This sudden capacity to rotate their faces through 270° is itself deeply unnerving. It reminds us perhaps of that most chilling of moments in the most chilling of films, *The Exorcist*, when the possessed she-devil Regan, with the man's voice and the green body fluids, writhes her head owl-like right round, from front to back, to face and terrify her prostrate mother.

THE GLOBAL DISTRIBUTION OF OWL FOLKLORE

It once was the case that people from Western backgrounds shared completely in this owl lore. In fact, the Brazilian ornithologist Helmut Sick blamed some of the wide distribution of these negative attitudes on European colonists, who carried them abroad wherever they settled. 'Owls merit our full protection', he wrote. 'We have to fight the bias against these birds: defamatory, baseless rumors brought in part from Europe, where they also lack a foundation. Such lies generate and spread antipathy to these most interesting creatures.' By contrast, Sick suggested that 'Indians revere owls, and backwoodspeople attribute to the pygmy-owl the power of bringing good luck'.[6]

Unfortunately, any singling out of Europeans as particularly susceptible to negative owl beliefs and, conversely, any claim that indigenous Americans are immune to them must be challenged. The wider truth is that the human fear of the owl family occurs on every continent and, while it inevitably varies from culture to culture, as it does from individual to individual, there are fundamental similarities around the world. Even today many communities

in the Americas retain some of these cultural attitudes. In the past they were widespread. Here are three examples of such indigenous owl anxieties.

Very often there is little written testimony on these matters and one has to rely, to some extent, on anecdotal evidence. Yet a typical account given to me in 1997 came from a conservation worker who had introduced owls to a classroom of Ojibwa Indians in Wisconsin, USA. Before showing an **Eastern Screech Owl** *Megascops asio* to these students he had to secure prior agreement from both the pupils and the pupils' parents, because of the owl's status as an omen of death for the Ojibwa. It was not surprising that some of the younger children were initially very frightened. Perhaps we should be even less surprised, given their concern for bravado, that the older teenagers actually identified the owl as a favourite bird.

There is a telling, albeit historical, anthropological account of similar concerns shown by the Creek people, originally of south-eastern USA. They were reported to have a fear of owls in general, but of the **Great Horned Owl** *Bubo virginianus* they were noted to have a 'great terror', believing it to be a 'spirit of the dead with potential to kill any who heard the wail or hoot'.[7] Similarly the Apache people of the American Southwest had a strong aversion to the birds. In 1883, during one of the final US campaigns to subdue the last renegade Chiricahua Apaches, an accompanying journalist found and took along a Great Horned Owl that he tied to the pommel of his saddle. The Apache scouts, who supported the expedition and without whose tracking skills there could be no hope of success, refused to continue until the bird was set free, because the owl represented *ch'ii dn*, a spirit or ghost of an evil person.[8] In 1902 it was still the custom after the death of an Apache to burn the house and inter the deceased, where it was believed that owls would visit the grave and call to the departed to take their spirit away.[9] (When I visited the Apache reservation at San Carlos, Arizona, in 1997, representatives revealed that owls were the birds to which they attached the deepest taboo.)

AFRICANS AND OWLS

Sometimes it is the parallels in human responses to owls, re-enacted by peoples who can have had no means of communication, that is so telling. A classic instance involves the method once used by Apache people to banish the owl's evil magic. Should a bird land in the vicinity of someone's home, thereby presaging disaster, the people could counteract its negative message by driving it away with a burning firebrand.

In South Africa the Reverend Robert Godfrey, writing in the first half of the twentieth century about the people of the Eastern Cape, published an account of how anyone confronted with an owl calling from a rooftop, 'seizes a firebrand . . . and throws the brand after the owl. The pity of it is that the owl, when caught, is soaked in paraffin and set alight. Off it flies, in a blaze, to fall down at a distance and die.'[10]

A Kenyan contributor adds the following:

Among my (Luhya) tribe an owl was an indication of bad things to come especially death. This is because the owl (called *Lihichichi* in the local language) was considered as halfway between a cat and a bird with very

In west Africa owls such as this Barn Owl are sold for their feathers and body parts, which are seen as items of immense magico-medicinal power.

scary eyes and therefore dreaded. If it was sighted or heard hooting near someone's homestead, it was a sign that someone in that home was going to die. As part of the defence by the people, the bird was sent away with a burning flame or even killed. Killing it would be a sign that life has triumphed over death.[11]

The fundamental similarities between the North American and South and east African scenarios all suggest how the malign symbolism of the bird, as well as the positive moral qualities attributed to fire, are reflex responses to external stimuli that were virtually hard-wired into our neurological system. (Nor are they just a thing of the past: in 1997 an owl that flew into a Malawian hospital caused pandemonium as patients fled the wards. The bird was eventually stoned to the ground, trussed up, doused with paraffin and set ablaze.)[12]

Today there are deep continuities in owl lore manifest

275

right across sub-Saharan Africa that suggest how viscerally deep and instinctive these reactions are still. A classic expression of the traditions is the role of owls in the magico-medicinal practices of west Africa (routinely referred to as gris-gris or ju-ju). Nigeria, Benin, Togo and Ghana are four key countries where owls are killed, collected and traded in fetish markets. The stalls selling animals for these purposes cluster together in much the same way that the fruit sellers or clothes merchants occupy their own particular quarters, and to most outsiders they are exotic and disturbing places. Part of our anxiety is the presence of so many dead animals or parts – gaping sharks' jaws, crocodile heads, pangolin skins, porcupine quills, dried snakes, heads of monkeys and chimpanzees, or their severed hands, shelves of desiccated chameleons, cat and dog skulls and, above all, scores, sometimes hundreds, of dead owls.

In Africa there is still a tendency to see ill health, financial difficulty or other wider misfortune as attributable to the agency of a witch or witch doctor. It is often assumed that the person with occult power is, in turn, employed by a third party who lacks the necessary knowledge of magic to inflict the distress upon the victim. In these supposed human exchanges owls play a fundamental part. In west Africa the standard pidgin English for 'owl' is 'witchbird'.

The sight and sound of a live owl is sometimes assumed to be the witch temporarily manifest in bird form.

> I once visited an aunt of mine during my postgraduate programme in Jos Plateau, Nigeria. I heard a Barn Owl calling in the evening so I jumped out to see it. To my surprise, my aunt ran for her Bible in her room and started praying. I asked what was wrong and she told me that a neighbour (pointing towards the direction of her residence) died the night she saw an owl (I guess a Barn Owl), implying that she was attacked by a witch that came in owl form.[13]

In Cameroon a discussion involving myself, an agricultural technician, a headmaster and a freelance journalist for the *Cameroon Post* centred on the precise call made by an owl that let the listener know whether the bird in question was actually a real owl or a witch temporarily in owl disguise.

However, owls are not just a means to inflict harm. They can also be used as a counteracting prophylactic. The dead birds sold in fetish markets form the basis of defensive spells or charms. Owl feathers or body parts are worn as an amulet and it is believed that any witch in owl form, or an owl under direction from a witch, would die instantly on contact with the person so protected. The owl's heart is particularly potent and can sell in Cameroon for the equivalent of the entire skin.[14]

What is so striking to an external observer is the coexistence of these ancient traditions in Africa alongside all the trappings and insignia of modern industrial twenty-first-century society, right down to the recreational amenities of a zoological garden, stocked with mammal and bird species that are among the most cherished exhibits elsewhere in the world:

> During a year teaching English in Sudan's Nuba Mountains region I spent many happy afternoons looking for birds around Dilling, the town where I lived.

My Sudanese friends were fascinated by my bird guide, especially with the notion that anyone had gone to the bother of identifying all the birds. Riffling through the pages they would stop at the section on owls and mutter, almost apologetically, something to the effect of 'very bad bird'. This, I already knew: friends had spoken of Khartoum Zoo where the pitiful owls on display were routinely cursed and venomously spat at by visitors.[15]

It is not just the way such conflicting ideas about owls coexist within a society that is remarkable, but also how an individual can encompass radically opposed ways of thinking. In 1999 I was told by a Swiss doctor about a highly educated Beninois academic, who had studied in Europe for years and was a philosophy professor at a university. One day the African academic revealed that he thought he was being pursued by a witch who visited his home as an owl (a woman who was otherwise well known to him in the village). He also suggested that he knew of sorcerers who could conjure the presence of the living bird by magical incantations over just a single feather. When confronted by the Swiss doctor with the laws of science that insisted on the impossibility of such an action, the owl-haunted professor refused to continue the conversation.[16]

In 1996–7 Heimo Mikkola conducted a sample survey in Malawi, Mozambique and Angola. He interviewed 189 people and of those questioned 81 per cent viewed owls as bad omens, while 46 per cent viewed all owls as representing a single entity. Almost all knew of traditional stories and belief about owls and roughly a quarter of respondents knew of someone who had killed or sacrificed them. Of the 51 birds slaughtered, more than a third had died so that the person could avoid the evil omen it represented or so they could use the owl to conduct magic.

Mikkola also interviewed five contemporary Malawian medicine men, who acknowledged that owl-based preparations were mainly for bewitching or killing people, rather than for protective purposes. The owl head or heart is pounded up and placed in the garden with a seedling among the bird tissue. Once the plants grows fully its roots are mixed with herbs that are often poisonous. The medicine man then sings to his preparation words that mean 'grow owl, grow, grow', and the bird will thus be resurrected. (This belief in a capacity to recreate the owl, incidentally, sheds light on the ideas held by the Beninois academic described above.) The reborn owl then flies to the home of the intended victim and hoots, after which the person eventually falls ill. Some of the medicine men, however, out of a curious kind of humanitarianism, felt that owls should not be used for this killing purpose because the victim took weeks to die. Using a lion, leopard, snake or crocodile vastly speeded up the death process and therefore greatly reduced the suffering.[17]

African owl lore is a belief system of huge diversity and in rapid flux, as people are affected by many influences – education, television, urban lifestyles and perhaps matters as mundane as street lighting. A Kenyan contributor gives a personal account of how the older ideas readily succumb to alternative ways of thinking. In fact, here, in microcosm, is our entire intellectual and emotional journey in relation to owls, not just in Africa but worldwide:

I grew up not far from the Aberdare/Nyandarua Mountains. In my community (Kikuyu), owls were feared and were believed to give a message of doom – persistent calls (we referred to these as cries/mourning; indeed we confused white spots of owl droppings found at the base of trees as tears) made by owls and ground hornbills (both groups were relatively common in those days) were immediately perceived to pass the message that someone would die in the next few days. People would then keep their ears to the ground to know who died next in the neighbourhood, and associate this with the owl calls. Our property has tall eucalyptus, juniper and olive trees. Owls and ground hornbills loved to spend time sitting on those trees and calling from there. We would be advised to chase them away – throwing objects from a distance. But would obviously not kill them for fear of the curse this would bring to us.

However, I liked to spend time, especially when grazing cattle in the field, appreciating the various types of birds, flowers, beetles and butterflies I observed. I also spent Sunday afternoons with friends chasing around hares and duikers and of course killing some to eat. Not that there was no other food, but we found fun in these activities; in fact our parents wouldn't allow us to cook the meat in the family kitchen. We cooked them in the fields. This interaction with wildlife made me start appreciating wildlife, including owls. However, what completely changed my attitude towards owls was my life as a university student. There were some Barn Owls nesting in the ceiling of my hostel room and making strange noises for weeks. It was only after the university workers removed the young birds from the ceiling that I realized that I had been sharing a room with owls – and was not harmed. The young were really cute. Later I started my career as an ornithologist and had very close encounters with owls, including handling some for ringing. I also interacted with a group of scientists who were studying the impacts of owls on pest rodents in Nakuru, Kenya. These experiences have made a big difference in changing my perception of owls.[18]

THE WISE AND THE GOOD OWL

We should not assume that the older and darker responses to owls are extinct among Western societies. As recently as the 1960s in northern France and Switzerland, Barn Owls were nailed to the doors of farm buildings as a means of warding off the evil eye.[19] When asked if they still thought the birds frightening, almost two-fifths of a modern British audience of 300 people over 15 years old said they thought they were scary.[20] Owls are capable of evoking a residue of all their ancient associations, but these are usually within a self-conscious frame, so that they inspire excitement and a sense of mystery, but seldom fear.

This is a true story. The funeral was over. The undertaker's car drove the family back from the church to the locked house. It was November. The afternoon was cold, numb with the death of a beloved wife, mother, companion. The son walked to the sitting room and opened the door. On the back of an armchair sat a bird. A white bird, perched motionless, looking at him with unblinking dark eyes, with no sign of fear

or distress. A young Barn Owl, a juvenile. He looked around: how . . . ? All the windows were closed, the fireplace undisturbed. He walked towards the owl, which remained completely calm. Gently he picked it up in both hands. It didn't struggle. It looked at him thoughtfully and he gazed back wondering what to do with this little bird. Carefully he went over to the window to open it. He opened his hands. The young bird waited, in no hurry to leave. Eventually it flapped slowly away across the garden and settled in a tree. There it stayed on a bare branch during the funeral tea, until the light failed and night came.[21]

More often our experiences of owls are moments that bring a mixture of fascination, awe, humour, joy, affection and perhaps a dash of make-believe:

The tiled silo of our old red bank barn in the mountains of northern Virginia, USA, is a haven for Barn Owls. Their ghostly night flights as they circle above the corn crib, their rasping cries, and their impassive heart-shaped faces as they stare down from the feed-chute rungs enrich our lives as does all the resident wildlife. I love everything about the owls – their eerie, silent cruising in the evening sky, the scolding of the adults as they encourage the first flights of the owlets. Best of all is the sight of the youngsters lined up right above my head as I crane my neck to see up into the long-empty silo. There they perch, wing to wing like somber judges on the bench, staring fixedly down at me as I talk softly and cheerfully to them. Tendrils of webby dust cling to the yellow tiles, and pellets encasing the tiny skeletons of mice crunch under my feet. I sneeze. They tilt their heads ever so slightly. 'What kind of music would you like this morning?' I ask. 'Mozart,' one says. 'Rap,' counters another. 'Classical rock,' the third insists. So I select a CD before I start to feed the horses. Ten minutes later, I check to see if the owlets are still there. No one has moved so much as a feather. 'Do you like what I picked out?' I ask. I swear I see them give an affirmative nod.[22]

People of Western background at least had a head start in shedding negative perceptions of owls, because there has long been a tradition portraying them as creatures of benign wisdom. It is often assumed that all owls were embraced by this countervailing mythology, but this surely overlooks the pre-eminent role played by a single species, the **Little Owl** *Athene noctua*, which has a massive range across north Africa and Europe as well as south-west and north-east Asia.

The country where the Little Owl's visual image is still omnipresent, and whose inhabitants once possessed an ancient empire spanning a good deal of the bird's range, is Greece. In exactly the way that other classical deities were represented by birds (see Guineafowl family, page 36 and Peacocks in the West, page 76), so Pallas Athene, the goddess of war and protectress of the city of Athens, was symbolised by a Little Owl. The bird's scientific name, indeed, enshrines the ancient religious connection.

As a principal deity of the arts and intellectual affairs, Athene was thought to have bestowed on humankind a range of blessings from ship-building and the ox-yoke to the flute and trumpet. She was a goddess of natural bounty, bringer

The Little Owl featured on the four-drachma coin was an emblem of Athens' patron deity, the goddess Athene.

of the plough and of olive cultivation.[23] The identification of this owlish deity with material wealth and generic cultural prosperity was manifest in Greek money. For hundreds of years across the Hellenic Mediterranean there were coins bearing images of Little Owls. They were even known as 'owls'.[24] (The modern Greek one-euro coin still bears an image of the bird, which was copied from the four-drachma piece of 500 BC.)[25]

It is surely this long-standing, profound connection between one owl species and the Greek goddess of wisdom that has given rise in Western society to the (eventually) indiscriminate association of owls with intelligence. Other supportive details may have been the birds' generic gifts of foresight, albeit often of a malign nature, or their all-seeing eyes, but we should not overlook how being wide-eyed is not always a sign of wisdom. There are long traditions linking owls with stupidity in Europe and Asia. I recall vividly in Madhya Pradesh a group of Indian forest guards at Bandhavgarh National Park, who delighted in ribbing one of their colleagues because his owl-like face singled him out as slow-witted.

> In India dull or stupid people are almost always compared with owls. In fact, the Hindi word for such a person is the word for an owl, *Ullu*.[26]

> In India owls are considered as stupid birds, particularly the **Spotted Owlet** *Athene brama*, which people generally see around houses and orchards. Actually there is a term of abuse *Ullu ka patha* or 'son of a lovely owl' which, if you say it to someone, he will get upset. This is particularly so as one is imputing that they are not even a big owl, but its smaller cousin (son).[27]

A question prompted by the anomalous Greek symbolism is why should one of the most influential city-states of the ancient world represent one of its pre-eminent deities with the Little Owl? One assumed source of Athene's owl-shaped divinity is Sumeria, where baked-clay relief plaques dating to about 1750 BC have been found depicting a female deity (or demon) with owl's feet and wings, flanked by owls and usually identified with Ishtar (or Lilith of the Old Testament). Yet, how this goddess travelled from the banks of the Tigris to Greece and where are her intermediary forms are questions that are not easily answered.

▶ Owls may be feared as agents of darkness in many parts of the world, but diurnal species, such as this Spotted Owlet, are sometimes as famous for their aura of comedy.

A more local suggestion is that real Little Owls once favoured Athene's temple on the Acropolis in Athens and the identification flowed from this coincidental habitat choice.[28] Another rather ingenious and precise explanation centred on the fact that Athene was said to have been born from Zeus' head, when it was split open by his son Hephaistos, the blacksmith to the gods. Since Zeus was traditionally represented by the oak tree, and Hephaistos by lightning, the Little Owl housed in a storm-cleft hole in an oak would symbolise Athene emerging from her father's crown.[29]

These answers overlook and fail to address the negative associations engendered by other members of the family, which were commonplace in the ancient world. Pliny, for example, wrote of the powerful funereal associations engendered by the Eurasian Eagle-Owl.[30] Yet perhaps one major reason why the Little Owl was eligible for a very different set of cultural responses is its diurnal lifestyle. Although the species is active by night, it is commonplace to find it during the day. Sunlight can strip owls of their fearsome and otherworldly qualities. In fact, the Little Owl often presents a reverse character. The great British nature writer J A Baker once wrote:

> One must try not to be anthropomorphic, yet it cannot be denied that little owls are very funny to watch. In flight, they are just owls, but at rest they seem to be natural clowns. They do not know it, of course. And that makes them much funnier, for they always appear indignant, outraged, brimming over with choler . . . whenever I see one close, in a tree, I laugh aloud.[31]

It is interesting that other pocket-sized diurnal owls share in these more positive, or, perhaps one should say, less threatening and fearful, responses. Spotted Owlets in India are a good example. Equally, when Helmut Sick wrote that 'backwoodspeople' attribute good luck to the **Ferruginous Pygmy Owl** *Glaucidium brasilianum*, it seems significant that this tiny Brazilian owl is often active by day.[32]

It is striking how when viewed in bright light – either of solar origin or of the intellectual variety – that the other key properties of owls also become apparent. One is the roundness of their shape, which is even more emphasised in small species and has a fundamental impact on human attitudes towards any animal. Roundness plays a core role in our frequently humorous but always immensely positive perceptions of birds as various as penguins and auks, thrushes and pittas. Stripped of their inner and outer darkness, owls readily become endearing, even loveable, creatures; hence the omnipresence of owls of the fluff-filled variety in many modern toyshops.

Little Owls enjoyed just such a place in people's affections both in the ancient and modern worlds. As long ago as the fifth century BC Aristotle described how 'birdcatchers use the owl as a decoy for catching little birds of all kinds'.[33] This is one of the oldest references to a long-standing tradition in Europe and Asia of trappers keeping smaller owl species as working decoys, which they placed in proximity either to nets or to lime-smeared sticks. It trades on a common reaction among songbirds, when they discover an owl, to flutter around it and call excitedly. While distracted in this mobbing behaviour the birds eventually expose themselves to capture.

Little Owls have been a favourite decoy bird probably since the Bronze Age. This form of domestication would have helped to break down any residual folkloric barrier between owls and their owners. Eventually in countries such as France, Germany and Belgium, but especially in Italy, where it was known as *civetta* (also as *sieta* and *zivetta*), it was a much-cherished kind of pet. There were special fairs, said to date back into antiquity, near the Italian city of Florence and later in the Tuscan town of Crespina (*La Fiera delle Civette*) that were held every September, where the tradition of hunting with decoy Little Owls was celebrated and the captive birds traded in large numbers.[34]

It is a measure of the deep affection lavished on these pet Little Owls that Renaissance poets such as Agnolo Firenzuola wrote verse celebrating their beloved 'Civetta', while other writers described how the birds were reared from birth and taken from the roofs of the houses, where they naturally bred and were clearly tolerated. The diminutive form of the bird's name *civettazza* was also once a term of affection meaning 'a little dear'.[35] (*Civetta*, used in reference to a woman, means a 'flirt' or 'coquette' although this too is probably archaic.) However, in France today, the parallel word for a Little Owl, *chouette*, has similar associations of endearment:

> *Chouette* literally means an 'owl', and is used as an adjective to mean friendly or nice (a thing or person) or as an exclamation (Chouette!), meaning 'great'. This is a very common expression in France.[36]

(It also seems significant that while the word 'owl' in French (*hibou*) and Italian (*gufo*) is a masculine noun, the name for Little Owl in both languages is feminine.)

Such is the gloriously contradictory nature of bird folklore that we should not dismiss the idea that wild Little Owls, when heard and seen at night (even by those who lavished affections on their pet Little Owls by day), could still have functioned as birds of ill omen in the past. Yet by the same token we should not underestimate the capacity of people, especially before the modern era, to conflate all owls as one owl. So the benign and wholesome threads of association that entwined about the Little Owl would have slowly become entangled round the whole family. We may have lost sight of the gradual chain of muddle and confusion that brought us to this point, but we all recognise its consequences. The Western idea that owls are good and wise is now the stuff of cliché.

Perhaps the most telling expression of the larger mental journey we have undertaken in the West in relation to these birds is the frequent presence of their images – particularly of Barn, Snowy and **Northern Saw-whet Owl** *Aegolius acadicus* – on the mantelpiece of late December, alongside more traditional birds of the Christmas card, such as the white dove of peace. It is so commonplace (at least in the UK and USA; rarely in Sweden) that we probably never stop to reflect upon it.[37] (The Barn Owl's church-dwelling habits in many countries may be a subliminal link in this Christmas-card tradition. In fact, in Brazil it is sometimes known as *Coruja-católica*, the 'Catholic Owl'.)[38] Yet imagine the psychological impact of sending an owl's image on a Christmas card in a country where the creatures are known generically as 'witchbirds'? In the West, however, it is received as it is intended – as an image of something beautiful and blessed.

What is striking about these Christmas-card birds – the white owl and the white dove – is the radical difference between their respective histories. White doves have remained a consistent image of goodness and of life for 5,000 years or more. The owl's symbolism, by contrast, has orbited across that same period, and the bird has gone from the black fowl of night to a cherished creature akin to the dove itself.

OWL FOOD

One stranger aspect to our encounters with owls is the inclusion of the birds in the human diet. There is a petroglyph in the cave called Les Trois Frères in southern France that is at least 13,000 years old. It depicts three owls and a common assumption is that the birds, like the other animals whose images appear in cave paintings, were eaten during the last ice age. Certainly thousands of bones from large owl species have been found in association with Palaeolithic tools.[39] In the Arctic, the Snowy Owl, which the Trois Frères image is thought to depict, remained a part of the Inuit diet for thousands of years.[40]

Once again, however, one finds that our deeply schismatic responses to owls were writ large in the matter of their consumption. For many communities the birds' overarching malignancy fed through into their flesh. Fear of the birds made them taboo as food. In Deuteronomy and Leviticus of the Old Testament, Judaic law forbade owl flesh along with that of kites and crows. In fact, better understanding of the original Hebrew and Aramaic texts has allowed recent clarification of the intensity of this prohibition. The *King James Bible* merely noted how the ban extended to 'the owl . . . And the little owl, and . . . great owl'. But in *The New English Bible* the owlish prescriptions have expanded:

> These are the birds you shall regard as vermin, and for this reason they shall not be eaten . . . the desert-owl, the short-eared owl, the long-eared owl and every kind of hawk; the tawny owl, the fisher-owl, and the screech-owl; the little owl, the horned owl . . . and the bat. (Leviticus, 11:13)

(It is deeply ironic that the reviled owl of the Jews later became a key Christian metaphor for the Jewish race, because in denying Jesus they were seen as preferring darkness to light. It is this anti-Semitic symbolism that explains the presence of medieval owl images in Christian churches, e.g. Gloucester Cathedral, UK.)[41]

The Greeks and Romans had no such qualms about consuming owls, except to note that some were inedible only because of their awful flavour. Yet Aristotle noted how other unspecified migrant owls were 'regarded as a table delicacy'.[42] As always, the Romans were not to be outdone in matters of eating wild-caught birds, but they did add a medicinal rationale to their owl-dining habits. They believed that owls' eggs were a cure for drunkenness and ate them to ward off a hangover.[43] In parts of Europe the idea survived well into the early modern period and there are German beer tankards made in owl form. (One wonders, incidentally, if there is an intriguing although, as yet, unresolved link between this magico-medicinal belief about owls and owl-shaped flasks found in ancient China. From as early as 1500 BC the Chinese made bronze wine vessels in the shape of owls. Is it possible that people in the Far East shared these notions of owl-induced sobriety?)

The eating of owls is still commonplace in some regions. In peninsular Malaysia, just north of Singapore, major seizures in 2008–9 of illegal bushmeat included more than 1,500 owls, which were thought to be for export to China.[44] It is a mark of the fundamental contradictions coexisting in owl lore that Africa is also one of the regions where the birds are still eaten regularly. This is not merely to imbibe the dark powers ascribed to them, but rather because some African communities find them tasty and nutritious. The following anecdote illuminates this, but it also highlights the curiosity that such behaviour arouses from the rest of the world.

While birdwatching near Weppa in central Nigeria, I and a friend, Tasso Leventis, spent the morning looking for a fishing owl which I had seen on a previous visit. Unfortunately, we were unable to find any trace of it. As we were packing up to leave, a young boy happened to pass by so I dug out the field guide, showed him a photo of the fishing owl and asked him if he ever saw it in the area. His said, yes, they often saw them around and, in fact, he had just eaten one for breakfast!

At this juncture, we followed him to his village where, sure enough, there were the remains of the owl, the claws, head and feathers. I submitted a short report on it to the African Bird Club and thought nothing more about it. Unbeknown to me, whilst I was away in northern Nigeria, somebody had got hold of my report and submitted it to numerous newspapers in the UK. It received remarkable publicity including half a page on the front page of *The Times* and was covered by the press all over the world. Unaware of all this, I eventually returned to Lagos, and was immediately contacted by

the BBC and ended up doing a ten-minute interview on *Newshour*. While I was out of contact, the BBC in the UK had even managed to track down my mother who was interviewed even though she was totally oblivious of the whole story. The final chapter occurred about a year later; I was on board an internal flight in Brazil and there in the in-flight magazine I was confronted by the words, 'you will have all heard about the story of Philip Hall and his Fishing Owl'.

(This bird turned out to be the **Vermiculated Fishing Owl** *Scotopelia bouvieri*, one of the least studied owls in Africa.)[45]

The vast majority of prey for the owls themselves are precisely those creatures least loved by humans – rats and mice. Larger owl species such as the Eurasian Eagle-Owl, however, can take young cattle or sheep, as well as wild boar, deer, wildcats and full-grown foxes. In sub-Saharan African the Verreaux's Eagle-Owl will occasionally eat warthog piglets or monkeys, while the nestlings of eagles, vultures and hawks are more common fare.[46] In fact the eating of birds of prey and even other smaller owls, which combines nutrition with the elimination of predatory rivals, is something of a speciality across the entire genus *Bubo*. These formidable night predators will also invade our home space and the Great Horned Owl of North America has been known to take poultry as large an adult hen turkey. It is even credited with the occasional pet cat, while the Eurasian Eagle-Owl has been known to have a taste for small domestic dogs.[47]

There has, as yet, never been an authenticated case of any owl killing or eating a human.

This misericord from Gloucester Cathedral features an owl being mobbed by small birds. It was there as an anti-Semitic reference since the Jews were thought to have preferred the darkness to the light of Jesus Christ.

Frogmouth family *Podargidae*

The 13 species of frogmouth are highly nocturnal, mainly insectivorous birds found across southern or south-east Asia and Australasia, with a collective range that centres on the island of Borneo (where six species occur). Like their close relatives, the potoos and nightjars, frogmouths are striking in appearance, with huge bright staring eyes, subtly mottled plumages and a vast amphibian's maw, whose downturned sides give the birds a rather lugubrious expression. Not that one often sees frogmouths in detail: by day they rely upon their extraordinary lichen-like camouflage to avoid detection.

Yet to encounter a frogmouth asleep, when it sits absolutely stationary, eyes clamped shut, head thrust heavenwards and tail flexed against the tree so that the whole thing resembles the gnarled end of a dead snag, is to experience one of the strangest birds in the region. That death-in-life immobility, as well as the eerie quality of their nocturnal vocalisations, has made frogmouths into mysterious night spirits for some of their human neighbours.

Oilbird family *Steatornithidae*

Among the various nightjar-like bird groups around the world, the **Oilbird** *Steatornis caripensis* is remarkable for its highly communal, cave-dwelling lifestyle. Yet what renders the species unique – and it enjoys a family all to itself – is its status as the planet's only nocturnal fruit-eating bird. Oilbirds occur across large parts of Central and South America, with outposts on the Caribbean island of Trinidad.

Adding to the Oilbird's sense of distinction is its capacity to manoeuvre in total darkness using echo-location. The technique, more usually associated with bats (and some swift species), involves the emission of high-frequency sounds that bounce off the bird's environment and create a sonar-like 'sound-picture' of the surrounding topography. Since nest colonies can involve thousands of pairs, some Oilbird caves mount an extraordinary assault upon human senses. The humid tropical darkness is filled with a cacophony of the birds' high-pitched clicking noises, but also a deafening, echoic barrage of 'harsh screams, snarls,

The Oilbird is the world's only nocturnal fruit-eating bird.

shrieks and snoring sounds'.[1] It has few parallels in the world of birds and is as unforgettable as it is difficult to convey. Yet one particular noise has a curiously slurping or gurgling quality and for me invokes some sort of satanic conclave avid for blood. Even modern science-hardened naturalists feel assailed and disoriented by the experience, especially as the birds, disturbed from their rocky ledges, will loom back and forth out of the gloom.

Small wonder, perhaps, that Oilbirds were once steeped in superstition. In parts of their range they are still called *Guácharo*, 'one who cries or moans loudly'.[2] The birds were seen as lost souls condemned to a tortured life inside the cave until their sins were purged.[3] Quite what part of this original mythology, if any, has survived is difficult to judge, but the birds' eeriness is indisputable. Their departure at nightfall in search of fruiting trees, when they rise screaming out the ground in loose groups, 'is an impressive and never-to-be-forgotten sight'.[4]

Oilbirds will fly as much as 150 km (93 miles) to rich feeding areas, where they clamber around the trees devouring fruits, especially those of laurels and palms. It is this oil-rich diet that accounts for the long history of exploitation and also for the name, 'oilbird'. The young acquire thick layers of fat that once made them enormously valuable to local people. Some caves have probably been exploited for millennia and it was just such an historic site that supplied the first scientific description of the bird. In 1799, the explorers Alexander von Humboldt and Aimé Bonpland travelled to Caripe (a word now enshrined in the scientific name) to see a series of caves and its *Guácharo* colony, which were famous throughout Venezuela even then. Humboldt and Bonpland wrote an account of their visit and of the Oilbird harvest, describing the bird itself as the size of a chicken, with the mouth of a goatsucker (see page 288) and the carriage of a vulture:

> The shrill and piercing cries of the guacharoes strike upon the vaults of the rocks, and are repeated by the echo in the depth of the cavern. The Indians showed us the nests of these birds, by fixing torches to the end of a long pole. These nests were fifty or sixty feet above our heads, in holes in the shape of funnels, with which the roof of the grotto is pierced like a sieve . . .
>
> The Indians enter the Cueva del Guacharo once a year, near midsummer, armed with poles, by means of which they destroy the greater part of the nests. At this season several thousands of birds are killed; and the old ones, as if to defend their brood, hover over the heads of the Indians, uttering terrible cries. The young, which fall to the ground, are opened on the spot. Their peritoneum is extremely loaded with fat, and a layer of fat reaches from the abdomen to the anus, forming a kind of cushion between the legs of the bird . . . At the period which is commonly called at Caripe *the oil harvest*, the Indians build huts with palm leaves, near the entrance, and even in the porch of the cavern . . . There, with a fire of brush-wood, they melt in pots of clay the fat of the young birds just killed. This fat is known by the name of butter or oil (*manteca* or *aceite*) of the guacharo. It is half liquid, transparent, without smell, and so pure that it may be kept above a year without becoming rancid. At the convent of Caripe no other oil is used in the kitchen of the monks.[5]

The Oilbird's occult reputation was clearly not a barrier to this exploitation. Yet one small benefit of the fears aroused by the birds was that collectors refused to enter the deepest parts of the caves. Some nest chambers are as much 800 m (2,600 ft) from the entrance and it ensured that enough pairs survived to maintain the colony's viability. Indeed, Caripe, 'the mine of fat' as the local people once called it, is now a tourist attraction and a national park, with a display housed in the local Humboldt Museum.

The threat from human harvests has largely receded across the Oilbird's range, and the loss of the bird's forested feeding habitat is intensifying, but locals have discovered new ways to make profit from Oilbirds that could have knock-on benefits for their conservation. As the following makes clear, Oilbirds are assailed by modernity in all its forms, yet they are sometimes able to persist in the most unlikely places.

> After driving through mountainous countryside for several hours we finally came to rest at a section of unopened motorway ruthlessly sliced through the rainforest. It seemed an unprepossessing place to find a bird I had fantasised about seeing for decades. We scrambled down towards a cleft in the rock running under the road. There was rubbish strewn everywhere and a black plastic water pipe emerging from the cleft made it obvious that if this was where the oilbirds were, they were not undisturbed: this was far from pristine. We walked into the left and our eyes had barely adjusted to the dim light when a huge shape noisily launched itself off a nearby ledge. I hadn't imagined they would be so close to the entrance.
>
> Shrieking and flapping, the Oilbird disappeared round a corner out of sight. We stood still, and the dimly lit cleft emerged slowly from the gloom. The ledge where the bird had been sitting was clean, compressed mud, underneath which was a colourful array of fruit remains. Elsewhere in the gorge I began to see other Oilbirds perched lengthways along the ledges, their huge eyes peering sleepily down at us. The most striking features were the tiny rows of white, heart-shaped spots on their wings, and the array of rictal bristles round the huge, hooked beak. Once or twice a bird launched itself into the air, emitting a retching, clicking scream – similar I assumed to the clicking they use to echo-locate when they happen to live in completely dark caves. With a one-metre wingspan these huge birds reminded me of a cross between a raptor and a nightjar, yet remarkably they feed on fruit found through a well-developed sense of smell.[6]

Potoo family *Nyctibiidae*

These seven species of Central and South America partake of the strangeness that seems to touch all the world's night birds. They have long tails and slender nightjar-like bodies with huge heads and immense mouths. The potoos' open gape, 'like that of a gigantic toad', is big enough in the **Great Potoo** *Nyctibius grandis* to accommodate a man's clenched fist.[1] Their disembodied voices also have an eerie and evocative quality, particularly the call of the widespread **Common Potoo** *Nyctibius griseus* which produces a drawn-out melancholic wail that falls in pitch and volume to its close.

The birds were once a strong focus of Amerindian and Brazilian folklore, especially the Great Potoo, whose plumage was used – and it may be still – in rituals intended to ensure chastity among newly pubescent girls. It seems likely that these rites draw on the birds' deep links to that ultimate virgin, the moon. The local name for potoos in Brazil is *mãe-de-lua* ('mother of the moon').[2]

The potoos' collective capacity for mystery and their power to evoke superstition are clearly demonstrated by the recent history of an as yet unnamed species in the Amazon. Over a three-year period, American naturalist Mario Cohn-

A Common Potoo
in its classic daytime
disguise as a dead
snag. Occasionally
when people are
walking in potoo
country they go
to reach for a
convenient tree
stump, only for the
'stump' to fly away.

Haft repeatedly heard an unfamiliar call that he likens to the long descending whistle of a falling bomb. Other people had ascribed the sound to another bird, the Sunbittern (see page 175), but Cohn-Haft eventually managed to see the source of the call and initially identified it as **White-winged Potoo** *Nyctibius leucopterus*, a species undetected since its discovery in 1821.

Twenty years later and after much detailed study, Cohn-Haft now recognises that his mystery bird – an exclusively Amazonian inhabitant – although very similar to the White-winged Potoo of coastal Brazil, is actually a species still unnamed by scientists. If the bird's physical presence had gone entirely unnoticed, its vocalisations had not, since the calls had been familiar to many local people. However, they had attributed them to a creature called the *curupira*, a figure of Amazonian folklore characterised as a hairy dwarf-like trickster who deceives hunters and other visitors to the forest. Cohn-Haft notes:

> It turns out that this potoo species is all over the Amazon Basin, despite never having been collected by scientists prior to 1989. Who would have guessed that a large bird, occurring even at the outskirts of major cities, could have been overlooked for centuries? Local people were also unaware of this bird's existence, but many of them know its song and believe it is the whistling of the much-feared *curupira*. Paying attention to local folklore and listening carefully to stories of rural residents of the Amazon and to the sounds of the woods around them, we can still discover new species of animal. I wonder what else we've missed?[3]

Nightjar family *Caprimulgidae*

These long-winged, slender-bodied night birds are found across almost the Earth's entire land surface south of about 60° N (excluding Antarctica and New Zealand), where they demonstrate a remarkable catholicity in habitat, from rainforest and burning desert to the inner city.

Yet their ubiquity disguises the family's real home territory. In Eurasia just a singleton (**European Nightjar** *Caprimulgus europaeus*) extends to that furthest northern latitude, and much the same occurs in North America, where the range of **Common Nighthawk** *Chordeiles minor* creeps into southern Alaska. At least three other resonantly named birds (**Chuck-will's-widow** *Caprimulgus carolinensis*, **Whip-poor-will** *Caprimulgus vociferus* and **Common Poorwill** *Phalaenoptilus nuttallii* occur as far north as southern Canada, but nightjars are really creatures of tropical warmth. Most of the family's 88 species are in the southern hemisphere, especially in South America (29 species) and Africa (26 species).

While many of us probably live in proximity to at least a single species, humans and nightjars are largely mutual strangers because of the birds' other key heartland – the darkness. As the great US nature writer Henry Thoreau

With their otherworldly vocalisations, erratic flight and wing-clapping displays, members of the nightjar family, like this European Nightjar, partake of the wider mystery of dusk.

At dusk it may be a creature of supremely fluid movement, but by day the European Nightjar assumes the stillness of stone.

once wrote, 'It is not nightfall till the whip-poor-wills begin to sing.'[1] His comment on this well-loved North American bird is true of the whole family. Nightjars come alive with a loss of light or, at least, when the world is reduced to the half-light of dusk. They have minute droplets of oil behind the retina surface – known as the tapetum lucidum – that enhance the light-gathering capability of their eyes. It is this layer, incidentally, which accounts for the bright pink, red, or fierce-orange glow of nightjars' eyes when they are caught in the car headlights or beam of a torch. Otherwise the most one normally glimpses is a flickering silhouette sweeping and twisting as the bird chases insects, before merging back into the shadows.

It is partly because they are so difficult to see that some nightjars are ranked among the world's least-known birds. The ultimate mystery is perhaps the **Nechisar Nightjar** *Caprimulgus solala*, which was discovered in its eponymous region of southern Ethiopia only in 1990. It was named as new to science solely on the basis of one wing – the dismembered remains found at the scene of a road accident. A live individual was not knowingly observed until 19 years later.[2]

Slightly better documented is **Prigogine's Nightjar** *Caprimulgus prigoginei*. It was first discovered in 1955 in the eastern forests of the Democratic Republic of the Congo and in more recent times there has been a string of sightings and sound recordings in west Africa of birds presumed to be this species. Unfortunately so little is known about its vocalisations, or, indeed, any aspect of the lifestyle of Prigogine's Nightjar, that none of the observers has been absolutely certain of their claims. There is but a single complete skin available to science.[3]

It is tempting to ascribe our deep sense of the nightjars' mysteriousness to the birds' sheer inaccessibility. Yet, ironically, it is perhaps when we observe them most closely

that they seem strangest of all. Occasionally nightjars can be found at their daytime roosts, when they rely on their wonderful crypsis to escape detection. In these rare moments the viewer is allowed to appreciate the subtle, soft, usually sombre colours and the exquisitely obliterative patterns that enable the birds to blend to their lichen-mottled rocks or the dead vegetation on which they rest. One of the best descriptions of how and why nightjars affect us so profoundly was written by Thoreau, when he stumbled on a brooding Common Nighthawk at Walden in Massachusetts. On 7 June 1853 he wrote:

> Visited my nighthawk on her nest. Could hardly believe my eyes when I stood within seven feet and beheld her sitting on her eggs, her head to me. She looked so Saturnian, so one with the earth, so sphinx-like, a relic of the reign of Saturn which Jupiter did not destroy, a riddle that might cause a man to go dash his head against a stone. It was not an actual living creature, far less a winged creature of the air, but a figure in stone or bronze, a fanciful production of art, like the gryphon or phoenix. In fact, with its breast toward me and owing to its color or size no bill perceptible, it looked like the end [of] a brand, such as are common in a clearing, its breast mottled or alternately waved with dark brown and gray, its flat, grayish, weather-beaten crown, its eyes nearly closed, purposely, lest those bright beads should betray it, with the stony cunning of the sphinx . . . It was enough to fill one with awe. The sight of this creature sitting on its eggs impressed me with the venerableness of the globe. There was nothing novel about it. All the while, this seemingly sleeping bronze sphinx, as motionless as the earth, was watching me with intense anxiety thorough those narrow slits in its eyelids.

The strange pink lining to the mouth of the European Nightjar may help to explain why the bird was once accused of sucking milk from goats' udders.

Another step, and it fluttered down the hill close to the ground, with a wabbling [*sic*] motion . . .[4]

Thoreau articulates our wider expectation that birds, whose collective metabolism is so supercharged compared with our own, should somehow be vital, alive and mobile. Yet his nighthawk was the inverse of all these qualities. In Thoreau's words, it was 'so one with the earth . . . a figure in stone or bronze'. The bird did eventually morph into an aerial and supple creature and it is perhaps this transformation from an absolute, corpse-like stillness to liquid dynamism that underscores Thoreau's other main reflection.

The bird not only changed into a creature quick with life, it also shifted into being part of the living moment out of an immense past. Writing in 1853 and before geologists and biologists had a full understanding of the age of the Earth and the 4-billion-year heritage of its life forms, Thoreau articulated his sense of the nighthawk's ancientness by invoking a time of classical gods, Jupiter and Saturn. Elsewhere he noted that his encounter with the nighthawk had been a 'fit prelude to meeting Prometheus bound to his rock on Caucasus'. We now know how accurate Thoreau's instinct was, because in France proto-nightjars have been unearthed which date to the late Eocene, 40 million years ago. This is ten times longer than the history of humankind.[5] In meeting these otherworldly creatures are we perhaps made more intensely aware of the long evolutionary journeys they have undertaken? Is it this indefinable but ancient aura possessed by some birds that moves us so deeply? (See also Hoatzin family, page 259.)

More generally humans have honoured these unknowable aspects of nightjars in the names they have coined for them or in the beliefs and ideas woven around them. Rather like owls, they could be omens that presage ill luck and this association is almost worldwide. In Costa Rica, for example, the bones of some species were said to be ground up and introduced into cigarettes as a sure way of inducing death in the unfortunate soul who then smoked them.[6] Such nightjar magic could be defensive as well as offensive. On the Mediterranean island of Malta old-time hunters will still carry one of the bird's dried legs as an amulet to ward off the evil eye.[7] (Yet European Nightjars are still trapped and shot as food on Malta and, more generally, the family is said to furnish excellent meat. In Africa, the birds are widely eaten today.)[8]

What is more difficult to judge about these decaying or obsolete superstitions is the seriousness, or otherwise, with which they were treated. Birds of darkness, indeed, all nocturnal creatures such as bats and even moths, still have a psychological edginess for diurnal primates like ourselves. This has not been banished even from the most modern of Western communities. Sometimes these older strata of belief or association are retained, if only in a self-consciously playful form:

> I was brought up in Kenya and there is a legend that the nightjar is a bird to be respected. If you kill one, or damage the egg, bad luck follows. I accidentally killed a nightjar in Ghana, I hit it with my motorcycle while driving at night, and I was bitten next day by a venomous snake![9]

Wes Craven, American film director of the classic *A Nightmare on Elm Street*, has also appealed to this atavistic response within us, and used Whip-poor-will vocalisations to heighten moments of tension in his horror movies. 'Probably inappropriately,' as he acknowledges, 'but it's such a haunting sound, and I do remember the sound from being a kid in the woods of Ohio.'[10]

One generalisation to be made about nightjars is that the full spectrum of responses is overall less dark than that inspired by owls (see page 271). For most humans, nightjars were at worst birds of mystery, or they were linked with the feelings of sadness and inward reflection induced by the setting sun. The connections are clearly demonstrated in the trio of onomatopoeic names coined for North America's widespread species. 'Chuck-will's-widow', 'Whip-poor-will' and 'poorwill' all imply some degree of human pain. Otherwise the birds have been linked with that other great inhabitant of darkness – and the ultimate source of emotional hurt – romantic love. Here are two stories respectively from Uganda and Nicaragua:

> At Murchison Falls National Park, Uganda, I was escorted by an exceptionally friendly, knowledgeable ranger called Kaphu George. On one journey back to our accommodation we travelled through the bush as darkness descended. The drive was made all the longer because of the nightjars we encountered sitting in the track. Of the six species, the male **Standard-winged Nightjar** *Macrodipteryx longipennis* was the most impressive. The bird looks small and stout on the ground, but its peculiar-shaped wings make it far more spectacular and memorable than many of its relatives. It has a single long wire-like extension protruding from the primaries that ends in a square block of feathering, giving the impression that a flag (or standard) is attached to each wing. In flight it looks bizarre – like a bird that has two large moths as constant companions chasing after it! George told us a wonderful tale that originated from his village close to Murchison Falls. In his teenage years it was a custom for young men with affections for a certain young lady to go out into the bush in search of a male Standard-winged Nightjar. Whoever was able to acquire the wire-like extension, the 'standard', would then present it to his intended lover and she would be instantly impressed. George told us how the youth of the village would be captivated in observing the displaying male nightjars (a ritual in which the male flies around quivering and flapping his 'standards') and as it always worked for the male nightjar, any lad who was able to present a girl with the feather would never fail in his quest! [11]

The Nicaraguan campesino farmers have incorporated the bird known as the 'pocoyo' (this name refers to all members of the nightjar family) into a song of the north-western region of the country (Chinandega province, near Consigüina volcano). It tells of a pocoyo personified as a man, who is sad and sings to his compañeros, the other pocoyos. His song goes something like: 'I am a sad pocoyo without fortune, who is looking for his love under the light of the moon, for a sweet young pocoyita who suddenly left, suddenly on her way to Tonalá' (a rural village in the north). The pocoyo goes on to ask his friends to tell their other friends of his sad situation, and then their songs evoke the crater walls of the great volcano Consigüina that are struck with torrential rains. These storms deepen the sadness because the sweet young pocoyita will remain for ever lost under those gloom-filled rains.

This story reflects both the behavior of the pocoyo (its repeated calls, as well as its preference for open space and dry nights) and also the lives and laments of the campesinos. While the pocoyo is not a bright or colorful bird, it is one that is present daily in the lives of the campesinos and whose song accompanies them nearly every rainless night. [12]

The note of sadness detected in nightjar voices has appealed to modern songwriters too, most famously the American country singer Hank Williams. In his 1949 classic 'I'm So Lonesome I Could Cry', he deploys not only the song of a nightjar, but also that other stock motif of American loneliness, the passing train. The singer finds his own doleful mood mirrored in the whistle of the midnight express and in the lonesome calling of a whippoorwill that seems too blue to fly. Nightjars have a similarly melancholic role in a lesser-known song of the British artist Elton John. In 'Come Down In Time' (1970), however, the lyrics evoke a softer note than Williams', mingling just a hint of lost love into the wider mood of tender reflection.

Finally there is a sense if not of love lost then certainly of love unfulfilled in an old game once played by the people of the southern Allegheny Mountains in Pennsylvania, USA.

> The whippoorwill reveals how long it will be before marriage – as many years as its notes are repeated: as I have heard the bird reiterate its cry more than 800 times without taking breath, this must often be a discouraging report to an anxious maid or bachelor.' [13]

THE MYTH OF THE GOATSUCKER

Perhaps the strangest idea that has been associated with nightjars is one of the oldest and most persistent. The scientific name for the genus, *Caprimulgus*, draws on the Latin words *capra*, 'goat', and *mulgere*, 'to milk'. It has been translated as 'goatsucker' and the anglicised name is still sometimes used for the group in North America. In Europe, nightjars are known as *ziegenmelker* (German), *chotacabras* (Spanish), *succiacapre* (Italian) and *Lelek kozodój* (Polish), all four names having the same goat connections. 'Goatsucker' was also an old name for European Nightjar in Britain until the eighteenth century, while in France it was called *Tettechèvre*, with an identical sense. All drew on the old belief that nightjars actually did feed by sucking the teats of goats. The idea was widespread for thousands of years. The pioneer British naturalist William Turner recorded it in central Europe in the sixteenth century, writing:

> When I was in Switzerland I saw an aged man, who fed his goats upon the mountains . . . I asked him whether he knew a bird . . . which in the dark is wont to suck goats' udders, so that afterwards the animals go blind. Now he replied that he himself had seen many in the Swiss mountains fourteen years before, that he had suffered many losses from those very birds, so that he had once had six she-goats blinded by Caprimulgi, but that one and all they had now flown away from Switzerland to Lower Germany, where nowadays they did not only steal the milk of she-goats . . . but killed the sheep besides.

In fairness to Turner, we should note that while he reported this conversation, he had an inkling the old boy was teasing him. If this were the case, then it demonstrates how the goatsucker myth was regarded with playful distrust by rural folk even in an age when we might assume it to have passed for fact.[14]

Yet in the late eighteenth century the nature diarist Gilbert White certainly knew of European Nightjars being blamed for a condition in young cattle (an illness that was caused by a species of fly). 'Puckeridge' was the countryman's name for the nightjar and for the fly-borne malady. In France, Georges Comte de Buffon noted that while the 'goatsucker' name was contradicted by the facts, it was nevertheless ancient and generally accepted. In the Tirol region of Austria an old folk name for European Nightjar was also 'cowmilker', *Kuhmelker*.[15] It seems that once the maleficent impact of nightjars had been established, the category of affected livestock was broadened to include almost any milk-yielding beast.

The earliest known reference to the supposed behaviour is in Aristotle's *History of Animals*:

> The so-called goat-sucker lives on mountains . . . it lays two eggs or three at most, and is of a sluggish disposition. It flies up to the she-goat and sucks its milk, from which habit it derives its name; it is said that, after it has sucked the teat of the animal, the teat dries up and the animal goes blind. It is dim-sighted in the day-time, but sees well enough by night. [16]

Most classical authors followed this lead. Aelian, for instance, stripped out the genuine natural history – such as Aristotle's reference to the bird's love of mountain landscapes and the laying of two eggs – and simply embellished its more sensational claim.

It seems that the Goatsucker is the most audacious of creatures, for it despises small birds but assails goats with the utmost violence, and more than that, it flies to their udders and sucks out the milk without any fear of vengeance from the goatherd, although it makes the basest return for being filled with milk, for it makes the dug 'blind' and staunches its flow. [17]

Few have bothered to enquire how the belief and name acquired currency and why they should have persisted for so long. One point to clarify from the outset is that, while goats' ceasing to give milk has many causes, there are few conditions which result in their blindness. The Honorary Veterinary Surgeon for the British Goat Society, himself a goat breeder, suggests that its rarity may have actually predisposed early goatherds to seek causes outside their commonplace experience to explain the affliction. [18]

In attempting to answer how the belief arose, I suggested in *Birds Britannica* (see page 295) that one persistently overlooked element in the goatsucker myth is the extent to which cyclical or unpredictable products derived from domestic animals – eggs, milk, etc. – were once steeped in ritual, taboo and superstition. It was precisely this psychological context that predisposed early goatherds to be hypersensitive about their animals. It was also this mindset that led them to ascribe changes in yield to all kinds of factors or unrelated causes. Yet this does not address why exactly they should blame a moth- and beetle-eating insectivore for stealing milk, a substance that the bird could not even genuinely digest.

The myth was certainly first recorded by Aristotle but one can see that, even in this brief passage, he was himself responding to pre-existing ideas ('so-called goatsucker . . . from which habit it derives its name; it is said that'). While

T. 8.

Caprimulgus.
The Goat-sucker.

Mark Catesby's eighteenth-century etching is thought to depict a Chuck-will's-widow. The bird's striking name comes from its plaintive four-note song, which can be repeated 834 times without pause.

289

he appears to have treated the beliefs as genuine, he was merely passing on what was well established in his day. The most we can assert is that the idea of the goatsucker arose some time between the origins of goat domestication (roughly 9000–8000 BC) and approximately 400 BC, well before Aristotle encountered and recorded it.

What supports the claim that it arose in the area close to Aristotle's own eastern Mediterranean is the myth's absence from other cultural traditions. Nightjar names seem to have no livestock connections in traditional African, Islamic, Hindu or Chinese thought. In Arabic it is known as *Sabed*, while in Egypt the various local names include:

Subad: a generic name for nightjars
Abu an-nawn: father of sleep
Ibb lay ir: unknown
Lubbaada: unknown
Qirra: possibly connected with a small female donkey
Tayr al-mawt: bird of death[19]

I learned that in Syria they also call it *Mesas*. I think that these Arabic names have to do with the fact that this bird rests and is very calm during the day, resuming flight at sunset and early morning.[20]

In Ki-Somali (the language of Somalians) the bird is *Habas*: meaning 'the squatter' (the one that flies a bit and suddenly and quickly drops to squat on the ground).[21]

In Iran I don't know of any links between nightjars and goats or livestock but there is a similar story for the lizard the Desert Monitor *Varanus griseus*, which in Farsi is called *Boz-maje* ('Goat sucker'). However *Shab-gard* ('Night roamer') is the common name for nightjars in Farsi.[22]

There are apparently no old names among these other cultures that indicate a direct connection with domestic animals. (While goatsucker-type names occur in the Americas, these are imports carried across the Atlantic by European colonists.) The only region where nomenclatural evidence does occur outside Europe is in Turkey and the Kurdish areas of Iraq and Iran (Kurdistan). There, the bird is known even today as *Çobanaldatan* and *Shwan-halkhalatena* (*Shwan*: 'shepherd', and *halkhalatena*: 'deceiver') respectively. Both have the same meaning, 'shepherd's deceiver'.[23] (There is an intriguing analogue of these words among the Spanish vernacular names for European Nightjar and **Red-necked Nightjar** *Caprimulgus ruficollis*. It is *engañapastores*, also meaning 'shepherd's deceiver'. How it came about is unknown.)[24]

While these names might appear to have similar kinds of association to the goatsucker tag, they probably have no links to the notion of stealing milk, as the following explanation of the Kurdish version emphasises:

The local people told me a story about *Shwan-halkhalatena* that goes as follows. One day a shepherd went out with a herd of sheep and goats, and seeing a nightjar, he tried to catch it. However, each time he attempted to get close, it moved a short distance. With each fresh attempt the shepherd believed he might finally get it, but he never did and after a long chase he realised he had failed. Too late he tried to get back to his herd, only to find that they had all been attacked and eaten by wolves.[25]

The fundamental connections that exist between the European Nightjar and the goatsucker name are significant because the habitat of this species and the places where goats are grazed strongly overlap. It is a bird of poor, thin-soiled, rocky country or rough heathland – exactly the landscape where goats would be pastured and confined for the night.

Two details, which might help to place the bird at the scene of the crime, are that goat pens are places of accumulated dung and probably of night-time fires maintained by herders for protection and cooking. Dung is a draw for beetles and possibly flies, while fires and light are an attractant for moths, all of which are important prey for European Nightjar. What is more difficult to identify is the specific link between the birds and the goats' udders.

There is, however, one piece of circumstantial evidence that might have predisposed original goatherds to blame nightjars – the birds' extraordinarily wide gape. The interior of the mouth even has a soft fleshy pink quality reminiscent of a teat and it is possible that early pastoralists mistakenly linked this wideness of gape and its pink fleshy lining to the task of sucking the pink fleshy udders of their stock. These are mere suppositions and the only widespread modern observations of nightjars that link them ecologically to livestock are similar to the following:

I used to see mainly Standard-winged Nightjars (and some **Long-tailed Nightjar** *Caprimulgus climacurus*) swooping near night-time tying places for N'dama cattle in The Gambia from time to time – especially at Keneba in Lower River Division of the country. The cattle are individually tied at night by their horns to short pegs, spaced close together in their respective herds around west African villages. I saw no evidence of the nightjars approaching the animals, but it seemed probable that insects were the main attraction.[26]

The one compelling piece of eyewitness testimony that squarely places the poor old goatsucker in the frame is a snippet from a British nineteenth-century naturalist, Charles Waterton, in his book *Wanderings in South America*:

Here I had a fine opportunity of examining several species of the caprimulgus. I am fully persuaded that these innocent little birds never suck the herds; for when they approach them, and jump up at their udders, it is to catch the flies and insects there. When the moon shone bright, I would frequently go and stand within three yards of a cow, and distinctly see the caprimulgus catch the flies on its udder. On looking for them in the forest, during the day, I either found them on the ground, or else invariably sitting longitudinally on the branch of a tree, not crosswise, like all other birds.[27]

While clearly linking nightjars only with cattle, it does at least suggest that the birds (albeit of an unspecified South American species) might feed inside livestock enclosures in a manner that would account for the goatsucking myth.

However, it leaves many questions unanswered and the most likely scenario is that once the myth took hold, based on these kinds of circumstantial observations, subsequent herders of livestock needed little empirical evidence to reconfirm the charge. The mere presence of goatsuckers flickering around their animals in the half-light would have been enough to indict them of the milk-drinking crime. Indeed once the idea had taken root it is likely that no additional confirmation at all was needed to perpetuate both the myth and the negative attitudes towards nightjars. Birds of mystery are exactly that. They are repositories for unexplained phenomena and they are blamed for things for which we cannot account. In short, they are scapegoats much more frequently than they are goatsuckers.

NIGHTJARS ON ROADS AND ROOFS

If we have falsely accused nightjars of crimes they could never commit, then we have at least gifted them one key benefit. Nightjars love roads and cleared tracks of almost any kind. There are references from the early nineteenth century that suggest European Nightjars had a liking for these thoroughfares even when they were merely for horse-drawn vehicles.[28] The behaviour is almost universal. There is, for example, an old Tamil name (*Pathekai-kuruvi*) in Sri Lanka for the Long-tailed Nightjar that means 'roadside bird'. One author noted 'its habit – which it shares with [**Indian Nightjar** *Caprimulgus asiaticus*] – of sitting in the middle of the road, its eyes gleaming red in the glare of the headlights, until the vehicle is nearly upon it.'[29]

As we know from the earlier part of this family account, nightjars do not always get out of the way in time and collisions with cars (or motorbikes) are a major source of mortality, especially in places like Africa. This is clearly proven by the history of the Nechisar Nightjar. There is also a description of a Zimbabwean truck coming to a halt after a night drive with 18 dead nightjars stuck to its radiator grille.[30]

Quite why the birds love roads is more difficult to prove, but speculation centres on the roads' latent warmth, and the presence of insects, live and dead, that are drawn in themselves by the heat or the lights of any cars. One adjacent piece of evidence is that both moths and nightjars are attracted to white sheets laid out on the ground or draped over bushes. Perhaps it is this issue of a light source – associated with roads or even linen – that in all cases draws the nightjars, because it first lures their principal prey, moths.

Another development in nightjar behaviour that seems extraordinary in birds of such pronounced 'otherness' is their willingness to nest in highly urban settings close to humans. From about 1869, Common Nighthawks were found to be using the flat gravel roofs in North American cities such as Boston and Cleveland, USA, and Montreal, Canada. Today the habit is widespread and has been adopted by other members of the family, including the **Lesser Nighthawk** *Chordeiles acutipennis* which nests on flat-topped adobe dwellings in Central America.[31]

Even more remarkable, in some ways, is the invasion of downtown Rio de Janeiro by **Band-winged Nightjar** *Caprimulgus longirostris* (a species that had gone unnoticed in Brazil from 1823–1940). Yet by the early 1950s this formerly 'lost' bird was found to be breeding in many districts of the country's second-largest city, including the world-famous beach district, Copacabana. One of its feeding strategies is to catch termites that are attracted to the lights shining from city-centre windows. Another favourite tactic is to hawk for insects as they swarm around street lamps in the darkness.[32] In all these instances of nightjars adapting to metropolitan life, one gains an impression of them not so much getting used to human presence, but rather being completely oblivious to it, like their relatives, the swifts (see page 294).

Swift family *Apodidae*

A straight 100 species are spread evenly around the world on all continents (except Antarctica), with Latin America (30 species), Africa (25 species) and the Oriental region (21 species; see Glossary) having the lion's share. Yet the family also has a tendency to occur on some of the world's most remote islands. There are places such as Atiu in the Cook Archipelago (**Atiu Swiftlet** *Aerodramus sawtelli*) or Babelthaup in the Palau Islands (**Palau Swiftlet** *Aerodramus pelewensis*) that appear on a map as specks in the Pacific's vast blue maw. These pinpricks have species of swift that breed nowhere else, except perhaps the neighbouring islands of comparable smallness.

Yet the notion of terrestrial distribution in this family needs to be qualified instantly. Swifts are so completely citizens of the air that to talk of the landscape below is almost meaningless. Over the vast majority of their lives the birds require merely that the breeze be warm enough to drift their insect diet into the heavens. Temperature, therefore, rather than landform or habitat, is a key constraint imposing a limit of 70° N in Eurasia, while in the other hemisphere swifts venture little further than 33° S in southern Africa (and its equivalent in South America and Australia). The birds are largely absent from New Zealand and the southern two-thirds of Argentina and Chile.

Swifts come to 'ground' only for breeding purposes. Before they start to nest, young birds may fly continuously for years at a stretch and make non-stop journeys totalling 500,000 km (300,000 miles).[1] A Swiss-ringed **Common Swift** *Apus apus* was shown to be breeding 21 years after it was first caught. Over a lifetime it may have spent less than six months (brooding eggs) anchored to any form of terra firma; the other 20-plus years were all airborne.[2] In fact, it is sometimes helpful to think of swifts as like seabirds: so adapted to another medium that they have no need of dry land. The wind-wafted insects on which they feed are even referred to as 'aerial plankton'. There are sometimes maritime connections in our names for them: the Germans, for instance, call the Common Swift *Mauersegler*, 'wall sailor'.

An individual swift's lifelong sky journey may rival in terms of distance the cumulative millions of kilometres performed by ocean-going albatrosses. (It is worth noting, however, that for a Wandering Albatross to enjoy the same wing-length/weight ratio as a Common Swift, it would have to have wings of 96 m: 315 ft. A 50 kg: 7.9 stone human, on the other hand, would require wings that were 547 m: 1,795 ft long.)

The proportions of the Common Swift typify the family's supreme adaptation to a life in the air. Most humans would need wings that were more than 500 m long to have the same wing-length/weight ratio as the bird.

SWIFTS AS EMBLEMS OF SUMMER

There are only five widespread species in North America and three in mainland Europe, with the **Chimney Swift** *Chaetura pelagica* and Common Swift the most abundant on their respective continents. Yet these eight species of the northern hemisphere may well make the largest psychological impact of all their family. The birds' universal dependence upon airborne insects means that they only return to colder latitudes when these unseen billions of invertebrates reach a critical mass. That often does not happen until late spring, and migrant swifts frequently return only in May, sometimes June. Conversely they leave again by August (Common Swift) or September (Chimney Swift). Their arrival and departure inscribe the very boundaries of summer in the north.

Often one feels that the brevity of the season compels a kind of emotional and physical intensity in swifts. It is as if their lives were held under immense pressure. In truth, the whole family shares in this same thrilling aura, for they are not only the most aerial of all birds, they are creatures of immense speed and grace. The **White-throated Needletail** *Hirundapus caudacutus* of China and the Himalaya (breeding season) and Australasia (non-breeding) is one of the fastest animals on Earth, and has been recorded at 170 kph (106 mph).[3] To compound the overall impression of surplus energy, swifts possess rasping, twittering or strangely clicking voices that we cannot easily reproduce or simply describe. The sounds are frequently evoked as high, shrill, scream-like even, but they always sound intense and to some people the swifts' reckless and frenzied brilliance embodies the whole spirit of the season.

> Swifts somehow manage to be both the very essence of wildness and the ultimate urban bird. Great travellers and wonderful aviators, they are without a doubt my favourite bird – nothing else comes close. For city dwellers like me, they mark the imminent arrival of summer better than anything. One swallow does not a summer make, perhaps . . . but a swift does.[4]

> Swifts vocalising (I don't like to use the word 'screaming') through a summer sky, aerial masters gracing me with their close proximity, are the epitome of summer for me and all too brief. I simply have to stand and soak them up.[5]

Swifts delineate not just the beginning and heart of summer, but also its close:

> Then one day you realise that you haven't heard the swifts today, and perhaps not yesterday either. And you become aware that they've all vanished and are now embarking on a treacherous journey thousands of miles away from your sleepy suburbia, where they seemed just as at home as they presumably feel in the dusty plains of Africa. But there's always the certain hope that that familiar cry will ring out again soon enough as another year passes.[6]

Many people find ways to honour this symbolic quality in swifts; some of us in more permanent ways than others.

> Swifts were one of the first birds I learnt to identify, and watching them from my childhood skylight, they heralded the start of summer. They became a symbol of the freedom of school holidays and home-made ice lollies, and long evenings. Even at university (where life, according to my parents, is one long holiday), swifts still carry a sense of liberation, and never more so than on my first holiday alone. I had gone to visit my best friend, and we spent three idyllic weeks working on an organic farm in the middle of the wilderness on Vancouver Island, Canada. The heat, the contact with nature (including my first bear!) and the overriding sense of freedom culminated in my swift tattoo. This, I hope, will always serve as a reminder on dark rainy days, that summer is never far away.[7]

SWIFTS AS BIRDS OF CONFUSION AND MYSTERY

Not everyone shares a delight in swifts or, at least, they do not attribute the pleasure solely to these birds, primarily because they do not genuinely recognise them. There are many people who never learn to separate swifts from the other predominantly aerial group, swallows and martins, known collectively as hirundines. The two families have no close relationship and to a trained eye they are instantly separable. Yet both include aerial species of small cigar-shaped body and long wings, which are frequently held in long elliptical glides free of wingbeats. That shared action is probably at the heart of the confusion.

The issue of mixing up swifts and swallows is thousands of years old. There is a famous, frequently quoted reference in Jeremiah in the Old Testament that touches on the migration of birds through present-day Israel and Palestine: 'Yea the stork in the heaven knoweth her appointed times; and the turtle and the crane and the swallow observe the time of their coming' (8:7). Although the translation in the *King James Bible* talks of swallows, the actual Hebrew word is *Sis* which, even today, is the name for Common Swift. ('*Sis* is an accurate rendering of the screaming call of this species.')[8]

Both the bird and the sound evoked by the Hebrew word have ancient resonances in the region, as one Jerusalem resident describes:

> We think that the swift is an important species that joined the urban bird assemblage when civilisations started erecting monumental buildings, such as the Temple Mount in Jerusalem, or fortifications in the Mediterranean. One of the oldest recorded Common Swift colonies still nests (around 80 pairs) in the Western Wall, known as the Wailing Wall. Every spring they arrive and start their communal aerobatics over the heads of the people who come to pray at first light. It is one of the most impressive bird-and-religion scenes I've ever witnessed (and I'm a total atheist). Devout Jews are covered with the white and blue *tallit*, swaying in rhythm, while above, as the sun shines over the roofs of the old city, swarms of circling swifts are crying over their heads. It gives you goose pimples. Aaah . . . Funnily, the lowest swift nests are at the end of the note line. When visitors insert their notes with messages to God it seems as if the shooting swifts are the messengers taking the notes directly to the target.[9]

The ancient Greeks gave us a root word from which came the family's current scientific name (*apous* roughly means 'footless', which describes the rather short limbs in most swifts), but they were somewhat loose in its application.

Aristotle's description of this particular bird clearly indicates that it was both resident in Greece and nested in long cells made of mud and placed beneath a rock or in a cavern. These attributes belong not to any swift but to the Eurasian Crag Martin, a member of the hirundine family.[10] The word of Greek origin also gave rise to a rather strange and somewhat muddled association in European culture. In heraldry a bird's image was used to denote the condition of the last-born scion of a landed family, who was himself 'footless' in the sense that he had no property of his own on which to plant his boot. However, the bird depicted was not, as we might have expected, *apus* the swift, but a martin (or martinet).

In truth this kind of confusion is universal. The current Portuguese or Brazilian name for swift is *andorinhão-preto.* (The latter derives from *andorinha*: 'swallow'; *andorinhão* means literally 'big swallow'.) Helmut Sick pointed out with regard to landscape features across Brazil that there are places called *gruta das andorinhas* ('swallow cave'), or *cachoeira das andorinhas* ('swallow falls'), or the more famous Saltos das Andorinhas e de Dardanelos ('the Falls of Swallows and Dardanelles') in Mato Grosso state. Yet they have nothing to do with hirundines. They are all sites notable for swifts. In the case of the latter it is the clouds of **Great Dusky Swift** *Cypseloides senex* and **White-collared Swift** *Streptoprocne zonaris*, which can number up to 1.5 million, that give the place its title. (To cement their intimate connections with such landscapes, Great Dusky Swifts will sometimes build their nests behind the falls and fly directly into the smoking curtain of tumbling water to access them.)[11]

It is not just that people are confused about swifts. The birds are themselves inherently mysterious, and several family members are past masters at eluding attention. The **White-chested Swift** *Cypseloides lemosi* of southern Colombia (and possibly Ecuador) is a fairly distinctive-looking bird, but it is almost completely unknown. It has been recorded on just a handful of occasions since the 1960s. Next to nothing is known about its ecology or movements and there are no photographs or sound recordings. If anything, **Schouteden's Swift** *Schoutedenapus schoutedeni* of the eastern forests in the Democratic Republic of the Congo is even more obscure. Named after a Belgian biologist, Henri Schouteden (1881–1972), it is known from just five skins and modern sight records are at best tentative. Its habitat, biology, range and even how it might be separated from other similar species are very poorly understood.[12]

Even the lives of many abundant swifts seem wrapped in secrecy. A wonderfully evocative old name for the Common Swift in Iran (*Bad Khorak*) 'means "wind-eater" because no one sees them on the ground feeding and they don't know these birds catch insects in the sky'.[13] In the past almost any creature that aroused a sense of mystery was often an object of suspicion. There are archaic names that indicate how the black creature with screaming cry was barely one remove from hell. 'Devil bird' or 'diveling' ('little devil') were old country names in Britain and the USA.[14] The negative associations find an echo in the highlands of Papua New Guinea, where during periods of inter-tribal war, a warrior would signify that times were bad by wearing a softwood ornament on his forecrown shaped like the wings of one of the island's five swiftlet species. The design was selected specifically because swiftlets were birds of ill omen and war was inevitably a period of disruption and death.[15]

Our modern freedom from this type of fearful response does not lessen the birds' inherent otherness. In fact one of the elements that cements their status as perhaps the most mysterious and captivating of all abundant avian inhabitants across the entire northern hemisphere is that swifts live so completely among us, yet somehow they remain unassailably separate. They are, at once, all around but out of reach. As the contributor above noted: they somehow manage to be 'both the very essence of wildness and the ultimate urban bird'. The celebrated British novelist Jim Crace illuminates this strange duality in swifts and how so much about these glorious creatures passes literally and figuratively over our heads.

I am most used to the swifts of the English Midlands, no more than a dozen at a time and so distant above our garden in early summer that even binoculars barely diminish their remoteness. But still I crane my neck and track them at every opportunity, hoping I suppose to requite their deep indifference for me with my high regard for them. They are a bird neither friendly nor unfriendly, but unforthcoming certainly and conspicuously uninvolved with the earthbound world below them. *Aloof* (originally a boating term meaning 'away and to windward') is the exact word for my swifts; it captures perfectly their yachting wings, their epic, weather-driven restlessness, their teasing fickle seasonality. It's hard to not feel wonderstruck by swifts.

So what am I to make of my birds' alpine cousins [**Alpine Swift** *Tachymarptis melba*]. Here, this evening, in Grasse in the Alpes Maritimes of southern France, the noise trapped in the dilapidated, medieval, traffic-free alleyways and courtyards is deafening and eerie. At least a thousand screaming swifts have condescended to spend an hour close to me. I could almost catch one with a butterfly net if I stretched high enough and if they weren't such whizz-kids of the wing, celebrating every duck and dive and every taken bug with their falsetto palaver. In the final shadows of the evening, these Alpine Swifts are closer to my head than either starlings or bats would ever dare to come. They are as close as gnats. I'm standing in the eye of the swarm. But still I cannot claim any intimacy with them. Despite this tumultuous proximity, they are not sharing any of their world with me. There is no interface, no common ground. They're still aloof. My love for them is vain. All they know about is bugs and air, feeding, flying, moving on. They leave me gaping at an empty sky.[16]

SWIFTS AND HUMAN ARCHITECTURE

With the **Mottled Swift** *Tachymarptis aequatorialis* of east and southern Africa, the Alpine Swift is among the largest species (the Portuguese name for the latter is *Andorinhão-real*, 'royal swift'), with a wingspan comparable to that of a small falcon (60 cm: 24 in). Yet like almost all the family, Alpine Swifts collapse down to a creature of mouse-like girth that slips into the smallest crannies in high walls or roofs. It is this routine cohabitation with ourselves that so emphasises the swift's essential remoteness.

How and when the transference took place from natural to man-made holes is difficult to pinpoint. As Amir Balaban noted above, it was probably associated with monumental

These Glossy Swiftlets in the Philippines are one of many species of swift that now exploit human structures for nest sites.

architecture (fortifications, religious buildings, etc.) and the earliest shift may well date back to Sumerian civilisation as much as 7,000 years ago. Today in many parts of the world swift hordes display a sense of high style. They have become a routine part of our experience of a country's most exalted architectural structures, such as the Parthenon in Greece, or the medieval walls encircling the labyrinthine old city of Fez in Morocco. Swifts also show strong ecclesiastical tastes:

> Once, in southern Spain at Easter, squadrons of swifts screamed around Seville's cathedral and Plaza Virgen de los Reyes. There had been no sign of them the previous day; clearly, they had just arrived and were showing off like avian joyriders, carving up the air around the Giralda bell tower like Moorish scimitars. [17]

Many swifts have now so completely taken to human artefacts that they are virtually dependent upon us. However, in some birds the transition has been remarkably recent and has been monitored accurately on several continents.

The **White-rumped Swift** *Apus caffer* was a beneficiary of colonial government in southern and eastern Africa, where it took to man-made structures in the 1930s, including culverts and railway bridges, mission buildings, hospitals, blocks of flats, hotels and even verandahs of private residences. Even more remarkable was the incremental spread of the **Little Swift** *Apus affinis*. During the same period this species also moved into urban accommodation across a vast area of the continent, from the Democratic Republic of the Congo in the west to Mozambique in the east and right down to South Africa, where it had been once confined to localised cave sites. Little Swifts assemble communal-style nest clusters, with up to 60 pairs all crammed together in untidy grass-and-feather agglomerations that are plastered to eaves or concrete overhangs. Roadside petrol stations are a classic favourite for them, where the constant human traffic of pedestrians and motor vehicles is no deterrent. However,

the record may well belong to a single building in Ghana, which was found to have 1,000 birds on it, while one bridge in the Democratic Republic of the Congo over the Lulua River had 5,000 nests. [18]

In the New World a similar pattern has occurred. The very name of North America's Chimney Swift proclaims the species' cultural odyssey into man-made interiors from tree-hole nest sites, which it may previously have used for tens, if not hundreds, of thousands of years. Yet it started to switch as early as the mid seventeenth century and now it is virtually dependent upon buildings, to the point where use of a 'natural' site is a noteworthy event. [19] The species can somehow manoeuvre down the tight circumference inside a smokestack to nest 6.4 m (21 ft) from the top. Yet the birds have acquired domestic habits other than just chimneys, and now particularly favour modern urban buildings. They

The agglomerations of feathers and other wind-blown detritus that comprise the communal nests of Little Swifts are regular adornments on buildings and bridges in parts of Africa.

This Common Swift has become bedraggled in a rainstorm. It is in such circumstances that these supreme birds of the skies occasionally fall to Earth.

have also been recorded in the walls of an old well, in barns, outbuildings, uninhabited dwellings, in a blacksmith's shop just 4.6 m (15 ft) from the forge, and by a communal children's bed in the upstairs of a family home.[20]

In South America the move to urban locations by relatives of the Chimney Swift has taken place only in the last 70 years. Both the **Grey-rumped Swift** *Chaetura cinereiventris* and **Ashy-tailed Swift** *Chaetura meridionalis* of Brazil were first noted to use residential chimneys only after World War Two and in parts of Amazonia it did not happen until the 1960s. There seems something curiously perverse in the idea that these swifts have benefited from the destruction of the original forest habitat in which they formerly bred. Once again, however, it points to the fact that these are not habitats for the birds in the fullest sense. They are nesting and sleeping quarters. The critical components are hole-nesting locations and these may have even increased with the replacement of Amazonian rainforest by urban settlement.[21]

EXPLOITATION OF SWIFTS

The dependence of swifts upon human structures meant that people could actually design buildings to give them ready access to the birds. Quite why anyone would want to catch a creature that routinely weighs less than 28 g (1 oz) might seem a mystery. Yet at one time young swift pulli were highly rated as food and in parts of Italy birdcatchers maintained purpose-built swift towers in domestic houses in order to harvest them for the table.[22] In Liberia in west Africa local people still build special swift houses 'looking

like half-closed umbrellas, 3–5 m high', which attract nesting **African Palm Swift** *Cypsiurus parvus*. These are lured to nest 'partly for fun, partly to eat the young'.[23]

It might seem stranger still to learn that the nests of swifts, which are often flimsy structures composed of wind-blown detritus seized in mid-air, can be as highly prized as the birds themselves. In fact some swift nests represent the most valuable single product yielded by any bird on Earth. At the heart of this remarkable cultural story are two tiny (11–14 cm: 4.3–5.5 in) cave-dwelling species found in south-east Asia, the **Edible-nest Swiftlet** *Aerodramus fuciphagus* and **Black-nest Swiftlet** *Aerodramus maximus*.

Small and brown, the Asian swiftlets, of which there are almost 30 species, are birds of baffling similarity and many are separable only on the closest inspection. One recurring characteristic is their love of deep caves as nest sites, some of which are among the most compelling avian spectacles. The Niah Caves in Sarawak (a Malaysian-owned state on Borneo) once held as many as 4.5 million swiftlets of various species. At dawn a great sweeping dragon's tail of birds exited the cave mouth to feed by day. At dusk the process was reversed, when there was a comparable outpouring of cave bats moving against the incoming tide of birds. (Alas, deforestation and over-harvesting of nests has seen the vast swiftlet flocks fall to 150,000 birds, while the bats have also declined in recent years.)

In the subterranean darkness of their nest chambers, swiftlets navigate using echo-location: clicking calls that bounce off the walls and, like sonar, help to create a sound-

picture of their environment. Their nests can be anything up to 400 m (1,300 ft) from the entrance. It means that on their maiden flight, young swiftlets must negotiate in total darkness the network of humid bird-congested tunnels, dense with the clicking sounds of other birds, to find the sunlight for their first time. Apparently, they seldom fail.

Since the seventeenth century and probably much earlier humans have slithered into these airless tunnels to harvest what seems the most unlikely of foods. The swiftlets make nests of various materials, but always anchor and cement the structures to the cave walls with their highly adhesive saliva. Some of the birds, such as the Edible-nest Swiftlet, make nests composed wholly from this material and these so-called 'white nests' are the most sought after. A mucin-like glycoprotein, the saliva hardens into colourless layers – described by one ornithologist as 'a substance resembling icing-glass' – and these are the essential ingredient of birds'-nest soup.[24] Quite how it was first added to the human diet is a mystery, but the discovery may date back into the Palaeolithic period.[25] Today, however, it is more than a food: the saliva is assumed to contain a virtual pharmacopoeia of health-enhancing agents. One accredited power is that of sexual stimulant, although the more prosaic abilities to dissolve phlegm and alleviate gastric trouble are high in its list of health benefits.

At one time it was believed that the nest material was a kind of algal foam gathered by the birds from the sea surface. A residue of the fancy is still embedded in modern nomenclature, because the word *fuciphagus* in the scientific

name of the Edible-nest Swiftlet means 'seaweed eating'.[26] John Ray reported on this same belief in the 1670s, referring to the birds as 'Chinese swallows', which reflected not so much their origins, but the principal market for swiftlet nests.[27] (It also illuminates once more the ancient swift / swallow confusion. There are many restaurants in China and elsewhere – I knew one in Norwich – that are called Swallow's Nest, probably because of the culinary celebrity of swiftlet saliva.)

The enduring reputation of swiftlet nests means that their key sources in caves across south-east Asia and countries such as Vietnam (once also in the Indian-controlled Nicobar Islands) are jealously guarded and highly prized as economic assets. Local collectors hold rights over sections of the cave wall as part of an elaborate system of ownership and management. However, many of the most important caves, such as the Niah Caves in Sarawak, contain large subterranean chambers, where the actual nests are high above the cave floor. To reach them is an enormously dangerous business, especially in the past when collectors had to climb to them via a network of bamboo ladders or walkways. Very often they had to balance precariously while simultaneously handling a long bamboo-handled tool to scrape the nests off the walls. An additional issue is the high value of the cave substrate, which is rich in swiftlet guano and utilised as fertiliser. As the floor's layers are mined, so reaching the cave roof becomes ever more difficult. Rather than enjoy the enhanced security of permanent access platforms the collecting teams feel it necessary very often

The nests of various Asiatic swiftlet species are one of the most expensive avian products in the world.

297

to dismantle their scaffolds each season, so that poachers cannot take advantage in their absence.

Many of the caves have probably been visited on an annual basis for hundreds of years without ever causing the swiftlet population to fail completely. Even in the most intensively managed caves, some birds are always able to bring off young in the more remote parts of the underground system. However, the ongoing harvest could sometimes reduce overall breeding success and formerly there was little regulation to ensure the swiftlets benefited from a closed season. Nest production by the birds is by no means an easy or rapid process. It can take swiftlets anything up to 127 days to rebuild a new saliva nest and replace the lost clutch of eggs.[28] However, the huge appetite for birds'-nest products, especially in China, creates its own kind of economic logic that has often bypassed considerations of the harvest's sustainability.

Once they are taken from the caves, the white nests of Edible-nest Swiftlets require almost no processing. The few feathers entangled in the salival weave are carefully extracted and then the nests are bound into moulds that retain the cup-shaped structure. The equivalent items derived from Black-nest Swiftlets are far more labour intensive. The so-called 'black nests' contain a high degree (roughly 50 per cent) of feathers and other material and this unwanted matter is carefully picked out of the water-softened nests in a painstaking business. These are teased apart and then reconstituted into bird-nest chips. It takes a skilled worker eight hours to process just 150 g (5.3 oz) of these raw black nests.

It is the high degree of labour required to prepare the products from this latter species that explains the enduring economic differential between white nests and black nests. Regardless of the disparity, however, the overall prices for what is in effect dried swiftlet mucus are nothing short of jaw dropping. In Sarawak from 1996–2001 freshly collected white nests were selling at $1,315–$1,790 per 1 kg (2.2 lb). In Kalimantan (Indonesian Borneo) the 2001 price per 1 kg for freshly collected black nests was $105–$395. By 1996 the total harvest taken from natural cave sources in Indonesia had risen to 110,000 kg (242,508 lb).[29]

However, a major development, an innovation that may well spare and even enhance the fortunes of these economically important birds, is the production of swiftlet nests from man-made sources. It was discovered that swiftlets could be enticed to nest and colonise human buildings in exactly the way that other family members have switched to anthropogenic sites all over the world. The economic potential from this cultural shift in swiftlet affairs was not lost on the enterprising peoples of south-east Asia.

In theory it means that nests could be more easily harvested and processed, but the birds themselves might actually receive a double benefit, in the foundation of new, sustainable nest colonies, often in urban environments, and also in the release of harvest pressure upon existing natural colonies. The building interiors are structured to mimic cave conditions with low-light and an often water-based cooling system, while a hormone-derived 'Love Potion' is being marketed to get the swiftlets into the 'mating mood'.[30] Purpose-built swiftlet houses are the strangest of human structures, as one unsuspecting observer notes:

I first saw swiftlet houses when I was travelling to Pangandaran on the south coast of Java. It's a long, winding journey, mostly through a pleasant landscape of rice paddies, bamboo groves, small fields and simple houses with red clay tile roofs. It was a shock to see a giant, grey box of a building, three or more storeys high, windowless, with walls of unpainted concrete. My first thought was that it was a prison, but closer to I could see a row of small holes the size of drainpipes near the top of the wall, where swiftlets occasionally dived in and out. The only other feature was a low metal door in one corner, locked shut with formidable bolts and padlocks. To add to the eerie presence of the building, a constant shrill twittering came from inside, audible several hundred metres away. Later I learned that the twittering was a recording of swiflet calls, played to attract the birds when the building is first established. Since then I've seen these grey, square buildings in many places in Java and Sumatra, sometimes growing incongruously out of the green rice fields, sometimes as an extra few floors on top of a house in the middle of a provincial town. Recently I have seen some swiftlet houses with roofs modelled on more traditional lines, with tiles and gables, but the walls are still gaunt, featureless rock faces.[31]

These buildings not only replicate the structure and purpose of commercial banks, but they are also patrolled very often by armed guards. The key difference is that the precious assets they contain are not banknotes or bullion, but bird saliva.

There is one last glorious gift we derive from swifts, but it is of a less material nature. The quintessential birds of air are sometimes unable to take off if they accidentally hit the ground. It occasionally happens. Young birds can be especially helpless and I remember vividly how once in the spring of 1983 I found a **House Swift** *Apus nipalensis* lying in the gutter of Freak Street, the famous hippy hangout in the heart of Kathmandu, Nepal. I also recall the instant sense of well-being once I tossed the bird lightly up and it resumed its place in the sky. Apparently it is a feeling we often share:

The greatest honour I have ever received was a thank you from a swift. It had been grounded and I picked up what at first I thought was a log of wood; it clung to me like a brooch. I examined it for obvious signs of injury then carefully launched it from an attic window, first stationing my mother, father and brother in the garden below to catch it if it fell. It swooped away exultantly then circled back round right past the window to thank us.[32]

Hummingbird family *Trochilidae*

A Route of Evanescence
With a revolving Wheel –
A Resonance of Emerald –
A Rush of Cochineal –
And every Blossom on the Bush
Adjusts its tumbled Head –
The mail from Tunis, probably,
An easy Morning's Ride –

In the poem by the nineteenth-century American writer Emily Dickinson we have many of the key themes in our engagements with these wonderful birds. Perhaps before everything else we notice the hummingbird's speed; a flight often so fast that much of the movement happens beyond the range of human vision. All we see is an ethereal mist of wingbeats ('a Route of Evanescence') which, blended with that intense colour ('A Resonance of Emerald / A Rush of Cochineal'), means that hummingbirds almost invite an element of fantasy.

In truth, the birds have never crossed the Atlantic, as Dickinson suggested, and certainly have never flown in a morning from Tunis. It just *seems* as if they might move that quickly. In fact, hummingbirds have never flown anywhere from Africa, because all 347 species are creatures entirely of the New World. There they inhabit almost every landscape, from Alaska to Tierra del Fuego, and from the snow-topped slopes of the Andes – at 5,200 m (more than 17,000 ft) in the

case of the **Bearded Helmetcrest** *Oxypogon guerinii* – to the skeleton-dry coasts of the Atacama Desert. However, the highest concentration, the centre of hummingbird evolution, is in the Andes. Ecuador, for example, has about 135 species, while the USA has just 19, of which six are only occasional visitors.[1]

As if to underscore how special hummingbirds are, Emily Dickinson suggests that we are not alone in our benign attitudes towards them. Even the blossoms turn their tumbled heads to please the passing bird. There is a story recorded by an American author, Bradford Torrey, of a hummingbird once caught in a spider's web. An unnamed informant told him that he was in the house

> when he heard the familiar squeaking notes of a hummer [a common colloquial name for a hummingbird], and thinking that their persistency must be occasioned by some unusual trouble, went out to investigate. Sure enough, there hung the bird in a spider's web attached to a rosebush, while the owner of the web, a big yellow-and-brown, pot-bellied bloodthirsty rascal, was turning its victim over and over, winding the web about it. Wings and legs were already fast, so that all the bird could do was cry for help. And help had come. The man at once killed the spider, and then, little by little, for it was an operation of no small delicacy, unwound the mesh in which the bird was

A Rufous-tailed Hummingbird of Latin America. In many members of the family the wings move at 70–80 beats a second and are visible as little more than a blurry halo around the flying bird.

entangled. The lovely creature lay still in his open hand till it had recovered its breath, then flew away. Who would not be glad to play the good Samaritan in such guise?[2]

What is most striking is the way that the uneven distribution of human sympathies is taken for granted. The slaughter of the web's true owner and the time-consuming extraction of its natural prey are perceived as the absolutely normal things to have done. More, they are presented as a moral duty ('Who would not play the good Samaritan') that we would all perform and consider apt.

As the ornithologist Karl-Ludwig Schuchmann astutely observes, 'Man's attitude to hummingbirds is a very unusual one within the context of his relations with the whole of the Animal Kingdom. It is wholly characterized by positive emotions.'[3] The birds are so small that they are barely worth catching and eating. (Yet young Latin American scamps kill them in flight with catapults, believing that eating a hummer's raw heart will improve their sight and aim.) Nor do they do anything that competes with our interests. On the contrary, they feed almost entirely on nectar, serving incidentally as valuable pollinators of flowers and plants. What little protein they take invariably comprises insects, many of which are harmful to us.

Yet our overwhelming sense of joy derives not from their utility, but from their beauty. W H Hudson proposed that they 'are perhaps the very loveliest things in nature'.[4] If they are not, then they certainly stand in the front rank, with butterflies, coral reefs (and their fish), meadows of spring flowers, the world's pheasants and its birds-of-paradise.

Hummingbird beauty is fantastic and even, sometimes, incredible. The colour range is vast and the intensity of hue has a lapidary brilliance. As Alfred Newton once wrote, there is a barely a precious stone – ruby, amethyst, sapphire, emerald, or topaz – that has not been invoked to convey their glamour.[5] In so many of the hummingbird family their colours have a metallic radiance determined by the microstructure of individual feathers, which refract light rather like a diamond or a film of oil. The plumage is often arranged in exquisite formations – breast or facial shields, extendible gorgets, glittering whiskers, winged collars, enormous crests, sumptuous trains, or paired tail plumes that, in the case of the **Marvelous Spatuletail** *Loddigesia mirabilis* and **Black-tailed Trainbearer** *Lesbia victoriae*, are three to four times longer than the birds themselves. Then there are birds with white powder-puff anklets on each leg (**Booted Racket-tail** *Ocreatus underwoodii*) or lance-like bills greater in length than the whole body and tail (**Sword-billed Hummingbird** *Ensifera ensifera*).

Yet all of this only captures one part of a much wider allure, which draws on the whole being of the birds, including their biology and basic biometrics. They are, for instance, among the smallest warm-blooded animals on Earth. Most of them are between 6.35–12.7 cm (2.5–5 in). The **Bee Hummingbird** *Mellisuga helenae* found in Cuba is, by general consent, the very smallest and is truly on an invertebrate scale. In length it is far less than many insects (less also than an ostrich's eye) and weighs under 2 g (0.07 oz).

Hummingbird kinetics provide another catalogue of superlatives. In fact, the birds are little more than two wing muscles suspended on a skeletal frame as fragile as dried grasses. In most migratory birds those muscles are disproportionately large in order to power their flight, amounting to roughly one-fifth of body weight. Yet hummingbird mass is almost one-third wing muscle. If their invertebrate thrum is slowed down to a rate that humans might observe, then it is revealed as a figure-of-eight rotation running at 70–80 beats a second. In the largest of the family, the **Giant Hummingbird** *Patagona gigas*, which is something of a misnomer when one calculates that it weighs just 20 g (0.7 oz), the pace is a moderate ten beats a second. However, in certain flight modes some hummingbirds attain extraordinary rates that are 20 times faster than this.[6]

Within this electric fizz of movement, the creature enjoys supreme control. Hummingbirds can fly forwards, up, down, backwards and very often a combination of these, or they can flip completely upside down. The other speciality is to hover in mid-air, the wings no more than a vague aura around it, so that the creature appears not to be moving at all and to be completely weightless. One acute observer reflects upon this effect:

> While they are prolific in this area of California, it still feels like a treat when I see one. A recent and unexpected encounter involved coming literally face to face with an **Anna's Hummingbird** *Calypte anna* as I emerged from my studio into a drizzly afternoon. Between the smudged blur of the wings that throbbed a few feet from me, the tiny body seemed almost motionless as it hung suspended in the air. It looked at me with its black ink-drop eye and I looked at it. Time also seemed suspended, every detail and feather coming into exquisite focus. Even in the low light, the slight swaying of its tail made iridescent colours wash over each other: rose red merging with emerald green with hints of blue and gold before it whirred off, into the rain.
>
> Hummingbirds often resemble insects as they zip about at high velocity. However, with close encounters such as these, I am also struck by a faintly aquatic look. There is a fish-scale sheen to the feathers. The wings, translucent with speed, can take on an almost fin-like appearance. The element of air itself seems momentarily transformed, making me feel like a diver encountering a dazzling fish emerging from a coral reef.[7]

The respiratory system underpinning a hummingbird's movements is no less astonishing. A vast pea-sized heart, proportionately four or five times greater than our own, can function at 20 beats a second. At rest the bird breathes about 300 times a minute and under hot conditions this can rise to 500. Compare this with our own average rate of 14–18 inhalations, while the speed at which our blood travels around our bodies is 100 times slower than in a hummingbird.[8] All of these comparative statistics can start to seem a little overwhelming, but one large salient truth emerges from them. Hummingbirds carry the possibility of warm-blooded life, of which we and the birds are common inheritors, to one of its outermost limits (see also Penguin family, page 92). The family represents one extreme boundary to all creation, a living intensity that is both scientifically proven yet also rich in symbolic possibilities.

HUMMINGBIRDS
IN PRE-COLUMBIAN MYTH

One of the striking things about almost all cultural portrayals of hummingbirds is that they honour this miraculous quality in their lives. The birds are writ large in the mythologies and story cycles of almost all those pre-Columbian peoples with whose range the birds overlapped. One can only cover a sample of this huge corpus of cultural association but in many a common thread is at work.

For the Akimel O'odham (Pima) people of southern Arizona and Mexico, a hummingbird came to the rescue of their ancestors in a time of severe drought. The bird twisted a magic thong around the rain and wind spirits, which had taken refuge in a hidden cave, and led them back to the supplicant and desperate people. Thereafter the hummingbird pledged that he and the rains and wind would all return to the O'odham lands together at the same season.

This linkage of hummingbirds with the coming of rain (and, thus, fertility) is found across much of the arid south-west region of the USA, most notably among the Hopi, Zuni and other Pueblo groups.[9] For their near-neighbours the Navaho, if not a bringer of rain, then the hummingbird was a bearer of food. One of their own origin myths described how the bird – one of four totem animals – brought them their corn with multicoloured grains.[10] Perhaps even more compelling, for its deep parallels to these North American tales, is a Yahgan story from Chile's Tierra del Fuego. In this the **Green-backed Firecrown** *Sephanoides sephaniodes* (*Sámakéär* or *Omora* in their language), the most southerly distributed of all its family, causes the mountain streams to flow and relieve the drought-stricken Yahgan.[11]

Another strand of stories that spanned a range of geographically associated cultures linked hummingbirds with tobacco. Rather than the abhorrent carcinogen that it is to modern society, tobacco had an almost sacred status for pre-Columbian peoples. Its use was framed within and mediated by a cradle of ritual, and the nicotine-rich leaves were hugely valued for their magico-medicinal properties, especially their trance-inducing power (see also Parrots and Amerindians, page 256). Along the northern coastline of South America (now Venezuela and Guyana) the Carib, Arawak and Warao peoples shared a myth that they had received the plant from hummingbirds. It is striking that the Cherokee, once located at the northern limit of its indigenous cultivation (in south-eastern USA), similarly honoured the hummingbird as a bringer of this gift.[12] For some communities the issues of rain, fertility and tobacco all subtly intermeshed. In order to induce the rains, Pueblo Indians would blow tobacco smoke to the four directions to summon those other moisture-bearing clouds.[13]

In all of the stories one can surmise a real-life context that underpinned the hummingbird associations. For North American peoples the birds are migrants that largely arrive in spring. They were ever likely, therefore, to carry with them connections to fertility or new life. Similarly the long tubular flowers of plants in the genus *Nicotiana*, from which tobacco is derived, are favourite sources of nectar for hummingbirds. Today there are commercial seed mixes of flowering *Nicotiana* that are advertised precisely for their ability to draw hummingbirds into the garden.

While we can see the genuine ecological linkages that help to account for the tribal stories, an underlying subtext

in them all is the birds' role as bringer of something precious and life enhancing – medicine, rain, or fertility. The point is even more emphatically made in the creation story of the Mohave people from southern California. At their beginning their ancestors lived in a place of darkness far underground. It was only with the help of a hummingbird, who pioneered the route towards the sunlight through a crack in the Earth's surface, that the Mohave were able to make their journey to the upper world, where they have lived ever since.[14] Here the hummingbird's gift is nothing less than sun-blessed terrestrial life itself.

One senses in all these human portraits that pre-Columbian Americans intuitively understood what biological science has unearthed: hummingbirds represent life distilled to a kind of ultimate essence. A bird so rich in the gift of life was the one best suited to endow human culture with life's richest gifts.

Perhaps the people for whom hummingbirds held the most prominent spiritual place were the Mexica, the rulers of pre-Cortesian Mexico and often called the Aztecs. In the vast pantheon of this god-haunted, war-obsessed

Diamonds shaken from a jewel – a White-necked Jacobin in the rain is part of a world that is beyond material price.

The name of the Mexican (Aztec) deity Huitzilopochtli means literally 'hummingbird of the left', but here he is shown swathed in the plumes of Resplendent Quetzals (see page 310).

civilisation was a figure called Huitzilopochtli. He contained elements of both culture hero and supreme being, and was also thought to have drawn on the older Mesoamerican god Quetzalcoatl (see also The Importance of Quetzals to Pre-Columbian Society, page 310). In the myth of their rise to power, the Mexica believed that they had once been led by a great warrior called Huitzitzil. Both a founder and defender of their great capital, Tenochtitlan (now Mexico City), this hero eventually fell in battle. As he expired the body vanished but his spirit was manifest as a hummingbird, whose feathers Huitzitzil had always worn on his left wrist as a sign of reverence for the creature.[15]

The name Huitzilopochtli translates as 'hummingbird of the left', or 'of the south', and draws on a name for the bird in Nahuatl, *huitzilin* or *huitzitzil*. As the Mexican Empire expanded, Huitzilopochtli eventually emerged as the central deity.[16] Rapacious and bloodthirsty, he was frequently honoured with human sacrifice. Yet, as well as a god of war and of the chase, he was also an incarnation of the sun. On the temple mount at the heart of Tenochtitlan, the two great shrines opposite one another were those of Huitzilopochtli and Tlaloc, god of rain. They embodied the two primary forces from which all life emanated, but they also represented the two human archetypes on which Mexican power was founded, the soldier and the farmer.

Tlaloc was equated with rain and the creative productivity of the agriculturalist; Huitzilopochtli stood for the sun and the glorious deeds of the warrior.[17] Those who were killed in battle, and even those whose lives were sacrificed on those terrible bloodstained stones at the summit of Tenochtitlan's temple mount – the place where their hearts were ripped out – were reincarnated after four years as hummingbirds.[18] The afterlife of Mexico's fallen braves was in some ways similar to that on offer to the Muslim martyr: a heaven of terrestrial pleasures. In the case of the Aztec soldier he was said to drink nectar in the flower-filled gardens of paradise, just like a real hummingbird.

The Mexican symbolism initially seems out of harmony with the wider pre-Columbian tradition that connected the birds to life's most cherished bounties. Linking them to war and to a deity that can look, to our eyes, like a blood-soaked demon seems almost a reversal of this pattern. Yet there

were profound underlying similarities. For one imaginary duty of the warriors reincarnated as hummingbirds was to aid Huitzilopochtli in his ultimate celestial battle. Every day the god warred with the forces of darkness and each dawn he prevailed by returning the world to light. What better symbol for the triumph of day over night than these jewelled birds of radiant colour?[19]

MODERN RESPONSES TO HUMMINGBIRDS

One area of deep continuity between pre-Columbian engagements with hummingbirds and those by people of European descent was the exploitation of the birds' plumage. The Mexica deployed the glittering colours of hummingbirds in ceremonial costumes, but also in what have been described as feather mosaics – images composed of minute feather fragments. In Mexican hands the craft was elevated to a level of technical accomplishment that has never been surpassed.[20] Unfortunately of all the treasures that were plundered and shipped to Europe, these artworks were inherently the most fragile. Very few still exist and among the most famous is a feathered shield – said to belong to a former ruler, Ahuitzotl – that was given personally by the Mexican emperor Moctezuma II to the conquistador Hernán Cortés in 1519. It is held today in the Museum of Ethnology in Vienna, Austria.

Hummingbird skins were later exported to Europe to be used in commercially manufactured ornaments. As late as the 1960s there was a thriving cottage industry in Brazil that involved the production of artificial flowers from hummingbird plumes. However, the slaughter involved with this production was probably on a small scale compared with that triggered by the worldwide craze for fashion garments featuring bird feathers (see also Herons and the Feather Industry, page 131). The natural colour range and ornamentation of hummingbird plumages made them obvious targets.

This particular harvest is difficult to quantify accurately, but even the fragmentary data suggest an export trade involving many millions of birds. A single London-based merchant, for example, in one year during the early 1800s imported 400,000 hummingbird skins from the Antilles alone. Hats, in which the birds were often displayed perched on artificial flowers, were a second major cause of their slaughter. One dealer was reported in the 1880s to have handled two million small birds of all kinds for use in the hat business.[21] Another compelling detail on the whole fashion trade was the existence of a shawl in 1905 that had involved 8,000 hummingbird skins (see also Hawaiian Honeycreeper family, page 507).[22]

However reluctantly, one must acknowledge that even this baleful expenditure of hummingbird lives was predicated upon an appreciation of the birds' exquisite beauty. As W H Hudson lamented so eloquently, however, it was also predicated upon a fallacy that the living vitality of the real bird could be truly conveyed either through the dried and disembodied feathers or even through words. The first sighting of the genuine article, he argued, 'comes like a revelation to the mind'.

To give any true conception of it by means of mere word-painting is not more impossible than it would be to bottle up a supply of the 'living sunbeams' themselves,

and convey them across the Atlantic to scatter them in a sparkling shower over the face of England. ... The special kind of beauty which makes the first sight of a humming-bird a revelation depends on the swift singular motions as much as on the intense gem-like and metallic brilliancy of the plumage.

The minute exquisite form, when the bird hovers on misty wings, probing the flowers with its coral spear, the fan-tail expanded, and poising motionless ... this forms a picture of airy grace and loveliness that baffles description. All this glory disappears when the bird is dead ...[23]

THE NAMES OF HUMMINGBIRDS

Hudson may have been right that language fails to convey the full impact of these birds. Yet the names coined by the early naturalists did at least involve a linguistic extravagance that is both memorable and rich in cultural association. The titles are dense with allusion to historical characters (**Humboldt's Sapphire** *Hylocharis humboldtii* and **Black-crested Coquette** *Lophornis helenae*; after Hélène Princesse d'Orléans, 1814–1858), or to classical mythology (**Mexican Woodnymph** *Thalurania ridgwayi* and **Violet-tailed Sylph** *Aglaiocercus coelestis*), to imaginary beings (**Lucifer Sheartail** *Calothorax lucifer* and **Black-eared Fairy** *Heliothryx auritus*) and even to the realms of astrophysics (**Bronze-tailed Comet** *Polyonymus caroli*).

In fact one problem with their names is that they are so outlandish they are rather unpractical. One commentator notes:

> Hummingbird names are the most obtuse bird names I know. Of all birds, their names stand apart for their oddness. Hummingbirds – and only hummingbirds as far as I know – appear to be named by a completely different tribe. Their names sit more comfortably in the province of precious jewels or ornamental flowers. If you said to someone, today we saw some great Mangos, Emeralds and Brilliants, would they have any clue you were referring to birds?[24]

Their utility is certainly at issue, but the nineteenth-century naturalists who dreamed up these titles also gave rise to a glorious kind of incidental poetry. As a whole body they are probably the most beautiful and suggestive set of names for any group of living organisms in the language.

Two personal favourites, for their blend of intense evocation and lyrical concision – referring to Colombian species that I have never seen – are **Tourmaline Sunangel** *Heliangelus exortis* and **Lazuline Sabrewing** *Campylopterus falcatus*. However, as the following contributions make plain, there are many glorious alternatives.

> Wow, there are lots, but here are a few of my favourites: **Dot-eared Coquette** *Lophornis gouldii*, **Frilled Coquette** *Lophornis magnificus*, **Racket-tailed Coquette** *Discosura longicaudus*,

The Rufous-crested Coquette of Central America is a bird as beautiful as its name.

The long curved bill of the Green Hermit reflects a nectar diet from plants such as heliconias, which the hummingbirds repay by effecting their pollination.

Fork-tailed Woodnymph *Thalurania furcata*, **Blossomcrown** *Anthocephala floriceps*, **Bronze-tailed Plumeleteer** *Chalybura urochrysia*, **Blue-throated Mountaingem** *Lampornis clemenciae*, **Amethyst-throated Sunangel** *Heliangelus amethysticollis*, **Red-tailed Comet** *Sappho sparganura*, **Bearded Mountaineer** *Oreonympha nobilis*, Bearded Helmetcrest, **Long-tailed Sylph** *Aglaiocercus kingi*, **Hyacinth Visorbearer** *Augastes scutatus*, **Purple-crowned Fairy** *Heliothryx barroti*, Marvelous Spatuletail. Whoever named some of these, incidentally, must have been stoned![25]

For pure hummer joy I don't think you can top **Shining Sunbeam** *Aglaeactis cupripennis*, although at the other end of the spectrum there is always Bearded Helmetcrest – which sounds like a character from a far-away Star Wars galaxy. And then there are the sexy Coquettes – Frilled, **Festive Coquette** *Lophornis chalybeus* and **Peacock Coquette** *Lophornis pavoninus*. It's hard to choose![26]

One issue facing those who see them regularly is the way that the pleasures of these real encounters subtly infuse the imaginative response to their titles.

If I limit myself to species I've seen – and I can't entirely separate my opinion of the appearance of the bird from its name, so taking this into account – I'd vote for **Horned Sungem** *Heliactin bilopha*, **Gould's Jewelfront** *Heliodoxa aurescens*, **Brazilian Ruby** *Clytolaema rubricauda*, **Crimson Topaz** *Topaza pella*, **Fiery-tailed Awlbill** *Avocettula recurvirostris*, and Festive Coquette. However, one other that leaps to mind is probably a favorite for lots of folks. I've never even seen the bird personally, but between the name, the appearance, and the story surrounding it, I can't help but vote for Marvelous Spatuletail.[27]

(The latter is endemic to one valley, the Utcubamba Valley in northern Peru, where the population is no more than 1,000 birds. It is threatened with extinction partly from habitat loss and partly from hunting. The birds' dried hearts are thought to be an aphrodisiac. W H Hudson called it perhaps 'the most wonderful humming-bird known'.)[28]

The inventiveness found in the English names is easily matched in other languages. One of the most evocative and, incidentally, probably among the oldest for any hummingbird, is a word of Brazilian Amerindian origin, *Guaracigaba*.[29] It is particularly powerful for the way it envisions the morphology of light and for its metaphysical yoking of such disjunct phenomena. It means 'the hair of the sun', which was subsequently rendered in English translation as 'tresses of the day star'. However, perhaps the most romantic of all generic names among modern languages is that of the Brazilians, who call hummingbirds *beija-flor*, 'flower kisser'.

In Brazil the names for hummingbirds are particularly descriptive or allusive to aspects of their behavior. We use, for example, *besourinho* ('small beetle') as a name for the very small ones (**Reddish Hermit** *Phaethornis ruber* and **Minute Hermit** *Phaethornis idaliae*) to suggest the way they hum. The **Planalto Hermit** *Phaethornis pretrei* is called *limpa-casa* ('clean house') for the way it catches spiders on the ceiling inside the houses. Yet my favorite is the *chifre-de-ouro* ('horn-of-gold') for Horned Sungem.[30]

Spanish names can also match their English equivalents. The Bee Hummingbird, for instance, is known in its native land as *Zunzuncito* which, as Graeme Gibson notes, 'strikes me as marvellously Cuban'.[31] It also has its etymological

---

roots in original Aztec and Mayan names for hummingbirds, respectively *Zunzon* and *Zumzum*.[32]

The dominance of hummingbird movement and associated wing noise in the coinage of generic names (if not the specific titles) is a striking aspect across a number of languages. 'Hummingbird' itself is, of course, a reflection of the pattern and was first used (in the form of 'hum-bird') as early as the 1640s.[33] One possible reason why it is so often highlighted is the poverty of the birds' vocalisations. Many of their calls are metallic and high-pitched and, as Helmut Sick noted, suggestive of insects or bats rather than birds.[34] Equally, while the particular colours and patterns vary from species to species, the zizz of their wings is common to all the family.

A typical example of a family name that draws on this buzzing sound of hummers in flight is the Nahuatl name encountered earlier, *huitzilin*. Its similarity to the word 'whizz' is surely more than coincidence and suggestive of the common origins of so much human speech. Another language where the name draws on the sound is found right at the tip of the Americas, among the Mapuche people of Chile. Their various versions for two species, the Giant Hummingbird and Green-backed Firecrown, are *pinda*, *pinguera*, *pigda* and *piñuda*. All draw on the verb *pigudcun* ('to rub together').[35]

HUMMERS AND HUMMINGBIRD FEEDERS

One striking aspect of the buzz is its occasionally threatening character. You can be in the rainforest and suddenly find a hummingbird right in front of your face. The intensity and even minatory quality of that beetle's whine just a wingbeat from your eyes would be unnerving if the encounter were any more prolonged. Yet they are gone in a second. Routinely the birds have an aura of complete fearlessness that suggests outright aggression. One thinks, incidentally, not only of that fundamental linkage running from Huitzilopochtli to the hummingbird warriors of the Mexica, but also, on a lighter note, of YouTube films entitled 'Attack of the Killer Hummingbird' that show people being 'buzzed' in their gardens by these fairy-sized mites.

There is a form of aggression inbuilt into the birds' very ecology because their metabolism requires fresh food supplies all the time. Hummingbirds have reached the smallest size possible for warm-blooded existence. If they were any smaller they simply could not meet their own insatiable dietary needs. Perched, or rather hovering, at the very brink of starvation on an almost daily basis, they are intensely territorial and will fight fiercely to defend precious nectar supplies. Or they find other means to feed constantly:

> Perhaps 40–50 years ago, Len Hill, the late owner of a bird zoo in Bourton-on-the-Water in the Cotswolds, UK, was flying back to London from the West Indies on the airline BOAC. Every half-hour or so he disappeared to the toilet. He was in first class and after a while the attentive stewardesses asked if he was feeling all right. He said that he was, but after the fifth or sixth visit and the third or fourth expression of concern by the stewardesses he came clean: in his pocket, in metal cigar tubes with the tops off and the bottoms cut off, he had hummingbirds for his walk-in aviary at his zoo. They needed to be fed sugar solution regularly and he

knew that he should not have taken live animals into the cabin at all. The stewardesses, officer and captain were entranced by the birds, encouraged Len to feed them at his seat, and insisted on photographs on arrival at Heathrow. For some years BOAC featured a hummingbird as a logo in the bottom corner of their advertisements. It was one of Len Hill's stowaways on their plane.[36]

The feats that hummingbirds accomplish on what seem like minuscule quantities of energy are astonishing. The **Ruby-throated Hummingbird** *Archilochus colubris* can migrate annually from eastern North America and in so doing fly non-stop across the Gulf of Mexico, a distance of 800 km (500 miles), nourished by 2 g (0.07 oz) of stored body fat. Theoretically the bird could fly right round the whole planet fuelled by nothing more than 100 g (3.5 oz) of fat, or the equivalent of 940 calories.

This sounds very little, but what people often overlook is the food a hummingbird requires proportionate to its own weight. A species weighing 5 g (0.2 oz) consumes daily the nectar of 1,000–2,000 flowers, which includes the water equivalent to 160 per cent of its body mass. The American ornithologist Alexander Skutch was once having lunch in the mountains of Guatemala when his host took him to task for the small amount on his plate, remarking that he had an appetite like a hummingbird. To this Skutch replied, 'If I did you might not invite me to visit you again. I would eat more than 300 pounds of food daily.'[37] The actual figure is less, but not much less. To eat the equivalent of a hummer consuming half its weight in sugar, would require a grown man to devour 59 kg (130 lb) of bread.[38]

By meeting the birds' burning demands for high-energy food, people have been able to exploit hummers, and bring what is often a difficult family to observe closely right into

The Ruby-throated Hummingbird is routinely lured into North American gardens with special sugar-water feeders.

Rufous-tailed Hummingbirds and Booted Racket-tails gather at a feeder in Ecuador. There are c.135 species of hummingbird in this country and occasionally such dispensers can become enveloped by a thrumming halo of jewel-like birds.

the garden and even on to the porch. The technique involves hanging out bottles of sugared water. The plastic holders, with access holes that mimic the shape and red colour of genuine flowers, dispense a solution of one part sugar (not honey, which ferments and can cause mycosis of the hummingbird's tongue that may be fatal) to between four and six parts water. Around this simple technology has arisen a sophisticated commercial business, especially in North America, but also a transcontinental practice that is hugely beneficial to both the hummingbirds and to the people who love them.

A resident of Venezuela describes how you can convert a domestic environment into a place of dazzling beauty and constant entertainment:

> I soon strung a taut wire the length of the balcony and hung a couple of hummingbird feeders. Within hours, a male **Copper-rumped Hummingbird** *Amazilia tobaci* had found them, and fed from both. He immediately included the balcony in his trap line and visited us often. Very soon **Black-throated Mango** *Anthracothorax nigricollis* and other copper-rumps found the feeders and, as if drawn by magic, the original male would turn up and fiercely chase them away. The regular Spanish name for hummingbirds is *colibri*, but here in northern Venezuela they are known as *tucusitos*.
>
> I found a reliable supplier in the US and bought half-a-dozen more feeders and strung them along the line. The number of local hummers that came to feed soon proved to be too much for the original discoverer

of this hummingbird Garden of Eden, and within weeks the balcony had become a sort of no-man's-land, where territories were not recognised and the birds learned there was always enough food for all. The feeders were taken down every evening, washed and dried and hung up at dawn refilled with fresh sugar water. Numbers increased continually, and on some days we actually had to refill some feeders in the afternoon.

> My mother-in-law, an elderly and ailing person with incipient Alzheimer's disease, would come to the room regularly to see the birds. She would stand in the open French windows, with the birds flying, their wings buzzing and whirring, less than two metres away. On one occasion when we had brought her to see, not only were there several birds at every feeder, but I counted 16 birds perched in the acacia, patiently waiting for a slot. There were always at least a few visitors at any moment, but at peak feeding times I could count up to 50 and possibly 60 birds either feeding or waiting a turn.[39]

What is so striking about the last part of this story, and so typical of many individual engagements with birds, is how they can serve us in all sorts of private ways, as well as at the level of a society or culture. (See also Oystercatcher family, page 197.) The personal value and meaning of these encounters cannot be easily quantified. Nevertheless we sense their importance; a point re-emphasised in the following:

> I never had a good relationship with my father – I could probably count how many 'normal' conversations I've had with him – he didn't care for me too much.

But a year before he died he said something about hummingbirds – the sound they make so you know there's one near – and we shared about three sentences. I then mailed him a feeder. I never mailed him anything before. And it gave us something. Not much, but a little something to share, a few more conversations:

'See many hummingbirds lately?'

Oh yeah, every day.'

'Me too.'

'Sure are pretty.'

'Yep.'[40]

Many people who put out hummer feeders become hugely attached to 'their' birds, sometimes designing the whole garden to meet their demands for flower nectar. There is also an ancillary industry in hummingbird products, many of them feminine in orientation – jewellery, ornaments, garments – as well as internet-based networks (http:// hummingbirdworld.com). In some gardens the owner's passion becomes so dominant the entire house can be festooned in feeders drawing in dozens of birds at any one time.

Another standard, especially in the hummingbird-rich landscapes of South America, is the tourist lodge well-stocked with bottles of sugared water. Some of the best sites include Septimo Paraiso Ecolodge in Ecuador, Amazonia Lodge in Manu Biosphere Reserve of Peru, and the privately owned Sitio Folha Seca, at Ubatuba in São Paulo State, Brazil.[41] However, perhaps the ultimate are in north-western Ecuador. Two renowned sites, the Tandayapa Lodge and Bellavista Cloud Forest Lodge, are among the finest places on Earth to see hummingbirds for diversity of species (31 and 28 species respectively), but also for sheer numbers. At any one time there can be scores of hungry birds, sometimes enveloping the feeders in a brilliant and dramatic hornet's nest of colour and sound.[42]

Although these super-sites are hugely impressive, there is a moment in all our lives when just a single one of these fantastic mites is enough to reduce any of us to speechlessness.

She'd always been a city girl. She lives downstairs from my friend in the projects. She's pretty sometimes, and sometimes she's on a run. She has a bad drug habit that comes and goes. Although she's an adult, Rosa has never roller skated or ridden a bike or been camping. Never swum in a lake or in the ocean, only stuck her toes in the pool. Sometimes she has a nice shy smile and hello, and sometimes she's furtive, sly, but at least she'll nod hi to me. One time she saw me filling the hummingbird feeder on the porch, and she got so excited she could hardly speak. 'I saw a . . . it went like . . .' and here she held up her hand and it quickly flew sideways, hovered, and flew forward and fluttered, hovering again. 'It was a . . . it was like . . .' Her eyes were wide, excited.

I smiled at her. 'You saw a hummingbird!' I said.

She pointed at me, 'Jess! A little bird!' She grinned. 'Hummingbird. It was a hummingbird?'

She was a 42-year-old city girl, and she saw her first hummingbird.[43]

Mousebird family *Coliidae*

The six species of mousebird are inhabitants of savannah bush and woodland in sub-Saharan Africa, with a northern limit in central Sudan. They comprise one of only two endemic bird orders in Africa (the other is the turacos, the Musophagiformes) and they are sometimes described as 'living fossils'. Skeletal remains remarkably similar to those of today's mousebirds have been found in 20-million-year-old deposits. Regardless of this tag, they are birds of such glorious vitality that few creatures could seem less fossil-like.

A key aspect of their behaviour is their intense sociability and the name, 'mousebird', is a reference to their rather furtive scuttling manners. They are invariably in parties of 3–15 birds and a perpetual barrage of sharp, sometimes explosive or rasping flight-calls reinforces the impression of their busy personalities. The most widespread of all the species, the **Speckled Mousebird** *Colius striatus*, has names in the Zulu, Xhosa and Tsonga languages (respectively *iNdlazi*, *Indlazi*, *Ndlazi*) which draw on its repeated call note, *dlatsi*, *dlatsi*.[1]

All six species are highly striking in shape, with massively elongated tails, but bodies that are not much bigger than a sparrow's. The average mousebird is about 33 cm (13 in) in length, two-thirds of which is tail. In flight they have a short-winged whirring action that is characterised by brief flurries of vigorous effort followed by dipping glides. The overall effect has been compared to a rocket.[2]

The family's scientific name, *Coliidae*, has become something of a mystery. It was assumed to derive from the ancient Greek word *koloios*, which was originally used either for the jackdaw or green woodpecker.[3] Neither of the European birds has any obvious relevance to the mousebirds themselves and another suggestion is that *Colius* comes from the Greek *koleos*, meaning 'scabbard', a reference to the sword-like shape of the tail.[4] The fact that modern ornithology has lost sight of the name's origins is intriguing, because 'coly' (plural 'colies') is still used as an alternative name for mousebird, especially in east and southern Africa.

They are primarily vegetarian and the family is renowned for a capacity to eat highly toxic berries. The **Red-faced Mousebird** *Urocolius indicus* of southern Africa is apparently tolerant of *Melia azedarach*, a member of the mahogany family whose fruits contain a neurotoxin poisonous to humans and poultry alike.[5] Speckled Mousebirds have been recorded feeding upon a South African fruit called *Acokanthera oblongifolia*, which is also known as 'bushman's poison', because indigenous hunters once used an extract from this plant to tip their arrows.[6]

However, the habit that brings mousebirds into sharpest focus for many people is their love of fruits and flowers that we also cherish. In east and southern Africa the family has adapted to living in suburban or agricultural areas, where they are, or were once, severely persecuted for their

The Speckled Mousebird of sub-Saharan Africa is a bird of great character and occasional horticultural mischief.

depredations on orchard fruit and garden plants. In 1956, the east African ornithologist V D van Someren recalled the retribution once inflicted in Kenya:

> At one time, I knew of organized 'drives'; several householders banded together and, armed with shotguns, they patrolled several valleys or had the birds driven towards them at fixed stances. Hundreds of birds were slain. Not long ago the Agricultural Department issued a note on how to get rid of these birds. It advocated putting out poisoned water and poisoned bait, netting the birds at their sleeping quarters and destroying their eggs. It also suggested that rewards be given for so many head and/or eggs – all rather diabolical, to my way of thinking.[7]

Martin Woodcock, the artist whose paintings appear in the seven-volume *The Birds of Africa*, adds an illuminating anecdote: 'Anyone with a garden strangles mousebirds. We have recently been speaking to someone who was brought up in Kenya who wanted to buy the mousebird plate from *The Birds of Africa*, as he remembered killing them as a boy!'[8]

The bird can eat their entire weight in vegetable matter

in a day (36–80 g: 1.3–2.8 oz) and they love leaves as much as they love fruit, a point emphasised in the following:

> Everyone I know who has gardened in Kenya (or at least the Nairobi/Limuru areas) found mousebirds to be dreadful pests in their gardens. They eat most things and it is very common knowledge. You'd be hard put to find a gardener who had not had a problem with them! I think the only way to stop them is to have the plants covered with netting. An odd bit of behaviour we noticed in our Langata garden was that they ate all the green leaves (leaving just the rachis) of pawpaw (papaya) trees. These trees did not do well at Langata but we did get a fairly regular supply of small fruits in spite of the trees having no leaves! The mousebirds never attempted to peck the fruits.[9]

Another Kenyan confirms the problem with mousebirds but puts their damage into perspective: 'They certainly are a nuisance in the garden, coming in large numbers to eat any soft fruits, tomatoes, etc. At my place we have a large framed area of what's called "bird net" to keep them away. We also have a 9,000-volt electric fence – but that's more to keep the elephants out!'[10]

Trogon family *Trogonidae*

The wonderfully named **Resplendent Quetzal** *Pharomachrus mocinno*, which occurs across Central America from southern Mexico to Panama, is a creature of renowned beauty and 'considered by many the most spectacular New World bird'.[1] Even within its family, however, it faces stiff competition. There are 42 trogons in all, spread through the forests of Africa (three species), Asia (12 species), Central and North America (14 species, including two Caribbean representatives that are endemic to their respective islands, the **Hispaniolan Trogon** *Priotelus roseigaster* and **Cuban Trogon** *Priotelus temnurus*) and South America (17 species, four of which extend into the northern continent). All of them are birds of extraordinary beauty and, as Helmut Sick noted, 'worthy of symbolizing the exuberance of the tropics'.[2]

They may occur worldwide, but trogons are remarkably consistent in their possession of shimmering green backs and tails, then underparts of intense red, orange, yellow or blue (or a combination of these) and finished very often with chequered or zigzag lines of black and white. Another rather odd unifying characteristic is their capacity to be birds of dazzling colour and yet also difficult to see. Trogons have a habit of sitting stock-still, sometimes for several minutes, in the dappled middle storey of a forest, before suddenly flicking off to the next perch. All one really detects is their departure. People who see them regularly also note how trogons somehow contrive to sit with their backs to the observer, often watching over their shoulders, so that the brighter underparts are always concealed. (The Xhosa of southern Africa were so struck by the seeming lethargy in trogon behaviour that their name for the local **Narina Trogon** *Apaloderma narina*, *Inshatshongo*, was also a nickname for a lazy woman.)[3]

That immobility is a little more difficult to accomplish for the male Resplendent Quetzal during the breeding season. Not only is he a mixture of iridescent emerald and crimson, he also possesses a tail that is up to 1 m (3.3 ft) long and more than twice the length of his body. Actually they are not true tail feathers but upper-tail coverts that overlay the rectrices and then spread and dance behind the tail tip for as much as 61 cm (24 in). The plumes are so incredible that when he first saw the bird, the French naturalist Baron Cuvier was inclined to think them a man-made hoax.[4] Today these fantastic plumes, which billow and waft in the breezes of the cloud-forest, make the Resplendent Quetzal a candidate for the region's most sought-after species, and among the most important wild creatures in a cultural context.

It is the national bird of Guatemala and an omnipresent symbol in the country's official iconography (on the doors of police vehicles), in business advertisements (for petrol stations) and in cultural life. The country's highest civic award for artistic, humanitarian or scientific endeavour is the *Orden del Quetzal*, the Order of the Quetzal. Guatemala's second city, Quetzaltenango, is named after the species

The Resplendent Quetzal has a justified reputation as one of the most spectacular birds in all the Americas.

The cultural prominence and high economic value of quetzal feathers in pre-Columbian Guatemala are reflected in the name of the nation's currency.

and there are two Mexican towns that bear similar trogon connections – Quetzalapa, San Miguel Quetzaltepec. At times the bird's link with the region descends to cliché. For example, there is barely a tourist-oriented shop that does not sell knick-knacks and textiles with the bird's image emblazoned upon them.

Yet these kitsch quetzals should not disguise the fact that it is also a symbol of immense political, intellectual and emotional significance. Typically, the species has given its name to the Guatemalan currency, the quetzal. The bird appears on all the coins and denominations of the modern banknotes, which are artefacts of great beauty, combining both a rectilinear Roman typography and the exquisite complexity of original Mayan hieroglyphs. Through the centre of all this intricate state symbolism sails a male Resplendent Quetzal in all his finery.

THE IMPORTANCE OF QUETZALS TO PRE-COLUMBIAN SOCIETY

This modern Guatemalan deployment of the bird may seem like a high honour, but it probably does little more than glance at the exalted status which quetzals once held for the ancient civilisations of Central America. The birds' primary role was to supply those fabulous tail plumes, said to be more valuable even than gold, which were then worn by religious authorities and the upper eschelons of Mesoamerican society. The modern name for the species comes from the Aztec (Nahuatl) word *Quetzal-tototl*, which meant roughly the fowl with the long green feathers.[5]

The plumes were gathered and arrayed into a spectacular tall feather crown that must have swayed and gestured above the head of the person wearing it. Feathers from all sorts of birds played a fundamental part in the ceremonial life of Central America. One can only guess at the colour and splendour of these occasions, and perhaps only the modern Brazilian carnivals or the festivals in the central highlands of New Guinea can give us any idea of this Mesoamerican feather-based pageantry.

The best evidence for the central role played by quetzal plumes is the highly complex relief images of the nobility and its historical achievements, which survive abundantly in Mayan and Aztec ruins and which are also a staple item of museums worldwide. Above the heads of these stone kings and carved priests sprout what look like long stalks of grass arrayed in a slightly flexed corolla. They were meant to indicate quetzal feathers. The ubiquity of this stylistic feature in Central American statuary hints at the huge numbers of quetzals that were pressed into service.

Despite the inherent fragility of the genuine article, there

are a handful of Aztec feather artefacts that have survived the ravages of time. The most important is a magnificent quetzal-feather crown, said to have been Moctezuma II's own headdress, and sometimes ranked among the world's greatest human treasures. It was taken by the Spaniards to give to Charles V, after which it eventually arrived in Austria, where it is presently housed in the Vienna Museum of Ethnology. It is now a source of some controversy between the Austrian and Mexican governments, since the latter claims its return as an inseparable part of the nation's heritage. Although the exact identity of the piece is now questioned (did it ever appear on the head of Moctezuma?), its beauty, workmanship and its implied consumption of quetzal feathers are all beyond dispute. There are 450 plumes in the piece, and since the tail of the living bird yielded only four of the longest feathers, it may have taken more than 112 quetzals to complete it.

To furnish themselves with these plumes, not to mention the other luxuries of aristocratic life – gold, turquoise, jade, liquidambar and jaguar skins – the Aztec authorities demanded material booty from a wide array of subject peoples. It was said that Moctezuma II himself had authorised the conquest of Soconusco (on the Pacific coast in modern Chiapas state) precisely in order to secure an adequate personal supply of quetzal feathers. The tribute goods were then transported back to Tenochtitlan from all corners of the empire by merchants known as *pochteca*.[6]

Examining indigenous documents drawn up shortly after the Spanish conquest, modern scholars have been able to assess this flow of tribute from the Mexican highlands and beyond. They estimate that the total annual harvest was 2,480 bunches of feathers. Unfortunately what constituted a bunch – depicted in Mexican glyphs as an open fist clamped round a sheath of plumes – is ambiguous. However, it is calculated that a man's hand might enclose between ten and 50 quetzal plumes and therefore the total number transported each year for Aztec usage alone was 6,200–31,000 feathers.[7] This takes no account of other Mayan states within the range of Resplendent Quetzal who commandeered their own parallel, if smaller, supplies of the magical birds.

Had collecting methods involved the death of the quetzals then such levels of harvest would probably have been unsustainable, even with the greater extent of forest in that period. However, most accounts confirm that the trappers who actually took the birds were forbidden to kill them, theoretically on pain of death. One such description of their methods occurs in Francisco Hernández's sixteenth-century work *Historia Avium Novae Hispaniae* (*A History of the Birds of New Spain*), a translation of which appears in John Ray's *The Ornithology of Francis Willughby*:

> These Birds live in the Province of Tecolotlan beyond *Quauhtemallam* [Guatemala] towards *Honduras*, where great care is taken that no man kill them . . . The Fowlers . . . betake themselves to the Mountains, and there hiding themselves in small Cottages, scatter up and down boil'd Indian Wheat, and prick down in the ground many rods besmeared with Birdlime, wherewith the Birds intangled become their prey . . . They have by the instinct of nature such knowledge of their riches, that once sticking to the Birdlime, they remain still and quiet, not struggling at all, that they may not mar or

The way in which the plumage of the Resplendent Quetzal changes colour according to the light was central to the bird's historic importance to the Mayan and Aztec civilisations.

▶ The Lilac-breasted Roller of east and southern Africa is a bird of great beauty and aerial grace, but occasionally an old elephant turd will serve it nicely as a perch from which to hunt for insects.

injure their feathers. The beauty whereof they are so in love with, that they chuse rather to be taken and killed, than by endeavouring to get their liberty do any thing that may deface or prejudice them.[8]

Hernández's somewhat contradictory statement that the quetzals, in their overweening vanity, preferred to die rather than risk the glories of their plumage may actually be the innate response of a bird family renowned for 'extremely thin skin, like silk paper', whose dense plumage falls 'out at the least touch'.[9] (The scientific name of Narina Trogon, *Apaloderma*, means 'delicate skin'.)[10] Perhaps quetzals do not struggle because they risk injury. Whatever the answer they are said to be rare in captivity and all trogons are apparently difficult to keep.

There is a strange paradox at the heart of the Western world's rather limited understanding of indigenous attitudes towards quetzals. We manage somehow both to overstate their significance and to underestimate the birds' importance for societies such as the Maya and Aztecs. On the one hand, quetzals have become, in the Western imagination, birds of legend. As the biogeographer Mark Bonta argues: 'While outsiders may think of it as mysterious, exotic, rare, or endangered, local [Honduran] farmers know it to be a common bird that nests in dead snags in their coffee farms, or wherever else it encounters its favorite food *aguacatillos* (wild avocados).'[11]

On the other hand, we have tended to gloss over, and may never truly recover, the full significance of the symbolic bird for pre-Columbian society. One fact, however, that is well established is the link between it and the deep-rooted Mesoamerican deity and culture hero Quetzalcoatl. (The Maya called the same god Kukulcan; *Kuk* was their name for the quetzal.) In indigenous sculpture, this supernatural being was frequently depicted as a dragon-like creature completely enwrapped in quetzal feathers. He was a god that encapsulated all terrestrial life, yoking together the airiness of a bird and the subterranean earthiness of a serpent (see also Albatross family and Coleridge's *The Rime of the Ancient Mariner*, page 99).

Another part of the complex symbolism attaching to quetzals has been investigated by the director of the Mexican Museum of Anthropology, Diana Magaloni-Kerpel. It concerns the bird's famously glittering iridescence, which is largely unexpressed in modern paintings and poses an intriguing challenge to contemporary photographers, as David Tipling explains:

When I went to photograph them in Costa Rica I would arrive each day at the nest at dawn. I was amazed at the colours this one male quetzal could morph through during the day, depending on the angle and quality of light that hit his plumage. One moment he could be lime green, the colour I associate with quetzals, but then the next minute he had changed to a shade of mauve, sometimes almost purple and often blue. I never liked photographing him during those 'weird' colour moments as he only looked like what I think of as a 'proper' quetzal when he was green.[12]

Magaloni-Kerpel examined a series of famous Mayan paintings at the ancient ruins of Bonampak in modern Chiapas, Mexico. She discovered that in representing quetzal feathers in paint the Mayan artists used a double-layered technique of blue on green against an original red background. She argues that this strict representational method was deployed not merely for aesthetic purpose or to achieve accuracy but because the luminous, shimmering quality of quetzal feathers was loaded with meaning for both the Maya and the Aztecs.

When their leaders, such as Moctezuma, donned a garment made from the iridescent feathers of quetzals, hummingbirds and other dazzlingly coloured species, a very precise idea was contained in the costume. The way the feathers' appearance moved chromatically from green through even to purple was analogous to how the Aztec leader himself was transformed from being merely human. The wearing of such precious feathers enveloped Moctezuma in the essence of his gods. Magaloni-Kerpel suggests that such a garment, and even painted representations of it, would become a part of the divine and 'a window into another realm'.[13]

Roller family *Coraciidae*

Rollers are medium-sized (c.30 cm: 12 in), broad-winged, big-headed, thick-billed birds of Old World grassland. There are 12 species and while they show a strong bias towards Africa (seven are endemic), the **European Roller** *Coracias garrulus* migrates from there to breed from Portugal east to the Mongolian steppe. Another wide-ranging species is the **Oriental Dollarbird** *Eurystomus orientalis* (named for the coin-sized azure spots on its wings), which occurs from northern China almost to the outskirts of Melbourne in southern Australia.

Rollers are famous for two things: their beauty and their remarkable aerial displays, which can suggest an almost ecstatic and self-delighting pleasure in flight. The name 'roller' draws precisely on this distinctive behaviour, which was said to be 'somewhat after the fashion of a Tumbler-Pigeon'.[1] More specifically ornithologists have described how the European Roller 'rockets up in the air vertically, flaps

about erratically in steep wave-crests and performs a series of fantastic evolutions – tumbling, somersaulting, nose-diving, looping the loop and rolling from side to side'.[2] Several other species, notably an endemic African trio – **Racket-tailed Roller** *Coracias spatulatus*, **Lilac-breasted Roller** *Coracias caudatus* and **Abyssinian Roller** *Coracias abyssinicus* – possess hugely elongated outer tail feathers, so that their physical beauty and aerial grace coalesce.

The family's wider aesthetic renown centres on a single colour – blue. When perched many roller species can look like crow-sized birds of moderate hue. Yet when they take wing they unfold a kaleidoscope of blue shades across their wings. Although roller plumage seldom includes the red and yellow parts of the colour spectrum one can understand how this moment of suddenly revealed brilliance led one nineteenth-century author to write, 'when flying in the sun it [the European Roller] looks like a moving rainbow'.[3]

This beauty once motivated widespread trapping for the plume trade. An old Italian method was to catch the European Roller in spring-traps or trap-cages baited with grasshoppers.[4] (There is a remarkable and rare ancient Egyptian image of a European Roller on a tomb at Beni Hasan. It depicts a trapper in his orchard – the inference being that the birds were stealing his fruit – trying to catch a roller using much the same methods as the Italians, but more than 3,500 years earlier.)[5] The widespread Asian species, the **Indian Roller** *Coracias benghalensis*, was also caught in 'thousands upon thousands . . . to supply the demand for gaudy feathers to bedizen ladies' dresses'.[6]

If the rollers' gift to us is their beauty, then our main offering to them has been our worldwide complex of telegraphic and electrical poles, wires and pylons. Wherever these towering artefacts march across areas of featureless steppe country they supply the rollers' favourite perches and often their only perches. In a number of countries this network is supplemented with other modern donations in the form of artificial nestboxes. However, the birds once exploited grander human artefacts. In Morocco, during the early twentieth century, European Rollers nested in holes along the city walls at Larache, Marrakesh, Meknes and the capital, Rabat. While the birds still use cavities in isolated rural buildings as substitute tree holes, our provision of nests sites has not prevented a major slump in European Roller numbers across at least 20 countries, from Portugal to Russia.

Our secondary gift to the world's rollers is fire. Grass fires are widely used in Africa and parts of Asia to clear old bush and stimulate the growth of fresh green vegetation for livestock grazing. These landscape-sized blazes are magnets for a spectrum of birds, including several roller species. Up to 5,000 European Rollers have been recorded to come from far and wide to attend bush fires in Tanzania.[7] The birds dash around the margins and occasionally into the path of the flames to hunt for large insects and other edible evacuees. In Sri Lanka, for this same reason, the Indian Roller is known as 'the one who inhales smoke'.[8]

An intriguing piece of folklore has been recorded in the Indian state of Kerala. The Indian Roller is apparently trapped and then cooked in a kind of broth that is meant to have therapeutic value in cases of whooping cough.[9] One might imagine that the birds' strong lungs and renowned tolerance of smoke and fire might be at the root of this practice, but its origins lie in ancient Sanskrit literature. The Rig Veda (a cycle of sacred hymns and one of the core texts of Hinduism) explicitly recorded how the sympathetic magic projected on to the Indian Roller (or possibly the Stork-billed Kingfisher) hinged upon the bird's harsh guttural cough-like call note. The broth was assumed to cause the bronchial illness suffered by a human patient to pass to the bronchial-voiced bird.[10]

In northern India the Indian Roller has a wider sacred status with some protective value:

> In Jharkhand province, which borders Bihar (north) and West Bengal (south) the Indian Roller, known as *Neelkanth* (meaning 'blue throated'), is not killed or, at least, I've never heard of it. Rather Hindus see it as the god Shiva, who drank poison during Samudramanthan to save the world and kept it in his throat, which turned it blue. For this reason people worship the roller as Shiva's representative. In Jharkhand, especially in tribal areas, the roller is saluted and people say *Teshe Raja Theshkumkum Maharaja salam*. It means 'revered Emperor'.[11]

Rajat Bhargava adds the following detail:

> During the Hindu festival Dussehra, prior to Diwali, the Indian Roller is trapped by certain traditional communities and then shown live to other Hindu spectators, who think it is auspicious to see this bird on Dussehra. In turn the bird trappers are given tips by these onlookers. Some wealthy people also pay to release the captive birds. The birds are originally caught using a type of cricket tied with cotton thread to diagonally placed dome-shaped twigs coated with glue prepared from *Ficus* tree sap. The bird flies to catch the cricket and becomes glued to the sticks. As Dussehra is in the month of October, a few European Rollers (which are passage migrants) are also trapped with the larger catch of Indian Rollers.
>
> In north-east India, Indian Rollers (race *affinis*) are collected as chicks or as adults (which are hunted using a catapult) and sold for food. Rollers are also eaten as a traditional medicine for various ailments that include coughs. In south India the Indian Roller is caught but the practice is not widespread and restricted to certain pockets where there are traditional-medicine healers and bird trappers.[12]

Kingfisher family *Alcedinidae*

Perhaps it is their blueness (see also Swallow and Martin family, page 416), a colour repeated in many species of kingfisher, that accounts for the family's special aura. Whatever the factor may be, our encounters with these birds are frequently touched by a sense of occasion. Some occasions – clearly – are more important than others:

> Way back in March 1982 my younger daughter, Lisa, was killed in a car crash whilst driving in the course of her job. She was 22, vivacious and lovely. Some weeks after Lisa's funeral, I was again at home on my own, this time unpacking shopping. 'Something' told me to stop what I was doing and to walk through the house to my little music room, which had French windows on to the back garden. Sitting just outside – to my great joy – was a **Common Kingfisher** *Alcedo atthis*. I carefully opened the other side, and was able to bend down and stroke the little bird. She then flew off, and that was that. There have been many occasions when winged visitors seem determined to be noticed and spoken to! That kingfisher has been a sort of mystifying solace to me over the years.[1]

Kingfishers vary greatly in size, from Australia's celebrated mascot, the **Laughing Kookaburra** *Dacelo novaeguineae* – the giant in the family at 47 cm (19 in) – to its elfin forest-dwelling relative the **African Dwarf Kingfisher** *Ispidina lecontei*, which measures just 10 cm (4 in). Yet their shared characteristics – long straight bill, huge head, stocky wedge-shaped body and (normally) stub tail – mean that all 95 species are easily recognisable as members of one family. They are justly famous worldwide for their beauty, and most species bear upon their backs one or several intense shades of blue that cement the birds' associations – like the word 'kingfisher' itself – with water. In truth, many are either inhabitants of forest or savannah-type bush and have almost no connection with aquatic environments or, indeed, with fish.

Europeans and North Americans are so familiar with their own highly charismatic representatives of the family that they can overlook how few kingfishers actually dwell in northern latitudes. America north of the Mexican–USA border has only one widespread species (**Belted Kingfisher** *Megaceryle alcyon*) and two other more restricted relatives (**Green Kingfisher** *Chloroceryle americana* and **Ringed Kingfisher** *Megaceryle torquata*). The situation is similar in Europe, where the Common Kingfisher is almost universal, but the **White-throated kingfisher** *Halcyon smyrnensis* and **Pied Kingfisher** *Ceryle rudis* are confined to the region's eastern fringe. South America holds just five species and Africa has 19, but the group's real home is the vast

swathe of islands between the south-east Asian mainland and Australia. Indonesia and New Guinea, for instance, each hold more than a quarter of all kingfishers, and as a whole the region has 53 of the 96 species.

In their habits kingfishers are largely loners – an exception is the Pied Kingfisher, whose roosts in tropical Africa can number many hundreds – and this solitariness (often at low densities) may explain why these birds of such lovely hue have been spared the usually dismal history of exploitation for their feathers.[2] However, one persistent antagonist was the 'selfish fisherman, who wants all the fish for himself and begrudges the poor bird an honest living'. A strategy that exploited the family's characteristic bent for open perches near rivers was to place traps on poles appropriately sited near the water's edge. In North America it was once the case that hundreds of Belted Kingfishers were 'caught and killed in this way along private trout streams', while 5,568 of this species were killed in 1937 at fish hatcheries near Lake Michigan.[3] In Europe an alternative was to dangle fine-meshed silk nets over the width of a stream or suspended from a bridge. The method took advantage of the way Common Kingfishers, when moving about their territories, invariably follow the line of a watercourse, and so would go straight into the nets.[4]

At the height of the great nineteenth-century mania for birds in women's fashions (see Herons and the Feather Industry, page 131) not even the kingfishers' antisocial lifestyle could spare them completely from the trade. In India

Despite the associations of their name and the tiddler-snatching habits of some, like this Common Kingfisher, there are many species in this family that seldom go near water or fish.

315

This remarkable Chinese headdress from the Qing Dynasty (AD 1644–1912) includes real kingfisher feathers.

For all their renown as birds of glorious blue, kingfishers are less associated with human ideals of beauty than of tranquillity. The connection is proverbial in some European languages and stems from ancient Greek mythology. Halcyon (also spelled Alcyone) was the daughter of the god of the wind, Aeolus, and she married Ceyx of Trachis, a son of the Morning Star. But these confirmed lovers vexed the first couple in the Greek pantheon when they dared to style themselves Hera and Zeus. As punishment for this presumption, the real Zeus sent a thunderstorm and shipwrecked Ceyx as he sailed to consult an oracle, and Halcyon, inconsolable at her husband's drowning, threw herself also into the sea.[7] Out of pity for their fate, Zeus then turned the doomed pair into kingfishers. Every year Halcyon and Ceyx built their nest on the surface of the sea and placed in it their eggs. Aeolus then stilled the winds for the period of their chick-rearing and that fortnight became known as the 'Halcyon Days', a spell of dead calm in the midst of winter.

What is extraordinary – and to some modern commentators more like 'wild lunacy' – is how this beautiful, if extravagant, fable became entangled in works of supposedly genuine natural history.[8] Aristotle is the author normally cited as illustrative of the way the tale became embedded in classical thought, but it was repeated by subsequent writers on nature, such as Pliny and Aelian (see Appendix II). In his account of kingfisher behaviour, Aristotle wrote:

> The halcyon breeds at the season of the winter solstice. Accordingly, when this season is marked with calm weather, the name of 'halcyon days' is given to the seven days preceding, as to as many following, the solstice . . . And these days are calm, when southerly winds prevail at the solstice . . . The halcyon is said to take seven days for building her nest, and the other seven for laying and hatching her eggs. In our country there are not always halcyon days about the time of the solstice, but in the Sicilian seas this season of calm is pretty regular. The bird lays about five eggs.[9]

Not content with this hearsay, Aristotle investigated the myth as if it were true and felt he had found material evidence of the nest (which actual marine creature supplied this 'nest' is unclear) to prove some of the legend. What is remarkable about Aristotle's passage on the kingfisher is the conflation of outright fantasy and real biology. His claim that the Common Kingfisher laid about five eggs is close enough (six or seven is usual) to suggest the statement rested on some genuine observation. But then how could he go on to elaborate the nest-on-the-sea-surface idea, if he had encountered a real nest burrow? (Common Kingfishers dig tunnels into riverbanks of *c.*50 cm: 20 in length and lay in a bare chamber that can become cluttered with regurgitated fish bones.)

However Aristotle arrived at his version of the kingfisher's reproductive behaviour, it is the case that 'halcyon days' entered European consciousness as an expression for a spell of tranquil weather. Eventually it also became a figurative description for any period of perfect conditions and, strangely, it is now most associated not with the winter solstice, but with the idealised summer days of our childhoods.

The Greek myth had a number of intriguing consequences for the roles ascribed to kingfishers for

bird trappers used live decoy birds placed near a small net to catch White-throated Kingfishers. The intense territorial behaviour of the resident pair meant that the birds would often be ravelled in the mesh even before the man had finished setting it. One witness in colonial India described how he was once attracted by 'a patch of cobalt blue on the countryside', only to find that 'several thousand skins of the White[-throated] Kingfisher were drying in the Indian sunshine.' As well as being funnelled into the international feather market, many kingfishers were apparently shipped to China where the blue plumes were used to make 'pretty ornaments for the ladies'.[5]

One method (known as *tian tsui*: 'embellish with kingfishers' and still occasionally practised) involves the inlay of tiny fragments of the bird's aquamarine feathers into ornaments, furniture and silver jewellery pieces that are often themselves of flower, bird or butterfly design. These were then painted with a hard enamel coating. Sometimes the turquoise of the White-throated Kingfisher was used alongside the richer navy of another family member, **Black-capped Kingfisher** *Halcyon pileata*, to create a gloriously complex blue patterning. One of the key historical sources of the various kingfishers that supplied the huge Chinese demand for this ancient technique was the extensive wetlands of Cambodia.

In the West the feathers were used whole and inserted into hats or other fashion accessories. As in China, the manufacturers were not averse to the wholesale wastage of the kingfishers' lives. At the collapse of the European market in bird plumes, partly because of the timely American anti-trade legislation, massive shipments of feathers were left unsold in British showrooms. These withdrawn lots included the skins of 90,000 birds, of which 22,000 were kingfishers.[6]

centuries in European culture. The idea that the bird was an indicator of weather, or could in some way influence climatic conditions, gave rise to a number of bizarre uses for dried kingfisher skins. For example, French and British fishermen were said to hang them on their boats because the corpse would spin and wherever the bill pointed was said to indicate from which direction the wind would blow. They were also kept as a handy talisman that could avert the effects of thunderstorms.[10]

Ever rigorous in their pursuit of facts, the British ornithologists John Ray and Francis Willughby noted, with heavy irony, in 1678 that: 'It is a Vulgar persuasion, that this bird, being hung up on an untwisted thread by the Bill, in any room, will turn its Breast to that quarter of the Heaven whence the wind blows: They that doubt it may try it.'[11] Their friend Sir Thomas Browne had, in fact, doubted it, hung up two birds side by side and, when each pointed in completely different directions, proved it to be the nonsense it was.[12] Yet earlier in the century, Shakespeare, who was never one to ruin a good metaphor with the facts, refers to the wind-divining legend of the kingfisher in *King Lear* (Act 2, Scene 2). In the play Kent describes the behaviour of certain rogues who will 'turn their halcyon beaks / With every gale and vary of their masters'.

The weather associations are similarly embedded in the nomenclature for Common Kingfishers elsewhere in Europe. There is, for instance, a Serbian name for the bird – *Zimorod* – which 'literally means "born in winter"'.[13] In France the same species is called *Martin-pècheur d'Europe* (an older local alternative from Normandy was *Oiseau de Saint Martin*), while in Spanish it is *Martín pescador*.[14] The significance of Martin, or St Martin, is made clearer by the Common Kingfisher's name in Malta. (Incidentally this Mediterranean island lies squarely in that zone of sea where the supposed period of calm of the halcyon days was said to be most conspicuous.) Maltese ornithologist John J Borg explains the connection:

> In Malta the Common Kingfisher is also associated with calm weather. Its Maltese name is *Ghasfur ta' San Martin* ('St Martin's Bird'). The feast of St Martin is held on the 11 November and that week is usually characterised by calm weather which, in fact, is known as *Is-sajf ta' San Martin* ('the summer of St Martin'). Although Common Kingfishers start appearing as early as mid July some believe that it's around November when they are really plentiful. Incidentally the original halcyon days, the days following the 21 December (up to 28–29 December), are also usually characterised by calm weather, although we had instances of rough weather in some years.[15]

It seems that, while the fundamental association of this bird's breeding season with a period of tranquil winter weather has remained intact over two and a half millennia, the details have been Christianised. St Martin has replaced the pagan daughter of Aeolus in kingfisher nomenclature.

One striking aspect of the myth of the halcyon and its effect on the understanding of real kingfishers is the durability of hearsay and inherited error in the face of real empirical observations. Aristotle's authority was such that he went almost unchallenged until the end of the Middle

The Common Kingfisher is one of the most widespread of its family, occurring from Portugal to Papua New Guinea.

Ages, but what is intriguing is how these falsehoods endured right into the modern period and the age of science. The British writer Charlotte Smith, in a book published in 1807, noted how she had seen a kingfisher 'hung up to the beam of a cottage ceiling', and was reassured that this weathervane 'never failed' to show changes of wind direction.[16]

A final overarching point emerging from the saga of Halcyon and her entanglement with kingfishers is the extent to which Greek mythology – that strange and wonderful cycle of stories, whose origins probably date back to the Bronze Age and even earlier – is still so much a living part of the world of letters and science, however subliminal the link may be. There are even today two genera in the kingfisher family named *Halcyon* (11 species) and *Ceyx* (four species). The Greek tales of divine lives, loves, labours and betrayals are implicit in ornithology's lexicon wherever birdwatchers might go. To give just a single example, the **Chameleon Dwarf Kingfisher** *Ceyx lepidus*, as its name suggests, is a creature of massive variability across its range from the Philippines to the Solomon Islands. Should one encounter the shy, solitary bird of royal blue and pale cinnamon by some shade-enlaced pool deep in the New Guinean rainforest, one carries into that tropical encounter, however involuntarily and however remote that moment may seem from the herb-scented mountains of Hellas, some fragment of its ancient legends.

One species not so touched by European culture is the largest of the family. The name used for this striking, crow-sized, mainly brown and white kingfisher is of Aboriginal origin. In fact there are four kookaburra species in the genus *Dacelo* (an anagram of *alcedo*, the Latin for kingfisher): two in Australia – the Laughing Kookaburra and the **Blue-winged Kookaburra** *Dacelo leachii* – while the **Rufous-bellied Kookaburra** *Dacelo gaudichaud* and **Spangled Kookaburra** *Dacelo tyro* (also of the Aru Islands) are found mainly in New Guinea. However, the bird that has made the name famous worldwide is the Laughing Kookaburra. This Australian endemic is found widely in open dry woodland, gardens, parks and eucalyptus-scattered farmland predominantly in the eastern half of the country. Colonists were so enamoured of the bird that they introduced it successfully to Western Australia, Tasmania and other islands, as well as to New Zealand (where a small population of about 500 individuals persists today).[17]

The species' four-syllable name is a fairly accurate rendering of the loud, cheerful and echoic voice, but it describes merely a 'snapshot' of sound that one can sometimes isolate momentarily within the species' more general outpourings. In full flow a Laughing Kookaburra better suggests the hilarious hooting noise produced by a pantomime ape with hands tucked into its armpits. The full cacophonous effect derives also from the fact the birds often 'laugh' in concert. This wonderful sound has accounted for a huge range of Aboriginal names across Australia's original human and cultural mosaic. As well as the now standard spelling there are Kowburra, Kangroburra, Kakaburri, Akkaburra, Kakaburra, Arkoburra, Kouburra, Kocaburra, Kakooburra, Karkoburra, Karconbur, Kookooburry, Kokoparra, Googooburra, Cowur-burra, Kowkargar, Gurgara, Gingarga, Kamminmalli, Toones, Doowal, Kaggoo, Greggoom, Karkungoon, Koaka, Gragon, Kakorim, Gookergaka, Koori, Kooree, Kulkyne, Konga, Koorungal, Krongkrong, Kooartang, Tarakook, Kron,

Koonet, Korung-korung, Kangoo, Wokook, Burndigan, Wook-wook and Coarg.[18]

Some of this variation must surely be a matter simply of how the spoken Aboriginal word struck the ear of the European who transcribed a particular version. However, it is notable that many of the different names converge in a consistent repetition of hard consonantal sounds. A well-known English alternative – laughing jackass – evokes the element of humour and the volume, but really gives little indication of the sound's true quality. Other historic vernacular names – 'alarm bird', 'breakfast bird', 'settler's clock' and 'bushman's clock' – at least reflect the way in which kookaburras start to vocalise before it is even properly light.

With the advent of television and cinema, kookaburra calls acquired a secondary function as sounds that could announce a programme's inherently exotic setting, some of which had no genuine Australian connections. The classic example was the kookaburra used in the (Africa-located) Tarzan films. The tame individual which made many of these early recordings became one of the most famous of all Australian birds. Jacko began life as a rather eccentric family pet, but his ability to break into the species' glorious laughing call at will meant that when he died, aged 15, in 1939, he had become a national celebrity. He appeared regularly on the radio, in live stage performances and in a fictionalised biography, *Jacko – The Broadcasting Kookaburra*.[19]

The way in which the public took this hugely charismatic bird to heart was also matched by the increased deployment of the species' image as a metaphor for Australia as a country, and as a symbol for its people as a whole. Laughing Kookaburras have appeared on the national currency – a square penny and halfpenny piece that have now become collectors' items, some of them worth up to AUS $57,000 – on stamps, in the names of ships, in the logos and advertisements for a huge spectrum of commercial products, as a military mascot for the Australian forces, and as a nickname for the national men's hockey team.[20]

However, perhaps the one kookaburra appearance that has secured the bird widest global recognition is in the song written by Marion Sinclair in the 1930s, entitled 'Kookaburra Sits in the Old Gum Tree'. This merry tune was once familiar to almost every English-speaking child, not just in the bird's home country but on both sides of the Atlantic. It was a stock tune as much for post-war Canadian Brownies as it was for British and American schoolchildren. One of the latter (from 1960s Nebraska) recalls 'quite clearly having sung it in music classes when I was very young ("music classes" in the early grades consisted mostly of sitting in a circle and singing)'.[21]

The song is still an engrained part of Australian popular culture and more recently became the centre of controversy that seems out of keeping with its quaint and dated innocence. In 2010 the rock band Men at Work were sued for breach of copyright for their use of a flute line (that drew on the Kookaburra song) in their 1980s hit single 'Down Under'. Larrikin Music, the owner of copyright in the kingfisher-inspired tune, claimed a substantial percentage of the band's recent profits.[22]

The real kookaburra's kingship of the bush is founded on more than mere merriness and vocal talent. It is a formidable predator and regularly catches and kill lizards and snakes,

some of the latter up to 1 m (3.3 ft) in length. The proportion of reptiles in the bird's diet may have been exaggerated, but it is certainly substantial (35 per cent) and these serpent-killing services encouraged colonists to spread kookaburras to other parts of Australia. However, the species also regularly takes nestlings of small birds and while this has been lamented, particularly in Tasmania, where the species was introduced in *c.*1905, it seems an accepted part of the bird's overall personality elsewhere in Australia. 'They do it with such humour!' was a defence offered, when I asked several Queensland women about the species' predation of songbirds. Yet not everyone is quite as sanguine:

> We've seen a kookaburra swallowing a native Bush Rat whole and another time one grabbed a juvenile **Forest Kingfisher** *Todiramphus macleayii* in front of a group of Japanese guests. They came running into the reception absolutely mortified asking us to stop it but we tried to explain this was a natural occurrence and there was nothing we could do to stop it.[23]

A standard practice when a kookaburra catches dangerous or highly mobile prey – a behaviour found in kingfishers generally – is to beat the potential food item vigorously sideways on a branch in order to immobilise it. Variations on this theme have been recorded:

> We had a cabin on the Yarra River in East Warburton [Victoria] and whenever we had a barbecue the kookaburra would swoop down and take a sausage off the hot coals of the barbecue. It would then take it up to the roof of the shack and then whack it hard on the roof before eating it.[24]

> We had a similar experience in the Conondale Range west of Queensland's Sunshine Coast. Several kookaburras were perching around the camping area watching a group of us cook up breakfast on the barbecue and only swooped down when the sausages were cooked. In fact they swooped as one guy picked up one on his fork and stole it from in front of his face! I think this behaviour is quite common around camping and picnic areas.[25]

In 2010 a kookaburra in a Sydney park ate so many sausages it weighed 565 g (20 oz), almost 40 per cent heavier than a normal adult bird, and was unable to fly. 'Mama Cass', as the female kookaburra became known (after the voluminous singer in the 1960s pop band, The Mamas & the Papas), was taken into custody and put on a diet.[26]

The Laughing Kookaburra is now a much-loved symbol of all things Australian.

319

Motmot family *Momotidae*

This family's ten species are birds of exceptional colour and shape, and are restricted to the Neotropics, with the highest diversity in Central America. Honduras has seven of the ten and more than any other country. In neighbouring Nicaragua the **Turquoise-browed Motmot** *Eumomota superciliosa* is the national bird.

Motmots are medium-sized birds of about 37 cm (14.6 in), with long dark bills, black facial masks and body colours dominated by deep rich greens or blues above and rusty tones below. Although they are primarily inhabitants of forest, some species, such as the Turquoise-browed Motmot, survive well in secondary growth and even areas that have been largely cleared for cultivation. The equally magnificent **Rufous Motmot** *Baryphthengus martii* will occasionally come to feed in domestic gardens in Panama (see also Tanager family, page 525).

The strange name is thought to derive from an original Nahuatl word (the language of the Mexica or Aztecs) that was onomatopoeic of one species' deep and rather owl-like hooting notes. The most likely candidate is the **Blue-crowned Motmot** *Momotus momota*, which occurs from northern Argentina to Mexico. Its local name in what is now British Guiana – *houtou* – is similarly suggestive of the call, and the French name for this same species contains a double echo of the voice – *Motmot houtouc*.

When accounts of the Blue-crowned Motmot first reached Europe in 1651, via the writings of the Spanish naturalist Francisco Hernández (in his *Historia Avium Novae Hispaniae: A History of the Birds of New Spain*), they were treated with deep scepticism. In his own book, the British ornithologist John Ray placed the 'momot' (as he called it) in a separate appendix that dealt with 'Such Birds as we suspect for fabulous'. The issue arousing suspicion was explained as follows (with Ray's comments on Hernández's work in square brackets):

> What is rare and extraordinary in this Bird is, that it hath in its Tail one quil longer than the rest, and which is feathered only at the end [This is, I dare say, more strange than true: For the Tails of all Birds I ever yet saw have their feathers growing by pairs, that is, two of a sort, on each side one,] and that so beautiful a Bird should be of no use, but for its feathers.[1]

Ray may have doubted Hernández's account but it was indubitably correct and it highlighted the most striking detail of motmot plumage. All but one of the family (the **Tody Motmot** *Hylomanes momotula*) have extremely long tails and in most species they account for half the birds' entire length. In addition to this, several species, including the Rufous, Blue-crowned and Turquoise-browed Motmots, also possess a pair of spoon-shaped racket tips or spatulae at the end of their tails.

Even when these birds are perched the whole rear end seems to be in constant motion, flicking laterally or vigorously up and down. In Brazil the **Rufous-capped Motmot** *Baryphthengus ruficapillus* is known as the 'pendulum-bird', *passáro-péndulo*, for its endlessly wagging appendage. In the Yucatán Peninsula the local name *pájaro reloj* ('clock bird') for Turquoise-browed Motmot honours the same characteristic.[2] The racket tips probably enhance the tail's function as an emotional indicator, but one key impact on the human observer is to increase the impression of aerial panache. When motmots fly the racket-tipped tail trails behind like a vast streamer and, among birdwatchers, motmots are some of the most sought-after species in Central and South America.

Controversy came to centre on exactly how the birds acquired these spoon-shaped features. Early naturalists suggested that the tail, as Charles Waterton put it, 'undergoes the same operation as our hair in a barber's shop'. Using its bill, the motmot trimmed down the central plumes to leave merely a pair of naked quills with just their feathered tips.[3] However, subsequent examination of the birds has shown that the vanes are especially weak on the middle portions of these plumes and the appearance of deliberate self-beautification is merely the bird preening away naturally delicate parts, or those bits simply falling off under normal wear and tear.[4]

When medieval Europeans were first told about the spatulate tail tips on the Blue-crowned Motmot, they thought they were being hoodwinked.

It was not only Western naturalists who felt the need to account for these strange features. In the Mato Grosso of central Brazil, the Pareci people explained their own possession of fire with a story about the magnificently flame-coloured Rufous Motmot. The bird carried its precious gift to their ancestors, the embers nestled at the end of that fabulous, smouldering tail.[5]

It is intriguing to see how birds and their vocalisations, in addition to acting as a motif for a natural environment, can come to stand as an emblem for an entire regional culture (see also Symbolic Turkeys, page 42). While travelling in the Yucatán region of Mexico, the great American artist and naturalist Louis Agassiz Fuertes (1874–1927) reflected upon this mysterious process in the context of the motmot. 'Most of the natives have sound-names for Motmots,' he wrote, 'and the Maya Indians of Yucatan call the brilliant little *Eumomota*

"Toh", and, as an appreciation of the interest, he has come to nest and roost familiarly in the age-long deserted ruins of their former glory.'

Indeed, these mysterious, gentle, shy, little birds came to me, at least, to be the living symbol of this great lost magnificence; for the present-day Mayas know naught of the art and history of their great forefathers, whose temples and beautiful buildings are now in utter oblivion and disuse, except as the shelters and dwellings of little 'Toh', the Motmot, and his soft *hoot* is the only sound that ever issues from their carved portals.[6]

Even today, Turquoise-browed Motmots (the *Toh* of the Maya people) can be seen in the vicinity of the Sacred Cenote, the vast natural well from which the grandest of all Mayan ruins in the Yucatán, Chichén Itzá, takes its name.

Bee-eater family *Meropidae*

There are 26 species of bee-eater spread across the tropical Old World, with an outlying singleton that reaches as far south as southern Australia (**Rainbow Bee-eater** *Merops ornatus*). In the other hemisphere another representative (**European Bee-eater** *Merops apiaster*) pushes the family's northernmost limits into France and Russia, breeding in areas roughly equivalent to the latitudes of Paris and Moscow respectively.

While it is assumed that bee-eaters first arose in Asia, where there are nine species today, their main centre of distribution and diversity is undoubtedly Africa. Sixteen of the family occur nowhere else. As many as 1 million European Bee-eaters spread to breed across 40 countries in a swathe of Eurasia from Kazakhstan west to the Atlantic coast. Yet even this vast flock returns en masse in winter and presses down into Africa like a rainbow inside a small box.

Every spring about a million European Bee-eaters bring a dash of tropical Africa to a vast swathe of Eurasia.

The species also has a resident breeding population in the southernmost part of that continent.

Bee-eaters are often to be found in the same kind of open savannah or tree-studded farmland habitats as the rollers (see page 312), and they also share with the latter family a dual reputation for physical beauty and exceptional abilities in flight. Their speciality is to seize insects in mid-air, the birds sometimes describing crazy snaking lines as they pursue their invisible prey. Just as impressive is a capacity to spot the 1–2 cm (0.4–0.8 in) insects. European Bee-eaters are thought to be able to identify bees, possibly sexing them, at 100 m (328 ft) range.[1]

Bees of all types are an important component of the bee-eater diet, but they are by no means their exclusive prey. Some specialise in ants (**White-throated Bee-eater** *Merops albicollis* of central Africa) or dragon- and damselflies (**Blue-cheeked Bee-eater** *Merops persicus* and **Olive Bee-eater** *Merops superciliosus* from south Asia and central Africa respectively) and all tend to take insects across a broad spectrum, even sometimes catching fish. However, it is their love of honeybees – the distribution of the whole bee-eater family, in fact, broadly overlaps with the original world range of honeybees, before beekeeping was discovered – that brought the birds to earliest attention.

The ancient Greeks knew them well and Aristotle showed extraordinary insight into aspects of the European Bee-eater's behaviour. He knew, for instance, that they nested at the end of tunnels that the birds excavate for up to 2 m (6.6 ft) into loose earth or sandy banks. He also got the clutch size exactly right (he said six to seven eggs, which is cited as the average in the scientific literature).[2] However, what seems most extraordinary was Aristotle's passing on of received wisdom that bee-eater adults, while breeding, were fed and cared for by their own offspring.[3]

Ornithologists have since discovered that a number of bee-eaters, notably the **White-fronted Bee-eater** *Merops bullockoides* and **Red-throated Bee-eater** *Merops bullocki* of Africa, are assisted in their breeding cycles by one to five young helpers. Almost two-thirds of breeding pairs among the first species and a fifth of pairs in the second receive this assistance.[4] While it is a little-studied phenomenon in the European Bee-eater, it is estimated that 20 per cent of breeding pairs receive similar extra-parental help from younger birds.[5] Modern audiences are often staggered by the level of ornithological misunderstanding in the ancient world (see, for example, Kingfisher family, page 316) but this Aristotelian statement is testament to the remarkable accuracy of some of their observations.

It seems rather unusual that while the Greeks were completely familiar with the birds' bee-devouring habits, their name – *Merops* – for the European species had no connection to the diet. It was a reference to the beautifully soft murmuring voice.[6] Yet Aristotle was well aware of the bird's pest status and said that beekeepers routinely killed them.[7] Similarly the Roman poet Virgil, in book four of his pastoral poem *The Georgics*, advocated that his apiarist discourage not only bee-eaters (he called them *Meropes*) but also swallows and lizards.[8]

A single bee-eater can eat 225 bee-sized insects a day, and just ten pairs could potentially account for 126,000 bees in a month.[9] Small wonder that bee-eaters are routine victims of apiarists today and, at one time, people even used to eat the birds as food. In southern Spain it was common practice to flood bee-eaters out of their nest holes and then snare them in nets as they escaped.[10] In Egypt an old name for them was *Melinoorghi*, 'the bees' enemy', and while this has lapsed with time, the antagonism of modern Egyptian beekeepers has not.[11]

The response of commercial honey producers may be easy to understand but so too is a deep, wide and ancient appreciation of bee-eaters. They are birds of great beauty and have long been held in human affection. For the ancient Egyptians bee-eaters were said to be birds of magical virtue (although they actually appear little in Egyptian art). In medical papyrus dating to the second millennium BC there are prescriptions recommending bee-eater fat as an ointment to stop flies biting. While one can at least recognise the rationale that might have led to this remedy it is more difficult to understand how a female patient, suffering from an unspecified feminine complaint, might benefit from having her eyes fumigated with bee-eater shanks. Perhaps the birds vaunted eyesight was already a thing of legend.[12]

The birds also enjoyed exalted status in the Sanskrit texts of early Hinduism. In flight bee-eaters have slender tapering wings with fine tails that can be rendered even longer and finer by the possession of central tail pins. The overall flight shape was taken to resemble a bow, and the sharp aim of the bird while chasing insects was seen as arrow-like. Together these led to connections with archery – an ancient Sanskrit name for the bee-eater was 'Vishnu's bow' – the birds being dedicated to deities associated with marksmanship.[13]

Another interesting Hindu association was the notional punishment meted out to scandalmongers. Since they spread bitter words with their tongues, the human slanderer was said to be reincarnated as a bee-eater in the next life. They would then suffer a fate assumed to befall the bird itself: namely to be stung upon its tongue. Early Hindu sages had clearly failed to notice that bee-eaters routinely take their sting-bearing prey to a perch and beat it repeatedly until the poison sac is removed. The birds may even be largely immune to bee venom.[14]

Modern lovers of bee-eaters may have uncoupled the birds from religious sentiment, but we have lost none of our deep feeling for them. The Rainbow Bee-eater of Australia (often known simply as the 'rainbow bird') is widely valued today as a bright-hued herald of spring. The European Bee-eater is routinely identified as the continent's 'most brilliantly coloured bird'.[15] Many of the species have gentle and pleasing calls that are difficult to transliterate, but approximate to softly rolled strings of Rs. Since bee-eaters are invariably colonial breeders, their nest sites are enveloped in these gloriously soothing calls. They create a soundscape that seems all of a piece with heat, stillness and the scent of wild herbs.

In species such as the exquisitely coloured **Southern Carmine Bee-eater** *Merops nubicoides* or **Northern Carmine Bee-eater** *Merops nubicus* of Africa there can be anything up to 1,000 nest holes at a single riverbank or earth mound. These crimson-splashed sites are places of immense colour and vibrancy, but the birds' love for feeding in the vicinity of bush fires (a common management tool among cattle-herding communities) engenders another kind of aesthetic experience. These scenarios involve a quintessentially African blend of flaming heat, dazzling beauty, a hint of danger and the maddening sting of grass-fire smoke.

Yet perhaps the ultimate bee-eater spectacle occurs in the context of nest colonies created by the **Rosy Bee-eater** *Merops malimbicus* in west Africa. They are described as one of 'the seven wonders of the bird world'.[16] As many as 23,000 pairs can be present at some of these super-colonies, which are located in sand bars on great rivers during the dry season, where the substrate is riddled with their burrows. Above the honeycombed riverbed waft great clouds of aerial birds, whose shocking-pink underparts flare intermittently as they sway and twist in flight. Such a vision is nothing short of astonishing.

Hoopoe family *Upupidae*

This beautiful dove-sized bird is found widely across most of Africa and vast areas of Eurasia, from Portugal to China. Gill and Wright divide the birds' various populations into three, according specific status to the sub-Saharan African birds (*Upupa africana*) and to the Madagascan birds (*Upupa marginata*), but I have chosen to retain it as a single taxon, **Eurasian Hoopoe** *Upupa epops*.

The unique combination of cinnamon-pink body, tall crest and long decurved bill, which are visible as the bird waddles across the ground probing incessantly, make it familiar to almost all of its human neighbours. Yet in flight the geometric black-and-white patterns across the upperparts and the slow-motion eloquence of its leisured butterfly action render the hoopoe unmistakable.

A common denominator across most of the bird's range is our fixation with its soft, curiously ventriloquial song and call, which resemble the mellow sounds produced by blowing into the neck of a bottle. Many names for the species, whether in the Pashto-speaking area near Kabul (*poppoo*), or across the Arab world (*hud-hud*), or among the

In 2008 Israelis elected the hoopoe as their national bird.

in any genuine aspect of behaviour or lifestyle. The hoopoe also demonstrates extremely well how one looks in vain in bird folklore for consistency or logic. A bird that is reviled in one story, is cherished as god-like in the next; it can have important medicinal status for one culture, yet be taboo to eat it for the neighbours.

HOOPOE MYTHS

Some of the European associations have their origins in what is indubitably among the darkest of all Greek myths. If now largely forgotten by modern ornithology, the story is extremely old and even Homer in the eighth century BC alluded to it in *The Odyssey* (XIX:518). It recounts the affairs of Tereus, King of Thrace, who, while married to Procne, falls madly in love with her sister, Philomela. The impassioned Tereus rapes the latter while disposing of his wife, confining her to slave quarters and silencing her by cutting out her tongue.

In order to let Philomela know what has transpired, the now mute Procne weaves into a robe an account of her fate and sends it secretly to her sister. Once liberated, Procne then kills her own son, Itys, and serves him up as dinner for Tereus. The unwitting cannibal eventually discovers how he has been punished and pursues both Philomela and Procne with an axe, but before he can add to the catalogue of slaughter, the gods turn them all into birds. Philomela becomes a nightingale and Procne a swallow, while Tereus is transformed into a hoopoe.[1] (There are various renderings of this story and in the well-known version by the Roman poet Ovid – in his *Metamorphoses* – Philomela is imprisoned and has her tongue cut out, and then weaves the garment that informs her sister, Procne, of her fate.)

Quite what psychological truth this terrible myth is intended to dramatise – other than the obvious, dreadful consequences of lust and sexual violence – is difficult to pinpoint. What is striking is the way that the humans' transformation into birds just before the point of even deeper tragedy is an element found in many bird-centred myths. To give just one example, among the stories of the Yahgan people of Tierra del Fuego in southernmost Chile, there is a tale of incest between a brother and sister. The boy attempts to lure the girl into the woods, promising her a rich crop of edible red berries as reward. They are then transformed into Magellanic Woodpeckers after their own illicit coupling. In these two tales, which are widely separated both in geography and cultural context, this same metamorphosis seems a way of dramatising the abnormality of the human behaviour. Death and release of their souls in bird form is, in both cases, a way of resolving tragedy but without all of its attendant misery.

What is equally striking is how the birds that feature in the stories continue to bear witness in real life to the underlying moral in their respective tales. In the case of the South American story, the Yahgan ascribed the red heads of Magellanic Woodpeckers to contact with the red berries in the myth. Similarly, genuine hoopoes were said to invoke the story of Tereus, because when the birds called they were assumed (in Greek) to be saying *pou-pou*. The vocalisation translates as 'where, where?' – Tereus' despairing cry as he searched for his wife and lover. Perhaps it is this perpetual link between the details of the story and our own experiences that is the main function of such tales. In both contexts, the

With its long curved beak, pied and salmon-pink plumage and soft pooping call notes, the hoopoe must be one of the most easily recognised of all the Old World birds.

Xhosa of South Africa (*ubhobhoyi*) or in Europe (*poup* in Portuguese and 'hoopoe' in English), are onomatopoeic. Even the often desiccated traditions of scientific Latin cannot avoid reproducing a version of this wonderfully resonant sound: both parts of the name, *Upupa epops*, and even the family name, *Upupidae*, carry an echo of the real call.

The French version is intriguing for the way it illuminates how words are coined and then later gain fresh associations. Their name for the bird is *huppe*, which is clearly onomatopoeic. However, it acquired a secondary sense of a 'crest' (or 'crested': *huppé*); a reference to the hoopoe's extraordinary headgear. The same word was then subsequently applied to other birds with that feature (e.g. Northern Lapwing: *Vanneau huppé*).

One wonders if it is the unique quality of the bird's sound, or perhaps the regal shape of that glorious crown, which helps to explain why hoopoes were once so steeped in ancient folklore. This is especially the case across its Muslim territories (and most Islamic nations fall within the species' range). These beliefs have a diminishing role in contemporary attitudes towards the hoopoe, and have no influence upon Western observers, but they are still hugely fascinating.

They demonstrate the complex cultural journeys undertaken over the centuries by some birds. They illuminate how a wild species can become freighted with complex ideas, often without many of them being rooted

myths' respective audiences were made mindful at each fresh acquaintance with the living bird of the fundamental moral truths embedded in the associated story. Thus, our random encounters with birds (the hoopoe or the woodpeckers) are imbued with cultural significance and ethical instruction.[2]

Another important strand of hoopoe lore draws on its status as a bird of powerful medicine and general virtue. Some of this tradition dates back at least to the ancient Egyptians. The hoopoe was a hieroglyph (denoting the phonetic value 'db') and its image featured regularly in Egyptian wall paintings or relief carvings.[3] Yet it was also an ingredient used in medicine and hoopoes are mentioned in a manuscript known as the Demotic Magical Papyrus of London and Leiden, dating to the second or third century AD. The document was found at Thebes (in Egypt) and includes magico-medicinal cures and spells. Hoopoe blood was recommended for use in prescriptions that were smeared on the patient's eyes to inspire visions.

These early usages of its body parts slowly expanded over the centuries until the hoopoe became a virtual pharmacopoeia by itself. An older Arabic name for the bird translated simply as 'the doctor' and it is still reputed to be used as medicine by the Hausa people of west Africa.[4] Even one short section, derived from a late-medieval medical text known as the Syriac Book of Medicine, gives a flavour of the hoopoe's broad-spectrum application.

> The left pinion is good for the man who is in thrall to his wife; remove one section of the bird and set it in oil, and let the man drink it, and he shall be free. Tie up the right shoulder in a piece of new rag, and hang it up over a woman who is ill in her body, and she shall have relief. Steep its tongue in rose-water for five days, and tie it up in buffalo skin, and hold it in thy hand, and the dogs will not bark at thee. Dry its skull, and macerate it in oil, and rub it on any part of the body thou wishest, and it will destroy the hair . . . Having salted the heart of this bird with Indian Salt, tie it in a lion's skin, and give it to a woman whose child will not come forth from her. Let her grasp it in her left hand, and her child will descend from her womb straightway.[5]

What seems to have cemented the bird's long-standing reputation as a virtuous creature, among Jews and Muslims alike, and perhaps even guaranteed its enduring magico-medicinal value – hoopoe skins were sold as medicine in Egyptian markets as recently as the 1980s and their dried skins placed over a child's room as a good luck charm – are its connections to King Solomon.[6] It is still known in parts of Afghanistan as *Suleimanai murg*, 'Solomon's bird'.[7]

There are two very striking stories that have ongoing ramifications. One tells of how the hoopoe was able to open its sealed nest chamber with a herb that magically cleft the stone in two. The hoopoe's special powers, which were often transferred in later Christian stories to the woodpecker (see page 270), were placed at Solomon's disposal as he built the Temple of Jerusalem. It enabled the king to undertake the construction without disobeying God's edict that it should take place without the use of iron tools. As a contributor notes: 'The name for the Eurasian Hoopoe in Aramaic (an ancient language of the Middle East) is *Nagar-tura*, meaning 'the stone-cutter'!'[8]

The hoopoe simply used its stone-cutting magic on

Solomon's behalf and the name given to this plant – in Hebrew accounts it is often described as a kind of worm – was *Shamir*. Some authorities link *Shamir* with a genuine cultivar from Asia, the sesame plant (known in Hebrew as *shumshma*). The notion of a magical stone-cleaving herb is perhaps best known to modern Western audiences through its subsequent appearance in the story of 'Ali Baba and the Forty Thieves' in the *Arabian Nights*. The secret incantation used to gain access to the robbers' cave is 'Open Sesame'.[9]

King Solomon also appears in the Qur'an (*Surah An-Naml*, v. 17–45), where there is a story of how the hoopoe acted as an important messenger between him and his bride-to-be, the Queen of Sheba. The tale became the subsequent basis for much more elaborate and positive cultural representations of the hoopoe in Islamic literature. Perhaps the most famous and exalted of these is the bird's appearance in a poem by the Persian Farid ud-Din Attar (little is known with certainty about Attar – meaning 'the perfumer' – but he was born about AD 1145 and died around AD 1220). Entitled *Mantiq Ut-Tair* and widely regarded as Attar's masterpiece, the poem is known in English as *The Conference of the Birds*. Like much Persian poetry, it has a religious theme as a flock of 30 birds, guided by the hoopoe, sets out to achieve union with the divine spirit, the great bird-like godhead referred to in the translated poem as the *Simurgh*.

As they discuss their quest, each bird in turn – sparrow, nightingale, parrot, partridge, peacock, etc. – expresses its

This painted cover to Farid ud-Din Attar's *The Conference of the Birds* is one example of the exalted cultural place that the hoopoe holds among Muslims.

individual thoughts and fears. Each is then answered by the hoopoe, which also recounts moral fables that illuminate the initial remarks of the other species. The entire poem draws upon a finely crafted pun, for *Simurgh* is a metaphor for God, while si *murgh* can mean '30 birds', the number that actually complete the hoopoe-led journey. Attar's verse deploys in magnificent form that ancient and universal imagery which identifies the human soul as a bird in flight. The hoopoe announces at one point:

> When the Simurgh manifested himself outside the veil, radiant as the sun, he produced thousands of shadows on earth. When he cast his glance on these shadows there appeared birds in great numbers. The different types of birds that are seen in the world are thus only the shadow of the Simurgh. Know then, O ignorant ones, that when you understand this you will understand exactly your relation to the Simurgh. [10]

This is the primary lesson imparted both to the birds in the tale and to the wider audience for Attar's great poem: that the divine we seek is already within us from the start. We are but fragments – scattered bird-like shadows – of God's all-embracing wholeness.

According to Islamic tradition the Prophet Muhammad forbade Muslims to kill hoopoes, but there is still dispute about whether their flesh is permitted or not. Here, finally, the bird's ancient folkloric status coincides with aspects of the species' genuine behaviour. The reason that its flesh was controversial for Muslims, and categorically proscribed for Jews and Christians alike, is the hoopoe's well-known tendency to foul its own nest.

One explanation for why the birds are such conspicuous neighbours to many human communities is their love of breeding in the many crevices created by domestic brickwork, sometimes in the midst of towns or busy villages. Hoopoes are somehow able to squeeze into the tiniest crannies and the nest cavity eventually becomes cramped, dirty and very smelly. (It is the use of such rock-bound nesting situations, incidentally, that presumably explains some of the myth of the *Shamir*, the hoopoe's secret stone-cutting herb.) The young birds have a genuine defence mechanism against predators that involves hissing snake-like and squirting malodorous droplets from their enlarged oil glands. The highly noxious stink has been likened to rotten meat and bird ringers apparently 'hate handling hoopoes because they squirt large amounts of smelly bird shit'. [11]

The ancient Greeks embellished these genuine aspects of hoopoe natural history by suggesting that the birds deliberately harvested human excreta to smear around the brood chamber. [12] The Romans even honoured the hoopoe by making it the patron saint of manuring. [13] However, one highly beneficial aspect of this behaviour was that hoopoes were officially banished as unclean from the dining tables of many human communities.

There were inevitably exceptions. In parts of southern Europe and among the Christian communities in Turkish-controlled Constantinople (Istanbul), the bird was said to have been a delicacy. [14] Yet the reverse attitude was more frequent. Hoopoes were to be avoided and are specifically mentioned in the Old Testament (Leviticus 11, and Deuteronomy 14) as birds that were unfit for human consumption, along with the vulture, the owl and the crow. A rather bizarre and persistent error of translation that confused the hoopoe with another species of high crest, rounded wings and slow-flapping flight – the Northern Lapwing – meant that it was this latter species named in the *King James* version of the Bible. However, it is correctly given as the hoopoe in *The New English Bible*.

What is striking is that these Old Testament lessons in hygiene seem to have had little bearing on modern Israelis when they came to the selection of their national bird in 2008. The event achieved huge media coverage and featured ten candidates, including Eurasian Hoopoe, Graceful Prinia and Palestine Sunbird (see also pages 429 and 482). Regardless of the scatological details in its private life, the hoopoe eventually emerged triumphant. One would like to imagine that its election as the chief avian totem offers the possibility of fresh cultural meanings to add to the hoopoe's long history of association. Could it become a token of reconciliation between the two great traditions in that small country – Islam and Judaism?

One of the competition organisers suggests that the hoopoe (known in Hebrew as *duchifat*) won 1.1 million votes not only because of the simple pleasures many derive from the bird's exquisite patterns and that gloriously emollient bottle-blown song of early spring. Another factor was its many historical connections, including references in the Qur'an and the bird's role in building the Temple of Jerusalem. [15] Amir Balaban, however, a co-originator of the project, whose own choice was the White-spectacled Bulbul, suspects that there were far more prosaic reasons for the election. The hoopoe won, he writes, 'because Israelis prefer blonds!' [16]

Hornbill family *Bucerotidae*

Hornbills are remarkable creatures. Some of the larger examples, such as the **Great Hornbill** *Buceros bicornis* of the south Asian mainland and Sumatra, are 1 m (3.3 ft) in length and are among the biggest birds in the forest. Almost all the family have disproportionately massive and decurved bills, often featuring a protruding casque atop the upper mandible, while their voices are loud and raucous, rising in some species to discordant screams ('between the protestations of a . . . chicken seized by the cook and the squeals of a three-quarters grown pup receiving punishment'). [1] Their heads, if observed clearly, sport long,

rather feminine eyelashes, but these are often combined with loose spiky 'Mohican' crown feathers, bare swollen wattles or pouches and wrinkled facial skin, all of which lend them an indefinable aura of prehistoric comedy.

When hornbills fly, however, the broad wings of the big species unleash a woodwind music that is both extraordinary and unforgettable. I can vividly recall a moment in Korup Forest in central Cameroon. Sealed off completely by the dense canopy from any sight of the **Black-casqued Wattled Hornbill** *Ceratogymna atrata* flying overhead, I could follow their progress by the noise. The wingbeats

sounded like someone pounding solemnly upon a huge medieval wooden door. Alfred Russel Wallace suggested that the thrum of some species in flight could be heard 1 mile (1.6 km) away. If they gather in large numbers, then the volume can be 'deafening'. A flock of 120 **Knobbed Hornbill** *Aceros cassidix* in Sulawesi, Indonesia, suddenly bursting out of a vast strangler fig, were said to recall 'an international airport' as 'jet planes take off'.[2] A regional name for the Great Hornbill in southern India is *malamorakki*, 'mountain shaking'.[3]

There are 50 species divided more or less equally between Africa (23) and Asia (27), with one of the latter, the **Blyth's Hornbill** *Rhyticeros plicatus*, extending the family's range into the western Pacific as far as the Solomon Islands. The birds are almost all large to very large fruit-eating inhabitants of dense forest, although the **African Grey Hornbill** *Tockus nasutus* and **Indian Grey Hornbill** *Ocyceros birostris* buck most of these family trends in their respective regions. They measure just 50 cm (19.7 in) or less. They are also wide-ranging inhabitants of open thorn woodland and even parks and gardens. Along with Africa's equally widespread **Red-billed Hornbill** *Tockus erythrorhynchus*, **Southern Yellow-billed Hornbill** *Tockus leucomelas* and **Northern Yellow-billed Hornbill** *Tockus flavirostris*, they are the species most likely to be seen by Western observers. Several of them will routinely enter safari campsites in countries like Kenya, Tanzania and South Africa, where they become remarkably tame, fossicking in the dust for leftover food scraps.

If encounters with hornbills are, for most Westerners, the preserve of a well-travelled minority, then many more of us will have made the family's acquaintance in the cartoon character from the massively popular musical and Disney film *The Lion King* (1994). Named Zazu (which may have been based on an African name for the Greater Honeyguide, *Sazu*), he is a slightly pompous royal attendant, who advises and chaperones the young lion king, Simba. His plumage is vaguely suggestive of a Northern Yellow-billed Hornbill, but the feature found on a real bird that truly qualifies Zazu

for cartoon stardom is the outsized banana beak with all its inherent humour.[4]

Early European observers, however, were often less amused by the hornbill's vast appendage than they were outraged. The Comte de Buffon, for instance, the great eighteenth-century French naturalist, thought it a cruel injustice by nature that hindered the birds from finding food. A century later the British cleric Bishop Stanley was even more uncharitable, referring to their 'seemingly deformed and monstrous bills'.[5] Even John Ray, usually immune to these prejudices, said that the bird 'hath a foul look'.[6] These judgements say little about hornbills, but a great deal about Europeans' innate sense of historical superiority, and about their restricted notions of how nature 'should' be and the 'norms' it should adhere to, which the extravagance of tropical life somehow violated.

THE SYMBOLIC AND CULTURAL VALUE OF HORNBILLS IN AFRICA AND ASIA

The hornbills' immediate human neighbours in their tropical homelands were usually more impressed, even if only with the birds' flavour. They have long been valued as a wonderful source of flesh ('superior to any fowl or pheasant').[7] In fact they are now threatened in parts of west Africa by the international trade in bushmeat. The birds in some ways lend themselves to easy capture.

One remarkable aspect of their breeding cycle is the way the female hornbill immures herself to brood the eggs within a tree hole, sometimes for several months, sealing up the entrance with mud until it is no more than a slit wide enough for beaks to pass in and out for feeding purposes; wide enough also that the female can maintain sanitary conditions by firing her jet of faeces clean out of the nest. During this incarceration, the females in many species undergo a full moult of their main wing and tail feathers. Finally both adults will break open the mud walls to enable the fledged young to emerge.

The hornbill breeding cycle depends upon intense cooperation between the adults. One male of the African

It is not difficult to see why the Great Hornbill has been held in such esteem by many of its human neighbours.

The distinctive bill of the Blyth's Hornbill is still widely worn for ceremonial purposes in New Guinea.

White-thighed Hornbill *Bycanistes albotibialis* was recorded to bring his partner 24,000 fruits during one such confinement.[8] The downside of these extraordinary arrangements is the vulnerability of the whole family unit to human hunters. In effect, the birds can be caught in traps of their own making, and they are taken not just for eating but also for a whole range of cultural purposes.

The sheer life force expressed by the hornbills' size, voice and the grandiose facial armoury of the larger species has made a strong impact on many communities. In west Africa they are birds of great power and their skins appear in markets from Togo to Cameroon, sometimes being traded internationally to meet demand in countries where they otherwise do not occur. Both the magnificent Black-casqued Wattled Hornbill and the **Yellow-casqued Wattled Hornbill** *Ceratogymna elata* are used in this way, and probably yield a double profit, the carcass going for bushmeat while the head is traded for magico-medicinal purposes.

The full spectrum of engagements with the family has been very little studied, but in Cameroon hornbills are used in traditional preparations for protection against witchcraft, the casque presumably being ground up and added to a wide variety of treatments.[9] In the Nigerian markets of Ibadan in 2011 the casques of both species named above were on sale at 2,500 naira each (£10: $15), which is a significant sum locally. The stallholder claimed that while supplies were decreasing, dead hornbills arrived weekly in the market and were included in preparations that brought success at work or in business, especially enhanced profitability.[10]

One dominant element emerging in many cultural contexts in Asia is the association of the birds with human masculinity. There is an undeniably phallic quality to the bird's horn beak. Occasionally the link could not be more direct. In Papua New Guinea some traditionally dressed men wear the actual beak of Blyth's Hornbill as a penis sheath: that striking protective tube which is placed round their member and is often made of hollowed gourd. A further Papuan expression of the same deep connections seems contained in the remarkable sculptures from the country's north-eastern Sepik region. These feature a hornbill-headed male figure whose elongated beak extends down into his own groin, so that the two organs are represented in a single appendage. Quite what these powerful wooden images signify is unclear, but some degree of gender or sexual connection is self-evident. (Indeed, one wonders if it was the submerged connotations suggested by the hornbill's beak that so offended the likes of Bishop Stanley?)

One recurrent theme in this male-oriented hornbill symbolism is the association of the birds with martial virility. Sometimes the link is entirely practical. In parts of Papua New Guinea the sharp lower mandibles of Blyth's Hornbills were used as spear points.[11] However, a more symbolic appropriation of the birds' vigour occurs in Nagaland, the state in north-east India that was once dominated by hill-dwelling communities known as the Naga. The people have long since abandoned their headhunting practice, but at one time they were hugely feared by their neighbours for this terrifying form of tribal warfare. Some of the most chilling images of their past depict bamboo display racks stacked high with row upon row of naked skulls taken from their victims.

A variety of animals, especially the wide-horned bovid called the 'mithan', a hybrid derived from the interbreeding of male gaur (a wild species of forest buffalo) and domestic cattle, were incorporated into Naga costume and ceremonial dress. Yet among the most important birds were – and, indeed, still are – Great Hornbills. In addition to the massive yellow bill and double-pronged casque, the Naga prize the birds' white tail plumes, which sport a broad subterminal black bar and measure anything up to 46 cm (18 in). They were once worn on people's heads at key ceremonies, rather like the eagle feathers beloved of Native Americans, and had

The Iban people of Borneo once used extraordinarily stylised carvings of Rhinoceros Hornbills in a form of symbolic warfare.

multiple meanings, but were centrally connected with high social status in both men and women.

Members of Naga families who hosted ceremonial feasts were entitled to wear hornbill feathers or headdresses. The daughter of a man offering one of his precious mithan bulls in sacrifice was similarly entitled to wear the ornaments. Yet the plumes were also integrally linked to the Naga practice of headhunting, the number of feathers often indicating the number of enemies slain during their raids. British colonial control eventually suppressed the tradition. Equally, increases in the Naga population, combined with pressures of excess hunting, have also reduced hornbill numbers and, while modern Naga ceremonies still feature serried lines of dancing youths or women, the long white 'plumes' sprayed above these performers are likely to be made from paper or other substitute materials.[12] Nevertheless, there are many magnificent photographs, often taken by early anthropologists and dating to the mid twentieth century, which have captured the ancient Naga engagement with the Great Hornbill.

Another place where hornbills were deeply connected to tribal warfare was on Borneo, the large south-east Asian island divided politically between Malaysia (Sarawak and Sabah), Indonesia (Kalimantan) and the independent state of Brunei. Borneo is home to eight hornbill species, including two of the most spectacular of the whole family, the **Helmeted Hornbill** *Rhinoplax vigil* (the state bird of Kalimantan) and **Rhinoceros Hornbill** *Buceros rhinoceros* (the state bird of Sarawak). Both were widely hunted and eaten, but the Rhinoceros Hornbill was invoked physically and symbolically in the context of headhunting. In a manner reminiscent of Naga practices, the bird's long white, black-banded tail feathers were worn in helmets and other regalia as an insignia of the warrior.

The birds were also deployed in the business of spiritual warfare. The Dayak, a dominant Bornean group, carved

exquisitely beautiful and elaborate wooden images of the bird as an invocation to one of their most important deities, Singalang Burong, the god of war. The hornbill effigy was endowed with magical powers and sent on ahead of the actual attack to wreak symbolic destruction on the enemy's camp. These carvings – some of them measuring as much as 2 m x 1 m (6.6 ft x 3.3 ft) and created in *plai*, a local wood of immense plasticity – are among the great bird artefacts of the region. They are famous not only for their vivid colour but also for their gloriously sweeping lines. The upward curl of the real horn on a Rhinceros Hornbill has become fantastically elaborate in the sculptures, to the point where the bird image is lost almost in the carvings' complexity of rococo detail and abstracted shapes.

When the sculpture was completed it became the centrepiece of elaborate rituals, during which it was anointed with sweet oils, sung to and plied with rice wine, until finally placed on the top of a ceremonial pole that could be 15.2 m (50 ft) high. The warlike Iban, a branch of the Dayak group, once ascribed their military dominance to the deployment of their special spirit hornbill.[13]

HELMETED HORNBILL IVORY

The Helmeted Hornbill, the largest of all the world's species on account of two extra-long central tail plumes, which Bornean warriors valued as a symbol of lethal prowess in battle, also yielded a hugely valuable kind of ivory. The casque on this species is a raised solid block of immensely hard material that is reputed as 'virtually imperishable'.[14] Of a rich warm yellow colour with an attractive red outer margin, this inherently rare substance takes a high polish and was carved into a wide range of decorative and practical items. In Borneo various tribes used the material particularly for ear ornaments, chest pendants and belt or sword toggles.

It was also traded as far as China at least from the fourteenth century (Ming Dynasty), where it was known as

The raised dense 'ivory' casque of the Helmeted Hornbill was once elaborately carved by Chinese craftsmen and considered more valuable than jade.

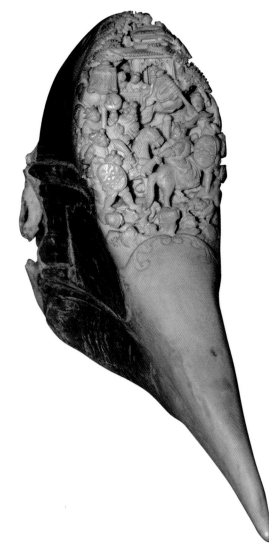

ho-ting and was more highly valued than jade. It was judged a perfect medium for delicate carving and sometimes the whole casque was used to depict exquisitely detailed court tableaux (while still attached to the bird's beak and desiccated head). As well as these relief scenes, the Chinese also used it for belt buckles and feather holders, both of which were signifiers of male rank in the Chinese court hierarchy. (The feathers themselves, often derived from peafowl or pheasant species – see also page 59 – were marks of distinction in exactly the same way as the pieces of carved hornbill ivory. It is intriguing to see how natural display in all kinds of birds, whether in the form of the hornbill casque or the pheasant plume, has so frequently been appropriated by humans, mainly men, as a means of conferring on themselves visual prowess and social distinction. One thinks ultimately, in this context, of the huge significance ascribed elsewhere to quetzal feathers or those of birds-of-paradise.)

HORNBILLS AND DEFORESTATION

Sadly many hornbill species are now in a state of potential crisis, partly because of losses inflicted by some of these exploitative activities, but largely as a result of deforestation. No fewer than 22 species, all but two of them in Asia, including the Rhinoceros and Helmeted Hornbills, are at some risk of extinction.[15] One of the fundamental issues is

the wholesale conversion of native tropical forests to palm oil plantations. They yield a product that is the second most consumed vegetable oil on Earth, used in almost everything, from biofuels in our cars to shampoo in the shower. The industry employs millions of people in a region where a third of the population (living within the range of Asia's hornbills) subsist below the poverty line. Average income per capita is often between $800–$1,000 (£490–£610) a year. It is a business undergoing massive expansion. In Indonesia and Malaysia, 6.77 million ha (16.7 million acres) were converted to palm oil plantations in the 12 years to 2002. Of this almost half involved clearing forests.[16]

This does not take into account the compound problems arising from weak governments, illegal logging and the ongoing expansion of Asia's human population; nor the question of deforestation and plantation development for timber and pulp, as well as a multitude of other land uses. The result is that ten Asian hornbills each have just 25,000 km^2 (9,650 miles^2) of their optimum habitat left; an area roughly equivalent to the US state of Massachusetts or the Italian island of Sardinia.[17]

Against this backdrop of loss, the multifarious cultural engagements with hornbills described above, which in some cases have been practised for thousands of years, start to look both destructive and unsustainable. How long can these magnificent birds be sold in the markets of Nigeria as remedies, in whose efficacy few non-Africans would have any faith? Yet these exploitative uses of hornbills are not solely to blame.

As Margaret Kinnaird and Timothy O'Brien argue in their book *The Ecology and Conservation of Asian Hornbills*, 'If we choose to continue altering our climate, felling our forests, and turning hornbills into fillets, medicines, and bangles, the outlook is bleak.'[18] To that catalogue of actions they might have added simple domestic Western behaviours, such as washing your hair or filling your tank with biofuel in downtown Derby or Detroit. The truth is hornbills are now on a frontline created by us all.

What is intriguing is the way that cultural expressions of a community's relationship with hornbills continue long after the birds themselves have been completely extirpated from a region. On the island of Java a contributor describes one such artefact:

In Bogor I bought a beautiful small wooden slit drum featuring a carving of Rhinoceros Hornbill. I was told it was for a street vendor. These merchants are very common in Indonesia and they have little hand-carts with two wheels and then a wooden stump at one end so that the cart balances when standing still. They use these for selling prepared ready-to-eat foods, such as *mie baso* (noodles with meatballs) or, sometimes, fresh fruits; but not fruits by the kilo – things like a slice of watermelon for eating now. Each vendor has his own sound so that people know when they are around, rather like an ice cream van in the UK. Some shout, and some bash a dish or a hollowed-out wooden drum like this one. I haven't seen such a lovely specimen in use but have seen quite decorative ones. The street vendors are known as *kaki lima* in Java, which means five legs made up from the two wheels, the stump and the two legs of the person pushing it. Unfortunately I don't know where it came from but it wasn't local to Bogor. Also I think it would be too heavy for one of the *kaki lima* vendors to lug around so I would think it must have been used for a more permanent food stall. [19]

A drum made in the image of a hornbill used by a street vendor may sound trivial in itself. But these small individual responses are the very fabric creating each distinct human culture.

In many ways the drum symbolises everything – all the cultural riches worldwide that derive from these birds – which we shall forfeit if we lose them. True, artefacts such as this will continue to be made and enjoyed for a time, perhaps for centuries, yet they will be like the light travelling from a star that has long since been extinguished. They will be without source and they will be lost finally in total darkness. And we will lose the hornbills and we will lose everything that hornbills have ever meant to us.

Ground Hornbill family *Bucorvidae*

These two turkey-sized black-bodied birds (adults weigh about 4 kg: 8.8 lb) are among the grandest of all the hornbills. In fact, with their booming voices that can be heard for up to 5 km (3 miles), their lurid bare-skin pouches of either cobalt blue or bright scarlet, and then their huge dark ox-horn-shaped beaks (yet also their wonderfully long feminine eyelashes that would be 'the envy of a mannequin'), the **Abyssinian Ground Hornbill** *Bucorvus abyssinicus* and **Southern Ground Hornbill** *Bucorvus leadbeateri* are among the most impressive of all Africa's birds.[1] They have now been accorded a family of their own because of subtle physiological distinctions from the other hornbills, but they differ further in their terrestrial lifestyles, while their tree-hole nest chambers lack the sealed mud walls used by their relatives.

Both ground hornbills were once widespread and common across larger areas of sub-Saharan Africa, but these ambling giants of the savannah – where they occur in close-knit family parties of two to five birds – are in retreat because of human impacts. The Southern Ground Hornbill has now been classified as at risk of extinction. Agricultural intensification and inadvertent poisoning are key issues, especially in countries like Zimbabwe and South Africa, where it has disappeared from 70 per cent of its historic range. However, both species were once spared many direct forms of persecution because of the powerful aura of magic that encircled them.

They are highly auspicious birds and are the focus of a complex folklore, in a way that is reminiscent of another singular African endemic, the Hamerkop (see page 137).

The Southern Ground Hornbill is one of the most magnificent of all Africa's birds.

In fact, some of the lore attaching to the two bird families overlaps, such as their shared connections with weather. Ground hornbill calls are said to foretell rain for many traditional communities (as is the sound of the Red-billed Hornbill for the Marakwet people of Kenya).[2] The Zulu call the Southern Ground Hornbill *Ingududu* (an onomatopoeic rendering of the rather dull-sounding boom), but it was also known historically as *Intaka Yemvula* ('the bird of rain') and to kill one was to risk potentially harmful downpours.

The death of a ground hornbill was also thought to have other damaging consequences. The Fingoes (a people closely related to the Zulu) believed that killing the bird could cause disease among their cattle. More widely the bird's presence in the village is taken as an ill omen, especially to the household on whose roof it might chance to rest.[3] Yet recent lore can also be rather dismissive of the birds, as revealed by a modern Zulu correspondent. Sakhamuzi Mhlongo writes:

> Among many Zulu village people a common form of insult for a person thought not to be very bright is to call them *Ingududu*, which is our name for the ground hornbill. The birds are always walking in small groups and since these are assumed to be of the same sex, they are thought also to be gay or lesbian. Among some Zulu communities, such as the Nyoni people, if one of the birds approaches you it is a cause of concern, because it's a sign that you too are gay![4]

Yet Southern Ground Hornbills can still be regarded as dangerously taboo – ideas of death and blood are especially associated with the crimson throat wattles – and in times of drought it was traditional practice to bring on the rains by catching one and ritually dispatching it in the river.[5] Today the formulae may have changed, but the resulting slaughter of ground hornbills has probably intensified. Ironically the species' increased scarcity is part of a downward synergy. Difficulty of supply has naturally raised the price for body parts. Yet the cost increase only seems to reinforce a belief among customers that the birds must have great magical potency, and so further fuels the international trade.

The birds are widely used in the southern African practices known as muti (while the heads of Abyssinian Ground Hornbills also turn up in west African fetish markets) and have various applications. Ground hornbills are thought to aid successful game hunts or quests for honey, the ash from their charred heads being smeared into lacerations on a witch doctor's face. He or she will then have the power to predict the best places to look.[6] Another usage involves the birds' powdered bone being rubbed into incisions on the shoulderblades to prevent the patient being struck by lightning.[7] In Ethiopia Abyssinian Ground Hornbills are hunted and their tail feathers plucked to use as insignia of (male) courage, either being worn by the distinguished individual or placed on the site of his grave.[8]

Ground hornbills are also susceptible to other forms of modern hazard. The presence of glass windows in domestic and civic buildings has triggered a strange kind of identity crisis for these highly territorial birds. They mistake their own reflections for a rival male and strike at it with their huge beaks, often smashing 'the glass to smithereens', which can lead to retribution by an irate homeowner. Farmers will sometimes shoot the entire family group. Various remedies have been tried over the years, including covering the windows with mud or paint, or protecting them with wire mesh, yet it remains a severe problem in some places.[9] Nineteen of 23 schools and a further 11 private farmsteads that surround a Zimbabwean reserve holding ground hornbills all had windows broken by the birds.[10] Those premises where the glass was subsequently painted over avoided the problem thereafter.

Another issue is that ground hornbills are predominantly carnivorous and formidable predators, and have been accused of taking chickens, even small goats. However, their larger prey are more likely to be scavenged carcasses, the birds even taking some of the leftovers at old lion kills. They will also steal animals originally caught by eagles or will kill the eagle itself. Yet ground hornbills can move freely among native herds of antelope and other ungulates without triggering alarm. Hunters, particularly in west Africa and southern Sudan, have learned to exploit this trust between the birds and the game in order to get closer to the latter. They fashion a rudimentary kind of disguise featuring the Abyssinian Ground Hornbills' distinctive head and beak, borne on a neck-like pole above their own heads. They then mimic the birds' foraging behaviour while stalking their true quarry.[11]

Toucan and Barbet family *Ramphastidae*

This bird tribe embraces two distinctive groups. The toucans are exclusively birds of Central and South America (40 species) with a northern limit in Mexico's Yucatán Peninsula. Barbets occur across much of the tropics with the majority in Africa (40 species) and south Asia (26 species), and a further 16 in South America.

Some authorities treat barbets and toucans as two separate families, but there are connections across all 122 species. They are predominantly frugivorous, they all nest in tree holes and they are almost all inhabitants either of tropical forest or woodland. Toucans are undoubtedly better known for their colours, but barbets are often birds of bright plumage and characterised by strong greens and frequent reds. It is intriguing to see how in Africa (barbets) and South America (toucans) the striking shapes and bright hues in both groups have lent themselves to the design of carved wooden and soapstone items for the tourist trade.

The toucans are in general the more familiar to a larger number of people. In fact, together with the large macaws, they are often considered *the* quintessential emblems of tropical rainforest. Typically, the beautiful **Keel-billed Toucan** *Ramphastos sulfuratus* is the national bird in Belize. The most striking feature on many species, of course, is that remarkable bill. 'Of all the many excesses in the bird world', wrote one admirer, 'none seem[s] quite so illogical as the large, colourful, and flamboyant beaks of toucans.'[1] This extraordinary appendage can be half the length of the bird's entire body and its massive size can lead to an impression of weight. Yet the beak is, in truth, exceedingly light and hollow but very strong, with internally crossing

rigid struts that act as an armature for the outer plate-like sheaths.

Exactly what purpose the toucan's bill serves is still debated and the question once led to some wild theorising by early naturalists. Even the great eighteenth-century German Alexander von Humboldt proposed that the birds used their downward-angled extremities to haul out passing fish while seated on the riverbank. In truth toucans are not piscivores and seldom even land on the ground.[2] They are arboreal fruit eaters (they can be occasional pests of orchards or planted crops). While the beak's extreme length enables toucans to reach berries otherwise difficult of access, it is thought that the colours and large size serve mainly as a sexual advertisement for breeding adults (immature birds have smaller, less colourful beaks) and as an intimidatory device to deter possible predators or to overawe rivals. The colour patterns on the bills of some species even give an impression of formidable jagged teeth, which enhances this threatening quality.[3]

Whatever function it may have for toucans, that huge beak suggested to humans all sorts of possibilities. It may, incidentally, have given us the birds' name. Walter Skeat, the Victorian philologist, suggested that 'toucan' was of Amerindian origin: the Guaraní word *tucā* derived from *ti* ('nose') and *cáng* ('bone') – signifying the bird with the bone nose.[4] (The compilers of the *Oxford English Dictionary*, however, reflect the more widespread view that 'toucan' is in some ways onomatopoeic of the birds' harsh calls.)

Toucan beaks were undoubtedly once used as a kind of medicine, presumably ground up into powder, and were also displayed whole as a body adornment. Lightweight and brightly patterned, they were often threaded on to elaborate chest ornaments, further coloured with clumps of scarlet and black toucan plumes. There is an extraordinary example from

the Jivaro people of eastern Peru in the Pitt Rivers Museum (Oxford, UK) that incorporates 19 toucans' upper mandibles and eight near-intact skins of either **Channel-billed Toucan** *Ramphastos (vitellinus) culminatus* or **White-throated Toucan** *Ramphastos (tucanus) cuvieri*, not to mention great lengths of hollow bird bone and the single skin of a Black-necked Red Cotinga. Another spectacular Jivaro ornament is held in the American Museum of Natural History (New York). This last item was draped over the wearer's back and comprises long sections of Oilbird bones from which depend bunches of toucan and cotinga feathers, finished with the glittering elytra of some huge iridescent beetles. Nor was it just Amerindian sensibilities that were moved by the colour in toucan plumage. The Brazilian emperors Pedro I (1798–1834) and Pedro II (1825–1891) wore a ceremonial cape that had been made from the breasts of Channel-billed Toucans.[5]

The birds' bright plumages and multicoloured bone noses almost certainly contributed to the family's long history in captivity. The indigenous inhabitants of Amazonia routinely keep them in their villages even today, partly for the high quality of their flesh, but also as attractive and entertaining trophies. In the early colonial period, Europeans caught the habit and it became a custom for wealthy individuals to acquire exotic creatures like toucans for their private zoos. Sometimes this was out of genuine scientific curiosity, but often it was no more than an early expression of conspicuous consumption.

In turn these captive toucans ended up in the works of European artists, where they served as quirky symbols of tropicality and the manifold novelties of Mother Nature. A classic example is Jan Brueghel's early-seventeenth-century painting *The Garden of Eden* where, in a landscape of pastoral tranquillity reminiscent of northern Europe, a toucan of unclear identity shares a perch with a Greater Bird-of-

The bird was shown with a pint pot perched on its gloriously golden beak. It cemented an impression of these birds as homely, humorous, fun-loving creatures, which owners of real pet toucans readily endorse – 'a tame bird likes nothing more than a gentle caress and an expression of affection'.[6] Yet there is a darker side to the tradition of keeping toucans in captivity, because many die in transit to their lives of solitary incarceration. There is also a less homely side to the birds themselves. In the wild they can be formidable predators of other birds and their nestlings. Walter Bates, the nineteenth-century British naturalist, kept one during his time in the Amazon and described how it devoured everything the human household ate:

> beef, turtle, fish, farinha, fruit, and was a constant attendant at our table . . . His appetite was most ravenous, and his powers of digestion quite wonderful. He got to know the meal hours to a nicety, and we found it very difficult . . . to keep him away from the dining-room . . . We tried to shut him out by enclosing him in the backyard, which was separated by a high fence from the street on which our front door opened, but he used to climb the fence and hop round by a long circuit to the dining-room, making his appearance with the greatest punctuality as the meal was placed on the table.[7]

Robin Restall, who kept a Toco Toucan at his Madrid home in Spain during the 1970s, adds the following details:

> It happily ate all sorts of fruit, and we very soon discovered how a toucan's digestive system works. As you know, fruit is a lot easier to digest and process than, say, meat . . . and the bird ate little and often. It seems as if the pipe from bill to the other end is always full, because no sooner is a strawberry swallowed, than a squirt of processed fruit is ejected from the other end. And that's when one appreciates the drawback of an all-wire cage. The hall wall became a mural of modern art!
>
> It was a charming and obviously intelligent creature and would gently take food from one's fingers, including mealworms and grasshoppers. But it was equally obviously not a house pet. So I wrote to the curator of birds/head keeper at the Zoological Society of London to ask if he'd like it. Within a week, I had crated the bird and entrusted it to British Airways. I also placed a Calandra Lark in a small box inside the crate as the zoo hadn't had one for decades and John was delighted to receive that as well – or would have been. Within an hour I had a phone call from Barajas airport saying there had been an accident with the toucan. I raced back and found the toucan had smashed the lark's travel box open, and torn the lark to shreds, eating all but the primaries![8]

BARBETS

The barbets, whose name derives from the coarse hairs – the rictal bristles – prominent around the birds' beaks, might be visually less striking and altogether more culturally unobtrusive than toucans, but they do have rather wonderful voices. This is especially true of some smaller species, such as the brightly coloured south Asian **Coppersmith Barbet** *Megalaima haemacephala*. The name of this rotund

The links between Irish stout and the Toco Toucan may not be instantly apparent, but the bird was part of Guinness advertisements for decades.

Paradise (exclusively from New Guinea), while below them a Jackass Penguin (from the southern Atlantic) exchanges glances with a Fallow Deer (from Europe).

These early representations of toucans, stripped of genuine context or any natural-historical veracity, have given rise to a long tradition of almost surreal imagery. Most famous in northern Europe was the enduring link made by advertisements in the 1930s and 1940s with Guinness. This black beer with its delicious creamy white head was then little more than a local stout ale, but it has since become a global brand and almost a sacred symbol of all things Irish. The advertisements that helped launch Guinness on its way to international fame deployed images of the **Toco Toucan** *Ramphastos toco*, which is the largest of its family. The bird's simple colours echoed the graphic black-and-white nature of the drink itself, but otherwise there were no authentic connections. These, however, were quickly added by the playful art of the copywriter. One advert featured a happy jingle that ran:

> Toucans in their nests agree
> Guinness is good for you
> Try some today and see
> What one or toucan do

sparrow-sized bird of Indian woodlands, villages and inner-city gardens gives a clue to its call.

Rhythmic, metallic and also strangely ventriloquial, it has been likened to the sound of the time-signal pips on All India Radio or, in Pakistan, to the exhaust of single-stroke engines in tubewells or village flour mills.[9] Yet the bird was named for the call's resemblance to the *tuk tuk* hammering of a busy metal worker. One remarkable aspect of the voice is its intensification as the summer temperatures rise. An average of 90 notes a minute is typical, but it can increase to 120 per minute when the bird is in full flow (sudden rainstorms apparently silence them instantly). Sometimes the noise can seem to continue for hours on end and while it has inspired charges of monotony, the coppersmith's unrelenting and largely subconscious impact can eventually triumph over our affections.

> The Coppersmith Barbet and the Common Hawk-Cuckoo (Brain-fever bird) are birds that are still mostly heard rather than seen. The *took took* sound still reverberates through the green patches of the city all summer. We had an 'Ashoka tree' (*Saraca asoca*) in our Calcutta garden where the Coppersmith Barbet used to frequent with the mynas, starlings and crows. For me, along with the peacock, it's the most beautiful common bird here.[10]

> Across the entire span of my birding life, its earthy, two-note call has kept me connected with the heartbeat of the Earth. I roll down the window of my car at a traffic signal and, distinctly, above all the din that *Homo sapiens* can conjure, the urgent two-note pulsing call of the barbet, the timekeeper of my buzzing world, floats through the air. For me, the coppersmith is a top-class bird. [11]

In Africa a very similar vocal effect is created by a suite of nine finch-sized barbets all known as tinkerbirds (and at one time simply as 'tinker', 'anvil-bird' and even 'Johnny Blacksmith').[12] They are often residents in wooded habitats in villages or towns, where they are creatures of the treetops and difficult to spot. Yet their relentless percussive calls can become, rather like those of Coppersmith Barbets in India, a perpetual part of African village life. Somehow the heat and the light and the ventriloquial tinkerbird sounds partake of one another to create an indefinable but enveloping sensory atmosphere.

To the francophone people of west Africa the **Yellow-fronted Tinkerbird** *Pogoniulus chrysoconus* (and possibly also the similar **Yellow-rumped Tinkerbird** *Pogoniulus bilineatus*) is a creature of auspicious power. Known as *le musicien*, in honour of its rhythmic *ponk-ponk-ponk* sound, the bird is believed by the Betamaribe (or Ditamari) people of northern Benin never to come to ground and to drink only drops of water (represented by the monotonous 'dripping' notes) caught directly from the creator in the skies.[13]

However, the bird itself is caught (probably in its tree-hole nest) and then offered for sale in the fetish markets of Benin and maybe in other parts of its wide sub-Saharan range. Prior to performance, especially at cultural events or important celebrations, musicians, dancers and other entertainers buy the dried skins of *le musicien*. These are either cooked and eaten or ground up into powder, especially the bird's tongue, to be added to food, drink or to soap (and used in a ritual bath or shower). All of these forms of consumption are thought to lead to an enhanced performance by the human musician. In the late 1990s it was one of the most valuable trade items in the fetish markets and each skin was priced at CFA 5,000 (£5: $8), which is a very significant sum for the Beninois. At that time, skilled tradesmen earned a daily wage of CFA 2,000.[14]

Honeyguide family *Indicatoridae*

These small drab birds are famous almost worldwide for their habit of guiding human honey hunters to bees' nests. Yet the family is remarkable for other reasons. There are 17 species in total, with two in Asia and the remaining 15 exclusively in sub-Saharan Africa. All are brood parasites in the manner of some cuckoos, with honeyguides specialising in hosts that are tree-hole nesting, such as woodpeckers and barbets. A further familial eccentricity is a collective habit of eating wax (known as cerophagy), a substance indigestible to all other birds and, indeed, most other living organisms. Yet it is highly nutritious, yielding seven times more calories than honey. One curious problem flowing from the birds' diet only arose with the advent of Christians in the honeyguides' realm. From the sixteenth century onwards, African clerics complained that honeyguides entered their churches and ate the candles.[1]

It is the relationship of the **Greater Honeyguide** *Indicator indicator* (and reportedly also the **Scaly-throated Honeyguide** *Indicator variegatus*, although proof is lacking) with human seekers of wild bees' nests that has given the family its greatest cultural celebrity. This bird has a distinctive chattering call (its Zulu names have acquired the secondary sense of a scolding wife), a slowly

undulating flight and bright white outer tail feathers, all of which it deploys in an attention-grabbing display as prelude to any shared bee-hunting foray.[2] The bird's favoured partners are human, but it may also cooperate with the large African mustelid the Ratel, sometimes known as the honey badger (the folklore associating the two is strong, but scientific proof of the bird guiding Ratels is very scant and possibly non-existent).[3]

Once a collaborator has been attracted, the bird flies in stages towards the bees' nest, moving 5–15 m (16–49 ft) in front of its partners. As the location of the nest draws close the bird makes shorter and shorter flights, until eventually it circles the nest area and falls silent, simply awaiting the partner's raid upon the bee colony. Their breaking open of the nest is accompanied by the insertion of a smouldering brand, whose smoke serves to stupefy and calm the angry bees. The nest finally yields rewards for both parties, the humans obtaining the precious stores of sweetness, while the honeyguide takes both the wax comb and the larvae it contains. Ironically, and despite the family's name, the honey is almost entirely ignored by the birds.

This remarkable relationship, which probably dates back thousands of years, is still surrounded by a rich body of lore.

A Kenyan environmentalist, Hussein Isack, has studied interactions between traditional Boran honey hunters and Greater Honeyguides (which they call *Simpirre-Damma*, 'honey bird') and has concluded that the men are three times more efficient at finding nests when they receive avian assistance than they are without it. To lure in the honeyguide, the Boran, like other African tribes, advertise their presence to it by blowing special whistles and banging loudly on trees or creating fire and smoke.

In many ways the mutualism between human and bird is total because, while each seeks out the other to find and access a bee colony, once it is broken open the humans take from it that which the bird largely does not want – namely the honeycomb. Yet there is often a conscious element of reciprocity observed by some hunters, because they deliberately leave a portion of comb as an offering for the bird's services. (However, not all do. Hussein Isack describes how the Boran hunters withhold any gift. They believe that the bird wants the bee products in order to get pregnant. Once it has them, it will no longer guide. By withholding these, the Boran assume the bird will continue to help them find fresh nests. As Isack also points out: 'the bird does not need any reward. There are always plenty of comb pieces that fall around the excavated bees' nest. And after the honey collectors are gone, the birds will enter the hole and feed on the combs.')[4]

THE SYMBOLISM OF HONEY HUNTING AND HONEYGUIDE INTERACTIONS

Aside from the actual physical interactions between Greater Honeyguides and African honey hunters, which are extraordinary and fascinating, there are several secondary cultural elements that are worth exploring. One is the simple sense of awe that this collaboration has inspired in a much wider modern audience. As one commentator noted:

> It would be difficult to find in all nature a more astonishing relationship . . . We are used to seeing pets that will beg for food or pester their master . . . But where among the creatures of the wild do we see an animal who has repeatedly been described as taking the initiative in coaxing its human neighbors into making a journey to an otherwise unprocurable source of food?[5]

Photographs and film footage of the interactions between bird and man have been intermittently aired to Western audiences since the 1950s. For hundreds of years the interactions have also been a staple of books of African travel, as well as of the literature of the modern tourist industry (in-flight magazines, etc.). One can detect in these constant repetitions an increasing if latent symbolic importance. In an age assailed by human ravages of the natural world, this is a rare story of cooperation, of harmonious interconnection and, perhaps, even one of hope. Yet this wholly positive symbolism loses sight of one intrinsic facet.

We might like to bear theoretical witness to honeyguide–honey hunter quests, but not actually to participate ourselves. The enterprise requires the kind of courage that few non-Africans possess. For the bee opposing the bird-and-human teamwork has itself become a symbol for nature. Yet, in this instance, it is an emblem of nature's inimical and treacherous power. In the form released on to the American continents it is known not so much as the honey bee *Apis mellifera*

scutellata, but as the 'African killer bee'. Indeed its legendary aggression is the stuff of sensationalist journalism and of horror movies. Those robust and remarkable men who place its extracted honeycomb with all its thick, dark sweetness into their baskets must also withstand repeated stings from this formidable insect, which can occasionally kill both inexperienced honeyguides and honey-hunting Ratels.

HONEYGUIDES AND WESTERN WRITERS

Another intriguing secondary element in the honeyguide–honey hunter partnership concerns the moment that the humans take their fill of the bees' ambrosial foodstuff. The act of leaving wax comb as reward for the honeyguide has been draped with a complex moral mythology.

Some honey hunters themselves do it out of simple gratitude, but also, it is said, to ensure that the bird does not take revenge in future by leading honey gatherers to waiting lions, leopards or venomous snakes instead of to bees' nests.[6] In fact it was the supposed wealth of anecdote among indigenous Africans relating the bird's tendency to mislead people that inspired some nineteenth-century naturalists to doubt the possibility of a symbiotic relationship at all.[7]

The Scottish explorer David Livingstone was so exercised about the truth of this charge that he asked each of 114 African men in his entourage about their own experiences. He established that only one of them claimed to have been misled by the bird (he was led to an elephant). One striking revelation from Livingstone's inquiry is the former prevalence of the relationship between African people and honeyguides in the nineteenth century. All of them had joined at some time in bird-led forays for honey. Needless to say, Livingstone also concluded that honeyguides guided men not to dangerous predators, but to the bees' nests that they were seeking.[8]

However, a writer who came to a very different conclusion after investigating the tale of the unrewarded honeyguide was the South African novelist and travel writer Laurens van der Post (1906–1996). In the second half of last century, van der Post was treated almost as a prophet-like sage with answers for all human woes and consulted alike by British royalty and right-wing prime ministers. His central authorial theme was of world crisis derived from a damaging imbalance of reason and the unconscious in modern humankind. The male and female elements of our personalities, which he characterised as Europe and Africa, needed to find a fresh reconciliation. He has since been shown to be a fantasist on a grand scale, inflating the bare facts of his life story to the level of mythic adventure.[9]

Yet he was also deeply fascinated by honey and by honeyguide interactions with humans, writing of their symbolism on several occasions. He claimed that as a small infant his San nurse, Klara, had interpreted the Greater Honeyguide's advertising calls for him as meaning, 'Quick! Quick! Honey! Quick!'[10] Later he claimed to hear directly from San hunters the mythic tale of how honeyguides had once collaborated with people, only to find that the latter 'took most for themselves and left the least and the worst' for the bird. In revenge, the honeyguide induced its old friend the Ratel to track the men to their sleeping places and bite off their testicles. In this supposedly ancient African story, van der Post sensed that there resided 'the truth of a parable that has passed the test of time'. He also divined a deep cultural significance in the honey presumed to be the final prize for the Ratel and honeyguide alike. For 'in the first language of things,' he wrote, 'honey is the supreme symbol of wisdom, since wisdom is the sweetness of the strength that comes to the spirit dedicated to the union of warring elements'. What happened to the men who had their balls bitten off by a honey badger was 'an accurate description of what happens to the human spirit which uses one opposite to deny the other'. [11]

Alas for van der Post's thesis, there is, as we have seen, little proof that Greater Honeyguides actually lead Ratels to bees' nests. Worse still for his ethical conclusions based on honey is the fact that the honeyguide does not eat it. In some ways, worst of all for his credibility is the absence of any evidence that he had ever had a San nurse called Klara to make sense of the honeyguide's vocalisations. He was dishonest about the small things of life as well as its grander ideas. [12]

Sadly, for all of those who cherish the idea of birds and humans working in collaboration, the facility of shop-bought sugar is undermining the relationship between honeyguides and honey hunters. It has even been suggested that the behaviour will die out altogether. However, not all is lost yet. Hussein Isack has worked with Lemusii hunter-gather communities in Ngurnit in the Ndoto Mountains in northern Kenya.

This involved getting the young children to accompany honey hunters in the field and to learn how these adults locate bees' nests with and without honeyguides and experience how the bird helps the hunters save lots of time and energy by guiding them. Secondly, we are seeking to develop bee-product-based entrepreneurship to provide incentives to the honey hunters. We also established a 'young honey hunters club' in the local school. [13]

Woodpecker family *Picidae*

The world's largest woodpecker at 51 cm (20 in) is the giant serpentine **Great Slaty Woodpecker** *Mulleripicus pulverulentus* of south Asia (the magnificent but now extinct **Imperial Woodpecker** *Campephilus imperialis* of northern Mexico was even bigger at 57 cm: 22.4 in). Woodpeckers then run a size spectrum right down to the miniature **Bar-breasted Piculet** *Picumnus aurifrons* (7.5 cm: 3 in) of Amazonia, which is smaller than a wren. Yet almost all 220 species have a basic and instantly recognisable form – thickset bodies, large heads, long chisel-like beaks and strong feet with zygodactylous toes (two forward and two behind).

In all regions where they occur they have a special place in people's affections. In the West they are favoured recipients at bird tables and backyard feeders. Among indigenous peoples worldwide they were – and are still – the object of complex folkloric beliefs and myths. Some of this popularity is undoubtedly owing to the birds' graphic (and once magical) colours, which are often boldly finished with red and yellow details – crowns, crests, nuchal patches, facial masks and bright 'moustaches'. Our attention is also drawn by the dramatic manner of their movements: the broad, rounded wings and the arrow-straight line of their flight, completed in undulating bounds, as well as that mammalian way they hug the tree and clamber around the trunk in sudden awkward jerks, propped up on the stiff board of their tail feathers.

They have a collective range that reflects the distribution of forest and woodland. Although in southern Africa (**Ground Woodpecker** *Geocolaptes olivaceus*) and South America (**Campo Flicker** *Colaptes campestris*) there are family members that have dispensed with tree cover, woodpeckers are largely absent from extensive arid regions, such as the Sindo–Saharan belt across Africa and Asia. Nor are there any woodpeckers at all in Australia, New Zealand or, perhaps more surprising, in New Guinea and Madagascar. Africa (26 species) and Asia (43 species) hold just 13 and 20 per cent respectively of the total, and the family's true heartland is Latin America (103 species). Brazil

alone holds 46 species. This diversity decreases as one moves from the tropics; there are just 22 woodpeckers in the USA and Canada, but in Europe and North Africa the equivalent latitudes hold only 11 species.

The aspect of woodpeckers that has perhaps most captured our imaginations is their ability to break open and excavate standing timber. The word 'woodpecker' itself acknowledges the capacity, and in Spanish (Latin America) and French (west Africa) there are names that are strongly anthropomorphic. *Carpintero* and *charpentier* both mean 'carpenter'. Other west African versions have associations that are even more arresting. Among the people of northern Benin the birds are called 'coffin makers'. [1] In truth, woodpeckers are more frequently the makers of nurseries, because the tree cavities they hollow out are crucial nest sites for a suite of families, including ducks, falcons, pigeons, parrots, owls, swifts, toucans, barbets, cotingas, tyrant flycatchers, starlings, tits and corvids.

For humans some of this natural carpentry has been less welcome, especially in an age or in regions of the world where houses are made of timber. I can testify to the problem, having clear memories of the demolition work performed one dawn by a pair of **Scaly-bellied Woodpecker** *Picus squamatus* on the bedroom wall of our shingle-built hotel in Kashmir, India. A species found almost Europe-wide, the huge and powerful **Black Woodpecker** *Dryocopus martius*, measures up to 47 cm (18.5 in) and is among the largest in the world. Its capacity for timber damage is well established and in several Scandinavian countries the birds are shot if people's houses are at risk. [2]

In Britain one long-standing form of damage placed woodpeckers outside the law as early as 1566. The Tudor legislation was mainly targeted at species accused of stealing grain, but the authorities had reasons for adding the **European Green Woodpecker** *Picus viridis* to the list of the proscribed. In the mid sixteenth century many ecclesiastical structures were partly made of timber and church-going woodpeckers were blamed for drilling holes in wooden towers and roofs. In his classic study *Silent Fields*, the

This image of a Grey-headed Woodpecker expresses the curiously jerky, almost reptilian, character to the movements of many woodpeckers.

338

author Roger Lovegrove records parish payments made on woodpecker heads across southern England throughout the early modern period (killing them is now illegal). In some places the persecution was not without occasional cause: a church steeple in Kent was so full of holes it was said to resemble 'gruyere cheese', while the 800-year-old church at Ashampstead, Berkshire, had 130 cavities. In the same county the replacement of shingles on a church at Old Windsor cost £23,000 in 2003.[3]

Another favourite woodpecker activity is drilling electricity poles, sometimes until they are so weakened that they snap. A number of species are partial to these man-made structures, possibly lured in by the buzzing sounds produced by the electric current, which suggests to the birds the presence of wood-boring prey. In Europe, the **Great Spotted Woodpecker** *Dendrocopos major* and **Grey-headed Woodpecker** *Picus canus* are significant pests, while the **Syrian Woodpecker** *Dendrocopos syriacus* apparently has a penchant for irrigation pipes.[4] In North America the scourge of utility poles are the **Pileated Woodpecker** *Dryocopus pileatus* and **Red-headed Woodpecker** *Melanerpes erythrocephalus*, with the **Golden-fronted Woodpecker** *Melanerpes aurifrons* and **Ladder-backed Woodpecker** *Picoides scalaris* doing damage in the southern states. In California and Arizona a very specific kind of injury is inflicted by the **Acorn Woodpecker** *Melanerpes formicivorus*, which riddles the poles not in its search for insects, but as a storage place for sometimes thousands of acorns (some trees have 50,000 separate holes where the birds store their nuts).[5]

One wonders if the damage inflicted by the Acorn Woodpecker on human structures has in any way been compensated by the pleasures given during many decades of television appearances. For the species was said to be one source of inspiration for the celebrated cartoon character Woody Woodpecker, who enjoyed a screen life between 1940–1972. (He even has a star on the Hollywood Walk of Fame: one wonders if any other species of bird has ever been so honoured?) Legend has it that the creator, Walter Lantz, was so incensed by a woodpecker hammering on his wooden cabin during his Californian honeymoon he wanted to kill the beast. His bride, however, counselled a more creative response, and so was born the feisty yellow-footed, blue-bodied bird with the dashing red quiff and the unmistakable trademark five-note laugh. Although Woody's colours and shape owe almost everything to human invention – he even has a distinctly upturned beak rather similar to that other legend of the silver screen Daffy Duck – his actual call note is strikingly similar to a real Acorn Woodpecker. Indeed, the links between the fictional and real birds, while they may be mere coincidence, are noted in modern field guides, where the authors sometimes mention the Acorn Woodpecker's 'raucous "Woody Woodpecker" calls'.[6] In real life, Woody's signature sound ended up as no laughing matter: Lantz was sued by the actor who created it and the men eventually settled out of court.[7]

As well as drilling into wood, many woodpeckers perform a repeated rapping action with their bills that exploits the resonating effects of standing timber. The sound, which serves in lieu of song for breeding and territorial purposes, is produced by strike rates of 30–40 blows a second. In fact, the action is so forceful that woodpeckers have special

musculature in the head and neck to protect them from potential shock damage. It has a somewhat un-avian, even mechanical, quality that suggests similarities to the roll of drums or even the crash of thunder. Yet it is, in essence, unique to this bird family. The power, clarity and sudden drama of drumming has intrigued humans for millennia and the fact that the authors often possess vivid red heads further predisposed early societies to the notion that the sound had great psychological significance.

Almost universally woodpeckers have been birds of strong omen, and this was especially the case among the ancient Latins, who identified one of their deities, Mars, the god of war, with a woodpecker. The connection is still enshrined in modern nomenclature: the Black Woodpecker's specific name (*Dryocopus*) *martius* means 'Martian' or 'relating to Mars'. Another fragment of evidence suggesting woodpeckers' importance in classical times is the old name for a region of central Italy bordering the Adriatic Sea – Picenum (the Latin for woodpeckers was *picus*). Building upon such evidence, but also upon other scattered and more tenuous material, a number of early-twentieth-century folklorists – notably the British poet Robert Graves – elevated the ancient Latin lore associated with woodpeckers to the idea of a formal cult in which the birds were themselves venerated as a god.[8]

There is little evidence to support these more grandiose speculations but, nevertheless, for thousands of years

One of the family's largest members, the Black Woodpecker can occasionally cause serious damage to wooden houses and buildings.

The Acorn Woodpecker of the Americas is well known for its laughing, Woody Woodpecker-like calls and its intense industry, some birds storing away as many as 50,000 acorns.

woodpeckers were undoubtedly omens of storm and rainfall. The most likely link was with the birds' drumming and its evocation of thunder. What is striking is the near universality of such ideas. Among east African communities, such as the Maasai, woodpeckers are birds of high cultural importance, and can be even invoked as a curse on one's enemies. The calls are also taken as an omen of success, or for a journey, but equally as a herald of rain (there is dispute over which species is intended, but the most likely is the **Nubian Woodpecker** *Campethera nubica*, a bird found widely across east Africa).[9]

In Europe a similar folklore centred on the European Green Woodpecker. The loud ringing calls may even now in some remote rural areas be taken as a sign of rain, but in historical times the idea was firmly embedded in folk belief. The bird had French nicknames such as *pic de la pluie* ('rain-pecker') or *pleu-pleu* ('rain-rain'), which was equally an onomatopoeic rendering of the loud high laughing note of this species (technically called a 'yaffle'). In Britain there were parallel vernacular names, such as 'thunderbird' and 'rain-maker'. In the seventeenth century, the naturalist John Aubrey wrote, 'To this day the country people doe divine of raine by their . . . cry.'[10] Finally in northern Italy there was an old proverb: *Quand el picozz picozza / O che l'e vent, o che l'e gozza* ('when the woodpecker taps, here comes the wind or the rain').[11]

Traditional beliefs among Native Americans reflect a number of these core threads of association. One such was a link with rain and deluge. A key creation myth for the Chitimacha people, who live in modern-day Louisiana, held that the world was overtaken by flood, except for a human couple protected inside a clay pot. A Red-headed Woodpecker also escaped inundation by clinging to the sky, all except for its tail, which turned black in the waters (the tail is black in this species). The species was also connected to war by some tribes, including the Cherokee. As the biological historian Shepard Krech notes, it is the one woodpecker famous for its genuine pugnacity.

THE IVORY-BILLED WOODPECKER

Perhaps the species that made the largest impression on Native Americans was itself one of the largest of all woodpeckers. The **Ivory-billed Woodpecker** *Campephilus principalis*, which is now very probably extinct, was once found on Cuba and along the American Gulf Coast states from east Texas to Florida, and then north as far as Arkansas and the southern edges of Illinois and North Carolina. One of the intriguing aspects of the bird is how it held significance across so many centuries and for so many different communities (now, after it has disappeared, also far beyond North American shores). One speculation flowing from this is whether, in each context, those widely separated peoples were somehow responding to the same intrinsic magic in the bird?

Whatever the answer, it was indisputably singled out for special treatment among large sections of indigenous America. The archaeological evidence includes the discovery of the bird's body parts, including that remarkable ivory-coloured bill, at Native American sites in Georgia, West Virginia, Alabama, Ohio and Illinois; and even archaeological remains in Nebraska, Colorado and the western Great Lake region, the last three locations way beyond the species' historical range.[12] Mark Catesby, the great pioneer of North American natural history (1682–1749), provided eyewitness testimony of this wide-ranging interest in ivory-bills, when he wrote:

> The bills of these birds are much valued by the *Canada Indians*, who make coronets of them for their Princes and great warriors, by fixing them round a wreath, with their points outward. The *Northern Indians* having none of these Birds in their cold country, purchase them of the Southern people at the price of two, and sometimes three buck-skins a bill.[13]

In a later period, Alexander Wilson (1766–1813) suggested that those Native Americans who wore various parts of the bird on their person assumed that they too would acquire the power and virtue of the creature itself. He added that since 'the disposition and courage of the Ivory-billed Woodpecker are well known . . . no wonder they should attach great value to it'.[14]

Perhaps it is Wilson's own personal experience of ivory-bill courage that best demonstrates why so many were touched by this bird. Near Wilmington, North Carolina, Wilson winged an ivory-bill that he then intended to keep alive in captivity. Unfortunately the creature had other plans. Its repeated calls (like 'the violent crying of a young child; which terrified my horse') alarmed the good ladies of Wilmington, who turned to watch in horror as Wilson arrived in town with his screaming captive. When the naturalist finally got the wounded beast to his hotel bedroom and left temporarily, he returned to find it had already made a big advance in its escape plans and had hacked through the wall down to the weather-boards. In under an hour, Wilson reckoned, the bird would have finished its tunnel.

> I now tied a string round his leg, and, fastening it to the table, again left him . . . in search of suitable food for him. As I reascended the stairs, I heard him again hard at work, and on entering had the mortification to perceive that he had almost entirely ruined the mahogany table to which he was fastened, and on which he had wreaked his whole vengeance. While engaged in taking a drawing, he cut me severely in several places, and, on the whole, he displayed such a noble and unconquerable spirit, that I was frequently tempted to restore him to his native woods. He lived with me nearly three days, but refused all sustenance, and I witnessed his death with regret.[15]

Few descriptions have better revealed the bird's formidable spirit. Sadly many notable naturalists in the ensuing 150 years – Audubon, Robert Ridgway, William Brewster, Frank Chapman, William Hornaday – followed Wilson's personal approach. They lamented the loss of Ivory-billed Woodpecker as a species, but continued their own piecemeal slaughter of the birds. However, the killing that really placed the creature in jeopardy was more of a business transaction. After the American Civil War ended in 1865, the defeated South was economically prostrate, while the rapidly industrialising North bought up vast tracts of virgin swamp forest from Florida to Louisiana to convert to pulp and timber. One commentator calls the 'complete consumption of the vast cypress forests (and simultaneously the long-leaf forests in the uplands surrounding the cypress swamps)' in less than a century 'one of the greatest feats of resource gluttony in American history'.[16]

By the 1930s the woodpecker that Wilson had called 'the king or chief of his tribe' was in dire need of a secure refuge. Fearing the very worst for the species, the Audubon Society financed a young researcher from Cornell University called James Tanner to investigate the ecology of this imperilled bird. Beginning in 1937, Tanner based himself in an area of virgin bottomland forest in Louisiana called the Singer Tract, owned by the sewing machine company of the same famous name. Comprising 328 km² (127 miles²) of sweet gum, oak and ash, the Singer Tract was a glorious wilderness; a last refuge for cougars, wolves and bears, and the only place where Ivory-billed Woodpeckers could be studied in anything

like normal conditions (Tanner estimated a population of between one and seven pairs over the period 1933–9).[17] His doctoral thesis, eventually published in 1942, is the only detailed study of the bird based on field observations of a wild population.

Tanner argued that the species was dependent not only upon virgin bottomland forest, but it needed large supplies of recently killed mature trees. Its peculiar feeding strategy, which focused on wood-boring larvae of longhorn beetles concentrated just beneath the surface, was reflected by its distinctive bill shape, which had a laterally flattened, almost spatulate tip for chiselling off the outer bark.[18] Ivory-bills nomadically followed the temporary abundance of these beetle larvae, which would once have been triggered by periodic, large-scale storm or hurricane damage and by natural forest fires. In the early stages of tree decay, ivory-bills moved into these areas and thrived, but as the decayed timber became older, they abandoned it and moved on.[19]

Alongside Tanner's investigation of its ecology, he also undertook a one-man 72,000 km (45,000 mile) transect in search of all remaining survivors, criss-crossing eight states and focusing particularly in the Mississippi Delta region and the forested river basins of its main tributaries. The results of his odyssey were not encouraging. The only long-term viable

Mark Catesby illustrated the Ivory-billed Woodpecker in his eighteenth-century book on North American wildlife and noted how its bill was enormously valued by Native Americans.

sites with recent populations of Ivory-billed Woodpeckers were the Singer Tract in Louisiana, the Big Cypress and Apalachicola River Forests in Florida and the Santee Swamp in South Carolina. The only one of these where Tanner had personally seen them was the first.[20]

While Tanner with his Audubon and Cornell superiors made their devastating conclusions and recommendations for the future of the USA's most impressive and endangered woodpecker, the forces of commerce were plotting its actual fate. The owners of the Singer Tract, the Singer Corporation, refused to intervene with its principal lessee, the Chicago Mill and Lumber Company, and they in turn were deaf to the pleas of the conservationists and to the interventions of four state governors (of Louisiana, Arkansas, Mississippi and Tennessee).[21] Their emphatically negative response was then accompanied by the sound of giant trees crashing to the ground. By December 1941, they had logged out 30 per cent of the Singer Tract and two years later, when the conservationists renewed their request for a pause in logging operations, the company responded by quickening its pace, the work being done by German prisoners of war, who themselves expressed distaste at the waste and destruction.[22] In April 1944, an artist, Don Eckelberry, sent to paint the final survivors, is regarded as the last indisputable witness to an Ivory-billed Woodpecker in the USA. The Singer Tract was eventually bought for conservation, but only in 1980 when the species had been extinct in the area for almost 40 years.[23]

THE MODERN CONTROVERSY SURROUNDING IVORY-BILLED WOODPECKER

This was not the final scene in the ivory-bill's tragic drama. For another half-century there were slender hopes for the species' salvation centred on the relict population in the pine forests of eastern Cuba. As recently as 1985, Ivory-billed Woodpeckers were observed on a handful of occasions. Environmentalists argued that if logging and hunting (the species was eaten by locals, as it had once been eaten in mainland USA) ceased forthwith, there was a slim chance for the bird's survival. Sadly, logging and hunting continued in Castro's communist Cuba, although the bird's numbers were probably already too low to be sustainable. By the end of the millennium all hope was finally lost.

The fifty years after the felling of the Singer Tract was a limbo period on the American mainland, during which there were periodic instances of people claiming to have seen Ivory-billed Woodpecker somewhere across its extensive former range. None of the records was ever verified. The locations of several of the most widely reported included Florida (1950, 1955), Georgia (1958) and east Texas (1966), but for many years the most controversial was one made at the Atchafalaya Swamp in Louisiana, where the record appeared to be supported by two photographs. Unfortunately, when the pictures were exhibited at a meeting of the American Ornithologists' Union in 1971, by a man who had himself been president of that organisation, they were widely dismissed as fakes.

The incident set a pattern and context for subsequent claimed sightings. The record was either dismissed as a hoax, or the observers themselves refused to go public with their story, for fear of social humiliation and rejection. It

was into this fraught atmosphere that Tim Gallagher, editor of *Living Bird*, a magazine of the Cornell Laboratory of Ornithology, and his friend Bobby Harrison went in search of this increasingly mythical species in the bayous of eastern Arkansas at the Cache River National Wildlife Refuge. Following an associate's earlier tip-off and just as they were stopping for lunch on 27 February 2004, a large black-and-white woodpecker flew past them at about 24 m (80 ft) range, showing white all along the trailing edge of its long black wings.

This configuration of white on the flying bird is deeply significant because, while the only other North American species of comparable size and colour to the ivory-bill, the Pileated Woodpecker, has a large area of white on the middle and *front* edge only on the underwing, the ivory-bill was white on both the upper and lower surfaces and that white extended across much of the *rear* edge of the wing. On a Pileated Woodpecker, a species still common in that area, that same part of the hind wing would have been black.

That expanse of white was what made Gallagher and Harrison cry out in unison, 'Ivory-bill!' In a sense it was this same white patch that later inspired a paper published in 2005 in the journal *Science*, co-authored by no fewer than 17 people. Just three pages long, it carried an electrifying message in its title: 'Ivory-billed Woodpecker (*Campephilus principalis*) persists in continental North America.' Within a very short time it had given rise to what one commentator called 'the greatest debate in ornithological history'. If that remark contains an element of exaggeration of the kind that permits Americans to define their Major League Baseball competition as the 'World Series', then this much is indisputably true. The question of whether Ivory-billed Woodpeckers survive in mainland USA has, without any hint of overstatement, 'polarized the [American] birding community like perhaps no other event in our history'.[24] It is the world's biggest woodpecker drama and a constant staple for television and radio news reports, and has engaged a huge general audience way beyond the confines of natural history.

There were two reasons why this particular sighting, which was ostensibly just one in a long sequence, was distinct from its predecessors. The observations by Gallagher and Harrison were backed by the full prestige of the Cornell Laboratory of Ornithology, one of the country's leading bird organisations and the very institution that had overseen Tanner's work all those decades ago. The first author on the all-important *Science* paper of 2005 was the Cornell director, John Fitzpatrick. In effect, the claim had academia's formal stamp of approval. Yet what really seemed to add weight to the record was the fact that someone had finally obtained what nobody had achieved hitherto – corroborative photographic evidence. It was a digital sequence of a woodpecker, taken by David Luneau, one of the Cornell team whose work followed in the wake of the original Cache River sighting in February 2004.

Unfortunately this somewhat blurry, shaky, very brief footage of what was purported to be an Ivory-billed Woodpecker in flight became as mired in debate as the whole question of the species' survival. In a sense, it became the epicentre of the controversy. For those supporting its identity as an ivory-bill, it was proof positive for the original Gallagher and Harrison sighting. Unfortunately, for the sceptics it resolved nothing. Where one party saw a woodpecker with a white trailing edge to its *upperwing*, the others saw the white middle and leading edge to the *underwing*. In short, the first side argued that the film was of an Ivory-billed Woodpecker, while the second recognised it as a Pileated Woodpecker. The footage sent the debate spinning into a series of secondary channels about the flight style of ivory-bills, about bird flight in its entirety, about perspective and digital technologies. The original paper in *Science* was followed by a rebuttal in the same journal in 2006. A counter rebuttal came shortly after, but elicited a second challenge, propelling the controversy on and on, round and round, without resolution. One of the more unusual subsequent pieces of analysis looked at the statistical spread of belief in the continued existence of the ivory-bill, almost as if unanimity of convictions would somehow corroborate the species' genuine survival.

Nine years after the initial moment of revelation on the bayous of eastern Arkansas, the story of this remarkable bird and its possible sighting is as complex and divisive as ever. Yet this much is probably agreed by all parties. There has been a massive ongoing search for the species. There have been repeated and, in some cases, tantalising woodpecker records in northern Florida, Arkansas, Louisiana and elsewhere. Yet nobody has improved on the Luneau film footage as 'evidence' of the species' continued existence. The last sighting of the bird on mainland North America which is universally acknowledged, remains that made by Don Eckelberry at the Singer Tract in April 1944. Sixty-nine years later the necessary and universally accepted proof of the survival of Ivory-billed Woodpecker is still hoped for, but still missing.

Exactly why people should wish this wonderful woodpecker to have somehow persisted, against the odds, is easy enough to understand. One need only recall Wilson's remarkable story to appreciate this. The possibility of its complete extinction was a calamity, as Arthur Bent expressed it, 'to all Americans who have any pride in the natural resources of their country'.[25] His contemporary Arthur Allen wrote in the preface to James Tanner's original study:

> Where is the man who knowingly would stand by and watch a marvelous creation of nature – harmless to man's interests, and of no intrinsic commercial value – be forced into the vortex of extirpation without even raising his voice in protest? Surely no intelligent human being could be indifferent to the passing of the last Ivory-billed Woodpecker . . .[26]

The deeper and, in some ways, more compelling questions are as follows. Why has a belief in its survival in mainland USA, despite a lack of irrefutable evidence for more than three generations, remained so strongly rooted among North Americans? Why has this particular bird occasioned such deep emotional commitment by those who, like Gallagher and Harrison, are still self-confessed 'ivory-bill chasers' and have hunted after its elusive ghost for decades?[27] The answers are less about the intrinsic magic of the woodpecker and more about the dismal human circumstances of its passing.

When Arthur Allen asked of his readers, 'Surely no intelligent human being could be indifferent to the passing of the last Ivory-billed Woodpecker,' in truth, a precise and devastating rebuttal of that question had been made. The Chicago Mill and Lumber Company had given an answer by the early 1940s to all who wished to save the Singer Tract. Its unspoken riposte announced that felled timber and profits

from lumber were what really mattered. (Actually it may well have already been too late for the continental Ivory-billed Woodpecker even before the company took its miserable decision to fell the area. The bird had possibly passed the critical threshold of no return. Yet this more complex picture has now largely been obscured. What remains is the simple, unequivocal, mean-spirited gesture of a commercial organisation. When asked to play the role of the god-emperor on the issue of life or death, the Chicago Mill and Lumber Company had raised its fist with the thumb down.)

The other devastating element in the woodpecker's extinction was that it had not been an isolated event. Its passing came at the end of a sequence of birds succumbing, one by one, to the forces of development and profit. These included the Great Auk, the Passenger Pigeon (see pages 227 and 241), the Carolina Parakeet, the Eskimo Curlew (see page 210) and, to a lesser extent, (since it was only a race of the Greater Prairie Chicken), the Heath Hen. Unlike these other birds, the Ivory-billed Woodpecker was not

The Ivory-billed Woodpecker may have been extinct for decades but in 2005 it inspired the greatest debate in American ornithological history.

lost without anyone quite understanding the consequences of their actions until it was too late. By the 1940s the USA had enjoyed a policy of conserving wildlife in national parks for almost 70 years. The National Audubon Society was nearly 50 years old. So, when the Chicago Mill and Lumber Company chose profit before the woodpecker's survival it was a calculated dismissal of all that conservation history.

It was precisely this wilful denial of the Ivory-billed Woodpecker's importance by a section of American society that now exercises and remains at the heart of this story for the rest of the nation. It is surely why a modern searcher for the ivory-bill, when trying to articulate his sense of personal mission, writes:

> It was inconceivable to me that a nation as proud and as prosperous as ours could not show enough restraint to protect just a few sites for this jewel of Creation. Perhaps it is a personality trait of my own, but I spent way too much time dwelling on the sad story of this bird.[28]

It also seems as if the fate contrived for the bird by a commercial timber company has since become the responsibility of all who have inherited the consequences of its historic actions. Another modern witness to the story describes how, 'When the news broke about the Arkansas bird, I actually got goose bumps. I photocopied the article, scrawled "Nature Wins" in bold black letters across the top of it, and taped it to the door of my office.'[29] Is it this sense of collective responsibility that helps explain why, as the noted birder and writer Rick Wright observes, the near-instantaneous reaction of many of those who have claimed sightings of the woodpecker is not to scream in delight, but to break down and weep? Wright further recounts how a week after the Cornell University's announcement, a preacher in Philadelphia, giving an Ascension sermon, found hope in the possibility that 'if even the woodpecker can return we humans aren't so impossible after all'. In Ohio a Lutheran seminarian was similarly 'moved to find in the rediscovery "a sign that humanity's sin . . . is not yet final and complete"'. A third commentator described how the story illuminates the deepest human 'desires for the natural and the sacred within us'.[30]

The story of the Ivory-billed Woodpecker, which is sometimes referred to as the 'Lazarus bird' or the 'Grail bird', has acquired elements of a religious myth or parable, encompassing the notions of mortal sin but also of collective redemption through the bird's rediscovery. It is these centrally important human ideas that have come to infuse the ornithological story over the years, and which continue to enhance the drama and to enlarge its significance above and beyond the realms of ornithological study. In short the Ivory-billed Woodpecker is a symbol that speaks about the very heart of modern American society, its values and aspirations. These were ideas not lost to Arthur Allen, then director of the Cornell Laboratory, when he wrote in the 1940s:

> The American way of life is worth anything we have to pay to preserve it, and the Ivory-billed Woodpecker is one little guide post on our way of life, a reminder of that pioneering spirit that has made us what we are, a people rich in resourcefulness and powerful to accomplish what is right. The Ivory-bill is a product of the great force of evolution acting on American bird life in ages past, to produce in our southeastern United States the noblest woodpeckers of them all . . . Is it worth ten dollars to save it? Is it worth ten million dollars? It is worth whatever we must pay to preserve it before it is too late.[31]

The exact figure that has actually been spent since 2004 is impossible to quantify, but the frequently quoted sum is $27 million. Bearing in mind that the woodpecker's bottomland swamp forest is an enormously rich and important habitat, one could argue that the Ivory-billed Woodpecker, even if it were already lost, has served as an immensely positive symbol for conservation effort. Indeed the recent purchases in the areas of Arkansas where the sightings took place were the final fruits of 20-year-old acquisition policies. However, if one assumes that a primary goal of these conservation dollars was to secure this glorious bird, then it would be the largest sum spent anywhere in the world on any animal that was already extinct.

Together with several colleagues, the distinguished author David Sibley has argued that the deepest meaning to be drawn from this bird lies in viewing the Ivory-billed Woodpecker not so much as 'a symbol of failed environmental decisions in the past', but as a lesson for the present and future. They write:

> The unsustainable harvest that doomed the Ivory-billed last century continues in other habitats today . . . One of the best things we can do now is to learn from the Ivory-bill's history, and focus on saving habitat and reducing pressure on that habitat, so that other species won't share its fate.
>
> We need to accept the loss of the Ivory-billed Woodpecker in order to have the determination and clarity needed to tackle the pressing real-world challenges that are all too plentiful.[32]

New Zealand Wren family *Acanthisittidae*

This ancient family is endemic to New Zealand and has no relationship whatsoever to the widespread wren family of the northern hemisphere and the Americas (see page 448). Yet the New Zealand birds share the same basic form and personality. They are minuscule creatures, rounded and virtually tailless, with strong legs and feet that reflect a largely ground-dwelling lifestyle. They are lovers of dense vegetation, crevices and shadow, and seem almost rodent-like in their incessantly furtive manner. While two birds – the **Rifleman** *Acanthisitta chloris* (Maori name, *Titipounamu*) and **New Zealand Rockwren** *Xenicus gilviventris* – are still widespread and common, a third, the **Bushwren** *Xenicus longipes* (Maori name, *Matuhi*), has not been seen since 1972 and is probably extinct.[1]

To a fourth species, **Stephens Island Wren** *Xenicus lyalli*, attaches a melancholy tale even more affecting than that of its recently lost sibling. It was found on just one tiny islet in the Cook Strait, at the north-eastern tip of New Zealand's South Island, and was first described when a lighthouse keeper called David Lyall noted a cat returning to his quarters with a tiny flightless bird in its jaws. It proved to be a species unknown to humans (although it may once have been familiar to Maoris, they appear to have had no name for it). Unfortunately the customary formalities surrounding the announcement of its existence in December 1894 (at a London meeting of the British Ornithologists' Club) were marked by the bitter and jealous acrimony of the two 'men of science' (one in New Zealand and one in the UK,

respectively Walter Buller and Walter Rothschild) who vied for first place in the discovery.

Another aspect that rather ruined the celebrations was the increasing realisation that the Stephens Island Wren had almost immediately slipped into oblivion.[2] This had probably occurred by 1895 and had been caused by predation by feral cats. One curious anomaly is how such a flightless bird, which is now known to have occurred on the mainland and where it was probably eliminated by introduced rats, had ever found its way to its final island refuge. The theory is that it sailed the short distance on rafts of floating vegetation.[3]

Pitta family *Pittidae*

Although pittas are eaten and kept as cagebirds in some parts of Asia, such as the Philippines and Vietnam, they have very little wider cultural status, especially in Europe or the Americas. There is one notable exception, however. Among the community of globetrotting birdwatchers, pittas rank among the most sought-after creatures on the planet.

There are 33 species concentrated in the forested regions of Asia from the central Himalaya eastwards to Papua New Guinea, with just two in tropical Africa (**African Pitta** *Pitta angolensis* and **Green-breasted Pitta** *Pitta reichenowi*), three in Australia (**Red-bellied Pitta** *Pitta erythrogaster*, **Noisy Pitta** *Pitta versicolor* and **Rainbow Pitta** *Pitta iris*) and a single bird (**Black-faced Pitta** *Pitta anerythra*) found on Bougainville and the Solomon Islands in the south-west Pacific. However, the pitta capitals of the world are Sabah and Thailand with at least six species each.[1]

One explanation for their status as the birding world's

ultimate objects of desire is their blend of rare beauty, difficulty of access and numerical scarcity (14 species are now deemed at some risk of extinction). Their names alone – Rainbow, **Garnet Pitta** *Pitta granatina*, **Superb Pitta** *Pitta superba*, **Fairy Pitta** *Pitta nympha* and **Elegant Pitta** *Pitta elegans* – evoke the brilliant plumage details and also the exquisite colour combinations on many of them. Another factor in their fame could well be their shape. At times they can look almost spherical but they are always rounded, full-bellied birds (see also Thrush family, page 467), and an old alternative name was 'jewel thrush'. A third element in their exalted status must be, as the ultimate pitta devotee makes clear, connected to their impenetrable, ill lit and often vexing place on the forest floor (see also Tapaculo family, page 354).

Briton Chris Gooddie, in order to see all of the pittas in a single year (2009) – the first and, to date, only person ever to have done so – gave up his job; spent over £20,000

Members of this family such as the Noisy Pitta are among the most sought after of all the world's birds.

The colours on the Blue-winged Pitta of south-east Asia help to explain why birds in this family were sometimes known as 'jewel thrushes'.

($32,500); travelled 196,340 km (122,000 miles) by aeroplane, boat (paddle- and engine-powered), motorbike, taxi or on foot; and lost 13 kg (2 stone) in weight during his one-man mission.

Why did I become obsessed with pittas? At its root, my obsession is a part of that whole adolescent collecting 'thing': the search for the missing football card, the elusive Hungarian Magyar Posta first-day cover stamp that will complete the set. Not just any old stamp will do, though; the one you really want is the one no one else has. The value lies in exclusivity.

At a deeper level I think birdwatching is a sanitised form of hunting. At its heart, it is predatory, carnivorous, red in tooth and claw, and nowhere does this become more apparent than inside the rainforest. Within this uncivilised other world, perhaps the most hostile environment known to us, the greatest challenge of all is to stalk the shyest creatures on the forest floor. To see them before they see you; to make a clean kill. I've always thought that it's no coincidence that the verb applied to the act of taking a photograph is 'to shoot'. The rest of my mania is pure logic; the shyest and most beautiful birds on the rainforest floor? No contest; the pittas rule supreme.

I can remember my first – a Noisy Pitta on Mount Whitfield in Cairns, Australia, September 1995 – and can still feel the hairs on the back of my neck standing up when I heard its distant whistle, the adrenalin rush when it finally, hesitantly, bounced on to the trail behind me and stood there weighing me up, a riot of colour packed into a tiny frame. Only I had seen it. No one else was there to share the moment. I was smitten.[2]

To raise money for what was assumed then to be the most endangered of all, the **Gurney's Pitta** *Pitta gurneyi*, Gooddie ran the London Marathon twice, in 2001 and 2002, and raised £4,000 ($6,500) for a conservation project in Thailand. The extent to which other birdwatchers share at least some of this fixation is manifest in the disproportionate use of pitta images in advertisements for wildlife tour companies and on the covers of bird books (*A Field Guide to the Birds of Borneo* by Susan Myers and *Birds of South-East Asia* by Craig Robson).

The keeping of caged pittas is widely condemned by environmentalists and illegal in many countries. However, this lends an ironic twist to the rediscovery of Gurney's Pitta in 1986 (after a 60-year lack of wild sightings), because it was an American zoo professional who tipped off environmentalists after he had seen live Gurney's Pittas in a dealer's shop in Bangkok. This led eventually to the detection of Thailand's last wild birds.[3] Since that date it has happily transpired that the 20 pairs of the species found in that country are merely the tip of a much larger population (*c*.20,000 pairs) in neighbouring Myanmar. Nevertheless Gurney's Pitta remains vulnerable to the enormous and biologically devastating conversion of Asian rainforest to palm oil plantations (see also Hornbills and Deforestation, page 330).[4]

The electronic buzzing noise made by the male Club-winged Manakin is typical of the many quirky manakin displays that have captivated people for centuries.

Manakin family *Pipridae*

Flame-crested, Scarlet-horned, Red-capped, Golden-headed, White-bearded, Blue-rumped – even the English nomenclature for this intriguing family of 44 birds gives a broad clue to their striking appearance and character. Manakins are exclusively Latin American birds – just three species reach as far north as south Mexico – and most of them are inhabitants of humid South American rainforest.

The males' plumages are highly distinctive for their bright colours, but these are invariably arranged in discrete and often relatively small patches. The strongest hue is frequently confined to the tops of their crowns. The females, by contrast, are almost all dull green. Aside from this strong sexual dimorphism, a second common denominator is the manakins' smallness, a quality that seems emphasised by their rotund shapes, stubby bills and short legs. The biggest species are just 14 cm (5.5 in) and some, like the **Blue-rumped Manakin** *Lepidothrix isidorei* (8 cm: 3 in), are among the tiniest birds in Amazonia.

The family name is itself a reference to the birds' dimensions and is said to derive from an old Dutch word *manneken* (famously used for the seventeenth-century bronze sculpture called *Manneken Pis* – literally 'the little man peeing' – in Brussels).[1] This gave us the English word 'manikin', meaning a 'dwarf' or 'small man', but today it is more commonly spelled 'mannequin' and has come to be associated with a shop's dummy or model. However, a further connotation to the initial Dutch word was 'little bird' or 'pretty little thing' and *manneken* was apparently used until the eighteenth century in reference to other European birds.[2] Incidentally, the South American manakins should not be confused with African and Asian mannikins. The latter is

just an alternative spelling of the same word, but the birds themselves are small finch-like species in the Waxbill and Munia family (see page 492).

The Neotropical manakins may be small, but their behaviour has long been a cause of deep human interest. The Brazilian naturalist Helmut Sick thought the gloriously beautiful **Blue Manakin** *Chiroxiphia caudata* of southern Amazonia among the best-known species in his country and described how even colonists in the sixteenth century were captivated by its behaviour.[3] This interest centres on the bird's breeding rituals. Those bright colours are deployed by the males as part of their courtship behaviour, in which an arena or space is specially selected and even cleared of obstructive vegetation, and known today as a 'lek' (see also Grouse Display and Human Dance, page 50). This is occupied by competing cocks as they display to catch the attention of females.

Their performances can be as captivating as they are amusing. The **Western Striped Manakin** *Machaeropterus striolatus*, for example, which is found across north-western Amazonia and the Orinoco basin, swings upside down on his perch or rotates rapidly right round it, while making a buzzing insect-like noise.[4] In the Blue Manakin the display can involve several males performing at one time. If there are just two they rotate in a double act of constant Catherine-wheel-like motion, each bird jumping up, fluttering back and behind his male dance partner. However, if there are more than two – sometimes as many as six take part – then they line up in sequence on a branch, bodies quivering, feet tapping and their fiery-red caps raised. Each male moves along the line closer to the onlooking female, and when he is immediately adjacent, he leaps up and flutters at her, purring rhythmically, then leapfrogs back over his male competitors to take a place at the rear of the queue.[5]

South American nomenclature for these birds makes several references to the manakins' choreography. In Brazil the Blue Manakin is called *Dançador*, 'dancer', while an old name was said to be 'the Fandango bird', after its elaborate footwork.[6] The three members of the family that occur in Argentina, including Blue Manakin, are also known as *Bailarín*, 'dancer'.

Perhaps the weirdest of all the dance moves deployed belongs to the **Red-capped Manakin** *Pipra mentalis* of northern South and Central America. A witness in the 1940s described its cavorting like 'a ballet dancer on tip-toe'.[7] This barely does justice to both the strangeness and inherent humour of the display. Through a super-fast sequence of tiny, almost trembling and (to the human eye) invisible foot movements, the bird seems to glide back and forth along a horizontal branch as if the motion were not of its volition or doing.

More recently these dazzling manoeuvres have been compared to the most celebrated of all modern dance steps, the 'moonwalk' performed by the late Michael Jackson. As if this link were not strong enough, the Red-capped Manakin possesses saffron-coloured thighs – 'yellow pantaloons' according to one author – that have a touch of the Jacksonesque fashion sense.[8] The bird's display has been widely featured on television and on YouTube, where the link with Jackson's own electrifying performance has been further cemented by the footage of the bird's display being set to the scintillating rhinestone sound of Jackson's 1983 hit 'Billie Jean'. The bird now has a reflected fame as the 'Moonwalking Bird' or the 'Bird Michael Jackson'.

There is one last feature to manakin displays that reinforces their overall weirdness, because many of the sounds incorporated are actually instrumental rather than vocal. The wings have specially thickened shafts in the secondaries, while the primaries are curved or oddly shaped. In combination these enable manakins to produce strange rattles, thrums, snaps, pops or whip-cracking noises. The **Club-winged Manakin** *Machaeropterus deliciosus*, so named for its apparently misshapen flight feathers, can produce 'an unusual insectlike or "electronic" buzz preceded by two dry tipping sounds'.[9] Another of the family, the **White-bearded Manakin** *Manacus manacus*, has a Brazilian name (*Rendeira*) that makes reference to these mechanical notes. *Rendeira* means 'lacemaker' and draws on the strange clicking noise that the male makes during his dance display. This sound was said to resemble the rattling of a bobbin during lacemaking.[10] More modern interpretations note the 'firecrackerlike snaps' and the sound's distinct similarity to the rude gesture known as a raspberry or a 'bronx cheer'.[11]

Cotinga family *Cotingidae*

These 98 species comprise one of the great New World bird families. They are famous for their beauty, including two species that are entirely deep blue and purple (**Blue Cotinga** *Cotinga nattererii* and **Spangled Cotinga** *Cotinga cayana*) as well as two of the very few pure-white land birds on Earth (**White Bellbird** *Procnias albus* and **Bare-throated Bellbird** *Procnias nudicollis*).

Yet cotingas are perhaps best known for being such an oddly mixed assemblage. Ornithologists frequently allude to the quality: 'a taxonomic potpourri'; 'impossible to characterize concisely'; 'an amazing avian family of controversial limits'.[1] Three broadly unifying characteristics are their frugivorous diet, their preference for arboreal habitats and their exclusively American distribution. In fact, they are predominantly South American. Just 11 family members occur in Mexico and only a single representative, the **Rose-throated Becard** *Platypsaris aglaiae* ('becard' roughly means 'big-beak'), creeps across the border into southern USA, where it has a small breeding presence in Arizona.[2]

The family's variety is greatest in Amazonia and exemplified by the size differences between the largest and smallest. The **Buff-throated Purpletuft** *Idopleura pipra* (9.5 cm: 3.7 in) of eastern Brazil is less than one-fifth the length of the huge and oddly adorned **Amazonian Umbrellabird** *Cephalopterus ornatus*. The male of this last species measures as much as 51 cm (20 in) and is one of the biggest passerines on the continent. Another oddly unifying aspect to cotingas is the frequency with which their beauty is enhanced – as in the case of the umbrellabirds – by fancy 'extras': wattles, frills, crests or patches of naked skin.

The **Bare-necked Fruitcrow** *Gymnoderus foetidus* of the Amazonian rainforest has an almost lizard-like lappet of cobalt flesh round the throat. The **Three-wattled Bellbird** *Procnias tricarunculatus* of Central America has what look like three black worms dribbling from its bill, and the **Long-wattled Umbrellabird** *Cephalopterus penduliger* of the northern Andes possesses two such features. Hanging over its face and beak, like a rakishly angled cap, is a forward-leaning crest, and at the throat droops a scarf-like extension almost like a feather boa, that can 'grow' during display until it is sometimes as long as the bird itself (46 cm: 18 in).

The ultimate cotingas for extravagance of colour and body shape, as well as for their captivating strangeness of display, are the jay-sized pair **Guianan Cock-of-the-rock** *Rupicola rupicola* and **Andean Cock-of-the-rock** *Rupicola peruvianus* (the national bird of Peru). While the females are essentially a shade of brown with darker flight feathers, the males have silk-sheened black tails and wings with bodies of either deep, almost fluorescent, tangerine (Guianan Cock-of-the-rock and also the eastern race of the Andean Cock-of-the-rock, *aequatorialis*) or brilliant blood red (Andean Cock-of-the-rock). One eyewitness of the latter species in display conveys this sumptuous colour:

> From the viewing platform on the valley side, the birds were surprisingly difficult to see. The vegetation was dense, and although the males were actively chasing

each other, they came into view only occasionally and rarely remained long enough in one place to register a satisfying image on my retina. I kept willing them to perch in the sun so I could see them properly. Eventually when one did, it was like a fleck of glowing magma in a field of green lava.[3]

It is almost inevitable that birds of such beauty would be incorporated into the Amerindian tradition of body decoration. Equally the dominant colours in these two brilliant birds were almost bound to have symbolic value. The Wai-Wai people of both Guyana and northern Brazil make circular diadems from the orange feathers of Guianan Cock-of-the-rock. On rainy days, these sun-coloured crowns are offered by shamans to the sun itself in the hope that it might be persuaded to shine.[4]

The Jivaro people, who live at the junction of the Amazonian forests and the eastern Andean slopes of Peru and Ecuador, achieved greatest notoriety for their custom of shrinking the skulls of their human enemies. Surviving examples of these macabre trophies are still sometimes adorned with fresh cock-of-the-rock feathers. However, a more innocuous facet of their cultural life was a sensual dance performed by the Jivaro women in imitation of displaying Andean Cock-of-the-rock males. To this suggestive performance they sang these words:

Being the wife of the cock-of-the-rock,
Being the wife of the little *súmga*,
I jokingly sing to you thus:
Cock-of-the-rock, my little husband,
Wearing your many-coloured dress of feathers,
Graceful in your movements!
I know I am useless myself,
But still I rejoice,
For I am the wife of the *súmga* –
So I jokingly sing.[5]

The Jivaro were (and are still) skilled exponents of feather art. One striking technique was to dry the entire skins of brightly coloured birds – especially toucans (see page 333) – and tie them into a complex 'necklace' of hollow bones and toucan mandibles. The piece would then have been draped across the whole of the upper body. Both Andean Cock-of-the-rock and the gloriously scarlet **Black-necked Red Cotinga** *Phoenicircus nigricollis* were incorporated into these breastplates (examples are on display in the Pitt Rivers Museum, Oxford, UK, and also in the American Museum of Natural History in New York; the latter artefacts feature tanagers and toucans). Sometimes as many as eight whole examples of the Black-necked Red Cotinga would be incorporated into chest adornments made by distant neighbours of the Jivaro, the Tikuna people of the Solimões River in the Colombian–Brazilian border region.[6]

Nor is it just Amerindians who covet the beauty of this family. Among Western aviculturalists the two species of cock-of-the-rock are 'almost revered by advanced bird fanciers'.[7] The very name of the **Pompadour Cotinga** *Xipholena punicea* also hints at a curious history entailed in its discovery and its initial christening by Europeans. The bird's glorious dark claret plumes were being shipped to Madame de Pompadour (1721–1764), the mistress of the French king Louis XV. However, her intended cargo fell into the hands of

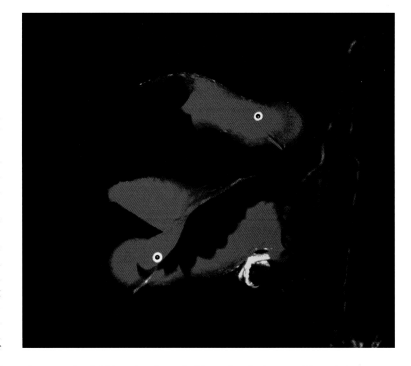

a buccaneering British cruiser. Instead of the cotinga feathers being worked into costumes for her ladyship, they were re-routed to the British naturalist George Edwards. At least he did Madame de Pompadour the honour of naming his new species after her.[8]

Although a direct encounter with living cotingas is a preserve mainly for those dwelling or travelling in South American rainforest, every human on Earth who has ever watched wildlife television has probably heard at least one member of the family.

The male Andean Cock-of-the-rock has the hot colours of molten magma.

As beautiful as any metallic jewellery, this neck pendant of the Urubú-Kapoor people of the Brazilian Amazon is made from the feathers of tanagers (turquoise), toucans (yellow), macaws (red) and Spangled Cotingas (purple).

The thing that sends shivers down my spine and takes me right back to the Manu National Park in Peru is not an image of any of the hundreds of exotic birds found there – the clay-eating macaws, dancing manakins, bejewelled hummingbirds or tanagers – but a sound: that of the **Screaming Piha** *Lipaugus vociferans*. Its tri-tone *weee weee-ah* call has the urgency, polyphonic shrillness and ear-splitting power of a police siren. Like so many loud birds, the piha is no pin-up – it's a dowdy grey-brown creature slightly bigger than a thrush – but its call instantly conjures up the experience of being in the rainforest. It has become a kind of audio shorthand for the place itself. But more widely it is an essential part of any soundtrack to documentaries and films set in the Amazon.[9]

The species' name and its label as the 'noisiest of all Amazonian birds' really do little justice to the atmospheric quality of that voice. It can drill through 300 m (985 ft) of dense forest and has a terminal whip-crack quality suggestive of the rising high-pitched interference as one turns the dial on an old-style radio.[10]

Another notion routinely associated with Screaming Piha calls is that they have a lingering, faintly haunting and enticing quality. In Guyana it is known as the 'gold bird', because the sound, 'if followed leads to places where gold could be found, while in Bolivia and Brazil it is known as "seringueros", the bird that led one to rubber trees'.[11] (The raw latex used in rubber was once immensely valuable.) In Brazil the bird is known as *Cricrió*, a trisyllable that contains a rudimentary echo of the sound. Yet the more suggestive title (there are at least five others) is *Tropeiro*, meaning 'muleteer', evoking that stock character's whistled commands to his pack-carrying train.[12]

Almost as famous are the voices of the four bellbird species. Their names are self-explanatory. The calls vary among the quartet but all resemble a hammer striking metal and they have a shared reputation as some of the farthest-carrying vocalisations of any bird. A range of 5 km (3 miles) has been claimed although a carrying distance of just 1 km (0.6 miles) has been proven. Most remarkable, perhaps, is the sound of the beautiful White Bellbird, described by one authority as 'like the metallic ringing clang of a gong'.[13]

Tyrant Flycatcher family *Tyrannidae*

This is the largest bird family on Earth and includes a total of 432 species. While they span the western hemisphere from the Arctic to Tierra del Fuego, they are predominantly birds of forest. In some tropical habitats they are the largest component of the whole avifauna and, in the words of one author, represent the 'most remarkable radiation and diversification . . . of any bird group anywhere in the world'.[1]

Ironically the vast majority of tyrant flycatchers are as marginal in cultural terms as they are important in a biological context. They are nearly all insectivorous and are insignificant as 'pests' of human crops; they are small to very small in size and so fall outside the usual target for wild protein, and most lie somewhere on a green-to-brown colour spectrum. For these reasons, they tend to pass a modest and blameless life, flycatching for insects high in the treetops, beyond the range of human ken.

Yet a small number of them buck the family trend. They have either bright colours or extravagant plumes, combined with boldly dynamic behaviour, and have been able to adapt to human-dominated landscapes. These few have sometimes become our most conspicuous bird neighbours in a huge variety of American settings.

Perhaps the best known is a group of 13 species, eight of which are regular summer migrants to North America, where the early settlers named them kingbirds. Two species, **Eastern Kingbird** *Tyrannus tyrannus* and **Western Kingbird** *Tyrannus verticalis*, are widespread and common almost continent-wide. They are quintessentially birds of farmland or open bushy habitats, where they sit on elevated perches to wait for aerial insects. The standard technique is to sally out from a wire and sometimes pursue an invisible prey in prolonged and twisting aerobatics. Some kingbird species even benefit from street lamps, which draw in the prey and then illuminate their nocturnal feeding.[2]

Kingbirds are among the key beneficiaries of the network of utility poles and wires that entwine most landscapes. It has multiple value for them, supplying both feeding station and breeding site. In a British Columbian study of Eastern Kingbirds, they were found to use man-made structures including pylons in almost a quarter of all nesting attempts.[3] They are also very much birds of that other dominating geometry of modern life, the road network, where they exploit the associated corridors of open space in which to forage. Unfortunately car collisions are a major cause of mortality, but their combined inclinations towards the open highway and power lines mean that kingbirds often bring a sense of grace and beauty to the otherwise relentless linear landscape of tarmac, white lines and roadside grime.

Bees were once thought – incorrectly – to be a major food for them. It earned the Eastern Kingbird two old vernacular names, 'bee-bird' or 'bee-martin', as well as widespread persecution from apiarists and farmers during the nineteenth and early twentieth centuries.[4] However, the 'kingbird' title suits them best. It was perhaps in part a reflection of their preference for elevated positions, but it drew even more on the birds' intensely aggressive behaviour. Its scientific equivalent, *Tyrannus*, demonstrates how animal nomenclature can sometimes carry political inflections. In this case it was said to be a commentary by early US citizens on a despotic English monarchy.[5] A modern equivalent occurs in the Caribbean: 'Cuban ornithologists jokingly refer to their endemic **Giant Kingbird** as the 'Castro bird', for its scientific name: *Tyrannus cubensis*!'.[6]

There may also have been a dash of respect in the original label, because kingbirds will take on opposition far larger and traditionally more regal than themselves. The American statesman Benjamin Franklin, when deliberating the suitability of the Bald Eagle as a national symbol for the fledgling state, complained that he (the eagle) is 'a rank coward; the little kingbird, not bigger than a sparrow, attacks him boldly and drives him out of the district. He is therefore by no means a proper emblem for the brave and honest

Tyrant flycatchers such as this Western Kingbird bring a dash of colour and zest to that otherwise harsh rectilinear landscape of roads, overhead wires and utility poles.

Cincinnati of America [a society of army officers], who have driven all the kingbirds from our country.'[7]

In truth the Eastern Kingbird is bigger than most sparrows, and its eagle-chasing habits have been questioned. Yet they are well known to chase species as large as herons, vultures, hawks and crows. Dogs, cats and humans are just as readily assaulted, but the ultimate in kingbird character was reported in 1935: 'The courage and audacity of this bird in attacking a noisy and relatively huge airplane was certainly extraordinary' (see also The Black Kite, page 159).[8]

The assaults are not just gratuitous violence – they are a defence of the eggs or young in their nest, although kingbirds often pursue victims way beyond the breeding territory. A regular strategy is to fly directly behind and then actually land on an opponent's back, pecking at it while hitching a ride. In some parts of the USA, these attacks are so routine they become a form of entertainment.

They haunt every hot July ballfield on the Great Plains, gray and yellow birds perched nervously on the chain link or fluttering low over the arena. The spectators don't notice them at all until a housecat or fox squirrel emerges from the grass. The squirrel's ancestral memories send it scurrying back to the safety of bur oak or cottonwood, but the housecat, evolutionarily unaware of the risk it's running, tries to slink across the field – and suddenly all tyrannid hell breaks loose. The quiet sputtering of the kingbirds becomes a chorus of shrieks, and the befuddled feline finds itself with a passenger, a fury of tiny talons and stout bill scratching and hammering at the same soft spot where the cat was once carried so gently by its mother. Fur and feathers fly as the housecat runs across the field, its body twisting and bucking in the effort to rid itself of the violent hitchhiker; and half-raised bats sink, gloves dangle, fingers point, as players and spectators turn their attention, for just a moment, to the battle enacted in front of them. Finally the cat cringes and crouches under the bleachers, and the kingbirds return to their

fence-line perches, rousting themselves and exchanging soft chirps, sure that they've done their part to make a July afternoon safe once again for softball.[9]

Another kingbird that occurs from Argentina to Mexico (and accidentally further north into the USA and Canada) is the **Fork-tailed Flycatcher** *Tyrannus savana*. Of all the family it is perhaps the ultimate combination of beauty and aggression. The male's deeply forked tail is considerably longer than the whole body and in flight the outermost feathers 'stream out behind like a pair of black ribbons'. Adding to the notion of formal performance is the bird's hard percussive call, which has been likened to 'the snapping of castanets'.[10] In his memoir of his Argentinian childhood, *Far Away and Long Ago*, W H Hudson described a local Fork-tailed Flycatcher and its unceasing battle with a hawk called the Chimango Caracara. (Hudson knew the flycatcher as the 'scizzor-tail'; not to be confused, incidentally, with its congener, the similarly beautiful **Scissor-tailed Flycatcher** *Tyrannus forficatus* of Mexico and central USA.)

> The scizzor-tail is one of the most courageous of that hawk-hating, violent-tempered tyrant-bird family, and every time a *chimango* appeared, which was about forty times a day, he would sally out to attack him in mid-air with amazing fury. The marauder driven off, he would return to the tree to utter his triumphant rattling castanet-like notes . . . then to settle down again to watch the sky for the appearance of the next *chimango*.[11]

In Brazil and other parts of tropical South America another tyrant flycatcher, the thrush-sized **Great Kiskadee** *Pitangus sulphuratus*, enjoys much the same conspicuous position as the kingbirds elsewhere. The Brazilian ornithologist Helmut Sick suggested that it is the best known and most popular bird in the whole country and, at times, becomes so accustomed to human presence, it is semi-domesticated.[12] Tameness towards us, however, does not preclude aggression towards almost everything else.

Its heavy pickaxe bill is a formidable weapon and extends

In parts of its vast Latin American range the Great Kiskadee is sometimes so habituated to people it can become semi-domesticated.

the range of prey well beyond the usual insect diet of most flycatchers. W H Hudson suggested that 'it seems to have studied to advantage the various habits of the Kestrel, Flycatcher, Kingfisher, Vulture, and fruit-eating Thrush'.[13] Kiskadees have been known to eat lizards, frogs and small mammals, sometimes plucking fish and tadpoles straight out of the water or searching for marine prey under stones in the intertidal zone. The contents of other birds' nests, municipal dumps, the interior of air-conditioning vents, around street lamps and voodoo shrines (for their edible offerings) in downtown Rio de Janeiro are all part of the kiskadee's extensive territory. As one Rio resident notes, 'it is one of the first birds to sing in urban areas and also one of the very few that you'd hear as a dawn chorus in a *favela* (slum)'.[14]

The modern Spanish name, *Luis Grande*, trades on

the kiskadee's dominance, but the rather strange English equivalent is a very close rendering of the bird's grating three-note call. One wonders also if the generic name *Pitangus*, which derives from an original Tupi word for the species, was equally a play on the voice. Certainly its Brazilian name and an older Spanish American version, respectively *Bem-Te-Vi* and *Bien-Te-Veo* ('I saw you well' and 'I see you well'), are onomatopoeic in origin, although they must also refer to the bird's penchant for high perches and its all-seeing adaptability.

In turn the *Bem-Te-Vi* gave its name to another all-seeing dweller of the streets. The late Erismar Rodrigues Moreira was a legendary drug dealer whose career was as brief as it was violent. A life of crime began at the age of 14 and reached its apogee in April 2004, when he assumed leadership of the

Amigos dos Amigos ('Friends of Friend'), the top gang in Rocinha, Rio's largest *favela*, after the previous incumbent was gunned down by police special forces. Aside from *Bem-Te-Vi*'s gold-plated guns, his contacts in high places, the lavish generosity of his street parties and a cocaine distribution business worth $9 million a year, he relied upon a *favela*-wide network of informants and lookouts. As one contributor notes, 'The gangs are constantly on the watch in the slums. One of the first things you notice when you go to

Rio is all the kids' kites over poor areas of the city. These are actually used as signalling devices by the gangs to let people know about police arriving, etc., rather than being indicative of their popularity with children.'[15]

On 29 October 2005 both the life and the lifestyle came to a bitter end. *Bem-Te-Vi* was gunned down in a street fight with 150 police. 'Subsequently both of his "concubines" were captured, on different days, at Rio airport trying to leave the country with large stashes of jewellery and money.'[16]

Antbirds such as this Ocellated Antbird often follow hunting swarms of army ants in order to pick off some of the bow-wave of fleeing invertebrates.

Antbird family *Thamnophilidae*

This is a large family of suboscine passerines (213 species) found exclusively in Central and South America. Almost all of them are small birds and residents of deep forest or dense secondary vegetation. As one author notes, 'Theirs is a half-lit world of vines, dim forest floor, dappled thickets and clearing edge.'[1] For these reasons they are seldom if ever hunted, eaten or even seen and, thus, enjoy few cultural associations, having a reputation mainly as birders' birds. Their habitual preference for thick cover and shade helps explain why many species are dark plumaged. However, while the males are predominantly grey or black often with white spots or bars, females are usually some shade of brown.

Three similar species found in Panama – the **Checker-throated Antwren** *Myrmotherula fulviventris*, **White-flanked Antwren** *Myrmotherula axillaris* and **Dot-winged Antwren** *Microrhopias quixensis* – are often seen together in mixed-species flocks and have acquired a nickname, 'the three amigos'.

I heard this first from a North American birdwatcher and it draws on that comedy film starring Chevy Chase and Steve Martin called the *¡Three Amigos!*. You often find them around the Soberania National Park [near

Panama City]. The Dot-winged and Checker-throated Antwrens are always together, but the white-flanked is one that comes and goes. Sometimes you don't see it, but most times when I'm birding I see the first two and by looking carefully I can invariably find a couple of white-flanked. They like to hang around together and I have not seen them fight or chase each other away. They seem to work quite well as a team, with the checker-throated specialising on insects from the dead leaf litter, while the other two get insects from the green leaves.[2]

The family name is slightly misleading. Antbirds do not feed, or very seldom feed, directly on ants; rather they feed on the same prey as the ant themselves. Many have evolved a close relationship with swarm-raiding forest species, such as *Eciton burchellii*, commonly known as army ants. These nomadic raiders live in temporary bivouacs and feed in a blanket-like formation that swarms en masse across the forest floor. Every arthropod or vertebrate animal that cannot elude this frenzied assault – it is said to include even humans, with horror stories of babies being eaten in their cots – is smothered, eventually killed and carried back whole, or dismembered for return to the colony.

The Ocellated Tapaculo of the northern Andes reflects the family's tendency towards creeping, furtive, ground-hugging lifestyles on the forest floor, but also its gift for unexpected beauty.

Tapaculo family *Rhinocryptidae*

This small (56 species) family is found exclusively in the Neotropics, with a single bird reaching as far north as Costa Rica and larger concentrations in the Andes and the southern third of South America, particularly Chile. Many species have tiny ranges, and are often restricted by narrow altitudinal limits or habitat preferences. The **Tacarcuna Tapaculo** *Scytalopus panamensis*, for instance, is known from just a single mountain ridge on the border of Panama and Colombia, and even the name of the **Tall-grass Wetland Tapaculo** *Scytalopus iraiensis* (also called Marsh Tapaculo) suggests the very specific requirements of this southern Brazilian species (of which there are possibly fewer than 1,000 birds).[1]

A lighter aspect to the group is its name. It derives from two Spanish words – *tapa* from *tapar*, 'to cover', and *culo*, 'arse'. It translates as 'cover up your arse', and is an injunction that stems from the habit of carrying their tails cocked. Charles Darwin recorded the name as long ago as the 1830s, offering a bowdlerised translation ('cover your posterior'), adding: 'well does the shameless little bird deserve its name; for it carries its tail more than erect, that is, inclined backwards towards its head'.[2] The word's ribald associations have widened today: it now serves as a South American slang term for gay men.

Many species are tiny in size and remarkably cryptic both in appearance – they can be difficult to identify even in the hand – and in habit. Tapaculos creep about in the dense shade of thick undergrowth and elicit a consistent set of descriptions in field guides: 'Secretive little forest-dwellers, who move about like mice on the forest floor . . . never straying far from cover'; 'often secretive and difficult to observe'.[3] It seems contradictory to state, but the family is most conspicuous for its obscurity. This invisibility accounts for the near-complete absence of cultural reference, and yet also their appeal to keen birders, who relish the challenges of seeing and separating them.

There is a further dimension to the tapaculos' allure, which is strongly linked to the dense, shadowed micro-landscapes they inhabit. These obscure and inaccessible crannies, which are often places of dead or decomposing vegetation and invertebrate life, often feel deeply inimical not just to human presence but to any kind of higher life form. To see one of these tiny, yet somehow perfect, birds slowly emerge and to be allowed to appreciate their subtle colours and patterns – many have bright rufous patches and sometimes intensely barred or squamated underparts – is often to experience a profound sense of privilege. Encounters with a number of deep-forest bird families (see also Pitta family and Antpitta family, pages 345 and 355) have this same aura of revelation.

A poem by the Chilean Nobel Laureate Pablo Neruda, entitled 'Tapaculo', which describes the **White-throated Tapaculo** *Scelorchilus albicollis*, invokes something of the impact.

It pops up hopping about the stones	*Surge saltando entre las piedras*
Above the parched grass	*sobre la hierba chamuscada*
And pick pick pecks	*y pica pica picotea:*
With a quick rap it dropped	*con rápido golpe bajó*
its round eyes, the beak	*los ojos redondos, el pico*
A yellow lightning bolt.	*es un relámpago amarillo*
And it changed the landscape:	*Y se trasladó de paisaje:*
Its long vertical tail,	*su larga cola vertical,*
The recalcitrant feathers	*con las plumas recalcitrantes*
Pointing at high noon	*que señalan el mediodía*
Raised above its rump.	*Enarboladas en el culo*

One of Neruda's lines – 'And it changed the landscape' – touches on a theme more completely explored in the poem 'Anecdote of the Jar', by the American poet Wallace Stevens.

I placed a jar in Tennessee,
And round it was, upon a hill.
It made the slovenly wilderness
Surround that hill.

The wilderness rose up to it,
And sprawled around, no longer wild.

Both poems tap into a psychological process relevant to a number of ground-dwelling birds of the deep forest. In exactly the way that the jar seems an absolute contradiction of the 'slovenly wilderness' – each therefore serving to define the very nature of the other – so the sheer living intensity of birds, such as tapaculos, stand in powerful contrast to the dark and inanimate disorder of their habitat. This encounter with unexpected beauty in the most forsaken places can give to the moment of observation a quality of startling epiphany.

Antthrush and Antpitta family *Formicariidae*

The feelings of privilege associated with seeing tapaculos are even more powerful in the case of antpittas. The whole family of 65 species is exclusively found in the New World (the northern extremity of their range is about the same latitude as Mexico City). They fit the common suboscine pattern, having acquired few if any cultural connections for anyone other than bird specialists. Yet for the latter they represent a compelling desideratum. Ground dwelling with large heads and almost spherical bodies, they range in size from the **Great Antpitta** *Grallaria excelsa* (25.5 cm: 10 in) to the miniature **Ochre-breasted Antpitta** *Grallaricula flavirostris* (10 cm: 4 in) which, when singing its melancholy song, inflates the entire body like a tiny blow-up ball.

One correspondent tries to illuminate the family's mysterious appeal.

I can't fully explain why birders are fascinated by antpittas. It may be that they combine the general interest in antbirds with some associated magic of the Asian pittas [see page 345]. I wouldn't describe them as beautiful in the sense that most ordinary people would recognise beauty. They look rather like out-of-proportion thrushes, with usually grey and brown plumage, huge eyes, long legs and almost non-existent tails. But for keen birders they have a magical understated quality. This, combined with the challenge of simply seeing them in dense forest with very low light levels, makes them highly sought after. Many are not particularly rare, but it is their elusiveness that provides the challenge. Robert Dean, the artist who illustrated the Costa Rican bird guide, charmingly reveals on the inside cover that the tiny Ochre-breasted Antpitta is his favourite bird – this in a country with the Resplendent Quetzal and dozens of stunning hummingbirds to compete with!

Once in Venezuela we camped among dense forest near Mount Roraima (Conan Doyle's 'Lost World') for three weeks, and used mist nets to catch and ring a range of rare and beautiful species. We never caught an antpitta, despite setting nets very close to the forest floor, and began to think we would miss them. Then one afternoon I heard a rustling just off the path and after some time located a recently fledged **Tepui Antpitta** *Myrmothera simplex* (found only in this area), being fed by its parents. I was able to watch the family group at close range for some three hours, until dusk, with them apparently oblivious to my presence. I noted the adults making a considerable noise and 'paddling' in the leaf litter to disturb prey. The challenge of finding the birds, combined with such a long period of observation, made them one of the highlights of the whole trip.[1]

In northern Ecuador a farmer from the Mindo area, the resonantly named Angel Paz (*paz* is Spanish for peace), has somehow succeeded in persuading several antpittas to eat worms from his own hand. Three either rare or beautiful species – **Giant Antpitta** *Grallaria gigantea* (successive individuals known as 'Maria'), **Moustached Antpitta** *Grallaria alleni* ('Manuel') and **Yellow-breasted Antpitta** *Grallaria flavotincta* ('Willy') – can all be seen (at a small charge) at Angel's farm (now renamed Paz de las Aves; 'peace of the birds').[2] A fourth species, the tiny Ochre-breasted Antpitta, has a strange but characteristic shimmying action that has inspired a personal name with links to the belly-dancing moves of another shapely South American. 'We call her Shakira', says Angel Paz's brother, Rodrigo, 'because she wiggles her butt like the Colombian singer.'[3]

Angel Paz of northern Ecuador displays models of the various antpittas that he has trained to come for worms at his prompting.

In his poem 'Angel Paz Talks to the Birds', Mark Roper dwells on the extraordinary personal relationship between these individual antpittas and this remarkable Ecuadorian, but also on the powerful if ill-defined emotions awakened by the simple intimacy of exchange between man and bird.

Golden rusty barred breast.
Sloe-grey shoulders.

The giant antpitta,
awkward in daylight

but there, charmed from
the shadow it inhabits,

somehow responding,
shiest, wariest bird,

to something like love
in Angel's voice.

When it feels it's been there
long enough, it leaves.

Angel folds away his voice.
And whatever that voice

has allowed to emerge
inside we too fold away.[4]

Staff at the Fundación Jocotoco, an organisation established to protect the globally endangered **Jocotoco Antpitta** *Grallaria ridgelyi*, heard of Angel's extraordinary achievements and learned the feeding technique directly from him in 2007. The bird at the heart of their project is notable not simply for its beauty and extreme rarity; Jocotoco Antpitta was only discovered as recently as 1997. The staff have now used the worm-luring method as part of efforts to raise awareness and encourage visitors. Two birds ('Pancho' and 'Vivi') respond to the calls of the Angel-trained employee and they emerge to feed at point-blank range, usually to the heavenly delight of the accompanying tourists.[5]

Ovenbird family *Furnariidae*

The English name for this exclusively Neotropical family is, in many ways, deeply misleading, since 'ovenbird' is applicable to only a handful of the 248 species. Yet any alternative would be just as arbitrary, given that furnariids, a more technical term for the group, are famous for their 'unparalleled heterogeneity and diversity in nest architecture, structural morphology, foraging behaviour and physiological tolerance'.[1] While their physical forms and lifestyles may be hugely varied, ovenbirds have one thing in common: 'the overwhelming majority . . . are basically brown . . . perhaps to a greater degree than . . . any other of the world's major bird families'.[2]

W H Hudson suggested another strand of continuity between them, commenting that they are 'mostly small, inconspicuous, thicket-frequenting birds, shy and fond of concealment to excess'.[3] Petite, coy and sombre-toned, ovenbirds were not destined to make a large mark on the cultural life of South America. Yet a hint of richer colour lies in their wonderful English names. Some are so complex and implausible they seem like the exaggerations that writers occasionally invent to parody the arcane dottiness of ornithology. These include the **Buff-breasted Earthcreeper** *Upucerthia validirostris*, the **Scribble-tailed Canastero** *Asthenes maculicauda*, the **Itatiaia Spinetail** *Oreophylax moreirae*, **Pink-legged Graveteiro** *Acrobatornis fonsecai*, the **Guttulated Foliage-gleaner** *Syndactyla guttulata*, **Scaly-throated Leaftosser** *Sclerurus guatemalensis* and **Sharp-tailed Streamcreeper** *Lochmias nematura*.

It would be wrong to suggest that no ovenbird has made a mark on us. The **Rufous Hornero** *Furnarius rufus* is the notable exception. Its cultural impact stems in part from its huge personality, which encompasses a deep tolerance of humans, extraordinarily loud calls which are delivered often in an excited duet, and a rather bizarre, almost dance-like, halting gait. The species is the national bird in Uruguay and also in Argentina, where the choice was made in 1928 following a poll of schoolchildren. Throughout its Spanish-speaking range the bird is known as *el hornero*, 'the baker'. This refers to the domed mud nest, which strongly resembles the outdoor adobe oven that was once widespread in an older Argentina (whence came, of course, the ovenbird name used for the entire family). The scientific version draws equally on associations with the *panaderia*: the Latin for an oven is *furnus*.

The birds themselves are common across open savannah country almost from Patagonia north to Bolivia, Paraguay and southern Brazil, where it is also well known and numerous. In Brazil it is similarly named for its nest: *Joao*

An Argentinian stamp features the widespread and hugely charismatic national bird, the Rufous Hornero.

de barro can be translated as 'John clay'. However, *barro* also means 'mud house' (*Joao* is a common personalised name for several Brazilian species). W H Hudson recalled similarly personalised and affectionate names in Argentina's northern Corrientes province and in Paraguay, including *Alonzo Garcia* and a diminutive, *Alonzito*. He was unable to account for that specific name except as an obvious term of affection, in the manner of 'Tom tit' and 'Jenny wren'.[4]

The nest can have walls 4–5 cm (1.6–2 in) thick and weigh up to 5 kg (11 lb): 50 times the combined weight of its construction team. The hornero pair operates with enormous speed, building up the sides with dung or wet mud and straw once the previous layer is dry. Work is stimulated by rain and the availability of the raw materials, and to complete a single nest can take as little as a fortnight. It is divided into two parts and this slender resemblance to the rooms of a human house elicited a stock set of anthropomorphic and often erroneous responses in older nature books: 'The nest . . . is divided into two rooms; the outer is the common room, and the inner is the nursery.'[5]

Each hornero territory can contain numerous old or untenanted nests – they will construct several simultaneously and use one – and sometimes they build new structures on the remnants of an abandoned predecessor, occasionally until they are six and even 11 units high. The abundance of horneros in open habitats and the durability of their ovens – Hudson recorded examples that survived for two to three years – mean that their works have a prominent place in the overall character and contour of many South American landscapes.[6]

> Travelling around Argentina in search of birds, I had frequent opportunity to admire the local architecture from magnificent Hispanic cathedrals to primitive mud huts in the Andean foothills. But the adobe buildings that I noticed most were the work of birds. Across huge areas of open country, the sturdy, football-sized hornero nests were impossible to miss, in places appearing to crown every fence-post, telephone pole or wall. Providing such snug security for the nestlings, they reminded me of the ancient cottage in which I lived at the time, whose wattle-and-daub walls protected my own family.[7]

These little mud houses also become a major source of nest or roosting locations for other birds, including members of the furnariid family, but also for lizards, small mammals, snakes, frogs and insects.

The horneros' ubiquity both cements their place in popular affection among southern South Americans and then, in turn, accounts for the birds' deep tolerance of human presence. They are present even in the heart of Buenos Aires, one of the largest cities in South America. The Brazilian authority Helmut Sick suggested that the bird 'seeks human neighbours'.[8] Horneros regularly make their nests on the sides of man-made buildings and other structures. The English film-maker David Attenborough describes finding one on a well-used gate, where it must have been swung through 90° several times a day.[9] A popular alternative is on the top or arms of utility poles, which can lead to complications. The ovens regularly cause shorting in the electricity that occasionally ends in fires or blackouts. 'In a census by the state electric company in Rio Grande do Sul [southern Brazil] in December 1987, there were 580 *F. rufus* nests on company structures, with 265 in risk of provoking short circuits.'[10] A second study in the state of Santa Catarina during 2002 found 1,546 nests on 2,234 power poles and in places hornero occupancy rose to almost 70 per cent of poles.[11]

These hazards have not lessened the bird's appeal to its human neighbours. It has given its name, for instance, to one of the foremost ornithological journals in South America (*El Hornero*, published under that name since 1917). It also features as a motif in commercial advertising by building merchants and developers: 'I recently saw a Brazilian property dealer with the name Hornero, and using a logo of a Rufous Hornero and its nest. It actually came up as the first "hit" when doing an online search for the journal of the same name!'[12] Another strand of *el hornero*'s commercial usage is in the titles of restaurants, especially pizzerias where the clay-oven nest has obvious relevance.

An older stratum of folklore still survives in South America, such as the notion that, like all good Catholics, horneros never work on the sabbath. 'In the small Argentinian town of Carlos Pellegrini I saw a hornero's nest that had actually been built on the head of Jesus in a sculpture of the Madonna and infant. In the same town there were also hornero nests on the top of the two posts which held up the town sign.'[13] One wonders if the bird's national significance and 'religious' personality ensured that a nest like this was permitted to remain in such a sensitive spot, when other nests would have been removed.

A slightly darker myth concerns the male bird's capacity to seal in an unfaithful spouse, immuring her unto death within the very walls of their defiled nest. The idea may stem from the discovery of occasional ovens where horneros have closed up the nest entrances with dead young left inside.[14]

W H Hudson recorded a variation on this theme:

> A pair of Oven-birds built their oven on a beam-end projecting from the wall of a ranch. One morning one of the birds was found caught in a steel trap . . . and both of its legs were crushed . . . On being liberated it flew up to and entered the oven, where it bled to death . . . Its mate remained two days, calling incessantly . . . and it eventually disappeared. Three days later it returned with a new mate, and immediately the two birds began carrying pellets of mud to the oven, with which they plastered up the entrance. Afterwards they built a second oven, using the sepulchre of the dead bird for its foundation, and here they reared their young.[15]

Another furnariid of high industry and associated power cuts is this seemingly insignificant resident of southern South America, the **Firewood-gatherer** *Anumbius annumbi*.

> When I first saw the huge stick nests of this aptly named species in the Argentinian savannahs, I thought the birds that had produced them would be at least the size of crows. They turned out to be drab brown weak-flying birds smaller than a starling. Almost as noticeable as the nests themselves were the piles of sticks dropped on the ground by the builders, as if they were planning to light a series of beacons.[16]

The nests can be 2 m (6.6 ft) across and frequently incorporate bits of metal in their construction. When

David and Goliath – a Blackish Cinclodes causes considerable distress to a Southern Elephant Seal as it tries to pick at open wounds on the mammal's neck.

this happens in nests assembled on power lines it can also cause electricity short circuits. On a more cooperative note, Firewood-gatherers often unwittingly act as house builders for a host of secondary tenants, including hundreds of species of invertebrate.[17]

A small all-dark family member confined to the Falklands and islands south of Tierra del Fuego, **Blackish Cinclodes** *Cinclodes antarcticus* is one of the best examples not only of the tameness associated with its family, but also of the extraordinary innocence displayed by many insular bird populations. In the 1830s Charles Darwin witnessed the behaviour, although he suggested that the bird might have been even tamer at one time, citing the experience of the French traveller Antoine-Joseph Pernety. In the 1760s Pernety killed ten of them with a small stick in half an hour and had them perch on his finger.[18]

If the birds had changed by Darwin's day, then they have now reverted to type. On the Falklands their bold and inquisitive manner is famous. They will readily perch on

your shoulders or walk across your boots, searching for food off the clothes and immediately around the body of anyone sitting down. They will also fly just offshore to feed on small boats or dinghies that are passing, even sometimes entering houses where they 'come to the dining table for titbits' at mealtime.[19]

Their boldness is not confined to humans. They routinely feed among the excreta of sea mammals and hop among the gigantic beached bodies of sun-dozing elephant seals, occasionally 'perching on the long deflated noses and picking at them'.[20] Another favourite technique is to probe into the deep, raw lacerations which encircle the necks of elephant seals. These wounds are inflicted by the massive canines of other bulls during the months of violent conflict that accompany the breeding season. To see a 18 cm (7 in) cinclodes harassing and causing distress to a 3-tonne seal is to witness one of the strangest David-and-Goliath confrontations in all nature.

Lyrebird family *Menuridae*

The family contains only two species – the **Superb Lyrebird** *Menura novaehollandiae* and the slightly smaller **Albert's Lyrebird** *Menura alberti* – but these twins must rank among the most captivating of all Australia's birds. Technically they are classified as passerines yet in shape, colour and in their shy, ground-dwelling, solitary,

forest-stalking habits lyrebirds rather resemble tawny-coloured gamebirds. In fact, 'mountain pheasant' was an old colonial name, and one nineteenth-century commentator felt they possessed no more beauty than a 'dusky colour'd Barn Door Fowl'.[1]

The judgement overlooks one glorious refinement in the

lyrebird's plumage. Massively elongated tail plumes, framed by a pair of distinctive lyrate outer feathers, are present on the males of both species and account for at least one of the superlatives attaching to the family. (The two outer tail feathers also gave the bird its scientific name: *Menura* means literally 'moon tail' and refers to the patterning – the transparent lunules – on the outer webs of these feathers.)[2] The Northern Raven may be heavier, but the cock Superb Lyrebird measures over 1 m (3.3 ft) and is among the longest passerines on Earth.

An early fanciful misconception, which probably had more to do with the bird's renown as a musician than any genuine observation, held that the tail was carried in the precise configuration of a human lyre. Many early colonial and European paintings cemented the falsehood in popular imagination, especially beyond Australian shores. In truth, during display the lacy, filamentous, spreading feathers are held widely as in an open fan, and at the height of a male's performance they are thrown forward so that they drape down over his head – nothing like a lyre, but like a rather coquettish bridal veil.

The lyrebird's peculiarity of dress drew widespread colonial admiration with all its customary and dismal consequences in terms of trophy hunting. The tail was displayed in Australian houses as an attractive curio, or individual feathers were used to adorn female headgear. In 1907 one eyewitness recorded men bearing baskets of up to 50 tails, hawking them through the streets of Sydney. There was also a brisk export trade from that city, with a single company shipping out 800 tails in 1911. Another

Sydney dealer handled 498 birds in the same year.[3] Together with habitat loss, these pressures weighed heavily on both species. Superb Lyrebird now occurs only in a forest belt from eastern Victoria to New South Wales. Its relative is even more confined, cleaving to drier higher-altitude forests straddling the Queensland–New South Wales border. A population of just 3,500 Albert's Lyrebird is deemed vulnerable to extinction.[4]

Scarcity has added lustre to the family's reputation but its real fame rests squarely on the extraordinary voice. The technical classification of lyrebirds in what are called the suboscine passerines is based on peculiarities of their vocal organ. These muscles, in turn, derive their name from Syrinx, the daughter of the river god Ladon. In Greek mythology she was the Arcadian nymph who was turned into a reed during her flight from the enamoured Pan, her body becoming the hollow stem from which pan pipes were fashioned. In no other bird family are such divine associations with the organ of sound more appropriate.

The lyrebird's syrinx confers on the two species a gift for imitation of exquisite accuracy. About three-quarters of their song output is mimicry. Both birds routinely incorporate pitch-perfect renderings of many of their avian forest neighbours, such as whipbirds, catbirds, parrots, owls and bowerbirds (see also Scrubbird family, page 361). Yet these straightforward borrowings are no more than a single strand in a vast repertoire. There was once a popular belief that the lyrebird could not reproduce the equally famous laughing call of a Laughing Kookaburra. In fact, as the Australian author Alec Chisholm noted, 'he can imitate, with perfect

Technically classified among the songbirds, the Albert's Lyrebird of eastern Australia wanders across the forest floor looking rather like a long-legged gamebird.

A linocut of Superb Lyrebird by Australian artist Narelle Oliver depicts the bird in singing mode.

ease, several Kookaburras in chorus, just as he can imitate the polyglot calling of a whole flock of Parrots'.[5]

Nor is the lyrebird's mimetic range limited to other birds' calls. The bird can copy bill snapping, the sound of young birds being fed, the rustle of a parrot's feathers, even the sound of wood being torn by a cockatoo, as well as a suite of non-avian creatures: croaking frogs, barking or howling dogs, the yapping of foxes, Dingo sounds, the calls of pademelons (a small kangaroo relative), the screams of fighting possums or their relatives, Koala grunts and a pig being killed. Individuals have been known to incorporate the clip-clop of horses hooves on stone, the random noises from a horse and dray, as well as useful human phrases such as 'Gee up Bess'. A tame bird called Jack (1885–1905), whose passing earned an obituary in Australia's foremost ornithological journal, *Emu*, when addressed by humans with the phrase, 'Poor Jack,' would reply, 'Not poor Jack, fat Jack.'[6]

> I've had some incredible experiences with lyrebirds of late in Sydney's south-west . . . But my most startling experience was last Christmas morning, about 7 a.m. From a group of three or four lyrebirds arose a distinct call of 'Fire! Fire!' It seems that one bird must have overheard this cry on some earlier danger-fraught occasion.[7]

A modern captive lyrebird, Chook, in Adelaide Zoo, inserted into his own performance a medley of noises that had originated with construction workers operating in the vicinity of his pen. These note-perfect renditions included the sounds of electric drills, hammering, manual sawing, an idling engine and human voices. In some ways the most remarkable aspect is that the latter comprise, not clearly enunciated words, but a rendering of casual verbal exchanges that are just beyond human earshot.[8]

Claims of lyrebird mimicry of man-made objects are legion and possibly exaggerated, but they undoubtedly occur. They range from car engines (including identifiable makes such as Porsche and Ferrari), car alarms, rattling chains, hydraulic rams, rock crushers, rifle shots, axes chopping, chainsaws and the motor drive on cameras, as well as the crackling of bush fires. Incidentally, the last five items narrate, in their inferential way, part of the biography of the whole

lyrebird family. Imitation has also resulted in delightful moments of human confusion. A bird learned to reproduce a timber mill's three-blast whistle that was used to summon the staff, but one day it caused havoc when it repeated the sound, thereby inadvertently creating the mill's six-blast signal for reporting fatalities.[9] An Australian backwoodsman recalled once how he had searched for a lost 'soul' whose *coo-ee* calls echoed through the forest. He eventually tracked down the person to a lyrebird in the bush.[10]

> Mervyn Bill, a forest surveyor . . . has written that when he was camped at Hell's Gates (Victoria), he was annoyed to see, through the theodolite telescope, his men doing certain field operations without the usual instructions. The fact became revealed, subsequently, that they had obeyed 'instructions' from a Lyrebird in an adjacent gully, which faultlessly imitated the surveyor's shrill, staccato code of signals.[11]

Perhaps the most affecting aspect of lyrebird mimicry is the way it can arc through time, connecting contemporary audiences with historical incidents, sometimes of exquisite poignancy. An example involves birds living in a park in New South Wales that were heard in 1969 to copy what seemed like flute music. Careful detective work eventually revealed that a flute player, living on a farm next to the same park, had been accustomed in the 1930s to play to his pet lyrebird before it was released back to the wild. That individual's descendants, or perhaps its neighbours and their offspring, had adopted the flute motifs and they were still being reproduced more than 30 years later. Analysis of the inherited sounds showed that they were versions of two popular thirties' songs, 'The Keel Row' and 'Mosquito's Dance'. The lyrebirds could produce both tunes simultaneously.[12]

An example which, if true, is even more moving, involves an Albert's Lyrebird found in Lamington National Park, Queensland, that has been heard and filmed producing a sequence of repetitive, highly syncopated sounds. The performance, which it coordinates with a foot-stomping movement on favourite vine stems, closely resembles a mixture of beating clap-sticks, rhythmic human voices and the 'tonal qualities of the didgeridoo wind instrument' produced as a part of an Aboriginal corroboree. Glen

Threlfo, the creator of a film entitled *Albert Lyrebird: Prince of the Rainforest*, suggests that it might be a version of indigenous human music, and that it possibly dates to the nineteenth century, when Aboriginal presence in the area was last recorded. However, Threlfo adds:

> Aboriginal Elders were consulted about these similarities. Their response was that they themselves were uncertain as to whether the bird copied it from the Aborigines or whether the local Aborigines copied it from the bird! Aboriginal dances often involve mimicry of animal calls and their movements. Examples may include other bird species like the courting dance of the Brolga, a large Sarus Crane of Northern Australia.[13]

We are deeply familiar with situations in which our artefacts record and perpetuate the memory of a lost bird. A classic instance is the early phonograph recording of a Maori hunter, who knew and could imitate the sounds of the extinct New Zealand species the Huia (see page 369). In the case of the lyrebirds of Lamington, however, it could be a reversal of that situation. There, the birds, not ourselves, are the archivists, the keepers of memory for their former neighbours (see also Parrot family, page 252).[14]

Such instances beg questions about quite how old the song of a lyrebird can be. Spontaneous, zany and as if extemporised in that very moment one hears it, the bird's music might, in truth, contain elements that have been passed down, generation to generation, for hundreds, even thousands, of years. Lyrebird vocalisations challenge us to reflect upon the whole nature of birdsong. If the sounds produced by this pair of species are not among the most pleasing avian performances because of their resemblance to human music, then they are, nevertheless, some of the most affecting and remarkable of all bird vocalisations. The level of mimesis can leave us aghast at the sophistication of the avian syrinx – as a medium to record the workings of a bird's entire neurological system, and as an instrument for reproducing a bird's inner world.

Some of our wider sense of awe at lyrebird vocalisations is surely manifest in the Australian deployment of the bird as a national motif in stamps, coats of arms and as a carved symbol in an arch celebrating the opening of the federal parliament in May 1901. Lyrebird images appear on the obverse of an Australian 10-cent coin and in the clear window ('a bit stylised but definitely a lyrebird') present on the AUS $100 bill.[15] There is a lyrebird in the logo of the New South Wales National Parks and Wildlife Service and, until recently, in that for the Queensland Conservatorium of Music. The song itself has given rise to a number of national audio-historical firsts: the first live radio broadcasts of a bird (1932-4) and the first live gramophone recording (1931) both featured the species with the divine syrinx.[16]

Scrubbird family *Atrichornithidae*

These exclusively Australian, thrush-sized birds with chequered brown upperparts, long tails and supremely elusive, almost rodent-like habits are relatives of the lyrebirds and are fellow suboscine passerines (see Glossary). There are just two species: the **Rufous Scrubbird** *Atrichornis refuscens* of northern New South Wales and south Queensland; and the **Noisy Scrubbird** *Atrichornis clamosus* found in only a tiny area of coastal Western Australia near the town of Albany and 3,000 km (1,850 miles) from its sibling.

The Noisy Scrubbird became an Australian and ornithological cause célèbre when it vanished for 70 years, was assumed to have gone extinct and was then rediscovered by a schoolteacher, Hargreaves Webster, in 1961. He reported his momentous find to the *West Australian* newspaper, which broke the story on Christmas morning.[1] Since then it has been the subject of a continuous, intensive, high-profile conservation effort, largely focused on rehabilitating the fire-damaged sedge-scrub habitat. It remains one of the country's rarest birds, despite these efforts and the establishment of new colonies through translocation.[2]

Like its closest relative, the Noisy Scrubbird has loud ringing vocalisations. In the words of its original European discoverer, John Gilbert, 'the notes were so exceedingly loud and shrill as to leave a ringing sensation in the ears'.[3] To local Aborigines it was known as *Jeemuluuk*, an onomatopoeic rendering of a three-note call, which has been interpreted by Europeans as *zip da dee*.

The scrubbirds share the gift for mimicry possessed by their more illustrious cousins, the lyrebirds. Each family, indeed, borrows sounds from the other, leading to occasional confusion about which bird is performing the specific vocalisation. It led the author Elspeth Huxley to the following tongue-in-cheek observation:

> The Rufus Scrub-bird [*sic*] is a mimic too. Half the birds in the forest seem to be mimics. I still have a memory of Gus [a wildlife guide] . . . halting in the path like an alerted pointer with his head on one side while a positive cacophony of sounds came to us from all sides: whistles, whiplashes, cackles, screeches, warbles and twitterings. He was trying to identify a strong, high-pitched whistle repeated several times with a slightly different pitch on each occasion. The possibilities were that it could be
> (a) a Rufus Scrub-bird *au naturel*;
> (b) a lyre-bird imitating a Rufus Scrub-bird;
> (c) a Bower-bird imitating a lyre-bird imitating a Rufus Scrub-bird;
> (d) a lyre-bird imitating a Bower-bird imitating a Rufus Scrub-bird;
> (e) a Catbird imitating a Bower-bird imitating a lyre-bird imitating . . .
> But I have forgotten the rest. Only an Australian bird-man could take all this without succumbing to a nervous breakdown.[4]

There are more serious ornithological speculations underlying Huxley's joke: about where birds acquire their mimicked phrases and for how long these borrowed motifs might have been passed down, like a sound torch from one songster to another, through the generations. The implication may be that one is hearing not just a ringing endorsement of the present moment, but also an immeasurably ancient past.

Bowerbird family *Ptilonorhynchidae*

The great American scholar of New Guinean birds Tom Gilliard once wrote, 'It is perhaps not too much to say that . . . of all living creatures . . . short of man himself, bower birds are the most bizarre.'[1] Human fascination with the family probably dates back tens of thousands of years and rests largely on the birds' habit of creating special structures as part of their breeding behaviour.

These artefacts are not nests, as is so often and falsely claimed even today. They are, in the pithy words of the author David Rothenberg, 'love shacks' – specially cleared arenas or arrangements of leaves, moss, grass stems, twigs or small branches where male bowerbirds court and display to their prospective mates.[2] They are often located in clearings in the forest, and some of them are of complex and beautiful construction, resembling even miniature wickerwork arbours or thatch-roofed pagodas, and rather like something humans themselves might make. And if not quite human, then in the words of one bowerbird devotee, certainly they look like a 'fit abode for Oberon and Titania'.[3]

Some species of bowerbird go to inordinate lengths to decorate the bowers further, bringing back a treasure trove of natural or anthropogenic objects. These can include flowers and bones, quartz stones and berries, feathers and plastic bottle tops, even used condoms and fragments of sloughed

A female or young male Archbold's Bowerbird from New Guinea. The adult male loves to decorate his maypole bower with the extraordinary head plumes of King of Saxony Birds-of-Paradise. Not only do rival birds pinch them from each other, but covetous male humans also steal them from the birds.

snakeskin. In some of the most elaborate structures the walls may be smeared with coloured pigments. In one or two species the medium may be applied with a wad of vegetable material. This action certainly constitutes one of the few examples of tool use among birds, but in the eyes of some people it represents a performance more akin to an artist with a brush.

It is telling that when Europeans first encountered these bird-built chambers, they refused to believe the assertions of local people that they were of avian origin. Instead they attributed their manufacture to women intending them as toys to amuse their children. That incredulity, which is so typical of colonial Europeans towards 'the natives', took exactly the same form in Australia and New Guinea.[4] Yet it is perhaps understandable. Among the world's 10,000 or so bird species, bowerbirds are the only ones to build in this way.

Regardless of whether their actions are informed by aesthetic considerations and are genuinely analogous to human creativity, or whether such language is an obstacle that hinders our real understanding of their behaviour, this much is undisputed. Bowerbirds, in the words of one commentator, 'raise difficult questions, questions that penetrate to the very foundation of our biological theories'.[5]

The 19 species (some authorities propose a total of 20) are divided between Australia and New Guinea. Twelve are found on the latter island, and nine in Australia, with two species common to both places. Several bowerbirds have minuscule ranges. The **Golden Bowerbird** *Prionodura newtoniana* and **Tooth-billed Bowerbird** *Scenopoeetes dentirostris* are confined to the Atherton Tableland region of tropical north Queensland in Australia. **Archbold's Bowerbird** *Archboldia papuensis* is found in a scatter of tiny areas of high-altitude moss forest in the central mountain ranges of New Guinea.

This latter species was not knowingly seen by a person of European descent until 1940: the last bowerbird to be 'discovered' for science. However, the story of how Tom Gilliard later obtained a pair of fresh skins demonstrates how well the bird had been studied by local Papuans. The American ornithologist gave one trapper a steel axe, two gold-lip shells, a machete, a table knife, a mirror, assorted small shells, beads, matches, tobacco, salt and a newspaper – in all the equivalent of twelve months' income – to lay his hands on two birds in 1950. He offered a similar price for any subsequent finds and the same Papuan then promptly caught nine more all at the same bower.[6]

It was more than a century earlier that the British artist and naturalist John Gould coined the name 'bowerbird', probably referring to the **Satin Bowerbird** *Ptilonorhynchus violaceus*, the one species that has good claims to be the best known of its entire family.[7] It is found widely in eastern Australia from Victoria to northern Queensland, and will visit even large gardens on the forest-fringed outskirts of major cities, such as Sydney and Canberra. In some areas they can become back-garden familiars that their human residents take almost for granted. The Australian poet Judith Wright, in her work 'Satin Bower-birds', dwells on this apparent ordinariness: 'somehow comic / begging

A Satin Bowerbird in Lamington National Park, Queensland, Australia, decorates his 'love shack' with a strange miscellany of blue objects.

their bread. A domestic, / quarrelling, amateur troupe' that is 'as uninteresting as pigeons'.[8]

Gould's coinage of the original 'bowerbird' name is perfectly apt and draws on an historical horticultural feature – the secluded garden spot enclosed by curving walls of foliage, where an earlier form of human courtship was often conducted. Scientific investigation of the bower's function for the birds suggests it serves as a mode of display not too dissimilar to those of their spectacular New Guinean neighbours, the birds-of-paradise, except that in bowerbirds the form of exhibition is external to the birds' anatomy. Secondly it has been demonstrated in some species that males with the greatest range of display objects in their bowers achieve the most mating success.[9] Bowerbirds have

been shown to have bigger brains than their similar-sized relatives (yet not as large as members of the crow family; see Clever Corvids, page 392), and studies have also indicated that there is a positive correlation between bower complexity and brain size. The part that was enlarged in builders of elaborate bowers was the cerebellum, mainly responsible for coordinating movement.[10]

There are usually considered to be four distinct forms of bower (two species, the **White-eared Catbird** *Ailuroedus buccoides* and **Green Catbird** *Ailuroedus crassirostris*, do not build a structure of any kind). The first and most simple is the work of the Tooth-billed Bowerbird and is no more than an area of forest floor meticulously cleared of obstacles – an older name for that bird, which is still used, is 'stagemaker' – and then decorated with large conspicuous leaves, whose thick stems are sawn through by the bird's serrated bill (hence the name).[11] A further development on the Tooth-billed Bowerbird's cleared court is the raised oval or circular mat of Archbold's Bowerbird. This represents the accumulated mass of fern fronds brought over time by its owner to the one spot. On the elevated perches above the mat, the male then lays orchid stems, while the mat itself is enhanced with a range of decorative materials including beetles' iridescent elytra, snail shells, fungi, fruits and charcoal.

A third bower form is the structure from which Gould took the family name. Technically it is known as an 'avenue' and in the case of Satin Bowerbird it comprises two parallel walls of grass stems or fine sticks planted into a raised mat of vegetation by the bird, with each wall curving gently outwards just above half its height. The curvature of these bower walls mimics to some extent the rounded body shape of the birds themselves. In many species the owners sometimes 'paint' the upper walls with partly masticated vegetable or fruit materials or charcoal, the sticky paste adhering and drying on the upright sticks.

The fourth and last bower structure is known as a 'maypole', which is often an extensive climbing fabric of sticks, mounting around a central support vine or trunk, with the stick ends radiating outwards in all directions. An equally complex alternative, perhaps the one that most closely approximates to our own notions of a building, is the 'maypole' built by the **Vogelkop Bowerbird** *Amblyornis inornata*. This remarkable, dull-brown bird belongs to a genus of the family known sometimes as the 'gardeners', in honour of their elaborate works in earth and vegetation. What is most striking among Vogelkop Bowerbirds, which are confined to the westernmost parts of Papua, is that separate populations build very different types of bower. Some assemble the more standard rising 'Christmas tree' of outward-pointing sticks. However, perhaps the one most compelling in form and complexity is that constructed by the Vogelkop Bowerbirds dwelling in the Tamrau, Arfak and Wandammen Mountains. Roofed and hut-like in design, sometimes with double entrances and what look like covered porches at their fronts, these bowers are among the most improbable and magical of all avian structures: the abodes truly fit for Shakespeare's fairy king and queen. To crown their sense of mystery, the birds assemble around them mounds of natural objects that are chosen for their colour and texture.

A layperson's almost unavoidable assumption is that the birds are aware of the beauty of which they are the authors. However, the idea of a single bird making aesthetic choices hovers dangerously close to a simple case of projection: attributing to bowerbirds the self-critical processes of a human artist. This much, however, is clear. Birds seem to have some sense of overall composition in their designs, often moving objects, replacing dead flowers or clearing natural obtrusions such as falling leaves. Birds whose bowers are disrupted by deliberately meddling humans can deal forcefully and with great speed to amend the unwanted changes. Bowerbirds, in short, seem to be more than automata acting under instinct and have at least some sense of individual judgement, even taste.

In many ways the clipped language of scientific reportage on the hoards of treasure gathered by Vogelkop Bowerbirds

seems only to add to their inherent strangeness and beauty. In their major work, Clifford and Dawn Frith, the family's most devoted students, outline the materials recorded during their detailed field observations:

> Commonest and largest decoration on all bowers was black bracket fungus *Aphyllophorales*, placed in 1–2 piles up to 20 cm high and 50 cm dia 1–5 m out from the aperture and thus usually downhill . . . Common on 7 bowers were 4–32 dark brown or blackish beetle elytra beneath (5 bowers) or on the mat beyond the hut. Seven bowers also had blue fruit decorations, always beneath the hut when present but also beyond it on 3. Next most common decoration were orange and red fruits, red leaves, other black fungi, black fruits and orange flowers . . . Infrequently used items, including butterflies, beetle heads, amber beetles, acorns, orange bark, and orange jelly-like fungus, placed within the 'hut'.[12]

It is in the miscellany of gathered objects, deployed to catch the admiring attention of a possible partner – or partners, since bowerbirds are promiscuous and males play no part in incubation or chick rearing – where the link between the cultural lives of humans and bowerbirds is at its deepest. (While it might seem also anthropomorphic to write of a bird's 'cultural life', these are truly cultural entities, whose construction is a learned tradition passed on from bird generation to generation, in much the same ways that traditional Papuan men inherit the designs of their spectacular feather adornments. It is notable, for example, that in the case of the Satin Bowerbird, males take seven years to reach sexual maturity. That immature phase is spent acquiring the techniques and skills necessary for successful bower construction.)

Many objects seem to be chosen partly for their rarity value, as if to demonstrate the hunting prowess and surplus 'leisure' time enjoyed by the fittest males. As a result of living often in close proximity to human neighbours, Satin Bowerbirds collect an astonishing array of man-made products including blue bags, matchboxes, cigarette packets, envelopes, marbles, glass, while one male in a national park near Sydney selected as ornamentation a synthetic condom.[13] As Clifford and Dawn Frith have pointed out there is a wonderful wry irony in this selection, given that a bower's real purpose is sexual reproduction.

In the case of the Satin Bowerbird the objects have the added allure of being largely blue and often a shade of lavender that matches the exquisite eyes of the female. An example I encountered in the Lamington National Park of southern Queensland was surrounded by the following collection: a frayed piece of blue nylon twine, a blue wrapper from a cornetto ice cream, a blue plastic peg and another darker blue peg, a blue plastic biro, a girl's lavender-coloured hair band, a blue plastic spoon, a metal blue bottle top, a blue pen top, a blue milk carton, Vicks VapoDrops sweet wrappers ('Original Flavour'), the blue tail feathers from Crimson Rosella parrots, bones (probably from a pademelon, a small type of kangaroo-like marsupial) and blue flowers. The last might seem a natural addition to the total, and reflect no human agency, but it is intriguing that the blooms are obtained from a shrub called 'wild tobacco' (elsewhere known as Woolly Nightshade *Solanum mauritianum*), a non-native plant brought originally from colonial South

America.[14] While its flower might match the Satin Bowerbird's eyes fairly closely and therefore seem an obvious item for the bird to collect, it is there only by dint of its human introduction.

Another larger bower nearby contained a similar array, but also included 25 bottle tops (all blue and one bearing the brand name Sprite), 20 drinking straws of various blue shades, some papery skin off bulbs of garlic, lavender-coloured raffia paper, the split body cases of emerging cicadas, a gold plastic pine cone (possibly from a Christmas decoration) and two bits of sloughed snakeskin. One notable characteristic of this particular bower was the close proximity of a coin-operated barbecue, a highly odorous outdoor lavatory and, at times, numerous visitor coaches and their evacuating human contents. Bowers are one remarkable physical spot where the cultural lives of humans and birds intersect. Yet this last example demonstrates how their respective sense of the surrounding space and the dominant function made of it by each species can diverge radically. Similarly intriguing is the way in which the blue bower ornaments are meaningless detritus casually discarded by one of these parties, when they become objects of great significance to the other.

There are moments, however, where exactly the same object is prized equally by both, but for quite separate reasons. One of the most striking instances occurred near Alice Springs and involved a species called the **Western Bowerbird** *Chlamydera guttata*. The Australian ornithologist Michael Sharland took a portrait of its bower (complete with a small plastic child's toy) only to find later that the blue flash bulb he had used in creating the photograph had been added to the very same display site.[15]

There are very rare occasions where the identical object is valued in precisely the same way by man and bird. The classic instance involves the extraordinary pair of crown feathers on a King of Saxony Bird-of-Paradise. Beautiful in both colour and form, they rise out of the male's head like a pair of insane horns, sometimes 50 cm (20 in) long and more than twice the length of the bird itself. An adult grows just two such plumes a year and after they have moulted off their original owners, male Archbold's Bowerbirds search for them or steal them from each other in order to adorn their bowers. Likewise, Papuan men take the very same feathers to use in their elaborate head ornaments (see also page 401). Rarity and ostentation are surely at work in the choice of these plumes made by the males of both species as a means to impress their respective females.[16] We should also recognise that the same behaviour is by no means confined to the mist-enshrouded forests of New Guinea. A socialite of modern Mayfair or the Manhattan fashionista partakes of the same deep fundamental tradition when they choose boldly adorned hats, often completed with bird feathers.

Other family members that make extensive use of man-made items are two species, found respectively in northern and eastern Australia, the **Great Bowerbird** *Chlamydera nuchalis* and **Spotted Bowerbird** *Chlamydera maculata*. They are avenue builders but their choice of ornaments, which are heaped all around sometimes like mounds of food at a banquet, are compelling for their eccentric range and sheer quantity. The items that command the headlines are those taken at various times by the latter species – a diamond ring, a man's glass eye stolen from a cup of water,

and sets of keys filched from the ignition switches of parked cars. In fact it is said that if anything goes missing within the known territory of a 'spotty', the place to begin the search is in its bower.[17] Further routine additions include cartridge cases, nails, spoons, coins, wire, foil, plastic, glass and the pull tags from aluminium cans.[18] In Australia it is now virtually proverbial to refer to a person with a tendency to hoard as 'a bit of a bowerbird'.[19]

Animal bones, stones and snail shells often form the greatest mass of decorations for Spotted and Great Bowerbirds. One spotted was recorded to have collected 2,500 land shells, while another assembled 1,320 bones (hence an old name for the species, 'sepulchre-bird').[20] A notable aspect to these collections is that some can have significant archaeological implications. It was shown that of 767 decorations at one Great Bowerbird site, there were 186 bones that may have originated from human meals, while more than half of 189 stones showed evidence of having been worked by people. These modified pieces may have been chosen because they sparkled more and were more attractive to potential mates. One intriguing speculation on how the birds might influence archaeological studies arose at a site where there was an abundance of Dugong bone fragments. Among the 253 pieces from the carcasses of this marine mammal there were notable absentees including small bones from the flippers. The suggestion was that these had possibly been removed by bowerbirds, thereby influencing any scholarly interpretation. [21]

It is intriguing to compare the response of some Australian Aborigines to that of African communities when confronted with the equally extreme and eccentric acquisitive habits of the stork-like bird the Hamerkop (see page 137). In the case of both that species and Great and Spotted Bowerbirds, their sepulchral tastes for bits of bone, skin and human possessions of all kinds have led to claims of the birds' sorcery. Aborigines apparently fear male Spotted and Great Bowerbirds as 'custodians of ceremonies involving secret "business" (rites) of their own'. It is assumed that some bowerbirds steal human bones for just such magical purposes.[22]

If the birds borrow some of their 'magic' from us, then their human neighbours sometimes reciprocate. In parts of New Guinea, Papuan men deliberately place a stray leaf on the bower of a **Macgregor's Bowerbird** *Amblyornis macgregoriae* and then observe the way that he removes it from his plot. These actions will indicate in which direction the young beaus should travel in order to seek their own brides. Even more impressive and tantalising as a cultural loan from bird to human is the manner in which New Guinean communities lay out their ceremonial grounds for their 'sing sing' events (see Bird-of-paradise family, page 400 for a fuller account). These ritual spaces are planted with parallel lines of trees and other linear assemblages of vegetation that undoubtedly suggest the structures of bowerbirds, even if the resemblance is merely coincidental. Frederick Mayer, a noted naturalist in New Guinea, 'once said to a man at Mt Hagen [site of a famous sing sing ground], "You people must have copied your dancing grounds from the Gardener [Macgregor's] Bower Bird."

"Oh, no," the native said. "The bird copied us."'[23]

Honeyeater family *Meliphagidae*

The honeyeaters are a large family (178 species) of small- to medium-sized songbirds with elongated body shapes, often with bright yellow or occasionally red plumage detail, and usually long, sickle-shaped bills. The birds are found across a vast zone, from Indonesia out into the most remote parts of the central Pacific. Several now extinct species, once of massive cultural significance, occurred even in Hawaii. This represents the eastern limit to the honeyeater's historic range, but their key centres of distribution are New Guinea (62 species) and Australia (73 species).

In the latter country, honeyeaters have radiated out to occupy a wide spectrum of habitats, but they are routinely found in woodland or forest, where a single area can hold several species – as many as ten in 1 ha (2.5 acres).[1] One veteran ornithologist suggested that he could not name 'any part of the continent, or scarcely an island, where one could go without seeing at least one of the . . . honeyeater tribe'.[2] Since they are also nectar- and fruit-eating birds, they will all gather to exploit the same food source. At these places of transient abundance the honeyeaters' loud, ringing, intensely sociable or playful, frequently metallic, occasionally aggressive and even insanely persistent calls can dominate the entire landscape.

Their aura of busyness means that they regularly occupy much the same psychological space in the west Pacific as the greenbuls do in Africa, or the bulbuls in Asia (see pages 430 and 433, respectively). Some of the most vocal and zany in manner – not to mention bizarre in appearance – are Australia's four species of friarbird (such as the **Noisy**

Friarbird *Philemon corniculatus*) whose name derives from the bare black skin on the head and 'the semblance of a hood about its shoulders ... And the sad hue of its plumage'.[3] These features were thought to suggest the friar's habit and his bald pate but, in truth, the birds often look weirdly reptilian. A rather appropriate and once widespread alternative name was 'leatherhead'.[4]

The friarbirds typify the family's wider adaptations to their diet. Like other honeyeaters, they possess fine, flexible, brush-tipped tongues that enable them to access the nectar in flowers. In fact, they are such persistent attendants at blossom-laden trees or bushes, such as eucalypts, acacias and banksias, that they play an important role in pollinating Australasian plant life. In Australia specifically, where honeyeater distribution mimics a similar human bias towards the eastern half of the country, several family members are among the most conspicuous and populous birds in the country. Gardeners will deliberately plant favoured flowering shrubs to lure them in, but the common alternative is a special nectar dispenser of sugar water (or a recommended mix of one part honey, to nine parts water).[5] One ornithologist, noting the predilection among some honeyeaters for wild sources of fermented nectar, took to adding sweet sherry to his feeders, and described how 'They just relished it!'[6]

One of the best-known family members is the thrush-sized **Blue-faced Honeyeater** *Entomyzon cyanotis*, which has adapted extremely well to both agricultural environments and suburbia. It is a routine attendant at many

The Blue-faced Honeyeater is a familiar bird of Australian woodland but also now city suburbs and town parks.

human gathering sites, such as campsites, outdoor cafes and parks. It is an immensely handsome bird (and occasional fruit pest) with silky white belly, golden-olive upperparts and a cobalt patch on the face, from which it derives an older name, 'blue eye'. More intriguing is another vernacular alternative, the 'gympie'. The coastal town in southern Queensland of the same title claims to derive it from an Aboriginal word for a local tree with stinging leaves. Gympie was used commonly for the honeyeater until the 1950s – and is occasionally used still – but what link it might have to the town is not clear.[7]

Another species rich in vernacular names is the hugely characterful and perhaps overly abundant **Noisy Miner** *Manorina melanocephala*, a starling-sized bird with mealy-brown plumage and a black bandit's mask. It thrives in parkland habitats created by Australian suburbia, and is sometimes known as the 'Mickey bird' for reasons that are explained here:

> The term 'mickey' comes from the expression, 'take the mickey' – to tease or take the rinse out of someone. This comes from their very nature, where they are always getting in each others' faces and playing. They don't restrict this play to their own kind and will do the same to practically any other bird and the larger the bird the better, particularly crows and kookaburras. When it is magpie-nesting season and the magpies attack our Silver-backed Butcherbirds [see also page 372], the Mickey birds will then attack the magpies with impunity.[8]

The 'mickey' connections may possibly pre-date the expression 'to take the mickey' (1950s), and could derive from another Australian colloquialism 'to chuck a micky', which means to throw a fit, or make a fuss – a conceivable reference to the hullabaloo raised by mobbing miners.[9] Alternatively, it may simply be a personal name to alliterate nicely with the word 'miner', hence the alternative, 'Mickey miner'.[10] Another piece of vernacular was 'soldier bird', although as the Australian author Alec Chisholm noted, 'they, perhaps, should be regarded as sentries rather than fighters'.[11] The miner's incessant vocalisations are aroused by almost any predator with a specific reputation for warning human neighbours of snakes (in fact yet another old name was 'snake bird'). Their alarm calls are also taken as a warning by other birds, but sometimes things are not as they seem:

> A favourite scenario – witnessed by myself – was at a local wildlife park were flocks of Rainbow Lorikeets (by the way, now the commonest species in Brisbane, Sydney and Melbourne suburban areas) were attracted to trays of bread and honey and seed held by tourists. The birds would perch over the tray – and arms and heads of the people. The local Noisy Miner flock would turn up, suddenly give an alarm call (to nothing that we could detect), watch the crowd of lorikeets fly off in a panic, which caused huge spillage of the foods, then calmly fly down and feast on the mess. True story.[12]

A more recent concern is the large increase in Noisy Miners, partly because of council planting policies in urban areas. The bureaucratic preference for wide, open lawned spaces with light eucalyptus tree cover has allowed Noisy Miners to thrive in suburbia and their highly aggressive behaviour is partly blamed for the decline of smaller songbirds, including several other honeyeater species.[13]

The Noisy Miner is one of the most successful members of its family in Australia.

RED FEATHER MONEY

Although honeyeaters may be most diverse and common in the western portion of their collective range, it is the small number of species spread through the scattered island groups and vast ocean spaces of the Pacific that have acquired a remarkable social and cultural importance. One bird of huge former significance is the **Cardinal Myzomela** *Myzomela cardinalis*. It occurs from the Caroline Islands, which are due east of the Philippines, as far as the central-south Pacific island of Samoa – a distance of more than 6,000 km (3,700 miles) – but the population in the Melanesian archipelago of Santa Cruz, south-east of the main Solomon Island chain, was uniquely prized for its bright feathers. The males were trapped on sticky perches and their tiny, if gloriously scarlet, plumes were plucked and woven into narrow belts of bark cloth.[14] At one time this practice was possibly killing at least 20,000 birds a year and 12 per cent of the main island's total population of Cardinal Myzomelas.

The cloth strips may have been just 5 cm (2 in) in width, but the weave could continue until the piece measured 10 m (32.8 ft) in length. A double coil can hold 50,000–60,000 feathers and represent not only a large number of dead birds (one estimate is between 345 and 500 per roll), but a massive investment of human time and skill. In a year the weavers were thought to finish off only about five rolls, each of which would have been in various stages of completion. When finalised and in pristine condition the beautiful scarlet-feathered strips look to a Western eye like bands of gorgeously red, deep-pile carpet. They are known as *tevau*, and when wound up into bulky coils they were used as precious trade items, but also as a symbol of wealth that functioned once as a kind of money.[15]

While it was immensely precious and carefully stored and protected in palm leaves or trade cloth, *tevau* was an inherently transient currency that lost colour and condition. It is thought that the red feathers were unlikely to last more than a few decades, at most, in prime condition. Very old examples on display in museums are often just fibre 'skeletons' devoid of both feathers and their all-important red hue. A classic example is a piece in the Great North Museum: Hancock in the British city of Newcastle upon Tyne.

At one time feather money was a major component of bride price (when the male suitor's family reinburses the relatives of the intended female partner) or was used to settle land agreements and compensation payments. Until the 1960s the price for a bride was ten rolls. However, they were also used for buying goods, such as pigs and canoes, while fines for misbehaviour, including extra-marital sex, were also paid in coils of red feathers. With the encroachment of a more conventional system of exchange (i.e. the Australian dollar) in the Santa Cruz Islands, feather-money production declined and probably died out completely in the 1960s, and all that remains today of these traditions are small stick-sized feather decorations for the tourist industry.[16]

While the manufacture of feather money was a speciality of the Solomon Islands, it reflects an historical and almost Pacific-wide tradition of utilising bird feathers, especially crimson feathers, for making objects and often important ceremonial garments as a means to convey heightened spiritual and political status. One thinks especially of the deep symbolic importance attached to cloaks made from kiwi feathers or the plumes of the now extinct Huia by the Polynesian inhabitants of New Zealand, the Maoris (see pages 30 and 369). In Tahiti also (and more widely in the Society Islands, now French Polynesia) special girdles made of bird feathers were at the heart of indigenous political and religious ritual.

However, these cultural practices and the accompanying exploitation of bird feathers reached their most exalted form or their most hypertrophied and destructive condition – depending on your point of view – in the Hawaiian Islands. Several species of honeyeater were central to these practices. The full story of Hawaiian and wider Polynesian use of feathers involves a much wider suite of birds, including frigatebirds, tropicbirds, parrots and pigeons, but especially, and most confusingly, an endemic Hawaiian family called the honeycreepers. It is under this quite separate and unrelated family that the story of pan-Pacific feather art, which produced some of the region's most beautiful and extraordinary artefacts, is best unfolded (see page 504).

Wattled Crow family *Callaeatidae*

This exclusively New Zealand family includes three species (one of them now extinct) of medium-to-large, long-tailed passerines with stout legs and short wings that reflect the birds' preference for scrambling or leaping among forest branches, rather than deploying their weak powers of flight. In many ways the family typifies the environmental crisis visited on the country after European settlement.

Since the nineteenth century two of the trio, the **Kokako** *Callaeas cinerea* and **Saddleback** *Philesturnus carunculatus*, have slumped towards extinction, despite neither being especially valued by Maori or European hunters as food. Yet both species have succumbed to a mixture of habitat loss (the widespread felling of native forest) and predation from introduced mammals (rats, stoats, possums). Today there are just *c*.1,400 Kokakos and 5,650 Saddlebacks, mainly confined to mammal-free offshore sites such as Little Barrier Island. The policy of translocation, one of the most intensive conservation efforts anywhere in the world, is a backstop policy for much of New Zealand's threatened avifauna.

While Saddlebacks are 'renowned for their innovative melodic line', the Kokako has an international reputation as a songster.[1] The well-known US birder Kenn Kaufman rates it above all others: 'It sings rich musical chords, and sounds like someone sitting in the forest playing an organ, slowly picking out thoughtful phrases. It's the world's greatest bird song.'[2] A volunteer at the Kokako stronghold on Little Barrier Island muses on this issue of comparative quality among birdsongs:

> At the bunkhouse we are drawn into endless argument: which bird sings the most beautiful song? I play them my favourite, the Pied Butcherbird [see page 372].
> But my kiwi friends won't be beaten by an Australian bird, and stick with the Kokako. Judgement is entirely

subjective, comparison perhaps equally so, but nonetheless interesting.

Both songs are difficult to describe. The Pied Butcherbird's is a melody of pure notes arranged in short, repeated phrases. The Kokako's has no melody. It contains sharp *mee-ews* that rise then fall, soft whistles, low brassy notes, sharper *tok-toks*. The butcherbird plays the flute, but includes trills that would defeat a human flautist. The Kokako plays the clarinet, the saxophone, the organ, the castanets. Both are masters of the perfect pause.

The Pied Butcherbird is Elgar, a traditionalist, a lover of melodic themes – the opening bars of the *Enigma Variations* are pure butcherbird. The tunes are predictable, their structure self-evident; they know where they are going and take you with them. A few moments' listening and you could sing along, if you had the voice for it. There is pleasure in knowing what comes next, as well as in the purity of the notes and the quality of their phrasing. The Kokako is Messiaen, a modernist (ironically, Messiaen knew and was inspired by the butcherbird). Their song has structure but no tune, and the structure is more complex, harder to detect. After hours of patient listening it is possible to anticipate the next sound or the length of a pause, but never with complete accuracy. There is pleasure too, in this dimension of surprise and in the questions it provokes. How do they decide what to sing next? And

when two Kokako sing together, how does one decide how to answer the other?

There is no meaningful answer to the question of which is more beautiful. A Pied Butcherbird fluting on the desert air. A Kokako duet echoing down a cool green valley. Both are peak experiences. Both are worth crossing the world for.[3]

A singing Kokako has an intriguing if largely subliminal role in the film *The Piano* (1993) by the kiwi writer and director Jane Campion. In this cinematic masterpiece about love, sexuality, repression and colonial New Zealand, the sounds of Kokako can be heard in the context of the largely wordless courtship between the central characters, Ada McGrath (Holly Hunter) and George Baines (Harvey Keitel). In their strange but compelling scenes of lovemaking, Baines sells back to Ada (who is a mute), one key at a time, her own piano in exchange for her performances upon the instrument. Each occasion that Ada approaches Baines' cabin to transact their mixture of music and passion, we hear the Kokako itself performing. The bird's song, whose power and impact is so much determined by the silence that seems somehow to wrap around its sparse, beautiful phrases, is perfectly matched to the couple's unspoken relationship.

The third in the wattled crow family, the **Huia** *Heteralocha acutirostris*, before being driven over the edge into complete oblivion, was a bird of huge cultural importance for the Maoris – a source of place and family names, of

The Kokako of New Zealand has a reputation as one of the world's finest songsters.

An unknown Maori photographed in the late nineteenth century sports Huia plumes in his hair and a cloak made partly from kiwi feathers.

fluted distress note was that it served to betray the birds' presence to hunters. Worse, the species responded inquisitively to human imitation making it easier for the Maori trappers to lure it within range. Their goal was not the meat, though this is said to have been delicious, but the Huia's white-tipped tail feathers of iridescent black. Sometimes the half-metre-long birds were kept in captivity and then intermittently plucked live. The plumage was a mark of high status among New Zealand's indigenous people, who used it to create two striking forms of feather decoration. A *pōhoi* was a rosette of body feathers, complete with head, wattles and all, worn on the ear, and signifying chiefly rank. A conspicuous aspect of this ornament was the female's elongated, finely decurved bill. (This, incidentally, was completely different to the male's stoutly pointed chisel, and was one of the most marked examples of separate bill morphology between the sexes of any bird species.) The other Huia adornment was an impressive circlet of 12 tail feathers across the crown, known as a *marereko*, and worn in times of war.

Maori attachment to Huia feathers and their high status as trade items inflicted serious losses upon the species. However, Huia skins acquired fatal popularity only after European colonists came to share a taste for them. The expanded market caused systematic hunting in many areas. Just 11 indigenous catchers took 646 birds in a single month of 1883.[5] The combined impact of this persecution, habitat loss and predation by non-native mammals caused the Huia to become extinct by the early twentieth century. All that now survives of the species are a few skins and eggs in international museums, while in institutions in New Zealand itself there are Maori ornaments of Huia feathers, such as the *pōhoi* and *marereko*. All that survives to remind the world of a Huia's unforgettable, penetrating whistle is merely the echo of an echo: an early recording of Henare Haumana, a member of a 1909 search party, who knew and could imitate the bird accurately.

proverbs and poetry, but also of feather adornments that signified prestige and social status.[4] The bird itself shared several distinct features with its surviving relatives, not least the brightly coloured orange wattles at the base of its bill (orange-red in the Saddleback and blue in Kokako) and also a loud clear whistling call.

However, the salient fact about the Huia's own softly

Helmetshrike and Bushshrike family *Malaconotidae*

This heterogeneous group of 55 species is almost entirely restricted to a single continent. Just one of them, the **Black-crowned Tchagra** *Tchagra senegalus*, has an outlying population along the Mediterranean coasts of Morocco, Algeria and Tunisia (and in Arabia). All the others are found exclusively in sub-Saharan Africa.

At one time they were assumed to be part of, or closely allied to, the shrike family *Laniidae*, and many of them superficially resemble shrikes – medium-sized songbirds of 18–26cm (7–10 in) with long tails and thick hook-tipped beaks. Today, however, they are now deemed to be quite separate groups, and even within the family the helmet- and bushshrikes are considered to be distinct by some authorities.

One common factor across many is a tendency to bright colours, especially among the bushshrikes. They can have striking red or yellow underparts that contrast smartly with black facial masks or dark colours on the upper body. The exemplars are the **Black-headed Gonolek** *Laniarius erythrogaster* (central Africa) and **Crimson-breasted Shrike** *Laniarius atrococcineus* (southern Africa), which

are deep blood red below and black above. One aspect that is quite unlike true shrikes is the family tendency towards shyness. All that glorious colour is often only glimpsed, as the birds dive into dense bush or forest cover.

Fortunately the family is as famous for its remarkable vocalisations as it is for beauty. The most celebrated for their voices are the 18 bushshrikes belonging to the genus *Laniarius*, which produce antiphonal duets involving both the male and female. The loud, ringing, sometimes bell-like and often hauntingly beautiful sounds account for the striking array of onomatopoeic titles for these family members, including the gonoleks (three species) and the boubous (ten species). The **Brubru** *Nilaus afer* is another bushshrike that owes its odd-seeming title to its voice, but the most strangely named and one of the most highly reputed songsters is the **Bokmakierie** *Telophorus zeylonus* (also once called Bakbakiri), which is found widely in open habitats including towns and gardens across South Africa and Namibia. The birds' loud and far-carrying duets occasionally spell out their own singular name.[1]

Butcherbird and Allies family *Cracticidae*

This family of 14 species includes a number of highly charismatic birds of the Australasian region, as well as a solitary, rare Oriental representative, whose name even hints at its singularity. With a heavy black body, massive bill and red pate crowned by a tonsure of straw-coloured 'hairs', the **Bornean Bristlehead** *Pityriasis gymnocephala* (found in peninsular Malaysia as well as on its eponymous island) is exceptional. It has baffled taxonomists for decades, who previously placed it with various families from shrikes to starlings and now with the butcherbirds. Yet this fascination among ornithologists, who view it as one of the ultimate must-see forest birds of Asia, is in inverse proportion to a general cultural indifference.

The bristlehead's overall form, particularly its bulky build and formidable hook-tipped bill, suggests the physical characters of other butcherbirds. Yet many of the family differ in being highly adaptable and among the most common and conspicuous of all wild animals in the Australian landscape. Three genera of medium-sized black or pied crow-like birds dominate our attention: five species of true butcherbirds (*Cracticus*), three species of currawong (*Strepera*) and the **Australian Magpie** *Gymnorhina tibicen*.

The last is among the best-known birds in the country (it also occurs naturally in New Guinea), acquiring a totemic role in 1904 as a state bird for South Australia, initially under the name 'piping shrike'. It is also known subliminally to many millions of non-Australians, because magpie vocalisations were and are a routine part of the soundtrack to *Neighbours*.[1] The longest-running drama in Australian television history was once part of daytime TV schedules around the world.

Like the bristlehead, the Australian Magpie has had a confused taxonomic past. As well as its similarity to shrikes, early ornithologists were struck by its superficial resemblance to the magpies of Eurasia and North America. The Australian bird's pied plumage and size, not to mention its bold personality, all suggested its northern namesake, but the likeness is coincidence. They are not closely related.

One major difference is the extraordinary musicality of Australian Magpies (unlike the grating machine-gun chatter of the other species). When the English mariner William Dampier made landfall in 1688 in what he called New Holland, he wrote about the western Australian birds 'all singing with great variety of fine shrill notes'.[2] One cannot help wondering whether Dampier was offering

A male Australian Magpie in attack mode is a routine source of suburban anxiety and not infrequent bloodshed.

The Australian Magpie's reputation for aggression may be well founded, but so too is its renown as a vocalist.

a first European eulogy on the sound of New Holland's magpie. The bird's scientific name *tibicen* means 'flautist' in Latin, a reference to the loud rich, rather throaty flute-like yodelling or warbling. Several birds will routinely sing together performing an antiphonal chorus with their heads and long straight pale bills pointed skywards. These concerts have earned the highest praise. The great naturalist Alfred Russel Wallace, co-discoverer of evolution through natural selection, thought it unequalled by any European songbird.[3] It is an immensely atmospheric song and somehow perfectly expressive of the Australian landscape.

The qualities have given rise to a range of vernacular names – 'organbird', 'flutebird', 'piper' and 'bell-magpie' – as well as various literary interpretations.[4] The best known, ironically, come from New Zealand, where Australian Magpies were introduced in the nineteenth century and are now locally common (it was also successfully introduced to Fiji). In his poem 'The Magpies', the writer Denis Glover (1912–1980) contrasted the robust persistence of the natural world with the frailties of human aspiration and endeavour. While the poem's central figures, Elizabeth and Tom, toil on their land to no genuine end – she dies, he goes 'light in the head' and the farm is repossessed by the mortgage company – so in each stanza the land's most mellifluous birds deliver a blithely indifferent chorus: *Quardle oodle ardle wardle doodle*. As a stab at the Australian Magpie's inexpressible melody, which seems beautifully rounded or quavering in shape, it isn't bad. Perhaps less accurate if more comedic is a recent rendition by fellow kiwi and children's author Pamela Allen: 'waddle, giggle, gargle'.

It is a justifiably celebrated songster, but the magpie's reputation as the continent's finest is not undisputed. Remarkably its relative, the slightly smaller but similarly coloured **Pied Butcherbird** *Cracticus nigrogularis*, is, if anything, even more highly regarded and must rank with North America's Hermit Thrush and Europe's Common Nightingale as possessor of the world's most beautiful birdsong. A notable feature shared by all three is their propensity to sing by night on a full moon. An admirer perfectly conveys the bird's ability to move us:

> It was a scorching day in July 2005, somewhere near the Mary River in Australia's Northern Territory. We were looking for Gouldian Finches, following up a reported sighting of the previous day, scanning the open bush – red earth, spiky grey foliage, shimmering heat. Our air-conditioned car beckoned enticingly, but I was drawn in a different direction by the most beautiful sound I have ever heard. A flute-like song piercing the air, phrases repeated in turn, punctuated by considered pauses, an occasional trill. Not just a song, but an unfolding composition. I had to find the musician. It took a while, but this was not one of those high, thin bird calls designed to fool a searcher; this was a proud song that said, 'Here I am!' And eventually, there he was, a Pied Butcherbird. The discovery brought an additional pleasure, for as he sang, as he composed, carefully choosing each note and phrase, he moved his head – up for the high notes, down for the low notes – and bowed, and spread his wings. Not just an aural performance, but a visual one. The beauty of it moved me to tears. I looked around for someone to share the magic, but my

companions were distant and preoccupied, so I offered a silent 'Thank you', and turned reluctantly away.[5]

One area of behaviour in which the Australian Magpie out-competes its relatives and, in fact, most of the world's birds is in the matter of aggression. As a commentator notes, 'Almost everyone in Australia has a "magpie story".'[6] Studies conducted in suburban Brisbane by Darryl Jones, a leading expert on the species, found that 85 per cent of people questioned had been attacked at some point in their lives. A survey in Queensland over a four-year period found that 99 per cent of those reporting injuries had bleeding head wounds. According to Darryl Jones, the number of serious eye injuries across the whole of Australia 'may be appallingly high'.[7] There are two claimed fatalities: one in 1946 when a 13-year old girl from New South Wales was struck in the head and died of tetanus.[8] A second story – widely believed and not dismissed by Jones despite its whiff of urban legend – occurred in Queensland and involved a middle-aged man struck so hard in the back of the neck that the beak penetrated the spinal cord and caused instant death to man and bird.[9]

Other members of the family known to attack humans include the **Pied Currawong** *Strepera graculina*, Pied Butcherbird and **Grey Butcherbird** *Cracticus torquatus*. In fact the proportion of butcherbird incidents that result in injury is higher than those for Australian Magpie, but the overall number of attacks is much smaller. In Brisbane, for example, 40 reports of aggressive butcherbirds per year compare with about 250 magpies.[10] More generally the family has a reputation if not for violence, then at least for mischief. Old settlers sometimes complained that currawongs entered their tents to steal food or any kind of portable object such as cutlery. On Tasmania, however, the human victims were known to respond by converting the thieves into a passable stew.[11]

What is beyond dispute in modern Australia is that magpie attacks upon people are frequent, dangerous and potentially traumatising. Some infamous birds have been featured on state and national television. Response teams of Brisbane wildlife officers have occasionally arrived at a suburban school's gates to find crowds of angry, distressed parents all urging their children to run into the yard where a medical officer awaits armed with the first-aid kit. Then as each infant makes haste across the intervening no-man's-land, he or she is greeted by a swooping bird. Before being shot or removed magpies have been known to chalk up more than 100 injuries during one of these schoolyard reigns of terror.[12]

Recent studies by Brisbane-based ecologists have uncovered that it is a perfectly 'natural' part of magpie behaviour and is intended to deter predators from the nest and its precious contents. The real danger period is at the height of the breeding season from August to October. Most of the aggression comes from males (99 per cent), but only a small percentage of breeding pairs contain such 'rogue' magpies (18 per cent). The frequency and severity of attacks is correlated to distance from the nest tree and the state of the development of the chicks, with the violence intensifying as they reach the point of fledging. Remarkably the birds can become fixated on certain human individuals, having a particular dislike for postmen and cyclists. While pedestrians are assaulted within 100 m (328 ft) of the nest tree, cyclists can be pursued for 150 m (492 ft) and even well beyond the bird's territory. Speed of passage, it appears, is one of the triggers for their aggressive response, so when cyclists dismount the attacks often cease.[13]

The classic method of dealing with such magpies has been to shoot them, although there is an underlying ecological relationship between ourselves and the species that makes this an increasingly inappropriate course of action. The bird thrives best in the mixture of open-grassland-with-trees that is the classic habitat of suburban Australia, and is one of the few native species to flourish under European colonisation. Magpies tend to gather where we also congregate and shotguns, therefore, become as dangerous to the victims of magpie attacks as the bird itself. The point is well illustrated by a log book entry by an agency staff member sent to sort out a 'problem' bird:

14 August–11 September 1997. Swooping in the Plaza, subsequently attacking. Many complaints. Police borrow agency shotgun to shoot bird, missed bird but peppered colleague with No. 8 shot instead. Shotgun impounded, inquiry held, bird escaped. Embarrassment all round![14]

A non-lethal alternative to killing the magpie, an option favoured by many, is to catch and remove it to a substantial distance from the scene of its crimes. While birds seldom find their way back and may routinely die, studies of what happens to the fatherless broods have revealed a remarkable aspect of magpie behaviour. Sometimes a 'stepfather' replaces the removed bird within hours of the latter being caught. Rather than killing the offspring of his predecessor, which is a classic pattern in many animals (for example, when a new male lion takes over a pride), these surrogate parent magpies are actually more attentive to the needs of their stepchildren than the original male. It seems the acquisition of a territory is the prime motive and the incentive to prove himself a worthy partner.

The almost unavoidable anthropomorphic perception of the male bird as the 'good father' is sometimes a part of people's response to magpie incidents. There have been cases where individual witnesses have harangued the authorities for removing a bird that was doing no more than any devoted parent.[15] This same positive feeling towards the birds may be at work in the public's preferred solution to problem magpies. The vast majority of people surveyed on how the wildlife agencies should tackle the issue favoured the erection of signs or to do nothing, while just 3 per cent thought the bird should be killed humanely. Preventive measures include use of umbrellas, wearing of hats and attaching flexible poles to the back of bicycles. One such deterrent widely deployed among schoolchildren, and now a rather striking feature of suburban Australia, is a sun hat that sports a pair of bright piercing 'eyes' on the back. It works on the assumption that the magpies do not attack while being 'watched'. However, their real efficacy as a deterrent may not justify the hat's popularity.

Humans may be the most frequently reported victims but they are not the only targets. Australian Magpies routinely attack other predatory birds, and there are reliable reports of horses, sheep and dogs all losing eyes to their pale dagger-like bills. Possums and Koalas are regularly injured. One highly telling piece of anthropomorphism – if not, at

the same time, completely understandable – involves the human rescue of Koalas when they inadvertently stray too close to magpie nests. There is a hospital in Brisbane where these much-loved marsupials are treated and it holds several animals blinded during magpie attacks.

There is also a wider sense in Australia that the butcherbird family, which is overall such a prominent beneficiary of suburban expansion, has acted collectively to oust other and perhaps more highly regarded songbirds. The eviction, which is sometimes characterised as a conflict between the 'little guys' and the 'big, nasty, domineering . . . gangs and thugs', is described by one contributor:

When we moved to live on the edge of the rainforest in Northern New South Wales in 1980 we were amazed at the dawn chorus of birds. We taped and forgot about it until 25 years later, when we replayed the tape and were amazed – the chorus is perhaps a twentieth of what it was and many birds are missing, especially the lyrebirds with their amazing ability to mimic sounds like chainsaws and motorbikes. We have a Coolamon tree on our property, which is at the moment covered in red flowers – usually we have flocks of drunk parrots falling out of the tree and this year none. Here the magpies, the currawongs, crows and butcherbirds dominate the scene.[16]

Members of the butcherbird family, such as this Pied Currawong, are widely accused of ousting smaller songbirds from Australian gardens.

Cuckooshrike family *Campephagidae*

This family of Old World tropical forest – they are predominantly Australasian (42 species), Asian (28 species) and African (12 species) – is well named. Many of the 89 species have the long tail and general slim build of a small cuckoo, but with the thick-billed, dark-masked mien of a large shrike. Another quality that foreshadows the cuckooshrikes' predatory behaviour is a frequent colour combination (grey, black and white) reminiscent of a smart military uniform. In fact the birds seldom eat anything much larger than caterpillars and other invertebrates picked from the foliage of the forest canopy.

There is something in this routine preference for the high treetops that foreshadows the cuckooshrikes' almost universal cultural anonymity. Somehow they seem remote from human attention. A few species may well be hunted and eaten on occasions (in New Guinea, the Papuans will take the **Hooded Cuckooshrike** *Coracina longicauda* and **Black-bellied Cuckooshrike** *Coracina montana*, which the Kalam people give the rather resonant names *snen twn* and *snen skoy* respectively, but they are not highly regarded as food).[1] The fruit diet of others may bring them into disrepute in commercial orchards, but otherwise cuckooshrikes go largely unnoticed.

A key exception is a handful of birds among the 13 Asian species belonging to the genus *Pericrocotus*. This is an oddly named group. The scientific name means 'very' or 'all around golden-yellow', but this describes only the plumage of female birds, since males are often bright red.[2] All 13 species have the same strange English name – minivet – which is of unknown origin and of obscure meaning. The compilers of the *Oxford English Dictionary* were completely without ideas, but the lexicographer A F Gotch has suggested some association with the birds' diminutive size. Unfortunately minivets are not particularly small (they average about 20 cm: 8 in).[3] One possibility is that it is, in part, an anglicisation of an original scientific name, *miniata*, given to them in the early nineteenth century. *Miniata* derives from the Latin *minium*, 'red lead', and means 'painted vermilion'.[4]

It is this immediate impression of intense and unexpected red colour that first strikes anyone catching sight of these fairly common, widespread but glorious birds as they flutter through the treetops of Asian forests. In India their Bengali name translates as 'little girl friends' or 'seven girl friends', a reference to the minivets' collective lifestyle and the way that small parties of them move in a playful follow-my-leader fashion through the canopy.[5] One particular people who were captivated by the sheer redness of minivets were the Naga, the remarkable and ethnically diverse communities living in the forested hills of north-eastern India and north-western Myanmar, and from whom derives the name of the Indian state Nagaland.

Although the Nagas were formerly infamous for their headhunting practices, they are better known today for the richness of their material culture, especially the beauty and quality of their cotton weavings and their jewellery. Birds, animals and insect body parts, as well as seeds and plants, were all once major components of their ceremonial dress, and the items used included tiger's teeth, boars' tusks, pangolin skins, bulls' horns, shells and the bill casques and tail feathers of Great Hornbill (see page 328). However, the **Scarlet Minivet** *Pericrocotus flammeus*, **Long-tailed Minivet** *Pericrocotus ethologus* and **Short-billed Minivet** *Pericrocotus brevirostris* were the source of beautiful vermilion and yellow feathers (are they still?) used by Naga craftsmen and -women in their earrings, headdresses and other smaller decorative pieces. The earrings, like those exhibited in the Pitt Rivers Museum, in Oxford, UK, are of intricate construction, with metal coils holding small sheaves of plaited fibres, from each of which depends a minivet flight feather.

Almost everything the Naga used in their decorative and symbolic arts was instinct with rich meanings and minivet feathers must have carried specific associations. Unfortunately the larger and more glamorous animals deployed in their symbolic lives have received all the attention and the beautiful if humble minivets have been neglected. Yet red is an immensely important and auspicious colour in all Naga artefacts and must have partly inspired their attachment to the birds.[6]

Piopio family *Turnagra*

The curious and extinct **Piopio** *Turnagra capensis* is part of the wider catalogue of tragedy associated with New Zealand's birdlife (see also Moa family, page 27, and the Wattled Crow family, page 368). It was brown and robust like a huge thrush. It had a massive bill and rather menacing pale eyes. However much it might have looked aggressive, the Piopio was, in truth, trusting and unwary, hopping in the vicinity of human settlement and its occupants. In the mid nineteenth century one colonial geographer recorded 40 pottering about his camp. Cats and dogs were part of a suite of introduced mammals that simply helped themselves to this once common and widespread species. Their predation was probably central to its extinction by 1902.[1]

The rather beautiful Maori name draws on the bird's loud ringing vocalisations. Yet there is something deeply telling about the involved history of error and confusion that lies behind its scientific equivalent. The man who coined it, Anders Sparrman, the Swedish naturalist aboard Captain James Cook's second expedition of 1772, somehow muddled up his skins and on naming the Piopio designated it as a species from the African Cape (hence *capensis*). *Turnagra* was used to suggest the bird's affinities with the tanagers of the Americas (see page 522). Yet, the Piopio was neither a tanager nor was it a 'thrush' as the white colonists of New Zealand liked to think.[2] Even now its real affinities are unclear and in the full list of bird species it enjoys that ambiguous taxonomic status – *Incertae sedis*, 'of uncertain placement'. There is, however, a genuine geographical location called Piopio, a small town on the central-west coast of New Zealand's North Island.

Shrike family *Laniidae*

These 31 colourful predatory songbirds are usually inhabitants of open country with scattered trees or bushes, and are primarily found in the Old World tropics with a particular concentration in Africa. Two-thirds of the shrikes either have their main wintering grounds or breed exclusively on the continent. The African endemics include the largest of the family, the gloriously pied **Magpie Shrike** *Urolestes melanoleucus* of the eastern and southern savannahs (43 cm: 17 in), whose tail can be twice the length of the whole body.

Yet shrikes are also well represented in Eurasia, where there are 13 species. Among these the remarkable **Great Grey Shrike** *Lanius excubitor* has one of the most extensive distributions of any northern passerine and occurs around the entire hemisphere. It is one of only two family representatives in North America, the other being its New World twin, the endemic **Loggerhead Shrike** *Lanius ludovicianus*.

The shrikes' modern classification among the songbirds would have intrigued our ornithological forebears, since historically they were considered to be pocket-sized relatives of the birds of prey. In his nine-volume summary of ornithology, *The Natural History of Birds*, the eighteenth-century Frenchman Comte de Buffon sandwiched them between the falcons and owls. One can understand his rationale. Great Grey Shrikes, for instance, will eat animals that are renowned for being as equally fierce as themselves (e.g. stoats and weasels), or for taking prey far bigger than themselves. Great Grey Shrikes have been recorded to attack egrets and grouse, or to finish off a wounded sandgrouse by drilling a hole through its skull (the sandgrouse was of unspecified species but was probably three or four times the weight of its assailant).[1]

In Alaska a major food item for Great Grey Shrike is the Snow Bunting, which is about two-thirds the former's own weight. Henry Thoreau possibly witnessed this predator–prey encounter near Concord, Massachusetts, on Christmas Eve 1850. 'Saw a shrike pecking to pieces a small bird,' he wrote, 'apparently a snow bird [Snow Bunting?]. At length he took him up in his bill . . . and flew slowly off with his prey dangling from his beak. I find that I had not associated such actions with my idea of birds. It was not birdlike.'[2] If not quite *un-bird-like*, it is certainly exceptional behaviour among such small species and one can readily understand Thoreau's sense of a natural order being somehow subverted.

Yet not all shrikes are quite so formidable and threatening, as the following contribution from east Africa makes plain:

I was once amazed to see a **Northern White-crowned Shrike** *Eurocephalus rueppelli* fly down from a bush and land on an African hare. The hare simply sat there and then, even more unbelievably, another shrike, and then two more, and then a fifth, all flew down and landed on the hare, which still just sat motionless. At this point one could hardly see the hare for shrikes, which were all over it and preening through its fur – presumably taking some sort of lice.[3]

Shrikes often impale their more substantial prey items on thorns or wedge them into the crook of forked branches. The storage is partly a response to the fact that shrikes cannot easily grip food in their feet and tear it apart, and the thorns serve in lieu of talons. Yet early observers likened the action to a butcher hanging his wares on meat hooks. The scientific name *Lanius*, the genus to which all but four of the family belong, means 'butcher' and on both sides of the Atlantic they were once known as 'butcher-birds'.[4]

Throughout history humans have been fixated by the

One of the masterpieces of Egyptian art, the painted tomb chapel of Khnumhotep II features remarkable images of Masked and Red-backed Shrikes (see also page 82).

shrikes' apparent aggression and have often judged them negatively. In the 1920s, in a year of exceptional winter numbers, various bird-banding groups along the east coast of the USA caught 70 Great Grey Shrikes. Instead of banding and releasing them with all the other migrants, 62 of the shrikes were deliberately killed.[5] Even today, the beautiful **Masked Shrike** *Lanius nubicus* of the eastern Mediterranean is almost never allowed to breed around Damascus, because Syrian hunters shoot them.[6] Why, one might ask, do we behave in this way?

Part of the answer lies in the names that we have used historically for shrikes. In his vast masterwork, *A Thesaurus of Bird Names* – one of the most important modern cultural studies of birds – Michel Desfayes has assembled a huge European synonymy for the Great Grey Shrike alone, comprising in excess of 700 names from 34 European and Asiatic languages or dialects (the book contains in total more than 100,000 bird names!). Desfayes' work emphasises how names are not neutral appendages that we pin to birds merely to facilitate recognition or discussion. They are a vocabulary loaded with meaning and value. And it says as much about ourselves as it does about the birds.

Desfayes analysed the shrike names and identified a number of root concepts behind their construction, including notions of cruelty, violence, sadism and danger. It is surely the attitudes underlying these folk names that help us to understand how American bird banders of yesteryear could have inherited an emotional response to an entirely innocent species that entailed its senseless slaughter.

One intriguing and hugely revealing story concerns a German name *neuntöter*. It was translated (and used in the past both in England and the USA) as 'nine-killer' or 'nine-murderer' and was said to refer either to the Great Grey Shrike's habit of killing nine times before it ceased a bout of serial slaughter, or to the nine times it killed in any single day.[7] In fact, Desfayes suggests that *neun* is not 'nine', but a corruption of *negen* and refers simply to *nagel*, 'nail'. The bird was a 'nail' killer, a reference to the thorn-based

storage behaviour of shrikes.[8] The English mistranslation demonstrates how inherited attitudes embedded in bird names can license further exaggeration or embellishment.

Another classic instance of the process occurs with a widespread African shrike known as the **Common Fiscal** *Lanius collaris* (five other African endemics have this same English name). The nineteenth-century British ornithologist Alfred Newton opted for a rather droll theory for how it got the somewhat odd 'fiscal' name. He suggested it was based on the bird's 'rapacity, which no revenue-officer could exceed'.[9] In fact it derived from similarities between the smartly pied birds and the smart black-and-white costume once worn by senior legal figures in South Africa.[10]

Not all our responses to shrikes have been so bloodstained. A good example is the remarkable painting at Beni Hasan in central Egypt. One of the burial chambers in this ancient cemetery housed a high-ranking official called Khnumhotep and on the walls of his tomb are scenes of ancient Egyptian fowlers catching scores of duck in clap nets. (A facsimile of the whole frieze is in the Metropolitan Museum of Art in New York; see also page 82.) The border detail in this painting includes images of four Masked Shrikes and a single adult **Red-backed Shrike** *Lanius collurio*. The presence in the same tableau of an adult male Common Redstart in autumn plumage corroborates the theory that it was executed in about October, when the wildfowl also returned in huge numbers to the banks of the Nile.[11]

Yet most remarkable of all and perhaps a little overlooked is the detailed representation of a Masked Shrike in flight. The fact that the image is of an immature bird is unusual in itself. For the adults are beautiful creatures with elaborately pied plumages distinguished by rich peachy flank patches and, one might assume, more likely candidates for decorative detail. The immature is less colourful but more subtle and the hugely talented artist has depicted it with extraordinary accuracy. Not only has he caught the salient features – the white outer tail feathers, the white bases to the outstretched primaries and the vestigial black bandit's mask through the eye – he has also included minute aspects that could only be appreciated after very careful scrutiny of the bird.

He has incorporated, for example, the pale-edged lesser and median coverts, the whitish fringes to the greater coverts and, by utilising a rather Picassian sense of perspective, has combined all these elements of the open upperwing with the squamated bars visible on the lower flanks. Crowning our sense of forensic precision is the pale base to the bird's lower mandible, which he has deliberately included, in contrast to the all-dark bill of the adult Masked Shrike painted next to it.

This image of an immature migrant bird, born that year and probably seen by the artist as it moved down the Nile to winter quarters in the Horn of Africa, is hugely impressive. Yet it was completed in the XII Dynasty and is at least 3,800 years old. It is possibly the most accurate human representation of any shrike for the next three and a half millennia and shows a deeper understanding of bird topography than that possessed, for example, by Leonardo da Vinci or Michelangelo. Since the Masked and Red-backed Shrikes are shown alongside two more of the region's most colourful migrants (Eurasian Hoopoe and Common Redstart) can we assume that they were not painted because they were eaten or trapped, like the ducks in the net, but because the artist thought them beautiful?

We too might now think shrikes beautiful and wonderful additions to the local landscape, but we seem powerless to halt their decline. The birds are particularly susceptible almost everywhere to the effects of agricultural intensification. Across most of Europe the **Woodchat Shrike** *Lanius senator*, **Lesser Grey Shrike** *Lanius minor*, Masked and Red-backed Shrikes are all in serious decline. The Loggerhead Shrike of North America has suffered a similar continent-wide shrinkage in range and numbers.[12] Even in Africa, a region not usually associated with intensive agriculture, there have been losses of species such as the Magpie Shrike in areas that have dense human populations.[13] However, elsewhere the birds may initially benefit from forest clearance and the expansion of agriculture.

Vireo and Greenlet family *Vireonidae*

There are 53 species found exclusively in the New World with a high concentration in Central and northern South America. Indeed the greenlets (15 species) occur no further north than the Yucatán Peninsula of Mexico, but at least 14 types of vireo breed in the USA and Canada. Some of them, such as the **Red-eyed Vireo** *Vireo olivaceus*, are long-distance migrants spreading from the Arctic Circle then south across both continents as far as Argentina, with all of the diverse populations converging in Amazonia during the non-breeding season. In the USA it is a common bird of many arboreal habitats, especially the broadleaf woods of the eastern states.

For all this ubiquity, the scientific name of the Red-eyed Vireo nicely explains the family's anonymity. The generic *Vireo* derives from the Latin verb *virere*, 'to be green'; *olivaceus* means 'olive-coloured'. The full title roughly translates as 'olive-coloured green bird'. As a result, vireos share the cultural profile of most small, sombre, insect-feeding creatures of the middle and upper canopy. They are largely overlooked and, if anything, the greenlets are even 'more nondescript'.[1]

The whole family is much more often heard than seen and their vocalisations provide one major claim on our attention. This is not so much for any quality of voice but for persistence. The Red-eyed Vireo, one of the most indefatigable of all New World songsters, is said to hold the North American record for most songs per unit of time: 22,197 in ten hours (the norm for most passerines is apparently 1,000–2,500 songs a day).[2] It works out at 37 of its short, variable and often rather slurred phrases every minute. It is perhaps not surprising that over the years a number of mnemonics have been devised for the bird's marathon performance. Several of the best, which double up as nice pointers on their behaviour, have a question-and-answer structure: 'Are you there? Here I am, Where are you?' Or: 'here-I-am, in the tree, look-up, at-the-top.'[3]

An older, now lost nickname for the bird was 'preacher', because the rising inflections at the end of each phrase suggested to some the delivery style of a parson's sermon. However, one wag, pointing to the endlessly repetitive character of the vireo's song, suggested that 'preacher' was a name devised by 'someone who had no very exalted opinion of the clergy'.[4]

The Red-eyed Vireo's song is by no means the only one that has been rendered as a mnemonic. There is a clever example for a widespread North American migrant, the **White-eyed Vireo** *Vireo griseus*, which takes account of the distinctive, metallic 'chic' notes that the bird appends to the beginning and end of most phrases: 'Quick! Give me the beer check!'[5] In the Caribbean, the **Black-whiskered Vireo** *Vireo altiloquus* has several personalised names, such

The distinctive song of the White-eyed Vireo has been nicely translated as 'Quick! Give me the beer check!'

as 'John-to-whit', 'John Philip', 'Whip-Tom-Kelly', 'Cheap-John-Stirrup', and *Bien-Te-Veo* (in Cuba) that echo the (usually trisyllabic) song.[6]

Some vireos are well known for their courage when sitting at the nest.[7] In the early twentieth century a naturalist, Ernest Baynes, described an occasion when he proffered ants' eggs at the end of a long weed stalk to a sitting female Red-eyed Vireo, and continued until she started to accept his gifts and a remarkable trust developed. His account illuminates the deep desire felt by many of us to overcome our species' baleful heritage – that instinctual fear we arouse in most wild animals. It also demonstrates how much pleasure there can be when the hope is realised, albeit briefly:

> Next day I returned and after she had promptly accepted a few more ants' eggs . . . I stepped up a little closer and offered one between my thumb and forefinger. After a little hesitation she took it, and from that moment we were on friendship's footing. She seemed much interested, if not actually pleased, whenever I approached . . . and did not mind in the least if I stroked her on the head or back with my finger. At first she was a little nervous when I stroked her throat, and when I persisted she slipped off the nest. But as she

got used to me she minded less and less and would even allow me to lift her off her eggs and put her gently back.

> In a day or two I felt sufficiently well acquainted with Madame Vireo to introduce my friends. Usually the introduction came as a surprise . . . Many people were introduced in this way, and children especially experienced ecstatic joy at the privilege of feeding and stroking a wild bird in her own home.

> One warm afternoon when some of us were paying her a visit, the little Vireo slipped away for a few minutes, and, flying to a bird-bath not far away, took a bath and returned, looking much refreshed and with her plumage damp and somewhat disarranged. Very soon she flew to the nest and looked rather astonished, I thought, to find my hand covering the little home. But she was not in the least afraid, and, forcing her way between my slightly parted fingers, went on to her eggs in the dark.[8]

Alas, there was no happy ending. One day Baynes returned to find the nest destroyed by some species of egg thief, presumably guided to the spot by the well-worn trail caused by repeated visits.

Figbird and Oriole family *Oriolidae*

This family comprises 30 slender thrush-like songbirds (24–30 cm: 9.5–12 in) of Old World forest, spread across Africa (nine species), Asia (12 species) and Australasia (ten species). Many orioles are birds of glorious colour, especially the males, which are often a crisp mixture of jet black and golden yellow. The family is essentially tropical in distribution although one species – the most widespread and successful, **Eurasian Golden Oriole** *Oriolus oriolus* – migrates from southern Africa to breed across a vast area from eastern Siberia and western China to the Atlantic shores of Spain and France. In northern latitudes the spring arrival of this bird introduces a rare note of exoticism to the temperate landscape.

> I'd longed to see a Eurasian Golden Oriole ever since receiving my first bird book as a child. So 50 years later, while visiting the Greek island of Kefalonia, I got up at dawn and waited in an olive grove, hoping my dream might come true. Just as the sun rolled back the pink mountain mists, I heard the fluting notes of *or-i-ole*, *or-i-ole*, then gasped as not one but two of these golden birds flew to a nearby mulberry tree, followed by a more modestly attired female. It was well worth the wait![1]

All but three of the family belong to one genus, *Oriolus*, with the additional trio – known as figbirds (*Sphecotheres*) – occurring in Indonesia and Australia. The best known is the **Australasian Figbird** *Sphecotheres vieilloti*, found predominantly in the coastal areas of Northern Territory and Queensland. While this species shares the size, shape and green plumage of some orioles, it differs markedly in its confiding behaviour. It is often an inhabitant of inner-city suburbs, especially where it can find its preferred fruiting fig trees (*Ficus*).

By contrast, the true orioles are infamous for their elusiveness. The authors of a recent monograph on the birds cite the virtues of their chosen subject – 'intelligent, beautiful, characterful, acrobatic, brave, diverse, successful and exciting' – but the first word in their list is 'frustrating'.[2] Anyone who has ever looked for an oriole will know why. Despite their bright colours, they are more often heard than seen and, unfortunately, the vocalisations themselves are as difficult to pin down. The loud, haunting, slowly fluted and almost yodelled song is strongly ventriloquial, and wherever the birds occur they assume much the same role: they are the beautiful disembodied sound of the high canopy.

Yet the songs of many orioles involve a compensatory kind of synaesthesia, the liquid tones seeming somehow to conjure the birds' appearance. The author Jonathan Elphick put it nicely: 'the mellow, lazily fluting [is] an aural equivalent of the sunny plumage'.[3] The English word 'oriole' is itself onomatopoeic of the song of Eurasian Golden Oriole. In turn, the word supplied a title for the New World orioles, part of a family technically known as the *Icteridae* (see page 511). They frequently possess some of the shape and colour, if not the voices, of their namesakes, but the two families are not remotely related. However, one habit they share is a great love for fruit.

One of the most memorable of all human images to feature the Eurasian Golden Oriole is a relief carving incised on to the walls of a burial chamber at Saqqara outside modern Cairo, Egypt. The anonymous artists managed somehow to give striking individuality to this 4,500-year-old tableau. It depicts two men, one of them clearly with dwarfism, pulling the strings to a net while a flock of birds flushes from a fig tree heavily burdened with fruit. It is a vision from a precise moment in the Egyptian autumn, when

The Australasian Figbird is a bird of rainforest and eucalyptus woodland but it will follow its love of fruit into suburban parks and gardens.

the figs ripen on the trees and the birds take advantage of the local abundance as they pass through the Nile valley back to sub-Saharan Africa. Among the clearly recognisable Eurasian Golden Orioles are three hoopoes, crests raised in alarm at their imminent capture (see page 325).[4]

This scenario was played out across the Mediterranean for thousands of years. It is striking, for instance, that the Eurasian Golden Oriole was known in Spain as the *becafigos* or *picafigo*, the 'fig pecker', while its modern Greek name (*Sykofágos*) means 'fig eater'.[5] In his classic Victorian work *A History of Fowling*, Hugh Macpherson described how fruit-eating golden orioles (known by the rather beautiful and onomatopoeic *rigogolo* or *rigolo*) were much sought after in Renaissance and early modern Italy for their exquisite flavour. If not caught in nets, they were shot after being lured with call whistles that mimicked the birds' liquid voice, or they were taken at night by means of a fowling lantern that dazzled them at their roosts.[6] John Ray described how he and Francis Willughby found many orioles in the poulterers' shops of late-seventeenth-century Naples adding, presumably from first-hand knowledge, that 'it feeds wonderfully fat, hath very delicate flesh and yields wholesome nourishment'.[7]

Even today Eurasian Golden Orioles may be shot for food or to feature in showy cabinets made up by taxidermists and displayed in Mediterranean living rooms. However, the scenes from the 1980s, when as many as 80,000 were killed on Malta alone, have finally ended.[8] Yet perhaps the most remarkable evidence for the longevity of these oriole traditions is the eyewitness account of birds being trapped in Port Said, Egypt, in 1984, using much the same methods represented on the Saqqara burial chamber just 200 km (125 miles away).[9]

Today orioles are more often victims of their beauty rather than their flavour. For aviculturists the birds possess the fateful combination of bright colour and melodious voice. In south-east Asia the equally lovely **Black-naped Oriole** *Oriolus chinensis* and **Black-hooded Oriole** *Oriolus xanthornus* are kept and traded as cagebirds. Yet outside the tropics, where the family's fruit-and-insect diet cannot be easily obtained, orioles had a reputation as a difficult group to keep captive. 'I do not know a single instance', wrote a nineteenth-century German author, 'of one [Eurasian Golden Oriole] having been preserved for more than three or four months.' Although he did encounter two birds reared from the nest, one of which had been taught to sing a minuet, while the other could imitate 'a flourish of trumpets'.[10]

Shrikethrush and Pitohui family *Colluricinclidae*

This small family of 14 rather thrush-like species are inhabitants of Australasia, especially of New Guinea. Two birds, the **Hooded Pitohui** *Pitohui dichrous* and **Variable Pitohui** *Pitohui kirhocephalus* from that island, are highly unusual for being poisonous. Their feathers and skin contain a potent neurotoxin (also found in poison dart frogs of South America), which they may well ingest from a type of beetle. Local people are alert to the characteristic, pointing out that if you lick the feathers of pitohuis, the tongue goes numb. In the interests of science, a former resident of Papua New Guinea explored the phenomenon:

> I was brought a fledgling Variable Pitohui when I lived in Tabubil, and being of an inquisitive turn of mind

what more natural thing to do than give it a lick to see if the reports were true, and also whether young birds have acquired the toxicity? It was a positive on both counts, I gave a tentative lick along the mantle and there was an immediate reaction via tingling of the lips and a slight numbness in the outer portion of my tongue. Sadly no hallucinations or visions of God, but definitely a reaction. It wore off very quickly and within three minutes had faded entirely, but I was glad to have had the chance to confirm it![1]

A local name for the Hooded Pitohui is *Wobob*, which is also a word for a type of skin disease.[2]

Drongo family *Dicruridae*

The drongos comprise 22 predominantly glossy black, medium-sized birds often with staring crimson eyes. They are inhabitants of the Old World tropics, occurring across sub-Saharan Africa and then from Iran eastwards through much of Asia to the Solomon Islands and eastern Australia. Two of the most widely appreciated species have ventured out of the family's usual forested habitats and are completely at home in open grassland and agricultural landscapes and even in the hearts of large cities. They are the **Fork-tailed Drongo** *Dicrurus adsimilis* ('one of the most familiar birds of the African savanna') and the **Black Drongo** *Dicrurus macrocercus* ('one of the commonest birds seen near dwellings in the Plains [of India]').[1]

The Black Drongo is one of the most characteristic common birds of the Indian and south-east Asian countryside.

While each of this widespread pair has a tail that makes up a third of its entire length, some drongos have much longer appendages. The generic name, *Dicrurus*, to which all but one of the family belongs, means 'forked tailed'.[2] Yet the ultimate is the **Greater Racket-tailed Drongo** *Dicrurus paradiseus* of south Asian forests, which measures 76 cm (30 in), half of which is the tail. In truth much of the latter is actually two naked outer-tail pins that terminate in twisted half spheres of feather. These small terminal blobs seem to have a life and mobility that is independent of their owner, one authority suggesting how they trail behind the bird like 'a pair of irate bumblebees in hot pursuit'.[3]

The grace and exaggerated curves of these wonderful plumes were not qualities lost on the hill people of north-eastern India. At least until the middle of the twentieth century they hunted both Greater and **Lesser Racket-tailed Drongo** *Dicrurus remifer* and used them to make striking head ornaments, further coloured with the rich-hued feathers of minivets and rollers.

These streamers add enormous panache to the racket-tailed drongos in flight, but the rest of the family are also noted for their aerial ability. The feeding behaviour is highly characteristic, with the birds choosing openly exposed perches – including the backs of grazing livestock and wild animals – from which to survey for insect prey. Drongos will then sally out suddenly at high speed, twisting and turning in pursuit before returning often to the original spot.

During the breeding season drongos cap these aerodynamic performances with intense aggression towards potential predators. Rather like the tyrant flycatchers of the New World (see page 350), drongos take on opponents well above their own weight division, including herons, cranes, hawks, buzzards, eagles, hornbills, crows, even mammals and large snakes. They have been known to soar above the 'victim' and then descend to attack, occasionally landing on the back of the larger bird. One recorded event involved **Square-tailed Drongo** *Dicrurus ludwigii* from west Africa chasing and pecking a White-necked Raven while riding on its rump, a species that is perhaps 40 times heavier than the assailant.[4]

It is this highly charged defence of their eggs and young that has earned the Black Drongo its enduring alternative name in India, 'king-crow'. More mysterious, however, is the origin of the name 'drongo'. It is widely reported to derive from a word among the Betsimasaraka and Sakalava peoples of northern Madagascar.[5] This was passed on to French naturalists during the early colonial period, who then transmitted it more widely until it was used for all 22 species in the family. Yet today the original Malagasy name seems to have lost currency with those who originally coined it.[6]

Fantail family *Rhipiduridae*

This family of 44 species is thought to belong within just a single genus, *Rhipidura*. They are mainly forest birds and are spread from India across to China and Japan and south to Australasia and the numerous archipelagos of the western and central Pacific, with a notable concentration in New Guinea (13 species). At just 7.5 cm (3 in) the **Yellow-bellied Fantail** *Rhipidura hypoxantha* of the Himalaya is the baby of the family, but almost all the rest conform to the same basic format. They are birds of about 16 cm (6.3 in) length with tails that are conspicuous for being constantly raised up and down like a tiny flag and often splayed open like a fan, hence the name.

The birds' restless tail waving is just a single part of a wider hyperactivity. Their movements often seem awkward and jerky, suggesting tiny clockwork toys. One manoeuvre, a neurotic swivelling to face different directions as the bird remains fixed to the spot, is a classic part of the repertoire. If excited they will pivot back and forth through a short, mechanical half turn, often coordinating the action to an irritated (and irritating) chatter. A few minutes' acquaintance with this intense behaviour is enough to confirm the family's core feature – they are birds of enormous vitality.

With all this 'joie de vivre', fantails can exhibit a remarkable tameness.[1] One species on New Guinea is even called the **Friendly Fantail** *Rhipidura albolimbata*. Perhaps the most accustomed to human presence is the rather misleadingly named **Willie Wagtail** *Rhipidura leucophrys* (found from eastern Indonesia, throughout New Guinea and across the whole of Australia). Wherever it occurs this striking black-and-white fantail of open country and tree-dotted farmland makes a big impression.

Typical of New Guinea lore is the response among the Kalam people of the highlands who know it as *konmayd* and exempt it as food because of its association with excrement (it is thought to feed in the vicinity of outside latrines and among pig turds). It is also deemed a valuable helper (and potentially the ghost of an ancestor reincarnated in bird form) and one special duty is its tending of domestic pigs.[2] In fact, fantails feed in close association with all livestock (goats, cattle and swine), sometimes riding on their backs and catching insects that are stirred up by the movements.[3] An old Australian name for the Willie Wagtail is 'shepherd's companion'.[4]

The bird's English name comes from Australia and reflects a European sensibility struggling to find a frame of reference for the birds of a 'new' continent. Yet at least one aspect is accurate: the bird, while cocking and waving the tail from side to side, does not actually spread it out like a fan. The personalised part, Willie, is explained by Darryl Jones:

> The homely name appears to relate to the bird's familiarity with early settlers in lonely places, as it almost instantly loses any fear of humans and is among the first wild birds to take advantage of the insects associated with farms and campsites. Pictures and stories of nests in hanging flowerpots, saddles and old boots in sheds and verandahs abound in early accounts, and every bush child learned to call it 'Sweet pretty creature' in imitation of its scolding call.[5]

◀ The personalised name Willie Wagtail reflects the great affection that this characterful little neighbour often inspires.

▼ The name of the Friendly Fantail from Indonesia and New Guinea says much about the species' confiding manner.

Monarch family *Monarchidae*

This group includes one of the best-known birds in all Australia, the **Magpielark** *Grallina cyanoleuca*. 'Mudlark', 'peewee', 'peewit', and 'Murray magpie' are just a sample of the many vernacular names given to this hugely popular species. It is now placed in the monarch family, but it has had a complex taxonomic past and, at one time, was accorded family status of its own (*Grallinidae*; alongside a single relative, the **Torrentlark** *Grallina bruijni* of New Guinea) or was closely linked with another all-Australian group, the mudnesters (see page 395). The present arrangement may prove to be accurate and enduring, but nevertheless the Magpielark remains an oddity among the monarchs, which are largely arboreal and flycatcher-like.

This species is ground loving with the broadest tolerance of open grassy habitats. It is only really excluded by the harshest deserts of the Australian interior, especially regions devoid of human society. That shared absence of bird and people is a measure of how the Magpielark has flourished alongside modern settlement and agriculture. The 'magpie'

associations in the name draw most obviously on the arresting black-and-white plumage, but a secondary reinforcement must be the bird's bold magpie-like demeanour. The birds are feisty residents of almost every Australian city, town, hamlet and their suburbs. They are birds of the roadside and lovers of telegraph wires. They will wander with a proprietorial coolness through the tarmacked forecourts of petrol stations and shopping malls, plucking dead insects off car windscreens and headlights.

The species also thrives near water of all kinds, often feeding along river or lake edges, where it behaves and looks rather like a small wader. It has long legs and broad, rounded wings so that in flight it appears like a floppy-winged pied plover. The resemblance in shape to the Northern Lapwing may well explain the peewee and peewit names (these are still vernacular names for that species; see page 200), but they are also undoubtedly onomatopoeic of the Magpielark's clear ringing calls.

The bird's aggression is legendary. It will fearlessly

Somewhere between a starling and a small pied plover in appearance, the Magpielark is one of the most widespread and conspicuous birds in Australia.

chase predators as large as eagles and even humans. Darryl Jones writes: 'The magpie-larks are especially vicious and persistent in their attacks and, despite their apparently delicate build, can inflict nasty wounds. Each year, wildlife agencies from throughout Australia are asked to deal with particular magpie-larks that have caused serious injuries.'[1] Another speciality – 'the peewee is definitely the bird most reported' – is battling with its own self-image. Magpielarks routinely attack their reflections either in house windows or car mirrors, mistaking them for territorial intruders. Sometimes individuals become so fixated on their self-generated opponent that they go to great lengths to find it. 'I once covered all of the ground level windows of a building with two layers of brown paper and the bird simply tore at the paper until the window was again exposed.'[2]

The rest of this rather heterogeneous family of 94 small-to medium-sized songbirds is largely Australasian (including New Guinea) or Pacific in distribution (75 species). Many of them conform to a specific physical blueprint and mode of behaviour. They are flycatchers with broad bills, big heads, often colourful or strikingly patterned plumages and a tendency towards inertia and silence and then sudden, dramatic flurries of activity. They perch upright in the middle storey of the forest, remaining still until the moment they burst forth, snatch some aerial insect prey and return to rest all in an instant.

The group includes two genera *Trochocercus* (five species) and *Terpsiphone* (12 species) that are African and Asian in distribution. Their predominantly forest-dwelling lifestyles ensure that they avoid most human attention, but the latter group, known as the paradise flycatchers, includes some species that are difficult to ignore. The **Asian Paradise Flycatcher** *Terpsiphone paradisi* and **African Paradise Flycatcher** *Terpsiphone viridis* have huge ranges across their respective continents and frequently find their way to the edges of towns or cities, and even into domestic gardens. Both are beautiful in colour and form. The head is deep charcoal grey, the upperparts a striking orange-chestnut and, in the males, the elongated central tail feathers extend for about one and a half times the length of the body.

The visual impact of these ribbon-like streamers is remarkable. They undulate and billow behind the birds like pennants, giving grace, impact and a strong dash of the bizarre to many observations of paradise flycatchers. Sometimes the effect is enhanced further because both species contain distinct white colour morphs, and these ivory-white individuals are birds of exquisite beauty.

No one has better evoked the family's occasionally surreal impact than the English travel author Redmond O'Hanlon, in his gloriously comic work of natural history *Into the Heart of Borneo*:

> My Balkan Sobranie tobacco, as 90 per cent humid as everything else, tasted as rich and wet as a good gravy, and the more arak I had, the less like fermented elastoplast it became. And it actually made one see things.
>
> A long white strip of silk chiffon detached itself from the tumultuous green tumble of trees and creepers on the opposite bank and undulated, as slowly as a lamprey in a lake, diagonally downstream. It was a very feminine apparition, redolent of everything I was beginning to miss, of silky rustles, lacy white knickers, of mysteriously intricate suspenders, of long, soft, white silk stockings dropped beside the bed. I looked at the arak with increased respect, and took some more.[3]

The suggestively feminine form that flowed towards O'Hanlon as he savoured his alcohol-softened evening in the Bornean forest was, in fact, a white-morph Asian Paradise Flycatcher with full streamers.

These floating airy qualities in paradise flycatchers have inspired some beautifully evocative local names in the Indian subcontinent, such as *Fhāmbāsīr* ('cotton flake') in the west Himalaya; *Tārwārio* ('swordsman') in Gujarati; *Redi-horā* ('cotton thief'; white morph), *Gini-horā* ('fire thief'; rufous morph) in Sinhalese.[4]

The closely related **Japanese Paradise Flycatcher** *Terpsiphone atrocaudata* is endemic to its eponymous archipelago. The almost calligraphic flourish to the male's streamers was ever likely to appeal to Chinese and Japanese artists, and the bird is a regular subject in Oriental bird-and-flower paintings, or a motif painted upon household screens, fans and other decorative objects.

Crow and Jay family *Corvidae*

Most people feel so familiar with this group of 123 species that it would be easy for them to assume the family needs no introduction. In truth, a large number of the crows and jays do not conform to our corvine stereotype – that large, often unloved, monochrome bird with the hoarse voice and the rogue's repertoire of survival skills. There are just 45 black species like this and all are in the genus *Corvus*. The majority of the family, however, comprise a whole suite of smaller and often much more colourful birds.

These include jays, magpies, treepies and magpie-jays, as well as true oddities, such as the endemic and now highly endangered **Stresemann's Bush Crow** *Zavattariornis stresemanni*. Rather like a starling in shape, it was first described for science only in 1938, it is mysteriously confined to three tiny areas of seemingly undistinguished park-like savannah of south-central Ethiopia, and has been judged one of the two 'most remarkable ornithological discoveries made in Africa [last] century'.[1] (The other was the Congo Peacock; see page 74.) Named after the great German ornithologist Erwin Stresemann, the bird is painful proof that not all corvids are over-abundant pests.

There is even one continent where black crows are absent entirely. South America has no native *Corvus* species, although the Americas as a whole are particularly rich in the other corvids (38 species) and especially jays. Just a small number of these birds share the family aura of sharp wits and suburban lifestyles. Many of the Neotropical jays, in fact, while being gregarious and highly vocal, are elusive birds of forest canopy and have little contact with humans at all.

On the other five continents the black crows are virtually

The Northern Raven has probably given rise to a larger body of human stories than any other bird on Earth.

ubiquitous and they are often familiar on a daily basis, whether we live in the Earth's biggest cities or its wildest landscapes. The following nine species fill much the same ecological niche (and have much the same cultural profile) in their respective regions: **Pied Crow** *Corvus albus* (sub-Saharan Africa), **American Crow** *Corvus brachyrhynchos* (North America), **Australian Raven** *Corvus coronoides* and **Torresian Crow** *Corvus orru* (Australia), **Carrion Crow** *Corvus corone* (Europe including much of Russia), **House Crow** *Corvus splendens*, **Large-billed Crow** *Corvus macrorhynchos* and **Jungle Crow** *Corvus levaillantii* (south Asia including much of China). A special place is reserved for the largest of them all, in fact the largest passerine (by weight) on Earth, the **Northern Raven** *Corvus corax*. Technically it should probably share this one superlative with an endemic Ethiopian relative, the **Thick-billed Raven** *Corvus crassirostris*. Yet a measure in which the first bird stands entirely alone is in the sheer wealth of its cultural resonances. Encircling the whole hemisphere from the Arctic Circle as far south almost as the Equator, the Northern Raven possibly has the richest human story of all birds.

OUR CONFLICTING RESPONSES TO CROWS

In exactly the same way that we have one dominant visual impression of crows, so could we be said to cleave to a single set of ideas about their cultural place. Crows have long been cast as the villains of the avian world. They are still viewed widely as destructive of our property, crops and livestock, as well as being undeservedly prosperous within nature itself

and vicious predators of their wildlife neighbours. They are particularly hated for thieving from songbird nests. In the past they were further condemned for possessing a kind of moral darkness. Simply to see or to encounter crows could be an ordeal unsettling our peace of mind and presaging misfortune. In short, crows were bad for us physically and psychologically. Few other groups of birds carry quite the same deep negative burden.

The only family that once inspired comparable hostility was the owls. I use the past tense because, while this last family still occasions anxiety in parts of the world, in many others and especially in the West, we have managed to slough off the older misapprehensions and have allowed owls to emerge as some of the most cherished of all birds (see page 271). Just as we have largely re-imagined our relationship to that family, so now belatedly we are beginning to reconsider corvids.

New research is proving an ancient strand of our mythology about them: that the birds are some of our most intelligent fellow creatures, with IQs comparable to primates or parrots, with sophisticated mastery of tools. In fact, we may well recognise that in corvids man the destroyer has more than met his match. The birds' remarkable persistence, in the teeth of our relentless opposition, merits respect. Ineradicable profiteers of landfill and human waste, crows are sometimes our most conspicuous wild neighbours in the most degraded landscapes. From these various elements we are fashioning a new kind of symbolism that casts crows as quintessentially modern and companionably tough, with a raw genius for the business of living.

We should also acknowledge that there has probably been

a small minority who has always loved crows. Today these corvophiles find fresh opportunities to celebrate not just the underrated black-winged beauty of crows, but also the dark euphony of their voices. One such contributor finds in the birds' shared vocalisations – those gravel-throated sounds from which, incidentally, so much crow nomenclature has been fashioned: *krähe* (German), *corneja* (Spanish), *kargassi* (Turkish), *qala rash* (Kurdish), *al ghurab* (Arabic), *kowwa* (Hindi) – genuine pleasure.[2] On reading my book *Crow Country*, one self-styled 'corvidologist' wrote to reprove me (gently):

> I thought I'd share with you that I don't find the Carrion Crow's voice as you wrote: 'hard, gnarled shrunken . . . the result of a force that comes close to pain'. I find it to be a comforting and endearing voice and I marvel at how much they appear to say with so few 'words'.[3]

An Italian devotee articulates her own profound feelings for them:

> My favourite birds are corvids. I don't know why, I mean, I didn't decide it. Maybe I find some sort of resonances in them, but I feel a big part of me is like a corvid: I see them as intelligent, curious and playful birds that no one really understands. Maybe I need to contact my wild and wise part. I like birds in an emotional and philosophical way, not in a scientific way. I like their colours, shapes and their sounds. They're symbolic . . . it's like they're the symbols of something deeper and they're there to communicate

with us. And corvids tell me a lot. If I see a flying bird I must have a look, not just to understand what kind of bird it is, but to let my spirit and thoughts go for a moment with it. Ravens are my favourite . . . it's like we understand each other. I feel excited when I hear the raven's sound. It would be great to have a raven or a rook as a free friend! There was a time when I totally fell in love with the Thick-billed Raven and I wanted to go to Ethiopia to see it.[4]

These newly strengthened positive views of crows complete a binary pattern of responses often as black and white as the plumage of some corvid species. It is the main theme of this essay and I present both sides, beginning with the dark.

BIRDS OF DARK DEEDS

In 2006 the *San Antonio Express-News* carried an article about a Wyoming town called Riverton that had become the site for a large roost of American Crows. The birds were arriving in thousands, possibly tens of thousands, and spending their nights in trees along Riverton's main streets, then leaving behind a voluminous shower of droppings each morning. They were said to be 'fearless and frightening', while the mayor likened their arrival at dusk to 'a black sky . . . moving over you'. Other residents used a vocabulary that was darker still – 'creepy', 'eerie', 'evil'.

The roost was judged no mere nuisance due only a measured response from the appropriate wildlife agency; it required an 'emergency decree' that had armed police units firing 12-gauge shotguns into the roost trees throughout

The House Crow is one of life's supreme opportunists and in the Indian subcontinent there is hardly an urban area where its plangent calls cannot be heard.

Rooks and Western Jackdaws are colonial species found widely together in Eurasia and sometimes their shared night-time roosts can swell to tens of thousands of birds.

the night. By morning Riverton's chief of police felt overwhelmed. 'We're killing the heck out of them,' he said, 'I just don't know if we're having much effect.' Unimpressed by these official operations, one frustrated local had already deployed his own shotgun, littering the floor with 'dead crows . . . amid smoking shell cases'. His use of a firearm in a public space was deemed technically illegal, but he was neither charged nor was he repentant. 'It just got down to where if the citizenry didn't try to protect themselves, their property would be just destroyed.' The reporter on the story agreed: 'Grandfathers and great-grandfathers carved a community out of hard-bitten land, and they aren't about to give it back.'[5]

In the account of this modern American skirmish one has many of the ingredients in a millennial-long warfare between people and corvids. In Riverton's sense of collective invasion, which seemed as much psychological as it was material, one detects the unconscious anxieties that such black birds can inspire. In the town's pursuit of swift and violent measures one has a classic expression of the knee-jerk intolerance and even of our visceral hatred for crows.

Corvids probably receive the least legal protection of any bird family worldwide. In the USA 'hunters across the country can kill [them] in open seasons with no bag limits', although jay species are protected everywhere and many states regulate the hunting season for crows.[6] Yet some historical assaults on crow roosts make the events in Riverton seem like child's play. In 1937 a posse of well-armed Texan corvocides, using a simultaneous detonation of 180 bombs over two nights, killed in the region of 70,000 birds. A couple of years later the state authorities in Illinois

slaughtered 328,000 corvids using 'festoons of dynamite bombs'. The event was broadcast so widely it made it into the pages of *Life* magazine.[7] Much the same treatment has been meted out to corvids in Europe. In the 27 states of the European Union the five commonest corvid species are still widely persecuted with an annual reported cull of 3.5 million birds.[8] However, the actual slaughter must be much higher and the least protected of all is the Carrion Crow.

By contrast, in Australia 'all five corvids are now legally protected and cannot be harmed without a permit'. Yet a Brisbane-based contributor adds:

Shooting crows is still common even if largely unsuccessful. Every farmer will tell you how hard they are to shoot, and that they can tell a rifle from a stick, etc. But there is nothing along the lines of the huge destruction of **Rook** *Corvus frugilegus* and Carrion Crows I saw first hand in Ireland; I have never heard of anyone actually applying for a permit to shoot crows in Oz although it may happen. One issue is that the only really large flocks are associated with roosts in urban areas, and that means no guns.[9]

In the past levels of persecution were, in some ways, even more intense. For if the methods were more primitive, the goal was outright annihilation. In Tudor Britain there were laws, not to authorise occasional culls, but to make it obligatory to persecute crows in exactly the manner demonstrated by the citizens of Riverton. Failure to kill them was punishable by fines. In 1544, for instance, George Amery of Barnton in the English county of Cheshire had to appear in court because he 'did permit them to build in his woods, to the injury of the country and contrary to the statute in such case made and provided'. Another Cheshire hamlet, Hunsterson, was fined 10 shillings and ninepence for failure to maintain nets that were used to catch and kill crows.[10] Nor was it just an issue of economic nuisance. They were also considered a psychological threat. In 1604 the British House of Commons rejected a parliamentary bill after the speech of its key sponsor was interrupted by the small corvid, a **Western Jackdaw** *Corvus monedula*, flying around the chamber. The omen was just too awful.[11]

This deep-seated fearfulness towards crows is by no means extinct. It is manifest in several women who, speaking to the Seattle-based author Lyanda Haupt, acknowledged that they would not walk 'in parks with their small children if there are too many crows'.[12] It is manifest in the language used by the reporter at Riverton, Wyoming: 'great-grandfathers carved a community out of hard-bitten land, and they aren't about to give it back'. However jocular his line, it evokes a sense of corvids as an elemental force threatening the very foundations of settled society. Finally it is manifest in that wonderful scene from Alfred Hitchcock's film *The Birds* (see also page 219), when a flock of Northern Ravens and other corvids assembles on the school climbing frame before the end of class.

In his deployment of corvids as agents of horror, the film's English director plumped for the one bird family most deeply associated with a sense of foreboding. In truth, however, by the time of *The Birds* (1963) the crow as a cinematic motif for evil had degenerated to cliché, or into comic characters ripe for animation (e.g. the crow companion to the Queen in Disney's *Snow White and the Seven Dwarfs*). Hitchcock found a way to revive their disturbing impact, partly by supplying as audio-backdrop to his scene a sublimely innocent, rollicking nonsense song. As the children chant ('rissledy-rossledy hey-Johnny-dossledy knickedy-knackedy', etc.), so they seem to conjure the brooding assembly until birds smother the playground in an ominous black mass. The scene has since become a kind of shorthand for any modern event involving public anxiety and big flocks of birds. Typically, the headline for the 2006 piece on Riverton was: 'Like in "The Birds", crows flocking to Wyoming town.'

What Hitchcock was drawing upon was a centuries-old linkage in European culture and languages of ravens and black corvids generally with death. In Germany *Rabenaas* ('raven's carrion') was a name once used for an evil villain; while a *Rabenstein* ('raven-stone' in English) was the place for a gibbet or gallows where just such a fellow ended his days. A further link was 'raven book', a euphemism for any list of the deceased. A 'raven's bill', on the other hand, was a form of surgical implement.[13] In turn, this medical expression echoes an ancient naval usage. On the prow of Roman triremes was a boarding plank tipped by a heavy metal spike. When this was dropped before the assault of another ship, the iron crashed deep into the enemy's deck timbers, fixing one vessel to the other. The Romans knew it as a *corvus*, a 'crow'.

Another death association was forged in the repressive ethos of the former Soviet Union:

In Stalin's time the black secret police cars that often 'disappeared' people, and which usually arrived in the dead of night, were known as *Voronok* – 'fast ravens'.

This slang hasn't been used since the 1950s, and police cars now are called *Abeisyanik*, 'a monkey cage'.[14]

All of this psychological alignment between corvids and death or menacing violence draws on a fundamental aspect of the birds' ecology. Many species, including even the treepies and magpies but especially black crows like the Northern Raven, are attracted to the rich sources of protein represented by livestock carcasses. Sometimes the dead meat included the bodies of humans. Ravens, in fact, would have been genuine attendees at those localities called raven-stones. Gradually the birds morphed from being merely associated with mortality to actual agents of death. As late as the eighteenth century the British were still blaming Northern Ravens for an ability to spread contagion.[15]

What cemented the birds' fundamental links not only to death but also to evil was their dominant hue. In the Christian vocabulary of colour, black is still indivisible from both mortality and moral corruption. Crows, even those whose ecology has little genuine connection to the eating of carrion such as the Eurasian Rooks and Western Jackdaws, were sometimes tarred with the same black brush. Yet it is salutary to remind ourselves how arbitrary is this Western linkage of crows with evil. Indian Hindus, by contrast, have deeply positive associations with the birds, as the following makes clear:

In his film *The Birds* Hitchcock made good use of the one bird family freighted with ancient associations of evil and foreboding – the crows.

The House Crow is commonly considered by Indians to be a representative of their dead relatives. Hence an orthodox, traditional south Indian would always first feed the crows some cooked rice in the morning before starting to partake of their food. Similarly on the anniversary of the death of their relatives, people make special balls of rice and feed them to the crows and this practice is an important ritual performed every year on that same date.[16]

We should further note that in certain areas where corvids are spring migrants, the birds manage to bypass their more demeaning connotations, and serve as welcome heralds of seasonal change. There is a painting by the nineteenth-century Russian landscape artist Aleksey Kondratievich Savrasov entitled *The Rooks have Returned*. In fact, the same species appears in several of his works and is always suggestive of life's final joyous release after the physical and emotional gridlock of the Russian winter.

In modern northern Alberta, Canada, the locals share similar sentiments:

'The crows are back!' he shouted as he burst twenty minutes late into the little log schoolhouse. 'Two crows, one perched on the big spruce at Wojack's place, the other on the ground peckin' at somethin'.' The teacher, who would usually demand a reason for late arrival by any pupil, broke into a huge smile and repeated, 'The crows are back.' Then he added, 'Spring is here at last.' The whole class was energised. It was mid April. The snow was disappearing fast, the ditches were surging with dirty water, winter was being pushed further north, but not without a fight. Like a jail sentence, winter seemed to last for ever here. We longed for spring. To the country folk living along the fringe of Alberta's boreal forest the American Crow was the true harbinger of spring. Not the robin, not the bluebird. The crows are back! [17]

Perhaps one form of compensation for our negative characterisation of the family is the presence of black corvids in some wonderfully evocative European artworks. A good example is Pablo Picasso's *Woman with a Raven*, which he completed in 1904. It captures an intimate moment as a young female caresses and leans in to kiss a pet raven standing on a table. The painting is typical of the Blue Period in Picasso's work, in that she is a skeletal beauty of ghostly pallor with bony shoulders, hollow cheeks and long fingers of such etiolated fragility they are barely thicker than the raven's legs.

The woman has been identified as Marguerite Luc, stepdaughter to the owner of Le Lapin Agile, the bohemian watering hole in the Montmartre district of Paris, where Picasso and his fellow artist friends met to drink and socialise. She may even have been Picasso's lover but, certainly, the raven was a pet of the premises, hopping among the tables to peck at crumbs and entertain the clients with its antics. The bird's striking presence in this avant-garde cafe reflected how ravens had come to be regarded as rather chic pets, expressing the individual mindset of their owner, someone who was at least publicly unafraid of the sinister connotations of the species.[18]

Domesticated ravens may have been fashionably quirky,

but they have also been celebrated for their huge personalities and an ability to develop deep emotional relationships with their owners. The American scientist and famous coracophile Bernd Heinrich, who has reared and kept many ravens, describes how he has never known anyone to refer to the birds as 'pets'. Rather they think of them as more like children or partners.[19] The extraordinary antics of one tame Victorian raven suggest its complex emotional world. It belonged to the owner of a coaching inn at the Elephant and Castle (now in central London), but the bird was also friendly with a number of the drivers and would set out on short happy excursions perched on the top of their coaches, switching vehicles whenever an inbound driver happened to pass to take him back to the inn. Once he was home, the raven's deepest intimacies were reserved for the stable's large pet dog.[20]

The practice of keeping ravens is extremely ancient. A key charm was noted during the Roman era, when Aelian described how they could be taught to speak like a human. 'For playful moods', he wrote, 'it has one voice, for serious moods another, and if it is delivering answers from the gods, then its voice assumes a devout and prophetic tone.'[21] Augustus (Octavian) was said to have been so enamoured of a raven (or crow) taught to say *ave Caesar victor imperator* ('Hail Caesar, victorious general') that he paid 20,000 sesterces for it.[22]

Sometimes tame ravens announce less formal greetings:

In London Zoo for some years there was a caged raven with a strong Cockney accent. He could wolf whistle and his repertoire included 'You aw ri?' (i.e. 'You all right?') and 'Woss a game, woss a game?' (i.e. 'What's the game?'). He was always our first port of call at the zoo.[23]

My grandfather had a raven who swore in Welsh. The raven's greeting to anyone who walked past was *Cau dy geg, Diawl* – 'Shut your Mouth, Devil' – especially if the visitor happened to be the vicar. As bad words go, *Diawl* is weightier than 'Devil', and certainly had a punch to it in 1940s north Wales.[24]

In Picasso's painting *Woman with a Raven* there is an obvious, tender intimacy between Marguerite Luc and her playfully croaking bird. In fact there are two versions of the subject – one in private American hands and the other in Spain's Toledo Museum of Art – and in the first there is a sense that she is actually smelling the creature, breathing in its apparently distinctive musky odour.[25] Yet there is also an unsettling quality to the preternaturally wan Marguerite. Both she and the raven are framed in an indeterminate space filled with the deepest mauve-blue. During his early years of personal hardship and poverty, Picasso was haunted by the violent suicide of his close friend Carles Casagemas in 1901. It is these circumstances that partly explain both the dominant melancholy hue and the despair-filled subject matter of the Blue Period. In the specific case of *Woman with a Raven* one cannot escape the idea that it depicts a real person kissing a real bird, but also an ethereal beauty embracing death.

Even more illustrative of the morbid associations long projected on to the birds is a painting by Vincent van Gogh. It is surely now the most famous image of the corvid family in Western art. It is entitled *Wheatfield with Crows* and has all the hallmarks of Van Gogh's late work: the rudimentary forms,

the vibrant primary colours, the thick impasto brushstrokes as the paint was almost wrestled into the canvas. It shows a sunshine-yellow cornfield under a rather heavy, brooding blue sky. Through the centre of the fields and up the middle of the whole painting runs a farmer's track, while above the fields is a flock of 40–45 corvids.

They are rendered in simple fashion as double curving lines to represent the outspread wings, like the letter 'M' that is the classic children's formula for flying birds in art. The flock is rather ambiguously portrayed and could be either vanishing into the blue yonder or beating rhythmically towards the artist. Nor is it straightforward to offer a judgement on their identity, although it can at least be attempted and the alternative suggestions could have deep implications for the significance of the work.

Firstly, however, we need to clarify that a couple of weeks after he painted it, Vincent van Gogh shot himself in the chest and died on 29 July 1890, aged just 37. The stock interpretation of *Wheatfield with Crows* (in French it is called *Champ de blé aux corbeaux*) is that it is a painting prefiguring the artist's death. The dwindling curve of the path shadowed by a host of ominous birds was seen as a metaphor of Van Gogh's self-selected end. The theory was given greater emphasis when it was assumed that this was actually his very last painting. Here in glorious colour was the artist's own suicide note. Subsequent research, however, has challenged that assumption and it is now thought that this was definitely *not* the final work.

Once we can set aside the idea of the suicide letter rendered in cornfield yellow and brooding blue, we can also re-examine the birds' presumed identity as Carrion Crows, heavily laden as they are with all those death associations.[26] The painting was executed just to the north-west of Paris in July 1890 in an area of cereal agriculture. At that season in that period and in that regional habitat the corvid species that was most likely to have been seen by Van Gogh in a post-breeding flock of over 40 birds is the Rook. This highly gregarious species is celebrated for its vibrant, even joyous, togetherness, which is in stark contrast to the territorial pair

that is the classic social unit for Carrion Crows. In fact the solitary Rook is such an anomaly it occasioned a sublimely terse Norfolk adage on corvid identification: 'when tha's crows, tha's rooks; and when tha's a rook, tha's a crow'. Rooky togetherness is particularly pronounced in the post-breeding period.

In the Carrion Crow's post-breeding period (i.e. July) the standard pattern is for parents to accompany their full-grown fledglings. Thus five or six birds would be a commonplace total for a crow flock. Larger groups do occur, but they are uncommon, they are most often seen in winter and are usually associated with temporary nocturnal roosts, when they come together as darkness descends and disperse by morning. In 1890 a summer flock of Carrion Crows numbering 40–45 birds to the north of the French capital would have been even less likely, given that the species was heavily persecuted and, therefore, far less numerous. An author on Parisian birds, Guilhem Lesaffre, suggests that, 'It would have been almost impossible for Carrion Crows to have congregated in the way that we see the birds flocking in Van Gogh's painting.'[27]

If we cannot pronounce on their identity with absolute certainty, we can at least say that it is much more likely that the birds seen by the artist were Rooks. It would also be more accurate and meaningful to call the painting *Wheatfield with Rooks*, rather than *Wheatfield with Crows*. Yet as soon as one applies the alternative title it immediately drains off some of the forbidding aura and the image assumes a more pastoral set of associations, because Rooks have very few of the macabre links long projected on to crows. They eat mainly grassland invertebrates. They seldom take carrion. They did not habitually frequent the gallows, nor peck out the eyes of fallen heroes on the battlefield. They were not symbols of evil, but background characters in farm landscapes. They were, and are still, motifs of the pastoral; scene-setting extras to rural idylls and nature's plenty. They did not appear in folklore or literature linked to witchcraft and malevolent forces. Nor were they prophets of doom, croaking of human death and disaster.

Van Gogh's *Wheatfield with Crows* is the most celebrated corvid image in Western art, but should it really be called *Wheatfield with Rooks?*

It is so abundant and often such a cheeky opportunist that we can overlook the Eurasian Magpie's glorious beauty.

Changing the title to *Wheatfield with Rooks* does not mean that the painting would lose all of its turbulent emotional content. The darkly brooding sky and the dwindling path may be enough by themselves to carry the submerged message of loneliness and terminal despair. Yet naming the birds as crows, as opposed to the much more likely Rooks, does demonstrate *our* predisposition to locate a particular symbolism in the work, and *our* preference for the buried, perhaps more convenient, connotations that are rooted in the 'crow' word and which the other name does not carry.

The whole issue demonstrates the power of paint to provoke the human imagination. After all, the matter revolves around 40–45 curving black lines. Equally it suggests the power of language. In a sense, the debate hinges on the difference between two four-letter names. Yet if we take both of these glorious bird-centred artworks by Van Gogh and Picasso, we can see how birds have a capacity to articulate our deepest thoughts and experiences. In a sense they are a kind of language all by themselves.

THE MAGPIE
FOR BETTER AND FOR WORSE

Another good illustration of the power of suggestion implicit in a bird's name is offered by the Australian Magpie of the butcherbird family (see page 371). Despite being completely unrelated to the **Eurasian Magpie** *Pica pica* of Europe, this Australian species has inherited some of the other bird's identity and often faces accusations commonly levelled against its namesake: that it is a thief of shiny objects. As one Australian ornithologist observes, 'It never happens!'[28]

The true magpies (involving 14 species in five genera) are relatively small corvids occurring across almost the whole northern hemisphere. They have sometimes escaped the odium heaped on black corvids, perhaps partly because they are birds of striking colour and beauty, often with long conspicuous tails. The Eurasian Magpie is no exception although superficially it can appear as a largely black bird with white underparts and shoulder patches. When seen well, as one contributor notes, the birds 'are white, black, blue-green, green-black, a rainbow of colour with the depth of shot silk'. [29]

One of the reasons that the species has not shaken off all of the customary corvid negativity is the modern issue of predation. Magpies have an unfortunate, seemingly ineradicable reputation as garden bullies that are undeserving of our charity.

Over the last ten years I believe my mother has spent less on feeding her own family than she has on enormous bags of bird food. As the daughter of an ornithologist [the celebrated conservationist Peter Conder] she has always felt passionate about her feathered friends. However, this passion exhibits itself in different ways. Eating breakfast one morning, she was sitting at her usual place, while numerous small birds were swirling around the garden and all was peaceful.

Suddenly my mother jumped out of her seat shrieking and I watched her doing laps of the garden waving her hands in the air like a maniac with five magpies, equally shocked, flying for their lives. This kind of behaviour is not uncommon in our home and, I fear, elsewhere in the UK.[30]

Another frequent charge is that Eurasian Magpies are responsible for killing songbird nestlings – which is true – and even for declines in some garden species – which is untrue. (It is intriguing to note that the same allegations are made of Australian Magpies; see page 373.) British ecologist Tim Birkhead, a leading authority on Eurasian Magpie, conducted a research project with the British Trust for Ornithology and found it had no major impact on songbird numbers. On the contrary, in those areas where magpies had increased so had songbird populations. Yet his experience suggests that once myths have taken root in popular consciousness, they are as difficult to extirpate as the corvids themselves.

> I once gave a talk about magpies to a Yorkshire bird group. They listened politely to all I had to say, including the fact that despite my years of research there was no evidence whatsoever that magpies have an effect on songbird numbers. When I'd finished they sat with arms folded and thanked me. The chairman then said that they didn't believe me, the entire audience nodding in agreement. So much for the power of science![31]

In the Far East perceptions of magpies soften considerably, just as the number of species increases. China holds an enormously handsome trio, the **Azure-winged Magpie** *Cyanopica cyanus*, **Yellow-billed Blue Magpie** *Urocissa flavirostris* and **Red-billed Blue Magpie** *Urocissa erythrorhyncha*, all of which regularly feature in Oriental visual arts and ceramics. A painting by the artist Cui Bai, entitled *Magpies and Hare*, was completed in AD 1061, and is one of the earliest dated works in all Chinese art (now in the National Palace Museum in Taiwan). It shows two Azure-winged Magpies caught in high winds as they shriek anxiously at a hare which, in turn, gazes serenely back at them. The painting's Chinese title, *Shauangxi tu* ('Picture of Double Happiness'), incorporates a pun since *xi* means both 'magpie' and 'happiness'. The full title can mean both 'double happiness' or simply 'two magpies'.[32]

It reflects how the Chinese continue to associate the birds with luck generally and deploy them as symbols of both fortune and fertility. Magpie images are frequent in wedding regalia. They are regular motifs in the art of Chinese paper cuts; those intricate decorative designs that are still a part of domestic life in the country. Paper cuts specifically associated with weddings frequently include magpies, while the pillows of newlyweds feature embroidered versions of the birds as symbols of harmony.[33]

We should recall that Eurasian Magpies have similar links to romantic fortune in the West, albeit of a more ambivalent character – for example, the old forecasting rhyme, 'One for sorrow / Two for joy', etc. Yet occasionally the birds can have an undisputed bearing on marital affairs:

> I'd been watching two [Eurasian] Magpies in the garden over several days as their nest was slowly taking shape high in the Scots pine opposite our bedroom window.

> Their economy and the way they worked together felt valiant, hopeful, as if they were not going to be toppled by high wind or foul weather. This quiet sustained nest building was going on at a time when I was preoccupied with deciding whether to marry again. It wasn't a question of love, but rather more whether I felt able to place my life within a relationship that could endure. As a migrant from an earlier marriage, it seemed unlikely. Now I had bought a house with my new partner and the question of marriage had become ever present. Neither thought nor feeling was guiding me. As I watched those magpies in their capacities to make a nest together, to prepare for the rearing of their young, I had a realisation if they can do it then so can I. Three months later we married. I had conceived my one and only child, my daughter who is now 22. I've watched the magpies every year since from the same window. My enduring joy![34]

The Eurasian Magpies that have offered the most enduring commentary on human marital relations are the 136 birds famously painted on to the ceiling of the Palácio Nacional in Sintra, Portugal. Avian images feature strongly

This costume by the late Alexander McQueen, which was photographed by chance in the display window of a Manhattan fashion house, expresses the exuberant talent of this young designer as well as his fascination for magpies.

in this ancient royal residence, with rooms that are full of swan and dove images, but the most intriguing is the Sala das Pegas ('the Magpie Room'). It dates from the fifteenth century and draws its significance from a story of King João, who was caught by his queen in the act of kissing and presenting a white rose to one of the maids. The somewhat embarrassed monarch is said to have reacted with the words *Por bem, por bem*, which translates loosely as 'it was all for the best' and indicated that his affections were harmless.

There are two versions of how the incident came to be expressed in 500-year-old paint. The modern official story is that João was so fed up with all the gossip stirred by his innocent gesture that he had the ceiling covered with as many chattering birds as there were maids of honour at court. Each magpie has a white rose in its left foot and in its beak a caption that reads *Por Bem*. An alternative story says that it was the queen herself who had the room painted and that the birds were a witty and ironic comment upon her husband's ambiguous behaviour and bland reassurances. Yet he was apparently so amused by the visual joke that he adopted *Por Bem* as his motto. The latter version draws some support from the fact that *pega* in Portuguese is a name for both the magpie but also another kind of faithless bird, a prostitute.[35]

CACHING CORVIDS

A few years ago a milk customer asked a local farmer about the honesty of his milk-delivery girl, as the customer had covered her bottle with a silver cup that had mysteriously disappeared. Why the customer had used such a valuable item we could never fathom, but she then replaced it with another silver cup, which also duly disappeared. The farmer said that he had always found the girl reliable, although one could never be sure of any child one did not know intimately. About a year later a tree in their garden was cut down as too big for its suburban space. It contained a magpie's nest which was found to contain the two silver cups.[36]

The thieving magpie is as familiar from Italian opera (Rossini's *La Gazza Ladra*) as it is from popular folk culture. Nor is the charge of larceny confined simply to the one species. In Roman times Pliny accused Western Jackdaws of having a fondness for stealing silver and gold.[37] Despite such evidence as the story above and the well-established habit among domesticated birds, a genuine predisposition to shiny objects in wild corvids is still a matter for dispute.

What is more certain is that the 'stealing' behaviour has its origins in the classic corvid trait of restless curiosity, and in the family's wider habit of caching surplus foods. Crows are inveterate hoarders, storing supplies that might be retrieved in harder times. Some species, such as the **Pinyon Jay** *Gymnorhinus cyanocephalus* and **Clark's Nutcracker** *Nucifraga columbiana* of North America, or the **Eurasian Jay** *Garrulus glandarius* and **Spotted Nutcracker** *Nucifraga caryocatactes* of Eurasia, show extraordinary providence, the adult birds storing thousands of seeds during the autumn. Each Spotted Nutcracker is thought to hide as many as 100,000. In any hectare of forested ground there may be as many as 25,000–40,000 corvid-sown tree seeds.[38] The birds also transport the crop large distances from where they first harvested it. Clark's Nutcrackers have

been recorded to carry pine nuts 22 km (13.7 miles) before burying them.[39]

Then in winter the birds visit their scattered larders to feed, exhibiting equally remarkable powers of memory in retrieving their stores. Clark's Nutcrackers and Pinyon Jays have been shown to have a recovery rate of 90 per cent.[40] Yet the birds are not always able to re-locate the concealed stocks. The lapses should surely be the cause of our deepening respect and admiration for corvids, since the 'lost' seeds can then germinate and develop as new trees. It is by these means that the birds serve as some of the most important foresters across the entire northern hemisphere, playing a fundamental role in the propagation of their own habitats. In an age of global warming we may yet learn to love these extraordinary tree-farming creatures for their role in husbanding forests on their slow retreat to the cooler climes of the north.

CLEVER CORVIDS

One characteristic shown by food-hoarding species is an enlargement of the part of the forebrain known as the hippocampus, an area that governs the capacity for spatial memory. Other parts of the 'avian prefrontal cortex', the nidopallium and mesopallium, which are densely packed with nerve cells, also show increased development in corvids.[41] Of all birds, in fact, with the exception of some parrots, corvids have the largest relative forebrain size. This area of the brain as a whole is responsible for learning and memory, and animals in which this portion is especially enlarged – a group that includes other primates, humans and crows – show increased ability to learn new skills and to forge new opportunities as circumstances change.

It is the capacity to improvise among corvids that has led people to marvel, if sometimes only grudgingly, at their sheer modernity and intelligence. One classic field of innovation is in the matter of their nest construction. In treeless areas where suitable wood products are in short supply, birds have been observed taking building materials from us. In fact, some of our products start to look purpose-made for homeless corvids. The **Chihuahuan Raven** *Corvus cryptoleucus* is a species of arid, often treeless landscapes in Mexico and south-west USA, where the birds use telegraph poles as a handy substitute for the nest tree. In the early part of last century they also used so much wire in nest construction that the telephone company had constantly to patrol certain stretches of the network, removing up to 363 kg (800 lb) of scrap metal annually.[42]

Sometimes the materials are more eccentric. In the nineteenth century Indian House Crows were known to make nests from the wires used in the stoppers for soda-water bottles.[43] In the early twentieth century one far-sighted couple of the same species was found constructing its home made entirely out of spectacle frames (supplied by the Simla branch of the Indian opticians Lawrence and Mayo).[44]

Yet it is in the business of finding fresh food that corvids show their real colours. Pliny the Elder marvelled at the birds' ability to drop nuts on roofs and among rocks to break open the otherwise impenetrable shells.[45] In modern Japan, Jungle Crows have developed the method to take advantage of more recent technologies. They drop walnuts on the pedestrian crossings over busy roads, where the passing traffic does the nut cracking for them. Then the periodic red lights at the crossing allow the birds to retrieve the processed walnut flesh in relative safety.

Another classic example of the family's eye for novelty is found among Torresian Crows, which have learned how to profit from the classic toxic scourge of the Australian outback. Cane Toads, introduced originally from Hawaii, are judged a major environmental issue in the country, because they routinely poison indigenous predators. Yet Torresian Crows have learned to avoid the venomous sacs located behind the amphibian's swollen head by flipping the toads on to their backs to expose their fleshy and edible bellies.

Corvids also collaborate with one another to catch prey far larger than themselves. Raven pairs can kill geese and gulls, or they steal the eggs of Ospreys and hawks from under their parents' very noses. In the Arctic, Northern Raven pairs have been observed working as a unit to cut off seal pups from their ice hole and then kill them as they try to escape. Corvid teamwork can also dispossess the most fearsome predators. Species as small as the **Black-billed Magpie** *Pica hudsonia*, the North American counterpart to the Eurasian Magpie, has been seen to mob a Golden Eagle, and when the raptor turned to ward off the feigned attack a second magpie seized the food item. Sometimes crows use other forms of assistance to overcome difficult prey. House Crows have been seen to catch a rat then deliberately push it underwater to drown it.[46] In Israel the local race of Carrion Crow has discovered other benefits of the 'drowning' technique:

> During the hot, dry summer we keep a bowl full of water in our backyard for birds, cats, dogs and even hedgehogs that are common in the urban environment. Very often, we also put out leftover bread for the birds. Lately we have observed frequent visits by Carrion Crows that show amazing behaviour. They take the bread, which is usually dry and hardly edible, and dip it in the water bowl several times until it's soaked and soft enough to be enjoyably eaten! It has been shown that this special behaviour has been developed to another stage. There is an observation of a Carrion Crow at the Yarkon River (Tel Aviv) that dropped the bread into the river and kept watching it until all of a sudden it dipped its beak into the water and pulled out a fish that was eating the bread. A fishing crow![47]

Cleverest of all, perhaps, is the crow that lets someone else do all the fishing:

> Until the 1990s I did a great deal of trout fishing and one time my friend bought me an American device called a 'stringer'. It involves over a metre of chain with eight to ten safety clips at the far end. Pegged in the bank or hung from the boat, and with your fish held on the clips, the chain is sunk into the water and keeps everything cool. No one to my knowledge was using this device in Britain and it caused much interest with other anglers. After a successful morning and with two bright silver Rainbow Trout around the 2 lb mark clipped and sunk on the stringer to the cool depths, we departed for lunch, as was our custom. As we walked back later that afternoon my friend immediately said, 'What's that Carrion Crow doing with your fish?' Hurrying across the dam to my gear I found that the crow, now staring moodily at me from a small ash tree, had seen the fish

in the clear water, associated them with the chain and, link by link, had eased them up until it could remove the eyes and had started on the gills of the topmost. This was a most remarkable feat because the bird could never have come across this puzzle before and had solved it within an hour.[48]

THE WISE CROW

Our growing capacity to appreciate the exceptional life skills possessed by corvids is, in many ways, not a learning process but a re-learning by the West of truths long appreciated elsewhere. For millennia the people dwelling around the upper third of our planet have celebrated the extraordinary capacity of the Northern Raven to live alongside them. In so doing they have woven this species into their arts and their cosmologies to make it one of the most culturally enriched birds on Earth. None has more fully expressed their admiration of the raven than the cluster of indigenous peoples from the American region known as the Pacific Northwest.

Arriving in the northern hemisphere from Asia about 15,000 years ago, these first Americans spread out to occupy a complex sequence of coastal bays, beaches and inlets, which are all flanked by dense evergreen forests and run through 15° of latitude from the south-east Alaskan Panhandle, along Canada's western seaboard, as far south as the Columbia River in Washington, USA. They have been divided into five basic linguistic groupings and while they share a modest number of words or word-sounds, the five communities speak languages that are as different from one another in structure and vocabulary as Arabic, English, Japanese, Persian and Finnish.[49]

However, this human mosaic, which includes the Tlingit, Haida and Tsimshian tribes (see also Loon family, page 98), shared to varying degrees elements of social structure and artistic heritage. A further common element was a condition of material affluence rooted in the richness of their marine ecosystem. The Northwest enjoyed extraordinary abundances of timber, game, fish and seafood, especially spawning salmon, seals and cetaceans. Their villages comprised substantial structures of cedar planking, often elaborately carved with animal motifs, as indeed were all their wooden artefacts including their whaling boats and ceremonial canoes. One part of this shared cultural tradition has become enmeshed in the world's collective sense of Native America with examples held in museums worldwide. The totem pole, that red-cedar monument covered in a fantastic bestiary of carved animal images which morph one into the other as they ascend the wooden column, is one of the most famous artefacts in all pre-Columbian America.

One portion of the peoples' collective world vision and central to their symbolic vocabulary was the mythic figure

This ceremonial rattle made by Native Americans of the Pacific coast portrays a Northern Raven carrying a human soul on its back and the sun in its beak.

This raven head by an unknown nineteenth-century sculptor of the Haida people from the Pacific Northwest once graced the top of a totem pole. Now it forms one of the largest exhibits in London's British Museum.

of the raven. The bird is everywhere in their art and in their cycles of stories, which were as important as a form of wealth as their racks of drying salmon or their stores of otter pelts. Sometimes the symbolic birds achieve monumental proportions. There is a vast raven motif, for instance, across the prow of a magnificent Tlingit canoe suspended from the ceiling of the American Museum of Natural History (New York). Equally impressive, in fact one of the largest artefacts on display in the British Museum (London), is the 1.6 m (5.2 ft) raven head that was once a crest from the summit of a Haida totem pole.

In the story cycles of the Tlingit and Haida we can recognise elements of our own modern perception of corvids as the arch survivors. For their mythic raven was a mischievous trickster and a cheat whose antics were a source of humour, shame and ridicule. Yet for the people of the Pacific Northwest there was a serious and magical side to raven, who possessed supernatural powers. One of the bird's cardinal achievements was to discover humankind itself, hidden away inside a clam shell. Having rescued men from their incarceration, raven then created woman and, in the case of the Haida, fashioned their home in the Queen Charlotte Islands from a pebble dropped into the sea.

Raven was the ultimate creative spirit, transforming life and bringing into existence whole landscapes and landscape features (the myth makers of the Pacific Northwest would surely not be surprised to learn of the jays' collective role in fashioning northern forests). Raven, however, was the source not only of the Milky Way and the moon, but also of the sun. The account of how raven gifted to all life the blessings of our light-bearing star is a story shared not only by the first peoples of the Pacific Northwest, but also by more distant communities in northern Siberia. Such creation stories could take whole days to relate in full and in their recounting touched upon themes fundamental to the world view of these communities.

Versions of how raven stole the sun are legion, but essentially they tell of an old man who, at the beginning of time, kept the sun tied in a bundle in his house. Through magical means raven managed to impregnate the man's only daughter by making himself very small and dropping into the water. The girl drank from the pool where raven was hidden and on swallowing this bird-cum-seed she eventually became pregnant. The birth of this baby boy made the girl's father very happy and wishing to please his grandson and heir, the old man allowed the child to play with all the possessions in the house. In turn, the child-raven opened various bundles setting free first the stars, then the moon and finally the sun. With the shining star in his beak the child turned back into a bird and flew out through the smoke hole, letting light into

the world. Yet the sun was so hot that as he escaped the fires burned raven and turned all his feathers black.[50]

As one commentator notes, this creation story was more than simply an account of how things came to be:

It also encapsulated the entire moral basis of generosity and exchange in Northwest Coast society. Raven presents the first gift – he gives himself as a child, the greatest of all treasures. His grandfather reciprocates by giving Raven . . . those treasures he had previously kept only for himself and which now benefit everyone. Raven gives himself as a sacrifice for the world, sacrificing his beauty for the benefit of the rest of the world. Raven's black feathers now remind us that we are part of that covenant, that we must give, must sacrifice. Nothing – not wealth, not beauty, not power, not status, not life itself – can be kept.[51]

The most extraordinary expression of this ethic of social giving was the central regional ceremony of the potlatch. The acts of generosity associated with the potlatch expressed the fundamental responsibility of persons of rank and power in Pacific Northwest society to share their wealth. (It is surely an expression of the Christian preference for keeping and hoarding over giving that the state authorities outlawed the potlatch and all its subversive philosophy.) Yet at one such event a tribal chief fed hundreds of guests for weeks and distributed 18,000 blankets, 700 carved silver bracelets, a dozen canoes (each equivalent in value to 3,000 blankets), sewing machines, outboard motors, pots and pans, hundreds of sacks of flour, sugar and other foods, as well as many other forms of wealth.[52]

Giving was a way for individuals and communities to align themselves with their overarching cosmology, which stressed the role and importance of change in life. The world was in a perpetual state of flux. Giving was a transaction that expressed that cycle. What was once yours became another's property, a process that carried on indefinitely, just as life and death were a kind of giving and receiving. To give was to take part in this flow of change. Many of these fundamental ideas seem manifest in the region's extraordinary artistic tradition, which is in many ways still dominated by a single two-dimensional motif, the rounded rectangle termed the 'ovoid'.[53]

Animals – bears, whales, birds, otters, fish – as well as mythical spirits and people were rendered in these interlocking patterns of curving lines and ovoids. Raven images in this format are both abundant and ubiquitous. In fact, they are among the most distinctive images of birds in all the Americas. Just as the entire regional aesthetic of the Pacific Northwest is itself instantly recognisable and flourishes today in the modern carved wooden artworks and textiles of exceptional artists. One dominant characteristic of Tlingit or Haida art, both in the present and in the past, is the way one form morphs into another. The ambiguous flow of images up and down a totem pole is, in many ways, a perfect expression of this constant life flux and the world's propensity to change.

That the Northern Raven should have been singled out for such a prominent place in Northwest art and culture surely expresses the peoples' recognition of the arch characteristic attributed to corvids. They are eternally predisposed to the new. They seem to flourish whatever happens. Their ability to survive unloved, unprotected and often in the teeth of violent opposition from us is itself an expression of their capacity to change and to adapt. As the Haida and the Tlingit and their neighbours recognised, corvids are *the* exemplars of a spirit running through all life. We would do well to recognise fully – and perhaps even to celebrate occasionally – their totemic place in the world.

Australian Mudnester family *Corcoracidae*

The **White-winged Chough** *Corcorax melanorhamphos* and **Apostlebird** *Struthidea cinerea* are endemic to eastern Australia and, while both are members of the same family, this species pair hardly looks alike. The larger all-black chough roughly resembles its Eurasian namesake in the crow family, but Apostlebirds – smaller, predominantly mealy grey-brown, ground dwelling and deeply social in habit – rather suggest the *Turdoides* babblers of Africa or Asia (see page 443). One common attribute of these Australian birds is their joint preference for open dry wooded or bush country. They have now also adapted to parks and suburban gardens.

Mudnesters share a highly gregarious social life and it is their communal behaviour which accounts for the name 'Apostlebird'. Their gatherings are seldom an exact analogue of the Messiah and his disciples – the typical party averaging nine birds with full parameters of three to 19. Yet the extended family operates as a single unit even sharing incubation, the feeding of nestlings and the construction of their beautifully sculpted open mud bowl, from which the family draws its name.

The intense sociability means that they are often enveloped in a babble of contact notes, especially Apostlebirds. It helps cement the idea that these are creatures possessed of huge personality.

> For character, my favourite must be the Apostlebirds (other name Happy Families); they are delightful birds that stroll around in family groups and, although they have dull plumage, they're so interesting to watch. If one bird goes to sit on a branch others will come and join it and huddle up close. In Cania Gorge [Queensland] when one bird decided to come and sunbathe by my feet, another came and cuddled up close and I couldn't move in case I frightened them. They genuinely give the impression they enjoy each other's company.[1]

Apostlebirds are routinely to be found fossicking in the dust about the tables at roadside rest stops, and easily convert into a cheeky circle of uninvited guests around any picnic spread. The aura of noisy togetherness has given rise to other nicknames, including (the somewhat sexist) 'CWA bird', from the all-female Australian organisation the Country Women's Association. In her poem 'Apostle-Birds' the Australian Judith Wright explores the humour of these wonderful creatures – their clannishness, their rudeness to the neighbours and their self-possession – but she also celebrates their aura of ancient belonging to the Earth's oldest landscapes.[2]

The Apostlebird is a 'gang member' and the intense togetherness of their family parties surrounds them in an aura of busyness and warm humour.

Bird-of-Paradise family *Paradisaeidae*

▶ The Raggiana Bird-of-Paradise shares fully in the family's wider reputation as some of the most beautiful organisms on Earth.

This family's reputation for including some of the most extravagantly colourful of all living organisms is widely appreciated and long established. Their main avian rivals for beauty's first prize on Earth are some of the pheasants (see page 58) and hummingbirds (see page 300). Yet much of our sense of familiarity with birds-of-paradise is a by-product of visual and written media – films, documentaries, books or magazine articles – and of all birds that have become fixtures in the Western imagination they must be the group that the smallest number of people has ever encountered in the wild.

The one community that is the glaring exception to our lack of direct contact is found on New Guinea. However, to speak of a single people in the context of this forested land is deeply misleading. The second largest island (after Greenland), it is also among the most culturally varied regions on the planet; and if language were the exclusive measure of diversity then it would be the most varied. More than 1,000 languages, one-sixth of all those used by the human race, are shared between just 7.5 million people.[1] Most of the Papuan languages are mutually unintelligible. Three of them are common to populations of more than 100,000, and about 50 are spoken by more than 10,000; but around 700 languages are the shared birthright of communities as small as a few dozen souls.[2] Many of these diverse groups had, and often still have, cultural lives in which birds-of-paradise play an integral part. The birds have been hunted and their body parts deployed in ceremonial dress for tens of thousands of years.

There are about 40 species in total, but unfortunately bird-of-paradise taxonomy has a deeply knotted history, and even now few authorities agree entirely. (A single example of the confusion involves a bird long known as Macgregor's Bird-of-Paradise. It is a species of bizarre beauty with circular, yellow fleshy wattles around its eyes that resemble half-melted plastic wheels from a child's toy. Some authorities now place this oddity among the honeyeaters – see page 366 – and have renamed it Macgregor's Lappetface.)

Of the family total, just eight are *not* found in New Guinea. Four occur only on adjacent islands to the west that are politically claimed by Indonesia, including the Raja Ampat group (**Wilson's Bird-of-Paradise** *Diphyllodes respublica* and **Red Bird-of-Paradise** *Paradisaea rubra*) and the northern Moluccas (**Paradise-crow** *Lycocorax pyrrhopterus* and **Standardwing** *Semioptera wallacii*). Two more species are island endemics in the D'Entrecasteaux Archipelago (**Goldie's Bird-of-Paradise** *Paradisaea decora* and **Curl-crested Manucode** *Manucodia comrii*), which is located off New Guinea's east coast and is politically part of Papua New Guinea, the nation forming the eastern half of the island.

A final two species occur along the east coast of Australia (two other largely New Guinean birds just make it to the northern tip of Australia's Cape York Peninsula, to give the country a total of four birds-of-paradise). They are the **Victoria's Riflebird** *Ptiloris victoriae* and **Paradise Riflebird** *Ptiloris paradiseus*, species named for the apparent resemblance of the males' iridescent green / blue-on-black plumage to the smart uniforms – 'the hanging pelisse and the jacket' – formerly worn by members of the British rifle

regiments.[3] They are perhaps the birds-of-paradise most routinely encountered by people of Western background. They are both forest dwellers, but Victoria's Riflebird will come to large gardens and even feed at bird tables. Although shyer in habit, the Paradise Riflebird occurs almost to the outer suburbs of Brisbane, while its population in New South Wales is the most southerly distributed of all its family.

Their relatives from further north – especially the seven members of the genus *Paradisaea*, the species which we probably think of today as most typical of their family – are creatures of gorgeous colour and improbable form. The adult males' heads are golden yellow. Their throats are iridescent emerald. At their rears, greater in apparent bulk than the rest of the whole bird, is a long, airy, curving 'bustle' of filamentous plumes. They look like tail feathers but they are, in fact, massively elongated flank feathers that emerge from under the wings and cascade behind their owners in shades – according to their species – of lemon, yellow, orange, burnt sienna or crimson. From the centre of their trains obtrude two further and even longer central tail pins, which can sway and quiver beyond the entire ensemble like a pair of narrow satin ribbons. On one of the most sought after of the paradiseids, the **Blue Bird-of-Paradise** *Paradisaea rudolphi*, all these same extravagances of shape and hue are repeated, but in tones of cerulean, cobalt and indigo.

During display the birds assault both the eye and the ear. A species such as **Greater Bird-of-Paradise** *Paradisaea apoda* gathers in special display leks, where the calls of the males – a loud, penetrating, echoic *waaaa-waaaa-waaaa* – convert the surrounding rainforest to a sound chamber of emotional intensity and sexual theatre. As soon as a drab brown-bodied female alights in the same tree as a male, he turns himself upside down and lets his train spray over his head and body as a cascading aura of brilliant yellow. In contrast to this airy net of colour, the male rhythmically pushes his dark wings forward and back as if rowing through the sunlit canopy. When he is confident of his effects, he returns to an upright posture and inches steadily towards her, sidling snake-like over her until she is cloaked in his ecstatic glamour. All the while he buffets either side of her head with his bill in a gesture that seems one part aggression, one part solicitous caress. Eventually they copulate, the wailing notes subside and the forest lapses into brief silence, except perhaps for the drone of cicadas and the hoarse pumping notes of unseen doves.

They are birds of such implausible radiance that one can perhaps understand how some of the first Europeans to witness bird-of-paradise skins disbelieved the evidence of their eyes. Instead they thought that they were being hoodwinked and that the birds had been made up by humans and stitched together from various parts of other animals.[4] What is generally regarded as the earliest European account of the family occurred in Cologne in 1523. Some skins of the **Lesser Bird-of-Paradise** *Paradisaea minor* had travelled west with the survivors of Ferdinand Magellan's first circumnavigation of the planet, after his crew had been gifted a small sample in the Molucca Islands. When the birds were given to the Spanish king, a young courtier reported the

details, his account referring to them by their Malay name: *Mamuco-Diata*, 'the bird of the gods'.[5] A modified version of this, 'manucode', is still used as part of the English name for four members of the family.

One thing that the Europeans acquired inadvertently from the Moluccan dignitaries who supplied these first bird-of-paradise skins was an understanding of their ecology that was fantastically indifferent to the truth. They were birds of the gods to the Malay-speaking traders and became, in turn, birds of paradise to Europeans, not only because they were so beautiful but also because they were assumed never to land on terra firma. Instead they dwelled in the upper ether, a claim confirmed for Europe's first over-credulous observers by the creatures' lack of legs and feet. In fact, in a time-honoured tradition the dead birds-of-paradise traded to Europe had simply had their limbs trimmed off for convenience. Often the wings were removed too.

Typical of the early European confusion are the words of a sixteenth-century Dutch merchant John Huyghen van Linschoten:

> In these Ilands onlie is found the bird which the Portingales [Portuguese] call *passaros de Sol*, that is Fowle of the Sunne, and the Latinists *Paradiseas*, and are by us called Paradice-birdes, for ye beauty of their feathers which pass all other birdes. These birdes are never seen alive but being dead they fall on the Ilands: they flie it is said alwaies into the Sunne and keep themselves continually in the ayre without lighting on the earth, for they have neither feet nor wings but only head and body . . .[6]

A writer called Tavernier was discontent even with this level of make-believe. His version of the birds had them flocking en masse to southern India, where they became intoxicated by the smell of nutmeg and in their spice-induced swoon were too drugged to notice the ants gnawing off their legs. It was this that explained the legless condition.[7]

Even in the late seventeenth century, the great English scientist John Ray felt it necessary to note the following:

> That Birds of Paradise want feet is not only a popular persuasion, but a thing not long since believed by learned men and great Naturalists . . . deceived by the birds dried or their cases, brought over into Europe out of the East Indies, dismembred, and bereaved of their Feet . . . This errour once admitted, the other fictions of idle brains, which seemed thence to follow, did without difficulty obtain belief; viz. that they lived upon the coelestial dew; that they flew perpetually without any intermission, and took no rest but on high in the Air, their Wings being spread; that they were never taken alive, but only when they fell down dead upon the ground . . .[8]

It was equally taken as fact that these creatures of perpetual motion bred by means of a hollow in the male's back and a matching cavity in his mate's breast. When they wanted to breed the female simply placed her frontal depression to his dorsal area, then laid her eggs and incubated the clutch while sitting upon his mantle and floating through the heavens.[9]

The various European and scientific names that were subsequently given to the birds-of-paradise are interesting for their insights into the history of ornithology. However, as a vocabulary to invoke some of the Earth's most beautiful creatures they seem to me personally to do less than justice to their 'owners'. This is in stark contrast to the extravagantly poetic but expressive English names coined for the hummingbirds of tropical America (see page 303).

A standard name construction for the birds-of-paradise was the patronymic. Even today there are ten in the English versions of their names (**Princess Stephanie's Astrapia** *Astrapia stephaniae* and Goldie's Bird-of-Paradise) and no fewer than 18 in the scientific nomenclature (**Ribbon-tailed Astrapia** *Astrapia mayeri* and **Black-billed Sicklebill** *Drepanornis albertisi*). They were largely chosen to honour the birds themselves, of course, but the individual Europeans behind the patronymic. It was they and their fellow nationals who, in this symbolic way, asserted a form of territorial possession even over the living treasures of the New Guinean forest. Occasionally the squabble over bird names mirrored precisely nineteenth-century Europe's colonial rivalries. The **Raggiana Bird-of-Paradise** *Paradisaea raggiana* (named in 1873 after the Marquis Raggi of Genoa, Italy) was simultaneously christened by northern European naturalists as the Empress of Germany's Bird-of-Paradise *Paradisaea augustavictoriae*. In this instance, however, a mere marquis eventually triumphed over her imperial highness.

The two name versions for the same species typify the formula by which early naturalists at least attempted to suggest the exalted physical character of the New Guinean birds. They were rendered special by being ascribed to people at the apex of Europe's deeply hierarchical society. The classic examples are the **Emperor Bird-of-Paradise** *Paradisaea guilielmi* and **King of Saxony Bird-of-Paradise** *Pteridophora alberti*, which refer respectively to Kaiser Wilhelm I (1797–1888) and King Albert (1828–1902). Mercifully, the latter species was spared the honour of Albert's full name – Frederick Augustus Albert Anton Ferdinand Joseph Karl Maria Baptist Nepomuk Wilhelm Xaver Georg Fidelis.

The huge linguistic diversity on the island of New Guinea means that for each of the individual birds-of-paradise there is an extraordinary synonymy of local names. These deserve a book in their own right. To give one example, Clifford Frith and Bruce Beehler, two foremost experts on the family, have assembled the following for the King of Saxony Bird-of-Paradise. The names run approximately east to west through the island's central cordillera: *Wárale* (Okapa), *Oretha* (Crater Mountain), *Kis-a-ba* (Kubor Mountains), *kis-ba* (Bismarck Mountains), *Nopd kolman* – the male – and *Nopd neb* – female or immature (Madang Province), *Leme* (Ialibu Mountain), *Gangade* or *Tima Gangade* (Tari Basin), *Kongbuk* – the male bird – and *Doongbi* – female or immature (Central Highlands), *Inem* (Hindenburg Range), *Wigelo* and *tat* (Ilaga Valley) and *Petre* (Weyland Mountains).[10]

The birds have filtered, via this rich indigenous cultural heritage, into the iconography of the modern nation of Papua New Guinea (PNG). The flag and the national coat of arms both bear a stylised male of a species that is appropriately endemic to the country, the Raggiana Bird-of-Paradise.[11]

> The Raggiana is the official bird of PNG, and the logo is everywhere in all sorts of formats and on the walls

at the entrance to Jacksons Airport in Port Moresby (a very nice stylised one). There is also a striking coat of arms on the gates to the Parliament House in Waigani, Port Moresby. And a large metal sculptural interpretation nearby at the roundabout by the Chinese Embassy. Some of the public logos look like there has been hanky-panky with the Lesser Bird-of-Paradise or the Greater Bird-of-Paradise, but what the hell! On the banknotes of the 2-kina [the Papuan currency] there is the Raggiana image from the coat of arms. The 10-kina note has a large Raggiana image on the back, while the 20-kina has a huge stylised version of the coat-of-arms image on the front. The 100-kina also has the coat-of-arms image. All have a further Raggiana logo on the clear plastic window on each note.[12]

There is a rather wonderful portrait of the Raggiana Bird-of-Paradise on the tail fins to aircraft owned by the national carrier, Air Niugini (it is also replicated on the company's website logo).[13] At the airport in the Papuan capital, Port Moresby, there are versions of paradise birds not just on the runway, but also in the departure-lounge bar: the tin cans and bottles of the country's popular beer South Pacific Export Lager have splendid pictures of the state bird on them.[14]

Ubiquitous though they may be, these motifs in modern Papuan life are nothing compared with the family's wider and former exploitation in traditional cultural settings. In the forested mountains of the country's interior, bird-of-paradise feathers formed a central part of extraordinary ceremonial practices. Historical descriptions of the public rites performed by pre-Cortesian Aztecs in Mexico (see Trogon family, page 310) suggest acts of display that were loaded with the same density of cultural meanings. Yet little in the modern era and certainly nothing from the contemporary fashion salons of Manhattan or Milan reflect an evolved aesthetic as ancient as the dress sense and colour codes of rural Papuans. Only perhaps the carnivals of Rio de Janeiro match New Guinean festivities for their blend of colour and raw spectacle. These Papuan events, known as *moka*, were, and possibly still are, one of the most extraordinary, lavish and captivating examples of human ritual found anywhere on Earth.

Usage of bird-of-paradise feathers was both ancient and, until recently, sustainable. Today, unfortunately, over-hunting bears heavily on two much-prized species. The Blue Bird-of-Paradise, which has an exceptionally high cultural status, is now at risk of extinction. So too is the **Black Sicklebill** *Epimachus fastuosus*, whose central tail plumes of iridescent blue-purple are among the longest of all bird-of-paradise adornments. A former Papuan hunter suggested that he could once have expected 200 kina (*c*.£50: $80) for a single tail feather from this species, and 50 kina (£12.50: $20) for a head plume of the King of Saxony Bird-of-Paradise.[15] Yet it should be noted that the primary factor assailing the family – a further nine species are now also deemed threatened or near-threatened – is loss of their forest habitats.[16]

The rituals themselves had their roots in the structure of Papuan society. Running for almost the entire length of the island, the central mountains of New Guinea are clothed in equatorial rainforest at lower levels but emerge eventually as alpine meadows with snow at altitudes above 5,000 m

Birds-of-paradise imagery is ubiquitous in Papua New Guinea and gives character to the nation's currency (the kina) and to its main airline.

(16,400 ft). However, the interior valleys of middle elevation are largely malaria free and were cleared or subjected to sophisticated swidden agriculture, based on the cultivation of taro, yams and, most especially now, the sweet potato. When groups of Australian gold prospectors encountered this central highland community of approximately half a million people (it has now doubled) in the 1930s, it was the first moment that the outside world knew anything of its existence.[17]

There are no large native mammals on New Guinea, and the flightless bird the cassowary (see page 19), represented the largest vertebrate other than ourselves until domesticated pigs were introduced from Indonesia. These eventually acquired paramount importance in Papuan society as a means of accumulating wealth and as a source of political prestige for the community's most powerful individuals, known with graphic simplicity as 'big men'. The swine acquired a third major role when, along with revenge killings and bride kidnap, they became a *casus belli* in New Guinea's perpetual cycle of warfare and temporary truce.[18]

The *moka* ceremonies were a way of conducting the intense competition of the big men by means other than naked violence. The aim of a community was to outdo their rivals and to give away more wealth, often in the form of pigs, but also other goods, including valuable shells, which served at one time as a form of money (kina, the Papuan currency, derives its name from a type of pearl shell). At the same time, *moka* ceremonies established patterns of reciprocity

The price of beauty – this sumptuous headdress on a young Papuan woman may have cost the lives of dozens of birds including birds-of-paradise and parrots.

and social obligation. The giving of wealth enhanced a big man's social standing and the prestige of his clan or tribe, but it also allowed them to resolve political differences, to rebuild alliances and to provide a means of compensation for injuries inflicted during war.[19] It has been estimated that 40–60 per cent of highland agricultural production was used to rear pigs for *moka*.[20]

When the colonial government exerted control over the warfare endemic in traditional society, it altered the nature of these ceremonies but it did not end their rationale. The *moka* event or, to use its modern pidgin name, 'sing sing' has simply adapted and remains an integral part of highland life in New Guinea, often in the form of an annual show. Dance, rather than more lethal forms of physical contest, may be the only medium left to express clan rivalry, but it involves intensely felt emotions. Today's gatherings are still treated with great seriousness by participants. Another fixture that survives from pre-colonial times in the modern sing sing is the value of these celebrations as a means for young people to meet their prospective partners. While bird-of-paradise feathers in head decorations may have decreased in proportion to the birds' own declines, they are a key element even now.

One of the most important portraits of *moka* is by the anthropologists Andrew and Marilyn Strathern in their book *Self-Decoration in Mount Hagen* (1971). It describes the ceremonies taking place in the Wahgi Valley at grounds specially laid out with lines of trees and other vegetation (whose resemblance to the avenues in a bowerbird's bower is remarkable; see also page 363). In addition to the competitive spirit driving the behaviour of the big men,

all the participants, even those there only as spectators, are expressing themselves – their status in society, their attractiveness as political allies or their allure as sexual partners – in the elaborate quality of their costume and adornment. In the words of the Stratherns:

> The act of decorating is symbolic: it is a gesture of self-display, and what is being displayed is a person in an enhanced or ideal state. On formal occasions the dancers assert group prosperity and health; when people dress up informally they assert their personal well-being. This is the general 'message' which decorations convey, and in a very real sense they are both the medium in which the message is communicated and the message itself.[21]

The materials used in highland ceremonies represent the natural products spanning the entire range of New Guinean ecosystems from the sea floor to the mountaintop. They include vegetation such as bark cloth, leaves, ferns, grasses, flowers, bamboo and wood for frames; pig bone (tusks especially) and cassowary quills or claws, animal furs, shells from a large variety of species, bird feathers and their soft parts, naturally occurring pigments or dyes, ochre, and natural oils (often hog fat) to make the whole ensemble glisten and shine. Another speciality, which has given identity and title to some New Guinean social groups (e.g. the Wigmen of Huli), are wigs made of hair, often including that of family and friends, as well as resin, bark cloth, hog grease and coloured pigments. The wigs are sculpted into forms more elaborate than the absurd headgear that once crowned admirals of the fleet in eighteenth-century Europe.

The feathers from a variety of bird species are used, but especially those of parrots, cassowaries and birds-of-paradise. Each wearer is helped by family members to blend the plumes into a wider design that may be half the height of the entire person. Some extreme examples have been recorded that were 4.9 m (16 ft) high.[22] These feather-based confections, radiant in tone, shaped often to sway and exaggerate the movements of the dancer, demonstrate an aesthetic understanding of contrast or complementary colour that has been evolving over hundreds, if not thousands, of years. Today one can see the influence of wider international access enjoyed by Papuans because peacock feathers routinely appear in sing sing headdresses, while another low-cost staple are synthetically dyed chicken feathers, which are then cut into zigzag patterns to enhance their impact.

Their lavishness of plumage, both in hue and structure, makes birds-of-paradise a key desideratum for participants. The standard Western impression, derived from photographs and documentary films, is of the filamentous 'tail-like' bustles obtained from the flanks of the paradiseid group, which sway flame-like above the heads of the dancing men. Yet several less-widely appreciated species play important roles, including the Blue, the King of Saxony and the **Superb Bird-of-Paradise** *Lophorina superba*.

The male of the latter, although a smallish species, has a fantastic, glittering, iridescent, aquamarine breast-shield, and the whole of the bird's underparts are often deployed as a frontal plate in the centre of any headdress. The King of Saxony Bird-of-Paradise is, if anything, more highly prized and is reserved for the most formal and important occasions

(see also Bowerbird family, page 365). The males possess two remarkable long ear-tufts that are more than twice the length of their owners. Recurring along the shafts of these incredible plumes are 40–50 flag-like sky-blue segments with an enamel-like sheen. These strips of shimmering colour are often used to divide and frame the whole head ornament and are described as running through the ensemble 'like streams of water'.[23] A measure of the bird's centrality in ritual ceremonies is that when an event is in preparation the people 'say "the bird is on its way", meaning "now the Saxony plumes will appear"'.[24]

Some of the most highly regarded species are almost inevitably scarce or inaccessible, or the bird's range may simply lie outside a particular tribal area. The ability to lay hands on these otherwise difficult-to-obtain birds and their feathers thus signifies the wearer's array of political and familial contacts, because only someone with a wide social network can source such prestigious plumes. In the Strathern study only four of 14 big men owned the skins of five bird-of-paradise species. Most bought or borrowed them from friends, kinsmen or in-laws.[25] Yet having the feathers at their disposal during the festivities is the outward symbol of their personal influence.

Bird-of-paradise feathers have an intrinsic high value. Those who know the location of the birds' display grounds – and where they can be most easily shot – fiercely guard this intelligence. Ownership of such a lek is treated as a precious and inheritable commodity, where the harvest is monitored to ensure long-term productivity.[26] Those not so fortunate to possess these forest locations can obtain

The glittering turquoise shield on the front of this Papuan headdress is taken from a Superb Bird-of-Paradise.

Some of the most important feathers used in Papuan costume come from the King of Saxony Bird-of-Paradise, whose long fine electric-blue head plumes can be twice the length of the whole bird.

feathers through the ritual of gift giving on the occasion of a wedding: a payment made to the girl's family known as bride price. Records from the Wahgi Valley of a century ago recount how ten brides were once purchased with the plumage from 36 Raggiana Birds-of-Paradise, 30 Lesser Birds-of-Paradise, three Princess Stephanie's Astrapias, 24 pearl-oyster shells, seven giant baler shells, 48 pigs, 71 stone axes and three bundles of salt.[27]

Owners wrap and carefully store away their best and most precious feathers between ceremonial events and seek to protect them from children's prying hands, or even the passing shadows of wives and daughters. In this strongly patriarchal society, men believe that merely for females to step over their headdresses can cause them to lose their radiance. That glossy sheen is not assumed to be an inherent part of the feathers, but an aspect determined by ritual and, until European missionaries forbade the practice, the highlanders sacrificed pigs to the clan ancestors to ensure the plumes would be bright.[28] This reflects the importance of brightness as part of the overall display. It is synonymous with sexual allure and to shine, with the assistance of liberal quantities of pig grease, is a highly desirable end in itself. If one thinks of the Western world's own preoccupation with the same effect – often achieved with the help of sequins, lipstick or -gloss, hairspray and make-up – then we can appreciate just how alike we are to our highland Papuan neighbours.

Societies often far removed from New Guinea eventually came to share a taste for the plumage of these glorious birds. The trade in feathers to other parts of south-east Asia is probably more than 2,000 years old. By the 1540s the French

naturalist Pierre Belon had seen bird-of-paradise feathers that had been trafficked across the whole of Asia and incorporated into the headgear worn by Janissary guards at the Ottoman court in Istanbul.[29] Similarly in the remote and isolated Himalayan kingdom of Nepal, the feathers had been worn by its royal family for centuries. Eventually the West acquired its own bird-of-paradise habit, and skins began to arrive at European ports, especially in Dutch vessels trading out of their colonies in the East Indies. By the nineteenth century, at the height of feather use in female high fashion (see also Herons and the Feather Industry, page 131), birds-of-paradise had become hugely profitable.

In the early twentieth century it was claimed that a single white hunter could shoot up to 700 birds a season, with a unit price of between £3–£7 per skin. It gave a total of £2,100–£4,900, which roughly translates into an annual salary of £119,000–£278,000 ($178,500–$417,000) by 2006 values.[30] The men often took enormous risks to obtain their precious birds and, as they ventured into the densely forested interior, some Chinese, Malay and European hunters ended their short if prosperous lives as protein for New Guinea's cannibal inhabitants.[31]

Regardless of such risks, it has been suggested that 80,000 paradise birds were being exported annually by colonial governments before the First World War.[32] The wider campaign to halt this fashion-related devastation of all birds led eventually to legislation banning the feather trade by 1921. Yet until the 1930s a criminal few continued to hunt for the jewels of the New Guinean forest, including a young Australian-born adventurer called Errol Flynn, who later became the swashbuckling star of many a Hollywood B-movie. One crook, a crewman on a commercial liner, SS *Kroonland*, and part of a British smuggling operation, was intercepted in the 1920s wearing a belt that held 150 bird-of-paradise plumes. Further investigations led to the seizure of $100,000 worth of contraband feathers.[33]

While the trade in bird-of-paradise feathers might have had localised impact on some populations, overall the sheer inaccessibility of the island's interior meant that its most celebrated birds were probably inviolate. Yet the Western world and the vast concatenation of effects flowing from its relentless ecological demands have exerted major influence on New Guinea. One of the most ironic consequences stemming from the West's invasion of the island was the impact of colonial government upon its ever-warring inhabitants. Europe's intervention in tribal conflict meant that the forest ceased to be a dangerous no-go zone. As one old expatriate in New Guinea noted: 'In the old days a warrior would only dare to hunt . . . in the immediate neighbourhood of his hamlet. Now . . . everyone is at peace, the young men roam far and wide over the mountains hunting for birds . . . As a result the head-dresses, these days, are bigger and finer than they have ever been.'[34] In a curious twist of fate, birds-of-paradise used for Papuan headdresses were simultaneously the symbols of peace and one of the chief victims ensuing from that atmosphere of calm.

In his account of his eight-year journey through this Asiatic region, *The Malay Archipelago*, the great nineteenth-century naturalist Alfred Russel Wallace was moved to write on the first occasion that he saw the gloriously crimson, starling-sized bird called the **King Bird-of-Paradise** *Cicinnurus regius*. In the passage Wallace entirely dismissed the deep aesthetic appreciation shown by local people for the creatures. Nevertheless his observation on the effects of Western civilisation upon these world-famous birds demonstrated remarkable insight and prescience:

> I thought of the long ages of the past, during which the successive generations of this little creature had run their course – year by year being born, and living and dying amid these dark and gloomy woods, with

no intelligent eye to gaze upon their loveliness; to all appearances such a wanton waste of beauty. Such ideas excite a feeling of melancholy. It seems sad, that on the one hand such exquisite creatures should live out their lives and exhibit their charms only in these wild inhospitable regions, doomed for ages yet to come to hopeless barbarism; while on the other hand, should civilized man ever reach these distant lands, and bring moral, intellectual, and physical light into the recesses of these virgin forests, we may be sure that he will so disturb the nicely-balanced relations of organic and inorganic nature as to cause the disappearance, and finally the extinction, of these very beings whose wonderful structure and beauty he alone is fitted to appreciate and enjoy. This consideration must surely tell us that all living things were *not* made for man.[35]

Wallace, in reference mainly to himself, concluded that the conflicting 'emotions excited in the mind of a naturalist', by the sight of birds of such 'surpassing rarity and beauty', require the poetic faculty fully to express them'. The poet Judith Wright (1915–2000) is one who has risen in wonderful fashion to this precise challenge. In her poem entitled 'Lyrebirds', the Australian writer faced head on the fundamental dilemma that Wallace posed – our overwhelming desire to visit, observe, encounter and to know, set against the often baleful consequences of these unavoidably intrusive actions. In response to her own burning urge to see a lyrebird, that glorious songster of the Australian bush (see page 358), Wright resolved the issue thus:

> No, I have never gone.
> Some things – ought to be left secret, alone;
> some things – birds like walking fables –
> ought to inhabit nowhere but the reverence of the heart.

Perhaps the birds-of-paradise are creatures that are too precious for us all to see and know. We should agree together to hold them, like Wright's lyrebird, as one of the great secrets of the collective human heart.

Australasian Robin family *Petroicidae*

Despite its name this group of 46 species, found mainly in Australia and New Guinea, has no close relationship with the two much-loved 'robins' of Europe and North America, which are members of the chat and thrush families respectively (see also page 472 and page 464). Their southern counterparts exhibit many of the same characteristics – the round-bodied, large-headed shape, liquid dark eyes, rather lethargic perch-and-pounce forage strategy and insect diet, as well as plumages that are equally bright and often red – but these shared attributes are a result of convergent evolution, and not because of any common ancestry.

Their English names denote how white colonists, when confronted with the fauna of a new continent, simply drew on an old familiar vocabulary from home. Yet one can understand the impulse to find continuities between the two.

In Australia the males of **Flame Robin** *Petroica phoenicea* (mainly in Victoria and New South Wales), **Scarlet Robin** *Petroica boodang* (Victoria, New South Wales and southern Western Australia) and **Red-capped Robin** *Petroica goodenovii* (widespread across much of the country) have glorious orange-red or scarlet underparts. The first two were even known by the venerable and affectionate nickname used for the English bird, 'robin redbreast'.[1]

There are also three family members in New Zealand. Two species, the **New Zealand Robin** *Petroica australis* and **Tomtit** *Petroica macrocephala*, both of which are largely white and black or shades of charcoal grey, are widespread and confiding forest birds. Yet the one to which attaches the most extraordinary story is a species called the **Black Robin** *Petroica traversi*. It occurs exclusively on the Chatham Islands, a small archipelago 850 km (528 miles) east of

Old Blue in her prime – had it not been for the sheer life force packed into this tiny puff of black feathers, her entire species may have gone extinct.

mainland New Zealand. The bird had once been common and widespread across this entire island group (963 km²: 372 miles²) but it underwent a rapid and devastating decline. It was very probably the arrival of sheep (about 60,000 by 1901), together with cats, dogs, rats, as well as Western agricultural practice and the wholesale use of fire to clear the islands' forests that caused the Black Robin to vanish completely from the archipelago's main islands. By the late nineteenth century the species was confined to just 5 ha (12.4 acres) of scrub forest on the tiny islet of Little Mangere.²

Despite the island being free of mammal predators and uninhabited, its habitat deteriorated partly because those involved in illegal muttonbirding had cleared it to land helicopters (see page 108). In the 1970s a deep sense of crisis concerning the future of the Black Robin led to a last-ditch conservation initiative. This involved moving the last seven birds from Little Mangere to better-quality habitat on its near neighbour, Mangere Island. However, this simple statement of transfer gives no indication of the nerve-racking tension that marked the evacuation and, indeed, the whole of the ensuing campaign. Birds had to be caught and then

transferred to small cages that were carried on the backs of the team as they made a half-hour descent on ropes of the 180 m (590 ft) sheer cliffs to the awaiting boats.

By 1976 the species' entire fate rested on seven birds: five males and two females. This was the smallest known population of any bird on the planet at the time.³ By 1979 it had fallen further to five, and even this minuscule figure overstates the number of real participants. As the authors of a book about this remarkable bird-and-human partnership make clear, 'The story of the saving of the Black Robin is to a large extent the story of *Old Blue*.'⁴ She had acquired her name from a coloured plastic ring placed around her leg in 1972, along with an aluminium band bearing the legend B11384. In the year of transfer from one island to another, Old Blue was already exceptional for exceeding the life expectancy of a Black Robin. She went on to live for about 13 years, an extraordinary span that was twice the average for her species, and which leads one almost to imagine that she had an inkling into the acute predicament faced by her kind.

Yet in 1980 the human team striving to save the species from extinction had little to celebrate in her performance. Old Blue was nine before she started to breed successfully, sometimes producing three broods a year. It was partly the intensive and exceptional midwifery of her human support team that brought about the gradual increase in the species' numbers. The project relied upon taking eggs from the robins and placing them first under Chatham Gerygones that were nesting wild close by, and then later in the nests of the archipelago's endemic race of Tomtit (*chathamensis*). However, these surrogate Tomtit parents nested on an entirely different island (South East) that was a 20 km (12.4 mile) boat ride away. The precision timing of the journey from one island to another with partly incubated eggs was only one detail in the critical and delicate coordination involved in the entire operation. For example, the team had to ensure that the robins' eggs' development was carefully matched to the stage of incubation achieved by the Tomtit foster patents. Another part of the project involved actually destroying the now eggless nests of the Black Robins, because that would encourage them to build a new nest and lay fresh eggs and, thus, double or treble their productivity. One senses the deep grain of understatement present in the words of these rigorous men of science when they write:

> Removing the eggs and destroying the nests of one of the world's rarest birds, with no guarantee of success in fostering or encouraging re-laying, proved very stressful for the team. The men lost much sleep during those first critical days, for if the gamble failed, they would surely be blamed for hastening the extinction of the species.[5]

Yet it is measure of the acute objectivity maintained in an enterprise shot through with high emotion that when Old Blue's senescence finally started to affect her breeding performance and other important genes needed to be incorporated into the recovering Black Robin population, the leader of the project, Don Merton, evacuated this 'grand old lady' from her breeding territory on Mangere Island to South East Island. She was last seen there on 13 December 1983. Until his own death Don Merton kept the well-worn aluminium band bearing the number B11384 above his mantelpiece.[6]

Yet her part in the recovery of the Black Robin was pivotal. Had she not been so exceptional and bucked every trend manifest in her species, changing her mate and 'breeding effectively even in her geriatric years', then, ironically, her own kind would very probably not have survived.[7] Every Black Robin alive is descended from Old Blue and her mate 'Old Yellow', and genetically all are as alike as identical twins. No free-living bird has less genetic variability than this species. In 1990 her descendants numbered about 116 birds. By 2007 the figure was about 180 adults on Mangere and South East Islands.[8]

In New Zealand both Old Blue and Black Robins are well known and routinely appear on television (there have been three documentary films). In the Chatham Islands themselves, where wildlife was once little appreciated, the local people have taken the bird to their hearts. It is commemorated in the nickname for the rugby team, the local shipping company and in local produce, such as beer and honey.[9] Before he died in 2011, Don Merton received an award from the Royal Forest and Bird Protection Society of New Zealand honouring his outstanding contribution to conservation. It was called the 'Old Blue Award'.

◀ The late Don Merton, whose work to save the Black Robin earned him widespread respect and a special conservation honour – the appropriately named 'Old Blue Award'.

Picathartes family *Picathartidae*

These two west African endemics, the **White-necked Picathartes** *Picathartes gymnocephalus* and **Grey-necked Picathartes** *Picathartes oreas*, are birds of elusive identity. In their complex journey through ornithological systematics over the last two centuries they have been wrongly placed within the starling, babbler, and crow families.

We should probably forgive the earlier confusion. One ornithologist noted, somewhat mischievously, how the picathartes lay eggs that look like those of a crow, while their mud nest resembles a swallow's. The creatures themselves possess bald heads similar to that of a vulture (although according to another admirer it looks like 'a leather aviator's cap').[1] It is a reflection of their ongoing identity crisis (or, rather, *our* confusion) that these two birds are still referred to in various publications as rockfowl, bald crows or picathartes.

Today they are usually accorded a family all to themselves and are mainly known by the last of these three names, which is surely the one most suggestive of their glorious singularity (although even this translates roughly as 'magpie-vulture').[2] Among globetrotting birders they are considered two of the most sought-after birds on Earth. In a recent shortlist of the ten sexiest species, the White-necked Picathartes of rainforests in Guinea, Sierra Leone, Liberia and Côte d'Ivoire came in at number three and was proposed as 'the coolest bird in Africa'.[3] In truth, both family members can hardly be separated on matters of beauty, secretiveness or coolness. If anything the Grey-necked Picathartes, found in the rainforests of Nigeria, Cameroon and Gabon, is even more colourful than its twin, with underparts that are suffused by a glorious apricot wash.

For birdwatchers the Grey-necked Picathartes of west Africa – here painted by British illustrator Mark Andrews – is among the most sought after of all African birds.

A further aspect of the birds' allure is their behaviour. Largely silent, they bound through the trees and across the forest floor partly floating on broad wings and partly springing in airy hops with their long legs repeatedly flexed. It has been claimed that their strange and captivating agility explains their reputation as supernatural beings among local African communities. Sadly this folklore, which once had a protective function, is dying out across much of the birds' shared range, as both species plunge toward extinction. In Ghana, for instance, many people do not even know the bird's local name (*anamie*).

Picathartes build cup-shaped mud nests that are attached to the sides of large boulders or rock formations and caves in the forest interior. (Grey-necked Picathartes have recently been found to build even on concrete bridges in Gabon, regardless of the vibrations caused by the heavy traffic.)[4] Those people who occasionally visit these huge forest monoliths are among the very few humans to encounter picathartes regularly.

> In Ghana the majority of the people who have seen the bird are hunters, who usually use nest sites as resting places during their hunting expeditions in the night as well as in the day. The nest sites of the bird provide good shelter from rain. Interactions with people who have seen the birds before, especially hunters, indicate that the bird is regularly killed for food in many of the communities where it occurs.[5]

Alhaji Siaka explains the birds' former cultural status in Sierra Leone:

> White-necked Picathartes was widely recognised by

various rural communities and each ethnic group had its own name for it. For example, the Mende in the south-east where the species has a stronghold called it *Kplokondi*. The Koranko in the north-east border region of the Loma Mountains Forest Reserve refer to it as *Farako-duwee*. The Temne called it *Sokorikonoh*. All of these tribes once attached traditional beliefs to the bird. A Temne old man I spoke to said that their nesting sites were only located by special hunters who possessed magical powers. He said that the bird is mostly silent, but when it calls the people in those days used to carry out a special sacrifice to ensure bumper harvests of their crops. The Mende people in the Gola Forest region once respected the bird and its nesting sites as sacred areas. In the village called Perri Fefewabu in the Gaura Chiefdom of Kenema District, the community used to visit the picathartes colony and perform some form of ritual for barren women so that they might bear children. This divine site was kept sacred for adornment where the people would contact a supernatural being and the birds were believed to be guards of the site protecting this unseen spirit.[6]

Throughout their combined ranges, picathartes are severely affected by deforestation and disturbance and both species are thought to have populations of no more than 10,000 birds.

Waxwing and Allies family *Bombycillidae*

This is a curiously heterogeneous group of eight rather beautiful species, which are widely spread on separate continents. One of them is a true oddity of south-west Asian ornithology, the **Hypocolius** *Hypocolius ampelinus*. This long-tailed grey bird of Iran and the Fertile Crescent is reminiscent of a shrike or miniature jay, but the strange name, which is of Greek construction, translates roughly as 'somewhat mousebird-like' and refers to a completely unrelated and uniquely African family (see page 307).[1] Four other family members are the silky-flycatchers, which are mainly birds of upland forest in Central America, although the all-black **Phainopepla** *Phainopepla nitens* extends into south-west USA as far as northern California.

The family's best-known trio are the waxwings. The

It is hard now to think of these glorious birds as bringers of bad luck but Bohemian Waxwings were once considered creatures of ill omen.

Bohemian Waxwing *Bombycilla garrulus* breeds both in a 5,000 km (3,100 mile) swathe of Eurasia largely beyond latitude 60° N, but also in north-west North America. There it meets the more widespread bird of the New World, the **Cedar Waxwing** *Bombycilla cedrorum*, which occurs across much of the upper three-quarters of that continent. Then there is a third sibling, the **Japanese Waxwing** *Bombycilla japonica*, which is confined to north-east Asia.

Periodically waxwings break out from their boreal confines and undertake massive, sometimes continent-wide, migrations far to the south of their usual range. Cedar Waxwings, for instance, have been recorded in Colombia and Venezuela, while Bohemian Waxwings turn up occasionally in Algeria and Israel. It is only during these enforced wanderings, which are known as irruptive migrations, that the birds are seen by large numbers of people.

Waxwing invasions are one of those natural dramas that seem to force themselves upon our attention. In Europe they were recorded as early as 1552 in the vicinity of the Rhine by the Swiss naturalist Conrad Gesner.[2] Such was the impact of these sudden, inexplicable arrivals that Bohemian Waxwings were once loaded with sinister import (although none of these baleful associations seem to have attached to the Cedar Waxwing in America). Old names for the species included *Pestvogel* ('plague-bird') which is still the bird's name in Dutch, as well as *unglückvogel*, *pestilenzvogel* and *todtenvogel* in German-speaking areas (respectively, 'disaster-bird', 'pestilence-bird' and 'death bird').[3] A widely recorded waxwing invasion during the winter of 1913 / 14 was later assumed to be a foreboding omen for the calamity that ensued the following summer – the First World War.[4]

A measure of how long this symbolism had survived is an unusual painting by the German artist Georg Flegel (1566–1638) that features a Bohemian Waxwing, entitled *Still Life of Birds and Insects*. Placed on a table and surrounded at random by odd items including fruits, nuts, live insects, a mouse and two dead birds is an eclectic flock of eight living birds. The juxtaposition of seemingly disconnected animals makes the image a little disconcerting but essentially it seems nothing more than a rather decorative exercise in natural realism. In fact each creature is laden with medieval symbolism that would have been well known and carefully deciphered by its contemporary audience. Some of the emblematic creatures include a Eurasian Woodcock (stupidity), Northern Lapwing (treachery or uncleanliness), a partridge (lust), a parrot (virtue), and the Bohemian Waxwing itself (disaster).[5]

One wonders if the Russian-born author Vladimir Nabokov was also trading on this old European lore in his novel *Pale Fire* (1962), which is famous for its allusive structure as well as its elusive meanings. *Pale Fire* is about a fictional character, John Shade, a writer who is eventually murdered. Part of the novel is Shade's own 999-line poem which opens with the words: 'I was the shadow of the waxwing slain / By the false azure in the windowpane.' These lines are at once a reference to a 'real' waxwing that strikes the glass as Shade looks out the same window. Yet it also seems to be an autobiographical symbol for Nabokov's fictional author: the bird's scientific name is *cedrorum*, a near pun on the poet's surname. And since Shade is to be slain himself, Nabokov was perhaps making of the waxwing a composite omen of his character's fate.

Alas, none of these psychological associations with waxwings was rooted in anything more than coincidence. The issue that really drives their wanderings is not human calamity, but the failure of their home supplies of winter fruit. For they are frugivores almost without equal. They will eat their own body weight in fruit a day. They will eat it until they can eat no more and are fit to burst, or are unable to fly. They will eat it even when it is fermented and they become stone drunk in the process.

One warm day last fall, I was walking with a chum through the fields . . . Suddenly my friend . . . pointed to a twenty-foot chokecherry tree, which was loaded with birds, and asked what those birds were. I told him they were Cedar Waxwings. As we drew closer the birds looked as though their feathers had been drawn or brushed the wrong way . . . All the while the birds were eating berries ravenously. My companion was soon in a fit of laughter. 'Why, they're drunk!' he exclaimed. Sure enough the birds were evidently intoxicated by the over-ripe chokecherries. Their actions were very comical, for they were helpless . . . Their crests were erect and in the excitement of seeing us they all tumbled around. Some tumbled to the ground where with outspread wings they attempted to run away; still others tottered on the branches with wings continually flapping, as though for balance. All the time we were there they kept up a continual hissing noise, as a family of snakes might do.[6]

Sometimes waxwings become so intoxicated, the alcohol can kill them. However, it was not their taste for the demon drink that deterred aviculturists from keeping the birds in captivity. It was that insatiable appetite and all its consequences. The nineteenth-century bird keeper Johann Bechstein complained of a pet waxwing:

It is a stupid and lazy bird . . . It is the greatest eater

To us it may now look like an exercise in natural-historical realism but Georg Flegel's *Still Life of Birds and Insects* was an image steeped in symbolism. The Bohemian Waxwing on the top left connoted disaster.

among birds that I know, being able to devour in a day a quantity of food equal to its own weight. It consequently passes hardly half digested, and, what is very disgusting, it is seen, like the ostrich, to eat again this excrement, if it is destitute of fresh food . . . In consequence of this voraciousness it must be cleaned very often to be kept sweet.[7]

In Bechstein's day the bird's English name was 'Bohemian chatterer'. It is something of a misnomer for the soft, silvery, faintly rippling sounds produced by all three waxwing species. Yet the calls produced by small flocks do have a continuous, conversational quality and the bird's name in France (*jaseur*) has acquired a secondary sense of someone who 'gossips or chats endlessly'.[8]

If Bechstein did not appreciate the voice of his Bohemian chatterer, at least he was alive to the bird's beauty. Waxwings were once known as 'silktails' in honour of their soft lax plumage. They were also paid the dubious compliment of being skinned and inserted into women's hats on an industrial scale during the feather fashions of the late nineteenth century (see also page 132). The naturalist Frank Chapman, patrolling the streets of New York in 1886, noted that 542 of 700 women bore headgear containing various bird parts. Over two such surveys he was able to identify 40 bird species in the various millinery ensembles, recognising 24 waxwings among them, which was more than any other bird family.[9]

Almost all commentators have dwelled on the subtlety of waxwing beauty. It has something of the formal smartness and finishing touches of male military costume, such as pips, epaulettes and prominent headgear. Humans have even begun to have their own impact upon the beauty of waxwings. Non-native berry-bearing plants such as cotoneaster, pyracantha and various types of Eurasian honeysuckle are all favourite ornamental shrubs for gardeners on both sides of the Atlantic, and they are also well appreciated by waxwings as substitutes for their usual wild-fruit fare. These important food sources have turned them into backyard birds, and the strong carotenoids ingested from honeysuckle berries will occasionally convert the yellow-tipped tails of Cedar Waxwings to a nice shade of orange.[10]

Palmchat family *Dulidae*

The **Palmchat** *Dulus dominicus* is a singularly unusual bird. Not only does this one species have a family to itself, its world range comprises just a single Caribbean island, Hispaniola, and its adjacent satellites. Hispaniola is divided politically between the states of Haiti and the Dominican Republic, and it is the latter that has staked claim to the bird's endemic symbolism. The Palmchat has been elected as the country's national bird.

It is a fitting accolade, because the species has not only withstood the wholesale modification of the island, it may well have benefited from deforestation, thriving in the savannah habitats that have replaced the original vegetation. It is perhaps the commonest species on the island and even flourishes at the heart of the biggest settlements, such as the Dominican capital, Santo Domingo.[1]

About the size of a thrush with a deep straw-coloured bill, dense, thick streaks across its entire underparts and a dark sooty-brown upper body, the Palmchat forms noisy chattering congregations, and in character the birds rather resemble the social groups of babblers (*Turdoides*) or bulbuls of Africa and Asia. In truth, the Palmchat's nearest relatives are thought to be the waxwings (see page 406).

As its name suggests, this fruit-eating bird's key ecological association is with palm trees, especially the royal palm, in which groups assemble large ragged, bulging fortresses of twigs and vegetation, sometimes 1 m (3.3 ft) across, that serve as communal nests. One ornithologist has likened these shared breeding sites to 'a block of flats', each pair to one compartment.[2] In the absence of their favourite tree, Palmchats will occasionally build on telegraph poles.

One of the local Haitian names for the species is puzzling. The Creole version, *Zwazo-palmis*, simply means 'palm bird', but *Esclave palmiste* means 'palm slave'. Originally the bird was said to be called just *esclave* ('slave'), perhaps because Hispaniola itself was once a slave entrepôt.[3] Or possibly it is, as the eighteenth-century French naturalist Mathurin Brisson understood it, a reference to the bird's dark colour and its subservience when faced with the aggressive territorial behaviour displayed by several species of tyrant flycatcher (see page 350). The scientific name expresses the same link: *Doulus* means 'slave' in Greek.[4]

Tit and Chickadee family *Paridae*

These 55 inhabitants of woodland and forest, park and garden, backyard and window ledge are among a select group of avian midgets that evoke in us the deepest emotional responses. Tits and chickadees are indisputably one of the most popular of all bird families, especially in western Europe and North America.

They are absent from Australasia and South America, but occur on four other continents. The main areas of diversity are Africa (18 species, including 15 that only occur south of the Sahara), Eurasia (18 species) and the Oriental regions (13 species), while North America and Europe (by itself) hold 11 and nine species respectively. One bird overlaps the last two regions and nicely illuminates the geographical split in anglicised names: it is known as the **Grey-headed Chickadee** *Poecile cincta* on one side of the Atlantic, but Siberian Tit in Europe.

The word 'chickadee' is a classic onomatopoeic rendering of the vocalisations made by several species which, as one contributor observes so aptly, 'has a "blocked nose" sound to it'.[1] It is the name used for seven of the North American

The Grey-headed Chickadee (Siberian Tit) is one of the most northerly breeding of all small resident songbirds and during the winter nights can withstand −60° C.

family members. 'Tit', on the other hand, is a northern European monosyllable that honours the other captivating quality in the family – their smallness. It is possibly of Norse or Icelandic origin and denoted a small animal or object. Both 'titling' (a type of fish) and 'titmouse' (originally applied to this bird family and often spelled 'titmose') were known in medieval Britain, yet as a stand-alone word 'tit' came into use, like 'chickadee', only in the nineteenth century.[2] The brevity seems extremely apt.

The family giant, the grandly titled **Sultan Tit**

Melanochlora sultanea of Asian forests, measures 20 cm (8 in) but most of the family are just 12.5 cm (5 in) or less, and the majority of tits weigh no more than 14 g (0.5 oz). It is the punch packed into that tiny puff of feathers which enthrals the birds' many admirers. They are creatures of mercurial zest and spontaneity and they captivate us as much by their speed as by their acrobatics. Writing of the **Black-capped Chickadee** *Poecile atricapillus*, one of the most loved and best known of all North American birds, an ornithologist beautifully captured the family's overarching mobility:

Chickadee refuses to look down for long upon the world; or, indeed, to look at any one thing from any direction for more than two consecutive twelfths of a second. 'Any old side up without care,' is the label he bears; and so with anything he meets, be it a pine-cone, an alder catkin, or a bug-bearing branchlet, topside, bottomside, inside, outside, all is right side to the nimble Chickadee.[3]

A disadvantage of this hyperactivity was the family's former popularity as cagebirds. Tits were widely trapped in Europe, especially during autumn and winter when several species combine into mixed assemblies, occasionally numbering dozens and even scores of birds that rove through the otherwise sombre woods in vibrant and noisy parties. A favourite stratagem used by the old birdcatchers was to lure the flocks to their traps with a type of flute or whistle made from a goose's leg bone. The sound was said to be irresistible to the birds.

Once caged, they were trained to perform tricks, such as hauling up a chain, on which were suspended tiny buckets of food. Another food-bearing mechanism that tested the birds' acrobatic skill had a central hole, through which they were obliged to hop to get at a suspended nut. The devices involved real danger and were said to be a frequent cause of the tits' death.[4]

A rather unfamiliar aspect to the birds, which is often only revealed when they are held captive, is their aggression. The **Great Tit** *Parus major*, which is the most successful and widespread of all the family worldwide, is notorious for attacking other birds when held in close confinement, even killing species as large as quail. A speciality is to pierce the skull and eat the brains.[5] Today the people most familiar with this trait are those who attach metal rings to birds' legs in order to study migration. One veteran ringer recounts his own painful memories:

> I cannot pretend to have lost any digits, but tits, notably **Blue Tit** *Cyanistes caeruleus*, have an enviable ability to cause pain to ringers' fingers on frozen winter mornings. And they seem to be especially good at finding the finger-quick, and any recent cuts, or injuries, that reveal nerve endings. I have been left a-cursing and wincing with tear-filled eyes on many occasions.[6]

As another contributor notes, this family penchant has a peculiarly ironic ring in Sweden:

> The Swedish word for 'tit' is *mes* but the word is also used to mean a 'coward' or 'wimp'. That is silly indeed because tits are not cowardly, quite the opposite. The ringers at Falsterbo Bird Observatory get their cuticles pecked to bits and pieces when they handle Great Tits! The word's secondary meaning must have come from somebody who knew nothing about the inquisitive birds we have in our gardens.[7]

TIT AND CHICKADEE USE OF THE HUMAN DOMESTIC ENVIRONMENT

Several other small birds (hummingbirds, crests, kinglets, wrens) exhibit a very similar psychological approach to humans that tits seem to possess: that we are too large and they are too small for us to bear any mutual ill will. The birds often show great trust when approaching human habitation or people. While we have come to associate their confidences with the modern backyard feeder or garden nestbox, the birds' adaptations to the domestic environment are long-standing. Alfred Newton recorded how an earthen bottle suspended in a garden in Stockton-on-Tees, England, was used by successive pairs of Blue Tit from 1779 (or possibly 1785) until Newton himself saw the bottle in 1873. Aside from intermissions totalling six years, Blue Tits nested at the site continuously for 110 years.[8]

In Europe Great and Blue Tits utilise every conceivable man-made orifice: letter boxes, drains, post holes, or crevices in brickwork, under roof eaves and occasionally garage interiors or within the house itself. Perhaps the most remarkable of localities are those recorded by the ever-unreliable Bishop Stanley, who noted a Blue Tit pair that nested in the handle of a manual water pump. The incubating bird was so located that the handle's constant motion up and down caused the bird's tail tip to wear away. An expression of even deeper intimacy was the Blue Tit couple that opted for the slot between the grinding teeth of a skeleton, 'a man who had been [originally] hung in chains for murder'.[9]

Today the birds' domicile of choice is the pre-manufactured bird box, which was first developed in medieval Europe (see Starling family, page 463).[10] By the late Victorian period these structures were well covered in a British book of 1897, *Wild Bird Protection and Nesting Boxes*. They are now an integral part of western European gardens and in aggregate must supply accommodation for many millions of pairs of Blue and Great Tit (there are an estimated 4.3 million nestboxes in British gardens alone).[11] In turn, the access facilities provided to researchers by these purpose-built boxes have resulted in the Great Tit becoming one of the most intimately studied animals on Earth.[12]

THE MORAL QUALITIES OF TITS AND CHICKADEES

Very often we have credited tits and chickadees for their display of trust in us, but we have also marvelled at their wider courage. In 1867 the American poet and philosopher Ralph Waldo Emerson celebrated it in a poem called 'The Titmouse'. Despite the title, the species he honours is almost certainly the Black-capped Chickadee. It opens with a description of bitter winter conditions that are so severe they put the poem's narrator in fear of his life. Suddenly he encounters the nasal *Chic-chic-a-dee-dee!* call of a resident 'titmouse' and he gradually feels both humbled and fortified by the bird's extraordinary hardihood in the face of the same blizzard.

> Here was this atom in full breath,
> Hurling defiance at vast death;
> This scrap of valor just for play
> Fronts the north-wind in waistcoat gray,
> As if to shame my weak behavior;
> I greeted loud my little savior,
> 'You pet! What dost here? And what for?

The verse trades on the well-founded literary tradition of placing in sharp contrast an animal's outer appearance of fragility and smallness, with the observer's sense of an immense inner moral force. The acute size differences between human and bird emphasise our own comparative

The cuteness of baby tits in nestboxes – not to mention the miracle of their development from tiny eggs – has done much to foster a wider concern for nature in many countries.

deficiencies and Emerson's bird compels the author to re-attune himself to the winter conditions:

> For well the soul, if stout within,
> Can arm impregnably the skin;
> And polar frost my frame defied,
> Made of the air that blows outside.

This 150-year-old poem sinks a deep and illuminating shaft into our entire psychological encounter with the family. (In fact it is striking how many of the subsequent ornithological descriptions of Black-capped Chickadee seemed to owe a debt to the language and spirit of Emerson's poem. One even wonders if it had any part in the species' designation as state bird in Massachusetts, Emerson's own home state.) Yet the verse also reflects genuine truths about the ecology of these birds.

The Grey-headed Chickadee (Siberian Tit) is the most northerly small resident songbird on Earth (other species breed further north, but migrate south in autumn). It reaches beyond the 70th parallel and can withstand temperatures of –60 °C (–76 °F). In midwinter it may have just four hours of daylight to locate the requisite 7–8 g (0.25 oz) of nuts and frozen insects. To guarantee itself these life-saving supplies each bird can also cache for later consumption as many as

500,000 food items, a figure that fully proclaims the industry of these indefatigable birds. When it roosts in its tree hole, a Siberian Tit can also lower its body temperature by as much 10 °C (50 °F) from a norm of 42 °C (107.6 °F), a state of induced hypothermia shared by two other Arctic-dwelling residents, the Black-capped and **Boreal Chickadees** *Poecile hudsonica* of North America.

Two modern observers give a full sense of the heroic mettle of these tiny birds and also the impact that their large spirits can have upon us:

> I live in a vast forest in Alaska, which had been
> undergoing an infestation of the spruce bark beetle, so
> we've lost a large percentage of the older seed-bearing
> trees. This has caused a shortage of the favorite food for
> the Boreal and Black-capped Chickadees. Each week
> I would fill a knapsack full of seed and suet, strap on
> my snowshoes and trek a five-mile circuit through the
> deep cold and wind-blown snow to various bird-feeding
> stations. Within minutes of leaving my cabin . . . here
> they would come . . . chick chick-a-dee-dee-deeing and
> swarming over my head to welcome me with open
> wings, while accompanying me throughout my trek
> and beckoning to their comrades along the way that the

The feeding of birds, especially members of the tit and chickadee family, has become a worldwide industry worth billions.

bird cafes were opening. As I made my way from one feeder to the next I could see them come out of holes in the hanging snow-covered branches of the dead trees to greet me. They were hungry and joyous to be able to eat another day and save their precious energy stores to make it to the light and warmth of spring sun coming back up to the north.[13]

Our farmyard in south-east Saskatchewan, Canada, has an extensive shelter-belt of wonderful trees. Our province has very flat topography but thankfully the evergreens provide shelter for the little chickadees. Setting a visual scene is particularly important to emphasise why these birds are so important to us. We often have winter weather that dips to −40 °C and it's even worse when the wind is blowing! Often the chickadees, with the nuthatches and woodpeckers, are the only living things seen outside the kitchen window on a cold winter day. The chickadees hop from branch to branch then they fly to the bird feeder to peck at black sunflower seeds. All the while singing their sweet little song, chick~a~dee~dee~dee, chick~a~dee~dee~dee! Of all the birds in any season the Black-capped Chickadees are the most enjoyed simply because they stand along with us as we live through the winter. Their lovely song provides the comfort and warmth that a person needs to know that all is well with the world. Couple that with a hot cup of tea, a pot of soup on the stove and bread in the oven, and life is perfect! In them is found no wrong.[14]

TITS, CHICKADEES AND FEEDING BIRDS

The giving of food and shelter to birds is almost a defining activity of modern developed society and while it has become a major multi-million-dollar industry, it has its emotional mainspring in the simplest of human impulses. It is an opportunity to escape what the British writer J A Baker called the 'hot hoop of fear' that constantly encircles our predatory species. A poignant and revealing expression of our wish to escape this baleful human heritage was a double-decker bird house I witnessed that had been placed over a grave in upstate New York, carrying the legend 'Wilderness Welcome'. Even in death, it seems, we cherish the possibility of deeper intimacy with other life forms.

Tits and chickadees are among the most prominent beneficiaries of these evolving human traditions. In America, feeders and feeding stations have proliferated and it is estimated that between 135–150 million people, 45–50 per cent of the population, participate in the activity.[15] The practice has also given rise to a massive ancillary market in bird-related garden furniture and equipment, such as dispensers, water baths, predator-protected feeders and bird houses, whose architecture, according to the author Christopher Leahy, is so 'grand that one's house may suffer by comparison'.[16] In the USA alone, expenditure on feeders is estimated at $800 million, while the sales of food itself has reached $1 billion. The prevalence of feeding stations has in turn triggered shifts in the distribution of birds, including a northward extension of the **Tufted Titmouse** *Baeolophus bicolor*.

In Europe a similar pattern is replicated. The British

people spend an estimated £200 million on food and feeders and roughly 34–75 per cent of householders participate in dispersing 50,000–60,000 tonnes of seed and other feedstuffs annually.[17] One key difference between Europe and North America is that, while chickadees use man-made nest sites infrequently, Great and Blue Tits are major beneficiaries. Largely as a consequence of both nest-boxes and supplementary feeding, these two species are among the most commonplace birds in British gardens. The BTO Garden BirdWatch scheme, which has run since 1995, has consistently returned the Blue Tit as the second most frequent garden visitor of all British birds, outnumbered only by the Common Blackbird. The larger Great Tit consistently polls as the sixth most frequent visitor over 17 years.

Blue and Great Tits are also hugely popular in continental Europe, although their respective positions are reversed in several countries. In the Netherlands, for example, the Great Tit is the second and the Blue Tit the fourth most common garden bird, while in Sweden these same two species come in first and third positions respectively (in 2013).[18] The distinguished Swedish author and birdwatcher Lennart Nilsson adds the following:

> A friend of ours, who lives bang in the middle of Stockholm, consulted me about a suitable feeder for her kitchen window on the third floor of a huge block of flats (but with plenty of trees, shrubs and lawns around). I suggested a nut feeder and she put one up. She is delighted to have Great and Blue Tits constantly about two feet from her place at the kitchen table.[19]

It would be easy to assume that these special affections for tits are replicated across the continent. Yet this is by no means the case. It is interesting to compare the following Serbian contribution with the Swedish one above:

> Most of the people here have heard of tits, but do not even know what tits in general look like, let alone how they might separate one species from another. Those who feed birds are more familiar, but usually do not know names of the different species. And it should be added that not many people feed birds here. It is not popular among the rural population, and only the wealthy one per cent of the urban population has gardens. I used to put out bacon on my mother's terrace

and the birds were pretty active. At my flat, no bird has ever visited.[20]

For some people not even point-blank range is intimacy enough when it comes to tits and chickadees. The wild birds can be lured even to our hands, especially in North America. A resident of Massachusetts describes exactly how:

> Birds have very good eyes. What I do is put black oil sunflower seeds in the feeder, and keep the shelled seeds on my hand. They much prefer the seeds with no shells. Or I temporarily hide all the food except what's on my hand. Find a place where you can comfortably rest your hand. I use the top of a stepladder. Make a line of about seven seeds across your shelf, and rest your hand on the far edge, with a handful of seeds. If a chickadee comes for the farthest seed, you've got an excellent chance. He'll take them one by one, getting closer and closer to your hand. You're not allowed to move. This should be done for at least ten minutes at a stretch, and if you get tired take a break and come back. You can either talk softly to the birds or not, just be consistent. The bird would prefer not to have to land on your hand the first time he takes a seed. If it doesn't work the first day, don't give up. Sometimes the first chickadee helps you teach the rest. You can see them watching and learning. You can't tell me birds don't think. It does take a lot of time and patience, but there's nothing like the feel of those delicate little feet on your hand. I love them so much I can hardly stand it! And even if they don't come to you, the time spent close to them, watching and listening and just being near, has not been wasted.[21]

Sometimes these moments of extreme intimacy with a wild bird can have effects that last a lifetime.

> In about 1965 my Grandmother lived in Villeneuve in Vaud, Switzerland, in a three-storey block surrounded by vineyards. Every morning my Grandfather would bring her breakfast in bed: tea, toast with the crusts cut off! And a few pine nuts. He would then open her French windows in her bedroom and leave her sat up in bed eating her breakfast. In would come the Great Tits to eat from her hand. As a small child of about seven I was allowed to sit very still and watch. I believe that this is what started my love of watching birds.[22]

Penduline Tit family *Remizidae*

These 11 species are found mainly in Africa, with a single representative apiece in Europe (**Eurasian Penduline Tit** *Remiz pendulinus*) and North America (**Verdin** *Auriparus flaviceps*). The 'penduline' part of the family name (which means 'pendant' or 'hanging') could refer either to the upside-down antics of these tiny acrobatic tit-like birds, or to the pendulous nature of their glorious bag-shaped nests. The structures are famous for their downy felted texture and exquisite softness that were once put to practical purpose by

various communities. The Maasai of Kenya were said to use those of the local **Grey Penduline Tit** *Anthoscopus caroli* as a pouch or purse, while in Poland and Russia the nests of Eurasian Penduline Tits were placed in people's shoes to keep their feet cosy, or were worn by children as slippers. Two rather strange powers once credited to the nests were an ability to ward off lightning strikes (in northern Italy) and a capacity to cure sore throats (in Russia).[1]

Swallow and Martin family *Hirundinidae*

Swallows are as widely distributed as they are universally cherished. There are 86 species worldwide and all are known collectively as hirundines, from the Latin for swallow, *hirundo*. The alternate English names, 'swallow' and 'martin', are not truly indicative of two distinct bird types in the same family. Rather the names are interchangeable in the manner of 'pigeon' and 'dove'. To illustrate the point there is a small, brown, water-loving species found on both sides of the Atlantic, but it is known as the Bank Swallow in North America and **Sand Martin** *Riparia riparia* in Europe. A useful rule of thumb, however, relates to family members with long tail streamers: they are almost always called swallows, while species with shorter forked tails have either name.

Hirundines are all small birds with rather rounded, cigar-shaped bodies. Even the biggest of the family, the American **Purple Martin** *Progne subis*, is just 65 g (2.3 oz), while the longest is the beautiful, rare and range-restricted African **Blue Swallow** *Hirundo atrocaerulea*. Although it can measure 25 cm (9.8 in), two-fifths of this is the elegantly forked tail, a disproportion that recurs in many species. The birds' long, relatively broad wings and tails can make swallows seem bigger than they truly are and are themselves an adaptation to a life in the air catching insects (some species such as the North American **Tree Swallow** *Tachycineta bicolor* take seeds and berries during periods of low temperature or when invertebrate food is scarce or absent). For this reason they are birds of warm climates, with main centres of diversity in Africa (40 species) and tropical America (35 species).

The exception to this geographical concentration comes during the 'summer' months, when some swallows and martins expand their ranges towards the two poles. In the temperate latitudes of Europe (five species) and North America (eight species) the diversity of species may be much lower, but the cultural impact of these migrant hirundines is possibly greater. A bird common to both hemispheres – in fact, the world's most widespread songbird – is the **Barn Swallow** *Hirundo rustica*, which occurs on six continents. It is the species of greatest cultural importance, partly because of the bird's awe-inspiring passage between North and South America or Europe and Africa. In making these world-wrapping journeys every year, these 20 g (0.7 oz) creatures have become both an emblem for the entire phenomenon of bird migration and a central symbol for the northern spring.

The most obvious manifestation of this is the proverb, coined in ancient Greece and first recorded in the work of a largely lost, fifth-century BC playwright called Cratinus: 'One swallow makes not a spring.' Over 3,500 years, versions of this have been embraced by Europeans and then passed onwards to the very ends of the Earth. In fact, it is surely among the most widespread of all bird-related proverbs. I have recorded its living presence in the following diverse countries: Argentina, Australia, Brazil and USA. It is, of course, used throughout Europe including Belarus, Bulgaria, the Czech Republic, Croatia, Macedonia, Montenegro and Ukraine. (Yet it does not occur in Armenia, while in Iraq and Iran they say: 'One flower doesn't make a spring.')[1]

However, a Czech contributor, Lucie Hošková, makes an important point. 'We have as a common saying, "One swallow doesn't make a spring," but in reality people are very much looking forward to spotting their first swallow which, for them, is the moment when spring truly begins.'[2] In short, this is an ancient proverb whose cautionary note we delight in ignoring. She also explains how the adage has acquired additional meanings in her native language:

The nest chamber patiently chiselled out by Sand Martins (Bank Swallows) reflects the strange intimacy with mud that is shared by many members of the hirundine family.

The phrase 'first swallow' is very widely used as a Czech expression for something new and promising (for example: 'the new prototype is a first swallow for this car company', or 'this song is a first swallow on the new CD of such-and-such a singer'). It can be used for almost anything.[3]

It is intriguing that a version of the first-swallow metaphor made independent appeal to the African imagination. In Zulu and Xhosa-speaking areas of South Africa there is, or was, an expression that translates as 'the swallow anticipates summer', a mildly pejorative figure of speech for someone 'who has been in too big a hurry to speak or to act'.[4]

In Australia the swallow has also acquired a rather anomalous spring symbolism, as Darryl Jones explains:

Swallows are much loved and oh-so familiar around every garden and farm shed, with their endearing habit of building those neat and proper nests in highly visible places, including hanging old boots and verandah poles. The 'Welcome' part of the name for the best-known species, the **Welcome Swallow** *Hirundo neoxena*, would appear to be yet another example of a traditional British sentiment applied mistakenly to an antipodean bird. Just as our 'magpies' are widely accused of stealing shiny things – it never happens! – [see page 390] swallows are 'welcome' harbingers of spring on their supposed migratory return. The problem is, they are normally thoroughly sedentary while spring is just a slightly warmer period before the oppressive heat of summer.[5]

THE SPECIAL APPEAL OF HIRUNDINES

Why is it, however, that, with the exception of the cuckoos in the Old World, swallows and martins are the most important heralds of spring? Why have we singled them out from so many hundreds of other migrants worldwide? What is it about hirundines that makes them so universally loved? Alexander Wilson (1766–1813), the great North American naturalist, said that he never knew but one man who expressed disapproval of the birds. This penurious, close-fisted farmer hated Purple Martins because they ate his bees.[6] Another more famous critic was the mathematician Pythagoras (*c.*570–495 BC) who adjured his pupils never to allow swallows to nest in the house. The reasons behind his injunction are a 2,500-year-old mystery, but perhaps Pythagoras disliked what a modern African contributor notes wryly:

I have a pair of **Wire-tailed Swallow** *Hirundo smithii*, now on about their sixth brood, nesting in the bedroom corridor of my house. I've done everything I can to dissuade them, as their habit of flying through the sitting room then turning sideways and firing shit at some of my paintings, is, to say the least, a bit annoying.[7]

Their exuberant white splashes aside, few birds inspire more affection. One factor in the love affair is that their droppings mainly comprise the remains of aerial insects. For thousands of years swallows were our most beautiful and versatile insecticide. They eat precisely what we dislike and, unlike sparrows or other seed-eating birds that share our houses, they never touch what we consume. It is the

The Barn Swallow is among the most widespread small birds in the world.

A happy family of Barn Swallows is surely the most beautiful and life-enhancing insecticide that any household could possess.

perfect relationship (and this issue of complementary diets notably recurs in our abiding love for storks; see also page 120). In Ghana among the Anufo people the Barn Swallow is 'called the "bird with the closed mouth" and is deemed sacred because it does not eat their food like other birds'.[8]

Another element that permits hirundines their aerial diet is the scintillating elan of swallow movements. Flight attains one form of perfection with this family. As Henry Thoreau noted: 'He has more air in his bones than other birds.'[9] No widespread small songbird flies so much or as gracefully. In fact swallows are routinely confused with the ultimate birds of the wing, the swifts (see also page 293). Alexander Wilson, probably exaggerating the speed of its flight by a factor of two, proposed an equation to assess the distance covered in a Barn Swallow's lifetime. He calculated a mile a minute for ten hours a day over ten years. His conclusion was a life's journey of 2.19 million miles (3,524,463 km), or 87 times round the Earth. Even if we halve or quarter his figure, it is, at minimum, equal to the moon and back.[10]

A core element of swallow and martin flight is a capacity to soar, glide and swoop without wing movements, a capacity they share with few other small birds of the temperate latitudes (and in Europe no other small bird flies this way). It seems – it is – effortless, and it is rooted in the ecology of warm air. Gliding flight is an adaptation to a diet of aerial insects caught on the wing. When it is cold there are too few invertebrates for such flight to be meaningful. It is only with a rise in air temperature during our summers that the swallow's classic mode of flight is permitted. So when we see these swooping blue birds once again, subliminally we are told in the most elegant and unmistakable way that the air is warm. We can dispense with coats. Leisure will resume sway. Life has returned.

There is a third element in many swallows, which is

especially true of the three birds that have most captivated the people of the northern hemisphere, the Barn Swallow, **Red-rumped Swallow** *Cecropis daurica* and Purple Martin. They are blue. To my knowledge no one has completely or convincingly explained the central psychological power of blue upon humans and their cultures. Yet our civilisation endlessly demonstrates its effects. Suffice to say the colour is magical. Among birds – one thinks especially of swallows, kingfishers and bluebirds, then individual species such as the Spix's Macaw and Blue Bird-of-Paradise – this hue singles out some of the most special in the world. In hirundines it is frequently blue mixed with purple, itself a colour tone of profound importance, especially in the past (see Rail family, page 179), and it often shines with a metallic, almost iridescent quality (see Trogon family, page 312). All of these chromatic elements cement the swallows' privileged status.

Finally, and perhaps most importantly, in this relationship is the fact that swallows appear to choose to live with us and by us. 'It is friendly to man,' wrote Aelian, 'and takes pleasure in sharing the same roof with this being. It comes uninvited, and when it pleases and sees fit.'[11] Humans seem singled out for preferential treatment. In the process hirundines have often abandoned their former 'natural' nest locations in caves and tree hollows, or on rock surfaces, to build on man-made structures, even sometimes in the densest of city centres. Occasionally the man-made structure is moving:

I was in Gotland in Sweden and we were on the 15-minute car ferry to Fâro in the north-east part of the island. To my surprise we found swallows nesting on the framework of the car ferry. One nest was broken but the other three had a family in and they were being fed whilst the ferry moved from one part of the sea to the other.[12]

Common House Martins add their portion of colour, grace, soothing song and good luck to any house on which they choose to build.

Swallows had built a nest on the ferry across Kariba Lake, Zambia. They were building on this constantly moving boat and taking mud from different parts of the lake edge, so that the nest began to resemble a multicoloured layer-cake.[13]

The collective act of trust by breeding hirundines has made some species almost entirely dependent upon our hospitality. The relationship amounts to a kind of mutualism and, for some people, it helps shape their entire encounter with nature.

Hirundines probably began to surrender some of their fate into our hands in the mid Holocene. It seems fitting, therefore, that one of the most important images of the birds dates from the period. It is a mural, known as the Spring Fresco, unearthed by archaeologists on the island of Thira (also called Santorini). A set of glorious palace paintings was buried on the Greek island by a huge volcanic eruption, greater than Krakatoa, that devastated Minoan civilisation. What this catastrophe bequeathed to us is some of the oldest, best-preserved European art from the Bronze Age, including the 3,600-year-old image of Barn Swallows in flight. The birds are so intoxicated with the thrill of spring that one of them turns upside down in mid-air. Ancient, simple and anonymous, the painting has perfectly captured both the joy of these birds and their fundamental symbolism.

As if to cement the deep psychological links between swallows and us, the birds construct their own houses of mud and straw, much in the manner of human bricks. One of the most widespread ideas – and as true in Tanzania as it is in Estonia (where Barn Swallow is the national bird) – is that the presence of a swallow-built annex on our homes is a form of natural blessing and a sign of prosperity. In Tanzania it signals the arrival of human chicks, as well as baby hirundines.[14] In the Greek temples of the ancient world

the birds even had special dispensation to defecate on the gods' statues.[15] That licence partly arose because to disturb swallows was – and in many places still is – to invite bad luck. That idea survives today from southern Europe to South America:

In Bulgaria, people believe that swallows bring happiness and good luck. Especially appreciated are the white swallows, which are actually albinos. Because they are very rare, people believe that they are special messengers of good fortune. There is a novel – *По жицата*, which means 'On The Wire' – written by the famous Bulgarian writer Yordan Yovkov, in which the life of one young woman and her family is shaped by their belief in a white swallow.[16]

In Croatia swallows are symbols of life and appear in sayings in different ways, such as 'kuću kućom lastavice čine', which could be translated as 'the swallows make a house into a home'. The life of any swallow is sacred and if one kills a swallow he or she will die. In some parts of Croatia it's even worse: 'if you kill a swallow your mother will die' is sometimes said by elderly people. Swallow nests were appreciated on the house because people believed they would save the house from lightning strikes and you were advised not to scrape the nests off. The birds are among the most popular animals in folk or pop songs and often used as a symbol of returning love or of someone returning home.[17]

In Argentina swallows have a strong presence in our culture. Their migrant habits are well known and itinerant labourers, such as those who pick seasonal fruit, are called *trabajadores golondrina* ('swallow workers'). The device on fences that is used to keep the wire tense is called a *golondrina*, because it sits there like

Almost the entire world population of the Purple Martin is a non-paying tenant of the North American people.

a bird on the wire. A colleague of mine built her house in two stages and when she was going to place the light appliances to her balcony the workers refused to connect one because a **Southern Martin** *Progne elegans* was nesting there. She never actually fitted that light and the birds still visit her.[18]

In China swallows retain their status as lucky omens and until recently were widely protected. One extraordinary expression of the old attachments occurs in traditional Miao villages of Guizhou province, in southern-central China. The beautiful wooden houses of this region are clustered together on the steep hillsides and seem almost consciously designed to accommodate humans and hirundines alike. Virtually every home has one or more pairs of Red-rumped Swallows (they actually breed *inside* the house) and the Miao use the arrival date of these seasonal tenants to calculate the optimum day for the whole community to go out to the paddies and start sowing the new year's rice. Thus human crops and the swallows' return are still integrally linked.[19]

A residue of the older feeling was also manifest at the Beijing Olympics in 2008. China's capital was itself once known as the City of Swallows and one of the five official Olympic mascots, Nini, a golden swallow, drew on the ancient connection. Nini's design was based on children's kites, made in the shape of swallows, that were once hugely popular and flown above the city skyline to welcome the spring and its special birds.[20] One wonders if urban sprawl and Beijing's infamous smog have now banished the real swallows from Swallow City?

In Europe and elsewhere changes in air quality, pesticide use, architecture and even in basic human decency have altered our relations with hirundines. Some contributors asked that I mention 'the lack of tolerance of the mess below the nest and how many nests are now knocked down from public spaces, such as shopping-centre car parks

and parkland amenity buildings'.[21] Outside a takeaway restaurant in Queensland, Australia, I once saw a plastic snake strategically placed near an unwelcome swallow's nest. Equally, 'martins are not always welcome when nesting on the outside of buildings above balconies and terraces'.[22] Yet we should also recall that the endless geometry of power and telecommunication lines that interlace the modern world has been one of our most extensive recent gifts to hirundines; to the point that one now wonders where swallows once perched. Equally we should note that people still show extraordinary tenderness towards the birds, as the following extracts demonstrate:

One year, unnoticed by me, a pair of **Common House Martin** *Delichon urbicum* had extended a nest over the hinge of a fanlight window in the bathroom. Opening the window, I watched with horror as the whole nest flipped down to the garden. I discovered three barely fledged chicks blinking up at me from the ruins below. I found an old bag of plaster of Paris. I greased an upturned pudding basin and fashioned a new nest over it. Once it had dried and the feathered lining of the original had been installed the chicks looked reasonably safe. I then dashed to the local fishing shop and bought mealworms, which my daughter and a friend managed to feed to the babies with tweezers. An electrician friend with ladders helped to wire the nest back underneath the guttering. To my great relief the parent birds started feeding them again. Remarkably over a few days they renewed the edges to the plaster nest and the following year the same pair or their offspring returned to the nest, did further repairs and built an extension to it on the side![23]

Our Granny always said that swallows were her favourite bird, to the extent that when she died she wanted to come back as one. Since that time, every

Martin houses like these in Tony and Kay Miller's garden in New Jersey can be found right across North America.

spring, a single swallow arrives a little earlier at the farm and is always welcomed as Granny returning home. Not only does this arrival signal the end of winter but it reassures us and lifts our spirits that an important member of our family has returned safe and well. The lucky person making the discovery lets other immediate family members know with a simple text, 'Granny's back.' The new arrival's song seems to fill the air and you realise something that is important, which has been missing, has returned and life and the world feel more complete and a better place to be.[24]

PURPLE MARTINS IN NORTH AMERICA

Even in a bird family that enjoys such privileged status as the swallows, the loving attention shown to Purple Martins is extraordinary. It is a large broad-winged hirundine of sumptuous purple-glossed royal blue (in males), with matt brown-black wings and a soft chirrupy, gurgling liquid song. (Incidentally, the Purple Martin's scientific name, *Progne*, commemorates the chortling quality of the vocalisations. It derives from the terrible Greek myth of King Tereus who, in order to prevent his wife, Procne, from speaking of his terrible crimes, cut out her tongue. The gods eventually turned Procne into a swallow, whose voice was thought to resemble the queen's inarticulate mutterings. The ancient Greeks were equally rude about swallows when they suggested that the bird's song sounded like prattling gossips.)

Purple Martins are wide-ranging migrants that winter in Latin America as far south as Argentina and then spread to breed across the northern continent as far as the central Canadian territories. Its natural nest sites are in tree holes, but even in pre-colonial times Native Americans of south-east USA were accustomed to hang empty gourds on poles to attract Purple Martins to breed in the vicinity of their settlements. The Native American practices were recorded in the late seventeenth century and were subsequently adopted by black rural communities of the southern states, who were similarly convinced that Purple Martins acted as deterrents to hawks and crows that would otherwise harass the chickens.[25]

These modest beginnings eventually gave rise to an almost universal habit among colonial Americans to put up some form of nesting structure for Purple Martins. It should be stressed that this is not the same as the adventitious colonisation of human structures that takes place among so many of the world's swallows. Purple Martins are accommodated in houses that serve no other purpose. Today all but the most westerly populations, which still (partly) use natural tree sites, benefit from this act of national kindness. Virtually the entire species – an estimated 6 million birds in a million colonies – has become a rent-free tenant of the American people.[26] As one naturalist put it: 'It is beyond all doubt, the "bird box" species of this country.'[27] There is now a Purple Martin Society (1994) and a Purple Martin Conservation Association (1987), but the oldest is the Nature Society (1962), which is also dedicated to the one beloved bird.

Both private individuals and civic institutions – environmental organisations, managers of nature reserves, parks or, indeed, any public space, as well as hirundine-friendly town councils and even commercial companies – will put out houses for Purple Martins. They can still be as simple as gourds on poles, but more often today they are purpose-built structures with multiple nest holes. One wonders if any privately built martin property is larger than a condominium in Winnfield, Louisiana, which can theoretically accommodate 620 pairs? There is, however, a remarkable community-sponsored martin tower at Lake Charles, Louisiana, dedicated to the serving veterans of the Vietnam War, which has accommodation for 2,640 pairs.[28] Otherwise, most houses are much smaller – yet even a 24-room aluminium suite costs anything up to $600 – and often include plastic mouldings shaped like the original hollow gourds. Another common feature is the human host's effort to eliminate the unwanted attentions of non-native squatters, such as House Sparrows and Common Starlings, which are widely trapped and killed.

Tony and Kay Miller in Cape May, New Jersey, are typical of the many thousands of proud, attentive landlords to these glorious birds:

> We started with them more than ten years ago and today across the garden we have eight houses, all on 16-foot poles, and baffles around the bases to stop the raccoons, squirrels and other predators. The eight houses can accommodate a total of 132 pairs. But we never have as many as that. This year is a banner year; we have 25 couples. During the winter I take them down and wash them out with a power hose and have them all ready long before 1 April, which is when the birds start to return. Sometimes we come back especially from Florida to make sure the boxes are up. We love the birds – they are my favorite – and I look forward to their sounds. I come out at 'wine time' at 4 p.m. just to watch their acrobatics. It's beautiful.[29]

THE MIRACLE OF HIRUNDINE MIGRATION

The facts of long-distance migration are now so well established that it is hard to imagine how it perplexed and confounded some of our forebears. In the fourth century BC Aristotle had an inkling of the truth and yoked together as fellow migrants two of the most conspicuous birds of the Mediterranean spring, the swallow and turtle dove.[30] Although the great philosopher could never have suspected that the hirundines had flown almost the entire length of Africa, the Greeks did at least know that swallows passed the winter on that continent.

Unfortunately this basic understanding was thrown into deep confusion in the Late Middle Ages by a Swedish archbishop, Olaus Magnus, who pronounced that swallows were routinely hauled up by fishermen, 'hanging together like a conglomerated mass'. In fact, swallows can occasionally cling together in times of low temperature, but this is no more than a short-term measure. However, with the wind of Christian authority in its sail, Magnus' false notion of hibernation was set adrift to become 'one of the longest-running debates in the history of ornithology'.[31] That the idea survived so long is extraordinary, but the great British writer on nature Henry Williamson wrote that in 1912 he met a man in Norfolk, England, who adamantly believed that swallows buried themselves in mud each autumn.[32] Hirundine hibernation had long been disproved by 1912, but this was not so a century earlier.

If one person could be said to embody the heated scientific conflict between the proponents of migration and hibernation, then that person would have to be the gentle vicar of Selborne, Gilbert White (1720–1793). Acutely observant naturalist he may have been, and author of *The Natural History of Selborne*, one of the most popular and enduring British books ever written, but he could not make up his mind on this major question. Throughout his writings he constantly revisited the subject and, not unlike a swallow himself, spiralled with profound irresolution round and round the alternatives. His confusion is fascinating not just for what it reveals about hirundine ecology and how hirundines affect us psychologically, but also for the light it sheds on wider human reflections about animal migration.

We should first note that at least White's theory of hibernation was a small improvement on some authorities, who believed that hirundines flew to the moon in autumn.[33] Equally there were extenuating circumstances for White's confusion. Hirundines are the quintessential birds of the air, but they can have a strangely intimate relationship with soil. Many species make nests of mud, but some even dig holes in the bare ground. The bird with which White was familiar was the Sand Martin (Bank Swallow), which excavates a long brood chamber in the sandy earth of riverbanks or soft cliffs. On one occasion local workers near White's home claimed to find 'swallows' in a chalk cliff that had collapsed after a winter storm. These were almost certainly Sand Martins (Bank Swallows) from the previous nest season, and dead because of other natural causes, but such details only served to bamboozle White even more.

Another circumstance that helped to increase his muddle was the almost universal public confusion (which flourishes to this day) of swallows with swifts. The young of the latter birds can naturally enter a state of torpor in bad weather, when their body functions slow profoundly to reduce energy loss while their parents are absent, sometimes 1,000 km (620 miles) away feeding in more clement conditions. White, alas, came across examples of immature swifts, discovered during renovation work in a church, 'which were, at first appearance, dead but, on being carried toward the fire, revived'.[34] White naturally wondered if swallows could also enter a similar and prolonged torpid state.

Just weeks before he died, White saw Sand Martins (Bank Swallows) swooping around a traditional nest colony and, unable to shake off the old doubts, wrote:

> This . . . gives great reason to suppose that they do not leave their wild haunts at all, but are secreted amidst the clefts, & caverns of these abrupt cliffs where they usually spend their summers. The late severe weather considered, it is not very probable that these birds should have migrated so early from a tropical region thro' all these cutting winds and pinching frosts: but it is easy to suppose that they may, like bats & flies, have been awakened by the influence of the Sun, amidst their secret latebrae, where they have spent the uncomfortable foodless months in a torpid state, & the profoundest of slumbers.[35]

Perhaps we should not just see White as wrong, but also as absolutely typical. A fundamental response of humans worldwide to the disappearance of seasonally abundant wildlife was to imagine that the answers lay below our feet. Shepard Krech, for example, in his book *The Ecological Indian*, points out that a classic belief of many groups of buffalo-hunting Native Americans was that these thundering giants of the prairie, at some point in the autumn, careered into caverns and vanished beneath deep lakes to spend their winters underground.[36] In South Africa tribes of the Cape region thought that the seasonal disappearance of quail could be explained by their metamorphosis into frogs that crawled under the earth for the dry season.[37]

In the well-travelled world of the jet age it is not difficult for us to imagine the simultaneous existence on the other side of the world. But until recently most people, White included, lived deeply sedentary lives. When faced with the mysteries of their own immediate environment, their instinct was to solve them with reference only to their immediate environment. A fundamental human response towards almost all earthly life is to assume its origins lay within the primal darkness of the soil.

There is wonderful confirmation in many of the creation stories of first peoples. So often humans explained their own beginnings in the subterranean shadows of middle Earth (see also Hummingbirds in Pre-Columbian Myth, page 301). In the case of the Hopi they had two creation stories. In one the entire race was stuck deep within the ground and birds were sent ahead to find an 'exit onto the sunlit rain-showered earth'. One of their avian guides was a swallow. In another story the Hopi made it to the sun-blessed uplands of the American Southwest, but they had forgotten their seed. The God of Dew sent someone back to retrieve the precious corn grains that were – and are still – at the heart of Hopi life. The bearer was a swallow.[38]

Migrant hirundines grant modern humanity their own kind of life-enhancing gift. In autumn as they prepare to depart and also in their winter quarters in Africa, South America and elsewhere the birds form enormous communal roosts. The collective movements and burbling songs from vast clouds of swallows are one of the most affecting and beautiful avian spectacles on Earth. Yet they can be in the most unlikely situations, such as a 1984 gathering on the banks of the Rio Negro in Brazil. About 100,000 martins of mixed species, including **Grey-breasted Martin** *Progne chalybea* and Purple Martin (60 per cent), settled for the night on the pipes, tubing, wires, ladders and platforms of an oil refinery.[39]

They can also be in the middle of cities, such as a recent massive roost in tree-lined streets just by the Highland Mall in Austin, Texas. As one contributor observes these sudden and overwhelming influxes 'captivate scientists, newspaper reporters, tourists, and birdwatchers including myself'. She adds:

> The martins seem to exemplify a celebration of life, gleefully chattering, spiralling carefree through the sky, basking in a landscape with few predators and ample mosquitoes. Indeed, each bird forms the life of the party, an angular piece of confetti in a martin Mardi Gras. Such a sight can't help but refresh the human soul, showing me that birds can still thrive in utter abundance, that life itself is an exquisite miracle – and that the Purple Martin throws the best parties in all the animal kingdom.[40]

Another speciality of roosting swallows is to gather at sites near water – a choice that seemed to confirm our ancestors' suspicions of sub-aquatic hibernation. The largest Purple Martin roost in North America, possibly peaking at a million-strong, is on an island in Lake Murray in Louisiana. Yet perhaps the ultimate in hirundine gatherings is another wetland location in South Africa. The Mount Moreland Reedbed, near Durban, holds 5 million Barn Swallows, possibly as many as one in six of the breeding birds in all Europe. Horatio Clare, author of *A Single Swallow*, his account of his own trans-African odyssey following the species' migration to his native Wales, witnessed such a super-roost:

> They call them *Inkonjani* – 'the lightning birds' – but they do not know. No one knows how it feels to live as they do, at that speed, in a sky which is all direction. Remember their eye-view, that all-around wheeling world, and nothing ahead of them but the tiny beak, and the air flying at their faces. Two million swallows together, in various stages of moult, over a swamp at evening, in hurricanes, typhoons of birds. I saw them. I followed them, as the Zulus say you shouldn't, if you want to come back. Part of me has still not come back.[41]

Lark family *Alaudidae*

The cultural centrality that this family holds for so many people cannot be explained by the birds' appearance. Larks are small, dumpy creatures with colours that range through mud-brown to sandy beige. The earth tones may make many of them dull and difficult to identify, but they well reflect the family's ground-hugging lifestyle. Frequently they possess slender legs with spike-heels and toes tipped by long nails that enable them to move quickly over soft substrates. They are accomplished runners with a corresponding reluctance to fly.

There are 96 species worldwide and many are inhabitants of open, sparsely wooded country, while a family speciality is the capacity to thrive in desert conditions. Three lark genera – *Eremophila*, *Eremopterix* and *Chersophilus* – have names that enshrine the association. They derive from Greek terms, *eremos* and *chersos* (= *khersos*), that refer to types of dry, barren country.[1] It is telling that on the singularly forested continent of South America there is only one breeding lark, the gloriously adaptable **Horned Lark** *Eremophila alpestris*. In fact, in the entire American hemisphere there is just this lone species. Africa meanwhile, with 80 per cent of the entire family (77 species), is the birds' real home. The region with the second highest diversity is Eurasia (21 species), of which 12 species occur in Europe. One curious anomaly is the absence of larks from the other great desert continent, Australia, where **Horsfield's Bush Lark** *Mirafra javanica* is the sole resident.

When European colonists recognised Australia's lark 'deficiencies' they quickly compensated by deliberately releasing a much-cherished bird of the home country, the **Eurasian Skylark** *Alauda arvensis*. It has colonised a temperate swathe of southernmost Victoria and New South Wales, and has enjoyed other successful introductions in Tasmania, New Zealand, Hawaii and Vancouver Island (Canada).[2] Yet the reason that it is the most widespread of all larks is a native distribution from the Pacific shores of Russia, China and Japan, across the intervening 10,500 km (6,524 miles) to the Atlantic coasts of Ireland and Morocco.

This lark is in many ways *the* lark – the bird that gave rise to the Old English word, *lœwerce*, and to the Old Norse,

Horned Lark occurs at the Earth's northernmost polar rim where it produces a high sweet song of the Arctic summer. When slowed dramatically and lowered two octaves, however, a recording of this same lark creates the melancholy heart to the second movement of Rautavaara's *Cantus Arcticus*.

lævirke, which find their echo in several modern European names for the family, such as *lerche* (Danish), *leeuwerik* (Dutch), *lerche* (German), *laverca* (Portuguese) and *lärka* (Swedish).[3] According to Pliny the Elder, the Romans derived their name, *alauda* (which gives us the family version *Alaudidae*), from a Celtic word meaning 'great songstress'. In truth, the Celts may have had in mind either Eurasian Skylark or a common relative, the **Crested Lark** *Galerida cristata*. Both are renowned for their voices, but it is the former that undoubtedly wears the laurels and which would be included in any list of the world's most celebrated songsters.

CULTURAL CELEBRATIONS OF SKYLARK SONG

Technically the individual units in the vocalisations of Eurasian Skylark fall within a narrow band of shrill notes – 'like marbles squeezed in your fist' suggested poet Norman MacCaig (in 'Stonechat on Cul Beg'). They can sound

guttural and hard and can give the song a mechanically produced quality. What makes it such a powerfully evocative song is its flowing, modulated, almost undulating structure which, at times, seems an audible analogue of the softly contoured habitats that the species occupies. A Eurasian Skylark can sing uninterrupted for 30 minutes.

Writing of the British in particular, Alfred Newton noted of skylark song that 'there is hardly a poet . . . who has not made it his theme, to say nothing of the many writers of prose who have celebrated its qualities in passages that will be remembered so long as our language lasts'.[4] The Eurasian Skylark rivals even the Common Nightingale for the quantities of purple ink expended in its honour. It is intriguing to reflect upon the songs of both birds to understand why their reputations should be so exalted. Each creates a form of disembodied music; nightingales because they sing at night when they are virtually impossible to see. Eurasian Skylarks, by contrast, are the supreme diurnal

They may have honoured the Eurasian Skylark in poetry and music for centuries, but Europeans still trap and eat the birds in their millions.

songsters, yet as they sing they fly high over their open territories so that it is often impossible to spot them in the empty blueness, a challenge that is compounded by the song's ventriloquy.

In the case of the nightingale it is as if the bird's music upwells out of the very darkness, while the lark's melody seems to shower down from out of the daylight itself. A birdsong without an apparent author has lent itself to the human imagination as the most plastic of symbols and we have felt at liberty to take possession and invest it with all sorts of private meanings. From the earliest times, Christian Europe took lark song literally as a heaven-sent gift ripe with religious symbolism. Singing skylarks were originally interpreted as being in some ways reflections of divine grace, as holy birds or the embodiment of angels, and the song itself a hymn or matin offered in praise of God.[5] (A long-established collective term for a flock of the birds – an exaltation of larks – seems to reflect these religious associations.)

In William Blake's poem *Milton*, his invocation of lark song touches on many of the traditional themes, but he also demonstrates fully how writers since the Middle Ages had felt in no sense bound to describe a real flesh-and-blood bird: Blake's lark, however beautiful or affecting we may find the poetic sentiments it arouses, is part of a fantasy of human conjuring.

> His little throat labours with inspiration; every feather
> On throat and breast and wings vibrates with the
>   effluence divine.
> All Nature listens silent to him, and the awful sun
> Stands still upon the mountain, looking on this little
>   bird
> With eyes of soft humility and wonder, love and awe.

Blake's fellow Romantics – Coleridge, Wordsworth, Shelley – also made lark song a metaphor for the spontaneous, morally charged enterprise of human creativity and especially for the gift of poetic invention. In Shelley's 'To a Skylark', perhaps the most famous of all lark verse in the language, he described the bird as:

> Like a poet hidden
> In the light of thought,
> Singing hymns unbidden,
> Till the world is wrought
> To sympathy with hopes and fears it heeded not:

In an age more attentive to natural-historical veracity, the author W H Hudson, in his book *Nature in Downland*, wrote powerfully of lark song and drilled down with great insight into its structure.

> The song of the lark is a continuous torrent of
> contrasted guttural and clear shrill sounds and trills, so
> rapidly emitted that the notes, so different in character,
> yet seem to interpenetrate or to overlap each other; and
> the effect on the ear is similar to that on the eye of sober
> or dull and brilliant colours mixed and running into one
> another in a confused pattern. The acutest note of all, a
> clear piercing sound like a cry several times repeated, is
> like a chance patch of most brilliant colour occurring at
> intervals in the pattern.

Hudson reflected on something often overlooked by earlier poets, which helps to explain why the sound should make such an appeal to our sense of beauty.

> . . . here, on these sheep-fed hills . . . you hear the lark
> all day long – not one nor half a dozen, nor a score or
> two, but many scores, and I should say hundreds of

Plain-looking it may be, but the Eurasian Skylark would join any list of the world's most celebrated songsters.

larks. Go where you like . . . you are ringed about with that perpetual unchanging stream of sound. It is not a confused, nor a diffused, sound, which is everywhere, filling the whole air like a misty rain, or a perfume, or like the universal hum of a teeming insect life in a wood in summer; . . . and you are always in the centre of it; and the effect is as of an innumerable company of invisible beings, forming an unbroken circle as wide as the horizon, chanting an everlasting melody in one shrill, unchanging tone.[6]

Like few other birds, larks are at their best, as Hudson emphasised, when they are heard in this choral form, when there are numerous males in an interlocking pattern of mutual territory-holding competition. In optimum conditions Eurasian Skylarks can reach densities of 200 pairs per km^2 (and some desert-dwelling larks can reach levels of 1,250 pairs per km^2). In the presence of such numbers the entire heavens seem roofed over with their singing and we feel entirely immersed in lark music. In these moments we are as compelled by the adjacent, interpenetrating impacts of light, open sky and the subliminal pleasures of extensive rolling habitats as we are by the larks themselves. Hudson, striving to convey the synaesthetic effect of these multiple factors, likened lark song to 'sunshine translated into sound'.

A modern contributor shares a sense that the bird and its places are somehow part of an indivisible whole:

Only when they take to the wing and hover high up, trilling their complex and dipping cadenza does it properly become a skylark, filling the whole space and showing us why it's there. It shouts out to be admired and looked at and heard. Once it's in the air binoculars are useless, or rather they should be abandoned, in favour of taking in the whole of the picture: the fields, the crops, the grass, the big drifting sky and that sound. It is absolutely and indescribably part of the landscape.[7]

At the heart of all writings on lark song, even sometimes only by implication, there is a conviction that their music contains something invincibly joyous and morally good. Larks, in fact, have supplied an entire vocabulary – 'larking', 'to lark about', 'to skylark', 'a lark' (as in a spree or frolic) 'larkishness', 'larksome' – much of which connotes the ideas of light-heartedness and innocent pleasure. Not all of it, in truth, was entirely innocent: a lesser-known historical meaning of 'lark' was 'to masturbate', while 'larking' was a euphemism for cunnilinguis and fellatio.[8] Nor is the pattern confined to English: 'In Serbia skylarking – *ševa* (noun), *ševiti* (verb) – means "having sex" and is very common.'[9] The inherent lightness of being assumed to reside in larks has also been used on occasions with razor-edged irony. In Victor Hugo's vast and brilliant novel *Les Misérables* (1862), the central character, Cosette, the orphaned waif who is wretchedly abused by her vile and grasping guardians, is referred to by them as 'the lark', as if to emphasise the depths of Cosette's misery and of their own moral bankruptcy.

We should not imagine that the only lark with a beautiful song is Eurasian Skylark. Many species have a similar vocal range and tonal quality or song structure. The **Calandra Lark** *Melanocorypha calandra* of the Mediterranean and western Asia, whose own vocalisations are a darker, coarser, if similarly modulated, downpour of notes, were particularly cherished in Italy. 'To sing like a calandra' was a proverbial Italian expression meaning to sing well, while in Greece, where the birds are still illegally trapped and kept in cages, the bird's name, γαλιάντρα ('galiantra'), is used metaphorically for 'a young lady who never stops speaking'.[10] Another highly praised performance is the haunting flute-like song of the **Greater Hoopoe-Lark** *Alaemon alaudipes*, which is found across the largely desert Saharo-Sindian region from Morocco to India. The British ornithologist Richard Meinertzhagen suggested that 'with an audience of silence, solitude, and space, the music of that lark attains a rare perfection'.[11] Like many larks, however, the species sometimes takes little account of the background human context that might otherwise distract an admirer.

In 1991 while preparing in the Saudi Arabian desert for the Gulf War, I was woken every morning at around 5 a.m. by the sound of what I could only describe as someone playing a flute. It was a beautiful sound and I used to lie there just listening. This went on for several days and I began to wonder who could be playing. I wasn't aware that any of my men could play an instrument. I decided I would find out who it was, so at the end of my morning briefing I asked. 'OK, which one of you is playing a flute at five in the morning?' My men all looked at me as if I had well and truly lost it: 'Boss, has the war got to you already?' I insisted that someone was playing a flute and it was OK as I thought it was wonderful. 'Now we know you *have* lost it,' they said.

'OK', I said, 'I'll find out who it is,' and the next morning I awoke to this beautiful sound. I jumped out of my sleeping bag and I must have walked for about ten minutes, when I was drawn to look up and to my total astonishment I saw a Greater Hoopoe-Lark tumbling like a stone to the ground, singing as it fell. I concluded that 'the flute' was the larks' song being cast in all directions as it bounced off sand dunes. This has remained with me and without doubt is the most beautiful song I have ever heard. Such beauty in the midst of the horrors we were about to enter into was surreal.[12]

EXPLOITATION OF LARKS

One of the recurrent themes of this book, which is magnified in the context of larks, is our capacity to cherish the bird (or, at least, our internal image of it) and the song, but ruthlessly exploit the creature itself. This duality amounts in this instance almost to a form of schizophrenia. Larks were and, in some places, still are eaten in large numbers. Until the 1970s *c.*4 million Eurasian Skylarks were taken in France and the present legal harvest in that country is still 1.2–1.6 million birds, while the Italian total is 1.5 million.[13] However, these present figures are probably only a fraction of the lark free-for-all of the past.

The birds were caught in a variety of ways but the scale of the nets used in Germany give an indication of the harvest itself. The lengths of mesh stood 1.8 m (6 ft) tall but stretched for 274 m (900 ft). Twelve of them comprised a single wall, which were then arrayed in successive rows, all facing east and usually six in number, but occasionally with as many as nine walls altogether. At dusk the autumn stubbles were driven to flush the roosting larks into these vast traps.[14]

Another ruse was to allow the larks to go to roost and then in the night, with bells ringing as a reassurance (intended to mimic the clanging bell noises produced by grazing livestock) and often with lamps in hand to dazzle and confuse the resting birds further, the fowlers would drag nets and lay them over the top. However, the most famous and widespread strategy, especially in Britain, France and Italy, involved a device that has become known as a 'lark mirror'. They involve a central spindle on which is placed an arm that spins constantly. The spiralling cross-piece usually curves downwards at each extremity, and the whole length

One of the oldest mechanisms by which larks were drawn into traps or brought within range of the awaiting hunter is the lark mirror.

is studded with shining fragments of mirror or polished metal. There are references to them as early as the fourteenth century and many historical examples are now considered folk art of enormous beauty and desirability.

No one has convincingly explained why larks and other birds are so attracted to these glittering contraptions.[15] Yet the fact remains that birds are irresistibly drawn out of the skies towards lark mirrors, settling near them and presenting themselves as a target for the gun, net or other means of capture. Sometimes birds seem almost to queue up to die, indifferent to the close presence of hunters, the gunfire and the slaughter unfolding all around them. In France even today a lark mirror (*miroir-aux-alouettes*) is a proverbial expression for a false promise or illusory inducement.[16]

The actual structure may have been simple but across the large geographical territory where they were popular, lark mirrors inspired much local ingenuity, resulting in an almost infinite variety. However, there were some recurrent features, including the use of live or stuffed Little Owls, sometimes as an alternative to the mirrors but often in combination with them.[17] (This owl has been used for lark-hunting purposes since the time of the ancient Greeks.)[18] Another practice was to add red paint or fabric, which was thought to have a similar magnetic effect on the prey. Sometimes the hat and coat of the hunter were also adorned with red or had further fragments of mirror sewn into them.

In English the whole business of hunting larks with these devices was known as 'daring larks' and Shakespeare alludes to the practice in *Henry VIII*. In Act 3 he has the Earl of Surrey jibe at his enemy, Cardinal Wolsey:

My lords,
Can ye endure to hear this arrogance?
And from this fellow? If we live thus tamely,
To be thus jaded by a piece of scarlet,
Farewell nobility! Let his grace go forward
And dare us with his cap, like larks.

The red cap traditionally associated with his ecclesiastical office completes Shakespeare's image of the cardinal beguiling his political opponents with papal authority, like a hunter flashing his scarlet cloth at larks.

To give some sense of how long-standing was Europe's love affair with lark hunting, St Francis of Assisi (1181–1226) is reputed to have said that were the emperor Frederick II, himself a passionate falconer and celebrated student of birds, ever to grant him an audience, he would plead for a curb on the trapping of larks.[19] Yet the most convincing proof for the efficiency of lark mirrors and, indeed, all the old methods is the numbers of birds sold at market. The statistics are fragmentary, but at least they offer a glimpse of the slaughter in past centuries.

In the Paris market during 1832, total sales were 826,462 birds (thrush numbers, for comparison, were just 30,081). At Dieppe in the winter of 1867–8, the numbers were estimated at 1,255,500, while in October at Leipzig the German *Lerchenstreichen* was thought to yield a regular harvest of 500,000 larks and as many as 1.5 million over the whole autumn season.[20] English lark catching had its main commercial centres in the London markets of Leadenhall and Newgate, where the combined sales in the mid Victorian period involved *c.*300,000 birds.[21] The above figures, incidentally, offer no insight into the huge numbers taken for the cagebird trade. For one consequence of all that glorious lark-centred poetry was a wide passion for captive larks in the drawing rooms of Europe.

If we cannot recover an overall figure for historic lark slaughter, we can at least conclude that it was massive but, simultaneously, still only a fraction of the tens, and possibly hundreds, of millions of Eurasian Skylarks that poured across the continent every autumn. However substantial the lark harvest, humans exploited a natural redundancy inbuilt in the birds' population dynamics (a third of Eurasian Skylarks are thought to die naturally in their first year). As late as 1980 the British wintering population was still calculated to be 25 million birds.[22]

It is intriguing that Eurasian Skylarks, present historically in such incalculable, seemingly profligate numbers, became a metaphor for luxury and material superfluity for some Europeans. The expression 'larks will fall into one's mouth already roasted' was proverbial in French and English from the Middle Ages for a place, people or situation that enjoyed a condition of natural plenty. The phrase eventually acquired a secondary pejorative sense, denoting those who simply expected riches to fall to them without effort. (It is interesting to note that in Sweden much the same expression occurs, but the bird is the sparrow.)[23]

In a curious way the old saying perfectly summarises the collective attitude towards larks. Through the clearance of Europe's primeval wildwood, which would otherwise have served as an insuperable barrier to larks, Neolithic agriculturalists created the extensive grasslands in which the birds could eventually thrive. Their European abundance was thus, in part, a consequence of farming and a human artefact. If, without knowing it, we helped to create the larks' heaven-sent plenty, then without thinking we proceeded to exploit it – capturing, killing and incarcerating these one-ounce morsels by the million and, cumulatively, by the billion. More recently we have, with almost equal disregard, set about the dissolution of the once vast numbers. Modern intensive agro-industry has squeezed out the inefficiencies of an older agriculture. The result is a wholesale loss of farmland birds – plovers, waders, buntings and finches – across much of the continent. Now that these habitat losses have inflicted major declines on larks, even the present diminished levels of hunting in Europe have become themselves a threat to the birds.[24]

Between 1970 and 1990, losses of Eurasian Skylarks were reported across half of European countries and in the 35 years from 1980 the species has lost almost half its population. In Britain exclusively the decline is more than 60 per cent.[25] The species is still widespread, but almost nowhere can it be heard in the manner described by Hudson at the beginning of last century.

What are the consequences? What does it mean to lose this totem of European farmland on such a scale? Reflecting the grievous losses, the British poet Alistair Elliot has fashioned a new kind of lark poetics:

Suddenly larks are rare. A fertiliser kills
The reasons for their song. Their landscape fills
With whispers that some sharp-eared god enjoys,
Papery music, low botanical noise.

Friends give each other names of fields not drugged, where birds
Still practise their ascensions on transparent words,
Still disappear in light and silence where
Nobody else can hide: a span of air.

You think of following them. The sounds of summer now
Falls only from an aeroplane that echoes somehow
In the soft sky. I'll find and interview
A lark with my machine . . .
                              But will that comfort you?

Nature is leaving earth. The species one by one
Withdraw their voices. Soon the creatures shall have gone,
Leaving the subtle horns of rock for nitrogen
And oxygen and noble gas to play upon.

Elliot's 'Speaking of Larks' is a heartfelt poem of lament. Yet perhaps we need to tease out some of the subtler cultural consequences of these ecological changes. I inquired at four British educational establishments, and in three classrooms, one of 14-year-olds (12 children) and two of 16-year-olds (18 and 12 children) at a local fee-paying school, and not a single child had heard skylark song.[26] Among older biology students at two British universities the results were marginally better: with figures of five (from 18) and two (from 18). In a degree class of young adults studying creative writing, none (of 11) had ever knowingly listened to lark song.[27] What will it mean to read Shelley's 'To a Skylark' or to listen to Ralph Vaughan Williams' *The Lark Ascending* (judged to be Britain's most popular piece of classical music), but never actually hear the bird's 'harmonious madness' oneself? Even more troubling in some ways: how can you respond to the profound sense of loss in Alistair Elliot's wonderful poem, when you have lost all opportunity to be inspired by the living bird?

As one contributor notes, the presence of singing larks is not just an indicator of 'whether or not we've stuffed up our countryside completely'. The sound is also a measure of more private inner values. 'To me', he adds, 'it's also become a sign of whether I have my priorities right or wrong. Can I still make time to walk and sit and listen? If the answer is no then I'm in trouble.'[28]

Cisticola and Allies family *Cisticolidae*

This group of small, streaky warbler-like songbirds includes 127 species, all but 20 of which are entirely African in range. The largest genus, *Cisticola* (52 species), is even more loyal to the continent with just two occurring outside the region. In fact the only cisticola without an African population is the Asiatic **Golden-headed Cisticola** *Cisticola exilis*.

The cisticolas are notable for being as ubiquitous in sub-Saharan Africa as they are unrecognised by many of its human inhabitants. Small, dull, brown and streaked could serve as a description for most of them. To make matters more complicated, they often vary according to gender, season and region. Few would disagree that they pose one of the most complex tests in all bird identification, and while visitors to Africa are seldom equal to the brain-straining cisticola challenge, resident birders wear a mastery of the group as a badge of (well-deserved) merit.

One person who stands outside this general pattern is a Briton, Rear-Admiral Hubert Lynes (1874–1942), who was so obsessed he made three expeditions specifically to study them, including one in 1926–27 that covered the entire length of Africa, from Cape to Cairo, over seven and half months. In the course of this journey he and a friend, B B Osmaston, collected 1,100 cisticolas, sometimes with assistance at the highest levels. (In Kenya, for instance, it was very much cisticolas imperial-style with a 'luxurious saloon car' at their disposal, in which 'we lived and moved to and fro on the railway, stopping when and where we wished so as to have many of the species literally at our front door'.)[1]

The final publication, 'Review of the genus *Cisticola*', a two-part supplement running to 673 pages, is the longest single contribution in the 154-year history of the bird journal *Ibis* (see also page 128). Lynes financed the paper himself. It is a measure of the miasmic confusion swirling around cisticolas until Lynes' work that he reduced nearly 200 putative species to 40. On his return from his last African expedition in 1939, he was seriously ill and died three years later.[2]

The word 'cisticola' is intriguing. Many probably see the birds without appreciating that the strange name originates with their nests. It derives from two Latin words, *cista*, 'a box or basket often of woven twigs', and *colo*, 'I inhabit or dwell'.[3] The nest itself is often a closely stitched fabric of dried grass and spider's web, sometimes of exquisite construction and fashioned like a bottle or flask. The nest of one species, the **Zitting Cisticola** *Cisticola juncidis*, has been described as a 'pure gem ... Shaped, according to view, like a pear, a purse, a cocoon or even an old-style electric light bulb.'[4]

A good deal of the family's behaviour is revealed by a rather amusing but consistent pattern in their names. As well as the Zitting Cisticola there are **Whistling** *Cisticola*

The Zitting Cisticola is as plain in voice as it is in appearance and fulfils the family's wider reputation for including some of the ultimate 'little brown jobs'.

lateralis, **Trilling** *Cisticola woosnami*, **Chattering** *Cisticola anonymus*, **Bubbling** *Cisticola bulliens*, **Churring** *Cisticola njombe*, **Tinkling** *Cisticola rufilatus*, **Wailing** *Cisticola lais*, **Winding** *Cisticola marginatus*, **Chirping** *Cisticola pipiens*, **Croaking** *Cisticola natalensis* and **Wing-snapping Cisticolas** *Cisticola ayresii*. The repetitions emphasise several aspects of their genuine ecology: they are birds often heard rather than seen; the vocalisations are sometimes the best clue to their identity; while the string of present participles suggests birds that are almost unceasingly doing something. In fact, the restlessness is part of the challenge of their identification.

Martin Woodcock, sole artist for the massive seven-volume *The Birds of Africa*, recalled his co-author, the late Stuart Keith, inventing new additions: 'The aim was to get as close to existing names as possible, and I recall that the new species included Piffling, Whining, Whingeing, Poxy and Pinkling.' Another story that has now passed into legend centres on the **Rock-loving Cisticola** *Cisticola aberrans* (*emini*). A bird guide once walked up to a site for this rather localised species and proceeded, to the deep consternation of his clients, to play a tape of the American rock star Bruce Springsteen, claiming that the name derived, not from its habitat, but from its choice of music.[5]

A striking exception among cisticola nomenclature arises with a common and widespread bird of southern African bush and savannah called the **Neddicky** *Cisticola fulvicapilla*. The name derives firstly from the Afrikaans *Neddikkie*, which in turn was taken from an original version in various indigenous African languages, such as the Xhosa (*Incede*) and Zulu (*iNcede, uNcede*). 'I'm not sure what *uNcede* means but Zulu people sometimes used to say, when a person was looking as if they hadn't eaten, "you're looking as thin as an uNcede".'[6]

In his book *Bird-Lore of the Eastern Cape Province*, the Reverend Robert Godfrey suggested that the name *Incede* was an attempt to convey the bird's alarm call, which is a harsh ticking sound.[7] This repeated dry note finds its human equivalent in the click sound found in various African languages, particularly those of Khoisan origin among whom it originated. ('The *nc* gives a click sound. It is the same sound as when you reprimand a child – *tsk tsk*. So the imitation call of the bird *nci nci* would also be a clicking sound.')[8] *Nci nci* is a shortened form of the word 'help' (*nceda!*), and was interpreted as the cisticola's cry of alarm as it was chased by predators.

Although Neddicky seems a pale and impoverished facsimile of the vibrant, extraordinary Khoisan-derived click, nevertheless it is probably the only standardised English name in bird nomenclature that incorporates that uniquely African linguistic component. One final speculation: if this click-derived bird name was confirmed to have originated with the San people (now associated with the Kalahari Desert), the oldest surviving members of the human race, then this may be the oldest, widely used, extant bird name for any species on Earth.

Most cisticolas may not have any cultural profile, but it is their general insignificance which has placed emphasis on one of their number. The **Cloud Cisticola** *Cisticola textrix* occurs in a broad arc through the eastern half of South Africa and is widely known for its hard, rhythmic, percussive 'clappering' note – exceptional, in fact, in a bird so small –

which is delivered as it performs a remarkably high dancing flight. Sometimes it is so high it cannot even be seen with binoculars, and an old name was 'Cloud-scraping Cisticola'. The prominence of the song display led to its inclusion in a number of folk stories among various ethnic communities.

The best known of these tells of the king of the birds. It is an apparently traditional story found widely across southern Africa. In a version recorded in the Transkei region of the Eastern Cape in the early twentieth century, the central drama involves a competition organised by all the birds to find a suitable leader from among their number. With the jackal acting as overall judge, each species flies as high as possible. None can apparently fly higher than the vulture but, just as jackal asks him to return to Earth as victor, all the assembled birds are startled to observe the tiny silhouette of a Cloud Cisticola emerging from concealment in the vulture's plumage and briefly flying higher still.

The mite flies down and is duly crowned king, but some birds accuse him of cheating, at which he instantly vanishes into a hole. While owl is set to guard the crevice, the others go in search of something with which to dig him out and, when they finally return to discover that the cisticola has escaped, they are as angry with owl as they are with the initial fugitive. Owl then vanishes down the hole and to this day he is hated by other birds and obliged to fly by night.[9]

The tale is remarkable for its virtually identical structure to a European story of the Winter Wren and its own election as king of the birds. In fact it is so similar, it seems likely that one is the source for the other, and most probably the myth travelled from Europe to southern Africa (see Wren Legends, page 448). Yet the African account is notable for its close observance of genuine behaviour. The sky-scraping display of the Cloud Cisticola fits nicely with a story about a high flier. A second resonant detail is how the cisticola manages to elude the other birds, which seems a perfect example of the family's gift for escapology.

There is a final addendum to the tale. The Cloud Cisticola's Xhosa name – *Igqaza* – is the same as that for Wing-snapping Cisticola, and exactly which bird was intended in their version (Xhosa is the predominant language of the Transkei area) is a moot point.[10] Equally in a contemporary Zulu telling of this widespread tale another member of the family, the Neddicky, is clearly intended as the central character. Yet the story's underlying moral is unaffected, because all these cisticolas are tiny, 'insignificant' birds and each serves to reinforce the central message that outward appearances can be deceptive.

One oddity among the allies of the cisticolas is the **Grey-capped Warbler**, a species whose eponymous scientific name, *Eminia lepida*, honours a character noted for his extraordinary internationalism. Emin Pasha (1840-1892), as he became known, was born in Silesia (now in Poland) as Eduard Carl Oscar Theodor Schnitzer. A man of many talents, he spoke Albanian, German, French, English, Greek, Italian and Turkish, as well as Arabic and a number of African languages. He first worked as a medical doctor for the Turks in Albania, but later offered his services to the British colonial government in Egypt, becoming the governor of Equatoria (now in Sudan).[11] 'His' warbler occurs from the south of that country to northern Tanzania and has no cultural associations, but some birds seem determined to force themselves upon human attention:

These warblers are normally extremely shy and very difficult to see, so I was more than a little surprised when my wife, Val, told me that she was feeding a male Grey-capped Warbler with mealworms. A feature of Grey-capped Warblers is their very loud song and within a very short time 'Graham' would announce himself (with a burst of song) that he was ready for some mealworms. Eventually, this normally shy bird started entering the dining room and demanding food. After a year he would even pass through the dining room into the lounge and announce his presence. To see and hear Graham sitting on our coffee table was quite an experience both visually and audibly. We almost had to put our fingers in our ears as his demanding song was so loud in a confined space. Unfortunately, his 'wife' never became tame and although we could sometimes see her she would never approach closely to be fed. One year they started to build a nest close (3 m) to our kitchen but, unfortunately, bush squirrels found this nest and destroyed it. One year Graham started to introduce his two offspring to us and, although they would approach quite close to be fed, they never became quite as friendly as Graham. After about ten years he was obviously getting old and one day my wife actually picked him up and gave him some Rescue Remedy [a proprietary herbal essence for stress], this helped for a few days but eventually he disappeared.[12]

Another genus within the *Cisticolidae* family is *Prinia*, which includes 23 species that are split fairly evenly between Asia and Africa. These long-tailed warbler-like birds share the general cultural anonymity of cisticolas, but one species bucks the trend. The **Graceful Prinia** *Prinia gracilis* straddles both continents from the Horn of Africa eastwards across to Myanmar. It is a tiny streaky mite, half of whose length is made up by a tail that the bird holds erect and wags as it moves. In fact the striking disproportions in a Graceful Prinia's build make it seem at times more tail than bird.

In Israel it can be found everywhere including city gardens, and the blend of its jaunty manner, confiding behaviour and busy personality has made it popular with the public. Even the pleasing disyllable by which it is known in Hebrew, *pashosh*, suggests affection. 'The name was mentioned in ancient Jewish texts (by the way, in Arabic, which is close to Hebrew, it is called *fsisi*).'[13] In 2008 the *pashosh* was one of ten candidates for Israel's national bird (see also Hoopoe family, page 326) and, although it was not chosen, the bird is embedded in Israeli culture.

> *Pashosh* is a synonym for something very small and a frequent term of endearment especially for children. It is used regularly in the names of childcare centres or kindergartens. It was also the name of a children's magazine in Israel in the 1980s. The word appears in many children books and songs, but I think another reason for the success of the name is because mothers think it sounds so cute.[14]

The word has acquired status as a general term of affection even for adults, in the manner that 'hen' might be used in Scotland, 'duck' in northern England or *caille* ('quail') in France.

Tailorbird family *Orthotomus*

They are perhaps eclipsed by the weavers of Africa (see page 490) but the largely Asian tailorbirds are still well known, and were once even more famous, for the quality of their 'needlework'. These talents are manifest in their exquisitely stitched nests and are honoured in the generic name *Orthotomus*, which derives from a Greek verb meaning 'to cut straight'.[1] The 'wonderful nest', wrote one Victorian authority, 'may be seen in almost every museum and read of in many books'.[2] If it is not quite so familiar today, it is still regularly cited as one of the more remarkable creations in the Animal Kingdom.

The family comprises 18 small warbler-like species, the majority of which are Oriental in distribution with eight relatives found in sub-Saharan Africa. The best known and most widespread is the **Common Tailorbird** *Orthotomus sutorius*. It ranges from Pakistan east to China and south as far as Indonesia, but in the Indian subcontinent it is abundant almost nationwide, from dense forests to inner-city gardens and parks, where the bird's relentless loud, plaintive monosyllables are recognised as one of the signature sounds of the whole country.

The tailorbird nest is built during India's torrid pre-monsoon heat or at the time of the rains themselves.

Broad evergreen leaves are folded together by the female and threaded to one another using vegetable floss. The leaf forms a neat cone into which the bird inserts a tiny fibre nest meshed together with spider's web and occasionally threads of cotton, string, wool and other human debris.

These construction methods form the basis of their names in several Indian languages, such as Gujarati (*Darjido*: 'tailor'), Hindi (*Darzee*: 'tailor') and, most accurately, in Urdu (*Darza*: 'tailoress').[3] It is also known as *cháng-wei féng-yè-yīng* ('long-tailed sew-leaf warbler') in China, *o-naga saihō-chō* ('long-tailed sewing-bird') in Japan and *Chi Chích bông* ('cotton warbler') in Vietnam.[4]

Another Indian name for the bird is *Tuntuni*, which features in a series of traditional Bengali folk tales about the adventures of one of these endearing little birds. Both the name and the character of Tuntuni were popularised in a book published in 1911, *Tuntuni'r Boi*, by the writer and artist Upendrakishore Ray (father to the more famous author Sukumar Ray, and grandfather to the world-renowned film director Satyajit Ray). In these children's stories the bird has a pert, loud-voiced and rather cheeky personality in keeping with the manner and relentless vocalisations of the real species.[5]

Bulbul family *Pycnonotidae*

If there were a logical correlation between a bird family's cultural importance and its abundance in places where humans also congregate, then the bulbuls would be a group of major significance. What is striking is the way that they are numerous and familiar across major parts of Africa and Asia, including the interiors of many cities, yet with all this ubiquity goes our equally widespread indifference to them.

The exemplar is the **Common Bulbul** *Pycnonotus barbatus*, a species described as 'probably the most familiar bird in Africa'.[1] It occurs across most of the continent with the exception of two desert regions: the Sahara and Kalahari – a distribution that closely mirrors our own and probably says much about the species' remarkable adaptation to us. Yet its reception by its human neighbours is well summarised by the renowned Kenyan birdwatcher Terry Stevenson, who notes how the Common Bulbul 'is in the genus *Pycnonotus*, a name that people commonly modify to "take-no-notice"!'[2] (The odd-sounding name is derived from Greek and actually means 'thick-backed', a reference to the bulbul's dense plumage.)[3]

In fairness, many members of the bulbul family have good reason to enjoy their cultural anonymity. There are 132 species in total, split fairly evenly between two regions – Africa and its islands (69 species) and Asia (63 species). Of these a very high percentage are strictly inhabitants of forest. Not only are they outside human ken because of this choice of habitat, but the bulbuls themselves are among the most difficult to recognise of all birds. The most extreme are the so-called greenbuls, which are concentrated in African rainforest. With the cisticolas (see page 427) they rank among that continent's most impenetrable of identification challenges. More than 55 species cluster in a narrow size range of *c*.15–20 cm (6–8 in) and have plumages that fall within a colour spectrum of greenish brown to brownish green. The identification of greenbuls can be a nightmare in olive.

A more noteworthy characteristic of a good number of greenbuls, such as the **Red-tailed Bristlebill** *Bleda syndactylus* and **Green-tailed Bristlebill** *Bleda eximius*, is a habit of attending swarms of safari ants of the genus *Dorylus* (Bleda, incidentally, was both brother and murder victim of Attila the Hun, and one of the more unlikely sources of eponymous names for African endemic birds).[4] When hunting, these insects spread out across the forest in great susurrating carpets of black chitin, their pincers waving and intent on devouring most creatures in their path. The greenbuls follow them in the hope of cashing in on the invertebrate bow-wave that retreats from the ants' course across the forest floor. In fact, birds of all kinds follow ant swarms for this very reason. These extraordinary scenes of multiple killers – there can be 20 million ants in a single colony – and panic-stricken escapees are one of the most fascinating predation scenarios in all African nature, equal to a lion kill, or a cheetah running down its antelope prey. The greenbuls seem to partake of the atmosphere of intense life-and-death excitement and their vocalisations are loud and constant.

In fact, the sounds of greenbuls are among the best ways to identify them. Mercifully they can often be voluble birds even without the stimulus of ants. The song of a quintessentially olive species such as the east African **Sombre Greenbul** *Andropadus importunus* is described as 'persistent to the point of annoyance'.[5] The bird's scientific name actually means 'importunate'. (A somewhat suggestive mnemonic for the song is 'WILLIE, run around the bush and squeeze-me!')[6] However, it is the name of another Kenyan species, the **Joyful Greenbul** *Chlorocichla laetissima*, that better conveys the signature quality of bulbul sounds. They have an irrepressible jauntiness and while they might not be particularly beautiful or melodious, they are undeniably cheerful. *Chip, chop, chip* – often rendered as *quick, doctor, quick* – is a classic transliteration of the slovenly if jolly notes of the Common Bulbul.

The name 'bulbul' is itself often thought to be mimetic of birdsong. However, there is a fundamental complication, whose origins date back at least 1,500 years, that centres on which bird exactly this disyllable was intended to invoke. Regardless of which language or pronunciation is used (since the word is universal in Arabic, Persian, Urdu and Hindu and from these Asiatic languages it has been transferred almost worldwide), the name's simple repetition of two fulsome rounded syllables could easily be thought to evoke the merry notes of a real bulbul. The problem is that for many hundreds of years the word *bulbul* was used specifically in Persian poetry to evoke a very different species, the Common Nightingale. (*Bulbul* or *bolbol* is still used for that bird in Iran and *Bülbül* in Turkey. Another Iranian name for the Common Nightingale is *hazar dastan*.)[7]

There is an extraordinary tradition in classical Persian verse of works that dwell on the love affair between the nightingale (*bulbul*) and the rose (*gul*). Of all literary motifs drawing primarily upon birds, this is surely among the most important in the entire canon of human writings, yielding a subtle, complex imagery that in the hands of great Persian masters, such as the poets Rumi (1207–1273) or Hafiz (no birth date and died *c*.1388), allowed them to explore fundamental human experiences of love and religious faith. It is under the nightingale that this remarkable body of poetry is considered (see page 478).

However, the question of how 'bulbul' came to be applied both to a species of Old World chat (Common Nightingale) and to members of the family *Pycnonotidae*, and also the complications that this conflation has caused, are all dealt with here. The first thing to note is that this symbolic bird is deeply embedded in Islamic culture from Moorish Spain to Mogul India, but also across the whole of contemporary Muslim society. In Tunis' famous kasbah, where my wife once bought a silver bracelet several years ago, she was reassured by a dealer that the unidentifiable bird depicted in the intricate mosaic of natural motifs was a bulbul. The same bird is recurrent in Islamic craftworks.

There is a musical instrument, an Indian blend of strings and keyboard, known as the 'bulbul tarang' (literally 'waves of nightingales'). Artists, singers, writers are all commonly nicknamed 'bulbul' for the distinguished character of their respective performances. (The poet Hafiz was himself known as 'the bulbul of Shiraz'.) The bird is also constantly mentioned in musical lyrics. A perfect example is the bulbul

A saucy bird is the
Common Bulbul.

The White-eared Bulbul adds its portion of cheerful song and colour to many south Asian towns and gardens.

celebrated in the hauntingly beautiful traditional love song *Sakana Al Leyel*, performed by, among others, the Lebanese chantreuse Fairouz, the Middle East's most celebrated female vocalist. Two verses run:

> I hear the bulbul
> between the fields
> pouring its beautiful songs
> in a space
> where the hills exhale their basil fragrance
>
> Do not be afraid
> My baby girl
> Stars discreet keep their secrets
> And the mist of the night
> in these vineyards
> conceal secrets
> Do not be afraid . . .[8]

The second key observation is that these references to bulbuls are almost certainly the result of the Common Nightingale's initial fame in Persian and Arabic poetry. Only the vocalisations of the latter bird could have inspired this verse, with all its associative ideas of love as a source of profound personal and spiritual conflict, because only nightingale song has the kind of power, range and suggestive qualities to sustain such imaginative elaboration. 'Real' bulbul vocalisations, as previously noted, are pleasant but simple, irrepressibly cheerful, but without attributes to

excite either our own emotional intensity or its attendant artistic responses.

Before assessing how *the* bulbuls (*Pycnonotidae*) became so entangled with the *other* bulbul (Common Nightingale), we need to overlay the analysis with a further qualifying rider. All these birds of Persian and wider Arabic culture are really inhabitants of the imagination, appropriated to express human ideals or qualities. While the allusions once had direct reference to a real bird and a genuinely extraordinary song, the symbolism eventually floated free from any anchorage in observed natural history, especially as the motif has expanded its geographical range. The poetic *bulbul* is an idealised bird to suit human ends, and the poets or singers who invoked it may not always have cared which bird they were alluding to. Bulbul simply meant a wild creature of exquisite song. What an Iranian birdwatcher notes of his fellow citizens could probably be extended to the whole Islamic region: 'old people that knew less about birds used to call any good singing bird "bolbol"'.[9] At Xanthos, Turkey, a man told me that the bird in front of us was a 'bulbul'. It was actually a Western Rock Nuthatch.

The final point to make is that while Persian poets could easily and certainly did hear real nightingales, since the species breeds extensively in that country's central and northern areas, Muslim poets living elsewhere could not, or could not easily, have heard it. The bird breeds only in north Africa from Morocco to Tunisia, and occurs almost nowhere else in the Arab-speaking world except as a migrant. ('Common Nightingale is called *andaleb* or *muzghah* or *sifrid*, depending on the Arabic tribal area.'[10] An Iranian correspondent adds that '*Andalib* is a sort of old-fashioned name', still used also in Iran.) [11]

Yet Muslim poets could hear other birds called 'bulbul'. Members of the family *Pycnonotidae* are present across much of the region including major centres of Islamic culture, from Fez to Cairo, and from Damascus to Baghdad, Shiraz to Delhi. The three main species involved are the Common Bulbul (in north Africa; called *bulbul* or *balbool* in Arabic), the **White-spectacled Bulbul** *Pycnonotus xanthopygos* (found along the western Arabian Peninsula, north through Israel and southern Turkey; *bulbul asfar alagez* in Arabic) and the **White-eared Bulbul** *Pycnonotus leucotis* (found in eastern Arabia and through Iran into northern India; *bulbul abyad alagez* in Arabic, and *bulbul khorma*: 'date-tree bulbul' in Iran). Then across the Indian subcontinent there are two secondary representatives: the **Red-vented Bulbul** *Pycnonotus cafer* and **Red-whiskered Bulbul** *Pycnonotus jocosus*. The Arabic names for these two birds are respectively *bulbul ahmer alagez* and *bulbul ahmer alwigna*.[12]

The relative distributions of the two kinds of 'bulbul' (*Luscinia* and *Pycnonotus*) meant that what began in Persia as a response to nightingales, continued in the nightingale-free areas with a handy substitute. The creatures most likely to serve that end were the birds most intimately connected with human habitation, and if the songs of bulbuls were simpler, they were at least a solid understudy for the real voice of Persian verse.

In many parts of south Asia where bulbuls occur there is a widespread tradition of keeping them as cagebirds. Various species are held but in India the Red-vented and Red-whiskered Bulbuls are often the pets of choice for their lively songs and habits (the latter's scientific name, *jocosus*, means 'merry'). However, there was a further tradition of keeping bulbuls as fighting birds. Gambling on the outcome of organised contests was a major component of this activity.[13] Elsewhere in the Islamic world, they are also kept simply as attractive pets. A former resident of Baghdad describes the folkloric beliefs that attach to the birds:

> When I was a little girl we used to have a bulbul at home; an old lady used to work for us as a housekeeper and one of her jobs was to look after the bulbul. Every day in the morning she used to clean the cage, which was made of palm tree leaves, and also clean the small bowls of water and food and put out fresh water and new food. As I remember she used to finely cut parsley as food for the bulbul. One of the funniest things which I remember, she used to advise me and my sister to drink the leftover water of the bulbul in the morning before we went to school, as she used to say it would make us think better and answer all the questions in the exam. At that time they didn't know there was something called 'bird flu'.[14]

Often one does not need to keep bulbuls to achieve intimacy with them. The Common (Africa), White-spectacled or White-eared (Middle East) and Red-vented Bulbuls (India) can be so tame as to seem domesticated. They will routinely enter public buildings, boats, houses and their verandahs, or live almost permanently in the enclosed gardens and courtyards that are such a part of Islamic architecture. They are habitual attendees of any kind of al fresco activity, and especially love the tabletops of outdoor restaurants or cafes, where they and the human customers are often serenaded by Islamic popular music replete with its bulbul associations. Sometimes scores of birds will attend the leftovers and their diet is extraordinarily catholic. A single observer noted Common Bulbuls eating 50 types of fruit. 'I feed my Common Bulbuls in Arusha [Tanzania] over-ripe bananas; impaling them on a stick lengthways as a fiscal shrike might!'[15]

The following, however, speaks eloquently not just of bulbul catholicity but also the robustness of their alimentary system:

> When I lived at Baringo we grew many types of hot chillies that I collected from my travels around Africa and Madagascar. Some of these, particularly the tiny ones, were incredibly hot, and even serious chilli addicts found several of these virtually impossible to eat. The Common Bulbuls however would just sit on the bush and gulp down one after the other – quite extraordinary – talk about ring-sting![16]

In Liberia the species is known as the 'pepper bird' and is a national symbol.

The Common Bulbul's appetite for other types of human food is remarkable. A Kenyan ornithologist, who reared one as a chick, started 'Splat' ('for obvious reasons') on syringes full of banana and papaya, graduated to avocado pear and then moved to tomato, bread, butter, jam, cheese, biscuits, cake, egg and chips, raw mince and the lumps of peel out of marmalade. However, 'the quivering wings and wide open beak gave the most excited display when minced meat came by'.

Splat's keeper further noted that:

> A tame bulbul is no respector [*sic*] of persons, and apart from taking the food off your fork, will stick his beak in your eye, your ear, up your nose and even silence talk by waiting, poised for your mouth to open, and then stick his beak in and pick your teeth. The amateur ornithologist must feel deflated when a bulbul perches on the binoculars and peeps over the top, in through the lens. You wear spectacles, he sits on them. You don't wear spectacles, your nose will do, but he will talk to you all the time.

One small consolation in rearing bulbuls was that, while the bird ate the olives out of dry martinis, Splat left the alcohol.[17]

The frequent impression given by truly wild bulbuls of their habituation to humans needs to be qualified by adding that, rather like sparrows (see page 483), they will cheekily take advantage, but are invariably wary and watchful. This mixture of opportunism and aloofness may be one reason why, as we noted at the beginning, bulbuls exist at the periphery of human attention. Another factor may be that their penchant for urban life makes them seem too human in character and too lacking in a sense of otherness for us to be moved by them, and we simply take them for granted.

Yet it is this familiarity of bulbuls that can triumph over us and lead even to deep affection. In 2007, as the Israeli people debated their choice of a national bird symbol, the journalist Avirama Golan, in gloriously anthropomorphic style, made a plea for her candidate, the White-spectacled Bulbul.

> The bulbul . . . suits us because of its name – stolen from the Arabic like hummus and falafel, which became the 'Israeli national dish' exported in our name – and because of its distribution: it is present everywhere in Israel . . . People in the know attest to the fact that the bulbul's noise and chirping is varied: from the wakeful morning song . . . to the heated quarrelling of two bulbuls who were closest friends only a moment ago. And if that is not enough, the bulbul, unlike any other bird, does not limit itself to chirping and dancing as a form of communication. In other words, a handshake and polite greeting is not its style. Two bulbuls that meet are so overcome by affection that they trample each other's heads, touch, taunt each other, and jump around as if they ate from the same mess kit for years.

Those who object to the choice of the bulbul because of the sexual innuendos associated with its name (slang for 'penis' in Hebrew) are missing the main point. That folksy usage of the unpretentious bird's name to describe the male genital organ proves the extent to which the bird is loved by the masses. This is not a crude or insulting expletive, but a childish term of affection that illustrates how Israelis relate to themselves: oversized, pampered infants for ever. There is no doubt that the bulbul is ours: loud, quick to anger, lavishing gregarious affection, and in love with his friends. He makes noise as he brags to his pals about his exploits, and calls himself affectionate names. He doesn't stop singing even as he is joyfully robbing fruit from others in true bulbul style.[18]

Alas, the bulbul's role as Israel's classic double entendre for the male organ probably doomed it to third place although, as the originator of the competition notes darkly, 'I suspect foul play.'[19]

Old World Warbler family *Sylviidae*

This family of 281 mainly small species occurs right across the Old World, from the Atlantic islands off African shores to the numerous island chains in the Pacific Ocean. There are major concentrations in the southern hemisphere, with 55 and 89 species breeding respectively in the Oriental and Afrotropical regions. However, this understates to some extent their prevalence in these two areas. Africa is typical. Approximately 40 additional species of warbler breed in the higher latitudes of Eurasia, but before the winter months of the northern hemisphere they make intercontinental migrations back to Africa. Come December that one continent holds almost half the family.

WARBLERS WITH BEAUTIFUL SONGS

Compared to the rainbow colours of New World warblers, these African and Asian birds are dowdy creatures and often remarkably similar to one another. Old World warblers come in a wide range of browns and greys. To make them even more of an identification challenge they are also lovers of thick cover. The names of two genera – *Sylvia* (21 species) and *Phylloscopus* (58 species) – reflect these habitat preferences. The first means 'woodland sprite', while the second means 'leaf seeker', suggesting the way these hyperactive birds flit at the twig ends in search of insects.[1] To compensate for any physical anonymity (which is much cherished by birders), warblers can have distinctive and even beautiful songs.

The Common Grasshopper Warbler is one of the bird world's great escapologists. An individual may migrate back and forth through some of the most densely populated parts of Europe without ever being spotted by human eyes.

The Willow Warbler migrates out of Africa to breed across a vast swathe of Eurasia and brings with it a song as soft as summer rain.

It is often by voice that they are easiest to recognise and sometimes this is the only means of detecting them. The *Locustella* warblers (nine species) are the ultimate skulkers. In fact, the generic name means roughly 'little grasshopper'.[2] They both behave and sound like invertebrates, burrowing into dense vegetation where they are usually revealed only by the flow of softly undulating mechanical notes that resemble the stridulations of insects. A species such as the **Common Grasshopper Warbler** *Locustella naevia* is *the* classic avian escapologist. An individual of this largely invisible species may breed in southern Scandinavia and pass annually back and forth to its winter quarters in Senegal. Over the course of its short existence it may make this extraordinary journey eight times, and so traverse repeatedly some of the most populous human regions on Earth. Yet it may conduct its entire life without ever once being glimpsed by any of us.

Warbler voices can still manage to have a major impact upon people, softening the atmosphere of otherwise austere northern landscapes in a way that few Old World birds can match. It is perhaps a measure of the effect of these songs of the south that in Ireland and Scotland, where no true nightingale ever performed, the **Sedge Warbler** *Acrocephalus schoenobaenus* was known either as the 'Irish' or 'Scotch nightingale'.[3] The vernacular names accrued partly on account of the bird's nocturnal singing, but they also suggest the way in which the audience discerned in the bird's rich vocalisations a sense of the exotic and the foreign.

My own personal encounter with this warbler effect occurred during my childhood. The **Willow Warbler** *Phylloscopus trochilus* is an Afro-Palearctic migrant, wintering in a wide belt of sub-Saharan Africa then spreading to breed across the boreal regions of Eurasia, from easternmost Siberia to the Atlantic coasts of Ireland. In the 1970s I intercepted this momentous, two-way, intercontinental

wave of Willow Warblers – at one time possibly involving as many as 2 billion birds – in northern England during April.[4] The species produces a gently descending cadence and the songs of rival males perpetually overlap, so that the Willow Warblers' collective music falls on the post-winter world of Derbyshire's gritstone hills like a warm shower of rain.

Willow Warbler song, however, is such a ubiquitous sound in some landscapes that it is almost unavoidable. That, at least, was the experience of the makers of the film *Cold Mountain* (2003), directed by Anthony Minghella. Based on a novel by Charles Frazier and set at the time of the American Civil War in North Carolina, it involves battle scenes supposedly located at Petersburg in Virginia. Unfortunately there are Willow Warblers' voices to be heard – when they have never truly sung in Virginia – reflecting the fact that the action was shot *c.*7,732 km (*c.*4,800 miles) away from Petersburg in the Carpathian Mountains of Romania. It is one of the many examples of how birds betray the real places behind the fiction of cinematography (see Old World Partridge, page 52).

A more obvious consequence of the beautiful song of many warblers was the tradition of trapping and keeping them as household pets. During the nineteenth century the sweet voice of the **Eurasian Blackcap** *Sylvia atricapilla* made it one of the most popular cagebirds in continental Europe.[5] Another victim was the **Great Reed Warbler** *Acrocephalus arundinaceus*, whose history as a parlour bird reveals another characteristic of warbler vocalisations. Some birds, especially the *Acrocephalus* warblers (37 species), are brilliant mimics and often incorporate a large range of borrowed sounds into their performances. Young caged Great Reed Warblers were apparently placed in proximity to singing nightingales and soon added passages from these other incomparable songsters to their own repertoire.[6]

The illegal trapping of Old World warblers, such as this Eurasian Blackcap, is a scandal that blights the reputations of several Mediterranean countries.

TRAPPING AND EATING WARBLERS

It may surprise some to learn that the main cultural encounter with Old World warblers flowed not from their wonderful voices, but from their delicious flavours. Despite weighing no more than 25–50 g (*c*.1–2 oz), many of these birds are highly regarded as food. The practice of catching and eating them is ancient and survives still as a source of ever-intensifying bitter controversy between modern environmentalists and traditional bird trappers.

There are references to the birds in *The Art of Cooking* (*De Re Coquinaria*), Europe's oldest volume of recipes and once attributed to a bon viveur of the early imperial age called Marcus Apicius. In fact, the recipes date from the fourth or fifth century AD, but they illuminate a taste for what the Romans called *ficedula* and what many Europeans referred to historically as *beccafico* and alternately as *beccafigo* or *beccafiche*. (Today in Italy small warblers are known as *uccellini* and in the northern Italian region of Brescia, where the consumption of songbirds is still commonplace, they are known as *polenta osei*, the latter a dialect word for 'songbirds'.) The old names, *ficedula* and *beccafico*, mean 'figpecker' and echo an original word coined in ancient Greece. Aristotle, for instance, mentions what was presumably a species of *Sylvia* warbler (possibly Eurasian Blackcap) as *sykalis*, which means much the same as its Roman and modern Italian equivalent, a 'fig-eating bird'.[7] It derives from a habit among several warblers of feeding upon cultivated and wild fruits, especially figs, and particularly in autumn.

A good deal of ink has been spilt in trying to identify the original figpecker, as if it could be ascribed to a single entity that modern taxonomists would call a species. The two most likely candidates, each of them genuinely fond of fruit, are the Eurasian Blackcap and the **Garden Warbler** *Sylvia borin*.[8] Both birds are common across Europe in summer and concentrate in the Mediterranean region during their autumn migration, when they were harvested in large numbers. However, one needs to caution against over-precision.

The truth is that both of these warblers are part of a massive, two-way flow of small migrant birds that are funnelled by geography out of the vastness of Africa each spring, into the bottleneck of the Mediterranean, and then out again across the even greater vastness of Eurasia. Many of the species, including not just a dozen or more Old World warblers, but also shrikes, thrushes, chats, pipits, larks and buntings, are all trapped and eaten and have been so probably since the Neolithic and possibly earlier. To our ancestors this cataract of protein bursting through the region each spring and autumn was manna from heaven.

In an age when our own contact with avian flesh is often mediated by supermarkets and cling film and centres on just two or three domesticated birds, we can hardly grasp how indiscriminate were the appetites of the past. Only in places such as New Guinea can we possibly glimpse the same kind of undifferentiated palate. Today in remote parts of that extraordinary island one is still met with looks of complete confusion when its inhabitants are asked which birds do they eat. All birds, they reply, puzzled that the question should be necessary. Precisely the same breadth of harvest existed once in Europe, and it is the vestige of this wholesale killing and careless consumption that so exercises the modern world.

Given the uncritical nature of former tastes we should be reluctant to fix the term *beccafico* on to one single species. Those who coined it probably had in mind all small birds. True, they were usually made sweet by a diet of fruit, especially in autumn, and by the deposits of fat on their breasts accrued to undertake their migrations, but it was not essential. What made the bird a *beccafico* was the common fact that it had been caught for the pot. Today in Greek-

speaking Cyprus, where such scraps of wild protein are still trapped and consumed amid political controversy, an element of ambiguity is implicit in the catch-all name for the victims. They are known as *ambelopoulia*, 'vine birds'.

The attempts to stop this tragic harvest are now such an emotionally charged part of European conservation that it is difficult even to mention that *beccafico* once had the highest culinary reputation, or to acknowledge that the two recipes in *The Art of Cooking* sound – frankly – delicious. One involves mashed asparagus seasoned with wine, herbs and oil mixed with eggs and finely chopped *beccafico*, and baked in moulds. A second, known as the Apician dish, mixed pork belly with fish, chicken and breasts of figpeckers or thrushes finely minced, cooked with herbs and raisin wine and steamed in layers of meat and pancake.[9]

A common practice was for the *beccafico* to be minced together and stuffed into larger roasts, such as pigs or other birds. Or they were served as hors d'ouevres before the main dish. In *The Satyricon* (see also Eating Thrushes, page 468), Petronius describes how Trimalchio presents his guests with a wooden chicken under which are peahen eggs, encrusted in rich pastry and filled with figpeckers in seasoned egg yolks.[10]

It is hard now to recover just how integrated was the harvest of warblers and other small birds into the social and commercial life of the region. However, John Ray noted in the late seventeenth century:

> *Beccafigo's* abound in *Candy* [Crete] . . . and also in the Island of *Cyprus*, where they are salted up in great numbers, and transported into other Countries. With us in *England* they are called by a general name, *Cyprus-birds*, and are in no less esteem with our Merchants for the delicacy of their taste, than they were of old with the *Italians* . . . *Beccafigo's* are accounted best and most in

season in the Autumn, as being then fattest by reason of the plenty of meat that season affords them. At which time they are highly prized and coveted by the Italians even now adays.[11]

In his account of wartime Italy, *Naples '44*, the great English travel writer Norman Lewis described his own hunting excursion for *beccafiche*. The 18 birds they captured and subsequently ate were taken using a lark mirror and shotgun, and they included not only larks, but buntings, wheatears, chats and various warblers (see also Exploitation of Larks, page 425). He also illuminated the intense passion of Neapolitans for the sport and cuisine associated with these tiny birds. King Ferdinand (1751–1825) was reputed to have developed his palace at nearby Capodimonte and then built himself an access road from Naples at a cost of several million ducats, all because the hill site of his residence lay on the migration route for the warblers. It was said – probably more as a nice conceit than as a true appraisal of royal finances – that Ferdinand's precious birds, each weighing a few grams, had cost the nation a thousand ducats apiece.[12]

THE MODERN CONTROVERSIES OF *BECCAFICO* AND *AMBELOPOULIA*

The case for ending the consumption of Old World warblers in the Mediterranean region seems as simple and visceral as it is overwhelming. All the species consumed are protected by common European Union law and often by additional legislation at a national level. Opponents of the practices point out that they are not only covered by legal prohibition: the harvest is unnecessary and serves no subsistence function at all. What was once essential protein is today mere luxury.

Yet perhaps the most powerful part of the environmental

A plate of *ambelopoulia* is a dish steeped in controversy, flavoured with illegality and, for some Cypriots, laced with cultural significance.

case is the grimly indiscriminate nature of the cull. Two major techniques are employed to trap birds: firstly, nets of various kinds, including the large mesh walls normally used by bird ringers. The other method widely adopted on Cyprus involves sticks or poles, often cut from pomegranate bushes, smeared with a highly adhesive substance. In Cyprus this is invariably derived from the fruits of a non-native Asian tree known as Syrian Plum (*Cordia myxa*). The finished products are traditionally called limesticks, and are now deployed in conjunction with hi-tech sound-recordings of the vocalisations of target species such as Eurasian Blackcap. In practice they catch everything that has the misfortune to mistake the lethal glue traps for perches.

The birds become increasingly enmeshed as they struggle to escape and in high temperatures they sometimes expire of heat exhaustion. Even birds as large as Montagu's Harriers and species that have no food value (e.g. Eurasian Scops Owls) fall prey to this revolting gunk. Victims of all the various techniques now number 122 bird species on Cyprus alone.[13] This regularly includes not just ten to 15 species of Old World warbler, but also European Turtle Doves, European Rollers, European Bee-eaters, Eurasian Wrynecks, Eurasian Golden Orioles, Red-backed, Masked and Woodchat Shrikes, Common Nightingales and even chameleons. Unfortunately the trappers are susceptible to a superstition that if any birds are set free, the site at which they were caught would be ruined. As a consequence they kill everything without exception.

A core source of the high emotions against the practice is the fact that these birds are not resident in southern Europe. They are migrants on their way to higher latitudes. In those places they are not looked upon as potential titbits of food; they are cherished elements of the northern summer. One contributor emphasises his own deep attachment to a species long considered to be the definitive *beccafico*:

One of my favourite songs is by a real virtuoso that I hear less and less these days, the Garden Warbler. Its notes when in full flow are rich, fluty, varied, and have subtle modulations with mimicry. I've detected blackbird, chaffinch and Great Tit in the song and I've been quite mesmerised by a particular bird singing just above me in the top of a hedge in full sun and quite unconcerned by my presence. Surely the Garden Warbler is greatly underrated in the birding world.[14]

It is this sense of common connection to birds killed and eaten specifically in southern Europe that has inspired major campaigns among conservation organisations located in the north, such as the Committee Against Bird Slaughter (Germany) or the Royal Society for the Protection of Birds (UK). The Europe-wide scale of the opposition is an undoubted strength, but it is also in some ways a weakness. On the ground the German or British activists smashing down nets and dismantling the limestick death traps are all just 'foreigners' in the eyes of the Italian or Cypriot trappers.

To them this is outside interference in traditions that date back hundreds, if not thousands, of years. Nor, it has to be said, has such external pressure brought the results for which conservationists had hoped. A recent report on Cyprus noted that the local authorities and the British administration that oversees a small territory known as the Sovereign Base Areas were 'losing the battle against this illegal activity'.[15]

Sample surveys on Cyprus suggested that trapping hugely increased in 2011 compared to 2009 (a rise of 86 per cent) and the total number of casualties estimated for the island as a whole was 1.9 million birds. The authorised task forces and volunteer activists confiscated 582 nets and 4,288 limesticks just in the autumn of 2011, sparing the lives of an estimated 630,000 birds. Unfortunately, the tradition of eating 20 g warblers remains rooted in the hearts of some Cypriot people. Why?

One reason is that it is big business. Trappers are said to be able to earn the equivalent of £30,000 ($45,000) from a few weeks' work. In the restaurants these bite-sized scraps of fatty pleasure sell for the equivalent of £3 ($4.50) each. A full plate of 12 birds costs a small fortune. In the course of research an anonymous witness (who is, nevertheless, a passionate conservationist) sampled the forbidden pleasures of *ambelopoulia*:

> When the birds arrived – the traditional dozen, all naked and swimming in fat – I suddenly lost my appetite. As I was the guest the plate was offered to me first, so I took two birds, probably blackcaps, with some chips. I cut a small piece from the bird and the taste was a pleasant surprise, reminding me instantly of the liver my mother cooked for us as kids. Indeed, I could see why they were considered tasty by my hosts and after getting over my initial reticence because of their appearance I finished by tucking into half a dozen, including a Great Reed Warbler. I refrained from eating the whole bird, but my hosts crunched on the heads too, leaving just the gizzard on their plates. The old trapper whose birds these were seemed pleased that a foreigner was enjoying them and he talked of trapping being his life. He trapped every day putting out around 400 limesticks and supplying two local restaurants. He admitted to hiding his birds in a hole in his garden in case he was ever raided by the police.[16]

The high prices paid at the point of consumption clearly provide a major incentive for the trappers. Nor are there great risks associated with these financial rewards, given that the fines for those caught red-handed are relatively small (400 euros). Such amounts could easily be recouped by a single night's trapping. (However, a more permanent deterrent may be effected by the recent penalty of 10,000 euros imposed on one restaurant owner caught with 2,000 birds in his premises.)[17]

Then there is the further issue of administrative tolerance. Sometimes this amounts to outright collusion by the authorities. On the southern Italian island of Ponza, where trapping is intense and often unopposed, one of the main shooters of European Turtle Doves is apparently an ex-chief of police. On Cyprus the all-comers' record for most *ambelopoulia* eaten at one sitting was 54. The capacious stomach accommodating that flock of songbirds belonged to a popular local politician.[18] Even if the trapping of small migrant birds is acknowledged as a criminal activity, it is often judged to be of low priority and undeserving of hard-pressed official resources. On Cyprus trappers are also thought to exploit areas that are near the boundary between the British-run Sovereign Base Areas and the Republic of Cyprus. Pursuit of trapping gangs is then complicated by issues of jurisdiction and may even draw in its wake larger strategic considerations between the different authorities.

At the very core of the controversy, of course, are the pleasant flavour and the cultural texture of the birds themselves, which conservationists find it difficult even to acknowledge. Anyone seeking to end the practice must first recognise that the wish to eat small warblers and other songbirds continues to make its expensive appeal to substantial numbers of Mediterranean people. On Cyprus, for instance, the traditional plate of a dozen birds is known in thinly veiled restaurant code as 'The Special One'. Conservationists may even have to confront the possibility that their own intense opposition to the eating of *ambelopoulia* or to other songbird-eating traditions adds spice to an already tasty dish.

Those who kill and cook the birds emphasise that the food is often associated with events that are already highly ritualised and loaded with a sense of family and community importance, such as weddings, christenings or special anniversaries. Cleaving to the ways of the past, in the teeth of what they would characterise as 'outside' persecution, could then be justified as a righteous gesture of national defiance. Like oysters, caviar or pâté de foie gras (see page 88) in other parts of the world, this is food dense with all sorts of historical and social meanings. High price, ancient tradition and cultural taboo form a heady mixture and it is unlikely that the consumption of warblers will end any time soon. Nor, too, will the opposition of environmentalists.

One of the most active opponents of the illegal killing of European songbirds is Andrea Rutigliano, an officer of the Committee Against Bird Slaughter, who combats warbler trapping in Cyprus as well as in the islands of his native Italy (especially Capri, Ischia, Ponza and Procida). Rutigliano, a small and slightly built figure, who has been beaten up in more than one country including Cyprus, describes some of the risks that he and his colleagues face on a routine basis:

> I began my work in the late 1990s when much of the real violence had already ended. At that time there were hundreds of incidents when activists were beaten with sticks by Italian hunters, or were punched in the face, had their noses broken, and were taken to hospital with injuries. They also had their car windows smashed, tyres slashed or the whole vehicle destroyed. One of the early activists was Piergiorgio Candela, who was very well known in the Brescia region of northern Italy, where hunters account for 2–3 million small birds a year, many of them killed illegally. At one time Candela was shot in the face at fairly close range and he only avoided major injury by covering his face with his hands.
>
> Once when I was doing work at the Colle San Zeno, where I documented the slaughter on a video you can see at 'Zugvogel-Massaker Colle San Zeno'; http://www.youtube.com/watch?v=YvraTjbOdDo, I was just about to drive down the hill in the dark when we heard a *puff*, *puff* sound like tyres bursting. I got out the car and could see that it was bullets that were stuck in the rubber housing around the window. The man who shot at me could never have seen in the dark if I had the window down or not. But if it had been down he would have shot the driver, we would have undoubtedly crashed and it could have killed not just me but my four passengers as well.
>
> Another time I was in the chestnut woods of Brescia with a female colleague and we found a couple of bow traps with thrushes in them. We stopped to release these but the birds were screaming and they betrayed our position to the hunters. Suddenly while we were treating the birds we heard a stone come crackling through the leaves. My colleague looked at me wide-

eyed and went silent. A couple of seconds later there was another crackling of leaves as an orange-sized stone came thundering towards us. There was a dog barking and I realised instantly that the hunters knew we were there and were throwing stones at us. If one of those rocks had caught us we would have been very badly injured. As we ran there were more stones falling and crashing until we left the scene.[19]

Andrea Rutigliano proposes the following figures across the Mediterranean region as a whole:

For passerines trapped legally (because of derogations from the EU legislation) or illegally we estimate 2.6 million in Spain, 1 million in France, 500,000 in Malta, 2.5 million in Italy and 3 million in Cyprus. Passerines that are legally shot in the 27 EU States (almost all in the Mediterranean) number 37.2 million, mainly thrushes, larks and corvids. Take out 3.5 million if you want to leave the legally killed corvids. Then there is a question of how many passerines are killed but not declared. According to some observers these could amount to 30 per cent of the declared total.[20]

The minimum grand total of small songbirds killed annually in the region is 43.3 million.

Babbler family *Timaliidae*

The 281 species in this huge family are in many ways the Old World counterparts of the ovenbirds, or furnariids, of the Americas (see page 356), in the sense that the babblers include an enormously diverse spectrum of bird shapes and bird lifestyles.

The **Giant Laughingthrush** *Garrulax maximus* of high-altitude forest in China, for instance, is a pale-eyed scrambler of 33 cm (13 in) which, with its long tail and white-spangled plumage, can look more like a small pheasant than a songbird. At the other extreme is the secretive, tailless **Pygmy Wren-Babbler** *Pnoepyga pusilla*, a bird smaller than the Winter Wren (9 cm: 3.5 in) that bounds like a dark ping-pong ball around the shadows and moss-covered boulders deep within Asian montane forests. There are also highly conspicuous arboreal members of the family, such as the brightly coloured sibias. At certain altitudes in the Himalaya, as long as some vestige of native vegetation survives, the **Rufous Sibia** *Heterophasia capistrata* seems to be draped on every tree and it feels almost impossible to escape the birds' loud, incessant, ever more irritating calls.

One notable overarching theme that spans the babbler family is their concentration in Asia. There are a couple of striking anomalies. The **Wrentit** *Chamaea fasciata*, the New World's only representative of this amorphous family, is a drab long-tailed skulker confined to dense chaparral along the USA's Pacific coastline. Europe too has a singleton: the **Bearded Reedling** *Panurus biarmicus*, or 'bearded tit' as it is often still named, occurs from Spain to China, but specialises across this vast expanse at wetland sites with phragmites reedbed. Of the remaining 279 birds, all but 34 (which occur in Africa) are Asian in distribution with the vast majority resident in the Oriental region. The northern boundary of this zoogeographical zone undulates east from Pakistan to the same latitude on China's east coast at Shanghai, and then it includes all the lands south and east as far as New Guinea (itself part of the Australasian region).

Babblers are a major part of the Oriental avifauna but especially in densely vegetated habitats. Like many forest birds they have made little impression on us and have few cultural associations. The exceptions are some of the laughingthrushes, which are hugely popular cagebirds, while the intensely sociable lifestyle of babblers in the genus *Turdoides* has also given rise to a significant body of folklore. Our wider silence on the group is itself striking and odd, given the enormous personality that many possess. Their very name gives a clue to this quality of intensity.

Babblers often associate in mix-species flocks and attract other camp-followers, including drongos, woodpeckers and fantails. These avian caravans can involve hundreds of individual birds and they roll through the forest in a self-generated envelope of hectic movement and explosive calls. Birds dart back and forth all around an observer, battering the senses in a frenzy of colour and noise. Then just as quickly as it flourished, the flock passes on, abandoning any slow-moving biped to the forest's silence and to a powerful impression of having witnessed something immensely vital and special. Occasionally babbler flocks make such a disturbance to the vegetation that, if the birds are not immediately visible, you could mistake them for a large, possibly dangerous mammal. A classic cause of heart-pounding excitement is the **White-crested Laughingthrush** *Garrulax leucolophus*, found across Asian forests from Kashmir to Sumatra, whose clamorous din has been likened to the yelping of a hound pack in full cry.[1]

> Reddish-brown hob-goblins with shining white caps flit through the bamboo canes, turn somersaults on liana swings, or rustle through the ground vegetation. Everywhere there is cracking and creaking in the branches, a whispering and murmuring, a mysterious hidden life. We will assume that you have observed all this from dense cover and now step slowly from behind the sheltering tree – a sudden rustle and flurry, then dead silence. You may see in the background three or four little red-brown imps, their white crests bristling with indignation, sitting almost motionless in a row on a bent bamboo pole. This breathless pause only lasts a second however. Then a brief, low chattering can be heard and immediately after this preliminary there starts up a chorus of diabolical cackling laughter, uttered with a precision worthy of a great orchestral conductor, the volume and vehemence of which is almost alarming.[2]

(One aspect of laughingthrushes that might have predisposed the German ornithologist G Heinrich to his vocabulary of hobgoblins and imps is their possession of eyes of pale or piercingly bright colour.)

On rare occasions laughingthrushes can be lured to close quarters in more tranquil circumstances, especially in places

A family party of White-crested Laughingthrushes can produce a chorus that sounds like 'a hound pack in full cry'.

The Hwamei is one of the most cherished cagebirds in all Asia.

languages, including the Japanese and Vietnamese versions (ironically, in Singapore it is often known by an English name: 'China thrush'). It is the **Hwamei** *Garrulax canorus*, a bird found from east and central China south to Laos and Vietnam. It resembles a small mid-brown thrush and its old English name was 'Melodious Laughingthrush', although Hwamei well captures its most arresting feature. A line of blue encircles the eye and then extends along the sides of the crown as a narrow eyebrow. Hwamei means 'painted eyebrow', although it is the species' renown as a vocalist that accounts for its popularity as a cagebird. The song is a loud sweet jumble of ringing notes interspersed with more complex tremulous warbling. The performance is now harnessed as part of the widespread Asian tradition of song competitions, although at one time Hwameis were kept for a different kind of sport.

The rather intense, feisty spirit manifest in the behaviour of many laughingthrushes was once exploited in Hwamei trapping, which involved a singing decoy bird being held in one compartment of a wire trap. His vocal challenge then lured competitors to enter the other side of the cage and eventually to snare themselves.[4] Works of Chinese ornithology from the early twentieth century talk of the Hwamei as 'a pugilist par excellence' and describe how birds were even pitted against one another like miniature fighting cocks, with large sums of money changing hands on the outcome.

What seems now a rather quaint fashion (an innocuous version of owning 'trophy' dog breeds by modern gang members) was the way that local toughs, during the late Qing Dynasty, would apparently carry a Hwamei in a cage held by a hook at the end of a pole. The bully walked along with the hook end pointing forwards and 'in those days, as recently as 1905, it was not a bird for respectable Chinkiang people [in the lower Yangtse region] to carry about'.[5] The keeping of Hwameis is now a more sedate part of Chinese life.

For 22 years I lived in Hong Kong. The crowded streets, the market stalls, the language, the steamy tropical climate mixed together in an intimidating cocktail of unquenchable activity. Only in the early morning, close to dawn, was there any sense of calm and it was then that an age-old custom unfolded. As the town was waking, men, short in stature and elderly, more often than not dressed all in black, a tunic shirt with a classic high-necked collar and three-quarter length baggy trousers, shuffled towards the nearest park. There they performed tai chi but each carried a cage, usually domed in shape with exquisitely formed, miniature, earthenware bowls for water and food. Atop the cage was a hook, the size of which would have satisfied the most demanding of maimed, swashbuckling buccaneers. The cage was hung from the bough of a tree while the owner carried out his stylised movements as precisely and in the same order as he had the morning before and the morning before that. Oriental Magpie-Robins and Yellow-fronted Canaries were favoured cagebirds much admired for their songs, but most prized was the Hwamei. The cage had been carried to the park decked in a dark cloth cover that was only removed as it was lifted towards its bough. And then the Hwamei would

where both humans and birds face common challenges. One such location is the Choktse Gompa, a Buddhist temple in Sichuan province, China, which lies at an altitude of *c*.3,600 m (11,800 ft). The main beneficiary of charity at this sacred spot is the neighbouring population of White Eared Pheasants, which have religious significance (see page 60), but other locals enjoy the handouts.

The monk, sitting cross-legged, shelled peanuts into his apron and the White Eared Pheasant gobbled them up. Yet the monk was also in the habit of putting cooked barley on a flat stone in front of the main temple building. This 'bird table' was aimed at any and all comers. As well as squirrels, it attracted a steady procession of birds and we saw Giant Laughingthrush, **Elliot's Laughingthrush** *Garrulax elliotii*, **Chinese Babax** *Babax lanceolatus*, as well as Rufous-breasted Accentor, Pink-rumped and White-browed Rosefinches all eating the same fistfuls of barley.[3]

The most widely appreciated of all China's 32 laughingthrushes is the one and only species that actually bears a name whose Chinese origins are evident in almost all

The beady-eyed
Jungle Babbler
is a bird of great
character and
occasional mischief.

sing, challenging neighbouring Hwameis imprisoned in similar cages.

Tai chi concluded, the men made for their regular tea-houses to meet and drink tea with other bird-fancier friends. Maybe it was wishful thinking but it was tempting to imagine these groups discussed little else but their birds, such was their preoccupation with them. A cage would be raised, held high from its base and twirled to demonstrate how calm and steady was the Hwamei inside. A fluttering bird had much to learn while a placid one was studied, admired and envied. A fascinating aspect of it all was that it prevailed as an entirely male preserve.[6]

The Hwamei-keeping habit has been exported to other countries in the region, including China's former colony Vietnam. A resident of the Vietnamese capital, Hanoi, describes the bird's place in national life:

I suspect most Hwameis are caught and sold locally, but it is possible they enter international trade in China or countries with large Chinese communities elsewhere in the region (Indonesia for example). The Vietnamese are incredibly brand conscious so, despite there being about 20 species of laughingthrush in Vietnam, only two are preferred as cagebirds, especially in the north: the Hwamei and **Black-throated Laughingthrush** *Garrulax chinensis* (southerners go for the White-rumped Shama). I suspect these two species account for 90 per cent of the trade. Both are great songsters, of course, and I am sure all laughingthrushes are kept for their songs rather than beauty. While it is rare to see other species in captivity, my neighbour in Hanoi keeps a solitary White-crested Laughingthrush not knowing that this

species sings a compound song requiring five to ten birds.[7]

The habit of keeping Hwameis in captivity has led to the establishment of feral populations in several countries including Japan and the USA (Hawaii). Their introduction to the latter archipelago was said to be a result of a fire in 1900 in the Chinese quarter of Honolulu, a story that has about it a whiff of urban myth.[8] There were certainly deliberate releases of Hwameis on a number of islands and the birds are still common on Hawaii, Kauai and Maui.[9]

Another non-native babbler, the strikingly beautiful **Red-billed Leiothrix** *Leiothrix lutea* ('leiothrix' is of Greek construction meaning 'smooth hair'), has also colonised some of the Hawaiian archipelago following deliberate releases, especially Hawaii, Maui and Oahu.[10] The species is cherished even by non-Asian bird fanciers, often under its old Europeanised sobriquet, 'Pekin robin', which alludes to the apricot suffusion on its breast. There is even a small free-flying population of this delightful bird in southern France.

The 29 species of babbler in the genus *Turdoides* (a word meaning 'thrush-like') have a wide distribution including much of Africa, the Middle East, south and south-east Asia. Predominantly brown with long tails and often with bright pale eyes, the birds are ground-dwelling lovers of brush and dry thickets. They are highly gregarious and are usually found in parties of six to 12 birds. In fact the *Turdoides* babblers are in many ways the meerkats of the bird world and have an intense, fascinating, highly developed social life.

This deeply rooted togetherness is expressed in collaborative breeding, the offspring and subordinate members of a clan helping to rear the young of the alpha female, but also in bouts of mutual preening or in roosting huddles, when all the birds nuzzle together in one long line on a traditional perch (the same spot can be used for years).[11] They also perform elaborate dance ceremonies and hold collective territories that they defend against rival babbler clans or potential predators. My earliest memory of seeing any babbler species – involving a group of **Fulvous Babbler** *Turdoides fulva* in southern Morocco in August 1979 – is dominated by the hullabaloo they raised at the sight of a 1.5 m (4.9 ft) black snake. Had it not been for the birds' feverish alarm I may never have detected what was very probably an Egyptian Cobra slithering across a grove metres from where I sat.

In India the rich communality expressed by this group of birds has led to several species acquiring the nickname the 'seven sisters'. These are the **Common Babbler** *Turdoides caudata*, **Jungle Babbler** *Turdoides striata* and **Large Grey Babbler** *Turdoides malcolmi*, which are widespread and numerous across large parts of the subcontinent. The original Hindi name is, in fact, *saath bhai*: *saath* meaning 'seven' and *bhai* meaning 'brothers'. With the prejudice typical of his age, a British ornithologist of the early twentieth century noted how 'in English for some reason (possibly their loquacity) the birds change their gender and

become the "Seven Sisters". It is often wrongly assumed that the parties always consist of seven birds; but "sath" is only a reflection of the phrase "panch sath" (5 or 7) an approximate phrase like "half a dozen".'[12]

The sex change performed on the original 'brothers' may, in fact, have had more to do with the familiar British name of 'Seven Sisters' for the constellation the Pleiades. The second point about seven being a casual round number in Hindu culture may be in error, as an Indian contributor explains.

There is a lot of symbolism with the number seven in Hinduism. There are the seven worlds in the universe, seven seas in the world; there are the seven sages or holy men, known as 'Saptarshi', that are the patriarchs of the Vedic religion and represent seven facets of wisdom and spiritual awareness. Also the stars of the Big Dipper are said to be the seven sages. Furthermore there are the 'Sapta Sindhu', the seven sacred rivers in Indian mythology, which gave birth to the word 'Hindu'. There are also the seven promises or vows, taken during the seven rounds that happen during a typical Hindu wedding ceremony around the sacred fire.[13]

White-eye family *Zosteropidae*

It is one of the many unexpected sights to assail a visitor on the streets of urban China. At a street corner or in the busy park, a person stands with his arm extended so that he holds a tiny birdcage and its minuscule green-and-yellow occupant roughly at eye level. While the traffic and ceaseless hubbub of inner-city China roar all around, the man seems to stand in a quiet pocket of contemplation, focused on his pet and its thin twittering cadence of sweet and occasionally buzzing notes.

The bird in the cage is a white-eye, an inconspicuous warbler-like species that, when seen high up in the tropical forests or densely vegetated habitats of Asia, hardly seems to warrant a second glance. Indeed, for much of humanity white-eyes are birds that blend effortlessly into the background. It is, strangely, in these moments on the streets of Hong Kong or Beijing, where the white-eye is unexpected and out of context, that one senses how delightful a little bird it is.

There are 99 species spread mainly across the tropical Old World – they are entirely absent from the Americas – of which just a handful enjoy large continental ranges. These are probably the best-known species and include the **African Yellow White-eye** *Zosterops senegalensis*, which is abundant over much of sub-Saharan Africa. The birds held captive in China are likely to be one of three species widespread in Asia – the **Oriental White-eye** *Zosterops palpebrosus* (from Pakistan and Tibet to Borneo), the **Chestnut-flanked White-eye** *Zosterops erythropleurus* (from Russia south and east through China to Vietnam) or the **Japanese White-eye** *Zosterops japonicus* (east China, Japan and south-east Asia).

Despite the wide occurrence of these few, white-eyes are well known for having established themselves on remote

tropical islands, from south-east Asia out into the heart of the Pacific Ocean. Yet one isolated place they did not reach without help was Hawaii. There the Japanese White-eye was deliberately introduced in 1928 and again in 1937. Within a short time these releases precipitated a veritable explosion in numbers and now the species is among the most abundant land birds with densities of 500 per km² (0.38 miles²).[1] As a modern resident notes, the bird retains a close relationship with humans in Hawaii.

The Mejiro, as many local people like to refer to it, is a fairly common bird from sea level up to the highest area where there is forest. This is true on all islands. They are not necessarily very easy to see. They are quiet and move about with minimal excitement. However, if you turn on a water sprinkler in your yard any bush that is getting wet is apt to have two or more white-eyes visit it to bathe. They materialise out of nowhere and disappear just as quickly. The islands are going through an extremely long dry spell – close to five years and this year is forecast to be the driest in a long, long time. That will do more harm to honeycreepers [see page 504] as they stay in the higher elevations whereas the white-eyes will come down to sea level and people's gardens to feed.[2]

For all their scattered distribution, many white-eyes exhibit a remarkable physical uniformity and the 75 species in the single genus *Zosterops* are even more consistent. Both sexes are alike and show no seasonal variation. They average about 12 cm (4.7 in). They are green above, usually with some yellow detail below, but their most notable feature is a ring of silky white feathers round the eyes that creates a pair of distinctive 'goggles' and accounts for the English

name. It is striking how this one feature has dominated our imaginations almost regardless of where we have encountered them. It is as true of the Zulus with the **Cape White-eye** *Zosterops pallidus* (their name is *umehlwane*, 'eyes') as it is of the inhabitants of the Indian state Maharashtra: 'in my mother tongue i.e. Marathi we call the Oriental White-eye *Chashmewala* which means "the bird with spectacles"'.[3]

The scientific name, *Zosterops*, similarly derives from two Greek words (*zōstēr*: 'a girdle or band', and *ops*: 'eye').[4] In German, as a native speaker notes, 'the name is *Brillenvogel*: – *Brille*, meaning "glasses" or "spectacles", and *Vogel* meaning "bird"'.[5] The Dutch name is *brilvogel*, which means 'a bird with glasses'.[6] The Chinese version, indicating how the bird's eye-rings seem almost to stand proud from the rest of the facial plumage, is *xiù-yan* – 'embroidery eye' – or *xiù-yan-niao* – 'embroidery eye bird'. Similarly the Japanese is *me-jiro*, comprising the words *me* – 'eye' – and *shiro* – 'white'.[7]

The name has also given rise to a Japanese expression that means to be 'crowded together'.

> The phrase *mejiro-oshi* is well known to all Japanese people and we say it regularly. A good example of where it is used is to describe the conditions on a train at morning rush hour when the coach is very crowded and it is impossible to find any space.[8]

The phrase draws on another notable feature of white-eyes – their lifestyle of intense togetherness. They have a habit of moving in groups of up to 50 through the vegetation and their collective aura of almost insect-like busyness seems mirrored in the high-pitched metallic contact notes that ricochet back and forth among the flock. It is the more elaborate and sweeter twittering songs of white-eyes that are the prime motivation for the Chinese and also a wider Asian tradition of keeping them as cagebirds. In places like Singapore devotees of the *mata puteh* (the Malay name also means 'white eye') hold song competitions and judge the individual songster by his volume and clarity, but also by subtle differences in the structure of the performance.[9]

A corollary of their popularity as cagebirds is the appearance of white-eyes in Chinese and Japanese art, especially in the long tradition of bird-and-flower paintings. The graphic simplicity of the birds – rounded in shape, reducible to just one or two colours and with a singular diagnostic mark – is beautifully evoked in works by Ando Hiroshige, such as an 1830s panel of a Japanese White-eye on the branch of a persimmon tree.[10]

In south-east Asia several species of white-eye are cherished as pets but they are also at the heart of songbird competitions, which are a major cultural activity across the region.

The black line on a Goldcrest's face can give it a rather glum expression but its needle-thin song is a high-pitched sprightly ditty.

Goldcrest and Kinglet family *Regulidae*

There are six of these feathered mites worldwide – a pair each in Europe and North America and two widely spaced single-island endemics, the **Madeiracrest** *Regulus madeirae*, confined to this one Atlantic island, and the **Flamecrest** *Regulus goodfellowi* of Taiwan. The most widespread is the **Goldcrest** *Regulus regulus*, which occurs right across Eurasia from Ireland to northern Japan. Both of the North American species are also distributed continent-wide and, with the Goldcrest, they wrap the family's distribution around almost the entire northern hemisphere.

The Goldcrest is among the smallest of all birds. At just 9 cm (3.5 in) in length and 6 g (0.2 oz) in weight it is outdone only by a number of the tiniest hummingbirds. Perhaps because of the miniature size, the family has left a large enduring impression upon our imaginations. Aristotle wrote of the Goldcrest, noting that it was 'little larger than a locust, has a crest of bright red, and is in every way a beautiful and graceful bird'.[1] (It is worth noting that he probably did not distinguish between Goldcrest and its European cousin, the **Firecrest** *Regulus ignicapilla*.)

The history of the generic name, *Regulus*, is as fascinating as it is complex. Essentially the word means 'little king' and is precisely translated in the common names for the two Americans, the **Ruby-crowned Kinglet** *Regulus calendula* and **Golden-crowned Kinglet** *Regulus satrapa*. The royal strand in the nomenclature derives in part from the bright crown on their heads.

Unfortunately for ornithologists over the last 2,400 years,

another mighty scrap from the northern hemisphere, the Winter Wren of the genus *Troglodytes*, also had a reputation as 'the king of birds'. The story of how the wren outsmarted the eagle to acquire the title is very ancient. It is at least 2,500 years old and probably much older. Aside from its beautifully symmetrical moral content, it is hard to explain the story's origins, but in his *History of Animals* Aristotle clearly showed awareness of it. He noted that the Winter Wren was often nicknamed 'old man' or 'king' and for that reason 'the eagle is at war with him' (see Wren Legends, page 448).[2]

The Greek philosopher distinguished between Goldcrest (his word was *tyrannos*, 'ruler') and Winter Wren (*trochilos*: 'runner').[3] Unfortunately thereafter the shared association with kingship and the tiny size of both species baffled many authors and unleashed a skein of confusion and overlap between the two. Some of the folkloric conflation of these birds is manifest in modern ornithology. Today in Swedish the Goldcrest is known as *Kungsfågel*, 'king bird' (the Swedish version of the king-of-birds tale actually features this species, rather than Winter Wren). In Spanish the Goldcrest's name is *Reyezuelo*, 'little king', and in French *Roitelet huppé*, 'crested wren / kinglet', while the modern Greek name for Goldcrest is *Chrysovasiliskos* ('golden kinglet').[4]

The six species of *Regulus* may lack the forceful personality of the other 'king of birds', and certainly do not possess the Winter Wren's volcanic song, but there is still something large-spirited and impressive about them. Luxembourg – a nation of just 400,000 citizens in an area of

2,586 km² (998 miles²), and squeezed between two European giants, France and Germany – has embraced the pocket-sized power of their own *Regulus* and adopted the Goldcrest as their national bird. In 1954 the Lëtzebuerger Natur- a Vulleschutzliga ('Luxembourg Birds and Nature Protection League') followed suit and changed the super-sized name of their journal (*Bulletin de la Ligue Luxembourgeoise pour l'Etude et la Protection des Oiseaux*) to the punchier *Regulus*.[5]

All the crests are associated with coniferous trees and both Ruby-crowned Kinglet and Goldcrest breed in boreal forests even beyond the Arctic Circle on each side of the Atlantic. The capacity to survive in such hostile environments is extraordinary, particularly since, in the case of the Goldcrest, 'Tolerance of hunger (in captivity) [is] so low that 1hr of food deprivation may be fatal.'[6] They are almost entirely insectivorous and, hitherto, have been unaffected by our modern bird-feeding habits. Yet this may change:

> Golden-crowned Kinglets come to feeders around here on occasion. At my old Nebraskan house they would come to a block of suet that hung from my porch. They seem nervous as they are always moving and flitting around.[7]

> In Sweden Goldcrests migrate but the majority stay to endure the snow and the many hours of darkness. In large parts of the country, the winter temperatures at night are often –20 °C. So far they have been rare visitors to bird tables, but in the last few years they are more and more discovering fat balls in gardens. It will probably mean better times for Scandinavian Goldcrests if they carry on.[8]

Despite their capacity to withstand more than 18 hours of frosted darkness each night, crests and kinglets succumb in their millions during harsh winters. In southern Finland as much as 90 per cent of the total resident Goldcrest population is estimated to be lost in some years.[9]

The family's ability to migrate over open water is well documented. Goldcrest crossings of the North Sea are routine. However, the occurrence of both Ruby-crowned Kinglet and Goldcrest as vagrants on Iceland is astonishing, given that the distance for the former is 4,275 km (2,656 miles) – albeit with a potential route via Greenland – and for the latter is at least 1,852 km (1,151 miles). It is possible that each bird sailed part of the way by boat from its respective continent.

Goldcrests are widely recorded to take advantage of human assistance, especially when the weather is foggy or misty. In an earlier age 'light vessels and boats off the coast and on the fishing grounds . . . are thronged with these birds, which are well known to the fishermen as "Herring Spinks", coming as they do in the middle of the herring harvest'.[10] ('Spink' was an old English name for the Common Chaffinch.) Its modern equivalent is the use made by Goldcrests of the various rigs and oil platforms scattered across the North Sea. There is something moving in the idea of such tiny birds finding succour in the middle of the night on these industrial maritime giants. (One reference, incidentally, which seems to draw on the birds' night-time wanderings is the wonderful name for Goldcrest in Malta – *Bufula tal-Qamar*, 'Moon Warbler'.)[11]

In times of stress crests and kinglets show remarkable

tameness, behaving as if they sense themselves to be too small to warrant human attention. They regularly search for food inside buildings or actually on human bodies. However, the following description of Golden-crowned Kinglets is exceptional: 'they allowed me to approach them and even to stroke them. Even when I patted them and stroked their beautiful crest or parted their wings. They even sat on my hands or lit on my coat. They were incredibly friendly.'[12]

Given the birds' pygmy dimensions, it is remarkable that migrant crests were once exploited by birdcatchers. One nineteenth-century ornithologist noted: 'I was surprised to find whole bunches of Goldcrests, with an occasional Firecrest, in the Italian markets; not indeed, in the same numbers as the Common Wren (*Troglodytes europaeus*), but still far from uncommonly.'[13] Not only were Goldcrests an unlikely item for the dining table, they were also caught, caged and sold as songbirds. The practice was recorded as long ago as the sixteenth century by the French author Pierre Belon, and remained widespread for hundreds of years.

One technique was to touch the bird with a long pole or fishing rod tipped with strongly adhesive lime, to which they would become stuck. Another method was to lure them towards limed twigs either with a decoy Goldcrest housed in a cage, or, in the case of Italian catchers, with an owl (see page 278). A third strategy was to shoot them with water:

> . . . that is, by first putting into a gun the common charge of powder, then a wadding of silk, then, as soon as the bird is within reach, two spoonfuls of water are poured in and covered with a second wadding of silk. This load, discharged at the distance of twenty paces, is capable of

The Firecrest weighs no more than 10 g but it was once kept as a cagebird in Europe, despite the relentless and finicky demands of its super-fast metabolism.

wetting the bird so completely that it may be taken by the hand.[14]

Given the furious pace of the kinglet metabolism, the need to feed the captive birds so regularly was an exacting regime. Yet the birds were valued for their minute voices, which produce a high-pitched tinkling ditty with an accelerated terminal flourish. Unfortunately it is frequently lost to human hearing in middle age.

> Goldcrests were one of the first to go, maybe 25 years ago. It only really hurt when I could see their bills moving with nothing apparently coming out. Being with someone who *does* hear them is a mixed blessing. It is oddly reassuring, knowing the bird is there but

not hearing it, and somehow confirms its essential otherness. But at the same time it can be exasperating and sad, even humiliating. No hearing aid can get the very high frequency songs back.[16]

The voice of the Ruby-crowned Kinglet is deceptively strong and clear.

> It's *loud*. The song starts off with rich, repetitious whistles. Then it rolls into a chant. And it ends with an effervescent mumbo-jumbo of trills and stutters. Surely, this must be the song of a big bird – a thrush or grosbeak or something? No, it is the song of Ruby-crowned Kinglet, a tiny little stub of a bird, yet one of our most talented vocalists.[16]

Wren family *Troglodytidae*

It says much about the elfin stature of most of this family that the **Giant Wren** *Campylorhynchus chiapensis* of Mexico's Pacific coast is so named but actually measures no more than 22 cm (8.7 in). Wrens are almost all very small, and predominantly brown birds of New World forest and woodland. They are particularly concentrated in Central America (Mexico alones holds 30 species), although another strong trend in their distribution is towards high-altitude landscapes, with 14 species almost entirely confined to the Andes and adjacent mountain ranges of South America. Several, such as the **Mountain Wren** *Troglodytes solstitialis*, **Santa Marta Wren** *Troglodytes monticola* and **Merida Wren** *Cistothorus meridae*, are all found above the 3,500 m contour (11,500 ft).

While they are largely associated with forests it would be truer to say that wrens love a particular kind of micro-habitat within areas of dense tree cover. It is that rather mysterious and (to humans) completely inaccessible labyrinth of crevices, holes and tunnels formed among tangled roots and dense undergrowth. Wrens live not so much *in* but *under* the vegetation.[1] Their family name, indeed, *Troglodytidae*, has come to mean 'cave-dweller', although in ancient Greek it meant literally 'a hole' or 'hollow burrower'.[2]

The name comes from the one bird, the **Winter Wren** *Troglodytes troglodytes*, among the family's 80 species that somehow found a way to tunnel out of the Americas and across the narrow Pacific straits to Asia. The escapee then crept its way through chinks and crannies over thousands of years all the way to the Atlantic shores of Europe (there is even a strong population in Iceland, where it is known as *rindill*). The bird pops up in north Africa, the continent's only representative, and occurs widely across central Asia (Turkey, Iran, Kazakhstan) and through the Himalaya. In fact, the Winter Wren is truly the mountaineer of the family, reaching altitudes of 5,500 m (18,000 ft) in Tibet. The other great wandering troglodyte is the **House Wren** *Troglodytes aedon*. From Canada's British Columbia province to the very tip of Chile and Argentina's Tierra del Fuego, it has spread across the entire Americas. (Winter Wrens even survive the cold season further north in Alaska or Canada's Yukon.) House Wren and Winter Wren both weigh about 12 g (0.4 oz).

WREN LEGENDS

While the family's subterranean lifestyle makes them sometimes difficult to observe, wrens are by no means shy. Rather like rails (see page 177), they have an eccentric capacity to alternate a creeping mouse-like furtiveness with astonishing assurance. They will sometimes approach us to within touching distance as if nothing were more normal. Partly as a consequence the birds have made an impact upon us that is out of all proportion to their size. Wrens, or at least the Winter Wren, are wreathed in human story. An old Greek name for the bird was *basileus*, 'the king', although in his own reference to the species Aristotle called it *trochilos*, 'runner'.[3] His account in the *History of Animals* makes clear that the bird was already a creature of folklore:

> The wren lives in brakes and crevices; it is difficult to capture, keeps out of sight, it is gentle of disposition, finds its food with ease, and is something of a mechanic. It goes by the nickname of 'old man' or 'king'; and the story goes that for this reason the eagle is at war with him.[4]

Aristotle's reference to the wren's enmity with the eagle almost certainly concerns an even older fable that tells of an ancient avian summit at which all the birds agreed to elect a leader or king. It was decided that whoever could fly the highest deserved the laurels and in the closing stages of the contest all were about to declare the eagle the obvious and expected victor. Just at the last moment, however, this anticipated end was completely confounded by a wren who popped out from beneath the eagle's plumage and flew just a little bit higher, declaring himself the 'king', much to the consternation of his audience. At the core of the tale are moral lessons about size being a deceptive measure of intrinsic worth and about the value of intelligence in the struggle of life.

The story was said by Plutarch to be one of Aesop's fables, although this particular parable does not occur in that ancient anthology. More certain is the fact that the tale became a stock part of European literature and culture and even occurs in parallel forms in other regions. In Africa, for instance, the myth resurfaces (possibly borrowed from European sources) but with the main characters replaced by the vulture and a tiny, rather insignificant warbler called a cisticola (see also page 428).

The Winter Wren is the mite with a machine-gun song and well deserves its legend as 'the king of birds'.

As the previous family account of crests and kinglets makes plain, there is even a major contender for the central role of the bird king in many European versions of the story. A source of great confusion in classical literature and ever afterwards was the closeness in name and physiology of another mighty midget. In Greek the Goldcrest was known as *basiliskos* ('little king' or 'kinglet') and regularly acquired the monarch's role in some versions of the story (see page 446). Goldcrests even possess narrow golden-coloured crown stripes as if to confirm their regal status.

However, the idea that the Winter Wren was a bird of exalted cultural importance was given a renewed lease of life in northern Europe, especially in France, Wales, western England and Ireland. During the seventeenth century until modern times, a linked pattern of local Christmas ceremonies centred on the public parade of captured or recently killed Winter Wrens often decked out with winter greenery in special 'wren houses'. The ceremony still occurs in modified form in western Ireland, although the dead wren has been replaced by an empty cage through which the bird is metaphorically invoked (see *Birds Britannica* for a fuller account of these wren-centred festivities in the UK and Ireland; pages 331–2).

Much has been made of the activities, including the idea that 'hunting the wren', or 'wrenning' as it is called, is a surviving relic from a pagan cult, which featured the seasonal scapegoat-type sacrifice of a tiny bird that was freighted with ancient religious importance. Edward Armstrong, for example, in *The Folklore of Birds* (1958) claimed that the 'Wren Cult reached the British Isles during the Bronze Age and was carried by megalith builders whose cultural inspiration came from the Mediterranean region'.[5]

Alas for those who have viewed the custom as a fragment of Neolithic culture alive and well in the age of cyberspace, no

evidence of any kind substantiates the existence of hunting-the-wren-style rituals before the modern age. Its earliest documented occurrence was the seventeenth century. The only significant 'proof' before these modern ceremonies that the Winter Wren was the 'king of the birds' and a creature possibly loaded with religious meaning comes from the existence of names such as the ancient Greek *basileus*. Yet how significant is that? Today in Germany and the Netherlands the Winter Wren is known as *Zaunkönig* ('hedge king') and *Winterkoning* ('winter king') respectively, but do these imply anything more than large affection for a tiny sprite?

As we have already discussed, evidence derived from the nomenclature for Winter Wren is rendered dubious, if not meaningless, by the persistent confusion of wrens and goldcrests in the ancient imagination. There is therefore a gap in the trail of evidence from at least the age of Rome to the seventeenth century. In short, writers like Edward Armstrong or Elizabeth Lawrence (*Hunting the Wren*, 1997), however fascinating and rich in associated detail their work, have built complex cultural theories on somewhat fragile foundations.[6]

THE PLEASURES OF WRENS

This is not to deny that there is something extraordinarily captivating about wrens. Like many such feathered scraps – one thinks of hummingbirds or tits and chickadees, as well as crests – they seem to possess a magnificent life force completely disproportionate to their size. One aspect of this in wrens is the often lion-sized power of the voice. The exemplar is the Winter Wren, although in North America the House Wren and **Bewick's Wren** *Thryomanes bewickii* are hardly less exuberant. The signature for the trio is the high pitch and penetrating suddenness of their phrases. The author Bradford Torrey expressed it perfectly when he said that the song had 'a martial fife-like character'.[7]

It is part of the unsubstantiated general lore about the Winter Wren that Celtic pagan priests treated the bird and its vocalisations as powerful omens. If this is unproven then certainly the Welsh name for wren has druidic associations as the author and scholar Jim Perrin explains: 'the Welsh for wren is *dryw*, plural *drywod*, which is also the Welsh for a seer, though the plural becomes *drywon*. They are both quite close to *derwydd*, which is a druid or wizard, and no doubt derive from the same ur-goidelic root'.[8] The unforgettable word used by Ted Hughes (in his poem 'Wren') to convey the seeming power of annunciation conveyed by wren song is 'glossolalia', the gift of speaking in tongues.

Wrens often cap these vocal powers with remarkable industry. In fact it is their capacity for construction of multiple nests that possibly explains Aristotle's curious reference to the bird being 'a mechanic'. Before a female chooses in which nest to lay her eggs, male wrens of many species prepare a number of options and sometimes as many as a dozen such structures. Yet the all-comers' record surely belongs to a race of the North American **Marsh Wren** *Cistothorus palustris* which may assemble 25–35 nests in a three-month nesting season.[9]

One of the deep human pleasures of wren nests is the glorious eccentricity of their locations. As if to confirm the bird's overarching religiosity, the nineteenth-century Bishop Stanley recorded several Winter Wren pairs nesting in British churches and building even on the parish bible. Equally amusing in terms of placement are the House Wren nests found in old or sometimes used hornet and wasps' nests, in fish creels, hanging fish baskets, watering cans, rusty tins, a clothes-peg bag hanging in a house, the pockets and sleeves of garments left in sheds, on old threshing machines, in the fold of an unused horse blanket, in the felt hat of an old scarecrow, in a leather mitten on a shop shelf, in a soap dish and in a human skull in a doctor's house.[10] As if to prove

that these foibles are actually shared across the entire species there was an occasion when 24 cow skulls were once collected and, typical of those rather macabre rustic displays that are sometimes made of livestock bones, they were hung up individually along the trees and bushes. Almost immediately 23 of them had nesting House Wrens.[11]

The ultimate wren whimsy – and perhaps the occasions when these birds or, indeed, any birds are most moving for us – is the moment when they choose to perceive humans as just one more odd-shaped perch on which to conduct their busy and mysterious lives:

It was a beautiful still afternoon with grasshoppers singing and a buzzard circling in the blue sky above. Sitting in the field – drawing on a pad on my lap – a hat pulled down to shield my face from the sun, I felt a tiny fluffy bundle land on my shoulder. Not daring to turn my head, I continued to sit until another of these brown objects did the same on my other shoulder. They were two baby wrens trying out their first flights from the hedge to the nearest object in the field. Another three launched themselves off, clumsily landing and clinging to my hat. At this point the worried mother was twittering and trilling anxiously from the hedge. Her shrill concerns got her offspring to desert me, only for them to crash-land into the grass.[12]

I live remote on Afognak Island in the Kodiak Archipelago in Alaska in a tiny little shanty. Some of my happiest moments are when the Winter Wrens fly in my window with a whirring sound where I sleep, land on my pillow and look at their reflections in my eyes, cocking their heads from side to side. Then they belt out their long thirty-note song with puffs of their little breath coming out their tiny bodies fogging up my vision.[13]

Nuthatch and Wallcreeper family *Sittidae*

Nuthatches are small to medium-sized, mainly arboreal songbirds with robust almost wedge-shaped bodies, short broad wings and long chisel-like beaks. In the manner of woodpeckers they cleave to the trunks of trees, but their most singular behaviour is an ability to defy gravity and walk head-first downwards as well as up.

There are 25 species worldwide and they are almost entirely inhabitants of the northern hemisphere, with concentrations in China (11 species), south-east Asia (nine species) and the Mediterranean with adjacent areas (seven species). There are just three in North America, and two marginal residents in Africa. However, this last pair exemplifies the extremes in nuthatch distribution.

On the one hand, the **Algerian Nuthatch** *Sitta ledanti* occurs in the forests of just one mountain, Djebel Babor, and three other small forests in coastal Algeria. The total range is 300 km² (115 miles²). (If anything the **Corsican Nuthatch** *Sitta whiteheadi*, found on the Mediterranean island to the north, has a smaller range still, occurring across 24,000 ha: 59,300 acres of ancient montane pine forest.) At the other extreme is the second African bird, the **Eurasian**

Nuthatch *Sitta europaea*. It may be represented in Africa by a single enclave in the Atlas Mountains of Morocco, but its full world range includes most of the Eurasian landmass, from Cornwall in England to Kamchatka in Russia. It is one of three species with almost continent-wide distributions, the other two being the North American **White-breasted Nuthatch** *Sitta carolinensis* and **Red-breasted Nuthatch** *Sitta canadensis*.

Many nuthatches possess large personalities that are expressed in their loud ringing calls and the sheer vigour of their actions. A classic bit of behaviour involves wedging food items – nuts and seeds – into tree holes and then whacking them with their awl-like bills. The nut-splitting operation seems to utilise the power of the bird's whole body, and the 'nuthatch' part of the family name refers to this intense labour. In the nineteenth century a specialist on captive birds noted that the nuthatch 'must be kept in a cage made entirely of wire, as wood cannot resist the strength of its beak'.[1]

The birds are famously indifferent to human presence and are routine attendees at garden bird feeders across much of their range. A speciality of the North American species

The gloriously beautiful Wallcreeper has a decided taste for grandiose architecture, from Lhasa's Potala Palace to Paris' Notre Dame Cathedral.

is a willingness to feed from people's hands. The Cherokees called nuthatches *tsuliena* ('deaf'), because of their seeming indifference to disturbance.[2] Clearly some individuals are more 'deaf' than others.

> I took some of the good nut mix with my arm stretched out in front of me, and a Red-breasted Nuthatch landed on it, looked at the nuts for a moment, and then he turned, giving me his back. He looked around the yard, he looked to the left, to the right. He looked up, he looked down. He'd never done this before. Thirty seconds went by. I admired his small feathers, how they shine. The way the feathers fit together, how, when he moves his head, some go under and some go over. How shiny his black cap is. I have always loved the way the black on his head blends into the blue of his back. Gorgeous. I was in love. This beautiful wild creature could perch anywhere he wants to, and he's perched on me.[3]

The odd one out of the family, the only member not in the genus *Sitta*, is the remarkably beautiful **Wallcreeper** *Tichodroma muraria*. When shuffling almost mouse-like over rock it appears grey and black. But when it takes flight a Wallcreeper is suddenly transformed by the brilliant rosette of intense crimson and a row of white 'eyes' on each of its broad butterfly's wings. It is an inhabitant of remote crags and on the map the species' distribution looks like a long chain of 'islands', but they represent the mountain ranges of Eurasia: the Tien Shan, the Himalaya and Hindu Kush, the Caucasus, Pontic Alps, the Pindos of Greece, the Dolomites, Alps and Pyrenees.

In winter Wallcreepers leave these inaccessible parts and descend to lower altitudes where they will feed in boulder-strewn riverbeds. Another substitute for natural crags are human structures, in which the species seems to show a particular tendency towards buildings of exalted character. In truth there may be solid ecological grounds for these architectural tastes. Our most imposing physical structures, often on high ground and standing proud of their neighbours, tend to be those fulfilling our deepest aspirations: military security, political power and religious faith. They are often old, even ancient, structures with monumental stonework that is full of Wallcreeper-friendly crevices. The sites often become hallowed ground, and any human visitors tend to show deep respect for the surroundings, including its beautiful rose-winged visitor.

> At the Covadonga Shrine in a wooded valley in the Picos de Europa, northern Spain, as hundreds of worshippers streamed into the massive building for Sunday morning Mass and the great bells rang out shaking the pink marble walls, and crag martins flew up and down fluttering, a Wallcreeper flew straight towards me and my wife before veering off on to the high wall of the Basilica. Something about the devotional atmosphere of the occasion as well as the somewhat hectic milling of the crowds, made this sighting particularly memorable – that conjunction of holiness, worship and the beauty of the spot seemed so appropriate to so extraordinary a bird.[4]

The Potala Palace in the Tibetan capital, Lhasa, is

the most spectacular of all Wallcreeper haunts. Yet other grandiose or historically important sites that well suit such a sought-after bird include: the magnificent eighth-century Chinese Buddha at Leshan, in southern Sichuan, where the bird favours the 28 m (92 ft) chest of the carved stone figure; the Leh Palace in Ladakh, India; the fourth-century Orthodox monastery built into the high cliff face at Sumela in Turkey's Pontic Alps; the massive cubist edifice at Shumen in Bulgaria, which is intended as a history of the nation expressed in monumental concrete; Esztergom Cathedral in northern Hungary, one of the largest Christian structures in the world; the 'fairy tale' medieval castle on the island in the middle of Lake Bled, Slovenia; Notre Dame Cathedral in Paris; the seventeenth-century citadel of Besançon in the French province of Franche-Comté; the 2,000-year-old Roman aqueduct, the Pont du Gard, as well as the spectacular hilltop castle and village of Les Baux, both of which are in Provence. (And finally, and perhaps not unexpected for so refined a species, a Wallcreeper – in tattoo form – creeps up the arm of French-based wildlife artist Nick Derry.) [5]

Rather at odds with the noble architectural associations we tend to deflect on to this glorious little bird is the individual Spanish Wallcreeper that was observed building its own structure: a nest partly assembled from the soft nicotine-stained fibres extracted from the filter tips of cigarette butts.[6]

Mockingbird and Thrasher family *Mimidae*

These 34 species are often bold, engaging birds that rather resemble big thrushes. A species like the widespread North American **Brown Thrasher** *Toxostoma rufum* even has prominent black breast streaks like a thrush. Yet all of them have long tails, fine long legs and often long curving beaks, while the staring pale irides give some thrashers a rather fierce, mean-eyed expression. In fact, an alternative name – 'trashers' – has been coined by some amused enthusiasts for the birds, 'because they toss a lot of bark, dirt and stuff around with their bills in their search for insects and grubs and other food below the soil surface. In the process they "trash" our sidewalks and patio with the tossed materials'.[1]

All of the family are exclusively found in the New World with a high concentration in Central America (Mexico holds 18 species) and a diminishing diversity at higher latitudes. Ten species breed north of the Mexican border, but just four cross into Canada, while at the other end of the Americas, Chile and Argentina have only five mockingbirds. Yet a family speciality has been the ability to reach and then thrive on tiny islands. They are found widely across the many archipelagos of the Caribbean, with the **Cozumel Thrasher** *Toxostoma guttatum* limited just to Cozumel Island off Mexico's Yucatán Peninsula, where it is critically threatened with extinction. Off the country's west coast the **Socorro Mockingbird** *Mimodes graysoni* is almost as endangered and is equally confined. Its entire range comprises the Mexican-owned Isla Socorro measuring 132 km^2 (51 miles^2).

However, the ultimate range-restricted birds occur on the Galápagos, where the diversity of mockingbirds is also remarkable. An ancestral bird somehow reached the islands from South America and gave rise to four separate species: the **Floreana Mockingbird** *Nesomimus trifasciatus*, **Hood Mockingbird** *Nesomimus macdonaldi*, **San Cristobal Mockingbird** *Nesomimus melanotis* and **Galapagos Mockingbird** *Nesomimus parvulus* (the last is further divided into seven subspecies, each occurring on seven separate islands). The first, however, Floreana Mockingbird, was once widespread across its eponymous island. Yet it subsequently went extinct on Floreana, which measures just 173 km^2 (67 miles^2), possibly because of cat and rat predation, and now the entire range for the surviving 250 birds is two minuscule satellite outcrops with a combined area of 0.9 km^2 (0.35 miles^2).

At least the Galápagos mockingbirds typify the family in their bold and feisty spirit. It is commonplace for tourists to arrive on an island and find themselves greeted by birds that perch on their shoulders, or (as happened to me) tug at their boot laces, inspect their water bottles or their picnics and, if no resistance is offered, help themselves to choice morsels. The Hood Mockingbird is so tame it is the 'bane of scientists working' on the island (now called Española) and caps its pushiness with raw aggression, eating seabird and iguana eggs, and killing or digging flesh wounds into seabird nestlings to drink their blood. They even show interest in blood trickling from scratches on human legs.[2]

THE RENOWNED VOICE OF MOCKINGBIRDS

Fortunately the characteristic for which mockingbirds are better known is the gentle art of music. In truth, not all are equally gifted – the Galápagos birds are noted exceptions – but several are often singled out as the most accomplished musicians on their respective continents. In South America, Helmut Sick credited the **Tropical Mockingbird** *Mimus gilvus* with inspiring the best-known lines of verse in Brazil. They are the opening couplet in *Canção do exílio*, the 'song of exile', by the Romantic author Gonçalves Dias, written in 1843 while he was studying in Portugal:

> My land has palm trees,
> Where the thrush sings
> The birds that sing in here
> Do not sing as they do there.

Sick suggested that the bird in the palm was no thrush, but a Tropical Mockingbird.

However, he went on to propose a close relative, the **White-banded Mockingbird** *Mimus triurus*, as the one attaining 'a perfection matched with difficulty by any other' songster.[3] W H Hudson agreed. Listening to the same species in Argentina, he felt it excelled all other songbirds he had ever heard. 'I can think of no other way', he wrote, 'to describe the surpassing excellence of its melody, which delights the soul beyond all other bird-music, than by saying that this bird is among song-birds like the diamond among stones'.[4]

453

Although its current name is Northern Mockingbird the species was once intimately associated with the states of the American South.

NORTHERN MOCKINGBIRD

The reputation of mockingbirds is striking for the way it transcends cultural boundaries. In Mexico, the sixteenth-century Spanish naturalist Francisco Hernández de Toledo called the widespread North American species and perhaps the best known of the family – the **Northern Mockingbird** *Mimus polyglottos* – 'the Queen of all singing birds'. He also noted how, in the original Nahuatl of Mexico, it was known as *Cencontlatolly*, meaning 'four hundred voices'.[5] That particular name is intriguing for the way it echoes the Persian, *hazar dastan* ('a thousand songs'), for another versatile songster, the Common Nightingale (see also page 478). In a number of Caribbean islands the Northern Mockingbird was itself known (and possibly still is) simply as the 'nightingale' (Jamaica) or the French and Spanish equivalents, *rossignol* and *ruiseñor* (Haiti and the Dominican Republic respectively).[6]

Among Native American communities the vocal abilities of Northern Mockingbirds were entwined with creation stories that explained the origins of human speech. Often the bird handed out a language to the different peoples as they first emerged, and to the Hopi the bird was the source of their ritual songs. These associative patterns were repeated in the bird's medicinal value, because its tongue or heart was eaten to aid the retentive powers of children or to correct defects of voice and memory.[7]

The song itself is a prolonged outpouring of boldly repeated phrases, occasionally alternating with quieter sotto voce passages and then even louder, almost ringing, declamatory notes. The signature emotion is one of bright, almost invincible optimism. Along with the joyous vigour of the delivery, is the mockingbird's repeated adjustment of the long loose tail and floppy white-barred wings, especially if the bird is balanced on a pole or wire, when the raising and lowering of body parts seem an element of the overarching variation. Another classic feature is the way the dark bill is held wide to reveal a yellow-pink mouth lining and the head tilts backwards to broadcast the whole performance. The ceaseless volley of music posts an invisible no-entry sign around the male's territory and has the power to bring his mate into reproductive condition and, during the nest-building stage, to enhance her receptivity to mating.[8]

One form of song that mockingbirds have carried to a level of perfection is the cover version. In fact, the word 'mockingbird' – and at one time it was called 'mock-bird' – derives from an old definition of 'mock' meaning 'to ridicule by imitation'.[9] Northern Mockingbirds are brilliant mimics, copying, according to Mark Catesby, one of the first to describe the species, almost anything 'from the Humming Bird to the Eagle'.[10] A famous Northern Mockingbird that sang in a Boston park for more than five years from 1914 was reputed to copy 39 other birdsongs and 50 calls, as well as the notes of frogs and crickets.[11] Another in South Carolina was credited with reproducing 32 other birdsongs in a ten-minute virtuoso passage, while a description by Edward Forbush noted how the species:

> improves upon most of the notes that he reproduces, adding also to his varied repertoire the crowing of chanticleer, the cackling of the hen, the barking of the house dog, the squeaking of the unoiled wheelbarrow, the postman's whistle, the plaints of young chickens and turkeys and those of young wild birds, not neglecting to mimic his own offspring. He even imitates man's musical inventions.[12]

CULTURAL REPRESENTATIONS OF NORTHERN MOCKINGBIRD

Such vocal powers once won the family an unfortunate reputation as cagebirds and Helmut Sick describes how mockingbirds are still favourite pets in Brazil, where they are trained sometimes to sing the national anthem.[13] In the USA even Thomas Jefferson had a pet mockingbird and was apparently so enamoured of it that, after his wife died, it slept in his bed every night.[14] The whole of the USA seems to have taken its cue from the third president in electing the bird as a backyard favourite. The ornithologist Frank Chapman suggested that it was 'our national songbird . . . famous the world over'.[15] Arthur Bent added that only the American Robin could rival it for popularity.

One ingredient in the mocker's cherished status is the bird's courage. They are well known for fiercely defending their nests and young from all-comers including humans, but also from birds of prey, cats, raccoons and snakes. Sometimes the species extends these violent assaults to almost any small bird straying into its territory. In a glorious celebration ('The Mockingbird') of this strange dual personality – the sweet, many-voiced neighbour and the aggressive sociopath – the poet Randall Jarrell (1914–1965) noted how:

> Hour by hour, fighting hard
> To make the world his own, he swooped
> On thrushes, thrashers, jays, and chickadees –
> At noon he drove away a big black cat.
>
> Now, in the moonlight, he sits here and sings.
> A thrush is singing, then a thrasher, then a jay –
> Then, all at once, a cat begins meowing.
> A mockingbird can sound like anything.
> He imitates the world he drove away
> So well that for a minute, in the moonlight,
> Which one's the mockingbird? Which one's the world?

Mockingbirds are sometimes so aggressive they can even kill snakes by pecking out their eyes.[16] Perhaps the most iconic image of this confrontation is the painting in Audubon's *Birds of America*. The tableau includes four adult Northern Mockingbirds bravely challenging a thick-waisted Timber Rattlesnake as it malignly entwines their nest. At the very epicentre of this magnificent portrait is the bold eye of one heroic parent perfectly aligned with the evil orb of the serpent. What cements the painting's reputation as one of the most famous in Audubon's entire oeuvre is the fact that rattlers do not genuinely climb trees. Yet, as Darryl Wheye and Donald Kennedy argue in their study of bird art, Audubon's rare mistake has functioned like the errors

found in stamps, coins and artists' prints: it has increased the painting's value. Audubon's image of the Brown Thrasher is a similar portrait of four birds confronting a predatory snake (a scene he actually witnessed), but this original print sells for less than half the sums paid for his misconceived mockers ($30,000–$60,000).[17]

One possible consequence of Audubon's image, however, is the election of the Northern Mockingbird as the state bird for Texas in 1927. Aside from the glorious voice, the citation specifically mentions its role as 'a fighter for the protection of his home, falling, if need be, in its defense, like any true Texan'.[18] It would be more accurate to view the Northern Mockingbird not just as a citizen of the Lone Star State, but of the entire southern region. Repeatedly ornithologists emphasised how the quintessential place to see and appreciate this remarkable bird was the South. Audubon himself felt that one should hear a mocker '*only* amid the magnolias of Louisiana'. Waxing lyrical on this theme, ornithologist Arthur Bent agreed wholeheartedly:

> Can one visualise it . . . without mental pictures of moss-bannered live oaks or towering magnolias, where the yellow jessamine climbs aloft to burst in golden glory among the pines and cypresses and the immaculate discs

This painting of Northern Mockingbirds fearlessly defending their nest from a Timber Rattlesnake is justifiably famous but it actually enshrines an error by Audubon. The snake doesn't climb trees.

of Cherokee roses reflect the moonlight? . . . Here, amid the crimson clusters of cassina and holly the mocker lives, or is equally at home in a moon-drenched old city whose garden walls and graceful spires reflect the golden civilization of a vanished era . . . to Charlestonians and other Carolinians, the entire scope of ornithology might be summed up . . . in a single species . . . the mockingbird![19]

Despite its name and the species' gradual expansion northwards, partly because of its favoured status among human neighbours, the Northern Mockingbird is still deeply connected to the South. As well as Texas, the bird is the state symbol in Arkansas, Florida, Mississippi and Tennessee (a close relative, the Brown Thrasher, is the state bird in Georgia). A resident of Arkansas expounds on the bird's emblematic complexities:

> As ubiquitous as sweet tea in the South, the mockingbird serves as Arkansas' official bird and is the namesake of many roads and local businesses within the state, such as Mockingbird Hill Water, Mockingbird Bay Resort, and Mockingbird Creative, Inc. The bird is much appreciated for eating farmers' pests and, of course, its uncanny ability to imitate a diverse repertoire of sounds: car alarms, washing machines, frogs, creaking gates, and other birds, confusing even the best of birders. Unbeknownst to a lot of slumbering Southerners, the maniacal bird singing outside their windows at 2 a.m. is most likely an unmated male, trying in earnest to attract a mate by the light of the moon, or street lights as the case may be. Without a doubt, the 'sleep-murdering mockingbird', as an editor of the *Arkansas Democrat-Gazette* calls it, exudes a colorful personality despite its drab plumage.[20]

The southern state to which the bird now has the deepest symbolic links is possibly Alabama, as a consequence of Harper Lee's acclaimed novel on race and human justice in the Deep South, *To Kill a Mockingbird* (1960). Lee's book is famous as a key text of the early US civil rights movement. Yet it is not just a restatement of the prejudice and bigotry that bedevilled the region in the twentieth century. It is an expression of all that is good and decent and true about the South, as exemplified by its lead adult characters: the lawyer, Atticus Finch (and father to the book's narrator, young 'Scout' Finch), and Tom Robinson, the black man who is unjustly convicted of rape and is shot while attempting to escape.

The title of the novel comes from a passage when Atticus Finch teaches his children a discriminatory ethics while shooting with a rifle. 'I'd rather you shoot at tin cans in the back yard,' says the lawyer, 'but I'll know you'll go after birds. Shoot all the blue jays you want, if you can hit 'em, but remember it's a sin to kill a mockingbird.'[21] Later a neighbour explains that this particular bird 'don't do one thing but make music for us to enjoy'. It is precisely this fundamental innocence and virtue that renders it such a crime to kill one. The wrongly accused and tragically slain Tom Robinson is himself symbolised by the mockingbird, since he is a figure who does nothing but try to help another human in need. Yet the deep generic links between mockingbirds and the

whole southern USA hint at a wider kind of symbolism. In blaming the innocent and defeating the virtuous, the citizens of Maycomb County, Alabama, implicate and condemn their whole region. The killing of the songbird invoked in the book's title foreshadows the manner in which they snuff out something precious within all of their lives.

It is ironic that a bird with the voice of invincible optimism has acquired such a melancholy symbolism. The artwork that perhaps best and most fully taps into the emotional register contained within mockingbird song was written 100 years earlier than Lee's novel. The sheer life-affirming music and declamatory passion of Walt Whitman's verse found an almost exact analogue in the unceasing outpourings of this bird. The poet echoed its voice with enormous effect in a famous declaration of his artistic identity, entitled 'Out of the Cradle Endlessly Rocking'.

In the poem Whitman recalls how a pair of Northern Mockingbirds (notably referred to as 'feather'd guests from Alabama' and, at that time, a rare breeding species in New York state) set up territory at Paumanok, near his childhood home on Long Island. However, the female bird dies, but rather than abandon their nesting place by the Atlantic shore, the male keeps a summer-long vigil. In his passionate and sustained song of hope towards the pitiless sweep of the ocean, the mockingbird offers the child poet a metaphor for his own poetic calling and a symbol for the mysterious birthplace of all creativity. Even just the extraordinary first sentence of this poem suggests Whitman's brilliant ability to capture the surging repetitive phrases of a mocker and the powerful sense of joy with which it almost bursts:

> Out of the cradle endlessly rocking,
> Out of the mocking-bird's throat, the musical shuttle,
> Out of the Ninth-month midnight,
> Over the sterile sands and the fields beyond, where the
>   child leaving his bed wander'd alone, bareheaded,
>   barefoot,
> Down from the shower'd halo,
> Up from the mystic play of shadows twining and
>   twisting as if they were alive,
> Out from the patches of briers and blackberries,
> From the memories of the bird that chanted to me,
> From your memories sad brother, from the fitful risings
>   and fallings I heard,
> From under that yellow half-moon late-risen and
>   swollen as if with tears,
> From those beginning notes of yearning and love there
>   in the mist,
> From the thousand responses of my heart never to cease,
> From the myriad thence-arous'd words,
> From the word stronger and more delicious than any,
> From such as now they start the scene revisiting,
> As a flock, twittering, rising, or overhead passing,
> Borne hither, ere all eludes me, hurriedly,
> A man, yet by these tears a little boy again,
> Throwing myself on the sand, confronting the waves,
> I, chanter of pains and joys, uniter of here and hereafter,
> Taking all hints to use them, but swiftly leaping beyond
>   them,
> A reminiscence sing.

Starling family *Sturnidae*

Depending on your point of view the Common Myna is a well-groomed, clarion-voiced bird of lawns and fields, or an unwanted invader with an arrogant walk.

It is claimed that in western Turkey, when flocks of the lovely **Rosy Starling** *Sturnus roseus* wandered across the region, the locals had different names for them depending on when they arrived and what they were eating. They were 'holy birds' when taking locusts and insect pests in May, but 'devil birds' when it was grapes in July.[1] That contrast in the Rosy Starling's reception perfectly summarises our Janus-faced attitudes towards this family. They can be treasured as some of the most beautiful, sought after and helpful of birds; just as easily they can be hated as a plague-like scourge.

There are 116 species and they were once concentrated in the Old World tropics, but such is the extraordinary human-induced spread of some starlings, and particularly the 'evil twins', **Common Starling** *Sturnus vulgaris* and **Common Myna** *Acridotheres tristis*, that the group is now almost global in range. South America is the last starling-free continent (although even this may change). The family's primary home is Africa with 50 species, while the Oriental and Australasian regions each have 26 species. (Australia itself, however, has just a single native starling, although both Common Starling and Common Myna have been introduced.) Many of those Australasian birds, as well as eight other species, reflect a common pattern among the family.

They are inhabitants of remote Pacific islands or archipelagos and have tiny world ranges. Classic examples are the **Pohnpei Starling** *Aplonis pelzelni* and **Rarotonga Starling** *Aplonis cinerascens*. The former is confined to the 345 km² (133 miles²) of its eponymous island (one of the Micronesian group); while the latter occurs on just one extinct volcano (called Rarotonga) in the Cook Archipelago, with an area of 67 km² (26 miles²). Not only are these two birds marooned on tiny scraps in the middle of the ocean, they are exceptionally rare. The Rarotonga Starling numbers 500, while the Pohnpei Starling has been considered extinct by some since the 1970s, although the discovery of a single skin in 1995 has raised hopes of continued survival. In each case, one of the major problems is the classic scourge of tropical-island environments – the impact of non-native organisms introduced either inadvertently or deliberately by humans.[2]

One of the places where a non-native animal has had a devastating effect on local starlings is on US-administered Guam, a Pacific island due east of the Philippines. Cheryl Calaustro explains both the environmental impact and the unforeseen human consequences:

The lilting whistle of the **Micronesian Starling** *Aplonis opaca* or *sáli* can easily be heard on a tiny offshore island called Cocos. But this is dramatically different to the jungles of Guam, which are deadly silent and where no forest birds sing. The explanation for this hush is the accidental introduction of the Brown Tree Snake, a formidable invasive species. Forest birds like the *ko'ko'* or Guam Rail once numbered thousands but owing to the voracious appetite of the snake, ten out of 12 native forest birds became extinct. Only the locally endangered *såli* and *chachaguak* (Island Swiftlet) remain. A whole generation of islanders has grown up not knowing that the forests of their ancestors should be alive with birdsong. This is a great loss to their cultural history and traditions. Guam's children have little interaction with native species and unknowingly turn a deaf ear and blind eye to nature. However I spend much time on a predator-free Cocos Island where the *såli* can still be found. The first time a child hears its song is a beautiful sight. One can see their eyes light up and on their faces a look of realisation when they understand what they have lost. This moment reinvigorates me and gives me hope for the future. I've done my part to keep the birds alive, not only through traditional science, but also by awakening the community's mind, spirit and memory. I know that one day Guam's forests will sing again.[3]

STARLINGS AS PETS

It seems deeply ironic that one of our commonest interactions with starlings is our frequent release of them where they should never occur. Humans have cherished the birds and kept them as pets all over the world, and then, sadly, set them free. They were frequent cagebirds not just because many starlings are beautiful – their speciality is a gloriously iridescent gloss – but they are also among the select few birds able to pronounce words.

The **Common Hill Myna** *Gracula religiosa* is a good candidate for the world's most articulate bird. Its mimicry of human speech can be uncannily accurate but it is also an impressive creature and the size of a small crow. It ranges from India to the Philippines where it inhabits dense jungle and at dawn and dusk groups gather to indulge in an extraordinary array of vocalisations, including bizarre wails or harsh gurgling and screech notes that can seem intensely human, or whistles reminiscent of the oscillating interference heard on old-style radios. Hill mynas favour the topmost canopy so that these incredibly loud calls are broadcast right through the forest and in their natural settings they create a spine-tingling sense of place.

However, in captivity, which is how most of us encounter these birds, those same wonderful voices express a bathetic comedy. Often hill mynas are trained to swear, or to sound like sirens or telephones and to utter banal phrases with the clearest diction. Tens of thousands of the birds are trafficked annually out of the wild and into conditions of solitary confinement. Young trained captive-bred mynas can sell for thousands of dollars. In the case of the family giant, the **Nias Hill Myna** *Gracula robusta* (30–36 cm: 12–14 in) from islands off the coast of Sumatra, the wild population is encouraged to breed in nestboxes where it can be more easily harvested for the pet trade.[4]

Starling species of more modest vocal talent also have a long pedigree as cagebirds. Pliny recorded that Common Starlings were welcome pets even in the most exalted households of ancient Rome. During the reign of Emperor Claudius (AD 41–54) both his son, Britannicus, and his eventual heir, Nero, had starlings that could pronounce Greek and Roman words.[5] This tradition of keeping them survived in Europe for 2,000 years, but perhaps the most celebrated individual bird was a Common Starling belonging to Wolfgang Amadeus Mozart. For three years it was his constant companion and when it died in 1787, the composer held a funeral for it, complete with formal mourners, and wrote a short commemorative poem that suggests his writing was not the true measure of his genius:

> He was not naughty, quite,
> But gay and bright,
> And under all his brag
> A foolish wag.
> This no one can gainsay
> And I will lay
> That he is now on high,
> And from the sky,
> Praises me without pay
> In his friendly way.
> Yet unaware that death
> Has choked his breath,
> And thoughtless of the one
> Whose rime is thus well done.

Common Starling song has a mixed reputation. To its detractors it is 'raucous and rather chaotic', and the fact that in France the bird's name (*étourneau*) is slang for a scatterbrained person is surely a reference to its vocal muddle.[6] Yet the sound is also, as Mozart implied, light, jazzy and zestful. In spring the song can have a rather inward quality as if the bird is trialling parts of its free-form medley for its own amusement. One author likened several in chorus to 'an orchestra tuning up'.[7]

This same sound may have inspired Mozart during his composition of a very strange piece, K522, that is known as 'A Musical Joke'. Discordant, at times off-key, rambling and awkwardly structured, the work was thought to be Mozart's satire on his less-talented contemporaries, but modern American scholars Andrew P King and Meredith J West believe that it was in part an attempt by the great composer to reproduce the zany, wheezing, chuffing song of his pet bird.[8]

More usually with captive starlings the borrowing was the other way round: the birds were trained to copy human melodies. In fact, what attracted Mozart to his own bird in the shop where he bought it was the creature's rendition of a tune that was highly similar to a piece he had himself just composed (a piano concerto, K453). A fellow German, Johann Bechstein, celebrated this aspect of their companionship:

> The starling becomes wonderfully familiar in the house; as docile and cunning as a dog, he is always gay, wakeful, soon knows all the inhabitants of the house, remarks their motions and air, and adapts himself to their humours. . . . He learns to pronounce words without having his tongue cut [it was once customary to split the tongue] which proves the uselessness of this cruel operation. He repeats correctly the airs which are taught him . . . imitates the cries of men and animals, and the songs of all the birds in the room with him.[9]

This capacity for mimicry is not confined to the drawing room. Wild starlings are famous for a rather humorous imitation of all kinds of other birds, bringing to the urban rooftop a sense of the much wilder spaces that they encompass. In Britain and Sweden the haunting modulated songs of Eurasian Curlews, Northern Lapwings and Tawny Owls, or the high mewing notes of Common Buzzards, are routine elements of their chimney-pot repertoire.[10] Another staple in Austria, Germany and France is the glorious liquid fluting of Eurasian Golden Orioles.[11] This penchant for oriole song even transcends species. According to one contributor:

> The **Spotless Starling** *Sturnus unicolor* [in Spain] tends to imitate orioles a lot! I've also heard them copying Black Redstart and Blue Rock Thrush incredibly well. But the mimicry varies according to the region. They also copy Azure-winged Magpies, especially around the Coto Doñana National Park.[12]

In North America Common Starlings have abandoned their old European imitations and learned a fresh vocabulary from their new avian neighbours. There is a widely held view that New World Common Starlings are less given to mimicry. However, the author Bill Thompson III offers a glorious inventory of the bird's American borrowings:

> I've heard them do the following: Carolina Wren, Eastern Meadowlark, Upland Sandpiper, Purple Martin, Northern Cardinal, Red-shouldered Hawk, Blue Jay, American Goldfinch. Plus (over the years): truck back-up beeper, construction worker's wolf whistle at a passing pretty woman, ringing telephone, cell-phone ringtone, car alarm, my son Liam calling 'Mommy?' (Julie [Zickefoose] has a chapter about this in her *Letters from Eden*.) There are starlings starting to nest in our front yard. I'll go listen a bit to see what else they mimic. Just now: Great Crested Flycatcher (don't migrate back for another 40 days), Northern Flicker, Red-winged Blackbird ('chack' call), Killdeer, Red-bellied Woodpecker, firetruck siren.[13]

As Thompson makes clear, often the copied sounds are not even those of birds. Other contributors add to the list: 'I remember one starling regularly imitated the 'tinkle-tinkle' call of a railway crossing, the sound when the red lights start flashing and the gates go down, but such dangerous road / railway crossings are now rare in Sweden.'[14]

> I once employed a man to run my small farm. His name was Brian, a cheerful soul with only one irritating habit. He whistled. He did so very well, but endlessly and it was always the same tune. Brian left to go to a job with better prospects and on my first day after he had gone, I was working in the yard at dawn feeding the animals, when I heard Brian whistling. I was sure I wasn't mistaken and searched the buildings but there was no one about. I heard the whistle again on several mornings. I was convinced Brian was playing tricks, as it was undoubtedly his whistle. It was most unnerving. After a few mornings of this nonsense, I happened to look up to see a starling perched on the gutter. I had found the culprit, making a perfect imitation of 'the whistle'.[15]

Rarer are those occasions when the starling mimicry is not an echo of the bird's immediate soundscape, but expresses both the history of a place and its lost human residents. (See also Lyrebird family, page 360 and Parrot family, page 252.)

> I was in the Outer Hebrides and I came across an abandoned derelict croft. It had no roof, but very substantial walls and in the gaps between the stonework was a starlings' nest. I could hear the birds inside, and eventually one of the starlings came to defend its territory. I heard straight away that it wasn't just the usual rambling song. It started to mimic a Corncrake, a species that is very rare in mainland Britain. It did this bird's buzzing repetitive song, but then it immediately went into other sounds that seemed familiar and had a strong rhythm to them. As I was listening I was looking around and could see the remnants of farm machinery, including an ancient tractor that had not moved for 20–30 years. I realised this bird was singing the song of some of this machinery. It was singing the song of a mechanical pump that had obviously been active around this farm and used by the people who had lived here.
>
> I wasn't listening to the same starling that heard those original sounds. These copied sounds are usually passed on from parents or neighbouring birds so that a young bird absorbs and then duplicates them. The strange thing was that I was recording the sounds in what had been somebody's living room, a place that had obviously been full of the conversations of family life over generations and which had passed into history. Yet the birds had returned and taken it back – claimed this space and these rocks – and were singing their own song. And they were singing the songs that were around when the people were here.[16]

STARLINGS AS AVIAN SCOURGE

In a roundabout way it is this same mimetic genius that launched the Common Starling on one of the most extraordinary invasions of any non-native bird. In 1890 a businessman from the Bronx called Eugene Schieffelin took it upon himself to introduce to North America all of the birds mentioned in Shakespeare's plays. The Common Starling has a walk-on part in *Henry IV, Part One*, when Harry Hotspur, eager to see his brother-in-law, Mortimer, restored to the favours of the king, announces: 'I'll have a starling shall be taught to speak / Nothing but "Mortimer", and give it him [the king] / To keep his anger still in motion.'

Schieffelin thus released into New York's Central Park about 100 Common Starlings over the two springs of 1890 and 1891. In their first seasons the arrivistes took to roosting on the American Museum of Natural History. Within short order, however, they were venturing much further afield: New Jersey and Connecticut (1900), Massachusetts (1908), New Hampshire and Pennsylvania (by 1910), Maine and Virginia (by 1916). Within half a century the thing had gone viral. From Oregon to Quebec, it had occupied an area estimated at over 7 million km^2 (2.7 million miles^2). Within 90 years it was among the most abundant birds on the continent, with outposts from Alaska to Mexico.[17]

The burgeoning numbers brought repeated complaints. One commentator noted that the bird is 'disliked by almost

everybody'.[18] Others put it in much stronger terms: 'it is vehemently hated wherever it occurs in the United States'.[19] Even the great E O Wilson has described it as 'a plague across America'.[20] Exactly how many Common Starlings are in the region is difficult to calculate, but the world population is sometimes estimated at 600 million – occasionally as high as 1.5 billion – with a third of these in the New World.[21]

Nor is North America the Common Starling's only territorial conquest. Parallel introductions were made in New Zealand (1862; now 'probably one of the most numerous species'), Australia (at least since 1881 and now common in the south-eastern two-fifths of the country), South Africa (since 1897 and now abundant), the West Indies (1903–4; locally common) and Fiji (since the mid twentieth century and common in agricultural areas).[22] It also has further outposts in the Bahamas, the Virgin and Cayman Islands, as well as the coastal fringe of Venezuela. An environmental assessment agency called the Invasive Species Specialist Group has nominated the bird as one of the '100 World's Worst' invaders.

If anything the Common Myna, the most abundant and successful of several urban-dwelling starlings in the Indian subcontinent, raises the possibility of an even wider expansion. It is larger than the Common Starling – up to 50 per cent heavier – with a louder and more assertive falsetto voice. Like their Eurasian counterparts, Common Mynas have been similarly cherished as cagebirds for their vocal ability, which encompasses human speech, and for their

'familiar, perky, well groomed' demeanour.[23] Although the human-induced territorial gains have been largely restricted to tropical latitudes, the myna's potential for global spread is extraordinary.

It is now found widely on archipelagos across the Atlantic, Indian and Pacific Oceans. It is precisely in these localities that it has become a potential competitor for rare and vulnerable endemics, including the Rarotonga Starling (mentioned above), but also the Seychelles Magpie-Robin, whose world population was just 178 birds in 2006. The Common Myna has also established outposts throughout the Middle East, China and Japan, but especially in Australia, New Zealand, South Africa, Botswana and even parts of southern Europe.[24] There is a well-established population in southern Florida, USA, where, incidentally, the more pleasantly spoken Common Hill Myna sustains a small enclave (25–99 pairs).[25] Given its commensal habits and capacity to thrive in warmer latitudes, the Common Myna surely has a potential to invade the agricultural and human-dominated parts of South America. The starling's collective range would then almost match our own.

STARLINGS AS MORALITY PLAY

Therein, of course, lies one of the more perverse truths about these evil twins of the family. They may be condemned for a whole host of genuine ecological and economic reasons, but they flourish where we also have flourished. In fact, they usually flourish only where we have flourished first. They

The improvised medley produced by a Common Starling in full flow is a sound that may well have inspired Mozart to write music.

461

Common Starling roosts were once an urban scourge in many parts of Europe; now they are often tourist attractions.

have reached many of the places in which they thrive solely because we have released them there and encouraged them to thrive. Often they were introduced because of their famed appetite for insects and it was thought they would control the local pests. The blame – if blame or moral judgement is appropriate to such issues – lies as much with us as it does with the Common Myna and the Common Starling. The British in particular bear a heavy responsibility, especially in Australia, New Zealand, Jamaica and South Africa. Eugene Schieffelin, however, was a member of an old and wealthy New York family with a house on Madison Avenue. Yet perhaps even he should not be identified as the starling's sole sorcerer's apprentice. Others tried repeatedly to introduce the bird to North America; they were just not as successful as Schieffelin.[26]

One recurrent feature of the spread is the birds' preference for urban settings or for areas that mix human settlement with arable agriculture and grazing pasture. However, this adaptation to the standard, heavily modified, fertilised landscapes of the Western world is a relatively recent phenomenon. In the early nineteenth century Common Starlings were anything but common in large parts of Britain (Scotland, west Wales, northern and south-west England). By the end of that century, however, they had become abundant everywhere except the Scottish Highlands. Over exactly the same period the human population had risen from 10–35 million.[27]

Starlings were as much the beneficiaries of the modern landscape as were people. When Eugene Schieffelin conjured the genie in Central Park and loosed Common Starlings upon the New World, the birds were almost pre-adapted to flourish in a countryside recently reshaped and made

fertile by (an originally European) white settler community. In precisely the same ways that the bird's stock rose in an ever more intensively humanised Britain, so in America it increased 'to excessive numbers in a cultivated, fertile country'. Yet it was 'rarely seen in unsettled regions'.[28]

Pointing out that their fortunes have been closely tied to our own is not to diminish the deleterious impact that Common Starlings are proven to have. In North America their agricultural impact is calculated at $800 million annually.[29] In France during the 1980s the losses to livestock farmers alone (through starling consumption of corn sileage) was estimated at 10 million euros.[30] As well as feedstuffs supplied to livestock, the birds predate many other crops, including olives, fruits of all kinds, particularly grapes and cherries, and germinating cereals. In 1960 a flock of about 500 birds managed even to take human life. They were sucked into the engines of a Lockheed Electra in Boston, USA, and caused a crash with 62 fatalities. A similar incident at Eindhoven (the Netherlands) killed another 34 passengers in 1996.[31]

Nor can one overlook the baleful ecological impact that non-native starlings have worldwide on all sorts of indigenous fauna. In North America the Common Starling has been particularly blamed for ousting hole-nesting species, from the Eastern Bluebird even to the Wood Duck (although a more recent review of this effect on native hole-nesting birds has shown the starling's impact to be less significant, except in the case of several woodpeckers).[32] Equally, Common Starlings are renowned for the stinking layers of guano deposited by their roosting hordes, which can in turn bring about human cases of infection, including a fungal condition called histoplasmosis.

Condemnation of the Common Starling has been a keynote in our relationship with the species whether the birds in question are native or non-native populations. Typically the British ornithologist W E Collinge, who postulated that the UK could hold 51 million breeding starlings (a fivefold exaggeration) in the 1920s, called the species 'a plague in the land and a source of great natural loss'.[33] Often the profound antipathy that the bird arouses is rooted simply in its abundance and success. When it is characterised in field guides as 'largely noxious', or 'jaunty, garrulous' and 'quarrelsome' one senses that subliminally these are transferred epithets (the Common Myna has even been accused of having an 'arrogant' walk).[34] Yet for some people it is this sheer humanity in starlings that is key to their sympathies: 'Starlings always remind me of human societies – opportunistic, squabbling and dependent on each other. I'm full of admiration for these birds for surviving and thriving.'[35]

Whether one loves them or hates them, however, we should all perhaps acknowledge that their seemingly relentless ecological triumph is nothing if not a reflection of our own. Mingled with our adverse judgements is a form of double standards. As an American ecologist has suggested, 'when we look at [starlings], to some extent we're looking at a morality play of ourselves'.[36]

When we laud the indigenous and condemn the alien should we not also reflect that these are the sentiments of a primate whose original home is Africa?

THE USEFUL STARLING

There was once an English proverb: '"Thou art a bitter bird," said the raven to the starling.' It meant much the same as the pot calling the kettle black.[37] There is more than a grain of truth to the old adage, and not just because we have hated starlings for doing exactly what our own species has done. It is also true because Common Starlings are apparently bitter tasting.

The seventeenth-century ornithologist John Ray suggested that their flavour was one reason why the birds were not eaten in Britain.[38] Yet they were consumed both in the past – James Boswell ate them in the Hebrides and declared them delicious – and in extremis.[39] During the Siege of Kut in Mesopotamia in 1916 (at which 1,600 British troops died and 13,000 surrendered) the hungry soldiers killed roosting starlings by the thousand, eliminating the bitter taste, it was said, by removing the heads. Starlings on toast was apparently a favoured recipe.[40]

The birds were also widely enjoyed on the European continent, from Silesia to Flanders. Since the Middle Ages householders had encouraged them to nest by placing earthen pots on their walls, from which the birds could be more conveniently harvested.[41] Examples of these proto-nestboxes, with what look like Common Starlings emerging from them, can be seen in Pieter Bruegel's gloriously surreal painting known as *Dulle Griet* ('Mad Meg') of 1562.[42] The ready-made nests have now vanished, but in France *pâté d'étourneau* is still apparently enjoyed.

Perhaps the most valuable aspect to starlings is not that they can be eaten, but what they eat themselves. The family member most widely trumpeted for its usefulness is the one mentioned at the beginning of this account, the Rosy Starling. Its ecology is closely tied to the abundance of locusts, which it can eat in massive quantities. A breeding colony of 1,500 pairs is said to consume up to 3 tonnes a day.[43] (Nor

A globular pre-roost flock formed by Common Starlings looks like a vast amoeba twisting and pulsing in the sky.

should one overlook the Common Starling's pest-disposal services. The ecologist Chris Feare estimated that Britain's population, while rearing a single spring brood, consumed 10,000 tonnes – mostly insects and including many injurious to agriculture. On that same basis, North America's birds could be eliminating 286,000 tonnes of largely invertebrate food for their collective nestlings.)[44]

Pliny and Aelian both mention the inhabitants of western and central Turkey praying for deliverance from ruinous insect swarms, and the first author described how Jupiter answered their appeals with what were known as 'birds of Seleucis'.[45] They have been identified as Rosy Starlings, which make irruptive migrations from central Asia sometimes as far as Europe. Alfred Newton recorded four such invasions in 1844 (Odessa, Russia, now in Ukraine), 1856 (Smyrna, now called Izmir, western Turkey), 1867 (Bulgaria) and 1875 (Verona, Italy). In each case the Rosy Starling flocks apparently coincided closely with the arrival of locust swarms, and the latter were then 'greedily devoured' by the former.[46]

In Georgia and Armenia, at least until the twentieth century, Muslim and Christian communities were convinced of the birds' ability to deliver them from locusts.[47] They also believed they could be conjured with specially blessed water that was brought from sacred wells and sprinkled with much religious ceremony. Although the references in Pliny and Aelian relate to ancient practices in what is now Turkey, the use of religious invocation in nearby Georgia was strikingly similar, and people in Asia Minor may have been praying continuously for starlings for thousands of years.[48]

At least in Russia Common Starlings are still birds of auspicious status. An estimated 25 million nestboxes have been provided to encourage the species, which is viewed as deeply benign to agriculture. A Russian ornithologist comments:

Common Starlings are very well loved in Russia, particularly as a harbinger of spring (they are migratory throughout most of Russia). Virtually every village has numerous boxes for starlings, and it was once compulsory for young pioneers to make them, going back to Stalin's time (and perhaps before). There were often school competitions for the best box, mainly among boys. There are also some boxes in cities, such as Novosibirsk. Sadly starlings have been declining in Russian cities, as in the West.[49]

It is this last development that may yet earn Common Starlings a wider blossoming of human sympathies. For the species has declined dramatically in large parts of Europe. In Britain and Ireland both breeding numbers and wintering migrants have more than halved in 30 years (in Britain alone breeding numbers have fallen by 80 per cent). In France the winter birds dropped from 60 million in 1975 to 20 million by the late 1980s.

With these losses have vanished old British urban roosts, which was a habit that Common Starlings acquired in their main century of expansion (the first was in Dublin in 1845). By the 1960s there were 69 such roosts in 39 British conurbations.[50] Today there are almost no large British urban roosts. Yet gatherings that involve millions of starlings are still not exceptional. One such famous example was in Rome, Italy, with a lineage stretching back almost 60 years, and final estimates of 10 million birds. Single streets held sub-groups of 100,000. Unfortunately the deluge of guano – apparently 7 tonnes per night – was so severe and destructive that environmentalists helped to disperse the roost during a 12-year experiment, by playing constant loud broadcasts of the species' own distress calls.

However, it is when these vast congregations are located in natural settings, especially in reedbeds or woods, where Common Starlings can be appreciated fully and without concern for damage. Vast and complex, the birds' amoebic slow-folding aerial manoeuvres have inspired multiple forms of research – how do so many individual organisms coordinate so beautifully without any overarching control or direction? – but also simple awe at their calming beauty and cumulative energy. Starlings have finally become major public attractions, even for people with no special ornithological interest.

Thrush family *Turdidae*

Thrushes are surely among the most popular birds on Earth. At one time they would have been even more so. The family was once considered to include a suite of smaller, beautiful and angelic-voiced relatives, such as the chats, shamas, robins and nightingales (see also page 472). In total that enlarged family embraced many of the world's most cherished songsters. Now the two groups have to divide the honours. Yet even as they stand today, the thrushes are almost as uniformly treasured as they are universally distributed.

There are 177 species worldwide, with high concentrations in Asia (63 species) and Latin America (52 species). The northern hemisphere is less rich in diversity. Just 18 thrushes have been recorded in Europe, of which 12 are rare migrants; while North America (north of the Rio Grande) has 24 species, including 11 occasional visitors. The one continent largely omitted from the thrushes' range is Australia, where there are only four species. However, the birds' popularity with humans has tended to make good any natural deficiencies: two of the Australian quartet are the result of deliberate introductions.

Nineteenth-century colonists in Australia and New Zealand, homesick for the melodies of Old World favourites, began a campaign of releases from the 1860s onwards. In the ensuing decades both the **Song Thrush** *Turdus philomelos* and the **Common Blackbird** *Turdus merula* flourished. Today in New Zealand both birds are present throughout the country including the outlying Kermadec, Chatham, Snares, Auckland and Campbell Islands. The Common Blackbird, in fact, has been called the most widespread species in New Zealand.[1] Even in the drier landscapes of mainland Australia, it has spread over a swathe of Victoria and New South Wales, from Adelaide to Sydney. The less catholic Song Thrush is confined to the southern extremity of this area.

The American Robin is one of the most successful species in all North America and vies with just a handful of others as the region's most popular bird.

There are several factors at work cementing the thrushes' popularity. In many areas of the world there are species, especially in the genus *Turdus*, that are among the most familiar of all garden inhabitants: the Common Blackbird (Europe), **American Robin** *Turdus migratorius* (North America), **Clay-colored Thrush** *Turdus grayi* (Central America), **American Bare-eyed Thrush** *Turdus nudigenis* (northern South America), **Rufous-bellied Thrush** *Turdus rufiventris* (western South America), **Olive Thrush** *Turdus olivaceus* (south and east Africa), **African Thrush** *Turdus pelios* (west and central Africa) and **Island Thrush** *Turdus poliocephalus* (spread from Sumatra eastwards across numerous islands into the western Pacific, with no fewer than 50 separate subspecies!). One factor running through all of these representatives is their confiding manner. Thrushes seem almost to thrust themselves upon our attentions and demand a sense of interaction.

Here are responses to thrushes on three separate continents. Note in each case the personalisation of the birds' identities and the sense of a reciprocal relationship between human and bird.

We live part-time in a cottage in the Muthaiga suburb of Nairobi, Kenya. The sitting room has French windows opening on to a small garden. My husband noticed an Olive Thrush peering in the window almost every day, and then one day the thrush walked in the open door. This became an everyday occurrence, so we put down a small plate of food. It would come in even if we had visitors, finding its way through the jumble of legs to the plate, eat its meal and then go. We are away several months of the year and on our return, as we opened the French windows, the thrush appeared and the feeding process went on as before. This continued for several

Nineteenth-century colonists to Australia and New Zealand were so homesick for the comforting sights and sounds of Common Blackbirds that they took the birds with them to both countries.

years and then it came no more. However, what must have been his progeny were around. One had damaged its foot. I started to feed him mincemeat and biscuit crumbs. It waited to be fed every day and whenever I went outside it appeared. If I was late it would 'tut' loudly expressing its displeasure, eventually it was almost feeding from my hand. This thrush (Whitey) was easy to identify as it had a white feather in its tail. Despite our long absences it always appeared on our return and we think this shows how long and accurate a bird's memory is and how it learns whom it can trust. If we were around it felt the area was safe even if we had strangers with us. This took place over a 12-year period.[2]

I joyfully welcome Mr and Mrs Robin's [American Robin] return as they are, for me, the first sign of spring. As a child each spring in London, Ontario, Canada, they would greet me as if to say, 'see, we're back, now winter is over, time to get out your bike and join us on our flights around this neighbourhood'. Their joyous songs have followed me through into the evening of my life. I now live in a very large city, where it is difficult to hear and see my family of birds, but thanks to the internet I can access their songs and pictures so I can have their constant encouragement around me 24 hours a day. Bliss![3]

A Common Blackbird was resident in our garden in Newmarket, UK, for five to six years. We named him

Brian and could recognise him immediately just by his mannerisms and, dare I say it, facial expressions. He became a fully fledged member of our family and loved nothing better than to listen to me waffling on about how wonderful he was, sitting on the fence and cocking his head on one side. He raised at least two broods a year in our garden and we marvelled at what a good parent he was, working tirelessly to feed his children. We also became 'guardians' when the youngsters were hopping about the garden, rushing out like screaming banshees to chase off various enemies like jackdaws, the neighbours' cat and the odd sparrowhawk and he seemed to know that we were looking after his interests and never flew off during these episodes. The fateful day arrived when, after returning from a week's holiday, I went straight into the garden and out came Brian from under his favourite bush near the house. Unfortunately he was trailing a wing which was obviously broken. He spent the night under the bush and on rising the next day I went out only to find his lifeless body. It was heartbreaking and I am not ashamed to say that I shed lots of tears. It almost seemed that he had waited for us to return from holiday before he died. Brian is now buried under his favourite bush. This season has seen a new kid on the block, duly named Bert who, for all we know, could be an offspring of Brian. He has had three broods this summer and all fledged, so the story starts again and will continue I am sure for many years.[4]

One largely subliminal but key element in our attachments to thrushes is surely their shape. Almost all have beautifully rounded lower parts, with a sweet ellipse around the belly and if they fluff themselves up they can look virtually spherical. This property of roundedness taps into what is assumed to be our innate response to the plumpness of babies, small children and pregnant women. (My wife and I recall our feelings of exquisite tenderness generated by my younger daughter's gloriously rounded stomach when she was a toddler!) One thinks also of our deep responses to other gravid forms, such as those wonderfully rotund statues of the laughing Buddha, or even simply the tactile sensuality of pots, mugs, glasses and cups of all kinds. It is surely no coincidence that we prefer to savour the effects upon our palate of vintage brandy or wine, and even hot cocoa, from such pot-bellied equivalents. Thrushes partake of our fundamental predisposition to the ripe sphere in all its myriad forms.

However warm our feeling for thrushes, the birds themselves are still capable of an authentically wild spirit. Even their worldwide commitment to the domestic garden is fuelled by a love for its invertebrate residents. There can be something powerfully other about their predatory stealth and, although it is usually on a pocket scale – the victims often worms and snails – it is not always so. The large **Blue Whistling Thrush** *Myophonus caeruleus* of south Asia is among the most impressively barrel-chested of the family. At 33 cm (13 in) and 180 g (6.3 oz) it is larger and heavier than many small hawks. I remember once seeing a Blue Whistling Thrush carrying a freshly killed mouse in its claws. Large thrushes will sometimes take and eat fish, young birds, newts, crabs and other animals:

> We have at least two pairs of fairly tame Common Blackbirds nesting in our garden and visiting our bird tables throughout the day. Recently I watched in amazement as a female blackbird attacked a medium-sized frog (about 30 mm body length) that had migrated from our garden pond into the nearby periwinkles. The frog was initially injured by repeated stabs from the bird, then shaken violently but not beaten. The attack lasted just three minutes until the frog appeared to be dead, at which moment the bird snatched it up and flew into thicker cover.[5]

Conversely, the great Brazilian naturalist Helmut Sick reported a giant South American frog of the genus *Leptodactylus* with a Rufous-bellied Thrush in its mouth. It says much about the uneven distribution of human affections across the natural world that the witness to this event rescued the bird from its amphibian death.[6]

EATING THRUSHES

One suspects that the same roundness that nourishes our affection for these birds was once at work in our parallel desire for them as food. Quite simply thrushes look good enough to eat. They have probably been part of the human diet wherever they occur and their bones have been retrieved from European cave deposits dating to the last ice age.[7] Even 12,000 years later they are still eaten in parts of the continent, although sometimes with a little more guilt than was previously the case.

These Spanish thrushes had been cooked for about four hours and so the bones had disintegrated. Thus we ate the whole bird. Despite the fact that they were presented as an entirely normal dish, although eaten infrequently as a treat, we were aware of an element of our own guilt which, alas, was quite overcome by the fact that they were absolutely delicious, accompanied by a good Rioja reserva.[8]

One of the earliest literary references to thrush catching occurs in Homer's *The Odyssey*. When Ulysses finally reveals his presence on Ithaca and wreaks terrible vengeance on his traitorous subjects, there is a passage describing how he dispatches a number of female slaves. Ulysses lashes a ship's hawser over a column and, 'like doves or long-winged thrushes caught in a net across the thicket where they come to roost and meeting death where they had only looked for sleep,' the women are hauled up and throttled.[9] Homer's detailed knowledge of netting thrushes suggests that he himself pursued the practice.

Thrushes were almost inevitably part of the vast spread served at Roman banquets; and the birds were not just on the table, but on the walls and floors. At the ancient ruins of Pompeii in southern Italy there are surviving paintings of both Common Blackbird and Song Thrush. In many cases the birds are shown in horticultural scenes, often in association with fruit, which remains even now a key food item said to yield thrush flesh of the finest flavour.[10]

In the Bardo Museum in Tunis there is an impressive third century AD mosaic (originally from Thuburbo Maius in Tunisia) with twelve medallions of edible animals, including what look like swans, ducks, partridge and pheasant. One, however, features four thrushes trussed in a bundle for the pot. Another Roman mosaic discovered near Ingolstadt in Germany, dating to *c.* AD 150, shows hunters catching the

This mosaic fragment of the second century AD, originally from El Jem, Tunisia, features five thrushes destined for the Roman dining table.

strikingly beautiful – and, from all accounts, deliciously tasty – **Fieldfare** *Turdus pilaris*.[11] This thrush-eating custom survived for almost 2,000 years in parts of Germany. In the seventeenth century Prussian trappers were said to have caught 600,000 birds during one season, although another historian put the annual total of Fieldfare killed with slingshots at 1.2 million birds in eastern Prussia alone.[12]

> I am from the hilly region east of Cologne, called *Bergisches Land*. There used to be a tradition to trap Fieldfares and other winter thrushes (**Redwing** *Turdus iliacus*, **Mistle Thrush** *Turdus viscivorus* and migratory **Ring Ouzel** *Turdus torquatus*; Blackbirds and Song Thrushes were usually released) in special traps. This practice was very widespread throughout the region until the early twentieth century. The tradition of hunting Fieldfares is commemorated in some local names and fairs. In the village of Bergisch Born, there is still an annual leisure fair called *Krammetsvogelfesttage* ('Fieldfare celebration days'), held, for example in 2007, from 21–24 September. A paper in a local journal from 1936 recalled the thrush trapping in the *Bergisches Land*. It ceased with an animal protection law in 1929. In 1936, in the (small and patchy) woods in the *Bergisches Land*, one could still find square pits in which the trappers set their huts. The trapped thrushes were killed and eaten; most of them, however, were sold to shops and restaurants in the nearby major towns and cities such as Cologne. A regional German ruler, Heinrich der Vogler (Henry the Bird Man; tenth century), carried a reference to his habit of trapping birds in his name. The trapping of *Krammetsvögel* is also known from other regions of Germany.[13]

There is a further intriguing classical reference to a thrush dish in *The Satyricon*, the work of the Roman author Petronius, who was an infamous voluptuary and habitual attendee at the court of Emperor Nero. In his book, one of the assembled gluttons sticks a knife into a roasted boar and out of the opening flutters a small flock of live thrushes that are then caught and handed to the guests by *The Satyricon*'s central character, the sensualist Trimalchio, with the words, 'You now see what fine acorns this woodland boar has been eating.'[14] The passage demonstrates just how long-standing was this culinary tradition, for many readers will be familiar with the dish, but in its more innocent guise as part of the children's nursery rhyme.

> Sing a song of sixpence, a pocket full of rye;
> Four and twenty blackbirds baked in a pie.
> When the pie was opened the birds began to sing
> Wasn't that a dainty dish to set before a king?

For more than 1,500 years these bizarre pastries containing live animals were a staple of European cuisine-as-entertainment. An Italian cookbook of 1549 provides the basic recipe:

> Make the coffin of a great Pie or pasty in the bottome whereof make a hole as big as your fist, or bigger if you will, let the sides of the coffin bee somewhat higher than ordinary pies, which done, put it full of Flower and bake it, and being baked, open the hole at the bottome, and take out the Flower.

Into the resulting cavity could be placed any manner of creature to elicit the necessary sense of novelty and surprise. Live frogs were one favourite, which were wont to 'make the Ladies skip and scamper'. Thrushes were another. These simultaneous eruptions from the food were said to cause a 'diverting Hurley-burley amongst the Guests in the Dark'.[15]

The more usual way to prepare thrushes was to take the tiny scraps of meat off each minuscule spotted breast and to bind it together (a Roman recipe recommended suckling pig stuffed with minced thrush). Thrush pâté is even now a celebrated luxury (but also, at one time, a rustic staple) in parts of Europe, while in Sardinia they are eaten as *grive*, a local form of barbecue. One revelatory statistic on the popularity of thrush meat appears in Natalino Fenech's book *Fatal Flight: The Maltese Obsession with Killing Birds* (1992). He suggested that the yearly bag, mainly of Song Thrushes, on the small Mediterranean island was 240,000–550,000 birds. Apparently the overall Maltese harvest is little changed today. In neighbouring Italy the annual total was estimated at 3–7 million and this figure is considered highly conservative.[16]

The French also allow trapping of thrushes in places such as the Massif Central. However, the slaughter is a highly contested issue and, like so many modern conservation stories, reveals a major psychological fault-line in our attitudes to nature. One method is the *tendelle*, a stone trap, which involves a bird coming to a fruit bait and then dislodging the support twigs that hold up a large flat stone (up to 10 kg: 22 lb). This then falls on top either crushing the bird outright or sealing it in a shallow pit beneath. As recently as 2009, permission was granted for the use of 20,000 *tendelles*, much to the horror of environmentalists, who view it as 'Stone Age' poaching.[17] French hunters, meanwhile, insist it is the maintenance of an ancient tradition, which dates back to ancient Greece.

If many are appalled by this modern European slaughter, they may be consoled by the fact that humans are often inadvertently kind to thrushes. Bialowieza National Park on the Polish–Belarusian border is an area of pristine forest that offers insights into Europe's wooded habitats prior to the advent of Neolithic agriculture and deforestation. Using bird population data from this glorious central-European landscape, ecologists have concluded that Britain's Common Blackbirds are now more than twice as numerous as in the mid Holocene. In short, suburban gardens and fertiliser-fed lawns are more to the Common Blackbird's taste than primeval wildwood.[18] And the UK's 4.5 million pairs of Common Blackbird represent merely a tenth of the much larger Europe-centred population.

THRUSH SONG

'Everyone likes thrushes' proclaimed Helmut Sick, and he went on to suggest that their 'songs are praised everywhere on earth, each country pointing with pride to the species that is the best singer in its area, claiming it is superior to all others'.[19] The following response to Europe's Common Blackbird could serve as a statement of our affections for the whole family: 'When a local bird starts singing at dusk I switch the radio off, sit still and listen. Their pre-dawn song is one of the few things that makes me glad to be losing sleep.'[20]

The sounds of the family members in the genera *Myadestes* and *Catharus* are familiar primarily to Americans on both

continents. Several of them, which are known in English as nightingale-thrushes (a name that evokes the purity of voice) or solitaires, have slow-fluted and hauntingly beautiful songs and reputations for being among the most accomplished of all bird vocalists.

> One of my two favourite songs is **Black-faced Solitaire** *Myadestes melanops*. The species is a highly prized cagebird in Costa Rica. It is known as the 'rusty-hinge bird' and listening to one of these singing in the cloud-forest at dawn when I was photographing Resplendent Quetzals almost moved me to tears it was so beautiful![21]

Black-faced Solitaires (called *Jilguero*) are so popular, in fact, that trapped birds exchange hands for as much as $300 each in Costa Rica, the trade in cagebirds potentially threatening the species' entire population.

Perhaps the best known among the group is a migrant species to North America, the **Hermit Thrush** *Catharus guttatus*, whose exquisite and slowly unfolded performance has acquired a reputation as the 'American Nightingale' and the continent's foremost songster.[22] It was commemorated in that hymn of desolation, T S Eliot's *The Waste Land* (in 'What the Thunder Said'), where the poet suggested a liquid quality to the sound: 'Drip drop drip drop drop drop drop'. To my own ears, the song of Hermit Thrush suggests something metallic, as if it has a hint of a tin whistle but played in the very highest part of its register. The pauses

are long and the notes have a pure, glassy, even icy, pitch. While many thrushes (especially in the genus *Turdus*) have some of the warmth and casualness of human song, the Hermit Thrush seems outside the range of any of our own vocalisations and it is this very inhumanity that speaks so powerfully to us. Aldo Leopold's memorable description of the song of Hermit Thrush is 'pouring silver chords from impenetrable shadows'.[23]

Henry Thoreau almost certainly heard it in the woods of Concord but never truly separated this species from its close relative the **Wood Thrush** *Hylocichla mustelina*, a bird almost as highly regarded for its song. Thoreau's commentary on his 'Wood Thrush' may refer to either bird, but this ambiguity is immaterial. For he pays homage to a fundamental optimism that seems intrinsic to so many thrush vocalisations:

> The wood thrush's is no opera music; it is not so much the compositions as the strain, the tone, – cool bars of melody from the atmosphere of everlasting morning or evening . . . The thrush alone declares the immortal wealth and vigor that is in the forest . . . Whenever a man hears it, he is young, and Nature is in her spring. Wherever he hears it, it is a new world, and a free country, and the gates of heaven are not shut against him.[24]

The quality of hopefulness is especially evident in the songs of the many thrushes in the genus *Turdus* (72

The song of the Black-faced Solitaire of Central America is so beautiful and affecting that it can move the photographer of this book almost to tears.

469

species), which are often characterised by full, rounded, softly burred notes that are best expressed by the letter 'R', rolled and repeated in short phrases, usually at an even pace comparable to that of a speaking human voice. Sometimes they also include complex mimicry. The most skilled is probably the **Lawrence's Thrush** *Turdus lawrencii* of central Amazonia, which is thought to include the sounds of about 50 other species in its repertoire, as well as the noises made by frogs and insects.[25] Often thrush phrases strongly suggest themselves to our ears as snippets of speech, as if they borrowed them directly from us. Sometimes it is not just speech that they take. A thrush in Edinburgh, Scotland:

> Sang a complexity of fragments, trills and whistles, a vast repertoire, each phrase repeated before another theme was seized and tossed into the mix. And then, the bird did something strange. It started to produce oddly 'electronic' sounds: the 'pow! pow!' of digitised noise before it reverted to more typical bird-like song. The place was near where children play. I'd seen them on Saturdays with those toy *Star Wars* light-sabres, waving them, glowing lurid colours, in the spring air, dramatic spaceship laser-gun noises ringing out. I made a connection then and wondered if it was this the bird was mimicking. I liked the thought – that I and my Song Thrush shared a sound secret.[26]

Perhaps it is because of these extraordinary note-perfect repetitions characterised by Song Thrush song that the species' melodies have proved one of the most tempting to render in verse. Poets (including Robert Browning, Edward Thomas and Ted Hughes) repeatedly returned to it for inspiration. Yet the best and most precise evocation of the bird's voice is by Alfred Tennyson in 'The Throstle'.

> 'Summer is coming, summer is coming.
> I know it, I know it, I know it.
> Light again, leaf again, life again, love again,'
> Yes, my wild little poet.
>
> Sing the new year in under the blue.
> Last year you sang it as gladly.
> 'New, new, new, new!' Is it then *so* new
> That you should carol so madly?
>
> 'Love again, song again, nest again, young again,'
> Never a prophet so crazy!
> And hardly a daisy as yet, little friend,
> See, there is hardly a daisy.
>
> 'Here again, here, here, here, happy year!'
> O warble unchidden, unbidden!
> Summer is coming, is coming, my dear,
> And all the winters are hidden.

Tennyson caught almost to perfection the staccato rhythms and the repeat phrases with occasional minute variations among them, but also managed to explore the intrinsically hopeful quality of the sound. The effect is reinforced by its occurrence during the season of lengthening days, increased warmth and natural growth. However, it is often the capacity of thrushes to sing, as Tennyson noted, when there is so little sign of obvious regeneration ('hardly a daisy as yet') that moves us.

All bird song is infused with this wider sense of rebirth,

but the fact that thrushes themselves are often omnipresent in many landscapes means that their sounds acquire dominance in the wider chorus. Thrush song is, in fact, virtually inescapable in some regions, assailing us even at night. The Rufous-bellied Thrushes of South America, just like the American Robins of central New York or Toronto and the Common Blackbirds of Madrid or Berlin, will sing in the hours of darkness by artificial light. A contributor offers her take on this insatiable canorous quality: 'To me it sounds like blackbirds just love to sing, they sing in the day and sing in the night like a fanfare, in a beautiful, rounded, throaty whistle.'[27]

The Beatles celebrated one of these nocturnal performances in their symbolic hymn to racial harmony, 'Blackbird', which is unusual among modern pop music for incorporating the real sound of the thrush into the song. However, not everyone loves these pre-dawn thrushes.

> The Rufous-bellied Thrush is pretty common in northern Argentina and my friend was once telling me about his New Year's Eve excesses and then topped it with . . . 'and then, I got home at 5.30 in the morning . . . you'd think I'd fall fast asleep? Well, no . . . there was a bloody bird that couldn't stop singing . . . drove me crazy!' A couple of years ago, while attending university in La Plata (60 km from Buenos Aires) a friend of mine mentioned the same problem, but in his case he'd drift asleep, only to dream he was actually killing the bird. So it seems that thrushes do not get along with insomniacs.[28]

The ubiquity of thrushes in many parts of the world carries powerful implications for our deepest responses to their songs. For we build up our relationship with bird sounds over years, even decades. Each bird that we hear, in some sense, taps into other buried memories of the same species, so that we experience not just the sound of any spring day, but the sounds of all the springs (and all the thrushes) we have ever known. Thrush song thus becomes a kind of audio-map for our whole lives, and it is this autobiographical awakening that is so moving and so important.

This impact of thrush song, indeed, illuminates a key part of our entire relationship with birds. For they are the omnipresent fixtures by which we order and measure our unfolding lives. They supply the quotidian furniture and raw materials out of which we fashion a sense of ourselves through recollection and self-reflection. Birds' songs help to mark the passage of time and the seasonal round, but also to give shape to the unfolding moment – what it means, in short, to be here, alive, on this Earth, right now.

There is another quality in thrush song that is directly related to the birds' abundance in the vicinity of humans. As Edward Forbush put it so beautifully about the American Robin, which is surely one of the world's commonest thrushes: 'On every vernal morning a wave of Robin song rises on the Atlantic coast to hail the coming day, and so, preceding the rising sun, rolls across the land until at last it breaks and dies away upon the distant shores of the Pacific.'[29]

Many thrushes sing most vigorously at dawn and a similar oceanic chorus of Common Blackbirds (my favourite thrush) swells every spring morning and floods across all Europe (in Sweden it is the national bird). In truth it transcends Europe, because the dawn tide of their song passes from the Elburz Mountains of Iran, right down into the oleander-filled valleys of Andalusia and even on into the Anti-Atlas of Morocco and those thick fig-shadowed wadis of the pre-desert. Blackbirds are present continuously across an area vaster than the empire of Rome at its greatest. Rather like an empire of song, we should perhaps think of it as one place, and the song as one song. Those dwelling within that musical territory, composed perhaps by 60–100 million voices, should celebrate a Common Blackbird heritage. Very few birds are so adaptable or so ubiquitous across continents to create a chorus on such a scale (yet see also The Call of the Cockerel, page 67).

THRUSHES AS SYMBOLS OF SUBURBIA

An aspect of our attachment to thrushes is their extraordinary capacity to thrive alongside us, despite often our complete re-ordering of the natural environment. The American Robin is perhaps the exemplar. It is the most abundant and widespread thrush in suburban USA and Canada, and proposed by some authorities as perhaps 'the most successful of all native birds'. There have been occasions when 'the legions of Robins, blanketing the sky above', numbered as many 1.25 million over one weekend in a single US county (Cape May, New Jersey).[30] These migrant thrushes spread to occupy almost every open space that humans have created, and are as much at home on school playing fields, interstate rest areas, in parks, gardens, or any flat, open, reasonably grassy spot, as they are in their once native forest.

As Edward Forbush suggested, the companionability seems to be enjoyed as much by the birds as by ourselves: 'All through the Northern States Robin ushers in the day with song. Hot or cold, wet or dry, the Robin sings. He makes himself at home in the back yard; he hops on the lawn; he knows all the folks and they all know him.'[31]

The bird's status as an archetype of suburban America was exploited with magnificent irony by the film director David Lynch in his chilling exploration of small-town corruption, *Blue Velvet* (1986). The film includes one of the most acutely observed dramatisations of violence in all cinema history, in Dennis Hopper's monstrously brilliant portrayal of the psychopathic Frank Booth. However, Lynch's real theme is the coexistence of innocence and horror, middle-class normality and Dantesque hellishness, drug dealing and murder in neighbourhoods of swing seats on front porches.

In the final scenes, which take place at the home of the young couple after they have triumphed over Booth's nightmarish reign, we are restored to what seems a world of middle-class propriety. All the insignia of this comforting landscape are emphasised in super-real colour – the manicured lawn, the red roses by the white picket fence and, presiding over all, the deeply ambivalent normality of an American Robin eating a bug. Or, at least, it is a model of an American Robin. Its arch falseness confirms the film's concluding message of hollow reassurance.

THE BLUEBIRDS OF HAPPINESS

If any thrush could displace the American Robin in the hearts of its human neighbours, then it could only be the bluebirds. They are three migrant species. The **Eastern Bluebird** *Sialia sialis* and **Western Bluebird** *Sialia*

mexicana show a bias in their North American ranges that is suggested by their names, while the **Mountain Bluebird** *Sialia currucoides* inhabits the uplands of the American West as far north as Alaska. Collectively the trio occupies vast areas of the whole continent, except central and north-eastern Canada.

The deep human feeling for them pre-dates white America. For the Navaho the birds were the heralds of the sun.[32] For the Hopi and Zuni peoples, bluebirds were associated with spring and female fertility, while their colour linked them psychologically with the west.[33] This symbolic importance has continued today. The Eastern Bluebird is the state bird in Missouri and New York, while its mountain sibling has been chosen by Nevada and Idaho.

The popularity of all three flows partly from the thrush family's shared assets of rounded shape, sweet song and confiding manners. Yet there is also something ineffably endearing in the 'personality' of this large-eyed trio. As Frank Chapman wrote of the Eastern Bluebird, its 'disposition is typical of all that is sweet and amiable'.[34] Even in the sixteenth century its friendliness was noted by the first settlers at the Plymouth Colony. To them it was 'the blue robin', a name deeply indicative of immediate affection.[35]

However, the other core reason for the bluebirds' popularity is surely the universal magic of blue in bird plumages. The colour undoubtedly exercises an especially powerful appeal to our imaginations (see also Parrot family, page 254 and Bird-of-paradise family, page 396). One thinks of the exalted place enjoyed by kingfishers and swallows, both of whose plumages are often dominated by blue. In Britain the Blue Tit has similarly galvanised a nation's affections (see page 410). The significance of blue in birds is perhaps

The Eastern Bluebird has benefited from a nationwide nestbox scheme in the USA.

▶ The European Robin's long-standing affair with people's gardens is largely cupboard love, but the British especially have wreathed the bird's back-door familiarity with a vast body of story and folklore.

most fully expressed in that species of no fixed identity – the proverbial 'bluebird of happiness', a mythic creature which has become almost a cross-cultural symbol of human hope and has its origins in a truly multinational scattering of folk sources.

If any genuine species could be said to have acquired the mantle of the imaginary symbol, then it is perhaps the North American bluebirds. The element that cemented this linkage was a genuine drama of life and death. In nature bluebirds utilise as their nest sites old cavities and excavations made by woodpeckers and other species. In the twentieth century they faced acute competition for holes from two undesirable aliens, the non-native House Sparrow (often once referred to as the 'English Sparrow'; see page 485) and the Common Starling. If left to run their natural course, the contests for nest sites are often won by the more aggressive newcomers. People therefore began to intervene to improve the odds in favour of bluebirds and the innate human sympathy for the underdog added an additional layer of affection for the much-loved favourite.

The idea of a bluebird trail was first floated in 1926 by Thomas Musselman of Quincy, Illinois, who used a nestbox of his own design. Setting up his lines of boxes along the

roads in Adams County of his home state, Musselman publicised the measures and his efforts eventually caught the imagination of an entire nation.[36] There is now a dedicated North American Bluebird Society, while bluebird trails are universal across the country involving tens of thousands of boxes. Illustrative of their ubiquity – not to mention the universal presence of the human devotees who build, erect and service them – were the 8,699 in the state of Wisconsin alone in 2009. From these human structures emerged 28,814 bluebird fledglings.

Common Starlings and House Sparrows are often killed to halt their competition. However, the boxes now supply nest sites for a range of other native birds, including House Wrens, Violet-Green Swallows and Tree Swallows. Bluebird boxes have helped secure the three species they were intended to assist, but they have also become a key instrument in the awakening of American concern for the whole natural world. Arguably, only a blue bird and, perhaps more than that, a blue thrush – described by the founder of the North American Bluebird Society as 'a symbol of love, hope and happiness' – could have galvanised a nation's affections in quite the same way.

Chat and Old World Flycatcher family *Muscicapidae*

This huge group comprises 294 species and is larger than all but a handful of bird families. They are small birds, mainly found in tropical Asia and Africa, and many of them have beautiful colours that are both bright and exquisitely complementary – powdery blue with buff, peach, orange or red are regular combinations. Yet Old World chats are frequently shy birds and are seldom seen without the conscious efforts of the observer.

They are almost all insectivores and many are lovers of dense vegetation, particularly forests, which are factors further calculated to exclude them from human attention. The obvious exceptions are birdwatchers, for whom some Old World chats are among the most elevated and sought-after birds. **Swynnerton's Robin** *Swynnertonia swynnertoni* of southern Africa and Asia's **Siberian Rubythroat** *Luscinia calliope* are classic examples. Yet for most people a high percentage of this bird family, particularly the 122 species of flycatcher, enjoy an anonymous life in the treetops, where they pass literally and figuratively over our heads. In short, many are creatures of marginal cultural significance.

Before addressing the exceptions to this rule we should first note that several distinctive groups within the Old World chats also buck the family trends towards shyness and dense habitats. They are the bush chats (12 species), rock (or cliff) chats (20 species), rock thrushes (14 species) and wheatears (23 species). These birds prefer open, often treeless, stony landscapes, a point emphasised by the fact that 48 species (70 per cent) of them breed or winter in Africa's savannahs and deserts. The wheatears can persist in the most inhospitable, waterless places, where their vivid white rumps and tails ('wheatear' is a bowdlerisation of their original Anglo-Saxon name, 'white arse'), flare when they suddenly take wing and serve as flags for their extraordinary resilience in such arid wastes.

Wheatears are also migrants and provide their family with its one substantial bridgehead in the Americas (the gorgeous **Bluethroat** *Luscinia svecica* also crosses the Bering Strait to breed in Alaska, while about a dozen other chats have appeared as wind-blown vagrants). The **Northern Wheatear** *Oenanthe oenanthe* traverses the whole of Asia to breed in northern Alaska, while another population of the same species has steadily leapfrogged from Iceland to Greenland and then into northern Canada. This pincer movement into the American Arctic involves Northern Wheatears in two extraordinary long-distance journeys. The Alaskan birds fly 26,000 km (16,155 miles) there and back to Africa each year, but some of the returning Canadian population reach west Africa after completing a 30-hour non-stop flight between Greenland and western Europe (2,500 km: 1,550 miles).[1] Northern Wheatears weigh about 30 g (1 oz).

THE BRITISH AND THE EUROPEAN ROBIN
If the chats have made any impression on humanity then it is partly as a consequence of their striking shapes. A number of them, the Northern Wheatear included, possess sweetly rounded body forms very similar to another hugely popular family, the thrushes, with which they are still sometimes linked taxonomically. In fact, many chats look like thrushes in miniature. Both bird groups make a claim on human affection not just for these delightful curves; they also possess disproportionately large heads with liquid dark eyes (see also Australasian Robin family, page 403). Creatures with big staring eyes – one thinks particularly of our own hard-wired responsiveness to newborn infants – are invariably viewed with special tenderness. Rather in the manner of characters in the Japanese tradition of manga comics, the owners of prominently large eyes often appear deeply soulful, innocent yet intelligent and deserving of sympathy.

The classic bird beneficiary of this stock response to large eyes is the **European Robin** *Erithacus rubecula*. 'The sprightly air of this species, the full dark eye and the sidelong turn of the head', wrote Victorian naturalist William Yarrell, 'give an appearance of sagacity and inquiry to their character.'[2] Such qualities, not to mention its fearless personality, have cemented the bird as a national mascot for the British and made it a source of endless story (see also *Birds Britannica*, pages 335–9).

> When my Grandad died we had a strange incident on the day of his funeral, when a robin spent the entire day sitting in the spot where Grandad used to sunbathe in his deckchair. It kept tapping at the window. We decided it was Grandad saying his goodbyes to us.[3]

> When I was 36 years old a robin kept coming into the house. Worried about the cats, I kept encouraging it to go out. But it refused and, even when I shut all the windows and doors, it kept flying up at the window. At the time we had a plumber in the house inspecting the tank. Smelling smoke, I went upstairs to investigate. The plumber had gone off for lunch but where he had kept his blowtorch some sparks had set fire to the felting on the roof . . . Because all the water pipes had been shut off I had to rush outside to find some water to douse the flames. I've heard how robins can presage fires, illness or death and this seems to be true. I love robins and feed the one in the garden, but birds, I believe, really can be messengers of the Gods.[4]

It is a perfect illustration of the deeply contradictory nature of bird omens that not all robin visits are regarded as positive:

> When I was seven or eight years old I had a robin land on the front of my dress, which refused to budge. I went into the house and showed it to my grandfather who warned me that it was a bad omen and that I should go outside with it, which I did. That day the police came round later to tell the family that my uncle had been killed in an accident.[5]

The clichéd image of the British robin, which is at variance with the personality in mainland Europe where the same species is often a curiously introverted creature, is the bold bird perched on the gardener's fork. Robins will sometimes summon the courage to follow us indoors, with a strong taste for churchgoing (see also *Birds Britannica*, page 338) that has only confirmed the bird's place as the ultimate avian emblem of Christmas. Occasionally the reputation seems deserved:

> After sprinkling bird food in the garden one afternoon and returning indoors, I was walking past our sitting room when a bird flew down the length of the room and plopped into the Christmas tree. He snuggled there quite happily among the lights looking like a bright red Christmas bauble. We worked out that in order to find his way to our tree, he must have hopped inside the utility-room door when it was open, flown through another door into the kitchen, negotiated a third into the hall and through a final set of doors into the sitting room. A real Christmas treat.[6]

THE VOICES OF OLD WORLD CHATS

One factor in the robin's cherished status is the quality of the voice and its willingness to sing in the twilight zones at both ends of the night. In Sweden the bird's early-rising habit earned it a well-known nickname.

> The European Robin is the first singer before the morning light breaks, still in full darkness, and his tunes are a cascade of very fine notes, silvery and like recently melted water trickling between moss-clad stones. Often it has just arrived from spending the winter further south, away from the bitterly cold and snow-covered north. In Sweden's wilder rural areas, the robin was for centuries believed to start singing early in order to wake up the capercaillies. Many people knew him simply as the 'capercaillie's alarmclock'.[7]

The ultimate voice among the family, however – the one that has given rise to what is surely the most important suite of avian motifs in all world literature – is the **Common Nightingale** *Luscinia megarhynchos*. Before attempting to deal with this theme it is worth pausing to note that the bird is actually one of several highly regarded songsters among the Old World chats.

A point not always appreciated is that there are even two species of nightingale. The Common Nightingale is widespread from the Atlantic coast of Morocco, through the Mediterranean and the Middle East, as far as the oases of western China. Further north, however, it is replaced by the **Thrush Nightingale** *Luscinia luscinia*. This species is much loved by Scandinavians as if it were *the* nightingale, although the renowned Swedish ornithologist Lars Svensson describes its song as 'more loud than beautiful' and suggests that it is a 'less vocally pleasing substitute for the "real" nightingale'.[8] Apparently when the Swedish novelist and playwright August Strindberg 'first had a Thrush Nightingale pointed out to him by a friend in Denmark, he initially thought it was a Song Thrush they were hearing. He was utterly disappointed, and wrote in his diary: "The Nightingale? Was that all there was to it!!"'[9]

Yet Scandinavia also possesses another highly reputed relative. One contributor notes that 'a singing Bluethroat on top of a low-growing mountain birch in Lapland, under the midnight sun, is unforgettable'.[10] In Asia other members of the same genus make a similar appeal to people.

> When I was travelling repeatedly to China in the late 1990s I regularly came across bird markets in Beijing and Qinhuangdao in Hebei province, about 300 km further east. Some stalls would have as many as 100 Siberian Rubythroats for sale, together with a handful of **Siberian Blue Robin** *Luscinia cyane* and **Red-flanked Bluetail** *Tarsiger cyanurus*. All of these are beautiful species, but they were almost certainly kept for their lovely songs.[11]

In Asia the **White-rumped Shama** *Copsychus malabaricus*, which is a long-tailed beauty combining white, red and charcoal grey, is among the country's most celebrated songsters. The bird is widely kept in captivity and in countries such as Singapore it is a focus of birdsong competitions. 'Shama' is also commonly used as a girls' name in India, although as one contributor notes, 'shama in Urdu is also the word for "flame" and used in poetry in the sense of a

"lighted candle". The latter association is as often the source for the human name as is its link with the Old World chat.'[12]

Irrespective of the high regard shown for these other species, the Common Nightingale remains the gold standard by which all birdsong is measured. Testimony to this is the use of its name as a way of honouring other vocalists. In Latin America there are two sweet-voiced troglodytes called the Northern and Southern Nightingale-Wrens and also seven species of thrush known as nightingale-thrushes. Several are renowned for their slow liquid flute-like songs, including the Spotted Nightingale-Thrush of the northern Andes. Then there is the extensive use of 'nightingale' in vernacular nomenclature. Sweden's Bluethroat, for example, is popularly known as 'the nightingale of the mountains'.[13] A common construct was to use 'nightingale' in the names of birds where the real thing did not occur, as if to indicate it served in lieu. An example is an old name for the Northern Cardinal ('Virginia nightingale'; see page 527) or the Northern Mockingbird (in Jamaica it was known simply as 'nightingale'). The latter is one of the nightingale's chief rivals as the world's top avian virtuoso.

Another regular pattern was to give the bird's name to famous human voices. Perhaps the best known of all is the 'Nightingale of Shiraz', applied to the Persian poet Muslihuddin Sa'di in the thirteenth century and then again to one of the greatest of all Persian writers, Muhammad Shamsuddin Hafiz, in the fourteenth. Science then returned the compliment when a well-read ornithologist named the central Asian race of Common Nightingale *Luscinia megarhynchos hafizi*. (One suspects Hafiz himself would have

▲ Abdul Rahman of Singapore says of his White-rumped Shama: 'My bird is worth around 2,000 Singapore dollars. The length of its tail, how it sings and the slenderness of its body make it worth this, but there's a local man here who breeds shamas with fifteen-inch tails and they're worth $12,000.'

◄ A bird dealer in the old Beijing bird market with a Siberian Rubythroat in the cage above his head.

cherished the circular nature of this conceit. He once wrote: 'Look at the smile on the Earth's lips this morning, she laid again with me last night.') Even poets who had probably never heard the bird sometimes acquired its name. The fourteenth-century Welsh lyric poet Dafydd ap Gwilym was known as *eos Dyfed*, the 'Dyfed nightingale', despite Dyfed (a district in southern Wales) seldom hosting the real creature.[14]

THE LITERARY NIGHTINGALE

The Common Nightingale has undoubtedly been more versified than any other bird on Earth. Perversely, these human celebrations create their own kind of difficulties. One of the core challenges is to respond freshly to the living creature without being affected by the sheer weight of expectation created by all the poetry, music and literature that, in some ways, entrap the experience in a thorn forest of cultural reference. Suffice to say that to hear the song by night is usually a powerful enough encounter to dispel any sense of cliché or disappointment, as Strindberg felt on hearing its close relative.

Common Nightingale song is remarkable for its volume and range. Many have tried to convey the experience through precise description of the sounds. One of the best, if allowances are made for its time and place, was by the French Comte de Buffon in the late eighteenth century. He wrote:

[The nightingale] succeeds in all styles, he renders all expressions . . . and he also augments their effect by contrast . . . he begins by a timid prelude, by faint uncertain sounds, as if he would try his instrument and interest his audience; then gaining courage he becomes gradually animated, warmed, and he soon displays in their plenitude all the resources of his incomparable organ, brilliant bursts, lively delicate trills, volleys of notes whose distinctness equals their volubility; an internal dull murmur, not itself pleasing to the ear, but very fit to enhance the brilliancy of the agreeable strains, sudden, brilliant and rapid runs . . . plaintive accents, tender cadences; sounds dwelt on without art, but swelling with sentiment; enchantingly penetrating notes, the true sighs of voluptuousness and love, which seem to come from the heart.[15]

Buffon's description is typical for its recourse to purple, but the great French naturalist genuinely captured the almost physical shape and power of the song, and its matchless alternation with passages of silence and exquisite vocal tenderness. The signature sound is a quickening and intensifying sequence of monosyllables that surge with bullet-like velocity and impact. Sometimes the phrases can be heard from several kilometres away. In the diction of Western poetry they were represented as *jug, jug*. Yet Buffon also conveys the other core human experience when listening to this bird: that somehow it is aware of the intense emotional charge contained within its performance and transmitted to the audience. As he notes, it is a song 'swelling with sentiment'.

In trying to understand why this particular species has had such impact before all others, there is a fundamental truism that bears repetition. In the case of most birds it is possible to watch it as it vocalises and, however wonderful that might be, the fact fixes and delimits the range of its psychological impact. Yet nightingales, in true chat tradition,

are classic skulkers. In addition they regularly – although do not exclusively – sing at night, so observing them is often impossible. The song is thus a disembodied music. One must assume the whereabouts and character of the author. In a sense this lack of fixity gives fullest rein to the human imagination and its appeal is deeper and richer (see also Lark family, page 422).

It is very difficult to summarise the full spectrum of ideas that the bird and its music have been impelled to express, but it has been wreathed intimately around those two human nocturnal enterprises – love and sex. Another keynote is intense and soulful emotion, whether it be exhilarating happiness (as in John Keats' famous 'Ode to a Nightingale', 1819) or intoxicating passion (as implied by Buffon's reference to 'the true sighs of voluptuousness and love'). All too often, however, it has expressed extreme emotion stained with melancholy, especially in the Western tradition, where Greek myth long supplied a tragic backcloth to nightingale references.

Two powerful, viscerally dark stories were embedded in Hellenic culture long before the likes of Aristotle or Pliny the Elder ever wrote about the real bird. One was the story of Aëdon. She was mother to Itylus, but so consumed by jealousy of her sister, Niobe, a mother of six sons and six daughters, that she attempted to kill Niobe's eldest-born child. In error, however, Aëdon murders her one and only offspring. She is so transfixed by grief at Itylus' death that, out of pity, Zeus transforms her into the sad-songed bird of the night.

Even more blood soaked is the myth already recounted in the context of the hoopoe (see page 324): the tragic tale of King Tereus and the two queen sisters, Procne and Philomela. Suffice to say here that the myth embraces extreme cruelty, murder, mutilation and cannibalism. Two important details that helped shape literary nightingales ever afterwards are that Tereus is inspired to his terrible crimes partly by the enchanting voice of his sister-in-law, Philomela. Secondly, after she is raped by Tereus, she is revenged by her mutilated sister, Procne, in the most visceral fashion, when Procne serves Tereus with his own son, Itys, as a dish at dinner. Thereafter Zeus conjures all into birds: Tereus as a hoopoe, Procne as a swallow and Philomela as a nightingale forever sobbing the name of the murdered nephew *Itu, Itu*.[16]

It is worth pausing to note that even if only subliminally the characters from these stories live on in the nomenclature of modern ornithology. Aëdon is part of the scientific name for Thick-billed Warbler and for House Wren, Philomela is found in the name for the Song Thrush, while Procne has given title to a genus of swallows (see page 419). The word 'Philomel' also became the stock literary alternative for the nightingale. Yet what survived most potently from the ancient world is an underlying sense that the song is a song of sadness. Even today it is commonplace to talk of nightingale vocalisations as 'sobbing'. The other classic inheritance from Greek myth which has been recycled by Western writers for more than two millennia is the idea that the singing bird whose heavenly voice draws all our responses is a female, like Philomela. All these elements, rooted in the cultural world of ancient Greece, are manifest in the works of writers 2,000 years later, such as William Shakespeare. In *The Rape of Lucrece*, for example, he wrote:

> Come, Philomel, that sing'st of ravishment,
> Make thy sad grove in my dishevell'd hair.
> As the dank earth weeps at thy languishment,
> So I at each sad stain will strain a tear,

The same Shakespearean error of gender – since the real songster is a territorial male – surfaces even in the most famous English poem on the bird, Keats' 'Ode to a Nightingale'.[17]

> My heart aches, and a drowsy numbness pains
>   My sense, as though of hemlock I had drunk,
> Or emptied some dull opiate to the drains
>   One minute past, and Lethe-wards had sunk:
> 'Tis not through envy of thy happy lot,
>   But being too happy in thine happiness, –
>   That thou, light-winged Dryad of the trees,
>   In some melodious plot
> Of beechen green, and shadows numberless,
>   Singest of summer in full-throated ease.

Alas, 200 years of recycled reference and repetition – including the classroom chore of committing it to memory – separate us from Keats' great poem. It has set in train a pattern of adverse reaction, which is sometimes felt towards the real birdsong itself. In a perverse way, we are so familiar and perhaps jaded in our response to Keats' heightened language and Romantic sentiment that it takes an effort of will to re-excavate the poem's wonderful originality.

Keats' eight stanzas summarise so much of the European tradition of nightingale verse, particularly the ideas that it is a song steeped in myth, but also a song of intense, almost unbearable emotion; that it is a kind of artistic ideal and a measure of human art, especially that of the poet; and that hearing it invites thoughts of death and a recognition of our own deep conscious separation from the world of nature where this sublime music so miraculously arises. Keats' ode is often deemed the work that unleashed our love affair with the bird, when perhaps it should be seen with greater justice not as the beginning but as the end of a long lineage of nightingale-inspired verse.

Certainly what followed was the bird's almost inevitable descent towards cliché. In his book *Say Goodbye to the Cuckoo*, Michael McCarthy argues that after Keats' encounter with a genuine *Luscinia megarhynchos* as he sat under a plum tree in his garden on Hampstead Heath, London, in May 1819, 'nightingales became "poetic". They were plonked into that toolbox of handy lyrical spare parts which also contained roses, kisses, dreams, moonlight and rainbows.'[18] He points out that within 90 years, modernism had turned the symbolism of this Old World chat on its head. The bird of romance had become tawdry and embittered, its song of love a sound of modern alienation, and of mechanical joyless sex. As T S Eliot noted in *The Waste Land*, Philomel's exquisite strains are nothing more than '"Jug Jug" to dirty ears'.

Fortunately the new art of cinema was able to bypass this cultural cul-de-sac and extend the bird's symbolic life for another century, if only because the real song, even as part of a soundtrack, is so powerful and so beautiful that it transcends any burden of human thought. Perhaps the most precise, effective and poignant usage of nightingale in modern cinema occurs in the French film *Jean de Florette*, by director Claude Berri, starring Gérard Depardieu and Yves

Montand. The film is set in Provence, a place with a long tradition of literary nightingales. (Keats himself made the connection when he asked for a draught of wine, 'Tasting of Flora and the country green / Dance, and Provençal song, and sunburnt mirth!')

In *Jean de Florette* (1986) the song of nightingales is a constant background to the dialogue and action. Not only is its usage natural historically apt, it also serves like a Greek chorus, summarising the plot and annotating the exquisite ironies unfolding as we watch. The film, based on the two great novels of Marcel Pagnol, tells the story of a malign farmer (Yves Montand) who, in connivance with his nephew, oversees the tragic demise of a hunchback neighbour (Gérard Depardieu) by secretly blocking up the only spring on the latter's farm. The two grasping rustics then watch Depardieu – his dreams, his farm and his life – slowly die

The meaning of those heavenly notes pouring from the saffron-lined mouth of a Common Nightingale is one of the most versified mysteries in all nature.

for want of water. Only at the end of the film's sequel, called *Manon des Sources* (1986), does the farmer come to realise the agonising pain of his circumstance. The hunchback he ruined was actually his only child by the only woman he had ever loved. If the character is not, like Tereus, doomed to eat his own son, he has at least slowly watched him die of thirst and is a figure supremely suited to Greek myth, and to the sobbing song of nightingales.

NIGHTINGALES IN PERSIAN POETRY

The claim that this is the most versified of all birds could be advanced on the basis solely of its place in European literature. What converts the nightingale to the avian symbol that is surely the richest in all writing is its role in Middle Eastern literature. The love affair between the rose and the nightingale is an ancient motif, whose central part in Persian verse long pre-dates the best-known nightingale poems in the European canon. In fact it is so much at the heart of Persian lyric verse that it has occasionally been called 'somewhat condescendingly, "rose-and-nightingale poetry"'.[19]

The bird classically appears in the short Persian verse form known as the *ghazal*, which not only adheres to strict rules of structure – line length, metre, rhyming patterns, etc. – it also draws upon a treasure hoard of poetic symbols. The nightingale and the rose are just two, albeit centrally important, motifs in a large catalogue. Each poet is expected to master the rigorous compositional tradition and then find ways to develop or respond afresh to the repertoire of stock images. The *ghazal* is thus dense with puns, allusions and references to earlier works, but the aim is to inhabit the formal architecture without it intruding or obstructing the natural flow of sense and feeling, and to infuse private emotion and experience into a preordained body of symbols. However, a leading modern Urdu critic observes that the *ghazal*, which has been described as 'one of the great artistic forms of world literature', is not meant 'to explain and illuminate the poet's feelings; on the contrary it is meant to veil them'.[20] Ambiguity is therefore central to the entire canon.

The Persian word for nightingale, *bulbul*, has itself become a source of separate confusion, having long been applied to the nocturnal songbird, but also more recently to the completely different bird family the bulbuls *Pycnonotidae* (for consideration of this ornithological muddle see page 430). In Farsi the name *bulbul* finds a convenient sound echo in the name for the rose (*gul*), a rhyme that has been endlessly exploited by poets. Although these are central elements in Persian verse and there is an epic work, *Gül u bülbül*, by the Turkish poet Mohammed Faźli (1506–1563), Persian poets seldom dwell exclusively on this single theme in the manner of Keats in his famous ode. Rather the nightingale/ rose relationship is drawn in tangentially as one of many recurrent motifs. A typically fleeting reference occurs in what is perhaps the best-known, and often the *only* known, Persian verse throughout the Western world, the *Rubáiyát* of Omar Khayyám. The sixth verse of Edward FitzGerald's famous translation (fifth edition) reads:

> And David's lips are lockt; but in divine
> High-piping Pehleví, with 'Wine! Wine! Wine!
> Red Wine!' – the Nightingale cries to the Rose
> That sallow cheek of hers to' incarnadine.[21]

At the core of the coupling of the flower and the bird is the idea that the nightingale sings to its beloved rose, rather than to any female bird partner. In *The Conference of the Birds*, the twelfth-century poem of Farid ud-Din Attar, the nightingale is asked by the hoopoe to go in search of God (the *Simurgh*) and is introduced thus:

> He poured emotion into each of the thousand notes of his song; and in each was to be found a world of secrets. When he sang of these mysteries the birds became silent. 'The secrets of love are known to me,' he said . . . 'So deep in love am I with the Rose that I do not even think of my own existence; but only of the Rose and the coral of her petals. The journey to the Simurgh is beyond my strength; the love of the Rose is enough for the Nightingale.'[22]

As Annemarie Schimmel argues in her masterly account of Persian verse *The Two-Colored Brocade*, so much of the poetry's multi-layered complexity is lost in translation. Yet very little that may seem casual is as it appears. Even the thousand notes of the nightingale's song (and often it is rendered as a thousand voices) is, in fact, a precise number assumed to comprise the bird's full musical repertoire. An alternative name for the species in Farsi is *hazar dastan*. An Iranian contributor explains that the name 'means "a thousand hands"! It comes from a tale that describes how this species can imitate one thousand songs and *hazar dastan* refers to this unbelievable ability. *Hazar dast* in Farsi means a juggler who can do anything.'[23] (In fact, acoustic analysis has shown that 1,000 voices is a little on the high side. A singing male produces in unique and unrepeated sequences a basic 600 different unit-types of sound, which it orders into 400 phrases per hour of song, with five to 20 unit-types per phrase.)[24]

Equally the heartfelt devotion expressed by the nightingale for the rose was itself an echo of human love, which is often a major subject of the Persian *ghazal*. And, rather like the literary conventions that shaped the verse itself, this emotional attachment felt by the poet for their own beloved was fettered by similarly strict cultural rules. The passion, which was as often expressed for another man as for a woman, was ideally a chaste and selfless devotion, rather in the manner of the courtly love that was such a part of European life in the Middle Ages (it is routinely suggested that the medieval troubadour tradition was deeply influenced and shaped by Islamic poetry). It was often presented as an unrequited affair and the sad strains of the bird for the beautiful but unobtainable rose mirror the thwarted condition of the poet's own relationship.

Yet the poetry's recourse to images of nature (nightingales and roses) and of other worldly pleasures (wine, drinking, tavern life, etc.) emphasises that this was a real and passionate love that admitted of the possibility of physical union. Attar's reference to 'the coral of her petals', for example, is not a casual allusion simply to the flower's form. Rather the opened rose, touched by the warm spring breeze, carried implicit suggestions of erotic fulfilment. The red of the rose is linked metaphorically to the red wine of earthly pleasure and to the red blood of real experience. Perhaps it is the strong materialist tradition of the West that wishes to find correspondence in Persian verse, but European translators have often overemphasised the worldliness of this Islamic poetry. Typically FitzGerald's famous translation of Omar Khayyám's *Rubáiyát* is cherished precisely for its celebration of sense and 'sin' – wine, women and song – over strict religious orthodoxy.

Yet, as is always the case in Persian verse, nothing is ever that simple. The garden, which is itself so much one of the great inventions of Persian civilisation, is both a real earthly place where a bird and flower might meet, but it is also the physical embodiment of Islamic paradise. Similarly, for Muslims the garden's most precious inhabitant, the rose, has special connotations, the flower traditionally arising from a drop of perspiration that fell from the Prophet as he ascended heavenwards. The name of the flower recurs in mystical works – such as *The Rose Garden* by the 'Nightingale of Shiraz' Muslihuddin Sa'di, and *The Rose Garden of Mystery* by Mahmud-Shabistari – reiterating its metaphoric linkage as the seat of God and the place of divine presence.

Finally the singing nightingale should not be seen as just a real bird, but also as an emblem of the poet, who himself performs a kind of song, and thirdly as the stock symbol for the human soul. In equal parts, the love expressed by a poetic bird for its poetic flower is a metaphoric echo of the soul's own longing for union with the divine. The ultimate ambiguity implicit within Persian love poetry is that it is at once a celebration of passion and pleasure, flowers and birds, but it is also a language of the spirit and of faith, particularly of Sufi mysticism.

Here is one of the best-known poems by the nightingale of nightingales, Hafiz, where all the disparate elements are perfectly united. (Musella, incidentally, is the beautiful garden in which he is now buried and Ruknabad is the real stream running through it.)

Come, bearer of the shining cup,
Bring the red grape into the sun,
That we may drink, and drink it up,
Before our little day is done;
For Ruknabad shall run and run,
And each year, punctual as spring,
The new-born nightingale shall sing
Unto Musella's new-born rose;
But we shall not know anything,
Nor laugh, nor weep, nor anywise
Listen or speak, fast closed our eyes
And shut our ears – in Paradise![25]

Hafiz's poem is both a celebration of physical intoxication but also of spiritual ecstasy. Through the exquisitely complex machinery of the *ghazal* these apparent opposites are brought into a near-perfect linguistic harmony and aesthetic reconciliation.

It would not be exaggerating to suggest that when handled with such consummate skill by generations of Persian poets, this apparently simple linkage of two natural symbols opens out to express ideas at the very heart of human civilisation. The challenge, and some would say the dilemma, confronting us is to enjoy and to explore and to celebrate experience in all its sensuous immediacy – the brief, unrepeatable pleasures of daily life: a glass of wine, the touch of a lover, a bird singing in a flowering thorn – while yet striving to fulfil the ultimate spiritual and ethical possibilities with which we are all endowed. In Persian lyric poetry love and law, heart and soul, sense and spirit are all united through the allegorical passion of a nightingale for a rose.

Dipper family *Cinclidae*

On the map the two Old World species in this family, the **White-throated Dipper** *Cinclus cinclus* and **Brown Dipper** *Cinclus pallasii*, are shown to occur in huge, if disjunct, areas right across Eurasia. These regions are more or less consistent with the distribution of the many mountain systems, from the Atlantic hill slopes of Ireland to the vast high plateaux in China and Tibet. Similarly in the Americas, the ranges of the three other species – **American Dipper** *Cinclus mexicanus*, **White-capped Dipper** *Cinclus leucocephalus* and **Rufous-throated Dipper** *Cinclus schulzi* – create what looks like a broad swathe running south from Arctic Alaska down to a narrow tail in the high Andes of northern Argentina.

As always, the maps simplify the real picture. If one genuinely attempted to show dipper distribution it would appear as a myriad sequence of thread-like lines all following the courses of a million rivers. For the birds are some of the most water loving of all passerines and specialise in boulder streams of high places. Dippers are so attached to running water that even when flying through their inevitably linear territories, they seem loath to deviate from its course and will follow a river's every twist and meander. They build their large moss nests on rocks near water, but will sometimes attach them to human structures that cross or bound the river's edge – bridges, culverts, water mills, etc.

They have a remarkable capacity to swim and walk (except apparently the White-capped Dipper of the northern Andes) under fast-flowing torrents, and show many adaptations that facilitate these sub-aquatic feats, including a very dense, heavily oiled plumage, rounded 'brawny-looking' bodies, strong feet and legs, as well as amphibious vision. In imitation of the river's undulating flow they also constantly flex their legs to dip and bob in sympathy, while a short scut-like tail is often held aloft like a miniature flag.[1]

Most people who know dippers well invariably love them for their buoyancy that seems as much psychological as it is physical. They display a self-reassuring cheerfulness and seem completely impervious to gloom, shadow, even pounding rain. All five species produce high shrill rambling songs, which are themselves burbling and stream-like in structure, and which possess the necessary pitch and power to be heard through the loudest background rush of water. And sometimes they receive a little help:

In late October I was walking over one of the many bridges across a river where houses are actually built over it, so that the water passes in a tunnel beneath. To my surprise, I heard a sweet, prolonged birdsong. Another resident stopped to remark on it too. It was clearly a dipper. At first, I thought it was underneath the road bridge, but it wasn't. Instead, the song was coming from the tunnel and the singer impossible to see. Clearly,

White-throated Dippers – with their blinking white eyelids, their ceaseless bobbing actions and high rambling sweet songs – are part of the very soul of upland streams across Eurasia.

the strength of the song was amplified considerably by the echo chamber formed by the tunnel. What a delight this was at a generally bird-silent time of year.[2]

The great American environmentalist John Muir, famous for his lifelong relationship with the Sierras of California, was a particular devotee of this bird. In his book *The Mountains of California* he wrote a whole chapter on the region's native American Dipper. It includes some of the most telling and insightful comments on these large-spirited creatures and their impact upon ourselves:

> Among all the countless waterfalls I have met in the course of ten years' exploration in the Sierra, whether among the icy peaks, or warm foot-hills, or in the profound yosemitic canyons of the middle region, not one was found without its ouzel [an old name for the

White-throated and American Dippers]. No canyon is too cold for this little bird, none too lonely, provided it be rich in falling water . . .

> He is the mountain streams' own darling, the humming-bird of blooming waters, loving rocky ripple-slopes and sheets of foam as a bee loves flowers, as a lark loves sunshine and meadows. Among all the mountain birds, none has cheered me so much in my lonely wanderings – none so unfailingly. For both in winter and summer he sings, sweetly, cheerily, independent alike of sunshine and of love, requiring no other inspiration than the stream on which he dwells. While water sings, so must he, in heat or cold, calm or storm, ever attuning his voice in sure accord; low in the drought of summer and the drought of winter, but never silent.[3]

Sunbird family *Nectariniidae*

Flaming, Amethyst, Malachite, Golden-winged, Regal, Beautiful, Shining, Splendid, Superb, Elegant, Flame-breasted and Fire-tailed – although the vocabulary used in the English nomenclature for sunbirds lacks all the glorious overblown poetry that is such a feature of hummingbird names (see page 303), there is no doubting a dominant aspect of this family. They are creatures of such loveliness that it is remarkable they do not have a stronger presence in human cultures.

The reputation for beauty is undoubtedly greater in the case of hummingbirds, but sunbirds have attributes that the others do not. One striking advantage is that the human eye has more time and opportunity to enjoy sunbirds. On hummingbirds the fabulous colour range is often physical rather than pigmental and, therefore, dependent upon light hitting the birds at certain angles for it to be properly revealed. The birds can often just look dark or black. Another issue with the New World's most beautiful

The Hunter's Sunbird has all the colour and fizzing sugar-fuelled energy for which this exclusively African bird family is famous.

family is the hummingbirds' sheer intensity of movement. They have a thrumming invertebrate-like electricity to their flight that frequently makes them seem a dazzling blur and little more. While sunbirds possess a fizzing kinesis of their own and while some of their iridescence is similarly light-dependent, they are generally just a little larger and slower, and our modest eyesight is enough to gain full measure of their radiance.

One other facet that this family shares with hummingbirds is ecological. Both are nectar-feeding specialists that play a key role in tropical-plant pollination, but sunbirds are exclusively Old World birds. There are 131 species spread largely across the tropics, although they are unevenly distributed across their vast range. Africa possesses two-thirds (87) of all species and is truly the sunbird continent, but within it the Democratic Republic of the Congo is the family's main stronghold (45 species). Yet if this concentration were measured relative to surface area – the DRC is a country that is three-quarters the size of India at 2.34 million km² (903,500 miles²) – then Uganda would perhaps be the sunbird seeker's main destination. This central African state, a tenth the size of the DRC, possesses more than a quarter of the world's total (37 species).

Most sunbirds have long decurved bills and extensible brush-tipped tongues that are adapted to a specialist nectar diet. For all these reasons the birds love highly developed tropical gardens where many of the largest and showiest blooms, chosen to please the human eye, also support the high-energy demands of sunbird respiration. In parts of Africa, especially among expatriate communities, there is a

tradition of supplying sugar solution from special dispensers, much in the way that hummingbirds are fed in the Americas. One such Kenyan gardener describes her family's efforts to attract sunbirds:

> We feed them with sugar water and, at times, especially when the aloes are not flowering, we have masses of them, and they can get through a litre a day! Many of our friends also feed them. The ones we have are **Collared Sunbird** *Hedydipna collaris*, **Green-headed Sunbird** *Cyanomitra verticalis*, **Amethyst Sunbird** *Chalcomitra amethystina* (inclined to chase the others off!), **Scarlet-chested Sunbird** *Chalcomitra senegalensis*, **Variable Sunbird** *Cinnyris venustus*, **Northern Double-collared Sunbird** *Cinnyris reichenowi* and **Bronzy Sunbird** *Nectarinia kilimensis*. We have a pair of very tame Bronzy Sunbirds that fly in and out of the house, sit on the silver and fight their reflections on glass or silver surfaces. We also have Baglafecht Weavers and Common Bulbul's drinking the sugar water, while the **Golden-winged Sunbird** *Drepanorhynchus reichenowi* and **Malachite Sunbird** *Nectarinia famosa* feed on the aloes and leonotis when they are in flower.[1]

Not only are sunbirds lured to feed in gardens, they will also breed on occupied buildings, and sometimes inside them. They show a particular fondness for garden trellises, washing lines, ropes and chains – all sites that reflect the very peculiar architecture of sunbird nests. They are often intricately woven and elongated, with the egg chamber merely a small purse-shaped bag (sometimes with a porch-like projection above its entrance) that is suspended within a longer rope of vegetation extending both above and below. In the astonishing nest of the **Blue-throated Brown Sunbird** *Cyanomitra cyanolaema* of central Africa the whole thing can be over 1 m (3.3 ft) long and is often filled with mammal hairs and, in some areas, especially with those of wild gorillas.[2]

The exterior of a sunbird nest can then be carefully disguised with fragments of lichen or caterpillar frass and, in the nest of the widespread Indian species **Purple Sunbird** *Cinnyris asiaticus*, with bits of paper, string and other litter, so that 'it may easily pass for a casual wind-blown collection of cobwebs and rubbish'.[3] The overall effect of the nest exterior is one of carefully engineered dishevelment to deflect predatory attention. This protection is almost certainly enhanced by the nest's location close to human habitation. For the Purple Sunbird the full suite of nesting opportunities in Indian gardens is striking and examples include on an old-style punkah (hand-driven fan) pulling rope, the flush chain for an outside lavatory, the pocket of a nightgown, inside the folds of some canvas suspended on a washing line and on an outside light with the nest chamber resting on the bulb. (The incubating bird flew out every time the light was switched on and eventually abandoned its two eggs.)[4]

The **Grey Sunbird** *Cyanomitra veroxii* is a 10 g (0.35 oz) species confined to the eastern coastal areas of southern Africa, but in Kenya specifically it builds almost entirely on human buildings. The nest itself can be 50 cm (19.6 in) long and suspended from house roofs, verandahs, porches, garages and in the interiors of rooms, even bedrooms, such as on the wires from which mosquito nets are hung.[5] Other sunbirds clearly share some of these habits: 'When we lived at Diani on the Kenyan south coast, the **Eastern Olive Sunbird** *Cyanomitra olivacea* frequently nested on the cords for hanging mosquito nets and other similar suitable places. This is common in coastal houses, which often have openings for ventilation through which the birds gain access.'[6]

An intriguing sunbird story concerns one of the only two species that reaches as far north as the Mediterranean shore. The **Palestine Sunbird** *Cinnyris osea* is a characteristically beautiful representative of its family. The male possesses iridescent turquoise upperparts and a throat patch of intense glossy purple. The species has a strangely disjunct range with small isolated pockets in Cameroon, Chad, Sudan and the Central African Republic and then a second population running the entire length of the western Arabian Peninsula as far north as Lebanon. It was named by the French naturalist Charles Bonaparte (his uncle was the emperor Napoleon) in 1856 and was particularly associated with the plains around Jericho.

In 2007, on Israel's sixtieth anniversary and inspired by an idea of Amir Balaban, director of the Jerusalem Bird Observatory, the Israeli people mounted a competition to name their national bird (see also Bulbul family, page 433 and Hoopoe family, page 326). One of the contenders was the Palestine Sunbird, which is common, widespread and much loved in Israel, bringing a dash of tropical colour to the often pastel-toned landscapes of the Middle East. Many Israelis now put out sugar-water dispensers to attract Palestine Sunbirds into their gardens. Yet few people are as devoted to the species as one remarkable woman.

The mother of sunbird feeders in Israel – 'Saint Nectarine' – was a South African lady named Ziva Altman, who immigrated to Israel and made Jerusalem her home. She fed hundreds of sunbirds with an array of makeshift feeders: small bottles, water bottles for mice, recycled roll-on deodorant bottles and more. She wrote a great children's book about her adventures with sunbirds. I had the honour of documenting her before she died; she was very ill with cancer. She prepared her famous nectar recipe (1 kg of sugar cooked in a litre of water). It was a rare snowy morning in a cold Jerusalem winter and there were more than 50 sunbirds drinking like there was no tomorrow on her kitchen window. Without her they would have surely perished during the freezing night. Some of them had on Jerusalem Bird Observatory rings. They had travelled a distance of about 2–3 km to her house. She was the best sunbird city bar and she is missed to this day by sunbirds and birders alike.[7]

The Palestine Sunbird's name has obvious geopolitical ramifications not just in English, but also in the Dutch (*Palestijnse Honingzuiger*), French (*Soui-manga de Palestine*), Spanish (*Suimanga palestina*), Swedish (*Palestinasolfågel*) and Turkish versions (*Filistin Nektarkuşu*). This almost certainly disqualified it from Israel's choice as national bird, although it is significant that in Hebrew the species' name has no Palestinian connection. It is simply called *tzufit*, 'little nectar bird'. Before this might be accused of stripping the species of any Islamic symbolism, it should be noted that in Arabic the name may be pure poetry, but it actually has no more patriotic connotations. It is *Abu Al Zahar*, 'The father of the brilliant'.

While the Israelis finally opted for the Eurasian Hoopoe as their state symbol, Palestinian environmentalists have semi-officially adopted the resonantly named sunbird as their own national bird. However, therein lies a curious irony. For the sunbird was once not at all widespread in the region as it is now.[8] Its population has gradually extended northwards since the 1930s and it is assumed to be a key beneficiary of the many kibbutzim and moshavim established by pioneer Zionists, and especially after the 1960s.[9] These collective farms were characterised by the creation of gardens rich in nectar-bearing blooms – plants that were destined to aid the spread of the Palestine Sunbird. The species' northward extension as far as Syria and Lebanon is closely linked with this new and important food source. So, while it is a geographical emblem of Arabic Palestine, the region's glorious sunbird is also, as Amir Balaban himself suggests, 'rather a good Zionist'.[10]

Old World Sparrow and Snowfinch family
Passeridae

There are 45 species in this family and more than half are found exclusively or largely in Africa, although one part of the group, the eight species of snowfinch, are entirely confined to the montane regions of Eurasia. They are birds of such remote places that only infrequently do they come into contact with people. An exception is the **White-winged Snowfinch** *Montifringilla nivalis*, which is spread across a scatter of high-altitude 'islands' from Mongolia to Spain. In the west of its range, however, the bird has acquired a habit of nesting in the walls to Alpine ski-lifts and other recreational structures, or foraging for scraps among the snow-goggled customers at mountaintop restaurants.

It is this capacity to exploit such human opportunities that has enabled one species to free itself from the family's original range and embark on a remarkable global colonisation. The seemingly ordinary but, in truth, completely extraordinary **House Sparrow** *Passer domesticus* vies with the Common Pigeon to be the planet's most widespread and abundant bird. The Old World distribution encompasses the Indian subcontinent, most of the Middle East and much of the remaining Eurasian landmass from Russian Siberia to the Atlantic shores of Europe and north Africa. During the course of the last 170 years it has added an area of almost equal extent: including all of North and South America (except Alaska, Arctic Canada and the Amazon–Orinoco rainforest basin), southern Africa and the eastern two-fifths of Australia.

According to its indefatigable nonagenarian biographer, the British ornithologist Denis Summers-Smith, the House Sparrow began its journey towards domesticity in the Fertile Crescent in the early Holocene. He speculates that the gradual development made by our Neolithic ancestors from a harvest of wild grass seeds to the deliberate cultivation of primitive cereals was a process carefully monitored by this finch-like bird. Our crops supplied much of its dietary needs, while our early excursions into house building created cavities that were tailor-made for its hole-nesting habits.[1]

Sparrows gradually adjusted themselves to civilisation, becoming more thoroughly acquainted with humans in a way that is matched (among birds) only by the Common Pigeon. Yet one of the striking characteristics of House Sparrows is their curious double personality. We think of them as hugely confiding and almost impertinent in their opportunism, and many people will have experienced moments such as this one recorded in Egypt:

> In Luxor I have regularly seen sparrows taking sugar wrapped in long packets, attacking the paper to open it and then threshing it about to release the granules. In Italy, on Isola Madre in Lake Maggiore, the sparrows

The House Sparrow is a worldwide citizen of our gardens, towns and cities.

This House Sparrow had successfully built a nest inside a Purple Martin house in Florida, USA, but very often people evict the birds as unwelcome squatters.

around the little restaurant are particularly tame, and I have seen a sparrow steal a strand of spaghetti from a fork that was on its way to somebody's mouth. Last year my husband was putting a piece of croissant into his mouth, when it was stolen by a swooping sparrow! I noticed that when my husband and I were both sitting at a table, the Egyptian House Sparrows would visit, but when one of us left to stock up with more breakfast from inside the restaurant, sparrows were much bolder, coming on to the table in greater numbers. They also appeared to be able to monitor the focus of my attention. On several occasions I was sitting at the table when I was drawn by some activity elsewhere. I picked up my camera and looked through the viewfinder to take photos. On turning back to my table I'd find it covered with sparrows, tucking into my croissant, etc.![2]

While few birds better deserve the scientific name *domesticus* (it means 'belonging to the house' or 'familiar'), the species has never lapsed into outright domestication or lost an inherent wariness. It has remained, in a very genuine sense, wild and this separates it from its great commensal companion, the Common Pigeon.

GLOBAL COLONISATION BY HOUSE SPARROW

It is conventional among environmentalists to view the introduction and spread of non-native species, from the water-hyacinth to the one-humped camel, as a process that brings deeply unwelcome consequences. The House Sparrow's global spread falls squarely within that tradition, but we should pause before considering its 'alien' status across half the world, to ask ourselves in which places exactly should it be classified as a native and in which others as a non-native invader.

Denis Summers-Smith speculates that the earliest sparrows were probably African in origin, but House Sparrows had long colonised the Middle East and southern Europe during the Pleistocene. However, their steady progress through northern Europe was achieved only gradually with the Neolithic expansion of agriculture. He suggests that they may have reached Britain at about the same time as the arrival of the Romans (who could have aided the birds' British invasion, given that these conquerors liked to keep and eat sparrows). Whatever the precise means by which the species occupied these islands, we would never now think of the British population, nor birds in any other part of its Old World range, as colonists and 'non-native'.[3] Yet in many areas of Eurasia that is exactly what they were.

What the species possessed from the very outset of its world-wrapping expansion was a *potential* to occupy almost any habitat as long as there was a pre-existing human settlement on which to fasten. This enormous plasticity in the House Sparrow's tastes is exemplified by its occupancy of the Dead Sea region of Jordan, at 377 m (1,236 ft) below sea level, to mountain settlements in the Himalaya above 4,500 m (14,763 ft), and of the rainless moonscape in Chile's Atacama Desert, to the lush Amazonian cities of Brazil. In all places it is our presence that licenses the sparrow's own. Once that precondition is met, it is perhaps a question only of the time that it takes for House Sparrows to assume their 'natural' place alongside us. In short we have made the whole world into their habitat, and dividing the bird's range into places where it can be approved or condemned is arbitrary and possibly even meaningless.

The point is underscored when one observes the ingenious tactics used by House Sparrows to further their range. Moreover, their methods seem all the more impressive when one realises that most House Sparrows are the supreme stay-at-home birds, passing their entire lives just 1 mile (1.6 km) from the roof hole where they were born. In Brazil, a country that the species has now widely occupied and where it was first released in 1906, Helmut Sick noted sparrows following the railway lines or taking passage on large boats along the main river systems. In 1973 he saw them sailing on one vessel down the São Francisco River and speculated that this was how the species colonised new towns that were at least 1,360 km (845 miles) further downstream.[4] On the Falkland Islands, 20 House Sparrows were recorded to have taken a ride there in a whaling ship from Montevideo, Uruguay. They arrived in the archipelago in 1919 and quickly set up residence in the main settlements, where they have thrived ever since.[5]

Similarly in 1970 the bird is thought to have reached Senegal and Gambia in west Africa by taking unofficial passage aboard a ship. In the Azores, meanwhile, wild sparrows have even been seen on inter-island aeroplane flights. However, perhaps the most remarkable stowaways were the sparrows observed boarding a ship in Bremerhaven, Germany, which they did not disembark until they reached Melbourne, Australia.[6] Given this kind of innovation and flexibility, one starts to think that the sparrow's global dominion was as unstoppable as our own. And if they are non-native 'aliens' across half their range, then so are we.

Often, however, their spread was not just an event waiting to happen. Settlers in North America, Australia, South Africa, Brazil and elsewhere deliberately facilitated the birds' colonisation by releasing them. One of the core motives was a hope that House Sparrows would serve as a cheap insecticide and clear out key irritants, such as the mosquitoes they were intended to devour in Brazil.[7] During the 1850s in North America it was hoped that they would resolve New York's various invertebrate problems with defoliating moths, armyworms and Hessian flies.[8]

While the species does indeed eat copious insects, especially in spring when breeding, it does not eat them exclusively. In these situations people failed – as Aldo Leopold, the great American ecologist, once urged us – to think like a mountain. Or they failed, at least, to think in terms of a complete ecosystem. Instead the pattern of reasoning behind sparrow introductions on four continents and numerous islands was two-dimensional and linear. We hoped that the wild creatures would obey our neatly devised plans, but somehow do nothing else.

SPARROWS AS PESTS

The consequences were growing populations of a new species that was considered a problem as often as it was ever deemed a solution. The classic instance of a moment's folly followed by lifetimes of regret was in North America. Not even the meteoric rise of Common Starlings on that continent equalled the earlier spread of the humble sparrow (see also pages 460). In the 1850s the American poet William Cullen Bryant celebrated the birds' arrival with a poem. Within 36 years sparrows had reached the west coast and colonised 35 US states and five Canadian territories in between. By 1889 a list had been compiled of 70 species that were said to suffer in competition with House Sparrows. Looking back from a vantage point of the mid twentieth century, Edward Forbush noted how, 'The English Sparrow … has been stigmatized as injurious, pernicious, disreputable, salacious, quarrelsome

and even murderous. It has been branded as thief, wretch, feathered rat, etc.'[9]

The name originally coined – 'English Sparrow' – came increasingly to carry connotations of the boorish foreigner forcing itself upon its New World hosts. In fact the British ornithologist Alfred Newton lamented as early as 1896 that, 'Having found their new colonist a failure, it seems too bad of them to distinguish it emphatically as the "English" Sparrow.' Almost 120 years later the sparrow spat among the English-speaking peoples has lost none of its potential for a rather rough-edged form of comic banter. An expatriate Briton working in the USA adds:

> I get exactly this about 'English Sparrows', as they like to call them, all the time. I usually have one of two responses; I either offer willingly to take as many as I can back to the UK, since it is now on the red list in the UK owing to severe population declines. Or I agree to take back sparrows so long as they agree to take back all the Canada Geese [a non-native immigrant in Europe] that we have spoiling ponds in the UK. As it happens, they are all blissfully unaware of either issue.[10]

The more fundamental problem is that however much some admired the 'sturdy, upstanding little fowl', as Edward Forbush once called it, the House Sparrow had long been recognised as a pest. Nor is it the only one in the family. Several species have extensive criminal records for depredations upon crops. The **Spanish Sparrow** *Passer hispaniolensis*, for instance, can occur in enormous colonies, one 60 ha (148 acre) plot in Morocco containing an estimated 125,000 pairs (a super-colony in Kazakhstan, meanwhile, had 1.3 million nests over 1 km^2: 0.38 miles^2). The latter species is known to inflict serious agricultural damage in Morocco and Tunisia, where they are caught in their tens of thousands with funnel traps.[11] In Egypt it is rice fields that suffer from House Sparrows, while in Turkey both the last species and the **Eurasian Tree Sparrow** *Passer montanus* do damage to wheat. Finally in Pakistan a mixed flock involving sparrows, doves and parakeets caused losses to cereals estimated at $31 million in the 1980s.[12]

It seems deeply ironic that the place where the bird's pest status was recorded in greatest detail was in the home territory of the 'English Sparrow' itself. For centuries the British clergy paid small bounties on the heads of a wide range of proscribed wildlife species and kept an audit of their payments for centuries. More money was distributed for the slaughter of sparrows than for all other so-called 'vermin' put together. Through a meticulous search of these historical records across the southern grain-growing counties of England, Roger Lovegrove has produced (in his classic book *Silent Fields*) a wonderfully detailed portrait of human warfare with this irrepressible bird.

One extraordinary set of data stands out – the accounts on the Isle of Wight off England's south coast. In one of the island's small parishes, an area measuring just 1,092 ha (2,700 acres), they caught c.428,000 over a 70-year period between 1758–1835. In the 1790s alone, catchers across the entire Isle of Wight are known to have dispatched 275,000 birds. The millions of sparrows killed on the island over the centuries are incalculable, but Lovegrove does offer an estimate for the total sparrow cull across England overall: a 'realistic figure for the minimum number of sparrows killed

In countries such as China where House Sparrows are absent, the Eurasian Tree Sparrow takes over the role of backyard familiar.

and eggs taken between *c.*1700 and *c.*1930 is probably well in advance of 100,000,000'.[13]

Yet it is a mark of this bird's extraordinary resilience that the population was probably little affected throughout all this piecemeal slaughter, even possibly increasing and certainly remaining stable until long after the Second World War, when there were an estimated 25 million birds for Britain as a whole. It is only in an era of clean agro-industry – free of spillage or waste and heavy on the use of chemical pesticides – and with the loss of green space and sparrow-friendly architecture in towns and cities that we have really found a way to reduce the species by more than half in the last 40 years. Today our anxieties for this steep decline rest oddly on a bird best noted for being cocky, abundant and workaday.[14]

SYMBOLIC SPARROWS

The sheer ubiquity of the sparrow, especially in the Old World, has long cemented its status as *the* standard small bird and even a measure of the entire class Aves. In fact the word 'passerine', which describes the perching songbirds (technically the order is called the Passeriformes) and embraces well over half the avian species on Earth, comes from the word *passer*, the Latin for sparrow. It is typical of the bird's capacity to stand for all its kind that there is even now a World Sparrow Day (20 March) – developed by the Indian conservation group Nature Forever – which is both a celebration of our 10,000-year-old relationship with the family *Passeridae*, but also, as its website announces, an attempt 'to kick off a conservation movement to save the common flora and fauna of the world'.[15]

Sparrows have also come to stand for people. The bird's name was used initially as a nickname to describe small, chirpy, cheerful souls, and eventually it gave us a suite of European surnames. These include Sperck, Sparling,

Sperling, Spurling (as in the British author Hilary Spurling), Spark, Speer (as in the wartime German leader Albert Speer) and possibly also Sprague, Spragg (as in the American novelist Mark Spragg), Sprake and Sparkes.[16] 'Sparrow' was also the source of a stage name for the renowned French chanteuse Edith Piaf. Her real name was Gassion, but she adopted Piaf, which was a vernacular version of sparrow (*moineau* is more typical) and which well suited this elfin singer's fragile, if feisty, persona.

More widely the sparrow has also given us both an endearing diminutive in English for small and often undernourished children, while 'the people in Bavaria use the word *Spatzl* a lot – I suppose like "darling" – but it means "little sparrow"'.[17] In France *un vilain moineau* was once a 'disreputable fellow' (it is largely unknown today).[18]

The hard edge to this last human version of the bird, as well as the living creature's reputation for being over-sexed – 'The male suffers from satyriasis, the female from nymphomania' – are both deeply embedded in a fascinating suite of connections that link the old cock sparrow with human sexuality.[19] The association is truly ancient. Aphrodite was thought to drive a chariot drawn by sparrows, while Cupid rode them bareback.[20] In the sixteenth century sparrow meat was viewed as an aphrodisiac – 'The Sparrow is a full hot bird and lecherous, and the flesh of them oft taken in meat exciteth to carnal lust' – while the seventeenth-century herbalist Culpeper placed a particular health warning on the boost to the libido delivered by sparrows' brains. Until recently in China sparrows' eggs were recommended as a cure for male impotence.[21]

Perhaps most famously, the bird has a central role in a poem by the Roman writer Catullus (84–54 BC), entitled 'To Lesbia's Pet Sparrow'. It is *the* classic model of the poetic bird employed as sexual symbol. The poem is a mock plea by the writer to be allowed to exchange places with the small pet belonging to a high-born lover Lesbia (Clodia Metelli). As she fondles the sparrow in her lap, Catullus' audience of the late Republican period would have readily understood its richly erotic subtext. Sparrows, or, at least, small birds generically described as *passer*, were kept as the playthings of wealthy courtesans. In modern Italian *passerina* (from the Italian *passero*, 'sparrow') is an equivalent to the English sexual slang 'pussy' (in modern Portuguese the same word is *pássara* or *passarinha*); in Catullus' day, the word *sinus*, referring to the bird's place in Lesbia's lap or bosom, could also imply the female sex organ. *Passer*, on the other hand, was then a synonym for 'penis'.[22]

Before returning specifically to sparrow symbolism, it is worth exploring this avian vocabulary for sex a little further. In contemporary Italian the *passer* / penis link has passed to *l'uccello*, a word simply meaning 'bird', which nevertheless indicates how the double entendre has survived for more than 2,000 years. In Spanish the same sexual associations attach to *polla*, a 'chick' or 'pullet', or to *pajaro*, another word for 'bird'. We also find that in Dutch (*vogelen*) and in German (*vögeln*) 'to go birding' came to mean, and still mean today, 'to have sex', which is why modern birdwatchers in these countries are often confronted with knowing smiles and barely suppressed innuendo when they tell people about their field passions.[23] Finally, in the English language, the bird-genital double entendre has been transferred to a different kind of backyard familiar. 'Cock' is the male member or an avian male of any kind, but especially that arch exemplar of farmyard testosterone, the cockerel (hence the Howlin' Wolf and Rolling Stones' classic song 'Little Red Rooster').

Almost all of this European vocabulary looks and sounds male in origin and draws upon that macho sense of women and birds as stock objects of the predatory hunt. (In England even today a common northern word for a woman is a 'bird'.) It is invariably an oral tradition outside of polite society that appeals to men and is, possibly in equal measure, unappealing to women. It is striking that recent additions to the bird / sex vocabulary – for example, the Australian expression 'budgie smugglers' for the visible bulge in tight swimming trunks – suggest the same sort of origin. So too does a modern Australian term for the vagina, 'spadger', which is an old vernacular name for the sparrow.[24] (It is equally noteworthy that in one of the languages where birds don't serve as a synonym for women, other classic prey species have been found as substitute. In the Serbian language and also Croatian and Bosnian, attractive young females are *riba*, 'fish', or another archetype of femininity, *macka*, 'cats'.)[25]

Despite the strong gender accent in bird-related terms for sex or sexual parts, I suspect that the psychological alignment between birds and sex / love cannot solely be accounted for as a male preserve. There seems to be a deeper substratum of connection between the two that is not gender specific and draws upon a fundamental commonality. Sex and love, like birds, are elusive, flighty, desirable, precious, vulnerable. Birds are capable of movements between different elements, and here one thinks particularly of their instantaneous gravity-defying passage from earth to air. This transformational quality inherent in birds, even those as sedentary as sparrows, maps the fleeting and joyous transport offered by love in all its forms.

SPIRITUAL SPARROWS

From the very beginning of our encounters with sparrows it seems almost that we have felt compelled to view them as if through both ends of a telescope simultaneously. They were at once small, familiar and mundane; yet we could also discern in these apparently humble little creatures, with their busy, self-absorbed parallel lives, something large and possibly momentous. (Incidentally that double perspective seems inextricably entailed in the sexual symbolism discussed above. Is the sparrow not a tailor-made emblem for the body parts down there that are small and hidden, yet profound and important?)

Just as the modern eco-group Nature Forever has used the sparrow as an icon for nature as a whole, so others previously deployed it as a metaphor for the interconnectedness of all things. No reference is more famous than that by the founder of the Christian faith. Both St Matthew (10:29–31) and St Luke (12:6–7) recalled how Jesus used sparrows to express God's all-encompassing grace. The Book of Matthew reads:

> Are not two sparrows sold for a farthing? And one of them shall not fall on the ground without your Father. But the hairs of your head are all numbered. Fear ye not therefore, ye are of more value than many sparrows.

Picking up on this biblical reference, the eighth-century monastic historian Bede explored the sparrow's universal symbolism in his *Ecclesiastical History of the English Nation*. The passage occurs as King Edwin agrees to convert to Christianity and one of his advisors endorses the royal decision with this supportive observation:

> The present life of man, O king, seems to me, in comparison of that time which is unknown to us, like to the swift flight of a sparrow through the room wherein you sit at supper in winter, with your commanders and ministers, and a good fire in the midst, whilst the storms of rain and snow prevail abroad; the sparrow, I say, flying in at one door, and immediately out at another, whilst he is within, is safe from the wintry storm; but after a short space of fair weather, he immediately vanishes out of your sight, into the dark winter from which he had emerged. So this life of man appears for a short space, but of what went before, or what is to follow, we are utterly ignorant.[26]

It is perhaps the most powerfully poetic image of this everyman bird and its strange ability to illuminate the commonplace magic that touches all earthly life.

The same benign and positive portrayal of the birds is to be found in the art of another sparrow-infested region – China. However, in that country it is not the House Sparrow that dwells alongside 1.3 billion Chinese people, but its daintier, arguably more beautiful, relative, the Eurasian Tree Sparrow. Wherever the two *Passer* species occur together the House Sparrow is dominant, but in the absence of the latter the other species flourishes and comes to occupy the same commensal space around people's homes. It is partly the intense sibling rivalry, incidentally, that has helped confine introduced populations of Eurasian Tree Sparrows in Australia and North America respectively to a narrow wedge largely in the state of Victoria and to a small enclave around the city of St Louis, Missouri.

In China, however, Eurasian Tree Sparrows enjoy free rein and they are still stock birds of the urban landscape and rural villages alike. In Chinese art the species has also long enjoyed an important role in numerous bird-and-flower paintings, where the sparrow's simple lines and graphic colours seem perfectly adjusted to the stylistic conventions of this classic artistic tradition. Tree Sparrows have appeared in these artworks for more than 1,000 years, a perfect example being a scroll called *Three Friends and One Hundred Birds* (painted by Bián Jingzhào in 1413 and now housed in the National Palace Museum in Taipei, Taiwan). Despite the title, the painting depicts 97 birds clustered in an imaginary flock. They include numerous different species such as doves, redstarts, Azure-winged Magpies, Japanese Waxwings, Black-throated Laughingthrush, Red-billed Leiothrix and Crested Mynas. Dominant, however, is a turbid mass of 25 Eurasian Tree Sparrows.

As an example of meticulously observed bird painting it has few equals for its age in all Western art. Yet along with its detailed naturalism the work is also richly symbolic. The 'three friends' refer to a trio of plants of central importance in Oriental cultures – the pine, bamboo and plum blossom. It is on these three friends that the avian assemblage is arrayed. The muster of so many birds in one spot is unlikely in real life, but it is itself an emblem of a wider idea – that of peace and harmony in the world of nature.

So often in other bird-and-flower paintings the Eurasian Tree Sparrows are the sole representatives of their kind, while the plants with which they are coupled are austere and leafless (e.g. Cui Bai's *Winter Sparrows* from the Song Dynasty, 960–1127). The birds are shown on the arthritic branches of plum in winter or on the sparse broken foliage of winter bamboo. Yet the busy, chirping sparrows are self-contained and blithely indifferent to the human world or its emotional complexities and somehow suggest everyday life – in fact, nature as a whole – continuing endlessly. This ancient Oriental idea is perfectly captured in parallel in the words of the American ornithologist Arthur Bent. Reflecting in the early twentieth century on the irritating pest status of 'English Sparrows' in the USA, Bent felt compelled to concede this much. 'We must admit,' he wrote, 'that, no matter how much we dislike them, they add a little cheer to the bleak winter landscape.'[27] It is surely this quality before all others – this indefatigability, this unremitting commitment to the business of living – that triumphs finally over us and lends to the supreme bird of ordinariness a kind of nobility.

◀ Easy to overlook in this glorious bird-and-flower painting, *Three Friends and One Hundred Birds* by Bián Jingzhào, is the playful scrum of Eurasian Tree Sparrows at the foot of the image.

Weaver and Widowbird family *Ploceidae*

These 109 finch-like birds are specialists of grassland habitats in sub-Saharan Africa (Kenya alone holds almost half the family). Just nine species occur outside Africa – five in south Asia and three in the islands of the Indian Ocean, with one other, the **Rüppell's Weaver** *Ploceus galbula*, extending its range across the Red Sea into the Arabian Peninsula. There are, in addition, nine weavers that have escaped captivity in parts of the Middle East, especially in the United Arab Emirates.

The stowaway of the family is the **Village Weaver**

The Northern Red
Bishop acquired the
name from its colour
combination, which
resembles the garb of
a Catholic cleric.

Ploceus cucullatus. This beautiful bird is widely held in captivity
and escapees have established feral populations in parts of
Europe, and especially in the Caribbean, where it was carried
by slaving vessels from west Africa.[1] It was well distributed in
Haiti and the Dominican Republic by the eighteenth century,
and was at one time a serious pest of cereal crops, although its
nuisance status is apparently declining.[2]

The factor that explains the wide export of captive
weavers is their lovely colours. The male Village Weaver's
bright sulphurous yellow underparts with black detail is
a common combination across many of the family. Yet the
highest renown for beauty undoubtedly belongs to the 17
species in the genus *Euplectes*, which are known either as
'bishops' (nine species) or 'widowbirds' (eight species). Both
names reflect the gorgeous, velvety textured plumages of the
breeding males. The former group, such as the **Northern
Red Bishop** *Euplectes franciscanus* of east Africa, is often
black and scarlet and the colours were thought to echo

A male Southern Masked Weaver begins to construct its beautifully domed, pot-like woven nest.

those of a bishop's cape and cassock. The widowbirds are equally bright but several, including the **Long-tailed Widowbird** *Euplectes progne* of south and east Africa, possess black tails twice as long as the whole bird. These sweeping extensions reminded early observers of the ostentatious black garments once worn by human widows in mourning. (The name of the whydahs in the family *Viduidae* shares this set of associations; see page 494.)

Many of the family cap their arresting physical appearances with hugely atmospheric vocalisations that often include weird drawn-out wheezing or buzzing notes. They are very much part of the background soundscape in the African savannah. Equally characteristic of that landscape are the beautiful nests in weaver breeding colonies. The scientific name (*Ploceus*) refers to these skilful textiles and derives from the Greek *plokeus*, 'a weaver', while *Euplectes* comes from the same root word, with the prefix *eu* meaning 'well' or 'nicely' (plaited).[3]

There is huge variety in nest construction across all 64 *Ploceus* species. Village Weavers make relatively simple inverted woven 'pots', but a number of species, including the **Black-necked Weaver** *Ploceus nigricollis* found in a wide belt across central Africa, create a globular bag-like chamber to which they append an additional narrow tube as an entrance. En masse and often swaying in the breeze as they dangle at the twig ends, the nests in weaver colonies look like scores of carefully fabricated decorations adorning some totem tree or bush. Some nests, however, are less decorative. The great stick fortresses assembled by **Red-billed Buffalo Weaver** *Bubalornis niger* can be 1 m (3.3 ft) across and so heavy that when built on the wind pumps used to raise water on African farms, they can stop the mechanism.[4]

South African ornithologist Dieter Oschadleus has studied how weavers have started to build their nests on human structures. He writes:

One of the earliest examples I found was **Southern**

Masked Weaver *Ploceus velatus* nesting on barbed wire fences in 1986 near my hometown Dundee in KwaZulu-Natal. I observed the same site being used every time I visited, so it has probably been used for more than two decades. Sometimes weavers build directly on houses. At one colony of **Cape Weaver** *Ploceus capensis* at Silverstroomstrand in the Western Cape, the nests were suspended from the eaves of the roof, the burglar guards surrounding windows and under the shed roof behind the house. I found another case of the same species nesting under a shed roof on a farm near Lamberts Bay, Western Cape. Again the weavers were actively breeding. A more unusual case is of Cape Weavers that built their nests for more than ten years under the service walkways over sewage ponds in Cape Town. In July 2010 I started a citizen science project called PHOWN (Photos of Weaver Nests; http://weavers.adu.org.za/phown.php), where birders and the general public can submit photos of weaver colonies online to study various aspects of their behaviour. Many more examples of weaver nests built on man-made structures may be viewed at http://weavers.adu.org.za/phown_query.php?ask=man-made.[5]

RED-BILLED QUELEA

Occasionally weaver nests achieve very high densities, and none is more concentrated than the breeding assemblages of **Red-billed Quelea** *Quelea quelea*. Their colonies can involve 30,000 nests per hectare (2.5 acres), with hundreds on every bush.[6] Among its many beautiful relatives, this 13 cm (5 in) bird has little to distinguish it except a tawny suffusion on the breasts of breeding males and the black masks and conical wax-red bills present on all age groups. Yet this species is one of the most remarkable in Africa and has a reputation as the 'avian locust' and the most serious bird pest on the continent.

The population is impossible to calculate, but in the 1960s two quelea experts proposed that it was between 1–100 billion. That upper limit, like much that has been written about the bird, is definite hyperbole. Yet any overestimate of Red-billed Queleas is easy to understand. Eyewitnesses have routinely encountered flocks of several millions. Weighing just 30 g (1 oz) apiece, queleas in these congregations resemble dark rainstorms and sound like thunder. Sometimes they are so numerous they are genuinely mistaken for locusts. In truth, the best estimate for their total post-breeding population, which is spread across sub-Saharan Africa except the rainforest areas of the Congo Basin, is 1.5 billion, a little more than there are people in China (1.33 billion).[7]

The species' parallel reputation as a devastating curse that blights the agriculture of Africa like an Old Testament plague is another strand of quelea mythology involving an element of fancy. One of the leading experts, the African ornithologist Sir Clive Elliott, suggested that its overall impact on harvests is not dissimilar to that of avian pests on other continents, such as the Red-winged Blackbird and Common Starling in North America. However, as Elliott points out, the impact of quelea damage is totally different.[8]

Starlings and blackbirds may depress profits for American farmers, but queleas can make the difference between Africans having enough to eat and a state of poverty and hunger. In many part of the quelea's range the people are subsistence agriculturalists, and any crop losses are serious. In the late nineteenth century one episode of quelea depredations in central Tanganyika (modern Tanzania) caused local famine.[9] The bird can become a problem for growers of standard Western cereals, such as rice, wheat, barley, oats and triticale, but also for those cultivating indigenous varieties – sorghum, teff, bulrush and finger millet. When a survey was conducted across the quelea's range, 24 countries rated it as an intermediate or major pest, with Botswana, Chad, Ethiopia, Kenya, Malawi, Mali, Sudan and Tanzania ranking it in the higher category.[10]

Africans have long had strategies for dealing with granivorous birds, including the employment of human scarers armed with slings, cracking whips and clanking cans, but the quelea's own distinctive breeding strategy can sometimes overcome all defences. Essentially the birds are nomadic and make complex short-range migrations in search of fresh rainfall and new growth. They are adapted to respond quickly to unpredictable and very short-lived abundances of native grass seeds which, rather than human crops, are actually their preferred foods. Their numbers concentrate where they find optimum conditions and a super-colony can assemble almost overnight. At just nine or ten days, they have one of the shortest incubation periods of any bird and the entire breeding cycle, from nest construction to abandonment of young, can be completed in six weeks.[11]

If one had the luxury of detachment from their impact, or the opportunity of experiencing these flocks simply as a phenomenon of African nature, like an elephant herd or wildebeests on migration, then they are remarkable concentrations of life, as one eyewitness makes plain.

> The passage of tens of millions of birds to and from their communal night roosts in the pink light of sunset and sunrise seem like twisting clouds of smoke on the horizon. As they approach closer they can be heard as a whooshing rush of air as the flock uncoils in alarm into different strands overhead that coalesce again farther on.

The giant and pygmy exchange places as an African Elephant is engulfed by a thundercloud of Red-billed Queleas.

Their vast breeding colonies, perhaps covering several square kilometres of thorn bushes with a hundred nests in each, are hot humid places of still air and a cloying smell of guano and drying grass. When the chicks have hatched the ground beneath the bushes is covered with eggshells like pale blue snow. The hubbub is immense and can be heard from far off, the chattering of chicks in the nests swelling and dying away, and a continuous sound of wings. Night roosts are even more densely packed and just as noisy; roosting birds chatter for hours after dusk, suddenly falling instantly silent only to start up again to the same volume as before.

Feeding flocks of tens of thousands of birds in long grass can be invisible and almost silent, but then it seems that the grassland itself is alive and moving, with a soft sound of wings and rustling grass stems. Birds continually fly up and over those still feeding on the ground and land beyond them, followed by those they have just leapfrogged. The entire mass of birds seems to unroll and re-roll across the landscape. The slightest disturbance will cause the flock to erupt from the grass with a sudden roar like a storm-force wind and the birds boil out of the ground in wave after wave. They may not go far, the whole mass now chattering excitedly, collapsing like a brown blanket to smother the grass again and then vanish.[12]

As well as the genie-like swirl of the queleas themselves, the flocks can attract a trailing caravan of predators. Even lions and leopards do not spurn the bounty of their prodigious numbers, but certain flesh-eating birds including storks, egrets, kites and eagles are habitual in quelea colonies. In the Kruger National Park, South Africa, one was said to hold 1,200 Tawny Eagles and 300 Marabou Storks. At another in the Sudan, Marabou Storks were estimated to have eaten a million young queleas.[13] One of the ways in which the species copes with this predation is to breed all at once, so that the whole colony is at the same stage in the breeding cycle. This close synchronisation has the effect of swamping predators with sheer numbers and ensures that some at least will be successful.

The downside of this reproductive simultaneity is that queleas descend on ripening crops and simply overwhelm most forms of traditional deterrence. The young ones especially are so hungry and indifferent to humans that they have to be almost shaken from the sorghum plants to be dislodged. In Sudan they are known as the 'deaf ones' because of this apparent indifference.[14] On some quelea-affected crops, the 'losses amounted to tens or sometimes hundreds of tonnes; a few involved thousands of tonnes'.[15]

For decades the answer to queleas has been some form of modern mass-killing strategy, which has included blowing up the breeding colony or the roost with gelignite or similar explosives, or spraying with chemicals such as the organophosphate fenthion (the brand name is Queletox). These can kill millions of birds almost instantly. The unfortunate knock-on effect of such poisons is that they kill anything else that eats the dead queleas. One such cull in Mali caused the deaths of 400 Black Kites, which is one more measure, incidentally, of how quickly this raptor can locate concentrations of 'food' (see also page 159).[16] Even more serious is the fact that local people often gather tonnes of dead birds to eat, exposing themselves to the same potential poisons.

Harvesting and eating queleas is just one of the many minor benefits that accrue from this superabundant bird. A single control operation in Ethiopia that was estimated to kill 70 per cent of the adults in a colony yielded 37 tonnes of flesh.[17] Another bonus is the opportunity to collect the guano from beneath their nests. In Somalia a group of citrus farmers were so pleased with the fertilising effect of a quelea roost in their orchards that they even hindered pest-control measures.[18] Another small gift from the massive numbers was the brief development in Senegal of an export trade in queleas for the cagebird market, while in the 1950s there was an attempt at selling the meat to the French. It was advertised as *Ortolan du Sénégal*. Alas the experiment failed when one shipment was contaminated with diesel oil.

Yet the raw product is not without reputation. The scientific researchers who do perennial combat with this pest have often been grateful for its culinary blessings to their bush diet. When the breasts are skewered and seasoned and placed over hot coals, or marinated in oil and herbs then grilled with a bacon wrap, they are apparently comparable in savour to large gamebirds. An omelette, meanwhile, made from their 1.7 g (0.06 oz) eggs (of which 30 would equal a single chicken's egg) has been judged positively delicious.[19] Yet the boiled equivalent has been declared by one experimental palate as 'disgusting and somehow not eggy'.[20]

Waxbill, Munia and Allies family *Estrildidae*

This family is predominantly tropical in range and comprises small to tiny finch-like birds. At just 7.5 cm (3 in), for instance, the aptly named **Locust Finch** *Ortygospiza locustella* of southern Africa is not much bigger than the invertebrate in its name. They are often highly sociable and move around grassland habitats or agricultural crops in mobile globular flocks that look 'like small swarms of large bees'.[1] Their capacity to vanish into the shortest vegetation as well as the accompanying vapour of tiny, nasal, buzzing calls rather compound their similarities to insects. There are 138 species worldwide largely confined to Africa (79), southern and south-east Asia (16), and the Australasian region (41).

Many of them are birds of glorious colour, with the rare **Gouldian Finch** *Erythrura gouldiae* of northern Australia singled out by some admirers as 'one of the most beautiful of all the birds in the world'.[2] The bright colours account for many of the waxbills' wide spectrum of wonderfully suggestive names, such as **Orange-winged Pytilia** *Pytilia afra*, **Purple Grenadier** *Uraeginthus ianthinogaster*, **Cinderella Waxbill** *Estrilda thomensis*, **African Firefinch** *Lagonosticta rubricata* and **Beautiful Firetail** *Stagonopleura bella*. The colours also explain our long tradition of keeping waxbills and munias as cagebirds. They are bred and traded widely and in some places they are readily kept as large flocks in what seem disproportionately minuscule quarters. In the bird market in Hong Kong I once saw 70–100 **White-rumped Munia** *Lonchura striata* housed in a wire cage no more than 70 x 30 x 30 cm (2 x 1 x 1 ft), while in India I encountered an enclosure of *c*.2 m^2 (21.5 ft^2) that held what were probably in excess of 1,000 birds.

A common development with captive-held species is for them to escape this incarceration and then to establish free-flying feral populations in countries far beyond their native ranges. A classic instance is the strangely named **Red Avadavat** *Amandava amandava*. The male of this glorious little bird is congealed-blood red covered with tiny white star-like spots (among aviculturists a quaint nickname is 'Indian strawberry').[3] Both the scientific name, Amandava, and the anglicised form, 'avadavat' (alternative spellings once included 'amidavad', 'amadavat' and 'avaduvat'), are corruptions of the Indian city Ahmedabad, where the species was first encountered by Europeans (the capital of Gujarat state is still known in colloquial Gujarati as Amdavad).[4] Ahmedabad's eponymous bird occurs across most of the Indian subcontinent as far east as China and Indonesia. However, this native distribution has been vastly expanded with the establishment of feral populations in Italy, Portugal, Spain, Egypt, Bahrain, United Arab Emirates, Japan, Singapore, West Indies, Fiji, and Hawaii.[5]

In some ways even more remarkable is the wide diaspora achieved by the **Java Sparrow** *Lonchura oryzivora*. This smart grey-and-black finch with a massive pink bill originally occurred only on the islands of Java and Bali, but it is now found across large areas of Asia, including southern China, Malaysia, Vietnam, Thailand, other parts of the Indonesian archipelago, the Philippines and Japan.[6] This Asian conquest was fuelled by the birds' attractions as a caged pet, whence it frequently absconded. While Java Sparrows may be creatures of pleasing graphic colour, they have also long been reputed as major pests of grain crops. The bird's older scientific name, *Padda*, refers to a love of paddies, while the present word *oryzivora* means 'rice eater'.[7] Another name for the species was 'rice bird'. It was, in turn, eaten by locals, much as Europeans once ate sparrows, and presumably for much the same reason: to reduce its impact on the harvest.[8] Yet the birds' feral status is clearly ancient: the species appears as a wild bird in Chinese paintings as early as the eleventh century and there is a particularly beautiful portrait by the Chinese artist Wang Yuan who lived in the fourteenth century.[9]

One of the qualities that has made the waxbill family such a popular group among aviculturists is their 'amiable disposition, and the affection they show to everyone indiscriminately'.[10] A flock of captive Java Sparrows was held by the British naturalist Tom Harrisson in the same cage as some Spotted Doves. The Java Sparrows carried the 'munia love for cuddling and canoodling to excess' and would climb under and over the doves and even on to their heads, one dove eventually becoming 'the comforter for up to eight Java Sparrows' each night.[11]

The same tractability has helped make one species, the beautiful Australian **Zebra Finch** *Taeniopygia guttata*, the avian equivalent of the laboratory white mouse, and the subject of many important ornithological experiments. It is the first passerine species, for example, whose entire genome has been sequenced. One infallible virtue, from the

scientist's perspective, is the brevity of the Zebra Finch's life. In one colour-ringed study in Australia, no individual lived more than 12 months (canaries, by contrast, can live for seven to eight years). This 'live fast, die young' pattern allows researchers to observe the species full life cycle in fairly short order.

Another 'virtue' possessed by this scientific favourite is a willingness to breed all year round and feed entirely on seed. Despite its tiny size – as one scientist put it, a Zebra Finch weighs 'the same as three regular-sized sugar cubes' (12 g: 0.4 oz) – it is an incredibly tough creature.[12] In the wild Zebra Finches cope with the intensely arid conditions of the Australian interior, where the traits noted above allow them to breed opportunistically, responding quickly to the occurrence of rain and fresh grass growth. One extraordinary facet of these adaptations is an ability to survive without fluids. In one laboratory study lasting 18 months Zebra Finches never once drank water.[13]

The Black-headed Munia is a widespread bird in Asia.

The Java Sparrow was originally confined to Indonesia but its attractiveness as a cagebird has led eventually to its release in many other Asian countries.

Indigobird and Whydah family *Viduidae*

These 20 species are small finch-like birds of grassland and open habitats in sub-Saharan Africa. Many of the males in breeding plumage have striking dark glossy colours, and nine species also acquire tails of sumptuous shape and size. In the case of the five paradise whydahs, some of the feathers have webs that are enormously widened as well as elongated, so that the full appendage drapes behind like the train on a peacock, but on a miniature scale (the whole bird in full fig is just 30 cm: 12 in). One of the first European accounts of the birds – by the great French scholar Michel de Montaigne, who saw them near Florence in 1580 – described them as 'little birds like goldfinches, which have two long feathers in their tail like those of a big capon'.[1] In the case of the widespread **Long-tailed Paradise Whydah** *Vidua paradisaea*, the male's tail is two to three times the length of his sparrow-sized body.

The curvaceous grace of these black tail plumes was deeply appealing to African people. Communities such as the Lozi and Lovali, now of modern-day Zambia, once made striking head garments from them, and may also have used the very similar tails of the Long-tailed Widowbird. Examples of these beautiful items are held in several anthropological institutions, including the Pitt Rivers Museum (Oxford, UK) and the American Museum of Natural History (New York).

The names given to the birds are a source of interest, but also of ongoing confusion and puzzlement. The word 'whydah' (sometimes spelled 'whidah' in the eighteenth century) is probably an alternative version of 'widow' or 'widow-bird', which they were so named because their predominantly dark plumages and long black tails were thought to resemble the rather grandiose costumes worn by bereaved wives in former centuries, the proverbial 'widow's weeds'. The scientific name, *Vidua*, the genus to which all but one of the whydahs belong, actually means 'widow' in Latin. (This, of course, overlooked the fact that the black birds were actually males in breeding dress. At all seasons the females are dull and streaky brown.) An alternative theory is that 'whydah' derived from Ouidah, the once-infamous slave entrepôt on the west African coast in the old kingdom of Dahomey (now in Benin), where the birds were first observed.[2] As a consequence some still pronounce the birds' name in the same way as the town (i.e. 'wee-dah'), instead of the more usual 'why-dah'.[3]

The more puzzling and intriguing part of the name is the adjectival 'paradise'. There is a deep sense of luxury and extravagance in a tail that exceeds in size and apparent bulk that of the whole bird. Yet why exactly should we – or why should those who first gave names to these birds (such as Carl Linnaeus) – think of paradise as a habitat where birds should naturally possess such features? It surely says less about the creatures and more about our own (European) imaginings of the paradisiacal ecosystem. Paradise is a place where all the fundamental ordinariness of our own mortal selves will be transformed by the extraordinariness of our natural surroundings.

The early ornithologists may have been less inclined to these heavenly associations had they known some of the genuine behaviour of whydahs. The males are, in fact, highly polygamous and try to attract multiple females in exuberant flight displays, when they flaunt their fantastic tails to advantage. One species in west Africa is called the **Exclamatory Paradise Whydah** *Vidua interjecta* because it is said to resemble 'a flying exclamation mark!'[4] An old name in several parts of Africa for the species called the **Pin-tailed Whydah** *Vidua macroura* was 'King-of-Six', because each male was said to possess as many partners.

Another unusual aspect of whydah breeding behaviour is that they are brood parasites. (One species is called the **Cuckoo Weaver** *Anomalospiza imberbis*.) Often they are highly host specific, exploiting a single species of estrildid finch. The Long-tailed Paradise Whydah, for example, lays eggs in the nest of the Green-winged Pytilia. The American ornithologist Robert Payne, the world's great authority on this group who has studied whydahs for 48 years, undertaking 20 trips to Africa totalling 65 months, suggests that the males even produce a song strongly mimetic of the host's fizzing trill.[5]

This nineteenth-century lithograph of Long-tailed Paradise Whydah is from a late edition of Alfred Brehm's *Life of Animals*. Yet living examples of this remarkable bird were seen in Europe at least 300 years earlier.

WEBERVÖGEL

This copying of the foster-parent's song ensures that he will only attract females who have themselves grown up in pytilia nests. Another characteristic of the brood parasitism among whydahs is that their offspring possess complex mouth patterns that look extremely like those of the host chicks. By mating only with partners of the same genetic stock as themselves, the adult Long-tailed Paradise Whydahs will, in turn, ensure that they produce offspring with the same deceptively similar mouthparts.[6]

The bright colours of adult whydahs have made them popular cagebirds, but one other factor predisposing collectors towards them is the way that the males switch seasonally to their flamboyant breeding dress from a plumage of sparrow-like streakiness. The transformation has been likened to the metamorphosis of 'the lowly caterpillar to the lovely butterfly'.[7] Their popularity with bird fanciers has also led to deliberate releases. A non-native population of Pin-tailed Whydahs has persisted on the Caribbean island of Puerto Rico for 40 years, but only because of the prior release of its preferred African host species, the Orange-cheeked Waxbill and Black-rumped Waxbill (see Waxbill family, page 493).[8]

Wagtail and Pipit family *Motacillidae*

This family of 67 species is found almost worldwide and, while it is absent from Antarctica, some pipits are among the most southerly distributed of all small birds, occurring in New Zealand (**New Zealand Pipit** *Anthus novaeseelandiae*; *pihoihoi* in Maori), on the subantarctic island of South Georgia (**South Georgia Pipit** *Anthus antarcticus*) and at the tip of Tierra del Fuego (**Correndera Pipit** *Anthus correndera*). Most, however, are subtropical inhabitants with a strong bias towards Africa (38 species) and Eurasia (19 species). By contrast, North America is home to five breeding species, with ten in Europe.

The family comprises three main groups: the pipits (46 species), wagtails (13 species) and longclaws (eight species; all in Africa). They are essentially small birds (12–20 cm: 5–8 in), and most are inhabitants of grassland or open country with sparse tree cover, although they show frequent attachment to water, whether it is in upland streams (**Grey Wagtail** *Motacilla cinerea* or **Mountain Wagtail** *Motacilla clara*), lakes or marshes (**Citrine Wagtail** *Motacilla citreola* and **Western Yellow Wagtail** *Motacilla flava*), or by rocky coastlines (**Eurasian Rock Pipit** *Anthus petrosus*). Sometimes just the spillage around a leaking tap or well is enough to draw them (**White Wagtail** *Motacilla alba*).

While pipits tend to be drab brown, streaky and difficult

The South Georgia Pipit is restricted to its eponymous archipelago and is among the most southerly of all songbirds.

Amid a gentle rainfall of their *chizzick* and *swi-soo* contact notes, a roost of White Wagtails in a neon-lit city street brings a touch of natural magic to the urban landscape.

to identify, wagtails and longclaws are boldly coloured, often with areas of yellow, pink and red. All the family is highly vocal, although the songs, especially those of the pipits, can be more notable for quantity rather than quality. They often deliver them during high-rising song flights, which they sustain for long periods: the North American **Sprague's Pipit** *Anthus spragueii* has been known to persist for three hours without a break. The word 'pipit' itself is probably onomatopoeic of the flat repetitive notes.

Small size and dull colours may have confined pipits to the cultural margins, but they were once considered good enough to eat. In fact, the birds are targets for European

hunters even in the twenty-first century. In 2001 five Italians were arrested in possession of a truck containing 58,000 mixed pipits and 10,000 Eurasian Skylarks, part of a haul captured in Serbia but intended for an illegal market in Italy.

Wagtails have more successfully commanded our attention, partly because of their glorious dynamism. They tend to be aggressive and highly vocal birds, but a great deal of their emotional life is expressed through their perpetually wagging tails. In a poem called 'Health', a complex exploration of the paradoxical nature of human desire and imagination, the poet Edward Thomas offers us a perfect image of a feeding wagtail.

I could not be as the wagtail running up and down
The warm tiles of the roof slope, twittering
Happily and sweetly as if the sun itself
Extracted the song
As the hand makes sparks from the fur of a cat:

His portrait captures all of the birds' nimbleness, but it also suggests the buoyancy of spirits so often manifest in wagtail kinetics, as if their metabolism possessed an inbuilt surplus that required a natural outlet. At one time this aura of flirtatiousness gave us a figurative use of 'wagtail' as a term of abuse for a lightweight young man or promiscuous woman. Shakespeare uses it in the former sense in *King Lear* (Act 2, Scene 2) when Kent says to Oswald: 'Spare my grey beard you wagtail?' Another contemporary who found moral deficiency in the bird was the Renaissance humanist Erasmus. In a text on civility and bodily comportment, the great Dutch teacher recommended that you 'don't move your whole body when speaking, like a wagtail'.[1]

The birds never look more flirtatious or nimble than when they are feeding in the presence of what seem, by contrast, lumbering giants. Wagtails love to follow the trampling hooves of livestock – and will also dash in the wake of migrating wildebeests and zebras – when they snap up anything that is disturbed by the movement. Old vernacular names for Western Yellow Wagtail include 'cow bird' (Britain), *vachette* ('little cow', France), and *Kuhstelze* ('cow wagtail', Germany, but *Schafstelze*, 'sheep wagtail', is now the official German name).[2]

Similar associations also occur in Africa. For the Marakwet people of Kenya the **African Pied Wagtail** *Motacilla aguimp* is known as 'akwano', literally meaning 'to look after the goats'.[3] In South Africa the **Cape Wagtail** *Motacilla capensis* was known among some pastoralist communities as 'the bird of the cattle'. Yet it was also viewed as a guardian spirit – another name was 'bird of good fortune' – because its presence in the kraal was an omen of the herd's well-being. It was considered taboo to kill or harm one.[4]

There was a third strand of African connections that linked the birds (possibly both African Pied and Cape Wagtails) with a fondness for 'being beside the washerwoman'. It reflected how the old sites for doing the laundry were also perfect for wagtails.[5] What is most moving and remarkable about this African triad of associations between livestock, washerwomen and wagtails is its replication in Europe. At the same time that the Western Yellow Wagtail was characterised as the 'cow bird' or 'cow kloot' (literally 'cow's hoof'), its relative, the White Wagtail, was also known as 'Molly washdish'.[6] In France the same trinity coexisted: names for wagtails included *vachette* and *lavandière* ('washerwoman').[7] In Spain various wagtails are still known in official nomenclature as *lavandera* ('laundress'). What is compelling is not just how the birds repeat the same ecological associations from continent to continent, but the way in which our imaginations seem impelled towards the same kinds of associative patterns regardless of time and distance.

Another way in which wagtails almost force themselves upon us is through their habit of forming collective roosts at night. Some of the largest gatherings in Africa can be truly extraordinary. An example on Lake Chad in Nigeria included 50,000 birds, but a roost at the Kazinga Channel at Mweya, in Queen Elizabeth National Park, Uganda is said to involve 750,000 Western Yellow Wagtails. A highly experienced witness at this super-roost qualifies his estimate: 'my guess would be that back then in the 1990s there were countless millions of [Western] Yellow Wagtails. I think that the reedbed at Mweya was a special roost, but given the massive swathes of reed all along the Kazinga Channel, I'd be surprised if there were not other massive roosts along the 40 km length of both banks.'[8]

It is perhaps when roosts occur in city centres, often in what appear the most unprepossessing locations, that they are most conspicuous. A recent example was a roost of about 3,000 White Wagtails just outside London's Heathrow Terminal 5 in 2012.[9] What made this twittering mass of neon-lit birds particularly special was that the trees they had chosen had been 'bird-proofed' to prevent any avian presence at the capital's main airport.

Amir Balaban describes equally intransigent wagtails in Jerusalem:

An original roost was destroyed when a new Calatrava bridge was built at the city entrance. The old poplars were chopped down, but trust the good old wagtails, they relocated a few streets westward to Vulture's Wing Street, which has all that the birds need: warm street lights, bus fumes and protective buildings. This street is also home to the ministry of the environment and the national parks headquarters – a very good neighbourhood indeed. The roost peaks at about 5,000 birds and in the whole metropolitan area we have another three roosts that have a few thousand more. In fact this phenomenon is widespread all over Israel where the main city streets serve as winter roosts for thousands of European wagtails.[10]

It does not always require vast flocks for us to be affected by these vivacious little birds. Occasionally breeding wagtails seek out places that involve extraordinary levels of intimacy. Nest sites have included an historical brass foundry, where a pair of White Wagtails reared four young 'within a foot of the wheel of a lathe, in the midst of the din of hammers and braziers'.[11] Another brood was reared on the deck of a pleasure boat that was repeatedly in use. However, the nest at a commercial peat-digging works surely involved the deepest level of cooperation.

As I was leaving, the peat company's site manager said he had something to show me. He pushed forward the driver's seat of his truck to reveal a White Wagtail's nest complete with a clutch of warm eggs. The birds' entry was from under the vehicle, through a hole in its metal floor. He took immense pride in the secret nest. I gathered that the same thing had happened successfully in the previous year. 'She lets me go for about fifteen minutes,' the manager said. 'Then I have to get back and park in exactly the same place.' He had organised his routine in a way he knew would suit the wagtail family. At weekends and in the evenings the birds had their strange mobile home to themselves, in perfect security. As we moved away to continue talking, the bird flicked down from the roof and, sure enough, disappeared under the truck. It had been strangely satisfying to see such a relationship of trust and respect, between safeguarded bird and protecting man.[12]

Finch family *Fringillidae*

It seems deeply emblematic of our vision of the Renaissance as a great infusion of humanitarian spirit into the cramped mindset of medieval Europe that one of our most cherished stories about Leonardo da Vinci has him pacing the markets of Florence, buying up caged birds and freeing them on the spot. The informant does not specify which species, but we can suggest with a degree of certainty that the birds liberated by one of the world's most celebrated artists would have included a fair sprinkling of this family. For thousands of years finches have been the cagebirds of choice to half of humanity.

There are 179 species in total, spread fairly evenly across five continents, with southern latitudes claiming the greatest diversity. Latin America holds 52 and Africa 44 species. The only tropical region where finches are under-represented is Australia, which is occupied by a finch-like family called the estrildids (see page 492). The northern latitudes, including da Vinci's Italy, have a much smaller finch selection – 25 species in Europe and 17 in America north of the Mexican / USA border – but these few embrace the qualities that have made finches some of the most cherished of all birds.

A factor in their popularity both as modern backyard familiars and as cagebirds throughout history is their tendency towards bright colour. The family is rich in reds and yellows. One genus, the *Carpodacus* finches whose members are largely known as rosefinches, are often intense deep dark crimson, about the colour of congealed blood. They are specialists of high-altitude landscapes – the

American Goldfinches on a bird feeder; underpinning this common-or-garden scene is a larger transaction that involves an exchange of seed, nuts and other foods for colour, beauty and distinct feelings of human well-being.

Himalayan country of Nepal has 13 of the 21 species – but one of their number is among the commonest species in the American backyard, the appropriately named **House Finch** *Carpodacus mexicanus*.

If anything, shades of yellow are even more dominant among finches and are particularly eye-catching on many species of siskin, serin and, perhaps most famous of all, on the canaries. The **Atlantic Canary** *Serinus canaria*, which originates in the Spanish-speaking archipelago of the same name, is the bird that has given us *the* 'canary'. Originally known as the 'canary-bird' it is probably the best known of all avian pets and once took Europe by storm as a kind of cagebird sensation. A much later rival during the nineteenth century was a small Australian parrot, but it says much about the canary as our default image of the avian pet that before the Budgerigar was known universally by its Aboriginal name, it was sometimes called the 'canary-parrot'.[1]

Another famous finch group dominated by yellows are the four goldfinches: **American Goldfinch** *Carduelis tristis*, **Lawrence's Goldfinch** *Carduelis lawrencei*, **Lesser Goldfinch** *Carduelis psaltria* and **European Goldfinch** *Carduelis carduelis*. Their collective range, the first three in North America (the Lesser Goldfinch extends through Central America as far south as Peru) and the last species across Eurasia, encircles two-thirds of the entire northern landmasses. Russian Siberia and China are the only goldfinch-free zone. The most widespread of the three New World birds, the American Goldfinch, is among the most beautiful of its entire family. The male is pure saffron yellow with black wings and forecrown. The European Goldfinch has a more intense golden colour but only across the outspread wings, while the face on both sexes is shining crimson bordered with white and slashed with black.

What the Comte de Buffon suggested of this last bird could easily be extended to the goldfinch quartet. He wrote: 'Beauty of plumage, softness of voice, quickness of instinct, remarkable cleverness, proved docility, tender affection, are all united in this delightful little bird; and if it were rare, or if it came from a foreign country, it would then be valued as it deserves.'[2] That 'softness of voice' celebrated by the French naturalist explains much about the popularity of many finches as cagebirds. All four goldfinches produce a sweet rambling song whose individual notes rather resemble the sound of glass fragments or tiny metal shards loosely striking against one another. When fused seamlessly together they create an almost liquid, soothing vocalisation that one imagines the word 'twitter' was invented to describe.

Beautiful birds with beautiful voices were ever likely to appeal to human cupidity, but what cemented finches as the cagebirds of choice was an aspect of their wider ecology. The family is primarily granivorous, finches possessing broad, deep conical bills adapted to cracking open the hard outer shells with great efficiency. A diet based on seed that could be easily sourced and stored throughout the year meant that finches had a massive advantage in terms of household convenience. With rivals such as the Common Nightingale – migratory and insectivorous but also a hugely popular cagebird for its song – the keepers had somehow to source daily quantities of invertebrate protein such as ants' eggs. Almost inevitably, many nightingales died. Yet finches could thrive on corn or millet.

Another practical plus was the opportunity to breed finches readily in captivity, without the need constantly to renew stocks from the wild. The **Common Linnet** *Carduelis cannabina*, a widespread Eurasian finch, was once enormously popular as a cagebird, partly for the gloriously airy, bubbling song. (This has given rise, incidentally, to a French saying: 'In Normandy I've come across the expression "to have a head like a linnet" (*tête de linotte*), which is a light-hearted way of saying someone is forgetful or scatty.')[3] It is commonplace even among granivorous birds to start their chicks on invertebrate food until they fledge, but the Common Linnet is exceptional for being able to feed their young only on seed.[4]

What sealed the status of finches as the classic birds for the parlour and dining room was an additional speciality of their feeding behaviour. A number of them, notably the smaller and more agile species such as the European Goldfinch, **Eurasian Siskin** *Carduelis spinus* and **Common Redpoll** *Carduelis flammea*, are able to manipulate seed heads, bending them or pulling them nearer or holding them underfoot so that they can more easily extract the edible parts. This coordination of feet and beak is precisely what Buffon was referring to when he wrote of the goldfinch's 'remarkable cleverness'. And it was these same skills that brought an additional layer of pleasure and entertainment for their owners. A common practice was to insert between the birds and their sustenance a suite of 'amusing' trials to test this physical dexterity. Often they could feed or drink only by manipulating tiny pulleys or chains on which were suspended finch-sized buckets of seed and water.

Cruellest of all practices with regard to finches, a tradition rooted in the false notion that it improved vocal ability, was the habit of blinding birds. (The barbarous ritual later supplied powerfully emotive arguments for the early campaigners seeking to end finch keeping.) While blinding had no provable impact on song production it may, ironically, have had a tenderising effect upon the owner's feelings for their sightless wards. A modern bird keeper suggests how this may have worked:

> The idea that anyone would deliberately blind a bird in order to make it sing more readily is utterly appalling. However, my view was somewhat modified by the experience of having a blind Zebra Finch as a pet for several years. 'Billie', who hatched blind and was hand-reared by my daughter, lived in a cage on the landing. He was perfectly capable of finding his food and water and enjoyed a bath; he especially liked being allowed outside on to the lawn to peck about for seeds. Billie was intensely social and loved human company, bursting into song at the sound of my daughter's footsteps or voice, and he relished having his neck tickled. His apparent affection for his human owners was utterly endearing, and the affection was mutual, Billie was a family favourite. Nonetheless, I could never quite decide whether his was a genuine affection or a dependency motivated by sightless desperation. This in turn made me wonder whether those bird keepers who blinded birds felt the same affection for their charges as we did towards Billie. I suspect they did, which suggests the bizarre contradictions in human behaviour.[5]

THE PLACE OF THE GOLDFINCH
IN RENAISSANCE ART

Even if we have no wish now to incarcerate birds in our living rooms, let alone blind them, we can at least appreciate the background factors that drove the historical popularity of captive finches. Yet when it comes to another aspect of their cultural significance in the Late Middle Ages, we are perhaps made aware not of what we share with our ancestors but how little we have in common.

It concerns the recurrence of European Goldfinches in a huge body of paintings, and especially in devotional images of the Madonna and holy child. Sometimes the bird was inserted unobtrusively into the backgrounds or at the feet of the human figures, but more often it occupies a central place, perched on Mary's fingers or nestled in Christ's outstretched hands. At least 486 paintings from a period spanning the Late Middle Ages and the Renaissance (roughly AD 1260–1500), and from a geographical area that included Russia, Bohemia, Bavaria, France, Spain, Portugal, the Low Countries and England, include the same finch motif. These images were all tracked down as part of painstaking detective work by an American ornithologist and art scholar, Herbert Friedmann,

At the heart of Leonardo da Vinci's *Litta Madonna* is the rather unexpected but equally unmistakable image of a European Goldfinch.

and documented in his book *The Symbolic Goldfinch* (1946). More than anything he showed that the symbolism was a phenomenon of Italian painting. Of the 254 artists he found to have illustrated the same bird, 214 of them were Italians and the names include some of the greatest artists of the age – Leonardo da Vinci, Michelangelo, and Raphael.[6]

The painting by da Vinci is, in many ways, typical of the genre. Dominated chromatically by the gorgeous lapis lazuli blue of the Madonna's robe and her crimson dress, the image portrays a moment of great tenderness between a mother and her suckling baby. What is, to modern eyes, exceptional in the biblical scene is the presence of a small bird at the painting's epicentre. Nestled within the shadows created by their close-pressed bodies, and almost perched on Jesus' fleshy thigh, is an unmistakable European Goldfinch.

In truth the image, which is known as the *Litta Madonna*, after its nineteenth-century owner, Duke Antonio Litta, is not a 'real' Leonardo. Although the maestro produced a preparatory study (now in the Louvre, Paris) and although the lambent curls of the infant Christ suggest his inimitable touch, the work is thought to come from the inferior hand of Leonardo's Milanese assistant Marco d'Oggiono, or possibly a colleague, Giovanni Boltraffio, or both, and probably in the 1480s. It now hangs in the Hermitage Museum in St Petersburg, Russia.[7]

Yet the painting's provenance is here secondary to the issue of why a small European passerine should have found its way at all into the image. And what was it about the bird that warranted inclusion in hundreds of other paintings of similar nature? Strangely, the answers begin in the account of the stone-curlew family found on page 195. It explains how the Eurasian Stone-curlew came to be identified as the *charadrios* of the ancient Greeks, a creature to which they once attached sovereign medicinal powers. These curative properties were vested in the bird's weirdly piercing yellow eyes. (It should be noted that the myth of the *charadrios* was not solely linked to this wader. Pliny the Elder suggested the medicinal bird was another yellow beauty, the Eurasian Golden Oriole. Friedmann himself linked the legend of the *charadrios* to the European Golden Plover and was almost certainly in error, given that the bird has liquid dark eyes.)

The ancients believed that simply by looking into those bright golden orbs of this admittedly rather compelling bird a human sufferer from jaundice would be cured of their ailment. Later the anonymous author (or authors) of a Greek Christian text from the second century AD, known as the *Physiologus*, divined in the myth of the *charadrios* a version of Christ's central mission to save mankind. (In similar bizarre fashion the same author(s) identified the story of Jesus in the brood care of pelicans; see page 141). In exactly the way that the yellow jaundice had been drawn mysteriously from the human patient by the gaze of the bird, so had the sins of humanity been absorbed inexorably by the suffering of Christ on the cross. From these rather tenuous beginnings the *charadrios* story subsequently morphed into a fully fledged metaphor for Christ's gift of redemption.

Friedmann identified French and Italian paintings (and sculptures) from the 1260s as the earliest works on this theme. Yet one later example, which sheds important light on medieval treatment of the *charadrios* myth, is a painting by a Venetian artist Carlo Crivelli. Active in the late fifteenth century, Crivelli produced several bird-centred images of the Madonna and Child. There is a fine work by him of Christ holding a goldfinch with outstretched wings that is now in New York's Metropolitan Museum of Art. Yet in another devotional image (in the Brera Gallery of Milan, Italy), Crivelli showed Christ holding not the last-named species but a Eurasian Golden Oriole.

Recall first that this was actually Pliny the Elder's original choice for the legend of the curative bird. Then note that to these three candidates must also be added a fourth. Medieval Europeans also credited larks with comparable medicinal power. Leonardo da Vinci himself mentioned the bird's supposed ability to cure the sick and to give wider prognosis for the patient's chances of recovery. 'The lark is a bird', he wrote, 'of which it is told that when it is taken into the presence of a sick person, if the sick man is going to die, the bird turns away its head and never looks at him. But if the sick person is going to recover the bird never loses sight of him and is the cause of curing all sickness.'[8]

Crivelli's painting of an oriole and Leonardo's reference to the lark emphasise how, for the artists, what truly mattered was not any underlying natural-historical veracity, but the symbolic charge invested in the bird. Really any bird with, and even without, yellow body parts was perfectly adequate to their ends; because what counted in the story of the *charadrios* was the Christian-inflected message. As one commentator wrote, there was a 'ceaseless sweep of allegory through men's minds. They felt and thought and dreamed in allegories; … the Middle Ages did not demand that allegory should have its feet planted on the earth so long as its head nodded high among the clouds …'[9] To give just one telling instance of the extraordinary dominance of symbolism over earthy realities – in medieval painting and literature, the two breasts of the Madonna were no mere teats to give suckle. Christian art had long looked upon the holy bosom as the 'two Testaments, from which flows the Milk of Doctrine'.[10]

What secured the goldfinch its place as the most important and widely reproduced version of the *charadrios* motif were other supportive symbolic associations that flowed from aspects of its plumage and lifestyle. Clearly the bar of gold across the wings was an important linkage with the root myth, but equally significant was the splash of crimson on the cheeks. It was a practice among medieval scholars to write birds into the Christian story and several cherished species with red breasts or faces, including the European Robin, Barn Swallow and the European Goldfinch, were retrospectively incorporated into the story of the Passion. Each was said to have acquired blood-coloured feathers while attempting to remove the thorn crown from the crucified head of the king of men. The red details were a permanent badge of their virtue in offering help to Christ.

A secondary supportive detail flowed from the bird's linkage to thistles (which had, incidentally, their own symbolic connection to the crucifixion). Thistle seeds are food for at least three of the four goldfinch species, but for European Goldfinches they are central. In fact the bird is still known in Italian as *cardellino*, from the Latin for thistle, *carduus*. Yet thistles were themselves blessed and curative, hence the name Holy Thistle for one species (*Cnicus benedictus*) that was long credited as a medicinal ingredient to combat the plague.[11] Through association with the plant, the goldfinch was itself invested with powers of defence against pestilence.

Like his father before him, Albert Dimech is a breeder of canaries and has kept alive this ancient Maltese tradition for many decades.

Herein lies the other key motive leading to the goldfinch images in the Middle Ages. The bird was present in all those devotional paintings not just as a symbol reminding us of the Christian story in a far-off land more than a millennium ago. It was there also to address local concerns that were peculiar to each painter's own time and place. A dominant feature of the age was the recurrent nightmare of plague, and by incorporating European Goldfinches into paintings the artists were invoking the curative powers of the *charadrios* on behalf of their contemporary audience. Each painting was intended as a form of visual good-luck charm, warding off contagion and bestowing symbolic health both upon those who viewed it and upon the person who owned it. Friedmann found that the greatest single production peak of these pictures coincided roughly with the time of the Black Death in the second quarter of the fourteenth century. In those 25 years almost as many goldfinch paintings were made as in the entire fifteenth century.[12]

The goldfinch's recurrent part in so many artworks between the thirteen and sixteenth centuries is a fascinating theme in its own right. Yet the same story is also as strong a candidate as any to illuminate how vastly different were our ancestors' views of nature. In many ways the medieval approach to birds differs from our own in much the same way that their Earth-centred Ptolemaic vision of the celestial spheres differs from our heliocentric universe. Until relatively recently people genuinely thought birds existed to fulfil very specific human ends. 'Singing birds,' wrote one author in the early eighteenth century, '. . . were undoubtedly designed by the Great Author of Nature on purpose to entertain and delight mankind.'[13] Birds revolved around us just as the Sun orbited the Earth. Had not the Book of Genesis explicitly authorised mankind's dominion over nature? Was it not rational, therefore, to assume that birds were a kind of natural text, in which God had laid clues to explain His moral purposes for us.

Later Darwin's theory of evolution would completely disassemble this human-centred, God-given version of the natural world and recreate it afresh, just as Copernicus revolutionised understanding of the medieval cosmos. The interconnectedness of all things may still have been in place after Darwin, but we now know that we are only part of life's purpose in a cast numbering millions of species. And the existence of a bird with a red face and golden wing bars owes nothing to us.

MODERN POPULARITY OF CAGED FINCHES

If we cannot now subscribe to the magical powers of the *charadrios*, we can at least appreciate how birds such as finches do have subtly therapeutic value. In fact modern Russian researchers claim that, among other species:

> The **Common Chaffinch** *Fringilla coelebs* can relieve frequent palpitation and arrhythmia. The sonorous cheerful melodies of the goldfinch and the siskin are helpful in cases of neuroses, activating the function of the whole organism. Sound vibrations produced by the European Robin remove head, heart and joint pains, and spasms in the liver, stomach, heart and vessels.[14]

It is intriguing to recall, in the light of these claims, the nineteenth-century recommendation to parents of a sullen child: 'my advice is, buy him a chaffinch'.[15]

In an age of unending white noise from electronica, and especially the relentless tinny beat leaking from a million earphones, it is hard for us to recover the deeper silences

Its pleasant twittering song means that the European Greenfinch is still a popular cagebird.

that once enveloped human societies as little as a century ago. Birds, with all their beautiful, complex vocalisations, were the most easily attained background music that people could enjoy. Sometimes they used cagebirds almost exactly as we might deploy electrically generated sound. In the early nineteenth century the organisers of balls and other public events would rent singing finches by the cageful, and just as the guests of honour appeared the covers would be whipped off so that the birds would instantly burst into song and serenade the new arrivals.[16] Relatively recently on the Mediterranean island of Malta, where finch trapping was once big business and cagebirds remain deeply rooted in popular culture, men could be seen walking the streets with a finch 'under their arm, as if it were a portable radio'.[17]

In the past, not only did people expect to enjoy the various vocalisations belonging to each species, they manipulated finches so that the living birds produced a synthesised music that was deemed an improvement on a bird's native voice. A classic object of the measures was the **Eurasian Bullfinch** *Pyrrhula pyrrhula*, a rotund soft-mannered species found right across the continents from Japan to western Europe. The male has a beautiful deep-pink breast, but his sad monotonous piping note has a modest reputation as music. Bird keepers learned to exploit the fact that young male finches acquire their songs from listening to adults of the same species. Rather than letting nature take its course, breeders isolated fledgling bullfinches and then exposed them to human melodies played often on dedicated bird organs or flutes that were adapted to the species' own voice. German keepers in the region of Hesse excelled in this schooling of bullfinches and exported them across Germany, Holland and Britain. It could be an immensely lucrative business. One nineteenth-century dealer was reputed to

send 100–200 birds trained in this manner to Berlin and London ever year, where he could expect to make several pounds for each one. A freshly caught wild bird, by contrast, could change hands for a few pence.[18]

Germany was also a major source of the finch that was once the most popular of all, the canary. In a sense this strange monopoly was a by-product of another industry. Mining communities in the Harz Mountains of northern Germany had long reared small birds to accompany them while they worked underground. In the airless shafts the sudden silences or changes in behaviour of their caged finches were the miners' best defence against the risk of carbon monoxide poisoning. Initially the German species of choice had been the Common Chaffinch, but canaries had been a fashionable cagebird since the sixteenth century and steadily German production and sales of these yellow finches exceeded all others. By the 1880s the Harz Mountain roller was a breed famed worldwide for its voice and German bird keepers were rearing and selling 150,000 birds a year.[19]

Changed tastes in entertainment have seen the steady decline of finch keeping in the modern era. One of the last bastions of trapping on a grand scale was the island of Malta, where three separate estimates of the total catch between 1982 and 1993 suggested a figure of 1–3 million finches.[20] What is most troubling about this huge harvest is the trappers' own admissions of the percentages dying shortly after capture: Common Linnet (75 per cent), European Goldfinch (80 per cent) and **European Serin** *Serinus serinus* (70 per cent).[21] However, change has come even to a place long regarded as the continent's worst black spot. Today, while the breeding and exhibition of captive-bred finches remain commonplace activities in Malta, the taking of wild finches has dramatically declined. In the 1980s there were 5,300 known trapping sites.

Now the Maltese police deal with about 30 cases of illegal catching annually.[22]

Yet we should not assume that the finches have finally been freed from all their cages. An Arab love of the species has seen prices for European Goldfinches in Israel soar. A fine singing male can 'reach a few thousand shekels' (1,000 shekels equals £160 or $256). Amir Balaban notes:

The authorities are fighting trappers but they are hard to catch and the punishment is light. The trappers usually use hidden compartments in car doors or floors to conceal the contraband. In some areas, such as Jerusalem, goldfinches have completely disappeared. They can be still seen in cages in stores all over the old city. [23]

Hawaiian Honeycreeper family *Drepanididae*

Although few people have heard of them and a far smaller number has ever actually seen the living creatures on Hawaii, the small, rather finch-like yellow-green and red birds called honeycreepers must possess one of the most compelling stories of all bird groups. (NB: there are six species from Latin America called honeycreepers, but these birds are all in the tanager family – see page 522 – and have no connection with Hawaii's endemic family.) The present condition of the Hawaiian honeycreepers is a tale dominated by the nightmare of imminent extinction and, at best, it is one of acute threat and conservation crisis. Of the 23 recognised species, six are critically threatened, five endangered, seven vulnerable, one near-threatened, while another is now deemed extinct (the **Kakawahie** *Paroreomyza flammea* was last seen in 1963). Just three are currently secure.

Yet their recent past was a saga of sophisticated exploitation by the islands' original Polynesian inhabitants. During the centuries that the Hawaiians fashioned honey-creeper feathers into ceremonial garments of the most glorious colour and form, they created some of the most beautiful objects in all Oceanic art. One of these items is arguably the most remarkable avian artefact that humans have ever made.

Even the very deepest past of this extraordinary family and the manner in which it came into being reads like a great romance of avian evolution. The eminent American naturalist and author E O Wilson has suggested that all the honeycreepers were probably descended many thousands of years ago from a single flock of primitive finch-like birds, which were somehow swept up by a storm out of mainland America or Asia and transported to the most remote heart of the Pacific Ocean. Finding few competitors on Hawaii, the honeycreepers radiated out after this single event to occupy a huge range of ecological niches, almost covering the entire 'spectrum of passerine bird adaptations'.[1] Some like the **Maui Parrotbill** *Pseudonestor xanthophrys* came to resemble tiny versions of the parrots. Others such as the culturally important **Iiwi** *Vestiaria coccinea* and **Hawaii Mamo** *Drepanis pacifica* (extinct since 1899) behave(d) like African sunbirds, while loose groups of the beautiful **Apapane** *Himatione sanguinea* sound like twittering canaries and resemble crimson warblers.

Extinction has decimated the family of honeycreepers. Perhaps half of all historical forms – twelve species and a whole suite of distinct subspecies – vanished prior to the mid twentieth century.[2] Despite this catastrophe, E O Wilson argues that the 'sweep of the radiation even among the surviving honeycreepers is the greatest of any closely related group of birds in the world'.[3] This variation far exceeds, for instance, that exhibited in the much better-known Darwin's finches of the Galápagos (see page 526).

Perhaps the honeycreepers' 'textbook display of radiation' and their appalling history of extinction are equally unfamiliar to the vast majority of us not just because of Hawaii's remoteness, but also because of the birds' remarkable yet somehow impenetrable nomenclature. The honeycreepers are the only substantial family of birds whose names in English – and indeed in all European languages – are largely borrowed directly from the indigenous versions (18 of the 23 species). This pattern is a welcome exception to the usual colonial trend of disregarding local languages and riding roughshod over non-European taxonomies.

Recent attempts have been made to simplify these lovely Hawaiian words and to eliminate the additional complexity of multiple diacritic marks, such as those that cluster about the name **Ou** *Psittirostra psittacea*. (Technically it is 'Ō'ū.) Yet the orthography used to transcribe the local honeycreepers, not to mention the baffling riot of diphthongs and multiple vowel sounds, is indisputably exotic. For once, words such as **Anianiau** *Hemignathus parvus* or **Akiapolaau** *Hemignathus munroi* or **Ula-ai-Hawane** *Ciridops anna* are probably more unwilling to stick in our memories than their Latin equivalents. Just as striking is their similarity to one another: **Akekee** *Loxops caeruleirostris* and **Akepa** *Loxops coccineus* and **Akohekohe** *Palmeria dolei*.

In some ways it is remarkable that the Hawaiians had such clearly differentiated names for the honeycreepers. Small songbirds that are considered individually inconsequential as protein are often dismissed even now under a single generic catch-all term. One thinks of the Italian word *beccafico* or the Cypriot *ambelopoulia* for any avian scrap that can be pickled and popped in the mouth, bones and all (see also page 436). Yet the honeycreepers were exceptional because of their importance as individual sources of yellow and crimson feathers. The Hawaiians converted the birds into extraordinary garments that were associated with high political office and spiritual status. However, honeycreepers were by no means the only source of these plumes. Nor was Hawaii the only place where Polynesians deployed feathers as an important part of their art.

To make the specifically Hawaiian context even more complicated, the other key group used in these cultural practices was the honeyeater family. Honeycreepers and honeyeaters bear a number of striking similarities. They show a convergence towards bright colour, they have a common nectar diet and share adaptations to that food source, such as hollow, brush-tipped tongues. Modern ornithologists, in fact, now consider the two groups entirely unrelated, but one can understand how in the taxonomy of pre-European Hawaiians these birds were all of a piece. For them, they were not an object of study, they were a ready supply of feathers.

For that reason the islands' honeyeaters and their suite of endemic honeyeaters (all five species of which are now extinct) are treated here together as part of a single subject. (For the rest of the honeyeater family see page 366.) In addition, I think it important to convey how the Hawaiian story is actually part of a much larger bird-centred cultural pattern and to cover something of this wider story, even though honeycreepers had no part in practices elsewhere in the Pacific.

These historic Hawaiian feather items took a variety of forms, and perhaps the best known is the *lei*. This item is part of the classic stereotyped image of Hawaii: that moment when some grass-skirted *hula*-dancing beauty greets the stranger and places a garland of flowers around their neck. The *lei* is worn by Hawaiian women as a necklace or in their hair and at one time some of the most special and symbolically important were made from birds' feathers. However, two of the most impressive feather items were worn on the head and round the shoulders. The first is a type of close-fitting, cloche-like helmet that bears a tall central crest throughout its entire curvature, rather like the helmet on a Roman general, or perhaps a cockerel's comb. The specific shape and style of these crests varied according to the island of origin. Sometimes fringed with yellow and patterned with radial lines of black feathers, the helmets are invariably bright scarlet and even 200 years after their original manufacture they glow in their museum cases like something illuminated from within.

The other primary costume piece, known as an *'ahu 'ula*, was worn round the shoulders and either extended as a full-length cloak, or it could be much shorter and cover only the upper torso, rather like a small cape. Although women occasionally wore *'ahu 'ula*, they were primarily reserved for men and all who possessed them were exclusively of high aristocratic rank. Like the helmets, the cloaks have a super-structure of coconut or vegetable fibres that was then intricately woven with tiny feathers in crescentic patterns of gold and crimson. Surviving examples, of which there are approximately 160 in institutions and private collections all over the world, such as the Great North Museum: Hancock in Newcastle, UK, and the American Museum of Natural History in New York, have almost certainly dimmed with time.[4] Yet, like the helmets, they retain sufficient colour and enough of their gorgeous velvety texture to suggest how, in the context of the living rituals for which they were first made, these robes must have shone with special brilliance.

While the Hawaiian garments represent a final development of an almost pan-Pacific feather art, many of the spiritual ideas and traditions informing their creation originated more than 4,000 km (2,500 miles) away to the south-west in the scattered archipelagos that now comprise French Polynesia.[5] The first colonists settling Hawaii in the seventh or eight century AD probably navigated from one of these island clusters, such as the Society Islands, whose capital is Tahiti. The anthropologist Nicholas Thomas suggests that for the Tahitians 'feathers were associated directly with … divine fecundity'. The first mythic being of the Polynesian pantheon was Ta'aroa, who not only created the other gods, he also shook out the red and yellow feathers covering his body and scattered them over the Earth as trees and verdure upon the land.[6]

Feathers were thus a key part of Tahitian ritual and

The woven feather capes worn by indigenous Hawaiian aristocracy and royalty were as sumptuously beautiful as they were often wasteful of avian lives.

red feathers were especially prized. It is a striking measure of their sacred importance, and also an illustration of the trans-Pacific trade in red birds and their plumages, that when Captain James Cook made his third voyage to Tahiti in August 1777, he called at Tonga and acquired quantities of scarlet plumes that he knew would be of great commercial and diplomatic value once he sailed further east to Tahiti. These Tongan feathers were possibly taken from the extraordinarily beautiful Maroon Shining Parrot, a bird that was originally native to Fiji but which had been introduced to the Tongan archipelago, almost certainly for the ritual significance of its plumage. When Cook arrived in Tahiti with a large store of the plumes, the news of this had an electrifying effect on the locals. Cook suggested that they were 'the most Valuable thing that can be carried to the island'.[7] He added:

> The news of red feathers being on board the Ships having reached the shore … day no sooner broke the next Wed[nesday] morning than we were surrounded by a Multitude of Canoes filled with people with hogs and fruit to barter; not more feathers than might be got from a Tom tit would purch[ase] a hog of 40 or 50 pound weight, but as every one in the Ships had some they fell in their value above five hundred per cent before night but even than [*sic*] the ballance of trade

505

A Hawaii Mamo
painted by William
Ellis during Captain
James Cook's voyage
to the Hawaiian
archipelago in 1778.

27.

was much in our favour and they never lessened in their value afterwards.[8]

Before returning to the subject of Hawaiian art, it is worth pausing to note some of the more extraordinary purposes to which these feathers were put in Tahiti itself. They were specially used in the construction of ritual girdles, which were known as *maro* and worn round the waist like the Tahitians' everyday loincloth, but donned only during key state ceremonies, such as the marriage of the heir apparent, the arrival and meeting of great guests, or before war and at the conclusion of peace. Rather like the Hawaiian garments, they had a woven vegetable fibre (flax) frame. The feathers were then stitched into this fabric with human-bone needles, which were themselves later inserted into the girdle.

A *maro* was both a signifier of high political rank, reserved exclusively for members of the Tahitian nobility, and a form of genealogy and mnemonic all in one, linking and reminding the present wearer of his chiefly ancestors and even of his divine forebears.[9] In a sense, these sacred pieces were never considered to be complete because they were added to with each new generation of ritual deployment. Some of the stages in the *maro*'s further elaboration might even be marked with human sacrifice.[10] The most exalted form of the girdle, stitched with red feathers, was known as a *maro ura*, of which one particularly important example extended for 6.4 m (21 ft). Since each hand's breadth signified a separate reign, the making of this whole *maro ura* was thought to have involved the death of hundreds of people.[11]

The garment itself was sacred and loaded with extraordinary power. Anyone inadvertently or deliberately violating its taboo status was liable to bring disaster upon themselves, such as illness or blindness. Similarly the ceremonial winding of such a garment around a noble during his royal consecration was as perilous as it was significant, since the wearer was profoundly, even dangerously, sacred. In order to neutralise this hazardous state sometimes his subjects danced wildly around him, urinating and defecating upon the royal person as a way of diffusing his powers.[12]

Almost inevitably the nineteenth-century Christian missionaries working in the Society Islands were appalled by the practices and strove to drive them out. Ironically, while there are many contemporaneous descriptions both of *maro* and the rituals in which they were central, no single example of the girdle itself has survived. One of the few fragments of material evidence of their structure is a drawing (now in the Mitchell Library in Sydney, Australia) by an English mariner, Captain William Bligh, a name made infamous by the mutiny aboard his ship, *The Bounty*. [13]

Some of this Tahitian tradition was diffused across the vast stretches of ocean that separated Hawaii from the Society Islands. However, the Hawaiians had no need of traded feathers, since their archipelago possessed birds of spectacular hue, albeit species the size of the endemic honeycreepers and honeyeaters. These birds were incorporated not only into the Hawaiian cloaks and helmets but also other ritual artefacts, none of which is more impressive than their effigies of their war god Ku. In these sculptural artworks there is an underlying skeleton or armature made of vegetable fibres from the vine-like aerial roots of *Freycinetia arborea*. Even this wicker frame – with its columnar neck, its large hollowed-out oval eyes, and the grim downturn of the mouth, made menacing by hundreds of jagged dogs' teeth – is powerful enough. Yet once this was smothered with a shimmering skin of red feathers, these sculptural forms looked nothing less than magnificent.[14]

A bird often exploited to supply the all-important crimson was the honeycreeper species known as the Iiwi. (Incidentally the Iiwi's scientific name, *Vestiaria coccinea*, enshrines the bird's former utilitarian value, because it loosely translates as 'of the scarlet-coloured clothing'.)[15] The sheer volume of feathering required to meet the relentless demands of various Hawaiian art forms speaks volumes about the levels of abundance once enjoyed by some members of this perilously threatened family. It also suggests that the caste of professional birdcatchers (known as *po'e hahai manu*) were kept permanently busy.[16] Theoretically the birds were protected by royal decree. While the whole body of an Iiwi was scarlet and therefore suitable for use, some birds had appropriate colours only on fragments of their plumage. Technically these species could be plucked of those desired parts and then released.[17] However, trappers often took the requisite feathers and then, applying pressure to their breasts, killed the birds, wrapped them in the outer sheaf of a banana stalk and placed them in a bag. Some of these tiny scraps of yellow feathers were said to be delicious when fried in their own fat.[18]

A classic victim of such treatment was the beautiful Hawaii Mamo. This honeycreeper's predominantly black plumage contrasted brilliantly with yellow shoulders and a bright-yellow rump. It was only these latter patches that were valued, and the minuscule yield on this species had a number of interlocking consequences. The professional hunters had to catch many more mamos than, for example, they did of Iiwis to yield the same volume of feathers. The species was also supposedly under royal protection for its cultural importance. However, a legendary rebuke made by one monarch to his birdcatchers – 'the feathers belong to me, but birds themselves belong to my heirs' – suggests that the law was honoured more in the breach than in its observance. Habitat loss was almost certainly another major factor in the bird's decline, but the mamo had become extinct by 1899.[19]

The other consequence of an individual mamo's micro-yield of feathers was the proportionately high premium placed on its head by the Hawaiian elite. Of all forms of Hawaiian property these feathers were said to be the most highly valued.[20] One commentator noted:

> The Mamo bird [was] the most highly prized for the yellow in a cloak … As yellow does not appear in Hawaiian myths as synonymous with royalty, nor does the Mamo bird appear in any tale that would give it such symbolic importance, its value therefore stood in direct relation to the labour involved rather than to any mythological account.[21]

In short, the mamo was a symbol of economic exclusivity. This situation contrasted sharply with the values attaching to the Iiwi. Although this bird was the colour most associated with divinity for Polynesians, the sheer abundance of this red species meant that it had a lower economic value than the other honeycreepers.

During the early period of Hawaiian contact with the colonial powers, an interesting shift took place in the political life of the indigenous inhabitants, which eventually found expression in the nation's symbolic garments made from red and yellow feathers. The anthropologist Tom Cummins has argued that the coming of Europeans in 1778 stripped away the old religious values that had formerly served to portray political power as a privilege ordained by divine right. The chiefs remained in control after the arrival of whites but the indigenous class system was exposed for what it was – a structure of control maintained through material wealth and military might.[22]

As wealth became the measure of all political power, so red feathers, despite their colour being the standard signifier of royalty and symbolic of traditional morals and religious values, came to lose some of their social prestige among the islands' aristocracy. Yellow feathers, by contrast, while historically less significant, came to acquire new symbolic importance because of their additional and enhanced connotations of wealth. This shift in cultural values led to increased harvest pressure upon birds with yellow in their plumages.

The most extraordinary outcome of this equating of kingship with wealth was a cloak belonging to the king Kamehameha I (*c*.1758–1819). He had been a minor chief in 1778, at the time of Captain James Cook's visit to the archipelago (Cook was later killed in a fracas on the beach at Kealakekua on the island of Hawaii in 1779). Kamehameha had eventually managed to assert himself over the other three main chiefdoms in the islands. This consolidation of power in one supreme ruler found its pre-eminent symbolic expression in a garment now housed in the Bishop Museum

in Honolulu. Aside from a border round the neck made from a few red Iiwi feathers, the whole fabric of this *'ahu 'ula* is yellow. It has been claimed that the manufacture of the garment had been started even in the reign of Kamehameha's predecessors.[23] Each mamo used to make it yielded only an estimated six or seven feathers, and it is calculated that the whole garment of 450,000 feathers was derived from approximately 80,000 birds.[24]

As anthropologist Nicholas Thomas has suggested of Hawaiian cloaks, nothing like them 'could have been produced in any other Oceanic society, because nowhere else did chiefs have the power to enforce such onerous demands upon their subjects'.[25] Kamehameha's all-yellow version – sumptuously textured, extravagantly beautiful and representative of the most extreme exploitation of Hawaii's natural resources – is their ultimate expression. It is hard to imagine any other single human garment ever involving that level of destruction of so many birds. This fantastic artefact, which in some ways represents the subordination of all Hawaiian cultural expression to a single hypertrophied value – wealth – speaks eloquently not only of its particular island context. It is a garment that carries implications for all humanity. As an expression of glittering technical achievement that involves simultaneously a reckless denial of ecological consequences, Kamehameha's cloak seems to symbolise the wonderful and tragic story of modern humanity and its impact upon the Earth's natural resources.

It is surely more than coincidence that not only the mamo (and a close relative, the **Black Mamo** *Drepanis funerea*) but also the suite of Hawaiian honeyeaters, including the Hawaii Oo *Moho nobilis* (1934), the Oahu Oo *Moho apicalis* (1837) and the Bishop's Oo *Moho bishopi* (1915) – all bearers of precious but limited yellow plumes – are now extinct. However, excessive harvest for feather art was by no means the only, or even the main, cause. Human arrival in Hawaii, by both Polynesians and Euro-Americans, has inflicted massive ecological disruption upon the archipelago. While different commentators sometimes like to divide the blame between the two cultural groups, assigning more to one or the other according to their political bias, the underlying truth is that all human occupancy has wrought wholesale change.

One of the critical factors is the introduction of non-native species. This problem afflicts almost all island communities. Yet in Hawaii this hazard has run riot. Of its 1,935 free-living flowering plant species, 902 are aliens. E O Wilson suggests that of the grand total (22,070 species) of organisms present in the islands, 4,373 are non-native invaders. Among these he identifies the arch destroyers of indigenous Hawaiian life as a species of insect, the big-headed ant, and the common pig.[26]

In the context specifically of the honeycreepers he might have added the mosquito and its accompanying protozoan parasites responsible for avian malaria. Many of the extinct honeycreepers, whose populations were weakened by hunting pressure, were trapped between the effects of habitat loss (through both logging and replacement of native forest with invasive trees and plant species) and alien introductions. Foreign mosquito-borne disease often issued a final *coup de grâce*. This remorseless triad of pressures now bears down on the islands' surviving honeycreepers with devastating force.

New World Warbler family *Parulidae*

The Chestnut-sided Warbler typifies the striking plumages possessed by many of its family.

These 118 species are found exclusively in the Americas and while they share some of the characteristics of Old World warblers – small size, delicate proportions, intense, busy insect-searching lifestyles – there is no relationship between the two groups. One area where they are completely divergent is on the issue of colour. While Old World warblers are famous for their drabness, their American counterparts are renowned for beauty. The family also presents one of those rare occasions when the birds occurring in temperate latitudes are as brilliant as their relatives in the tropics. In fact, in some ways the many warblers that migrate to breed in North America are the most highly regarded of the whole group.

More than 50 species occur north of the USA–Mexican border and many breed in Canada's great stretches of boreal forest. During April and May as they pour across the continent in their hundreds of millions these birds unleash an intense spring rainbow of colour that is one of the great natural spectacles of the region. A 'warbler wave' is one name for the drama and birdwatchers routinely claim that it is the highlight of their wildlife year.[1]

The chromatic range is extraordinary. Birds like the increasingly scarce **Cerulean Warbler** *Dendroica cerulea* or the **Black-throated Blue Warbler** *Dendroica caerulescens*, which both breed in the eastern USA, have

upperparts of intense 'heavenly-blue'.[2] Yet another bird of eastern woodland – and among the most highly regarded of all – is the **Blackburnian Warbler** *Dendroica fusca*, with crown and facial stripes of bright gold and a throat of flaming orange. A species breeding mainly in the swamp woods of the Mississippi basin is the **Prothonotary Warbler** *Protonotaria citrea*. The male possesses a brilliance of yellow that is unmatched across its family – 'radiant beauty' was the judgement of one admirer – and, for once, the singularity of the hue seems somehow enshrined in the strangely un-American name.[3] It refers to the golden-yellow robes worn by an official – known as a *protonotarius* – of the late Roman Empire in Byzantium.[4]

If any generalisations can be offered about the sheer spectrum of beauty in the group, then it is the preponderance of yellows, blacks and whites, but also the frequency with which the colours are arrayed in compelling juxtaposition. On one glorious little bird the lines of contrasting colour are blended in crisp, curving patterns. Perhaps the most extraordinary is the **Black-and-white Warbler** *Mniotilta varia*, a common species found widely across central and eastern North America, that is an intricate skein of alternating dark-and-light. Theoretically the vividly pied plumage should stand out against the green of deciduous woodland, but Black-and-white Warblers feed by clambering creeper-like along trunks and branches and somehow they blend perfectly with the mottled bark and their wider setting.

Another common thread across the group is the extent to which their impact is auditory as well as visual. Few New World warblers are noted for the richness of their voices, and many have songs that are intense, high-pitched and, occasionally, even rather insect-like (in the case of the Black-and-white Warbler). Yet some of the short ditties have been turned into mnemonics, one example being the song of the **American Yellow Warbler** *Dendroica petechia*, a species breeding almost continent-wide. The bird's shrill phrases with their abrupt terminal flourish have long been rendered as 'sweet, sweet, sweet, I'm so sweet', while the similarly structured notes of the **Chestnut-sided Warbler** *Dendroica pensylvanica* are committed to memory as 'pleased, pleased, pleased to meetcha'.[5] Perhaps the most characteristic note associated with these many migrant species is a tiny, seemingly inarticulate 'chip' sound that is their shared contact call. Brief and simple it may be, but it can have enormous impact.

New World warblers are nocturnal migrants and if they encounter adverse weather or natural geographical obstacles in the course of their passage – mountains, large lakes, coastlines, etc. – they will descend to feed and refuel. There are locations now famed for these mass arrivals, such as Cape May (New Jersey), High Island (Texas), Magee Marsh (Ohio) and Point Pelee (Ontario). But there are also much wider, if lesser, influxes at other places, the most famous of which is probably Central Park amid the unlikely skyscraper canyons of Manhattan. At first light on the occasions of these dramatic waves, the chipping contact notes and the snatches of fast-paced melody are the observer's initial indication that a real warbler spectacle is about to unfold.

A further facet of these migration dramas is rooted in the ecology of the family. For New World warblers offer a classic illustration of adaptive radiation, with various species occupying subtly different niches across the woodland complex. Some, such as the continent-wide **Ovenbird** *Seiurus aurocapilla* or the **Northern Waterthrush** *Seiurus noveboracensis* and **Louisiana Waterthrush** *Seiurus motacilla*, are ground-dwelling birds that walk across the woodland floor, and in the case of the two streak-chested waterthrushes they often feed along the margins of streams and rivers or standing water rather like diminutive sandpipers. Other relatives, however, such as the continent-wide **Common Yellowthroat** *Geothlypis trichas* or the similarly yellow-breasted **Mourning Warbler** *Oporornis philadelphia* prefer low-standing thickets or scrub. Then there is a suite of species, often the most highly prized in the group, which occupy the high canopy.

An occupational hazard of the warbler wave is a condition widely known as 'warbler neck', a dull ache in the cervical vertebrae as the observer scours the treetops for hours on end.[6] Two classic agents of this ornithological ailment are the Blackburnian and Cerulean Warblers. Yet if conditions are absolutely perfect for a major warbler arrival then 'warbler neck' is only one part of a wider pathology. At their very best, these migration influxes induce an almost feverish anxiety. For birds are simultaneously everywhere, and a key part of the experience is not knowing where to look next. Yet we should emphasise that these glorious little birds are affliction and therapy all in one:

Few things delight my heart more than a summer stroll through the boreal forest, which seemingly extends from the Arctic Circle to my family's cottage in northern Wisconsin. Soon a cacophony resonates above my head. My husband, Dan, identifies the voices as warblers. I peer through my binoculars and admire their technicolor plumages: a Chestnut-sided Warbler washed in yellow, russet-red, and a black malar stripe; a **Blue-winged Warbler** *Vermivora pinus* exhibiting black eyeliner and cobalt-blue wingtips; and finally, an **American Redstart** *Setophaga ruticilla* clad in Halloween black and orange. As Dan whistles like a Screech Owl, more birds approach and scold him with their *zee-zee-zee* and *chicka-dee-dee-dee* alarm calls because they think a predator is in their midst. The warblers' swirling colors spin me into a state of euphoria, and I am oblivious to my watch and my smartphone's allure of email and Internet. Those can wait; for now, I am detoxing in the best way I know how.[7]

Proof of the human joy in these glorious birds are the occasions when 15,000 observers, including people from all around the world, converge on a hotspot such as Magee Marsh. In 2010 this increasingly celebrated site held a bird-based event from 7–16 May. With wry humour the organisers of this Ohio festival named it 'The Biggest Week in American Birding' (it spanned 10 days). Using rhetoric of similar stamp, devotees of Magee Marsh now call it the 'warbler capital of the world', based on the 30-plus species during the peak May period.

These tiny birds represent only a minuscule fraction of the biotic mass in any woodland environment, yet their imaginative and psychological impact upon us is out of all proportion to their mathematical share in the landscape. Henry Thoreau touched upon a part of this mysterious effect when he wrote of a May morning filled with New World warblers:

Think how thoroughly the trees are thus explored by various birds. You can hardly sit near one for five minutes now, but either a woodpecker or creeper [Thoreau's name for the Black-and-white Warbler] comes and examines its bark rapidly, or a warbler – a summer yellowbird [American Yellow Warbler] for example – make a pretty thorough exploration about all its expanding leaflets, even to the topmost twig. The whole North American forest is thus explored for insect food now by several hundred species of birds.[8]

All birds have a powerful ability to transport us beyond any immediate scene and allow us to reflect on a wider shared context. In the case of intensely active species such as warblers this is doubly so, because we only ever see them for moments. Then they are gone and they pass deeper into the vegetation beyond our reach. We can only stand and imagine their lives restlessly, endlessly continuing in other parts of the wood – and in all woods – where we shall never follow.

Yet through them, especially in the approach to their breeding season when the birds' colours seem freshly minted, we are made deeply aware of the wider surging renewal of life. Warblers in dazzling new plumages amid the startling greenery of new foliage dramatise the advent of spring like few other organisms, except perhaps that full-bodied mass of blossom on fruit trees.

Mystery of the Missing Migrants is one of the most famous and surely among the most beautiful of images by the American artist Charley Harper.

ARTISTIC REPRESENTATIONS OF NEW WORLD WARBLER MIGRATION

If anyone could be said to have summarised this rather intangible set of feelings and experiences triggered by warbler migration, then it is the great modernist painter Charley Harper (1922–2007), arguably the most original artist of North American wildlife since John James Audubon. His style is instantly recognisable, while his work is the diametric opposite of that produced under North America's dominant wildlife tradition of natural realism. Instead of micro-feather detail, Harper's birds have an almost child-like graphic simplicity, with forms rendered down to pure lines and abstracted shapes filled with single colours. The images are dominated by colour, but they are also humorous, witty, subtle and they manage to convey almost as much information about the species they represent as anything by Roger Tory Peterson or Robert Bateman.

One of Harper's most famous images is *Mystery of the Missing Migrants*. Set within a gorgeous plane of star-studded twilight blue are 46 Neotropical birds, including 27 species of New World warbler. All are migrants. All face left to right – except his Swallow-tailed Kite, whose arresting red eyes make direct contact with the viewer's own – and all are presented in a tangled matrix of colour and pattern. Unpicking all of the birds, in fact, some of which are only represented by the ends of their tails (they are, after all, mysteriously missing) is rather like the challenge of real field birding. The image is an environmental plea for the loss of North America's wildlife heritage. Yet it is also a celebration of migrant birds. No single painting has better captured the collective brilliance, variety and shimmering

now-you-see-me, now-you-don't lives of the continent's wood warblers.

Right at the very heart of *Mystery of the Missing Migrants* is a Cerulean Warbler, one of the most rapidly disappearing of all its family. However, its going is no real mystery. This species typifies the plight of many migrant birds, and not just those in Harper's magnificent serigraph, but right around the world. Across these numerous examples, the precise threats differ but all of them have a human face. Almost everywhere birds are victims of our relentless consumption of resources. In 2010 the American novelist Jonathan Franzen made the Cerulean Warbler and its plight a central motif for his novel *Freedom*. The book is exceptional and groundbreaking for the way it places the enterprise of wildlife conservation and the ethical values that underpin it in literary fiction. *Freedom* is surely the first occasion that any writer has attempted to marry 'the great American novel' and modern ornithology.

Ecological research into the Cerulean Warbler's transcontinental lifestyle has exposed how habitat losses are now inflicting a population loss of 3 per cent per annum. Overall since 1966 it has declined by more than 80 per cent.[9] One pressure assailing it is the conversion of its winter quarters in South American forest to agricultural plantation. (A partial solution has also been identified in the promotion of shade-grown coffee, a crop that combines a high-quality commercial product with the preservation of most of a forest ecosystem. This habitat holds three to 14 times the density of Cerulean Warblers found in neighbouring primary forest.)

Yet the second core threat that is literally grinding Cerulean Warblers into carbon dust is the destruction of its breeding habitat in the USA. The species' distribution is tied to increasingly fragmented old-growth deciduous forests within a latitudinal belt spanning from Arkansas to Minneapolis and eastwards to the Atlantic. Unfortunately the warbler's highest densities are in the coal-mining regions of three states (West Virginia, Kentucky and Tennessee) where the classic model of excavation is known as mountaintop removal (MTR). The operation inflicts a double habitat loss, smashing the mountaintops down to their bare substrate and burying the valleys below under mining spoil. In the ten-year period to 2002, more than 1,500 km² (*c*.600 miles²) of forest were lost at the heart of the Cerulean Warbler's range.

Franzen manages to splice the specifics of Cerulean Warbler conservation into a wider examination of American consumption, especially its relentless quest for carbon-based energy, and the deeply compromised ethics of its industrial-military complex. More ambitious still, he makes all of these broad themes of American public life the background to a story of one nuclear family. Walter Berglund, the conservationist with a mission to save New

World warblers, is the archetypal middle-class male with wife (Patty) and two kids (Joey and Jessica). The book charts the fraught and fragmented but somehow always elasticated relationships of this family quartet, and at one level the book is a simple domestic drama. In fact commentators upon *Freedom*, unaccustomed to wildlife conservation as a meet theme for literary fiction, are so surprised or baffled by its ornithological content that they ignore it almost completely and describe the book as the account of a family at war with itself.

Yet Franzen is himself a birder. His novel is called *Freedom*. A bird is nothing if not the stock human motif for freedom. Through the story of the Cerulean Warbler the author is able to examine the multiple layers of liberty that modern Americans enjoy and demand of right. Franzen also assesses how those diverse forms of political liberty and private indulgence carry a cost. He invites us to consider how freedom affects both the humans that claim it and the world that bears its consequences.

A Montezuma Oropendola performs its distinctive 'falling' display.

New World Blackbird family *Icteridae*

This family is as wide-ranging across the Americas as it is heterogeneous in physical form. There are 105 species and they encompass an enormous size range, from the beautiful and migratory **Orchard Oriole** *Icterus spurius* of North America, measuring just 16 cm (6.3 in), to the family giants, including the **Montezuma Oropendola** *Psarocolius montezuma* and **Olive Oropendola** *Psarocolius yuracares*, which are up to 53 cm (21 in) in length. These two are found in the Central and South American rainforests respectively and are among the largest of all songbirds, with males weighing as much as 528 g (1.1 lb).

The group is at its most diverse in the tropics, with countries such as Mexico and Colombia holding more than 30 species apiece. The diversity declines with latitude so that a country like Canada holds only 13 breeding icterids, with just two – the **Red-winged Blackbird** *Agelaius phoeniceus* and **Rusty Blackbird** *Euphagus carolinus* – summering in Alaska. The northern pair is among the 24 species breeding regularly in the USA. At the other end of the Americas, only the **Long-tailed Meadowlark** *Sturnella loyca* reaches the tip of Tierra del Fuego, but it has also colonised the Falkland Islands, where it is often

The slurred nasal song display of the Red-winged Blackbird is one of the first signs of the North American spring.

known as the 'military starling', a name that nicely evokes the regimental crimson on the breast, as well as the bird's waddling starling-like gait and shape.

The colour that better characterises the family is yellow. 'Icterids', another generic name for New World blackbirds, comes from a Greek word technically meaning 'jaundice yellow', but here it reflects the preponderance of brilliant gold or orange in their plumages. The exemplars are the 30 species in the genus *Icterus* (they are mainly known as 'orioles' but their physical similarities to the unrelated Old World orioles of Africa and Eurasia are superficial; see page 378). Some orioles have become much-loved garden birds that have been drawn to close quarters, especially in North America, by the provision of fresh fruit and other sugar-rich foods.

The **Baltimore Oriole** *Icterus galbula* is a special visitor. I lure them in with oranges, or perhaps a cup of marmalade. They dart as a welcome blaze of orange and black into our everyday lives from that edge where the wild and the backyard blur. Once almost unknown to us here in Nebraska, the birds have increased and we're happy to welcome them.[1]

AMBIVALENT ATTITUDES TOWARDS NEW WORLD BLACKBIRDS

The orioles may be much loved and welcomed for their beauty, but overall the New World blackbirds have a highly mixed reputation. The family includes some of the most successful and populous birds in all the Americas, but it is often the curious fate of superabundant organisms to endure widespread human dislike. Perhaps the most unpopular family member, and surely a candidate as the most unloved native bird in all North America, is the **Brown-headed Cowbird** *Molothrus ater*. A beast that is black of plumage, destructive of crops and bellicose of manner was never likely to be the nation's most cherished, but to these demerits the poor cowbird adds the lifestyle of a shiftless freeloader. It is an aggressive brood parasite, laying eggs in the nests of more than 220 other bird species, including even shorebirds and ducks.[2]

The cowbird is not alone in its role as outcast. Several New World blackbirds have inspired a hatred that is both ancient and international. The environmental historian Mark Bonta tells a rather amusing tale about the rapidly changing cultural status of the large, aggressive **Great-tailed Grackle** *Quiscalus mexicanus* in ancient Mexico. This long-tailed bird is now an habitué of urban environments from Ecuador to Iowa, but it was originally absent from central Mexico. The inhabitants introduced the bird they called *teuzanatl* to an area around their capital, Tenochtitlan, because of the enormous desirability of its iridescent purple plumage. The sumptuous tail plumes were in particular demand by Mexico's celebrated feather artists (see also Trogon family, page 310) and the grackles initially enjoyed imperial protection because of this special function. Unfortunately the species quickly resorted to type when its numbers exploded and it exchanged the status of cultural pet for that of abundant pest.[3]

Very little has changed today. An ornithologist recently made a plea for the Great-tailed Grackle based not on its invariably overlooked beauty, but on the atmospheric power of the voice. 'Despite its reputation for obnoxiousness,' he writes, 'it produces one of the most remarkable vocal arrays of any North American bird.'[4] Perhaps its intelligence will also win it more sympathy:

When I lived in Texas for four years there were two pecan trees in my yard. The grackles would take pecans from the ground in their massive beaks, hop into the road and the parking lot next door, leave the pecans, and wait for cars to crush them. Then they would eat them. I never once saw a dead grackle there, and I never saw that behavior anywhere else even though the grackles and pecan trees were quite plentiful. Very smart birds![5]

Across the Americas, the exact blackbird species may vary from country to country, but the family's overarching status as avian enemy number one remains constant. In Honduras it is an all-dark bird known as *huachír*, the **Melodious Blackbird** *Dives dives*, which is a target of scarecrows and slingshot-wielding boys and which is regarded as a devastating pest on maize crops.[6] In Brazil it is a relative known as the **Chopi Blackbird** *Gnorimopsar chopi* that is persecuted – and eaten – for its habit of pulling up recently planted corn. Its strange name is said to be onomatopoeic of its voice, but rural folk have another deeply resonant mnemonic for the ringing vocalisations. The bird is said to sing, 'You plant, Joaquim, You plant, Joaquim, I'll pull it out, I'll pull it out.'[7]

The bad reputation of some North American blackbirds long pre-dates white colonisation. The nineteenth-century naturalist Alexander Wilson recorded how Red-winged

Blackbirds descended on Native American cornfields 'like vast clouds, wheeling and diving … and … darkening the air with their numbers'.[8] European settlers quickly adopted both the defensive measures and the attitudes of their indigenous neighbours. In the mid eighteenth century Mark Catesby wrote:

The red wing'd starling [Red-winged Blackbird] and Purple-Daw [**Common Grackle** *Quiscalus quiscula*] . . . are most voracious corn-eaters. They seem combined to do all the mischief they are able and to make themselves most formidable, both kinds unite in one flock, and are always together . . . They are the boldest and most destructive Birds in the Country.[9]

As if their reputation were not dark enough, the early naturalists discovered other reasons to dislike New World blackbirds. They often possess a rather unusual musky bouquet, said to resemble the odour of cockroaches and instrumental in making the birds completely unpalatable.[10]

In North America three New World blackbirds – the Common Grackle, Red-winged Blackbird and Brown-headed Cowbird – pool their status as least-loved bird with that of another common hate figure, the Common Starling. The quartet gathers in vast mixed-species assemblies, when the differences of size and colour are lost in the general mass of all-dark birds. They are deemed the most economically significant avian pests in the USA, and do particular damage around cattle feedlots or in other agricultural environments where grain is available.[11]

In the mid twentieth century pest-control teams used funnel nets to catch huge numbers of them. One such programme took 672,000 blackbirds and starlings in 101 operations, with as many as 120,000 birds trapped in the course of a single night.[12] Yet in proportion to the overall size of the flocks these figures are actually insignificant. One roost at Millers Lake in southern Louisiana, which surely must rank among the largest individual bird congregations in the Americas, numbered 38 million in 1986.[13] Seldom to be outdone on the issue of size, Texas produced a roost in the mid 1970s that was estimated at 50 million. During the same period field workers for the US Fish and Wildlife Service found 723 roosts nationwide that held an estimated 537 million blackbirds and starlings.[14]

Perhaps the one species that best expresses our Janus-faced responses to the whole family is the **Bobolink** *Dolichonyx oryzivorus*. It is in some ways an oddity among the group, not just for its remarkable long-distance pan-American migration, which involves some populations travelling 20,000 km (12,000 miles) from breeding grounds in Canada as far south as Argentina. Most New World blackbirds, regardless of all their physical heterogeneity, possess long, straight dagger-like beaks that rather resemble a pair of fine sharp-nosed pincers, but the Bobolink has a stubby finch's bill to match the dumpy sparrow-like shape.

However, the male in breeding plumage is remarkably handsome, with his sooty face and breast, white wing panels and creamy 'shawl' across the rear crown. He also possesses a short sweet song that has been much versified, although no one has perhaps bettered Thoreau's single line of overheard conversation between a boy and his mother: 'What makes he sing so sweet, Mama? Do he eat flowers?'[15] Thoreau captured the exquisite liquid quality of Bobolink song when he wrote:

'It is as if he touched his harp within a vase of liquid melody, and when he lifted it out, the notes fell like bubbles from the trembling springs.'[16]

For all the cherished connections with vernal North America and fresh-flushed grassland habitats, Bobolinks were also hated and much persecuted as a pest of grain crops. An old name was 'rice bird', while the second part of the scientific name means 'rice eater'. It reflects a time when south-bound Bobolinks arrived in their millions among the rice-growing states around the Gulf of Mexico, where they were trapped and shot relentlessly. It was also kept as a caged songbird and harvested for food. A local name in Jamaica is 'butter bird', reflecting the fat-rich condition of their migrant flocks.[17] Today it is more a victim of habitat loss, especially the disappearance of species-rich native grasslands.

NEW WORLD BLACKBIRDS AS SYMBOLS OF LANDSCAPE

Not all New World blackbirds have dark or even mixed reputations. Classic exceptions are two beautiful inhabitants of open grassland habitats, the **Western Meadowlark** *Sturnella neglecta* and **Eastern Meadowlark** *Sturnella magna*. Each has an extensive North American range – the latter species also occurs as far south as the cerrado savannahs of northern Brazil – with a broad area of overlap between the two running from northern Mexico, through Texas and Oklahoma to Wisconsin. Wherever they occur the two are famous for their short sweet songs, which has a slow fluted quality in the Western Meadowlark. Both birds often deliver their vocalisations from roadside fence posts, when the intermittent snatches of wild melody enter the car's open window and become a glorious part of journeys through many types of farm country.

The sounds have international impact, if only subliminally, because meadowlarks are a staple background sound in Western films or American television programmes with outdoor settings. The symbolism was made official in one of the great prairie regions of the USA, when the Western Meadowlark was elected state bird for Nebraska in 1929. (There is a deeper piece of ornithological history embedded in the choice because the species was first recognised by Audubon in 1843 along the Missouri River of eastern Nebraska.) A devotee both of meadowlarks and of Nebraskan prairie expands on the bird's emblematic role in his home area:

The meadowlark is a huge part of symbolism here. It appears officially on car license plates and in the names of businesses statewide. There's a Meadowlark coffee shop in Lincoln, an elementary school and a golf course in Kearney, a retirement home in Deshler, a hotel in Bridgeport, and storage facility in Omaha. My most impressive find, however, was a two-foot-high hand-painted meadowlark on a farm building north of Burwell. It is so large that, like the living bird's song, it seems to call out to you for acknowledgement. People across the state know the meadowlark, even those that don't take the time to look, because it calls boldly into our ears as we ride by on the highway. It is a symbol of our state that is much like the prairie itself – subdued but immensely beautiful – and we are proud to have it as our bird.[18]

The 24 species of oropendola and cacique from Central and South America may be at the other end of a spectrum both in terms of their size and also in terms of the habitats that they occupy, but they share with the meadowlarks that same capacity to symbolise their wider environment. They are hugely striking creatures, with many possessing vivid patches of golden yellow, while a speciality is long sulphurous tails or stripes of this colour along the tail's outer margins. The Spanish name 'oropendola' actually means 'golden plumes'. Male caciques and oropendolas are often much bigger and twice as heavy as their female partners. Indeed, the strange name 'cacique' is thought to be of Taíno origin, the language spoken by the now extinct Arawak people of Hispaniola. It meant 'chief' and referred, in the ornithological sense, to the apparent social dominance of the male birds.[19]

Just as remarkable as the birds themselves are their nests. Many oropendolas and caciques weave long pendulous structures with a brood pouch suspended on a 'rope' that is often constructed of fibres taken from straggling epiphytes or bromeliads, such as the Spanish moss that drapes down in vast curtains over some rainforest trees. These woven nests can be anything up to 2 m (6.6 ft) long and cluster together in the canopy, sometimes involving several dozens together, where they look like weird swaying sculptural textiles. Yet, as one commentator notes, the nests 'are easily seen but virtually impossible to reach'.[20]

Sometimes they are located in huge trees near places with heavy human traffic. The ornithologist Bennett Hennessey describes how Bolivian oropendolas show a strong predilection for public spaces:

I lived in the tropical Bolivian town of Rurrenabaque for a year, where **Russet-backed Oropendola** *Psarocolius angustifrons* would make a point of breeding in trees around the town. It was not so obvious as some weaver birds in Africa, but there did appear to be an association between human habitation and the colony's choice of nearby isolated trees.

Icterids are such intelligent birds and one thing I've seen is **Dusky-green Oropendola** *Psarocolius atrovirens* on the road to the Chapare lowlands in Cochabamba. They arrive at around 6 a.m. every morning to seek out bugs drawn by the lights of the 24-hour police drug-check roadblock. The place has a big two-lane raised tin roof of about 120 m x 80 m in the middle of the cloud-forest at 2,000 m above sea level. The support beams for the roof involve a matrix of thin welded metal rods with lots of crannies for hiding insects. The oropendolas come in groups of ten to 15 and search through the lot, with all the great foraging postures of icterids, upside down, hanging, probing, etc. They will slowly move up a beam sticking their heads around each rod then up and over. This fabulous show lasts for about ten minutes and then the birds disappear for the day into the cloud-forest.[21]

The oropendolas' acrobatic skills are perhaps at their most dramatic in the breeding colonies. The males vocalise loudly, but they also simultaneously drop forward as if about to fall from their perches and occasionally swing upside down or perform a complete somersault round the branch, with their wings quivering and yellow-plumed tails spread. The sounds they make during these 'falling'

displays are equally unforgettable and often comprise high, loud, liquid wailing or glugging and gurgling notes that cleave the surrounding rainforest with enormous impact. In ornithological literature they are often referred as 'slashing' or 'whip-like' notes.[22] In their way these oropendola displays, amid the richly suggestive architecture of their nests, are as redolent of the New World tropics as the glittering whirr of hummingbirds, or the scintillating colours of tanagers, or the misshapen eccentricity of toucans. Occasionally, as if aware of their wider powers of evocation, oropendolas choose the most symbolic of locations to nest. There is a good-sized Montezuma Oropendola colony, for instance, at the heart of the magnificent Mayan ruins at Tikal, Guatemala.

The Amerindians of South America respond widely to the sheer spectacle and to the atmosphere of intense breeding competitiveness associated with oropendola colonies. They eat the birds but they also gather their plumes, especially the tail feathers, for personal display. Among the Desana people of Colombia, for instance, there is an hereditary lineage of shamans known as the 'sons of the oropendola'. The Desana people link the distinctive dangling globes of the nests with human fertility, for their resemblance both to the human scrotum and to the interior form of the female uterus. The shamans made, and possibly still make, striking circular headdresses from the male tail plumes, whose shape and golden colour were associated with the ultimate source of fertility, the sun.[23]

Although various Amerindian communities have drawn on the fertility symbolism suggested by oropendola colonies, they could never have appreciated just how truly extraordinary are these breeding arrangements. Many species are not only highly polygynous, with males competing to mate with the more numerous females; in turn, hens also seek to copulate with multiple partners. Females then vie with one another to build their nests at the heart of the colony, with the optimum positions being taken by older dominant birds.

Oropendolas have also evolved to site their nest colonies in the close vicinity of bees' or wasps' nests, because these aggressive colonial insects deter the presence of possible nest predators. In cases where the wasps and bees have been removed, it is found that the oropendolas themselves desert the site.[24]

The Bananaquit (at top and bottom left) of Latin America is a bird with a sweet tooth and a definite taste for alcohol.

Bananaquit family *Coerebidae*

The **Bananaquit** *Coereba flaveola* may weigh just 10 g (0.35 oz) and measure less than 11 cm (4.3 in), but it is one of the most captivating midgets in Latin America's vast avifauna. It now occupies a monotypic family after the South American honeycreepers, with which it was once associated, were reassigned to the tanager family *Thraupidae*. Despite its current lack of close relatives, the Bananaquit is itself enormously diverse and has been split into as many as 41 different races that occur from Mexico and the many islands of the Caribbean (except Cuba) south as far as northern Argentina. It also encompasses great physical variation, with some Bananaquits being almost entirely black, right through to the more typical dark-backed form, with long white eyebrow and bright sulphurous-yellow underparts.

One constant feature is the decurved awl-like beak, with which it pierces flower petals to rob plants of their nectar.

A love of showy blooms has made it a common inhabitant of gardens, although it seems also to favour coastal areas and achieves especially high densities on islands. In some parts of the Caribbean, such as on Trinidad and Tobago, it is among the commonest songbirds. In these places it caps its bright colours and abundance with immense personality. One author called it 'a fearless little busybody', while in his *Birds of the West Indies* the ornithologist James Bond (whence, incidentally, the novelist Ian Fleming found inspiration to name his celebrated fictional character Agent 007) listed 14 different local names.[1] These vernacular versions reflect not only the Bananaquit's familiarity to many people (e.g. Bessie Coban and *reinita*, 'little queen'), but also the bird's great love of sugar (sugar bird, *sucrier*). At outdoor restaurants and in private gardens the Bananaquit will readily come to the dining table and indulge in what are often voluntary donations of sugar or jam and, if feeders have been put out to attract hummingbirds, then it also readily takes over these sugar dispensers.[2]

Yet its strangest dietary penchant is a taste for alcohol. Professor Cedric Smith has studied the drinking habits of Bananaquits and after various experiments concluded that the birds had a preference for beverages containing 4–6 per cent alcohol (similar to strong beer), but refused those of 8 per cent or over (their revulsion was expressed by vigorous shaking of the head). Best of all tipples was a mixture of 4–6 per cent proof sweetened with sugar or strawberry jam. This is not the only species to enjoy alcohol, but one striking aspect of the Bananaquit's own consumption is a seeming ability to drink copiously without any ill effects (see also pages 249 and 407).[3]

The bird's conviviality has given it a symbolic place at the Caribbean bar, although many of the cultural associations draw first on a well-loved calypso song, 'Yellow Bird', that was originally Haitian but was later popularised worldwide by the likes of the singer Harry Belafonte. The bird sat high in the banana tree is, in fact, a Bananaquit. It has now been transferred into the titles of many restaurants or hotels, but also to a delicious Yellow Bird cocktail (rum, Galliano, crème de bananes and orange juice). Alas it is probably too strong a drink for the eponymous bird's own alcoholic tastes.

Bunting and New World Sparrow family
Emberizidae

This large family of 170 finch-like birds is predominantly found in the Americas with a high percentage on the northern continent. Some, however, such as the brush finches (33 species) are boldly coloured inhabitants of scrub or forest-edge mainly in South America, with just five occurring as far north as Mexico. The one other key exception to the family's concentration in the New World is the 40 species of bunting in the genus *Emberiza*, which all have their main breeding ranges in Eurasia (31 species) or Africa (nine species), specialising in open bushy country and grasslands.

By far the largest contingent of the family is the 64 species that all bear the name 'sparrow'. They are completely unrelated to the small brown global citizen which has made that name commonplace the world over, the House Sparrow (see page 483). They are also different to the latter in temperament and lifestyle, and are as often noted for modesty and shyness as the House Sparrow is for its brazen familiarity.

SPARROWS AND THEIR OBSCURITY
What the New World sparrows indubitably share with House Sparrows are their smallness of size and the predominance of brown in their plumages. Many are the quintessential 'little brown jobs' – dull, streaky and obscure. There are 34 sparrows north of Mexico and the diversity compounds an impression for many people that they are difficult to separate and hardly worth the effort. Adding to this anonymity is a habit among several, such as three widespread birds of North American farmland, the **Savannah Sparrow** *Passerculus sandwichensis*, **Vesper Sparrow** *Pooecetes gramineus* and **Grasshopper Sparrow** *Ammodramus savannarum*, of running mouse-like through the grasses and only taking flight when almost stepped upon. The ornithologist Frank Chapman wrote of the last species, 'Few common birds

may be more easily overlooked.' He went on to describe an occasion when he introduced an ornithological friend to this bird and its song, only for the friend to return home and find that Grasshopper Sparrows were abundant all around his own house. Until that point he had overlooked them completely.[1]

His omission is understandable. The songs of the Grasshopper Sparrow and also of the **Le Conte's Sparrow** *Ammodramus leconteii* of central Canada are often mistaken for the stridulations of insects. Meanwhile the song of the poor little **Henslow's Sparrow** *Ammodramus henslowii*, another mouse-like creeper of weedy meadows in eastern USA and south-east Canada, has been labelled as the 'poorest vocal efforts of any bird': a hiccupping 'tsi-lick'.[2]

The more highly renowned **Song Sparrow** *Melospiza melodia*, which is a common bird across almost all North America and which will sing at night by moonlight, underscores a third factor in the group's reputation for obscurity. Some sparrows are enormously diverse: the Song Sparrow, for instance, has been redivided into at least 39 separate subspecies, while the **Fox Sparrow** *Passerella iliaca* and Savannah Sparrow have 18 and 21 races respectively. Some of the Song Sparrow forms are so distinct from one another it is hard to credit that they all belong to the same species.

Before considering the challenges posed by sparrows we should note that not all the family are quite so obscure or inhibited. The dapper **Chipping Sparrow** *Spizella passerina*, which is a common bird from Alaska to Nicaragua, has been described as 'the little brown-capped pensioner of the dooryard and lawn, that comes about farmhouse doors to glean crumbs shaken from the tablecloth'.[3] Others are even more domesticated.

The remarkable **Rufous-collared Sparrow**

The Song Sparrow
is found widely in
North America and
is also hugely variable
across its range.

Zonotrichia capensis is found across much of South America, and even the names used for this bright, perky inhabitant of farms, towns and roadsides suggest the affection that it inspires: *tico-tico* (Brazil), *chesyhasy* (Paraguay), *chingolo* (from Mexico to Argentina). A contributor from the latter country adds: 'Chingolo is a well-loved bird here. Most people use the diminutive *chingolito*. In rural areas House Sparrows are generally not liked, but no one seems to mind the *chingolos*.'[4] (The family member that is perhaps most adapted to living alongside us is the **House Bunting** *Emberiza striolata*, which occurs from India to the Atlantic shores of north Africa. The western races of this gloriously modest bird fulfil their name by dwelling both around human habitations and frequently inside them.)

STUDIES OF SPARROWS

If many New World sparrows have a reputation for being elusive and challenging, it has certainly not been a barrier to their intensive study. In fact their obscurity has become its own slightly perverse incentive for scientists, as one modern sparrow devotee explains:

'Tell me again', this from my Mom, 'why you stopped studying those pretty warblers with bright colors to study these birds that are hard to find (in the winter), hard to tell apart, and whose nests are also so difficult to find?' 'Mom,' I said, 'I started studying sparrows for exactly all the reasons/questions you just mentioned.'[5]

An earlier pioneer of sparrow research was the remarkable Margaret Morse Nice who, while rearing her own brood of five children aged between seven and 18, spent nine years from 1928–36 monitoring a population of Song Sparrows in Ohio. Through her work she made this one species among the most closely observed of all the world's birds. The research involved colour banding more than 500 adults and placing aluminium rings on 353 nestlings, as well as hand-rearing a number of the chicks. Morse, a rare woman in a male-dominated field, combined an impressive grasp of developments in behavioural ecology, especially key contemporary work emerging from Europe, with a groundbreaking field study of her own. She is important for helping to redirect ornithology from a consideration of

general taxa to the life of an individual organism, following a Song Sparrow in minute and intimate detail from its emergence as an egg to the mortality of the adult bird.[6]

Another great student of the sparrows was Oliver Austin Jr. He edited and compiled, with the aid of more than 100 collaborators, the last parts of Arthur Cleveland Bent's *Life Histories of North American Birds*. The section on the buntings and New World sparrows runs to three volumes – there were 1,345 pages on the sparrows alone – which is more material than for any other group of birds in this monumental series. Finally published in 1968 by the Smithsonian Institution with gloriously understated sand-grey card covers – a colour not unlike the birds described within – and with uncut pages in the manner of old antiquarian works, these three richly detailed books have the feel now of ancient texts.

On page 1335 one finds mention of remarkable experiments undertaken by Richard Mewaldt in the winter of 1961–2, when he took 414 birds of two migratory sparrow species, the **Golden-crowned Sparrow** *Zonotrichia atricapilla* and **White-crowned Sparrow** *Zonotrichia leucophrys*, and flew them to Baton Rouge, Louisiana. Twenty-six of these released birds eventually found their way back to Mewaldt's study area in San Jose, California – a minimum of 2,900 km (1,800 miles). The following winter 660 sparrows (22 of which had already completed the previous season's epic) were flown to Maryland and released. Just 15 birds covered the 3,862 km (2,400 miles) coast-to-coast back to San Jose, but they did include four White-crowned Sparrows that had completed both odysseys.[7]

THE SYMBOLISM OF NEW WORLD SPARROWS

Occasionally this remarkable migrant has even been able to pass across the Atlantic to Europe, with records in France, Iceland and the Netherlands. One such wanderer, only the fifth ever recorded White-crowned Sparrow in Britain, turned up in a garden in Cley, Norfolk, in January 2008. True to family tradition this particular sparrow was shy and elusive, but it was lured into view by careful manipulation of the bird-feeding regimes in all the surrounding gardens. Thousands of people eventually got to see it and donations collected from these happy observers raised £6,500 ($10,500). It is a measure of how individual birds can sometimes leave their small traces among whole communities that this rather lost but world-wandering White-crowned Sparrow was commemorated in church services and now features in the stained-glass window of Cley's beautiful medieval church.[8]

Another person who tried to unravel this capacity of New World sparrows to move us was Henry Thoreau. Listening to the sweet ditty of a little grey Vesper Sparrow, which he could hardly spot on its grey song post, set among the grey ploughland of Massachusetts, Thoreau reflected on the bird's power, like Proust's madeleines, to awaken long, rich sequences of memory:

As the baywing [an old name for Vesper Sparrow] sang many a thousand years ago, so sang he tonight
. . . It reminded me of many a summer sunset, of many miles of gray rails, of many a rambling pasture, of the farmhouse far in the fields, its milk-pans and well-sweep, and the cows coming home from pasture.[9]

Years later he wrote on hearing this same species: 'Only think how finely our life is furnished in all its details, – sweet wild birds provided to fill its interstices with song!'[10] It is this occupation of life's mere 'interstices' that is central to the sparrows' effect. The act of discriminating tiny details in birds of such plainness calls forth our highest powers of observation. And that process is both moving and fundamental, because it entails our higher gifts of consciousness, surely the defining quality of our species. So

Part of the heaving melee of birders who made pilgrimage to the Norfolk village of Cley-next-the-Sea to see a White-crowned Sparrow in 2008. The locals honoured their American visitor by enshrining its image in their church window.

The White-crowned Sparrow is a handsome familiar of the North American landscape. Yet this vagrant individual was photographed in Cley-next-the-Sea, Norfolk, UK.

in a sense we are rendered most human when recognising the most humble of birds. Janet Ruth, a contemporary researcher of New World sparrows in south-eastern Arizona, explains the birds' capacity to move her, but also why they should move us all:

> I defy you to hold a Grasshopper Sparrow in your hand and look at the lemon yellow at the bend of its wing and over its eye, and the chestnut, gray, and black on its back, or a **Baird's Sparrow** *Ammodramus bairdii* and look at the amazing ochre color washing over its face and the nape of its neck, and then call those birds 'little brown jobs'.

> To me these and other sparrow species are the biological representatives of the grasslands in the American West. There is something about the wide-open spaces with rolling hills and waves of grass and nothing to get in the way of my view. And there is something about the little bundles of energy that inhabit these grasslands that has captured my heart – taking on the multiple colors and shades of cured grasses – golds, chestnut, grays, black, and more shades of brown than you can imagine. They live in a landscape without much vertical vegetative structure, so they forage on the ground and build their nests on the ground or in grass clumps. They perch on sparse shrubs, or an extra-tall grass clump, or the odd fence post or cholla to sing, and if they aren't satisfied with the elevation of these terrestrial song perches, they evolve aerial ones. Take the beautiful display of the so-called 'drab' **Cassin's Sparrow** *Aimophila cassinii* who launches himself into the air from a shrub, and when he reaches the zenith of his arc of flight, he throws his head back, flares his wings and, emitting his plaintive

song, flutters back to earth like an angel on grass-colored wings.

> What is the cultural value of sparrows and do they have a message for us? In my winter sparrow research, I often employ groups of local volunteers to help flush sparrows into mist nets for banding (or ringing as they say 'across the pond'). On occasions the volunteers are schoolchildren. I still remember the group that came out through a program for inner-city kids; they'd never seen the grasslands within 60 miles of their homes. They helped chase sparrows, watched me band them and record data, asked intelligent and funny questions about sparrows, took pictures with the point-and-shoot cameras, and got to hold out their hand so that a sparrow could fly off after we were done. The looks on their faces as that sparrow flashed away were worth all the struggles of 'herding kids'. And I overheard one of them say, 'These grasslands rock!' That is the message of the sparrows and the kids. Sparrows rock and their habitat rocks and we need them both.[11]

THE CULT OF THE ORTOLAN

The buntings of Europe and Africa share much of the cultural anonymity of their New World relatives, but there is one glaring exception. The **Ortolan Bunting** *Emberiza hortulana* is an Afro-Palearctic migrant that spreads to breed across the middle latitudes of Eurasia, from Portugal to Russian Siberia. It has been celebrated for centuries, not for the sweet tristesse of the song, nor the bird's delicate beauty, but for its exquisite flavour.

The rather odd name derives from an old Italian version, *hortulane*, which associated the species with gardens.[12] More recently in France the bird acquired local names such as *vigneron* or *vignerot*, suggesting a preference for wine-making

country.[13] In fact, ortolans are largely found in upland pasture, where they can occur at high densities and where their summer songs can become the defining soundtrack of the landscape. The bird produces a series of rasping notes – with a hint of metal being filed gently – which resembles the opening motif of Beethoven's Fifth Symphony. Yet rather than the uplifting drama of those notes, the ortolan adds a melancholic downward twist. (The Tunisians were said to trap them, not to eat, but to savour the sad music.)[14]

Like a number of small migrant birds (see also Old World Warbler family, page 436) the Ortolan Bunting acquired an early culinary reputation among Europeans and has been hunted, trapped, fattened and eaten ever since, latterly in the teeth of international condemnation. The Roman writer of the first century BC Marcus Terentius Varro is assumed to have intended this species in his reference to rearing *miliaria* (although it was once the scientific name for another widespread European bunting, **Corn Bunting** *Emberiza calandra*) in his work *On Farming*.[15] Certainly little has changed since Varro's day in ortolan husbandry. Trapped in nets or small wooden traps called *matoles*, the ortolans are transferred to fattening sheds where they are sometimes blinded or kept in semi-darkness to focus their minds on food. They are over-supplied with oats, millets and water and in a matter of weeks put on two to three times their normal weight. It is alleged even that they die sometimes of suffocation from so much fat. Killed and plucked, the Italian suppliers once packed them in boxes crammed with meal or bran that preserved the bodies for as long as 20 days.[16]

For the diner the heart of the ortolan experience is the sensory rush delivered when the bird is bitten open and out floods a burst of hot fat. Additional allure came from the claim that this molten bunting was also an aphrodisiac.[17] French gastronomes added a further Gallic twist to the

moment by having the birds drowned in Armagnac, so that on being crushed in the diner's mouth the little lungs release a further 'liqueur-scented flower' of taste.[18] The variations in preparation and the rococo pattern of ritual that has sprouted and thoroughly entwined ortolan eating would rival any of the comparable junkies' lore surrounding opium or cocaine. And like Class A drugs, ortolans have now acquired the additional guilt-rich rush of illegality and sin.

Even in former times the relative scarcity of the raw product ensured that the birds were almost always a delicacy for the super-rich. Today they can sell for 100 euros apiece. French monarchs were often extreme devotees and Louis XVIII devised his own ortolan dishes and even prepared them himself. A frequent element in the recipe is a double dose of avian suffering that combines a bunting drowned in spirit with a goose whose liver is enlarged by force feeding (see also page 88). The name of one recipe, which involves inserting the bird's fat little carcass into an even bigger Périgord truffle, is called 'ortolan-in-the-coffin'.[19]

A further significant variable in the ortolan cult is the manner in which the bird is eaten. One technique was outlined in the novella *Gigi* (1944) by the French author Colette. As Aunt Alicia trains the eponymous Gigi in the sexual wiles and social mores of Parisian high society, the teenage beauty is exhorted to slice her ortolans smartly in two, without grating blade on plate, and eat each half, bones and all.[20] More commonly the initiate eats the whole thing with only the head extruding from the lips. Another standard rite is to cover the face, as you consume your ortolan, with a napkin.

This detail was an innovation of an eighteenth-century cleric-cum-epicure and a friend of the culinary author Jean Brillat-Savarin. The latter's volume on food, known in English as *The Physiology of Taste* or *Gastronomy as a Fine Art*

Beloved of epicures, scholars, royalty and rugby players, the Ortolan Bunting of Eurasia may possess the most expensive flesh of any bird on Earth.

(1825) which is one part cookbook, one part medical and philosophical treatise, is still influential today and reflective of French society's religious devotion to the dining table. The purpose of the napkin was to concentrate the senses on the emergent ortolan vapours. More recently it has been suggested that the cloth is there out of shame: to hide one's gluttony from God.

This is especially the case now that the killing and eating of Ortolan Buntings, which is a severely declining species in its European range, are against the law. Unfortunately a minority, including a number of prominent public figures, takes a perverse pride in flouting the ban. The slaughter therefore continues with an estimated 50,000 birds trapped

annually. One anonymous source gave us an account of one such gourmet meal in the town of Dax, at the heart of France's ortolan-catching country. A local restaurant held a dinner to honour the Dax rugby team, one of the country's foremost clubs. If one assumes that the ortolan dish maintained the customary rule of one bird per diner (in 1995 President Mitterrand is said to have permitted himself a final indulgence of two, *only* when days away from his own death), and if one assumes that, aside from the 15 players, there were the trainers, subs and coaches, then the entire Dax club consumed somewhere in the region of 3,000 euros' worth of ortolan – for about 1.5 kg (3.3 lb) of roasted wild bird.[21]

Tanager and Allies family *Thraupidae*

The tanagers vie with that other vast assemblage of Neotropical birds, the tyrant flycatchers (see page 350), to be the world's largest bird family. Their taxonomy is still in a state of flux, but the group is now considered to include 395 small, to very small (9.5–24 cm: 3.7–9.4 in), predominantly forest species, which often associate in mixed flocks. Three-quarters of them are found only in South America, with just four breeding widely north of the USA–Mexican border.

If the birds seem physically fairly homogenous, the range of genera embraced by the tanager family is striking, with a comparably wide spectrum of lifestyles. This includes the bush tanagers (nine species), ant tanagers (five), hemispingus (15), dacnis (11), honeycreepers (six), conebills (11), flowerpiercers (18), warbling finches (14) and seedeaters (39). One common strand across the groups is their beauty. Like the hummingbirds, the tanagers are in many ways the epitome of tropical exoticism. This loveliness has inspired superlatives or rare moments of poetry even in the parched language of modern ornithology: 'wildly colorful forest birds'; 'brilliant and often kaleidoscopic colours', 'one of the great groups of American birds . . . tanagers contribute decidedly to the reputation for beauty held by Neotropical avifauna'.[1]

The bright colours supply another thread of continuity through the group. Their English names are remarkably similar. They divide into four basic types (NB: I have omitted from the analysis the 13 species that are found on the Galápagos archipelago, and which have achieved worldwide fame as Darwin's finches; see below). Nine species have patronymics (e.g. **Passerini's Tanager** *Ramphocelus passerinii*); 50 are named after places, geographical features or habitat forms (e.g. **Brazilian Tanager** *Ramphocelus bresilius*, **Huallaga Tanager** *Ramphocelus melanogaster*, **Marsh Seedeater** *Sporophila palustris*); and 15 have names derived from their dimensions or physical attributes (e.g. **Lesser Seed Finch** *Oryzoborus angolensis*, **Parrot-billed Seedeater** *Sporophila peruviana*).

The vast majority, however – approximately 300 – have names based on their colours, which are often pinpointed to a particular body part. The consistency is striking (e.g. **Black-capped Hemispingus** *Hemispingus atropileus*, **Flame-rumped Tanager** *Ramphocelus flammigerus*, **Golden-backed Mountain Tanager** *Buthraupis aureodorsalis*, **Scarlet-thighed Dacnis** *Dacnis venusta*, **Red-legged Honeycreeper** *Cyanerpes cyaneus*). The

quest to construct variations on this theme has occasionally led to a form of found poetry (e.g. **Black-goggled Tanager** *Trichothraupis melanops*, **Glistening-green Tanager** *Chlorochrysa phoenicotis*, **Gilt-edged Tanager** *Tangara cyanoventris*, **Viridian Dacnis** *Dacnis viguieri*). The rotation of different colour-to-body-part combinations has also led to an element of confusing overlap (**Red-crowned Ant Tanager** *Habia rubica*, **Red-throated Ant Tanager** *Habia fuscicauda*, **Crimson-backed Tanager** *Ramphocelus dimidiatus*, Flame-rumped Tanager). This is especially the case when all the birds occur at a single locality, as these last four species sometimes do.

One needs to stress a central caveat that they are the English versions for a bird group mainly found in Spanish- or Portuguese-speaking areas, where the local names are older, more varied and richer in association. (As one contributor notes 'the boringly named, but beautiful **Cherry-throated Tanager** *Nemosia rourei*, a long-lost (until recently) endemic of the Atlantic forest, is called the *saíra-apunhalada*, "the tanager with wounded neck", from *apunhalar*, the verb "to stab"!')[2] Before the colonial period such birds would have found identity in a mosaic of indigenous languages; as they do still. That said, the dominant pattern in the anglicised names reveals the extent to which they have grown up in a very shallow cultural soil.

They are names predominantly devised by specialists, with little or no input from a wider community. Yet it is interesting to compare them with the nomenclature for the hummingbirds, which was also invented by ornithologists (see page 303). The English titles for the latter family are among the most beautiful and imaginatively coined for any group of living organisms. The tanagers are comparably impressive as birds – in some ways more so, because hummingbird pigmentation is often physical and the colours frequently invisible to a human observer, while tanager colour is 'often reinforced by a metallic or opalescent sheen' – yet they have names that, by and large, lack texture.[3]

There is a number of intriguing addenda to the subject. The two oddly named groups, hemispingus and dacnis, seem to hold out promise of some deeper cultural or linguistic connection with the Americas. In fact there is none. 'Hemispingus' is of Greek construction – *hemi*, 'like', and *spingos*, 'a small bird' (it probably originally referred to the Common Chaffinch, which had an old English name,

The Blue-grey Tanager is one of the most familiar and widespread birds in South America.

'spink'). *Dacnis* is also a Greek word and simply refers to an unidentifiable small bird.[4]

The one and only tanager that does at least carry a name of Hispanic origin is the recently discovered **Pardusco** *Nephelornis oneilli*, which is confined to small areas of elfin woodland on the eastern slopes of the central Peruvian Andes. Unique it may be in tanager nomenclature, yet the word is Spanish for 'grey-brown'. The singularity of the Pardusco is that it is 'devoid of really distinctive marks'.[5]

There is a last irony to note: the word 'tanager' itself is derived from the Tupi, one of the important indigenous languages of Amazonia. In Tupi, *tangará* is a name for a brightly coloured bird and was probably originally intended to designate not a tanager at all, but a manakin (see page 347). The early natural historians in Brazil used the name with reference to two highly conspicuous and colourful dancing birds, the Blue Manakin and Blue-backed Manakin. However, the German naturalist Georg Marcgrave, working in Brazil during the seventeenth century (or possibly his editor, Jan de Laet, who had never set foot in the country), misapplied the same name to the gloriously colourful **Seven-colored Tanager** *Tangara fastuosa*. The error was perpetuated and the name passed from its rightful owners (the manakins) to the other bird family.[6] The same word (*tangará*) has since been appropriated as the Latin name for the largest genus in the family (50 species) and is used in the Spanish names for tanagers. Yet, oddly, the original Tupi has not found its way into the current Brazilian names for the group, although the Blue Manakin is still known as *tangará*.

If the English names for these wonderful birds are curiously limited in range, it is not the case in their native lands. To give an example of the plethora of local names attaching to tanagers, one need only consider the **Sayaca Tanager** *Thraupis sayaca* and its very close relative – they may indeed be two forms of one species – the **Blue-grey Tanager** *Thraupis episcopus*. Together they span the entire continent, except Chile and southern Argentina, and are among the region's most abundant and familiar birds. This pair is habituated to human presence, thriving even in parks or gardens. Blue-grey Tanagers are known variously as *Viuditas* (Honduras; 'little widows'), *Azulejos* (Panama and Guatemala; 'bluish'), *Azulillo* or *Pito* (Guatemala) and *Violinistas* (Peru; 'violin players', from the fast squeaky song).[7]

With regard to the Blue-grey Tanager's twin, the word 'Sayaca' is itself derived from two Tupi words: *say* (any frugivorous colourful bird) and *açu* ('large').[8] Across its range it is known as *Sanhaço-cinzento* (Brazil; *cinzento*: 'greyish'), *Sai hovy*, *Chovy*, and *Celestino* (Paraguay; first and second names unknown, probably Guaraní in origin; *Celestino*: 'sky blue'), *Sayubú oscuro* (Bolivia; *Sayubú*: unknown, *oscuro*: 'dark') and *Frutero celeste* (Uruguay; 'sky-blue fruit-eater').[9]

As the last name indicates, one place where tanagers and humans regularly meet is in the vicinity of fruit, sometimes as competitors for the produce of commercial orchards. While they can be considered pests, they are also welcome guests whenever bird tables are stocked to attract these noted frugivores. The four species of North American tanager – **Hepatic Tanager** *Piranga hepatica*, **Summer Tanager** *Piranga rubra*, **Scarlet Tanager** *Piranga olivacea* and **Western Tanager** *Piranga ludoviciana* – are now all popular attendants at backyard feeders if fruit is on offer.

The practice also occurs more sparingly in the Caribbean, Central and South America where the spectacle engendered can be astonishing in terms of its beauty and for the intensity

The Shining
Honeycreeper
typifies the tanagers'
reputation for
tropical radiance.

of their feeding behaviour. Tanagers come and go constantly and, if several species are involved, they traffic to the fruit piles a parade ground of brilliant colour, dominated very often by a military crimson. On such feeders, tanagers can seem at times like an embodiment of the entire tropics. Throughout the squabble they maintain a soundtrack of often harsh vocalisations. One can understand why European writers, like the Victorian explorer Henry Bates, wrote: 'In their habits they . . . resemble the common house-sparrow of Europe . . . They are just as lively, restless, bold, and wary; their notes are very similar, chirping and inharmonious, and they seem to be almost as fond of the neighbourhood of man.'[10]

The following contributions suggest that the feeding of tanagers occurs most often where Western influence is strong, or where Western visitors are anticipated.

Smart lodges put out bird feeders. Los Tucanes lodge in the middle of the cloud-forest on the road to Manu in Peru has a great set of feeders, attracting many of the *Tangara* tanagers down for fruit. They must have at least ten species. Many lodges are doing this in countries like Ecuador. In a Pantanal lodge they put out rice along carved-out palm trunks, attracting a plethora of birds including **Silver-beaked Tanager** *Ramphocelus carbo*. It certainly is not a common custom in Bolivia,

Colombia, Ecuador and Peru and probably not in most of hot Amazonian Brazil. The only experience I have with people using feeders in South America is in the larger cities in Brazil.[11]

Another contributor adds detail to the last point: 'One does see fruit put out for tanagers in Brazil, usually at places where locals like to see tourists visit.'[12]

Raúl Arias de Para, the pioneering Panamanian environmentalist, describes his feeders at the Canopy Lodge in the extinct volcanic crater at El Valle:

It is quite common to put fruit out for the birds. The uncommon thing is to have a wide variety of species. We stock the bird feeders repeatedly while the guests are around. When we have no guests we stock them twice a day, morning and afternoon. Sometimes we put papayas and oranges, but banana is their favourite. I once put apples and they ignored them, and I thought they would like melons but they only nibbled at them. In El Valle we can buy 100 bananas for $5 – we spend approximately $1,250 a year on bananas, which comes out to 25,000 bananas per year. I estimate four to five bananas make a pound so our little feathered friends consume between 5,000 and 6,250 pounds of bananas every year! That is a lot of bananas!

I enjoy sitting and looking at the feeders. Especially to see how the tanagers defend the bananas aggressively from the Clay-colored Thrushes. Some individuals of the Blue-grey, Crimson-backed, Flame-rumped, or **Dusky-faced Tanagers** *Mitrospingus cassinii* will resist and even scare away the much bigger thrushes, others will not. Aggression among the family seems to be an individual trait not a species trait. However, all bets are off when the big guys show up, by this I mean the Rufous Motmot or the Chestnut-headed Oropendolas. When they come, everybody scrambles.[13]

It is inevitable that the bright plumages of some tanagers have been incorporated into the complex feather art that was once a major feature of indigenous Amazonian cultures. The small size of tanager plumes means that they are seldom the most eye-catching or easily recognised part of any item. However, sometimes they have acquired specific purpose.

One of the best examples involves the endangered and range-restricted monotypic **Orange-throated Tanager** *Wetmorethraupis sterrhopteron* of southern Ecuador and northern Peru. The Amerindian communities in the area – Aguaruna – call the bird *Inchituch* from its song. The story goes that if a man in the tribe falls for a girl, he can assure her devoted attention and love if he hunts an *Inchituch*, uses the orange throat feathers to make an earring(s) and presents it to the girl as a gift of affection. If she accepts it she is then spellbound and falls madly in love with the offerer.[14]

Another expectation one might have of such exquisitely plumed birds is that they would be widely kept as decorative pets. Fortunately many of them have been blessed in this matter by a lack of vocal ability. They have very harsh, coarse

or simple songs, sometimes even insect-like or notes that 'bring to mind the squeak of a bat'.[15] Another decided asset has been the specialised fruit or nectar-based diets that have discouraged all but the most dedicated aviculturists. However, some of the birds are so attractive that all obstacles have been overcome. A major victim of the cagebird trade is also among the most beautiful of the family. The Seven-colored Tanager of Brazil's Atlantic coastal forest has been traded for centuries and was once exported to Europe for use in the fashion trade. It was still being sold over wide areas of northern Brazil until the 1980s, when a single bird could fetch as much as $30. Now the numbers are fewer than 10,000 and the species is thought at risk of extinction.[16]

Perhaps the most seriously affected of the group are the *Sporophila* seedeaters. No fewer than 11 species of the 32 in this genus are thought to be threatened or near-threatened, primarily because of trapping for the cagebird trade. Unlike many of the family, they are granivorous and often have attractive, sweetly whistled or trilling songs. They are especially popular in southern Brazil and Argentina, where they are known as *capuchinos* for the distinctly capped appearance of several species (the word *capucho*, 'hood', was derived from the tonsure on the heads of Capuchin monks). The ultimate victim is the **Entre Rios Seedeater** *Sporophila zelichi*, found only in the Argentinian province of the same name and in southern Paraguay (seedeaters are sometimes called *paraguayitos* in honour of their presumed provenance). Relentless trapping of the species has reduced the wild population possibly to as few as 50 pairs.[17]

The habit of keeping seedeaters in cages is widespread and traditional in poorer rural areas of northern Argentina. In some villages in Entre Ríos province almost every household has its cage of these delightful birds. Ironically this widespread folk attachment to the species has led to some becoming immensely valuable commodities.

A Jivaro headdress from northern Peru featuring ten tanagers of various species.

525

The British artist Tolly Nason has made cast-glass models of the beaks of various Darwin's Finches. At 20 times their natural size, these sculptures give luminous power and emphasis to tiny bird parts that have become draped with human story.

DARWIN'S FINCHES

These 13 species found only on the Galápagos archipelago are perhaps the most celebrated of all the tanager family. (There is one other member of this subfamily – technically called Geospizinae – the **Cocos Finch** *Pinaroloxias inornata*, on the island of the same name 650 km: 400 miles to the north.) In fact they are among the most famous animals on the entire planet. As one author notes, 'There are few text books of biology that fail to make some reference to these sparrow-like birds.'[18]

Their celebrity rests partly on the extraordinary adaptive radiation manifest in their varying bill shapes, which run a gamut from the nut-cracking pincers of a small parrot, to the tiny needle of a warbler. Primarily, however, the fame rests on their encounter with the world's most celebrated biologist in September 1835. A 26-year-old Charles Darwin called at the Galápagos during his voyage as ship's naturalist aboard the HMS *Beagle*. In his journal account of the weeks ashore, Darwin recorded how he obtained skins of the islands' land birds, including nine of the 13 distinctive finches. He noted only rudimentary details of appearance, but went on to speculate in his book *The Voyage of the Beagle*:

> The most curious fact is the perfect gradation in the size of the beaks in the different species of Geospiza, from one as large as that of a hawfinch to that of a chaffinch, and (if Mr. Gould is right . . .) even to that of a warbler. . . . Seeing this gradation and diversity of structure in one small intimately related group of birds, one might really fancy that from an original paucity of birds in this archipelago, one species had been taken and modified for different ends.[19]

Here in embryonic form is the concept of speciation that Darwin worked on for a further 15 years and finally propounded in his book on evolution through natural selection, *The Origin of Species*. However, the extent of Darwin's exploration of his ideas through specific consideration of the Galápagos finches needs careful qualification. The passage above did not appear in his private diary, nor in the first edition of *The Voyage of the Beagle*. It was added retrospectively to an edition of 1845.[20]

Furthermore there is absolutely nothing on the birds in *The Origin of Species*. Darwin, in fact, did not initially appreciate the close relationships between the finches. As he himself noted, it was the young John Gould who brilliantly worked out their taxonomy and corrected Darwin's misconception that they were a heterogeneous collection of finches, tanagers and warblers. In his defence, it is worth noting that the variation among the 13 birds is huge and baffling. One old Galápagos hand noted: 'It is only a very wise man or a fool who thinks he is able to identify all the finches which he sees.'[21]

Despite the patchiness of Darwin's original work and the absence of any fundamental link between him, *Geospiza* and his subsequent world-changing theory, the man and his finches are now irrevocably bound together. The American scientist Stephen J Gould called this 'the Galapagos myth' and pointed out that Darwin 'had missed the story of the finches entirely, because he had been fooled by their convergences and had not recognized the underlying taxonomic unity'.[22] Gould also pointed out that the Galápagos finches were 'widely but wrongly believed to be Darwin's principal inspiration'.[23] In fact, the debunking of the story has now become almost as frequent as the original falsehood, but it is symptomatic of the irresistible power of myth over the human imagination that the spurious connection between Darwin and so-called Darwin's finches remains unassailable.

Partly because of the myth, 'his' birds are today 'among the most thoroughly studied wild animals in existence'.[24] In some ways their behaviour facilitates close scrutiny. One scientist working on the group noted that, 'In Kenya, finches flush as much as 30 meters away. In the Galápagos, the birds land on the rim of your coffee cup. If there's only a little coffee left in there, they will land right inside and take a sip . . . On the really isolated islands like Wolf, you could catch the birds by hand.'[25] In Darwin's day the birds were probably tamer.

Yet a detail of their feeding behaviour which escaped his notice was that of the **Sharp-beaked Ground Finch** *Geospiza difficilis*. On the island of Wolf the species puts its dagger-like appendage to macabre use, when it pecks the backs of incubating boobies and drinks their blood. It will even drink the blood of its own dead. The habit has earned it a widespread nickname, 'vampire finch'.

Another detail unappreciated by Darwin but unearthed by a Darwin lookalike, the British biologist Peter Grant, is the sheer speed of evolution exhibited in some populations of the birds. Grant and his wife, Rosemary, have devoted a lifetime to the study of Darwin's finches. (At the Charles Darwin Research Station on the island of Santa Cruz the staff have a saying: 'Only God and Peter Grant can recognize Darwin's finches.')[26] During their studies there was a severe drought on the island of Daphne Major and the Grants found that it had killed off all but 180 of the island's population of **Medium Ground Finch** *Geospiza fortis*. The survivors were all discovered to have marginally larger beaks because, it appears, the bigger-billed minority had been able to access some of the island's only food, the tough seeds belonging to a plant called *Tribulus*.

Not only had 180 Medium Ground Finches survived, but of these 150 were males. It meant that there was fierce competition for the 30 females. The biggest males (with the biggest bills) triumphed, ensuring that the genes for this particular trait were even more emphasised in the next generations. The difference between survival and death had been a matter of about half a millimetre in bill length and depth. Yet it was evolution in action before the Grants' very eyes. They subsequently calculated that 23 such bouts of drought were all that were needed to convert the Medium Ground Finch into its parrot-billed bigger brother, the **Large Ground Finch** *Geospiza magnirostris*.[27]

Grosbeak, Saltator and Allies family *Cardinalidae*

These 42 chunky seed-eating birds form a rather heterogeneous group – or as one author writes 'a hodgepodge family' – that has inspired much uncertainty over their true relationships.[1] Several of them have previously been assigned to other closely related families, such as the buntings and New World sparrows (*Emberizidae*) or the tanagers (*Thraupidae*). The whole group is still undergoing review, another authority suggesting that we should 'expect to see a fair bit of checklist shuffling' even now.[2]

At least one unifying factor is their exclusive distribution in the New World, where grosbeaks are spread from Canada to Argentina. Some species like the beautiful **Rose-breasted Grosbeak** *Pheucticus ludovicianus* are long-distance pan-American migrants, reaching a northern limit in Canada's Northwest Territories but with some populations moving during the northern winter to Amazonian forests as far south as Peru. (Occasionally Rose-breasted Grosbeaks have even been blown to Europe, with records scattered from Norway to Malta.) The family's highest diversity is found in Central America – Mexico alone holds almost half the species – but the numbers dwindle outside the tropical region, with just 13 species in the USA and five in Canada.

Another strongly unifying family element is the birds' great beauty, especially the males. No fewer than nine are completely, or largely, deep indigo or cobalt blue. More striking still are the species that combine this glorious colour with patches of red or yellow, such as the **Painted Bunting** *Passerina ciris*. It breeds in Mexico and the southern states of the USA and is one of the most celebrated of the whole family. It was avidly trapped for centuries (it continues illegally) and enjoyed an unenviable soubriquet among bird fanciers, the 'nonpareil', a beauty without equal. In fact many of the most attractive family members are still widely caught and kept as cagebirds, including the near-threatened Mexican endemic, the **Rose-bellied Bunting** *Passerina rositae*.

THE CHRISTMAS BIRD OF NORTH AMERICA

Another grosbeak trio that is famous for colour is the **Vermilion Cardinal** *Cardinalis phoeniceus*, **Northern Cardinal** *Cardinalis cardinalis* and **Pyrrhuloxia** *Cardinalis sinuatus*. The strange-sounding name of this last bird, which is largely Mexican in range with outlying populations spread from Texas to Arizona, also refers to the group's redness. 'Pyrrhuloxia' is a word of Greek construction denoting a flame-coloured finch.[3] The colour is so dominant in the Northern Cardinal that when it was first encountered by early colonial naturalists they just called it the 'red-bird'. (In fact only males are red; females are a warm, red-tinged buff-brown.)

This actually understates the beauty of Northern Cardinals, because the male possesses a black facial mask, while both sexes have orange-red bills and striking conical crests. (The name 'cardinal' derives from the assumed similarity of the bird's own tall red 'hat' to the Catholic cleric's crimson garb and his bishop's mitre.) At one time the species was kept worldwide for its colours and also for the cheerfully atmospheric song. Other old names included 'Virginia' or 'Carolina nightingale'.[4] Cardinal song is highly varied but a common phrase is a repeated *chop-chop-chop-chop-chop* sequence that is reminiscent of the hard *jug-jug* notes characteristic of nightingales.

One striking feature in cardinal vocalisations is the performance of duets by breeding couples. Another endearing aspect of their pair bond is the attentiveness of the male towards his mate during courtship, when he will feed her directly. The cardinals' togetherness was well noted by Native Americans, and Cherokee men, keen to exert the same kind of hold over prospective partners, had a magical incantation that included the lines, 'I am as handsome as the Redbird / I am as masculine as the Redbird' (see also Nightjar family, page 288).[5]

For all the geographical associations of the bird's modern

The logo for the Arizona Cardinals football team has turned a beloved denizen of the North American backyard into a turbo-charged sports bird.

name, the cardinal was actually thought to be a southerner. In 1754 Mark Catesby called it the 'summer red-bird' because in winter it appeared to abandon Carolina and Virginia and migrate elsewhere.[6] However, as the population of colonial settlers increased during the nineteenth century, so the bird began a long steady expansion of its own. In the 1880s it was assumed to reach a northern limit in Kentucky ('Kentucky cardinal' was another old nickname), but by 1895 it was noted as far north as the Great Lake region, and within another 15 years it had extended eastwards as far as the lower Hudson River. By 1958 it was established in Massachusetts, and Maine by 1969.[7]

This range extension and the bird's huge popularity are part of a larger pattern of interaction between cardinals and their many human admirers. Of all North American birds it is one of the easiest to identify, a point well made by this telling observation: 'I have even recognised a dead male cardinal by the side of the highway, perfect in form but freshly crestfallen, like a discarded Christmas tree decoration.'[8] Its singularity ensured it preferential treatment in the backyard, especially when the bird-feeding habit took hold among North Americans. It was also most welcome when natural food was scarcest. Winter is the season when those cardinal colours make their greatest appeal.

The composer and birder Eric Salzman summarises the bird's interlocking virtues in the following terms: 'Northern Cardinal is a dooryard species. It comes to feeders and it's bright red. And it's there all winter and you can see it against the snow. How can you beat that?'[9] Few contemporary Americans would disagree. As one observer noted, 'its plumage seems to shine with unusual brilliancy in the reflected light from the snow'.[10] Another admirer calls it 'a show-stopper type of bird', and adds:

> Where I grew up in southwest Iowa, United States of America, the Northern Cardinal was always noticed and especially in the winter months when the branches were bare and snow on the ground. Their welcome, glorious red plumage would stand out like neon signs blinking, 'Here I am, watch me now!'[11]

During the larger silence of the dead season even its song seems sweeter. The well-known US author and birder Bill Thompson III names among his ten favourite North American vocalisations 'a cardinal song on a sunny winter's day'.[12] Around the solstice the bird even assumes a form of religious significance, for it is one of the most abundant species on the Christmas mantelpiece. Perhaps only the Christian dove of peace features on as many greetings cards, where the cardinal has come to fill exactly the same symbolic niche as the European Robin in the UK.

The near-perfect alignment of this grosbeak with the conditions of winter have helped to elevate it to a state of popularity equalled by just a handful of other North American species, such as the American Robin and Northern Mockingbird. It is the bird emblem in no fewer than seven states (more than any other species): Illinois, Indiana, Kentucky, North Carolina, Ohio, Virginia and West Virginia. However, this civic symbolism only glances at the cardinal's ubiquity in man-made North America. It is the staple bird of kitchen accessories (on tablecloths, linen, mugs, crockery and place mats), but also much further afield in the domestic environment, from garden pots and ornaments, stained-glass windows to body tattoos.[13] A somewhat scary swept-crested Northern Cardinal – the diametric opposite, in fact, of its classic homely image – serves as logo for a football team, the Arizona Cardinals. In Missouri there is a baseball team that has been known as the St Louis Cardinals since 1900. (It is interesting that the birds depicted in the logos for both of these teams have had their red bills replaced with yellow ones.) However, as one contributor notes, these reflected humanised versions are all fine, but nothing quite compares with the living presence of the red bird itself.

> Every morning when I walk out the back door of this old stone house in the Blue Ridge Mountains, the flashes of red put a smile on the face of the day. The bird feeders hang from the trees by the woodshed, and the cardinals and myriad other songbirds are there having breakfast as I head for the barn. Some license plates for cars feature the cardinal; these are the specialty plates that cost a little more than the standard variety. Cardinals are almost like a signature on many Christmas cards and on holiday advertisements. But cardinals are best out there flitting through the trees or hopping on the ground searching for sunflower seeds fallen from the feeders.[14]

BIRDS, PEOPLE, AND BIRDLIFE INTERNATIONAL

As Mark Cocker makes abundantly clear in his introduction, *Birds and People* is as much about people as it is birds, and it is the people who care deeply about birds and nature that lie at the heart of this extraordinary book.

For the 17 years that Cocker has researched and written on the themes explored in *Birds and People*, a global correspondence has flowed across his desk in Norfolk. Already the author of several books, including *Birds Britannica*, that stress the cultural significance of birds, his most recent, *Crow Country*, is subtitled a 'meditation on birds, landscape and nature'. It celebrates the countryside around his home, with a focus on the comings and goings of Rooks, notably a spectacular winter roost which, at its height, can number 40,000 individuals.

In Britain Rooks are extremely commonplace birds of farmland, but the subtle trick within *Crow Country* is to reveal the seemingly familiar and ordinary features of a landscape in ever deeper layers. Nature and human society are explored to uncover close interdependencies, and expose how we have shaped and been shaped by place. This is the approach deployed in *Birds and People* where Cocker's wide-ranging text, set alongside David Tipling's beautiful, evocative pictures, builds a firm foundation for a new cultural insight into the world's birds.

In the late 1980s, Mark Cocker worked for BirdLife International (then still the International Council for Bird Preservation), and he has maintained a long-standing fellowship with the conservationists who work for the Partnership. His journalism consistently addresses the environmental crisis, and he has been catalytic in a forum, New Networks for Nature, which brings together a wide range of thinkers and actors from the arts and sciences to promote the intrinsic value of nature in contemporary society.

In the early days, the BirdLife offices were a series of Portakabins in the corner of a Cambridgeshire field, and correspondence with the world was undertaken by letter, joined later by the clatter of telex, then the warbling fax, and now, of course, the internet, email and Skype. Although the means of communication have changed since Cocker first worked with BirdLife, and the scale of engagement has grown exponentially, the commitment sown by the first collaborators remains undiminished; and the expertise and assistance of BirdLife Partners worldwide has helped the creators of *Birds and People* to conduct a truly global orchestra of voices – each one locally distinct – and collate that essence. Perhaps the book's most important aspect is the live contemporary dialogue thronging the text, bringing a sense of how nature is still such a vital force in shaping all our lives.

Mark Cocker makes the point that *Birds and People* is not a book of conservation alone, even though a relationship with the BirdLife Partnership has provided much fuel for the initiative, and conservation is a familiar element in the cultural life of many communities. Critically, however, the international chorus demonstrates and celebrates the diverse ways in which we address our concern for birds and nature; and represents a host of people who need to be included in any future action for our environment. Throughout the world the conservation community runs a real risk of alienating parts of society by invariably proposing doom-laden agenda, often created within an environmental silo that fails to acknowledge the genuine aspirations of the poor and dispossessed. For sure the global crisis of overuse is acute, but by reaching out to new players across a wide range of disciplines, by working at local scale, the BirdLife Partnership is successfully challenging a doggedly negative orthodoxy. Solutions lie in collaborative approaches that acknowledge complexity, take a long-term view and empower local people. Indeed, most of the voices in *Birds and People* are not those of conservationists per se, but of people from all walks of life, who have been transformed by their own encounters with birds.

For obvious reasons, people identify most with their own backyards, their own nature, and with the birds that share their space. Celebrating the fiftieth anniversary of Rachel Carson's *Silent Spring*, Margaret Atwood – who, with her husband, Graeme Gibson, is Honorary President of BirdLife's Rare Bird Club – writes that Carson knew how to explain science so readers would understand, and that she also believed 'if you don't love a thing you won't save it'.

A love of birds runs through the pages of *Birds and People*, and similarly throughout the BirdLife network. It is the lifeblood, the oxygen that drives a commitment to saving birds, both rare and commonplace, from further decline. BirdLife supports those at the grassroots, giving them the information, tools and resources they need to make a difference, to have a real influence.

Although BirdLife International was established in 1922 (as the International Council for Bird Preservation) its metamorphosis into a worldwide constituency of national non-government organisations in 1994 marked the creation of an extraordinary Partnership that now includes NGOs in 116 countries, and is active, at the time of writing, in 155. BirdLife is invariably referred to as a family, and it is true that the network is alive with close friendships and working relationships based on a passionate concern for the future.

Mark Cocker writes that 'birds are not just ubiquitous upon our physical planet', but 'are fellow travellers of the human spirit, and have colonised our imaginations'. In many ways, BirdLife is a response to this colonisation, and to the sober realisation that a world without birds, without their songs, their effervescent parallel lives, would be a barren and lifeless thing.

From the beginning, BirdLife has worked closely on globally threatened species at risk for a wide variety of reasons, from wetland and forest loss to the depredations of invasive species, like rats and cats. Some 1,313 bird species are red-listed and, of these, 197 are considered critically at risk, and are the focus of our work on preventing extinctions: one of a suite of Partnership-wide programmes that address threats to migratory birds, forests and seabirds, climate change, invasive species, urbanisation and a growing range of other issues.

At the heart of these initiatives are the sites essential to birds, places known within the BirdLife Partnership as Important Bird Areas (or IBAs) – each identified by one or more of four criteria: the presence of a threatened or restricted range species, a key habitat, or a place where birds congregate, including the spectacular migration bottlenecks where tens of thousands of birds mass as they make the seasonal movements that so inspire us.

Each IBA is, of course, unique, and contains a community of birds, and other animals, that is the backdrop to people's daily lives. This is the nature with which our existence is entwined. The animal landscape that surrounds and nurtures us is special to every human society, from 'remote' thinly populated habitats such as the great tropical forests of the Congo Basin, to frenetic, dense urban spaces, like that surrounding New York's Central Park.

Worldwide there are over 12,000 IBAs, and associated with them is a dynamic grassroots constituency of Local Conservation Groups (LCGs) – growing steadily, place by place, IBA by IBA, catalysed by country Partners and a worldwide local empowerment programme. From the Curry Upland Farmers' Cooperative in the Philippines, to Upper Shire Association for the Conservation of Liwonde National Park in Malawi, the Voluntarios Comunitarios de Jaragua in the Dominican Republic and Salmon Arm Bay Nature Enhancement Society in British Columbia, Canada, all these groups are championing conservation at site level, galvanising an array of responses to pressure on the environment.

At any IBA, complex local circumstances demand singular solutions. And it is the inhabitants of these places who are, like Mark Cocker in his own Norfolk landscape, best placed to articulate those solutions. In an oft-jaded realm of 'development fatigue', LCGs are energised and focused on delivering real conservation.

Coordinating these local constituencies are the national Partners of BirdLife ranging from the well-established NGOs like Audubon in the United States, the UK's Royal Society for the Protection of Birds, the RSPB, and Vogelbescherming Nederland to newer, equally passionate and effective organisations like Guyra Paraguay, Nature Fiji and Burung Indonesia.

Together these NGOs caucus in six regions, and elect a representative, democratic global council which employs a Secretariat based in Cambridge, and in six regional offices in Brussels, Quito, Nairobi, Suva, Singapore and Amman. Secretariat staff support the activities of the Partnership, particularly in science, policy and advocacy, in individual and institutional capacity development and in responding to local and national demands.

In many instances, this work means lobbying international institutions, such as the World Bank and United Nations, or multilateral environmental conventions on biological diversity, climate change and migratory species. A marine programme works at the cutting edge of high seas conservation, addressing the crisis of birds caught as by-catch in longline and trawl fisheries, and championing new marine protected areas. As a family, the peerless albatrosses are some of the most threatened birds in the world.

In recent years, BirdLife has also initiated a series of collaborations, like *Birds and People*, with musicians, authors and visual artists, channelling the enduring impact that birds have on our creative lives. A great panoply of sculpture and painting, writing (notably poetry), storytelling and music is influenced by the songs, colours and behaviours of birds. Throughout the world, the arts community has a major role to play in witnessing, describing and celebrating nature, and joining scientists, conservation practitioners and all those concerned about the crisis of biodiversity loss that we face at every level.

In his introduction, Cocker writes how we are all 'indebted to birds for their life-enhancing gifts' and, in turn, BirdLife owes him, David Tipling, their indefatigable researcher, Jonathan Elphick, and the cast of hundreds who have contributed stories to *Birds and People* a great debt of gratitude for this groundbreaking book. Its pages demonstrate the almost infinite ways in which birds inspire people, and present a dynamic, live conversation, in much the same way that BirdLife embodies a constantly evolving and responsive conservation movement.

Readers who would like to learn more about the BirdLife Partnership can visit the website: www.birdlife.org. Links within the site will lead you to any national BirdLife Partner and to a wide range of stories, case studies and examples of the reality – in terms of challenges and successes – of undertaking bird conservation work around the world.

John Fanshawe,
BirdLife International

Great Egret

APPENDIX I: **GLOSSARY**

A number of words highly familiar in the world of ornithology present some difficulty to a non-specialist audience. The most frequently used technical terms are listed below.

Congener A bird of the same genus. For example, Cooper's Hawk *Accipiter cooperii* is a congener of the Northern Goshawk *Accipiter gentilis*.

Endemic A bird species or race that occurs exclusively in one area, region or, most often, a single country. It is used as an adjective or noun.

Galliform The anglicised name for any member of the bird order Galliformes ('chicken shaped'), a large, predominantly Old World group including turkeys, pheasants, partridges, grouse, quail, and junglefowl, the wild ancestor of the domestic fowl.

Jizz A twentieth-century English coinage (spelled gizz in the US) to convey the overall 'personality' and impression made by a bird, as opposed to its quantifiable details (i.e. wingbars, leg colour, etc.). Jizz takes into account factors such as subtlety of shape and proportion, as well as attitude and character of movements. Alas, jizz is also US slang for sperm, although perhaps the notion of some kind of essence is common to both meanings.

Monotypic A family or genus of birds that is represented by only a single species.

Neotropics / Neotropical The zoogeographical region embracing the Americas roughly south of Mexico City to the southern tip of South America. It is the most bird-rich region on the planet. (See also **zoogeography** below.)

Oriental The zoogeographical area roughly coinciding with tropical south Asia and extending as far north as 30° N in China. West to east it covers the area from the Indus Valley in Pakistan to Borneo.

Palearctic The zoogeographical zone that embraces all of Europe and all Asia north or west of the Oriental zone. It also includes Africa north of the Sahara.

Polyandrous A breeding arrangement in which the female bird has more than one male partner.

Ratite(s) Name used to describe the large flightless birds of the southern continents, including ostrich, rhea, kiwis and extinct species such as the elephant birds. The word comes from *ratis*, Latin for a raft or boat without a keel. Being flightless, this group of birds lacks the protruding bone ridge which anchors the wing muscles.

Rectrix (-ces) Technical name for the main tail feather(s).

Suboscine / oscine passerines A name used in taxonomy to describe a group of birds within the order Passeriformes or passerines. They are characterised by having four toes emerging from the foot at the same point, with three pointing forwards, one backwards, and are often called 'perching birds'. Passerines represent about 60 per cent of the 10,500 avian species in the world. They are further divided into the oscine (also known simply as 'songbirds') and suboscine passerines, which have differing vocal apparatus, particularly the structure of the syrinx. Suboscines comprise 12 families (including the ovenbirds, tyrant flycatchers and antbirds, as well as several Australian bird families). As their name suggests, the suboscines are considered to be more primitive than their oscine relatives. One commentator notes:'While the oscine passerines are for the most part extremely similar in terms of their bodily structure . . . The suboscines seem the tiniest bit "goofier" – a bit long-legged, or tall-headed, or large-eyed, or barely odd in some other way.'

Taxon (plural **taxa**) A general term used for any category of classification. However, the fundamental unit is the species and taxon is often used as a synonym or alternative for that word.

Zoogeography Natural scientists divide the world into six faunal regions, based on studies of the distribution and relationships of animal species (as well as plants, etc.) within a particular area. The six regions are: Afrotropical, Australasia, Nearctic, Neotropical, Oriental and Palearctic.

APPENDIX 2: **BIOGRAPHICAL DETAILS**

Here are some biographical details for the ornithologists who feature
most regularly in the text and may be unfamiliar to the general reader.

Aelian, or **Claudius Aelianus** (AD *c*.175–*c*.235) An Italian author who lived in Rome but wrote in Greek, now best known for a 17-book study of animals and nature, which (ironically) is usually referred to by its Latin title *De natura animalium*, or in English simply as *On Animals*. It is a somewhat quirky, over-credulous miscellany of facts, half-truths and complete fantasy. It is, however, fascinating, and all the more revealing of the beliefs and attitudes of the classical world for Aelian's faithful copying of other Greek writers on these themes.

Salim Ali (1896–1987) This diminutive and rather bird-like Indian bird man is one of the great figures of twentieth-century ornithology and is still revered in his home country. He wrote extensively on the nation's huge avifauna, made numerous expeditions to all parts of the subcontinent and is perhaps best known for the ten-volume *Handbook of the Birds of India and Pakistan* (co-authored with the American Dillon Ripley). Ali is also notable for the quality of his writing. While deeply rooted in ornithological science, he was also alive to the human 'story' in the lives of birds and his observations are full of colour, feeling, wide scholarship and good humour.

Aristotle (384–322 BC) This Greek intellectual and teacher (his pupils included Alexander the Great) must have burned for most of his 62 years with an almost insatiable desire for knowledge about almost every aspect of human experience. In addition to his writings on art, ethics, politics and metaphysics, Aristotle was a founder of Western science and a restless interrogator of the natural world. His four works on animals are rich in detail, much of it highly accurate and all of it illuminating of Greek responses and beliefs about birds. He lived for several years on the island of Lesbos (close to Turkey), which is still an outstanding place for migratory birds. Yet we can only dream about its ornithological riches in Aristotle's day. Without reading the works of this towering genius one cannot even begin to understand classical attitudes, nor those of medieval Europe and, in some instances, even modern responses to the natural world.

William Beebe (1877–1962) American naturalist, explorer and author whose centrifugal interests took him in a multitude of geographical and scientific directions. He wrote extensively on his foreign journeys, producing many books of wildlife travel such as *Our Search for a Wilderness*, which was written by the author with his first wife, Mary Blair. A prolonged journey across Asia in search of gamebirds resulted in his four-volume *A Monograph of the Pheasants* (1918–22). His other great passion was oceanographic exploration, which he pursued in his 'bathysphere' in the waters off Bermuda. He was the first person to descend below 900 m (3,000 ft).

Arthur Cleveland Bent (1866–1954) An American ornithologist brought up in Massachusetts. When he was 44 he was commissioned by the Smithsonian Institution to write a book on his country's ornithology. The final part of *Life Histories of North American Birds* did not appear until after his death. It is usually referred to as a 21-volume work but in fact it comprises 24 books, since several parts were split in two or into three. Somewhat rambling and discursive, it is also a glorious, hugely entertaining and massively informative work. Bent had at his disposal a continent-wide network of informants whom he quoted at length. His *Life Histories* has long been superseded by more rigorous works of ornithology, but none has the human appeal, nor the wide-ranging scholarship of Bent's original.

W H Hudson (1841–1922) A writer and naturalist of huge range and achievement. His nationality is complex. His parents were citizens of the USA, but he was brought up on the Argentinian pampas just south of Buenos Aires (his house, now a museum and environmental centre, has been engulfed by the city suburbs). Yet he passed most of his adult life in England. The nation of his childhood and his adopted country vie for his reputation. In turn his international readership is, in some sense, a measure of the enduring qualities of Hudson's pantheistic philosophy and his literary gifts for evoking wildlife, especially birds. He wrote almost 30 books, from novels (*Green Mansions*, 1904) to serious ornithology (*Birds of La Plata*, 1920). Many, such as his rhapsodic evocation of his Argentinian childhood, *Far Away and Long Ago* (1918), are still in print.

Allan Octavian Hume (1829–1912) One of the Victorian founders of Indian ornithology (but also a civil servant of liberal bent, who helped create the institution that became the Indian Congress Party. President Jawaharlal Nehru eventually led the party to India's independence in 1947). He amassed a bird skin collection numbering 80,000 birds and published extensively, latterly in his own journal, *Stray Feathers*. In his Himalayan retreat known as Rothney Castle he assembled a truly mountainous collection of papers and writings, most of which were lost when his servant sold the lot in the Simla market as waste paper.

Aldo Leopold (1887–1948) A pioneer American ecologist and academic who also managed and rehabilitated an environmentally exhausted farm in Wisconsin. The goal was to put into practice his philosophy of how humans could work the land in a way that was not damaging to the underlying ecology or its natural inhabitants. The place is now both an environmental centre and a shrine to the man. Leopold is viewed very much as a prophet for modern conservationists. He was also the author of the posthumously published (he died fighting a fire on the farm) *A Sand County Almanac* (1949), a work of lyrical prose that combines simple reflections upon nature with more theoretical ideas about our relationships to wild places and wild creatures.

Pliny the Elder (AD 23–79) Landowner, soldier and scholar from northern Italy. Of his voluminous writings, only the 37-book *Historia Naturalis* survives. It is an unreliable but fascinating encyclopedia on Roman knowledge including a compendium on matters natural historical, that blends a great deal of fiction with the facts. Today, however, the falsehoods are almost as valuable and illuminating of his age as the examples of genuine observation. Testament to his scientific bent is the fact that during the eruption of Vesuvius which buried Pompeii, Pliny was sailing past offshore, landed in order to study the phenomenon and was killed by its impact.

John Ray (1627–1705) In many ways the 'father' of British ornithology if not all natural science. This seventeenth-century polymath was educated at Cambridge and trained for the church, but allowed his cyclopean 360-degree curiosity to lead him astray into the realms of natural science. With the financial support and collaboration of the wealthier and landed Francis Willughby (who died at the appallingly young age of 36), Ray largely wrote and saw through publication their joint *Ornithology* (1678). He also wrote on fish, insects, mammals and plants, including a groundbreaking three-volume botanical work, *History of Plants*, as well as other diverse books on his foreign travels and lexicology. His whole career helped establish the study of nature in Britain on its first systematic foundations.

Helmut Sick (1910–1991) German-born naturalist who travelled to the Brazilian rainforest in the late 1930s to study birds and became marooned by the outbreak of World War Two. He was among the foremost naturalists in his adopted country and one of the greats of twentieth-century ornithology. He eventually rose to become the Curator of Birds at the National Museum in Rio de Janeiro but he also undertook numerous lengthy expeditions to all corners of this vast country in search of its unparalleled birdlife. His extensive publications culminated in the *Ornitologia Brasileira* (*Birds in Brazil*), a glorious compendium of humane scholarship that expresses a lifetime's relentless enquiry and acute observation.

Henry David Thoreau (1817–1862) American writer and naturalist, who studied at Harvard before returning to his home in Concord, Massachusetts, where he lived almost all his days. Despite a friendship with the transcendentalist poet and author Ralph Waldo Emerson, and the publication of works such as *Walden* – a description of years spent living in the woods by the now celebrated pond – Thoreau was not especially noted or successful in his lifetime. However, after his premature death from tuberculosis at just 44, he acquired a worldwide reputation as a writer and thinker. He had a substantial impact on global politics through his essay on civil disobedience and became a major influence on people like Mahatma Gandhi. He also remains among the finest writers and most important voices on one of the central themes of our age – human relationships with, and responsibilities towards, the whole of nature.

APPENDIX 3: **UNTREATED FAMILIES**

These are bird families with limited cultural profiles or with cultural profiles that overlap squarely with several or many others. The bracketed figure is the number of species in the family.

Magpie Goose *Anseranatidae* (1)
Shoebill *Balaenicipitidae* (1)
Mesites *Mesitornithidae* (3)
Flufftails *Sarothruridae* (9)
Buttonquails *Turnicidae* (16)
Crab-plover *Dromadidae* (1)
Ibisbill *Ibidorhynchidae* (1)
Painted Snipe *Rostratulidae* (2)
Plains-wanderer *Pedionomidae* (1)
Seedsnipe *Thinocoridae* (4)
Owlet-Nightjars *Aegothelidae* (9)
Treeswifts *Hemiprocnidae* (4)
Ground rollers *Brachypteraciidae* (5)
Cuckoo Roller *Leptosomatidae* (1)
Todies *Todidae* (5)
Wood hoopoes *Phoeniculidae* (9)
Jacamars *Galbulidae* (18)
Puffbirds *Bucconidae* (35)
Broadbills *Eurylaimidae* (15)
Asities *Philepittidae* (4)
Sapayoa *Sapayaoidae* (1)
Uncertain family *Piprites, Calyptura* (4)
Gnateaters *Conopophagidae* (9)
Woodcreepers *Dendrocolaptidae* (51)
Australasian treecreepers *Climacteridae* (7)
Australasian wrens *Maluridae* (28)
Bristlebirds *Dasyornithidae* (3)
Pardalotes *Pardalotidae* (4)
Australasian warblers *Acanthizidae* (62)
Australasian babblers *Pomatostomidae* (5)

Logrunners *Orthonychidae* (3)
Satinbirds *Cnemophilidae* (3)
Berrypeckers *Melanocharitidae* (12)
Whipbirds, jewel-babblers *Eupetidae* (10)
Quail-thrushes *Cinclosomatidae* (5)
Wattle-eyes, batises *Platysteiridae* (29)
Uncertain family *Tephrodornis, Philentoma* (4)
Boatbills *Machaerirhynchidae* (2)
Vangas *Vangidae* (21)
Woodswallows *Artamidae* (11)
Ioras *Aegithinidae* (4)
Sittellas *Neosittidae* (3)
Shriketits *Falcunculidae* (4)
Whistlers *Pachycephalidae* (44)
Uncertain family *Melampitta, Ifrita* (3)
Rockjumpers *Chaetopidae* (2)
Bushtits *Aegithalidae* (11)
Uncertain family *Neolestes, Nicator*, etc. (9)
Uncertain family *Myzornis, Malia*, etc. (4)
Sugarbirds *Promeropidae* (2)
Fairy-bluebirds *Irenidae* (2)
Gnatcatchers *Polioptilidae* (15)
Treecreepers *Certhiidae* (8)
Philippine creepers *Rhabdornithidae* (3)
Leafbirds *Chloropseidae* (8)
Flowerpeckers *Dicaeidae* (45)
Accentors *Prunellidae* (13)
Olive Warbler *Peucedramidae* (1)
Uncertain family *Zeledonia Icteria*, etc. (6)

SELECT BIBLIOGRAPHY

All titles are published in London unless otherwise stated.
All references listed in the endnotes appear in full in the bibliography apart from
website sources and those given in full in the list of abbreviations at the beginning of the notes.
Reference details in the notes include author(s), publication date and page number(s).
However, in the case of classical sources we have followed the usual
convention of citing book and chapter numbers.

Aelian, *On Animals*, Books 1–3, Heinemann, 1959.

Alderfer, Jonathan (ed), *Complete Birds of North America*, National Geographic, Washington, DC, 2006.

Aldrovandi, Ulisse, *Aldrovandi on Chickens* (trans. L R Lind), University of Oklahoma Press, Norman, 1963.

Ali, Salim, *The Fall of a Sparrow*, Oxford University Press, Oxford, 1985.

Ali, Salim, and Ripley, Dillon, *Handbook of the Birds of India and Pakistan*, Oxford University Press, Oxford, 1983.

Allen, Durward (ed), *Pheasants in North America*, Stackpole Books, Harrisburg, 1956.

Allen, Mark, *Falconry in Arabia*, Orbis, 1980.

Allen, Stewart, *In the Devil's Garden*, Canongate, 2002.

Amirsadeghi, Hossein, *Sky Hunters: The Passion of Falconry*, Thames and Hudson, 2008.

Anderson, Cary, *The Eagle Lady*, Eagle Eye, Anchorage, 2003.

Anon, 'Secrets of Christmas seabird revealed', *World Birdwatch* 28(1):9, 2006.

Anon, 'Pheasants an unexpected help', *BTO News*, May–June 2008.

Arberry, A J, *Immortal Rose: An Anthology of Persian Lyrics*, Luzac and Co, 1948.

Archer, Geoffrey, Sir, and Godman, Eva, *The Birds of British Somaliland*, Gurney and Jackson, 1937.

Arentsen, Herman, and Fenech, Natalino, *Lark Mirrors: Folk Art from the Past*, self-published, 2004.

Arguedas, José María, *Yawar Fiesta* (trans. Frances Horning Barraclough), University of Texas Press, Austin, 1985.

Armstrong, Edward, *Bird Display*, Cambridge University Press, Cambridge, 1942.

——, *The Folklore of Birds*, Collins, 1958.

——, *The Life and Lore of the Bird*, Crown, New York, 1975.

Arnott, W Geoffrey, *Birds in the Ancient World From A to Z*, Routledge, Abingdon, 2007.

Ashley, Lisa, Major, Richard, and Taylor, Charlotte, 'Does the presence of grevilleas and eucalypts in urban gardens influence the distribution and foraging ecology of Noisy Miners?', *Emu* 109:135–42, 2009.

Attar, Farid ud-Din, *The Conference of the Birds* (trans. Garcin de Tassy), Routledge and Kegan Paul, 1971.

Attenborough, David, *Quest in Paradise*, Lutterworth, 1959.

——, *The Zoo Quest Expeditions: Travels in Guyana, Indonesia and Paraguay*, Lutterworth, 1980.

——, *Life on Air*, BBC Books, 2002.

Baha El Din, S M, and Salama, W, *The Catching of Birds in North Sinai* (Study Report No 45), International Council for Bird Preservation, Cambridge, 1991.

Baicich, Paul, 'Tanner Trails', *Birding* 39(2):28–9, 2007.

——, 'Snowcock Release: The Beginnings', *Birding* 41(6):66–7, 2009.

——, 'Bird Clubs and Bluebird Trails: Early 1960s', *Birding* 42(2):58–9, 2010.

Bainbrigge Fletcher, T, and Inglis, C M, *Birds of an Indian Garden*, Thacker, Spink and Co, Calcutta, 1924.

Baker, J A, *The Peregrine, The Hill of Summer and Diaries* (eds Mark Cocker and John Fanshawe), HarperCollins, 2010.

Ball, Stanley, 'Jungle Fowls from Pacific Islands', *Bernice P. Bishop Museum Bulletin*, 108, 1933.

Balogh, Greg, 'Raising Shorties', *Audubon*, January–February 2008, pages 27–30.

Barbeau, Marius, *Totem Poles*, Vol 1, National Museum of Canada, Ottawa, 1950.

Barber, Theo, *The Human Nature of Birds*, Bookman Press, Melbourne, 1993.

Barnes, Keith, 'The World's 10 Sexiest Birds', *Winging It* 20(1):1–5, 2008.

Bartley, Glenn, 'Ecuador Adventure', *Birding* 42(3):54–5, 2010.

Bates, Henry, *The Naturalist on the River Amazon*, Dent, 1969.

Bates, Henry, and Busenbark, Robert, *Finches and Soft-billed Birds*, TFH Publications, Neptune City, 1970.

Batty, J, *Domesticated Ducks and Geese*, Saiga Books, Hindhead, 1979.

Baughman, Mel (ed), *National Geographic Reference Atlas to the Birds of North America*, National Geographic, Washington, DC, 2003.

Baynes, Ernest, 'A Vireo as Hostess', *Bird-Lore* 24:256–9, 1922.

Beaglehole, J C (ed), *The Voyage of the Endeavour, 1768–1771*, Boydell Press, Woodbridge, 1999.

Bechstein, J M, *The Natural History of Cage Birds*, Groombridge, 1888.

Bede, *The Ecclesiastical History of the English Nation*, Dent, 1910.

Beebe, Mary, and Beebe, William, *Our Search for a Wilderness*, Henry Holt, New York, 1910.

Beebe, William, *A Monograph of the Pheasants*, Vols 1–4, Dover, 1990.

——, *Pheasant Jungles*, World Pheasant Association, Reading, 1994.

Beeton, Isabella, *The Book of Household Management*, Jonathan Cape, 1968.

Bell, Cathie, 'Row over bird's rise from ashes', *Guardian Weekly*, 27 September 1998, page 25.

Belshaw, R H H, *Guinea Fowl of the World*, Nimrod, Liss, 1985.

Benson, C E, 'Egret Farming in Sind', *Journal, Bombay Natural History Society* 28:748–50, 1922.

Berlo, Janet, and Wilson, Lee Anne, *Arts of Africa, Oceania, and the Americas*, Prentice Hall, New Jersey, 1993.

Betrò, M C, *Hieroglyphics: The Writings of Ancient Egypt*, Abbeville, New York, 1996.

Bewick, Thomas, *A History of British Birds*, Vol 1, Longman, 1826.

Birch, G, 'Egret Farming in Sind', *Journal, Bombay Natural History Society* 21:161–3, 1914.

——, 'Egret Farming in Sind', *Journal, Bombay Natural History Society* 27:944–7, 1921.

Bircham, Peter, *A History of Ornithology*, HarperCollins, 2007.

Bird, D, Varland, D, and Negro, J, *Raptors in Human Landscapes: Adaptations to Built and Cultivated Environments*, Academic Press, 1996.

Birkhead, Tim, *The Magpies*, Poyser, Calton, 1991.

——, *Great Auk Islands*, Poyser, 1993.

——, *The Red Canary*, Weidenfeld and Nicolson, 2003.

——, *The Wisdom of Birds*, Bloomsbury, 2008.

——, *Bird Sense*, Bloomsbury, 2012.

Blackwood, Beatrice, *The Kukukuku of the Upper Watut*, Pitt Rivers Museum, Oxford, 1978.

Blüchel, Kurt, *Game and Hunting*, Könemann, Cologne, 1997.

Bodsworth, Fred, *Last of the Curlews*, Counterpoint, Washington, DC, 1995.

Boehrer, Bruce, *Parrot Culture*, University of Pennsylvania Press, Philadelphia, 2004.

Bond, James, *Birds of the West Indies*, Collins, 1990.

Bonnefoy, Yves, *Asian Mythologies* (trans. Wendy Doniger), University of Chicago Press, Chicago, 1993.

Bonser, A E, *Cassell's Natural History for Young People*, Cassell, 1905.

Bonta, Mark, *Seven Names for the Bellbird*, Texas A&M University Press, College Station, 2003.

Bourke, John, *An Apache Campaign in the Sierra Madre*, Charles Scribners, 1958.

Boyce, Mary, *Zoroastrians: Their Religious Beliefs and Practices*, Routledge and Kegan Paul, 1979.

Boyd, A W, 'Early Natural History Records in Cheshire and South Lancashire', *The North Western Naturalist* 21:227, 1946.

Bringhurst, Robert, *A Story as Sharp as a Knife*, Douglas and McIntyre, Vancouver, 1999.

Britton, Dorothy, and Hayashida, Tsuneo, *The Japanese Crane: Bird of Happiness*, Kodansha International, Tokyo, 1993.

Brooke, Michael, *Albatrosses and Petrels across the World*, Oxford University Press, Oxford, 2004.

Brown, Andy, and Grice, Phil, *Birds in England*, Poyser, 2005.

Brown, Leslie, *The Mystery of the Flamingos*, Country Life, 1959.

Brown, W J, *The Gods Had Wings*, Constable, 1936.

Browne, Thomas, Sir, *Notes and Letters on the Natural History of Norfolk*, Jarrolds, 1902.

Bruce Wilmore, Sylvia, *Swans of the World*, Taplinger, New York, 1974.

Bruggers, Richard, and Elliott, Clive, *Quelea quelea, Africa's Bird Pest*, Oxford University Press, Oxford, 1989.

Buffon, Georges-Louis Leclerc, Comte de, *The Natural History of Birds*, Vol 1, Cambridge University Press, Cambridge, 2010.

Burenhult, Goran (ed), *People of the Past*, Fog City Press, San Francisco, 2003.

Burfield, Ian, and van Bommel, Frans (eds), *Birds in Europe: Population estimates, trends and conservation status*, BirdLife International, Cambridge, 2004.

Butchart, Stuart, 'Birds to find: a review of "lost", obscure and poorly known African bird species', *Bull ABC* 14:145, 2007.

Butler, David, and Merton, Don, *The Black Robin*, Oxford University Press, Oxford, 1992.

Butvill, David, 'In-flight meal', *BBC Wildlife*, December 2010.

Cairncross, Frances, 'Connecting Flights', *Conservation in Practice* 7(1):16–21, 2006.

Caldwell, Harry, and Caldwell, John, *South China Birds*, Hester May Vanderburgh, Shanghai, 1931.

Cammann, Schuyler, 'Chinese carvings in Hornbill Ivory', *Sarawak Museum Journal* 5:393–9, 1951.

Campbell, Bruce, and Lack, Elizabeth (eds), *A Dictionary of Birds*, Poyser, Calton, 1985.

Campbell, Joseph, *The Masks of God: Primitive Mythology*, Arkana, 1987.

Caro, Mark, *The Foie Gras Wars*, Simon and Schuster, 2009.

Carter, Paul, *Parrot*, Reaktion, 2006.

Casement, M B, 'Migration across Mediterranean observed by radar', *Ibis* 108:461–91, 1966.

Catesby, Mark, *The Natural History of Carolina, Florida and the Bahama Islands*, Marsh, Wilcox and Stichall, 1754.

Chancellor, Alexander, 'Bankers are too embarrassed to shoot game. This can only be a positive development', *Guardian G2*, 17 April 2009.

Chantler, Phil, and Dreissens, Gerald, *Swifts*, Pica Press, Sussex, 1995.

Chapin, J P, 'The Congo Peacock', *Proceedings of the IX International Ornithological Congress*, 1938, pages 101–9.

Chapman, Frank, *Handbook of Birds of Eastern North America*, Appleton-Century, New York, 1934.

Cheke, Robert, Mann, Clive, and Allen, Richard, *Sunbirds*, Helm, 2001.

Cherry, Peter, and Morris, Trevor, *Domestic Duck Production: Science and Practice*, CABI, Wallingford, 2008.

Cherry-Garrard, Apsley, *The Worst Journey in the World*, Picador, 1994.

Chevenix Trench, C C, 'Egret Farming in Sind', *Journal, Bombay Natural History Society* 28:751–2, 1922.

Chisholm, Alec, *Bird Wonders of Australia*, Angus and Robertson, Sydney, 1956.

Chisholm, Graham, 'King of Scream', *Audubon*, September–October 2008, page 204.

Chiweshe, N, 'The current conservation status of the Southern Ground Hornbill *Bucorvus leadbeateri* in Zimbabwe', in Kemp, A C, and Kemp, M I (eds), *The Active Management of Hornbills and their Habitats for Conservation*, CD-ROM, Proceedings of the 4th International Hornbill Conference, Mabula Game Lodge, Bela-Bela, South Africa, 2007, pages 252–66.

Choate, Ernest, *The Dictionary of American Bird Names*, Gambit, Boston, 1973.

Clark, Grahame, 'Fowling in Prehistoric Europe', *Antiquity* 22:116–30, 1948.

Clay, Rob (ed), *101 Aves Communes del Paraguay*, Asociación Guyra Paraguay, Asunción, 2002.

Cleere, Nigel, and Nurney, David, *Nightjars*, Pica Press, Sussex, 1998.

Clement, Peter, Harris, Alan, and Davis, John, *Finches and Sparrows*, Helm, 1993.

Cloudsley-Thompson, J L, 'Wildlife massacres in Sudan', *Oryx* 26:202–4, 1992.

Cocker, Mark, *Loneliness and Time*, Secker and Warburg, 1992.

——, *Rivers of Blood, Rivers of Gold*, Jonathan Cape, 1998a.

——, 'The Magic, Myth and Folklore of Birds in West Africa', unpublished report for Winston Churchill Memorial Trust, London, 1998b.

——, 'African birds in traditional magico-medicinal use – a preliminary survey', *Bull ABC* 7:60–65, 2000.

——, *A Tiger in the Sand*, Jonathan Cape, 2006.

——, *Crow Country*, Jonathan Cape, 2007.

Cocker, Mark, and Mabey, Richard, *Birds Britannica*, Chatto and Windus, 2005.

Cocker, Mark, and Mikkola, Heimo, 'Magic, myth and misunderstanding: cultural responses to owls in Africa and their implications for conservation', *Bull ABC*, 8:31–5, 2001.

Colette, *Gigi and The Cat*, Vintage, 2003.

Collar, Nigel, and Stuart, Simon, *Threatened Birds of Africa and Related Islands*, International Council for Bird Preservation, Cambridge, 1985.

Collar, Nigel, and Andrew, Paul, *Birds to Watch*, International Council for Bird Preservation, Cambridge, 1988.

Collar, N, Gonzaga, L, Krabbe, N, Madrono Nieto, A, Naranjo, L, Parker III, T, and Wege, D, *Threatened Birds of the Americas*, International Council for Bird Preservation, Cambridge, 1992.

Collings, Mark, *A Very British Coop*, Macmillan, 2008.

Conder, Peter, *The Wheatear*, Christopher Helm, Bromley, 1989.

Cook, James, *The Journals* (ed Philip Edwards), Penguin, 2003.

Cott, Hugh, 'The Exploitation of Wild Birds for their Eggs', *Ibis* 95:409–49, 643–75, 1953.

——, 'The Exploitation of Wild Birds for their Eggs', *Ibis* 96:130–49, 1954.

Cowles, R B, 'The life history of *Scopus umbretta bannermani* C. Grant in Natal, South Africa', *Auk* 47:159–76, 1930.

Crabbe, George, *The Poetical Works of George Crabbe*, Henry Frowde, 1908.

Cranbrook, Earl, 'Report on the Birds' Nest Industry in the Baram District and at Niah, Sarawak', *Sarawak Museum Journal* 33:145–70, 1984.

Crewe, Mike, 'Some observations on Wallcreeper nest material', *British Birds* 100: 444–5, 2007.

Croxall, John, 'Conservation of Southern Ocean Albatrosses', *Bird Conservation International* 18(Supplement 1):13–29, 2008.

Cruickshank, Helen (ed), *Thoreau on Birds*, McGraw Hill, New York, 1964.

Cumpston, John, *Macquarie Island*, Department of External Affairs, Canberra, 1968.

Curtis, Edward, *The North American Indian*, Taschen, Cologne, 2005.

Cuthbertson, Margaret, 'African Game 400 Years Ago', *African Wild Life* 3(2):148–50, 1949.

da Vinci, Leonardo, *Notebooks*, Oxford University Press, Oxford, 2008.

Damas, David (ed), *Handbook of North American Indians: Arctic*, Smithsonian Institution, Washington, DC, 1984.

Darwin, Charles, *The Voyage of the Beagle*, Vintage, 2009.

——, *Animals and Plants under Domestication*, Vols 1–2, John Murray, 1890.

——, *The Descent of Man*, John Murray, 1901.

Dave, K N, *Birds in Sanskrit Literature*, Motilal Banarsidass, Delhi, 2005.

Davidson, Alan, *The Oxford Companion to Food* (ed Tom Jaine), Oxford University Press, Oxford, 2006.

Davies, Nick, *Cuckoos, Cowbirds and Other Cheats*, Poyser, 2000.

Davies, S J J F, *Ratites and Tinamous*, Oxford University Press, Oxford, 2002.

Davies, Z, Fuller, R, Loram, A, Irvine, K, Sims, V, and Gaston, K, 'A national scale inventory of resource provision for biodiversity within domestic gardens, *Biological Conservation* 142:761–71, 2009.

Davis, Lloyd, and Renner, Martin, *Penguins*, Poyser, 2003.

Dawkins, Richard, *The Ancestor's Tale*, Weidenfeld and Nicolson, 2004.

Dawson, W R, 'The Lore of the Hoopoe (*Upupa epops*)', *Ibis* 67:31–9, 1925a.

——, 'The Bee-eater (*Merops apiaster*) from the Earliest Times, and a further Note on the Hoopoe,' *Ibis* 67:590–94, 1925b.

de Gubernatis, Angelo, *Zoological Mythology*, Vol 2, Trubner, 1872.

de Kay, Charles, *Bird Gods of Ancient Europe*, Harry Allenson, 1898.

de la Peña, Martín, and Rumboll, Maurice, *Birds of Southern South America and Antarctica*, HarperCollins, 1998.

Dee, Tim, *The Running Sky*, Jonathan Cape, 2009.

Dekker, René, 'Megapodes – from Fairy Tale to Reality', *Bull OBC* 7(1):10–13, 1988.

Delacour, Jean, *The Waterfowl of the World*, Vol 4, Country Life, 1964.

Delacour, Jean, and Amadon, Dean, *Curassows and Related Birds*, American Museum of Natural History, New York, 1973.

Demey, Ron, 'Africa Round-up', *Bull ABC* 11:93–100, 2004.

Demey, Ron, and Kirwan, Guy, 'Africa Round-up', *Bull ABC* 11:10, 2004.

Demey, Ron, Kirwan, Guy, and Lack, Peter, 'Africa Round-up', *Bull ABC* 14:134–5, 2007.

——, 'Africa Round-up', *Bull ABC* 15:17, 2008.

Demey, Ron, Kirwan, Guy, and Lucking, Rob, 'Africa Round-up', *Bull ABC* 5:89, 1998.

Derwent Sue, and Mander, Myles, 'Twitchers Bewitched', *Africa – Birds and Birding* 2:22–5, 1997.

Desfayes, Michel, *A Thesaurus of Bird Names*, Vols 1–2, Musée cantonal d'histoire naturelle, Sion, Switzerland, 1998.

Diamond, A W, and Filion, F L, *The Value of Birds*, International Council for Bird Preservation, Cambridge, 1987.

Diamond, Jared, *Guns, Germs and Steel*, Norton, New York, 1999.

Diaz, Bernal, *The Conquest of New Spain* (trans. J M Cohen), Folio Society, 1974.

Dixon, R B, *Oceanic Mythology*, Harvard University Press, Cambridge, Massachusetts, 1916.

Dohner, Janet, *The Encyclopedia of Historic and Endangered Livestock and Poultry Breeds*, Yale University Press, 2001.

Donald, Paul, *The Skylark*, Poyser, 2004.

Doughty, Robin, *Feather Fashions and Bird Preservation*, University of California Press, Berkeley, 1975.

——, 'Eider husbandry in the North Atlantic: trends and prospects', *Polar Record* 19:447–59, 1979.

——, *The Mockingbird*, University of Texas Press, Austin, 1988.

——, *Return of the Whooping Crane*, University of Texas Press, Austin, 1989.

Doughty, Robin, and Fergus, Rob, *The Purple Martin*, University of Texas Press, Austin, 2002.

Douville de Franssu, P, Gramet, P, Grolleau, G, and Such, A, 'Aerial Treatments against Starling Roosts in France with Chloro-para-toluidin (CPT): Results of eight years of experiments', *Proceedings of the Thirteenth Vertebrate Pest Conference*, Paper 55, 1988, pages 272–6.

du Maurier, Daphne, 'The Birds', in *Murmurations* (ed Nicholas Royle), Two Ravens Press, Isle of Lewis, 2011.

Ducey, James, *Birds of the Untamed West: The History of Birdlife in Nebraska, 1750 to 1875*, Making History, Omaha, 2000.

Dupree, Nancy, 'An Interpretation of the Role of the Hoopoe in Afghan Folklore and Magic', *Folklore* 85(3):173–93, 1974.

Durrell, Gerald, *The Drunken Forest*, Rupert Hart-Davis, 1956.

Eastman, Maxine, *The Life of the Emu*, Angus and Robertson, 1969.

Eastwood, Ken, 'Who's a naughty boy then?', *Australian Geographic*, October–December 2005.

Efe, Márcio Eferim, and Filippini, Alexandre, 'Nidificação do João-de-barro, *Furnarius rufus* (Passeriformes Furnariidae) em estruturas de distribuição de energia eléctrica em Santa Catarina', *Ornithologia* 1(2):121–4, June 2006.

Egremont, Pamela, and Rothschild, Miriam, 'The Calculating Cormorants', *Biological Journal of the Linnean Society* 12:181–6, 1979.

Ellis, Hattie, *Planet Chicken: The Shameful Story of the Bird on Your Plate*, Sceptre, 2007.

Elphick, Jonathan, *Birds: The Art of Ornithology*, Scriptum, 2004.

——, *John Gould, The Family of Toucans*, Taschen, Cologne, 2011.

Elphick, Jonathan, and Tipling, David, *Great Birds of Britain and Europe*, Duncan Baird, 2008.

Emery, Nathan, and Clayton, Nicola, 'The Mentality of Crows: Convergent Evolution of Intelligence in Corvids and Apes', *Science* 306:1903–7, 2004.

Engers, Joe, *The Great Book of Wildfowl Decoys*, Swan Hill Press, Shrewsbury, 2000.

Estes, Richard, *The Behavior Guide to African Mammals*, California University Press, Berkeley, 1991.

Evans, Mike, *Important Bird Areas in the Middle East*, BirdLife International, Cambridge, 1994.

Ewans, Martin, *Bharatpur: Bird Paradise*, H F and G Witherby, 1989.

Farley, Jack, *The Misericords of Gloucester Cathedral*, Jack Farley, Gloucester, 1981.

Feare, Chris, *The Starling*, Oxford University Press, Oxford, 1984.

Feare, Chris, and Craig, Adrian, *Starlings and Mynas*, Helm, 1998.

Fedducia, Alan, *The Origins and Evolution of Birds*, Yale University Press, New Haven, 1996.

Fee, William, 'The Parsees and the Towers of Silence at Bombay, India', *National Geographic Magazine* 16(12):529–54, 1905.

Feest, Christian, *Native Arts of North America*, Thames and Hudson, 1992.

Fenech, Natalino, *Fatal Flight: The Maltese Obsession with Killing Birds*, Quiller Press, 1992.

——, *A Complete Guide to the Birds of Malta*, Midsea Books, Valletta, 2010

Finn, Frank, *Indian Sporting Birds*, Francis Edwards, 1915.

Fisher, James, *The Fulmar*, Collins, 1952.

Fisher, James, and Lockley, Ronald, *Sea-Birds*, Collins, 1954.

Fishpool, Lincoln, and Evans, Michael, *Important Bird Areas in Africa and Associated Islands*, Pisces Publications and BirdLife International, Cambridge, 2001.

Fitter, Richard, *Wildlife for Man*, Collins, 1986.

Fitter, Richard, and Richardson, Richard, *The Pocket Guide to British Birds*, Collins, 1952.

FitzGerald, Edward, *Rubáiyát of Omar Khayyám*, Collins, 1953.

Fitzpatrick, John, Lammertink, Martjan, Luneau Jr, David, Gallagher, Tim, Harrison, Bobby, Sparling, Gene, Rosenberg, Kenneth, Rohrbaugh, Ronald, Swarthout, Elliott, Wrege, Peter, Swarthout, Sara, Dantzker, Marc, Charif, Russell, Barksdale, Timothy, Remsen Jr, J V, Simon, Scott, and Zollner, Douglas, 'Ivory-Billed Woodpecker (*Campephilus principalis*) Persists in Continental North America', *Science* 308:1460–62, 2005.

Flannery, Tim, *Throwim Way Leg*, Penguin, 1998.

Fleming, Andrew, *St Kilda and the Wider World*, Windgather Press, Macclesfield, 2005.

Fleming, Ian, *You Only Live Twice*, Penguin, 2004.

Flood, Bob, 'The New Zealand Storm-petrel is not extinct', *Birding World* 16:479–82, 2003.

Floyd, Ted, 'The Ivory-billed Woodpecker', *Birding* 39(2):26, 2007.

——, *Smithsonian Field Guide to the Birds of North America*, HarperCollins, New York, 2008.

Forbes, W A, 'Eleven Weeks in north-eastern Brazil', *Ibis* 23:312–62, 1881.

Forbush, Edward, *A Natural History of American Birds of Eastern and Central North America*, Bramhall, New York, 1955.

Foreshaw, Joseph, and Cooper, William, *Parrots of the World*, Blandford, 1989.

Forrester, Ron, and Andrews, Ian (eds), *The Birds of Scotland*, Vols 1–2, Scottish Ornithologists' Club, Aberlady, 2007.

Forsberg, Michael, *On Ancient Wings: The Sandhill Crane of North America*, Michael Forsberg Photography, Lincoln, Nebraska, 2004.

Franzen, Jonathan, *Freedom*, Fourth Estate, 2010.

——, 'Emptying the Skies', *New Yorker*, 26 July 2010.

Freeman, J D, 'A Note on the Gawai Kenyalang, or Hornbill Ritual of the Iban of Sarawak', in Smythies, B E, *The Birds of Borneo*, Oliver and Boyd, 1960.

Friedland, Susan, *Food and Morality*, Prospect Books, Totnes, 2008.

Friedmann, Herbert, *The Symbolic Goldfinch*, Pantheon, New York, 1946.

Frith, Clifford, and Beehler, Bruce, *The Birds of Paradise*, Oxford University Press, Oxford, 1998.

Frith, Clifford, and Frith, Dawn, *The Bowerbirds*, Oxford University Press, Oxford, 2004.

——, *The Bowerbirds: Nature, Art, History*, Frith & Frith, Malanda, 2008.

Fry, Hilary, Fry, Kathie, and Harris, Alan, *Kingfishers, Bee-Eaters and Rollers*, Helm, 1992.

Fuller, Errol, *Extinct Birds*, Viking/Rainbird, 1987.

——, *The Lost Birds of Paradise*, Swan Hill Press, Shrewsbury, 1995.

——, *The Great Auk*, self-published, Southborough, 1999.

——, *Dodo: From Extinction to Icon*, Collins, 2002.

Gallagher, Tim, 'The Dawn of Recovery', *Birds*, no issue number:55–9, 1990.

——, *The Grail Bird: The Rediscovery of the Ivory-billed Woodpecker*, Houghton Mifflin, New York, 2006.

Garnett, Richard, 'Defoe and the swallows', *Times Literary Supplement*, 13 February 1969.

Garrard, Garry, *A Book of Verse: The Biography of the Rubaiyat of Omar Khayyam*, Sutton, Stroud, 2007.

Gaskell, Jeremy, *Who Killed the Greak Auk?*, Oxford University Press, Oxford, 2000.

Gatter, Wulf, *Birds of Liberia*, Pica Press, Sussex, 1998.

Gattiker, Ernst, and Gattiker, Luise, *Die Vögel in Volkglauben*, Aula Verlag, Wiesbaden, 1989.

Gibbon, Edward, *The History of the Decline and Fall of the Roman Empire*, Vols 1–8 (ed Felipe Fernández-Armesto), Folio Society, 1990.

Gibbs, David, Barnes, Eustace, and Cox, John, *Pigeons and Doves*, Pica Press, Sussex, 2001.

Gibson, Graeme, *Perpetual Motion*, St Martin's Press, New York, 1982.

Gilliard, Thomas, *Birds of Paradise and Bower Birds*, Weidenfeld and Nicolson, 1969.

Gladstone, Hugh, *Record Bags and Shooting Records*, Witherby, 1922.

Glare, P G W (ed), *Oxford Latin Dictionary*, Oxford University Press, Oxford, 1982.

Glasier, Phillip, *Falconry and Hawking*, Batsford, London, 1998.

Godfrey, Robert, *Bird-Lore of the Eastern Cape Province*, Witwaterstrand University Press, Johannesburg, 1941.

Godfrey, W Earl, *The Birds of Canada*, National Museum of Canada, Ottawa, 1966.

Golding, F D, 'Nigerian Pets: The Ground Hornbill', *Nigerian Field* 4:123–6, 1935.

Gollop, J B, Barry, T W, and Iversen, E H, *Eskimo Curlew: A Vanishing Species?*, Saskatchewan Natural History Society, Regina, 1986.

Goodman, Jordan, 'Guano happens (sometimes)', *Geographical Magazine* 78(11), 2006.

Goodman, Steven, and Meininger, Peter (eds), *The Birds of Egypt*, Oxford University Press, Oxford, 1989.

Goodwin, Derek, *Crows of the World*, British Museum (Natural History), 1976.

——, *Birds of Man's World*, British Museum, 1978.

——, *Pigeons and Doves of the World*, British Museum (Natural History), 1983.

Goring, Rosemary (ed), *Dictionary of Beliefs and Religions*, Chambers, 1992.

Goriup, Paul, and Schulz, Holger, *Conservation Management of the White Stork: An International Opportunity*, International Council for Bird Preservation, Cambridge, 1990.

Gorman, Gerard, *Woodpeckers of Europe*, Bruce Colman, Devon, 2004.

Gotch, A F, *Latin Names Explained*, Cassell, 1995.

Gould, Stephen J, *The Structure of Evolutionary Theory*, Belknapp Press, 2002.

Grady, W, *Vulture: Nature's Ghastly Gourmet*, Sierra Club, 1997.

Graham, Victor, 'The Pelican as Image and Symbol', *Revue de Littérature Comparée* 36:235–43, 1962.

Grahame, Kenneth, *The Wind in the Willows*, Folio Society, 1995.

Graves, Gary, 'Avian commensals in Colonial America: when did Chaetura pelagica become the chimney swift?', *Archives of Natural History* 31(2):300–307, 2004.

Graves, Robert, *The Greek Myths*, Vols 1–2, Folio Society, 1996.

Green, Jonathon, *Slang Down the Ages*, Kyle Cathie, 1993.

——, *Cassell's Dictionary of Slang*, Cassell, 2000.

Greenoak, Francesca, *British Birds: Their Folklore, Names and Literature*, Helm, 1997.

Greenslade, Michael, 'Hunters of a Different Kind', *Paradise* 4, 2010, pages 34–7.

Greenway, James, *Extinct and Vanishing Birds of the World*, Dover, New York, 1967.

Greppin, John, *Classical and Middle Armenian Bird Names: A Linguistic, Taxonomic and Mythological Study*, Caravan Books, Delmar, New York, 1978.

Gretton, Adam, *The Ecology and Conservation of the Slender-billed Curlew*, International Council for Bird Preservation, Cambridge, 1991.

——, 'Where does the Slender-billed Curlew nest, and what future does it have?', *British Birds* 95:334–44, 2002.

Grieve, M, *A Modern Herbal*, Cresset Press, 1994.

Grigson, Geoffrey, *The Englishman's Flora*, Helicon, Oxford, 1996.

Grindol, Diane, and Roudybush, Tom, *Teaching Your Bird to Talk*, Howell Book House, New Jersey, 2004.

Grzimek, Bernard, *Grzimek's Animal Life Encyclopedia*, Vol 7, Van Nostrand Reinhold, New York, 1972.

Gurney, J H, *Early Annals of Ornithology*, Paul Minet, Chicheley, 1972.

Haag-Wackernagel, Daniel, *Die Taube*, Schwabe, Basel, 1998.

Hafiz, *New Nightingale, New Rose: Poems from the Divan of Hafiz* (trans. Richard Le Gallienne), Bardic Press, California, 2004.

Hagemeijer, W J M, and Blair, M, *The EBCC Atlas of European Breeding Birds*, Poyser, 1997.

Hancock, James, and Elliott, Hugh, *The Herons of the World*, London Editions, 1978.

Hancock, James, Kushlan, James, and Kahl, Philip, *Storks, Ibises and Spoonbills of the World*, Academic Press, 1992.

Hanks, Patrick, and Hodges, Flavia, *A Dictionary of Surnames*, Oxford University Press, Oxford, 1988.

Hansell, Jean, *The Pigeon in History*, Millstream Books, Bath, 1998.

Hansell, Mike, *Built by Animals*, Oxford University Press, Oxford, 2007.

Hansell, Peter, and Hansell, Jean, *Dovecotes*, Shire, Princes Risborough, 2001.

Hansen, Kjeld, *A Farewell to Greenland's Wildlife* (trans. Robin Worrall), Gads Forlag, Copenhagen, 2002.

Hansen, Snær, 'Where Have All The Puffins Gone?', *The Rejkjavik Grapevine*, 5 November –1 December 2011.

Harcourt, E S, and Phillott, D C (trans.), *Two Treatises on Falconry*, Bernard Quaritch, 1968.

Hardy, Thomas, *Tess of the d'Urbervilles*, Macmillan, 1974.

Hare, C E, *Bird Lore*, Country Life, 1952.

Harris, R, *Picus Who Is Also Zeus*, Cambridge University Press, Cambridge, 1916.

Harrison, Colin, *The History of the Birds of Britain*, Collins, 1988.

Harrison, Peter, *Seabirds*, Christopher Helm, 1983.

Harrison, T P, *They Tell of Birds*, Greenwood Press, Westport, Connecticut, 1956.

Harrisson, Tom, 'Humans and Hornbills in Borneo', *Sarawak Museum Journal* 5:400–413, 1951.

———, 'Food of Collocalia Swiftlets at Niah Cave on Borneo', *Journal, Bombay Natural History Society* 71:376–93.

Harting, J, *The Ornithology of Shakespeare*, Gresham Press, Old Woking, 1978.

Haupt, Lyanda, *Pilgrim on the Great Bird Continent*, Little, Brown, New York, 2006.

———, *Crow Planet*, Back Bay Books, New York, 2011.

Haverschmidt, François, *The Life of the White Stork*, E J Brill, Leiden, 1949.

Haynes, Ann, 'Human Exploitation of Seabirds in Jamaica', *Biological Conservation* 41:99–124, 1987.

Haynes, Cynthia, *Raising Turkeys, Ducks, Geese, Pigeons and Guineas*, Tab Books, Blue Ridge Summit, Pennsylvania, 1987.

Haynes-Sutton, Ann, 'The Value of Seabirds as a Socio-economic Resource in Jamaica', in *The Value of Birds*, A Diamond and F Filion (eds), Cambridge, International Council for Bird Preservation, 1987, pages 77–83.

Heather, Barrie, and Robertson, Hugh, *Field Guide to the Birds of New Zealand*, Oxford University Press, Oxford, 1997.

Hedges, John, *Tomb of the Eagles: A Window on Stone Age Tribal Britain*, John Murray, 1984.

Heinrich, Bernd, *Ravens in Winter*, Barrie and Jenkins, 1990.
———, *Mind of the Raven*, Ecco, 2002.

Heng, Natalie, 'Owls poached for exotic meat market', *The Star*, 13 September 2011.

Henry, G M, *A Guide to the Birds of Ceylon*, De Silva and Sons, Kandy, 1978.

Herodotus, *The Histories* (trans. Aubrey de Sélincourt), Penguin, Harmondsworth, 1975.

Hill, Frederick, 'Lyre Fire', *Australian Geographic*, July–September 2005, page 8.

Hill, Geoffrey, *Ivorybill Hunters*, Oxford University Press, Oxford, 2007.

Hilty, Steven, and Brown, William, *A Guide to the Birds of Colombia*, Princeton University Press, Princeton, 1986.

Hinnells, John, *The Zoroastrian Diaspora*, Oxford University Press, Oxford, 2005.

Hiroshige, Ando, *Birds and Flowers*, George Braziller, New York, 1988.

Holloway, Simon, *The Historical Atlas of Breeding Birds in Britain and Ireland 1875–1900*, Poyser, 1996.

Holmes, Richard, *Coleridge: Early Visions*, Hodder and Stoughton, 1989.

Holmgren, Virginia, *The Way of the Hummingbird: In Legend, History and Today's Garden*, Capra, Santa Barbara, 1986.

Homer, *The Iliad* (trans. E V Rieu), Penguin, Harmondsworth, 1950.

———, *The Odyssey* (trans. E V Rieu), Penguin, Harmondsworth, 1976.

Hooper, Stephen, *Pacific Encounters: Art and Divinity in Polynesia 1760–1860*, British Museum, 2006.

Hope, Annette, *Londoners' Larder: English Cuisine from Chaucer to the Present*, Mainstream, 1990.

Hosking, Eric, and Sage, Bryan, *Antarctic Wildlife*, Croom Helm, 1982.

Houlihan, Patrick, *Birds of Ancient Egypt*, Aris and Phillips, Warminster, 1986.

House, Adrian, *Francis of Assisi*, Chatto and Windus, 2000.

Howe, Bea, *Antiques for the Victorian Home*, Spring Books, 1973.

Howell, Steve, and Webb, Sophie, *A Guide to the Birds of Mexico and Northern Central America*, Oxford University Press, Oxford, 1995.

Huc, Évariste-Régis, and Gabet, Joseph, *Travels in Tartary, Thibet and China, 1844–1846*, Dover, New York, 1987.

Hudson, Nigel, et al, 'Report on rare birds in Great Britain in 2008', *British Birds* 102:528–601, 2009.

Hudson, W H, *Birds of La Plata*, Vols 1–2, Dent, 1920.
———, *The Naturalist in La Plata*, Dent, 1939.
———, *Adventures Among Birds*, Dent, 1951a.
———, *Nature in Downland*, Dent, 1951b.
———, *Far Away and Long Ago*, Eland, 1982.

Hughes, Janice, *Cranes: A Natural History of a Bird in Crisis*, Firefly, New York, 2008.

Hull, Robin, *Scottish Birds: Culture and Tradition*, Mercat Press, Edinburgh, 2001.

Hulme, F E, *Natural History Lore and Legend*, Bernard Quaritch, 1895.

Humboldt, Alexander, and Bonpland, Aimé, *Personal Narrative of Travels to the Equinoctial Regions of the New Continent During the Years 1799–1804*, Vol 3 (trans. Helen Maria Wiliams), Longman, Hurst, Rees, Orme and Brown, 1918.

Hutton, Ronald, *Stations of the Sun: A History of the Ritual Year in Britain*, Oxford University Press, Oxford, 1996.

Huxley, Elspeth, *Their Shining Eldorado*, Chatto and Windus, 1967.

Hyams, Edward, *Animals in the Service of Man*, Dent, 1972.

Ikram, Salima (ed), *Divine Creatures: Animal Mummies in Ancient Egypt*, The American University in Cairo Press, New York, 2005.

Impellusa, Lucia, *Nature and Its Symbols*, J. Paul Getty Trust, Los Angeles, 2004.

Ingersoll, Ernest, *Birds in Legend, Fable and Folklore*, Longmans Green, 1923.

Isack, H A, and Reyer, H-U, 'Honeyguides and Honey Gatherers: Interspecific Communication in a Symbiotic Relationship', *Science* 243:1343–6.

Jackson, Christine, *Great Bird Paintings of the World*, Antique Collectors' Club, Woodbridge, 1993.
———, *Peacock*, Reaktion, 2006.

Jackson, H D, 'A review of Afrotropical nightjar mortality, mainly road kills,' *Ostrich* 73:147–61, 2002.

Jackson, Jerome, *In Search of the Ivory-billed Woodpecker*, Smithsonian Books, Washington, DC, 2004.

Jackson, Michael, *Galapagos: A Natural History*, University of Calgary Press, Calgary, 1993.

Jacobs, Julian, *The Nagas: Hillpeoples of Northeast India*, Hansjörg Mayer, Stuttgart, 1990.

Jamandores, J, *Starting It Right (In Cockfighting)*, Bacchus, Manila, 2001.

Jarvis, M J F, 'Interactions between Man and South African Gannet *Sula capensis*', *Ostrich*, Supplement 8, 1970, pages 497–513.

Jashemski, Wilhelmina, and Meyer, Frederick, *The Natural History of Pompeii*, Cambridge University Press, Cambridge, 2002.

Jobling, J A, *Helm Dictionary of Scientific Bird Names*, Christopher Helm, 2010.

Johnsgard, Paul, *The Grouse of the World*, University of Nebraska Press, Lincoln, 1983.

———, *Crane Music: A Natural History of American Cranes*, Smithsonian Institution, Washington, DC, 1991.

———, *Cormorants, Darters, and Pelicans of the World*, Smithsonian Institution Press, 1993.

———, *The Avian Brood Parasites*, Oxford University Press, Oxford, 1997.

———, *Grassland Grouse and Their Conservation*, Smithsonian Institution Press, 2002.

Johnson, Alan, and Cézilly, Frank, *The Greater Flamingo*, Poyser, 2007.

Johnson, Murray, 'Feathered Foes: Soldier, Settlers and Western Australia's "Emu War" of 1932', *Journal of Australian Studies* 86:147–57, 2006.

Johnson, Walter (ed), *Gilbert White's Journals*, David and Charles, Newton Abbot, 1970.

Jones, Darryl, *Magpie Alert: Learning to Live with a Wild Neighbour*, University of New South Wales Press, Sydney, 2002.

Jones, Darryl, Dekker, René, and Roselaar, Cees, *The Megapodes*, Oxford University Press, Oxford, 1995.

Jones, Darryl, and Everding, S, 'Australian Brush-turkeys in a suburban environment: implications for conflict and conservation', *Wildlife Research* 18:285–97, 1991.

Jones, Darryl, and Reynolds, James, 'Feeding birds in our towns and cities: a global research opportunity', *Journal of Avian Biology* 39:265–71, 2008.

Jones, J D F, *Storyteller: The Many Lives of Laurens van der Post*, John Murray, 2001.

Jones, Stephen, *The Last Prairie*, University of Nebraska Press, Lincoln, 2006.

Jukema, Joop, Piersma, Theunis, and Hulscher, Jan B, *Goudplevieren en wilsterflappers*, Fryske Akademy, Utrecht, 2001.

Jukema, Joop, and Piersma, Theunis, 'Were Slender-billed Curlews *Numenius tenuirostris* once common in The Netherlands, and do they have patches of powder feathers?', *Ibis* 146:165–7, 2004.

Juniper, Tony, *Spix's Macaw*, Fourth Estate, 2002.

Kahl, M P, 'Observations on the behaviour of the Hamerkop *Scopus umbretta* in Uganda', *Ibis* 109:25–32, 1967.

Kassagam, J K, *What is this Bird Saying?: A study of names and cultural beliefs about birds amongst the Marakwet peoples of Kenya*, Binary Computer Services, Nairobi, 1997.

Katz, Solomon (ed), *Encyclopedia of Food and Culture*, Thomson Gale, New York, 2003.

Kaufman, Kenn, 'Endemics and Ecotourism', *Birding* 40(4):51, 2008.

Kear, Janet, *Man and Wildfowl*, Poyser, Berkhamsted, 1990.

——— (ed), *Ducks, Geese and Swans*, Vols 1–2, Oxford University Press, Oxford, 2005.

Keats, John, *John Keats* (ed Elizabeth Cook), Oxford University Press, Oxford, 1990.

Kemp, Alan, *The Hornbills*, Oxford University Press, Oxford, 1995.

Kerr, John, Sir, *A Naturalist in the Gran Chaco*, Cambridge University Press, Cambridge, 1950.

Keyte, Hugh, and Parrott, Andrew (eds), *The Shorter New Oxford Book of Carols*, Oxford University Press, Oxford, 1993.

Kiff, Lloyd, 'To the Brink and Back', *Terra* 28(4):7–18, 1990.

King, Warren, *Endangered Birds of the World*, Smithsonian Institution Press, Washington, DC, 1981.

Kingdon, Jonathan, *Island Africa*, Collins, 1990.

Kinnaird, Margaret, and O'Brien, Timothy, *The Ecology and Conservation of Asian Hornbills*, University of Chicago Press, Chicago, 2007.

Kiple, Kenneth, and Ornelas, Kriemhild, *The Cambridge World History of Food*, Vol 2, Cambridge University Press, Cambridge, 2000.

Kirke-Swann, H, *A Dictionary of English and Folk-Names of British Birds*, EP Publishing, Wakefield, 1977.

Kirwan, Guy, Boyla, K A, Castell, P, Demirci, B, Özen, M, Welch, H, and Marlow, T, *The Birds of Turkey*, Christopher Helm, 2008.

Kochmann, Karl, *Black Forest Clockmaker and the Cuckoo Clock*, Antique Clock Publishing, San Francisco, 1990.

Koford, Carl, *The California Condor*, National Audubon Research Report 4, New York, 1953.

Konter, André, *Grebes of Our World*, Lynx, Barcelona, 2001.

Koon, Lim Chan, and Cranbrook, Earl, *Swiftlets of Borneo*, Natural History Publications, Kota Kinabalu, 2002.

Kothari, Ashish, *Birds in Our Lives*, Universities Press, Hyderabad, 2007.

Krech, Shepard, *The Ecological Indian*, Norton, New York, 1999.

———, *Spirits of the Air: Birds and American Indians in the South*, University of Georgia Press, Athens, Georgia, 2009.

Kumerloeve, H, 'Vom Hortulanenfang bei Osnabrueck im 17. und 18. Jahrhundert', (About the catching of Ortolan Buntings near Osnabrück in the seventeenth and eighteenth centuries), *Veröff. Naturwiss. Ver. Osnabrueck* 26:67–130, 1953.

Lack, David, *Darwin's Finches*, Cambridge University Press, Cambridge, 1947.

———, *Robin Redbreast*, Clarendon Press, Oxford, 1950.

———, *Swifts in a Tower*, Methuen, 1956.

———, *The Life of the Robin*, Witherby, 1976.

Lack, Peter, *The Atlas of Wintering Birds in Britain and Ireland*, Poyser, Calton, 1986.

Laertius, Diogenes, *Lives of The Philosophers* (trans. R D Hicks), Harvard University Press, Cambridge, Massachusetts, 1925.

Lambert, Rob, 'Seabird control and fishery protection in Cornwall, 1900–1950', *British Birds*, 96:30–34, 2003.

Lampedusa, Giuseppe Tomasi di, *The Leopard*, Harvill Secker, 2010.

Landsborough Thomson, A (ed), *A New Dictionary of Birds*, Nelson, 1964.

Langley, Nick, 'The Lost and Found Bird', *World Birdwatch* 27(2):13–16, 2005.

La Touche, J D D, *A Handbook of the Birds of Eastern China*, Vol 1, Taylor and Francis, London, 1925.

Latta, S, et al, *Birds of the Dominican Republic and Haiti*, Christopher Helm, 2006.

Laubreaux, Alin, *The Happy Glutton*, Ivor Nicholson and Watson, 1931.

Laufer, Berthold, *Ostrich Egg-shell Cups in Mesopotamia and the Ostrich in Ancient and Modern Times*, Field Museum of Natural History, Chicago, 1926.

———, 'The domestication of the cormorant in China and Japan', *Field Museum of Natural History (Anthropological Series)* 18 (3):200–262, 1931.

Lawrence, Elizabeth, *Hunting the Wren: Transformation of Bird to Symbol*, University of Tennessee Press, Knoxville, 1997.

Leahy, Christopher, *The Birdwatchers' Companion*, Robert Hale, 1983.

Lee, David, and Vina, Nicasio, 'A Re-evaluation of the Status of the endangered Black-capped Petrel, *Pterodroma hasitata*, in Cuba', *Ornitologia Neotropical* 4:99–101, 1993.

Lee, Harper, *To Kill a Mockingbird*, Vintage, 2004.

Lefranc, Norbert, and Worfolk, Tim, *The Shrikes*, Pica Press, Sussex, 1997.

Legge, Sarah, *Kookaburra: King of the Bush*, CSIRO Publishing, Collingwood, 2004.

Lehmberg, Thomas, and Dinesen, Lars, 'The bright sides of stumbling over a new bird species', *Bull ABC* 1:24–5, 1994.

Leigh Fermor, Patrick, *Mani*, John Murray, 1958.

Leopold, Aldo, *A Sand County Almanac*, Ballantine, New York, 1970.

Leopold, A Starker, *The California Quail*, University of California Press, Berkeley, 1977.

Lever, Christopher, *Naturalized Birds of the World*, Poyser, 2005.

Lévi-Strauss, Claude, *Totemism* (trans. Rodney Needham), Beacon Press, Boston, 1963.

Lewis, Norman, *Naples '44*, Eland, 1983.

Lewis-Williams, David, *The Mind in the Cave*, Thames and Hudson, 2004.

Lewis-Williams, David, and Pearce, David, *Inside the Neolithic Mind*, Thames and Hudson, 2005.

Limbert, Martin, *The Uses and Curation of Birds' Egg Collections*, Peregrine Books, Leeds, 2003.

Liu, Fengwen, *Flower and Bird Painting in Ancient China*, China Intercontinental Press, Beijing, 2007.

Liu, He, and Grémillet, David, 'Great Cormorants (*Phalacrocorax carbo*) in China', *Bull OBC* in prep.

Livingstone, David, *Missionary Travels and Researches in South Africa*, Ward, Lock and Co, 1857.

Lockwood, W B, *The Oxford Dictionary of British Bird Names*, Oxford University Press, Oxford, 1993.

Long, John, *Introduced Birds of the World*, David and Charles, 1981.

Lonsdale, Steven, *Animals and the Origins of Dance*, Thames and Hudson, 1981.

Lopez, Barry, *Arctic Dreams*, Picador, 1987.

Lord, E A R, 'Notes on the Blue-faced Honeyeater', *The Emu* 50:100–101, 1950.

Love, John, *Penguins*, Colin Baxter, Grantown-on-Spey, 1997.

Lovegrove, Roger, *Silent Fields: The Long Decline of a Nation's Wildlife*, Oxford University Press, Oxford, 2007.

Lowes, John Livingston, *The Road to Xanadu: A Study in the Ways of the Imagination*, Houghton Mifflin, Boston, 1964.

Lutwack, L, *Birds in Literature*, University of Florida Press, Gainesville, 1994.

Lynch, Wayne, *Penguins of the World*, A&C Black, 2007.

Lynes, H, 'Review of the genus *Cisticola*', *Ibis*, Supplements 1 and 2, 1930.

Lynes, H, and Osmaston, B B, 'Our African Cisticola Tour', *Ibis*, Supplement 2, 1930, pages 1–673.

Maasdorp, Leslee, 'A campaign to highlight the plight of the Southern Ground Hornbill in Zimbabwe', in Kemp, A C, and Kemp, M I (eds), *The Active Management of Hornbills and their Habitats for Conservation*, CD-ROM, Proceedings of the 4th International Hornbill Conference, Mabula Game Lodge, Bela-Bela, South Africa, 2007, pages 225–30.

McCarthy, Michael, *Say Goodbye to the Cuckoo*, John Murray, 2009.

McConnell, R, *Land of Water: Explorations in the Natural History of Guyana, South America*, Book Guild, Lewes, 2000.

Macdonald, Helen, *Falcon*, Reaktion, 2006.

McEwan, Colin, Barreto, Cristiana, and Neves, Eduardo, *Unknown Amazon: Culture in Nature in Ancient Brazil*, British Museum, 2001.

McGirk, Jan, 'Royal falconers in search of bustards clash with tribesmen', *Independent*, 17 November 2003.

McKelvie, Colin, *The Book of the Woodcock*, Swan Hill Press, Shrewsbury, 1990.

Maclean, Gordon, *Robert's Birds of Southern Africa*, New Holland, 1988.

McLynn, Frank, *Stanley: The Sorcerer's Apprentice*, Constable, 1991.

McNulty, Faith, *The Whooping Crane*, Longmans, 1966.

Macpherson, Hugh, *A History of Fowling*, David Douglas, Edinburgh, 1897.

Madge, Steve, and McGowan, Phil, *Pheasants, Partridges and Grouse*, Christopher Helm, 2002.

Mails, Thomas, *The People Called Apache*, BDD Books, New York, 1993.

Majnep, Ian Saem, and Bulmer, Ralph, *Birds of My Kalam Country*, University of Auckland, Auckland, 1977.

Marchant, S, and Higgins, P J, *Handbook of Australian, New Zealand & Antarctic Birds*, Vol 1, Oxford University Press, Melbourne, 1990.

Marion, Remy, *Penguins*, Sterling, New York, 1999.

Martin, Brian, *The Glorious Grouse: A Natural and Unnatural History*, David and Charles, Newton Abbot, 1990.

Martin, Dan, 'On the Cultural Ecology of Sky Burial on the Himalayan Plateau', *East and West* (46):353–70, 1996.

Martin, Laura, *The Folklore of Birds*, Globe Pequot Press, Old Saybrook, 1993.

Marzluff, John, and Angell, Tony, *In the Company of Crows and Ravens*, Yale University Press, 2005.

Marzluff, John, and Balda, Russell, *The Pinyon Jay*, Poyser, 1992.

Masefield, John, *Wild Bird Protection and Nesting Boxes*, Taylor Brothers, Leeds, 1897.

Mason, Paul, and Allsop, Jake, *The Golden Oriole*, Poyser, 2009.

Massey Stewart, John, 'The "lily of birds": the success story of the Siberian White Crane', *Oryx* 21:6–10, 1987.

Matthews, Mitford (ed), *A Dictionary of Americanisms*, Vols 1–2, Oxford University Press, Oxford, 1951.

Matthiessen, Peter, *The Wind Birds*, Viking Press, New York, 1973.

———, *The Birds of Heaven*, Harvill Press, 2001.

———, *End of the Earth*, National Geographic, Washington, DC, 2003.

Mayhew, Henry, *London Life and the London Poor*, Vol 1, Henry Griffin, 1864.

Mead, Christopher, *The State of the Nation's Birds*, Whittet Books, Stowmarket, 2000.

Mearns, Barbara, and Mearns, Richard, *Biographies for Birdwatchers*, Academic Press, 1988.

Meiklejohn, M F M, 'The Use of Earthenware pots as nesting-holes for Starlings and House Sparrows', *British Birds* 47:95–6, 1954.

Meinertzhagen, Richard, *Nicoll's Birds of Egypt*, Vols 1–2, Hugh Rees, 1930.

———, *Pirates and Predators*, Oliver and Boyd, 1959.

Mellaart, James, *Catal Hüyük: A Neolithic Town in Anatolia*, McGraw Hill, New York, 1967.

Merrill, Linda, *The Peacock Room: A Cultural Biography*, Freer Gallery of Art, Washington, DC, 1998.

Mikkola, Heimo, 'Comparative study on general public owl knowledge in Malawi and in Eastern and Southern Africa', *Nyala* 20:25–35, 1997.

Millar, Ronald, *Kut: The Death of an Army*, Secker and Warburg, 1969.

Miller, Henry, *The Colossus of Maroussi*, Penguin, Harmondsworth, 1985.

Mitchell, Margaret, *Observations on Birds of Southeastern Brazil*, University of Toronto Press, Toronto, 1957.

Mithen, Steven, *After The Ice*, Phoenix, 2004.

Montaigne, Michel de, *The Complete Works*, Everyman, 2003.

Moore, Charles, 'Plastic Turning Vast Area of Ocean into Ecological Nightmare', *Winging It* 21(1), 2009, page 14.

Moreau, Reg, 'The British status of the Quail and some problems of its biology', *British Birds* 44:257–76, 1951.

———, *The Palaearctic-African Bird Migrations Systems*, Academic Press, 1972.

Morphy, Howard (ed), *Animals into Art*, Unwin Hyman, 1989.

Morus, R L, *Animals, Men and Myths*, Gollancz, 1953.

Mountfort, Guy, *Portrait of a Desert*, Collins, 1965.

Muigai, Francis, and Bennum, Leon, *Gikuyu Natural History*, no place or publisher, 1994.

Muir, John, *The Eight Wilderness-Discovery Books*, Diadem Books, 1992.

Mullarney, Killian, Svensson, Lars, Zetterström, Dan, and Grant, Peter, *Collins Bird Guide*, HarperCollins, 1999.

Mungure, S, 'The view of the commonmen of the conservation of birds and their habitats in Tanzania', *Proc. IV Pan-Afr. Orn. Congr.*, 1980, pages 367–72.

Murphy, Robert Cushman, *Oceanic Birds of South America*, Vols 1–2, Macmillan, New York, 1936.

Mynott, Jeremy, *Birdscapes*, Princeton University Press, Oxford, 2009.

Naoroji, Rishad, *Birds of Prey of the Indian Subcontinent*, Christopher Helm, 2006.

Nason, Anne, *Discovering Birds: An Introduction to the Birds of Nigeria*, Pisces, Newbury, 1992.

Nattrass, Ric, *Talking Wildlife*, Steve Parish Publishing, Queensland, 2004.

Negere, E, 'The effects of religious belief on conservation of birds in Ethiopia', *Proc. IV Pan-Afr. Orn. Congr.*, 1980, pages 361–5.

Nelson, Bryan, *The Atlantic Gannet*, Fenix Books, Great Yarmouth, 2002.

Newby, John, 'The Birds of the Ouadi Rimé – Ouaid Achim Faunal Reserve', *Malimbus* 1:104–5, 1979.

———, 'The slaughter of Sahelian wildlife by Arab royalty', *Oryx* 24:6–8, 1990.

Newton, Alfred, *A Dictionary of Birds*, A&C Black, 1896.

Nguyen Quang, P, Vo Quang, Y, and Voisin, J-F, *The White-nest Swiftlet and the Black-nest Swiftlet*, Boubée, Paris, 2002.

Nicholls, Charles, *Leonardo Da Vinci*, Penguin, 2005.

Nicholson, E M, *Birds and Men*, Bloomsbury, 1990.

Nice, Margaret Morse, *Studies in the Life History of the Song Sparrow*, Vols 1–2, Dover, New York, 1964.

Nielsen, John, *Condor*, Harper Perennial, New York, 2007.

Nightingale, Neil, *New Guinea: an island apart*, BBC Books, 1992.

Niles, Lawrence, et al, *Status of the Red Knot* (Calidris canutus rufa) *in the Western Hemisphere*, New Jersey Department of Environmental Protection, Trenton, 2007.

Nixon, Rob, *Dream Birds: The Strange History of the Ostrich in Fashion, Food and Fortune*, Picador, New York, 1999.

Novotny, Vojtech, *Notebooks from New Guinea*, Oxford University Press, Oxford, 2009.

Nully, Thomas, and Shane, Simon (eds), *Ratite Management, Medicine, and Surgery*, Krieger, Malabar, Florida, 1996.

O'Brien, E, 'Indian Grey Shrike (*Lanius lathora* [sic]) attacking wounded sandgrouse', *Journal, Bombay Natural History Society* 26:667, 1919.

Ogilvie, Malcolm, and Ogilvie, Carol, *Flamingos*, Sutton, Gloucester, 1986.

Ogilvie, Malcolm, and Rose, Chris, *Grebes of the World*, Bruce Coleman, Uxbridge, 2003.

O'Hanlon, Redmond, *Into the Heart of Borneo*, Salamander Press, Edinburgh, 1984.

Opie, Iona, and Opie, Peter, *The Oxford Dictionary of Nursery Rhymes*, Oxford University Press, Oxford, 1985.

Opie, Iona, and Tatem, Moira, *A Dictionary of Superstitions*, Oxford University Press, Oxford, 1989.

Orians, Gordon, *Blackbirds of the Americas*, University of Washington Press, Seattle, 1985.

Oschadleus, H D, 'New records of weavers using man-made structures for nesting', *Bull ABC* 12:31–6, 2005.

Pacheco, J F, 'Tangara – genero de uns, ainda que nome vulgar de outros!', *Tangara* 1(1):5–11, 2001.

Palmer, Ralph (ed), *Handbook of North American Birds*, Vol 5, Diurnal Raptors (Part 2), Yale University Press, 1988.

Parmelee, Alice, *All the Birds of the Bible: Their Stories, Identification and Meaning*, Lutterworth Press, 1959.

Payne, Robert, 'Field identification of the brood-parasitic whydahs *Vidua* and Cuckoo Finch *Anomalospiza imberbis*', *Bull ABC* 4:18–28, 1996.

Paz, Uzi, *The Birds of Israel*, Stephen Greene Press, Lexington, 1987.

Pearson, D L, and Beletsky, L, *The Ecotravellers' Wildlife*

Guide: *Brazil, Amazon and Pantanal*, Academic Press, San Diego, 2002.

Peat, Neville, *Kiwi: The People's Bird*, Otago University Press, Dunedin, 2006.

Pepperberg, Irene, *Alex and Me*, Collins, New York, 2008.

Perrins, C (ed), *The Encyclopedia of Birds*, Oxford University Press, Oxford, 2009.

Petersen, Aevar, 'Traditional Seabird Fowling in Iceland', in *Traditions of Seabird Fowling in the North Atlantic Region*, Island Book Trust, Lewis, 2005, pages 194–215.

Peterson, Amy, and Peterson, Townsend, 'Aztec exploitation of cloud forests: tributes of liquidambar and quetzal feathers', *Global Ecology and Biogeography Letters* 2:165–73, 1992.

Petronius, *The Satyricon* (trans. J P Sullivan), Penguin, 1986.

Pitches, Adrian, 'News and Comment', *British Birds* 102:289–90, 2009.

——, 'News and Comment', *British Birds* 102:474, 2009.

Pizzey, Graham, *A Field Guide to the Birds of Australia*, Collins, Sydney, 1980.

Pliny, *Natural History*, Books 8–11 (trans. H Rackham), Harvard University Press, Cambridge, Massachusetts, 1997.

Pollan, Michael, *The Botany of Desire*, Random House, New York, 2001.

Pollard, John, *Birds in Greek Life and Myth*, Thames and Hudson, 1977.

Polo, Marco, *The Travels* (ed Ronald Latham), Penguin, Harmondsworth, 1979.

Poole, A (ed), *The Birds of North America Online* (BNABO), Cornell Laboratory of Ornithology, Ithaca, 2002.

Porter, Joseph, *Paper Medicine Man: John Gregory Bourke and his American West*, University of Oklahoma Press, Norman, 1986.

Potts, G R, 'Urban Starling roosts in the British Isles', *Bird Study* 14:25–42, 1967.

Pratt, Douglas, Bruner, Phillip, and Berrett, Delwyn, *The Birds of Hawaii and the Tropical Pacific*, Princeton University Press, Princeton, 1987.

Preston, G, 'The Omnivorous Bulbul', *Bulletin of East African Natural History Society*, October–December, 1975, pages 112–13.

Price, Jennifer, *Flight Maps: Adventures with Nature in Modern America*, Basic Books, New York, 1999.

Pyle, R L, and Pyle, P, *The Birds of the Hawaiian Islands: Occurrence, History, Distribution, and Status*, Version 1, B.P. Bishop Museum, Honolulu, 31 December 2009; http://hbs.bishopmuseum.org/birds/rlp-monograph/

Queeny, Edgar, 'The Wandorobo and the Honeyguide', *Natural History* 61(9):392–6, 1952.

Rand, Austin, and Gilliard, Thomas, *Handbook of New Guinea Birds*, Weidenfeld and Nicolson, 1967.

Rao, Koka Mrutyumjaya, 'The Bandas and their Impact on the Population of Vultures in Guntur and Prakasam Districts', *Blackbuck* VIII(3): 60–63, 1997.

Ratcliffe, Derek, *The Peregrine Falcon*, Poyser, 1993.

Ray, John, *The Ornithology of Francis Willughby*, 1678.

Reader, John, *Man on Earth*, Perennial Library, New York, 1990.

Reardon, Mitch, 'Rainbows in Flight', *Australian Geographic*, July–September 2001, pages 86–99.

Reilly, Pauline, *The Lyrebird: A Natural History*, New South Wales University Press, Kensington, 1988.

——, *Penguins of the World*, Oxford University Press, Oxford, 1994.

Reina, Ruben, and Kensinger, Kenneth, *The Gift of Birds: Featherwork of Native South American Peoples*, University Museum of Archaeology and Anthropology, Philadelphia, 1991.

Restall, Robin, Rodner, Clamencia, and Lentino, Miguel, *Birds of Northern South America*, Vols 1–2, Christopher Helm, 2006.

Richardson, John, *A Life of Picasso*, Vol 1, Pimlico, 2009.

Ridgely, Robert, and Gwynne Jr, John, *A Guide to the Birds of Panama*, Princeton University Press, Princeton, 1989.

Ridgely, Robert, and Rivadeneira, Mercedes, 'The Worm Feeder', *Winging It* 19(3):6–7, 2007.

Ridgely, Robert, and Tudor, Guy, *The Birds of South America*, Vols 1–2, Oxford University Press, Oxford, 1989.

Riley, Michael, 'Like in "The Birds", crows flocking to Wyoming town', *San Antonio Express-News*, 19 February 2006.

Riley, Murdoch, *Maori Bird Lore*, Viking Sevenseas, Paraparaumu, New Zealand, 2001.

Roberts, Sonia, *Bird Keeping and Birdcages: A History*, David and Charles, Newton Abbot, 1972.

Roberts, Tom, *The Birds of Pakistan*, Vol 1, Oxford University Press, Oxford, 1991.

Robertson, Peter, *A Natural History of the Pheasant*, Swan Hill Press, Shrewsbury, 1997.

Robin, Libby, *The Flight of the Emu: A Hundred Years of Australian Ornithology 1901–2001*, Melbourne University Press, Carlton South, 2001.

Rose, Roger, *Symbols of Sovereignty: Feather Girdles of Tahiti and Hawai'i*, Bishop Museum, Honolulu, 1978.

Rothenberg, David, *Why Birds Sing*, Penguin, 2006.

Routh, Shelagh, and Routh, Jonathan, *Leonardo's Kitchen Note Books*, Collins, 1987.

Rowan, M K, 'The Great Shearwater Puffinus gravis at its Breeding Grounds', *Ibis* 94:97–121, 1952.

Rowland, Beryl, *Birds with Human Souls: A Guide to Bird Symbolism*, University of Tennessee Press, Knoxville, 1978.

Rowling, J K, *Harry Potter and the Chamber of Secrets*, Bloomsbury, 1999.

Rozzi, Ricardo, et al, *Multi-Ethnic Bird Guide of the Sub-Antarctic Forests of South America*, University of North Texas, Dallas, 2010.

Ryley Scott, George, *The History of Cockfighting*, Charles Skilton, 1957.

Savage, Christopher, 'Wildfowling in Northern Iran', *Wildfowl Trust Annual Report* 14:30–46, 1963.

Saville, Sav, Stephenson, Brett, and Southey, Ian, 'A possible sighting of an "extinct bird" – the New Zealand Storm-petrel', *Birding World* 16:173–5, 2003.

Sax, Boria, *Crow*, Reaktion, 2003.

Schimmel, Annemarie, *A Two-Colored Brocade: The Imagery of Persian Poetry*, The University of North Carolina Press, Chapel Hill, 1992.

Schorger, A W, *The Wild Turkey: Its History and Domestication*, University of Oklahoma Press, Norman, 1966.

——, *The Passenger Pigeon: Its Natural History and Extinction*, University of Oklahoma Press, Norman, 1955.

Schulenberg, Thomas S, Stotz, Douglas F, Lane, Daniel F, O'Neill, John P, and Parker III, Theodore, *Birds of Peru*, Christopher Helm, 2007.

Seddon, P J, et al, 'Restoration of houbara bustard populations in Saudi Arabia: developments and future directions', *Oryx* 29:136–42, 1995.

Seyffert, Oskar, *The Dictionary of Classical Mythology, Religion, Literature, and Art*, Gramercy Books, Avenel, 1995.

Sharland, Michael, *Birds of the Sun*, Angus and Robertson, 1967.

Shialis, Tassos, *BirdLife Cyprus Trapping Report Autumn 2011*, BirdLife Cyprus, 2011.

——, *BirdLife Cyprus Trapping Report Winter 2011/2012*, BirdLife Cyprus, 2012.

Shipman, Pat, *Taking Wing: Archaeopteryx and the Evolution of Bird Flight*, Phoenix, 1999.

Shirihai, Hadoram, *The Birds of Israel*, Academic Press, 1996.

——, *A Complete Guide to Antarctic Wildlife*, A&C Black, 2007.

Short, Lester, and Horne, Jennifer, *Toucans, Barbets and Honeyguides*, Oxford University Press, Oxford, 2001.

Shrubb, Michael, *The Lapwing*, Poyser, 2007.

Sibley, David, *The Sibley Guide to Birds*, Knopf, New York, 2000.

Sibley, David, Elphick, Chris, Bevier, Louis, and Patten, Michael, 'Ivory-billed Woodpecker Letters', *Birding* 39(6):11–13, 2007.

Sick, Helmut, *Birds in Brazil*, Princeton University Press, Princeton, 1993.

Siegfried, W R, 'On the nest of the Hamerkop', *Ostrich* 46:267, 1975.

Simms, Eric, *The Public Life of the Street Pigeon*, Hutchinson, 1979.

——, *British Warblers*, Collins, 1985.

Simon, André, *A Concise Encyclopedia of Gastronomy*, Penguin, Harmondsworth, 1983.

Simpson, Colin, *Adam in Plumes*, Angus and Robertson, Sydney, 1955.

Simpson, Ken, and Day, Nicolas, *Field Guide to the Birds of Australia*, Penguin, Victoria, 2004.

Sinclair, Ian, and Ryan, Peter, *Birds of Africa south of the Sahara*, Struik, Cape Town, 2003.

Skov, Henning, 'Danish White Storks in south-west England', *British Birds* 65:303–4, 1971.

Skutch, Alexander, *Hummingbird*, Crown, New York, 1973.

——, *Origins of Nature's Beauty*, University of Texas Press, Austin, 1992.

——, *Antbirds and Ovenbirds: Their Lives and Homes*, University of Texas Press, Austin, 1996.

Slifer, Dennis, *Signs of Life: Rock Art of the Upper Rio Grande*, Ancient City Press, Santa Fe, 1998.

Smith, Harry, *A Visit to Ancient Egypt: Life at Memphis and Saqqara*, Aris and Phillips, Warminster, 1974.

Smith, Malcolm, *Life with Birds*, Whittles, Dunbeath, 2011.

Smith, Page, and Daniel, Charles, *The Chicken Book*, North Point Press, San Francisco, 1982.

Smith, William, *The Oxford Dictionary of English Proverbs*, Oxford University Press, Oxford, 1980.

Smythies, B E, *The Birds of Burma*, Oliver and Boyd, Edinburgh, 1953.

——, *The Birds of Borneo*, Oliver and Boyd, Edinburgh, 1960.

Snow, David, *The Cotingas*, British Museum (Natural History), 1982.

Snyder, Noel, and Snyder, Helen, *The California Condor*, Academic Press, 2000.

Soustelle, Jacques, *The Daily Life of the Aztecs*, Weidenfeld and Nicolson, 1961.

Stanley, Edward, *A Familiar History of Birds*, John Parker, 1851.

Steadman, David, *Extinction & Biogeography of Tropical Pacific Birds*, University of Chicago Press, Chicago, 2006.

Steel, Tom, *The Life and Death of St Kilda*, HarperCollins, 1994.

Stefferud, Alfred (ed), *Birds in Our Lives*, The US Department of the Interior, Washington, DC, 1966.

Stein, Sarah, *Plumes: Ostrich Feathers, Jews and a Lost World of Global Commerce*, Yale University Press, 2008.

Steinbeck, John, *The Grapes of Wrath*, Everyman, 1993.

——, *The Log from the Sea of Cortez*, Penguin, 2000.

Stevenson, Henry, *The Birds of Norfolk*, Vol 2, John Van Voorst and Gurney and Jackson, 1870.

Stevenson, Terry, and Fanshawe, John, *Field Guide to the Birds of East Africa*, Poyser, 2002.

Stewart, Hilary, *Looking at Indian Art of the Northwest Coast*, University of Washington Press, Seattle, 1979.

Steyn, Peter, *Breeding Birds of Southern Africa*, Fernwood Press, Vlaeberg, 1996.

Stokes Donald, and Stokes, Lilian, *The Stokes Field Guide to the Birds of North America*, Little Brown, New York, 2010.

Stonor, C R, 'Fishing with the Indian Darter (*Anhinga melanogaster*) in Assam', *Journal, Bombay Natural History Society* 47:746–7, 1948.

Strange, Ian, *A Field Guide to the Wildlife of the Falkland Islands and South Georgia*, HarperCollins, 1992.

Strathern, Andrew, and Strathern, Marilyn, *Self-Decoration in Mount Hagen*, Duckworth, 1971.

Striffler, Stephen, *Chicken: The Dangerous Transformation of America's Favourite Food*, Yale University Press, 2005.

Strong, Roy, *Feast: A History of Grand Eating*, Jonathan Cape, 2002.

Stuart Baker, E C, 'The Game Birds of India, Burma and Ceylon, Part IX', *Journal, Bombay Natural History Society* 22:1–12, 1913a.

——, 'The Game Birds of India, Burma and Ceylon, Part X', *Journal, Bombay Natural History Society* 22:219–29, 1913b.

Summers-Smith, Denis, *The Sparrows*, Poyser, Calton, 1988.

——, *On Sparrows and Man*, self-published, Guisborough, 2005.

Sun, Bingshan, *Chinese Paper-Cuts*, China International Press, Beijing, 2007.

Sunquist, F, Sunquist, M, and Beletsky, L, *Florida: The Ecotravellers' Wildlife Guide*, Academic Press, 2002.

Sutton, Clay, and Sutton, Pat, *Birds and Birding at Cape May*, Stackpole Books, Mechanicsburg, 2006.

Swainson, Charles, *The Folklore and Provincial Names of British Birds*, Llanerch Publishers, Felinfach, 1998.

Sweeney, William, 'My Ivory-bill Encounter', *Birding* 39(2):68–71, 2007.

Tait, William, *The Birds of Portugal*, Witherby, London, 1924.

Tanner, James T, *The Ivory-billed Woodpecker*, Dover, Minnesota, 2003.

Tapper, Stephen, *Game Heritage: An Ecological Review from Shooting and Gamekeeping Records*, Game Conservancy Trust, Fordingbridge, 1992.

———— (ed), *A Question of Balance*, Game Conservancy Trust, Fordingbridge, 1999.

Taylor, Barry, and van Perlo, Ber, *Rails*, Pica Press, Sussex, 1998.

Taylor, Moss, Seago, Michael, Allard, Peter, and Dorling, Don, *The Birds of Norfolk*, Pica Press, Sussex, 1999.

Tegetmeier, W B, *Pheasants: Their Natural History and Practical Management*, Horace Cox, 1897.

Thomas, Hugh, *The Conquest of Mexico*, Hutchinson, 1993.

Thomas, Keith, *Man and the Natural World*, Allen Lane, 1983.

Thomas, Nicholas, *Oceanic Art*, Thames and Hudson, 1995.

————, *Discoveries: The Voyages of Captain Cook*, Allen Lane, 2004.

Thompson, Della (ed), *The Oxford Compact English Dictionary*, Oxford University Press, Oxford, 1996.

Thompson, Peter, *A Natural History of the Pheasant*, Swan Hill Press, Shrewsbury, 1997.

Thomsen, Kai-Michael, and Höder, Hermann, 'The Sixth International White Stork Census, 2004–2005', in *Waterbirds around the World*, Scottish Natural Heritage, Edinburgh, 2006, pages 403–5.

Thoreau, Henry, *Thoreau on Birds* (ed Francis Allen), Beacon Press, Boston, 1993.

Ticehurst, Claud, *The Birds of Suffolk*, Gurney and Jackson, 1932.

Ticehurst, Norman, *The Mute Swan in England*, Cleaver-Hulme, 1957.

Tickell, W L N, *Albatrosses*, Pica Press, Mountfield, 2000.

Tidemann, Sonia, and Gosler, Andrew, *Ethno-ornithology: Birds, Indigenous Peoples, Culture and Society*, Earthscan, 2010.

Todd, Kim, *Tinkering with Eden: A Natural History of Exotics in America*, Norton, New York, 2001.

Torrey, Bradford, *The Clerk of the Woods*, Houghton Mifflin, New York, 1903.

Toynbee, Jocelyn, *Animals in Roman Life and Art*, Thames and Hudson, 1973.

Treuenfels, Carl A von, *The Magic of Cranes*, Abrams, New York, 2007.

Tucker, Graham, and Heath, Melanie, *Birds in Europe: Their Conservation Status*, BirdLife International, Cambridge, 1994.

Turbott, E G (ed), *Buller's Birds of New Zealand*, Macdonald, 1967.

Turner, Angela, *The Barn Swallow*, Poyser, 2006.

Turner, William, *Turner on Birds* (ed A H Evans), Cambridge University Press, Cambridge, 1903.

Tweti, Mira, *Of Parrots and People*, Viking, New York, 2008.

Tyler, Hamilton, *Pueblo Birds and Myths*, University of Oklahoma Press, Norman, 1979.

Tyson, Peter, *The Eighth Continent: Life, Death and Discovery in the Lost World of Madagascar*, HarperCollins, New York, 2000.

Ucko, Peter, and Dimbleby, G W, *The Domestication and Exploitation of Plants and Animals*, Duckworth, 1969.

Underhill, D, and Sunderland, S K, *Australia's Dangerous Creatures*, Reader's Digest, Sydney, 1987.

van der Post, Laurens, *The Lost World of the Kalahari*, Odhams, Watford, 1958.

————, *The Heart of the Hunter*, Hogarth Press, 1961.

Van Nieuwenhuyse, Dries, Génot, Jean-Claude, and

Johnson, David, *The Little Owl*, Cambridge University Press, Cambridge, 2008.

van Someren, V D, *A Bird Watcher in Kenya*, Oliver and Boyd, Edinburgh, 1958.

Varro, M T, *Varro on Farming* (trans. Lloyd Storr-Best), G Bell and Sons, 1912.

Vaughan, Richard, and Vaughan, Nancy, *The Stone Curlew*, Isabelline Books, Falmouth, 2005.

Verdi, Richard, *The Parrot in Art*, Scala, 2007.

Virgil, *The Eclogues, The Georgics* (trans. C Day Lewis), Oxford University Press, Oxford, 1983.

Voous, Karel, *Atlas of European Birds*, Nelson, London, 1960.

Walker, Adrian, *The Encylopedia of Falconry*, Swan Hill Press, Shrewsbury, 1999.

Wallace, Alfred Russel, *The Malay Archipelago*, John Beaufoy, Oxford, 2009.

Walmsley, Andrew, 'Kea Capers', *BBC Wildlife*, January 2010.

Wamiti, W, and Muigai, F, 'Birds' Inspiration in the Proverbs and Sayings of the Agikuyu People of Kenya', in Harebottle, D M, Craig, A J F K, Anderson, M D, Rakotomanana, H, and Muchai, M (eds), *Proceedings of the 12th Pan-African Ornithological Congress*, 2008, Animal Demography Unit, Cape Town, 2009, pages xx–xxx.

Wang, Nan, 'Cultural conservation of pheasants in Daocheng County, Sichuan province, China', *World Pheasant Association Annual Review*, 2006/7.

Warren, Louis, *The Hunter's Game: Poachers and Conservationists in Twentieth Century America*, Yale University Press, 1999.

Waterton, Charles, *Wanderings in South America*, Fellowes, 1828.

Watson, Adam, and Moss, Robert, *The Grouse*, HarperCollins, 2008.

Waylen, Kerry, 'Drumsticks, dancing and divinity: the value of Galliformes to humankind', *World Pheasant Association Annual Review*, 2006/7.

Weaver, Mary Anne, 'Hunting With The Sheikhs', *New Yorker*, 14 December 1992.

Weiner, Jonathan, *The Beak of the Finch: Evolution in Real Time*, Jonathan Cape, 1994.

Werness, Hope (ed), *The Continuum Encyclopedia of Animal Symbolism in Art*, Continuum, New York, 2004.

Wernham, Chris, Toms, Mike, Marchant, John, Clark, Jacquie, Siriwardena, Gavin, and Baillie, Stephen (eds), *The Migration Atlas*, Poyser, 2002.

Wheeler, Sara, *Cherry: A Life of Apsley Cherry-Garrard*, Jonathan Cape, 2001.

Wheye, Darryl, and Kennedy, Donald, *Humans, Nature, and Birds*, Yale University Press, 2008.

Whinnom, Keith, *A Glossary of Spanish Bird-Names*, Tamesis Books, 1966.

Whistler, Hugh, *Popular Handbook of Indian Birds* (ed Norman Kinnear), Gurney and Jackson, 1949.

White, Gilbert, *The Natural History of Selborne* (ed R Kearton), Arrowsmith, 1924.

————, *Gilbert White's Journals* (ed Walter Johnson), David and Charles, Newton Abbot, 1970.

Wienholt, Michael, 'Ivory-billed Woodpecker Letters', *Birding* 39(4):10–11, 2007.

Wilkes, G, *A Dictionary of Australian Colloquialisms*, Sydney University Press, Sydney, 1978.

Williams, Jeni, *Interpreting Nightingales*, Sheffield Academic Press, Sheffield, 1997.

Williams, Tony, *The Penguins*, Oxford University Press, Oxford, 1995.

Williamson, Henry, *The Story of a Norfolk Farm*, Clive Holloway Books, 1986.

Williamson, Kenneth, 'Birds in Faeroe Folk-Lore', *The North Western Naturalist* 21:7–19, 155–66, 1946.

———, *The Atlantic Islands*, Routledge and Kegan Paul, 1948.

———, 'The Antiquity of the Calf of Man Manx Shearwater Colony', *Bird Study* 20:310, 1973.

Wilson, C A, *Food and Drink in Britain from the Stone Age to Recent Times*, Constable, 1991.

Wilson, Edward O, *The Diversity of Life*, Belknapp Press, Cambridge, Massachusetts, 1992.

———, *The Future of Life*, Abacus, 2003.

Wilson, Emily, 'Sparrows and Scrubbers', *New Republic* (online), 22 December 2005; http://www.powells.com/review/2005_12_22.html

Witherby, Harry, 'Obituary: Admiral Hubert Lynes', *British Birds* 36:156–8, 1943.

Witherby, H, Jourdain, F C R, Ticehurst, N, and Tucker, B, *The Handbook of British Birds*, Vols 1–5, Witherby, 1938–41.

Wolfe, Richard, *Moa*, Penguin, 2003.

Wood, Casey, and Fyfe, Marjorie (eds), *The Art of Falconry of Frederick II of Hohenstaufen*, Charles Branford, Boston, Massachusetts, 1955.

Woods, Robin, *Guide to Birds of the Falkland Islands*, Anthony Nelson, Oswestry, 1988.

Wordsworth, Dora, *A Journal of a Few Months' Residence in Portugal and Glimpses of the South of Spain*, Vol 2, Edward Moxon, 1847.

Wright, Judith, *Birds*, National Library of Australia, Canberra, 2003.

Wright, Rick, 'Taking it Personal: Where the Ivory-bill Survives', *Birding* 39(2):48–52, 2007.

Xin, Yang, Barnhart, Richard, Chongzheng, Nie, Cahill, James, Shaojun, Lang, and Hung, Wu, *Three Thousand Years of Chinese Painting*, Yale University Press, 1997.

Yalden, D W, and Albarella, U, *The History of British Birds*, Oxford University Press, Oxford, 2009.

Yarrell, William, *A History of British Birds*, Vols 1–3, John Van Voorst, 1845.

Yeatman, Marwood, *The Last Food of England*, Ebury, 2007.

Yésou, P, and Clergeau, P, 'Sacred Ibis: a new invasive species in Europe', *Birding World* 18:517–26, 2005.

Yfantis, Stavros, 'The extinction of white storks in southern Greece: an unknown aspect of Greek–Turkish relations' (trans. Dimitris Vavylis), *Oikotopia* 14, May–June 1999.

Zeuner, Frederick, *A History of Domesticated Animals*, Hutchinson, 1963.

Zino, Frank, 'A Short History of the Shearwater Hunt on The Great Salvage and Recent Developments on the Island', *Bocagiana* 84:1–9, 1985.

———, 'The Madeiran Freira Conservation Project', *World Birdwatch*, June 1991.

NOTES

Abbreviations
The numbered references listed in these notes comprise the author, year and page number(s) of the publication. The full bibliographic reference for each title is presented in the Select Bibliography. Several extensively used books and journals have been abbreviated to the following:

Aristotle, *HoA* – Aristotle, *History of Animals* in *The Complete Works of Aristotle*, Vol 1 (ed Jonathan Barnes), Princeton University Press, Chichester, 1995.

Bannerman – Bannerman, David, *Birds of the British Isles*, Vols 1–12, Oliver and Boyd, Edinburgh, 1953–63.

Bent – Bent, Arthur, *Life Histories of North American Birds*, Dover, New York, 1961–5. A 26-volume work but the volumes are not numbered sequentially, many were published in the same year and there have been many editions and reprints. Here individual volumes are listed (without date) using only the first bird family featured in the main title, with a volume number if that specific title comprised more than a single volume.

BoA – Brown, L H, Fry, H, Keith, S, Newman, E K and Urban, E K, *The Birds of Africa*, Vols 1–7, Academic Press, Cambridge, 1982–2004.

BWP – Cramp, S, Simmons, K and Perrins, C (eds), *Handbook of the Birds of Europe, the Middle East and North Africa*, Vols 1–9, Oxford University Press, Oxford, 1977–95.

COED – *The Compact Edition of the Oxford English Dictionary*, Oxford University Press, Oxford, 1971.

HBW – del Hoyo, Josep, Elliott, Andrew and Sargatal, Jorgi (eds), *Handbook of the Birds of the World*, Vols 1–15, Lynx, Barcelona, 1992–2012.

SOED – Onions, C T (ed), *The Shorter Oxford English Dictionary*, Oxford University Press, Oxford, 1992.

TBW – BirdLife International, *Threatened Birds of the World*, Lynx and BirdLife International, Barcelona and Cambridge, UK, 2000.

Introduction
1 Arnott, 2007, page 189.
2 Lévi-Strauss, 1963, page 89.
3 Shipman, 1999, page 275.
4 Fiona Clark, Hampshire, UK.
5 Anthony Ward, Durham, UK.
6 Wilson, 1992, pages 132–40.

Tinamous *Tinamidae*
1 *HBW* 1:122; Gotch, 1995, page 182.
2 Hilty and Brown, 1986, page 42.
3 Restall, Rodner and Lentino, 2006, Vol 1, page 27.
4 Campbell and Lack, 1985, page 595.
5 *HBW* 1:113.
6 Sick, 1993, page 100.
7 Sick, 1993, page 100.
8 *HBW* 1:125.

Ostriches *Struthionidae*
1 Richard Knocker, Arusha, Tanzania.
2 Kassagam, 1997, page 12.
3 Laufer, 1926, page 3.
4 *BoA* 1:32.
5 Parmelee, 1959, page 208.
6 Amir Balaban, Jerusalem, Israel.

7 *BoA* 1:32.
8 Negere, 1980, page 364.
9 John Fanshawe, Cornwall, UK.
10 Aristotle, *Parts of Animals*, Bk IV, 697.
11 Zeuner, 1963, pages 476–7.
12 Laufer, 1926, page 27.
13 Nixon, 1999, page 12.
14 Houlihan, 1986, pages 2–3.
15 Birkhead, 2008, page 313.
16 Kassagam, 1997, page 11.
17 Laufer, 1926, pages 36–7.
18 Daudi Peterson, Arusha, Tanzania.
19 Richard Knocker, Arusha, Tanzania.
20 Doughty, 1975, page 1.
21 Parmelee, 1959, page 208.
22 Nixon, 1999, page 59.
23 Nixon, 1999, page 96.
24 Nixon, 1999, pages 86–8; Laufer, 1926, page 44.
25 Nixon, 1999, page 74.
26 Laufer, 1926, page 44.

Rheas *Rheidae*
1 Hudson, 1920, Vol 2, page 230.
2 Gabriel Swinton Stott, Boliqueime, Portugal.
3 Haupt, 2006, pages 88–110.
4 Sick, 1993, page 107; Perrins, 2009, page 38.
5 *TBW*, page 630.
6 Sick, 1993, page 109.
7 Davies, 2002, page 61.
8 David Tipling, Norfolk, UK.
9 Mark Pearman, Buenos Aires, Argentina.

Cassowaries *Casuariidae*
1 Sue Gregory, Queensland, Australia.
2 Joseph Ando, Mount Hagen, Papua New Guinea.
3 *TBW*, page 32.
4 Sue Gregory, Kuranda, Australia.
5 Blackwood, 1978, page 7.
6 Blackwood, 1978, pages 7, 82–3.
7 Sue Gregory, Kuranda, Australia.
8 Blackwood, 1978, pages 128, 132.
9 Flannery, 1998, page 64.
10 Sue Gregory, Kuranda, Australia.
11 Campbell and Lack, 1985, page 82.
12 Underhill and Sunderland, 1987, page 14.
13 Nightingale, 1992, page 58.
14 Chisholm, 1956, page 205.
15 Underhill and Sunderland, 1987, page 15.
16 Phil Gregory, Kuranda, Australia.

Emu *Dromaiidae*
1 Marchant and Higgins, 1990, pages 47–8.
2 *COED*, page 852; Jobling, 2010, page 145.
3 Robin, 2001, page 16.
4 Burenhult, 2003, pages 158–9, 163, 423.
5 Dixon, 1916, pages 288–300.
6 Eastman, 1969, page 44.
7 Nully and Shane, 1996, page 41.
8 Davies, 2002, page 58.
9 Stanley, 1851, page 322.
10 Robin, 2001, page 159.
11 Johnson, 2006, pages 147–57.
12 Robin, 2001, pages 338–9.
13 Chisholm, 1956, page 231.
14 http://www.aea-emu.org

Elephant Birds *Aepyornithidae*
1 Dawkins, 2004, pages 235–45.
2 Campbell and Lack, 1985, page 178.
3 Ingersoll, 1923, page 202.

4 Polo, 1979, page 300.
5 Fuller, 1987, page 18.
6 Fedducia, 1996, page 284.

Moas *Dinornithidae*
1 Wolfe, 2003, page 181.
2 Wolfe, 2003, page 178.
3 Fuller, 1987, pages 22–3.
4 http://www.stuff.co.nz/4347914a10.html
5 Dawkins, 2004, pages 235–45.
6 Bell, 27 September 1998.

Kiwis *Apterygidae*
1 Attenborough, 2002, page 361.
2 Attenborough, 2002, pages 361–2.
3 Peat, 2006, page 53.
4 Peat, 2006, page 52.
5 Narena Olliver, Wairarapa, New Zealand.
6 Hokimate Harwood, Wellington, New Zealand.
7 Peat, 2006, pages 146–7.
8 http://www.adb.online.anu.edu.au/biogs
9 http://kiwi-fruit.info/kiwi-fruit
10 Peat, 2006, page 131.
11 Riley, 2001, page 138.
12 http://collections.tepapa.govt.nz
13 *HBW* 1:108.
14 Hokimate Harwood, Wellington, New Zealand.

Megapodes *Megapodiidae*
1 *TBW*, pages 124–7.
2 Collar et al, 2008, page 122.
3 *HBW* 2:287.
4 *HBW* 2:281.
5 Dekker, 1988, page 13.
6 *HBW* 2:298.
7 Greenslade, 2010, pages 34–7.
8 Diamond, 1987, pages 84–5.
9 *TBW*, page 124.
10 Paul Jepson, Oxford, UK.
11 Sue Gregory, Kuranda, Australia.
12 *HBW* 2:284–5.

Chachalacas, Curassows and Guans *Cracidae*
1 Restall, Rodner and Lentino, 2006, Vol 1, page 42.
2 Gotch, 1995, page 241.
3 Hilty and Brown, 1986, page 122; Bent, Gallinaceous Birds, page 351.
4 Sick, 1993, pages 190, 196.
5 Rob Cahill, Alta Verapaz, Guatemala.
6 James Lowen, Buenos Aires, Argentina.
7 Barry Walker, Cuzco, Peru.
8 Restall, Rodner and Lentino, 2006, Vol 1, page 42.
9 Sick, 1993, page 195.
10 *TBW*, page 131.
11 Elizabeth Cabrera, Ypacaraí, Paraguay.
12 Bates, 1969, page 232.
13 Sick, 1993, page 195.
14 Sick, 1993, page 196.
15 Delacour and Amadon, 1973, page 109.
16 Raúl Arias de Para, El Valle, Panama.
17 Bent, Gallinaceous Birds, page 347; Sick, 1993, page 196.
18 *TBW*, page 132.

Guineafowl *Numididae*
1 Seyffert, 1995, page 387.

2 Graves, 1996, pages 246–50.
3 Houlihan, 1986, pages 82–3; Betrò, 1996, page 105.
4 Belshaw, 1985, page 9.
5 COED, page 3435.
6 Harting, 1978, pages 176–9.
7 Rosalind Ford, Newfoundland, Canada.
8 http://www.lymediseasepa.com/GuineaHens.htm
9 Godfrey, 1941, page 41.
10 Belshaw, 1985, page 11.
11 Malcolm Green, Newcastle, UK.

New World Quails *Odontophoridae*
1 Tyler, 1979, page 85.
2 Lever, 2005, pages 27–32.
3 Bent, Gallinaceous Birds, page 27.
4 Alan Bartels, Nebraska, USA.
5 Bent, Gallinaceous Birds, page 20.
6 Bonta, 2003, page 141.
7 Bent, Gallinaceous Birds, page 26.
8 Rick Halcott, Nebraska, USA.
9 Stefferud, 1966, page 125.
10 http://bna.birds.cornell.edu/bna/species/397
11 Muir, 1992, page 548.
12 Bent, Gallinaceous Birds, page 68.
13 Martin, 1993, page 153.
14 Bella Bigsby, California, USA.
15 Bella Bigsby, California, USA.

Pheasants, Fowl and Allies *Phasianidae*
1 Forbush, 1955, page 155.
2 Harting, 1978, page 179; Burak Sanyürek, Kalkan, Turkey.
3 Schorger, 1966, page 14.
4 Schorger, 1966, pages 354–5.
5 Frank Portman, California, USA.
6 SOED, page 2631.
7 Haynes, 1987, page 5.
8 Green, 1993, page 58.
9 http://www.webexhibits.org/80/daylightsaving/franklin2.html
10 Frank Portman, California, USA.
11 David Cobham, Norfolk, UK.
12 Bewick, 1826, page 326.
13 Katz, 2003, page 120.
14 Isabelle Charmantier, Montpellier, France.
15 Peter Herkenrath, Cambridge, UK.
16 Dimitris Vavylis, Trikala, Greece.
17 Angela Mancino, Milan, Italy.
18 Svetlana Gretton, Suffolk, UK.
19 Vesna Goldsworthy, London, UK.
20 Lennart Nilsson, Lund, Sweden.
21 Schorger, 1966, pages 354–68.
22 Kiple and Ornelas, 2000, page 581.
23 Tyler, 1979, pages 85–105.
24 Schorger, 1966, pages 10–12.
25 Matthews, 1951, page 1721.
26 Bella Bigsby, California, USA.
27 B Widener, Georgia, USA.
28 Schorger, 1966, page 365.
29 Schorger, 1966, page 374.
30 Krech, 2009, page 17.
31 Bent, Gallinaceous Birds, page 327.
32 Forbush, 1955, page 155.
33 Kiple and Ornelas, 2000, page 579.
34 Dohner, 2001, page 443.
35 Rick Halcott, Nebraska, USA.
36 http://advocacy.britannica.com/blog/advocacy/2010/11/consider-the-turkey-3/
37 Leopold, 1970, page 146.
38 Martin, 1990, page 71.
39 Bent, Gallinaceous Birds, page 159.
40 Watson and Moss, 2008, pages 33, 78.
41 TBW, pages 135–6.

42 Johnsgard, 2002, page 40.
43 TBW, page 639.
44 Jones, 2006, page 173.
45 Tapper, 1992, page 100; Mead, 2000, page 162.
46 Martin, 1990, page 71.
47 Forrester and Andrews, 2007, page 294.
48 Johnsgard, 1983, pages 369–75; however, I have ignored the author's British figure for Willow Ptarmigan (Red Grouse) of 2.5 million birds and used the much lower, authoritative figure of Stephen Tapper, which is 500,000 at the end of the 1980s. Tapper, 1992, page 100.
49 http://bna.birds.cornell.edu/bna/species/051 and http://bna.birds.cornell.edu/bna/species/369
50 HBW 2:396.
51 Margaret Atwood, Toronto, Canada.
52 Jon Farrar, Nebraska, USA.
53 Alan Bartels, Nebraska, USA.
54 Ray Collier, Highland, UK.
55 Ray Collier, Highland, UK.
56 Lockwood, 1993, page 75.
57 COED, pages 1216–20.
58 SOED, page 894.
59 http://www.ceantar.org/Dicts/MB2/mb38.html; Lockwood, 1993, page 121.
60 COED, pages 2348, 3265.
61 Forbush, 1955, page 135.
62 Rosalind Ford, Ontario, Canada.
63 Bent, Gallinaceous Birds, page 126.
64 Bent, Gallinaceous Birds, page 140.
65 COED, pages 1561, 1601.
66 Bent, Gallinaceous Birds, page 291.
67 Armstrong, 1942, page 208.
68 Stefferud, 1966, page 469.
69 Leopold, 1970, page 13.
70 Johnsgard, 1983, page 336.
71 Rick Wright, Arizona, USA.
72 Alan Bartels, Nebraska, USA.
73 Bent, Gallinaceous Birds, page 292; Jones, 2006, page 172.
74 http://www.wheatoncollege.edu/flett/george_flett.html
75 Armstrong, 1975, page 75.
76 Lonsdale, 1981, page 72.
77 Witherby et al, 1941, Vol 5, page 210.
78 Stefferud, 1966, page 351.
79 Baicich, 2009, pages 66–7; Rick Wright, Arizona, USA.
80 Lever, 2005, pages 27–66; Pratt, Bruner and Berrett, 1987, pages 116–23.
81 Tapper, 1999, page 145.
82 Opie, 1985, pages 122–6; Keyte and Parrott, 1993, page 229.
83 Margaret Samuel, Glamorgan, UK; Howe, 1973, page 60.
84 Dimitris Vavylis, Trikala, Greece; Ali and Ripley, 1983, page 99; Arnott, 2007, page 82.
85 Ali and Ripley, 1983, page 99.
86 Roberts, 1991, page 230.
87 Mynott, 2009, page 83.
88 Ali and Ripley, 1983, page 100.
89 Stephen Spawls, Norfolk, UK.
90 Nigel Winser, Oxfordshire, UK.
91 Lehmberg and Dinesen, 1994, pages 24–5.
92 Davidson, 2006, page 641.
93 Houlihan, 1986, page 76.
94 Pliny, Bk X, XXXIII.
95 Pollard, 1977, page 62.
96 Gladstone, 1922, page 59.
97 Macpherson, 1897, page 363.
98 Beeton, 1968, page 530.
99 Baha El Din and Salama, 1991, pages 5–17.
100 Meinertzhagen, 1930, page 80.
101 Moreau, 1951, pages 265–6.

102 Hagemeijer and Blair, 1997, page 215.
103 Casement, 1966, pages 461–91.
104 Meinertzhagen, 1930, page 649.
105 Greenoak, 1997, page 74.
106 Ray, 1678, page 170.
107 Harting, 1978, page 218.
108 COED, page 2381.
109 Laertius, Bk I, 51 (trans. Jeremy Mynott).
110 Robertson, 1997, page 98.
111 Beebe, 1990, Vol 4, page 31.
112 Elphick, 2004, page 239.
113 Finn, 1915, page 213; Ananda Banerjee, Delhi, India.
114 Beebe, 1994, page 184.
115 Liu, 2007, page 64.
116 Gibbon, 1990, Vol 8, page 246.
117 TBW, pages 145–57, 640–41.
118 Madge and McGowan, 2002, page 326.
119 Beebe, 1990, Vol 2, page 134.
120 Beebe, 1990, Vol 3, page 16.
121 Beebe, 1990, Vol 2, page 181.
122 HBW 2:466.
123 Polo, 1979, page 105.
124 Beebe, 1990, Vol 3, page 15.
125 Roberts, 1991, page 241; Waylen, 2006/7, page 19.
126 Yub Raj Basnet, Kathmandu, Nepal.
127 Beebe, 1990, Vol 3, page 197.
128 Beebe, 1990, Vol 3, pages 176–80.
129 Darwin, 1901, pages 606–10.
130 Beebe, 1990, Vol 4, pages 124–5.
131 Beebe, 1990, Vol 1, page 134; Doughty, 1975, page 143.
132 Wang, 2006/7, page 23.
133 Lu Xin, Hubei, China.
134 Gavin Maxwell, Somerset, UK.
135 Lever, 2005, pages 50–63.
136 Arnott, 2007, page 186.
137 Harting, 1978, page 212.
138 Harrison, 1988, page 192.
139 Hudson, 1951a, page 87.
140 Tapper, 1992, page vii.
141 Tapper, 1992, page 7.
142 Lever, 2005, page 54.
143 Anon, May–June 2008.
144 Tapper, 1992, page 151.
145 HBW 2:468.
146 Stefferud, 1966, page 348.
147 Lever, 2005, pages 54–6.
148 Stefferud, 1966, page 125.
149 Allen, 1956, page 205.
150 Allen, 1956, page 16.
151 Robertson, 1997, page 124.
152 Chancellor, 17 April 2009.
153 Jon Farrar, Nebraska, USA.
154 Alan Bartels, Nebraska, USA.
155 Casey Pheiffer, Washington, DC, USA.
156 Beebe, 1990, Vol 1, page xlviii.
157 Katz, 2003, page 120.
158 http://www.fao.org/docrep/010/ah876e/ah876e08
159 Ellis, 2007, page 40.
160 Ellis, 2007, pages 42–5.
161 Ellis, 2007, page 38.
162 Striffler, 2005, page 32.
163 Ellis, 2007, page 26.
164 Striffler, 2005, page 2.
165 Ellis, 2007, page 85.
166 http://www.dailymail.co.uk/health/article-301419/Fat-Britain-Tackling-obesity-epidemic.html
167 http://www.nytimes.com/2006/01/25/international/europe/25obese.html
168 Striffler, 2005, page 17.
169 Ellis, 2007, page 85.

170 Striffler, 2005, page 30.
171 Houlihan, 1986, pages 80–81.
172 Parmelee, 1959, pages 122–3; Pollard, 1977, page 88.
173 Arnott, 2007, page 10.
174 http://www.nytimes.com/2007/06/05/science/05chic
175 Ball, 1933, pages 3–22.
176 Pliny, Bk X, XXIV.
177 Brown, 1936, page 134.
178 Stephen Spawls, Norfolk, UK.
179 Gattiker and Gattiker, 1989, page 416.
180 Smith and Daniel, 1982, page 16.
181 Yossi Leshem, Tel Aviv, Israel.
182 Aldrovandi, 1963, page 4.
183 Amir Balaban, Jerusalem, Israel.
184 Stephen Spawls, Norfolk, UK.
185 HBW 2:466.
186 Sun, 2007, page 20.
187 Thoreau, 1993, page 489.
188 Aelian, Bk 3, 31.
189 Rowling, 1999, pages 215–16.
190 HBW 2:466; Gattiker and Gattiker, 1989, page 447.
191 Thoreau, 1993, pages 490–91.
192 Miller, 1985, pages 247–8.
193 Leigh Fermor, 1958, pages 125–6.
194 Alan Bartels, Nebraska, USA; Rick Wright and Jennie Duberstein, Arizona, USA; Andrew Dobson, Warwick, Bermuda; Olga Hazard, Atitlán, Guatemala; Mark Bonta, Mississippi, USA; Raúl Arias de Para, El Valle, Panama; Barry Walker, Cuzco, Peru; Bennett Hennessey, Santa Cruz, Bolivia; James Lowen, Buenos Aires, Argentina.
195 Malcolm Green, Northumberland, UK; James Wolstencroft, Arusha, Tanzania; Jane Gaithuma, Nairobi, Kenya; Abdi Jama, Djibouti City, Djibouti; Martin Walsh, Cambridge, UK.
196 Lucy Pearce, Cork, Ireland; Peter Herkenrath, Cambridge, UK; Arne Ohlsson, Lund, Sweden; Jari Peltomäki, Liminka, Finland; Leszek Wysocki, Norfolk, UK, Angela Mancino, Milan, Italy; John J Borg, Valletta, Malta; Dragan Simic, Belgrade, Serbia; Boris Barov, Sofia, Bulgaria; Nada Tosheva, Sofia, Bulgaria; Svetlana Gretton, Suffolk, UK; Dimitris Vavylis, Trikala, Greece; Amir Balaban, Jerusalem, Israel; Elsadig Bashir, Doha, Qatar; Nariman Nouri, Tehran, Iran; Greg Pringle, Beijing, China; Jonathan Eames, Hanoi, Vietnam; Harry Boedi Mranata, Jakarta, Indonesia; John Koi, Morobe Province, Papua New Guinea; Michael Kiu, New Britain, Papua New Guinea; Gerhard Veit, New South Wales, Australia; Hokimate Harwood, Wellington, New Zealand.
197 Arnott, 2007, pages 10–11; Ryley Scott, 1957, page 57.
198 Ryley Scott, 1957, page 20.
199 Janet Robbins, California, USA.
200 Ryley Scott, 1957, page 112.
201 Ryley Scott, 1957, page 105.
202 Ryley Scott, 1957, page 101.
203 David Tipling, Norfolk, UK.
204 Janet Robbins, California, USA.
205 David Tipling, Norfolk, UK.
206 COED, page 571.
207 Ryley Scott, 1957, page 42.
208 Ryley Scott, 1957, pages 40–50.
209 Jamandores, 2001, pages 42–3.
210 Crabbe, 1908, pages 53–4.
211 Ryley Scott, 1957, pages 165–6.
212 Ali and Ripley, 1983, page 126.
213 COED, page 2102.

214 Jackson, 2006, page 40.
215 http://www.time.com/time/magazine/article/0,9171,770931,00.html
216 Chapin, 1938, pages 101–9.
217 David Tipling, Norfolk, UK.
218 Suvash Barman, Dhaka, Bangladesh.
219 Ananda Banerjee, Delhi, India.
220 Roberts, 1991, page 247.
221 http://www.christies.com/LotFinder/lot_details.aspx?intObjectID=5157017
222 Armstrong, 1975, page 140; Ingersoll, 1923, page 144.
223 Armstrong, 1975, page 140.
224 Arnott, 2007, pages 235–6.
225 Davidson, 2006, page 590.
226 Pliny, Bk X, XXIII; Arnott, 2007, page 236.
227 Gibbon, 1990, Vol 1, page 94.
228 Strong, 2002, page 37.
229 Arnott, 2007, page 236.
230 Dimitris Vavylis, Trikala, Greece.
231 Angela Mancino, Milan, Italy.
232 Vesna Goldsworthy, London, UK.
233 Hanks and Hodges, 1988, page 411.
234 Beebe, 1990, Vol 4, page 179.
235 Ananda Banerjee, Delhi, India.
236 Lisa Goddard, Norfolk, UK.
237 Opie and Tatem, 1989, page 300.
238 Garrard, 2007, pages 152–7.
239 Armstrong, 1975, page 140.
240 de Kay, 1898, page 133.
241 Hyams, 1972, page 36.
242 Beebe, 1990, Vol 4, page 178.
243 Parmelee, 1959, page 124; Ingersoll, 1923, page 141.
244 Patrick Claffey, Dublin, Ireland; http://www.youtube.com/watch?v=gB6uQXuSizw&feature=fvw
245 Jackson, 2006, pages 154–5.
246 Merrill, 1998, pages 219–21.
247 Merrill, 1998, pages 243–5.
248 http://www.asia.si.edu/exhibitions/online/peacock/7.htm

Screamers *Anhimidae*

1 Sick, 1993, page 165.
2 Beebe and Beebe, 1910, page 381.
3 McConnell, 2000, page 9.
4 Sick, 1993, page 165; Restall, Rodner and Lentino, 2006, Vol 1, page 34.
5 Hudson, 1939, page 228.
6 Gabriel Castresana, Samborombón, Argentina.
7 James Lowen, Buenos Aires, Argentina.
8 Sick, 1993, page 165; Kear, 2005, Vol 1, page 182.
9 James Lowen, Buenos Aires, Argentina.

Ducks, Geese and Swans *Anatidae*

1 Nancy Hillstrand, Alaska, USA.
2 Aristotle, *HoA*, Bk III 509b.
3 Werness, 2004, page 149.
4 Houlihan, 1986, page 68.
5 Houlihan, 1986, pages 62–3; Richard Parkinson, London, UK.
6 Sick, 1993, page 158.
7 Ewans, 1989, pages 9–10.
8 Gladstone, 1922, page 94.
9 Evans, 1994, page 67.
10 Savage, 1963, pages 30–46.
11 Evans, 1994, page 89.
12 Savage, 1963, pages 30–46.
13 Gladstone, 1922, page 89; Newton, 1896, page 170.
14 Kear, 2005, page 10.
15 Gladstone, 1922, page 90. The author does not specify how many decoys were involved or in what year, and his ambiguous syntax makes

it difficult to understand exactly what he intended.
16 Engers, 2000, page 14.
17 Engers, 2000, pages 11, 119.
18 Sutton and Sutton, 2006, page 427.
19 Simon, 1983, pages 563, 590–91; Yeatman, 2007, page 205.
20 Clay Sutton, New Jersey, USA.
21 Sutton and Sutton, 2006, page 426.
22 Rick Halcott, Nebraska, USA.
23 Leopold, 1970, page 25.
24 Desfayes, 1998, Vol 1, pages 178–9.
25 Sick, 1993, page 163; Simon, 1983, page 556.
26 Haynes, 1987, page 233; Kear, 2005, page 453.
27 Jobling, 2010, page 83.
28 Cherry and Morris, 2008, page 7.
29 Terry Stevenson, Rift Valley Province, Kenya.
30 Doughty, 1979, page 449.
31 Damas, 1984, pages 482–3.
32 Smith, 2011, pages 48–9.
33 Doughty, 1979, page 450.
34 http://eiderdown.com/files/eider_article.pdf
35 http://www.nordicstore.net/eiderdown_duvets_from_iceland_1429_ctg.htm
36 Houlihan, 1986, page 55.
37 Kear, 1990, page 51.
38 Toynbee, 1973, page 263.
39 Pliny, Bk X, XXVII; Batty, 1979, page 151.
40 Pliny, Bk X, XXVII.
41 Houlihan, 1986, page 84.
42 Ucko and Dimbleby, 1969, page 309; Zeuner, 1963, page 421.
43 Kaufman in Friedland, 2008, page 125; Kear, 1990, pages 46–7.
44 Caro, 2009, pages 166–70; Kaufman in Friedland, 2008, page 129.
45 Beeton, 1968, page 450.
46 Caro, 2009, page 86.
47 Caro, 2009, page 86.
48 Caro, 2009, pages 33, 111.
49 http://www.folklore.ee/folklore/vol18/pa06.pdf
50 Burenhult, 2003, page 282.
51 Bruce Wilmore, 1974, page 46.
52 Lever, 2005, pages 78–9.
53 Aristotle, *HoA*, Bk IX, 615b.
54 Pliny, Bk X, XXXII.
55 Bent, Wild Fowl II, page 288.
56 Graves, 1996, page 196.
57 Nicholls, 2005, pages 396–8.

Penguins *Spheniscidae*

1 Abdi Jama, Djibouti City, Djibouti.
2 Nariman Nouri, Tehran, Iran.
3 Reilly, 1994, page 108.
4 Love, 1997, page 16.
5 Lynch, 2007, page 11; Reilly, 1994, page ix.
6 Guy Kirwan, Norfolk, UK.
7 Fernando Pacheco, Rio de Janeiro, Brazil.
8 Hosking and Sage, 1982, page 91.
9 Marion, 1999, page 38; Williams, 1995, pages 152–60.
10 Williams, 1995, page 156.
11 Sara Wheeler, London, UK.
12 Heart of the Great Alone (exhibition), Edinburgh, October 2009.
13 Wheeler, 2001, page 107.
14 Cherry-Garrard, 1994, page 240.
15 Cherry-Garrard, 1994, pages 253–4.
16 Cherry-Garrard, 1994, pages 285–6.
17 Sara Wheeler, London, UK.
18 Marion, 1995, page 114.
19 Gaskell, 2000, pages 48–9.
20 Strange, 1992, page 38.
21 Marion, 1995, page 118.

22 Cook, 2003, pages 409–10.
23 Marion, 1995, page 120.
24 Strange, 1992, pages 36–8.
25 Cumpston, 1968, pages 270, 305.
26 Cumpston, 1968, page 221.
27 Cumpston, 1968, page 309.
28 Williams, 1995, page 131.
29 Davis and Renner, 2003, page 161.
30 Williams, 1995, page 128.
31 Davis and Renner, 2003, page 163; http://www.birdlife.org/datazone/species/index.html?action=SpcHTMDetails.asp&sid=3861
32 Davis and Renner, 2003, page 169.
33 http://www.lds.org.au/newsroom/article.asp?id=FF77010E-CFB2-473B-952D-F286A5E1F766; http://www.tct.org.au/jumper.htm

Loons (Divers) *Gaviidae*
1 Yarrell, 1845, Vol 3, page 429.
2 Cruickshank, 1964, page 30.
3 *BWP* I:58.
4 *COED*, page 1661.
5 Christine Muir, Orkney, Scotland.
6 Lockwood, 1993, page 97.
7 Leahy, 1983, page 420.
8 Adrienne Bagwell, Surrey, UK.
9 Floyd, 2008, page 71.
10 Graeme Gibson, Ontario, Canada.
11 Godfrey, 1966, page 10.
12 Armstrong, 1958, pages 63–70.
13 Bonnefoy, 1993, page 352.
14 Armstrong, 1958, pages 63–70; Lewis-Williams and Pearce, 2005, page 71.
15 Lewis-Williams and Pearce, 2005, pages 70–71.
16 http://www.youtube.com/watch?v=DfUmSFVncPk

Albatrosses *Diomedeidae*
1 *COED*, page 52.
2 Matthiessen, 2003, page 12.
3 Bonser, 1905, page 179.
4 Shirihai, 2007, page 84.
5 Grahame, 1995, page 9.
6 Holmes, 1989, page 173.
7 Thompson, 1996, page 23.
8 Matthiessen, 2003, page 12.
9 Leahy, 1983, page 23.
10 Lowes, 1964, page 206.
11 Murphy, 1936, page 544.
12 Tickell, 2000, pages 357–8.
13 Murphy, 1936, page 495.
14 Murphy, 1936, page 495.
15 Opie and Tatem, 1989, page 1.
16 Brooke, 2004, page 156.
17 Murphy, 1936, page 563.
18 Brooke, 2004, page 157.
19 http://www.rspb.org.uk/ourwork/policy/marine/international/publications.asp
20 Croxall, 2008, page 17.
21 Croxall, 2008, page 17.
22 Shirihai, 2007, page 103.
23 Shirihai, 2007, page 82.
24 Ben Lascelles, Cambridge, UK.
25 Moore, 2009, page 14.
26 Balogh, 2008, page 27.
27 Shirihai, 2007, page 89.
28 http://www.birdlife.org/datazone/species/index.html

Petrels and Shearwaters *Procellariidae*
1 Newton, 1896, page 710; Murphy, 1936, page 586.
2 Stanley, 1851, page 446.
3 Latta et al, 2006, page 36.

4 Latta et al, 2006, page 36.
5 Guy Kirwan, Norfolk, UK; Lee and Vina, 1993, pages 99–101.
6 Zino, 1991, page 8.
7 http://fas-history.rutgers.edu/clemens/Jamestown/Strachey.html
8 Williamson, 1973, page 311.
9 Jonas Ellerström, Lund, Sweden.
10 Christine Muir, Orkney, Scotland. One other intriguing relationship at work on Rum is between the Manx Shearwaters and the substrate into which they dig their burrows. The slopes where they nest comprise alternating bands of hard resistant gabbro and softer friable layers of peridotite. It is the latter exclusively that the birds are able to excavate. Yet both rock types are products of an extinct volcano, of which Trollaval is a vestige. It is surely one of the more awe-inspiring ecological complexities that this bird, an inhabitant of open ocean, should be so intimately, perhaps irrevocably, connected to the life of a volcano that existed at least 60 million years ago. Shearwaters have found the same optimum conditions for their burrows at a handful of sites, most notably Skomer and Skokholm off Wales (165,000 pairs). Between them, the three islands hold more than two-thirds of the world's manxies.
11 Dick Ashford, Oregon, USA.
12 Fisher, 1952, pages 89–91; Bannerman 8:183.
13 Rowan, 1952, pages 97–121.
14 Zino, 1985, pages 1–9.
15 Diamond, 1999, page 312.
16 Cocker, 1998a, pages 182–3; Diamond and Filion, 1987, pages 63–75.
17 http://www.parks.tas.gov.au/index.aspx?base=5100
18 *TBW*, page 65.
19 Bent, Petrels, page 116; David Wingate, Bermuda.
20 Collar et al, 1992, page 48.
21 David Wingate, Bermuda.
22 Eamon de Buitlear, *Bermuda's Treasure Island*, DVD, 2006.

Storm Petrels *Hydrobatidae*
1 *COED*, page 2147.
2 Gotch, 1995, page 94.
3 Fernando Pacheco, Rio de Janeiro, Brazil.
4 Williamson, 1946, page 155.
5 Demey and Kirwan, 2004, page 10.
6 Wernham et al, 2002, page 124.
7 Murphy, 1936, page 738.
8 Forbush, 1955, page 15.
9 Shirihai, 2007, pages 215–17; Saville, Stephenson and Southey, 2003, pages 173–5; Flood, 2003, pages 479–82.
10 Murphy, 1936, page 738.
11 John J Borg, Rabat, Malta.

Diving Petrels *Pelecanoididae*
1 Philip Jones, Cornwall, UK.

Grebes *Podicipedidae*
1 Gotch, 1995, page 188; *COED*, page 117.
2 Sick, 1993, page 110.
3 Routh and Routh, 1987, page 73.
4 Pablo Rojas, Samborombón, Argentina.
5 Yarrell, 1845, Vol 3, page 404; *COED*, page 1199.
6 *COED*, page 3331.
7 Holloway, 1996, page 46.
8 Bent, Diving Birds, page 4.
9 Doughty, 1975, page 143.
10 Hagemeijer and Blair, 1997, page 9.

11 Konter, 2001, page 47.
12 Ogilvie and Rose, 2003, page 45.
13 Armstrong, 1975, page 166.
14 Konter, 2001, pages 135–8.
15 Maurice Rumboll, Buenos Aires, Argentina.
16 http://en.wikipedia.org/wiki/Hesketh_Hesketh-Prichard

Flamingos *Phoenicopteridae*
1 Ogilvie and Ogilvie, 1986, page 17.
2 Brown, 1959, pages 52–4.
3 Marcos Baltuska, Chubut Province, Argentina.
4 Bent, Marsh Birds, page 10.
5 Rowland, 1978, page 134.
6 Herodotus, Bk II, 73.
7 Pliny, Bk X, II; Arnott, 2007, pages 191–2; Ingersoll, 1923, pages 191–8.
8 *COED*, page 1015.
9 Landsborough Thomson, 1964, pages 265–6.
10 Houlihan, 1986, pages 15–16; Betrò, 1996, page 108.
11 Marcel Marée, Assistant Keeper (Curator), Department of Ancient Egypt and Sudan, the British Museum, London, UK.
12 Houlihan, 1986, page 16.
13 Johnson and Cézilly, 2007, page 11.
14 Alan Johnson, Arles, France.
15 Strong, 2002, page 37.
16 Arnott, 2007, page 189.
17 Price, 1999, page 130.
18 Bill Pranty, Florida, USA.

Storks *Ciconiidae*
1 Hancock, Kushlan and Kahl, 1992, page 109.
2 Abdi Jama, Djibouti City, Djibouti.
3 Vesna Goldsworthy, London, UK.
4 Sick, 1993, page 144.
5 Abdi Jama, Djibouti City, Djibouti.
6 Bent, Marsh Birds, page 70.
7 *BWP* I:332.
8 Hancock, Kushlan and Kahl, 1992, page 77.
9 Hancock, Kushlan and Kahl, 1992, page 100.
10 Hancock, Kushlan and Kahl, 1992, page 131.
11 Ali and Ripley, 1983, page 26, Hancock, Kushlan and Kahl, 1992, page 131.
12 Hancock, Kushlan and Kahl, 1992, page 136.
13 *TBW*, pages 84–6.
14 John Fanshawe, Cornwall, UK.
15 Demey, Kirwan and Lack, 2007, pages 134–5.
16 Opie and Tatem, 1989, page 379.
17 Mhorag Candy, Western Australia, Australia.
18 Vesna Goldsworthy, London, UK.
19 Angela Mancino, Milan, Italy.
20 Nada Tosheva, Sofia, Bulgaria.
21 Gattiker and Gattiker, 1989, pages 523–33.
22 Haverschmidt, 1949, page 30.
23 Simone Himenez, La Rioja, Spain.
24 Skov, 1971, pages 303–4.
25 Yarrell, 1845, Vol 2, page 557.
26 Ray, 1678, page 287.
27 Stanley, 1851, pages 342–3.
28 Kirwan et al, 2008, page 113.
29 Nariman Nouri, Tehran, Iran.
30 Yfantis, May–June 1999 (trans. Dimitris Vavylis).
31 Goriup and Schulz, 1990, pages 2–6; Hagemeijer and Blair, 1997, page 59.
32 Nigel Fletcher, Berlin, Germany.
33 Thomsen and Höder, 2006, pages 403–5.
34 Demey, 2004, page 95.
35 Cairncross, 2006, pages 16–21.
36 Yossi Leshem and Dan Alon, Tel Aviv, Israel.
37 Cairncross, 2006, pages 16–21.

Ibises and Spoonbills *Threskiornithidae*

1 Maaike Manten, Nairobi, Kenya.
2 Godfrey, 1941, page 20.
3 Kassagam, 1997, page 51.
4 Stephen Spawls, Norfolk, UK.
5 Yésou and Clergeau, 2005, pages 517–26.
6 Arnott, 2007, page 73.
7 Betrò, 1996, page 76.
8 Herodotus, Bk II, 75–6.
9 Hancock, Kushlan and Kahl, 1992, pages 166, 214.
10 Sick, 1993, page 140.
11 Hancock, Kushlan and Kahl, 1992, page 194.
12 Pollard, 1977, page 67.
13 Yésou and Clergeau, 2005, pages 517–26.
14 Dr Neal Spencer, Assistant Keeper (Curator), Department of Ancient Egypt and Sudan, the British Museum, London, UK.
15 Ikram, 2005, page 9.
16 Ikram, 2005, page 134.
17 Smith, 1974, page 27.
18 Ikram, 2005, pages 152–5.
19 Ikram, 2005, page 156.
20 Houlihan, 1986, page 30.

Herons and Bitterns *Ardeidae*

1 Restall, Rodner and Lentino, 2006, Vol 1, page 69.
2 Hardy, 1974, pages 170–71.
3 Thoreau, 1993, pages 72–3, 79–80.
4 Restall, Rodner and Lentino, 2006, Vol 1, page 70.
5 Werness, 2004, page 214.
6 Liu He, Beijing, China.
7 Sun, 2007, page 58.
8 Ray, 1678, page 278.
9 Ali and Ripley, 1983, page 15; Roberts, 1991, page 93. One intriguing but now mostly forgotten story in the larger narrative of worldwide heron slaughter was the temporary domestication of Little Egrets for their plumes by these extraordinarily talented hunter-gatherers. In the early part of the twentieth century several British officers investigated this remarkable achievement. It was a true domestication, not merely taming, because the birds bred and replenished their own stocks in captivity. Although the economic potential and efficiency of their methods were noted – including their harvest of aigrettes four times a year – none of the colonial witnesses bothered to ask how quickly they had managed to achieve egret domestication. It can be only one of a small number of occasions where we achieved the enormously difficult enterprise of domestication, then abandoned its fruits within decades. Birch, 1914, pages 161–3; Birch, 1921, pages 944–7; Benson, 1922, pages 748–9; Chevenix Trench, 1922, pages 751–2.
10 Houlihan, 1986, pages 13–15.
11 Ray, 1678, page 279.
12 Stanley, 1851, page 339; Ray, 1678, page 282.
13 Doughty, 1975, page 1.
14 Ali and Ripley, 1983, page 18.
15 Doughty, 1975, page 74.
16 Doughty, 1975, page 25.
17 Doughty, 1975, page 27.
18 Bent, Marsh Birds, page 142.
19 Doughty, 1975, page 16.
20 Doughty, 1975, page 74; *HBW* 1:396.
21 Price, 1999, page 64.
22 Bannerman 6:89.
23 Hancock and Elliott, 1978, page 31.
24 Houlihan, 1986, page 18; Elsadig Bashir, Doha, Qatar.

25 Hancock and Elliott, 1978, page 31.
26 Hancock and Elliott, 1978, page 31.
27 Swainson, 1998, page 146; Hancock and Elliott, 1978, page 40.
28 Guy Kirwan, Norfolk, UK; Fernando Pacheco, Rio de Janeiro, Brazil.
29 Thoreau, 1993, page 70.
30 Hancock and Elliott, 1978, page 42.
31 Albert Martinez Vilalta, Barcelona, Spain.

Tropicbirds *Phaethontidae*

1 *BWP* 1:182.
2 Murphy, 1936, page 799.
3 *HBW* 1:286.

Frigatebirds *Fregatidae*

1 Harrison, 1983, page 307.
2 Anon, 2006.
3 Bent, Petrels, pages 307–12.
4 Thomas, 1995, pages 91–2; Waite in Morphy, 1989, pages 318–42.
5 Waite in Morphy, 1989, pages 318–42.
6 Patrick Pikacha, Marovo Lagoon, Solomon Islands.
7 Thomas, 1995, page 90.

Hamerkop *Scopidae*

1 Kahl, 1967, pages 25–32.
2 Cowles, 1930, pages 159–76.
3 Cowles, 1930, pages 159–76.
4 Steyn, 1996, page 39.
5 Venetia Lang, London, UK.
6 Godfrey, 1941, pages 11–17; Cowles, 1930, pages 159–76.
7 Cowles, 1930, pages 159–76.
8 Steyn, 1996, page 39.
9 David Moyer, Iringa, Tanzania.
10 *BoA* 1:170.
11 Cowles, 1930, pages 159–76.
12 Stephen Spawls, Norfolk, UK.
13 Godfrey, 1941, page 15.
14 Siegfried, 1975, page 267.
15 Godfrey, 1941, pages 16–17.
16 *BoA* 1:169.
17 Peter Steyn, Cape Town, South Africa.
18 Claire Spottiswoode, Cambridgeshire, UK.
19 Martin Walsh, Cambridge, UK.

Pelicans *Pelecanidae*

1 Ali and Ripley, 1983, page 7.
2 Bent, Petrels, pages 286–7.
3 Armstrong, 1975, page 84.
4 Ingersoll, 1923, page 148; Graham, 1962, page 235.
5 Ingersoll, 1923, page 59.
6 Isabelle Charmantier, Exeter, UK.
7 Newton, 1896, page 6.
8 *HBW* 1:306.
9 Dragan Simic, Belgrade, Serbia.
10 Bonser, 1905, page 179.
11 Johnsgard, 1993, page 348.
12 *BoA* 1:123.
13 Fitter, 1986, page 88.
14 Fitter, 1986, pages 70, 88.
15 Dimitris Vavylis, Trikala, Greece.
16 Houlihan, 1986, page 11.

Gannets and Boobies *Sulidae*

1 Nelson, 2002, page 52.
2 Patrick Pikacha, Marovo Lagoon, Solomon Islands.
3 Nelson, 2002, page 69.
4 Bannerman 8:33.
5 Nelson, 2002, page 70.
6 Nelson, 2002, page 74.

7 Armstrong, 1975, page 177.
8 Birkhead, 1993, page 118.
9 Nelson, 2002, page 87; Fisher and Lockley, 1954, page 79.
10 Nelson, 2002, page 95.
11 Nelson, 2002, pages 87, 95.
12 Fleming, 2005, page 59.
13 Bannerman 8:25.
14 Steel, 1994, page 187.
15 Nelson, 2002, page 361.
16 Steel, 1994, pages 150–55.
17 Goodman, 2006, pages 40–44.
18 Landsborough Thomson, 1964, pages 346–8; Murphy, 1936, pages 286–95.
19 Nelson, 2002, page 344.
20 Campbell and Lack, 1985, page 265.
21 Johnsgard, 1993, page 126.
22 *TBW*, pages 42, 72.
23 *TBW*, page 80.
24 *TBW*, page 73.
25 Williamson, 1948, pages 136–7.

Cormorants *Phalacrocoracidae*

1 COED, page 559.
2 Ali and Ripley, 1983, page 9; Laufer, 1931, pages 200–262.
3 Armstrong, 1975, page 121.
4 Liu He, Beijing, China.
5 Laufer, 1931, pages 200–262.
6 Egremont and Rothschild, 1979, pages 181–6.
7 Laufer, 1931, pages 200–262; Armstrong, 1975, pages 121–3.
8 Fleming, 2004, page 139.
9 Mark Brazil, Hokkaido, Japan.
10 Laufer, 1931, pages 200–263.
11 Zeuner, 1963, page 473; Armstrong, 1975, page 123.
12 Harting, 1978, pages 262–4.
13 Ray, 1678, pages 331–2.
14 Liu He, Beijing, China.
15 Lambert, 2003, pages 30–34.
16 Stefferud, 1966, page 235.
17 http://bna.birds.cornell.edu/bna/species/441

Anhingas *Anhingidae*

1 Sick, 1993, page 127.
2 Stonor, 1948, pages 746–7.
3 Amir Balaban, Jerusalem, Israel.

Birds of Prey *Cathartidae, Falconidae* and *Accipitridae*

1 Ratcliffe, 1993, page 363; Baker, 2010, page 45; Birkhead, 2012, page 19.
2 Buffon, 2010, page 139.
3 Snyder and Snyder, 2000, page 146.
4 Reina and Kensinger, 1991, page 106.
5 Molly Bennett, Roger Peart and Brian Richmond, Dorset, UK.
6 Shan Egerton, Powys, UK.
7 Naoroji, 2006, page 25; Ali and Ripley, 1983, page 85.
8 Pliny, Bk X, IV.
9 Axel Bräunlich, Berlin, Germany.
10 Bent, Birds of Prey I, page 335.
11 Palmer, 1988, pages 218–20.
12 Forrester and Andrews, 2007, Vol 1, page 485.
13 *TBW*, page 118.
14 Rob Williams, Cuzco, Peru.
15 Rob Williams, Cuzco, Peru; Newton, 1896, page 101.
16 Werness, 2004, page 103.
17 Arguedas, 1985, page 34.
18 Rob Williams, Cuzco, Peru.
19 Snyder and Snyder, 2000, pages 32–5.
20 Houlihan, 1986, page 37.

21 Demey, 2004, page 99.
22 Meinertzhagen, 1959, page 85.
23 Ray, 1678, page 75.
24 Nigel Redman, London, UK.
25 Ray, 1678, page 75.
26 David Tipling, Norfolk, UK.
27 Naoroji, 2006, page 240.
28 Koford, 1953, page 129.
29 Snyder and Snyder, 2000, pages 45–7.
30 Kiff, 1990, pages 7–18.
31 Kiff, 1990, pages 7–18; Snyder and Snyder, 2000, pages 225–30.
32 Ratcliffe, 1993, page 382.
33 Macdonald, 2006, page 129.
34 Nielsen, 2007, page 189.
35 Snyder and Snyder, 2000, page 65.
36 Amirsadeghi, 2008, page 39.
37 Evans in Harcourt and Phillott, 1968, page v.
38 Amirsadeghi, 2008, page 35.
39 Evans in Harcourt and Phillott, 1968, page vi.
40 Harcourt and Phillott, 1968, page 33.
41 Baker, 2010, page 149.
42 Harcourt and Phillott, 1968, page 115; Allen, 1980, page 80.
43 Jobling, 2010, page 183.
44 Glasier, 1998, page 22.
45 Naoroji, 2006, page 26.
46 Blüchel, 1997, page 170.
47 Naoroji, 2006, page 26.
48 Naoroji, 2006, page 26.
49 Polo, 1979, page 143.
50 Roberts, 1991, page 219–20.
51 Glasier, 1998, page 10.
52 Dal Han, Bayan-Ulgii, Mongolia.
53 Michael Kiu, New Britain, Papua New Guinea; Macdonald, 2006, page 107.
54 Rao, 1997, pages 60–63.
55 Aelian, Bk 10, 22.
56 Rowland, 1978, pages 176–8.
57 Houlihan, 1986, page 40.
58 COED, page 3662.
59 Mellaart, 1967, pages 92–3.
60 Mithen, 2004, pages 93–5.
61 Mithen, 2004, page 564.
62 Lewis-Williams and Pearce, 2005, page 117.
63 Lewis-Williams and Pearce, 2005, page 77.
64 Houlihan, 1986, page 42.
65 Boyce, 1979, page 157.
66 Rishad Naoroji, Mumbai, India.
67 Boyce, 1979, page 157.
68 Smith, 2011, page 73.
69 Hinnells, 2005, page 750.
70 Fee, 1905, page 553.
71 Rishad Naoroji, Mumbai, India.
72 Leahy, 1983, page 754.
73 Martin, 1996, page 367.

Bustards *Otidae*

1 Mountfort, 1965, page 62.
2 *TBW*, page 187.
3 Pliny, Bk X, XXIX.
4 Lockwood, 1993, pages 37–8.
5 http://www.greatbustard.org
6 Pliny, Bk X, XXIX.
7 Arnott, 2007, page 167.
8 Mithen, 2004, page 564.
9 Ali and Ripley, 1983, page 142.
10 David Moyer, Iringa, Tanzania.
11 Beaglehole, 1999, pages 325–6.
12 Aelian, Bk 2, 28.
13 Pollard, 1977, page 85.
14 David Moyer, Iringa, Tanzania.
15 Ali, 1985, page 200.
16 Stevenson, 1870, pages 23–4.
17 Macpherson, 1897, pages 436–7.

18 Archer and Godman, 1937, page 340.
19 Harcourt and Phillott, 1968, pages 57–8.
20 Newby, 1979, pages 104–5.
21 Weaver, 14 December 1992.
22 http://www.endangeredspecieshandbook.org/persecution_trophy2.php
23 Weaver, 14 December 1992.
24 Weaver, 14 December 1992.
25 Weaver, 14 December 1992.
26 Cloudsley-Thompson, 1992, pages 202–4.
27 Newby, 1990, pages 6–8.
28 Cloudsley-Thompson, 1992, pages 202–4.
29 Seddon et al, 1995, pages 136–42.
30 McGirk, 17 November 2003.
31 Abdi Jama, Djibouti City, Djibouti.
32 Elsadig Bashir, Doha, Qatar.
33 Harcourt and Phillott, 1968, page 119.
34 David Moyer, Iringa, Tanzania.

Seriemas *Cariamidae*

1 Mitchell, 1957, page 72.
2 Durrell, 1956, page 137.
3 John Hemming, London, UK.
4 Forbes, 1881, page 358.
5 Sick 1993, page 218.
6 Fernando Pacheco, Rio de Janeiro, Brazil.
7 *HBW* 3:238; Perrins, 2009, page 222.
8 Kathleen Lowrey, Alberta, Canada.
9 Kerr, 1950, page 88.

Kagu *Rhynochetidae*

1 Guy Dutson, Cambridge, UK.
2 Greenway, 1967, page 253.
3 *TBW*, page 185.
4 Vivien Chartendrault, Nouméa, New Caledonia.

Sunbittern *Eurypygidae*

1 Barnes, 2008, page 1.
2 Campbell and Lack, 1985, page 568.
3 *HBW* 3:232; Sick, 1993, page 216.
4 Bennett Hennessey, Santa Cruz, Bolivia.
5 Fernando Pacheco, Rio de Janeiro, Brazil.

Rails, Crakes and Coots *Rallidae*

1 Chapman, 1934, page 257.
2 Taylor and van Perlo, 1998, page 42.
3 Sick, 1993, page 209.
4 Yarrell, 1845, Vol 3, page 93.
5 Whinnom, 1966, page 52.
6 Ali and Ripley, 1983, page 138; http://birdbase.hokkaido-ies.go.jp/rdb/rdb_en/frangula.pdf
7 Taylor and van Perlo, 1998, page 457.
8 Bent, Marsh Birds, page 344.
9 Jeremy Mynott, Suffolk, UK.
10 Seyffert, 1995, pages 528–9.
11 Aelian, Bk 3, 42; Pollard, 1977, page 23; Arnott, 2007, page 197.
12 Jashemski and Meyer, 2002, page 391.
13 Toynbee, 1973, page 281; http://sights.seindal.dk/sight/481_Vestibule_of_the_Small_Circus.html
14 Houlihan, 1986, pages 88–91.
15 Whinnom, 1966, pages 51–2; *BWP* 2:578.
16 Lockwood, 1993, page 66.
17 Sick, 1993, page 204.
18 Sick, 1993, page 214.
19 Arnott, 2007, page 183.
20 Goodman and Meininger, 1989, pages 76–85, 221; Houlihan, 1986, page 88.
21 Taylor and van Perlo, 1998, page 530.
22 Roberts, 1991, page 268.
23 Taylor and van Perlo, 1998, page 538.
24 Taylor and van Perlo, 1998, page 274.
25 Bent, Marsh Birds, page 303.

26 Whinnom, 1966, page 51; *BWP* 2:570.
27 *TBW*, pages 178–84.
28 Turbott, 1967, pages 162–7.
29 Taylor and van Perlo, 1998, pages 463–73.
30 Taylor and van Perlo, 1998, page 59.

Finfoots *Heliornithidae*

1 *HBW* 3:214.
2 Ali and Ripley, 1983, page 140.
3 *TBW*, page 185.

Trumpeters *Psophiidae*

1 Restall, Rodner and Lentino, 2006, Vol 1, page 110.
2 Campbell and Lack, 1985, page 611.
3 Barry Walker, Cuzco, Peru.
4 Pearson and Beletsky, 2002, page 141.
5 Restall, Rodner and Lentino, 2006, Vol 1, page 110.
6 Katharine Milton, California, USA.
7 James Lowen, Buenos Aires, Argentina.
8 *HBW* 3:104.

Cranes *Gruidae*

1 Leopold, 1970, page 102.
2 *HBW* 3:81.
3 Philip Hall, Lagos, Nigeria.
4 *TBW*, page 165.
5 The occurrence of more easily recognisable crane images at other sites in the region supports the idea that cranes had wide symbolic importance for Near-Eastern Neolithic communities. However, the carved images at Göbekli Tepe are not accurate enough to be beyond dispute. They may be Common Cranes, but the rudimentary features could possibly be construed as those of ostrich, storks or even geese. Lewis-Williams and Pearce, 2005, page 128.
6 Homer, 1950, Bk II, 544.
7 Pollard, 1977, page 111.
8 Aelian, Bk 1, 44, Aelian, Bk 3, 14; Aelian, Bk 7, 7.
9 Håkan Karlsson, Lund, Sweden.
10 Jari Peltomäki, Liminka, Finland.
11 Pollard, 1977, page 133.
12 Houlihan, 1986, page 84.
13 http://www.hornborga.com/eng/crane_stat.asp
14 Håkan Karlsson, Lund, Sweden.
15 Ananda Banerjee, Delhi, India.
16 Britton and Hayashida, 1993, page 60.
17 David Tipling, Norfolk, UK.
18 Treuenfels, 2007, pages 175–6.
19 McNulty, 1966, page 27.
20 McNulty, 1966, page 32.
21 The exact number of surviving whoopers in the late 1930s is a slightly vexed question. Most authorities usually cite a figure between narrow parameters of 14–18, which was the estimated total at Aransas in 1938. In fact there were an additional 11 wild whoopers in Louisiana that year, making a grand total of 29: the number cited, for example, by Robin Doughty in *Return of the Whooping Crane*. However, the Louisiana birds were doomed and, after increasing to 13 in 1939, they slowly dwindled, until in 1950 the last one was taken into custody and re-released at Aransas as a pinioned bird. In practical terms the Louisiana contingent played no role in the recovery of the species, and authors have reflected this by effectively ignoring them. Collar et al, 1992, page 1014.
22 Hughes, 2008, page 118.
23 Hughes, 2008, pages 145–67.

24 Matthiessen, 2001, pages 113–19; Massey Stewart, 1987, pages 6–10.
25 Hughes, 2008, page 205.
26 McNulty, 1966, page 25.
27 Joanne Luyster, Kentucky, USA.
28 Alan Bartels, Nebraska, USA.

Limpkin *Aramidae*
1 Sunquist, Sunquist and Beletsky, 2002, page 126.
2 Howell and Webb, 1995, page 248; Schulenberg et al, 2007, page 76.
3 Bent, Marsh Birds, page 258.
4 HBW 3:92.
5 Bent, Marsh Birds, page 254.

Stone-curlews and Thick-knees *Burhinidae*
1 Gill Ainsworth, Northern Territory, Australia.
2 Darryl Jones, Queensland, Australia.
3 Landsborough Thomson, 1964, page 816; Latta et al, 2006, page 73.
4 Vaughan and Vaughan, 2005, page 7.
5 Sherif Baha El Din, Cairo, Egypt.
6 Mary Dungan Megalli, Cairo, Egypt.
7 Mary Dungan Megalli, Cairo, Egypt.
8 Sherif Baha El Din, Cairo, Egypt.
9 Aelian, Bk 17, 13.

Sheathbills *Chionidae*
1 Murphy, 1936, page 1000.
2 Harrison, 1983, page 320; Murphy, 1936, page 1000.
3 James Lowen, London, UK.
4 Sue Gregory, Queensland, Australia.
5 Murphy, 1936, page 1001.
6 Vic Tucker, Devon, UK.

Oystercatchers *Haematopodidae*
1 Karen Acton, Swansea, Wales.

Stilts and Avocets *Recurvirostridae*
1 Newton, 1896, pages 913–14.
2 http://www.birdlife.org/datazone/species
3 Forbush, 1955, page 209.

Plovers *Charadriidae*
1 Burfield and van Bommel, 2004, page 116.
2 Darryl Jones, Queensland, Australia.
3 Ali and Ripley, 1983, page 147.
4 Sherif Baha El Din, Cairo, Egypt.
5 Sick, 1993, page 225.
6 de la Peña and Rumboll, 1998, unpaginated.
7 Tait, 1924, pages 189–90.
8 Maaike Manten, Nairobi, Kenya; Peter Herkenrath, Cambridge, UK; Dragan Simic, Belgrade, Serbia; Svetlana Gretton, Suffolk, UK; Arne Ohlsson, Lund, Sweden.
9 Jones, 2002, page 56.
10 Darryl Jones, Queensland, Australia.
11 James Lowen, London, UK.
12 Sick, 1993, page 225.
13 Marcos Baltuska, Chubut Province, Argentina.
14 Pablo Rojas and Gabriel Castresana, Buenos Aires Province, Argentina.
15 Hudson, 1982, page 200.
16 Hudson, 1939, page 21.
17 Swainson, 1998, page 180.
18 Gotch, 1995, page 202.
19 COED, page 2212.
20 Marcos Baltuska, Chubut Province, Argentina.
21 Shrubb, 2007, page 36.
22 Jukema and Piersma, 2004, pages 165–7.
23 Jukema, Piersma and Hulscher, 2001, pages 236–46.

24 Fenech, 1992, page 75.
25 Fenech, 2010, pages 272–5.
26 Simon, 1983, page 592.
27 HBW 3:406.
28 Newton, 1896, pages 504–5.
29 Shrubb, 2007, pages 33–6.
30 Lars Karlsson, Tidaholm, Sweden.
31 Ash Harrison, Derbyshire, UK.

Jacanas *Jacanidae*
1 Ray, 1678, page 317.
2 Ali and Ripley, 1983, page 144.

Sandpipers and Snipe *Scolopacidae*
1 COED, page 816.
2 Wernham et al, 2002, pages 297–9.
3 Matthiessen, 1973, pages 16–17.
4 Phil Battley, Palmerston North, New Zealand.
5 Butvill, 2010, page 77.
6 Islay McLeod, Christchurch, New Zealand.
7 Hudson, 1982, pages 324–5.
8 Matthiessen, 1973, page 17.
9 Clive Minton, Victoria, Australia.
10 Fishpool and Evans, 2001, page 573.
11 Niles et al, 2007, pages 1–236.
12 Gretton, 1991, page 16.
13 Collar and Andrew, 1988, page 55.
14 Tucker and Heath, 1994, page 276.
15 Gretton, 2002, page 341.
16 Adam Gretton, Suffolk, UK.
17 Bent, Shore Birds II, page 129.
18 Gollop, Barry and Iverson, 1986, page 37.
19 Gollop, Barry and Iverson, 1986, page 83.
20 Gollop, Barry and Iverson, 1986, page 52.
21 Bent, Shore Birds II, page 133.
22 Gollop, Barry and Iverson, 1986, page 109.
23 Graeme Gibson, Toronto, Canada.
24 Gollop, Barry and Iverson, 1986, page 109.
25 Burfield and van Bommel, 2004, page 126.
26 Gerry Cotter, Lancashire, UK.
27 Dee, 2009, page 27.
28 Cruickshank, 1964, page 92.
29 Bent, Shore Birds I, pages 72–3.
30 Matthiessen, 1973, page 23.
31 Sutton and Sutton, 2006, page 134.
32 Gladstone, 1922, page 74.
33 Chapman, 1934, page 271.
34 Macpherson, 1897, pages 448–9.
35 Macpherson, 1897, page 453.
36 Gladstone, 1922, page 77.
37 Lampedusa, 2010, pages 177–8.
38 Bent, Shore Birds I, page 61.
39 Matthiessen, 1973, page 33.
40 Bent, Shore Birds I, page 68.
41 McKelvie, 1990, page 69.
42 Anonymous, Sweden.
43 Jim Irons, Norfolk, UK.

Coursers and Pratincoles *Glareolidae*
1 Herodotus, Bk II, 63.
2 Newton, 1896, page 733.
3 Stanley, 1851, pages 362–5.
4 Meinertzhagen, 1959, pages 224–5.
5 BoA 2:207.

Gulls and Terns *Laridae*
1 Christian Cadot, Lower Normandy, France.
2 Conor Jameson, Hertfordshire, UK.
3 Sick, 1993, page 235.
4 Gotch, 1995, page 273.
5 Cruickshank, 1964, page 98.
6 Jim Perrin, Ariège, France.
7 Cruickshank, 1964, page 98.
8 Andrew Bloomfield, Norfolk, UK.
9 Ann Kelley, Cornwall, UK.

10 du Maurier, 2011, page 222.
11 Ray Tipper, Algarve, Portugal.
12 Ruth Brompton-Charlesworth, York, UK.
13 Bella Bigsby, California, USA.
14 Browne, 1902, pages 9–10.
15 Cott, 1953, page 670; Taylor et al, 1999, page 309.
16 Limbert, 2003, page 38.
17 HBW 3:696.
18 Cott, 1953, page 426; Cott, 1954, page 130.
19 COED, page 1934.
20 Gotch, 1995, page 276.
21 Haynes, 1987, pages 99–124; Haynes-Sutton, 1987, page 78.

Skuas *Stercorariidae*
1 Williamson, 1946, page 159.
2 Whinnom, 1966, page 57.
3 Murphy, 1936, page 1032.
4 Murphy, 1936, pages 1032–3.
5 James Lowen, London, UK.
6 Hosking and Sage, 1982, page 125.
7 Murphy, 1936, page 1023.

Auks *Alcidae*
1 Newton, 1896, page 304.
2 COED, page 1879.
3 Desfayes, 1998, Vol 1, page 266.
4 Bent, Diving Birds, page 94.
5 Williamson, 1946, page 164.
6 Williamson, 1948, page 154.
7 Fisher and Lockley, 1954, page 63.
8 Bent, Diving Birds, page 216.
9 Bent, Diving Birds, pages 220–21.
10 Bethan Evans, Cardiff, UK.
11 Lopez, 1987, page 121.
12 Birkhead, 1993, pages 80–90.
13 Burenhult, 2003, pages 118–21.
14 Birkhead, 1993, page 89.
15 Gaskell, 2000, page 169.
16 Gaskell, 2000, pages 146–7.
17 Birkhead, 1993, page 84.
18 Cott, 1953, page 418.
19 Macpherson, 1897, page 494.
20 Damas, 1984, page 298.
21 Damas, 1984, page 193.
22 Macpherson, 1897, page 487.
23 Williamson, 1948, pages 145–6.
24 Petersen, 2005, pages 194–215.
25 Hansen, 5 November–1 December 2011.
26 Hansen, 2002, pages 36–40.
27 Hansen, 2002, page 64.
28 Hansen, 2002, page 35.

Sandgrouse *Pteroclididae*
1 Jobling, 2010, page 322.
2 BoA 2:424.
3 Elsadig Bashir, Doha, Qatar.
4 Ali and Ripley, 1983, page 201.
5 Stuart Baker, 1913b, page 227.
6 Stuart Baker, 1913a, pages 1–12.
7 Stuart Baker, 1913a, pages 1–12.
8 Ali and Ripley, 1983, pages 201–2.
9 Gladstone, 1922, page 111.
10 Demey, Kirwan and Lucking, 1998, page 89.
11 Long, 1981, page 204.
12 HBW 4:48; Long, 1981, pages 202–4.
13 Pyle and Pyle, 2009.
14 Polo, 1979, page 103.
15 Long, 1981, page 204.
16 Huc and Gabet, 1987, pages 191–2.
17 Brown and Grice, 2005, page 412.

Pigeons and Doves *Columbidae*
1 Maaike Manten, Suva, Fiji.

2 COED, page 781.
3 Gibbs, Barnes and Cox, 2001, pages 172–3.
4 Gibbs, Barnes and Cox, 2001, page 173.
5 Fuller, 2002, page 123.
6 Jackson, Christine, 1993, pages 54–7.
7 Fuller, 2002, page 40.
8 Kingdon, 1990, page 31.
9 Jobling, 2010, pages 135, 204.
10 Isabelle Charmantier, Devon, UK; Angela Mancino, Milan, Italy; Peter Herkenrath, Cambridge, UK.
11 Vesna Goldsworthy, London, UK.
12 Maaike Manten, Suva, Fiji.
13 Svetlana Gretton, Suffolk, UK.
14 Rick Wright, Arizona, USA.
15 TBW, pages 210–30.
16 Haag-Wackernagel, 1998, page 32.
17 Rowland, 1978, page 42.
18 Angela Mancino, Milan, Italy.
19 Rowland, 1978, page 42–6.
20 Sherif and Mindy Baha El Din, Cairo, Egypt; Wael M Shohdi, Kafr el Sheikh, Egypt.
21 Werness, 2004, page 144.
22 Pollard, 1977, page 140; Rowland, 1978, page 48; Green, 1993, page 42.
23 Pollard, 1977, page 133.
24 Hansell, 1998, page 154; Haag-Wackernagel, 1998, page 198.
25 Jim Crace, Birmingham, UK.
26 Goodwin, 1983, page 61.
27 HBW 4:102.
28 Houlihan, 1986, page 103.
29 Sherif and Mindy Baha El Din, Cairo, Egypt; Wael M Shohdi, Kafr el Sheikh, Egypt.
30 Hansell and Hansell, 2001, page 10.
31 Hansell, 1998, page 55; Hansell gives the date of this event as 1260 BC, but Egyptian chronologies have since changed.
32 Pliny, Bk X, LII.
33 Hansell, 1998, page 131.
34 Suzanne Padfield, Ceredigion, Wales.
35 Tamadhur Jamil Al-Khishali, Norwich, UK.
36 Anoushka Alexander, London, UK.
37 Collings, 2008, pages 87.
38 Collings, 2008, pages 58–63.
39 Collings, 2008, page 94.
40 Katrina Porteous, Northumberland, UK.
41 Collings, 2008, page 34.
42 Schorger, 1955, page 205.
43 Stephen Moss, Somerset, UK.
44 Steinbeck, 2000, page 152.
45 Steve Howell, California, USA.
46 Voislav Vasic, Belgrade, Serbia.
47 Peter McDermott, Dublin, Ireland.
48 Hagemeijer and Blair, 1997, page 389.
49 Alderfer, 2006, page 301.
50 Sick, 1993, page 245.
51 http://www.dovehunting.us/argentina-dove-hunt-testimonials.html
52 Muir, 1992, page 73.
53 Bent, Gallinaceous Birds, page 390.
54 Schorger, 1955, page 14.
55 Schorger, 1955, page 54.
56 Schorger, 1955, page 12.
57 Schorger, 1955, page 51.
58 Schorger, 1955, page 133.
59 Schorger, 1955, page 92.
60 Schorger, 1955, page 79.
61 Schorger, 1955, pages 78–86.
62 Schorger, 1955, page 135.
63 Schorger, 1955, page 138.

64 Schorger, 1955, pages 129–32.
65 Schorger, 1955, page 148.
66 Schorger, 1955, page 142.
67 Schorger, 1955, pages 157–66.
68 Price, 1999, pages 42–3.
69 Price, 1999, pages 53–4.
70 Leopold, 1970, page 116.
71 Gibson, 1982, page 83.
72 Graeme Gibson, Ontario, Canada.
73 Price, 1999, page 54.
74 Cocker, 2006, page 74.
75 Houlihan, 1986, page 105.
76 Bannerman 8: 367.
77 Fenech, 1992, pages 73–9.
78 Fenech, 1992, page 10.
79 http://ec.europa.eu/environment/nature/conservation/wildbirds/hunting/docs/turtle_dove.pdf

Cockatoos and Parrots *Psittacidae*

1 Darryl Jones, Queensland, Australia.
2 Heather and Robertson, 1997, page 356; Walmsley, 2010, pages 68–71.
3 Sick, 1993, page 251.
4 TBW, pages 235–82.
5 Lever, 2005, pages 124–30.
6 Ananda Banerjee, Delhi, India.
7 Ali and Ripley, 1983, page 222.
8 Foreshaw and Cooper, 1989, page 360; HBW 4:330.
9 Darryl Jones, Queensland, Australia.
10 Reardon, 2001, page 94.
11 Margaret Samuel, Glamorgan, UK.
12 Darryl Jones, Queensland, Australia.
13 Newton, 1896, page 93.
14 Keith and Lindsay Fisher, Queensland, Australia.
15 Darryl Jones, Queensland, Australia.
16 Darryl Jones, Queensland, Australia.
17 Eastwood, 2005, pages 94–5.
18 Aristotle, HoA, Bk VIII, 597.
19 Marian King, Queensland, Australia.
20 Jashemski and Meyer, 2002, page 322.
21 Newton, 1896, page 685; Boehrer, 2004, page 20.
22 Sick, 1993, page 251.
23 Verdi, 2007, page 18.
24 Rowland, 1978, page 121; Jackson, Christine, 1993, page 106; Impellusa, 2004, page 302.
25 Boehrer, 2004, page 55.
26 COED, page 2229.
27 Isabelle Charmantier, Devon, UK; Angela Mancino, Milan, Italy.
28 HBW 4:327.
29 Sick, 1993, page 252.
30 Boehrer, 2004, page 178.
31 Sick, 1993, page 255.
32 Pepperberg, 2008, page 7.
33 Sick, 1993, page 258; Ali and Ripley, 1983, page 221; Bainbrigge Fletcher and Inglis, 1924, page 153.
34 Ananda Banerjee, Delhi, India.
35 June Holmes, Tyne and Wear, UK.
36 Margaret Quigley, Lancashire, UK.
37 Grindol and Roudybush, 2004, page 39.
38 Graeme Gibson, Ontario, Canada.
39 Juniper, 2002, page 45.
40 Mira Tweti, California, USA.

41 Collar et al, 1992, page 304.
42 Tyler, 1979, pages 26–7.
43 Sick, 1993, page 263.
44 Boehrer, 2004, page 153.
45 Tweti, 2008, page 149.
46 HBW 4:328.
47 Collar et al, 1992, pages 241–9; TBW, page 258.
48 Tweti, 2008, page 217.
49 Sick, 1993, page 263.
50 Collar et al, 1992, pages 241–9.
51 Collar et al, 1992, page 268; Juniper, 2002, pages 89–123.
52 Rowland, 1978, page 120.
53 Sick, 1993, page 262.
54 Darryl Jones, Brisbane, Australia.
55 Boehrer, 2004, page 55; Robert Prys-Jones, Hertfordshire, UK.
56 Tweti, 2008, pages 54–6.
57 Bill Pranty, Florida, USA; Lever, 2005, pages 123–42.
58 Reina and Kensinger, 1991, pages 94–5.
59 Reina and Kensinger, 1991, pages 26–39.
60 Reina and Kensinger, 1991, pages 37–8.
61 Sick, 1993, pages 253–4; Reina and Kensinger, 1991, page 112.
62 Bennett Hennessey, Santa Cruz, Bolivia.

Hoatzin *Opisthocomidae*

1 Restall, Rodner and Lentino, 2006, Vol I, page 154.
2 Armstrong, 1975, page 263.
3 Newton, 1896 page 421.
4 Sick, 1993, page 204.
5 Schulenberg et al, 2007, page 186.
6 Sick, 1993, page 205.
7 Newton, 1896, page 424.
8 Jobling, 2010, page 193.
9 Ray, 1678, page 389.
10 Sick, 1993, page 205.
11 Bennett Hennessey, Santa Cruz, Bolivia.
12 HBW 3:30.

Turacos *Musophagidae*

1 Newton, 1896, page 519; Gotch, 1995, page 292.
2 Stevenson and Fanshawe, 2002, page 186.
3 Andrea Eames, Christchurch, New Zealand.
4 Landsborough Thomson, 1964, page 843.
5 Christian Azenui Asanga, Bamenda, Cameroon.
6 Clement Toh, Bamenda, Cameroon.
7 Kadiri Serge Bobo, Ngaoundéré, Cameroon.
8 Henry Nkwain, Bamenda, Cameroon.

Cuckoos *Cuculidae*

1 Claire Stares, Hampshire, UK.
2 Davies, 2000, page 28; Lefranc and Worfolk, 1997, page 137.
3 Aristotle, HoA, Bk IX, 618.
4 Newton, 1896, page 119.
5 Bircham, 2007, page 116.
6 Vesna Goldsworthy, London, UK.
7 Isabelle Charmantier, Devon, UK.
8 Anne Charmantier, Languedoc, France.
9 Katia Tsikhno, Minsk, Republic of Belarus.
10 Lennart Nilsson, Lund, Sweden.
11 Green, 1993, pages 38, 63.
12 COED, page 619.
13 Harting, 1978, page 149.

14 Christine Muir, Orkney, UK.
15 Lucie Hošková, Roztoky, Czech Republic.
16 Mary Crane, Wiltshire, UK.
17 Clive Fairweather, Devon, UK.
18 Håkan Karlsson, Lund, Sweden.
19 Nick Elton and Anabelle Legrix, Cornwall, UK.
20 Peter Herkenrath, Cambridge, UK.
21 Anna Staneva, Varna, Bulgaria.
22 Lucie Hošková, Roztoky, Czech Republic.
23 Kalliopi Stara, Ioannina, Greece.
24 Zoryana Lukyanchuk, Vinitzia, Ukraine; Yulia Moroz, Vinitzia, Ukraine.
25 Tsovinar Hovhannisyan, Yerevan, Armenia.
26 Grigson, 1996, pages 44–5.
27 Sarah Muir, East Lothian, UK.
28 Gattiker and Gattiker, 1989, page 265; Kalliopi Stara, Ioannina, Greece.
29 Kassagam, 1997, pages 32–3.
30 Muiruri and Maundu in Tidemann and Gosler, 2010, page 287.
31 Sakhamuzi Mhlongo, KwaZulu-Natal, South Africa.
32 Davies, 2000, page 110.
33 Ananda Banerjee, Delhi, India.
34 Kochmann, 1990, page 199.
35 Kochmann, 1990, page 4; http://en.wikipedia.org/wiki/Cuckoo_clock
36 Kochmann, 1990, pages 7, 102.
37 Bent, Cuckoos, page 37.
38 Slifer, 1998, page 154.
39 Werness, 2004, page 409; Tyler, 1979, pages 257–64.
40 Steyn, 1996, page 109.
41 Patrick Claffey, Dublin, Ireland.
42 Nason, 1992, page 91.
43 Tarun Chhabra, Tamil Nadu, India.
44 Aelian, Bk 1, 45.
45 Rowland, 1978, page 181.
46 Ali and Ripley, 1983, page 240.

Barn Owls Tytonidae **and Owls** Strigidae
1 Steinbeck, 1993, pages 148–9.
2 Mikkola, 1997, page 25.
3 Lewis-Williams, 2004, page 82; Wheye and Kennedy, 2008, page 7.
4 Gary Mock, Devon, UK.
5 Perrins, 2009, pages 322–35.
6 Sick, 1993, page 292.
7 Krech, 2009, page 146.
8 Porter, 1986, page 155; Bourke, 1958, page 74.
9 Mails, 1993, page 219.
10 Godfrey, 1941, page 61.
11 George Eshiamwata, Nairobi, Kenya.
12 Mikkola, 1997, page 29.
13 Ademola Ajagbe, Nairobi, Kenya.
14 Cocker, 2000, pages 60–65.
15 Laurence Mitchell, Norfolk, UK.
16 Cocker, 1998b, page 5.
17 Mikkola, 1997, pages 25–35; Cocker and Mikkola, 2001, pages 30–35.
18 Paul Kariuki Ndang'ang'a, Nyandarua, Kenya.
19 Cocker, 1998b, page 2.
20 HBW 5:136.
21 Rosamond Richardson, Essex, UK.
22 Cornelia Hutt, Virginia, USA.
23 Seyffert, 1995, pages 80–82.
24 Arnott, 2007, page 55.
25 Clairie Papazoglou, Nicosia, Cyprus.

26 Aasheesh Pittie, Andhra Pradesh, India.
27 Asad Rahmani, Maharashtra, India.
28 Asad Rahmani, Maharashtra, India.
29 Brown, 1936, pages 25–6.
30 Pliny, Bk X, XVI.
31 Baker, 2010, page 145.
32 Sick, 1993, page 296.
33 Aristotle, HoA, Bk IX, 609a.
34 van Nieuwenhuyse, Génot and Johnson, 2008, pages 17–18.
35 Macpherson, 1897, pages 173–5.
36 Marie Demoulin, Namur, Belgium.
37 Arne Ohlsson, Lund, Sweden; David Johnson, Virginia, USA.
38 Sick, 1993, page 288.
39 Wheye and Kennedy, 2008, page 43.
40 Bent, Birds of Prey II, page 366.
41 Farley, 1981, page 18.
42 Aristotle, HoA, Bk IX, 618a.
43 de Gubernatis, 1872, page 247.
44 Heng, 13 September 2011.
45 Philip Hall, Lagos, Nigeria.
46 BoA 3:132.
47 Bent, Birds of Prey II, page 308; BWP 4:470–71.

Oilbird Steatornithidae
1 Cleere and Nurney, 1998, page 113.
2 Newton, 1896, page 638.
3 Ingersoll, 1923, page 16.
4 Restall, Rodner and Lentino, 2006, Vol 1, page 210.
5 Humboldt and Bonpland, 1918, pages 125–8.
6 Tim Birkhead, Sheffield, UK.

Potoos Nyctibiidae
1 Sick, 1993, page 300.
2 Sick, 1993, page 302.
3 Mario Cohn-Haft, Manaus, Brazil.

Nightjars Caprimulgidae
1 Cruickshank, 1964, page 115.
2 Pitches, 2009, page 474.
3 Butchart, 2007, page 145.
4 Cruickshank, 1964, pages 116–17.
5 HBW 4:302.
6 Ingersoll, 1923, page 6.
7 Fenech, 2010, page 321.
8 Jackson, 2002, pages 147–61.
9 Stephen Spawls, Norfolk, UK.
10 Chisholm, 2008, page 24.
11 Andrew Bloomfield, Norfolk, UK.
12 Martín Lezama-López and Sarah Otterstrom, Managua, Nicaragua.
13 Ingersoll, 1923, page 6.
14 Turner, 1903, pages 49–51.
15 Gattiker and Gattiker, 1989, page 243.
16 Aristotle, HoA, Bk IX, 618b.
17 Aelian, BK 3, 39.
18 John Matthews, Essex, UK.
19 Goodman and Meininger, 1989, page 331; Diana and Hassan Qasrawi, Somerset, UK.
20 Elsadig Bashir, Doha, Qatar.
21 Abdi Jama, Djibouti City, Djibouti.
22 Mohammad Tohidifar, Tehran, Iran.
23 Kirwan et al, 2008, page 258; Korsh Ararat, Sulaymaniyah, Iraq.
24 Whinnom, 1966, page 62; Montserrat Fenwick, Norfolk, UK.

25 Korsh Ararat, Sulaymaniyah, Iraq.
26 Tim Wacher, London, UK.
27 Waterton, 1828, page 223.
28 Yarrell, 1845, Vol 2, page 272.
29 Henry, 1978, page 160.
30 Jackson, 2002, pages 147–61.
31 Bent, Cuckoos, page 211.
32 Sick, 1993, page 309.

Swifts Apodidae
1 Perrins, 2009, page 346.
2 Fenech, 2010, page 323.
3 Roberts, 1991, page 503.
4 Laurence Mitchell, Norfolk, UK.
5 Lusie Ambler, Sussex, UK.
6 Leah Pilmer, Middlesex, UK.
7 Lizzy Denning, Cambridge, UK.
8 Yossi Leshem, Tel Aviv, Israel.
9 Amir Balaban, Jerusalem, Israel.
10 Aristotle, HoA, Bk I, 487b, Bk IX, 618b.
11 Sick, 1993, pages 312–16.
12 Butchart, 2007, pages 145–6.
13 Mohammad Tohidifar, Tehran, Iran.
14 Graves, 2004, pages 300–307.
15 Strathern and Strathern, 1971, page 101.
16 Jim Crace, Birmingham, UK.
17 Laurence Mitchell, Norfolk, UK.
18 BoA 3:227–34.
19 Graves, 2004, pages 300–307.
20 Bent, Cuckoos, page 274.
21 Sick 1993, page 314; Chantler and Driessens, 1995, pages 163, 172–3.
22 Macpherson, 1897, page 155.
23 Gatter, 1998, page 151.
24 Ray, 1678, page 215.
25 Nguyen Quang, Vo Quang and Voisin, 2002, page 223.
26 Jobling, 2010, page 165.
27 Ray, 1678, page 215.
28 Cranbrook, 1984, page 148.
29 Koon and Cranbrook, 2002, pages 74–91.
30 http://swiftletfarmer.blogspot.com/2010/08/swiftlet-farms-visiting.html
31 Pete Wood, East Java, Indonesia.
32 Rosamund Young, Worcestershire, UK.

Hummingbirds Trochilidae
1 Robert Ridgely, New Hampshire, USA.
2 Torrey, 1903, page 88.
3 HBW 5:523.
4 Hudson, 1939, page 205.
5 Newton, 1896, page 446.
6 Perrins, 2009, page 354.
7 Bella Bigsby, California, USA.
8 Sick, 1993, page 323.
9 Holmgren, 1986, pages 54–7; Tyler, 1979, pages 117–20.
10 Holmgren, 1986, pages 70–71.
11 Rozzi et al, 2010, pages 168–9.
12 Holmgren, 1986, pages 44–52.
13 Tyler, 1979, page 117.
14 Holmgren, 1986, pages 32–3.
15 Holmgren, 1986, pages 64–5.
16 Thomas, 1993, page 11.
17 Soustelle, 1961, pages 52–3, 106.
18 Soustelle, 1961, page 107.
19 Holmgren, 1986, pages 65–7.
20 Soustelle, 1961, pages 68–9.

21 Doughty, 1975, page 30.
22 Sick, 1993, page 337.
23 Hudson, 1939, pages 205–6.
24 Bennett Hennessey, Santa Cruz, Bolivia.
25 Barry Walker, Cuzco, Peru.
26 Eric Salzman, New York, USA.
27 Mario Cohn-Haft, Manaus, Brazil.
28 Hudson, 1939, page 215.
29 Ray, 1678, page 232.
30 Fernando Pacheco, Rio de Janeiro, Brazil.
31 Graeme Gibson, Ontario, Canada.
32 Holmgren, 1986, page 164.
33 Newton, 1896, page 441.
34 Sick, 1993, page 323.
35 Rozzi et al, 2010, page 168.
36 Richard Gozney, Bermuda.
37 Skutch, 1973, page 33.
38 Sick, 1993, page 324.
39 Robin Restall, Caracas, Venezuela.
40 Karen Buchinsky, Massachusetts, USA.
41 Barry Walker, Cuzco, Peru; Fernando Pacheco, Rio de Janeiro, Brazil.
42 Robert Ridgely, New Hampshire, USA.
43 Karen Buchinsky, Massachusetts, USA.

Mousebirds *Coliidae*
1 Maclean, 1988, page 369; Godfrey, 1941, page 62.
2 Godfrey, 1941, page 62.
3 Arnott, 2007, page 106.
4 Jobling, 2010, page 113.
5 *BoA* 3:244.
6 Perrins, 2009, page 364.
7 van Someren, 1958, pages 203–4.
8 Martin Woodcock, Norfolk, UK.
9 Graeme Backhurst, Kent, UK.
10 Terry Stevenson, Rift Valley Province, Kenya.

Trogons *Trogonidae*
1 Howell and Webb, 1995, page 436.
2 Sick, 1993, page 352.
3 Godfrey, 1941, page 63.
4 Newton, 1896, page 760.
5 Newton, 1896, page 758.
6 Thomas, 1993, page 45.
7 Peterson and Peterson, 1992, pages 165–73.
8 Ray, 1678, page 392.
9 Sick, 1993, page 353.
10 Jobling, 2010, page 50.
11 Bonta, 2003, pages 129–30.
12 David Tipling, Norfolk, UK.
13 http://nuevomundo.revues.org/1462

Rollers *Coraciidae*
1 Newton, 1896, page 793.
2 Ali and Ripley, 1983, page 289.
3 Yarrell, 1845, Vol 2, pages 214–15.
4 Macpherson, 1897, page 149.
5 Houlihan, 1986, page 113.
6 Newton, 1896, page 794.
7 *BWP* 4:769.
8 Fry, Fry and Harris, 1992, page 190.
9 Fry, Fry and Harris, 1992, page 290.
10 Dave, 2005, page 157.
11 Mithlesh Dwivedi, Bihar, India.
12 Rajat Bhargava, Delhi, India.

Kingfishers *Alcedinidae*
1 Patricia Girdler, Wiltshire, UK.
2 *BoA* 3:299.
3 Bent, Cuckoos, page 124; *HBW* 6:186.
4 Macpherson, 1897, page 151.
5 Macpherson, 1897, page 151.
6 Robin, 2001, page 97.
7 Graves, 1996, page 159.
8 Arnott, 2007, page 12.
9 Aristotle, *HoA*, Bk V, 542a.
10 Newton, 1896, page 486; Ingersoll, 1923, page 22.
11 Ray, 1678, page 146.
12 Birkhead, 2008, pages 17–18.
13 Vesna Goldsworthy, London, UK.
14 Swainson, 1998, page 104.
15 John J Borg, Rabat, Malta.
16 Yarrell, 1845, Vol 2, page 228.
17 Fry, Fry and Harris, 1992, page 134.
18 Chisholm, 1956, page 226.
19 Legge, 2004, page 12.
20 Legge, 2004, pages 7–9.
21 Margaret Atwood and Graeme Gibson, Ontario, Canada; Rick Wright, Arizona, USA; Eric Salzman, New York, USA.
22 http://en.wikipedia.org/wiki/Men_at_Work
23 Keith and Lindsay Fisher, Queensland, Australia.
24 Gael Patterson, Queensland, Australia.
25 Keith and Lindsay Fisher, Queensland, Australia.
26 http://www.metro.co.uk/weird/829080-obese-kookaburra-sent-to-fat-camp-after-eating-too-many-sausages

Motmots *Momotidae*
1 Ray, 1678, page 386.
2 Howell and Webb, 1995, page 440.
3 Newton, 1896, page 595; Waterton, 1828, page 126.
4 Sick, 1993, pages 359–60.
5 Sick, 1993, page 361.
6 Armstrong, 1975, page 260.

Bee-eaters *Meropidae*
1 *BWP* 4:752.
2 *BWP* 4:761.
3 Aristotle, *HoA*, Bk IX, 615a.
4 *BoA* 3:316–22.
5 *BWP* 4:744–5.
6 Jeremy Mynott, Suffolk, UK.
7 Aristotle, *HoA*, Bk IX, 626.
8 Virgil, *The Georgics*, Bk IV, 14.
9 Perrins, 2009, page 376.
10 Macpherson, 1897, page 150.
11 Sherif Baha El Din, Cairo, Egypt.
12 Dawson, 1925b, pages 590–91.
13 Dave, 2005, pages 149–50.
14 *BWP* 4:752.
15 Pollard, 1977, page 47.
16 Perrins, 2009, page 374.

Hoopoe *Upupidae*
1 Graves, 1996, page 161.
2 Pollard, 1977, pages 164–6; Rozzi et al, 2010, page 50.
3 Betrò, 1996, page 106.

4 Adam Manvell, Norfolk, UK; Swainson, 1998, page 106.
5 Dawson, 1925a, pages 31–9.
6 Amir Balaban, Jerusalem, Israel.
7 Dupree, 1974, page 176.
8 Yossi Leshem, Tel Aviv, Israel.
9 *COED*, page 2743; Aelian, Bk 3, 26.
10 Attar, 1971, page 30.
11 Amir Balaban, Jerusalem, Israel; *BWP* 4:794.
12 Aristotle, *HoA*, Bk IX, 616b.
13 Dupree, 1974, page 173.
14 Newton, 1896, page 432.
15 Yossi Leshem, Tel Aviv, Israel.
16 Amir Balaban, Jerusalem, Israel.

Hornbills *Bucerotidae*
1 Ali and Ripley, 1983, page 295.
2 Kinnaird and O'Brien, 2007, page xiv.
3 Ali and Ripley, 1983, page 295.
4 Cuthbertson, 1949, page 149.
5 Newton, 1896, page 436; Stanley, 1851, page 190.
6 Ray, 1678, page 117.
7 Ali and Ripley, 1983, page 296.
8 Landsborough Thomson, 1964, page 379.
9 Henry Nkwain, Bamenda, Cameroon.
10 Christine Peacock, Ibadan, Nigeria.
11 Majnep and Bulmer, 1977, page 129.
12 Jacobs, 1990, page 108.
13 Freeman, 1960, pages 99–102.
14 Harrisson, 1951, page 403.
15 *TBW*, pages 331–5.
16 Kinnaird and O'Brien, 2007, page 193.
17 Kinnaird and O'Brien, 2007, page 208.
18 Kinnaird and O'Brien, 2007, page 235.
19 Helen Taylor, Cambridge, UK.

Ground Hornbills *Bucorvidae*
1 van Someren, 1958, page 13.
2 Kassagam, 1997, pages 31–2.
3 Godfrey, 1941, pages 66–7.
4 Sakhamuzi Mhlongo, KwaZulu-Natal, South Africa.
5 Ingersoll, 1923, pages 16–17.
6 Maasdorp, 2007, page 227.
7 Derwent and Mander, 1997, pages 22–5.
8 Yilma Dellelegn Abebe, Addis Ababa, Ethiopia.
9 van Someren, 1958, page 13.
10 Chiweshe, 2007, page 262.
11 Kemp, 1995, pages 4, 93.

Toucans and Barbets *Ramphastidae*
1 Bates and Busenbark, 1970, page 445.
2 Elphick, 2011, page 7; Bates, 1969, page 361.
3 Sick, 1993, pages 372–3.
4 Newton, 1896, page 976.
5 Sick, 1993, page 378.
6 Bates and Busenbark, 1970, page 448.
7 Bates, 1969, page 362.
8 Robin Restall, Caracas, Venezuela.
9 Ali and Ripley, 1983, page 300; Roberts, 1991, page 538.
10 Ananda Banerjee, Delhi, India.
11 Aasheesh Pittie, Andhra Pradesh, India.
12 Godfrey, 1941, page 69.
13 Patrick Claffey, Dublin, Ireland.
14 Patrick Claffey, Dublin, Ireland; Cocker, 2000, pages 63–4.

Honeyguides *Indicatoridae*
1 Cuthbertson, 1949, page 149; Short and Horne, 2001, page 96.
2 Godfrey, 1941, page 70.
3 *HBW* 7:286; Estes, 1991, page 436; Short and Horne, 2001, page 478.
4 Hussein Isack, Nairobi, Kenya.
5 Queeny, 1952, page 392.
6 Godfrey, 1941, page 70.
7 Newton, 1896, page 429.
8 Livingstone, 1857, page 471.
9 Cocker, 1992, pages 72–95.
10 van der Post, 1958, pages 25, 103.
11 van der Post, 1961, pages 72–6.
12 Jones, 2001, page 103.
13 Hussein Isack, Nairobi, Kenya.

Woodpeckers *Picidae*
1 Patrick Claffey, Dublin, Ireland.
2 Gorman, 2004, page 167.
3 Lovegrove, 2007, pages 140–43.
4 Perrins, 2009, page 413.
5 Perrins, 2009, page 412.
6 Alderfer, 2006, page 365.
7 http://en.wikipedia.org/wiki/Woody_Woodpecker
8 Pollard, 1977, pages 172–7.
9 Ng'weno in Tidemann and Gosler, 2010, pages 103–13; Kassagam, 1997, pages 28–30.
10 Rowland, 1978, page 182.
11 Swainson, 1998, page 100.
12 Krech, 2009, pages 186–7.
13 Catesby, 1754, page 16.
14 Krech, 2009, page 187.
15 Armstrong, 1975, page 252.
16 Hill, 2007, page 6.
17 Tanner, 2003, page 39; Gallagher, 2006, page 90.
18 Hill, 2007, pages 155–6.
19 Tanner, 2003, pages 46–53.
20 Tanner, 2003, pages 90–93.
21 Baicich, 2007, page 29; Gallagher, 2006, pages 15–16.
22 Jackson, 2004, pages 144–6.
23 Jackson, 2004, page 151.
24 Floyd, 2007, page 26.
25 Bent, Woodpeckers, page 1.
26 Tanner, 2003, page vii.
27 Gallagher, 2006, page 157.
28 Sweeney, 2007, page 70.
29 Wienholt, 2007, pages 10–11.
30 Wright, 2007, pages 48–52.
31 Tanner, 2003, page viii.
32 Sibley et al, 2007, pages 11–13.

New Zealand Wrens *Acanthisittidae*
1 Heather and Robertson, 1997, pages 164, 371–4.
2 Fuller, 1987, pages 192–6.
3 http://en.wikipedia.org/wiki/Stephens_Island_Wren

Pittas *Pittidae*
1 Chris Gooddie, London, UK.
2 Chris Gooddie, London, UK.
3 Langley, 2005, pages 13–16.
4 http://www.birdlife.org/news/news/2009/10/gurneys_pitta.html

Manakins *Pipridae*
1 Newton, 1896, page 531; Maaike Manten, Nairobi, Kenya.
2 COED, page 1716.
3 Sick, 1993, page 487; Guy Kirwan, Norfolk, UK.
4 Hilty and Brown, 1986, page 435.
5 Sick, 1993, pages 497–8; also see fabulous YouTube footage entitled 'Blue Manakins lekking'.
6 Newton, 1896, page 533; Fernando Pacheco, Rio de Janeiro, Brazil.
7 Armstrong, 1942, page 228.
8 Skutch, 1992, page 110.
9 Hilty and Brown, 1986, page 435.
10 Sick, 1993, page 499.
11 Hilty and Brown, 1986, page 435.

Cotingas *Cotingidae*
1 Leahy, 1983, page 157; Howell and Webb, 1995, page 519; Skutch, 1992, page 127.
2 Choate, 1973, page 6.
3 Tim Birkhead, Yorkshire, UK.
4 Reina and Kensinger, 1991, page 58.
5 Armstrong, 1942, page 201.
6 McEwan, Barreto and Neves, 2001, pages 8–9.
7 Bates and Busenbark, 1970, page 427.
8 Newton, 1896, page 86.
9 Ben Hoare, Bristol, UK.
10 Hilty and Brown, 1986, page 445.
11 Snow, 1982, page 114.
12 Sick, 1993, pages 512–13.
13 Restall, Rodner and Lentino, 2006, Vol 1, page 539.

Tyrant Flycatchers *Tyrannidae*
1 Ridgely and Gwynne Jr, 1989, page 282.
2 Latta et al, 2006, page 146.
3 *HBW* 9:233.
4 Bent, Flycatchers, page 25; Forbush, 1955, page 308.
5 Forbush, 1955, page 308.
6 Guy Kirwan, Norfolk, UK.
7 http://www.webexhibits.org:80/daylightsaving/franklin2.html
8 Bent, Flycatchers, page 21.
9 Rick Wright, Arizona, USA.
10 Hudson, 1920, Vol 1, page 191.
11 Hudson, 1982, page 47.
12 Sick, 1993, pages 449, 481.
13 Hudson, 1920, Vol 1, page 176.
14 Guy Kirwan, Norfolk, UK.
15 Guy Kirwan, Norfolk, UK.
16 Guy Kirwan, Norfolk, UK.

Antbirds *Thamnophilidae*
1 Restall, Rodner and Lentino, 2006, Vol 1, page 379.
2 Carlos Bethancourt, Panama City, Panama.

Tapaculos *Rhinocryptidae*
1 *TBW*, pages 377–8.
2 Darwin, 2009, page 283.
3 Restall, Rodner and Lentino, 2006, Vol 1, page 439; Schulenberg et al, 2007, page 392.

Antthrushes and Antpittas *Formicariidae*
1 Adam Gretton, Suffolk, UK.
2 Bartley, 2010, page 54.

3 Rodrigo Paz, Mindo, Ecuador.
4 Mark Roper, Co Kilkenny, Ireland.
5 Ridgely and Rivadeneira, 2007, pages 6–7.

Ovenbirds *Furnariidae*
1 *HBW* 8:162.
2 *HBW* 8:193.
3 Hudson, 1939, page 235.
4 Hudson, 1920, Vol 1, page 197.
5 Bonser, 1905, page 168.
6 Hudson, 1920, Vol 1, page 201.
7 Jonathan Elphick, London, UK.
8 Sick, 1993, page 431.
9 Attenborough, 1980, page 306.
10 Sick, 1993, page 431.
11 Efe and Filippini, 2006, pages 121–4.
12 Guy Kirwan, Norfolk, UK.
13 Amir Balaban, Jerusalem, Israel.
14 Sick, 1993, page 432.
15 Hudson, 1920, Vol 1, page 202.
16 Jonathan Elphick, London, UK.
17 Sick, 1993, page 430.
18 Darwin, 2009, pages 411–12.
19 Skutch, 1996, page 248.
20 Sue Gregory, Kuranda, Australia.

Lyrebirds *Menuridae*
1 Robin, 2001, page 169.
2 Jobling, 2010, page 250.
3 Chisholm, 1956, page 22.
4 *TBW*, page 407.
5 Chisholm, 1956, page 23.
6 Robin, 2001, page 171.
7 Hill, 2005, page 8.
8 http://www.youtube.com/watch?v=WeQjkQpeJwY
9 Chisholm, 1956, page 175.
10 Chisholm, 1956, page 24.
11 Chisholm, 1956, page 175.
12 Reilly, 1988, page 47.
13 Glen Threlfo and Tane Gravatt, Queensland, Australia.
14 Glen Threlfo, *Albert Lyrebird: Prince of the Rainforest*, DVD, 2000.
15 Sue Gregory, Queensland, Australia.
16 Robin, 2001, pages 174–5.

Scrubbirds *Atrichornithidae*
1 Robin, 2001, pages 258–9.
2 *TBW*, page 408.
3 Robin, 2001, page 257.
4 Huxley, 1967, page 362.

Bowerbirds *Ptilonorhynchidae*
1 Gilliard, 1969, page xvii.
2 Rothenberg, 2006, page 40.
3 Skutch, 1992, page 182.
4 Frith and Frith, 2004, page 11; Chisholm, 1956, page 4.
5 Gilliard, 1969, page xii.
6 Frith and Frith, 2008, page 123.
7 Frith and Frith, 2008, page 114.
8 Wright, 2003, page 56.
9 Hansell, 2007, page 224.
10 Hansell, 2007, page 244; Perrins, 2009, page 458.
11 Pizzey, 1980, page 389.

12 Frith and Frith, 2004, page 294.
13 Frith and Frith, 2004, page 373.
14 Tane Gravatt, Queensland, Australia.
15 Sharland, 1967, page 37.
16 Frith and Frith, 2008, page 142.
17 Chisholm, 1956, page 14.
18 Pizzey, 1980, page 388; Frith and Frith, 2008, page 270.
19 Frith and Frith, 2004, page 8.
20 Chisholm, 1956, pages 13–14.
21 Frith and Frith, 2004, page 8.
22 Frith and Frith, 2004, page 7.
23 Simpson, 1955, page 183.

Honeyeaters *Meliphagidae*
1 Perrins, 2009, page 466.
2 Sharland, 1967, page 44.
3 Newton, 1896, page 292.
4 Rand and Gilliard, 1967, page 573.
5 Nattrass, 2004, page 99.
6 Sharland, 1967, page 45.
7 Lord, 1950, page 100; Pizzey, 1980, page 322.
8 Malcolm and Caroline Taylor, Queensland, Australia.
9 Wilkes, 1978, page 218.
10 COED, page 2643.
11 Chisholm, 1956, page 72.
12 Darryl Jones, Queensland, Australia.
13 Ashley, Major and Taylor, 2009, pages 135–42.
14 Landsborough Thomson, 1964, pages 565–6.
15 http://www.britishmuseum.org/explore/highlights/highlight_objects/aoa/f/feather_money_tevau.aspx
16 Houston in Tidemann and Gosler, 2010, pages 55–66.

Wattled Crows *Callaeatidae*
1 Perrins, 2009, page 495.
2 Kaufman, 2008, page 53.
3 Kay Milton, Auckland, New Zealand.
4 Hokimate Harwood, Wellington, New Zealand.
5 Fuller, 1987, page 229.

Helmetshrikes and Bushshrikes
Malaconotidae
1 BoA 6:413.

Butcherbirds and Allies *Cracticidae*
1 Tim Birkhead, Yorkshire, UK.
2 Chisholm, 1956, page 222.
3 Jones, 2002, page 12.
4 Pizzey, 1980, page 405.
5 Kay Milton, Auckland, New Zealand.
6 HBW 14:331.
7 Jones, 2002, pages 50–51.
8 Chisholm, 1956, page 73.
9 Jones, 2002, page 52.
10 Jones, 2002, page 130.
11 Sharland, 1967, page 163.
12 Jones, 2002, pages 82–3.
13 Jones, 2002, pages 37–41.
14 Jones, 2002, page 114.
15 Jones, 2002, page 83.
16 Gerhard Veit, New South Wales, Australia.

Cuckooshrikes *Campephagidae*
1 Majnep and Bulmer, 1977, page 82.

2 Jobling, 2010, page 298.
3 Gotch, 1995, page 374.
4 Jobling, 2010, page 256.
5 Dave, 2005, page 58.
6 Jacobs, 1990.

Piopio *Turnagra*
1 Heather and Robertson, 1997, pages 422–3.
2 Fuller, 1987, pages 200–204.

Shrikes *Laniidae*
1 O'Brien, 1919, page 667.
2 Thoreau, 1993, page 384. Thoreau used the name 'snowbird' for both the Snow Bunting and the Dark-eyed Junco.
3 Terry Stevenson, Rift Valley Province, Kenya.
4 Jobling, 2010, page 219.
5 Bent, Wagtails, page 125.
6 Lefranc and Worfolk, 1997, page 30.
7 Ray, 1678, page 87.
8 Desfayes, 1998, Vol 1, page 894.
9 Newton, 1896, page 253.
10 Lefranc and Worfolk, 1997, page 17.
11 Houlihan, 1986, pages 126–8.
12 http://bna.birds.cornell.edu/bna/species/231
13 BoA 6:376.

Vireos and Greenlets *Vireonidae*
1 Restall, Rodner and Lentino, 2006, Vol 1, page 567.
2 Leahy, 1983, page 659.
3 Eric Salzman, New York, USA; Sibley, 2000, page 342.
4 Bent, Wagtails, page 343.
5 Stokes and Stokes, 2010, page 487.
6 Bond, 1990, page 185.
7 Bent, Wagtails, page 232.
8 Baynes, 1922, pages 256–9.

Figbirds and Orioles *Oriolidae*
1 Yvette Verner, Sussex, UK.
2 Mason and Allsop, 2009, page 9.
3 Elphick and Tipling, 2008, page 221.
4 Houlihan, 1986, page 129.
5 Whinnom, 1966, page 68; Desfayes, 1998, Vol 1, page 805.
6 Macpherson, 1897, page 17.
7 Ray, 1678, page 199.
8 Fenech, 1992, page 79; Natalino Fenech, Valletta, Malta.
9 Houlihan, 1986, page 131.
10 Bechstein, 1888, pages 47–8.

Shrikethrushes and Pitohuis *Colluricinclidae*
1 Phil Gregory, Queensland, Australia.
2 Majnep and Bulmer, 1977, page 103.

Drongos *Dicruridae*
1 BoA 5:528; Bainbrigge Fletcher and Inglis, 1924, page 32.
2 Jobling, 2010, page 135.
3 Ali and Ripley, 1983, page 359.
4 BoA 5:523.
5 Campbell and Lack, 1985, page 156.
6 HBW 14:201.

Fantails *Rhipiduridae*
1 Smythies, 1960, page 438.

2 Majnep and Bulmer, 1977, page 100.
3 Ali and Ripley, 1983, page 504.
4 Pizzey, 1980, page 264.
5 Darryl Jones, Queensland, Australia.

Monarchs *Monarchidae*
1 Jones, 2002, page 57.
2 Nattrass, 2004, page 26.
3 O'Hanlon, 1984, page 50.
4 Ali and Ripley, 1983, pages 506–8.

Crows and Jays *Corvidae*
1 Collar and Stuart, 1985, page 687.
2 Korsh Ararat, Sulaymaniyah, Iraq; Ananda Banerjee, Delhi, India.
3 Lindsey Ingham, London, UK.
4 Angela Mancino, Milan, Italy.
5 Riley, 19 February 2006.
6 Haupt, 2011, page 197.
7 Bent, Jays, pages 252–6.
8 Andrea Rutigliano, Milan, Italy.
9 Darryl Jones, Queensland, Australia.
10 Boyd, 1946, page 227.
11 Thomas, 1983, page 78.
12 Haupt, 2011, page 20.
13 COED, page 2423; Heinrich, 1990, page 23.
14 Adam and Svetlana Gretton, Suffolk, UK.
15 Boyd, 1946, page 227.
16 Geetha Iyer, Tamil Nadu, India.
17 David Stirling, British Columbia, Canada.
18 Richardson, 2009, pages 295–307.
19 Heinrich, 2002, page 31.
20 Stanley, 1851, pages 203–4.
21 Aelian, Bk 2, 51.
22 Toynbee, 1973, page 274.
23 Ian Johnson, Norfolk, UK.
24 Sian Daffyd, Gwynedd, UK.
25 Heinrich, 2002, page 83.
26 http://www.vggallery.com/painting/p_0779.htm
27 Guilhem Lesaffre, Paris, France.
28 Darryl Jones, Queensland, Australia.
29 Sara Butler, Somerset, UK.
30 James Rhodes, Oxfordshire, UK.
31 Tim Birkhead, Yorkshire, UK.
32 Xin et al, 1997, pages 114–16.
33 Sun, 2007, pages 47, 60.
34 Karen Brember, Surrey, UK.
35 Wordsworth, 1847, pages 47–9; Tait, 1924, page xii.
36 David Swithinbank, Lancashire, UK.
37 Pliny, Bk X, XLI.
38 BWP 8:82.
39 Marzluff and Balda, 1992, page 39.
40 Marzluff and Angell, 2005, page 42.
41 Emery and Clayton, 2004, pages 1903–07; Marzluff and Angell, 2005, pages 42–3.
42 Bent, Jays, page 223.
43 Newton, 1896, page 118.
44 Meinertzhagen, 1959, page 169.
45 Pliny, Bk X, XXX.
46 Heinrich, 2002, page 133; Meinertzhagen, 1959, pages 36–8.
47 Shay and Yehoadan Tzur, Haifa, Israel.
48 Keith Clack, Oxford, UK.
49 Bringhurst, 1999, pages 159–60.
50 Barbeau, 1950, pages 324–52.
51 Walens in Berlo and Wilson, 1993, page 186.

52 Walens in Berlo and Wilson, 1993, page 183.
53 Stewart, 1979, pages 15–59.

Australian Mudnesters *Corcoracidae*
1 Margaret Samuel, Glamorgan, UK.
2 Wright, 2003, page 31.

Birds-of-Paradise *Paradisaeidae*
1 Diamond, 1999, page 306.
2 Reader, 1990, page 37.
3 Newton, 1896, page 789.
4 Frith and Beehler, 1998, page 4.
5 Newton, 1896, page 38.
6 Simpson, 1955, page 184.
7 Hulme, 1895, page 210.
8 Ray, 1678, page 90.
9 Frith and Beehler, 1998, page vii.
10 Frith and Beehler, 1998, page 305.
11 Frith and Beehler, 1998, page 152.
12 Phil Gregory, Queensland, Australia.
13 http://www.airniugini.com.pg
14 http://www.sp.com.pg/export_lager.html
15 Joseph Ando, Mount Hagen, Papua New Guinea.
16 *TBW*, pages 617–18, 688.
17 Simpson, 1955, page xvi.
18 Strathern and Strathern, 1971, page 102.
19 Strathern and Strathern, 1971, page 48.
20 Reader, 1990, page 45.
21 Strathern and Strathern, 1971, page 59.
22 Gilliard, 1969, page 28.
23 Strathern and Strathern, 1971, page 65.
24 Strathern and Strathern, 1971, page 63.
25 Strathern and Strathern, 1971, pages 28–32.
26 Frith and Beehler, 1998, page 145.
27 Novotny, 2009, pages 41–2.
28 Strathern and Strathern, 1971, page 31.
29 Newton, 1896, page 38.
30 Gilliard, 1969, pages 24–6.
31 Frith and Beehler, 1998, page 34.
32 Doughty, 1975, page 10.
33 Doughty, 1975, page 146.
34 Attenborough, 1959, page 39.
35 Wallace, 2009, pages 409–10.

Australasian Robins *Petroicidae*
1 Pizzey, 1980, pages 237–9.
2 Butler and Merton, 1992, page 12.
3 King, 1981, unpaginated.
4 Butler and Merton, 1992, page 30.
5 Butler and Merton, 1992, page 88.
6 Butler and Merton, 1992, pages 122–3.
7 the late Don Merton, Tauranga, New Zealand.
8 http://www.birdlife.org/datazone/species
9 Butler and Merton, 1992, page 254.

Picathartes *Picathartidae*
1 Barnes, 2008, page 2.
2 Gotch, 1995, page 396.
3 Barnes, 2008, page 2.
4 Demey, Kirwan and Lack, 2008, page 17.
5 Augustus Asamoah, Accra, Ghana.
6 Alhaji Siaka, Freetown, Sierra Leone.

Waxwings and Allies *Bombycillidae*
1 Gotch, 1995, page 381.
2 Macpherson, 1897, page 84.
3 Desfayes, 1998, Vol 1, page 913.

4 Gattiker and Gattiker, 1989, page 208.
5 Jackson, Christine, 1993, pages 30–31.
6 Forbush, 1955, page 394.
7 Bechstein, 1888, page 189.
8 Delphine Legrix-Balidas, Upper Normandy, France.
9 Mynott, 2009, pages 310–11.
10 Baughman, 2003, page 371.

Palmchat *Dulidae*
1 *HBW* 10:327.
2 Campbell and Lack, 1985, page 431.
3 Gotch, 1995, page 382.
4 Jobling, 2010, page 141.

Tits and Chickadees *Paridae*
1 Jo Ferranto, Colorado, USA.
2 *COED*, pages 3333–5.
3 Bent, Jays, page 329.
4 Bechstein, 1888, page 276.
5 Bechstein, 1888, page 275.
6 John Fanshawe, Cornwall, UK.
7 Arne Ohlsson, Lund, Sweden.
8 Newton, 1896, pages 553, 967.
9 Stanley, 1851, page 252.
10 Masefield, 1897, page 31.
11 Davies et al, 2009, pages 761–71.
12 Perrins, 2009, page 554.
13 Nancy Hillstrand, Alaska, USA.
14 Donnett Elder, Saskatchewan, Canada.
15 Jones and Reynolds, 2008, pages 265–71.
16 Leahy, 1983, page 69.
17 Tim Harrison, Norfolk, UK; Jones and Reynolds, 2008, pages 265–71.
18 Arne Ohlsson, Lund, Sweden; Bern de Bruijn, Utrecht, Netherlands; Maaike Manten, Nairobi, Kenya.
19 Lennart Nilsson, Lund, Sweden.
20 Dragan Simic, Belgrade, Serbia.
21 Karen Buchinsky, Massachusetts, USA.
22 Caroline (née Fontannaz) Goulden, Salzburgerland, Austria.

Penduline Tits *Remizidae*
1 Barber, 1993, page 55; Gattiker and Gattiker, 1989, page 198.

Swallows and Martins *Hirundinidae*
1 Marcos Baltuska, Chubut Province, Argentina; Darryl Jones, Queensland, Australia; Katia Tsikhno, Minsk, Republic of Belarus; Anna Staneva, Varna, Bulgaria; Håkan Karlsson, Lund, Sweden; Ksenija Putilin, Skopje, Republic of Macedonia; Marija Stanisic, Podgorica, Montenegro; Zoryana Lukyanchuk, Vinitzia, Ukraine; Tsovinar Hovhannisyan, Yerevan, Armenia; Korsh Ararat, Sulaymaniyah, Iraq.
2 Lucie Hošková, Roztoky, Czech Republic.
3 Lucie Hošková, Roztoky, Czech Republic.
4 Godfrey, 1941, page 73.
5 Darryl Jones, Brisbane, Australia.
6 Bent, Flycatchers, page 497.
7 Terry Stevenson, Rift Valley Province, Kenya.
8 Patrick Claffey, Dublin, Ireland.
9 Cruickshank, 1964, page 129.
10 Bent, Flycatchers, page 452.
11 Aelian, Bk 1, 52.

12 Vera Hicks, Kent, UK.
13 Richard Mabey, Norfolk, UK.
14 Mungune, 1980, page 369.
15 Pollard, 1977, page 127.
16 Anna Staneva, Varna, Bulgaria.
17 Vedran Lucić, with help from BIOM, Zagreb, Croatia.
18 Marcos Baltuska, Chubut Province, Argentina.
19 Phil Chapman, Bristol, UK.
20 Rowland, 1978, page 164; http://en.wikipedia.org/wiki/Fuwa
21 Darryl Jones, Brisbane, Australia.
22 Arne Ohlsson, Lund, Sweden.
23 Jennie Kuca, Oxfordshire, UK.
24 John Fergusson, Ayrshire, UK.
25 Doughty and Fergus, 2002, pages 14–15.
26 Doughty and Fergus, 2002, page 87.
27 Bent, Flycatchers, page 489.
28 Doughty and Fergus, 2002, pages 21, 72.
29 Tony Miller, New Jersey, USA.
30 Aristotle, *HoA*, Bk VIII, 597b.
31 Birkhead, 2008, page 143.
32 Williamson, 1986, page 25.
33 Garnett, 13 February 1969.
34 White, 1924, page 37.
35 White, 1970, page 428.
36 Krech, 1999, pages 148–9.
37 Godfrey, 1941, page 40.
38 Tyler, 1979, page 116.
39 Sick, 1993, page 523.
40 Samantha Scheiman, Arkansas, USA.
41 Horatio Clare, Veneto, Italy.

Larks *Alaudidae*
1 Gotch, 1995, pages 367–8.
2 Lever, 2005, pages 161–5.
3 *COED*, page 1572.
4 Newton, 1896, page 507.
5 Rowland, 1978, pages 97–101.
6 Hudson, 1951b, pages 151–4.
7 Colin Williams, Hampshire, UK.
8 Green, 2000, page 716.
9 Vesna Goldsworthy, London, UK.
10 Bechstein, 1888, page 185; Kalliopi Stara, Ioannina, Greece.
11 Landsborough Thomson, 1964, page 418.
12 Geoffrey McMullan, London, UK.
13 Donald, 2004, pages 168–9.
14 Macpherson, 1897, pages 62–3.
15 Arentsen and Fenech, 2004, page 27.
16 José Bico, Île-de-France, France.
17 Arentsen and Fenech, 2004, page 11.
18 Pollard, 1977, page 104.
19 House, 2000, page 25.
20 Arentsen and Fenech, 2004, page 24; Newton, 1896, page 508; Macpherson, 1897, page 65; Donald, 2004, page 224.
21 Mayhew, 1864, page 128.
22 Lack, 1986, page 290.
23 Smith, 1980, page 442; Arne Ohlsson, Lund, Sweden.
24 Donald, 2004, pages 169–70.
25 Donald, 2004, pages 67–71.
26 John Fisher, Norfolk, UK.
27 Tim Birkhead, Sheffield, UK; Nigel Brown, Bangor, UK; Charles Bennett, Leicestershire, UK.
28 Colin Williams, Hampshire, UK.

Cisticolas and Allies *Cisticolidae*
1 Lynes and Osmaston, 1930, page 608.
2 Witherby, 1943, pages 156–8.
3 Gotch, 1995, page 400; Glare, 1982, pages 247, 349.
4 Simms, 1985, page 172.
5 Martin Woodcock, Norfolk, UK; Nigel Redman, Kent, UK.
6 Sakhamuzi Mhlongo, KwaZulu-Natal, South Africa.
7 Godfrey, 1941, page 97.
8 Patricia Schonstein, Cape Town, South Africa.
9 Godfrey, 1941, pages 92–6.
10 Maclean, 1988, pages 579–80.
11 McLynn, 1991, page 139.
12 Dave Richards, Karen, Kenya.
13 Shay Tzur, Haifa, Israel.
14 Shay Tzur, Haifa, Israel.

Tailorbirds *Orthotomus*
1 Jobling, 2010, page 291.
2 Newton, 1896, page 942.
3 Aasheesh Pittie, Andhra Pradesh, India.
4 Aasheesh Pittie, Andhra Pradesh, India; Jonathan Eames, Hanoi, Vietnam.
5 Ananda Banerjee, Delhi, India.

Bulbuls *Pycnonotidae*
1 *BoA* 4:367.
2 Terry Stevenson, Rift Valley Province, Kenya.
3 Gotch, 1995, page 375.
4 Jobling, 2010, page 73.
5 *BoA* 4:299.
6 Sinclair and Ryan, 2003, page 418.
7 Kirwan et al, 2008, page 317; Mohammad Azhdeh and Jeni Williams, Carmarthen, UK.
8 translated by Tamadhur Jamil Al-Khishali, Norwich, UK.
9 Ali Sadr, Tehran, Iran.
10 Elsadig Bashir, Doha, Qatar.
11 Ali Sadr, Tehran, Iran.
12 Elsadig Bashir, Doha, Qatar.
13 Whistler, 1949, page 70.
14 Tamadhur Jamil Al-Khishali, Norwich, UK.
15 James Wolstencroft, Arusha, Tanzania.
16 Terry Stevenson, Rift Valley Province, Kenya.
17 Preston, 1975, pages 112–13.
18 Avirama Golan, Tel Aviv, Israel.
19 Amir Balaban, Jerusalem, Israel.

Old World Warblers *Sylviidae*
1 Jobling, 2010, pages 305, 375–6.
2 Gotch, 1995, page 398.
3 Swainson, 1998, page 28.
4 Moreau, 1972, pages 102–4.
5 Macpherson, 1897, page 128.
6 Bechstein, 1888, page 206.
7 Aristotle, *HoA*, Bk VIII, 592b; Arnott, 2007, page 233.
8 Arnott, 2007, pages 233–4; Ray, 1678, pages 216, 226–7; Newton, 1896, page 250.
9 Apicius, Bk 4, Ch 2, recipes 132, 141; see http://penelope.uchicago.edu/Thayer/E/Roman/Texts/Apicius
10 Petronius, 1986, 'Dinner with Trimalchio', section 33.
11 Ray, 1678, page 227.

12 Lewis, 1983, page 197.
13 Shialis, 2012, page 6.
14 Mark Turner, Worcestershire, UK.
15 Shialis, 2011, page 7.
16 Anonymous, UK.
17 Shialis, 2011, page 19.
18 Franzen, 26 July 2010.
19 Andrea Rutigliano, Milan, Italy.
20 Andrea Rutigliano, Milan, Italy.

Babblers *Timaliidae*
1 Ali and Ripley, 1983, page 456.
2 Smythies, 1953, page 51.
3 John Holmes, Hong Kong, China.
4 Caldwell and Caldwell, 1931, page 88.
5 La Touche, 1925, page 64.
6 Ray Tipper, Algarve, Portugal.
7 Jonathan Eames, Hanoi, Vietnam.
8 Lever, 2005, page 173.
9 Pratt, Bruner and Berrett, 1987, page 266.
10 Jobling, 2010, page 221; Pyle and Pyle, 2009.
11 *BWP* 7:117.
12 Whistler, 1949, page 41.
13 Ananda Banerjee, Delhi, India.

White-eyes *Zosteropidae*
1 Lever, 2005, page 177; Pratt, Bruner and Berrett, 1987, page 282.
2 Mike Ord, Oahu, Hawaii.
3 Godfrey, 1941, page 118.
4 Gotch, 1995, page 418.
5 Peter Herkenrath, Cambridge, UK.
6 Maaike Manten, Nairobi, Kenya.
7 Greg Pringle, Beijing, China.
8 Keiko Suzue, Tokyo, Japan.
9 http://pet-cockatiel.com/Dboard/viewforum.php?f=56
10 Hiroshige, 1988, unpaginated.

Goldcrests and Kinglets *Regulidae*
1 Aristotle, *HoA*, Bk VIII, 592b.
2 Aristotle, *HoA*, Bk IX, 615a.
3 Arnott, 2007, pages 20–21, 247.
4 Dimitris Vavylis, Trikala, Greece.
5 André Konter, Echternach, Luxembourg.
6 *BWP* 6:676.
7 Alan Bartels, Nebraska, USA.
8 Arne Ohlsson, Lund, Sweden.
9 *BWP* 6:670.
10 Ticehurst, 1932, page 114.
11 John J Borg, Rabat, Malta.
12 Bent, Thrushes, page 391.
13 Macpherson, 1897, page 130.
14 Bechstein, 1888, page 272.
15 Richard Mabey, Norfolk, UK.
16 Ted Floyd, Colorado, USA.

Wrens *Troglodytidae*
1 Nicholson, 1990, page 160.
2 Jobling, 2010, page 391; Gotch, 1995, page 383.
3 Arnott, 2007, pages 20–21.
4 Aristotle, *HoA*, Bk IX, 615a.
5 Armstrong, 1958, page 166.
6 Hutton, 1996, pages 97–8; Armstrong, 1958, pages 141–66.
7 Bent, Nuthatches, page 155.
8 Jim Perrin, Ariège, France.
9 Perrins, 2009, page 545.

10 Bent, Nuthatches, page 119; Forbush, 1955, page 358.
11 Bent, Nuthatches, page 118.
12 Kurt Jackson, Cornwall, UK.
13 Nancy Hillstrand, Alaska, USA.

Nuthatches and Wallcreeper *Sittidae*
1 Bechstein, 1888, page 86.
2 Martin, 1993, page 129.
3 Karen Buchinsky, Massachusetts, USA.
4 Roger Howard, Essex, UK.
5 Ananda Banerjee, Delhi, India; Chris Davis, Sussex, UK; Nick Derry, Franche-Comté, France; Milko Dimitrov, Bourgas, Bulgaria; Caroline (née Fontannaz) Goulden, Saltzburgerland, Austria; Colin Jones, Norfolk, UK; Ed Keeble, Suffolk, UK; Richard Sprakes, Yorkshire, UK; Dominique Tomasini, Besançon, France.
6 Crewe, 2007, pages 444–5.

Mockingbirds and Thrashers *Mimidae*
1 Janet Ruth, New Mexico, USA.
2 Jackson, Michael, 1993, pages 186–8; *HBW* 10:467.
3 Sick, 1993, pages 545, 549.
4 Hudson, 1920, Vol 1, page 12; Hudson, 1939, page 276.
5 Catesby, 1754, page 27.
6 Bond, 1990, page 166; Latta et al, 2006, page 166.
7 Tyler, 1979, pages 212-15; Martin, 1993, page 122.
8 Doughty, 1988, pages 36–7.
9 *COED*, page 1826.
10 Catesby, 1754, page 27.
11 Bent, Nuthatches, pages 311–12.
12 Chapman, 1934, page 409; Forbush, 1955, page 367.
13 Sick, 1993, page 550.
14 Tweti, 2008, page 25.
15 Chapman, 1934, page 408.
16 Krech, 2009, page 196.
17 Wheye and Kennedy, 2008, pages 122–3.
18 Doughty, 1988, page 68.
19 Bent, Nuthatches, page 296.
20 Samantha Scheiman, Arkansas, USA.
21 Lee, 2004, page 98.

Starlings *Sturnidae*
1 Voous, 1960, page 264.
2 Feare and Craig, 1998, pages 129–31; *TBW*, page 60.
3 Cheryl M Calaustro, Guam, USA.
4 Feare and Craig, 1998, pages 143–7.
5 Pliny, Bk X, LIX.
6 Leahy, 1983, page 681; Edith Cadot and Josette Canu, Upper Normandy, France.
7 Fitter and Richardson, 1952, page 55.
8 http://www.starlingtalk.com/mozart3.htm
9 Bechstein, 1888, page 183.
10 Arne Ohlsson, Lund, Sweden.
11 John Parker, Salzburg, Austria; Peter Herkenrath, Cambridge, UK; Dominique Tomasini, Besançon, France.
12 Byron Palacios, Dorset, UK.
13 Bill Thompson III, Ohio, USA.
14 Arne Ohlsson, Lund, Sweden.
15 Richard Wakeford, email contribution, UK.

16 Chris Watson, Tyne and Wear, UK.
17 Bent, Wagtails, pages 183–4.
18 Stefferud, 1966, page 247.
19 Bates and Busenbark, 1970, page 359.
20 Wilson, 2003, page 71.
21 Feare, 1984, page 62.
22 Heather and Robertson, 1997, page 414; Lever, 2005, pages 197–9; *BoA* 6:654.
23 Ali and Ripley, 1983, page 369.
24 Lever, 2005, pages 184–93.
25 Bill Pranty, Florida, USA.
26 Todd, 2001, pages 135–47.
27 Holloway, 1996, pages 392–3.
28 Forbush, 1955, page 399.
29 http://ddr.nal.usda.gov/ bitstream/10113/17532/1/IND44083370.pdf
30 Douville de Franssu et al, 1988, pages 272–6.
31 Feare and Craig, 1998, page 42.
32 Feare, 1984, page 40; *HBW* 14:702.
33 Feare, 1984, page 172.
34 Leahy, 1983, page 559; Pizzey, 1980, page 380; Simpson and Day, 2004, page 280.
35 Karen Lunt, Liverpool, UK.
36 Martin, 1993, page 177.
37 Swainson, 1998, page 73.
38 Ray, 1678, page 196.
39 Lovegrove, 2007, page 170.
40 Millar, 1969, pages 184–5.
41 *BWP* 8:239.
42 Meiklejohn, 1954, pages 95–6.
43 *BWP* 8:273.
44 Feare, 1984, page 160.
45 Pliny, Bk X, XXXIX; Aelian, Bk 17, 19.
46 Newton, 1896, page 698.
47 Greppin, 1978, pages 187–9.
48 Bannerman 1:75–6.
49 Dr A K Yurlov and Professor V Glupov, Novosibirsk, Russia.
50 Potts, 1967, pages 25–42.

Thrushes *Turdidae*
1 Heather and Robertson, 1997, page 384.
2 Dorothea Brass, Nairobi, Kenya.
3 Lynne Ross, Toronto, Canada.
4 Jean Skinner, Suffolk, UK.
5 John Beatty, Derbyshire, UK.
6 Sick, 1993, page 545.
7 Yalden and Albarella, 2009, pages 45–50.
8 Sebastian Thewes, Spain.
9 Homer, 1976, Bk XXII, 468.
10 Jashemski and Meyer, 2002, page 399; Yarrell, 1845, Vol 1, page 209.
11 Blüchel, 1997, page 88.
12 Wernham et al, 2002, page 529; Clark, 1948, page 116.
13 Peter Herkenrath, Cambridge, UK.
14 Petronius, 1986, 'Dinner with Trimalchio', section 40 (trans. Jeremy Mynott).
15 Rowland, 1978, page 12.
16 Fenech, 1992, page 79; Franzen, 26 July 2010.
17 Pitches, 2009, pages 289–90.
18 Yalden and Albarella, 2009, page 62.
19 Sick, 1993, pages 543–5.
20 Karen Lunt, Merseyside, UK.
21 David Tipling, Norfolk, UK.
22 Bent, Thrushes, pages 142, 156–7; Forbush, 1955, pages 379–80; Chapman, 1934, pages 414–15.

23 Leopold, 1970, page 57.
24 Thoreau, 1993, pages 428–9.
25 Restall, Rodner and Lentino, 2006, Vol 1, page 618.
26 Rachel Holmes, Edinburgh, UK.
27 Sam Lauren Smith, Leicestershire, UK.
28 Marcos Baltuska, Chubut Province, Argentina.
29 Forbush, 1955, page 373.
30 Sutton and Sutton, 2006, pages 20–22.
31 Forbush, 1955, page 373.
32 Martin, 1993, page 12.
33 Tyler, 1979, pages 161–7.
34 Chapman, 1934, page 419.
35 Bent, Thrushes, page 233.
36 Baicich, 2010, pages 58–9.

Chats and Old World Flycatchers
Muscicapidae
1 Conder, 1989, pages 35–48; *BWP* 5:776.
2 Yarrell, 1845, Vol 1, page 248.
3 Liz Hague, London, UK.
4 Stephanie Sorrell, Cumbria, UK.
5 Stephanie Sorrell, Cumbria, UK.
6 Elizabeth Reynaud, Surrey, UK.
7 Arne Ohlsson, Lund, Sweden.
8 Mullarney et al, 1999, page 258.
9 Lennart Nilsson, Lund, Sweden.
10 Arne Ohlsson, Lund, Sweden.
11 David Tipling, Norfolk, UK.
12 Aasheesh Pittie, Hyderabad, India.
13 Arne Ohlsson, Lund, Sweden.
14 Williams, 1997, page 65.
15 Bechstein, 1888, page 217.
16 Graves, 1996, pages 161–3.
17 Keats, 1990, pages 285–8, 603.
18 McCarthy, 2009, page 47.
19 Schimmel, 1992, page 178.
20 Arberry, 1948, page v; Schimmel, 1992, page 3.
21 FitzGerald, 1953, page 112.
22 Attar, 1971, pages 14–15.
23 Mohammad Tohidifar, Tehran, Iran.
24 *BWP* 5:634.
25 Hafiz, 2004, page 6.

Dippers *Cinclidae*
1 Restall, Rodner and Lentino, 2006, Vol 1, page 607.
2 John Barkham, Devon, UK.
3 Muir, 1992, page 410.

Sunbirds *Nectariniidae*
1 Liz Coverdale, Laikipia, Kenya.
2 *BoA* 6:172.
3 Ali and Ripley, 1983, page 663.
4 Ali and Ripley, 1983, pages 662–3; Cheke, Mann and Allen, 2001, page 317.
5 *BoA* 6:182; Cheke, Mann and Allen, 2001, page 226.
6 Liz Coverdale, Laikipia, Kenya.
7 Amir Balaban, Jerusalem, Israel.
8 Paz, 1987, page 227.
9 Shirihai, 1996, page 532.
10 Amir Balaban, Jerusalem, Israel.

Old World Sparrows and Snowfinches
Passeridae
1 Summers-Smith, 1988, pages 278–81.
2 Diana Qasrawi, Somerset, UK.

3 Summers-Smith, 1988, page 280.
4 Sick, 1993, page 638.
5 Woods, 1988, pages 231–2.
6 Clement, Harris and Davis, 1993, page 445; Summers-Smith, 2005, page 83.
7 Sick, 1993, page 638.
8 Todd, 2001, page 138.
9 Forbush, 1955, page 457.
10 Mike Crewe, New Jersey, USA.
11 *BWP* 8:313; Bruggers and Elliott, 1989, page 335.
12 Bruggers and Elliott, 1989, page 3.
13 Lovegrove, 2007, pages 171–8.
14 Tim Harrison, Norfolk, UK.
15 http://www.worldsparrowday.org/ themefor2011.html
16 Hanks and Hodges, 1988, page 503.
17 Thomas Muir, Frankfurt, Germany.
18 Nick Elton and Anabelle Legrix, Cornwall, UK.
19 Bent, Blackbirds, page 7.
20 Arnott, 2007, page 227.
21 Cott, 1954, page 139.
22 Wilson, 22 December 2005.
23 Birkhead, 2003, page 21.
24 Carter, 2006, page 86; Green, 2000, page 1115.
25 Dragan Simic, Belgrade, Serbia.
26 Bede, 1910, Ch 13.
27 Bent, Blackbirds, page 23.

Weavers and Widowbirds *Ploceidae*
1 Lever, 2005, pages 223–4.
2 Latta et al, 2006, page 215.
3 Gotch, 1995, pages 441–4.
4 Birkhead, 2012, page 100.
5 Dieter Oschadleus, Cape Town, South Africa; Oschadleus, 2005, pages 31–6.
6 Bruggers and Elliott, 1989, page 19.
7 Bruggers and Elliott, 1989, page 21.
8 Bruggers and Elliott, 1989, pages 33–4.
9 Landsborough Thomson, 1964, page 673.
10 Bruggers and Elliott, 1989, page 27.
11 Bruggers and Elliott, 1989, page 181.
12 Peter Jones, Sutherland, UK.
13 Bruggers and Elliott, 1989, pages 222–4.
14 Bruggers and Elliott, 1989, page 255.
15 Bruggers and Elliott, 1989, page 26.
16 Bruggers and Elliott, 1989, page 313.
17 Bruggers and Elliott, 1989, page 327.
18 Bruggers and Elliott, 1989, page 22.
19 Bruggers and Elliott, 1989, pages 328–30.
20 Peter Jones, Sutherland, UK.

Waxbills, Munias and Allies *Estrildidae*
1 Smythies, 1960, page 498.
2 Bates and Busenbark, 1970, page 94.
3 Bates and Busenbark, 1970, page 135.
4 Ali and Ripley, 1983, page 679; Newton, 1896, page 11.
5 Lever, 2005, pages 236–9.
6 Lever, 2005, pages 246–50.
7 Gotch, 1995, page 441.
8 Smythies, 1960, page 494.
9 Liu, 2007, page 64.
10 Bechstein, 1888, page 103.
11 Smythies, 1960, page 494.
12 Birkhead, 2008, page 332.
13 Tim Birkhead, Sheffield, UK.

Indigobirds and Whydahs *Viduidae*

1 Montaigne, 2003, page 1133.
2 Jobling, 2010, page 401.
3 COED, pages 3756, 3774.
4 Payne, 1996, page 24.
5 Robert Payne, Michigan, USA.
6 Payne, 1996, page 21.
7 Bates and Busenbark, 1970, page 159.
8 Lever, 2005, page 251.

Wagtails and Pipits *Motacillidae*

1 Thomas, 1983, page 37.
2 Swainson, 1998, page 45; Peter Herkenrath, Cambridge, UK.
3 Kassagam, 1997, page 48.
4 Godfrey, 1941, pages 100–101.
5 Godfrey, 1941, page 102.
6 Swainson, 1998, pages 44–5.
7 Newton, 1896, page 1018.
8 Malcolm Wilson, Johannesburg, South Africa.
9 Jeremy Mynott, Suffolk, UK.
10 Amir Balaban, Jerusalem, Israel.
11 Stanley, 1851, page 253.
12 Peter Walton, Cheshire, UK.

Finches *Fringillidae*

1 Newton, 1896, page 72.
2 Bechstein, 1888, page 146.
3 Nick Elton, Cornwall, UK.
4 BWP 8:610.
5 Tim Birkhead, Sheffield, UK.
6 Friedmann, 1946, pages 4–5.
7 Nicholls, 2005, pages 133–4, 238–9.
8 da Vinci, 2008, page 215.
9 Friedmann, 1946, page 26.
10 Friedmann, 1946, page 44.
11 Grieve, 1994, page 795.
12 Friedmann, 1946, page 66.
13 Birkhead, 2003, page 27.
14 Evgeny Karev, Ufa, Russia.
15 Cocker and Mabey, 2005, page 443.
16 Roberts, 1972, pages 57–9.
17 Fenech, 1992, pages 115–16.
18 Bechstein, 1888, pages 95–6.
19 Birkhead, 2003, page 9.
20 Fenech, 1992, pages 78–9.
21 Fenech, 1992, page 113.
22 Fenech, 1992, page 112; Natalino Fenech, Valletta, Malta.
23 Amir Balaban, Jerusalem, Israel.

Hawaiian Honeycreepers *Drepanididae*

1 Pratt, Bruner and Berrett, 1987, page 295.
2 TBW, page 706–7.
3 Wilson, 1992, page 97.
4 Cummins in Berlo and Wilson, 1993, page 167.
5 Hooper, 2006, page 15.
6 Thomas, 1995, page 154.
7 Cook, 2003, page 494.
8 Cook, 2003, page 495.
9 Rose, 1978, page 1.
10 Thomas, 1995, page 155.
11 Rose, 1978, pages 3–4.
12 Rose, 1978, page 4; Thomas, 1995, page 15.
13 Thomas, 1995, page 156.
14 Hooper, 2006, pages 80–83.
15 Jobling, 2010, page 400; Gotch, 1995, page 432.
16 Cummins in Berlo and Wilson, 1993, page 171.

17 Thomas, 2004, page 387.
18 Macpherson, 1897, page 140.
19 King, 1981, unpaginated.
20 Macpherson, 1897, page 136.
21 Cummins in Berlo and Wilson, 1993, page 172.
22 Cummins in Berlo and Wilson, 1993, page 181.
23 Macpherson, 1897, page 136.
24 Rose, 1978, page 57.
25 Thomas, 1995, page 164.
26 Wilson, 2003, pages 44–7.

New World Warblers *Parulidae*

1 Leahy, 1983, page 775.
2 Bent, American Wood Warblers, page 329.
3 Chapman, 1934, page 446.
4 Jobling, 2010, page 318.
5 Eric Salzman, New York, USA.
6 Mike Higgiston, New York, USA.
7 Samantha Scheiman, Arkansas, USA.
8 Cruickshank, 1964, page 160.
9 http://www.birdlife.org/datazone/speciesfactsheet.php?id=9120

New World Blackbirds *Icteridae*

1 Alan Bartels, Nebraska, USA.
2 Davies, 2000, page 145; Leahy, 1983, page 159.
3 Bonta, 2003, page 22.
4 Floyd, 2008, page 543.
5 Alan Bartels, Nebraska, USA.
6 Bonta, 2003, pages 15, 47.
7 Sick, 1993, page 629.
8 Krech, 2009, page 50.
9 Catesby, 1754, page 13.
10 Catesby, 1754, page 11; Sick, 1993, page 615.
11 Bruggers and Elliott, 1989, page 21.
12 Bruggers and Elliott, 1989, page 335.
13 Johnsgard, 1997, page 345.
14 Orians, 1985, page 56.
15 Leahy, 1983, page 101.
16 Cruickshank, 1964, page 172.
17 Bond, 1990, page 223.
18 Alan Bartels, Nebraska, USA.
19 Gotch, 1995, page 434; Sick, 1993, page 616.
20 Restall, Rodner and Lentino, 2006, Vol 1, page 747.
21 Bennett Hennessey, Santa Cruz, Bolivia.
22 Ridgely and Gwynne Jr, 1989, page 434; Restall, Rodner and Lentino, 2006, Vol 1, page 749.
23 Reina and Kensinger, 1991, page 99.
24 Sick, 1993, pages 618–19; Orians, 1985, pages 76–7.

Bananaquit *Coerebidae*

1 Restall, Rodner and Lentino, 2006, Vol 1, page 683; Bond, 1990, page 207.
2 Sick, 1993, page 562.
3 Professor Cedric Smith, New York, USA.

Buntings and New World Sparrows *Emberizidae*

1 Chapman, 1934, page 522.
2 Bent, Grosbeaks, page 784.
3 Forbush, 1955, page 523.
4 Marcos Baltuska, Chubut Province, Argentina.
5 Janet Ruth, New Mexico, USA.
6 Nice, 1964; Bent, Grosbeaks, pages 1513–23.
7 Stefferud, 1966, page 264.
8 Martin Woodcock, Norfolk, UK; Hudson et al, 2009, pages 592–3.

9 Cruickshank, 1964, page 193.
10 Cruickshank, 1964, page 194.
11 Janet Ruth, New Mexico, USA.
12 Ray, 1678, page 270.
13 Desfayes, 1998, Vol 1, page 1230.
14 Bannerman 1:281.
15 Varro, Bk 3, Ch 5:2.
16 Macpherson, 1897, page 53.
17 Kumerloeve, 1953, pages 67–130.
18 Allen, 2002, page 74.
19 Laubreaux, 1931, page 46.
20 Colette, 2003, page 33.
21 Anonymous, Corrèze, France.

Tanagers and Allies *Thraupidae*

1 Floyd, 2008, page 409; Restall, Rodner and Lentino, 2006, Vol 1, page 625; Sick, 1993, page 563.
2 Guy Kirwan, Norfolk, UK.
3 Sick, 1993, page 564.
4 Gotch, 1995, page 427; Arnott, 2007, pages 36, 221.
5 Ridgely and Tudor, 1989, Vol 1, page 207.
6 Pacheco, 2001, pages 5–11; Gotch, 1995, page 427.
7 Mark Bonta, Mississippi, USA; Raúl Arias de Para, El Valle, Panama; Claudia Burgos and Hugo Haroldo Toledo, Guatemala Province, Guatemala.
8 Fernando Pacheco, Rio de Janeiro, Brazil.
9 Clay, 2002, page 100; de la Peña and Rumboll, 1998, unpaginated.
10 Bates, 1969, page 7.
11 Bennett Hennessey, Santa Cruz, Bolivia.
12 Guy Kirwan, Norfolk, UK.
13 Raúl Arias de Para, El Valle, Panama.
14 Barry Walker, Cuzco, Peru.
15 Sick, 1993, page 565.
16 Collar et al, 1992, page 922; TBW, page 564.
17 Juan Ignacio Areta, Entre Ríos Province, Argentina.
18 Jackson, Michael, 1993, page 188.
19 Darwin, 2009, page 391.
20 Lack, 1947, page 9.
21 Jackson, Michael, 1993, page 189.
22 Gould, 2002, page 192.
23 Dawkins, 2004, page 220.
24 Dawkins, 2004, page 220.
25 Weiner, 1994, page 45.
26 Weiner, 1994, page 43.
27 Dawkins, 2004, pages 220–22.

Grosbeaks, Saltators and Allies *Cardinalidae*

1 Alderfer, 2006, page 597.
2 Floyd, 2008, page 445.
3 Choate, 1973, page 177.
4 Newton, 1896, page 76.
5 Krech, 2009, page 160.
6 Catesby, 1754, page 56.
7 Forbush, 1955, page 483; Bent, Cardinals I, page 1; Baughman, 2003, page 394.
8 Adrienne Bagwell, Surrey, UK.
9 Eric Salzman, New York, USA.
10 Forbush, 1955, page 483.
11 Donnett Elder, Saskatchewan, Canada.
12 Bill Thompson III, Ohio, USA.
13 Jo Ferranto, Colorado, USA.
14 Cornelia Hutt, Virginia, USA.

ACKNOWLEDGEMENTS

Over the eight calendar years that we have been working on *Birds and People* we have acquired many debts of gratitude. None is more significant than that owed to all the contributors whose words appear in the book. *Birds and People* would have been impossible without them.

Many of these contributors have become part of a network of constant informants and even friends. I was able to filter through their personal experiences the facts, ideas or claims that we found elsewhere in the literature. This worldwide support has been an immense gift and privilege. I would like to offer all of the following people our heartfelt thanks (an asterisk denotes those who made important multiple contributions): Yilma Dellelegn Abebe, Karen Acton, Abrar Ahmed, Gill Ainsworth, Ademola Ajagbe, Alan Aldous, Anoushka Alexander, Elisabeth Alington, Michael Allen, Dan Alon, Lusie Ambler, B Amos, Mark Anderson, Wicki Anderson, Joseph Ando, Korsh Ararat*, Juan Ignacio Areta, Raúl Arias de Para*, Augustus Asamoah, Christian Azenui Asanga, Dick Ashford*, Margaret Atwood, Augustine Azealor, Mohammad Azhdeh, Graeme Backhurst, Emma Bacon, Adrienne Bagwell*, Sherif and Mindy Baha El Din, Sarah Bakewell, Amir Balaban*, Michael Balter, Marcos Baltuska, Ananda Banerjee*, Anne Bannerman, Hem Baral, John Barkham, John Barlow, Suvash Barman, Boris Barov, Alan Bartels*, Elsadig Bashir*, Yub Raj Basnet, Phil Battley, John Beatty, Charles Bennett, Molly Bennett, Brinley Best, Carlos Bethancourt, Rajat Bhargava, José Bico, Bella Bigsby*, Tim Birkhead*, Ben and Theo Blackburn, Bryan Bland, Andrew Bloomfield, Kadiri Serge Bobo, Mark Bonta, John J Borg*, Kate Boreham, Dorothea Brass, Axel Bräunlich, Mark Brazil, Brandon Breen, Karen Brember, Ruth Brompton-Charlesworth, Joost Brouwer*, Nigel Brown, Karen Buchinsky, Ian Burfield, Claudia Burgos, Sara Butler, David Butvill, Elizabeth Cabrera, Christian Cadot, Edith Cadot, Rob Cahill, Cheryl M Calaustro, Sara Calhim, Jesus Calle, Andrew Campbell, Mhorag Candy, John Cantelo, Josette Canu, Gabriel Castresana, Claudio Celada, Phil Chapman, Anne Charmantier, Isabelle Charmantier*, Vivien Chartendrault, Bharati Chatuvedi, Anthony Cheke, Tarun Chhabra, Mand Christie, Keith Clack, Patrick Claffey*, Fiona Clark, Horatio Clare, Chris Clegg, Sacha Cleminson, David Cobham, Miriam and Rachael Cocker, Mario Cohn-Haft, Ray Collier, Alan Conreras, Oswaldo Contreras, Gerry Cotter, David Cottrell, Liz and Miles Coverdale, Peter Cowdrey, Jim Crace, Mary Crane, Mike and Megan Crewe*, Nicola Crockford, Mike and Ping Crosby, Michael Crow, Deborah Crowhurst, John Croxall, David Culley, Sian Daffyd, Henry Ole Dapash, Cuppam Dasarthy, Miriam Darlington, Chris Davis, Wayne Davis, Ian Dawson, Bern de Bruijn, Ian de Reybekill, Marie Demoulin, Lizzy Denning, Nick Derry, Pedro Develey, Rob Devereaux, Mohammed Dilawar, Milko Dimitrov, Marco Dinetti, Judy Dixon, Aline Dobbie, Andrew Dobson, Paul Doherty, Penny Dolby, Frankie Douglas, Jennie Duberstein, Andrew Duff, Maria Duff, Carolyn Duncan, Euan Dunn, Guy Dutson, Mithlesh Dwivedi, Andrea Eames, Jonathan Eames*, Mike Eatough, Joanna Eede, Shan Egerton, Donnett Elder, Jonas Ellerström, Alistair Elliot, Hattie Ellis, Nick Elton*, George Eshiamwata, Bethan Evans, Alison Fairchild, Clive Fairweather, Jon Farrar, Matt Feaviour, Natalino Fenech*, Montserrat Fenwick, John Fergusson, Jo Ferranto*, William Finch, Clem Fisher, John Fisher, Keith and Lindsay Fisher, James Fleming, Nigel Fletcher, Ted Floyd*, Brenda and John Ford, Rosalind Ford, Roger Fotso, C France, Paul Fretter, Laura Friend, Cliff and Dawn Frith, Anne Fromage-Mariette, Jane Gaithuma, Phil Gates, Robert Gerson, Sunetro Ghosal, Graeme Gibson, Gillian Gilbert, Patricia Girdler, Mitch and Patty Gliddon, V Glupov, Lisa Goddard, Avirama Golan, Chris Goldsmith, Vesna Goldsworthy*, Chris Gooddie, Robert Gosford, Caroline (née Fontannaz) Goulden, Richard Gozney, Tane Gravatt, Kathleen Gray, Jon Green, Malcolm Green, Diana Greenway, Lydia Greeves, Phil and Sue Gregory*, Adam, Svetlana and Jacob Gretton*, Joan Grimley, Richard Grimmett, Gill Hacon, Liz Hague, Rick Halcott*, Philip and Margaret Hall*, Dal Han, Kjeld Hansen, Kate Hardy, the late Tony Hare, Geoff and Anabel Harries, Merilyn Harris, Ash Harrison, Tim Harrison, Hokimate Harwood, Olga Hazard, Liu He, Martin Helicar, Penny Hemans, John Hemming, Nicola Hemmings, Bennett Hennessey*, Peter Herkenrath*, Vera Hicks, Mike Higgiston, Nancy Hillstrand*, Simone Himenez, Richard Hines, Ben Hoare, Ian Hodder, John and Jemi Holmes, June Holmes, Rachel Holmes, Lucie Hošková, Tsovinar Hovhannisyan, Matthew Howard, Roger Howard, Steve Howell, Sue Hughes, Linda Hunter, Cornelia Hutt, Mohammad Sajid Idrisi, Lindsey Ingham, Jim Irons, Hussein Isack, Pamela Ive, Alan Ives, Geetha Iyer, Kurt Jackson, Paul Jackson, Abdi Jama*, Conor Jameson, Tamadhur Jamil Al-Khishali, Girish Jathar, Matthew Jeffery, Paul Jepson, Paul Johnsgard, Alan Johnson, David Johnson, Ian Johnson, Jo Johnson, Chris Jones, Colin Jones, Darryl Jones*, Marianne Jones, Peter Jones, Philip Jones, Evgeny Karev, Paul Kariuki Ndang'ang'a, Håkan Karlsson, Lars Karlsson, Ed Keeble, Ann Kelley, Alan Kemp, Samuel Kepuknai, Angela King, Marian King, Mike Kings, Guy Kirwan*, Harrison Kitukung, Michael Kiu, Richard and Jules Knocker, John Koi, André Konter, Ashish Kothari, Jennie Kuca, Peter Lack, Clive Lane, Venetia Lang, Ben Lascelles, Chris Leahy, Rosemary Lee, Anabelle Legrix*, Delphine Legrix-Balidas, Guilhem Lesaffre, Yossi Leshem*, Debra Lesinski, Corinne Lewis, Gwyneth Lewis, Martín Lezama-López, Marisa Loach, James Lowen*, Kathleen Lowrey, Vedran Lucić, Zoryana Lukyanchuk, Karen Lunt, Joanne Luyster, Richard Mabey, John McAllister, Michael McCarthy, Peter McDermott, Phil McGowan, Colin Macintosh, John McKie, Islay McLeod, Geoffrey McMullan, Adam McNaughton*, Grahame Madge, Sonu Mahesh, Angela Mancino*, Maaike Manten*, Adam Manvell, Brian Marchant, Marcel Marée, Alwyn Marriage, Albert Martinez Vilalta, John Matthews, Gavin Maxwell, Mary Dungan Megalli, Manfred Meiners, Tim Melling, the late Don Merton, Sakhamuzi Mhlongo*, Heimo Mikkola, Katie Millard, Kay and Tony Miller, Graham Mills, Katharine Milton, Kay Milton*, Jane (Geniva) Minja, Clive Minton, Laurence Mitchell, Gary Mock, Stephen Montorian, Yulia Moroz, Brian Morris, Rick Morris, Stephen Moss, Andrew Motion, Dennis Moye, David Moyer, Harry Boedi Mranata and R Boedi Mranata, Peter and Elaine Mucci, Tommy and Christine Muir*, Sarah Muir, Thomas Muir, Polly Munro, Philip Murphy, Jeremy Mynott*, Kitkung Nampaso, Rishad Naoroji, Peter Newlands, Derek Niemann, Lennart Nilsson*, Mwai Njonjo, Henry Nkwain, Nariman Nouri, Pat Nutbrown, Rebecca O'Connor, Maurice Odhiambo Ongoro, Jen Ogilvie, Redmond O'Hanlon, Arne Ohlsson*, Narena Olliver, Mike Ord, Dieter Oschadleus, John O'Sullivan, Sarah Otterstrom, William Overal, Nick Owens, Fernando Pacheco*, Suzanne Padfield, Byron Palacios, Ann Panton, Clairie Papazoglou, John Parker, Richard Parkinson, Gael Patterson, Robert Payne, David Paynter, Rodrigo Paz, Christine Peacock, Lucy Pearce, Mark Pearman, David Pearson, Roger Peart, Jari Peltomäki, Jim Perrin*, Daudi Peterson, Casey Pheiffer, Patrick Pikacha, Leah Pilmer, Steve Piotrowski, Aasheesh Pittie*, Bob Pomfret, Katrina Porteous, Richard Porter*, Frank Portman, Bill Pranty, Greg Pringle, Robert Prys-Jones, Ksenija Putilin, Diana and Hassan Qasrawi, Bill and Rowena

Quantrill, Margaret Quigley, Abdul Rahman, Asad Rahmani*, Michael Rank, Mrutyumjaya Rao, Nigel Redman, Robin Restall, Elizabeth Reynaud, Arnaud Reynier, Deborah Reynolds, James Rhodes, Sarah Rhodes, David Richards, Rosamond Richardson, Susan Richardson, Brian Richmond, Robert Ridgely, Janet Ritchie, Patrick Roba, Janet Robbins, Scott K Robinson, Pablo Rojas, Mark Roper, Lynne Ross, David Rothenberg, Sandra Taylor Rouja, Paul Rouzer, Steve Rowland, Peter Rudman, Maurice Rumboll, Jon Russell, Janet Ruth, Andrea Rutigliano*, Ali Sadr, Eric and Lorna Salzman*, Margaret Samuel, Harkirat Sangha, Margaret Saunders, Sav Saville, Norbert Schaffer, Dan Scheiman, Samantha Scheiman*, Jack Schmitt, Patricia Schonstein, Shino Setsuda, Alex and Elwira Seymour-Cooper, Jevgeni Shergalin, Wael M Shohdi, Alhaji Siaka, Simona Sibirkaite, David Sibley, Dragan Simic, Lavrentis Sidiropoulos, Fred Silcock, Jean Skinner, Professor Cedric Smith, Macklin Smith, Phil Smith, Sam Lauren Smith, Steve Snelling, Burak Sonyürek, Stephanie Sorrell, José R Soto, Laura and Stephen Spawls*, Ken Spencer*, Neal Spencer, Claire Spottiswoode, Richard Sprakes, Anna Staneva, Marija Stanisic, Kalliopi Stara*, Claire Stares, Brent Stephenson, Terry Stevenson*, Peter Steyn, Chris Stimpson, David Stirling, Ollie Stone-Lee, Gabriel and Jill Stott, Marilyn Strathern, Terry Suchma, Alisha Sufit, Joe Sultana, Elchin Sultanov, Denis Summers-Smith, Clay and Pat Sutton*, Keiko Suzue, David Swithinbank, Brian and Margaret Sykes, Stephen Tapper, Jose and Ozlem Tavares, Caroline and Malcolm Taylor, Helen Taylor, Stephen Taylor, Sebastian Thewes, Glen Threlfo, Bill Thompson III*, Ray Tipper, Clement Toh, Mohammad Tohidifar, Hugo Haroldo Toledo, Dominique Tomasini, Mike Toms, Nada Tosheva*, Henrietta Towle, Rigas Tsiakiris, Katia Tsikhno, Vic Tucker, Mark Turner, Mira Tweti, Shay and Yehoadan Tzur, Gro Urstad, Hilary van de Watering, Voislav Vasic, Dimitris Vavylis*, Gerhard Veit, F Vere-Hodge, Yvette Verner, Julío Victoriano, Tim Wacher, Richard Wakeford, Barry Walker*, Pauline Wallace, Martin Walsh, Peter Walton, Wanyoike Wamiti, Anthony Ward, the late Robert Warren, Steve Warrington, Linda Waterman, Chris Watson, Sara Wheeler, Richard White, Simon Whitehead, B Widener, Jane Wight, Bill Wigram, Colin Williams, Jeni Williams*, Rob Williams, Dorothy Wilson, Malcolm Wilson, Sally-Ann Wilson, Simon Winder, David Wingate, Nigel and Shane Winser, James Wolstencroft*, Pete Wood, Martin Woodcock*, Malcolm Wright, Rick Wright*, Dave Wybrow, Leszek Wysocki, Lu Xin, Alberto Yanosky, Sandra Yeo, Gayda Young, Rosamund Young, A K Yurlov, Julie Zickefoose.

I wish to single out Darryl Jones (Australia), Bennett Hennessey (Bolivia), Amir Balaban (Israel), Ananda Banerjee, Aasheesh Pittie (India), Lennart Nilsson, Arne Ohlsson (Sweden), Tim Birkhead, Jeremy Mynott, my mother-in-law, Christine Muir (UK), and Alan Bartels (USA) for their services above and beyond the call of duty. I also give major thanks to polymathic birder Rick Wright for his expert reading of the entire text and for sparing me from many errors. Those that remain are mine alone.

We were able to bring our message about Birds and People to a much wider audience and to solicit for contributions because of the support of a number of media personnel. These include: Ted Floyd (American Birding Association and Birding), Delta Willis (Audubon Society), Neil Braidwood (Aurora), Ollie Stone-Lee, Brett Westwood, (BBC Radio 4), Ben Hoare (BBC Wildlife), Andrew Dobson (Bermuda Audubon Society), Fiona Barclay (Bird Guides), Adrian Long, Mike Rands (BirdLife International and World Birdwatch), Dominic Mitchell (Birdwatch), Sheena Harvey and Matt Merritt (Birdwatching), Adrian Pitches (British Birds), Claire Gogerty (Coast), Drusilla Beyfus (Daily Telegraph), Bob Gosford (Ethnoornithologists' Network), Sam Wollaston (Guardian), David Cobham (Hawk and Owl Trust), Michael McCarthy (Independent), Janet Robbins and Lyons Filmer (KWM Radio), Stephanie Cross (The Lady), James Lowen (Neotropical Bird Club), Rebecca Worsfold (Norfolk Wildlife Trust), Brian Sykes (Oriental Bird Club), Paul Herbert and Simon Wilkes (Random House's dedicated Birds and People website), Sophie Poklewski Koziell and Jo Oland (Resurgence), Simon Barnes (The Times), Judith Tooth (Wave), Pam Gardiner (Wikipedia), Phil McGowan (World Pheasant Association), Tony Henderson, Lennart Nilsson, Asad Rahmani and Anders Wirdheim.

The project drew its first lungfuls of clear Norfolk air on a walk I shared with John Fanshawe of BirdLife International in 2005. The vast flat marshes of Haddiscoe Island near my home, not to mention the immense skies of that place, seem ideally suited to imagining things on a big scale. Little did we know how long it would take us to turn the dream into reality. Yet John has been there every step of the way, as ambassador at large across the huge BirdLife network, enabling us to tap into the expertise and the private experiences of people worldwide. We owe him an enormous debt of gratitude for his diplomatic skills, not only in the UK, but especially in Argentina and the USA.

Jonathan Elphick has shared an almost unbroken partnership with the authors and with Random House spanning 15 years. He was the researcher not only on Birds and People, but also Birds Britannica. A close friend over three decades, he is a scrutiniser of ornithological fact without equal and a scholar of exceptional breadth. His expertise embraces all things living, as well as most of the arts, especially music, literature and cooking. To give one small indication of his centrifugal interests, the phrase 'and ninthly' became a kind of motif for our many prolonged, discursive telephone conversations over seven years. He is in many ways an unsung hero of Birds and People. If John Fanshawe was our roving ambassador on Earth, then I think of Jonathan as our man in the underworld, burrowing through London's library stacks in search of the killer fact. We cannot thank him enough.

Almost everything that I have achieved professionally in the last 20 years has involved my agent, Gill Coleridge of Rogers, Coleridge and White, and Dan Franklin, my editor at Jonathan Cape. They are the 'mother' and 'father' of my literary life and I give them immense thanks for being, as always, peerless professionals and for taking such risks on my behalf and on behalf of the birds. They have been wonderfully supported by two exemplary teams at both Rogers, Coleridge and White and Random House. We give special thanks to Alex Bowler, Neil Bradford, Roger Bratchell, Cara Jones, Joe Pickering, Vicki Robinson, Sally Sargeant, Ellie Steel and Claire Wilshaw. Ellie Steel has done a truly outstanding job of line editing such a complicated book, while Production Director Neil Bradford has smoothly coordinated the work of several exceptional professionals who have made important contributions to the finished product. These include Eric Bailey and his team at XY Digital and the designer Peter Ward.

None of the books I've written has taken a greater toll than this. I suspect it would have been impossible to bear, especially in the final 18 months, had it not been for the unflinching support of my 'gorgeous girls', Mary, Rachael (Rachy) and Miriam (Milly). In fact our two children have grown into young women under the shadow of this huge book. It has exerted its unavoidable gravitational pressure even upon their lives and they are probably as pleased to see it finished as anyone. Finally my partner, Mary, has been a tower of strength, a source of endless encouragement, of wise counsel and of loving company throughout all the difficult times. I offer her my deepest heartfelt thanks.

PHOTOGRAPHER'S ACKNOWLEDGEMENTS

The travel and logistics required to shoot this body of work have been a major undertaking. Over an eight-year period I travelled to 39 countries on all seven continents, visiting remote tribal communities from the Amazon to Papua New Guinea. I've stood in awe at thousands of Snow Geese lifting off at dawn in New Mexico, been deafened by parrots arriving at the world's largest clay lick in the heart of the Amazon, drunk vodka late into the night with Mongolian eagle hunters, and been privileged to photograph some of the finest antiquities in museums around the world. Few of these experiences would have been possible without the support, time and effort – often far beyond any expectation I may have had – given by tour companies, nature guides, researchers, biologists, fellow photographers and a multitude of other organisations.

For their expert help and camaraderie in the field I wish to thank Sue Gregory (Australia), Claudio Vidal, Yvonne Paeile Jordan (Chile), Zhou Li, Barry Wong (China), Noel Urena (Costa Rica), Martin Hellicar, Sergeant Kyriacos Elia, Panicos Panayides (Cyprus), Nestor Alban (Ecuador), Giorgi Darchiasvili (Georgia), Ana Smith, Olga Hazard (Guatemala), Jari Peltomäki (Finland), Babloo Khan, Vinod Goswami, Seva Ram (India), Andrea Rutigliano (Italy), Dave Richards, Harrison K Nampaso and Henry Ole Dapash (Kenya), Natalino Fenech, Albert Dimech (Malta), Dal Han, Gereltuv Dashdoorov (Mongolia), Brent Stephenson, Detlef and Carol Davies (New Zealand), Carlos Bethancourt, Raúl Arias de Para (Panama), Nellee Holland, Meike Lang, Daniel Wakra, Benson and Alus Hale, Timan Tumbo, Hale Johu, Pym Mamindl (Papua New Guinea), Guillermo Rodeigues Gomez, Silverio Duri Valdivia and Barry Walker (Peru), Domingo Ramon 'Chicoy' Enerio, Domingo Gutterez, Adri Constantino and Nicky Icarangal (Philippines), Willie Foo, Winston Loong, Abdul Rahman (Singapore), Carles Santana and Roger Sanmarti (Spain), Brydon Thomason (UK), Iain Nicolson, Mike Crewe, Dan Anvers, Julian Davis (USA) and Christian Savigny, Cheesemans' Ecology Safaris, Adventure Network (Antarctica, Falklands and South Georgia).

Many people gave valuable advice and often logistical support on reaching far-flung destinations; others offered opportunities closer to home. They include Chris Abrams, Heather Angel, Tim Appleton, Al Dawes, Frederic Desmette, Sophie Ellis, Mark Hancox, Roger Kass, Dave Kjaer, Chris Knights, Dave Leech, Tim Loseby, Wayne Lynch, Tolly Nason, Arni Olafsson, New Jersey Audubon, Ryan Nico, Papua Bird Club, Papua New Guinea Tourism Authority, Philippines Tourism, Philippines Wild Bird Club, Raj Singh, Brian Small, Bill Thompson III, David Waters and Barry Wright. John Macpherson and Andrew Midgley offered their expertise dealing with both film production and post-production work while putting the book together.

For the laughs and memories of great shared experiences in many locations I thank Roger Tidman, David Tomlinson and Jari Peltomäki. A special debt of thanks is due to John Fanshawe who facilitated many opportunities through BirdLife contacts around the world and to my agent, Pat White. Six years ago, when Mark Cocker asked if I would like to join him on this journey, I had no need to think twice. This project has given birth to a valued friendship. With much laughter along the way it has been an immense privilege working with Mark on *Birds and People*.

Finally, a huge debt of gratitude goes to my long-suffering family. Jayne in particular and our two children, James and Charlotte, have put up with my frequent absences often in far-flung corners of the world. Without their love and encouragement so many of the pictures within these pages would never have been taken.

CREDITS

We would like to thank the following for the use of the pictures and text extracts listed below according to page number.

Every effort has been made to trace the holders of copyright.

Should there be any inadvertent omissions or errors, the publishers will be pleased to correct them in a future edition.

PICTURE CREDITS

78 Whistler's peacocks, Freer Gallery of Art, Smithsonian Institution, D.C. Gift of Charles Lang Freer, F1904.61

103 *The end of an albatross*, Bruce Pearson

157 Yawar Fiesta, Rob Williams

190 Whooping Crane, Natural History Museum Picture Library

245 (right) Turtle Dove, Natalino Fenech

261 Bannerman's Turaco festival, Mark Edwards / BirdLife

275 Fetish market, Carolyn Hall

360 Lyrebird, Narelle Oliver / Scholastic Australia

404 Black Robin (left) Don Merton / New Zealand Department of Conservation; (right) New Zealand Department of Conservation

405 Picathartes, Mark Andrews

491 Quelea with elephant, Antero Topp

506 Mamo, Natural History Museum Picture Library

510 *Mystery of the Missing Migrants*, Estate of Charley Harper, www.charleyharperstudio.com

TEXT CREDITS

94 Apsley Cherry-Garrard, *The Worst Journey in the World*. Used by permission of the Scott Polar Research Institute, University of Cambridge

117 Rainer Maria Rilke, 'The Flamingos', *The Selected Poetry of Rainer Maria Rilke*, translated by Stephen Mitchell, translation copyright © 1980, 1981, 1982 by Stephen Mitchell. Used by permission of Random House, Inc.

130 Du Mu, 'Egrets', translated by Paul Rouzer for *Birds and People*. Used by permission of the translator

150 Du Fu, 'Country Cottage', translated by Paul Rouzer for *Birds and People*. Used by permission of the translator

179 Norman MacCaig, 'A Voice of Summer', *The Poems of Norman MacCaig*. Used by permission of Polygon

264, 289, 316, 448 Jonathan Barnes, *The Complete Works of Aristotle*, *Revised Oxford Translation*, copyright © 1985 by The Jowett Copyright Trustees. Used by permission of Princeton University Press

354 Pablo Neruda, 'Tapaculo', *Art of Birds*, translated by Jack Schmitt. Used by permission of Carmen Balcells Agencia Literaria, S.A. and the translator

355 Wallace Stevens, 'Anecdote of the Jar', *Collected Poems*. Used by permission of Faber & Faber and Random House, Inc.

362, 403 Judith Wright, 'Satin Bower-birds' and 'Lyrebirds', *Collected Poems*. Used by permission of HarperCollins Australia

455 Randall Jarrell, 'The Mockingbird', *The Complete Poems*, copyright © 1969, renewed 1997 by Mary von S. Jarrell. Used by permission of Faber & Faber and Farrar, Straus and Giroux

SPECIES INDEX

GENERAL INDEX